military	*Mil*	militar
music		
noun		
nautical		
oneself		
pejorative		
photography		
plural		
politics	*Pol*	
possessive	*poss*	posesivo
past participle	*pp*	participio pasado
preposition	*prep*	preposición
present participle	*pres p*	participio de presente
pronoun	*pron*	pronombre
past tense	*pt*	tiempo pasado
railroad	*Rail*	ferrocarril
religion	*Relig*	religión
school	*Schol*	enseñanza
singular	*sing*	singular
someone	*s. o.*	alguien
something	*sth*	algo
technical	*Tec*	técnico
university	*Univ*	universidad
verb	*vb*	verbo
intransitive verb	*vi*	verbo intransitivo
pronominal verb	*vpr*	verbo pronominal
transitive verb	*vt*	verbo transitivo
transitive & intransitive verb	*vti*	verbo transitivo e intransitivo

Oxford Spanish Mini Dictionary
Diccionario Oxford Mini

Spanish–English • English–Spanish
español-inglés • inglés-español

Diccionario Oxford Mini

CUARTA EDICIÓN

español-inglés
inglés-español

Oxford Spanish Mini Dictionary

FOURTH EDITION

Spanish–English
English–Spanish

OXFORD
UNIVERSITY PRESS

Great Clarendon Street, Oxford OX2 6DP

Oxford University Press is a department of the University of Oxford. It furthers the University's objective of excellence in research, scholarship, and education by publishing worldwide in

Oxford New York

Auckland Cape Town Dar es Salaam Hong Kong Karachi Kuala Lumpur Madrid Melbourne Mexico City Nairobi New Delhi Shanghai Taipei Toronto

With offices in
Argentina Austria Brazil Chile Czech Republic France Greece Guatemala Hungary Italy Japan South Korea Poland Portugal Singapore Switzerland Thailand Turkey Ukraine Vietnam

Published in the United States
by Oxford University Press Inc., New York

British Library Cataloguing in Publication Data

Data available

Library of Congress Cataloging in Publication Data
Data available

ISBN 978-0-19-953435-7
ISBN 978-0-19-954126-3 (US edition)
ISBN 978-0-19-953490-6 (Spanish cover edition)

10 9 8 7 6 5 4 3 2 1

Typeset by Interactive Sciences Ltd, Gloucester
Printed and bound in Italy by
Legoprint S.p.A.

Contents/Índice

Proprietary terms

This dictionary includes some words which have, or are asserted to have, proprietary status as trademarks. Their inclusion does not imply that they have acquired for legal purposes a non-proprietary or general significance, nor any other judgement concerning their legal status. In cases where the editorial staff have some evidence that a word has proprietary status this is indicated in the entry for that word by the symbol ®, but no judgement concerning the legal status of such words is made or implied thereby.

Marcas registradas

Este diccionario incluye algunas palabras que son o pretenden ser marcas registradas. Cuando al editor le consta que una palabra es una marca registrada, esto se indica por medio del símbolo ®. No debe atribuirse ningún valor jurídico ni a la presencia ni a la ausencia de tal designación.

Contributors/Colaboradores

Fourth Edition/Cuarta edición

Editors/Editores
Joanna Rubery
Nicholas Rollin

Phrasefinder/Frases útiles
Pablo Pérez D'Ors
Carol Styles Carvajal
Oriana Orellana Jordán

Data input/Entrada de datos
Susan Wilkin

Third Edition/Tercera edición

Nicholas Rollin
Carol Styles Carvajal

Second Edition/Segunda edición

Editors/Editores
Carol Styles Carvajal
Michael Britton
Jane Horwood

Phrasefinder/Frases útiles
Idoia Noble
Neil and Roswitha Morris

Data input/Entrada de datos
Susan Wilkin

First Edition/Primera edición

Editor/Editora
Christine Lea

Introduction

This new edition of the *Oxford Spanish Mini Dictionary* is designed as an effective and practical reference tool for the student, adult learner, traveller, and business professional.

The wordlist has been revised and updated to reflect recent additions to both languages. The *Phrasefinder* section has been expanded. It aims to provide the user with the confidence to communicate in the most commonly encountered social situations such as travel, shopping, eating out, and organizing leisure activities.

Another valuable feature of the dictionary is the special status given to more complex grammatical words which provide the basic structure of both languages. Boxed entries in the text for these *function words* provide extended treatment, including notes to warn of possible pitfalls.

The dictionary has an easy-to-use, streamlined layout. Bullets separate each new part of speech within an entry. Nuances of sense or usage are pinpointed by indicators or by typical collocates with which the word frequently occurs. Extra help is given in the form of symbols to mark the register of words and phrases. An exclamation mark [!] indicates colloquial language, and a cross [✖] indicates slang.

Each English headword is followed by its phonetic transcription between slashes. The symbols used are those of the International Phonetic Alphabet. Pronunciation is also shown for derivatives and compounds where it is not easily deduced from that of a headword. The rules for the pronunciation of Spanish are given on pages xii–xiii.

The swung dash (~) is used to represent a headword or that part of a headword preceding the vertical bar (|).

In both English and Spanish only irregular plurals are given. Normally Spanish nouns and adjectives ending in an unstressed vowel form the plural by adding s (e.g. *libro*, *libros*). Nouns and adjectives ending in a stressed vowel or a consonant add es (e.g. *rubí*, *rubíes*, *pared*, *paredes*). An accent on the final syllable is not required when es is added (e.g. *nación*, *naciones*). Final *z* becomes *ces* (e.g. *vez*, *veces*).

Spanish nouns and adjectives ending in o form the feminine by changing the final *o* to *a* (e.g. *hermano*, *hermana*). Most Spanish nouns and adjectives ending in anything other than final *o* do not have a separate feminine form, with the exception of those denoting nationality etc.; these add a to the masculine singular form (e.g. *español*, *española*). An accent on the penultimate syllable is then not required (e.g. *inglés*, *inglesa*). Adjectives ending in *án*, *ón*, or *or* behave like those denoting nationality, with the following exceptions: *inferior*, *mayor*, *mejor*, *menor*, *peor*, *superior*, where the feminine has the same form as the masculine. Spanish verb tables will be found at the end of the book.

The Spanish alphabet

In Spanish *ñ* is considered a separate letter and in the Spanish–English section, therefore, is alphabetized after *ny*.

Introducción

Esta nueva edición del *Diccionario Oxford Mini* ha sido concebida a fin de proporcionar una herramienta de referencia práctica y eficaz al estudiante, joven y adulto, al viajero y a la persona de negocios.

Se ha revisado la lista de palabras con el objeto de incorporar nuevos términos en ambos idiomas. La sección central contiene una lista de *Frases útiles*, que se ha ampliado, destinada a que el usuario adquiera la confianza necesaria para comunicarse en las situaciones más normales de la vida diaria, como las que se encuentran al viajar, hacer compras, comer fuera y organizar actividades recreativas.

Otro valioso aspecto del diccionario es la importancia especial que se da a palabras con una función más compleja dentro de la gramática y que proveen la estructura básica de ambos idiomas. Estos *vocablos clave* están contenidos en recuadros dentro del texto, donde se les da un tratamiento amplio y se incluyen notas para advertir sobre posibles escollos.

El diccionario tiene una presentación clara y es fácil de usar. Símbolos distintivos separan las diferentes categorías gramaticales dentro de cada entrada. Los matices de sentido y de uso se muestran con precisión mediante indicadores o por colocaciones típicas con las que la palabra se usa frecuentemente. Se encuentra ayuda adicional en los signos que indican el registro idiomático de las palabras y frases. Un signo de exclamación ! señala el uso coloquial y una cruz ✖ el uso argot.

Cada palabra cabeza de artículo en inglés va seguida de su transcripción fonética entre barras oblicuas. Los símbolos que se usan son los del Alfabeto Fonético Internacional. También aparece la pronunciación de derivados y nombres compuestos cuando no es posible deducirla de la palabra cabeza de artículo. Las reglas sobre pronunciación inglesa se encuentran en la página xiv.

La tilde (~) se emplea para sustituir la palabra cabeza de artículo o aquella parte de tal palabra que precede a la barra vertical (|).

Tanto en inglés como en español se dan los plurales solamente si son irregulares. Para formar el plural regular en inglés se añade la letra s al sustantivo singular, pero se añade es cuando se trata de una palabra que termina en *ch*, *sh*, *s*, *ss*, *us*, *x*, *o*, *z* (p.ej. *sash*, *sashes*). En el caso de una palabra que termine en *y* precedida por una consonante, la y se transforma en *ies* (p.ej. *baby*, *babies*). Para formar el tiempo pasado y el participio pasado se añade *ed* al infinitivo de los verbos regulares ingleses (p.ej. *last*, *lasted*). En el caso de los verbos ingleses que terminan en e muda se añade sólo la *d* (p.ej. *move*, *moved*). En el caso de los verbos Ingleses que terminan en *y*, se debe cambiar la *y* por *ied* (p.ej. *carry*, *carried*). Los verbos irregulares se encuentran en el diccionario por orden alfabético remitidos al infinitivo, y también en la lista que aparece en las últimas páginas del diccionario.

Pronunciation of Spanish

Vowels

a between pronunciation of *a* in English *cat* and *arm*

e like *e* in English *bed*

i like *ee* in English *see* but a little shorter

o like *o* in English *hot* but a little longer

u like *oo* in English *too*

y when a vowel is as Spanish **i**

Consonants

b (1) in initial position or after a nasal consonant is like English *b*
(2) in other positions is between English *b* and English *v*

c (1) before **e** or **i** is like *th* in English *thin*. In Latin American Spanish is like English *s*.
(2) in other positions is like *c* in English *cat*

ch like *ch* in English *chip*

d (1) in initial position, after nasal consonants and after **l** is like English *d*
(2) in other positions is like *th* in English *this*

f like English *f*

g (1) before **e** or **i** is like *ch* in Scottish *loch*
(2) in initial position is like *g* in English *get*
(3) in other positions is like (2) but a little softer

j like *ch* in Scottish *loch*

k like English *k*

l like English *l* but see also **ll**

ll like *lli* in English *million*

m like English *m*

n like English *n*

ñ like *ni* in English *opinion*

p like English *p*

q like English *k*

r rolled or trilled

s like *s* in English *sit*

t like English *t*

v (1) in initial position or after a nasal consonant is like English *b*
(2) in other positions is between English b and English *v*

w like Spanish **b** or **v**

x like English *x*

y like English *y*

z like *th* in English *thin*

Pronunciación inglesa

Símbolos fonéticos

Vocales y diptongos

iː	*s*ee	ɔː	s*aw*	eɪ	p*a*ge	ɔɪ	j*oi*n
ɪ	s*i*t	ʊ	p*u*t	əʊ	h*o*me	ɪə	n*ea*r
e	t*e*n	uː	t*oo*	aɪ	f*i*ve	eə	h*ai*r
æ	h*a*t	ʌ	c*u*p	aɪə	f*i*re	ʊə	p*oo*r
ɑː	*ar*m	ɜː	f*ur*	aʊ	n*ow*		
ɒ	g*o*t	ə	*a*go	aʊə	fl*ou*r		

Consonantes

p	*p*en	tʃ	*ch*in	s	*s*o	n	*n*o
b	*b*ad	dʒ	*J*une	z	*z*oo	ŋ	si*ng*
t	*t*ea	f	*f*all	ʃ	*sh*e	l	*l*eg
d	*d*ip	v	*v*oice	ʒ	mea*s*ure	r	*r*ed
k	*c*at	θ	*th*in	h	*h*ow	j	*y*es
g	*g*ot	ð	*th*en	m	*m*an	w	*w*et

El símbolo ' precede a la sílaba sobre la cual recae el acento tónico.

Aa

a *preposición*

Note that **a** followed by **el** becomes **al**, e.g. **vamos al cine**

....➤ (*dirección*) to. **fui a México** I went to Mexico. **muévete a la derecha** move to the right

....➤ (*posición*) **se sentaron a la mesa** they sat at the table. **al lado del banco** next to the bank. **a orillas del río** on the banks of the river

....➤ (*distancia*) **queda a 5 km** it's 5 km away. **a pocos metros de aquí** a few meters from here

....➤ (*fecha*) **hoy estamos a 5** today is the 5th. **¿a cuánto estamos?**, (*LAm*) **¿a cómo estamos?** what's the date?

....➤ (*hora, momento*) at. **a las 2** at 2 o'clock. **a fin de mes** at the end of the month. **a los 21 años** at the age of 21; (*después de*) after 21 years

....➤ (*precio*) **¿a cómo están las peras?** how much are the pears? **están a 3 euros el kilo** they're 3 euros a kilo. **salen a 15 euros cada uno** they work out at 15 euros each.

....➤ (*medio, modo*) **fuimos a pie** we went on foot. **hecho a mano** hand made. **pollo al horno** (*LAm*) roast chicken

....➤ (*cuando precede al objeto directo de persona*) *no se traduce*. **conocí a Juan** I met Juan. **quieren mucho a sus hijos** they love their children very much

....➤ (*con objeto indirecto*) to. **se lo di a Juan** I gave it to Juan. **le vendí el coche a mi amigo** I sold my friend the car, I sold the car to my friend. **se lo compré a mi madre** I bought it from my mother; (*para*) I bought it for my mother

➡ Cuando la preposición **a** se emplea precedida de ciertos verbos como **empezar, faltar, ir, llegar** etc., ver bajo el respectivo verbo

ábaco *m* abacus

abadejo *m* pollack

abadía *f* abbey

abajo *adv* (down) below; (*dirección*) down(wards); (*en casa*) downstairs. ● *int* down with. **~ de** (*LAm*) under(neath). **calle ~** down the street. **el ~ firmante** the undersigned. **escaleras ~** down the stairs. **la parte de ~** the bottom (part). **más ~** further down

abalanzarse 10 *vpr* rush (**hacia** towards)

abanderado *m* standard-bearer; (*Mex, en fútbol*) linesman

abandon|ado *adj* abandoned; (*descuidado*) neglected; (persona) untidy. **~ar** *vt* leave (un lugar); abandon (persona, cosa). ● *vi* give up. **~arse** *vpr* give in; (*descuidarse*) let o.s. go. **~o** *m* abandonment; (*estado*) neglect

abani|car [7] *vt* fan. **~co** *m* fan

abaratar *vt* reduce

abarcar [7] *vt* put one's arms around, embrace; (*comprender*) embrace

abarrotar *vt* overfill, pack full

abarrotes *mpl* (*LAm*) groceries; (*tienda*) grocer's shop

abast|ecer [11] *vt* supply. **~ecimiento** *m* supply; (*acción*) supplying. **~o** *m* supply. **no dar ~o** be unable to cope (**con** with)

abati|do *adj* depressed. **~miento** *m* depression

abdicar [7] *vt* give up. • *vi* abdicate

abdom|en *m* abdomen. **~inal** *adj* abdominal

abec|é *m* [!] alphabet, ABC. **~edario** *m* alphabet

abedul *m* birch (tree)

abej|a *f* bee. **~orro** *m* bumblebee

aberración *f* aberration

abertura *f* opening

abeto *m* fir (tree)

abierto *pp véase* ABRIR. • *adj* open

abism|al *adj* abysmal; (*profundo*) deep. **~ar** *vt* throw into an abyss; (*fig, abatir*) humble. **~arse** *vpr* be absorbed (**en** in), be lost (**en** in). **~o** *m* abyss; (*fig, diferencia*) world of difference

ablandar *vt* soften. **~se** *vpr* soften

abnega|ción *f* self-sacrifice. **~do** *adj* self-sacrificing

abochornar *vt* embarrass. **~se** *vpr* feel embarrassed

abofetear *vt* slap

aboga|cía *f* law. **~do** *m* lawyer, solicitor; (*ante tribunal superior*) barrister (*Brit*), attorney (*Amer*).

abolengo *m* ancestry

aboli|ción *f* abolition. **~cionismo** *m* abolitionism. **~cionista** *m & f* abolitionist. **~r** [24] *vt* abolish

abolla|dura *f* dent. **~r** *vt* dent

abolsado *adj* baggy

abomba|do *adj* convex; (*LAm, atontado*) dopey. **~r** *vt* make convex. **~rse** *vpr* (*LAm, descomponerse*) go bad

abominable *adj* abominable

abona|ble *adj* payable. **~do** *adj* paid. • *m* subscriber. **~r** *vt* pay; (*en agricultura*) fertilize. **~rse** *vpr* subscribe.

abono *m* payment; (*estiércol*) fertilizer; (*a un periódico*) subscription

aborda|ble *adj* reasonable; (persona) approachable. **~je** *m* boarding. **~r** *vt* tackle (un asunto); approach (una persona); (*Naut*) come alongside; (*Mex, Aviac*) board

aborigen *adj & m* native

aborrec|er [11] *vt* loathe. **~ible** *adj* loathsome. **~ido** *adj* loathed. **~imiento** *m* loathing

abort|ar *vi* have a miscarriage. **~ivo** *adj* abortive. **~o** *m* miscarriage; (*voluntario*) abortion. **hacerse un ~o** have an abortion

abotonar *vt* button (up). **~se** *vpr* button (up)

abovedado *adj* vaulted

abrasa|dor *adj* burning. **~r** *vt* burn. **~rse** *vpr* burn

abraz|ar *vt* [10] embrace. **~arse** *vpr* embrace. **~o** *m* hug. **un fuerte ~o de** (*en una carta*) with best wishes from

abre|botellas *m invar* bottle-opener. ~**cartas** *m invar* paper-knife. ~**latas** *m invar* tin opener (*Brit*), can opener

abrevia|ción *f* abbreviation; (*texto abreviado*) abridged text. ~**do** *adj* brief; (texto) abridged. ~**r** *vt* abbreviate; abridge (texto); cut short (viaje etc). • *vi* be brief. ~**tura** *f* abbreviation

abrig|ado *adj* (lugar) sheltered; (persona) well wrapped up. ~**ador** *adj* (*Mex*, *ropa*) warm. ~**ar** 12 *vt* shelter; cherish (esperanza); harbour (duda, sospecha). ~**arse** *vpr* (take) shelter; (*con ropa*) wrap up. ~**o** *m* (over)coat; (*lugar*) shelter

abril *m* April. ~**eño** *adj* April

abrillantar *vt* polish

abrir (*pp* **abierto**) *vt/i* open. ~**se** *vpr* open; (*extenderse*) open out; (el tiempo) clear

abrochar *vt* do up; (*con botones*) button up

abruma|dor *adj* overwhelming. ~**r** *vt* overwhelm

abrupto *adj* steep; (*áspero*) harsh

abrutado *adj* brutish

absentismo *m* absenteeism

absolución *f* (*Relig*) absolution; (*Jurid*) acquittal

absolut|amente *adv* absolutely, completely. ~**o** *adj* absolute. **en** ~**o** (not) at all. ~**orio** *adj* of acquittal

absolver 2 (*pp* **absuelto**) *vt* (*Relig*) absolve; (*Jurid*) acquit

absor|bente *adj* absorbent; (*fig*, *interesante*) absorbing. ~**ber** *vt* absorb. ~**ción** *f* absorption. ~**to** *adj* absorbed

abstemio *adj* teetotal. • *m* teetotaller

absten|ción *f* abstention. ~**erse** 40 *vpr* abstain, refrain (**de** from)

abstinencia *f* abstinence

abstra|cción *f* abstraction. ~**cto** *adj* abstract. ~**er** 41 *vt* abstract. ~**erse** *vpr* be lost in thought. ~**ído** *adj* absent-minded

absuelto *adj* (*Relig*) absolved; (*Jurid*) acquitted

absurdo *adj* absurd. • *m* absurd thing

abuche|ar *vt* boo. ~**o** *m* booing

abuel|a *f* grandmother. ~**o** *m* grandfather. ~**os** *mpl* grandparents

ab|ulia *f* apathy. ~**úlico** *adj* apathetic

abulta|do *adj* bulky. ~**r** *vt* (*fig*, *exagerar*) exaggerate. • *vi* be bulky

abunda|ncia *f* abundance. **nadar en la** ~**ncia** be rolling in money. ~**nte** *adj* abundant, plentiful. ~**r** *vi* be plentiful

aburguesarse *vpr* become middle-class

aburri|do *adj* (*con estar*) bored; (*con ser*) boring. ~**dor** *adj* (*LAm*) boring. ~**miento** *m* boredom; (*cosa pesada*) bore. ~**r** *vt* bore. ~**rse** *vpr* get bored

abus|ar *vi* take advantage. ~**ar de la bebida** drink too much. ~**ivo** *adj* excessive. ~**o** *m* abuse

acá *adv* here. ~ **y allá** here and there. **de** ~ **para allá** to and fro. **de ayer** ~ since yesterday. **más** ~ nearer

acaba|do *adj* finished; (*perfecto*) perfect. • *m* finish. ~**r** *vt/i* finish. ~**rse** *vpr* finish; (*agotarse*) run out; (*morirse*) die. ~**r con** put an end to. ~**r de** (+ *infinitivo*) have just (+ *pp*). ~ **de llegar** he has just arrived. ~**r por** (+ *infinitivo*) end up (+ *gerundio*). **¡se acabó!** that's it!

acabóse *m*. **ser el** ~ be the end, be the limit

a

a

acad|emia *f* academy. **~émico** *adj* academic

acallar *vt* silence

acalora|do *adj* heated; (persona) hot. **~rse** *vpr* get hot; (*fig, excitarse*) get excited

acampar *vi* camp

acantilado *m* cliff

acapara|r *vt* hoard; (*monopolizar*) monopolize. **~miento** *m* hoarding; (*monopolio*) monopolizing

acariciar *vt* caress; (animal) stroke; (idea) nurture

ácaro *m* mite

acarre|ar *vt* transport; (desgracias etc) cause. **~o** *m* transport

acartona|do *adj* (piel) wizened. **~rse** *vpr* (*ponerse rígido*) go stiff; (piel) become wizened

acaso *adv* maybe, perhaps. ● *m* chance. **~ llueva mañana** perhaps it will rain tomorrow. **por si ~** (just) in case

acata|miento *m* compliance (**de** with). **~r** *vt* comply with

acatarrarse *vpr* catch a cold, get a cold

acaudalado *adj* well off

acceder *vi* agree; (*tener acceso*) have access

acces|ible *adj* accessible; (persona) approachable. **~o** *m* access, entry; (*Med, ataque*) attack

accesorio *adj & m* accessory

accident|ado *adj* (terreno) uneven; (*agitado*) troubled; (persona) injured. **~al** *adj* accidental. **~arse** *vpr* have an accident. **~e** *m* accident

acci|ón *f* (*incl Jurid*) action; (*hecho*) deed; (*Com*) share. **~onar** *vt* work. ● *vi* gesticulate. **~onista** *m & f* shareholder

acebo *m* holly (tree)

acech|ar *vt* lie in wait for. **~o** *m* spying. **al ~o** on the look-out

aceit|ar *vt* oil; (*Culin*) add oil to. **~e** *m* oil. **~e de oliva** olive oil. **~te de ricino** castor oil. **~era** *f* cruet; (*para engrasar*) oilcan. **~ero** *adj* oil. **~oso** *adj* oily

aceitun|a *f* olive. **~ado** *adj* olive. **~o** *m* olive tree

acelera|dor *m* accelerator. **~r** *vt* accelerate; (*fig*) speed up, quicken

acelga *f* chard

acent|o *m* accent; (*énfasis*) stress. **~uación** *f* accentuation. **~uar** **21** *vt* stress; (*fig*) emphasize. **~uarse** *vpr* become noticeable

acepción *f* meaning, sense

acepta|ble *adj* acceptable. **~ción** *f* acceptance; (*éxito*) success. **~r** *vt* accept

acequia *f* irrigation channel

acera *f* pavement (*Brit*), sidewalk (*Amer*)

acerca de *prep* about

acerca|miento *m* approach; (*fig*) reconciliation. **~r** **7** *vt* bring near. **~rse** *vpr* approach

acero *m* steel. **~ inoxidable** stainless steel

acérrimo *adj* (*fig*) staunch

acert|ado *adj* right, correct; (*apropiado*) appropriate. **~ar** **1** *vt* (*adivinar*) get right, guess. ● *vi* get right; (*en el blanco*) hit. **~ar a** happen to. **~ar con** hit on. **~ijo** *m* riddle

achacar **7** *vt* attribute

achacoso *adj* sickly

achaque *m* ailment

achatar *vt* flatten

achicar **7** *vt* make smaller; (*fig, fam, empequeñecer*) belittle; (*Naut*) bale out. **~rse** *vpr* become smaller; (*humillarse*) be intimidated

achicharra|r *vt* burn; (*fig*) pester. **~rse** *vpr* burn

achichincle *m & f* (*Mex*) hanger-on

achicopalado *adj* (*Mex*) depressed

achicoria *f* chicory

achiote *m* (*LAm*) annatto

achispa|do *adj* tipsy. **~rse** *vpr* get tipsy

achulado *adj* cocky

acicala|do *adj* dressed up. **~r** *vt* dress up. **~rse** *vpr* get dressed up

acicate *m* spur

acidez *f* acidity; (*Med*) heartburn

ácido *adj* sour. • *m* acid

acierto *m* success; (*idea*) good idea; (*habilidad*) skill

aclama|ción *f* acclaim; (*aplausos*) applause. **~r** *vt* acclaim; (*aplaudir*) applaud

aclara|ción *f* explanation. **~r** *vt* lighten (colores); (*explicar*) clarify; (*enjuagar*) rinse. • *vi* (el tiempo) brighten up. **~rse** *vpr* become clear. **~torio** *adj* explanatory

aclimata|ción *f* acclimatization, acclimation (*Amer*). **~r** *vt* acclimatize, acclimate (*Amer*). **~rse** *vpr* become acclimatized, become acclimated (*Amer*)

acné *m* acne

acobardar *vt* intimidate. **~se** *vpr* lose one's nerve

acocil *m* (*Mex*) freshwater shrimp

acog|edor *adj* welcoming; (ambiente) friendly. **~er** **14** *vt* welcome; (*proteger*) shelter; (*recibir*) receive. **~erse** *vpr* take refuge. **~ida** *f* welcome; (*refugio*) refuge

acolcha|do *adj* quilted. **~r** *vt* quilt, pad

acomedido *adj* (*Mex*) obliging

acomet|er *vt* attack; (*emprender*) undertake. **~ida** *f* attack

acomod|ado *adj* well off. **~ador** *m* usher. **~adora** *f* usherette. **~ar** *vt* arrange; (*adaptar*) adjust. • *vi* be suitable. **~arse** *vpr* settle down; (*adaptarse*) conform

acompaña|miento *m* accompaniment. **~nte** *m & f* companion; (*Mus*) accompanist. **~r** *vt* go with; (*hacer compañía*) keep company; (*adjuntar*) enclose

acondicionar *vt* fit out; (*preparar*) prepare

aconseja|ble *adj* advisable. **~do** *adj* advised. **~r** *vt* advise. **~rse** *vpr.* **~rse con** consult

acontec|er **11** *vi* happen. **~imiento** *m* event

acopla|miento *m* coupling; (*Elec*) connection. **~r** *vt* fit; (*Elec*) connect; (*Rail*) couple

acorazado *adj* armour-plated. • *m* battleship

acord|ar **2** *vt* agree (upon); (*decidir*) decide; (*recordar*) remind. **~arse** *vpr* remember. **~e** *adj* in agreement; (*Mus*) harmonious. • *m* chord

acorde|ón *m* accordion. **~onista** *m & f* accordionist

acordona|do *adj* (lugar) cordoned off; (zapatos) lace-up. **~r** *vt* lace (up); (*rodear*) cordon off

acorralar *vt* round up (animales); corner (personas)

acortar *vt* shorten; cut short (permanencia). **~se** *vpr* get shorter

acos|ar *vt* hound; (*fig*) pester. **~o** *m* pursuit; (*fig*) pestering

acostar **2** *vt* put to bed; (*Naut*) bring alongside. • *vi* (*Naut*) reach

a

land. ~**se** *vpr* go to bed; (*echarse*) lie down. ~**se con** (*fig*) sleep with

acostumbra|do *adj* (*habitual*) usual. ~**do a** used to. ~**r** *vt* get used. **me ha ~do a levantarme por la noche** he's got me used to getting up at night. • *vi.* ~**r** be accustomed to. **acostumbro a comer a la una** I usually have lunch at one o'clock. ~**rse** *vpr* become accustomed, get used

acota|ción *f* (*nota*) margin note (*en el teatro*) stage direction; (*cota*) elevation mark. ~**miento** *m* (*Mex*) hard shoulder

acrecentar **1** *vt* increase. ~**se** *vpr* increase

acredita|do *adj* reputable; (*Pol*) accredited. ~**r** *vt* prove; accredit (diplomático); (*garantizar*) guarantee; (*autorizar*) authorize. ~**rse** *vpr* make one's name

acreedor *adj* worthy (**de** of). • *m* creditor

acribillar *vt* (*a balazos*) riddle (**a** with); (*a picotazos*) cover (**a** with); (*fig, a preguntas etc*) bombard (**a** with)

acr|obacia *f* acrobatics. ~**obacias aéreas** aerobatics. ~**óbata** *m & f* acrobat. ~**obático** *adj* acrobatic

acta *f* minutes; (*certificado*) certificate

actitud *f* posture, position; (*fig*) attitude, position

activ|ar *vt* activate; (*acelerar*) speed up. ~**idad** *f* activity. ~**o** *adj* active. • *m* assets

acto *m* act; (*ceremonia*) ceremony. **en el ~** immediately

act|or *m* actor. ~**riz** *f* actress

actuación *f* action; (*conducta*) behaviour; (*Theat*) performance

actual *adj* present; (asunto) topical. ~**idad** *f* present; (*de asunto*) topicality. **en la ~idad** (*en este momento*) currently; (*hoy en día*) nowadays. ~**idades** *fpl* current affairs. ~**ización** *f* modernization. ~**izar** **10** *vt* modernize. ~**mente** *adv* now, at the present time

actuar **21** *vi* act. ~ **de** act as

acuarel|a *f* watercolour. ~**ista** *m & f* watercolourist

acuario *m* aquarium. **A~** Aquarius

acuartelar *vt* quarter, billet; (*mantener en cuartel*) confine to barracks

acuático *adj* aquatic

acuchillar *vt* slash; stab (persona)

acuci|ante *adj* urgent. ~**ar** *vt* urge on; (*dar prisa a*) hasten. ~**oso** *adj* keen

acudir *vi.* ~ **a** go to; (*asistir*) attend; turn up for (a una cita); (*en auxilio*) go to help

acueducto *m* aqueduct

acuerdo *m* agreement. • *vb véase* **ACORDAR**. **¡de ~!** OK! **de ~ con** in accordance with. **estar de ~** agree. **ponerse de ~** agree

acuesto *vb véase* **ACOSTAR**

acumula|dor *m* accumulator. ~**r** *vt* accumulate. ~**rse** *vpr* accumulate

acunar *vt* rock

acuñar *vt* mint, coin

acupuntura *f* acupuncture

acurrucarse **7** *vpr* curl up

acusa|do *adj* accused; (*destacado*) marked. • *m* accused. ~**r** *vt* accuse; (*mostrar*) show; (*denunciar*) denounce; acknowledge (recibo)

acuse *m.* ~ **de recibo** acknowledgement of receipt

acus|ica *m & f* **I** telltale. ~**ón** *m*

[T] telltale

acústic|a *f* acoustics. **~o** *adj* acoustic

adapta|ble *adj* adaptable. **~ción** *f* adaptation. **~dor** *m* adapter. **~r** *vt* adapt; (*ajustar*) fit. **~rse** *vpr* adapt o.s.

adecua|do *adj* suitable. **~r** *vt* adapt, make suitable

adelant|ado *adj* advanced; (niño) precocious; (reloj) fast. **por ~ado** in advance.. **~amiento** *m* advance(ment); (*Auto*) overtaking. **~ar** *vt* advance, move forward; (*acelerar*) speed up; put forward (reloj); (*Auto*) overtake. ● *vi* advance, go forward; (reloj) gain, be fast. **~arse** *vpr* advance, move forward; (reloj) gain; (*Auto*) overtake. **~e** *adv* forward. ● *int* come in!; (*¡siga!*) carry on! **más ~e** (*lugar*) further on; (*tiempo*) later on. **~o** *m* advance; (*progreso*) progress

adelgaza|miento *m* slimming. **~r** [10] *vt* make thin; lose (kilos). ● *vi* lose weight; (*adrede*) slim. **~rse** *vpr* lose weight; (*adrede*) slim

ademán *m* gesture. **en ~ de** as if to. **ademanes** *mpl* (*modales*) manners.

además *adv* besides; (*también*) also; (*lo que es más*) what's more. **~ de** besides

adentr|arse *vpr*. **~arse en** penetrate into; study thoroughly (tema etc). **~o** *adv* in(side). **~ de** (*LAm*) in(side). **mar ~o** out at sea. **tierra ~o** inland

adepto *m* supporter

aderez|ar [10] *vt* flavour (bebidas); (*condimentar*) season; dress (ensalada). **~o** *m* flavouring; (*con condimentos*) seasoning; (*para ensalada*) dressing

adeud|ar *vt* owe. **~o** *m* debit

adhe|rir [4] *vt/i* stick. **~rirse** *vpr* stick; (*fig*) follow. **~sión** *f* adhesion; (*fig*) support. **~sivo** *adj & m* adhesive

adici|ón *f* addition. **~onal** *adj* additional. **~onar** *vt* add

adicto *adj* addicted. ● *m* addict; (*seguidor*) follower

adiestra|do *adj* trained. **~miento** *m* training. **~r** *vt* train. **~rse** *vpr* practise

adinerado *adj* wealthy

adiós *int* goodbye!; (*al cruzarse con alguien*) hello!

adit|amento *m* addition; (*accesorio*) accessory. **~ivo** *m* additive

adivin|anza *f* riddle. **~ar** *vt* foretell; (*acertar*) guess. **~o** *m* fortuneteller

adjetivo *adj* adjectival. ● *m* adjective

adjudica|ción *f* award. **~r** [7] *vt* award. **~rse** *vpr* appropriate. **~tario** *m* winner of an award

adjunt|ar *vt* enclose. **~o** *adj* enclosed; (*auxiliar*) assistant. ● *m* assistant

administra|ción *f* administration; (*gestión*) management. **~dor** *m* administrator; (*gerente*) manager. **~dora** *f* administrator; manageress. **~r** *vt* administer. **~tivo** *adj* administrative

admira|ble *adj* admirable. **~ción** *f* admiration. **~dor** *m* admirer. **~r** *vt* admire; (*sorprender*) amaze. **~rse** *vpr* be amazed

admi|sibilidad *f* admissibility. **~sible** *adj* acceptable. **~sión** *f* admission; (*aceptación*) acceptance. **~tir** *vt* admit; (*aceptar*) accept

adobar *vt* (*Culin*) pickle; (*condimentar*) marinade

a

adobe *m* sun-dried brick
adobo *m* pickle; (*condimento*) marinade
adoctrinar *vt* indoctrinate
adolecer 11 *vi.* **~ de** suffer from
adolescen|cia *f* adolescence. **~te** *adj* adolescent. ● *m & f* teenager, adolescent
adonde *adv* where
adónde *adv* where?
adop|ción *f* adoption. **~tar** *vt* adopt. **~tivo** *adj* adoptive; (hijo) adopted; (patria) of adoption
adoqu|ín *m* paving stone; (*imbécil*) idiot. **~inado** *m* paving. **~inar** *vt* pave
adora|ción *f* adoration. **~r** *vt* adore
adormec|er 11 *vt* send to sleep; (*fig, calmar*) calm, soothe. **~erse** *vpr* fall asleep; (un miembro) go to sleep. **~ido** *adj* sleepy; (un miembro) numb
adormilarse *vpr* doze
adorn|ar *vt* adorn (**con, de** with). **~o** *m* decoration
adosar *vt* lean (**a** against); (*Mex, adjuntar*) to enclose
adqui|rir 4 *vt* acquire; (*comprar*) purchase. **~sición** *f* acquisition; (*compra*) purchase. **~sitivo** *adj* purchasing
adrede *adv* on purpose
adrenalina *f* adrenalin
aduan|a *f* customs. **~ero** *adj* customs. ● *m* customs officer
aducir 47 *vt* allege
adueñarse *vpr* take possession
adul|ación *f* flattery. **~ador** *adj* flattering. ● *m* flatterer. **~ar** *vt* flatter
ad|ulterar *vt* adulterate. **~ulterio** *m* adultery
adulto *adj & m* adult, grown-up
advenedizo *adj & m* upstart
advenimiento *m* advent, arrival; (*subida al trono*) accession
adverbio *m* adverb
advers|ario *m* adversary. **~idad** *f* adversity. **~o** *adj* adverse, unfavourable
advert|encia *f* warning. **~ir** 4 *vt* warn; (*notar*) notice
adviento *m* Advent
adyacente *adj* adjacent
aéreo *adj* air; (foto) aerial; (ferrocarril) overhead
aeróbico *adj* aerobic
aerodeslizador *m* hovercraft
aero|ligero *m* microlight. **~lito** *m* meteorite. **~moza** *f* (*LAm*) flight attendant. **~puerto** *m* airport. **~sol** *m* aerosol
afab|ilidad *f* affability. **~le** *adj* affable
afamado *adj* famous
af|án *m* hard work; (*deseo*) desire. **~anador** *m* (*Mex*) cleaner. **~anar** *vt* ✖ pinch 🅸. **~anarse** *vpr* strive (**en, por** to)
afear *vt* disfigure, make ugly; (*censurar*) censure
afecta|ción *f* affectation. **~do** *adj* affected. **~r** *vt* affect
afect|ivo *adj* sensitive. **~o** *m* (*cariño*) affection. ● *a.* **~o a** attached to. **~uoso** *adj* affectionate. **con un ~uoso saludo** (*en cartas*) with kind regards. **suyo ~ísimo** (*en cartas*) yours sincerely
afeita|do *m* shave. **~dora** *f* electric razor. **~r** *vt* shave. **~rse** *vpr* shave, have a shave
afeminado *adj* effeminate. ● *m* effeminate person
aferrar *vt* grasp. **~se** *vpr* to

cling (**a** to)

afianza|miento *m* (*refuerzo*) strengthening; (*garantía*) guarantee. **~rse** [10] *vpr* become established

afiche *m* (*LAm*) poster

afici|ón *f* liking; (*conjunto de aficionados*) fans. **por ~ón** as a hobby. **~onado** *adj* keen (**a** on), fond (**a** of). • *m* fan. **~onar** *vt* make fond. **~onarse** *vpr* take a liking to

afila|do *adj* sharp. **~dor** *m* knife-grinder. **~r** *vt* sharpen

afilia|ción *f* affiliation. **~do** *adj* affiliated. **~rse** *vpr* become a member (**a** of)

afín *adj* similar; (*contiguo*) adjacent; (personas) related

afina|ción *f* (*Auto, Mus*) tuning. **~do** *adj* (*Mus*) in tune. **~dor** *m* tuner. **~r** *vt* (*afilar*) sharpen; (*Auto, Mus*) tune. **~rse** *vpr* become thinner

afincarse [7] *vpr* settle

afinidad *f* affinity; (*parentesco*) relationship by marriage

afirma|ción *f* affirmation. **~r** *vt* make firm; (*asentir*) affirm. **~rse** *vpr* steady o.s. **~tivo** *adj* affirmative

aflicción *f* affliction

afligi|do *adj* distressed. **~r** [14] *vt* distress. **~rse** *vpr* distress o.s.

aflojar *vt* loosen; (*relajar*) ease. • *vi* let up. **~se** *vpr* loosen

aflu|encia *f* flow. **~ente** *adj* flowing. • *m* tributary. **~ir** [17] *vi* flow (**a** into)

afónico *adj* hoarse

aforismo *m* aphorism

aforo *m* capacity

afortunado *adj* fortunate, lucky

afrancesado *adj* Frenchified

afrenta *f* insult; (*vergüenza*) disgrace

África *f* Africa. **~ del Sur** South Africa

africano *adj & m* African

afrodisíaco *adj & m* aphrodisiac

afrontar *vt* bring face to face; (*enfrentar*) face, confront

afuera *adv* out(side) **¡~!** out of the way! **~ de** (*LAm*) outside. **~s** *fpl* outskirts

agachar *vt* lower. **~se** *vpr* bend over

agalla *f* (*de los peces*) gill. **~s** *fpl* (*fig*) guts

agarradera *f* (*LAm*) handle

agarr|ado *adj* (*fig, fam*) mean. **~ar** *vt* grasp; (*esp LAm*) take; (*LAm, pillar*) catch. **~arse** *vpr* hold on; (*fam, reñirse*) have a fight. **~ón** *m* tug; (*LAm, riña*) row

agarrotar *vt* tie tightly; (el frío) stiffen; garotte (un reo). **~se** *vpr* go stiff; (*Auto*) seize up

agasaj|ado *m* guest of honour. **~ar** *vt* look after well. **~o** *m* good treatment

agazaparse *vpr* crouch

agencia *f* agency. **~ de viajes** travel agency. **~ inmobiliaria** estate agency (*Brit*), real estate agency (*Amer*). **~rse** *vpr* find (out) for o.s.

agenda *f* diary (*Brit*), appointment book (*Amer*); (*programa*) agenda

agente *m* agent; (*de policía*) policeman. • *f* agent; (*de policía*) policewoman. **~ de aduanas** customs officer. **~ de bolsa** stockbroker

ágil *adj* agile

agili|dad *f* agility. **~zación** *f* speeding up. **~zar** *vt* speed up

agita|ción *f* waving; (*de un lí-*

quido) stirring; (*intranquilidad*) agitation. **~do** *adj* (el mar) rough; (*fig*) agitated. **~dor** *m* (*Pol*) agitator

agitar *vt* wave; shake (botellas etc); stir (líquidos); (*fig*) stir up. **~se** *vpr* wave; (el mar) get rough; (*fig*) get excited

aglomera|ción *f* agglomeration; (*de tráfico*) traffic jam. **~r** *vt* amass. **~rse** *vpr* form a crowd

agnóstico *adj & m* agnostic

agobi|ante *adj* (trabajo) exhausting; (calor) oppressive. **~ar** *vt* weigh down; (*fig, abrumar*) overwhelm. **~o** *m* weight; (*cansancio*) exhaustion; (*opresión*) oppression

agolparse *vpr* crowd together

agon|ía *f* death throes; (*fig*) agony. **~izante** *adj* dying; (luz) failing. **~izar** 10 *vi* be dying

agosto *m* August. **hacer su ~** feather one's nest

agota|do *adj* exhausted; (*todo vendido*) sold out; (libro) out of print. **~dor** *adj* exhausting. **~miento** *m* exhaustion. **~r** *vt* exhaust. **~rse** *vpr* be exhausted; (existencias) sell out; (libro) go out of print

agracia|do *adj* attractive; (*que tiene suerte*) lucky. **~r** *vt* make attractive

agrada|ble *adj* pleasant, nice. **~r** *vt/i* please. **esto me ~** I like this

agradec|er 11 *vt* thank (persona); be grateful for (cosa). **~ido** *adj* grateful. **¡muy ~ido!** thanks a lot! **~imiento** *m* gratitude

agrado *m* pleasure; (*amabilidad*) friendliness

agrandar *vt* enlarge; (*fig*) exaggerate. **~se** *vpr* get bigger

agrario *adj* agrarian, land; (*política*) agricultural

agrava|nte *adj* aggravating. ● *f* additional problem. **~r** *vt* aggravate; (*aumentar el peso*) make heavier. **~rse** *vpr* get worse

agravi|ar *vt* offend; (*perjudicar*) wrong. **~o** *m* offence

agredir 24 *vt* attack. **~ de palabra** insult

agrega|do *m* aggregate; (*diplomático*) attaché. **~r** 12 *vt* add; appoint (persona). **~rse** *vpr* to join

agres|ión *f* aggression; (*ataque*) attack. **~ividad** *f* aggressiveness. **~ivo** *adj* aggressive. **~or** *m* aggressor

agreste *adj* country; (terreno) rough

agriar *regular, o raramente* 20 *vt* sour. **~se** *vpr* turn sour; (*fig*) become embittered

agr|ícola *adj* agricultural. **~icultor** *m* farmer. **~icultura** *f* agriculture, farming

agridulce *adj* bitter-sweet; (*Culin*) sweet-and-sour

agrietar *vt* crack. **~se** *vpr* crack; (piel) chap

agrio *adj* sour. **~s** *mpl* citrus fruits

agro|nomía *f* agronomy. **~pecuario** *adj* farming

agrupa|ción *f* group; (*acción*) grouping. **~r** *vt* group. **~rse** *vpr* form a group

agruras *fpl* (*Mex*) heartburn

agua *f* water; (*lluvia*) rain; (*marea*) tide; (*vertiente del tejado*) slope. **~ abajo** downstream. **~ arriba** upstream. **~ bendita** holy water. **~ corriente** running water. **~ de colonia** eau de cologne. **~ dulce** fresh water. **~ mineral con gas** fizzy mineral water. **~ mineral sin gas** still mineral water. **~ potable**

drinking water. ~ **salada** salt water. **hacer** ~ (*Naut*) leak. **se me hizo ~ la boca** (*LAm*) my mouth watered

aguacate *m* avocado pear; (*árbol*) avocado pear tree

aguacero *m* downpour, heavy shower

aguado *adj* watery; (*Mex, aburrido*) boring

agua|fiestas *m & f invar* spoil-sport, wet blanket. **~mala** *f* (*Mex*), **~mar** *m* jellyfish. **~marina** *f* aquamarine

aguant|ar *vt* put up with, bear; (*sostener*) support. ● *vi* hold out. **~arse** *vpr* restrain o.s. **~e** *m* patience; (*resistencia*) endurance

aguar 15 *vt* water down

aguardar *vt* wait for. ● *vi* wait

agua|rdiente *m* (cheap) brandy. **~rrás** *m* turpentine, turps I

agud|eza *f* sharpness; (*fig, perspicacia*) insight; (*fig, ingenio*) wit. **~izar** 10 *vt* sharpen. **~izarse** *vpr* (enfermedad) get worse. **~o** *adj* sharp; (ángulo, enfermedad) acute; (voz) high-pitched

agüero *m* omen. **ser de mal ~** be a bad omen

aguijón *m* sting; (*vara*) goad

águila *f* eagle; (*persona perspicaz*) astute person; (*Mex, de moneda*) heads. **¿~ o sol?** heads or tails?

aguileño *adj* aquiline

aguinaldo *m* Christmas box; (*LAm, paga*) Christmas bonus

aguja *f* needle; (*del reloj*) hand; (*de torre*) steeple. **~s** *fpl* (*Rail*) points

agujer|ear *vt* make holes in. **~o** *m* hole

agujetas *fpl* stiffness; (*Mex, de zapatos*) shoe laces. **tener ~** be stiff

aguzado *adj* sharp

ah *int* ah!, oh!

ahí *adv* there. ~ **nomás** (*LAm*) just there. **de ~ que** that is why. **por ~** that way; (*aproximadamente*) thereabouts

ahija|da *f* god-daughter, godchild. **~do** *m* godson, godchild. **~dos** *mpl* godchildren

ahínco *m* enthusiasm; (*empeño*) insistence

ahog|ado *adj* (*en el agua*) drowned; (*asfixiado*) suffocated. **~ar** 12 *vt* (*en el agua*) drown; (*asfixiar*) suffocate; put out (fuego). **~arse** *vpr* (*en el agua*) drown; (*asfixiarse*) suffocate. **~o** *m* breathlessness; (*fig, angustia*) distress

ahondar *vt* deepen. ● *vi* go deep. **~ en** (*fig*) examine in depth. **~se** *vpr* get deeper

ahora *adv* now; (*hace muy poco*) just now; (*dentro de poco*) very soon. **~ bien** however. **~ mismo** right now. **de ~ en adelante** from now on, in future. **por ~** for the time being

ahorcar 7 *vt* hang. **~se** *vpr* hang o.s.

ahorita *adv* (*esp LAm fam*) now. **~ mismo** right now

ahorr|ador *adj* thrifty. **~ar** *vt* save. **~arse** *vpr* save o.s. **~o** *m* saving. **~os** *mpl* savings

ahuecar 7 *vt* hollow; fluff up (colchón); deepen (la voz)

ahuizote *m* (*Mex*) scourge

ahuma|do *adj* (*Culin*) smoked; (*de colores*) smoky. **~r** *vt* (*Culin*) smoke; (*llenar de humo*) fill with smoke. ● *vi* smoke. **~rse** *vpr* become smoky; (comida) acquire a smoky taste

ahuyentar *vt* drive away; banish (pensamientos etc)

a

aimará *adj & m* Aymara. ● *m & f* Aymara indian

airado *adj* annoyed

aire *m* air; (*viento*) breeze; (*corriente*) draught; (*aspecto*) appearance; (*Mus*) tune, air. **~ acondicionado** air-conditioning. **al ~ libre** outdoors. **darse ~s** give o.s. airs. **~ar** *vt* air; (*ventilar*) ventilate; (*fig, publicar*) make public. **~arse** *vpr.* **salir para ~arse** go out for some fresh air

airoso *adj* graceful; (*exitoso*) successful

aisla|do *adj* isolated; (*Elec*) insulated. **~dor** *adj* (*Elec*) insulating. **~nte** *adj* insulating. **~r** 23 *vt* isolate; (*Elec*) insulate

ajar *vt* crumple; (*estropear*) spoil

ajedre|cista *m & f* chess-player. **~z** *m* chess

ajeno *adj* (*de otro*) someone else's; (*de otros*) other people's; (*extraño*) alien

ajetre|ado *adj* hectic, busy. **~o** *m* bustle

ají *m* (*LAm*) chilli; (*salsa*) chilli sauce

aj|illo *m* garlic. **al ~illo** cooked with garlic. **~o** *m* garlic. **~onjolí** *m* sesame

ajuar *m* furnishings; (*de novia*) trousseau; (*de bebé*) layette

ajust|ado *adj* right; (vestido) tight. **~ar** *vt* fit; (*adaptar*) adapt; (*acordar*) agree; settle (una cuenta); (*apretar*) tighten. ● *vi* fit. **~arse** *vpr* fit; (*adaptarse*) adapt o.s.; (*acordarse*) come to an agreement. **~e** *m* fitting; (*adaptación*) adjustment; (*acuerdo*) agreement; (*de una cuenta*) settlement

al = **a + el**

ala *f* wing; (*de sombrero*) brim. ● *m & f* (*deportes*) winger

alaba|nza *f* praise. **~r** *vt* praise

alacena *f* cupboard (*Brit*), closet (*Amer*)

alacrán *m* scorpion

alambr|ada *f* wire fence. **~ado** *m* (*LAm*) wire fence. **~e** *m* wire. **~e de púas** barbed wire

alameda *f* avenue; (*plantío de álamos*) poplar grove

álamo *m* poplar. **~ temblón** aspen

alarde *m* show. **hacer ~ de** boast of

alarga|do *adj* long. **~dor** *m* extension. **~r** 12 *vt* lengthen; stretch out (mano etc); (*dar*) give, pass. **~rse** *vpr* get longer

alarido *m* shriek

alarm|a *f* alarm. **~ante** *adj* alarming. **~ar** *vt* alarm, frighten. **~arse** *vpr* be alarmed. **~ista** *m & f* alarmist

alba *f* dawn

albacea *m & f* executor

albahaca *f* basil

albanés *adj & m* Albanian

Albania *f* Albania

albañil *m* builder; (*que coloca ladrillos*) bricklayer

albarán *m* delivery note

albaricoque *m* apricot. **~ro** *m* apricot tree

albedrío *m* will. **libre ~** free will

alberca *f* tank, reservoir; (*Mex, piscina*) swimming pool

alberg|ar 12 *vt* (*alojar*) put up; (vivienda) house; (*dar refugio*) shelter. **~arse** *vpr* stay; (*refugiarse*) shelter. **~ue** *m* accommodation; (*refugio*) shelter. **~ue de juventud** youth hostel

albino *adj & m* albino

albóndiga *f* meatball, rissole

albornoz *m* bathrobe

alborot|ado *adj* excited; (*aturdido*) hasty. **~ador** *adj* rowdy. • *m* trouble-maker. **~ar** *vt* disturb, upset. • *vi* make a racket. **~arse** *vpr* get excited; (el mar) get rough. **~o** *m* row, uproar

álbum *m* (*pl* **~es** *o* **~s**) album

alcachofa *f* artichoke

alcald|e *m* mayor. **~esa** *f* mayoress. **~ía** *f* mayoralty; (*oficina*) mayor's office

alcance *m* reach; (*de arma, telescopio etc*) range; (*déficit*) deficit

alcancía *f* money-box; (*LAm, de niño*) piggy bank

alcantarilla *f* sewer; (*boca*) drain

alcanzar **10** *vt* (*llegar a*) catch up; (*coger*) reach; catch (un autobús); (bala etc) strike, hit. • *vi* reach; (*ser suficiente*) be enough. **~ a** manage

alcaparra *f* caper

alcázar *m* fortress

alcoba *f* bedroom

alcoh|ol *m* alcohol. **~ol desnaturalizado** methylated spirits, meths. **~ólico** *adj & m* alcoholic. **~olímetro** *m* Breathalyser . **~olismo** *m* alcoholism

alcornoque *m* cork-oak; (*persona torpe*) idiot

aldaba *f* door-knocker

aldea *f* village. **~no** *adj* village. • *m* villager

alea|ción *f* alloy. **~r** *vt* alloy

aleatorio *adj* uncertain

aleccionar *vt* instruct

aledaños *mpl* outskirts

alega|ción *f* allegation; (*LAm, disputa*) argument. **~r** **12** *vt* claim; (*Jurid*) plead. • *vi* (*LAm*) argue. **~ta** *f* (*Mex*) argument. **~to** *m* plea

alegoría *f* allegory

alegr|ar *vt* make happy; (*avivar*) brighten up. **~arse** *vpr* be happy; (*emborracharse*) get merry. **~e** *adj* happy; (*achispado*) merry, tight. **~ía** *f* happiness

aleja|do *adj* distant. **~miento** *m* removal; (*entre personas*) estrangement; (*distancia*) distance. **~r** *vt* remove; (*ahuyentar*) get rid of; (*fig, apartar*) separate. **~rse** *vpr* move away

alemán *adj & m* German

Alemania *f* Germany. **~ Occidental** (*historia*) West Germany. **~ Oriental** (*historia*) East Germany

alenta|dor *adj* encouraging. **~r** **1** *vt* encourage. • *vi* breathe

alerce *m* larch

al|ergia *f* allergy. **~érgico** *adj* allergic

alero *m* (*del tejado*) eaves

alerta *adj* alert. **¡~!** look out! **estar ~** be alert; (*en guardia*) be on the alert. **~r** *vt* alert

aleta *f* wing; (*de pez*) fin

aletarga|do *adj* lethargic. **~r** **12** *vt* make lethargic. **~rse** *vpr* become lethargic

alet|azo *m* (*de un ave*) flap of the wings; (*de un pez*) flick of the fin. **~ear** *vi* flap its wings, flutter

alevosía *f* treachery

alfab|ético *adj* alphabetical. **~etizar** **10** *vt* alphabetize; teach to read and write. **~eto** *m* alphabet. **~eto Morse** Morse code

alfalfa *f* alfalfa

alfar|ería *m* pottery. **~ero** *m* potter

alféizar *m* (window)sill

alférez *m* second lieutenant

alfil *m* (*en ajedrez*) bishop

a

alfile|r *m* pin. **~tero** *m* pincushion; (*estuche*) pin-case

alfombr|a *f* (*grande*) carpet; (*pequeña*) rug, mat. **~ado** *adj* (*LAm*) carpeted. **~ar** *vt* carpet. **~illa** *f* rug, mat; (*Med*) type of measles

alforja *f* saddle-bag

algarabía *f* hubbub

algas *fpl* seaweed

álgebra *f* algebra

álgido *adj* (*fig*) decisive

algo *pron* something; (*en frases interrogativas, condicionales*) anything. • *adv* rather. **¿~ más?** anything else? **¿quieres tomar ~?** would you like a drink?; (*de comer*) would you like something to eat?

algod|ón *m* cotton. **~ón de azúcar** candy floss (*Brit*), cotton candy (*Amer*). **~ón hidrófilo** cotton wool. **~onero** *adj* cotton. • *m* cotton plant

alguacil *m* bailiff

alguien *pron* someone, somebody; (*en frases interrogativas, condicionales*) anyone, anybody

algún *véase* ALGUNO

alguno *adj* (*delante de nombres masculinos en singular* **algún**) some; (*en frases interrogativas, condicionales*) any; (*pospuesto al nombre en frases negativas*) at all. **no tiene idea alguna** he hasn't any idea at all. **alguna que otra vez** from time to time. **algunas veces, alguna vez** sometimes. • *pron* one; (*en plural*) some; (*alguien*) someone

alhaja *f* piece of jewellery; (*fig*) treasure. **~s** *fpl* jewellery

alharaca *f* fuss

alhelí *m* wallflower

alia|do *adj* allied. • *m* ally. **~nza** *f* alliance; (*anillo*) wedding ring. **~r** [20] *vt* combine. **~rse** *vpr* be combined; (*formar una alianza*) form an alliance

alias *adv & m* alias

alicaído *adj* (*fig, débil*) weak; (*fig, abatido*) depressed

alicates *mpl* pliers

aliciente *m* incentive; (*de un lugar*) attraction

alienado *adj* mentally ill

aliento *m* breath; (*ánimo*) courage

aligerar *vt* make lighter; (*aliviar*) alleviate, ease; (*apresurar*) quicken

alijo *m* (*de contrabando*) consignment

alimaña *f* pest. **~s** *fpl* vermin

aliment|ación *f* diet; (*acción*) feeding. **~ar** *vt* feed; (*nutrir*) nourish. • *vi* be nourishing. **~arse** *vpr* feed (**con, de** on). **~icio** *adj* nourishing. **productos** *mpl* **~icios** foodstuffs. **~o** *m* food. **~os** *mpl* (*Jurid*) alimony

alinea|ción *f* alignment; (*en deportes*) line-up. **~r** *vt* align, line up

aliñ|ar *vt* (*Culin*) season; dress (ensalada). **~o** *m* seasoning; (*para ensalada*) dressing

alioli *m* garlic mayonnaise

alisar *vt* smooth

alistar *vt* put on a list; (*Mil*) enlist. **~se** *vpr* enrol; (*Mil*) enlist; (*LAm, prepararse*) get ready

alivi|ar *vt* lighten; relieve (dolor, etc); (*arg, hurtar*) steal, pinch [!]. **~arse** *vpr* (dolor) diminish; (persona) get better. **~o** *m* relief

aljibe *m* tank

allá *adv* (over) there. **¡~ él!** that's his business! **~ fuera** out there. **~ por 1970** back in 1970. **el más ~** the beyond. **más ~** further on. **más ~ de** beyond. **por ~** that way

allana|miento *m.* ~**miento (de morada)** breaking and entering; (*LAm, por la autoridad*) raid. ~**r** *vt* level; remove (obstáculos); (*fig*) iron out (dificultades etc); break into (una casa); (*LAm, por la autoridad*) raid

allega|do *adj* close. ● *m* close friend; (*pariente*) close relative. ~**r** 12 *vt* collect

allí *adv* there; (*tiempo*) then. ~ **fuera** out there. **por** ~ that way

alma *f* soul; (*habitante*) inhabitant

almac|én *m* warehouse; (*LAm, tienda*) grocer's shop; (*de un arma*) magazine. ~**enes** *mpl* department store. ~**enaje** *m* storage; (*derechos*) storage charges. ~**enar** *vt* store; stock up with (provisiones)

almanaque *m* almanac

almeja *f* clam

almendr|a *f* almond. ~**ado** *adj* almond-shaped. ~**o** *m* almond tree

alm|íbar *m* syrup. ~**ibarar** *vt* cover in syrup

almid|ón *m* starch. ~**onado** *adj* starched; (*fig, estirado*) starchy

almirante *m* admiral

almizcle *m* musk. ~**ra** *f* muskrat

almohad|a *f* pillow. **consultar con la** ~**a** sleep on it. ~**illa** *f* small cushion. ~**ón** *m* large pillow, bolster

almorranas *fpl* haemorrhoids, piles

alm|orzar 2 & 10 *vt* (*a mediodía*) have for lunch; (*desayunar*) have for breakfast. ● *vi* (*a mediodía*) have lunch; (*desayunar*) have breakfast. ~**uerzo** *m* (*a mediodía*) lunch; (*desayuno*) breakfast

alocado *adj* scatter-brained

aloja|miento *m* accommodation. ~**r** *vt* put up. ~**rse** *vpr* stay

alondra *f* lark

alpaca *f* alpaca

alpargata *f* canvas shoe, espadrille

alpin|ismo *m* mountaineering, climbing. ~**ista** *m & f* mountaineer, climber. ~**o** *adj* Alpine

alpiste *m* birdseed

alquil|ar *vt* (*tomar en alquiler*) hire (vehículo), rent (piso, casa); (*dar en alquiler*) hire (out) (vehículo), rent (out) (piso, casa). **se alquila** to let (*Brit*), for rent (*Amer.*) ~**er** *m* (*acción — de alquilar un piso etc*) renting; (*— de alquilar un vehículo*) hiring; (*precio — por el que se alquila un piso etc*) rent; (*— por el que se alquila un vehículo*) hire charge. **de** ~**er** for hire

alquimi|a *f* alchemy. ~**sta** *m* alchemist

alquitrán *m* tar

alrededor *adv* around. ~ **de** around; (*con números*) about. ~**es** *mpl* surroundings; (*de una ciudad*) outskirts

alta *f* discharge

altaner|ía *f* (*arrogancia*) arrogance. ~**o** *adj* arrogant, haughty

altar *m* altar

altavoz *m* loudspeaker

altera|ble *adj* changeable. ~**ción** *f* change, alteration. ~**r** *vt* change, alter; (*perturbar*) disturb; (*enfadar*) anger, irritate. ~**rse** *vpr* change, alter; (*agitarse*) get upset; (*enfadarse*) get angry; (comida) go off

altercado *m* argument

altern|ar *vt/i* alternate. ~**arse** *vpr* take turns. ~**ativa** *f* alternative. ~**ativo** *adj* alternating. ~**o** *adj* alternate; (*Elec*) alternating

Alteza *f* (*título*) Highness

a

altibajos *mpl* (*de terreno*) unevenness; (*fig*) ups and downs

altiplanicie *f*, **altiplano** *m* high plateau

altisonante *adj* pompous

altitud *f* altitude

altiv|ez *f* arrogance. **~o** *adj* arrogant

alto *adj* high; (persona, edificio) tall; (voz) loud; (*fig, elevado*) lofty; (*Mus*) (nota) high(-pitched); (*Mus*) (voz, instrumento) alto; (horas) early. • *adv* high; (*de sonidos*) loud(ly). • *m* height; (*de un edificio*) top floor; (*viola*) viola; (*voz*) alto; (*parada*) stop. • *int* halt!, stop! **en lo ~ de** on the top of. **tiene 3 metros de ~** it is 3 metres high

altoparlante *m* (*esp LAm*) loudspeaker

altruis|mo *m* altruism. **~ta** *adj* altruistic. • *m & f* altruist

altura *f* height; (*Aviac, Geog*) altitude; (*de agua*) depth; (*fig, cielo*) sky. **a estas ~s** at this stage. **tiene 3 metros de ~** it is 3 metres high

alubia *f* (haricot) bean

alucinación *f* hallucination

alud *m* avalanche

aludi|do *adj* in question. **darse por ~do** take it personally. **no darse por ~do** turn a deaf ear. **~r** *vi* mention

alumbra|do *adj* lit. • *m* lighting. **~miento** *m* lighting; (*parto*) childbirth. **~r** *vt* light

aluminio *m* aluminium (*Brit*), aluminum (*Amer*)

alumno *m* pupil; (*Univ*) student

aluniza|je *m* landing on the moon. **~r** 10 *vi* land on the moon

alusi|ón *f* allusion. **~vo** *adj* allusive

alza *f* rise. **~da** *f* (*de caballo*) height; (*Jurid*) appeal. **~do** *adj* raised; (*Mex, soberbio*) vain; (precio) fixed. **~miento** *m* (*Pol*) uprising. **~r** 10 *vt* raise, lift (up); raise (precios). **~rse** *vpr* (*Pol*) rise up

ama *f* lady of the house. **~ de casa** housewife. **~ de cría** wetnurse. **~ de llaves** housekeeper

amab|ilidad *f* kindness. **~le** *adj* kind; (*simpático*) nice

amaestra|do *adj* trained. **~r** *vt* train

amag|ar 12 *vt* (*mostrar intención de*) make as if to; (*Mex, amenazar*) threaten. • *vi* threaten; (algo bueno) be in the offing. **~o** *m* threat; (*señal*) sign; (*Med*) symptom

amainar *vi* let up

amalgama *f* amalgam. **~r** *vt* amalgamate

amamantar *vt/i* breast-feed; (animal) to suckle

amanecer *m* dawn. • *vi* dawn; (persona) wake up. **al ~** at dawn, at daybreak. **~se** *vpr* (*Mex*) stay up all night

amanera|do *adj* affected. **~rse** *vpr* become affected

amansar *vt* tame; break in (un caballo); soothe (dolor etc). **~se** *vpr* calm down

amante *adj* fond. • *m & f* lover

amapola *f* poppy

amar *vt* love

amara|je *m* landing on water; (*de astronave*) splash-down. **~r** *vi* land on water; (astronave) splash down

amarg|ado *adj* embittered. **~ar** 12 *vt* make bitter; embitter (persona). **~arse** *vpr* become bitter. **~o** *adj* bitter. **~ura** *f* bitterness

amariconado *adj* [T] effeminate

amarill|ento *adj* yellowish; (tez) sallow. **~o** *adj & m* yellow

amarra|s *fpl*. **soltar las ~s** cast off. **~do** *adj* (*LAm*) mean. **~r** *vt* moor; (*esp LAm, atar*) tie. **~rse** *vpr LAm* tie up

amas|ar *vt* knead; (*acumular*) to amass. **~ijo** *m* dough; (*acción*) kneading; (*fig, fam, mezcla*) hotchpotch

amate *m* (*Mex*) fig tree

amateur *adj & m & f* amateur

amazona *f* Amazon; (*jinete*) horsewoman

ámbar *m* amber

ambici|ón *f* ambition. **~onar** *vt* aspire to. **~onar ser** have an ambition to be. **~oso** *adj* ambitious. • *m* ambitious person

ambidextro *adj* ambidextrous. • *m* ambidextrous person

ambient|ar *vt* give an atmosphere to. **~arse** *vpr* adapt o.s. **~e** *m* atmosphere; (*entorno*) environment

ambig|üedad *f* ambiguity. **~uo** *adj* ambiguous

ámbito *m* sphere; (*alcance*) scope

ambos *adj & pron* both

ambulancia *f* ambulance

ambulante *adj* travelling

ambulatorio *m* out-patients' department

amedrentar *vt* frighten, scare. **~se** *vpr* be frightened

amén *m* amen. • *int* amen! **en un decir ~** in an instant

amenaza *f* threat. **~r** 10 *vt* threaten

amen|idad *f* pleasantness. **~izar** 10 *vt* brighten up. **~o** *adj* pleasant

América *f* America. **~ Central** Central America. **~ del Norte** North America. **~ del Sur** South America. **~ Latina** Latin America

american|a *f* jacket. **~ismo** *m* Americanism. **~o** *adj* American

amerita|do *adj* (*LAm*) meritorious. **~r** *vt* (*LAm*) deserve

amerizaje *m véase* AMARAJE

ametralla|dora *f* machine-gun. **~r** *vt* machine-gun

amianto *m* asbestos

amig|a *f* friend; (*novia*) girl-friend; (*amante*) lover. **~able** *adj* friendly. **~ablemente** *adv* amicably

am|ígdala *f* tonsil. **~igdalitis** *f* tonsillitis

amigo *adj* friendly. • *m* friend; (*novio*) boyfriend; (*amante*) lover. **ser ~ de** be fond of. **ser muy ~s** be close friends

amilanar *vt* daunt. **~se** *vpr* be daunted

aminorar *vt* lessen; reduce (velocidad)

amist|ad *f* friendship. **~ades** *fpl* friends. **~oso** *adj* friendly

amn|esia *f* amnesia. **~ésico** *adj* amnesiac

amnist|ía *f* amnesty. **~iar** 20 *vt* grant an amnesty to

amo *m* master; (*dueño*) owner

amodorrarse *vpr* feel sleepy

amoldar *vt* mould; (*adaptar*) adapt; (*acomodar*) fit. **~se** *vpr* adapt

amonestar *vt* rebuke, reprimand; (*anunciar la boda*) publish the banns

amoniaco, amoníaco *m* ammonia

amontonar *vt* pile up; (*fig, acumular*) accumulate. **~se** *vpr* pile up; (gente) crowd together

a

amor *m* love. **~es** *mpl* (*relaciones amorosas*) love affairs. **~ propio** pride. **con mil ~es, de mil ~es** with (the greatest of) pleasure. **hacer el ~** make love. **por (el) ~ de Dios** for God's sake

amoratado *adj* purple; (*de frío*) blue

amordazar 10 *vt* gag; (*fig*) silence

amorfo *adj* amorphous, shapeless

amor|ío *m* affair. **~oso** *adj* loving; (cartas) love; (*LAm*), *encantador*) cute

amortajar *vt* shroud

amortigua|dor *adj* deadening. ● *m* (*Auto*) shock absorber. **~r** 15 *vt* deaden (ruido); dim (luz); cushion (golpe); tone down (color)

amortiza|ble *adj* redeemable. **~ción** *f* (*de una deuda*) repayment; (*de bono etc*) redemption. **~r** 10 *vt* repay (una deuda)

amotinar *vt* incite to riot. **~se** *vpr* rebel; (*Mil*) mutiny

ampar|ar *vt* help; (*proteger*) protect. **~arse** *vpr* seek protection; (*de la lluvia*) shelter. **~o** *m* protection; (*de la lluvia*) shelter. **al ~o de** under the protection of

amperio *m* ampere, amp 1

amplia|ción *f* extension; (*photo*) enlargement. **~r** 20 *vt* enlarge, extend; (*photo*) enlarge

amplifica|ción *f* amplification. **~dor** *m* amplifier. **~r** 7 amplify

ampli|o *adj* wide; (*espacioso*) spacious; (ropa) loose-fitting. **~tud** *f* extent; (*espaciosidad*) spaciousness; (*espacio*) space

ampolla *f* (*Med*) blister; (*de medicamento*) ampoule, phial

ampuloso *adj* pompous

amputar *vt* amputate; (*fig*) delete

amueblar *vt* furnish

amuleto *m* charm, amulet

amuralla|do *adj* walled. **~r** *vt* build a wall around

anacr|ónico *adj* anachronistic. **~onismo** *m* anachronism

anales *mpl* annals

analfabet|ismo *m* illiteracy. **~o** *adj & m* illiterate

analgésico *adj* analgesic. ● *m* painkiller

an|álisis *m invar* analysis. **~álisis de sangre** blood test. **~alista** *m & f* analyst. **~alítico** *adj* analytical. **~alizar** 10 *vt* analyze

an|alogía *f* analogy. **~álogo** *adj* analogous

anaranjado *adj* orangey

an|arquía *f* anarchy. **~árquico** *adj* anarchic. **~arquismo** *m* anarchism. **~arquista** *adj* anarchistic. ● *m & f* anarchist

anat|omía *f* anatomy. **~ómico** *adj* anatomical

anca *f* haunch; (*parte superior*) rump; (*fam, nalgas*) bottom. **en ~s** (*LAm*) on the crupper

ancestro *m* ancestor

ancho *adj* wide; (ropa) loose-fitting; (*fig*) relieved; (*demasiado grande*) too big; (*ufano*) smug. ● *m* width; (*Rail*) gauge. **~ de banda** bandwidth. **tiene 3 metros de ~** it is 3 metres wide

anchoa *f* anchovy

anchura *f* width; (*medida*) measurement

ancian|o *adj* elderly, old. ● *m* elderly man, old man. **~a** *f* elderly woman, old woman. **los ~os** old people

ancla *f* anchor. **echar ~s** drop anchor. **levar ~s** weigh anchor. **~r** *vi* anchor

andad|eras *fpl* (*Mex*) baby-walker. **~or** *m* baby-walker
Andalucía *f* Andalusia
andaluz *adj & m* Andalusian
andamio *m* platform. **~s** *mpl* scaffolding
and|anzas *fpl* adventures. **~ar** 25 *vt* (*recorrer*) cover, go. • *vi* walk; (máquina) go, work; (*estar*) be; (*moverse*) move. **~ar a caballo** (*LAm*) ride a horse. **~ar en bicicleta** (*LAm*) ride a bicycle. **¡anda!** go on!, come on! **~ar por** be about. **~arse** *vpr* (*LAm, en imperativo*) **¡andate!** go away! • *m* walk. **~ariego** *adj* fond of walking
andén *m* platform
Andes *mpl*. **los ~** the Andes
andin|o *adj* Andean. **~ismo** *m* (*LAm*) mountaineering, climbing. **~ista** *m & f* (*LAm*) mountaineer, climber
andrajo *m* rag. **~so** *adj* ragged
anduve *vb véase* ANDAR
anécdota *f* anecdote
anecdótico *adj* anecdotal
anegar 12 *vt* flood. **~se** *vpr* be flooded, flood
anejo *adj véase* ANEXO
an|emia *f* anaemia. **~émico** *adj* anaemic
anest|esia *f* anaesthesia; (*droga*) anaesthetic. **~esiar** *vt* anaesthetize. **~ésico** *adj & m* anaesthetic. **~esista** *m & f* anaesthetist
anex|ar *vt* annex. **~o** *adj* attached. • *m* annexe
anfibio *adj* amphibious. • *m* amphibian
anfiteatro *m* amphitheatre; (*en un teatro*) upper circle
anfitri|ón *m* host. **~ona** *f* hostess
ángel *m* angel; (*encanto*) charm
angelical *adj*, **angélico** *adj* angelic
angina *f*. **~ de pecho** angina (pectoris). **tener ~s** have tonsillitis
anglicano *adj & m* Anglican
angl|icismo *m* Anglicism. **~ófilo** *adj & m* Anglophile. **~ohispánico** *adj* Anglo-Spanish. **~osajón** *adj & m* Anglo-Saxon
angosto *adj* narrow
angu|ila *f* eel. **~la** *f* elver, baby eel
ángulo *m* angle; (*rincón, esquina*) corner; (*curva*) bend
angusti|a *f* anguish. **~ar** *vt* distress; (*inquietar*) worry. **~arse** *vpr* get distressed; (*inquietarse*) get worried. **~oso** *adj* anguished; (*que causa angustia*) distressing
anhel|ar *vt* (+ *nombre*) long for; (+ *verbo*) long to. **~o** *m* (*fig*) yearning
anidar *vi* nest
anill|a *f* ring. **~o** *m* ring. **~o de boda** wedding ring
ánima *f* soul
anima|ción *f* (*de personas*) life; (*de cosas*) liveliness; (*bullicio*) bustle; (*en el cine*) animation. **~do** *adj* lively; (sitio etc) busy. **~dor** *m* host. **~dora** *f* hostess; (*de un equipo*) cheerleader
animadversión *f* ill will
animal *adj* animal; (*fig, fam, torpe*) stupid. • *m* animal; (*fig, fam, idiota*) idiot; (*fig, fam, bruto*) brute
animar *vt* give life to; (*dar ánimo*) encourage; (*dar vivacidad*) liven up. **~se** *vpr* (*decidirse*) decide; (*ponerse alegre*) cheer up. **¿te animas a ir al cine?** do you feel like going to the cinema?
ánimo *m* soul; (*mente*) mind; (*valor*) courage; (*intención*) inten-

a

tion. ¡~! come on!, cheer up! **dar ~s** encourage

animos|idad *f* animosity. **~o** *adj* brave; (*resuelto*) determined

aniquilar *vt* annihilate; (*acabar con*) ruin

anís *m* aniseed; (*licor*) anisette

aniversario *m* anniversary

anoche *adv* last night, yesterday evening

anochecer 11 *vi* get dark. **anochecí en Madrid** I was in Madrid at dusk. • *m* nightfall, dusk. **al ~** at nightfall

anodino *adj* bland

an|omalía *f* anomaly. **~ómalo** *adj* anomalous

an|onimato *m* anonymity. **~ónimo** *adj* anonymous; (sociedad) limited. • *m* (*carta*) anonymous letter

anormal *adj* abnormal. • *m* & *f* 1 idiot. **~idad** *f* abnormality

anota|ción *f* (*nota*) note; (*acción de poner notas*) annotation. **~r** *vt* (*poner nota*) annotate; (*apuntar*) make a note of; (*LAm*) score (un gol)

anquilosa|miento *m* (*fig*) paralysis. **~rse** *vpr* become paralyzed

ansi|a *f* anxiety, worry; (*anhelo*) yearning. **~ar** 20 *vt* long for. **~edad** *f* anxiety. **~oso** *adj* anxious; (*deseoso*) eager

antag|ónico *adj* antagonistic. **~onismo** *m* antagonism. **~onista** *m* & *f* antagonist

antaño *adv* in days gone by

antártico *adj* & *m* Antarctic

ante *prep* in front of, before; (*frente a*) in the face of; (*en vista de*) in view of. • *m* elk; (*piel*) suede. **~anoche** *adv* the night before last. **~ayer** *adv* the day before yesterday. **~brazo** *m* forearm

antece|dente *adj* previous. • *m* antecedent. **~dentes** *mpl* history, background. **~dentes penales** criminal record. **~der** *vt* precede. **~sor** *m* predecessor; (*antepasado*) ancestor

antelación *f* (advance) notice. **con ~** in advance

antemano *adv*. **de ~** beforehand

antena *f* antenna; (*radio, TV*) aerial

antenoche *adv* (*LAm*) the night before last

anteoj|eras *fpl* blinkers. **~o** *m* telescope. **~os** *mpl* binoculars; (*LAm, gafas*) glasses, spectacles. **~os de sol** sunglasses

ante|pasados *mpl* forebears, ancestors. **~poner** 34 *vt* put in front (**a** of); (*fig*) put before, prefer. **~proyecto** *m* preliminary sketch; (*fig*) blueprint

anterior *adj* previous; (*delantero*) front. **~idad** *f*. **con ~idad** previously. **con ~idad a** prior to

antes *adv* before; (*antiguamente*) in the past; (*mejor*) rather; (*primero*) first. **~ de** before. **~ de ayer** the day before yesterday. **~ de que** + *subjuntivo* before. **~ de que llegue** before he arrives. **cuanto ~, lo ~ posible** as soon as possible

anti|aéreo *adj* anti-aircraft. **~biótico** *adj* & *m* antibiotic. **~ciclón** *m* anticyclone

anticip|ación *f*. **con ~ación** in advance. **con media hora de ~ación** half an hour early. **~ado** *adj* advance. **por ~ado** in advance. **~ar** *vt* bring forward; advance (dinero). **~arse** *vpr* be early. **~o** *m* (*dinero*) advance; (*fig*) foretaste

anti|conceptivo *adj* & *m* contraceptive. ~ **de emergencia** morning-after pill. ~**congelante** *m* antifreeze

anticua|do *adj* old-fashioned. ~**rio** *m* antique dealer

anticuerpo *m* antibody

antídoto *m* antidote

anti|estético *adj* ugly. ~**faz** *m* mask

antig|ualla *f* old relic. ~**uamente** *adv* formerly; (*hace mucho tiempo*) long ago. ~**üedad** *f* antiquity; (*objeto*) antique; (*en un empleo*) length of service. ~**uo** *adj* old; (ruinas) ancient; (mueble) antique

Antillas *fpl*. **las** ~ the West Indies

antílope *m* antelope

antinatural *adj* unnatural

antip|atía *f* dislike; (*cualidad de antipático*) unpleasantness. ~**ático** *adj* unpleasant, unfriendly

anti|semita *m & f* anti-Semite. ~**séptico** *adj & m* antiseptic. ~**social** *adj* antisocial

antítesis *f invar* antithesis

antoj|adizo *adj* capricious. ~**arse** *vpr* fancy. **se le** ~**a un caramelo** he fancies a sweet. ~**itos** *mpl* (*Mex*) snacks bought at street stands. ~**o** *m* whim; (*de embarazada*) craving

antología *f* anthology

antorcha *f* torch

ántrax *m* anthrax

antro *m* (*fig*) dump, hole. ~ **de perversión** den of iniquity

antrop|ología *f* anthropology. ~**ólogo** *m* anthropologist

anua|l *adj* annual. ~**lidad** *f* annuity. ~**lmente** *adv* yearly. ~**rio** *m* yearbook

anudar *vt* tie, knot. ~**se** *vpr* tie

anula|ción *f* annulment, cancellation. ~**r** *vt* annul, cancel. • *adj* (dedo) ring. • *m* ring finger

anunci|ante *m & f* advertiser. ~**ar** *vt* announce; advertise (producto comercial); (*presagiar*) be a sign of. ~**o** *m* announcement; (*para vender algo*) advertisement, advert [I]; (*cartel*) poster

anzuelo *m* (fish)hook; (*fig*) bait. **tragar el** ~ swallow the bait

añadi|dura *f* addition. **por** ~**dura** in addition. ~**r** *vt* add

añejo *adj* (vino) mature

añicos *mpl*. **hacer(se)** ~ smash to pieces

año *m* year. ~ **bisiesto** leap year. ~ **nuevo** new year. **al** ~ per year, a year. **¿cuántos** ~**s tiene?** how old is he? **tiene 5** ~**s** he's 5 (years old). **el** ~ **pasado** last year. **el** ~ **que viene** next year. **entrado en** ~**s** elderly. **los** ~**s 60** the sixties

añora|nza *f* nostalgia. ~**r** *vt* miss

apabulla|nte *adj* overwhelming. ~**r** *vt* overwhelm

apacible *adj* gentle; (clima) mild

apacigua|r [15] *vt* pacify; (*calmar*) calm; relieve (dolor etc). ~**rse** *vpr* calm down

apadrinar *vt* sponsor; be godfather to (a un niño)

apag|ado *adj* extinguished; (color) dull; (aparato eléctrico, luz) off; (persona) lifeless; (sonido) muffled. ~**ar** [12] *vt* put out (fuego, incendio); turn off, switch off (aparato eléctrico, luz); quench (sed); muffle (sonido). ~**arse** *vpr* (fuego, luz) go out; (sonido) die away. ~**ón** *m* blackout

apalabrar *vt* make a verbal agreement; (*contratar*) engage

apalear *vt* winnow (grano); beat

(alfombra, frutos, persona)

apantallar *vt* (*Mex*) impress

apañar *vt* (*arreglar*) fix; (*remendar*) mend; (*agarrar*) grasp, take hold of. **~se** *vpr* get along, manage

apapachar *vt* (*Mex*) cuddle

aparador *m* sideboard; (*Mex, de tienda*) shop window

aparato *m* apparatus; (*máquina*) machine; (*doméstico*) appliance; (*teléfono*) telephone; (*radio, TV*) set; (*ostentación*) show, pomp. **~so** *adj* showy, ostentatious; (caída) spectacular

aparca|miento *m* car park (*Brit*), parking lot (*Amer*). **~r** 7 *vt/i* park

aparear *vt* mate (animales).**~se** *vpr* mate

aparecer 11 *vi* appear. **~se** *vpr* appear

aparej|ado *adj*. **llevar ~ado, traer ~ado** mean, entail. **~o** *m* (*avíos*) equipment; (*de caballo*) tack; (*de pesca*) tackle

aparent|ar *vt* (*afectar*) feign; (*parecer*) look. ● *vi* show off. **~a 20 años** she looks like she's 20. **~e** *adj* apparent

apari|ción *f* appearance; (*visión*) apparition. **~encia** *f* appearance; (*fig*) show. **guardar las ~encias** keep up appearances

apartado *adj* separated; (*aislado*) isolated. ● *m* (*de un texto*) section. **~ (de correos)** post-office box, PO box

apartamento *m* apartment, flat (*Brit*)

apart|ar *vt* separate; (*alejar*) move away; (*quitar*) remove; (*guardar*) set aside. **~arse** *vpr* leave; (*quitarse de en medio*) get out of the way; (*aislarse*) cut o.s. off. **~e** *adv* apart; (*por separado*) separately; (*además*) besides. ● *m* aside; (*párrafo*) new paragraph. **~e de** apart from. **dejar ~e** leave aside. **eso ~e** apart from that

apasiona|do *adj* passionate; (*entusiasta*) enthusiastic; (*falto de objetividad*) biased. ● *m*. **~do de** lover. **~miento** *m* passion. **~r** *vt* excite. **~rse** *vpr* be mad (**por** about); (*ser parcial*) become biased

ap|atía *f* apathy. **~ático** *adj* apathetic

apea|dero *m* (*Rail*) halt. **~rse** *vpr* get off

apechugar 12 *vi*. I **~ con** put up with

apedrear *vt* stone

apeg|ado *adj* attached (a to). **~o** *m* I attachment. **tener ~o a** be fond of

apela|ción *f* appeal. **~r** *vi* appeal; (*recurrir*) resort (a to). ● *vt* (*apodar*) call. **~tivo** *m* (nick)name

apellid|ar *vt* call. **~arse** *vpr* be called. **¿cómo te apellidas?** what's your surname? **~o** *m* surname

apelmazarse *vpr* (lana) get matted

apenar *vt* sadden; (*LAm, avergonzar*) embarrass. **~se** *vpr* be sad; (*LAm, avergonzarse*) be embarrassed

apenas *adv* hardly, scarcely; (*Mex, sólo*) only. ● *conj* (*esp LAm, en cuanto*) as soon as. **~ si** I hardly

ap|éndice *m* appendix. **~endicitis** *f* appendicitis

apergaminado *adj* (piel) wrinkled

aperitivo *m* (*bebida*) aperitif; (*comida*) appetizer

aperos *mpl* implements; (*de labranza*) agricultural equipment; (*LAm, de un caballo*) tack

apertura *f* opening
apesadumbrar *vt* upset. **~se** *vpr* sadden
apestar *vt* infect. • *vi* stink (**a** of)
apet|ecer 11 *vi.* **¿te ~ece una copa?** do you fancy a drink? do you feel like a drink?. **no me ~ece** I don't feel like it. **~ecible** *adj* attractive. **~ito** *m* appetite; (*fig*) desire. **~itoso** *adj* appetizing
apiadarse *vpr* feel sorry (**de** for)
ápice *m* (*nada, en frases negativas*) anything. **no ceder un ~** not give an inch
apilar *vt* pile up
apiñar *vt* pack in. **~se** *vpr* (personas) crowd together; (cosas) be packed tight
apio *m* celery
aplacar 7 *vt* placate; soothe (dolor)
aplanar *vt* level. **~ calles** (*LAm fam*) loaf around
aplasta|nte *adj* overwhelming. **~r** *vt* crush. **~rse** *vpr* flatten o.s.
aplau|dir *vt* clap, applaud; (*fig*) applaud. **~so** *m* applause; (*fig*) praise
aplaza|miento *m* postponement. **~r** 10 *vt* postpone; defer (pago)
aplica|ble *adj* applicable. **~ción** *f* application. **~do** *adj* (persona) diligent. **~r** 7 *vt* apply. • *vi* (*LAm, a un puesto*) apply (for). **~rse** *vpr* apply o.s.
aplom|ado *adj* composed. **~o** *m* composure
apocado *adj* timid
apocar 7 *vt* belittle (persona). **~se** *vpr* feel small
apodar *vt* nickname
apodera|do *m* representative. **~rse** *vpr* seize
apodo *m* nickname
apogeo *m* (*fig*) height
apolilla|do *adj* moth-eaten. **~rse** *vpr* get moth-eaten
apolítico *adj* non-political
apología *f* defence
apoltronarse *vpr* settle o.s. down
apoplejía *f* stroke
aporrear *vt* hit, thump; beat up (persona)
aport|ación *f* contribution. **~ar** *vt* contribute. **~e** *m* (*LAm*) contribution
aposta *adv* on purpose
apostar[1] 2 *vt/i* bet
apostar[2] *vt* station. **~se** *vpr* station o.s.
apóstol *m* apostle
apóstrofo *m* apostrophe
apoy|ar *vt* lean (**en** against); (*descansar*) rest; (*asentar*) base; (*reforzar*) support. **~arse** *vpr* lean, rest. **~o** *m* support
apreci|able *adj* appreciable; (*digno de estima*) worthy. **~ación** *f* appreciation; (*valoración*) appraisal. **~ar** *vt* value; (*estimar*) appreciate. **~o** *m* appraisal; (*fig*) esteem
apremi|ante *adj* urgent, pressing. **~ar** *vt* urge; (*obligar*) compel; (*dar prisa a*) hurry up. • *vi* be urgent. **~o** *m* urgency; (*obligación*) obligation
aprender *vt/i* learn. **~se** *vpr* learn
aprendiz *m* apprentice. **~aje** *m* learning; (*período*) apprenticeship
aprensi|ón *f* apprehension; (*miedo*) fear. **~vo** *adj* apprehensive, fearful
apresar *vt* seize; (*capturar*) capture

a

aprestar *vt* prepare. **~se** *vpr* prepare

apresura|do *adj* in a hurry; (*hecho con prisa*) hurried. **~r** *vt* hurry. **~rse** *vpr* hurry up

apret|ado *adj* tight; (*difícil*) difficult; (*tacaño*) stingy, mean. **~ar** **1** *vt* tighten; press (botón); squeeze (persona); (*comprimir*) press down. ● *vi* be too tight. **~arse** *vpr* crowd together. **~ón** *m* squeeze. **~ón de manos** handshake

aprieto *m* difficulty. **verse en un ~** be in a tight spot

aprisa *adv* quickly

aprisionar *vt* trap

aproba|ción *f* approval. **~r** **2** *vt* approve (of); pass (examen). ● *vi* pass

apropia|ción *f* appropriation. **~do** *adj* appropriate. **~rse** *vpr.* **~rse de** appropriate, take

aprovecha|ble *adj* usable. **~do** *adj* (*aplicado*) diligent; (*ingenioso*) resourceful; (*oportunista*) opportunist. **bien ~do** well spent. **~miento** *m* advantage; (*uso*) use. **~r** *vt* take advantage of; (*utilizar*) make use of. ● *vi* make the most of it. **¡que aproveche!** enjoy your meal! **~rse** *vpr.* **~rse de** take advantage of

aprovisionar *vt* provision (**con**, **de** with). **~se** *vpr* stock up

aproxima|ción *f* approximation; (*proximidad*) closeness; (*en la lotería*) consolation prize. **~damente** *adv* roughly, approximately. **~do** *adj* approximate, rough. **~r** *vt* bring near; (*fig*) bring together (personas). **~rse** *vpr* come closer, approach

apt|itud *f* suitability; (*capacidad*) ability. **~o** *adj* (*capaz*) capable; (*adecuado*) suitable

apuesta *f* bet

apuesto *m* handsome. ● *vb véase* APOSTAR [1]

apuntalar *vt* shore up

apunt|ar *vt* aim (arma); (*señalar*) point at; (*anotar*) make a note of, note down; (*inscribir*) enrol; (*en el teatro*) prompt. ● *vi* (*con un arma*) to aim (**a** at). **~arse** *vpr* put one's name down; score (triunfo, tanto etc). **~e** *m* note; (*bosquejo*) sketch. **tomar ~s** take notes

apuñalar *vt* stab

apur|ado *adj* difficult; (*sin dinero*) hard up; (*LAm, con prisa*) in a hurry. **~ar** *vt* (*acabar*) finish; drain (vaso etc); (*causar vergüenza*) embarrass; (*LAm, apresurar*) hurry. **~arse** *vpr* worry; (*LAm, apresurarse*) hurry up. **~o** *m* tight spot, difficult situation; (*vergüenza*) embarrassment; (*estrechez*) hardship, want; (*LAm, prisa*) hurry

aquejar *vt* afflict

aquel *adj* (*f* **aquella**, *mpl* **aquellos**, *fpl* **aquellas**) that; (*en plural*) those

aquél *pron* (*f* **aquélla**, *mpl* **aquéllos**, *fpl* **aquéllas**) that one; (*en plural*) those

aquello *pron* that; (*asunto*) that business

aquí *adv* here. **de ~** from here. **de ~ a 15 días** in a fortnight's time. **~ mismo** right here. **de ~ para allá** to and fro. **de ~ que** that is why. **hasta ~** until now. **por ~** around here

aquietar *vt* calm (down)

árabe *adj* & *m* & *f* Arab; (*lengua*) Arabic

Arabia *f* Arabia. **~ Saudita**, **~ Saudí** Saudi Arabia

arado *m* plough. **~r** *m* ploughman

arancel *m* tariff; (*impuesto*) duty. **~ario** *adj* tariff

arándano *m* blueberry

arandela *f* washer

araña *f* spider; (*lámpara*) chandelier. **~r** *vt* scratch

arar *vt* plough

arbitra|je *m* arbitration; (*en deportes*) refereeing. **~r** *vt/i* arbitrate; (*en fútbol etc*) referee; (*en tenis etc*) umpire

arbitr|ariedad *f* arbitrariness. **~ario** *adj* arbitrary. **~io** *m* (free) will

árbitro *m* arbitrator; (*en fútbol etc*) referee; (*en tenis etc*) umpire

árbol *m* tree; (*eje*) axle; (*palo*) mast. **~ genealógico** family tree. **~ de Navidad** Christmas tree

arbol|ado *m* trees. **~eda** *f* wood

arbusto *m* bush

arca *f* (*caja*) chest. **~ de Noé** Noah's ark

arcada *f* arcade; (*de un puente*) arch; (*náuseas*) retching

arcaico *adj* archaic

arce *m* maple (tree)

arcén *m* (*de autopista*) hard shoulder; (*de carretera*) verge

archipiélago *m* archipelago

archiv|ador *m* filing cabinet. **~ar** *vt* file (away). **~o** *m* file; (*de documentos históricos*) archives. **~o adjunto** (email) attachment

arcilla *f* clay

arco *m* arch; (*Elec, Mat*) arc; (*Mus, arma*) bow; (*LAm, en fútbol*) goal. **~ iris** rainbow

arder *vi* burn; (*LAm, escocer*) sting; (*fig, de ira*) seethe. **estar que arde** be very tense

ardid *m* trick, scheme

ardiente *adj* burning

ardilla *f* squirrel

ardor *m* heat; (*fig*) ardour; (*LAm, escozor*) smarting. **~ de estómago** heartburn

arduo *adj* arduous

área *f* area

arena *f* sand; (*en deportes*) arena; (*en los toros*) (bull)ring. **~ movediza** quicksand

arenoso *adj* sandy

arenque *m* herring. **~ ahumado** kipper

arete *m* (*LAm*) earring

Argel *m* Algiers. **~ia** *f* Algeria

Argentina *f* Argentina

argentino *adj* Argentinian, Argentine. • *m* Argentinian

argolla *f* ring. **~ de matrimonio** (*LAm*) wedding ring

arg|ot *m* slang. **~ótico** *adj* slang

argucia *f* cunning argument

argüir **19** *vt* (*probar*) prove, show; (*argumentar*) argue. • *vi* argue

argument|ación *f* argument. **~ar** *vt/i* argue. **~o** *m* argument; (*de libro, película etc*) story, plot

aria *f* aria

aridez *f* aridity, dryness

árido *adj* dry. **~s** *mpl* dry goods

Aries *m* Aries

arisco *adj* unfriendly

arist|ocracia *f* aristocracy. **~ócrata** *m & f* aristocrat. **~ocrático** *adj* aristocratic

aritmética *f* arithmetic

arma *f* arm, weapon; (*sección*) section. **~ de fuego** firearm, **~s de destrucción masiva** weapons of mass destruction. **~da** *f* navy; (*flota*) fleet. **~do** *adj* armed (**de** with). **~dura** *f* armour; (*de gafas etc*) frame; (*Tec*) framework. **~mentismo** *m* build up of arms.

a

~mento *m* arms, armaments; (*acción de armar*) armament. **~r** *vt* arm (**de** with); (*montar*) put together. **~r un lío** kick up a fuss

armario *m* cupboard; (*para ropa*) wardrobe (*Brit*), closet (*Amer*)

armatoste *m* huge great thing

armazón *m & f* frame(work)

armiño *m* ermine

armisticio *m* armistice

armonía *f* harmony

armónica *f* harmonica, mouth organ

armoni|oso *adj* harmonious. **~zar** 10 *vt* harmonize. ● *vi* harmonize; (personas) get on well (**con** with); (colores) go well (**con** with)

arn|és *m* armour. **~eses** *mpl* harness

aro *m* ring, hoop

arom|a *m* aroma; (*de flores*) scent; (*de vino*) bouquet. **~ático** *adj* aromatic

arpa *f* harp

arpía *f* harpy; (*fig*) hag

arpillera *f* sackcloth, sacking

arpón *m* harpoon

arquear *vt* arch, bend. **~se** *vpr* arch, bend

arque|ología *f* archaeology. **~ológico** *adj* archaeological. **~ólogo** *m* archaeologist

arquero *m* archer; (*LAm, en fútbol*) goalkeeper

arquitect|o *m* architect. **~ónico** *adj* architectural. **~ura** *f* architecture

arrabal *m* suburb; (*barrio pobre*) poor area. **~es** *mpl* outskirts. **~ero** *adj* suburban; (*de modales groseros*) common

arraiga|do *adj* deeply rooted. **~r** 12 *vi* take root. **~rse** *vpr* take root; (*fig*) settle

arran|car 7 *vt* pull up (planta); pull out (diente); (*arrebatar*) snatch; (*Auto*) start. ● *vi* start. **~carse** *vpr* pull out. **~que** *m* sudden start; (*Auto*) start; (*fig*) outburst

arras *fpl* security; (*en boda*) coins

arrasar *vt* level, smooth; raze to the ground (edificio etc); (*llenar*) fill to the brim. ● *vi* (*en deportes*) sweep to victory; (*en política*) win a landslide victory

arrastr|ar *vt* pull; (*por el suelo*) drag (along); give rise to (consecuencias). ● *vi* trail on the ground. **~arse** *vpr* crawl; (*humillarse*) grovel. **~e** *m* dragging; (*transporte*) haulage. **estar para el ~e** ! be done in

arre *int* gee up! **~ar** *vt* urge on

arrebat|ado *adj* (*irreflexivo*) impetuous. **~ar** *vt* snatch (away); (*fig*) win (over); captivate (corazón etc). **~arse** *vpr* get carried away. **~o** *m* (*de cólera etc*) fit; (*éxtasis*) ecstasy

arrech|ar *vt* (*LAm fam, enfurecer*) to infuriate. **~arse** *vpr* get furious. **~o** *adj* furious

arrecife *m* reef

arregl|ado *adj* neat; (*bien vestido*) well-dressed; (*LAm, amañado*) fixed. **~ar** *vt* arrange; (*poner en orden*) tidy up; sort out (asunto, problema etc); (*reparar*) mend. **~arse** *vpr* (*solucionarse*) get sorted out; (*prepararse*) get ready; (*apañarse*) manage, make do; (*ponerse de acuerdo*) come to an agreement. **~árselas** manage, get by. **~o** *m* (*incl Mus*) arrangement; (*acción de reparar*) repair; (*acuerdo*) agreement; (*solución*) solution. **con**

~o a according to

arrellanarse *vpr* settle o.s. (**en** into)

arremangar 12 *vt* roll up (mangas); tuck up (falda). **~se** *vpr* roll up one's sleeves

arremeter *vi* charge (**contra** at); (*atacar*) attack

arremolinarse *vpr* mill about; (el agua) to swirl

arrenda|dor *m* landlord. **~dora** *f* landlady. **~miento** *m* renting; (*contrato*) lease; (*precio*) rent. **~r** 1 *vt* (*dar casa en alquiler*) let; (*dar cosa en alquiler*) hire out; (*tomar en alquiler*) rent. **~tario** *m* tenant

arreos *mpl* tack

arrepenti|miento *m* repentance, regret. **~rse** 4 *vpr* (*retractarse*) to change one's mind; (*lamentarse*) be sorry. **~rse de** regret; repent of (pecados)

arrest|ar *vt* arrest, detain; (*encarcelar*) imprison. **~o** *m* arrest; (*encarcelamiento*) imprisonment

arriar 20 *vt* lower (bandera, vela)

arriba *adv* up; (*dirección*) up(wards); (*en casa*) upstairs. ● *int* up with; (*¡levántate!*) up you get!; (*¡ánimo!*) come on! **¡~ España!** long live Spain! **~ de** (*LAm*) on top of. **~ mencionado** aforementioned. **calle ~** up the street. **de ~ abajo** from top to bottom. **de 10 euros para ~** over 10 euros. **escaleras ~** upstairs. **la parte de ~** the top part. **los de ~** those at the top. **más ~** higher up

arrib|ar *vi* (barco) reach port; (*esp LAm, llegar*) arrive. **~ista** *m & f* social climber. **~o** *m* (*esp LAm*) arrival

arriero *m* muleteer

arriesga|do *adj* risky; (person) daring. **~r** 12 *vt* risk; (*aventurar*) venture. **~rse** *vpr* take a risk

arrim|ar *vt* bring close(r). **~arse** *vpr* come closer, approach

arrincona|do *adj* forgotten; (*acorralado*) cornered. **~r** *vt* put in a corner; (*perseguir*) corner (*arrumbar*) put aside. **~rse** *vpr* become a recluse

arroba *f* (*Internet*) at (@); measure of weight

arrocero *adj* rice

arrodillarse *vpr* kneel (down)

arrogan|cia *f* arrogance; (*orgullo*) pride. **~te** *adj* arrogant; (*orgulloso*) proud

arroj|ar *vt* throw; (*emitir*) give off, throw out; (*producir*) produce. ● *vi* (*esp LAm, vomitar*) throw up. **~arse** *vpr* throw o.s. **~o** *m* courage

arrollar *vt* roll (up); (*atropellar*) run over; (*vencer*) crush

arropar *vt* wrap up; (*en la cama*) tuck up. **~se** *vpr* wrap (o.s.) up

arroy|o *m* stream; (*de una calle*) gutter. **~uelo** *m* small stream

arroz *m* rice. **~ con leche** rice pudding. **~al** *m* rice field

arruga *f* (*en la piel*) wrinkle, line; (*en tela*) crease. **~r** 12 *vt* wrinkle; crumple (papel); crease (tela). **~rse** *vpr* (la piel) become wrinkled; (tela) crease, get creased

arruinar *vt* ruin; (*destruir*) destroy. **~se** *vpr* (persona) be ruined

arrullar *vt* lull to sleep. ● *vi* (palomas) coo

arrumbar *vt* put aside

arsenal *m* (*astillero*) shipyard; (*de armas*) arsenal; (*fig*) mine

arsénico *m* arsenic

arte *m* (*f en plural*) art; (*habilidad*) skill; (*astucia*) cunning. **bellas ~s** fine arts. **con ~** skilfully. **malas**

a

~s trickery. **por amor al ~** for the fun of it

artefacto *m* device

arteria *f* artery; (*fig, calle*) main road

artesan|al *adj* craft. **~ía** *f* handicrafts. **objeto** *m* **de ~ía** traditional craft object. **~o** *m* artisan, craftsman

ártico *adj* Arctic. **Á~** *m*. **el Á~** the Arctic

articula|ción *f* joint; (*pronunciación*) articulation. **~do** *adj* articulated; (lenguaje) articulate. **~r** *vt* articulate

artículo *m* article. **~s** *mpl* (*géneros*) goods. **~ de exportación** export product. **~ de fondo** editorial, leader

artífice *m & f* artist; (*creador*) architect

artifici|al *adj* artificial. **~o** *m* (*habilidad*) skill; (*dispositivo*) device; (*engaño*) trick

artiller|ía *f* artillery. **~o** *m* artilleryman, gunner

artilugio *m* gadget

artimaña *f* trick

art|ista *m & f* artist. **~ístico** *adj* artistic

artritis *f* arthritis

arveja *f* (*LAm*) pea

arzobispo *m* archbishop

as *m* ace

asa *f* handle

asado *adj* roast(ed) • *m* roast (meat), joint; (*LAm, reunión*) barbecue. **~o a la parrilla** grilled meat; (*LAm*) barbecued meat

asalariado *adj* salaried. • *m* employee

asalt|ante *m* attacker; (*de un banco*) robber. **~ar** *vt* storm (fortaleza); attack (persona); raid (banco etc); (*fig*) (duda) assail; (*fig*) (idea etc) cross one's mind. **~o** *m* attack; (*robo*) robbery; (*en boxeo*) round

asamblea *f* assembly; (*reunión*) meeting

asar *vt* roast. **~se** *vpr* be very hot. **~ a la parrilla** grill; (*LAm*) barbecue. **~ al horno** (*sin grasa*) bake; (*con grasa*) roast

asbesto *m* asbestos

ascend|encia *f* descent; (*LAm, influencia*) influence. **~ente** *adj* ascending. **~er** **1** *vt* promote. • *vi* go up, ascend; (cuenta etc) come to, amount to; (*ser ascendido*) be promoted. **~iente** *m & f* ancestor; (*influencia*) influence

ascens|ión *f* ascent; (*de grado*) promotion. **día** *m* **de la A~ión** Ascension Day. **~o** *m* ascent; (*de grado*) promotion

ascensor *m* lift (*Brit*), elevator (*Amer*). **~ista** *m & f* lift attendant (*Brit*), elevator operator (*Amer*)

asco *m* disgust. **dar ~** be disgusting; (*fig, causar enfado*) be infuriating. **estar hecho un ~** be disgusting. **me da ~** it makes me feel sick. **¡qué ~!** how disgusting! **ser un ~** be disgusting

ascua *f* ember. **estar en ~s** be on tenterhooks

asea|do *adj* clean; (*arreglado*) neat. **~r** *vt* (*lavar*) wash; (*limpiar*) clean; (*arreglar*) tidy up

asedi|ar *vt* besiege; (*fig*) pester. **~o** *m* siege

asegura|do *adj & m* insured. **~dor** *m* insurer. **~r** *vt* secure, make safe; (*decir*) assure; (*concertar un seguro*) insure; (*preservar*) safeguard**~rse** *vpr* make sure

asemejarse *vpr* be alike

asenta|do *adj* situated; (*arraigado*) established. **~r** 1 *vt* place; (*asegurar*) settle; (*anotar*) note down; (*Mex, afirmar*) state. **~rse** *vpr* settle; (*estar situado*) be situated; (*esp LAm, sentar cabeza*) settle down

asentir 4 *vi* agree (**a** to). **~ con la cabeza** nod

aseo *m* cleanliness. **~s** *mpl* toilets

asequible *adj* obtainable; (precio) reasonable; (persona) approachable

asesin|ar *vt* murder; (*Pol*) assassinate. **~ato** *m* murder; (*Pol*) assassination. **~o** *m* murderer; (*Pol*) assassin

asesor *m* adviser, consultant. **~ar** *vt* advise. **~arse** *vpr*. **~arse con** consult. **~ía** *f* consultancy; (*oficina*) consultant's office

asfalt|ado *adj* asphalt. **~ar** *vt* asphalt. **~o** *m* asphalt

asfixia *f* suffocation. **~nte** *adj* suffocating. **~r** *vt* suffocate. **~rse** *vpr* suffocate

así *adv* (*de esta manera*) like this, like that. • *adj* such. **~ ~** so-so. **~ como** just as. **~ como ~**, (*LAm*) **~ nomás** just like that. **~ ... como** both ... and. **~ pues** so. **~ que** so; (*en cuanto*) as soon as. **~ sea** so be it. **~ y todo** even so. **aun ~** even so. **¿no es ~?** isn't that right? **si es ~** if that is the case. **y ~ (sucesivamente)** and so on

Asia *f* Asia

asiático *adj* & *m* Asian

asidero *m* handle; (*fig, pretexto*) excuse

asidu|amente *adv* regularly. **~o** *adj* & *m* regular

asiento *m* seat; (*en contabilidad*) entry. **~ delantero** front seat. **~ trasero** back seat

asignar *vt* assign; allot (porción, tiempo etc)

asignatura *f* subject. **~ pendiente** (*en enseñanza*) failed subject; (*fig*) matter still to be resolved

asil|ado *m* inmate; (*Pol*) refugee. **~o** *m* asylum; (*fig*) shelter; (*de ancianos etc*) home. **pedir ~o político** ask for political asylum

asimétrico *adj* asymmetrical

asimila|ción *f* assimilation. **~r** *vt* assimilate

asimismo *adv* also; (*igualmente*) in the same way, likewise

asir 45 *vt* grasp

asist|encia *f* attendance; (*gente*) people (present); (*en un teatro etc*) audience; (*ayuda*) assistance. **~encia médica** medical care. **~enta** *f* (*mujer de la limpieza*) charwoman. **~ente** *m* & *f* assistant. **~ente social** social worker. **~ido** *adj* assisted. **~ir** *vt* assist, help. • *vi*. **~ir a** attend, be present at

asm|a *f* asthma. **~ático** *adj* & *m* asthmatic

asno *m* donkey; (*fig*) ass

asocia|ción *f* association; (*Com*) partnership. **~do** *adj* associated; (socio) associate. • *m* associate. **~r** *vt* associate; (*Com*) take into partnership. **~rse** *vpr* associate; (*Com*) become a partner

asolar 1 *vt* devastate

asomar *vt* show. • *vi* appear, show. **~se** *vpr* (persona) lean out (**a, por** of); (cosa) appear

asombr|ar *vt* (*pasmar*) amaze; (*sorprender*) surprise. **~arse** *vpr* be amazed; (*sorprenderse*) be surprised. **~o** *m* amazement, surprise.

~**oso** *adj* amazing, astonishing

asomo *m* sign. **ni por ~** by no means

aspa *f* cross, X-shape; (*de molino*) (windmill) sail. **en ~** X-shaped

aspaviento *m* show, fuss. **~s** *mpl* gestures. hacer ~s make a big fuss

aspecto *m* look, appearance; (*fig*) aspect

aspereza *f* roughness; (*de sabor etc*) sourness

áspero *adj* rough; (sabor etc) bitter

aspersión *f* sprinkling

aspiración *f* breath; (*deseo*) ambition

aspirador *m*, **aspiradora** *f* vacuum cleaner

aspira|nte *m & f* candidate. **~r** *vt* breathe in; (máquina) suck up. ● *vi* breathe in; (máquina) suck. **~r a** aspire to

aspirina *f* aspirin

asquear *vt* sicken. ● *vi* be sickening. **~se** *vpr* be disgusted

asqueroso *adj* disgusting

asta *f* spear; (*de la bandera*) flagpole; (*cuerno*) horn. **a media ~** at half-mast. **~bandera** *f* (*Mex*) flagpole

asterisco *m* asterisk

astilla *f* splinter. **~s** *fpl* firewood

astillero *m* shipyard

astringente *adj & m* astringent

astr|o *m* star. **~ología** *f* astrology. **~ólogo** *m* astrologer. **~onauta** *m & f* astronaut. **~onave** *f* spaceship. **~onomía** *f* astronomy. **~ónomo** *m* astronomer

astu|cia *f* cleverness; (*ardid*) cunning trick. **~to** *adj* astute; (*taimado*) cunning

asumir *vt* assume

asunción *f* assumption. **la A~** the Assumption

asunto *m* (*cuestión*) matter; (*de una novela*) plot; (*negocio*) business. **~s** *mpl* **exteriores** foreign affairs. **el ~ es que** the fact is that

asusta|dizo *adj* easily frightened. **~r** *vt* frighten. **~rse** *vpr* be frightened

ataca|nte *m & f* attacker. **~r** **7** *vt* attack

atad|o *adj* tied. ● *m* bundle. **~ura** *f* tie

ataj|ar *vi* take a short cut; (*Mex, en tenis*) pick up the balls. ● *vt* (*LAm, agarrar*) catch. **~o** *m* short cut

atañer **22** *vt* concern

ataque *m* attack; (*Med*) fit, attack. **~ al corazón** heart attack. **~ de nervios** fit of hysterics

atar *vt* tie. **~se** *vpr* tie up

atarantar *vt* (*LAm*) fluster. **~se** *vpr* (*LAm*) get flustered

atardecer **11** *vi* get dark. ● *m* dusk. **al ~** at dusk

atareado *adj* busy

atasc|ar **7** *vt* block; (*fig*) hinder. **~arse** *vpr* get stuck; (tubo etc) block. **~o** *m* blockage; (*Auto*) traffic jam

ataúd *m* coffin

atav|iar **20** *vt* dress up. **~iarse** *vpr* dress up, get dressed up. **~ío** *m* dress, attire

atemorizar **10** *vt* frighten. **~se** *vpr* be frightened

atención *f* attention; (*cortesía*) courtesy, kindness; (*interés*) interest. **¡~!** look out!. **llamar la ~** attract attention, catch the eye; **prestar ~** pay attention

atender **1** *vt* attend to; (*cuidar*) look after. ● *vi* pay attention

atenerse 40 *vpr* abide (a by)
atentado *m* (*ataque*) attack; (*afrenta*) affront (**contra** to). ~ **contra la vida de uno** attempt on s.o.'s life
atentamente *adv* attentively; (*con cortesía*) politely; (*con amabilidad*) kindly. **lo saluda** ~ (*en cartas*) yours faithfully
atentar *vi*. ~ **contra** threaten. ~ **contra la vida de uno** make an attempt on s.o.'s life
atento *adj* attentive; (*cortés*) polite; (*amable*) kind
atenua|nte *adj* extenuating. ● *f* extenuating circumstance. ~**r** 21 *vt* attenuate; (*hacer menor*) diminish, lessen
ateo *adj* atheistic. ● *m* atheist
aterciopelado *adj* velvety
aterra|dor *adj* terrifying. ~**r** *vt* terrify
aterriza|je *m* landing. ~**je forzoso** emergency landing. ~**r** 10 *vt* land
aterrorizar 10 *vt* terrify
atesorar *vt* hoard; amass (fortuna)
atesta|do *adj* packed, full up. ● *m* sworn statement. ~**r** *vt* fill up, pack; (*Jurid*) testify
atestiguar 15 *vt* testify to; (*fig*) prove
atiborrar *vt* fill, stuff. ~**se** *vpr* stuff o.s.
ático *m* attic
atina|do *adj* right; (*juicioso*) wise, sensible. ~**r** *vt/i* hit upon; (*acertar*) guess right
atizar 10 *vt* poke; (*fig*) stir up
atlántico *adj* Atlantic. **el (océano) A**~ the Atlantic (Ocean)
atlas *m* atlas
atl|eta *m & f* athlete. ~**ético** *adj* athletic. ~**etismo** *m* athletics
atmósfera *f* atmosphere
atole *m* (*LAm*) boiled maize drink
atolladero *m* bog; (*fig*) tight corner
atolondra|do *adj* scatterbrained; (*aturdido*) stunned. ~**r** *vt* fluster; (*pasmar*) stun. ~**rse** *vpr* get flustered
at|ómico *adj* atomic. ~**omizador** *m* spray, atomizer
átomo *m* atom
atónito *m* amazed
atonta|do *adj* stunned; (*tonto*) stupid. ~**r** *vt* stun. ~**rse** *vpr* get confused
atorar *vt* (*esp LAm*) to block; (*Mex, sujetar*) secure. ~**se** *vpr* (*esp LAm, atragantarse*) choke; (*atascarse*) get blocked; (puerta) get jammed
atormentar *vt* torture. ~**se** *vpr* worry, torment o.s.
atornillar *vt* screw on
atosigar 12 *vt* pester
atraca|dor *m* mugger; (*de banco*) bank robber. ~**r** 7 *vt* dock; (*arrimar*) bring alongside; hold up (banco); mug (persona). ● *vi* (barco) dock
atracci|ón *f* attraction. ~**ones** *fpl* entertainment, amusements
atrac|o *m* hold-up, robbery. ~**ón** *m*. **darse un** ~**ón** stuff o.s. (**de** with)
atractivo *adj* attractive. ● *m* attraction; (*encanto*) charm
atraer 41 *vt* attract
atragantarse *vpr* choke (**con** on). **la historia se me atraganta** I can't stand history
atrancar 7 *vt* bolt (puerta). ~**se**

a

vpr get stuck

atrapar *vt* catch; (*encerrar*) trap

atrás *adv* back; (*tiempo*) previously, before. **años ~** years ago. **~ de** (*LAm*) behind. **dar un paso ~** step backwards. **hacia ~, para ~** backwards

atras|ado *adj* behind; (reloj) slow; (*con deudas*) in arrears; (país) backward. **llegar ~ado** (*esp LAm*) arrive late. **~ar** *vt* put back (reloj); (*demorar*) delay, postpone. • *vi* (reloj) be slow. **~arse** *vpr* be late; (reloj) be slow; (*quedarse atrás*) fall behind. **~o** *m* delay; (*de un reloj*) slowness; (*de un país*) backwardness. **~os** *mpl* (*Com*) arrears

atravesa|do *adj* lying across. **~r** 1 *vt* cross; (*traspasar*) go through (*poner transversalmente*) lay across. **~rse** *vpr* lie across; (*en la garganta*) get stuck, stick

atrayente *adj* attractive

atrev|erse *vpr* dare. **~erse con** tackle. **~ido** *adj* daring; (*insolente*) insolent. **~imiento** *m* daring; (*descaro*) insolence

atribu|ción *f* attribution. **~ciones** *fpl* authority. **~uir** 17 *vt* attribute; confer (función). **~irse** *vpr* claim

atribulado *adj* afflicted

atributo *m* attribute

atril *m* lectern; (*Mus*) music stand

atrocidad *f* atrocity. **¡qué ~!** how awful!

atrofiarse *vpr* atrophy

atropell|ado *adj* hasty. **~ar** *vt* knock down; (*por encima*) run over; (*empujar*) push aside; (*fig*) outrage, insult. **~arse** *vpr* rush. **~o** *m* (*Auto*) accident; (*fig*) outrage

atroz *adj* appalling; (*fig*) atrocious

atuendo *m* dress, attire

atún *m* tuna (fish)

aturdi|do *adj* bewildered; (*por golpe*) stunned. **~r** *vt* bewilder; (golpe) stun; (ruido) deafen

auda|cia *f* boldness, audacity. **~z** *adj* bold

audi|ble *adj* audible. **~ción** *f* hearing; (*prueba*) audition.**~encia** *f* audience; (*tribunal*) court; (*sesión*) hearing

auditor *m* auditor. **~io** *m* audience; (*sala*) auditorium

auge *m* peak; (*Com*) boom

augur|ar *vt* predict; (cosas) augur. **~io** *m* prediction. **con nuestros mejores ~ios para** with our best wishes for. **mal ~** bad omen

aula *f* class-room; (*Univ*) lecture room

aull|ar 23 *vi* howl. **~ido** *m* howl

aument|ar *vt* increase; magnify (imagen). • *vi* increase. **~o** *m* increase; (*de sueldo*) rise

aun *adv* even. **~ así** even so. **~ cuando** although. **más ~** even more. **ni ~** not even

aún *adv* still, yet. **~ no ha llegado** it still hasn't arrived, it hasn't arrived yet

aunar 23 *vt* join. **~se** *vpr* join together

aunque *conj* although, (even) though

aúpa *int* up! **de ~** wonderful

aureola *f* halo

auricular *m* (*de teléfono*) receiver. **~es** *mpl* headphones

aurora *f* dawn

ausen|cia *f* absence. **en ~cia de** in the absence of. **~tarse** *vpr* leave. **~te** *adj* absent. • *m & f* absentee; (*Jurid*) missing person. **~tismo** *m* (*LAm*) absenteeism

auspici|ador *m* sponsor. **~ar** *vt* sponsor. **~o** *m* sponsorship; (*signo*) omen. **bajo los ~s de** sponsored by

auster|idad *f* austerity. **~o** *adj* austere

austral *adj* southern

Australia *m* Australia

australiano *adj & m* Australian

Austria *f* Austria

austriaco, **austríaco** *adj & m* Austrian

aut|enticar 7 authenticate. **~enticidad** *f* authenticity. **~éntico** *adj* authentic

auto *m* (*Jurid*) decision; (*orden*) order; (*Auto, fam*) car. **~s** *mpl* proceedings

auto|abastecimiento *m* self-sufficiency. **~biografía** *f* autobiography

autobús *m* bus. **en ~** by bus

autocar *m* (long-distance) bus, coach (*Brit*)

autocontrol *m* self-control

autóctono *adj* indigenous

auto|determinación *f* self-determination. **~didacta** *adj* self-taught. • *m & f* self-taught person. **~escuela** *f* driving school. **~financiamiento** *m* self-financing

autógrafo *m* autograph

autómata *m* robot

autom|ático *adj* automatic. • *m* press-stud. **~atización** *f* automation

automotor *m* diesel train

autom|óvil *adj* motor. • *m* car. **~ovilismo** *m* motoring. **~ovilista** *m & f* driver, motorist

aut|onomía *f* autonomy. **~onómico** *adj*, **~ónomo** *adj* autonomous

autopista *f* motorway (*Brit*), freeway (*Amer*)

autopsia *f* autopsy

autor *m* author. **~a** *f* author(ess)

autori|dad *f* authority. **~tario** *adj* authoritarian

autoriza|ción *f* authorization. **~do** *adj* authorized, official; (*opinión etc*) authoritative. **~r** 10 *vt* authorize

auto|rretrato *m* self-portrait. **~servicio** *m* self-service restaurant. **~stop** *m* hitch-hiking. **hacer ~stop** hitch-hike

autosuficiente *adj* self-sufficient

autovía *f* dual carriageway

auxili|ar *adj* auxiliary; (*profesor*) assistant. • *m & f* assistant. • *vt* help. **~o** *m* help. **¡~o!** help! **en ~o de** in aid of. **pedir ~o** shout for help. **primeros ~os** first aid

Av. *abrev* (**Avenida**) Ave

aval *m* guarantee

avalancha *f* avalanche

avalar *vt* guarantee

aval|uar *vt* 21 (*LAm*) value. **~úo** *m* valuation

avance *m* advance; (*en el cine*) trailer. **avances** *mpl* (*Mex*) trailer

avanzar 10 *vt* move forward. **~ la pantalla** scroll up. • *vi* advance

avar|icia *f* avarice. **~icioso** *adj*, **~iento** *adj* greedy; (*tacaño*) miserly. **~o** *adj* miserly. • *m* miser

avasallar *vt* dominate

Avda. *abrev* (**Avenida**) Ave

ave *f* bird. **~ de paso** (*incl fig*) bird of passage. **~ de rapiña** bird of prey

a

AVE - Alta Velocidad Española A high-speed train service linking Madrid, Seville and Huelva via Cadiz, established in 1992 in time for the international exhibition, Expo 92 in Seville. Lines under construction include: Madrid-Barcelona, with an extension to France, and Barcelona-Valencia. An Ave service linking Madrid and Galicia is planned.

avecinarse *vpr* approach

avejentar *vt* age

avellan|a *f* hazelnut. **~o** *m* hazel (tree)

avemaría *f* Hail Mary

avena *f* oats

avenida *f* (*calle*) avenue

avenir 53 *vt* reconcile. **~se** *vpr* come to an agreement; (*entenderse*) get on well (**con** with)

aventaja|do *adj* outstanding. **~r** *vt* be ahead of; (*superar*) surpass

avent|ar 1 *vt* fan; winnow (grano etc); (*Mex, lanzar*) throw; (*Mex, empujar*) push. **~arse** *vpr* (*Mex*) throw o.s.; (*atreverse*) dare. **~ón** *m* (*Mex*) ride, lift (*Brit*)

aventur|a *f* adventure. **~a amorosa** love affair. **~ado** *adj* risky. **~ero** *adj* adventurous. • *m* adventurer

avergonzar 10 & 16 *vt* shame; (*abochornar*) embarrass. **~se** *vpr* be ashamed; (*abochornarse*) be embarrassed

aver|ía *f* (*Auto*) breakdown; (*en máquina*) failure. **~iado** *adj* broken down. **~iarse** 20 *vpr* break down

averigua|ción *f* inquiry; (*Mex, disputa*) argument. **~r** 15 *vt* find out. • *vi* (*Mex*) argue

aversión *f* aversion (**a, hacia, por** to)

avestruz *m* ostrich

avia|ción *f* aviation; (*Mil*) air force. **~dor** *m* (*piloto*) pilot

av|ícola *adj* poultry. **~icultura** *f* poultry farming

avidez *f* eagerness, greed

ávido *adj* eager, greedy

avinagra|do *adj* sour. **~rse** *vpr* go sour; (*fig*) become embittered

avi|ón *m* aeroplane (*Brit*), airplane (*Amer*); (*Mex, juego*) hopscotch. **~onazo** *m* (*Mex*) plane crash

avis|ar *vt* warn; (*informar*) notify, inform; call (médico etc). **~o** *m* warning; (*comunicación*) notice; (*LAm, anuncio, cartel*) advertisement; (*en televisión*) commercial. **estar sobre ~o** be on the alert. **sin previo ~o** without prior warning

avisp|a *f* wasp. **~ado** *adj* sharp. **~ero** *m* wasps' nest; (*fig*) mess. **~ón** *m* hornet

avistar *vt* catch sight of

avivar *vt* stoke up (fuego); brighten up (color); arouse (interés, pasión); intensify (dolor). **~se** *vpr* revive; (*animarse*) cheer up; (*LAm, despabilarse*) wise up

axila *f* armpit, axilla

axioma *m* axiom

ay *int* (*de dolor*) ouch!; (*de susto*) oh!; (*de pena*) oh dear! **¡~ de ti!** poor you!

aya *f* governess, child's nurse

ayer *adv* yesterday. • *m* past. **antes de ~** the day before yesterday. **~ por la mañana**, (*LAm*) **~ en la mañana** yesterday morning

ayuda *f* help, aid. **~ de cámara** valet. **~nta** *f*, **~nte** *m* assistant; (*Mil*) adjutant. **~r** *vt* help

ayun|ar *vi* fast. **~as** *fpl*. **estar en**

~as have had nothing to eat or drink; (*fig, fam*) be in the dark. **~o** *m* fasting

ayuntamiento *m* town council, city council; (*edificio*) town hall

azabache *m* jet

azad|a *f* hoe. **~ón** *m* (large) hoe

azafata *f* air hostess

azafate *m* (*LAm*) tray

azafrán *m* saffron

azahar *m* orange blossom; (*del limonero*) lemon blossom

azar *m* chance; (*desgracia*) misfortune. **al ~** at random. **por ~** by chance. **~es** *mpl* ups and downs

azaros|amente *adv* hazardously. **~o** *adj* hazardous, risky; (vida) eventful

azorar *vt* embarrass. **~rse** *vpr* be embarrassed

Azores *fpl*. **las ~** the Azores

azotador *m* (*Mex*) caterpillar

azot|ar *vt* whip, beat; (*Mex*, *puerta*) slam. **~e** *m* whip; (*golpe*) smack; (*fig*, *calamidad*) calamity

azotea *f* flat roof

azteca *adj* & *m* & *f* Aztec

> **Aztecas** A Náhuatl-speaking people who in the fourteenth century established a brilliant and tyrannical civilization in central and southern Mexico. Its capital was Tenochtitlán, built on reclaimed marshland, and which became Mexico City. The Aztec empire collapsed in 1521 after defeat by the Spaniards led by Hernán Cortés.

az|úcar *m* & *f* sugar. **~ucarado** *adj* sweet, sugary. **~ucarar** *vt* sweeten. **~ucarero** *m* sugar bowl

azucena *f* (white) lily

azufre *m* sulphur

azul *adj* & *m* blue. **~ado** *adj* bluish. **~ marino** navy blue

azulejo *m* tile

azuzar 10 *vt* urge on, incite

> **Año Nuevo** See ▷**NOCHEVIEJA**

Bb

bab|a *f* spittle. **~ear** *vi* drool, slobber; (niño) dribble. **caérsele la ~a a uno** be delighted. **~eo** *m* drooling; (*de un niño*) dribbling. **~ero** *m* bib

babor *m* port. **a ~** to port, on the port side

babosa *f* slug

babosada *f* (*Mex*) drivel

babos|ear *vt* slobber over; (niño) dribble over. ●*vi* (*Mex*) day dream. **~o** *adj* slimy; (*LAm*, *tonto*) silly

babucha *f* slipper

baca *f* luggage rack

bacalao *m* cod

bache *m* pothole; (*fig*) bad patch

bachillerato *m* school-leaving examination

bacteria *f* bacterium

bagaje *m*. **~ cultural** cultural knowledge; (*de un pueblo*) cultural heritage

bahía *f* bay

bail|able *adj* dance. **~aor** *m* Flamenco dancer. **~ar** *vt/i* dance. **ir a ~ar** go dancing. **~arín** *m* dancer.

b

~**arina** *f* dancer; (*de ballet*) ballerina. ~**e** *m* dance; (*actividad*) dancing. ~**e de etiqueta** ball

baja *f* drop, fall; (*Mil*) casualty. ~ **por maternidad** maternity leave. **darse de** ~ take sick leave. ~**da** *f* slope; (*acto de bajar*) descent; (*camino*) way down. ~**r** *vt* lower; (*llevar abajo*) get down; go down (escalera); bow (la cabeza). ● *vi* go down; (temperatura, precio) fall. ~**rse** *vpr* pull down (pantalones). ~**r(se) de** get out of (coche); get off (autobús, caballo, tren, bicicleta)

bajeza *f* vile deed

bajío *m* shallows; (*de arena*) sandbank; (*LAm, terreno bajo*) low-lying area

bajo *adj* low; (*de estatura*) short, small; (cabeza, ojos) lowered; (*humilde*) humble, low; (*vil*) vile, low; (voz) low; (*Mus*) deep. ● *m* lowland; (*Mus*) bass. ● *adv* quietly; (volar) low. ● *prep* under. ~ **cero** below zero. ~ **la lluvia** in the rain. **los** ~**s** (*LAm*) ground floor (*Brit*), first floor (*Amer*); **los** ~**s fondos** the underworld

bajón *m* sharp drop; (*de salud*) sudden decline

bala *f* bullet; (*de algodón etc*) bale. (*LAm, en atletismo*) shot. **como una** ~ like a shot. **lanzamiento de** ~ (*LAm*) shot put

balada *f* ballad

balan|ce *m* balance; (*documento*) balance sheet; (*resultado*) outcome. ~**cear** *vt* balance. ~**cearse** *vpr* swing. ~**ceo** *m* swinging. ~**cín** *m* rocking chair; (*de niños*) seesaw. ~**za** *f* scales; (*Com*) balance

balar *vi* bleat

balazo *m* (*disparo*) shot; (*herida*) bullet wound

balboa *f* (*unidad monetaria panameña*) balboa

balbuc|ear *vt/i* stammer; (niño) babble. ~**eo** *m* stammering; (*de niño*) babbling. ~**ir** 24 *vt/i* stammer; (niño) babble

balcón *m* balcony

balda *f* shelf

balde *m* bucket. **de** ~ free (of charge). **en** ~ in vain

baldío *adj* (terreno) waste

baldosa *f* (floor) tile; (*losa*) flagstone

bale|ar *adj* Balearic. ● **las (Islas) B**~**ares** the Balearics, the Balearic Islands. ● *vt* (*LAm*) to shoot. ~**o** *m* (*LAm, tiroteo*) shooting

balero *m* (*Mex*) cup and ball toy; (*rodamiento*) bearing

balido *m* bleat; (*varios sonidos*) bleating

balística *f* ballistics

baliza *f* (*Naut*) buoy; (*Aviac*) beacon

ballena *f* whale

ballet /ba'le/ (*pl* ~**s**) *m* ballet

balneario *m* spa; (*con playa*) seaside resort

balompié *m* soccer, football (*Brit*)

bal|ón *m* ball. ~**oncesto** *m* basketball. ~**onmano** *m* handball. ~**onvolea** *m* volleyball

balotaje *m* (*LAm*) voting

balsa *f* (*de agua*) pool; (*plataforma flotante*) raft

bálsamo *m* balsam; (*fig*) balm

i

balseros The name given to illegal immigrants who try to enter a country in small boats or on rafts. It applies particularly to Cubans who try to enter the US by sailing to

Florida and to immigrants attempting to enter Spain by crossing the Straits of Gibraltar.

baluarte *m* (*incl fig*) bastion
bambalina *f* drop curtain. **entre ~s** behind the scenes
bambole|ar *vi* sway. **~arse** *vpr* sway; (mesa etc) wobble; (barco) rock. **~o** *m* swaying; (*de mesa etc*) wobbling; (*de barco*) rocking
bambú *m* (*pl* **~es**) bamboo
banal *adj* banal. **~idad** *f* banality
banan|a *f* (*esp LAm*) banana. **~ero** *adj* banana. **~o** *m* (*LAm*) banana tree
banc|a *f* banking; (*conjunto de bancos*) banks; (*en juegos*) bank; (*LAm, asiento*) bench. **~ario** *adj* bank, banking. **~arrota** *f* bankruptcy. **hacer ~arrota**, **ir a la ~arrota** go bankrupt. **~o** *m* (*asiento*) bench; (*Com*) bank; (*bajío*) sandbank; (*de peces*) shoal
banda *f* (*incl Mus, Radio*) band; (*Mex, para el pelo*) hair band; (*raya ancha*) stripe; (*cinta ancha*) sash; (*grupo*) gang, group. **~ acha** broadband. **~ sonora** sound-track. **~da** *f* (*de pájaros*) flock; (*de peces*) shoal
bandeja *f* tray
bandejón *m* (*Mex*) central reservation (*Brit*), median strip (*Amer*)
bander|a *f* flag. **~illa** *f* banderilla. **~ear** *vt* stick the banderillas in. **~ero** *m* banderillero. **~ín** *m* pennant, small flag
bandido *m* bandit
bando *m* edict, proclamation; (*facción*) camp, side. **~s** *mpl* banns. **pasarse al otro ~** go over to the other side
bandolero *m* bandit
bandoneón *m* large accordion
banjo *m* banjo
banquero *m* banker
banquete *m* banquet; (*de boda*) wedding reception
banquillo *m* bench; (*Jurid*) dock; (*taburete*) footstool
bañ|ador *m* (*de mujer*) swimming costume; (*de hombre*) swimming trunks. **~ar** *vt* bath (niño); (*Culin, recubrir*) coat. **~arse** *vpr* go swimming, have a swim; (*en casa*) have a bath. **~era** *f* bath (tub). **~ista** *m & f* bather. **~o** *m* bath; (*en piscina, mar etc*) swim; (*cuarto*) bathroom; (*LAm, wáter*) toilet; (*bañera*) bath(tub); (*capa*) coat(ing)
baqueano (*LAm*), **baquiano** *m* guide
bar *m* bar
baraja *f* pack of cards. **~r** *vt* shuffle; juggle (cifras etc); consider (posibilidades); (*Mex, explicar*) explain
baranda, **barandilla** *f* rail; (*de escalera*) banisters
barat|a *f* (*Mex*) sale. **~ija** *f* trinket. **~illo** *m* junk shop; (*géneros*) cheap goods. **~o** *adj* cheap. ● *adv* cheap(ly)
barba *f* chin; (*pelo*) beard
barbacoa *f* barbecue; (*carne*) barbecued meat
barbari|dad *f* atrocity; (*fam, mucho*) awful lot [!]. **¡qué ~dad!** how awful! **~e** *f* barbarity; (*fig*) ignorance. **~smo** *m* barbarism
bárbaro *adj* barbaric, cruel; (*bruto*) uncouth; (*fam, estupendo*) terrific [!] ● *m* barbarian. **¡qué ~!** how marvellous!
barbear *vt* (*Mex, lisonjear*) suck up to
barbecho *m*. **en ~** fallow
barber|ía *f* barber's (shop). **~o** *m*

barber; (*Mex, adulador*) creep
barbilla *f* chin
barbitúrico *m* barbiturate
barbudo *adj* bearded
barca *f* (small) boat. **~ de pasaje** ferry. **~za** *f* barge
barcelonés *adj* of Barcelona, from Barcelona. • *m* native of Barcelona
barco *m* boat; (*navío*) ship. **~ cisterna** tanker. **~ de vapor** steamer. **~ de vela** sailing boat. **ir en ~** go by boat
barda *f* (*Mex*) wall; (*de madera*) fence
barítono *adj & m* baritone
barman *m* (*pl* ~s) barman
barniz *m* varnish; (*para loza etc*) glaze; (*fig*) veneer. **~ar** 10 *vt* varnish; glaze (loza etc)
barómetro *m* barometer
bar|ón *m* baron. **~onesa** *f* baroness
barquero *m* boatman
barquillo *m* wafer; (*Mex, de helado*) ice-cream cone
barra *f* bar; (*pan*) loaf of French bread; (*palanca*) lever; (*de arena*) sandbank; (*LAm, de hinchas*) supporters. **~ de labios** lipstick
barrabasada *f* mischief, prank
barraca *f* hut; (*vivienda pobre*) shack, shanty
barranco *m* ravine, gully; (*despeñadero*) cliff, precipice
barrer *vt* sweep; thrash (rival)
barrera *f* barrier. **~ del sonido** sound barrier
barriada *f* district; (*LAm, barrio marginal*) slum
barrial *m* (*LAm*) quagmire
barrida *f* sweep; (*LAm, redada*) police raid
barrig|a *f* belly. **~ón** *adj*, **~udo** *adj* pot-bellied
barril *m* barrel
barrio *m* district, area. **~s bajos** poor quarter, poor area. **el otro ~** (*fig, fam*) the other world. **~bajero** *adj* vulgar, common
barro *m* mud; (*arcilla*) clay; (*arcilla cocida*) earthenware
barroco *adj* Baroque. • *m* Baroque style
barrote *m* bar
bartola *f*. **tirarse a la ~** take it easy
bártulos *mpl* things. **liar los ~** pack one's bags
barullo *m* racket; (*confusión*) confusion. **a ~** galore
basar *vt* base. **~se** *vpr*. **~se en** be based on
báscula *f* scales
base *f* base; (*fig*) basis, foundation. **a ~ de** thanks to; (*mediante*) by means of; (*en una receta*) mainly consisting of. **~ de datos** database. **partiendo de la ~ de, tomando como ~** on the basis of
básico *adj* basic
basílica *f* basilica
básquetbol, **basquetbol** *m* (*LAm*) basketball

bastante

• *adjetivo/pronombre*

····➤ (*suficiente*) enough. **¿hay ~s sillas?** are there enough chairs? **ya tengo ~** I have enough already

····➤ (*mucho*) quite a lot. **vino ~ gente** quite a lot of people came. **tiene ~s amigos** he has quite a lot of friends **¿te gusta?- sí, ~** do you like it?

— yes, quite a lot

● *adverbio*

····➤ (*suficientemente*) enough. **no has estudiado ~** you haven't studied enough. **no es lo ~ inteligente** he's not clever enough (**como para** to)

····➤ **bastante** + *adjetivo/adverbio* (*modificando la intensidad*) quite, fairly. **parece ~ simpático** he looks quite friendly. **es ~ fácil de hacer** it's quite easy to do. **canta ~ bien** he sings quite well

····➤ **bastante** *con verbo* (*considerablemente*) quite a lot. **el lugar ha cambiado ~** the place has changed quite a lot

bastar *vi* be enough. **¡basta!** that's enough! **basta con decir que** suffice it to say that. **basta y sobra** that's more than enough

bastardilla *f* italics

bastardo *adj & m* bastard

bastidor *m* frame; (*Auto*) chassis. **~es** *mpl* (*en el teatro*) wings. **entre ~es** behind the scenes

basto *adj* coarse. **~s** *mpl* (*naipes*) clubs

bast|ón *m* walking stick; (*de esquí*) ski pole. **~onazo** *m* blow with a stick; (*de mando*) staff of office

basur|a *f* rubbish, garbage (*Amer*); (*en la calle*) litter. **~al** *m* (*LAm, lugar*) rubbish dump. **~ero** *m* dustman (*Brit*), garbage collector (*Amer*); (*sitio*) rubbish dump; (*Mex, recipiente*) dustbin (*Brit*), garbage can (*Amer*)

bata *f* dressing-gown; (*de médico etc*) white coat; (*esp LAm, de baño*) bathrobe

batahola *f* (*LAm*) pandemonium

batall|a *f* battle. **~a campal** pitched battle. **de ~a** everyday. **~ador** *adj* fighting. ● *m* fighter. **~ar** *vi* battle, fight. **~ón** *m* battalion.

batata *f* sweet potato

bate *m* bat. **~ador** *m* batter; (*cricket*) batsman. **~ar** *vi* bat

batería *f* battery; (*Mus*) drums. ● *m & f* drummer. **~ de cocina** kitchen utensils, pots and pans

baterista *m & f* drummer

batido *adj* beaten; (nata) whipped. ● *m* batter; (*bebida*) milk shake. **~ra** *f* (food) mixer

batir *vt* beat; break (récord); whip (nata). **~ palmas** clap. **~se** *vpr* fight

batuta *f* baton. **llevar la ~** be in command, be the boss

baúl *m* trunk

bauti|smal *adj* baptismal. **~smo** *m* baptism, christening. **~zar** 10 *vt* baptize, christen. **~zo** *m* christening

baya *f* berry

bayeta *f* cloth

bayoneta *f* bayonet

baza *f* (*naipes*) trick; (*fig*) advantage. **meter ~** interfere

bazar *m* bazaar

bazofia *f* revolting food; (*fig*) rubbish

beato *adj* blessed; (*piadoso*) devout; (*pey*) overpious

bebé *m* baby

beb|edero *m* drinking trough; (*sitio*) watering place. **~edizo** *m* potion; (*veneno*) poison. **~edor** *m* heavy drinker. **~er** *vt/i* drink. **~ida** *f* drink. **~ido** *adj* drunk

beca *f* grant, scholarship. **~do** *m* (*LAm*) scholarship holder, scholar.

~r **7** *vt* give a scholarship to. **~rio** *m* scholarship holder, scholar

b

beige /beis, beʒ/ *adj & m* beige

béisbol *m*, (*Mex*) **beisbol** *m* baseball

belén *m* crib, nativity scene

belga *adj & m & f* Belgian

Bélgica *f* Belgium

bélico *adj*, **belicoso** *adj* warlike

bell|eza *f* beauty. **~o** *adj* beautiful. **~as artes** *fpl* fine arts

bellota *f* acorn

bemol *m* flat. **tener (muchos) ~es** be difficult

bend|ecir **46** (*pero imperativo* **bendice**, *futuro, condicional y pp regulares*) *vt* bless. **~ición** *f* blessing. **~ito** *adj* blessed; (*que tiene suerte*) lucky; (*feliz*) happy

benefactor *m* benefactor

benefic|encia *f* charity. **de ~encia** charitable. **~iar** *vt* benefit. **~iarse** *vpr* benefit. **~iario** *m* beneficiary; (*de un cheque etc*) payee. **~io** *m* benefit; (*ventaja*) advantage; (*ganancia*) profit, gain. **~ioso** *adj* beneficial

benéfico *adj* beneficial; (*de beneficencia*) charitable

ben|evolencia *f* benevolence. **~évolo** *adj* benevolent

bengala *f* flare. **luz** *f* **de ~** flare

benigno *adj* kind; (*moderado*) gentle, mild; (tumor) benign

berberecho *m* cockle

berenjena *f* aubergine (*Brit*), eggplant (*Amer*)

berr|ear *vi* (animales) bellow; (niño) bawl. **~ido** *m* bellow; (*de niño*) bawling

berrinche *m* temper; (*de un niño*) tantrum

berro *m* watercress

besamel(a) *f* white sauce

bes|ar *vt* kiss. **~arse** *vpr* kiss (each other). **~o** *m* kiss

bestia *f* beast; (*bruto*) brute; (*idiota*) idiot. **~ de carga** beast of burden. **~l** *adj* bestial, animal; (*fig, fam*) terrific. **~lidad** *f* (*acción brutal*) horrid thing; (*insensatez*) stupidity

besugo *m* red bream

besuquear *vt* cover with kisses

betabel *f* (*Mex*) beetroot

betún *m* (*para el calzado*) shoe polish

biberón *m* feeding-bottle

Biblia *f* Bible

bibliografía *f* bibliography

biblioteca *f* library; (*mueble*) bookcase. **~ de consulta** reference library. **~rio** *m* librarian

bicarbonato *m* bicarbonate

bicho *m* insect, bug; (*animal*) small animal, creature. **~ raro** odd sort

bici *f* **I** bike. **~cleta** *f* bicycle. **ir en ~cleta** cycle. **~moto** (*LAm*) moped

bidé, **bidet** /bi'ðeɪ/ *m* bidet

bidón *m* drum, can

bien *adv* well; (*muy*) very, quite; (*correctamente*) right; (*de buena gana*) willingly. • *m* good; (*efectos*) property. **¡~!** fine!, OK!, good! **~... (o) ~** either... or. **¡está ~!** fine!, alright!; (*basta*) that is enough!. **más ~** rather. **¡muy ~!** good! **no ~** as soon as. **¡qué ~!** marvellous!, great! **I**. **si ~** although

bienal *adj* biennial

bien|aventurado *adj* fortunate. **~estar** *m* well-being. **~hablado** *adj* well-spoken. **~hechor** *m* benefactor. **~intencionado** *adj* well-

meaning
bienio *m* two year-period
bienvenid|a *f* welcome. **dar la ~a a uno** welcome s.o. **~o** *adj* welcome. **¡~o!** welcome!
bifurca|ción *f* junction. **~rse** 7 *vpr* fork; (*rail*) branch off
b|igamia *f* bigamy. **~ígamo** *adj* bigamous. ● *m* bigamist
bigot|e *m* moustache. **~ón** *adj* (*Mex*), **~udo** *adj* with a big moustache
bikini *m* bikini
bilingüe *adj* bilingual
billar *m* billiards
billete *m* ticket; (*de banco*) (bank) note (*Brit*), bill (*Amer*). **~ de ida y vuelta** return ticket (*Brit*), round-trip ticket (*Amer*). **~ sencillo** single ticket (*Brit*), one-way ticket (*Amer*). **~ra** *f*, **~ro** *m* wallet, billfold (*Amer*)
billón *m* billion (*Brit*), trillion (*Amer*)
bi|mensual *adj* fortnightly, twice-monthly. **~mestral** *adj* two-monthly. **~mestre** two-month period. **~motor** *adj* twin-engined. ● *m* twin-engined plane
binoculares *mpl* binoculars
biocarburante *m* biofuel
bi|ografía *f* biography. **~ográfico** *adj* biographical
bi|ología *f* biology. **~ológico** *adj* biological. **~ólogo** *m* biologist
biombo *m* folding screen
biopsia *f* biopsy
bioterrorismo *m* bioterrorism
biplaza *m* two-seater
biquini *m* bikini
birlar *vt* 🄸 steal, pinch 🄸
bis *m* encore. **¡~!** encore! **vivo en el 3 ~** I live at 3A
bisabuel|a *f* great-grandmother. **~o** *m* great-grandfather. **~os** *mpl* great-grandparents
bisagra *f* hinge
bisiesto *adj*. **año** *m* **~** leap year
bisniet|a *f* great-granddaughter. **~o** *m* great-grandson. **~os** *mpl* great-grandchildren
bisonte *m* bison
bisoño *adj* inexperienced
bisté, **bistec** *m* steak
bisturí *m* scalpel
bisutería *f* costume jewellery
bitácora *f* binnacle
bizco *adj* cross-eyed
bizcocho *m* sponge (cake)
bizquear *vi* squint
blanc|a *f* white woman; (*Mus*) minim. **~o** *adj* white; (tez) fair. ● *m* white; (*persona*) white man; (*espacio*) blank; (*objetivo*) target. **dar en el ~o** hit the mark. **dejar en ~o** leave blank. **pasar la noche en ~o** have a sleepless night. **~ura** *f* whiteness
blandir 24 *vt* brandish
bland|o *adj* soft; (carácter) weak; (*cobarde*) cowardly; (carne) tender. **~ura** *f* softness; (*de la carne*) tenderness
blanque|ar *vt* whiten; whitewash (paredes); bleach (tela); launder (dinero). ● *vi* turn white. **~o** *m* whitening; (*de dinero*) laundering
blasón *m* coat of arms
bledo *m*. **me importa un ~** I couldn't care less
blinda|je *m* armour (plating). **~r** *vt* armour(-plate)
bloc *m* (*pl* **~s**) pad
bloque *m* block; (*Pol*) bloc. **en ~** en bloc. **~ar** *vt* block; (*Mil*) blockade; (*Com*) freeze. **~o** *m* blockade; (*Com*) freezing
blusa *f* blouse

b

bob|ada *f* silly thing. **decir ~adas** talk nonsense. **~ería** *f* silly thing

bobina *f* reel; (*Elec*) coil

bobo *adj* silly, stupid. • *m* idiot, fool

boca *f* mouth; (*fig, entrada*) entrance; (*de buzón*) slot; (*de cañón*) muzzle. **~ abajo** face down. **~ arriba** face up

bocacalle *f* junction. **la primera ~ a la derecha** the first turning on the right

bocad|illo *m* (filled) roll; (*fam, comida ligera*) snack. **~o** *m* mouthful; (*mordisco*) bite; (*de caballo*) bit

boca|jarro. **a ~jarro** point-blank. **~manga** *f* cuff

bocanada *f* puff; (*de vino etc*) mouthful; (*ráfaga*) gust

bocata *f* sandwich

bocatería *f* sandwich bar

bocaza *m & f invar* big-mouth

boceto *m* sketch; (*de proyecto*) outline

bochinche *m* row; (*alboroto*) racket. **~ro** *adj* (*LAm*) rowdy

bochorno *m* sultry weather; (*fig, vergüenza*) embarrassment. **¡qué ~!** how embarrassing!. **~so** *adj* oppressive; (*fig*) embarrassing

bocina *f* horn; (*LAm, auricular*) receiver. **tocar la ~** sound one's horn. **~zo** *m* toot

boda *f* wedding

bodeg|a *f* cellar; (*de vino*) wine cellar; (*LAm, almacén*) warehouse; (*de un barco*) hold. **~ón** *m* cheap restaurant; (*pintura*) still life

bodoque *m & f* (*fam, tonto*) thick-head; (*Mex, niño*) kid

bofes *mpl* lights. **echar los ~** slog away

bofet|ada *f* slap; (*fig*) blow. **~ón** *m* punch

boga *f* (*moda*) fashion. **estar en ~** be in fashion, be in vogue. **~r** 12 *vt* row. **~vante** *m* (*crustáceo*) lobster

Bogotá *f* Bogotá

bogotano *adj* from Bogotá. • *m* native of Bogotá

bohemio *adj & m* Bohemian

bohío *m* (*LAm*) hut

boicot *m* (*pl* **~s**) boycott. **~ear** *vt* boycott. **~eo** *m* boycott. **hacer un ~** boycott

boina *f* beret

bola *f* ball; (*canica*) marble; (*mentira*) fib; (*Mex, reunión desordenada*) rowdy party; (*Mex, montón*). **una ~ de** a bunch of; (*Mex, revolución*) revolution; (*Mex, brillo*) shine

boleadoras (*LAm*) *fpl* bolas

bolear *vt* (*Mex*) polish, shine

bolera *f* bowling alley

bolero *m* (*baile, chaquetilla*) bolero; (*fig, fam, mentiroso*) liar; (*Mex, limpiabotas*) bootblack

bole|ta *f* (*LAm, de rifa*) ticket; (*Mex, de notas*) (school) report; (*Mex, electoral*) ballot paper. **~taje** *m* (*Mex*) tickets. **~tería** *f* (*LAm*) ticket office; (*de teatro, cine*) box office. **~tero** *m* (*LAm*) ticket-seller

boletín *m* bulletin; (*publicación periódica*) journal; (*de notas*) report

boleto *m* (*esp LAm*) ticket; (*Mex, de avión*) (air) ticket. **~ de ida y vuelta**, (*Mex*) **~ redondo** return ticket (*Brit*), round-trip ticket (*Amer*). **~ sencillo** single ticket (*Brit*), one-way ticket (*Amer*)

boli *m* T Biro (P), ball-point pen

boliche *m* (*juego*) bowls; (*bolera*) bowling alley

bolígrafo *m* Biro (P), ball-point pen

bolillo *m* bobbin; (*Mex, pan*) (bread) roll

bolívar *m* (*unidad monetaria venezolana*) bolívar

Bolivia *f* Bolivia

boliviano *adj* Bolivian. ● *m* Bolivian; (*unidad monetaria de Bolivia*) boliviano

boll|ería *f* baker's shop. **~o** *m* roll; (*con azúcar*) bun

bolo *m* skittle; (*Mex, en bautizo*) coins. **~s** *mpl* (*juego*) bowling

bols|a *f* bag; (*Mex, bolsillo*) pocket; (*Mex, de mujer*) handbag; (*Com*) stock exchange; (*cavidad*) cavity. **~a de agua caliente** hot-water bottle. **~illo** *m* pocket. **de ~illo** pocket. **~o** *m* (*de mujer*) handbag. **~o de mano**, **~o de viaje** (overnight) bag

bomba *f* bomb; (*máquina*) pump; (*noticia*) bombshell. **~ de aceite** (*Auto*) oil pump. **~ de agua** (*Auto*) water pump. **pasarlo ~** have a marvellous time

bombachos *mpl* baggy trousers, baggy pants (*Amer*)

bombarde|ar *vt* bombard; (*desde avión*) bomb. **~o** *m* bombardment; (*desde avión*) bombing. **~ro** *m* (*avión*) bomber

bombazo *m* explosion

bombear *vt* pump

bombero *m* fireman. **cuerpo** *m* **de ~s** fire brigade (*Brit*), fire department (*Amer*)

bombilla *f* (light) bulb; (*LAm, para mate*) pipe for drinking maté

bombín *m* pump; (*fam, sombrero*) bowler (hat) (*Brit*), derby (*Amer*)

bombo *m* (*tambor*) bass drum. **a ~ y platillos** with a lot of fuss

bomb|ón *m* chocolate; (*Mex, malvavisco*) marshmallow. **~ona** *f* gas cylinder

bonachón *adj* easygoing; (*bueno*) good-natured

bonaerense *adj* from Buenos Aires. ● *m* native of Buenos Aires

bondad *f* goodness; (*amabilidad*) kindness; (*del clima*) mildness. **tenga la ~ de** would you be kind enough to. **~oso** *adj* kind

boniato *m* sweet potato

bonito *adj* nice; (*mono*) pretty. **¡muy ~!**, **¡qué ~!** that's nice!, very nice!. ● *m* bonito

bono *m* voucher; (*título*) bond. **~ del Tesoro** government bond

boñiga *f* dung

boqueada *f* gasp. **dar la última ~** be dying

boquerón *m* anchovy

boquete *m* hole; (*brecha*) breach

boquiabierto *adj* open-mouthed; (*fig*) amazed, dumbfounded. **quedarse ~** be amazed

boquilla *f* mouthpiece; (*para cigarillos*) cigarette-holder; (*filtro de cigarillo*) tip

borbotón *m*. **hablar a borbotones** gabble. **salir a borbotones** gush out

borda|do *adj* embroidered. ● *m* embroidery. **~r** *vt* embroider

bord|e *m* edge; (*de carretera*) side; (*de plato etc*) rim; (*de un vestido*) hem. **al ~e de** on the edge of; (*fig*) on the brink of. ● *adj* (*Esp fam*) stroppy. **~ear** *vt* go round; (*fig*) border on. **~illo** *m* kerb (*Brit*), curb (*esp Amer*)

bordo. **a ~** on board

borla *f* tassel

borrach|era *f* drunkenness. **pegarse una ~era** get drunk. **~ín** *m* drunk; (*habitual*) drunkard. **~o** *adj* drunk. ● *m* drunkard. **estar ~o** be

b

drunk. **ser ~o** be a drunkard

borrador *m* rough draft; (*de contrato*) draft; (*para la pizarra*) (black)board rubber; (*goma*) eraser

borrar *vt* rub out; (*tachar*) cross out; delete (información)

borrasc|a *f* depression; (*tormenta*) storm. **~oso** *adj* stormy

borrego *m* year-old lamb; (*Mex, noticia falsa*) canard

borrico *m* donkey; (*fig, fam*) ass

borrón *m* smudge; (*de tinta*) inkblot. **~ y cuenta nueva** let's forget about it!

borroso *adj* blurred; (*fig*) vague

bos|coso *adj* wooded. **~que** *m* wood, forest

bosquej|ar *vt* sketch; outline (plan). **~o** *m* sketch; (*de plan*) outline

bosta *f* dung

bostez|ar 10 *vi* yawn. **~o** *m* yawn

bota *f* boot; (*recipiente*) wineskin

botana *f* (*Mex*) snack, appetizer

botánic|a *f* botany. **~o** *adj* botanical. ● *m* botanist

botar *vt* launch; bounce (pelota); (*esp LAm, tirar*) throw away. ● *vi* bounce

botarate *m* irresponsible person; (*esp LAm, derrochador*) spendthrift

bote *m* boat; (*de una pelota*) bounce; (*lata*) tin, can; (*vasija*) jar. **~ de la basura** (*Mex*) rubbish bin (*Brit*), trash can (*Amer*). **~ salvavidas** lifeboat. **de ~ en ~** packed

botella *f* bottle

botica *f* chemist's (shop) (*Brit*), drugstore (*Amer*). **~rio** *m* chemist (*Brit*), druggist (*Amer*)

botijo *m* earthenware jug

botín *m* half boot; (*de guerra*) booty; (*de ladrones*) haul

botiquín *m* medicine chest; (*de primeros auxilios*) first aid kit

bot|ón *m* button; (*yema*) bud; (*LAm, insignia*) badge. **~ones** *m invar* bellboy (*Brit*), bellhop (*Amer*)

bóveda *f* vault

boxe|ador *m* boxer. **~ar** *vi* box. **~o** *m* boxing

boya *f* buoy; (*corcho*) float. **~nte** *adj* buoyant

bozal *m* (*de perro etc*) muzzle; (*de caballo*) halter

bracear *vi* wave one's arms; (*nadar*) swim, crawl

bracero *m* seasonal farm labourer

braga(s) *f(pl)* panties, knickers (*Brit*)

bragueta *f* flies

bram|ar *vi* bellow. **~ido** *m* bellowing

branquia *f* gill

bras|a *f* ember. **a la ~a** grilled. **~ero** *m* brazier

brasier *m* (*Mex*) bra

Brasil *m.* **(el) ~** Brazil

brasile|ño *adj & m* Brazilian. **~ro** *adj & m* (*LAm*) Brazilian

bravío *adj* wild

brav|o *adj* fierce; (*valeroso*) brave; (mar) rough. **¡~!** *int* well done! bravo! **~ura** *f* ferocity; (*valor*) bravery

braz|a *f* fathom. **nadar a ~a** swim breast-stroke. **~ada** *f* (*en natación*) stroke. **~alete** *m* bracelet; (*brazal*) arm-band. **~o** *m* arm; (*de caballo*) foreleg; (*rama*) branch. **~o derecho** right-hand man. **del ~o** arm in arm

brea *f* tar, pitch

brebaje *m* potion; (*pej*) concoction

brecha *f* opening; (*Mil*) breach; (*Med*) gash. **~ generacional** generation gap. **estar en la ~** be in the thick of it

brega *f* struggle. **andar a la ~** work hard

breva *f* early fig

breve *adj* short. **en ~** soon, shortly. **en ~s momentos** soon. **~dad** *f* shortness

brib|ón *m* rogue, rascal. **~onada** *f* dirty trick

brida *f* bridle

brigad|a *f* squad; (*Mil*) brigade. **~ier** *m* brigadier (*Brit*), brigadier-general (*Amer*)

brill|ante *adj* bright; (*lustroso*) shiny; (persona) brilliant. ● *m* diamond. **~ar** *vi* shine; (*centellear*) sparkle. **~o** *m* shine; (*brillantez*) brilliance; (*centelleo*) sparkle. **sacar ~o** polish. **~oso** *adj* (*LAm*) shiny

brinc|ar **7** *vi* jump up and down. **~o** *m* jump. **dar un ~o, pegar un ~o** jump

brind|ar *vt* offer. ● *vi*. **~ar por** toast, drink a toast to. **~is** *m* toast

br|ío *m* energy; (*decisión*) determination. **~ioso** *adj* spirited; (*garboso*) elegant

brisa *f* breeze

británico *adj* British. ● *m* Briton, British person

brocha *f* paintbrush; (*para afeitarse*) shaving-brush

broche *m* clasp, fastener; (*joya*) brooch; (*Mex, para el pelo*) hairslide (*Brit*), barrete (*Amer*)

brocheta *f* skewer; (*plato*) kebab

brócoli *m* broccoli

brom|a *f* joke. **~a pesada** practical joke. **en ~a** in fun. **ni de ~a** no way. **~ear** *vi* joke. **~ista** *adj* fond of joking. ● *m & f* joker

bronca *f* row; (*reprensión*) telling-off; (*LAm, rabia*) foul mood. **dar ~ a uno** bug s.o.

bronce *m* bronze; (*LAm*) brass. **~ado** *adj* bronze; (*por el sol*) tanned. **~ar** *vt* tan (piel). **~arse** *vpr* get a suntan

bronquitis *f* bronchitis

brot|ar *vi* (*plantas*) sprout; (*Med*) break out; (líquido) gush forth; (lágrimas) well up. **~e** *m* shoot; (*Med*) outbreak

bruces: **de ~** face down(wards). **caer de ~** fall flat on one's face

bruj|a *f* witch. **~ería** *f* witchcraft. **~o** *m* wizard, magician. ● *adj* (*Mex*) broke

brújula *f* compass

brum|a *f* mist; (*fig*) confusion. **~oso** *adj* misty, foggy

brusco *adj* (*repentino*) sudden; (persona) brusque

Bruselas *f* Brussels

brusquedad *f* roughness; (*de movimiento*) abruptness

brut|al *adj* brutal. **~alidad** *f* brutality; (*estupidez*) stupidity. **~o** *adj* ignorant; (*tosco*) rough; (peso, sueldo) gross

bucal *adj* oral; (lesión) mouth

buce|ar *vi* dive; (*nadar*) swim under water. **~o** *m* diving; (*natación*) underwater swimming

bucle *m* ringlet

budín *m* pudding

budis|mo *m* Buddhism. **~ta** *m & f* Buddhist

buen *véase* **BUENO**

buenaventura *f* good luck; (*adivinación*) fortune

bueno *adj* (*delante de nombre mas-*

culino en singular **buen**) good; (*agradable*) nice; (tiempo) fine. ● *int* well!; (*de acuerdo*) OK!, very well! **¡buena la has hecho!** you've gone and done it now! **¡buenas noches!** good night! **¡buenas tardes!** (*antes del atardecer*) good afternoon!; (*después del atardecer*) good evening! **¡~s días!** good morning! **estar de buenas** be in a good mood. **por las buenas** willingly. **¡qué bueno!** (*LAm*) great!

Buenos Aires *m* Buenos Aires

buey *m* ox

búfalo *m* buffalo

bufanda *f* scarf

bufar *vi* snort

bufete *m* (*mesa*) writing-desk; (*despacho*) lawyer's office

buf|o *adj* comic. **~ón** *adj* comical. ● *m* buffoon; (*Historia*) jester

buhardilla *f* attic; (*ventana*) dormer window

búho *m* owl

buhonero *m* pedlar

buitre *m* vulture

bujía *f* (*Auto*) spark plug

bulbo *m* bulb

bulevar *m* avenue, boulevard

Bulgaria *f* Bulgaria

búlgaro *adj* & *m* Bulgarian

bull|a *f* noise. **~icio** *m* hubbub; (*movimiento*) bustle. **~icioso** *adj* bustling; (*ruidoso*) noisy

bullir 22 *vi* boil; (*burbujear*) bubble; (*fig*) bustle

bulto *m* (*volumen*) bulk; (*forma*) shape; (*paquete*) package; (*maleta etc*) piece of luggage; (*protuberancia*) lump

buñuelo *m* fritter

BUP *abrev* (**Bachillerato Unificado Polivalente**) secondary school education

buque *m* ship, boat

burbuj|a *f* bubble. **~ear** *vi* bubble; (vino) sparkle

burdel *m* brothel

burdo *adj* rough, coarse; (excusa) clumsy

burgu|és *adj* middle-class, bourgeois. ● *m* middle-class person. **~esía** *f* middle class, bourgeoisie

burla *f* taunt; (*broma*) joke; (*engaño*) trick. **~r** *vt* evade. **~rse** *vpr*. **~rse de** mock, make fun of

burlesco *adj* (*en literatura*) burlesque

burlón *adj* mocking

bur|ocracia *f* bureaucracy; (*Mex, funcionariado*) civil service. **~ócrata** *m & f* bureaucrat; (*Mex, funcionario*) civil servant. **~ocrático** *adj* bureaucratic; (*Mex*) (empleado) government

burro *adj* stupid; (*obstinado*) pigheaded. ● *m* donkey; (*fig*) ass

bursátil *adj* stock-exchange

bus *m* bus

busca *f* search. **a la ~ de** in search of. ● *m* beeper

buscador *m* search engine

buscapleitos *m & f invar* (*LAm*) trouble-maker

buscar 7 *vt* look for. ● *vi* look. **buscársela** ask for it; **ir a ~ a uno** fetch s.o.

búsqueda *f* search

busto *m* bust

butaca *f* armchair; (*en el teatro etc*) seat

buzo *m* diver

buzón *m* postbox (*Brit*), mailbox (*Amer*)

Cc

C/ *abrev* (**Calle**) St, Rd

cabal *adj* exact; (*completo*) complete. **no estar en sus ~es** not be in one's right mind

cabalga|dura *f* mount, horse. **~r** 12 *vt* ride. ● *vi* ride, go riding. **~ta** *f* ride; (*desfile*) procession

caballa *f* mackerel

caballerango *m* (*Mex*) groom

caballeresco *adj* gentlemanly. **literatura** *f* **caballeresca** books of chivalry

caballer|ía *f* mount, horse. **~iza** *f* stable. **~izo** *m* groom

caballero *m* gentleman; (*de orden de caballería*) knight; (*tratamiento*) sir. **~so** *adj* gentlemanly

caballete *m* (*del tejado*) ridge; (*para mesa*) trestle; (*de pintor*) easel

caballito *m* pony. **~ del diablo** dragonfly. **~ de mar** sea-horse. **~s** *mpl* (*carrusel*) merry-go-round

caballo *m* horse; (*del ajedrez*) knight; (*de la baraja española*) queen. **~ de fuerza** horsepower. **a ~** on horseback

cabaña *f* hut

cabaret /kaba're/ *m* (*pl* **~s**) night club

cabecear *vi* nod off; (*en fútbol*) head the ball; (caballo) toss its head

cabecera *f* (*de la cama*) headboard; (*de la mesa*) head; (*en un impreso*) heading

cabecilla *m* ringleader

cabello *m* hair. **~s** *mpl* hair

caber 28 *vi* fit (en into). **no cabe duda** there's no doubt

cabestr|illo *m* sling. **~o** *m* halter

cabeza *f* head; (*fig, inteligencia*) intelligence. **andar de ~** have a lot to do. **~da** *f* nod. **dar una ~da** nod off. **~zo** *m* butt; (*en fútbol*) header

cabida *f* capacity; (*extensión*) area; (*espacio*) room. **dar ~ a** have room for, accommodate

cabina *f* (*de pasajeros*) cabin; (*de pilotos*) cockpit; (*electoral*) booth; (*de camión*) cab. **~ telefónica** telephone box (*Brit*), telephone booth (*Amer*)

cabizbajo *adj* crestfallen

cable *m* cable

cabo *m* end; (*trozo*) bit; (*Mil*) corporal; (*mango*) handle; (*en geografía*) cape; (*Naut*) rope. **al ~ de** after. **de ~ a rabo** from beginning to end. **llevar a ~** carry out

cabr|a *f* goat. **~iola** *f* jump, skip. **~itilla** *f* kid. **~ito** *m* kid

cábula *m* (*Mex*) crook

cacahuate, (*Mex*) **cacahuete** *m* peanut

cacalote *m* (*Mex*) crow

cacao *m* (*planta y semillas*) cacao; (*polvo*) cocoa; (*fig*) confusion

cacarear *vt* boast about. ● *vi* (gallo) crow; (gallina) cluck

cacería *f* hunt. **ir de ~** go hunting

cacerola *f* saucepan, casserole

cacharro *m* (earthenware) pot; (*coche estropeado*) wreck; (*cosa inútil*) piece of junk; (*chisme*) thing. **~s** *mpl* pots and pans

cachear *vt* frisk

cachemir *m*, **cachemira** *f* cashmere

C

cacheo *m* frisking
cachetada *f* (*LAm*) slap
cache|te *m* slap; (*esp LAm, mejilla*) cheek. **~tear** *vt* (*LAm*) slap. **~tón** *adj* (*LAm*) chubby-cheeked
cachimba *f* pipe
cachiporra *f* club, truncheon
cachivache *m* piece of junk. **~s** *mpl* junk
cacho *m* bit, piece; (*LAm, cuerno*) horn
cachondeo *m* [F] joking, joke
cachorro *m* (*perrito*) puppy; (*de león, tigre*) cub
cachucha *f* (*Mex*) cup
caciqu|e *m* cacique, chief; (*Pol*) local political boss; (*hombre poderoso*) tyrant. **~il** *adj* despotic. **~ismo** *m* despotism
caco *m* thief
cacofonía *f* cacophony
cacto *m*, **cactus** *m invar* cactus
cada *adj invar* each, every. **~ uno** each one, everyone. **uno de ~ cinco** one in five. **~ vez más** more and more
cadáver *m* corpse
cadena *f* chain; (*TV*) channel. **~ de fabricación** production line. **~ de montañas** mountain range. **~ perpetua** life imprisonment
cadera *f* hip
cadete *m* cadet
caduc|ar [7] *vi* expire. **~idad** *f*. **fecha** *f* **de ~idad** sell-by date. **~o** *adj* outdated
cae|r [29] *vi* fall. **dejar ~r** drop. **este vestido no me ~ bien** this dress doesn't suit me. **hacer ~r** knock over. **Juan me ~ bien** I like Juan. **su cumpleaños cayó en martes** his birthday fell on a Tuesday. **~rse** *vpr* fall (over). **se le cayó** he dropped it
café *m* coffee; (*cafetería*) café; (*Mex, marrón*) brown. ● *adj*. **color ~** coffee-coloured. **~ con leche** white coffee. **~ cortado** coffee with a little milk. **~ negro** (*LAm*) expresso. **~ solo** black coffee
cafe|ína *f* caffeine. **~tal** *m* coffee plantation. **~tera** *f* coffee-pot. **~tería** *f* café. **~tero** *adj* coffee
caíd|a *f* fall; (*disminución*) drop; (*pendiente*) slope. **~o** *adj* fallen

> *i*
> **cafetería** In Spain, a place to have a coffee or other drinks, pastries and cakes. *Cafeterías* are frequently combined with *bares* and are very similar. However, *cafeterías* are usually smarter, and serve a wider variety of dishes.

caigo *vb véase* CAER
caimán *m* cayman, alligator
caj|a *f* box; (*de botellas*) case; (*ataúd*) coffin; (*en tienda*) cash desk; (*en supermercado*) check-out; (*en banco*) cashier's desk. **~a de ahorros** savings bank. **~a de cambios** gearbox. **~a de caudales**, **~a fuerte** safe. **~a negra** black box. **~a registradora** till. **~ero** *m* cashier. **~ero automático** cash dispenser. **~etilla** *f* packet. **~ita** *f* small box. **~ón** *m* (*de mueble*) drawer; (*caja grande*) crate; (*LAm, ataúd*) coffin; (*Mex, en estacionamiento*) parking space. **ser de ~ón** be obvious. **~uela** *f* (*Mex*) boot (*Brit*), trunk (*Amer*)
cal *m* lime
cala *f* cove
calaba|cín *m*, **|cita** *f* (*Mex*) courgette (*Brit*), zucchini (*Amer*). **~za** *f* pumpkin; (*fig, fam, idiota*) idiot.

dar ~zas a uno give s.o. the brush-off

calabozo *m* prison; (*celda*) cell

calado *adj* soaked. **estar ~ hasta los huesos** be soaked to the skin. • *m* (*Naut*) draught

calamar *m* squid

calambre *m* cramp

calami|dad *f* calamity, disaster. **~toso** *adj* calamitous

calaña *f* sort

calar *vt* soak; (*penetrar*) pierce; (*fig, penetrar*) see through; rumble (persona); sample (fruta). **~se** *vpr* get soaked; (zapatos) leak; (*Auto*) stall

calavera *f* skull; (*Mex, Auto*) tail light

calcar 7 *vt* trace; (*fig*) copy

calcet|a *f*. **hacer ~** knit. **~ín** *m* sock

calcetín *m* sock

calcinar *vt* burn

calcio *m* calcium

calcomanía *f* transfer

calcula|dor *adj* calculating. **~dora** *f* calculator. **~r** *vt* calculate; (*suponer*) reckon, think; (*imaginar*) imagine

cálculo *m* calculation; (*Med*) stone

caldear *vt* heat, warm. **~se** *vpr* get hot

caldera *f* boiler

calderilla *f* small change

caldo *m* stock; (*sopa*) clear soup, broth

calefacción *f* heating. **~ central** central heating

caleidoscopio *m* kaleidoscope

calendario *m* calendar; (*programa*) schedule

calent|ador *m* heater. **~amiento** *m* warming; (*en deportes*) warm-up. **~ar** 1 *vt* heat; (*templar*) warm. **~arse** *vpr* get hot; (*templarse*) warm up; (*LAm, enojarse*) get mad. **~ura** *f* fever, (high) temperature. **~uriento** *adj* feverish

calibr|ar *vt* calibrate; (*fig*) weigh up. **~e** *m* calibre; (*diámetro*) diameter; (*fig*) importance

calidad *f* quality; (*condición*) capacity. **en ~ de** as

calidez *f* (*LAm*) warmth

cálido *adj* warm

caliente *adj* hot; (habitación, ropa) warm; (*LAm, enojado*) angry

califica|ción *f* qualification; (*evaluación*) assessment; (*nota*) mark. **~do** *adj* (*esp LAm*) qualified; (*mano de obra*) skilled. **~r** 7 *vt* qualify; (*evaluar*) assess; mark (examen etc). **~r de** describe as, label

cáliz *m* chalice; (*en botánica*) calyx

caliz|a *f* limestone. **~o** *adj* lime

calla|do *adj* quiet. **~r** *vt* silence; keep (secreto); hush up (asunto). • *vi* be quiet, keep quiet, shut up [!]. **~rse** *vpr* be quiet, keep quiet, shut up [!] **¡cállate!** be quiet!, shut up! [!]

calle *f* street, road; (*en deportes, autopista*) lane. **~ de dirección única** one-way street. **~ mayor** high street, main street. **de ~** everyday. **~ja** *f* narrow street. **~jear** *vi* hang out on the streets. **~jero** *adj* street. • *m* street plan. **~jón** *m* alley. **~ón sin salida** dead end. **~juela** *f* back street, side street

call|ista *m & f* chiropodist. **~o** *m* corn, callus. **~os** *mpl* tripe. **~osidad** *f* callus

calm|a *f* calm. **¡~a!** calm down!. **en ~a** calm. **perder la ~a** lose one's composure. **~ante** *m* tranquilizer; (*para el dolor*) painkiller. **~ar** *vt* calm; (*aliviar*) soothe. • *vi* (viento) abate. **~arse** *vpr* calm down; (viento) abate. **~o** *adj* calm. **~oso** *adj* calm; (*fam, flemático*) slow

calor *m* heat; (*afecto*) warmth. **hace ~** it's hot. **tener ~** be hot. **~ía** *f* calorie. **~ífero** *adj* heat-producing. **~ífico** *adj* calorific

calumni|a *f* calumny; (*oral*) slander; (*escrita*) libel. **~ar** *vt* slander; (*por escrito*) libel. **~oso** *adj* slanderous; (cosa escrita) libellous

caluroso *adj* warm; (clima) hot

calv|a *f* bald head; (*parte sin pelo*) bald patch. **~icie** *f* baldness. **~o** *adj* bald

calza *f* wedge

calzada *f* road; (*en autopista*) carriageway

calza|do *adj* wearing shoes. • *m* footwear, shoe. **~dor** *m* shoehorn. **~r** 10 *vt* put shoes on; (*llevar*) wear. **¿qué número calza Vd?** what size shoe do you take? • *vi* wear shoes. **~rse** *vpr* put on

calz|ón *m* shorts. **~ones** *mpl* shorts; (*LAm, ropa interior*) panties. **~oncillos** *mpl* underpants

cama *f* bed. **~ de matrimonio** double bed. **~ individual** single bed. **guardar ~** stay in bed

camada *f* litter

camafeo *m* cameo

camaleón *m* chameleon

cámara *f* (*aposento*) chamber; (*fotográfica*) camera. **~ fotográfica** camera. **a ~ lenta** in slow motion

camarad|a *m & f* colleague; (*de colegio*) schoolfriend; (*Pol*) comrade. **~ería** *f* camaraderie

camarer|a *f* chambermaid; (*de restaurante etc*) waitress. **~o** *m* waiter

camarógrafo *m* cameraman

camarón *m* shrimp

camarote *m* cabin

cambi|able *adj* changeable; (*Com etc*) exchangeable. **~ante** *adj* variable; (persona) moody. **~ar** *vt* change; (*trocar*) exchange. • *vi* change. **~ar de idea** change one's mind. **~arse** *vpr* change. **~o** *m* change; (*Com*) exchange rate; (*moneda menuda*) (small) change; (*Auto*) gear. **~o climático** climate change. **en ~o** on the other hand

camello *m* camel

camellón *m* (*Mex*) traffic island

camerino *m* dressing room

camilla *f* stretcher

camin|ante *m* traveller. **~ar** *vt/i* walk. **~ata** *f* long walk. **~o** *m* road; (*sendero*) path, track; (*dirección, ruta*) way. **~o de** towards, on the way to. **abrir ~o** make way. **a medio ~o, a la mitad del ~o** half-way. **de ~o** on the way

cami|ón *m* truck, lorry; (*Mex, autobús*) bus. **~onero** *m* lorry-driver; (*Mex, de autobús*) bus driver. **~oneta** *f* van; (*LAm, coche familiar*) estate car

Camino de Santiago A pilgrimage route since the Middle Ages across north-western Spain to Santiago de Compostela in Galicia. The city was founded at a place where a shepherd is said to have discovered the tomb of St James the Apostle, and its cathedral reputedly houses the saint's relics.

camis|a *f* shirt. **~a de fuerza** strait-jacket. **~ería** *f* shirtmaker's.

~eta *f* T-shirt; (*ropa interior*) vest. **~ón** *m* nightdress

camorra *f* 🄸 row. **buscar ~** look for a fight

camote *m* (*LAm*) sweet potato

campamento *m* camp. **de ~** *adj* camping

campan|a *f* bell. **~ada** *f* stroke. **~ario** *m* bell tower, belfry. **~illa** *f* bell

campaña *f* campaign

campe|ón *adj & m* champion. **~onato** *m* championship

campes|ino *adj* country. • *m* peasant. **~tre** *adj* country

camping /'kampin/ *m* (*pl* **~s**) camping; (*lugar*) campsite. **hacer ~** go camping

camp|iña *f* countryside. **~o** *m* country; (*agricultura, fig*) field; (*de fútbol*) pitch; (*de golf*) course. **~osanto** *m* cemetery

camufla|je *m* camouflage. **~r** *vt* camouflage

cana *f* grey hair, white hair. **peinar ~s** be getting old

Canadá *m.* **el ~** Canada

canadiense *adj & m & f* Canadian

canal *m* (*incl TV*) channel; (*artificial*) canal; (*del tejado*) gutter. **~ de la Mancha** English Channel. **~ de Panamá** Panama Canal. **~ón** *m* (*horizontal*) gutter; (*vertical*) drainpipe

canalla *f* rabble. • *m* (*fig, fam*) swine. **~da** *f* dirty trick

canapé *m* sofa, couch; (*Culin*) canapé

Canarias *fpl.* **las (islas) ~** the Canary Islands, the Canaries

canario *adj* of the Canary Islands. • *m* native of the Canary Islands; (*pájaro*) canary

canast|a *f* (large) basket **~illa** *f* small basket; (*para un bebé*) layette. **~illo** *m* small basket. **~o** *m* (large) basket

cancela|ción *f* cancellation. **~r** *vt* cancel; write off (deuda)

cáncer *m* cancer. **C~** Cancer

cancha *f* court; (*LAm, de fútbol, rugby*) pitch, ground

canciller *m* chancellor; (*LAm, ministro*) Minister of Foreign Affairs

canci|ón *f* song. **~ón de cuna** lullaby. **~onero** *m* song-book

candado *m* padlock

candel|a *f* candle. **~abro** *m* candelabra. **~ero** *m* candlestick

candente *adj* (*rojo*) red-hot; (*fig*) burning

candidato *m* candidate

candidez *f* innocence; (*ingenuidad*) naivety

cándido *adj* naive

candil *m* oil lamp. **~ejas** *fpl* footlights

candor *m* innocence; (*ingenuidad*) naivety

canela *f* cinnamon

cangrejo *m* crab. **~ de río** crayfish

canguro *m* kangaroo. • *m & f* (*persona*) baby-sitter

caníbal *adj & m & f* cannibal

canica *f* marble

canijo *adj* weak; (*Mex, terco*) stubborn; (*Mex, intenso*) incredible

canilla *f* (*LAm*) shinbone

canino *adj* canine. • *m* canine (tooth)

canje *m* exchange. **~ar** *vt* exchange

cano *adj* grey. **de pelo ~** grey-haired

canoa *f* canoe

can|ónigo *m* canon. **~onizar** 10 *vt* canonize
canoso *adj* grey-haired
C
cansa|do *adj* tired; (*que cansa*) tiring. **~dor** (*LAm*) tiring. **~ncio** *m* tiredness. **~r** *vt* tire; (*aburrir*) bore. • *vi* be tiring; (*aburrir*) get boring. **~rse** *vpr* get tired
canta|nte *adj* singing. • *m & f* singer. **~or** *m* Flamenco singer. **~r** *vt/i* sing. **~rlas claras** speak frankly. • *m* singing; (*poema*) poem
cántaro *m* pitcher. **llover a ~s** pour down
cante *m* folk song. **~ flamenco, ~ jondo** Flamenco singing
cantera *f* quarry
cantidad *f* quantity; (*número*) number; (*de dinero*) sum. **una ~ de** lots of
cantimplora *f* water-bottle
cantina *f* canteen; (*Rail*) buffet; (*LAm, bar*) bar
cant|inela *f* song. **~o** *m* singing; (*canción*) chant; (*borde*) edge; (*de un cuchillo*) blunt edge. **~o rodado** boulder; (*guijarro*) pebble. **de ~o** on edge
canturre|ar *vt/i* hum. **~o** *m* humming
canuto *m* tube
caña *f* (*planta*) reed; (*del trigo*) stalk; (*del bambú*) cane; (*de pescar*) rod; (*de la bota*) leg; (*vaso*) glass. **~ de azúcar** sugar-cane. **~da** *f* ravine; (*camino*) track; (*LAm, arroyo*) stream
cáñamo *m* hemp. **~ indio** cannabis
cañ|ería *f* pipe; (*tubería*) piping. **~o** *m* pipe, tube; (*de fuente*) jet. **~ón** *m* (*de pluma*) quill; (*de artillería*) cannon; (*de arma de fuego*) barrel; (*desfiladero*) canyon. **~onera** *f* gunboat
caoba *f* mahogany
ca|os *m* chaos. **~ótico** *adj* chaotic
capa *f* layer; (*de pintura*) coat; (*Culin*) coating; (*prenda*) cloak; (*más corta*) cape; (*en geología*) stratum
capaci|dad *f* capacity; (*fig*) ability. **~tar** *vt* qualify, enable; (*instruir*) train
caparazón *m* shell
capataz *m* foreman
capaz *adj* capable, able
capcioso *adj* sly, insidious
capellán *m* chaplain
caperuza *f* hood; (*de bolígrafo*) cap
capilla *f* chapel
capital *adj* capital, very important. • *m* (*dinero*) capital. • *f* (*ciudad*) capital. **~ de provincia** county town. **~ino** *adj* (*LAm*) of/from the capital. **~ismo** *m* capitalism. **~ista** *adj & m & f* capitalist. **~izar** 10 *vt* capitalize
capit|án *m* captain; (*de pesquero*) skipper. **~anear** *vt* lead, command; skipper (pesquero); captain (un equipo)
capitel *m* (*de columna*) capital
capitulaci|ón *f* surrender. **~ones** *fpl* marriage contract
capítulo *m* chapter; (*de serie*) episode
capó *m* bonnet (*Brit*), hood (*Amer*)
capón *m* (*pollo*) capon
caporal *m* (*Mex*) foreman
capot|a *f* (*de mujer*) bonnet; (*Auto*) folding top; (*de cochecito*) hood. **~e** *m* cape; (*Mex, de coche*) bonnet (*Brit*), hood (*Amer*)
capricho *m* whim. **~so** *adj* capricious, whimsical

Capricornio *m* Capricorn
cápsula *f* capsule
captar *vt* harness (agua); grasp (sentido); capture (atención); win (confianza); (*radio*) pick up
captura *f* capture. **~r** *vt* capture
capucha *f* hood
capullo *m* bud; (*de insecto*) cocoon
caqui *m* khaki
cara *f* face; (*de una moneda*) heads; (*de un objeto*) side; (*aspecto*) look, appearance; (*descaro*) cheek. **~ a** facing. **~ a ~** face to face. **~ dura** *véase* **CARADURA**. **~ o cruz** heads or tails. **dar la ~ a** face up to. **hacer ~ a** face. **tener mala ~** look ill. **volver la ~** look the other way
carabela *f* caravel
carabina *f* carbine; (*fig, fam, señora*) chaperone
caracol *m* snail; (*de mar*) winkle; (*LAm, concha*) conch; (*de pelo*) curl. **¡~es!** Good Heavens!. **~a** *f* conch
carácter *m* (*pl* **caracteres**) character; (*índole*) nature. **con ~ de** as
característic|a *f* characteristic. **~o** *adj* characteristic, typical
caracteriza|do *adj* characterized; (*prestigioso*) distinguished. **~r** 10 *vt* characterize
caradura *f* cheek, nerve. ● *m & f* cheeky person
caramba *int* good heavens!
carambola *f* (*en billar*) cannon; (*Mex, choque múltiple*) pile-up. **de ~** by pure chance
caramelo *m* sweet (*Brit*), candy (*Amer*); (*azúcar fundido*) caramel
caraqueño *adj* from Caracas
carátula *f* (*de disco*) sleeve (*Brit*), jacket (*Amer*); (*de video*) case; (*de libro*) cover; (*Mex, del reloj*) face
caravana *f* caravan; (*de vehículos*) convoy; (*Auto*) long line, traffic jam; (*remolque*) caravan (*Brit*), trailer (*Amer*); (*Mex, reverencia*) bow
caray *int* ! good heavens!
carb|ón *m* coal; (*para dibujar*) charcoal. **~ de leña** charcoal. **~oncillo** *m* charcoal. **~onero** *adj* coal. ● *m* coal-merchant. **~onizar** 10 *vt* (*fig*) burn (to a cinder). **~ono** *m* carbon
carbura|dor *m* carburettor. **~nte** *m* fuel
carcajada *f* guffaw. **reírse a ~s** roar with laughter. **soltar una ~** burst out laughing
cárcel *f* prison, jail
carcelero *m* jailer
carcom|er *vt* eat away; (*fig*) undermine. **~erse** *vpr* be eaten away; (*fig*) waste away
cardenal *m* cardinal; (*contusión*) bruise
cardiaco, **cardíaco** *adj* cardiac, heart
cardinal *adj* cardinal
cardo *m* thistle
carear *vt* bring face to face (personas); compare (cosas)
care|cer 11 *vi*. **~cer de** lack. **~cer de sentido** not to make sense. **~ncia** *f* lack. **~nte** *adj* lacking
care|ro *adj* pricey. **~stía** *f* (*elevado*) high cost
careta *f* mask
carey *m* tortoiseshell
carga *f* load; (*fig*) burden; (*acción*) loading; (*de barco, avión*) cargo; (*de tren*) freight; (*de arma*) charge; (*Elec, ataque*) charge; (*obligación*) obligation. **llevar la ~ de algo** be responsible for sth. **~da** *f* (*Mex,*

C

Pol) supporters. **~do** *adj* loaded; (*fig*) burdened; (atmósfera) heavy; (café) strong; (pila) charged. **~mento** *m* load; (*acción*) loading; (*de un barco*) cargo. **~r** 12 *vt* load; (*fig*) burden; (*Elec, atacar*) charge; fill (pluma etc). ● *vi* load. **~r con** carry. **~rse** *vpr* (pila) charge. **~rse de** to load s.o. down with

cargo *m* (*puesto*) post; (*acusación*) charge. **a ~ de** in the charge of. **hacerse ~ de** take responsibility for. **tener a su ~** be in charge of

carguero *m* (*Naut*) cargo ship

caria|do *adj* decayed. **~rse** *vpr* decay

caribeño *adj* Caribbean

caricatura *f* caricature

caricia *f* caress; (*a animal*) stroke

caridad *f* charity. **¡por ~!** for goodness sake!

caries *f invar* tooth decay; (*lesión*) cavity

cariño *m* affection; (*caricia*) caress. **~ mío** my darling. **con mucho ~** (*en carta*) with love from. **tener ~ a** be fond of. **tomar ~ a** become fond of. **~so** *adj* affectionate

carisma *m* charisma

caritativo *adj* charitable

cariz *m* look

carmesí *adj & m* crimson

carmín *m* (*de labios*) lipstick; (*color*) red

carnal *adj* carnal. **primo ~** first cousin

carnaval *m* carnival. **~esco** *adj* carnival

carne *f* meat; (*Anat, de frutos, pescado*) flesh. **~ de cerdo** pork. **~ de cordero** lamb. **~ de gallina** goose pimples. **~ molida** (*LAm*), **~ picada** mince (*Brit*), ground beef (*Amer*). **~ de ternera** veal. **~ de vaca** beef. **me pone la ~ de gallina** it gives me the creeps. **ser de ~ y hueso** be only human

carné, **carnet** *m* card. **~ de conducir** driving licence (*Brit*), driver's license (*Amer*) **~ de identidad** identity card. **~ de manejar** (*LAm*) driving license (*Brit*), driver's license (*Amer*). **~ de socio** membership card

carnero *m* ram

carnicer|ía *f* butcher's (shop); (*fig*) massacre. **~o** *adj* carnivorous. ● *m* butcher

carnívoro *adj* carnivorous. ● *m* carnivore

carnoso *adj* fleshy; (pollo) meaty

caro *adj* expensive. ● *adv* dear, dearly. **costar ~ a uno** cost s.o. dear.

carpa *f* carp; (*LAm, tienda*) tent

carpeta *f* folder, file. **~zo** *m*. **dar ~zo a** shelve

carpinter|ía *f* carpentry. **~o** *m* carpinter, joiner

carraspe|ar *vi* clear one's throat. **~ra** *f*. **tener ~ra** have a frog in one's throat

carrera *f* run; (*prisa*) rush; (*concurso*) race; (*estudios*) degree course; (*profesión*) career; (*de taxi*) journey

carreta *f* cart. **~da** *f* cartload

carrete *m* reel; (*película*) film

carretear *vi* (*LAm*) taxi

carretera *f* road. **~ de circunvalación** bypass, ring road. **~ nacional** A road (*Brit*), highway (*Amer*)

carretilla *f* wheelbarrow

carril *m* lane; (*Rail*) rail

carrito *m* (*en supermercado, para equipaje*) trolley (*Brit*), cart (*Amer*)

carro *m* cart; (*LAm, coche*) car;

(*Mex, vagón*) coach. ~ **de combate** tank. ~**cería** *f* (*Auto*) bodywork

carroña *f* carrion

carroza *f* coach, carriage; (*en desfile de fiesta*) float

carruaje *m* carriage

carrusel *m* merry-go-round

cart|a *f* letter; (*lista de platos*) menu; (*lista de vinos*) list; (*mapa*) map; (*naipe*) card. ~**a blanca** free hand. ~**a de crédito** letter of credit. ~**a verde** green card. ~**earse** *vpr* correspond

cartel *m* poster; (*letrero*) sign. ~**era** *f* hoarding; (*en periódico*) listings; (*LAm en escuela, oficina*) notice board (*Brit*), bulletin board (*Amer*). **de** ~ celebrated

carter|a *f* wallet; (*de colegial*) satchel; (*para documentos*) briefcase; (*LAm, de mujer*) handbag (*Brit*), purse (*Amer*). ~**ista** *m & f* pickpocket

cartero *m* postman, mailman (*Amer*)

cartílago *m* cartilage

cartilla *f* first reading book. ~ **de ahorros** savings book. **leerle la** ~ **a uno** tell s.o. off

cartón *m* cardboard

cartucho *m* cartridge

cartulina *f* card

casa *f* house; (*hogar*) home; (*empresa*) firm. ~ **de huéspedes** boarding-house. ~ **de socorro** first aid post. **ir a** ~ go home. **salir de** ~ go out

casaca *f* jacket

casado *adj* married. **los recién** ~**s** the newly-weds

casa|mentero *m* matchmaker. ~**miento** *m* marriage; (*ceremonia*) wedding. ~**r** *vt* marry. ~**rse** *vpr* get married

cascabel *m* small bell; (*de serpiente*) rattle

cascada *f* waterfall

casca|nueces *m invar* nutcrackers. ~**r** **7** *vt* crack (nuez, huevo); (*pegar*) beat. ~**rse** *vpr* crack

cáscara *f* (*de huevo, nuez*) shell; (*de naranja*) peel; (*de plátano*) skin

cascarrabias *adj invar* grumpy

casco *m* helmet; (*de cerámica etc*) piece, fragment; (*cabeza*) scalp; (*de barco*) hull; (*envase*) empty bottle; (*de caballo*) hoof; (*de una ciudad*) part, area

cascote *m* piece of rubble. ~**s** *mpl* rubble

caserío *m* country house; (*poblado*) hamlet

casero *adj* home-made; (*doméstico*) domestic; (*amante del hogar*) home-loving; (reunión) family. ● *m* owner; (*vigilante*) caretaker

caseta *f* hut; (*puesto*) stand. ~ **de baño** bathing hut

casete *m & f* cassette

casi *adv* almost, nearly; (*en frases negativas*) hardly. ~ ~ very nearly. ~ **nada** hardly any. **¡**~ **nada!** is that all? ~ **nunca** hardly ever

casill|a *f* hut; (*en ajedrez etc*) square; (*en formulario*) box; (*compartimento*) pigeonhole. ~ **electrónica** e-mail address. ~**ero** *m* pigeonholes; (*compartimento*) pigeonhole

casino *m* casino; (*club social*) club

caso *m* case. **el** ~ **es que** the fact is that. **en** ~ **de** in the event of. **en cualquier** ~ in any case, whatever happens. **en ese** ~ in that case. **en todo** ~ in any case. **en último** ~ as a last resort. **hacer** ~ **de** take notice of. **poner por** ~ suppose

c

caspa *f* dandruff
casquivana *f* flirt
cassette *m & f* cassette
casta *f* (*de animal*) breed; (*de persona*) descent; (*grupo social*) caste
castaña *f* chestnut
castañetear *vi* (dientes) chatter
castaño *adj* chestnut; (ojos) brown. ● *m* chestnut (tree)
castañuela *f* castanet
castellano *adj* Castilian. ● *m* (*persona*) Castilian; (*lengua*) Castilian, Spanish. **~parlante** *adj* Castilian-speaking, Spanish-speaking. **¿habla Vd ~?** do you speak Spanish?

castellano In Spain the term *castellano*, rather than *español*, refers to the Spanish language as opposed to Catalan, Basque etc. The choice of word has political overtones; *castellano* has separatist connotations and *español* is considered neutral. In Latin America *castellano* is another term for Spanish.

castidad *f* chastity
castig|ar 12 *vt* punish; (*en deportes*) penalize. **~o** *m* punishment; (*en deportes*) penalty
castillo *m* castle
cast|izo *adj* traditional; (*puro*) pure. **~o** *adj* chaste
castor *m* beaver
castrar *vt* castrate
castrense *m* military
casual *adj* chance, accidental. **~idad** *f* chance, coincidence. **dar la ~idad** happen. **de ~idad**, **por ~idad** by chance. **¡qué ~idad!** what a coincidence!. **~mente** *adv* by chance; (*precisamente*) actually
cataclismo *m* cataclysm
catador *m* taster
catalán *adj & m* Catalan
catalizador *m* catalyst
cat|alogar 12 *vt* catalogue; (*fig*) classify. **~álogo** *m* catalogue
Cataluña *f* Catalonia
catamarán *m* catamaran
catapulta *f* catapult
catar *vt* taste, try
catarata *f* waterfall, falls; (*Med*) cataract
catarro *m* cold
cat|ástrofe *m* catastrophe. **~astrófico** *adj* catastrophic
catecismo *m* catechism
cátedra *f* (*en universidad*) professorship, chair; (*en colegio*) post of head of department
catedral *f* cathedral
catedrático *m* professor; (*de colegio*) teacher, head of department
categ|oría *f* category; (*clase*) class. **de ~oría** important. **de primera ~oría** first-class. **~órico** *adj* categorical
cat|olicismo *m* catholicism. **~ólico** *adj* (Roman) Catholic ● *m* (Roman) Catholic
catorce *adj & m* fourteen
cauce *m* river bed; (*fig, artificial*) channel
caucho *m* rubber
caudal *m* (*de río*) volume of flow; (*riqueza*) wealth. **~oso** *adj* (río) large
caudillo *m* leader
causa *f* cause; (*motivo*) reason; (*Jurid*) trial. **a ~ de**, **por ~ de** because of. **~r** *vt* cause
cautel|a *f* caution. **~oso** *adj* cautious, wary
cauterizar 10 *vt* cauterize

cautiv|ar *vt* capture; (*fig, fascinar*) captivate. **~erio** *m*, **~idad** *f* captivity. **~o** *adj & m* captive

cauto *adj* cautious

cavar *vt/i* dig

caverna *f* cave, cavern

caviar *m* caviare

cavidad *f* cavity

caza *f* hunting; (*con fusil*) shooting; (*animales*) game. ● *m* fighter. **andar a (la) ~ de** be in search of. **~ mayor** game hunting. **dar ~** chase, go after. **ir de ~** go hunting/shooting. **~dor** *m* hunter. **~dora** *f* jacket. **~r** 10 *vt* hunt; (*con fusil*) shoot; (*fig*) track down; (*obtener*) catch, get

caz|o *m* saucepan; (*cucharón*) ladle. **~oleta** *f* (small) saucepan. **~uela** *f* casserole

cebada *f* barley

ceb|ar *vt* fatten (up); bait (anzuelo); prime (arma de fuego). **~o** *m* bait; (*de arma de fuego*) charge

ceboll|a *f* onion. **~eta** *f* spring onion (*Brit*), scallion (*Amer*). **~ino** *m* chive

cebra *f* zebra

cece|ar *vi* lisp. **~o** *m* lisp

cedazo *m* sieve

ceder *vt* give up; (*transferir*) transfer. ● *vi* give in; (*disminuir*) ease off; (*romperse*) give way, collapse. **ceda el paso** give way (*Brit*), yield (*Amer*)

cedro *m* cedar

cédula *f* bond. **~ de identidad** identity card

CE(E) *abrev* (**Comunidad (Económica) Europea**) E(E)C

ceg|ador *adj* blinding. **~ar** 1 & 12 *vt* blind; (*tapar*) block up. **~arse** *vpr* be blinded (**de** by). **~uera** *f* blindness

ceja *f* eyebrow

cejar *vi* give way

celada *f* ambush; (*fig*) trap

cela|dor *m* (*de cárcel*) prison warder; (*de museo etc*) security guard. **~r** *vt* watch

celda *f* cell

celebra|ción *f* celebration. **~r** *vt* celebrate; (*alabar*) praise. **~rse** *vpr* take place

célebre *adj* famous

celebridad *f* fame; (*persona*) celebrity

celest|e *adj* heavenly; (vestido) pale blue. **azul ~e** sky-blue. **~ial** *adj* heavenly

celibato *m* celibacy

célibe *adj* celibate

celo *m* zeal; (*de las hembras*) heat; (*de los machos*) rut; (*cinta adhesiva*) Sellotape (P) (*Brit*), Scotch (P) tape (*Amer*). **~s** *mpl* jealousy. **dar ~s** make jealous. **tener ~s** be jealous

celofán *m* cellophane

celoso *adj* conscientious; (*que tiene celos*) jealous

celta *adj & m* (*lengua*) Celtic. ● *m & f* Celt

célula *f* cell

celular *adj* cellular. ● *m* (*LAm*) mobile, cellphone

celulosa *f* cellulose

cementerio *m* cemetery

cemento *m* cement; (*hormigón*) concrete; (*LAm, cola*) glue

cena *f* dinner; (*comida ligera*) supper

cenag|al *m* marsh, bog; (*fig*) tight spot. **~oso** *adj* boggy

cenar *vt* have for dinner; (*en cena ligera*) have for supper. ● *vi* have dinner; (*tomar cena ligera*) have supper

c

cenicero *m* ashtray

ceniza *f* ash

censo *m* census. **~ electoral** electoral roll

censura *f* censure; (*de prensa etc*) censorship. **~r** *vt* censure; censor (prensa etc)

centavo *adj & m* hundredth; (*moneda*) centavo

centell|a *f* flash; (*chispa*) spark. **~ar**, **~ear** *vi* sparkle

centena *f* hundred. **~r** *m* hundred. a **~res** by the hundred. **~rio** *adj* centenarian. • *m* centenary; (*persona*) centenarian

centeno *m* rye

centésim|a *f* hundredth. **~o** *adj* hundredth

cent|ígrado *adj* centigrade, Celsius. • *m* centigrade. **~igramo** *m* centigram. **~ilitro** *m* centilitre. **~ímetro** *m* centimetre

céntimo *adj* hundredth. • *m* cent

centinela *f* sentry

centolla *f*, **centollo** *m* spider crab

central *adj* central. • *f* head office. **~ de correos** general post office. **~ eléctrica** power station. **~ nuclear** nuclear power station. **~ telefónica** telephone exchange. **~ita** *f* switchboard

centraliza|ción *f* centralization. **~r** 10 *vt* centralize

centrar *vt* centre

céntrico *adj* central

centrífugo *adj* centrifugal

centro *m* centre. **~ comercial** shopping centre (*Brit*), shopping mall (*Amer*). **~ de llamadas** call centre

Centroamérica *f* Central America

centroamericano *adj & m* Central American

ceñi|do *adj* tight. **~r** 5 & 22 *vt* take (corona); (vestido) cling to. **~rse** *vpr* limit o.s. (a to)

ceñ|o *m* frown. **fruncir el ~o** frown. **~udo** *adj* frowning

cepill|ar *vt* brush; (*en carpintería*) plane. **~o** *m* brush; (*en carpintería*) plane. **~o de dientes** toothbrush

cera *f* wax

cerámic|a *f* ceramics; (*materia*) pottery; (*objeto*) piece of pottery. **~o** *adj* ceramic

cerca *f* fence; (*de piedra*) wall. • *adv* near, close. **~ de** *prep* close to, close up, closely

cercan|ía *f* nearness, proximity. **~ías** *fpl* vicinity. **tren** *m* **de ~ías** local train. **~o** *adj* near, close.

cercar 7 *vt* fence in, enclose; (gente) surround; (*asediar*) besiege

cerciorar *vt* convince. **~se** *vpr* make sure

cerco *m* (*asedio*) siege; (*círculo*) ring; (*LAm, valla*) fence; (*LAm, seto*) hedge

cerdo *m* pig; (*carne*) pork

cereal *m* cereal

cerebr|al *adj* cerebral. **~o** *m* brain; (*persona*) brains

ceremoni|a *f* ceremony. **~al** *adj* ceremonial. **~oso** *adj* ceremonious

cerez|a *f* cherry. **~o** *m* cherry tree

cerill|a *f* match. **~o** *m* (*Mex*) match

cern|er 1 *vt* sieve. **~erse** *vpr* hover. **~idor** *m* sieve

cero *m* nought, zero; (*fútbol*) nil (*Brit*), zero (*Amer*); (*tenis*) love; (*persona*) nonentity

cerquillo *m* (*LAm, flequillo*) fringe (*Brit*), bangs (*Amer*)

cerra|do *adj* shut, closed; (*espa-*

cio) shut in, enclosed; (cielo) overcast; (curva) sharp. **~dura** *f* lock; (*acción de cerrar*) shutting, closing. **~jero** *m* locksmith. **~r** **1** *vt* shut, close; (*con llave*) lock; (*cercar*) enclose; turn off (grifo); block up (agujero etc). • *vi* shut, close. **~rse** *vpr* shut, close; (herida) heal. **~r con llave** lock

cerro *m* hill

cerrojo *m* bolt. **echar el ~** bolt

certamen *m* competition, contest

certero *adj* accurate

certeza, **certidumbre** *f* certainty

certifica|do *adj* (carta etc) registered. • *m* certificate. **~r** **7** *vt* certify

certitud *f* certainty

cervatillo, **cervato** *m* fawn

cerve|cería *f* beerhouse, bar; (*fábrica*) brewery. **~za** *f* beer. **~za de barril** draught beer. **~za rubia** lager

cesa|ción *f* cessation, suspension. **~nte** *adj* redundant. **~r** *vt* stop. • *vi* stop, cease; (*dejar un empleo*) resign. **sin ~r** incessantly

cesárea *f* caesarian (section)

cese *m* cessation; (*de un empleo*) dismissal. **~ del fuego** (*LAm*) ceasefire

césped *m* grass, lawn

cest|a *f* basket. **~o** *m* basket. **~o de los papeles** waste-paper basket

chabacano *adj* common; (chiste etc) vulgar. • *m* (*Mex, albaricoque*) apricot

chabola *f* shack. **~s** *fpl* shanty town

cháchara *f* **I** chatter; (*Mex, objetos sin valor*) junk

chacharear *vt* (*Mex*) sell. • *vi* **I** chatter

chacra *f* (*LAm*) farm

chal *m* shawl

chalado *adj* **I** crazy

chalé *m* house (with a garden), villa

chaleco *m* waistcoat, vest (*Amer*). **~ salvavidas** life-jacket

chalet *m* (*pl* **~s**) house (with a garden), villa

chalote *m* shallot

chamac|a *f* (*esp Mex*) girl. **~o** *m* (*esp Mex*) boy

chamarra *f* sheepskin jacket; (*Mex, chaqueta corta*) jacket

chamb|a *f* (*Mex, trabajo*) work. **por ~a** by fluke. **~ear** *vi* (*Mex, fam*) work

champán *m*, **champaña** *m & f* champagne

champiñón *m* mushroom

champú *m* (*pl* **~es** *o* **~s**) shampoo

chamuscar **7** *vt* scorch

chance *m* (*esp LAm*) chance

chancho *m* (*LAm*) pig

chanchullo *m* **I** swindle, fiddle **I**

chanclo *m* clog; (*de caucho*) rubber overshoe

chándal *m* (*pl* **~s**) tracksuit

chantaje *m* blackmail. **~ar** *vt* blackmail

chanza *f* joke

chapa *f* plate, sheet; (*de madera*) plywood; (*de botella*) metal top; (*carrocería*) bodywork; (*LAm cerradura*) lock. **~do** *adj* plated. **~do a la antigua** old-fashioned. **~do en oro** gold-plated

chaparro *adj* (*LAm*) short, squat

chaparrón *m* downpour

chapopote *m* (*Mex*) tar

chapotear *vi* splash

chapucero *adj* (persona) slapdash; (trabajo) shoddy

chapulín *m* (*Mex*) locust; (*saltamontes*) grasshopper

chapurrar, **chapurrear** *vt* have a smattering of, speak a little

chapuza *f* botched job; (*trabajo ocasional*) odd job

chaquet|a *f* jacket. **cambiar de ~a** change sides. **~ón** *m* three-quarter length coat

charc|a *f* pond, pool. **~o** *m* puddle, pool

charcutería *f* delicatessen

charla *f* chat; (*conferencia*) talk. **~dor** *adj* talkative. **~r** *vi* ⊡ chat. **~tán** *adj* talkative. ● *m* chatterbox; (*vendedor*) cunning hawker; (*curandero*) charlatan

charol *m* varnish; (*cuero*) patent leather. **~a** *f* (*Mex*) tray

charr|a *f* (*Mex*) horsewoman, cowgirl. **~o** *m* (*Mex*) horseman, cowboy

chascar ◼7 *vt* crack (látigo); click (lengua); snap (dedos). ● *vi* (madera) creak. **~ con la lengua** click one's tongue

chasco *m* disappointment

chasis *m* (*Auto*) chassis

chasqu|ear *vt* crack (látigo); click (lengua); snap (dedos). ● *vi* (madera) creak. **~ con la lengua** click one's tongue. **~ido** *m* crack; (*de la lengua*) click; (*de los dedos*) snap

chatarra *f* scrap iron; (*fig*) scrap

chato *adj* (nariz) snub; (objetos) flat. ● *m* wine glass

chav|a *f* (*Mex*) girl, lass. **~al** *m* ⊡ boy, lad. **~o** *m* (*Mex*) boy, lad.

checa|da *f* (*Mex*) check; (*Mex, Med*) checkup. **~r** ◼7 *vt* (*Mex*) check; (*vigilar*) check up on. **~r tarjeta** clock in

checo *adj & m* Czech. **~slovaco** *adj & m* (*History*) Czechoslovak

chelín *m* shilling

chelo *m* cello

cheque *m* cheque. **~ de viaje** traveller's cheque. **~ar** *vt* check; (*LAm*) check in (equipaje). **~o** *m* check; (*Med*) checkup. **~ra** *f* cheque-book

chévere *adj* (*LAm*) great

chica *f* girl; (*criada*) maid, servant

chicano *adj & m* Chicano, Mexican-American

> **Chicano** *Chicanos* are Mexican Americans, descendants of Mexican immigrants living in US. For long looked down by Americans of European descent, Chicanos have found a new pride in their origins and culture. There are numerous Chicano radio stations and many universities and colleges now offer courses in Chicano studies.

chícharo *m* (*Mex*) pea

chicharra *f* cicada; (*timbre*) buzzer

chichón *m* bump

chicle *m* chewing-gum

chico *adj* ⊡ small; (*esp LAm, de edad*) young. ● *m* boy. **~s** *mpl* children

chicoria *f* chicory

chifla|do *adj* ⊡ crazy, daft. **~r** *vt* whistle at, boo. ● *vi* (*LAm*) whistle; (⊡, *gustar mucho*) **me chifla el chocolate** I'm mad about chocolate. **~rse** *vpr* be mad (**por** about)

chilango *adj* (*Mex*) from Mexico City

chile *m* chilli

Chile *m* Chile
chileno *adj & m* Chilean
chill|ar *vi* scream, shriek; (ratón) squeak; (cerdo) squeal. **~ido** *m* scream, screech. **~ón** *adj* noisy; (colores) loud; (sonido) shrill
chimenea *f* chimney; (*hogar*) fireplace
chimpancé *m* chimpanzee
china *f* Chinese (woman)
China *f* China
chinche *m* drawing-pin (*Brit*), thumbtack (*Amer*); (*insecto*) bedbug; (*fig*) nuisance. **~eta** *f* drawing-pin (*Brit*), thumbtack (*Amer*)
chinela *f* slipper
chino *adj* Chinese; (*Mex rizado*) curly. ● *m* Chinese (man); (*Mex, de pelo rizado*) curly-haired person
chipriota *adj & m & f* Cypriot
chiquero *m* pen; (*LAm, pocilga*) pigsty (*Brit*), pigpen (*Amer*)
chiquillo *adj* childish. ● *m* child, kid [!]
chirimoya *f* custard apple
chiripa *f* fluke
chirri|ar [20] *vi* creak; (frenos) screech; (pájaro) chirp. **~do** *m* creaking; (*de frenos*) screech; (*de pájaros*) chirping
chis *int* sh!, hush!; (*fam, para llamar a uno*) hey!, psst!
chism|e *m* gadget, thingumajig [!]; (*chismorreo*) piece of gossip. **~es** *mpl* things, bits and pieces. **~orreo** *m* gossip. **~oso** *adj* gossipy. ● *m* gossip
chisp|a *f* spark; (*pizca*) drop; (*gracia*) wit; (*fig*) sparkle. **estar que echa ~a(s)** be furious. **~eante** *adj* sparkling. **~ear** *vi* spark; (*lloviznar*) drizzle; (*fig*) sparkle. **~orrotear** *vt* throw out sparks; (fuego) crackle; (aceite) spit
chistar *vi*. **ni chistó** he didn't say a word. **sin ~** without saying a word
chiste *m* joke, funny story. **tener ~** be funny
chistera *f* top hat
chistoso *adj* funny
chiva|rse *vpr* tip-off; (niño) tell. **~tazo** *m* tip-off. **~to** *m* informer; (*niño*) telltale
chivo *m* kid; (*LAm, macho cabrío*) billy goat
choca|nte *adj* shocking; (*Mex desagradable*) unpleasant. **~r** [7] *vt* clink (vasos); (*LAm*) crash (vehículo). **¡chócala!** give me five! ● *vi* collide, hit. **~r con**, **~r contra** crash into
choch|ear *vi* be gaga. **~o** *adj* gaga; (*fig*) soft
choclo *m* (*LAm*) corn on the cob
chocolate *m* chocolate. **tableta** *f* **de ~** bar of chocolate
chófer, (*LAm*) **chofer** *m* chauffeur; (*conductor*) driver
cholo *adj & m* (*LAm*) half-breed
chopo *m* poplar
choque *m* collision; (*fig*) clash; (*eléctrico*) shock; (*Auto, Rail etc*) crash, accident; (*sacudida*) jolt
chorizo *m* chorizo
chorro *m* jet, stream; (*caudal pequeño*) trickle; (*fig*) stream. **a ~** (avión) jet. **a ~s** (*fig*) in abundance
chovinista *adj* chauvinistic. ● *m & f* chauvinist
choza *f* hut
chubas|co *m* shower. **~quero** *m* raincoat, anorak
chuchería *f* trinket
chueco *adj* (*LAm*) crooked

chufa *f* tiger nut
chuleta *f* chop
chulo *adj* cocky; (*bonito*) lovely (*Brit*), neat (*Amer*); (*Mex, atractivo*) cute. • *m* tough guy; (*proxeneta*) pimp
chup|ada *f* suck; (*al helado*) lick; (*al cigarro*) puff. **~ado** *adj* skinny; (*fam, fácil*) very easy. **~ar** *vt* suck; puff at (cigarro etc); (*absorber*) absorb. **~ete** *m* dummy (*Brit*), pacifier (*Amer*). **~ón** *m* sucker; (*LAm*) dummy (*Brit*), pacifier (*Amer*); (*Mex, del biberón*) teat
churrasco *m* barbecued steak
churro *m* fritter; 🅸 mess
chut|ar *vi* shoot. **~e** *m* shot
cianuro *m* cyanide
cibernética *f* cibernetics
cicatriz *f* scar. **~ar** **10** *vt/i* heal. **~arse** *vpr* heal
cíclico *adj* cyclic(al)
ciclis|mo *m* cycling. **~ta** *adj* cycle. • *m & f* cyclist
ciclo *m* cycle; (*de películas, conciertos*) season; (*de conferencias*) series
ciclomotor *m* moped
ciclón *m* cyclone
ciego *adj* blind. • *m* blind man, blind person. **a ciegas** in the dark
cielo *m* sky; (*Relig*) heaven; (*persona*) darling. **¡~s!** good heavens!, goodness me!
ciempiés *m invar* centipede
cien *adj* a hundred. **~ por ~** one hundred per cent
ciénaga *f* bog, swamp
ciencia *f* science; (*fig*) knowledge. **~s** *fpl* (*Univ etc*) science. **~s empresariales** business studies. **a ~ cierta** for certain
cieno *m* mud
científico *adj* scientific. • *m* scientist
ciento *adj & m* a hundred, one hundred. **~s de** hundreds of. **por ~** per cent
cierre *m* fastener; (*acción de cerrar*) shutting, closing; (*LAm, cremallera*) zip, zipper (*Amer*)
cierto *adj* certain; (*verdad*) true. **estar en lo ~** be right. **lo ~ es que** the fact is that. **no es ~** that's not true. **¿no es ~?** isn't that right? **por ~** by the way. **si bien es ~ que** although
ciervo *m* deer
cifra *f* figure, number; (*cantidad*) sum. **en ~** coded, in code. **~do** *adj* coded. **~r** *vt* code; place (esperanzas)
cigala *f* crayfish
cigarra *f* cicada
cigarr|illera *f* cigarette box; (*de bolsillo*) cigarette case. **~illo** *m* cigarette. **~o** *m* (*cigarrillo*) cigarette; (*puro*) cigar
cigüeña *f* stork
cilantro *m* coriander
cil|índrico *adj* cylindrical. **~indro** *m* cylinder
cima *f* top; (*fig*) summit
cimbr|ear *vt* shake. **~earse** *vpr* sway. **~onada** *f*, **~onazo** *m* (*LAm*) jolt; (*de explosión*) blast
cimentar **1** *vt* lay the foundations of; (*fig, reforzar*) strengthen
cimientos *mpl* foundations
cinc *m* zinc
cincel *m* chisel. **~ar** *vt* chisel
cinco *adj & m* five; (*en fechas*) fifth
cincuent|a *adj & m* fifty; (*quincuagésimo*) fiftieth. **~ón** *adj* in his fifties
cine *m* cinema; (*local*) cinema (*Brit*), movie theater (*Amer*). **~asta** *m & f*

film maker (*Brit*), movie maker (*Amer*). **~matográfico** *adj* film (*Brit*), movie (*Amer*)

cínico *adj* cynical. • *m* cynic

cinismo *m* cynicism

cinta *f* ribbon; (*película*) film (*Brit*), movie (*Amer*); (*para grabar, en carreras*) tape. **~ aislante** insulating tape. **~ métrica** tape measure. **~ virgen** blank tape

cintur|a *f* waist. **~ón** *m* belt. **~ón de seguridad** safety belt. **~ón salvavidas** lifebelt

ciprés *m* cypress (tree)

circo *m* circus

circuito *m* circuit; (*viaje*) tour. **~ cerrado** closed circuit. **corto ~** short circuit

circula|ción *f* circulation; (*vehículos*) traffic. **~r** *adj* circular. • *vi* circulate; (líquidos) flow; (*conducir*) drive; (*caminar*) walk; (autobús) run

círculo *m* circle. **~ vicioso** vicious circle. **en ~** in a circle

circunci|dar *vt* circumcise. **~sión** *f* circumcision

circunferencia *f* circumference

circunflejo *m* circumflex

circunscri|bir (*pp* **circunscrito**) *vt* confine. **~birse** *vpr* confine o.s. (a to). **~pción** *f* (*distrito*) district. **~pción electoral** constituency

circunspecto *adj* circumspect

circunstancia *f* circumstance

circunv|alar *vt* bypass. **~olar** *vt* **2** circle

cirio *m* candle

ciruela *f* plum. **~ pasa** prune

ciru|gía *f* surgery. **~jano** *m* surgeon

cisne *m* swan

cisterna *f* tank, cistern

cita *f* appointment; (*entre chico y chica*) date; (*referencia*) quotation. **~ a ciegas** blind date. **~ flash** speed dating. **~ción** *f* quotation; (*Jurid*) summons. **~do** *adj* aforementioned. **~r** *vt* make an appointment with; (*mencionar*) quote; (*Jurid*) summons. **~rse** *vpr* arrange to meet

cítara *f* zither

ciudad *f* town; (*grande*) city. **~ balneario** (*LAm*) coastal resort. **~ perdida** (*Mex*) shanty town. **~ universitaria** university campus. **~anía** *f* citizenship; (*habitantes*) citizens. **~ano** *adj* civic. • *m* citizen, inhabitant

cívico *adj* civic

civil *adj* civil. • *m & f* civil guard; (*persona no militar*) civilian

civiliza|ción *f* civilization. **~r** **10** *vt* civilize. **~rse** *vpr* become civilized

civismo *m* community spirit

clam|ar *vi* cry out, clamour. **~or** *m* clamour; (*protesta*) outcry. **~oroso** *adj* noisy; (*éxito*) resounding

clandestino *adj* clandestine, secret; (periódico) underground

clara *f* (*de huevo*) egg white

claraboya *f* skylight

clarear *vi* dawn; (*aclarar*) brighten up

clarete *m* rosé

claridad *f* clarity; (*luz*) light

clarifica|ción *f* clarification. **~r** **7** *vt* clarify

clar|ín *m* bugle. **~inete** *m* clarinet. **~inetista** *m & f* clarinettist

clarividen|cia *f* clairvoyance; (*fig*) far-sightedness. **~te** *adj* clairvoyant; (*fig*) far-sighted

claro *adj* clear; (*luminoso*) bright;

(colores) light; (líquido) thin. • *m* (*en bosque etc*) clearing; (*espacio*) gap. • *adv* clearly. • *int* of course! **¡~ que sí!** yes, of course! **¡~ que no!** of course not!

C

clase *f* class; (*tipo*) kind, sort; (*aula*) classroom. **~ media** middle class. **~ obrera** working class. **~ social** social class. **dar ~s** teach

clásico *adj* classical; (*típico*) classic. • *m* classic

clasifica|ción *f* classification; (*deportes*) league. **~r** 7 *vt* classify

claustro *m* cloister; (*Univ*) staff

claustrof|obia *f* claustrophobia. **~óbico** *adj* claustrophobic

cláusula *f* clause

clausura *f* closure

clava|do *adj* fixed; (*con clavo*) nailed. **es ~do a su padre** he's the spitting image of his father. • *m* (*LAm*) dive. **~r** *vt* knock in (clavo); stick in (cuchillo); (*fijar*) fix; (*juntar*) nail together

clave *f* key; (*Mus*) clef; (*instrumento*) harpsichord. **~cín** *m* harpsichord

clavel *m* carnation

clavícula *f* collarbone, clavicle

clav|ija *f* peg; (*Elec*) plug. **~o** *m* nail; (*Culin*) clove

claxon /'klakson/ *m* (*pl* **~s**) horn

clemencia *f* clemency, mercy

clementina *f* tangerine

cleptómano *m* kleptomaniac

clerical *adj* clerical

clérigo *m* priest

clero *m* clergy

clic *m*: **hacer ~ en** to click on

cliché *m* cliché; (*Foto*) negative

cliente *m* customer; (*de médico*) patient; (*de abogado*) client. **~la** *f* clientele, customers; (*de médico*) patients

clim|a *m* climate; (*ambiente*) atmosphere. **~ático** *adj* climatic. **~atizado** *adj* air-conditioned

clínic|a *f* clinic. **~o** *adj* clinical

cloaca *f* drain, sewer

clon *m* clone

cloro *m* chlorine

club *m* (*pl* **~s** *o* **~es**) club

coacci|ón *f* coercion. **~onar** *vt* coerce

coagular *vt* coagulate; clot (sangre); curdle (leche). **~se** *vpr* coagulate; (sangre) clot; (leche) curdle

coalición *f* coalition

coarta|da *f* alibi. **~r** *vt* hinder; restrict (libertad etc)

cobard|e *adj* cowardly. • *m* coward. **~ía** *f* cowardice

cobert|izo *m* shed. **~ura** *f* covering; (*en radio, TV*) coverage

cobij|a *f* (*Mex, manta*) blanket. **~as** *fpl* (*LAm, ropa de cama*) bedclothes. **~ar** *vt* shelter. **~arse** *vpr* (take) shelter. **~o** *m* shelter

cobra *f* cobra

cobra|dor *m* collector; (*de autobús*) conductor. **~r** *vt* collect; (*ganar*) earn; charge (precio); cash (cheque); (*recuperar*) recover. • *vi* be paid

cobr|e *m* copper. **~izo** *adj* coppery

cobro *m* collection; (*de cheque*) cashing; (*pago*) payment. **presentar al ~** cash

coca|ína *f* cocaine. **~lero** *adj* (of) coca farming. • *n* coca farmer

cocción *f* cooking; (*Tec*) firing

coc|er 2 & 9 *vt/i* cook; (*hervir*) boil; (*Tec*) fire. **~ido** *m* stew

coche *m* car, automobile (*Amer*); (*de tren*) coach, carriage; (*de bebé*) pram (*Brit*), baby carriage (*Amer*). **~-cama** sleeper. **~ fúnebre** hearse. **~ restaurante** dining-car. **~s de choque** dodgems. **~ra** *f* garage; (*de autobuses*) depot

cochin|ada *f* dirty thing. **~o** *adj* dirty, filthy. ● *m* pig

cociente *m* quotient. **~ intelectual** intelligence quotient, IQ

cocin|a *f* kitchen; (*arte*) cookery, cuisine; (*aparato*) cooker. **~a de gas** gas cooker. **~a eléctrica** electric cooker. **~ar** *vt/i* cook. **~ero** *m* cook

coco *m* coconut; (*árbol*) coconut palm; (*cabeza*) head; (*que mete miedo*) bogeyman. **comerse el ~** think hard

cocoa *f* (*LAm*) cocoa

cocodrilo *m* crocodile

cocotero *m* coconut palm

cóctel *m* (*pl* **~s** *o* **~es**) cocktail

cod|azo *m* nudge (with one's elbow). **~ear** *vt/i* elbow, nudge. **~earse** *vpr* rub shoulders (**con** with)

codici|a *f* greed. **~ado** *adj* coveted, sought after. **~ar** *vt* covet. **~oso** *adj* greedy

código *m* code. **~ de la circulación** Highway Code

codo *m* elbow; (*dobladura*) bend. **~ a ~** side by side. **hablar (hasta) por los ~s** talk too much

codorniz *m* quail

coeficiente *m* coefficient. **~ intelectual** intelligence quotient, IQ

coerción *f* constraint

coetáneo *adj & m* contemporary

coexist|encia *f* coexistence. **~ir** *vi* coexist

cofradía *f* brotherhood

cofre *m* chest; (*Mex, capó*) bonnet (*Brit*), hood (*Amer*)

coger **14** *vt* (*esp Esp*) take; catch (tren, autobús, pelota, catarro); (*agarrar*) take hold of; (*del suelo*) pick up; pick (frutos etc); (*LAm, vulgar*) to screw. **~se** *vpr* trap, catch; (*agarrarse*) hold on

cogollo *m* (*de lechuga etc*) heart; (*brote*) bud

cogote *m* nape; (*LAm, cuello*) neck

cohech|ar *vt* bribe. **~o** *m* bribery

cohe|rente *adj* coherent. **~sión** *f* cohesion

cohete *m* rocket

cohibi|do *adj* shy; (*inhibido*) awkward; (*incómodo*) awkward. **~r** *vt* inhibit; (*incomodar*) make s.o. feel embarrassed. **~rse** *vpr* feel inhibited

coima *f* (*LAm*) bribe

coincid|encia *f* coincidence. **dar la ~encia** happen. **~ir** *vt* coincide

coje|ar *vt* limp; (mueble) wobble. **~ra** *f* lameness

coj|ín *m* cushion. **~inete** *m* small cushion

cojo *adj* lame; (mueble) wobbly. ● *m* lame person

col *f* cabbage. **~es de Bruselas** Brussel sprouts

cola *f* tail; (*fila*) queue; (*para pegar*) glue. **a la ~** at the end. **hacer ~** queue (up) (*Brit*), line up (*Amer*)

colabora|ción *f* collaboration. **~dor** *m* collaborator. **~r** *vi* collaborate

colada *f* washing. **hacer la ~** do the washing

colador *m* strainer

colapso *m* collapse; (*fig*) standstill

colar [2] *vt* strain; pass (moneda falsa etc). • *vi* (líquido) seep through; (*fig*) be believed. **~se** *vpr* slip; (*en una cola*) jump the queue; (*en fiesta*) gatecrash

colch|a *f* bedspread. **~ón** *m* mattress. **~oneta** *f* air bed; (*en gimnasio*) mat

colear *vi* wag its tail; (asunto) not be resolved. **vivito y coleando** alive and kicking

colecci|ón *f* collection. **~onar** *vt* collect. **~onista** *m & f* collector

colecta *f* collection

colectivo *adj* collective

colega *m & f* colleague

colegi|al *m* schoolboy. **~ala** *f* schoolgirl. **~o** *m* school; (*de ciertas profesiones*) college. **~o mayor** hall of residence

cólera *m* cholera. • *f* anger, fury. **montar en ~** fly into a rage

colérico *adj* furious, irate

colesterol *m* cholesterol

coleta *f* pigtail

colga|nte *adj* hanging. • *m* pendant. **~r** [2] & [12] *vt* hang; hang out (ropa lavada); hang up (abrigo etc); put down (teléfono). • *vi* hang; (*teléfono*) hang up. **~rse** *vpr* hang o.s. **dejar a uno ~do** let s.o. down

colibrí *m* hummingbird

cólico *m* colic

coliflor *f* cauliflower

colilla *f* cigarette end

colina *f* hill

colinda|nte *adj* adjoining. **~r** *vt* border (**con** on)

colisión *f* collision, crash; (*fig*) clash

collar *m* necklace; (*de perro*) collar

colmar *vt* fill to the brim; try (paciencia); (*fig*) fulfill. **~ a uno de atenciones** lavish attention on s.o.

colmena *f* beehive, hive

colmillo *m* eye tooth, canine (tooth); (*de elefante*) tusk; (*de carnívoro*) fang

colmo *m* height. **ser el ~** be the limit, be the last straw

coloca|ción *f* positioning; (*empleo*) job, position. **~r** [7] *vt* put, place; (*buscar empleo*) find work for. **~rse** *vpr* find a job

Colombia *f* Colombia

colombiano *adj & m* Colombian

colon *m* colon

colón *m* (*unidad monetaria de Costa Rica y El Salvador*) colon

colon|ia *f* colony; (*comunidad*) community; (*agua de colonia*) cologne; (*Mex, barrio*) residential suburb. **~ia de verano** holiday camp. **~iaje** *m* (*LAm*) colonial period. **~ial** *adj* colonial. **~ialista** *m & f* colonialist. **~ización** *f* colonization. **~izar** [10] colonize. **~o** *m* colonist, settler; (*labrador*) tenant farmer

coloqui|al *adj* colloquial. **~o** *m* conversation; (*congreso*) conference

color *m* colour. **de ~** colour. **en ~(es)** (fotos, película) colour. **~ado** *adj* (*rojo*) red. **~ante** *m* colouring. **~ear** *vt/i* colour. **~ete** *m* blusher. **~ido** *m* colour

colosal *adj* colossal; (*fig, fam, magnífico*) terrific

columna *f* column; (*en anatomía*) spine. **~ vertebral** spinal column; (*fig*) backbone

columpi|ar *vt* swing. **~arse** *vpr* swing. **~o** *m* swing

coma *f* comma; (*Mat*) point. • *m*

(*Med*) coma

comadre *f* (*madrina*) godmother; (*amiga*) friend. **~ar** *vi* gossip

comadreja *f* weasel

comadrona *f* midwife

comal *m* (*Mex*) griddle

comand|ancia *f* command. **~ante** *m & f* commander. **~o** *m* command; (*Mil, soldado*) commando; (*de terroristas*) cell

comarca *f* area, region

comba *f* bend; (*juguete*) skipping-rope; (*de viga*) sag. **saltar a la ~** skip. **~rse** *vpr* bend; (viga) sag

combat|e *m* combat; (*pelea*) fight. **~iente** *m* fighter. **~ir** *vt/i* fight

combina|ción *f* combination; (*enlace*) connection; (*prenda*) slip. **~r** *vt* combine; put together (colores)

combustible *m* fuel

comedia *f* comedy; (*cualquier obra de teatro*) play; (*LAm, telenovela*) soap (opera)

comedi|do *adj* restrained; (*LAm, atento*) obliging. **~rse** 5 *vpr* show restraint

comedor *m* dining-room; (*restaurante*) restaurant

comensal *m* fellow diner

comentar *vt* comment on; discuss (tema); (*mencionar*) mention. **~io** *m* commentary; (*observación*) comment. **~ios** *mpl* gossip. **~ista** *m & f* commentator

comenzar 1 & 10 *vt/i* begin, start

comer *vt* eat; (*a mediodía*) have for lunch; (*esp LAm, cenar*) have for dinner; (*corroer*) eat away; (*en ajedrez*) take. ● *vi* eat; (*a mediodía*) have lunch; (*esp LAm, cenar*) have dinner. **dar de ~** a feed. **~se** *vpr* eat (up)

comerci|al *adj* commercial; (ruta) trade; (nombre, trato) business. ● *m* (*LAm*) commercial, ad. **~ante** *m* trader; (*de tienda*) shopkeeper. **~ar** *vi* trade (**con** with, **en** in); (*con otra persona*) do business. **~o** *m* commerce; (*actividad*) trade; (*tienda*) shop; (*negocios*) business. **~o justo** fair trade

comestible *adj* edible. **~s** *mpl* food. **tienda de ~s** grocer's (shop) (*Brit*), grocery (*Amer*)

cometa *m* comet. ● *f* kite

comet|er *vt* commit; make (falta). **~ido** *m* task

comezón *m* itch

comicios *mpl* elections

cómico *adj* comic; (*gracioso*) funny. ● *m* comic actor; (*humorista*) comedian

comida *f* food; (*a mediodía*) lunch; (*esp LAm, cena*) dinner; (*acto*) meal

comidilla *f*. **ser la ~ del pueblo** be the talk of the town

comienzo *m* beginning, start

comillas *fpl* inverted commas

comil|ón *adj* greedy. **~ona** *f* feast

comino *m* cumin. **(no) me importa un ~** I couldn't care less

comisar|ía *f* police station. **~io** *m* commissioner; (*deportes*) steward

comisión *f* assignment; (*organismo*) commission, committee; (*Com*) commission

comisura *f* corner. **~ de los labios** corner of the mouth

comité *m* committee

como *prep* as; (*comparación*) like. ● *adv* about. ● *conj* as. **~ quieras** as you like. **~ si** as if

cómo *adverbio*

····➤ how. **¿~ se llega?** how do you get there? **¿~ es de alto?** how tall is it? **sé ~ pasó** I know how it happened

> ! Cuando **cómo** va seguido del verbo **llamar** se traduce por *what,* p. ej. **¿~ te llamas?** *what's your name?*

····➤ cómo + *ser* (*sugiriendo descripción*) **¿~ es su marido?** what's her husband like?; (*físicamente*) what does her husband look like? **no sé ~ es la comida** I don't know what the food's like

····➤ (*por qué*) why. **¿~ no actuaron antes?** why didn't they act sooner?

····➤ (*pidiendo que se repita*) sorry?, pardon? **¿~? no te escuché** sorry? I didn't hear you

····➤ (*en exclamaciones*) **¡~ llueve!** it's really pouring! **¡~! ¿que no lo sabes?** what! you mean you don't know? **¡~ no!** of course!

cómoda *f* chest of drawers
comodidad *f* comfort. **a su ~** at your convenience
cómodo *adj* comfortable; (*conveniente*) convenient
comoquiera *conj.* **~ que sea** however it may be
compacto *adj* compact; (*denso*) dense; (líneas etc) close
compadecer **11** *vt* feel sorry for. **~se** *vpr.* **~se de** feel sorry for
compadre *m* godfather; (*amigo*) friend
compañ|ero *m* companion; (*de trabajo*) colleague; (*de clase*) classmate; (*pareja*) partner. **~ía** *f* company. **en ~ía de** with
compara|ble *adj* comparable. **~ción** *f* comparison. **~r** *vt* compare. **~tivo** *adj & m* comparative
comparecer **11** *vi* appear
comparsa *f* group. ● *m & f* (*en el teatro*) extra
compartim(i)ento *m* compartment
compartir *vt* share
compás *m* (*instrumento*) (pair of) compasses; (*ritmo*) rhythm; (*división*) bar (*Brit*), measure (*Amer*); (*Naut*) compass. **a ~** in time
compasi|ón *f* compassion, pity. **tener ~ón de** feel sorry for. **~vo** *adj* compassionate
compatib|ilidad *f* compatibility. **~le** *adj* compatible
compatriota *m & f* compatriot
compendio *m* summary
compensa|ción *f* compensation. **~ción por despido** redundancy payment. **~r** *vt* compensate
competen|cia *f* competition; (*capacidad*) competence; (*poder*) authority; (*incumbencia*) jurisdiction. **~te** *adj* competent
competi|ción *f* competition. **~dor** *m* competitor. **~r** **5** *vi* compete
compinche *m* accomplice; (*fam, amigo*) friend, mate **I**
complac|er **32** *vt* please. **~erse** *vpr* be pleased. **~iente** *adj* obliging; (marido) complaisant
complej|idad *f* complexity. **~o** *adj & m* complex
complement|ario *adj* complementary. **~o** *m* complement; (*Gram*) object, complement
complet|ar *vt* complete. **~o** *adj* complete; (*lleno*) full; (*exhaustivo*)

comprehensive

complexión *f* build

complica|ción *f* complication; (*esp AmL*, *implicación*) involvement. **~r** 7 *vt* complicate; involve (persona). **~rse** *vpr* become complicated; (*implicarse*) get involved

cómplice *m & f* accomplice

complot *m* (*pl* **~s**) plot

compon|ente *adj* component. ● *m* component; (*miembro*) member. **~er** 34 *vt* make up; (*Mus, Literatura etc*) write, compose; (*esp LAm*, *reparar*) mend; (*LAm*) set (hueso); settle (estómago). **~erse** *vpr* be made up; (*arreglarse*) get better. **~érselas** manage

comporta|miento *m* behaviour. **~rse** *vpr* behave. **~rse mal** misbehave

composi|ción *f* composition. **~tor** *m* composer

compostura *f* composure; (*LAm*, *arreglo*) repair

compota *f* stewed fruit

compra *f* purchase. **~ a plazos** hire purchase. **hacer la(s) ~(s)** do the shopping. **ir de ~s** go shopping. **~dor** *m* buyer. **~r** *vt* buy. **~venta** *f* buying and selling; (*Jurid*) sale and purchase contract. **negocio** *m* **de ~venta** second-hand shop

compren|der *vt* understand; (*incluir*) include. **~sión** *f* understanding. **~sivo** *adj* understanding

compresa *f* compress; (*de mujer*) sanitary towel

compr|esión *f* compression. **~imido** *adj* compressed. ● *m* pill, tablet. **~imir** *vt* compress

comproba|nte *m* proof; (*recibo*) receipt. **~r** *vt* check; (*demostrar*) prove

comprom|eter *vt* compromise; (*arriesgar*) jeopardize. **~eterse** *vpr* compromise o.s.; (*obligarse*) agree to; (novios) get engaged. **~etido** *adj* (situación) awkward, delicate; (autor) politically committed. **~iso** *m* obligation; (*apuro*) predicament; (*cita*) appointment; (*acuerdo*) agreement. **sin ~iso** without obligation

compuesto *adj* compound; (persona) smart. ● *m* compound

computa|ción *f* (*esp LAm*) computing. **curso** *m* **de ~ción** computer course. **~dor** *m*, **computadora** *f* computer. **~r** *vt* calculate. **~rizar**, **computerizar** 10 *vt* computerize

cómputo *m* calculation

comulgar 12 *vi* take Communion

común *adj* common; (*compartido*) joint. **en ~** in common. **por lo ~** generally. ● *m* **el ~ de** most

comunal *adj* communal

comunica|ción *f* communication. **~do** *m* communiqué. **~do de prensa** press release. **~r** 7 *vt* communicate; (*informar*) inform; (*LAm*, *por teléfono*) put through. **está ~ndo** (teléfono) it's engaged. **~rse** *vpr* communicate; (*ponerse en contacto*) get in touch. **~tivo** *adj* communicative

comunidad *f* community. **~ de vecinos** residents' association. **C~ (Económica) Europea** European (Economic) Community. **en ~** together

Comunidad Autónoma *i*

In 1978 Spain was divided into *comunidades autónomas* or *autonomías*, which have far greater powers than the old

C

regiones. The *comunidades autónomas* are: Andalusia, Aragon, Asturias, Balearic Islands, the Basque Country, Canary Islands, Cantabria, Castilla y León, Castilla-La Mancha, Catalonia, Extremadura, Galicia, Madrid, Murcia, Navarre, La Rioja, Valencia and the North African enclaves of Ceuta and Melilla.

comunión *f* communion; (*Relig*) (Holy) Communion

comunis|mo *m* communism. **~ta** *adj & m & f* communist

con *prep* with; (+ *infinitivo*) by. **~ decir la verdad** by telling the truth. **~ que** so. **~ tal que** as long as

concebir 5 *vt/i* conceive

conceder *vt* concede, grant; award (premio); (*admitir*) admit

concej|al *m* councillor. **~ero** *m* (*LAm*) councillor. **~o** *m* council

concentra|ción *f* concentration; (*Pol*) rally. **~r** *vt* concentrate; assemble (personas). **~rse** *vpr* concentrate

concep|ción *f* conception. **~to** *m* concept; (*opinión*) opinion. **bajo ningún ~to** in no way

concerniente *adj*. **en lo ~ a** with regard to

concertar 1 *vt* arrange; agree (upon) (plan)

concesión *f* concession

concha *f* shell; (*carey*) tortoiseshell

conciencia *f* conscience; (*conocimiento*) awareness. **~ limpia** clear conscience. **~ sucia** guilty conscience. **a ~ de que** fully aware that. **en ~** honestly. **tener ~ de** be aware of. **tomar ~ de** become aware of. **~r** *vt* make aware. **~rse** *vpr* become aware

concientizar 10 *vt* (*esp LAm*) make aware. **~se** *vpr* become aware

concienzudo *adj* conscientious

concierto *m* concert; (*acuerdo*) agreement; (*Mus, composición*) concerto

concilia|ción *f* reconciliation. **~r** *vt* reconcile. **~r el sueño** get to sleep. **~rse** *vpr* gain

concilio *m* council

conciso *m* concise

conclu|ir 17 *vt* finish; (*deducir*) conclude. • *vi* finish, end. **~sión** *f* conclusion. **~yente** *adj* conclusive

concord|ancia *f* agreement. **~ar** 2 *vt* reconcile. • *vi* agree. **~e** *adj* in agreement. **~ia** *f* harmony

concret|amente *adv* specifically, to be exact. **~ar** *vt* make specific. **~arse** *vpr* become definite; (*limitarse*) confine o.s. **~o** *adj* concrete; (*determinado*) specific, particular. **en ~o** definite; (*concretamente*) to be exact; (*en resumen*) in short. • *m* (*LAm, hormigón*) concrete

concurr|encia *f* concurrence; (*reunión*) audience. **~ido** *adj* crowded, busy. **~ir** *vi* meet; ; (*coincidir*) agree. **~ a** (*asistir a*) attend

concurs|ante *m & f* competitor, contestant. **~ar** *vi* compete, take part. **~o** *m* competition; (*ayuda*) help

cond|ado *m* county. **~e** *m* earl, count

condena *f* sentence. **~ción** *f* condemnation. **~do** *m* convicted person. **~r** *vt* condemn; (*Jurid*) convict

condensa|ción *f* condensation.

~**r** *vt* condense
condesa *f* countess
condescende|ncia *f* condescension; (*tolerancia*) indulgence. ~**r** 1 *vi* agree; (*dignarse*) condescend
condici|ón *f* condition. **a ~ón de (que)** on condition that. ~**onal** *adj* conditional. ~**onar** *vt* condition
condiment|ar *vt* season. ~**o** *m* seasoning
condolencia *f* condolence
condominio *m* joint ownership; (*LAm, edificio*) block of flats (*Brit*), condominium (*esp Amer*)
condón *m* condom
condonar *vt* (*perdonar*) reprieve; cancel (deuda)
conducir 47 *vt* drive (vehículo); carry (electricidad, gas, agua). • *vi* drive; (*fig, llevar*) lead. **¿a qué conduce?** what's the point? ~**se** *vpr* behave
conducta *f* behaviour
conducto *m* pipe, tube; (*en anatomía*) duct. **por ~ de** through. ~**r** *m* driver; (*jefe*) leader; (*Elec*) conductor
conduzco *vb véase* **CONDUCIR**
conectar *vt/i* connect
conejo *m* rabbit
conexión *f* connection
confabularse *vpr* plot
confecci|ón *f* (*de trajes*) tailoring; (*de vestidos*) dressmaking. ~**ones** *fpl* clothing, clothes. **de ~ón** ready-to-wear. ~**onar** *vt* make
confederación *f* confederation
conferencia *f* conference; (*al teléfono*) long-distance call; (*Univ*) lecture. **~ en la cima, ~ (en la) cumbre** summit conference. ~**nte** *m & f* lecturer
conferir 4 *vt* confer; award (premio)
confes|ar 1 *vt/i* confess. ~**arse** *vpr* confess. ~**ión** *f* confession. ~**ionario** *m* confessional. ~**or** *m* confessor
confeti *m* confetti
confia|do *adj* trusting; (*seguro de sí mismo*) confident. ~**nza** *f* trust; (*en sí mismo*) confidence; (*intimidad*) familiarity. ~**r** 20 *vt* entrust. •*vi.* **~r en** trust
confiden|cia *f* confidence, secret. ~**cial** *adj* confidential. ~**te** *m* confidant. •*f* confidante
configur|ación *f* configuration. ~**ar** *vt* to configure
conf|ín *m* border. ~**ines** *mpl* outermost parts. ~**inar** *vt* confine; (*desterrar*) banish
confirma|ción *f* confirmation. ~**r** *vt* confirm
confiscar 7 *vt* confiscate
confit|ería *f* sweet-shop (*Brit*), candy store (*Amer*). ~**ura** *f* jam
conflict|ivo *adj* difficult; (época) troubled; (*polémico*) controversial. ~**o** *m* conflict
confluencia *f* confluence
conform|ación *f* conformation, shape. ~**ar** *vt* (*acomodar*) adjust. • *vi* agree. ~**arse** *vpr* conform. ~**e** *adj* in agreement;(*contento*) happy, satisfied; (*según*) according (**con** to). **~e a** in accordance with, according to. • *conj* as. • *int* OK!. ~**idad** *f* agreement; (*tolerancia*) resignation. ~**ista** *m & f* conformist
conforta|ble *adj* comfortable. ~**nte** *adj* comforting. ~**r** *vt* comfort
confronta|ción *f* confrontation. ~**r** *vt* confront
confu|ndir *vt* (*equivocar*) mistake,

confuse; (*mezclar*) mix up, confuse; (*turbar*) embarrass. **~ndirse** *vpr* become confused; (*equivocarse*) make a mistake. **~sión** *f* confusion; (*vergüenza*) embarrassment. **~so** *adj* confused; (*borroso*) blurred

congela|do *adj* frozen. **~dor** *m* freezer. **~r** *vt* freeze

congeniar *vi* get on

congesti|ón *f* congestion. **~onado** *adj* congested. **~onarse** *vpr* become congested

congoja *f* distress; (*pena*) grief

congraciarse *vpr* ingratiate o.s.

congratular *vt* congratulate

congrega|ción *f* gathering; (*Relig*) congregation. **~rse** 12 *vpr* gather, assemble

congres|ista *m & f* delegate, member of a congress. **~o** *m* congress, conference. **C~o** Parliament. **C~o de los Diputados** Chamber of Deputies

cónico *adj* conical

conífer|a *f* conifer. **~o** *adj* coniferous

conjetura *f* conjecture, guess. **~r** *vt* conjecture, guess

conjuga|ción *f* conjugation. **~r** 12 *vt* conjugate

conjunción *f* conjunction

conjunto *adj* joint. • *m* collection; (*Mus*) band; (*ropa*) suit, outfit. **en ~** altogether

conjurar *vt* exorcise; avert (peligro). • *vi* plot, conspire

conllevar *vt* to entail

conmemora|ción *f* commemoration. **~r** *vt* commemorate

conmigo *pron* with me

conmo|ción *f* shock; (*tumulto*) upheaval. **~ cerebral** concussion. **~cionar** *vt* shock. **~ver** 2 *vt* shake; (*emocionar*) move

conmuta|dor *m* switch; (*LAm, de teléfonos*) switchboard. **~r** *vt* exchange

connota|ción *f* connotation. **~do** *adj* (*LAm, destacado*) distinguished. **~r** *vt* connote

cono *m* cone

conoc|edor *adj & m* expert. **~er** 11 *vt* know; (*por primera vez*) meet; (*reconocer*) recognize, know. **se conoce que** apparently. **dar a ~er** make known. **~erse** *vpr* know o.s.; (dos personas) know each other; (*notarse*) be obvious. **~ido** *adj* well-known. • *m* acquaintance. **~imiento** *m* knowledge; (*sentido*) consciousness. **sin ~imiento** unconscious. **tener ~imiento de** know about

conozco *vb véase* **CONOCER**

conque *conj* so

conquista *f* conquest. **~dor** *adj* conquering. • *m* conqueror; (*de América*) conquistador. **~r** *vt* conquer, win

consabido *adj* usual, habitual

Conquistadores The collective term for the succession of explorers, soldiers and adventurers who, from the sixteenth century onward led the settlement and exploitation of Spain's Latin American colonies.

consagra|ción *f* consecration. **~r** *vt* consecrate; (*fig*) devote. **~rse** *vpr* devote o.s.

consanguíneo *m* blood relation

consciente *adj* conscious

consecuen|cia *f* consequence; (*coherencia*) consistency. **a ~cia de** as a result of. **~te** *adj* consistent

consecutivo *adj* consecutive

conseguir 5 & 13 *vt* get, obtain; (*lograr*) manage; achieve (objetivo)

consej|ero *m* adviser; (*miembro de consejo*) member. **~o** *m* piece of advice; (*Pol*) council. **~o de ministros** cabinet

consenso *m* assent, consent

consenti|do *adj* (niño) spoilt. **~miento** *m* consent. **~r** 4 *vt* allow; spoil (niño). ● *vi* consent

conserje *m* porter, caretaker. **~ría** *f* porter's office

conserva *f* (*mermelada*) preserve; (*en lata*) tinned food. **en ~** tinned (*Brit*), canned. **~ción** *f* conservation; (*de alimentos*) preservation

conservador *adj & m* (*Pol*) conservative

conservar *vt* keep; preserve (alimentos). **~se** *vpr* keep; (costumbre) survive

conservatorio *m* conservatory

considera|ble *adj* considerable. **~ción** *f* consideration; (*respeto*) respect. **de ~ción** serious. **de mi ~ción** (*LAm, en cartas*) Dear Sir. **~do** *adj* considerate; (*respetado*) respected. **~r** *vt* consider; (*respetar*) respect

consigna *f* order; (*para equipaje*) left luggage office (*Brit*), baggage room (*Amer*); (*eslogan*) slogan

consigo *pron* (*él*) with him; (*ella*) with her; (*Ud, Uds*) with you; (*uno mismo*) with o.s.

consiguiente *adj* consequent. **por ~** consequently

consist|encia *f* consistency. **~ente** *adj* consisting (**en** of); (*firme*) solid; (*LAm, congruente*) consistent. **~ir** *vi*. **~ en** consist of; (*radicar en*) be due to

consola|ción *f* consolation. **~r** 2 *vt* console, comfort. **~rse** *vpr* console o.s.

consolidar *vt* consolidate. **~se** *vpr* consolidate

consomé *m* clear soup, consommé

consonante *adj* consonant. ● *f* consonant

consorcio *m* consortium

conspira|ción *f* conspiracy. **~dor** *m* conspirator. **~r** *vi* conspire

consta|ncia *f* constancy; (*prueba*) proof; (*LAm, documento*) written evidence. **~nte** *adj* constant. **~r** *vi* be clear; (*figurar*) appear, figure; (*componerse*) consist. **hacer ~r** state; (*por escrito*) put on record. **me ~ que** I'm sure that. **que conste que** believe me

constatar *vt* check; (*confirmar*) confirm

constipa|do *m* cold. ● *adj*. **estar ~do** have a cold; (*LAm, estreñido*) be constipated. **~rse** *vpr* catch a cold

constitu|ción *f* constitution; (*establecimiento*) setting up. **~cional** *adj* constitutional. **~ir** 17 *vt* constitute; (*formar*) form; (*crear*) set up, establish. **~irse** *vpr* set o.s. up (**en** as). **~tivo** *adj*, **~yente** *adj* constituent

constru|cción *f* construction. **~ctor** *m* builder. **~ir** 17 *vt* construct; build (edificio)

consuelo *m* consolation

consuetudinario *adj* customary

cónsul *m & f* consul

consulado *m* consulate

consult|a *f* consultation. **horas** *fpl* **de ~a** surgery hours. **obra** *f* **de ~a** reference book. **~ar** *vt* consult. **~orio** *m* surgery

C

consumar *vt* complete; commit (crimen); carry out (robo); consummate (matrimonio)

consum|ición *f* consumption; (*bebida*) drink; (*comida*) food. **~ición mínima** minimum charge. **~ido** *adj* (persona) skinny, wasted. **~idor** *m* consumer. **~ir** *vt* consume. **~irse** *vpr* (persona) waste away; (vela, cigarillo) burn down; (líquido) dry up. **~ismo** *m* consumerism. **~o** *m* consumption; (*LAm, en restaurante etc*) (*bebida*) drink; (*comida*) food. **~o mínimo** minimum charge

contab|ilidad *f* book-keeping; (*profesión*) accountancy. **~le** *m & f* accountant

contacto *m* contact. **ponerse en ~ con** get in touch with

conta|do *adj*. **al ~** cash. **~s** *adj pl* few. **tiene los días ~s** his days are numbered. **~dor** *m* meter; (*LAm, persona*) accountant

contagi|ar *vt* infect (persona); pass on (enfermedad); (*fig*) contaminate. **~o** *m* infection; (*directo*) contagion. **~oso** *adj* infectious; (*por contacto directo*) contagious

contamina|ción *f* contamination, pollution. **~r** *vt* contaminate, pollute

contante *adj*. **dinero** *m* **~** cash

contar **2** *vt* count; tell (relato). **se cuenta que** it's said that. ● *vi* count. **~ con** rely on, count on. **~se** *vpr* be included (**entre** among)

contempla|ción *f* contemplation. **sin ~ciones** unceremoniously. **~r** *vt* look at; (*fig*) contemplate

contemporáneo *adj & m* contemporary

conten|er **40** *vt* contain; hold (respiración). **~erse** *vpr* contain o.s. **~ido** *adj* contained. ●*m* contents

content|ar *vt* please. **~arse** *vpr*. **~arse con** be satisfied with, be pleased with. **~o** *adj* (*alegre*) happy; (*satisfecho*) pleased

contesta|ción *f* answer. **~dor** *m*. **~ automático** answering machine. **~r** *vt/i* answer; (*replicar*) answer back

contexto *m* context

contienda *f* conflict; (*lucha*) contest

contigo *pron* with you

contiguo *adj* adjacent

continen|tal *adj* continental. **~te** *m* continent

continu|ación *f* continuation. **a ~ación** immediately after. **~ar** **21** *vt* continue, resume. ● *vi* continue. **~idad** *f* continuity. **~o** *adj* continuous; (*frecuente*) continual. **corriente** *f* **~a** direct current

contorno *m* outline; (*de árbol*) girth; (*de caderas*) measurement. **~s** *mpl* surrounding area

contorsión *f* contortion

contra *prep* against. **en ~** against. ● *m* cons. ●*f* snag. **llevar la ~** contradict

contraata|car **7** *vt/i* counterattack. **~que** *m* counter-attack

contrabaj|ista *m & f* double-bass player. **~o** *m* double-bass; (*persona*) double-bass player

contraband|ista *m & f* smuggler. **~o** *m* contraband

contracción *f* contraction

contrad|ecir **46** *vt* contradict. **~icción** *f* contradiction. **~ictorio** *adj* contradictory

contraer **41** *vt* contract. **~ matri-**

monio marry. **~se** *vpr* contract
contralto *m* counter tenor. • *f* contralto
contra|mano. **a ~** in the wrong direction. **~partida** *f* compensation. **~pelo**. **a ~** the wrong way
contrapes|ar *vt* counterweight. **~o** *m* counterweight
contraproducente *adj* counterproductive
contrari|a *f*. **llevar la ~a** contradict. **~ado** *adj* upset; (*enojado*) annoyed. **~ar** 20 *vt* upset; (*enojar*) annoy. **~edad** *f* setback; (*disgusto*) annoyance. **~o** *adj* contrary (**a** to); (dirección) opposite. **al ~o** on the contrary. **al ~o de** contrary to. **de lo ~o** otherwise. **por el ~o** on the contrary. **ser ~o a** be opposed to, be against
contrarrestar *vt* counteract
contrasentido *m* contradiction
contraseña *f* (*palabra*) password; (*en cine*) stub
contrast|ar *vt* check, verify. • *vi* contrast. **~e** *m* contrast; (*en oro, plata*) hallmark
contratar *vt* contract (servicio); hire, take on (empleados); sign up (jugador)
contratiempo *m* setback; (*accidente*) mishap
contrat|ista *m & f* contractor. **~o** *m* contract
contraven|ción *f* contravention. **~ir** 53 *vt* contravene
contraventana *f* shutter
contribu|ción *f* contribution; (*tributo*) tax. **~ir** 17 *vt/i* contribute. **~yente** *m & f* contributor; (*que paga impuestos*) taxpayer
contrincante *m* rival, opponent
control *m* control; (*vigilancia*) check; (*lugar*) checkpoint. **~ar** *vt* control; (*vigilar*) check. **~arse** *vpr* control s.o.
controversia *f* controversy
contundente *adj* (arma) blunt; (argumento) convincing
contusión *f* bruise
convalec|encia *f* convalescence. **~er** 11 *vi* convalesce. **~iente** *adj & m & f* convalescent
convalidar *vt* recognize (título)
convenc|er 9 *vt* convince. **~imiento** *m* conviction
convenci|ón *f* convention. **~onal** *adj* conventional
conveni|encia *f* convenience; (*aptitud*) suitability. **~ente** *adj* suitable; (*aconsejable*) advisable; (*provechoso*) useful. **~o** *m* agreement. **~r** 53 *vt* agree. • *vi* agree (**en** on); (*ser conveniente*) be convenient for, suit; (*ser aconsejable*) be advisable
convento *m* (*de monjes*) monastery; (*de monjas*) convent
conversa|ción *f* conversation. **~ciones** *fpl* talks. **~r** *vi* converse, talk
conver|sión *f* conversion. **~so** *adj* converted. • *m* convert. **~tible** *adj* convertible. • *m* (*LAm*) convertible. **~tir** 4 *vt* convert. **~tirse** *vpr.* **~tirse en** turn into; (*Relig*) convert
convic|ción *f* conviction. **~to** *adj* convicted
convida|do *m* guest. **~r** *vt* invite
convincente *adj* convincing
conviv|encia *f* coexistence; (*de parejas*) life together. **~ir** *vi* live together; (*coexistir*) coexist
convocar 7 *vt* call (huelga, elecciones); convene (reunión); summon (personas)
convulsión *f* convulsion
conyugal *adj* marital, conjugal; (vida) married

C

cónyuge *m* spouse. **~s** *mpl* married couple

coñac *m* (*pl* ~s) brandy

coopera|ción *f* cooperation. **~r** *vi* cooperate. **~nte** *m & f* voluntary aid worker. **~tiva** *f* cooperative. **~tivo** *adj* cooperative

coordinar *vt* coordinate

copa *f* glass; (*deportes, fig*) cup; (*de árbol*) top. **~s** *fpl* (*naipes*) hearts. **tomar una ~** have a drink

copia *f* copy. **~ en limpio** fair copy. **sacar una ~** make a copy. **~r** *vt* copy

copioso *adj* copious; (lluvia, nevada etc) heavy

copla *f* verse; (*canción*) folksong

copo *m* flake. **~ de nieve** snowflake. **~s de maíz** cornflakes

coquet|a *f* flirt; (*mueble*) dressing-table. **~ear** *vi* flirt. **~o** *adj* flirtatious

coraje *m* courage; (*rabia*) anger

coral *adj* choral. ● *m* coral; (*Mus*) chorale

coraza *f* cuirass; (*Naut*) armour-plating; (*de tortuga*) shell

coraz|ón *m* heart; (*persona*) darling. **sin ~ón** heartless. **tener buen ~ón** be good-hearted. **~onada** *f* hunch; (*impulso*) impulse

corbata *f* tie, necktie (*esp Amer*). **~ de lazo** bow tie

corche|a *f* quaver. **~te** *m* fastener, hook and eye; (*gancho*) hook; (*paréntesis*) square bracket

corcho *m* cork. **~lata** *f* (*Mex*) (crown) cap

corcova *f* hump

cordel *m* cord, string

cordero *m* lamb

cordial *adj* cordial, friendly. ● *m* tonic. **~idad** *f* cordiality, warmth

cordillera *f* mountain range

córdoba *m* (*unidad monetaria de Nicaragua*) córdoba

cordón *m* string; (*de zapatos*) lace; (*cable*) cord; (*fig*) cordon. **~ umbilical** umbilical cord

coreografía *f* choreography

corista *f* (*bailarina*) chorus girl

cornet|a *f* bugle; (*Mex, de coche*) horn. **~ín** *m* cornet

coro *m* (*Mus*) choir; (*en teatro*) chorus

corona *f* crown; (*de flores*) wreath, garland. **~ción** *f* coronation. **~r** *vt* crown

coronel *m* colonel

coronilla *f* crown. **estar hasta la ~** be fed up

corpora|ción *f* corporation. **~l** *adj* (castigo) corporal; (trabajo) physical

corpulento *adj* stout

corral *m* farmyard. **aves** *fpl* **de ~** poultry

correa *f* strap; (*de perro*) lead; (*cinturón*) belt

correc|ción *f* correction; (*cortesía*) good manners. **~to** *adj* correct; (*cortés*) polite

corrector ortográfico *m* spell checker

corre|dizo *adj* running. **nudo** *m* **~dizo** slip knot. **puerta** *f* **~diza** sliding door. **~dor** *m* runner; (*pasillo*) corridor; (*agente*) agent, broker. **~dor de coches** racing driver

corregir 5 & 14 *vt* correct

correlación *f* correlation

correo *m* post, mail; (*persona*) courier; (*LAm, oficina*) post office. **~s** *mpl* post office. **~ electrónico**

e-mail. **echar al ~** post

correr *vt* run; (*mover*) move; draw (cortinas). ● *vi* run; (agua, electricidad etc) flow; (tiempo) pass. **~se** *vpr* (*apartarse*) move along; (colores) run

correspond|encia *f* correspondence. **~er** *vi* correspond; (*ser adecuado*) be fitting; (*contestar*) reply; (*pertenecer*) belong; (*incumbir*) fall to. **~erse** *vpr* (*amarse*) love one another. **~iente** *adj* corresponding

corresponsal *m* correspondent

corrid|a *f* run. **~a de toros** bullfight. **de ~a** from memory. **~o** *adj* (*continuo*) continuous

corriente *adj* (agua) running; (monedas, publicación, cuenta, año) current; (*ordinario*) ordinary. ● *f* current; (*de aire*) draught; (*fig*) tendency. ● *m* current month. **al ~** (*al día*) up-to-date; (*enterado*) aware

corr|illo *m* small group. **~o** *m* circle

corroborar *vt* corroborate

corroer 24 & 37 *vt* corrode; (*en geología*) erode; (*fig*) eat away

corromper *vt* corrupt, rot (materia). **~se** *vpr* become corrupted; (materia) rot; (alimentos) go bad

corrosi|ón *f* corrosion. **~vo** *adj* corrosive

corrupción *f* corruption; (*de materia etc*) rot

corsé *m* corset

corta|do *adj* cut; (carretera) closed; (leche) curdled; (*avergonzado*) embarrassed; (*confuso*) confused. ● *m* coffee with a little milk. **~dura** *f* cut. **~nte** *adj* sharp; (viento) biting; (frío) bitter. **~r** *vt* cut; (*recortar*) cut out; (*aislar, separar, interrumpir*) cut off. ● *vi* cut; (novios) break up. **~rse** *vpr* cut o.s.; (leche etc) curdle; (*fig*) be embarrassed. **~rse el pelo** have one's hair cut. **~rse las uñas** cut one's nails. **~uñas** *m invar* nail-clippers

corte *m* cut; (*de tela*) length. **~ de luz** power cut. **~ y confección** dressmaking. ● *f* court; (*LAm, tribunal*) Court of Appeal. **hacer la ~** court. **las C~s** the Spanish parliament. **la C~ Suprema** the Supreme Court

cortej|ar *vt* court. **~o** *m* (*de rey etc*) entourage. **~o fúnebre** cortège, funeral procession

cortés *adj* polite

cortesía *f* courtesy

corteza *f* bark; (*de queso*) rind; (*de pan*) crust

cortijo *m* farm; (*casa*) farmhouse

cortina *f* curtain

corto *adj* short; (*apocado*) shy. **~ de** short of. **~ de alcances** dim, thick. **~ de vista** short-sighted. **a la corta o a la larga** sooner or later. **quedarse ~** fall short; (*subestimar*) underestimate. **~circuito** *m* short circuit.

Coruña *f*. **La ~** Corunna

cosa *f* thing; (*asunto*) business; (*idea*) idea. **como si tal ~** just like that; (*como si no hubiera pasado nada*) as if nothing had happened. **decirle a uno cuatro ~s** tell s.o. a thing or two

cosecha *f* harvest; (*de vino*) vintage. **~r** *vt* harvest

coser *vt* sew; sew on (botón); stitch (herida). ● *vi* sew. **~se** *vpr* stick to s.o.

cosmético *adj & m* cosmetic

cósmico *adj* cosmic

cosmo|polita *adj & m & f* cosmo-

C

politan. ~s *m* cosmos
cosquillas *fpl*. **dar ~** tickle. **hacer ~** tickle. **tener ~** be ticklish
costa *f* coast. **a ~ de** at the expense of. **a toda ~** at any cost
costado *m* side
costal *m* sack
costar 2 *vt* cost. ● *vi* cost; (*resultar difícil*) to be hard. **~ caro** be expensive. **cueste lo que cueste** at any cost
costarricense *adj & m*, **costarriqueño** *adj & m* Costa Rican
cost|as *fpl* (*Jurid*) costs. **~e** *m* cost. **~ear** *vt* pay for; (*Naut*) sail along the coast
costero *adj* coastal
costilla *f* rib; (*chuleta*) chop
costo *m* cost. **~so** *adj* expensive
costumbre *f* custom; (*de persona*) habit. **de ~** usual; (*como adv*) usually
costur|a *f* sewing; (*línea*) seam; (*confección*) dressmaking. **~era** *f* dressmaker. **~ero** *m* sewing box
cotejar *vt* compare
cotidiano *adj* daily
cotille|ar *vt* gossip. **~o** *m* gossip
cotiza|ción *f* quotation, price. **~r** 10 *vt* (*en la bolsa*) quote. ● *vi* pay contributions. **~rse** *vpr* fetch; (*en la bolsa*) stand at; (*fig*) be valued
coto *m* enclosure; (*de caza*) preserve. **~ de caza** game preserve
cotorr|a *f* parrot; (*fig*) chatterbox. **~ear** *vi* chatter
coyuntura *f* joint
coz *f* kick
cráneo *m* skull
cráter *m* crater
crea|ción *f* creation. **~dor** *adj* creative. ● *m* creator. **~r** *vt* create
crec|er 11 *vi* grow; (*aumentar*) increase; (río) rise. **~ida** *f* (*de río*) flood. **~ido** *adj* (persona) grown-up; (número) large, considerable; (plantas) fully-grown. **~iente** *adj* growing; (luna) crescent. **~imiento** *m* growth
credencial *f* document. ● *adj*. **cartas** *fpl* **~es** credentials
credibilidad *f* credibility
crédito *m* credit; (*préstamo*) loan. **digno de ~** reliable
credo *m* creed
crédulo *adj* credulous
cre|encia *f* belief. **~er** 18 *vt/i* believe; (*pensar*) think. **~o que no** I don't think so, I think not. **~o que sí** I think so. **no ~o** I don't think so. **¡ya lo ~o!** I should think so!. **~erse** *vpr* consider o.s. **no me lo ~o** I don't believe it. **~íble** *adj* credible
crema *f* cream; (*Culin*) custard; (*LAm, de la leche*) cream. **~ batida** (*LAm*) whipped cream. **~ bronceadora** sun-tan cream
cremallera *f* zip (*Brit*), zipper (*Amer*)
crematorio *m* crematorium
crepitar *vi* crackle
crepúsculo *m* twilight
crespo *adj* frizzy; (*LAm, rizado*) curly. ● *m* (*LAm*) curl
cresta *f* crest; (*de gallo*) comb
creyente *m* believer
cría *f* breeding; (*animal*) baby animal. **las ~s** the young
cria|da *f* maid, servant. **~dero** *m* (*de pollos etc*) farm; (*de ostras*) bed; (*de plantas*) nursery. ● *m* servant. **~dor** *m* breeder. **~nza** *f* breeding. **~r** 20 *vt* suckle; grow (plantas); breed (animales); (*educar*) bring up

(*Brit*), raise (*esp Amer*). **~rse** *vpr* grow up

criatura *f* creature; (*niño*) baby

crim|en *m* (serious) crime; (*asesinato*) murder; (*fig*) crime. **~inal** *adj* & *m* & *f* criminal

crin *f* mane

crío *m* child

criollo *adj* Creole; (*LAm, música, comida*) traditional. ●*m* Creole; (*LAm, nativo*) Peruvian, Chilean etc

crisantemo *m* chrysanthemum

crisis *f invar* crisis

crispar *vt* twitch; (*fam, irritar*) annoy. **~le los nervios a uno** get on s.o.'s nerves

cristal *m* crystal; (*Esp, vidrio*) glass; (*Esp, de una ventana*) pane of glass. **limpiar los ~es** (*Esp*) clean the windows. **~ino** *adj* crystalline; (*fig*) crystal-clear. **~izar** 10 crystallize. **~izarse** *vpr* crystallize

cristian|dad *f* Christendom. **~ismo** *m* Christianity. **~o** *adj* Christian. **ser ~o** be a Christian. ●*m* Christian

cristo *m* crucifix

Cristo *m* Christ

criterio *m* criterion; (*discernimiento*) judgement; (*opinión*) opinion

cr|ítica *f* criticism; (*reseña*) review. **~iticar** 7 *vt* criticize. **~ítico** *adj* critical. ● *m* critic

croar *vi* croak

crom|ado *adj* chromium-plated. **~o** *m* chromium, chrome

crónic|a *f* chronicle; (*de radio, TV*) report; (*de periódico*) feature. **~ deportiva** sport section. **~o** *adj* chronic

cronista *m* & *f* reporter

crono|grama *m* schedule, timetable. **~logía** *f* chronology

cron|ometrar *vt* time. **~ómetro** *m* (*en deportes*) stop-watch

croqueta *f* croquette

cruce *m* crossing; (*de calles, carreteras*) crossroads; (*de peatones*) (pedestrian) crossing

crucial *adj* crucial

crucifi|car 7 *vt* crucify. **~jo** *m* crucifix

crucigrama *m* crossword (puzzle)

crudo *adj* raw; (*fig*) harsh. ●*m* crude (oil)

cruel *adj* cruel. **~dad** *f* cruelty

cruji|do *m* (*de seda, de hojas secas*) rustle; (*de muebles*) creak. **~r** *vi* (seda, hojas secas) rustle; (muebles) creak

cruz *f* cross; (*de moneda*) tails. **~ gamada** swastika. **la C~ Roja** the Red Cross

cruza|da *f* crusade. **~r** 10 *vt* cross; exchange (palabras). **~rse** *vpr* cross; (*pasar en la calle*) pass each other. **~rse con** pass

cuaderno *m* exercise book; (*para apuntes*) notebook

cuadra *f* (*caballeriza*) stable; (*LAm, distancia*) block

cuadrado *adj* & *m* square

cuadragésimo *adj* fortieth

cuadr|ar *vt* square. ● *vi* suit; (cuentas) tally. **~arse** *vpr* (*Mil*) stand to attention; (*fig*) dig one's heels in. **~ilátero** *m* quadrilateral; (*Boxeo*) ring

cuadrilla *f* group; (*pandilla*) gang

cuadro *m* square; (*pintura*) painting; (*Teatro*) scene; (*de números*) table; (*de mando etc*) panel; (*conjunto del personal*) staff. **~ de distribución** switchboard. **a ~s**, **de ~s** check. **¡qué ~!**, **¡vaya un ~!**

what a sight!

cuadrúpedo *m* quadruped

cuádruple *adj & m* quadruple

c **cuajar** *vt* congeal (sangre); curdle (leche); (*llenar*) fill up. ● *vi* (nieve) settle; (*fig, fam*) work out. **cuajado de** full of. **~se** *vpr* coagulate; (sangre) clot; (leche) curdle

cual *pron.* **el ~, la ~ etc** (*animales y cosas*) that, which; (*personas, sujeto*) who, that; (*personas, objeto*) whom. ● *adj* (*LAm, qué*) what. **~ si** as if. **cada ~** everyone. **lo ~** which. **por lo ~** because of which. **sea ~ sea** whatever

cuál *pron* which; (*LAm, qué*) what

cualidad *f* quality

cualquiera *adj* (*delante de nombres* **cualquier,** *pl* **cualesquiera**) any. ● *pron* (*pl* **cualesquiera**) anyone, anybody; (*cosas*) whatever, whichever. **un ~** a nobody. **una ~** a slut

cuando *adv* when. ● *conj* when; (*si*) if. **~ más** at the most. **~ menos** at the least. **aun ~** even if. **de ~ en ~** from time to time

cuándo *adv & conj* when. **¿de ~ acá?, ¿desde ~?** since when? **¡~ no!** (*LAm*) as usual!, typical!

cuant|ía *f* quantity; (*extensión*) extent. **~ioso** *adj* abundant. **~o** *adj* as much ... as, as many ... as. ● *pron* as much as, as many as. ● *adv* as much as. **~o antes** as soon as possible. **~o más, mejor** the more the merrier. **en ~o** as soon as. **en ~o a** as for. **por ~o** since. **unos ~os** a few, some

cuánto *adj* (*interrogativo*) how much?; (*interrogativo en plural*) how many?; (*exclamativo*) what a lot of! ● *pron* how much?; (*en plural*) how many? ● *adv* how much. **¿~ mides?** how tall are you? **¿~ tiempo?** how long? **¡~ tiempo sin verte!** it's been a long time! **¿a ~s estamos?** what's the date today? **un Sr. no sé ~s** Mr So-and-So

cuáquero *m* Quaker

cuarent|a *adj & m* forty; (*cuadragésimo*) fortieth. **~ena** *f* (*Med*) quarantine. **~ón** *adj* about forty

cuaresma *f* Lent

cuarta *f* (*palmo*) span

cuartel *m* (*Mil*) barracks. **~ general** headquarters

cuarteto *m* quartet

cuarto *adj* fourth. ● *m* quarter; (*habitación*) room. **~ de baño** bathroom. **~ de estar** living room. **~ de hora** quarter of an hour. **estar sin un ~** be broke. **y ~** (a) quarter past

cuarzo *m* quartz

cuate *m* (*Mex*) twin; (*amigo*) friend; (▯, *tipo*) guy

cuatro *adj & m* four. **~cientos** *adj & m* four hundred

Cuba *f* Cuba

cuba|libre *m* rum and Coke (P). **~no** *adj & m* Cuban

cúbico *adj* cubic

cubículo *m* cubicle

cubiert|a *f* cover; (*neumático*) tyre; (*Naut*) deck. **~o** *adj* covered; (cielo) overcast. ● *m* place setting, piece of cutlery; (*en restaurante*) cover charge. **a ~o** under cover

cubilete *m* bowl; (*molde*) mould; (*para los dados*) cup

cubis|mo *m* cubism. **~ta** *adj & m & f* cubist

cubo *m* bucket; (*Mat*) cube

cubrecama *m* bedspread

cubrir (*pp* **cubierto**) *vt* cover; fill

(vacante). **~se** *vpr* cover o.s.; (*ponerse el sombrero*) put on one's hat; (el cielo) cloud over, become overcast

cucaracha *f* cockroach

cuchar|a *f* spoon. **~ada** *f* spoonful. **~adita** *f* teaspoonful. **~illa**, **~ita** *f* teaspoon. **~ón** *m* ladle

cuchichear *vi* whisper

cuchill|a *f* large knife; (*de carnicero*) cleaver; (*hoja de afeitar*) razor blade. **~ada** *f* stab; (*herida*) knife wound. **~o** *m* knife

cuchitril *m* (*fig*) hovel

cuclillas: **en ~** *adv* squatting

cuco *adj* shrewd; (*mono*) pretty, nice. ● *m* cuckoo

cucurucho *m* cornet

cuello *m* neck; (*de camisa*) collar. **cortar(le) el ~ a uno** cut s.o.'s throat

cuenc|a *f* (*del ojo*) (eye) socket; (*de río*) basin. **~o** *m* hollow; (*vasija*) bowl

cuenta *f* count; (*acción de contar*) counting; (*cálculo*) calculation; (*factura*) bill; (*en banco, relato*) account; (*de collar*) bead. **~ corriente** current account, checking account (*Amer*). **dar ~ de** give an account of. **darse ~ de** realize. **en resumidas ~s** in short. **por mi propia ~** on my own account. **tener en ~** bear in mind

cuentakilómetros *m invar* milometer

cuent|ista *m & f* story-writer; (*de mentiras*) fibber. **~o** *m* story; (*mentira*) fib, tall story. **~ de hadas** fairy tale. ● *vb véase* CONTAR

cuerda *f* rope; (*más fina*) string; (*Mus*) string. **~ floja** tightrope. **dar ~ a** wind up (un reloj)

cuerdo *adj* (persona) sane; (acción) sensible

cuerno *m* horn

cuero *m* leather; (*piel*) skin; (*del grifo*) washer. **~ cabelludo** scalp. **en ~s (vivos)** stark naked

cuerpo *m* body

cuervo *m* crow

cuesta *f* slope, hill. **~ abajo** downhill. **~ arriba** uphill. **a ~s** on one's back

cuestión *f* matter; (*problema*) problem; (*cosa*) thing

cueva *f* cave

cuida|do *m* care; (*preocupación*) worry. **¡~do!** watch out!. **tener ~do** be careful. **~doso** *adj* careful. **~r** *vt* look after. ● *vi*. **~r de** look after. **~rse** *vpr* look after o.s. **~rse de** be careful to

culata *f* (*de revólver, fusil*) butt. **~zo** *m* recoil

culebr|a *f* snake. **~ón** *m* soap opera

culinario *adj* culinary

culminar *vi* culminate

culo *m* [!] bottom; (*LAm vulg*) arse (*Brit vulg*), ass (*Amer vulg*)

culpa *f* fault. **echar la ~** blame. **por ~ de** because of. **tener la ~** be to blame (**de** for). **~bilidad** *f* guilt. **~ble** *adj* guilty. ● *m & f* culprit. **~r** *vt* blame (**de** for)

cultiv|ar *vt* farm; grow (plantas); (*fig*) cultivate. **~o** *m* farming; (*de plantas*) growing

cult|o *adj* (persona) educated. ● *m* cult; (*homenaje*) worship. **~ura** *f* culture. **~ural** *adj* cultural

culturismo *m* body-building

cumbre *f* summit

cumpleaños *m invar* birthday

cumplido *adj* perfect; (*cortés*) polite. ● *m* compliment. **de ~** courtesy. **por ~** out of a sense of duty. **~r** *adj* reliable

cumpli|miento *m* fulfilment; (*de ley*) observance; (*de orden*) carrying out. **~r** *vt* carry out; observe (ley); serve (condena); reach (años); keep (promesa). **hoy cumple 3 años** he's 3 (years old) today. ● *vi* do one's duty. **por ~r** as a mere formality. **~rse** *vpr* expire; (*realizarse*) be fulfilled

cuna *f* cradle; (*fig, nacimiento*) birthplace

cundir *vi* spread; (*rendir*) go a long way

cuneta *f* ditch

cuña *f* wedge

cuñad|a *f* sister-in-law. **~o** *m* brother-in-law

cuño *m* stamp. **de nuevo ~** new

cuota *f* quota; (*de sociedad etc*) membership, fee; (*LAm, plazo*) instalment; (*Mex, peaje*) toll

cupe *vb véase* CABER

cupo *m* cuota; (*LAm, capacidad*) room; (*Mex, plaza*) place

cupón *m* coupon

cúpula *f* dome

cura *f* cure; (*tratamiento*) treatment. ●*m* priest. **~ción** *f* healing. **~ndero** *m* faith-healer. **~r** *vt* (*incl Culin*) cure; dress (herida); (*tratar*) treat; (*fig*) remedy; tan (pieles). **~rse** *vpr* get better

curios|ear *vi* pry; (*mirar*) browse. **~idad** *f* curiosity. **~o** *adj* curious; (*raro*) odd, unusual ●*m* onlooker; (*fisgón*) busybody

curita *f* (*LAm*) (sticking) plaster

curriculum (vitae) *m* curriculum vitae, CV

cursar *vt* issue; (*estudiar*) study

cursi *adj* pretentious, showy

cursillo *m* short course

cursiva *f* italics

curso *m* course; (*Univ etc*) year. **en ~** under way; (año etc) current

cursor *m* cursor

curtir *vt* tan; (*fig*) harden. **~se** *vpr* become tanned; (*fig*) become hardened

curv|a *f* curve; (*de carretera*) bend. **~ar** *vt* bend; bow (estante). **~arse** *vpr* bend; (estante) bow; (madera) warp. **~ilíneo** *adj* curvilinear; (mujer) curvaceous. **~o** *adj* curved

cúspide *f* top; (*fig*) pinnacle

custodi|a *f* safe-keeping; (*Jurid*) custody. **~ar** *vt* guard; (*guardar*) look after. **~o** *m* guardian

cutáneo *adj* skin

cutis *m* skin, complexion

cuyo *pron* (*de persona*) whose, of whom; (*de cosa*) whose, of which. **en ~ caso** in which case

Dd

dactilógrafo *m* typist

dado *m* dice. ● *adj* given. **~ que** since, given that

daltónico *adj* colour-blind

dama *f* lady. **~ de honor** bridesmaid. **~s** *fpl* draughts (*Brit*), checkers (*Amer*)

damasco *m* damask; (*LAm, fruta*) apricot

danés *adj* Danish. ● *m* Dane; (*idioma*) Danish

danza *f* dance; (*acción*) dancing. **~r** 10 *vt/i* dance

dañ|ar *vt* damage. **~se** *vpr* get

damaged. **~ino** *adj* harmful. **~o** *m* damage; (*a una persona*) harm. **~os y perjuicios** damages. **hacer ~o a** harm, hurt. **hacerse ~o** hurt o.s.

dar 26 *vt* give; bear (frutos); give out (calor); strike (la hora). ●*vi* give. **da igual** it doesn't matter. **¡dale!** go on! **da lo mismo** it doesn't matter. **~ a** (ventana) look on to; (edificio) face. **~ a luz** give birth. **~ con** meet (persona); find (cosa). **¿qué más da?** it doesn't matter! **~se** *vpr* have (baño). **dárselas de** make o.s. out to be. **~se por** consider o.s.

dardo *m* dart

datar *vi.* **~ de** date from

dátil *m* date

dato *m* piece of information. **~s** *mpl* data, information. **~s personales** personal details

de *preposición*

Note that **de** before **el** becomes **del**, e.g. **es del norte**

····➤(*contenido, material*) of. **un vaso de agua** a glass of water. **es de madera** it's made of wood (*pertenencia*) **el coche de Juan** Juan's car. **es de ella** it's hers. **es de María** it's María's. **las llaves del coche** the car keys (*procedencia, origen, época*) from. **soy de Madrid** I'm from Madrid. **una llamada de Lima** a call from Lima. **es del siglo V** it's from the 5th century (*causa, modo*) **se murió de cáncer** he died of cancer. **temblar de miedo** to tremble with fear. **de dos en dos** two by two

····➤(*parte del día, hora*) **de noche** at night. **de madrugada** early in the morning. **las diez de la mañana** ten (o'clock) in the morning. **de 9 a 12** from 9 to 12

····➤(*en oraciones pasivas*) by. **rodeado de agua** surrounded by water. **va seguido de coma** it's followed by a comma. **es de Mozart** it's by Mozart

····➤(*al especificar*) **el cajón de arriba** the top drawer. **la clase de inglés** the English lesson. **la chica de verde** the girl in green. **el de debajo** the one underneath

····➤(*en calidad de*) as. **trabaja de oficinista** he works as a clerk. **vino de chaperón** he came as a chaperon

····➤(*en comparaciones*) than. **pesa más de un kilo** it weighs more than a kilo

····➤(*con superlativo*) **el más alto del mundo** the tallest in the world. **el mejor de todos** the best of all

····➤(*sentido condicional*) if. **de haberlo sabido** if I had known. **de continuar así** if this goes on

➡ Cuando la preposición **de** se emplea como parte de expresiones como **de prisa, de acuerdo** etc., y de nombres compuestos como **hombre de negocios, saco de dormir** etc., ver bajo el respectivo nombre

deambular *vi* roam (**por** about)

debajo *adv* underneath. **~ de** under(neath). **el de ~** the one underneath. **por ~** underneath. **por ~ de** below

debat|e *m* debate. **~ir** *vt* debate

deber *vt* owe. ● *verbo auxiliar* have to, must; (*en condicional*) should. **debo marcharme** I must go, I have to go. ● *m* duty. **~es** *mpl* homework. **~se** *vpr.* **~se a** be due to

debido *adj* due; (*correcto*) proper. **~ a** due to. **como es ~** as is proper

débil *adj* weak; (sonido) faint; (luz) dim

debili|dad *f* weakness. **~tar** *vt* weaken. **~tarse** *vpr* weaken, get weak

débito *m* debit. **~ bancario** (*LAm*) direct debit

debut *m* debut

debutar *vi* make one's debut

década *f* decade

deca|dencia *f* decline. **~dente** *adj* decadent. **~er** 29 *vi* decline; (*debilitarse*) weaken. **~ído** *adj* in low spirits. **~imiento** *m* decline, weakening

decano *m* dean; (*miembro más antiguo*) senior member

decapitar *vt* behead

decena *f* ten. **una ~ de** about ten

decencia *f* decency

decenio *m* decade

decente *adj* decent; (*decoroso*) respectable; (*limpio*) clean, tidy

decepci|ón *f* disappointment. **~onar** *vt* disappoint

decidi|do *adj* decided; (persona) determined, resolute. **~r** *vt* decide; settle (cuestión etc). ● *vi* decide. **~rse** *vpr* make up one's mind

decimal *adj & m* decimal

décimo *adj & m* tenth. ● *m* (*de lotería*) tenth part of a lottery ticket

decir 46 *vt* say; (*contar*) tell. ● *m* saying. **~ que no** say no. **~ que sí** say yes. **dicho de otro modo** in other words. **dicho y hecho** no sooner said than done. **¿dígame?** can I help you? **¡dígame!** (*al teléfono*) hello! **digamos** let's say. **es ~** that is to say. **mejor dicho** rather. **¡no me digas!** you don't say!, really! **por así ~, por ~lo así** so to speak, as it were. **querer ~** mean. **se dice que** it is said that, they say that

decisi|ón *f* decision. **~vo** *adj* decisive

declara|ción *f* declaration; (*a autoridad, prensa*) statement. **~ción de renta** income tax return. **~r** *vt/i* declare. **~rse** *vpr* declare o.s.; (epidemia etc) break out

declinar *vt* turn down; (*Gram*) decline

declive *m* slope; (*fig*) decline. **en ~** sloping

decola|je *m* (*LAm*) take-off. **~r** *vi* (*LAm*) take off

decolorarse *vpr* become discoloured, fade

decora|ción *f* decoration. **~do** *m* (*en el teatro*) set. **~r** *vt* decorate. **~tivo** *adj* decorative

decoro *m* decorum. **~so** *adj* decent, respectable

decrépito *adj* decrepit

decret|ar *vt* decree. **~o** *m* decree

dedal *m* thimble

dedica|ción *f* dedication. **~r** 7 *vt* dedicate; devote (tiempo). **~rse** *vpr.* **~rse a** devote o.s. to. **¿a qué se dedica?** what does he do? **~toria** *f* dedication

dedo *m* finger; (*del pie*) toe. **~**

anular ring finger. ~ **corazón** middle finger. ~ **gordo** thumb; (*del pie*) big toe. ~ **índice** index finger. ~ **meñique** little finger. ~ **pulgar** thumb

deduc|ción *f* deduction. ~**ir** 47 *vt* deduce; (*descontar*) deduct

defect|o *m* fault, defect. ~**uoso** *adj* defective

defen|der 1 *vt* defend. ~**sa** *f* defence. ~**derse** *vpr* defend o.s. ~**sivo** *adj* defensive. ~**sor** *m* defender. **abogado** *m* ~**sor** defence counsel

defeño *m* (*Mex*) person from the Federal District

deficien|cia *f* deficiency. ~**cia mental** mental handicap. ~**te** *adj* poor, deficient. ● *m & f* ~**te mental** mentally handicapped person

déficit *m invar* deficit

defini|ción *f* definition. ~**do** *adj* defined. ~**r** *vt* define. ~**tivo** *adj* definitive. **en** ~**tiva** all in all

deform|ación *f* deformation; (*de imagen etc*) distortion. ~**ar** *vt* deform; distort (imagen, metal). ~**arse** *vpr* go out of shape. ~**e** *adj* deformed

defraudar *vt* defraud; (*decepcionar*) disappoint

defunción *f* death

degenera|ción *f* degeneration; (*cualidad*) degeneracy. ~**do** *adj* degenerate. ~**r** *vi* degenerate

degollar 16 *vt* cut s.o.'s throat

degradar *vt* degrade; (*Mil*) demote. ~**se** *vpr* demean o.s..

degusta|ción *f* tasting. ~**r** *vt* taste

dehesa *f* pasture

deja|dez *f* slovenliness; (*pereza*) laziness. ~**do** *adj* slovenly; (*descuidado*) slack, negligent. ~**r** *vt* leave; (*abandonar*) abandon; give up (estudios); (*prestar*) lend; (*permitir*) let. ~**r a un lado** leave aside. ~**r de** stop

dejo *m* aftertaste; (*tonillo*) slight accent; (*toque*) touch

del = **de** + **el**

delantal *m* apron

delante *adv* in front. ~ **de** in front of. **de** ~ front. ~**ra** *f* front; (*de teatro etc*) front row; (*ventaja*) lead; (*de equipo*) forward line. **llevar la** ~**ra** be in the lead. ~**ro** *adj* front. ● *m* forward

delat|ar *vt* denounce. ~**or** *m* informer

delega|ción *f* delegation; (*oficina*) regional office; (*Mex, comisaría*) police station. ~**do** *m* delegate; (*Com*) agent, representative. ~**r** 12 *vt* delegate

deleit|ar *vt* delight. ~**e** *m* delight

deletrear *vt* spell (out)

delfín *m* dolphin

delgad|ez *f* thinness. ~**o** *adj* thin; (*esbelto*) slim. ~**ucho** *adj* skinny

delibera|ción *f* deliberation. ~**do** *adj* deliberate. ~**r** *vi* deliberate (**sobre** on)

delicad|eza *f* gentleness; (*fragilidad*) frailty; (*tacto*) tact. **falta de** ~**eza** tactlessness. **tener la** ~ **de** have the courtesy to. ~**o** *adj* delicate; (*refinado*) refined; (*sensible*) sensitive

delici|a *f* delight. ~**oso** *adj* delightful; (sabor etc) delicious

delimitar *vt* delimit

delincuen|cia *f* delinquency. ~**te** *m & f* criminal, delinquent

delinquir 8 *vi* commit a criminal offence

delir|ante *adj* delirious. ~**ar** *vi* be delirious; (*fig*) talk nonsense. ~**io**

m delirium; (*fig*) frenzy
delito *m* crime, offence
demacrado *adj* haggard
demagogo *m* demagogue
demanda *f* demand; (*Jurid*) lawsuit. **~do** *m* defendant. **~nte** *m & f* (*Jurid*) plaintiff. **~r** *vt* (*Jurid*) sue; (*LAm, requerir*) require
demarcación *f* demarcation
demás *adj* rest of the, other. • *pron* rest, others. **lo ~** the rest. **por ~** extremely. **por lo ~** otherwise
demas|ía *f*. **en ~ía** in excess. **~iado** *adj* too much; (*en plural*) too many. • *adv* too much; (*con adjetivo*) too
demen|cia *f* madness. **~te** *adj* demented, mad
dem|ocracia *f* democracy. **~ócrata** *m & f* democrat. **~ocrático** *adj* democratic
demol|er 2 *vt* demolish. **~ición** *f* demolition
demonio *m* devil, demon. **¡~s!** hell! **¿cómo ~s?** how the hell? **¡qué ~s!** what the hell!
demora *f* delay. **~r** *vt* delay. • *vi* stay on. **~rse** *vpr* be too long; (*LAm, cierto tiempo*). **se ~ una hora en llegar** it takes him an hour to get there
demostra|ción *f* demonstration, show. **~r** 2 *vt* demonstrate; (*mostrar*) show; (*probar*) prove. **~tivo** *adj* demonstrative
dengue *m* dengue fever
denigrar *vt* denigrate
denominado *adj* named; (*supuesto*) so-called
dens|idad *f* density. **~o** *adj* dense, thick
denta|dura *f* teeth. **~dura postiza** dentures, false teeth. **~l** *adj* dental
dent|era *f*. **darle ~era a uno** set s.o.'s teeth on edge. **~ífrico** *m* toothpaste. **~ista** *m & f* dentist
dentro *adv* inside; (*de un edificio*) indoors. **~ de** in. **~ de poco** soon. **por ~** inside
denuncia *f* report; (*acusación*) accusation. **~r** *vt* report; (periódico etc) denounce
departamento *m* department; (*LAm, apartamento*) flat (*Brit*), apartment (*Amer*)
depend|encia *f* dependence; (*sección*) section; (*oficina*) office. **~encias** *fpl* buildings. **~er** *vi* depend (**de** on). **~ienta** *f* shop assistant. **~iente** *adj* dependent (**de** on). • *m* shop assistant
depila|r *vt* depilate. **~torio** *adj* depilatory
deplora|ble *adj* deplorable. **~r** *vt* deplore, regret
deponer 34 *vt* remove from office; depose (rey); lay down (armas). • *vi* give evidence
deporta|ción *f* deportation. **~r** *vt* deport
deport|e *m* sport. **hacer ~e** take part in sports. **~ista** *m* sportsman. • *f* sportswoman. **~ivo** *adj* sports. • *m* sports car
dep|ositante *m & f* depositor. **~ositar** *vt* deposit; (*poner*) put, place. **~ósito** *m* deposit; (*almacén*) warehouse; (*Mil*) depot; (*de líquidos*) tank
depravado *adj* depraved
deprecia|ción *f* depreciation. **~r** *vt* depreciate. **~rse** *vpr* depreciate
depr|esión *f* depression. **~imido** *adj* depressed. **~imir** *vt* depress. **~imirse** *vpr* get

depressed

depura|ción *f* purification. **~do** *adj* refined. **~r** *vt* purify; (*Pol*) purge; refine (estilo)

derech|a *f* (*mano*) right hand; (*lado*) right. **a la ~a** on the right; (*hacia el lado derecho*) to the right. **~ista** *adj* right-wing. • *m & f* right-winger. **~o** *adj* right; (*vertical*) upright; (*recto*) straight. • *adv* straight. **todo ~o** straight on. • *m* right; (*Jurid*) law; (*lado*) right side. **~os** *mpl* dues. **~os de autor** royalties

deriva *f* drift. **a la ~** drifting, adrift

deriva|do *adj* derived. • *m* derivative, by-product. **~r** *vt* divert. • *vi*. **~r de** derive from, be derived from. **~rse** *vpr*. **~rse de** be derived from

derram|amiento *m* spilling. **~amiento de sangre** bloodshed. **~ar** *vt* spill; shed (lágrimas). **~arse** *vpr* spill. **~e** *m* spilling; (*pérdida*) leakage; (*Med*) discharge; (*Med, de sangre*) haemorrhage

derretir **5** *vt* melt

derribar *vt* knock down; bring down, overthrow (gobierno etc)

derrocar **7** *vt* bring down, overthrow (gobierno etc)

derroch|ar *vt* squander. **~e** *m* waste

derrot|a *f* defeat. **~ar** *vt* defeat. **~ado** *adj* defeated. **~ero** *m* course

derrumba|r *vt* knock down **~rse** *vpr* collapse; (persona) go to pieces

desabotonar *vt* unbutton, undo. **~se** *vpr* come undone; (persona) undo

desabrido *adj* tasteless; (persona) surly; (*LAm*) dull

desabrochar *vt* undo. **~se** *vpr* come undone; (persona) undo

desacato *m* defiance; (*Jurid*) contempt of court

desac|ertado *adj* ill-advised; (*erróneo*) wrong. **~ierto** *m* mistake

desacreditar *vt* discredit

desactivar *vt* defuse

desacuerdo *m* disagreement

desafiar **20** *vt* challenge; (*afrontar*) defy

desafina|do *adj* out of tune. **~r** *vi* be out of tune. **~rse** *vpr* go out of tune

desafío *m* challenge; (*a la muerte*) defiance; (*combate*) duel

desafortunad|amente *adv* unfortunately. **~o** *adj* unfortunate

desagrada|ble *adj* unpleasant. **~r** *vt* displease. • *vi* be unpleasant. **me ~ el sabor** I don't like the taste

desagradecido *adj* ungrateful

desagrado *m* displeasure. **con ~** unwillingly

desagüe *m* drain; (*acción*) drainage. **tubo** *m* **de ~** drain-pipe

desahog|ado *adj* roomy; (*acomodado*) comfortable. **~ar** **12** *vt* vent. **~arse** *vpr* let off steam. **~o** *m* comfort; (*alivio*) relief

desahuci|ar *vt* declare terminally ill (enfermo); evict (inquilino). **~o** *m* eviction

desair|ar *vt* snub. **~e** *m* snub

desajuste *m* maladjustment; (*desequilibrio*) imbalance

desala|dora *f* desalination plant. **~r** *vt* to desalinate

desal|entador *adj* disheartening. **~entar** **1** *vt* discourage. **~iento** *m* discouragement

d

desaliñado *adj* slovenly
desalmado *adj* heartless
desalojar *vt* (ocupantes) evacuate; (policía) to clear; (*LAm*) evict (inquilino)
desampar|ado *adj* helpless; (lugar) unprotected. **~ar** *vt* abandon. **~o** *m* helplessness; (*abandono*) lack of protection
desangrar *vt* bleed. **~se** *vpr* bleed
desanima|do *adj* down-hearted. **~r** *vt* discourage. **~rse** *vpr* lose heart
desapar|ecer **11** *vi* disappear; (efecto) wear off. **~ecido** *adj* missing. ● *m* missing person. **~ición** *f* disappearance
desapego *m* indifference
desapercibido *adj*. **pasar ~** go unnoticed
desaprobar **2** *vt* disapprove of
desarm|able *adj* collapsible; (estante) easy to dismantle. **~ar** *vt* disarm; (*desmontar*) dismantle; take apart; (*LAm*) take down (carpa). **~e** *m* disarmament
desarraig|ado *adj* rootless. **~ar** **12** *vt* uproot. **~o** *m* uprooting
desarregl|ar *vt* mess up; (*alterar*) disrupt. **~o** *m* disorder
desarroll|ar *vt* develop. **~arse** *vpr* (*incl Foto*) develop; (suceso) take place. **~o** *m* development
desaseado *adj* dirty; (*desordenado*) untidy
desasosiego *m* anxiety; (*intranquilidad*) restlessness
desastr|ado *adj* scruffy. **~e** *m* disaster. **~oso** *adj* disastrous
desatar *vt* untie; (*fig, soltar*) unleash. **~se** *vpr* come undone; to undo (zapatos)
desatascar **7** *vt* unblock
desaten|der **1** *vt* not pay attention to; neglect (deber etc). **~to** *adj* inattentive; (*descortés*) discourteous
desatin|ado *adj* silly. **~o** *m* silliness; (*error*) mistake
desatornillar *vt* unscrew
desautorizar **10** *vt* declare unauthorized; discredit (persona); (*desmentir*) deny
desavenencia *f* disagreement
desayun|ar *vt* have for breakfast. ● *vi* have breakfast. **~o** *m* breakfast
desazón *m* (*fig*) unease
desbandarse *vpr* (*Mil*) disband; (*dispersarse*) disperse
desbarajust|ar *vt* mess up. **~e** *m* mess
desbaratar *vt* spoil; (*Mex*) mess up (papeles)
desbloquear *vt* clear; release (mecanismo); unfreeze (cuenta)
desbocado *adj* (caballo) runaway; (escote) wide
desbordarse *vpr* overflow; (río) burst its banks
descabellado *adj* crazy
descafeinado *adj* decaffeinated. ● *m* decaffeinated coffee
descalabro *m* disaster
descalificar **7** *vt* disqualify; (*desacreditar*) discredit
descalz|ar **10** *vt* take off (zapatos). **~o** *adj* barefoot
descampado *m* open ground. **al ~** (*LAm*) in the open air
descans|ado *adj* rested; (trabajo) easy. **~ar** *vt/i* rest. **~illo** *m* landing. **~o** *m* rest; (*del trabajo*) break; (*LAm, rellano*) landing; (*en deportes*) half-time; (*en el teatro etc*) interval
descapotable *adj* convertible

descarado *adj* cheeky; (*sin vergüenza*) shameless

descarg|a *f* unloading; (*Mil, Elec*) discharge. **~ar** 12 *vt* unload; (*Mil, Elec*) discharge; (*Informática*) download. **~o** *m* (*recibo*) receipt; (*Jurid*) evidence

descaro *m* cheek, nerve

descarriarse 20 *vpr* go the wrong way; (res) stray; (*fig*) go astray

descarrila|miento *m* derailment. **~r** *vi* be derailed. **~rse** *vpr* (*LAm*) be derailed

descartar *vt* rule out

descascararse *vpr* (pintura) peel; (taza) chip

descen|dencia *f* descent; (*personas*) descendants. **~der** 1 *vt* go down (escalera etc). ● *vi* go down; (temperatura) fall, drop; (*provenir*) be descended (**de** from). **~diente** *m & f* descendent. **~so** *m* descent; (*de temperatura, fiebre etc*) fall, drop

descifrar *vt* decipher; decode (clave)

descolgar 2 & 12 *vt* take down; pick up (el teléfono). **~se** *vpr* lower o.s.

descolor|ar *vt* discolour, fade. **~ido** *adj* discoloured, faded; (persona) pale

descomp|oner 34 *vt* break down; decompose (materia); upset (estómago); (*esp LAm, estropear*) break; (*esp LAm, desarreglar*) mess up. **~onerse** *vpr* decompose; (*esp LAm, estropearse*) break down; (persona) feel sick. **~ostura** *f* (*esp LAm, de máquina*) breakdown; (*esp LAm, náuseas*) sickness; (*esp LAm, diarrea*) diarrhoea; (*LAm, falla*) fault. **~uesto** *adj* decomposed; (*encolerizado*) angry; (*esp LAm, estropeado*) broken. **estar ~uesto** (*del estómago*) have diarrhoea

descomunal *adj* enormous

desconc|ertante *adj* disconcerting. **~ertar** 1 *vt* disconcert; (*dejar perplejo*) puzzle. **~ertarse** *vpr* be put out, be disconcerted

desconectar *vt* disconnect

desconfia|do *adj* distrustful. **~nza** *f* distrust, suspicion. **~r** 20 *vi*. **~r de** mistrust; (*no creer*) doubt

descongelar *vt* defrost; (*Com*) unfreeze

desconoc|er 11 *vt* not know, not recognize. **~ido** *adj* unknown; (*cambiado*) unrecognizable. ● *m* stranger. **~imiento** *m* ignorance

desconsidera|ción *f* lack of consideration. **~do** *adj* inconsiderate

descons|olado *adj* distressed. **~uelo** *m* distress; (*tristeza*) sadness

desconta|do *adj*. **dar por ~do (que)** take for granted (that). **~r** 2 *vt* discount; deduct (impuestos etc)

descontento *adj* unhappy (**con** with), dissatisfied (**con** with). ● *m* discontent

descorazonar *vt* discourage. **~se** *vpr* lose heart

descorchar *vt* uncork

descorrer *vt* draw (cortina). **~ el cerrojo** unbolt the door

descort|és *adj* rude, discourteous. **~esía** *f* rudeness

descos|er *vt* unpick. **~erse** *vpr* come undone. **~ido** *adj* unstitched

descrédito *m* disrepute. **ir en ~ de** damage the reputation of

descremado *adj* skimmed

descri|bir (*pp* **descrito**) *vt* describe. **~pción** *f* description

descuartizar [10] *vt* cut up
descubierto *adj* discovered; (*no cubierto*) uncovered; (vehículo) open-top; (piscina) open-air; (cielo) clear; (cabeza) bare. ● *m* overdraft. **poner al ~** expose
descubri|miento *m* discovery. **~r** (*pp* **descubierto**) *vt* discover; (*destapar*) uncover; (*revelar*) reveal; unveil (estatua). **~rse** *vpr* (*quitarse el sombrero*) take off one's hat
descuento *m* discount; (*del sueldo*) deduction; (*en deportes*) injury time
descuid|ado *adj* careless; (aspecto etc) untidy; (*desprevenido*) unprepared. **~ar** *vt* neglect. ● *vi* not worry. **¡~a!** don't worry!. **~arse** *vpr* be careless **~o** *m* carelessness; (*negligencia*) negligence
desde *prep* (*lugar etc*) from; (*tiempo*) since, from. **~ ahora** from now on. **~ hace un mes** for a month. **~ luego** of course. **~ Madrid hasta Barcelona** from Madrid to Barcelona. **~ niño** since childhood
desdecirse [46] *vpr.* **~ de** take back (palabras etc); go back on (promesa)
desd|én *m* scorn. **~eñable** *adj* insignificant. **nada ~eñable** significant. **~eñar** *vt* scorn
desdicha *f* misfortune. **por ~** unfortunately. **~do** *adj* unfortunate
desdoblar *vt* (*desplegar*) unfold
desear *vt* want; wish (suerte etc). **le deseo un buen viaje** I hope you have a good journey. **¿qué desea Vd?** can I help you?
desech|able *adj* disposable. **~ar** *vt* throw out; (*rechazar*) reject. **~o** *m* waste
desembalar *vt* unpack
desembarcar [7] *vt* unload. ● *vi* disembark
desemboca|dura *f* (*de río*) mouth; (*de calle*) opening. **~r** [7] *vi.* **~r en** (río) flow into; (calle) lead to
desembolso *m* payment
desembragar [12] *vi* declutch
desempaquetar *vt* unwrap
desempat|ar *vi* break a tie. **~e** *m* tie-breaker
desempeñ|ar *vt* redeem; play (papel); hold (cargo); perform, carry out (deber etc). **~arse** *vpr* (*LAm*) perform. **~arse bien** manage well. **~o** *m* redemption; (*de un deber, una función*) discharge; (*LAm, actuación*) performance
desemple|ado *adj* unemployed. ●*m* unemployed person. **los ~ados** the unemployed. **~o** *m* unemployment
desencadenar *vt* unchain (preso); unleash (perro); (*causar*) trigger. **~se** *vpr* be triggered off; (guerra etc) break out
desencajar *vt* dislocate; (*desconectar*) disconnect. **~se** *vpr* become dislocated
desenchufar *vt* unplug
desenfad|ado *adj* uninhibited; (*desenvuelto*) self-assured. **~o** *m* lack of inhibition; (*desenvoltura*) self-assurance
desenfocado *adj* out of focus
desenfren|ado *adj* unrestrained. **~o** *m* licentiousness
desenganchar *vt* unhook; uncouple (vagón)
desengañ|ar *vt* disillusion. **~arse** *vpr* become disillusioned; (*darse cuenta*) realize. **~o** *m* disillusionment, disappointment
desenlace *m* outcome

desenmascarar *vt* unmask
desenredar *vt* untangle. **~se** *vpr* untangle
desenro|llar *vt* unroll, unwind. **~scar** 7 *vt* unscrew
desentend|erse 1 *vpr* want nothing to do with. **~ido** *m*. **hacerse el ~ido** (*fingir no oír*) pretend not to hear; (*fingir ignorancia*) pretend not to know
desenterrar 1 *vt* exhume; (*fig*) unearth
desentonar *vi* be out of tune; (colores) clash
desenvoltura *f* ease; (*falta de timidez*) confidence
desenvolver 2 (*pp* **desenvuelto**) *vt* unwrap; expound (idea etc). **~se** *vpr* perform; (*manejarse*) manage
deseo *m* wish, desire. **~so** *adj* eager. **estar ~so de** be eager to
desequilibr|ado *adj* unbalanced. **~io** *m* imbalance
des|ertar *vt* desert; (*Pol*) defect. **~értico** *adj* desert-like. **~ertor** *m* deserter; (*Pol*) defector
desespera|ción *f* despair. **~do** *adj* desperate. **~nte** *adj* infuriating. **~r** *vt* drive to despair. **~rse** *vpr* despair
desestimar *vt* (*rechazar*) reject
desfachat|ado *adj* brazen, shameless. **~ez** *f* nerve, cheek
desfallec|er 11 *vt* weaken. • *vi* become weak; (*desmayarse*) faint. **~imiento** *m* weakness; (*desmayo*) faint
desfasado *adj* out of phase; (idea) outdated; (persona) out of touch
desfavorable *adj* unfavourable
desfil|adero *m* narrow mountain pass; (*cañón*) narrow gorge. **~ar** *vi* march (past). **~e** *m* procession, parade. **~e de modelos** fashion show
desgana *f*, (*LAm*) **desgano** *m* (*falta de apetito*) lack of appetite; (*Med*) weakness, faintness; (*fig*) unwillingness
desgarr|ador *adj* heart-rending. **~ar** *vt* tear; (*fig*) break (corazón). **~o** *m* tear, rip
desgast|ar *vt* wear away; wear out (ropa). **~arse** *vpr* wear away; (ropa) be worn out; (persona) wear o.s. out. **~e** *m* wear
desgracia *f* misfortune; (*accidente*) accident; **por ~** unfortunately. **¡qué ~!** what a shame!. **~do** *adj* unlucky; (*pobre*) poor. ●*m* unfortunate person, poor devil [I]
desgranar *vt* shell (habas etc)
desgreñado *adj* ruffled, dishevelled
deshabitado *adj* uninhabited; (edificio) unoccupied
deshacer 31 *vt* undo; strip (cama); unpack (maleta); (*desmontar*) take to pieces; break (trato); (*derretir*) melt; (*disolver*) dissolve. **~se** *vpr* come undone; (*disolverse*) dissolve; (*derretirse*) melt. **~se de algo** get rid of sth. **~se en lágrimas** dissolve into tears. **~se por hacer algo** go out of one's way to do sth
desheredar *vt* disinherit
deshidratarse *vpr* become dehydrated
deshielo *m* thaw
deshilachado *adj* frayed
deshincha|do *adj* (neumático) flat. **~r** *vt* deflate; (*Med*) reduce the swelling in. **~rse** *vpr* go down
deshollinador *m* chimney sweep

deshon|esto *adj* dishonest; (*obsceno*) indecent. **~ra** *f* disgrace. **~rar** *vt* dishonour

deshora *f.* a ~ out of hours. comer a ~s eat between meals

d **deshuesar** *vt* bone (carne); stone (fruta)

desidia *f* slackness; (pereza) laziness

desierto *adj* deserted. ● *m* desert

designar *vt* designate; (*fijar*) fix

desigual *adj* unequal; (terreno) uneven; (*distinto*) different. **~dad** *f* inequality

desilusi|ón *f* disappointment; (*pérdida de ilusiones*) disillusionment. **~onar** *vt* disappoint; (*quitar las ilusiones*) disillusion. **~onarse** *vpr* be disappointed; (*perder las ilusiones*) become disillusioned

desinfecta|nte *m* disinfectant. **~r** *vt* disinfect

desinflar *vt* deflate. **~se** *vpr* go down

desinhibido *adj* uninhibited

desintegrar *vt* disintegrate. **~se** *vpr* disintegrate

desinter|és *m* lack of interest; (*generosidad*) unselfishness. **~esado** *adj* uninterested; (*liberal*) unselfish

desistir *vi.* ~ **de** give up

desleal *adj* disloyal. **~tad** *f* disloyalty

desligar 12 *vt* untie; (*separar*) separate; (*fig, librar*) free. **~se** *vpr* break away; (*de un compromiso*) free o.s. (**de** from)

desliza|dor *m* (*Mex*) hang glider. **~r** 10 *vt* slide, slip. **~se** *vpr* slide, slip; (patinador) glide; (tiempo) slip by, pass; (*fluir*) flow

deslucido *adj* tarnished; (*gastado*) worn out; (*fig*) undistinguished

deslumbrar *vt* dazzle

desmadr|arse *vpr* get out of control. **~e** *m* excess

desmán *m* outrage

desmanchar *vt* (*LAm*) remove the stains from

desmantelar *vt* dismantle; (*despojar*) strip

desmaquillador *m* make-up remover

desmay|ado *adj* unconscious. **~arse** *vpr* faint. **~o** *m* faint

desmedido *adj* excessive

desmemoriado *adj* forgetful

desmenti|do *m* denial. **~r** 4 *vt* deny; (*contradecir*) contradict

desmenuzar 10 *vt* crumble; shred (carne etc)

desmerecer 11 *vi.* **no ~ de** compare favourably with

desmesurado *adj* excessive; (*enorme*) enormous

desmonta|ble *adj* collapsible; (armario) easy to dismantle; (*separable*) removable. **~r** *vt* (*quitar*) remove; (*desarmar*) dismantle, take apart. ● *vi* dismount

desmoralizar 10 *vt* demoralize

desmoronarse *vpr* crumble; (edificio) collapse

desnatado *adj* skimmed

desnivel *m* unevenness; (*fig*) difference, inequality

desnud|ar *vt* strip; undress, strip (persona). **~arse** *vpr* undress. **~ez** *f* nudity. **~o** *adj* naked; (*fig*) bare. ● *m* nude

desnutri|ción *f* malnutrition. **~do** *adj* undernourished

desobed|ecer 11 *vt* disobey. **~iencia** *f* disobedience

desocupa|do *adj* (asiento etc) vacant, free; (*sin trabajo*) unem-

ployed; (*ocioso*) idle. **~r** *vt* vacate; (*vaciar*) empty; (*desalojar*) clear
desodorante *m* deodorant
desolado *adj* desolate; (persona) sorry, sad
desorbitante *adj* excessive
desorden *m* disorder, untidiness; (*confusión*) confusion. **~ado** *adj* untidy. **~ar** *vt* disarrange, make a mess of
desorganizar 10 *vt* disorganize; (*trastornar*) disturb
desorienta|do *adj* confused. **~r** *vt* disorientate. **~rse** *vpr* lose one's bearings
despabila|do *adj* wide awake; (*listo*) quick. **~r** *vt* (*despertar*) wake up; (*avivar*) wise up. **~rse** *vpr* wake up; (*avivarse*) wise up
despach|ar *vt* finish; (*tratar con*) deal with; (*atender*) serve; (*vender*) sell; (*enviar*) send; (*despedir*) fire. **~o** *m* dispatch; (*oficina*) office; (*venta*) sale; (*de localidades*) box office
despacio *adv* slowly
despampanante *adj* stunning
desparpajo *m* confidence; (*descaro*) impudence
desparramar *vt* scatter; spill (líquidos)
despavorido *adj* terrified
despecho *m* spite. **a ~ de** in spite of. **por ~** out of spite
despectivo *adj* contemptuous; (sentido etc) pejorative
despedazar 10 *vt* tear to pieces
despedi|da *f* goodbye, farewell. **~da de soltero** stag-party. **~r** 5 *vt* say goodbye to, see off; dismiss (empleado); evict (inquilino); (*arrojar*) throw; give off (olor etc). **~rse** *vpr* say goodbye (**de** to)
despeg|ar 12 *vt* unstick. • *vi* (avión) take off. **~ue** *m* take-off
despeinar *vt* ruffle the hair of
despeja|do *adj* clear; (persona) wide awake. **~r** *vt* clear; (*aclarar*) clarify. • *vi* clear. **~rse** *vpr* (*aclararse*) become clear; (tiempo) clear up
despellejar *vt* skin
despenalizar *vt* decriminalize
despensa *f* pantry, larder
despeñadero *m* cliff
desperdici|ar *vt* waste. **~o** *m* waste. **~os** *mpl* rubbish
desperta|dor *m* alarm clock. **~r** 1 *vt* wake (up); (*fig*) awaken. **~rse** *vpr* wake up
despiadado *adj* merciless
despido *m* dismissal
despierto *adj* awake; (*listo*) bright
despilfarr|ar *vt* waste. **~o** *m* squandering
despintarse *vpr* (*Mex*) run
despista|do *adj* (*con estar*) confused; (*con ser*) absent-minded. **~r** *vt* throw off the scent; (*fig*) mislead. **~rse** *vpr* (*fig*) get confused
despiste *m* mistake; (*confusión*) muddle
desplaza|miento *m* displacement; (*de opinión etc*) swing, shift. **~r** 10 *vt* displace. **~rse** *vpr* travel
desplegar 1 & 12 *vt* open out; spread (alas); (*fig*) show
desplomarse *vpr* collapse
despoblado *m* deserted area
despoj|ar *vt* deprive (persona); strip (cosa). **~os** *mpl* remains; (*de res*) offal; (*de ave*) giblets
despreci|able *adj* despicable; (cantidad) negligible. **~ar** *vt* despise; (*rechazar*) scorn. **~o** *m* contempt; (*desaire*) snub
desprender *vt* remove; give off

(olor). **~se** *vpr* fall off; (*fig*) part with; (*deducirse*) follow
despreocupa|do *adj* unconcerned; (*descuidado*) careless. **~rse** *vpr* not worry
desprestigiar *vt* discredit
desprevenido *adj* unprepared. **pillar a uno ~** catch s.o. unawares
desproporcionado *adj* disproportionate
desprovisto *adj*. **~ de** lacking in, without
después *adv* after, afterwards; (*más tarde*) later; (*a continuación*) then. **~ de** after. **~ de comer** after eating. **~ de todo** after all. **~ (de) que** after. **poco ~** soon after
desquit|arse *vpr* get even (**de** with). **~e** *m* revenge
destaca|do *adj* outstanding. **~r** 7 *vt* emphasize. • *vi* stand out. **~rse** *vpr* stand out. **~rse en** excel at
destajo *m*. **trabajar a ~** do piece-work
destap|ar *vt* uncover; open (botella). **~arse** *vpr* reveal one's true self. **~e** *m* (*fig*) permissiveness
destartalado *adj* (coche) clapped-out; (casa) ramshackle
destello *m* sparkle; (*de estrella*) twinkle; (*fig*) glimmer
destemplado *adj* discordant; (nervios) frayed
desteñir 5 & 22 *vt* fade. • *vi* fade; (color) run. **~se** *vpr* fade; (color) run
desterra|do *m* exile. **~r** 1 *vt* banish
destetar *vt* wean
destiempo *m*. **a ~** at the wrong moment; (*Mus*) out of time
destierro *m* exile
destil|ar *vt* distil. **~ería** *f* distillery
destin|ar *vt* destine; (*nombrar*) post. **~atario** *m* addressee. **~o** *m* (*uso*) use, function; (*lugar*) destination; (*suerte*) destiny. **con ~o a** (going) to
destituir 17 *vt* dismiss
destornilla|dor *m* screwdriver. **~r** *vt* unscrew
destreza *f* skill
destroz|ar 10 *vt* destroy; (*fig*) shatter. **~os** *mpl* destruction, damage
destru|cción *f* destruction. **~ir** 17 *vt* destroy
desus|ado *adj* old-fashioned; (*insólito*) unusual. **~o** *m* disuse. **caer en ~o** fall into disuse
desvalido *adj* needy, destitute
desvalijar *vt* rob; ransack (casa)
desvalorizar 10 *vt* devalue
desván *m* loft
desvanec|er 11 *vt* make disappear; (*borrar*) blur; (*fig*) dispel. **~erse** *vpr* disappear; (*desmayarse*) faint. **~imiento** *m* (*Med*) faint
desvariar 20 *vi* be delirious; (*fig*) talk nonsense
desvel|ar *vt* keep awake. **~arse** *vpr* stay awake, have a sleepless night. **~o** *m* sleeplessness
desvencijado *adj* (mueble) rickety
desventaja *f* disadvantage
desventura *f* misfortune. **~do** *adj* unfortunate
desverg|onzado *adj* impudent, cheeky. **~üenza** *f* impudence, cheek
desvestirse 5 *vpr* undress
desv|iación *f* deviation; (*Auto*) diversion. **~iar** 20 *vt* divert; deflect (pelota). **~iarse** *vpr* (carretera)

branch off; (*del camino*) make a detour; (*del tema*) stray. **~ío** *m* diversion

desvivirse *vpr.* **~se por** be completely devoted to; (*esforzarse*) go out of one's way to

detall|ar *vt* relate in detail. **~e** *m* detail; (*fig*) gesture. **al ~e** retail. **entrar en ~es** go into detail. **¡qué ~e!** how thoughtful! **~ista** *m & f* retailer

detect|ar *vt* detect. **~ive** *m* detective

deten|ción *f* stopping; (*Jurid*) arrest; (*en la cárcel*) detention. **~er** 40 *vt* stop; (*Jurid*) arrest; (*encarcelar*) detain; (*retrasar*) delay. **~erse** *vpr* stop; (*entretenerse*) spend a lot of time. **~idamente** *adv* at length. **~ido** *adj* (*Jurid*) under arrest. ● *m* prisoner

detergente *adj & m* detergent

deterior|ar *vt* damage, spoil. **~arse** *vpr* deteriorate. **~o** *m* deterioration

determina|ción *f* determination; (*decisión*) decison. **~nte** *adj* decisive. **~r** *vt* determine; (*decidir*) decide

detestar *vt* detest

detrás *adv* behind; (*en la parte posterior*) on the back. **~ de** behind. **por ~** at the back; (*por la espalda*) from behind

detrimento *m* detriment. **en ~ de** to the detriment of

deud|a *f* debt. **~or** *m* debtor

devalua|ción *f* devaluation. **~r** 21 *vt* devalue. **~se** *vpr* depreciate

devastador *adj* devastating

devoción *f* devotion

devol|ución *f* return; (*Com*) repayment, refund. **~ver** 5 (*pp* **devuelto**) *vt* return; (*Com*) repay, refund. ● *vi* be sick

devorar *vt* devour

devoto *adj* devout; (amigo etc) devoted. ● *m* admirer

di *vb véase* DAR, DECIR

día *m* day. **~ de fiesta** (public) holiday. **~ del santo** saint's day. **~ feriado** (*LAm*), **~ festivo** (public) holiday. **al ~** up to date. **al ~ siguiente** (on) the following day. **¡buenos ~s!** good morning! **de ~** by day. **el ~ de hoy** today. **el ~ de mañana** tomorrow. **un ~ sí y otro no** every other day. **vivir al ~** live from hand to mouth

> **Día de la raza** In Latin America, the anniversary of Columbus's discovery of America, October 12. In Spain it is known as *Día de la Hispanidad*. It is a celebration of the cultural ties shared by Spanish-speaking countries.

diab|etes *f* diabetes. **~ético** *adj* diabetic

diab|lo *m* devil. **~lura** *f* mischief. **~ólico** *adj* diabolical

diadema *f* dladem

diáfano *adj* diaphanous; (cielo) clear

diafragma *m* diaphragm

diagn|osis *f* diagnosis. **~osticar** 7 *vt* diagnose. **~óstico** *m* diagnosis

diagonal *adj & f* diagonal

diagrama *m* diagram

dialecto *m* dialect

di|alogar 12 *vi* talk. **~álogo** *m* dialogue; (*Pol*) talks

diamante *m* diamond

diámetro *m* diameter

diana *f* reveille; (*blanco*) bull's-eye

diapositiva *f* slide, transparency

diario *adj* daily. • *m* newspaper; (*libro*) diary. **a ~o** daily. **de ~o** everyday, ordinary

diarrea *f* diarrhoea

dibuj|ante *m* draughtsman. • *f* draughtswoman. **~ar** *vt* draw. **~o** *m* drawing. **~os animados** cartoons

diccionario *m* dictionary

dich|a *f* happiness. **por ~a** fortunately. **~o** *adj* said; (*tal*) such. • *m* saying. **~o y hecho** no sooner said than done. **mejor ~o** rather. **propiamente ~o** strictly speaking. **~oso** *adj* happy; (*afortunado*) fortunate

diciembre *m* December

dicta|do *m* dictation. **~dor** *m* dictator. **~dura** *f* dictatorship. **~men** *m* opinion; (*informe*) report. **~r** *vt* dictate; pronounce (sentencia etc); (*LAm*) give (clase)

didáctico *adj* didactic

dieci|nueve *adj & m* nineteen. **~ocho** *adj & m* eighteen. **~séis** *adj & m* sixteen. **~siete** *adj & m* seventeen

diente *m* tooth; (*de tenedor*) prong; (*de ajo*) clove. **~ de león** dandelion. **hablar entre ~s** mumble

diestro *adj* right-handed; (*hábil*) skillful

dieta *f* diet

diez *adj & m* ten

diezmar *vt* decimate

difamación *f* (*con palabras*) slander; (*por escrito*) libel

diferen|cia *f* difference; (*desacuerdo*) disagreement. **~ciar** *vt* differentiate between. **~ciarse** *vpr* differ. **~te** *adj* different; (*diversos*) various

diferido *adj* (*TV etc*) **en ~** recorded

dif|ícil *adj* difficult; (*poco probable*) unlikely. **~icultad** *f* difficulty. **~icultar** *vt* make difficult

difteria *f* diphtheria

difundir *vt* spread; (*TV etc*) broadcast

difunto *adj* late, deceased. • *m* deceased

difusión *f* spreading

dige|rir **4** *vt* digest. **~stión** *f* digestion. **~stivo** *adj* digestive

digital *adj* digital; (*de los dedos*) finger

dign|arse *vpr* deign to. **~atario** *m* dignitary. **~idad** *f* dignity. **~o** *adj* honourable; (*decoroso*) decent; (*merecedor*) worthy (**de** of). **~ de elogio** praiseworthy

digo *vb véase* **DECIR**

dije *vb véase* **DECIR**

dilatar *vt* expand; (*Med*) dilate; (*prolongar*) prolong. **~se** *vpr* expand; (*Med*) dilate; (*extenderse*) extend; (*Mex, demorarse*) be late

dilema *m* dilemma

diligen|cia *f* diligence; (*gestión*) job; (*carruaje*) stagecoach. **~te** *adj* diligent

dilucidar *vt* clarify; solve (misterio)

diluir **17** *vt* dilute

diluvio *m* flood

dimensión *f* dimension; (*tamaño*) size

diminut|ivo *adj & m* diminutive. **~o** *adj* minute

dimitir *vt/i* resign

Dinamarca *f* Denmark

dinamarqués *adj* Danish. • *m* Dane

dinámic|a *f* dynamics. **~o** *adj*

dynamic

dinamita *f* dynamite

dínamo *m* dynamo

dinastía *f* dynasty

diner|al *m* fortune. **~o** *m* money. **~o efectivo** cash. **~o suelto** change

dinosaurio *m* dinosaur

dios *m* god. **~a** *f* goddess. **¡D~ mío!** good heavens! **¡gracias a D~!** thank God!

diplom|a *m* diploma. **~acia** *f* diplomacy. **~ado** *adj* qualified. **~arse** *vpr* (*LAm*) graduate. **~ático** *adj* diplomatic. ● *m* diplomat

diptongo *m* diphthong

diputa|ción *f* delegation. **~ción provincial** county council. **~do** *m* deputy; (*Pol, en España*) member of the Cortes; (*Pol, en Inglaterra*) Member of Parliament; (*Pol, en Estados Unidos*) congressman

dique *m* dike

direc|ción *f* direction; (*señas*) address; (*los que dirigen*) management; (*Pol*) leadership; (*Auto*) steering. **~ción prohibida** no entry. **~ción única** one-way. **~ta** *f* (*Auto*) top gear. **~tiva** *f* board; (*Pol*) executive committee. **~tivas** *fpl* guidelines. **~to** *adj* direct; (línea) straight; (tren) through. **en ~to** (*TV etc*) live. **~tor** *m* director; (*Mus*) conductor; (*de escuela*) headmaster; (*de periódico*) editor; (*gerente*) manager. **~tora** *f* (*de escuela etc*) headmistress. **~torio** *m* board of directors; (*LAm, de teléfonos*) telephone directory

dirig|ente *adj* ruling. ● *m & f* leader; (*de empresa*) manager. **~ir** **14** *vt* direct; (*Mus*) conduct; run (empresa etc); address (carta etc). **~irse** *vpr* make one's way; (*hablar*) address

disciplina *f* discipline. **~r** *vt* discipline. **~rio** *adj* disciplinary

discípulo *m* disciple; (*alumno*) pupil

disco *m* disc; (*Mus*) record; (*deportes*) discus; (*de teléfono*) dial; (*de tráfico*) sign; (*Rail*) signal. **~ duro** hard disk. **~ flexible** floppy disk

disconforme *adj* not in agreement

discord|e *adj* discordant. **~ia** *f* discord

discoteca *f* discothèque, disco **!**; (*colección de discos*) record collection

discreción *f* discretion

discrepa|ncia *f* discrepancy; (*desacuerdo*) disagreement. **~r** *vi* differ

discreto *adj* discreet; (*moderado*) moderate

discrimina|ción *f* discrimination. **~r** *vt* (*distinguir*) discriminate between; (*tratar injustamente*) discriminate against

disculpa *f* apology; (*excusa*) excuse. **pedir ~s** apologize. **~r** *vt* excuse, forgive. **~rse** *vpr* apologize

discurs|ar *vi* speak (**sobre** about). **~o** *m* speech

discusión *f* discussion; (*riña*) argument

discuti|ble *adj* debatable. **~r** *vt* discuss; (*contradecir*) contradict. ● *vi* argue (**por** about)

disecar **7** *vt* stuff; (*cortar*) dissect

diseminar *vt* disseminate, spread

disentir **4** *vi* disagree (**de** with, **en** on)

diseñ|ador *m* designer. **~ar** *vt* design. **~o** *m* design; (*fig*) sketch

disertación *f* dissertation

disfraz *m* fancy dress; (*para engañar*) disguise. **~ar** 10 *vt* dress up; (*para engañar*) disguise. **~arse** *vpr.* **~arse de** dress up as; (*para engañar*) disguise o.s. as.

disfrutar *vt* enjoy. • *vi* enjoy o.s. **~ de** enjoy

disgust|ar *vt* displease; (*molestar*) annoy. **~arse** *vpr* get annoyed, get upset; (dos personas) fall out. **~o** *m* annoyance; (*problema*) trouble; (*riña*) quarrel; (*dolor*) sorrow, grief

disidente *adj & m & f* dissident

disimular *vt* conceal. • *vi* pretend

disipar *vt* dissipate; (*derrochar*) squander

dislocarse 7 *vpr* dislocate

disminu|ción *f* decrease. **~ir** 17 *vi* diminish

disolver 2 (*pp* **disuelto**) *vt* dissolve. **~se** *vpr* dissolve

dispar *adj* different

disparar *vt* fire; (*Mex, pagar*) buy. • *vi* shoot (**contra** at)

disparate *m* silly thing; (*error*) mistake. **decir ~s** talk nonsense. **¡qué ~!** how ridiculous!

disparidad *f* disparity

disparo *m* (*acción*) firing; (*tiro*) shot

dispensar *vt* give; (*eximir*) exempt. • *vi.* **¡Vd dispense!** forgive me

dispers|ar *vt* scatter, disperse. **~arse** *vpr* scatter, disperse. **~ión** *f* dispersion. **~o** *adj* scattered

dispon|er 34 *vt* arrange; (*Jurid*) order. • *vi.* **~er de** have; (*vender etc*) dispose of. **~erse** *vpr* prepare (**a** to). **~ibilidad** *f* availability. **~ible** *adj* available

disposición *f* arrangement; (*aptitud*) talent; (*disponibilidad*) disposal; (*Jurid*) order, decree. **~ de ánimo** frame of mind. **a la ~ de** at the disposal of. **a su ~** at your service

dispositivo *m* device

dispuesto *adj* ready; (persona) disposed (**a** to); (*servicial*) helpful

disputa *f* dispute; (*pelea*) argument

disquete *m* diskette, floppy disk

dista|ncia *f* distance. **a ~ncia** from a distance. **guardar las ~ncias** keep one's distance. **~nciar** *vt* space out; distance (amigos). **~nciarse** *vpr* (dos personas) fall out. **~nte** *adj* distant. **~r** *vi* be away; (*fig*) be far. **~ 5 kilómetros** it's 5 kilometres away

distin|ción *f* distinction; (*honor*) award. **~guido** *adj* distinguished. **~guir** 13 *vt/i* distinguish. **~guirse** *vpr* distinguish o.s.; (*diferenciarse*) differ. **~tivo** *adj* distinctive. • *m* badge. **~to** *adj* different, distinct

distra|cción *f* amusement; (*descuido*) absent-mindedness, inattention. **~er** 41 *vt* distract; (*divertir*) amuse. **~erse** *vpr* amuse o.s.; (*descuidarse*) not pay attention. **~ído** *adj* (*desatento*) absent-minded

distribu|ción *f* distribution. **~idor** *m* distributor. **~ir** 17 *vt* distribute

distrito *m* district

disturbio *m* disturbance

disuadir *vt* deter, dissuade

diurno *adj* daytime

divagar 12 *vi* digress; (*hablar sin sentido*) ramble

diván *m* settee, sofa

diversi|dad *f* diversity. **~ficar** 7 *vt* diversify

diversión *f* amusement, entertainment; (*pasatiempo*) pastime

diverso *adj* different

diverti|do *adj* amusing; (*que tiene gracia*) funny. **~r** 4 *vt* amuse, entertain. **~rse** *vpr* enjoy o.s.

dividir *vt* divide; (*repartir*) share out

divino *adj* divine

divisa *f* emblem. **~s** *fpl* currency

divisar *vt* make out

división *f* division

divorci|ado *adj* divorced. ● *m* divorcee. **~ar** *vt* divorce. **~arse** *vpr* get divorced. **~o** *m* divorce

divulgar 12 *vt* spread; divulge (secreto)

dizque *adv* (*LAm*) apparently; (*supuestamente*) supposedly

do *m* C; (*solfa*) doh

> **DNI - Documento Nacional de Identidad** See ▷**DOCUMENTO DE IDENTIDAD**

dobl|adillo *m* hem; (*de pantalón*) turn-up (*Brit*), cuff (*Amer*). **~ar** *vt* double; (*plegar*) fold; (*torcer*) bend; turn (esquina); dub (película). ● *vi* turn; (campana) toll. **~arse** *vpr* double; (*curvarse*) bend. **~e** *adj* double. ● *m* double. **el ~e** twice as much (**de**, **que** as). **~egar** 12 *vt* (*fig*) force to give in. **~egarse** *vpr* give in

doce *adj* & *m* twelve. **~na** *f* dozen

docente *adj* teaching. ● *m* & *f* teacher

dócil *adj* obedient

doctor *m* doctor. **~ado** *m* doctorate

doctrina *f* doctrine

document|ación *f* documentation, papers. **~al** *adj* & *m* documentary. **~o** *m* document. **D~o Nacional de Identidad** identity card

> **documento de identidad** An identity card that all residents over a certain age in Spain and Latin America must carry at all times. Holders must quote their identity card number on most official forms. The card is also known as *carné de identidad*, and in Spain as the *DNI* (*Documento Nacional de Identidad*).

dólar *m* dollar

dolarizar *vt* dollarize

dol|er 2 *vi* hurt, ache; (*fig*) grieve. **me duele la cabeza** I have a headache. **le duele el estómago** he has (a) stomach-ache. **~or** *m* pain; (*sordo*) ache; (*fig*) sorrow. **~or de cabeza** headache. **~or de muelas** toothache. **~oroso** *adj* painful

domar *vt* tame; break in (caballo)

dom|esticar 7 *vt* domesticate. **~éstico** *adj* domestic

domicili|ar *vt*. **~ar los pagos** pay by direct debit. **~o** *m* address. **~o particular** home address. **reparto a ~** home delivery service

domina|nte *adj* dominant; (persona) domineering. **~r** *vt* dominate; (*contener*) control; (*conocer*) have a good command of. ● *vi* dominate. **~rse** *vpr* control o.s.

domingo *m* Sunday

dominio *m* authority; (*territorio*) domain; (*fig*) command

dominó *m* (*pl* **~s**) dominoes; (*ficha*) domino

don *m* talent, gift; (*en un sobre*) Mr. **~ Pedro** Pedro

donación *f* donation

donaire *m* grace, charm

dona|nte *m& f* (*de sangre*) donor. **~r** *vt* donate

doncella *f* maiden; (*criada*) maid

donde *adv* where

dónde *adv* where?; (*LAm, cómo*) how; **¿hasta ~?** how far? **¿por ~?** whereabouts?; (*por qué camino?*) which way? **¿a ~ vas?** where are you going? **¿de ~ eres?** where are you from?

dondequiera *adv.* **~ que** wherever. **por ~** everywhere

doña *f* (*en un sobre*) Mrs. **~ María** María

dora|do *adj* golden; (*cubierto de oro*) gilt. **~r** *vt* gilt; (*Culin*) brown

dormi|do *adj* asleep. **quedarse ~do** fall asleep; (*no despertar*) oversleep. **~r** 6 *vt* send to sleep. • *vi* sleep. **~rse** *vpr* fall asleep. **~r la siesta** have an afternoon nap, have a siesta. **~tar** *vi* doze. **~torio** *m* bedroom

dors|al *adj* back. • *m* (*en deportes*) number. **~o** *m* back. **nadar de ~** (*Mex*) do (the) backstroke

dos *adj & m* two. **de ~ en ~** in twos, in pairs. **los ~, las ~** both (of them). **~cientos** *adj & m* two hundred

dosi|ficar 7 *vt* dose; (*fig*) measure out. **~s** *f invar* dose

dot|ado *adj* gifted. **~ar** *vt* give a dowry; (*proveer*) provide (**de** with). **~e** *m* dowry

doy *vb véase* DAR

dragar 12 *vt* dredge

drama *m* drama; (*obra de teatro*) play. **~turgo** *m* playwright

drástico *adj* drastic

droga *f* drug. **~dicto** *m* drug addict. **~do** *m* drug addict. **~r** 12 *vt* drug. **~rse** *vpr* take drugs

droguería *f* hardware store

ducha *f* shower. **~rse** *vpr* have a shower

dud|a *f* doubt. **poner en ~a** question. **sin ~a (alguna)** without a doubt. **~ar** *vt/i* doubt. **~oso** *adj* doubtful; (*sospechoso*) dubious

duelo *m* duel; (*luto*) mourning

duende *m* imp

dueñ|a *f* owner, proprietress; (*de una pensión*) landlady. **~o** *m* owner, proprietor; (*de una pensión*) landlord

duermo *vb véase* DORMIR

dul|ce *adj* sweet; (agua) fresh; (*suave*) soft, gentle. • *m* (*LAm*) sweet. **~zura** *f* sweetness; (*fig*) gentleness

duna *f* dune

dúo *m* duet, duo

duplica|do *adj* duplicated. **por ~** in duplicate. • *m* duplicate. **~r** 7 *vt* duplicate. **~rse** *vpr* double

duque *m* duke. **~sa** *f* duchess

dura|ción *f* duration, length. **~dero** *adj* lasting. **~nte** *prep* during; (*medida de tiempo*) for. **~ todo el año** all year round. **~r** *vi* last

durazno *m* (*LAm, fruta*) peach

dureza *f* hardness; (*Culin*) toughness; (*fig*) harshness

duro *adj* hard; (*Culin*) tough; (*fig*) harsh. • *adv* (*esp LAm*) hard

DVD *m* (**Disco Versátil Digital**) DVD. **~teca** *f* DVD library

Ee

e *conj* and
Ébola *m* ebola
ebrio *adj* drunk
ebullición *f* boiling
eccema *m* eczema
echar *vt* throw; post (carta); give off (olor); pour (líquido); (*expulsar*) expel; (*de recinto*) throw out; fire (empleado); (*poner*) put on; get (gasolina); put out (raíces); show (película). **~ a** start. **~ a perder** spoil. **~ de menos** miss. **~se atrás** (*fig*) back down. **echárselas de** feign. **~se** *vpr* throw o.s.; (*tumbarse*) lie down
eclesiástico *adj* ecclesiastical
eclipse *m* eclipse
eco *m* echo. **hacerse ~ de** echo
ecolog|ía *f* ecology. **~ista** *m & f* ecologist
economato *m* cooperative store
econ|omía *f* economy; (*ciencia*) economics. **~ómico** *adj* economic; (*no caro*) inexpensive. **~omista** *m & f* economist. **~omizar** 10 *vt/i* economize
ecoturismo *m* ecotourism
ecuación *f* equation
ecuador *m* equator. **el E~** the Equator. **E~** (*país*) Ecuador
ecuánime *adj* level-headed; (*imparcial*) impartial
ecuatoriano *adj & m* Ecuadorian
ecuestre *adj* equestrian
edad *f* age. **~ avanzada** old age. **E~ de Piedra** Stone Age. **E~ Media** Middle Ages. **¿qué ~ tiene?** how old is he?
edición *f* edition; (*publicación*) publication
edicto *m* edict
edific|ación *f* building. **~ante** *adj* edifying. **~ar** 7 *vt* build; (*fig*) edify. **~io** *m* building; (*fig*) structure
edit|ar *vt* edit; (*publicar*) publish. **~or** *adj* publishing. ● *m* editor; (*que publica*) publisher. **~orial** *adj* editorial. ● *m* leading article. ● *f* publishing house
edredón *m* duvet
educa|ción *f* upbringing; (*modales*) (good) manners; (*enseñanza*) education. **falta de ~ción** rudeness, bad manners. **~do** *adj* polite. **bien ~do** polite. **mal ~do** rude. **~r** 7 *vt* bring up; (*enseñar*) educate. **~tivo** *adj* educational
edulcorante *m* sweetener
EE.UU. *abrev* (**Estados Unidos**) USA
efect|ivamente *adv* really; (*por supuesto*) indeed. **~ivo** *adj* effective; (*auténtico*) real. ● *m* cash. **~o** *m* effect; (*impresión*) impression. **en ~o** really; (*como respuesta*) indeed. **~os** *mpl* belongings; (*Com*) goods. **~uar** 21 *vt* carry out; make (viaje, compras etc)
efervescente *adj* effervescent; (bebidas) fizzy
efica|cia *f* effectiveness; (*de persona*) efficiency. **~z** *adj* effective; (persona) efficient
eficien|cia *f* efficiency. **~te** *adj* efficient
efímero *adj* ephemeral
efusi|vidad *f* effusiveness. **~vo** *adj* effusive; (persona) demonstrative
egipcio *adj & m* Egyptian
Egipto *m* Egypt

e

ego|ísmo *m* selfishness, egotism. **~ista** *adj* selfish

egresar *vi* (*LAm*) graduate; (*de colegio*) leave school, graduate (*Amer*)

eje *m* axis; (*Tec*) axle

ejecu|ción *f* execution; (*Mus*) performance. **~tar** *vt* carry out; (*Mus*) perform; (*matar*) execute. **~tivo** *m* executive

ejempl|ar *adj* exemplary; (*ideal*) model. ● *m* specimen; (*libro*) copy; (*revista*) issue, number. **~ificar** **7** *vt* exemplify. **~o** *m* example. **dar (el) ~o** set an example. **por ~o** for example

ejerc|er **9** *vt* exercise; practise (profesión); exert (influencia). ● *vi* practise. **~icio** *m* exercise; (*de profesión*) practice. **hacer ~icios** take exercise. **~itar** *vt* exercise

ejército *m* army

ejido *m* (*Mex*) cooperative

ejote *m* (*Mex*) green bean

el *artículo definido masculino* (*pl* **los**)

The masculine article **el** is also used before feminine nouns which begin with stressed **a** or **ha**, e.g. **el ala derecha, el hada madrina.** Also, **de** followed by **el** becomes **del** and **el** preceded by **a** becomes **al**

····➤the. **el tren de las seis** the six o'clock train. **el vecino de al lado** the next-door neighbour. **cerca del hospital** near the hospital

····➤*No se traduce en los siguientes casos:* (*con nombre abstracto, genérico*) **el tiempo vuela** time flies. **odio el queso** I hate cheese. **el hilo es muy durable** linen is very durable

····➤(*con colores, días de la semana*) **el rojo está de moda** red is in fashion. **el lunes es fiesta** Monday is a holiday

····➤(*con algunas instituciones*) **termino el colegio mañana** I finish school tomorrow. **lo ingresaron en el hospital** he was admitted to hospital

····➤(*con nombres propios*) **el Sr. Díaz** Mr Díaz. **el doctor Lara** Doctor Lara

····➤(*antes de infinitivo*) **es muy cuidadosa en el vestir** she takes great care in the way she dresses. **me di cuenta al verlo** I realized when I saw him

····➤(*con partes del cuerpo, articulos personales*) *se traduce por un posesivo.* **apretó el puño** he clenched his fist. **tienes el zapato desatado** your shoe is undone

····➤**el + de. es el de Pedro** it's Pedro's. **el del sombrero** the one with the hat

····➤**el + que** (*persona*) **el que me atendió** the one who served me. (*cosa*) **el que se rompió** the one that broke.

····➤**el + que** + *subjuntivo* (*quienquiera*) whoever. **el que gane la lotería** whoever wins the lottery. (*cualquiera*) whichever. **compra el que sea más barato** buy whichever is cheaper

él *pron* (*persona*) he; (*persona con prep*) him; (*cosa*) it. **es de ~** it's his

elabora|ción *f* elaboration; (*fabricación*) manufacture. **~r** *vt* elaborate; manufacture (producto);

(*producir*) produce
el|asticidad *f* elasticity. **~ástico** *adj & m* elastic
elec|ción *f* choice; (*de político etc*) election. **~ciones** *fpl* (*Pol*) election. **~tor** *m* voter. **~torado** *m* electorate. **~toral** *adj* electoral; (campaña) election
electrici|dad *f* electricity. **~sta** *m & f* electrician
eléctrico *adj* electric; (aparato) electrical
electri|ficar **7** *vt* electrify. **~zar** **10** *vt* electrify
electrocutar *vt* electrocute. **~se** *vpr* be electrocuted
electrodoméstico *adj* electrical appliance
electrónic|a *f* electronics. **~o** *adj* electronic
elefante *m* elephant
elegan|cia *f* elegance. **~te** *adj* elegant
elegía *f* elegy
elegi|ble *adj* eligible. **~do** *adj* chosen. **~r** **5** & **14** *vt* choose; (*por votación*) elect
element|al *adj* elementary; (*esencial*) fundamental. **~o** *m* element; (*persona*) person, bloke (*Brit, fam*). **~os** *mpl* (*nociones*) basic principles
elenco *m* (*en el teatro*) cast
eleva|ción *f* elevation; (*de precios*) rise, increase; (*acción*) raising. **~dor** *m* (*Mex*) lift (*Brit*), elevator (*Amer*). **~r** *vt* raise; (*promover*) promote
elimina|ción *f* elimination. **~r** *vt* eliminate; (*Informática*) delete. **~toria** *f* preliminary heat
élite /e'lit, e'lite/ *f* elite
ella *pron* (*persona*) she; (*persona con prep*) her; (*cosa*) it. **es de ~s** it's theirs. **~s** *pron* pl they; (*con prep*) them. **es de ~** it's hers
ello *pron* it
ellos *pron pl* they; (*con prep*) them. **es de ~** it's theirs
elocuen|cia *f* eloquence. **~te** *adj* eloquent
elogi|ar *vt* praise. **~o** *m* praise
elote *m* (*Mex*) corncob; (*Culin*) corn on the cob
eludir *vt* avoid, elude
emanar *vi* emanate (**de** from); (*originarse*) originate (**de** from, in)
emancipa|ción *f* emancipation. **~r** *vt* emancipate. **~rse** *vpr* become emancipated
embadurnar *vt* smear
embajad|a *f* embassy. **~or** *m* ambassador
embalar *vt* pack
embaldosar *vt* tile
embalsamar *vt* embalm
embalse *m* reservoir
embaraz|ada *adj* pregnant. ● *f* pregnant woman. **~ar** **10** *vt* get pregnant. **~o** *m* pregnancy; (*apuro*) embarrassment; (*estorbo*) hindrance. **~oso** *adj* awkward, embarrassing
embar|cación *f* vessel. **~cadero** *m* jetty, pier. **~car** **7** *vt* load (mercancías etc). **~carse** *vpr* board. **~carse en** (*fig*) embark upon
embargo *m* embargo; (*Jurid*) seizure. **sin ~** however
embarque *m* loading; (*de pasajeros*) boarding
embaucar **7** *vt* trick
embelesar *vt* captivate
embellecer **11** *vt* make beautiful
embesti|da *f* charge. **~r** **5** *vt/i* charge
emblema *m* emblem

e

embolsarse *vpr* pocket
embonar *vt* (*Mex*) fit
emborrachar *vt* get drunk. **~se** *vpr* get drunk
emboscada *f* ambush
embotar *vt* dull
embotella|miento *m* (*de vehículos*) traffic jam. **~r** *vt* bottle
embrague *m* clutch
embriag|arse **12** *vpr* get drunk. **~uez** *f* drunkenness
embrión *m* embryo
embroll|ar *vt* mix up; involve (persona). **~arse** *vpr* get into a muddle; (*en un asunto*) get involved. **~o** *m* tangle; (*fig*) muddle
embruj|ado *adj* bewitched; (casa) haunted. **~ar** *vt* bewitch. **~o** *m* spell
embrutecer **11** *vt* brutalize
embudo *m* funnel
embuste *m* lie. **~ro** *adj* deceitful. ● *m* liar
embuti|do *m* (*Culin*) sausage. **~r** *vt* stuff
emergencia *f* emergency
emerger **14** *vi* appear, emerge
emigra|ción *f* emigration. **~nte** *adj & m & f* emigrant. **~r** *vi* emigrate
eminen|cia *f* eminence. **~te** *adj* eminent
emisario *m* emissary
emi|sión *f* emission; (*de dinero*) issue; (*TV etc*) broadcast. **~sor** *adj* issuing; (*TV etc*) broadcasting. **~sora** *f* radio station. **~tir** *vt* emit, give out; (*TV etc*) broadcast; cast (voto); (*poner en circulación*) issue
emoci|ón *f* emotion; (*excitación*) excitement. **¡qué ~ón!** how exciting!. **~onado** *adj* moved. **~onante** *adj* exciting; (*conmovedor*) moving. **~onar** *vt* move. **~onarse** *vpr* get excited; (*conmoverse*) be moved
emotivo *adj* emotional; (*conmovedor*) moving
empacar **7** *vt* (*LAm*) pack
empacho *m* indigestion
empadronar *vt* register. **~se** *vpr* register
empalagoso *adj* sickly; (persona) cloying
empalizada *f* fence
empalm|ar *vt* connect, join. ● *vi* meet. **~e** *m* junction; (*de trenes*) connection
empan|ada *f* (savoury) pie; (*LAm, individual*) pasty. **~adilla** *f* pasty
empantanarse *vpr* become swamped; (coche) get bogged down
empañar *vt* steam up; (*fig*) tarnish. **~se** *vpr* steam up
empapar *vt* soak. **~se** *vpr* get soaked
empapela|do *m* wallpaper. **~r** *vt* wallpaper
empaquetar *vt* package
emparedado *m* sandwich
emparentado *adj* related
empast|ar *vt* fill (muela). **~e** *m* filling
empat|ar *vi* draw. **~e** *m* draw
empedernido *adj* confirmed; (bebedor) inveterate
empedrar **1** *vt* pave
empeine *m* instep
empeñ|ado *adj* in debt; (*decidido*) determined (**en** to). **~ar** *vt* pawn; pledge (palabra). **~arse** *vpr* get into debt; (*estar decidido a*) be determined (**en** to). **~o** *m* pledge; (*resolución*) determination. **casa** *f*

de **~s** pawnshop. **~oso** *adj* (*LAm*) hardworking

empeorar *vt* make worse. • *vi* get worse. **~se** *vpr* get worse

empequeñecer [11] *vt* become smaller; (*fig*) belittle

empera|dor *m* emperor. **~triz** *f* empress

empezar [1] & [10] *vt/i* start, begin. **para ~** to begin with

empina|do *adj* (cuesta) steep. **~r** *vt* raise. **~rse** *vpr* (persona) stand on tiptoe

empírico *adj* empirical

emplasto *m* plaster

emplaza|miento *m* (*Jurid*) summons; (*lugar*) site. **~r** [10] *vt* summon; (*situar*) site

emple|ada *f* employee; (*doméstica*) maid. **~ado** *m* employee. **~ar** *vt* use; employ (persona); spend (tiempo). **~arse** *vpr* get a job. **~o** *m* use; (*trabajo*) employment; (*puesto*) job

empobrecer [11] *vt* impoverish. **~se** *vpr* become poor

empoll|ar *vt* incubate (huevos); (*arg, estudiar*) cram [I]. • *vi* (ave) sit; (estudiante) [I] cram. **~ón** *m* [I] swot (*Brit, fam*), grind (*Amer, fam*)

empolvarse *vpr* powder

empotra|do *adj* built-in, fitted. **~r** *vt* fit

emprende|dor *adj* enterprising. **~r** *vt* undertake; set out on (viaje). **~rla con uno** pick a fight with s.o.

empresa *f* undertaking; (*Com*) company, firm. **~ puntocom** dotcom company. **~rio** *m* businessman; (*patrón*) employer; (*de teatro etc*) impresario

empuj|ar *vt* push. **~e** *m* (*fig*) drive. **~ón** *m* push, shove

empuña|dura *f* handle

emular *vt* emulate

en *prep* in; (*sobre*) on; (*dentro*) inside, in; (*medio de transporte*) by. **~ casa** at home. **~ coche** by car. **~ 10 días** in 10 days. **de pueblo ~ pueblo** from town to town

enagua *f* petticoat

enajena|ción *f* alienation. **~ción mental** insanity. **~r** *vt* alienate; (*volver loco*) derange

enamora|do *adj* in love. • *m* lover. **~r** *vt* win the love of. **~rse** *vpr* fall in love (**de** with)

enano *adj & m* dwarf

enardecer [11] *vt* inflame. **~se** *vpr* get excited (**por** about)

encabeza|do *m* (*Mex*) headline. **~miento** *m* heading; (*de periódico*) headline. **~r** [10] *vt* head; lead (revolución etc)

encabritarse *vpr* rear up

encadenar *vt* chain; (*fig*) tie down

encaj|ar *vt* fit; fit together (varias piezas). • *vi* fit; (*cuadrar*) tally. **~arse** *vpr* put on. **~e** *m* lace; (*Com*) reserve

encaminar *vt* direct. **~se** *vpr* make one's way

encandilar *vt* dazzle; (*estimular*) stimulate

encant|ado *adj* enchanted; (persona) delighted. **¡~ado!** pleased to meet you! **~ador** *adj* charming. **~amiento** *m* spell. **~ar** *vt* bewitch; (*fig*) charm, delight. **me ~a la leche** I love milk. **~o** *m* spell; (*fig*) delight

encapricharse *vpr*. **~ con** take a fancy to

encarar *vt* face; (*LAm*) stand up to (persona). **~se** *vpr*. **~se con** stand up to

e

encarcelar *vt* imprison
encarecer 11 *vt* put up the price of. **~se** *vpr* become more expensive
encarg|ado *adj* in charge. ● *m* manager, person in charge. **~ar** 12 *vt* entrust; (*pedir*) order. **~arse** *vpr* take charge (**de** of). **~o** *m* job; (*Com*) order; (*recado*) errand. **hecho de ~o** made to measure
encariñarse *vpr.* **~ con** take to, become fond of
encarna|ción *f* incarnation. **~do** *adj* incarnate; (*rojo*) red; (uña) ingrowing. ● *m* red
encarnizado *adj* bitter
encarpetar *vt* file; (*LAm, dar carpetazo*) shelve
encarrilar *vt* put back on the rails; (*fig*) direct, put on the right track
encasillar *vt* classify; (*fig*) pigeonhole
encauzar 10 *vt* channel
enceguecer *vt* 11 (*LAm*) blind
encend|edor *m* lighter. **~er** 1 *vt* light; switch on, turn on (aparato eléctrico); start (motor); (*fig*) arouse. **~erse** *vpr* light; (aparato eléctrico) come on; (*excitarse*) get excited; (*ruborizarse*) blush. **~ido** *adj* lit; (aparato eléctrico) on; (*rojo*) bright red. ● *m* (*Auto*) ignition
encera|do *adj* waxed. ● *m* (*pizarra*) blackboard. **~r** *vt* wax
encerr|ar 1 *vt* shut in; (*con llave*) lock up; (*fig, contener*) contain. **~ona** *f* trap
enchilar *vt* (*Mex*) add chili to
enchinar *vt* (*Mex*) perm
enchuf|ado *adj* switched on. **~ar** *vt* plug in; fit together (tubos etc). **~e** *m* socket; (*clavija*) plug; (*de tubos etc*) joint; (*fam, influencia*) contact. **tener ~e** have friends in the right places
encía *f* gum
enciclopedia *f* encyclopaedia
encierro *m* confinement; (*cárcel*) prison
encim|a *adv* on top; (*arriba*) above. **~ de** on, on top of; (*sobre*) over; (*además de*) besides, as well as. **por ~** on top; (*adj* la ligera) superficially. **por ~ de todo** above all. **~ar** *vt* (*Mex*) stack up. **~era** *f* worktop
encina *f* holm oak
encinta *adj* pregnant
enclenque *adj* weak; (*enfermizo*) sickly
encoger 14 *vt* shrink; (*contraer*) contract. **~se** *vpr* shrink. **~erse de hombros** shrug one's shoulders
encolar *vt* glue; (*pegar*) stick
encolerizar 10 *vt* make angry. **~se** *vpr* get furious
encomendar 1 *vt* entrust
encomi|ar *vt* praise. **~o** *m* praise. **~oso** *adj* (*LAm*) complimentary
encono *m* bitterness, ill will
encontra|do *adj* contrary, conflicting. **~r** 2 *vt* find; (*tropezar con*) meet. **~rse** *vpr* meet; (*hallarse*) be. **no ~rse** feel uncomfortable
encorvar *vt* hunch. **~se** *vpr* stoop
encrespa|do *adj* (pelo) curly; (mar) rough. **~r** *vt* curl (pelo); make rough (mar)
encrucijada *f* crossroads
encuaderna|ción *f* binding. **~dor** *m* bookbinder. **~r** *vt* bind
encub|ierto *adj* hidden. **~rir** (*pp* **encubierto**) *vt* hide, conceal; cover up (delito); shelter (delincuente)
encuentro *m* meeting; (*en depor-*

tes) match; (*Mil*) encounter
encuesta *f* survey; (*investigación*) inquiry
encumbrado *adj* eminent; (*alto*) high
encurtidos *mpl* pickles
endeble *adj* weak
endemoniado *adj* possessed; (*muy malo*) wretched
enderezar 10 *vt* straighten out; (*poner vertical*) put upright; (*fig, arreglar*) put right, sort out; (*dirigir*) direct. **~se** *vpr* straighten out
endeudarse *vpr* get into debt
endiablado *adj* possessed; (*malo*) terrible; (*difícil*) difficult
endosar *vt* endorse (cheque)
endulzar 10 *vt* sweeten; (*fig*) soften
endurecer 11 *vt* harden. **~se** *vpr* harden
enemi|go *adj* enemy. ● *m* enemy. **~stad** *f* enmity. **~star** *vt* make an enemy of. **~starse** *vpr* fall out (**con** with)
en|ergía *f* energy. **~érgico** *adj* (persona) lively; (decisión) forceful
energúmeno *m* madman
enero *m* January
enésimo *adj* nth, umpteenth I
enfad|ado *adj* angry; (*molesto*) annoyed. **~ar** *vt* make cross, anger; (*molestar*) annoy. **~arse** *vpr* get angry; (*molestarse*) get annoyed. **~o** *m* anger; (*molestia*) annoyance
énfasis *m invar* emphasis, stress. **poner ~** stress, emphasize
enfático *adj* emphatic
enferm|ar *vi* fall ill. **~arse** *vpr* (*LAm*) fall ill. **~edad** *f* illness. **~era** *f* nurse. **~ería** *f* sick bay; (*carrera*) nursing. **~ero** *m* (male) nurse
~izo *adj* sickly. **~o** *adj* ill. ● *m* patient
enflaquecer 11 *vt* make thin. ● *vi* lose weight
enfo|car 7 *vt* shine on; focus (lente); (*fig*) approach. **~que** *m* focus; (*fig*) approach
enfrentar *vt* face, confront; (*poner frente a frente*) bring face to face. **~se** *vpr.* **~se con** confront; (*en deportes*) meet
enfrente *adv* opposite. **~ de** opposite. **de ~** opposite
enfria|miento *m* cooling; (*catarro*) cold. **~r** 20 *vt* cool (down); (*fig*) cool down. **~rse** *vpr* go cold; (*fig*) cool off
enfurecer 11 *vt* infuriate. **~se** *vpr* get furious
engalanar *vt* adorn. **~se** *vpr* dress up
enganchar *vt* hook; hang up (ropa). **~se** *vpr* get caught; (*Mil*) enlist
engañ|ar *vt* deceive, trick; (*ser infiel*) be unfaithful. **~arse** *vpr* be wrong, be mistaken; (*no admitir la verdad*) deceive o.s. **~o** *m* deceit, trickery; (*error*) mistake. **~oso** *adj* deceptive; (persona) deceitful
engarzar 10 *vt* string (cuentas); set (joyas)
engatusar *vt* I coax
engendr|ar *vt* father; (*fig*) breed. **~o** *m* (*monstruo*) monster; (*fig*) brainchild
englobar *vt* include
engomar *vt* glue
engordar *vt* fatten, gain (kilo). ● *vi* get fatter, put on weight
engorro *m* nuisance
engranaje *m* (*Auto*) gear
engrandecer 11 *vt* (*enaltecer*) exalt, raise

engrasar *vt* grease; (*con aceite*) oil; (*ensuciar*) get grease on

engreído *adj* arrogant

engullir 22 *vt* gulp down

enhebrar *vt* thread

enhorabuena *f* congratulations. **dar la ~** congratulate

enigm|a *m* enigma. **~ático** *adj* enigmatic

enjabonar *vt* soap. **~se** *vpr* to soap o.s.

enjambre *m* swarm

enjaular *vt* put in a cage

enjuag|ar 12 *vt* rinse. **~ue** *m* rinsing; (*para la boca*) mouthwash

enjugar 12 *vt* wipe (away)

enjuiciar *vt* pass judgement on

enjuto *adj* (persona) skinny

enlace *m* connection; (*matrimonial*) wedding

enlatar *vt* tin, can

enlazar 10 *vt* link; tie together (cintas); (*Mex*, *casar*) marry

enlodar *vt*, **enlodazar** 10 *vt* cover in mud

enloquecer 11 *vt* drive mad. ● *vi* go mad. **~se** *vpr* go mad

enlosar *vt* (*con losas*) pave; (*con baldosas*) tile

enmarañar *vt* tangle (up), entangle; (*confundir*) confuse. **~se** *vpr* get into a tangle; (*confundirse*) get confused

enmarcar 7 *vt* frame

enm|endar *vt* correct. **~endarse** *vpr* mend one's way. **~ienda** *f* correction; (*de ley etc*) amendment

enmohecerse 11 *vpr* (*con óxido*) go rusty; (*con hongos*) go mouldy

enmudecer 11 *vi* be dumbstruck; (*callar*) fall silent

ennegrecer 11 *vt* blacken

ennoblecer 11 *vt* ennoble; (*fig*) add style to

enoj|adizo *adj* irritable. **~ado** *adj* angry; (*molesto*) annoyed. **~ar** *vt* anger; (*molestar*) annoy. **~arse** *vpr* get angry; (*molestarse*) get annoyed. **~o** *m* anger; (*molestia*) annoyance. **~oso** *adj* annoying

enorgullecerse 11 *vpr* be proud

enorm|e *adj* huge, enormous. **~emente** *adv* enormously. **~idad** *f* immensity; (*de crimer*) enormity

enraizado *adj* deeply rooted

enrarecido *adj* rarefied

enred|adera *f* creeper. **~ar** *vt* tangle (up), entangle; (*confundir*) confuse; (*involucrar*) involve. **~arse** *vpr* get tangled; (*confundirse*) get confused; (persona) get involved (**con** with). **~o** *m* tangle; (*fig*) muddle, mess

enrejado *m* bars

enriquecer 11 *vt* make rich; (*fig*) enrich. **~se** *vpr* get rich

enrojecerse 11 *vpr* (persona) go red, blush

enrolar *vt* enlist

enrollar *vt* roll (up), wind (hilo etc)

enroscar 7 *vt* coil; (*atornillar*) screw in

ensalad|a *f* salad. **armar una ~a** make a mess. **~era** *f* salad bowl. **~illa** *f* Russian salad

ensalzar 10 *vt* praise; (*enaltecer*) exalt

ensambla|dura *f*, **ensamblaje** *m* (*acción*) assembling; (*efecto*) joint. **~r** *vt* join

ensanch|ar *vt* widen; (*agrandar*) enlarge. **~arse** *vpr* get wider. **~e** *m* widening

ensangrentar 1 *vt* stain with blood

ensañarse *vpr.* **~ con** treat cruelly

ensartar *vt* string (cuentas etc)

ensay|ar *vt* test; rehearse (obra de teatro etc). **~o** *m* test, trial; (*composición literaria*) essay

enseguida *adv* at once, immediately

ensenada *f* inlet, cove

enseña|nza *f* education; (*acción de enseñar*) teaching. **~nza media** secondary education. **~r** *vt* teach; (*mostrar*) show

enseres *mpl* equipment

ensillar *vt* saddle

ensimismarse *vpr* be lost in thought

ensombrecer [11] *vt* darken

ensordecer [11] *vt* deafen. ● *vi* go deaf

ensuciar *vt* dirty. **~se** *vpr* get dirty

ensueño *m* dream

entablar *vt* (*empezar*) start

entablillar *vt* put in a splint

entallar *vt* tailor (un vestido). ● *vi* fit

entarimado *m* parquet; (*plataforma*) platform

ente *m* entity, being; (*fam, persona rara*) weirdo; (*Com*) firm, company

entend|er [1] *vt* understand; (*opinar*) believe, think. ● *vi* understand. **~er de** know about. **a mi ~er** in my opinion. **dar a ~er** hint. **darse a ~er** (*LAm*) make o.s. understood **~erse** *vpr* make o.s. understood; (*comprenderse*) be understood. **~erse con** get on with. **~ido** *adj* understood; (*enterado*) well-informed. **no darse por ~ido** pretend not to understand. ● *interj* agreed!, OK! [T]. **~imiento** *m* understanding

entera|do *adj* well-informed; (*que sabe*) aware. **darse por ~do** take the hint. **~r** *vt* inform (**de** of). **~rse** *vpr.* **~rse de** find out about, hear of. **¡entérate!** listen! **¿te ~s?** do you understand?

entereza *f* (*carácter*) strength of character

enternecer [11] *vt* (*fig*) move, touch. **~se** *vpr* be moved, be touched

entero *adj* entire, whole. **por ~** entirely, completely

enterra|dor *m* gravedigger. **~r** [1] *vt* bury

entibiar *vt* (*enfriar*) cool; (*calentar*) warm (up). **~se** *vpr* (*enfriarse*) cool down; (*fig*) cool; (*calentarse*) get warm

entidad *f* entity; (*organización*) organization; (*Com*) company; (*importancia*) significance

entierro *m* burial; (*ceremonia*) funeral

entona|ción *f* intonation. **~r** *vt* intone; sing (nota). ● *vi* (*Mus*) be in tune; (colores) match. **~rse** *vpr* (*emborracharse*) get tipsy

entonces *adv* then. **en aquel ~** at that time, then

entorn|ado *adj* (puerta) ajar; (ventana) slightly open. **~o** *m* environment; (*en literatura*) setting

entorpecer [11] *vt* dull; slow down (tráfico); (*dificultar*) hinder

entra|da *f* entrance; (*incorporación*) admission, entry; (*para cine etc*) ticket; (*de datos, Tec*) input; (*de una comida*) starter. **de ~da** right away. **~do** *adj*. **~do en años** elderly. **ya ~da la noche** late at night. **~nte** *adj* next, coming

entraña *f* (*fig*) heart. **~s** *fpl* entrails; (*fig*) heart. **~ble** *adj* (cariño) deep; (amigo) close. **~r** *vt* involve

entrar *vt* (*traer*) bring in; (*llevar*) take in. ● *vi* go in, enter; (*venir*) come in, enter; (*empezar*) start, begin; (*incorporarse*) join. **~ en**, (*LAm*) **~ a** go into

e

entre *prep* (*dos personas o cosas*) between; (*más de dos*) among(st)

entre|abierto *adj* half-open. **~abrir** (*pp* **entreabierto**) *vt* half open. **~acto** *m* interval. **~cejo** *m* forehead. **fruncir el ~cejo** frown. **~cerrar** 1 *vt* (*LAm*) half close. **~cortado** *adj* (voz) faltering; (respiración) laboured. **~cruzar** 10 *vt* intertwine

entrega *f* handing over; (*de mercancías etc*) delivery; (*de novela etc*) instalment; (*dedicación*) commitment. **~r** 12 *vt* deliver; (*dar*) give; hand in (deberes); hand over (poder). **~rse** *vpr* surrender, give o.s. up; (*dedicarse*) devote o.s. (**a** to)

entre|lazar 10 *vt* intertwine. **~més** *m* hors-d'oeuvre; (*en el teatro*) short comedy. **~mezclar** *vt* intermingle

entrena|dor *m* trainer. **~miento** *m* training. **~r** *vt* train. **~rse** *vpr* train

entre|pierna *f* crotch; *medida* inside leg measurement. **~piso** *m* (*LAm*) mezzanine. **~sacar** 7 *vt* pick out; (*peluquería*) thin out **~suelo** *m* mezzanine; (*de cine*) dress circle **~tanto** *adv* meanwhile, in the meantime **~tejer** *vt* weave; (*entrelazar*) interweave

entreten|ción *f* (*LAm*) entertainment. **~er** 40 *vt* entertain, amuse; (*detener*) delay, keep. **~erse** *vpr* amuse o.s.; (*tardar*) delay, linger. **~ido** *adj* (*con ser*) entertaining; (*con estar*) busy. **~imiento** *m* entertainment

entrever 43 *vt* make out, glimpse

entrevista *f* interview; (*reunión*) meeting. **~rse** *vpr* have an interview

entristecer 11 *vt* sadden, make sad. **~se** *vpr* grow sad

entromet|erse *vpr* interfere. **~ido** *adj* interfering

entumec|erse 11 *vpr* go numb. **~ido** *adj* numb

enturbiar *vt* cloud

entusi|asmar *vt* fill with enthusiasm; (*gustar mucho*) delight. **~asmarse** *vpr*. **~asmarse con** get enthusiastic about. **~asmo** *m* enthusiasm. **~asta** *adj* enthusiastic. ● *m & f* enthusiast

enumerar *vt* enumerate

envalentonar *vt* encourage. **~se** *vpr* become bolder

envas|ado *m* packaging; (*en latas*) canning; (*en botellas*) bottling. **~ar** *vt* package; (*en latas*) tin, can; (*en botellas*) bottle. **~e** *m* packing; (*lata*) tin, can; (*botella*) bottle

envejec|er 11 *vt* make (look) older. ● *vi* age, grow old. **~erse** *vpr* age, grow old

envenenar *vt* poison

envergadura *f* importance

envia|do *m* envoy; (*de la prensa*) correspondent. **~r** 20 *vt* send

enviciarse *vpr* become addicted (**con** to)

envidi|a *f* envy; (*celos*) jealousy. **~ar** *vt* envy, be envious of. **~oso** *adj* envious; (*celoso*) jealous. **tener ~a a** envy

envío *m* sending, dispatch; (*de*

mercancías) consignment; (*de dinero*) remittance. ~ **contra reembolso** cash on delivery. **gastos** *mpl* **de** ~ postage and packing (costs)

enviudar *vi* be widowed

env|oltura *f* wrapping. ~**olver** **2** (*pp* **envuelto**) *vt* wrap; (*cubrir*) cover; (*rodear*) surround; (*fig, enredar*) involve. ~**uelto** *adj* wrapped (up)

enyesar *vt* plaster; (*Med*) put in plaster

épica *f* epic

épico *adj* epic

epid|emia *f* epidemic. ~**émico** *adj* epidemic

epil|epsia *f* epilepsy. ~**éptico** *adj* epileptic

epílogo *m* epilogue

episodio *m* episode

epístola *f* epistle

epitafio *m* epitaph

época *f* age; (*período*) period. **hacer** ~ make history, be epoch-making

equidad *f* equity

equilibr|ado *adj* (well-)balanced. ~**ar** *vt* balance. ~**io** *m* balance; (*de balanza*) equilibrium. ~**ista** *m & f* tightrope walker

equinoccio *m* equinox

equipaje *m* luggage (*esp Brit*), baggage (*esp Amer*)

equipar *vt* equip; (*de ropa*) fit out

equiparar *vt* make equal; (*comparar*) compare

equipo *m* equipment; (*de personas*) team

equitación *f* riding

equivale|nte *adj* equivalent. ~**r** **42** *vi* be equivalent; (*significar*) mean

equivoca|ción *f* mistake, error. ~**do** *adj* wrong. ~**rse** *vpr* make a mistake; (*estar en error*) be wrong, be mistaken. ~**rse de** be wrong about. ~**rse de número** dial the wrong number. **si no me equivoco** if I'm not mistaken

equívoco *adj* equivocal; (*sospechoso*) suspicious ● *m* misunderstanding; (*error*) mistake

era *f* era. ● *vb véase* **SER**

erario *m* treasury

erección *f* erection

eres *vb véase* **SER**

erguir **48** *vt* raise. ~**se** *vpr* raise

erigir **14** *vt* erect. ~**se** *vpr.* ~**se en** set o.s. up as; (*llegar a ser*) become

eriza|do *adj* prickly. ~**rse** **10** *vpr* stand on end; (*LAm*) (persona) get goose pimples

erizo *m* hedgehog; (*de mar*) sea urchin. ~ **de mar** sea urchin

ermita *f* hermitage. ~**ño** *m* hermit

erosi|ón *f* erosion. ~**onar** *vt* erode

er|ótico *adj* erotic. ~**otismo** *m* eroticism

err|ar **1** (*la* **i** *inicial pasa a ser* **y**) *vt* miss. ● *vi* wander; (*equivocarse*) make a mistake, be wrong. ~**ata** *f* misprint. ~**óneo** *adj* erroneous, wrong. ~**or** *m* error, mistake. **estar en un** ~**or** be wrong, be mistaken

eruct|ar *vi* belch. ~**o** *m* belch

erudi|ción *f* learning, erudition. ~**to** *adj* learned; (palabra) erudite

erupción *f* eruption; (*Med*) rash

es *vb véase* **SER**

esa *adj véase* **ESE**

ésa *pron véase* **ÉSE**

esbelto *adj* slender, slim

esboz|ar **10** *vt* sketch, outline. ~**o**

e

m sketch, outline

escabeche *m* brine. **en ~** pickled

escabroso *adj* (terreno) rough; (asunto) difficult; (*atrevido*) crude

escabullirse 22 *vpr* slip away

escafandra *f* diving-suit

e

escala *f* scale; (*escalera de mano*) ladder; (*Aviac*) stopover. **hacer ~ en** stop at. **vuelo sin ~s** non-stop flight. **~da** *f* climbing; (*Pol*) escalation. **~r** *vt* climb; break into (una casa). ● *vi* climb, go climbing

escaldar *vt* scald

escalera *f* staircase, stairs; (*de mano*) ladder. **~ de caracol** spiral staircase. **~ de incendios** fire escape. **~ de tijera** step-ladder. **~ mecánica** escalator

escalfa|do *adj* poached. **~r** *vt* poach

escalinata *f* flight of steps

escalofrío *m* shiver. **tener ~s** be shivering

escalón *m* step, stair; (*de escala*) rung

escalope *m* escalope

escam|a *f* scale; (*de jabón, de la piel*) flake. **~oso** *adj* scaly; (piel) flaky

escamotear *vt* make disappear; (*robar*) steal, pinch

escampar *vi* stop raining

esc|andalizar 10 *vt* scandalize, shock. **~andalizarse** *vpr* be shocked. **~ándalo** *m* scandal; (*alboroto*) commotion, racket. **armar un ~** make a scene. **~andaloso** *adj* scandalous; (*alborotador*) noisy

escandinavo *adj* & *m* Scandinavian

escaño *m* bench; (*Pol*) seat

escapa|da *f* escape; (*visita*) flying visit. **~r** *vi* escape. **dejar ~r** let out **~rse** *vpr* escape; (líquido, gas) leak

escaparate *m* (shop) window

escap|atoria *f* (*fig*) way out. **~e** *m* (*de gas, de líquido*) leak; (*fuga*) escape; (*Auto*) exhaust

escarabajo *m* beetle

escaramuza *f* skirmish

escarbar *vt* scratch; pick (dientes, herida); (*fig, escudriñar*) pry (**en** into). **~se** *vpr* pick

escarcha *f* frost. **~do** *adj* (fruta) crystallized

escarlat|a *adj invar* scarlet. **~ina** *f* scarlet fever

escarm|entar 1 *vt* teach a lesson to. ● *vi* learn one's lesson. **~iento** *m* punishment; (*lección*) lesson

escarola *f* endive

escarpado *adj* steep

escas|ear *vi* be scarce. **~ez** *f* scarcity, shortage; (*pobreza*) poverty. **~o** *adj* scarce; (*poco*) little; (*muy justo*) barely. **~o de** short of

escatimar *vt* be sparing with

escayola *f* plaster

esc|ena *f* scene; (*escenario*) stage. **~enario** *m* stage; (*fig*) scene. **~énico** *adj* stage. **~enografía** *f* set design

esc|epticismo *m* scepticism. **~éptico** *adj* sceptical. ● *m* sceptic

esclarecer 11 *vt* (*fig*) throw light on, clarify

esclav|itud *f* slavery. **~izar** 10 *vt* enslave. **~o** *m* slave

esclusa *f* lock; (*de presa*) floodgate

escoba *f* broom

escocer 2 & 9 *vi* sting

escocés *adj* Scottish. ● *m* Scot

Escocia *f* Scotland

escog|er 14 *vt* choose. **~ido** *adj* chosen; (mercancía) choice; (clientela) select
escolar *adj* school. ● *m* schoolboy. ● *f* schoolgirl
escolta *f* escort
escombros *mpl* rubble
escond|er *vt* hide. **~erse** *vpr* hide. **~idas** *fpl* (*LAm*, *juego*) hide-and-seek. **a ~idas** secretly. **~ite** *m* hiding place; (*juego*) hide-and-seek. **~rijo** *m* hiding place
escopeta *f* shotgun
escoria *f* slag; (*fig*) dregs
escorpión *m* scorpion
Escorpión *m* Scorpio
escot|ado *adj* low-cut. **~e** *m* low neckline. **pagar a ~e** share the expenses
escozor *m* stinging
escri|bano *m* clerk. **~bir** (*pp* **escrito**) *vt/i* write. **~bir a máquina** type. **¿cómo se escribe...?** how do you spell...? **~birse** *vpr* write to each other. **~to** *adj* written. **por ~to** in writing. ● *m* document. **~tor** *m* writer. **~torio** *m* desk; (*oficina*) office; (*LAm*, *en una casa*) study. **~tura** *f* (hand)writing; (*Jurid*) deed
escr|úpulo *m* scruple. **~upuloso** *adj* scrupulous
escrut|ar *vt* scrutinize; count (votos). **~inio** *m* count
escuadr|a *f* (*instrumento*) square; (*Mil*) squad; (*Naut*) fleet. **~ón** *m* squadron
escuálido *adj* skinny
escuchar *vt* listen to; (*esp LAm*, *oír*) hear. ● *vi* listen
escudo *m* shield. **~ de armas** coat of arms
escudriñar *vt* examine
escuela *f* school. **~ normal** teachers' training college
escueto *adj* simple
escuincle *m* (*Mex fam*) kid Ⓕ
escul|pir *vt* sculpture. **~tor** *m* sculptor. **~tora** *f* sculptress. **~tura** *f* sculpture
escupir *vt/i* spit
escurr|eplatos *m invar* plate rack. **~idizo** *adj* slippery. **~ir** *vt* drain; wring out (ropa). ● *vi* drain; (ropa) drip. **~irse** *vpr* slip
ese *adj* (*f* **esa**) that; (*mpl* **esos**, *fpl* **esas**) those
ése *pron* (*f* **ésa**) that one: (*mpl* **ésos**, *fpl* **ésas**) those; (*primero de dos*) the former
esencia *f* essence. **~l** *adj* essential. **lo ~l** the main thing
esf|era *f* sphere; (*de reloj*) face. **~érico** *adj* spherical
esf|orzarse 2 & 10 *vpr* make an effort. **~uerzo** *m* effort
esfumarse *vpr* fade away; (persona) vanish
esgrim|a *f* fencing. **~ir** *vt* brandish; (*fig*) use
esguince *m* sprain
eslabón *m* link
eslavo *adj* Slavic, Slavonic
eslogan *m* slogan
esmalt|ar *vt* enamel. **~e** *m* enamel. **~e de uñas** nail polish
esmerado *adj* careful; (persona) painstaking
esmeralda *f* emerald
esmer|arse *vpr* take care (**en** over).
esmero *m* care
esmoquin (*pl* **esmóquines**) *m* dinner jacket, tuxedo (*Amer*)
esnob *adj invar* snobbish. ● *m & f* (*pl* **~s**) snob. **~ismo** *m* snobbery

esnórkel *m* snorkel

eso *pron* that. **¡~ es!** that's it! **~ mismo** exactly. **a ~ de** about. **en ~** at that moment. **¿no es ~?** isn't that right? **por ~** that's why. **y ~ que** even though

esos *adj pl véase* ESE

ésos *pron pl véase* ÉSE

espabila|do *adj* bright; (*despierto*) awake. **~r** *vt* (*avivar*) brighten up; (*despertar*) wake up. **~rse** *vpr* wake up; (*avivarse*) wise up; (*apresurarse*) hurry up

espaci|al *adj* space. **~ar** *vt* space out. **~o** *m* space. **~oso** *adj* spacious

espada *f* sword. **~s** *fpl* (*en naipes*) spades

espaguetis *mpl* spaghetti

espald|a *f* back. **a ~as de uno** behind s.o.'s back. **volver la(s) ~a(s) a uno** give s.o. the cold shoulder. **~ mojada** wetback. **~illa** *f* shoulder-blade

espant|ajo *m*, **~apájaros** *m invar* scarecrow. **~ar** *vt* frighten; (*ahuyentar*) frighten away. **~arse** *vpr* be frightened; (*ahuyentarse*) be frightened away. **~o** *m* terror; (*horror*) horror. **¡qué ~o!** how awful! **~oso** *adj* horrific; (*terrible*) terrible

España *f* Spain

español *adj* Spanish. • *m* (*persona*) Spaniard; (*lengua*) Spanish. **los ~es** the Spanish

esparadrapo *m* (sticking) plaster

esparcir **9** *vt* scatter; (*difundir*) spread. **~rse** *vpr* be scattered; (*difundirse*) spread; (*divertirse*) enjoy o.s.

espárrago *m* asparagus

espasm|o *m* spasm. **~ódico** *adj* spasmodic

espátula *f* spatula; (*en pintura*) palette knife

especia *f* spice

especial *adj* special. **en ~** especially. **~idad** *f* speciality (*Brit*), specialty (*Amer*). **~ista** *adj* & *m* & *f* specialist. **~ización** *f* specialization. **~izarse** **10** *vpr* specialize. **~mente** *adv* especially

especie *f* kind, sort; (*en biología*) species. **en ~** in kind

especifica|ción *f* specification. **~r** **7** *vt* specify

específico *adj* specific

espect|áculo *m* sight; (*de circo etc*) show. **~acular** *adj* spectacular. **~ador** *m* & *f* spectator

espectro *m* spectre; (*en física*) spectrum

especula|dor *m* speculator. **~r** *vi* speculate

espej|ismo *m* mirage. **~o** *m* mirror. **~o retrovisor** (*Auto*) rear-view mirror

espeluznante *adj* horrifying

espera *f* wait. **a la ~** waiting (**de** for). **~nza** *f* hope. **~r** *vt* hope; (*aguardar*) wait for; expect (vista, carta, bebé). **espero que no** I hope not. **espero que sí** I hope so. •*vi* (*aguardar*) wait. **~rse** *vpr* hang on; (*prever*) expect

esperma *f* sperm

esperpento *m* fright

espes|ar *vt/i* thicken. **~arse** *vpr* thicken. **~o** *adj* thick. **~or** *m* thickness

espetón *m* spit

esp|ía *f* spy. **~iar** **20** *vt* spy on. • *vi* spy

espiga *f* (*de trigo etc*) ear

espina *f* thorn; (*de pez*) bone; (*en anatomía*) spine. **~ dorsal** spine

espinaca *f* spinach

espinazo *m* spine
espinilla *f* shin; (*Med*) blackhead; (*LAm, grano*) spot
espino *m* hawthorn. **~so** *adj* thorny; (*fig*) difficult
espionaje *m* espionage
espiral *adj & f* spiral
esp|iritista *m & f* spiritualist. **~íritu** *m* spirit; (*mente*) mind. **~iritual** *adj* spiritual
espl|éndido *adj* splendid; (persona) generous. **~endor** *m* splendour
espolear *vt* spur (on)
espolvorear *vt* sprinkle
esponj|a *f* sponge. **~oso** *adj* spongy
espont|aneidad *f* spontaneity. **~áneo** *adj* spontaneous
esporádico *adj* sporadic
espos|a *f* wife. **~as** *fpl* handcuffs. **~ar** *vt* handcuff. **~o** *m* husband
espuela *f* spur; (*fig*) incentive
espum|a *f* foam; (*en bebidas*) froth; (*de jabón*) lather; (*de las olas*) surf. **echar ~a** foam, froth. **~oso** *adj* (vino) sparkling
esqueleto *m* skeleton; (*estructura*) framework
esquema *m* outline
esqu|í *m* (*pl* **~ís**, **~íes**) ski; (*deporte*) skiing. **~iar** [20] *vi* ski
esquilar *vt* shear
esquimal *adj & m* Eskimo
esquina *f* corner
esquiv|ar *vt* avoid; dodge (golpe). **~o** *adj* elusive
esquizofrénico *adj & m* schizophrenic
esta *adj véase* ESTE
ésta *pron véase* ÉSTE
estab|ilidad *f* stability. **~le** *adj* stable
establec|er [11] *vt* establish. **~erse** *vpr* settle; (*Com*) set up. **~imiento** *m* establishment
establo *m* cattleshed
estaca *f* stake
estación *f* station; (*del año*) season. **~ de invierno** winter (sports) resort. **~ de servicio** service station
estaciona|miento *m* parking; (*LAm, lugar*) car park (*Brit*), parking lot (*Amer*). **~r** *vt* station; (*Auto*) park. **~rio** *adj* stationary
estadía *f* (*LAm*) stay
estadio *m* stadium; (*fase*) stage
estadista *m* statesman. ● *f* stateswoman
estadístic|a *f* statistics; (*cifra*) statistic. **~o** *adj* statistical
estado *m* state; (*Med*) condition. **~ civil** marital status. **~ de ánimo** frame of mind. **~ de cuenta** bank statement. **~ mayor** (*Mil*) staff. **en buen ~** in good condition
Estados Unidos *mpl* United States
estadounidense *adj* American, United States. ● *m & f* American
estafa *f* swindle. **~r** *vt* swindle
estafeta *f* (*oficina de correos*) (sub-)post office
estala|ctita *f* stalactite. **~gmita** *f* stalagmite
estall|ar *vi* explode; (*olas*) break; (guerra etc) break out; (*fig*) burst. **~ar en llanto** burst into tears. **~ar de risa** burst out laughing. **~ido** *m* explosion; (*de guerra etc*) outbreak
estamp|a *f* print; (*aspecto*) appearance. **~ado** *adj* printed. ● *m* printing; (*motivo*) pattern; (*tela*) cotton print. **~ar** *vt* stamp;

e

(*imprimir*) print

estampido *m* bang

estampilla *f* (*LAm*, *de correos*) (postage) stamp

estanca|do *adj* stagnant. **~r** 7 *vt* stem. **~rse** *vpr* stagnate

e

estancia *f* stay; (*cuarto*) large room

estanco *adj* watertight. ● *m* tobacconist's (shop)

estanco In Spain, an establishment selling tobacco, stamps, bus and metro passes and other products whose sale is restricted. Cigarettes etc are sold in bars and cafés but at higher prices. *Estancos* also sell stationery and sometimes papers.

estandarte *m* standard, banner

estanque *m* pond; (*depósito de agua*) (water) tank

estanquero *m* tobacconist

estante *m* shelf. **~ría** *f* shelves; (*para libros*) bookcase

estaño *m* tin

estar 27

● *verbo intransitivo*

....> to be **¿cómo estás?** how are you?. **estoy enfermo** I'm ill. **está muy cerca** it's very near. **¿está Pedro?** is Pedro in? **¿cómo está el tiempo?** what's the weather like? **ya estamos en invierno** it's winter already

....> (*quedarse*) to stay. **sólo ~é una semana** I'll only be staying for a week. **estoy en un hotel** I'm staying in a hotel

....> (*con fecha*) **¿a cuánto estamos?** what's the date today? **estamos a 8 de mayo** it's the 8th of May.

....> (*en locuciones*) **¿estamos?** all right? **¡ahí está!** that's it! **~ por** (*apoyar a*) to support; (*LAm*, *encontrarse a punto de*) to be about to; (*quedar por*) **eso está por verse** that remains to be seen. **son cuentas que están por pagar** they're bills still to be paid

● *verbo auxiliar*

....> (*con gerundio*) **estaba estudiando** I was studying

....> (*con participio*) **está condenado a muerte** he's been sentenced to death. **está mal traducido** it's wrongly translated. **estarse** *verbo pronominal* to stay. **no se está quieto** he won't stay still

Cuando el verbo **estar** forma parte de expresiones como **estar de acuerdo, estar a la vista, estar constipado,** etc., ver bajo el respectivo nombre o adjetivo

estatal *adj* state

estático *adj* static

estatua *f* statue

estatura *f* height

estatuto *m* statute; (*norma*) rule

este *adj* (región) eastern; (viento, lado) east. ● *m* east. ● *adj* (*f* **esta**) this; (*mpl* **estos**, *fpl* **estas**) these. ● *int* (*LAm*) well, er

éste *pron* (*f* **ésta**) this one; (*mpl* **éstos**, *fpl* **éstas**) these; (*segundo de dos*) the latter

estela *f* wake; (*de avión*) trail; (*lápida*) carved stone

estera *f* mat; (*tejido*) matting

est|éreo *adj* stereo. **~ereofónico** *adj* stereo, stereophonic

estereotipo *m* stereotype

estéril *adj* sterile; (terreno) barren

esterilla *f* mat

esterlina *adj*. **libra** *f* **~** pound sterling

estético *adj* aesthetic

estiércol *m* dung; (*abono*) manure

estigma *m* stigma. **~s** *mpl* (*Relig*) stigmata

estil|arse *vpr* be used. **~o** *m* style; (*en natación*) stroke. **~ mariposa** butterfly. **~ pecho** (*LAm*) breaststroke. **por el ~o** of that sort

estilográfica *f* fountain pen

estima *f* esteem. **~do** *adj* (amigo, colega) valued. **~do señor** (*en cartas*) Dear Sir. **~r** *vt* esteem; have great respect for (persona); (*valorar*) value; (*juzgar*) consider

est|imulante *adj* stimulating. ● *m* stimulant. **~imular** *vt* stimulate; (*incitar*) incite. **~ímulo** *m* stimulus

estir|ado *adj* stretched; (persona) haughty. **~ar** *vt* stretch; (*fig*) stretch out. **~ón** *m* pull, tug; (*crecimiento*) sudden growth

estirpe *m* stock

esto *pron neutro* this; (*este asunto*) this business. **en ~** at this point. **en ~ de** in this business of. **por ~** therefore

estofa|do *adj* stewed. ● *m* stew. **~r** *vt* stew

estómago *m* stomach. **dolor** *m* **de ~** stomach ache

estorb|ar *vt* obstruct; (*molestar*) bother. ● *vi* be in the way. **~o** *m* hindrance; (*molestia*) nuisance

estornud|ar *vi* sneeze. **~o** *m* sneeze

estos *adj mpl véase* ESTE

éstos *pron mpl véase* ÉSTE

estoy *vb véase* ESTAR

estrabismo *m* squint

estrado *m* stage; (*Mus*) bandstand

estrafalario *adj* eccentric; (ropa) outlandish

estrago *m* devastation. **hacer ~os** devastate

estragón *m* tarragon

estrambótico *adj* eccentric; (ropa) outlandish

estrangula|dor *m* strangler; (*Auto*) choke. **~r** *vt* strangle

estratagema *f* stratagem

estrat|ega *m & f* strategist. **~egia** *f* strategy. **~égico** *adj* strategic

estrato *m* stratum

estrech|ar *vt* make narrower; take in (vestido); embrace (persona). **~ar la mano a uno** shake hands with s.o. **~arse** *vpr* become narrower; (*abrazarse*) embrace. **~ez** *f* narrowness. **~eces** *fpl* financial difficulties. **~o** *adj* narrow; (vestido etc) tight; (*fig, íntimo*) close. **~o de miras** narrow-minded. ● *m* strait(s)

estrella *f* star. **~ de mar** starfish. **~ado** *adj* starry

estrellar *vt* smash; crash (coche). **~se** *vpr* crash (**contra** into)

estremec|er 11 *vt* shake. **~erse** *vpr* shake; (*de emoción etc*) tremble (**de** with). **~imiento** *m* shaking

estren|ar *vt* wear for the first time (vestido etc); show for the first time (película). **~arse** *vpr* make one's début. **~o** *m* (*de película*) première; (*de obra de teatro*) first night; (*de persona*) debut

estreñi|do *adj* constipated. **~miento** *m* constipation

estrés *m* stress
estría *f* groove; (*de la piel*) stretch mark
estribillo *m* (*incl Mus*) refrain
estribo *m* stirrup; (*de coche*) step. perder los **~s** lose one's temper
estribor *m* starboard
estricto *adj* strict
estridente *adj* strident, raucous
estrofa *f* stanza, verse
estropajo *m* scourer
estropear *vt* damage; (*plan*) spoil; ruin (ropa). **~se** *vpr* be damaged; (*averiarse*) break down; (ropa) get ruined; (fruta etc) go bad; (*fracasar*) fail
estructura *f* structure. **~l** *adj* structural
estruendo *m* roar; (*de mucha gente*) uproar
estrujar *vt* squeeze; wring (out) (ropa); (*fig*) drain
estuario *m* estuary
estuche *m* case
estudi|ante *m & f* student. **~antil** *adj* student. **~ar** *vt* study. **~o** *m* study; (*de artista*) studio. **~oso** *adj* studious
estufa *f* heater; (*Mex, cocina*) cooker
estupefac|iente *m* narcotic. **~to** *adj* astonished
estupendo *adj* marvellous; (persona) fantastic; **¡~!** that's great!
est|upidez *f* stupidity; (*acto*) stupid thing. **~úpido** *adj* stupid
estupor *m* amazement
estuve *vb véase* ESTAR
etapa *f* stage. **por ~s** in stages
etéreo *adj* ethereal
etern|idad *f* eternity. **~o** *adj* eternal
étic|a *f* ethics. **~o** *adj* ethical
etimología *f* etymology
etiqueta *f* ticket, tag; (*ceremonial*) etiquette. **de ~** formal
étnico *adj* ethnic
eucalipto *m* eucalyptus
eufemismo *m* euphemism
euforia *f* euphoria
euro *m* euro. **~escéptico** *adj & m* Eurosceptic
Europa *f* Europe
euro|peo *adj & m* European. **~zona** *f* eurozone
eutanasia *f* euthanasia
evacua|ción *f* evacuation. **~r** **21** *vt* evacuate
evadir *vt* avoid; evade (impuestos). **~se** *vpr* escape
evalua|ción *f* evaluation. **~r** **21** *vt* assess; evaluate (datos)
evangeli|o *m* gospel. **~sta** *m & f* evangelist; (*Mex, escribiente*) scribe
evapora|ción *f* evaporation. **~rse** *vpr* evaporate; (*fig*) disappear
evasi|ón *f* evasion; (*fuga*) escape. **~vo** *adj* evasive
evento *m* event; (*caso*) case
eventual *adj* possible. **~idad** *f* eventuality
eviden|cia *f* evidence. **poner en ~cia a uno** show s.o. up. **~ciar** *vt* show. **~ciarse** *vpr* be obvious. **~te** *adj* obvious. **~temente** *adv* obviously
evitar *vt* avoid; (*ahorrar*) spare; (*prevenir*) prevent
evocar **7** *vt* evoke
evoluci|ón *f* evolution. **~onar** *vi* evolve; (*Mil*) manoeuvre
ex *prefijo* ex-, former
exacerbar *vt* exacerbate
exact|amente *adv* exactly. **~itud** *f* exactness. **~o** *adj* exact; (*preciso*) accurate; (*puntual*) punc-

tual. ¡~! exactly!

exagera|ción *f* exaggeration. **~do** *adj* exaggerated. **~r** *vt/i* exaggerate

exalta|do *adj* exalted; (*excitado*) (over)excited; (*fanático*) hotheaded. **~r** *vt* exalt. **~rse** *vpr* get excited

exam|en *m* exam, examination. **~inar** *vt* examine. **~inarse** *vpr* take an exam

exasperar *vt* exasperate. **~se** *vpr* get exasperated

excarcela|ción *f* release (from prison). **~r** *vt* release

excava|ción *f* excavation. **~dora** *f* digger. **~r** *vt* excavate

excede|ncia *f* leave of absence. **~nte** *adj* & *m* surplus. **~r** *vi* exceed. **~rse** *vpr* go too far

excelen|cia *f* excellence; (*tratamiento*) Excellency. **~te** *adj* excellent

exc|entricidad *f* eccentricity. **~éntrico** *adj* & *m* eccentric

excepci|ón *f* exception. **~onal** *adj* exceptional. **a ~ón de, con ~ón de** except (for)

except|o *prep* except (for). **~uar** 21 *vt* except

exces|ivo *adj* excessive. **~o** *m* excess. **~o de equipaje** excess luggage (*esp Brit*), excess baggage (*esp Amer*)

excita|ción *f* excitement. **~r** *vt* excite; (*incitar*) incite. **~rse** *vpr* get excited

exclama|ción *f* exclamation. **~r** *vi* exclaim

exclu|ir 17 *vt* exclude. **~sión** *f* exclusion. **~siva** *f* sole right; (*reportaje*) exclusive (story). **~sivo** *adj* exclusive

excomu|lgar 12 *vt* excommunicate. **~nión** *f* excommunication

excremento *m* excrement

excursi|ón *f* excursion, outing. **~onista** *m* & *f* day-tripper

excusa *f* excuse; (*disculpa*) apology. **presentar sus ~s** apologize. **~r** *vt* excuse

exento *adj* exempt; (*libre*) free

exhalar *vt* exhale, breath out; give off (olor etc)

exhaust|ivo *adj* exhaustive. **~o** *adj* exhausted

exhibi|ción *f* exhibition; (*demostración*) display. **~cionista** *m* & *f* exhibitionist. **~r** *vt* exhibit **~rse** *vpr* show o.s.; (*hacerse notar*) draw attention to o.s.

exhumar *vt* exhume; (*fig*) dig up

exig|encia *f* demand. **~ente** *adj* demanding. **~ir** 14 *vt* demand

exiguo *adj* meagre

exil|(i)ado *adj* exiled. ● *m* exile. **~(i)arse** *vpr* go into exile. **~io** *m* exile

exim|ente *m* reason for exemption; (*Jurid*) grounds for acquittal. **~ir** *vt* exempt

existencia *f* existence. **~s** *fpl* stock. **~lismo** *m* existentialism

exist|ente *adj* existing. **~ir** *vi* exist

éxito *m* success. **no tener ~** fail. **tener ~** be successful

exitoso *adj* successful

éxodo *m* exodus

exonerar *vt* exonerate

exorbitante *adj* exorbitant

exorci|smo *m* exorcism. **~zar** 10 *vt* exorcise

exótico *adj* exotic

expan|dir *vt* expand; (*fig*) spread. **~dirse** *vpr* expand. **~sión** *f* ex-

e

pansion. **~sivo** *adj* expansive

expatria|do *adj & m* expatriate. **~rse** *vpr* emigrate; (*exiliarse*) go into exile

expectativa *f* prospect; (*esperanza*) expectation. **estar a la ~** be waiting

e

expedi|ción *f* expedition; (*de documento*) issue; (*de mercancías*) dispatch. **~ente** *m* record, file; (*Jurid*) proceedings. **~r** **5** *vt* issue; (*enviar*) dispatch, send. **~to** *adj* clear; (*LAm, fácil*) easy

expeler *vt* expel

expend|edor *m* dealer. **~edor automático** vending machine. **~io** *m* (*LAm*) shop; (*venta*) sale

expensas *fpl* (*Jurid*) costs. **a ~ de** at the expense of. **a mis ~** at my expense

experiencia *f* experience

experiment|al *adj* experimental. **~ar** *vt* test, experiment with; (*sentir*) experience. **~o** *m* experiment

experto *adj & m* expert

expiar **20** *vt* atone for

expirar *vi* expire

explanada *f* levelled area; (*paseo*) esplanade

explayarse *vpr* speak at length; (*desahogarse*) unburden o.s. (**con** to)

explica|ción *f* explanation. **~r** **7** *vt* explain. **~rse** *vpr* understand; (*hacerse comprender*) explain o.s. **no me lo explico** I can't understand it

explícito *adj* explicit

explora|ción *f* exploration. **~dor** *m* explorer; (*muchacho*) boy scout. **~r** *vt* explore

explosi|ón *f* explosion; (*fig*) outburst. **~onar** *vt* blow up. **~vo** *adj & m* explosive

explota|ción *f* working; (*abuso*) exploitation. **~r** *vt* work (mina); farm (tierra); (*abusar*) exploit. ● *vi* explode

expone|nte *m* exponent. **~r** **34** *vt* expose; display (mercancías); present (tema); set out (hechos); exhibit (cuadros etc); (*arriesgar*) risk. ● *vi* exhibit. **~rse** *vpr.* **~se a que** run the risk of

exporta|ción *f* export. **~dor** *m* exporter. **~r** *vt* export

exposición *f* exposure; (*de cuadros etc*) exhibition; (*de hechos*) exposition

expres|ar *vt* express. **~arse** *vpr* express o.s. **~ión** *f* expression. **~ivo** *adj* expressive; (*cariñoso*) affectionate

expreso *adj* express. ● *m* express; (*café*) expresso

exprimi|dor *m* squeezer. **~r** *vt* squeeze

expropiar *vt* expropriate

expuesto *adj* on display; (lugar etc) exposed; (*peligroso*) dangerous. **estar ~ a** be exposed to

expuls|ar *vt* expel; throw out (persona); send off (jugador). **~ión** *f* expulsion

exquisito *adj* exquisite; (*de sabor*) delicious

éxtasis *m invar* ecstasy

extend|er **1** *vt* spread (out); (*ampliar*) extend; issue (documento). **~erse** *vpr* spread; (paisaje etc) extend, stretch. **~ido** *adj* spread out; (*generalizado*) widespread; (brazos) outstretched

extens|amente *adv* widely; (*detalladamente*) in full. **~ión** *f* extension; (*área*) expanse; (*largo*) length.

~**o** *adj* extensive
extenuar 21 *vt* exhaust
exterior *adj* external, exterior; (*del extranjero*) foreign; (aspecto etc) outward. ● *m* outside, exterior; (*países extranjeros*) abroad
extermin|ación *f* extermination. ~**ar** *vt* exterminate. ~**io** *m* extermination
externo *adj* external; (signo etc) outward. ● *m* day pupil
extin|ción *f* extinction. ~**guidor** *m* (*LAm*) fire extinguisher. ~**guir** 13 *vt* extinguish. ~**guirse** *vpr* die out; (fuego) go out. ~**to** *adj* (raza etc) extinct. ~**tor** *m* fire extinguisher
extirpar *vt* eradicate; remove (tumor)
extorsión *f* extortion
extra *adj invar* extra; (*de buena calidad*) good-quality; (huevos) large. **paga** *f* ~ bonus
extracto *m* extract
extradición *f* extradition
extraer 41 *vt* extract
extranjer|ía *f* (*Esp*) **la ley de** ~ immigration law. ~**o** *adj* foreign. ● *m* foreigner; (*países*) foreign countries. **del** ~ from abroad. **en el** ~, **por el** ~ abroad
extrañ|ar *vt* surprise; (*encontrar extraño*) find strange; (*LAm, echar de menos*) miss. ~**arse** *vpr* be surprised (**de** at). ~**eza** *f* strangeness; (*asombro*) surprise. ~**o** *adj* strange. ● *m* stranger
extraoficial *adj* unofficial
extraordinario *adj* extraordinary
extrarradio *m* outlying districts
extraterrestre *adj* extraterrestrial. ● *m* alien
extravagan|cia *f* oddness, eccentricity. ~**te** *adj* odd, eccentric
extrav|iado *adj* lost. ~**iar** 20 *vt* lose. ~**iarse** *vpr* get lost; (objetos) go missing. ~**ío** *m* loss
extremar *vt* take extra (precauciones); tighten up (vigilancia). ~**se** *vpr* make every effort
extremeño *adj* from Extremadura
extrem|idad *f* end. ~**idades** *fpl* extremities. ~**ista** *adj & m & f* extremist. ~**o** *adj* extreme. ● *m* end; (*colmo*) extreme. **en** ~**o** extremely. **en último** ~**o** as a last resort
extrovertido *adj & m* extrovert
exuberan|cia *f* exúberance. ~**te** *adj* exuberant
eyacular *vt/i* ejaculate

Ff

fa *m* F; (*solfa*) fah
fabada *f* bean and pork stew
fábrica *f* factory. **marca** *f* **de** ~ trade mark
fabrica|ción *f* manufacture. ~**ción en serie** mass production. ~**nte** *m & f* manufacturer. ~**r** 7 *vt* manufacture
fábula *f* fable; (*mentira*) fabrication
fabuloso *adj* fabulous
facci|ón *f* faction. ~**ones** *fpl* (*de la cara*) features
faceta *f* facet
facha *f* (*fam, aspecto*) look. ~**da** *f* façade
fácil *adj* easy; (*probable*) likely

facili|dad *f* ease; (*disposición*) aptitude. **~dades** *fpl* facilities. **~tar** *vt* facilitate; (*proporcionar*) provide

factible *adj* feasible

factor *m* factor

factura *f* bill, invoice. **~r** *vt* (*hacer la factura*) invoice; (*al embarcar*) check in

f

faculta|d *f* faculty; (*capacidad*) ability; (*poder*) power. **~tivo** *adj* optional

faena *f* job. **~s domésticas** housework

faisán *m* pheasant

faja *f* (*de tierra*) strip; (*corsé*) corset; (*Mil etc*) sash

fajo *m* bundle; (*de billetes*) wad

falda *f* skirt; (*de montaña*) side

falla *f* fault; (*defecto*) flaw. **~ humana** (*LAm*) human error. **~r** *vi* fail. **me falló** he let me down. **sin ~r** without fail. ● *vt* (*errar*) miss

fallec|er **11** *vi* die. **~ido** *m* deceased

fallido *adj* vain; (*fracasado*) unsuccessful

fallo *m* (*defecto*) fault; (*error*) mistake. **~ humano** human error; (*en certamen*) decision; (*Jurid*) ruling

falluca *f* (*Mex*) smuggled goods

fals|ear *vt* falsify, distort. **~ificación** *f* forgery. **~ificador** *m* forger. **~ificar** **7** *vt* forge. **~o** *adj* false; (*falsificado*) forged; (joya) fake

falt|a *f* lack; (*ausencia*) absence; (*escasez*) shortage; (*defecto*) fault, defect; (*culpa*) fault; (*error*) mistake; (*en fútbol etc*) foul; (*en tenis*) fault. **a ~a de** for lack of. **echar en ~a** miss. **hacer ~a** be necessary. **me hace ~a** I need. **sacar ~as** find fault. **~o** *adj* lacking (**de** in)

faltar *verbo intransitivo*

! cuando el verbo **faltar** va precedido del complemento indirecto **le** (o **les, nos** etc) el sujeto en español pasa a ser el objeto en inglés p.ej: **les falta experiencia** *they lack experience*

····➤(*no estar*) to be missing **¿quién falta?** who's missing? **falta una de las chicas** one of the girls is missing. **al abrigo le faltan 3 botones** the coat has three buttons missing. **~ a algo** (*no asistir*) to be absent from sth; (*no acudir*) to miss sth

····➤(*no haber suficiente*) **va a ~ leche** there won't be enough milk. **nos faltó tiempo** we didn't have enough time

····➤(*no tener*) **le falta cariño** he lacks affection

····➤(*hacer falta*) **le falta sal** it needs more salt. **¡es lo que nos faltaba!** that's all we needed!

····➤(*quedar*) **¿te falta mucho?** are you going to be much longer? **falta poco para Navidad** it's not long until Christmas. **aún falta mucho** (*distancia*) there's a long way to go yet **¡no faltaba más!** of course!

fama *f* fame; (*reputación*) reputation

famélico *adj* starving

familia *f* family; (*hijos*) children. **~ numerosa** large family. **~r** *adj* familiar; (*de la familia*) family; (*sin ceremonia*) informal; (lenguaje) colloquial. ● *m & f* relative. **~ridad** *f* familiarity. **~rizarse** **10** *vpr* be-

come familiar (**con** with)
famoso *adj* famous
fanático *adj* fanatical. • *m* fanatic
fanfarr|ón *adj* boastful. • *m* braggart. **~onear** *vi* show off
fango *m* mud. **~so** *adj* muddy
fantasía *f* fantasy. **de ~** fancy; (*joya*) imitation
fantasma *m* ghost
fantástico *adj* fantastic
fardo *m* bundle
faringe *f* pharynx
farmac|éutico *m* chemist (*Brit*), pharmacist, druggist (*Amer*). **~ia** *f* (*ciencia*) pharmacy; (*tienda*) chemist's (shop) (*Brit*), pharmacy
faro *m* lighthouse; (*Aviac*) beacon; (*Auto*) headlight
farol *m* lantern; (*de la calle*) street lamp. **~a** *f* street lamp
farr|a *f* partying. **~ear** *vi* (*LAm*) go out partying
farsa *f* farce. **~nte** *m & f* fraud
fascículo *m* instalment
fascinar *vt* fascinate
fascis|mo *m* fascism
fase *f* phase
fastidi|ar *vt* annoy; (*estropear*) spoil. **~arse** *vpr* (máquina) break down; hurt (pierna); (*LAm, molestarse*) get annoyed. **¡para que te ~es!** so there!. **~o** *m* nuisance; (*aburrimiento*) boredom. **~oso** *adj* annoying
fatal *adj* fateful; (*mortal*) fatal; (*fam, pésimo*) terrible. **~idad** *f* fate; (*desgracia*) misfortune
fatig|a *f* fatigue. **~ar** 12 *vt* tire. **~arse** *vpr* get tired. **~oso** *adj* tiring
fauna *f* fauna
favor *m* favour. **a ~ de, en ~ de** in favour of. **haga el ~ de** would you be so kind as to, please. **por ~** please
favorec|er 11 *vt* favour; (vestido, peinado etc) suit. **~ido** *adj* favoured
favorito *adj & m* favourite
fax *m* fax
faxear *vt* fax
faz *f* face
fe *f* faith. **dar ~ de** certify. **de buena ~** in good faith
febrero *m* February
febril *adj* feverish
fecha *f* date. **a estas ~s** now; (*todavía*) still. **hasta la ~** so far. **poner la ~** date. **~r** *vt* date
fecund|ación *f* fertilization. **~ación artificial** artificial insemination. **~ar** *vt* fertilize. **~o** *adj* fertile; (*fig*) prolific
federa|ción *f* federation. **~l** *adj* federal
felici|dad *f* happiness. **~dades** *fpl* best wishes; (*congratulaciones*) congratulations. **~tación** *f* letter of congratulation. **¡~taciones!** (*LAm*) congratulations! **~tar** *vt* congratulate
feligrés *m* parishioner
feliz *adj* happy; (*afortunado*) lucky. **¡Felices Pascuas!** Happy Christmas! **¡F~ Año Nuevo!** Happy New Year!
felpudo *m* doormat
fem|enil *adj* (*Mex*) women's. **~enino** *adj* feminine; (equipo) women's; (*en biología*) female. • *m* feminine. **~inista** *adj & m & f* feminist.
fen|omenal *adj* phenomenal. **~ómeno** *m* phenomenon; (*monstruo*) freak
feo *adj* ugly; (*desagradable*) nasty. •*adv* (*LAm*) (*mal*) bad

feria *f* fair; (*verbena*) carnival; (*Mex*, *cambio*) small change. **~do** *m* (*LAm*) public holiday

ferment|ar *vt/i* ferment. **~o** *m* ferment

fero|cidad *f* ferocity. **~z** *adj* fierce

férreo *adj* iron; (disciplina) strict

ferreter|ía *f* hardware store, ironmonger's (*Brit*). **~o** *m* hardware dealer, ironmonger (*Brit*)

ferro|carril *m* railway (*Brit*), railroad (*Amer*). **~viario** *adj* rail. ● *m* railwayman (*Brit*), railroader (*Amer*)

fértil *adj* fertile

fertili|dad *f* fertility. **~zante** *m* fertilizer. **~zar** 10 *vt* fertilize

ferv|iente *adj* fervent. **~or** *m* fervour

festej|ar *vt* celebrate; entertain (persona). **~o** *m* celebration

festiv|al *m* festival. **~idad** *f* festivity. **~o** *adj* festive. ● *m* public holiday

fétido *adj* stinking

feto *m* foetus

fiable *adj* reliable

fiado *m*. **al ~** on credit. **~r** *m* (*Jurid*) guarantor

fiambre *m* cold meat. **~ría** *f* (*LAm*) delicatessen

fianza *f* (*dinero*) deposit; (*objeto*) surety. **bajo ~** on bail

fiar 20 *vt* (*vender*) sell on credit; (*confiar*) confide. ● *vi* give credit. **~se** *vpr*. **~se de** trust

fibra *f* fibre. **~ de vidrio** fibreglass

ficción *f* fiction

fich|a *f* token; (*tarjeta*) index card; (*en juegos*) counter. **~ar** *vt* open a file on. **estar ~ado** have a (police) record. **~ero** *m* card index; (*en informática*) file

fidedigno *adj* reliable

fidelidad *f* faithfulness

fideos *mpl* noodles

fiebre *f* fever. **~ aftosa** foot-and-mouth disease. **~ del heno** hay fever. **~ porcina** swine fever. **tener ~** have a temperature

fiel *adj* faithful; (memoria, relato etc) reliable. ● *m* believer

fieltro *m* felt

fier|a *f* wild animal. **~o** *adj* fierce

fierro *m* (*LAm*) metal bar; (*hierro*) iron

fiesta *f* party; (*día festivo*) holiday. **~s** *fpl* celebrations

> **fiestas** A *fiesta* in Spain can be a day of local celebrations, a larger event for a town or city, or a national holiday to commemorate a saint's day or a historical event. Famous Spanish *fiestas* include The *Fallas* in Valencia, the *Sanfermines* in Pamplona, and the *Feria de Sevilla*. In Latin America *fiestas patrias* are a period of one or more days when each country celebrates its independence. There are usually military parades, firework displays, and cultural events typical of the country.

figura *f* figure; (*forma*) shape. **~r** *vi* appear; (*destacar*) show off. **~rse** *vpr* imagine. **¡figúrate!** just imagine!

fij|ación *f* fixing; (*obsesión*) fixation. **~ar** *vt* fix; establish (residencia). **~arse** *vpr* (*poner atención*) pay attention; (*percatarse*) notice. **¡fíjate!** just imagine! **~o** *adj* fixed; (*firme*) stable; (*permanente*) permanent. ● *adv*. **mirar ~o** stare

fila *f* line; (*de soldados etc*) file; (*en el teatro, cine etc*) row; (*cola*) queue. **ponerse en ~** line up

filántropo *m* philanthropist

filat|elia *f* stamp collecting, philately. **~élico** *adj* philatelic. ● *m* stamp collector, philatelist

filete *m* fillet

filial *adj* filial. ● *f* subsidiary

Filipinas *fpl.* **las (islas) ~** the Philippines

filipino *adj* Philippine, Filipino

filmar *vt* film; shoot (película)

filo *m* edge; (*de hoja*) cutting edge. **al ~ de las doce** at exactly twelve o'clock. **sacar ~ a** sharpen

filología *f* philology

filón *m* vein; (*fig*) gold-mine

fil|osofía *f* philosophy. **~ósofo** *m* philosopher

filtr|ar *vt* filter. **~arse** *vpr* filter; (dinero) disappear; (noticia) leak. **~o** *m* filter; (*bebida*) philtre. **~ solar** sunscreen

fin *m* end; (*objetivo*) aim. **~ de semana** weekend. **a ~ de** in order to. **a ~ de cuentas** at the end of the day. **a ~ de que** in order that. **a ~es de** at the end of. **al ~** finally. **al ~ y al cabo** after all. **dar ~ a** end. **en ~** in short. **por ~** finally. **sin ~** endless

final *adj* final. ● *m* end. ● *f* final. **~idad** *f* aim. **~ista** *m & f* finalist. **~izar** 10 *vt* finish. ● *vi* end

financi|ación *f* financing; (*fondos*) funds; (*facilidades*) credit facilities. **~ar** *vt* finance. **~ero** *adj* financial. ● *m* financier

finca *f* property; (*tierras*) estate; (*rural*) farm; (*de recreo*) country house

fingir 14 *vt* feign; (*simular*) simulate. ● *vi* pretend. **~se** *vpr* pretend to be

finlandés *adj* Finnish. ● *m* (*persona*) Finn; (*lengua*) Finnish

Finlandia *f* Finland

fino *adj* fine; (*delgado*) thin; (oído) acute; (*de modales*) refined; (*sutil*) subtle

firma *f* signature; (*acto*) signing; (*empresa*) firm

firmar *vt/i* sign

firme *adj* firm; (*estable*) stable, steady; (color) fast. ● *m* (*pavimento*) (road) surface. ● *adv* hard. **~za** *f* firmness

fisc|al *adj* fiscal, tax. ● *m & f* public prosecutor. **~o** *m* treasury

fisg|ar 12 *vi* snoop (around). **~ón** *adj* nosy. ● *m* snooper

físic|a *f* physics. **~o** *adj* physical. ● *m* physique; (*persona*) physicist

fisonomista *m & f.* **ser buen ~** be good at remembering faces

fistol *m* (*Mex*) tiepin

flaco *adj* thin, skinny; (*débil*) weak

flagelo *m* scourge

flagrante *adj* flagrant. **en ~** red-handed

flama *f* (*Mex*) flame

flamante *adj* splendid; (*nuevo*) brand-new

flamear *vi* flame; (bandera etc) flap

flamenco *adj* flamenco; (*de Flandes*) Flemish. ● *m* (*ave*) flamingo; (*música etc*) flamenco; (*idioma*) Flemish

flamenco Flamenco is performed in three forms: guitar, singing and dancing. Originally a gypsy art form, it also has Arabic and North African influences. Modern flamenco blends traditional forms with rock, jazz and salsa. In its pure form the music and lyrics are improvised, but tourists are more likely to see rehearsed performances.

flan *m* crème caramel
flaqueza *f* thinness; (*debilidad*) weakness
f
flauta *f* flute
flecha *f* arrow. **~zo** *m* love at first sight
fleco *m* fringe; (*Mex, en el pelo*) fringe (*Brit*), bangs (*Amer*)
flem|a *f* phlegm. **~ático** *adj* phlegmatic
flequillo *m* fringe (*Brit*), bangs (*Amer*)
fletar *vt* charter; (*LAm, transportar*) transport
flexible *adj* flexible
flirte|ar *vi* flirt. **~o** *m* flirting
floj|ear *vi* flag; (*holgazanear*) laze around. **~o** *adj* loose; (*poco fuerte*) weak; (*perezoso*) lazy
flor *f* flower. **la ~ y nata** the cream. **~a** *f* flora. **~ecer** 11 *vi* flower, bloom; (*fig*) flourish. **~eciente** *adj* (*fig*) flourishing. **~ero** *m* flower vase. **~ista** *m & f* florist
flot|a *f* fleet. **~ador** *m* float; (*de niño*) rubber band. **~ar** *vi* float. **~e**. **a ~e** afloat
fluctua|ción *f* fluctuation. **~r** 21 *vi* fluctuate
flu|idez *f* fluidity; (*fig*) fluency. **~ido** *adj* fluid; (*fig*) fluent. ● *m* fluid. **~ir** 17 *vi* flow
fluoruro *m* fluoride
fluvial *adj* river
fobia *f* phobia
foca *f* seal
foco *m* focus; (*lámpara*) floodlight; (*LAm, de coche*) (head)light; (*Mex, bombilla*) light bulb
fogón *m* cooker; (*LAm, fogata*) bonfire
folio *m* sheet
folklórico *adj* folk
follaje *m* foliage
follet|ín *m* newspaper serial. **~o** *m* pamphlet
follón *m* I mess; (*alboroto*) row; (*problema*) trouble
fomentar *vt* promote; boost (ahorro); stir up (odio)
fonda *f* (*pensión*) boarding-house; (*LAm, restaurant*) cheap restaurant
fondo *m* bottom; (*de calle, pasillo*) end; (*de sala etc*) back; (*de escenario, pintura etc*) background. **~ de reptiles** slush fund. **~s** *mpl* funds, money. **a ~** thoroughly
fonétic|a *f* phonetics. **~o** *adj* phonetic
fontanero *m* plumber
footing /'futin/ *m* jogging
forastero *m* stranger
forcejear *vi* struggle
forense *adj* forensic. ●*m & f* forensic scientist
forjar *vt* forge. **~se** *vpr* forge; build up (ilusiones)
forma *f* form; (*contorno*) shape; (*modo*) way; (*Mex, formulario*) form. **~s** *fpl* conventions. **de todas ~s** anyway. **estar en ~** be in good form. **~ción** *f* formation; (*educación*) training. **~l** *adj* formal; (*de fiar*) reliable; (*serio*) serious. **~lidad** *f* formality; (*fiabilidad*) reliability; (*seriedad*) seriousness. **~r** *vt* form; (*componer*) make up; (*enseñar*) train. **~rse** *vpr* form; (*desarrollarse*) develop; (*educarse*) to be educated. **~to** *m* format
formidable *adj* formidable; (*muy*

grande) enormous
fórmula *f* formula; (*sistema*) way. **~ de cortesía** polite expression
formular *vt* formulate; make (queja etc). **~io** *m* form
fornido *adj* well-built
forr|ar *vt* (*en el interior*) line; (*en el exterior*) cover. **~o** *m* lining; (*cubierta*) cover
fortale|cer 11 *vt* strengthen. **~za** *f* strength; (*Mil*) fortress; (*fuerza moral*) fortitude
fortuito *adj* fortuitous; (encuentro) chance
fortuna *f* fortune; (*suerte*) luck
forz|ar 2 & 10 *vt* force; strain (vista). **~osamente** *adv* necessarily. **~oso** *adj* necessary
fosa *f* ditch; (*tumba*) grave. **~s** *fpl* **nasales** nostrils
fósforo *m* phosphorus; (*cerilla*) match
fósil *adj & m* fossil
foso *m* ditch; (*en castillo*) moat; (*de teatro*) pit
foto *f* photo. **sacar ~s** take photos
fotocopia *f* photocopy. **~dora** *f* photocopier. **~r** *vt* photocopy
fotogénico *adj* photogenic
fot|ografía *f* photography; (*Foto*) photograph. **~ografiar** 20 *vt* photograph. **~ógrafo** *m* photographer
foul /faʊl/ *m* (*pl* **~s**) (*LAm*) foul
frac *m* (*pl* **~s** *o* **fraques**) tails
fracas|ar *vi* fail. **~o** *m* failure
fracción *f* fraction; (*Pol*) faction
fractura *f* fracture. **~r** *vt* fracture. **~rse** *vpr* fracture
fragan|cia *f* fragrance. **~te** *adj* fragrant
frágil *adj* fragile
fragmento *m* fragment; (*de canción etc*) extract
fragua *f* forge. **~r** 15 *vt* forge; (*fig*) concoct. • *vi* set
fraile *m* friar; (*monje*) monk
frambuesa *f* raspberry
franc|és *adj* French. • *m* (*persona*) Frenchman; (*lengua*) French. **~esa** *f* Frenchwoman
Francia *f* France
franco *adj* frank; (*evidente*) marked; (*Com*) free. • *m* (*moneda*) franc
francotirador *m* sniper
franela *f* flannel
franja *f* border; (*banda*) stripe; (*de terreno*) strip
franque|ar *vt* clear; (*atravesar*) cross; pay the postage on (carta). **~o** *m* postage
franqueza *f* frankness
frasco *m* bottle; (*de mermelada etc*) jar
frase *f* phrase; (*oración*) sentence. **~ hecha** set phrase
fratern|al *adj* fraternal. **~idad** *f* fraternity
fraud|e *m* fraud. **~ulento** *adj* fraudulent
fray *m* brother, friar
frecuen|cia *f* frequency. **con ~cia** frequently. **~tar** *vt* frequent. **~te** *adj* frequent
frega|dero *m* sink. **~r** 1 & 12 *vt* scrub; wash (los platos); mop (el suelo); (*LAm, fam, molestar*) annoy
freír 51 (*pp* **frito**) *vt* fry. **~se** *vpr* fry; (persona) roast
frenar *vt* brake; (*fig*) check
frenético *adj* frenzied; (*furioso*) furious
freno *m* (*de caballería*) bit; (*Auto*)

brake; (*fig*) check

frente *m* front. ~ **a** opposite. ~ **a** ~ face to face. **al** ~ at the head; (*hacia delante*) forward. **chocar de** ~ crash head on. **de** ~ **a** (*LAm*) facing. **hacer** ~ **a** face (cosa); stand up to (persona). ● *f* forehead. **arrugar la** ~ frown

f

fresa *f* strawberry

fresc|o *adj* (*frío*) cool; (*reciente*) fresh; (*descarado*) cheeky. ● *m* fresh air; (*frescor*) coolness; (*mural*) fresco; (*persona*) impudent person. **al** ~**o** in the open air. **hacer** ~**o** be cool. **tomar el** ~**o** get some fresh air. ~**or** *m* coolness. ~**ura** *f* freshness; (*frío*) coolness; (*descaro*) cheek

frialdad *f* coldness; (*fig*) indifference

friccí|ón *f* rubbing; (*fig, Tec*) friction; (*masaje*) massage. ~**onar** *vt* rub

frigidez *f* frigidity

frígido *adj* frigid

frigorífico *m* fridge, refrigerator

frijol *m* (*LAm*) bean. ~**es refritos** (*Mex*) fried purée of beans

frío *adj & m* cold. **tomar** ~ catch cold. **hacer** ~ be cold. **tener** ~ be cold

frito *adj* fried; (🅸, *harto*) fed up. **me tiene** ~ I'm sick of him

fr|ivolidad *f* frivolity. ~**ívolo** *adj* frivolous

fronter|a *f* border, frontier. ~**izo** *adj* border; (país) bordering

frontón *m* pelota court; (*pared*) fronton

frotar *vt* rub; strike (cerilla)

fructífero *adj* fruitful

fruncir 9 *vt* gather (tela). ~ **el ceño** frown

frustra|ción *f* frustration. ~**r** *vt* frustrate. ~**rse** *vpr* (*fracasar*) fail. **quedar** ~**do** be disappointed

frut|a *f* fruit. ~**al** *adj* fruit. ~**ería** *f* fruit shop. ~**ero** *m* fruit seller; (*recipiente*) fruit bowl. ~**icultura** *f* fruit-growing. ~**o** *m* fruit

fucsia *f* fuchsia. ● *m* fuchsia

fuego *m* fire. ~**s artificiales** fireworks. **a** ~ **lento** on a low heat. **tener** ~ have a light

fuente *f* fountain; (*manantial*) spring; (*plato*) serving dish; (*fig*) source

fuera *adv* out; (*al exterior*) outside; (*en otra parte*) away; (*en el extranjero*) abroad. ~ **de** outside; (*excepto*) except for, besides. **por** ~ on the outside. ● *vb véase* IR *y* SER

fuerte *adj* strong; (color) bright; (sonido) loud; (dolor) severe; (*duro*) hard; (*grande*) large; (lluvia, nevada) heavy. ● *m* fort; (*fig*) strong point. ● *adv* hard; (*con hablar etc*) loudly; (llover) heavily; (*mucho*) a lot

fuerza *f* strength; (*poder*) power; (*en física*) force; (*Mil*) forces. ~ **de voluntad** will-power. **a** ~ **de** by (dint of). **a la** ~ by necessity. **por** ~ by force; (*por necesidad*) by necessity. **tener** ~**s para** have the strength to

fuese *vb véase* IR *y* SER

fug|a *f* flight, escape; (*de gas etc*) leak; (*Mus*) fugue. ~**arse** 12 *vpr* flee, escape. ~**az** *adj* fleeting. ~**itivo** *adj & m* fugitive

fui *vb véase* IR, SER

fulano *m* so-and-so. ~, **mengano y zutano** every Tom, Dick and Harry

fulminar *vt* (*fig, con mirada*) look daggers at

fuma|dor *adj* smoking. • *m* smoker. **~r** *vt/i* smoke. **~r en pipa** smoke a pipe. **~rse** *vpr* smoke. **~rada** *f* puff of smoke

funci|ón *f* function; (*de un cargo etc*) duty; (*de teatro*) show, performance. **~onal** *adj* functional. **~onar** *vi* work, function. **no ~ona** out of order. **~onario** *m* civil servant

funda *f* cover. **~ de almohada** pillowcase

funda|ción *f* foundation. **~mental** *adj* fundamental. **~mentar** *vt* base (en on). **~mento** *m* foundation. **~r** *vt* found; (*fig*) base. **~rse** *vpr* be based

fundi|ción *f* melting; (*de metales*) smelting; (*taller*) foundry. **~r** *vt* melt; smelt (metales); cast (objeto); blend (colores); (*fusionar*) merge; (*Elec*) blow; (*LAm*) seize up (motor). **~rse** *vpr* melt; (*unirse*) merge

fúnebre *adj* funeral; (*sombrío*) gloomy

funeral *adj* funeral. • *m* funeral. **~es** *mpl* funeral

funicular *adj* & *m* funicular

furg|ón *m* van. **~oneta** *f* van

fur|ia *f* fury; (*violencia*) violence. **~ibundo** *adj* furious. **~ioso** *adj* furious. **~or** *m* fury

furtivo *adj* furtive. **cazador ~** poacher

furúnculo *m* boil

fusible *m* fuse

fusil *m* rifle. **~ar** *vt* shoot

fusión *f* melting; (*unión*) fusion; (*Com*) merger

fútbol *m*, (*Mex*) **futbol** *m* football

futbolista *m* & *f* footballer

futur|ista *adj* futuristic. • *m* & *f* futurist. **~o** *adj* & *m* future

Gg

gabardina *f* raincoat

gabinete *m* (*Pol*) cabinet; (*en museo etc*) room; (*de dentista, médico etc*) consulting room

gaceta *f* gazette

gafa *f* hook. **~s** *fpl* glasses, spectacles. **~s de sol** sunglasses

gaf|ar *vt* ⓘ bring bad luck to. **~e** *m* jinx

gaita *f* bagpipes

gajo *m* segment

gala *f* gala. **~s** *fpl* finery, best clothes. **estar de ~** be dressed up. **hacer ~ de** show off

galán *m* (*en el teatro*) (romantic) hero; (*enamorado*) lover

galante *adj* gallant. **~ar** *vt* court. **~ría** *f* gallantry

galápago *m* turtle

galardón *m* award

galaxia *f* galaxy

galera *f* galley

galer|ía *f* gallery. **~ía comercial** (shopping) arcade. **~ón** *m* (*Mex*) hall

Gales *m* Wales. **país de ~** Wales

gal|és *adj* Welsh. • *m* Welshman; (*lengua*) Welsh. **~esa** *f* Welshwoman

galgo *m* greyhound

Galicia *f* Galicia

galimatías *m invar* gibberish

gallard|ía *f* elegance. **~o** *adj* elegant

gallego *adj & m* Galician
galleta *f* biscuit (*Brit*), cookie (*Amer*)
gall|ina *f* hen, chicken; (*fig, fam*) coward. **~o** *m* cock
galón *m* gallon; (*cinta*) braid; (*Mil*) stripe
galop|ar *vi* gallop. **~e** *m* gallop
gama *f* scale; (*fig*) range
g
gamba *f* prawn (*Brit*), shrimp (*Amer*)
gamberro *m* hooligan
gamuza *f* (*piel*) chamois leather; (*de otro animal*) suede
gana *f* wish, desire; (*apetito*) appetite. **de buena ~** willingly. **de mala ~** reluctantly. **no me da la ~** I don't feel like it. **tener ~s de** (+ *infinitivo*) feel like (+ *gerundio*)
ganad|ería *f* cattle raising; (*ganado*) livestock. **~o** *m* livestock. **~o lanar** sheep. **~o porcino** pigs. **~o vacuno** cattle
gana|dor *adj* winning. • *m* winner. **~ncia** *f* gain; (*Com*) profit. **~r** *vt* earn; (*en concurso, juego etc*) win; (*alcanzar*) reach. • *vi* (*vencer*) win; (*mejorar*) improve. **~rle a uno** beat s.o. **~rse la vida** earn a living. **salir ~ndo** come out better off
ganch|illo *m* crochet. **hacer ~illo** crochet. **~o** *m* hook; (*LAm, colgador*) hanger. **tener ~o** be very attractive
ganga *f* bargain
ganso *m* goose
garabat|ear *vt/i* scribble. **~o** *m* scribble
garaje *m* garage
garant|e *m & f* guarantor. **~ía** *f* guarantee. **~izar** 10 *vt* guarantee
garapiña *f* (*Mex*) pineapple squash. **~do** *adj*. **almendras** *fpl* **~das** sugared almonds
garbanzo *m* chick-pea
garbo *m* poise; (*de escrito*) style. **~so** *adj* elegant
garganta *f* throat; (*valle*) gorge
gárgaras *fpl*. **hacer ~** gargle
garita *f* hut; (*de centinela*) sentry box
garra *f* (*de animal*) claw; (*de ave*) talon
garrafa *f* carafe
garrafal *adj* huge
garrapata *f* tick
garrapat|ear *vi* scribble. **~o** *m* scribble
garrote *m* club, cudgel; (*tormento*) garrotte
gar|úa *f* (*LAm*) drizzle. **~uar** *vi* 21 (*LAm*) drizzle
garza *f* heron
gas *m* gas. **con ~** fizzy. **sin ~** still
gasa *f* gauze
gaseosa *f* fizzy drink
gas|óleo *m* diesel. **~olina** *f* petrol (*Brit*), gasoline (*Amer*), gas (*Amer*). **~olinera** *f* petrol station (*Brit*), gas station (*Amer*)
gast|ado *adj* spent; (vestido etc) worn out. **~ador** *m* spendthrift. **~ar** *vt* spend; (*consumir*) use; (*malgastar*) waste; (*desgastar*) wear out; wear (vestido etc); crack (broma). **~arse** *vpr* wear out. **~o** *m* expense; (*acción de gastar*) spending
gastronomía *f* gastronomy
gat|a *f* cat. **a ~as** on all fours. **~ear** *vi* crawl
gatillo *m* trigger
gat|ito *m* kitten. **~o** *m* cat. **dar ~o por liebre** take s.o. in
gaucho *m* Gaucho

gaucho A peasant of the pampas of Argentina, Uruguay and Brazil. Modern gauchos work as foremen on farms and ranches and take part in rodeos. Traditionally, a gaucho's outfit was characterized by its baggy trousers, leather chaps, and *chiripá*, a waist-high garment. They also used *boleadoras* for catching cattle.

gaveta *f* drawer

gaviota *f* seagull

gazpacho *m* gazpacho

gelatina *f* gelatine; (*jalea*) jelly

gema *f* gem

gemelo *m* twin. **~s** *mpl* (*anteojos*) binoculars; (*de camisa*) cuff-links

gemido *m* groan

Géminis *m* Gemini

gemir 5 *vi* moan; (animal) whine, howl

gen *m*, **gene** *m* gene

geneal|ogía *f* genealogy. **~ógico** *adj* genealogical. **árbol** *m* **~ógico** family tree

generaci|ón *f* generation. **~onal** *adj* generation

general *adj* general. **en ~** in general. **por lo ~** generally. ●*m* general. **~izar** 10 *vt/i* generalize. **~mente** *adv* generally

generar *vt* generate

género *m* type, sort; (*en biología*) genus; (*Gram*) gender; (*en literatura etc*) genre; (*producto*) product; (*tela*) material. **~s de punto** knitwear. **~ humano** mankind

generos|idad *f* generosity. **~o** *adj* generous

genétic|a *f* genetics. **~o** *adj* genetic

geni|al *adj* brilliant; (*divertido*) funny. **~o** *m* temper; (*carácter*) nature; (*talento, persona*) genius

genital *adj* genital. **~es** *mpl* genitals

genoma *m* genome

gente *f* people; (*nación*) nation; (*fam, familia*) family, folks; (*Mex, persona*) person. ●*adj* (*LAm*) respectable; (*amable*) kind

gentil *adj* charming. **~eza** *f* kindness. **tener la ~eza de** be kind enough to

gentío *m* crowd

genuflexión *f* genuflection

genuino *adj* genuine

ge|ografía *f* geography. **~ográfico** *adj* geographical.

ge|ología *f* geology. **~ólogo** *m* geologist

geom|etría *f* geometry. **~étrico** *adj* geometrical

geranio *m* geranium

geren|cia *f* management. **~ciar** *vt* (*LAm*) manage. **~te** *m & f* manager

germen *m* germ

germinar *vi* germinate

gestación *f* gestation

gesticula|ción *f* gesticulation. **~r** *vi* gesticulate

gesti|ón *f* step; (*administración*) management. **~onar** *vt* take steps to arrange; (*dirigir*) manage

gesto *m* expression; (*ademán*) gesture; (*mueca*) grimace

gibraltareño *adj & m* Gibraltarian

gigante *adj* gigantic. ● *m* giant. **~sco** *adj* gigantic

gimn|asia *f* gymnastics. **~asio** *m* gymnasium, gym 1. **~asta** *m & f* gymnast. **~ástic** *adj* gymnastic

gimotear *vi* whine

g

ginebra *f* gin
ginec|ólogo *m* gynaecologist
gira *f* tour. **~r** *vt* spin; draw (cheque); transfer (dinero). ● *vi* rotate, go round; (en camino) turn
girasol *m* sunflower
gir|atorio *adj* revolving. **~o** *m* turn; (*Com*) draft; (*locución*) expression. **~o postal** money order
gitano *adj & m* gypsy
glacia|l *adj* icy. **~r** *m* glacier
glándula *f* gland
glasear *vt* glaze; (*Culin*) ice
glob|al *adj* global; (*fig*) overall. **~alización** *f* globalization. **~o** *m* globe; (*juguete*) balloon
glóbulo *m* globule
gloria *f* glory; (*placer*) delight. **~rse** *vpr* boast (**de** about)
glorieta *f* square; (*Auto*) roundabout (*Brit*), (traffic) circle (*Amer*)
glorificar 7 *vt* glorify
glorioso *adj* glorious
glotón *adj* gluttonous. ● *m* glutton
gnomo /'nomo/ *m* gnome
gob|ernación *f* government. **Ministerio** *m* **de la G~ernación** Home Office (*Brit*), Department of the Interior (*Amer*). **~ernador** *adj* governing. ● *m* governor. **~ernante** *adj* governing. ● *m & f* leader. **~ernar** 1 *vt* govern. **~ierno** *m* government
goce *m* enjoyment
gol *m* goal
golf *m* golf
golfo *m* gulf; (*niño*) urchin; (*holgazán*) layabout
golondrina *f* swallow
golos|ina *f* titbit; (*dulce*) sweet. **~o** *adj* fond of sweets
golpe *m* blow; (*puñetazo*) punch; (*choque*) bump; (*de emoción*) shock; (*arg, atraco*) job Ⓘ; (*en golf, en tenis, de remo*) stroke. **~ de estado** coup d'etat. **~ de fortuna** stroke of luck. **~ de vista** glance. **~ militar** military coup. **de ~** suddenly. **de un ~** in one go. **~ar** *vt* hit; (*dar varios golpes*) beat; (*con mucho ruido*) bang; (*con el puño*) punch. ● *vi* knock
goma *f* rubber; (*para pegar*) glue; (*banda*) rubber band; (*de borrar*) eraser. **~ de mascar** chewing gum. **~ espuma** foam rubber
googlear ® *vt/i* Ⓘ to google
gord|a *f* (*Mex*) small thick tortilla. **~o** *adj* (persona) (*con ser*) fat; (*con estar*) have put on weight; (carne) fatty; (*grueso*) thick; (*grande*) large, big. ● *m* first prize. **~ura** *f* fatness; (*grasa*) fat
gorila *f* gorilla
gorje|ar *vi* chirp. **~o** *m* chirping
gorra *f* cap. **~ de baño** (*LAm*) bathing cap
gorrión *m* sparrow
gorro *m* cap; (*de niño*) bonnet. **~ de baño** bathing cap
got|a *f* drop; (*Med*) gout. **ni ~a** nothing. **~ear** *vi* drip. **~era** *f* leak
gozar 10 *vt* enjoy. ● *vi*. **~ de** enjoy
gozne *m* hinge
gozo *m* pleasure; (*alegría*) joy. **~so** *adj* delighted
graba|ción *f* recording. **~do** *m* engraving, print; (*en libro*) illustration. **~dora** *f* tape-recorder. **~r** *vt* engrave; record (discos etc)
graci|a *f* grace; (*favor*) favour; (*humor*) wit. **~as** *fpl* thanks. **¡~as!** thank you!, thanks! **dar las ~as** thank. **hacer ~a** amuse; (*gustar*) please. **¡muchas ~as!** thank you

very much! **tener ~a** be funny. **~oso** *adj* funny. • *m* fool, comic character

grad|a *f* step. **~as** *fpl* stand(s). **~ación** *f* gradation. **~o** *m* degree; (*en enseñanza*) year (*Brit*), grade (*Amer*). **de buen ~o** willingly

gradua|ción *f* graduation; (*de alcohol*) proof. **~do** *m* graduate. **~l** *adj* gradual. **~r** [21] *vt* graduate; (*regular*) adjust. **~rse** *vpr* graduate

gráfic|a *f* graph. **~o** *adj* graphic. • *m* graph

gram|ática *f* grammar. **~atical** *adj* grammatical

gramo *m* gram, gramme (*Brit*)

gran *adj véase* GRANDE

grana *f* (*color*) deep red

granada *f* pomegranate; (*Mil*) grenade

granate *m* (*color*) maroon

Gran Bretaña *f* Great Britain

grande *adj* (*delante de nombre en singular* **gran**) big, large; (*alto*) tall; (*fig*) great; (*LAm, de edad*) grown up. **~za** *f* greatness

grandioso *adj* magnificent

granel *m*. **a ~** in bulk; (*suelto*) loose; (*fig*) in abundance

granero *m* barn

granito *m* granite; (*grano*) small grain

graniz|ado *m* iced drink. **~ar** [10] *vi* hail. **~o** *m* hail

granj|a *f* farm. **~ero** *m* farmer

grano *m* grain; (*semilla*) seed; (*de café*) bean; (*Med*) spot. **~s** *mpl* cereals

granuja *m & f* rogue

grapa *f* staple. **~r** *vt* staple

gras|a *f* grease; (*Culin*) fat. **~iento** *adj* greasy

gratifica|ción *f* (*de sueldo*) bonus (*recompensa*) reward. **~r** [7] *vt* reward

grat|is *adv* free. **~itud** *f* gratitude. **~o** *adj* pleasant **~uito** *adj* free; (*fig*) uncalled for

grava|men *m* tax; (*carga*) burden; (*sobre inmueble*) encumbrance. **~r** *vt* tax; (*cargar*) burden

grave *adj* serious; (voz) deep; (sonido) low; (acento) grave. **~dad** *f* gravity

gravilla *f* gravel

gravitar *vi* gravitate; (*apoyarse*) rest (**sobre** on); (peligro) hang (**sobre** over)

gravoso *adj* costly

graznar *vi* (cuervo) caw; (pato) quack; honk (ganso)

Grecia *f* Greece

gremio *m* union

greña *f* mop of hair

gresca *f* rumpus; (*riña*) quarrel

griego *adj & m* Greek

grieta *f* crack

grifo *m* tap, faucet (*Amer*)

grilletes *mpl* shackles

grillo *m* cricket. **~s** *mpl* shackles

gringo *m* (*LAm*) foreigner; (*norteamericano*) Yankee [!]

gripe *f* flu

gris *adj* grey. • *m* grey; (*fam, policía*) policeman

grit|ar *vi* shout. **~ería** *f*, **~erío** *m* uproar. **~o** *m* shout; (*de dolor, sorpresa*) cry; (*chillido*) scream. **dar ~s** shout

grosella *f* redcurrant. **~ negra** blackcurrant

groser|ía *f* rudeness; (*ordinariez*) coarseness; (*comentario etc*) coarse remark; (*palabra*) swearword. **~o** *adj* coarse; (*descortés*) rude

grosor *m* thickness

g

grotesco *adj* grotesque
grúa *f* crane
grueso *adj* thick; (persona) fat, stout. • *m* thickness; (*fig*) main body
grumo *m* lump
gruñi|do *m* grunt; (*de perro*) growl. **~r** 22 *vi* grunt; (perro) growl
grupa *f* hindquarters
grupo *m* group
gruta *f* grotto
guacamole *m* guacamole
guadaña *f* scythe
guaje *m* (*Mex*) gourd
guajolote *m* (*Mex*) turkey
guante *m* glove
guapo *adj* good-looking; (chica) pretty; (*elegante*) smart
guarda *m* & *f* guard; (*de parque etc*) keeper. **~barros** *m invar* mudguard. **~bosque** *m* gamekeeper. **~costas** *m invar* coastguard vessel. **~espaldas** *m invar* bodyguard. **~meta** *m* goalkeeper. **~r** *vt* keep; (*proteger*) protect; (*en un lugar*) put away; (*reservar*) save, keep. **~rse** *vpr*. **~rse de** (+ *infinitivo*) avoid (+ *gerundio*). **~rropa** *m* wardrobe; (*en local público*) cloakroom. **~vallas** *m invar* (*LAm*) goalkeeper
guardería *f* nursery
guardia *f* guard; (*policía*) policewoman; (*de médico*) shift. **G~ Civil** Civil Guard. **~ municipal** police. **estar de ~** be on duty. **estar en ~** be on one's guard. **montar la ~** mount guard. •*m* policeman. **~ jurado** *m* & *f* security guard. **~ de tráfico** *m* traffic policeman. •*f* traffic policewoman
guardián *m* guardian; (*de parque etc*) keeper; (*de edificio*) security guard
guar|ecer 11 *vt* (*albergar*) give shelter to. **~ecerse** *vpr* take shelter. **~ida** *f* den, lair; (*de personas*) hideout
guarn|ecer 11 *vt* (*adornar*) adorn; (*Culin*) garnish. **~ición** *m* adornment; (*de caballo*) harness; (*Culin*) garnish; (*Mil*) garrison; (*de piedra preciosa*) setting
guas|a *f* joke. **~ón** *adj* humorous. • *m* joker
Guatemala *f* Guatemala
guatemalteco *adj* & *m* Guatemalan
guateque *m* party, bash
guayab|a *f* guava; (*dulce*) guava jelly. **~era** *f* lightweight jacket
gubernatura *f* (*Mex*) government
güero *adj* (*Mex*) fair
guerr|a *f* war; (*método*) warfare. **dar ~a** annoy. **~ero** *adj* warlike; (*belicoso*) fighting. • *m* warrior. **~illa** *f* band of guerrillas. **~illero** *m* guerrilla
guía *m* & *f* guide. • *f* guidebook; (*de teléfonos*) directory
guiar 20 *vt* guide; (*llevar*) lead; (*Auto*) drive. **~se** *vpr* be guided (**por** by)
guijarro *m* pebble
guillotina *f* guillotine
guind|a *f* morello cherry. **~illa** *f* chilli
guiñapo *m* rag; (*fig, persona*) wreck
guiñ|ar *vt/i* wink. **~o** *m* wink. **hacer ~os** wink
gui|ón *m* hyphen, dash; (*de película etc*) script. **~onista** *m* & *f* scriptwriter
guirnalda *f* garland
guisado *m* stew

guisante *m* pea. ~ **de olor** sweet pea

guis|ar *vt/i* cook. **~o** *m* stew

guitarr|a *f* guitar. **~ista** *m & f* guitarist

gula *f* gluttony

gusano *m* worm; (*larva de mosca*) maggot

gustar

● *verbo intransitivo*

! Cuando el verbo **gustar** va precedido del complemento indirecto **le** (o **les, nos** etc), el sujeto en español pasa a ser el objeto en inglés. **me gusta mucho la música** *I like music very much*. **le gustan los helados** *he likes ice cream*. **a Juan no le gusta** *Juan doesn't like it* (or *her* etc)

····➤ **gustar** + *infinitivo*. **les gusta ver televisión** they like watching television

····➤ **gustar que** + *subjuntivo*. **me ~ía que vinieras** I'd like you to come. **no le gusta que lo corrijan** he doesn't like being corrected. **¿te ~ía que te lo comprara?** would you like me to buy it for you?

····➤ **gustar de algo** to like sth. **gustan de las fiestas** they like parties

····➤ (*tener acogida*) to go down well. **ese tipo de cosas que siempre gusta** those sort of things always go down well. **el libro no gustó** the book didn't go down well

····➤ (*en frases de cortesía*) to wish. **como guste** as you wish. **cuando gustes** whenever you wish

● *verbo transitivo*

····➤ (*LAm, querer*) **¿gusta un café?** would you like a coffee? **¿gustan pasar?** would you like to come in? **gustarse** *verbo pronominal* to like each other

gusto *m* taste; (*placer*) pleasure. **a** ~ comfortable. **a mi** ~ to my liking. **buen** ~ good taste. **con mucho** ~ with pleasure. **dar** ~ please. **mucho** ~ pleased to meet you. **~so** *adj* tasty; (*de buen grado*) willingly

gutural *adj* guttural

ha *vb véase* HABER

haba *f* broad bean

Habana *f* **La** ~ Havana

habano *m* (*puro*) Havana

haber *verbo auxiliar* 30 have. ●*v impersonal* (*presente s & pl* **hay**, *imperfecto s & pl* **había**, *pretérito s & pl* **hubo**). **hay una carta para ti** there's a letter for you. **hay 5 bancos en la plaza** there are 5 banks in the square. **hay que hacerlo** it must be done, you have to do it. **he aquí** here is, here are. **no hay de qué** don't mention it, not at all. **¿qué hay?** (*¿qué pasa?*) what's the matter?; (*¿qué tal?*) how are you?

habichuela *f* bean

hábil *adj* skilful; (*listo*) clever; (*día*) working; (*Jurid*) competent

habili|dad *f* skill; (*astucia*) cleverness; (*Jurid*) competence. **~tar** *vt* qualify

habita|ción *f* room; (*dormitorio*) bedroom; (*en biología*) habitat. **~ción de matrimonio**, **~ción doble** double room. **~ción individual**, **~ción sencilla** single room. **~do** *adj* inhabited. **~nte** *m* inhabitant. **~r** *vt* live in. ● *vi* live

hábito *m* habit

habitua|l *adj* usual, habitual; (cliente) regular. **~r** 21 *vt* accustom. **~rse** *vpr.* **~rse a** get used to

habla *f* speech; (*idioma*) language; (*dialecto*) dialect. **al ~** (*al teléfono*) speaking. **ponerse al ~ con** get in touch with. **~dor** *adj* talkative. ● *m* chatterbox. **~duría** *f* rumour. **~durías** *fpl* gossip. **~nte** *adj* speaking. ● *m & f* speaker. **~r** *vt* speak. ● *vi* speak, talk (**con** to); (*Mex, por teléfono*) call. **¡ni ~r!** out of the question! **se ~ español** Spanish spoken

hacend|ado *m* landowner; (*LAm*) farmer. **~oso** *adj* hard-working

hacer 31

● *verbo transitivo*

····▸ to do. **¿qué haces?** what are you doing? **~ los deberes** to do one's homework. **no sé qué ~** I don't know what to do. **hazme un favor** can you do me a favour?

····▸ (*fabricar, preparar, producir*) to make. **me hizo un vestido** she made me a dress. **~ un café** to make a (cup of) coffee. **no hagas tanto ruido** don't make so much noise

····▸ (*construir*) to build (casa, puente)

····▸ **hacer que uno haga algo** to make s.o. do sth. **haz que se vaya** make him leave. **hizo que se equivocara** he made her go wrong

····▸ **hacer hacer algo** to have sth done. **hizo arreglar el techo** he had the roof repaired

➡ Cuando el verbo **hacer** se emplea en expresiones como **hacer una pregunta, hacer trampa** etc., ver bajo el respectivo nombre

● *verbo intransitivo*

····▸ (*actuar, obrar*) to do. **hiciste bien en llamar** you did the right thing to call **¿cómo haces para parecer tan joven?** what do you do to look so young?

····▸ (*fingir, simular*) **hacer como que** to pretend. **hizo como que no me conocía** he pretended not to know me. **haz como que estás dormido** pretend you're asleep

····▸ **hacer de** (*en teatro*) to play the part of; (*ejercer la función de*) to act as

····▸ (*LAm, sentar*) **tanta sal hace mal** so much salt is not good for you. **dormir le hizo bien** the sleep did him good. **el pepino me hace mal** cucumber doesn't agree with me

verbo impersonal

····▸ (*hablando del tiempo atmosférico*) to be. **hace sol** it's sunny. **hace 3 grados** it's 3 degrees

····▸ (*con expresiones temporales*) **hace una hora que espero** I've been waiting for an hour.

llegó hace 3 días he arrived 3 days ago. **hace mucho tiempo** a long time ago. **hasta hace poco** until recently

- **hacerse** *verbo pronominal*

····➤ (*para sí*) to make o.s. (falda, café)

····➤ (*hacer que otro haga*) **se hizo la permanente** she had her hair permed. **me hice una piscina** I had a pool built

····➤ (*convertirse en*) to become. **se hicieron amigos** they became friends

····➤ (*acostumbrarse*) **~se a algo** to get used to sth

····➤ (*fingirse*) to pretend. **~se el enfermo** to pretend to be ill

····➤ (*moverse*) to move. **hazte para atrás** move back

····➤ **hacerse de** (*LAm*) to make (amigo, dinero)

hacha *f* axe; (*antorcha*) torch

hacia *prep* towards; (*cerca de*) near; (*con tiempo*) at about. **~ abajo** downwards. **~ arriba** upwards. **~ atrás** backwards. **~ las dos** (at) about two o'clock

hacienda *f* country estate; (*en LAm*) ranch; **la ~ pública** the Treasury. **Ministerio** *m* **de H~** Ministry of Finance; (*en Gran Bretaña*) Exchequer; (*en Estados Unidos*) Treasury

hada *f* fairy. **el ~ madrina** the fairy godmother

hago *vb véase* **HACER**

Haití *m* Haiti

halag|ar 12 *vt* flatter. **~üeño** *adj* flattering; (*esperanzador*) promising

halcón *m* falcon

halla|r *vt* find; (*descubrir*) discover. **~rse** *vpr* be. **~zgo** *m* discovery

hamaca *f* hammock; (*asiento*) deck-chair

hambr|e *f* hunger; (*de muchos*) famine. **tener ~e** be hungry. **~iento** *adj* starving

hamburguesa *f* hamburger

harag|án *adj* lazy, idle. ● *m* layabout. **~anear** *vi* laze around

harap|iento *adj* in rags. **~o** *m* rag

harina *f* flour

hart|ar *vt* (*fastidiar*) annoy. **me estás ~ando** you're annoying me. **~arse** *vpr* (*llenarse*) gorge o.s. (**de** on); (*cansarse*) get fed up (**de** with). **~o** *adj* full; (*cansado*) tired; (*fastidiado*) fed up (**de** with). ● *adv* (*LAm*) (*muy*) very; (*mucho*) a lot

hasta *prep* as far as; (*en el tiempo*) until, till; (*Mex*) not until. ● *adv* even. **¡~ la vista!** goodbye!, see you! **!** **¡~ luego!** see you later! **¡~ mañana!** see you tomorrow! **¡~ pronto!** see you soon!

hast|iar 20 *vt* (*cansar*) weary, tire; (*aburrir*) bore. **~iarse** *vpr* get fed up (**de** with). **~ío** *m* weariness; (*aburrimiento*) boredom

haya *f* beech (tree). ● *vb véase* **HABER**

hazaña *f* exploit

hazmerreír *m* laughing stock

he *vb véase* **HABER**

hebilla *f* buckle

hebra *f* thread; (*fibra*) fibre

hebreo *adj* & *m* Hebrew

hechi|cera *f* witch. **~cería** *f* witchcraft. **~cero** *m* wizard. **~zar** 10 *vt* cast a spell on; (*fig*) captivate. **~zo** *m* spell; (*fig*) charm

hech|o *pp de* **hacer**. ● *adj* (*manufacturado*) made; (*terminado*) done; (vestidos etc) ready-made; (*Culin*) done. ● *m* fact; (*acto*) deed; (*cuestión*) matter; (*suceso*) event. **de ~o** in fact. **~ura** *f* making; (*forma*) form; (*del cuerpo*) build; (*calidad de fabricación*) workmanship

hed|er **1** *vi* stink. **~iondez** *f* stench. **~iondo** *adj* stinking, smelly. **~or** *m* stench

hela|da *f* frost. **~dera** *f* (*LAm*) fridge, refrigerator. **~dería** *f* ice-cream shop. **~do** *adj* freezing; (*congelado*) frozen; (*LAm, bebida*) chilled. ● *m* ice-cream. **~r** **1** *vt/i* freeze. **anoche heló** there was a frost last night. **~rse** *vpr* freeze

h

helecho *m* fern

hélice *f* propeller

helicóptero *m* helicopter

hembra *f* female; (*mujer*) woman

hemorr|agia *f* haemorrhage. **~oides** *fpl* haemorrhoids

hendidura *f* crack, split; (*en geología*) fissure

heno *m* hay

heráldica *f* heraldry

hered|ar *vt/i* inherit. **~era** *f* heiress. **~ero** *m* heir. **~itario** *adj* hereditary

herej|e *m* heretic. **~ía** *f* heresy

herencia *f* inheritance; (*fig*) heritage

heri|da *f* injury; (*con arma*) wound. **~do** *adj* injured; (*con arma*) wounded; (*fig*) hurt. ● *m* injured person. **~r** **4** *vt* injure; (*con arma*) wound; (*fig*) hurt. **~rse** *vpr* hurt o.s.

herman|a *f* sister. **~a política** sister-in-law. **~astra** *f* stepsister. **~astro** *m* stepbrother. **~o** *m* brother. **~o político** brother-in-law. **~os** *mpl* brothers; (*chicos y chicas*) brothers and sisters. **~os gemelos** twins

hermético *adj* hermetic; (*fig*) watertight

hermos|o *adj* beautiful; (*espléndido*) splendid. **~ura** *f* beauty

héroe *m* hero

hero|ico *adj* heroic. **~ína** *f* heroine; (*droga*) heroin. **~ísmo** *m* heroism

herr|adura *f* horseshoe. **~amienta** *f* tool. **~ero** *m* blacksmith

herv|idero *m* (*fig*) hotbed; (*multitud*) throng. **~ir** **4** *vt/i* boil. **~or** *m* (*fig*) ardour. **romper el ~** come to the boil

hiberna|ción *f* hibernation. **~r** *vi* hibernate

híbrido *adj* & *m* hybrid

hice *vb véase* HACER

hidalgo *m* nobleman

hidrata|nte *adj* moisturizing. **~r** *vt* hydrate; (crema etc) moisturize

hidráulico *adj* hydraulic

hidr|oavión *m* seaplane. **~oeléctrico** *adj* hydroelectric. **~ofobia** *f* rabies. **~ófobo** *adj* rabid. **~ógeno** *m* hydrogen

hiedra *f* ivy

hielo *m* ice

hiena *f* hyena

hierba *f* grass; (*Culin, Med*) herb **mala ~** weed. **~buena** *f* mint.

hierro *m* iron

hígado *m* liver

higi|ene *f* hygiene. **~énico** *adj* hygienic

hig|o *m* fig. **~uera** *f* fig tree

hij|a *f* daughter. **~astra** *f* stepdaughter. **~astro** *m* stepson. **~o** *m* son. **~os** *mpl* sons; (*chicos y chicas*) children

hilar *vt* spin. **~ delgado** split hairs

hilera *f* row; (*Mil*) file

hilo *m* thread; (*Elec*) wire; (*de líquido*) trickle; (*lino*) linen
hilv|án *m* tacking. **~anar** *vt* tack; (*fig*) put together
himno *m* hymn. **~ nacional** anthem
hincapié *m*. **hacer ~ en** stress, insist on
hincar 7 *vt* drive (estaca) (**en** into). **~se** *vpr*. **~se de rodillas** kneel down
hincha *f* 1 grudge. • *m & f* (*fam, aficionado*) fan
hincha|do *adj* inflated; (*Med*) swollen. **~r** *vt* inflate, blow up. **~rse** *vpr* swell up; (*fig, fam, comer mucho*) gorge o.s. **~zón** *f* swelling
hinojo *m* fennel
hiper|mercado *m* hypermarket. **~sensible** *adj* hypersensitive. **~tensión** *f* high blood pressure
hípic|a *f* horse racing. **~o** *adj* horse
hipn|osis *f* hypnosis. **~otismo** *m* hypnotism. **~otizar** 10 *vt* hypnotize
hipo *m* hiccup. **tener ~** have hiccups
hipo|alérgeno *adj* hypoallergenic. **~condríaco** *adj & m* hypochondriac
hip|ocresía *f* hypocrisy. **~ócrita** *adj* hypocritical. • *m & f* hypocrite
hipódromo *m* racecourse
hipopótamo *m* hippopotamus
hipoteca *f* mortgage. **~r** 7 *vt* mortgage
hip|ótesis *f invar* hypothesis. **~otético** *adj* hypothetical
hiriente *adj* offensive, wounding
hirsuto *adj* (barba) bristly; (pelo) wiry
hispánico *adj* Hispanic

Hispanidad - Día de la
See ▷**DÍA DE LA RAZA**

Hispanoamérica *f* Spanish America
hispano|americano *adj* Spanish American. **~hablante** *adj* Spanish-speaking
hist|eria *f* hysteria. **~érico** *adj* hysterical
hist|oria *f* history; (*relato*) story; (*excusa*) tale, excuse. **pasar a la ~oria** go down in history. **~oriador** *m* historian. **~órico** *adj* historical. **~orieta** *f* tale; (*con dibujos*) strip cartoon
hito *m* milestone
hizo *vb véase* HACER
hocico *m* snout
hockey /'(x)oki/ *m* hockey. **~ sobre hielo** ice hockey
hogar *m* home; (*chimenea*) hearth. **~eño** *adj* domestic; (persona) home-loving
hoguera *f* bonfire
hoja *f* leaf; (*de papel, metal etc*) sheet; (*de cuchillo, espada etc*) blade. **~ de afeitar** razor blade. **~lata** *f* tin
hojaldre *m* puff pastry
hojear *vt* leaf through
hola *int* hello!
Holanda *f* Holland
holand|és *adj* Dutch. • *m* Dutchman; (*lengua*) Dutch. **~esa** *f* Dutchwoman. **los ~eses** the Dutch
holg|ado *adj* loose; (*fig*) comfortable. **~ar** 2 & 12 *vi*. **huelga decir que** needless to say. **~azán** *adj* lazy. • *m* idler. **~ura** *f* looseness; (*fig*) comfort
hollín *m* soot

hombre *m* man; (*especie humana*) man(kind). ● *int* Good Heavens!; (*de duda*) well. ~ **de negocios** businessman. ~ **rana** frogman

hombr|era *f* shoulder pad. ~**o** *m* shoulder

homenaje *m* homage, tribute. **rendir ~ a** pay tribute to

home|ópata *m* homoeopath. ~**opatía** *f* homoeopathy. ~**opático** *adj* homoeopathic

homicid|a *adj* murderous. ● *m & f* murderer. ~**io** *m* murder

homosexual *adj & m & f* homosexual. ~**idad** *f* homosexuality

hond|o *adj* deep. ~**onada** *f* hollow

Honduras *f* Honduras

hondureño *adj & m* Honduran

honest|idad *f* honesty. ~**o** *adj* honest

hongo *m* fungus; (*LAm, Culin*) mushroom; (*venenoso*) toadstool

hon|or *m* honour. ~**orable** *adj* honourable. ~**orario** *adj* honorary. ~**orarios** *mpl* fees. ~**ra** *f* honour; (*buena fama*) good name. ~**radez** *f* honesty. ~**rado** *adj* honest. ~**rar** *vt* honour

hora *f* hour; (*momento puntual*) time; (*cita*) appointment. ~ **pico**, ~ **punta** rush hour. ~**s** *fpl* **de trabajo** working hours. ~**s** *fpl* **extraordinarias** overtime. ~**s** *fpl* **libres** free time. **a estas ~s** now. **¿a qué ~?** (at) what time? **a última ~** at the last moment. **de última ~** last-minute. **en buena ~** at the right time. **media ~** half an hour. **pedir ~** to make an appointment. **¿qué ~ es?** what time is it?

horario *adj* hourly. ● *m* timetable. ~ **de trabajo** working hours

horca *f* gallows

horcajadas *fpl*. **a ~** astride

horchata *f* tiger-nut milk

horizont|al *adj & f* horizontal. ~**e** *m* horizon

horma *f* mould; (*para fabricar calzado*) last; (*para conservar su forma*) shoe-tree. **de ~ ancha** broad-fitting

hormiga *f* ant

hormigón *m* concrete

hormigue|ar *vi* tingle; (*bullir*) swarm. **me ~a la mano** I've got pins and needles in my hand. ~**o** *m* tingling; (*fig*) anxiety

hormiguero *m* anthill; (*de gente*) swarm

hormona *f* hormone

horn|ada *f* batch. ~**illa** *f* (*LAm*) burner. ~**illo** *m* burner; (*cocina portátil*) portable electric cooker. ~**o** *m* oven; (*para cerámica etc*) kiln; (*Tec*) furnace

horóscopo *m* horoscope

horquilla *f* pitchfork; (*para el pelo*) hairpin

horr|endo *adj* awful. ~**ible** *adj* horrible. ~**ipilante** *adj* terrifying. ~**or** *m* horror; (*atrocidad*) atrocity. **¡qué ~or!** how awful!. ~**orizar** 10 *vt* horrify. ~**orizarse** *vpr* be horrified. ~**oroso** *adj* horrifying

hort|aliza *f* vegetable. ~**elano** *m* market gardener

hosco *adj* surly

hospeda|je *m* accommodation. ~**r** *vt* put up. ~**rse** *vpr* stay

hospital *m* hospital. ~**ario** *adj* hospitable. ~**idad** *f* hospitality

hostal *m* boarding-house

hostería *f* inn

hostia *f* (*Relig*) host

hostigar 12 *vt* whip; (*fig, molestar*) pester

hostil *adj* hostile. **~idad** *f* hostility

hotel *m* hotel. **~ero** *adj* hotel. ● *m* hotelier

hoy *adv* today. **~ (en) día** nowadays. **~ por ~** at the present time. **de ~ en adelante** from now on

hoy|o *m* hole. **~uelo** *m* dimple

hoz *f* sickle

hube *vb véase* HABER

hucha *f* money box

hueco *adj* hollow; (palabras) empty; (voz) resonant; (persona) superficial. ● *m* hollow; (*espacio*) space; (*vacío*) gap

huelg|a *f* strike. **~a de brazos caídos** sit-down strike. **~a de hambre** hunger strike. **declararse en ~a** come out on strike. **~uista** *m & f* striker

huella *f* footprint; (*de animal etc*) track. **~ de carbono** carbon footprint. **~ digital** fingerprint

huelo *vb véase* OLER

huérfano *adj* orphaned. ● *m* orphan. **~ de** without

huert|a *f* market garden (*Brit*), truck farm (*Amer*); (*terreno de regadío*) irrigated plain. **~o** *m* vegetable garden; (*de árboles frutales*) orchard

hueso *m* bone; (*de fruta*) stone

huésped *m* guest; (*que paga*) lodger

huesudo *adj* bony

huev|a *f* roe. **~o** *m* egg. **~o duro** hard-boiled egg. **~o escalfado** poached egg. **~o estrellado, ~o frito** fried egg. **~o pasado por agua** boiled egg. **~os revueltos** scrambled eggs. **~o tibio** (*Mex*) boiled egg

hui|da *f* flight, escape. **~dizo** *adj* (*tímido*) shy; (*esquivo*) elusive

huipil *m* (*Mex*) traditional embroidered smock

> **huipil** A traditional garment worn by Indian and mestizo women in Mexico and Central America. *Huipiles* are generally made of richly embroidered cotton. They are very wide and low-cut, and are either waist- or thigh-length.

huir *vi* 17 flee, run away; (*evitar*). **~ de** avoid. **me huye** he avoids me

huitlacoche *m* (*Mex*) edible black fungus

hule *m* oilcloth; (*Mex, goma*) rubber

human|idad *f* mankind; (*fig*) humanity. **~itario** *adj* humanitarian. **~o** *adj* human; (*benévolo*) humane

humareda *f* cloud of smoke

humed|ad *f* dampness; (*en meteorología*) humidity; (*gotitas de agua*) moisture. **~ecer** 11 *vt* moisten. **~ecerse** *vpr* become moist

húmedo *adj* damp; (clima) humid; (labios) moist; (*mojado*) wet

humi|ldad *f* humility. **~lde** *adj* humble. **~llación** *f* humiliation. **~llar** *vt* humiliate. **~llarse** *vpr* lower o.s.

humo *m* smoke; (*vapor*) steam; (*gas nocivo*) fumes. **~s** *mpl* airs

humor *m* mood, temper; (*gracia*) humour. **estar de mal ~** be in a bad mood. **~ista** *m & f* humorist. **~ístico** *adj* humorous

hundi|miento *m* sinking. **~r** *vt* sink; destroy (persona). **~rse** *vpr* sink; (edificio) collapse

húngaro *adj & m* Hungarian

Hungría *f* Hungary

huracán *m* hurricane

h

huraño *adj* unsociable
hurgar 12 *vi* rummage (**en** through). **~se** *vpr.* **~se la nariz** pick one's nose
hurra *int* hurray!
hurtadillas *fpl.* **a ~** stealthily
hurt|ar *vt* steal. **~o** *m* theft; (*cosa robada*) stolen object
husmear *vt* sniff out; (*fig*) pry into
huyo *vb véase* HUIR

Ii

iba *véase* IR
ibérico *adj* Iberian
iberoamericano *adj & m* Latin American
iceberg /iθ'ber/ *m* (*pl* **~s**) iceberg
ictericia *f* jaundice
ida *f* outward journey; (*partida*) departure. **de ~ y vuelta** (billete) return (*Brit*), round-trip (*Amer*); (viaje) round
idea *f* idea; (*opinión*) opinion. **cambiar de ~** change one's mind. **no tener la más remota ~, no tener la menor ~** not have the slightest idea, not have a clue [!]
ideal *adj & m* ideal. **~ista** *m & f* idealist. **~izar** 10 *vt* idealize
idear *vt* think up, conceive; (*inventar*) invent
ídem *pron & adv* the same
idéntico *adj* identical
identi|dad *f* identity. **~ficación** *f* identification. **~ficar** 7 *vt* identify. **~ficarse** *vpr* identify o.s. **~ficarse con** identify with
ideol|ogía *f* ideology. **~ógico** *adj* ideological
idílico *adj* idyllic
idilio *m* idyll
idiom|a *m* language. **~ático** *adj* idiomatic
idiosincrasia *f* idiosyncrasy
idiot|a *adj* idiotic. ● *m & f* idiot. **~ez** *f* stupidity
idolatrar *vt* worship; (*fig*) idolize
ídolo *m* idol
idóneo *adj* suitable (**para** for)
iglesia *f* church
iglú *m* igloo
ignora|ncia *f* ignorance. **~nte** *adj* ignorant. ● *m* ignoramus. **~r** *vt* not know, be unaware of; (*no hacer caso de*) ignore
igual *adj* equal; (*mismo*) the same; (*similar*) like; (*llano*) even; (*liso*) smooth. ● *adv* the same. ● *m* equal. **~ que** (the same) as. **al ~ que** the same as. **da ~, es ~** it doesn't matter. **sin ~** unequalled
igual|ar *vt* make equal; equal (éxito, récord); (*allanar*) level. **~arse** *vpr* be equal. **~dad** *f* equality. **~mente** *adv* equally; (*también*) also, likewise; (*respuesta de cortesía*) the same to you
ilegal *adj* illegal
ilegible *adj* illegible
ilegítimo *adj* illegitimate
ileso *adj* unhurt
ilícito *adj* illicit
ilimitado *adj* unlimited
ilógico *adj* illogical
ilumina|ción *f* illumination; (*alumbrado*) lighting. **~r** *vt* light (up). **~rse** *vpr* light up
ilusi|ón *f* illusion; (*sueño*) dream; (*alegría*) joy. **hacerse ~ones** build up one's hopes. **me hace ~ón** I'm

thrilled; I'm looking forward to (algo en el futuro). **~onado** *adj* excited. **~onar** *vt* give false hope. **~onarse** *vpr* have false hopes

ilusionis|mo *m* conjuring. **~ta** *m & f* conjurer

iluso *adj* naive. • *m* dreamer. **~rio** *adj* illusory

ilustra|ción *f* learning; (*dibujo*) illustration. **~do** *adj* learned; (*con dibujos*) illustrated. **~r** *vt* explain; (*instruir*) instruct; (*añadir dibujos etc*) illustrate. **~rse** *vpr* acquire knowledge. **~tivo** *adj* illustrative

ilustre *adj* illustrious

imagen *f* image; (*TV etc*) picture

imagina|ble *adj* imaginable. **~ción** *f* imagination. **~r** *vt* imagine. **~rse** *vpr* imagine. **~rio** *m* imaginary. **~tivo** *adj* imaginative

imán *m* magnet

imbécil *adj* stupid. • *m & f* idiot

imborrable *adj* indelible; (*recuerdo etc*) unforgettable

imita|ción *f* imitation. **~r** *vt* imitate

impacien|cia *f* impatience. **~tarse** *vpr* lose one's patience. **~te** *adj* impatient

impacto *m* impact; (*huella*) mark. **~ de bala** bullet hole

impar *adj* odd

imparcial *adj* impartial. **~idad** *f* impartiality

impartir *vt* impart, give

impasible *adj* impassive

impávido *adj* fearless; (*impasible*) impassive

impecable *adj* impeccable

impedi|do *adj* disabled. **~mento** *m* impediment. **~r** 5 *vt* prevent; (*obstruir*) hinder

impenetrable *adj* impenetrable

impensa|ble *adj* unthinkable. **~do** *adj* unexpected

impera|r *vi* prevail. **~tivo** *adj* imperative; (*necesidad*) urgent

imperceptible *adj* imperceptible

imperdible *m* safety pin

imperdonable *adj* unforgivable

imperfec|ción *f* imperfection. **~to** *adj* imperfect

imperi|al *adj* imperial. **~alismo** *m* imperialism. **~o** *m* empire; (*poder*) rule. **~oso** *adj* imperious

impermeable *adj* waterproof. • *m* raincoat

impersonal *adj* impersonal

impertinen|cia *f* impertinence. **~te** *adj* impertinent

imperturbable *adj* imperturbable

ímpetu *m* impetus; (*impulso*) impulse; (*violencia*) force

impetuos|idad *f* impetuosity. **~o** *adj* impetuous

implacable *adj* implacable

implantar *vt* introduce

implementación *f* implementation

implica|ción *f* implication. **~r** 7 *vt* implicate; (*significar*) imply

implícito *adj* implicit

implorar *vt* implore

impon|ente *adj* imposing; I terrific. **~er** 34 *vt* impose; (*requerir*) demand; deposit (*dinero*). **~erse** *vpr* (*hacerse obedecer*) assert o.s.; (*hacerse respetar*) command respect; (*prevalecer*) prevail. **~ible** *adj* taxable

importa|ción *f* importation; (*artículo*) import. **~ciones** *fpl* imports. **~dor** *adj* importing. • *m* importer

importa|ncia *f* importance.

~nte *adj* important; (*en cantidad*) considerable. **~r** *vt* import; (*ascender a*) amount to. ● *vi* be important, matter. **¿le ~ría...?** would you mind...? **no ~** it doesn't matter

importe *m* price; (*total*) amount

importun|ar *vt* bother. **~o** *adj* troublesome; (*inoportuno*) inopportune

imposib|ilidad *f* impossibility. **~le** *adj* impossible. **hacer lo ~le para** do all one can to

i

imposición *f* imposition; (*impuesto*) tax

impostor *m* impostor

impoten|cia *f* impotence. **~te** *adj* impotent

impracticable *adj* impracticable; (*intransitable*) unpassable

imprecis|ión *f* vagueness; (*error*) inaccuracy. **~o** *adj* imprecise

impregnar *vt* impregnate; (*empapar*) soak

imprenta *f* printing; (*taller*) printing house, printer's

imprescindible *adj* indispensable, essential

impresi|ón *f* impression; (*acción de imprimir*) printing; (*tirada*) edition; (*huella*) imprint. **~onable** *adj* impressionable. **~onante** *adj* impressive; (*espantoso*) frightening. **~onar** *vt* impress; (*negativamente*) shock; (*conmover*) move; (*Foto*) expose. **~onarse** *vpr* be impressed; (*negativamente*) be shocked; (*conmover*) be moved

impresionis|mo *m* impressionism. **~ta** *adj & m & f* impressionist

impreso *adj* printed. ● *m* form. **~s** *mpl* printed matter. **~ra** *f* printer

imprevis|ible *adj* unforeseeable. **~to** *adj* unforeseen

imprimir (*pp* **impreso**) *vt* print (libro etc)

improbab|ilidad *f* improbability. **~le** *adj* unlikely, improbable

improcedente *adj* inadmissible; (conducta) improper; (despido) unfair

improductivo *adj* unproductive

improperio *m* insult. **~s** *mpl* abuse

impropio *adj* improper

improvis|ación *f* improvisation. **~ado** *adj* improvised. **~ar** *vt* improvise. **~o** *adj*. **de ~o** unexpectedly

impruden|cia *f* imprudence. **~te** *adj* imprudent

imp|udicia *f* indecency; (*desvergüenza*) shamelessness. **~údico** *adj* indecent; (*desvergonzado*) shameless. **~udor** *m* indecency; (*desvergüenza*) shamelessness

impuesto *adj* imposed. ● *m* tax. **~ a la renta** income tax. **~ sobre el valor agregado** (*LAm*), **~ sobre el valor añadido** VAT, value added tax

impuls|ar *vt* propel; drive (persona); boost (producción etc). **~ividad** *f* impulsiveness. **~ivo** *adj* impulsive. **~o** *m* impulse

impun|e *adj* unpunished. **~idad** *f* impunity

impur|eza *f* impurity. **~o** *adj* impure

imputa|ción *f* charge. **~r** *vt* attribute; (*acusar*) charge

inaccesible *adj* inaccessible

inaceptable *adj* unacceptable

inactiv|idad *f* inactivity. **~o** *adj* inactive

inadaptado *adj* maladjusted

inadecuado *adj* inadequate; (*inapropiado*) unsuitable
inadmisible *adj* inadmissible; (*inaceptable*) unacceptable
inadvertido *adj* distracted. **pasar ~** go unnoticed
inagotable *adj* inexhaustible
inaguantable *adj* unbearable
inaltera|ble *adj* impassive; (color) fast; (convicción) unalterable. **~do** *adj* unchanged
inapreciable *adj* invaluable; (*imperceptible*) imperceptible
inapropiado *adj* inappropriate
inasequible *adj* out of reach
inaudito *adj* unprecedented
inaugura|ción *f* inauguration. **~l** *adj* inaugural. **~r** *vt* inaugurate
inca *adj & m & f* Inca. **~ico** *adj* Inca

Incas Founded in the twelfth century, the Andean empire of the Quechua-speaking Incas grew and extended from southern Colombia to Argentina and central Chile. Its capital was Cuzco. The Incas built an extensive road network and impressive buildings, including Machu Picchu. The empire collapsed in 1533 after defeat by the Spaniards led by Francisco Pizarro.

incalculable *adj* incalculable
incandescente *adj* incandescent
incansable *adj* tireless
incapa|cidad *f* incapacity; (*física*) disability. **~citado** *adj* disabled. **~citar** *vt* incapacitate. **~z** *adj* incapable
incauto *adj* unwary; (*fácil de engañar*) gullible
incendi|ar *vt* set fire to. **~arse** *vpr* catch fire. **~ario** *adj* incendiary. ● *m* arsonist. **~o** *m* fire
incentivo *m* incentive
incertidumbre *f* uncertainty
incesante *adj* incessant
incest|o *m* incest. **~uoso** *adj* incestuous
inciden|cia *f* incidence; (*efecto*) impact; (*incidente*) incident. **~tal** *adj* incidental. **~te** *m* incident
incidir *vi* fall (**en** into); (*influir*) influence
incienso *m* incense
incierto *adj* uncertain
incinera|dor *m* incinerator. **~r** *vt* incinerate; cremate (cadáver)
incipiente *adj* incipient
incisi|ón *f* incision. **~vo** *adj* incisive. ● *m* incisor
incitar *vt* incite
inclemen|cia *f* harshness. **~te** *adj* harsh
inclina|ción *f* slope; (*de la cabeza*) nod; (*fig*) inclination. **~r** *vt* tilt; (*inducir*) incline. **~rse** *vpr* lean; (*en saludo*) bow; (*tender*) be inclined (**a** to)
inclu|ido *adj* included; (precio) inclusive. **~ir** 17 *vt* include; (*en cartas*) enclose. **~sión** *f* inclusion. **~sive** *adv* inclusive. **hasta el lunes ~sive** up to and including Monday. **~so** *adv* even
incógnito *adj* unknown. **de ~** incognito
incoheren|cia *f* incoherence. **~te** *adj* incoherent
incoloro *adj* colourless
incomestible *adj*, **incomible** *adj* uneatable, inedible
incomodar *vt* inconvenience; (*causar vergüenza*) make feel uncomfortable. **~se** *vpr* feel uncom-

fortable; (*enojarse*) get angry

incómodo *adj* uncomfortable; (*inconveniente*) inconvenient

incomparable *adj* incomparable

incompatib|ilidad *f* incompatibility. **~le** *adj* incompatible

incompeten|cia *f* incompetence. **~te** *adj & m & f* incompetent

incompleto *adj* incomplete

incompren|dido *adj* misunderstood. **~sible** *adj* incomprehensible. **~sión** *f* incomprehension

incomunicado *adj* cut off; (preso) in solitary confinement

inconcebible *adj* inconceivable

inconcluso *adj* unfinished

incondicional *adj* unconditional

inconfundible *adj* unmistakable

incongruente *adj* incoherent; (*contradictorio*) inconsistent

inconmensurable *adj* immeasurable

inconscien|cia *f* unconsciousness; (*irreflexión*) recklessness. **~te** *adj* unconscious; (*irreflexivo*) reckless

inconsecuente *adj* inconsistent

inconsistente *adj* flimsy

inconsolable *adj* unconsolable

inconstan|cia *f* lack of perseverance. **~te** *adj* changeable; (persona) lacking in perseverance; (*voluble*) fickle

incontable *adj* countless

incontenible *adj* irrepressible

incontinen|cia *f* incontinence. **~te** *adj* incontinent

inconvenien|cia *f* inconvenience. **~te** *adj* inconvenient; (*inapropiado*) inappropriate; (*incorrecto*) improper. • *m* problem; (*desventaja*) drawback

incorpora|ción *f* incorporation. **~r** *vt* incorporate; (*Culin*) add. **~rse** *vpr* sit up; join (sociedad, regimiento etc)

incorrecto *adj* incorrect; (*descortés*) discourteous

incorregible *adj* incorrigible

incorruptible *adj* incorruptible

incrédulo *adj* sceptical; (mirada, gesto) incredulous

increíble *adj* incredible

increment|ar *vt* increase. **~o** *m* increase

incriminar *vt* incriminate

incrustar *vt* encrust

incuba|ción *f* incubation. **~dora** *f* incubator. **~r** *vt* incubate; (*fig*) hatch

incuestionable *adj* unquestionable

inculcar **7** *vt* inculcate

inculpar *vt* accuse

inculto *adj* uneducated

incumplimiento *m* nonfulfilment; (*de un contrato*) breach

incurable *adj* incurable

incurrir *vi.* **~ en** incur (gasto); fall into (error); commit (crimen)

incursión *f* raid

indagar **12** *vt* investigate

indebido *adj* unjust; (uso) improper

indecen|cia *f* indecency. **~te** *adj* indecent

indecible *adj* indescribable

indecis|ión *f* indecision. **~o** *adj* (*con ser*) indecisive; (*con estar*) undecided

indefenso *adj* defenceless

indefini|ble *adj* indefinable. **~do** *adj* indefinite; (*impreciso*) undefined

indemnizar **10** *vt* compensate

independ|encia *f* independence. **~iente** *adj* independent. **~izarse** 10 *vpr* become independent

indes|cifrable *adj* indecipherable. **~criptible** *adj* indescribable

indeseable *adj* undesirable

indestructible *adj* indestructible

indetermina|ble *adj* indeterminable. **~do** *adj* indeterminate; (tiempo) indefinite

India *f.* la ~ India

indica|ción *f* indication; (*señal*) signal. **~ciones** *fpl* directions. **~dor** *m* indicator; (*Tec*) gauge. **~r** 7 *vt* show, indicate; (*apuntar*) point at; (*hacer saber*) point out; (*aconsejar*) advise. **~tivo** *adj* indicative. ● *m* indicative; (*al teléfono*) dialling code

índice *m* index; (*dedo*) index finger; (*catálogo*) catalogue; (*indicación*) indication; (*aguja*) pointer

indicio *m* indication, sign; (*vestigio*) trace

indiferen|cia *f* indifference. **~te** *adj* indifferent. **me es ~te** it's all the same to me

indígena *adj* indigenous. ● *m & f* native

indigen|cia *f* poverty. **~te** *adj* needy

indigest|ión *f* indigestion. **~o** *adj* indigestible

indign|ación *f* indignation. **~ado** *adj* indignant. **~ar** *vt* make indignant. **~arse** *vpr* become indignant. **~o** *adj* unworthy; (*despreciable*) contemptible

indio *adj & m* Indian

indirect|a *f* hint. **~o** *adj* indirect

indisciplinado *adj* undisciplined

indiscre|ción *f* indiscretion. **~to** *adj* indiscreet

indiscutible *adj* unquestionable

indisoluble *adj* indissoluble

indispensable *adj* indispensable

indisp|oner 34 *vt* (*enemistar*) set against. **~onerse** *vpr* fall out; (*ponerse enfermo*) fall ill. **~osición** *f* indisposition. **~uesto** *adj* indisposed

individu|al *adj* individual; (cama) single. ● *m* (*en tenis etc*) singles. **~alidad** *f* individuality. **~alista** *m & f* individualist. **~alizar** 10 *vt* individualize. **~o** *m* individual

indocumentado *m person without identity papers*; (*inmigrante*) illegal immigrant

índole *f* nature; (*clase*) type

indolen|cia *f* indolence. **~te** *adj* indolent

indoloro *adj* painless

indomable *adj* untameable

inducir 47 *vt* induce. **~ a error** be misleading

indudable *adj* undoubted

indulgen|cia *f* indulgence. **~te** *adj* indulgent

indult|ar *vt* pardon. **~o** *m* pardon

industria *f* industry. **~l** *adj* industrial. ● *m & f* industrialist. **~lización** *f* industrialization. **~lizar** 10 *vt* industrialize

inédito *adj* unpublished; (*fig*) unknown

inefable *adj* indescribable

ineficaz *adj* ineffective; (*sistema etc*) inefficient

ineficiente *adj* inefficient

ineludible *adj* inescapable, unavoidable

inept|itud *f* ineptitude. **~o** *adj* inept

inequívoco *adj* unequivocal

inercia *f* inertia

inerte *adj* inert; (*sin vida*) lifeless

I

inesperado *adj* unexpected
inestable *adj* unstable
inestimable *adj* inestimable
inevitable *adj* inevitable
inexistente *adj* non-existent
inexorable *adj* inexorable
inexper|iencia *f* inexperience. **~to** *adj* inexperienced
inexplicable *adj* inexplicable
infalible *adj* infallible
infam|ar *vt* defame. **~atorio** *adj* defamatory. **~e** *adj* infamous; (*fig, fam, muy malo*) awful. **~ia** *f* infamy
infancia *f* infancy
infant|a *f* infanta, princess. **~e** *m* infante, prince. **~ería** *f* infantry. **~il** *adj* children's; (población) child; (actitud etc) childish, infantile
infarto *m* heart attack
infec|ción *f* infection. **~cioso** *adj* infectious. **~tar** *vt* infect. **~tarse** *vpr* become infected. **~to** *adj* infected; ⊡ disgusting
infeli|cidad *f* unhappiness. **~z** *adj* unhappy
inferior *adj* inferior. ● *m & f* inferior. **~idad** *f* inferiority
infernal *adj* infernal, hellish
infestar *vt* infest; (*fig*) inundate
infi|delidad *f* unfaithfulness. **~el** *adj* unfaithful
infierno *m* hell
infiltra|ción *f* infiltration. **~rse** *vpr* infiltrate
ínfimo *adj* lowest; (calidad) very poor
infini|dad *f* infinity. **~tivo** *m* infinitive. **~to** *adj* infinite. ● *m*. **el ~to** the infinite; (*en matemáticas*) infinity. **~dad de** countless
inflación *f* inflation
inflama|ble *adj* (in)flammable. **~ción** *f* inflammation. **~r** *vt* set on fire; (*fig, Med*) inflame. **~rse** *vpr* catch fire; (*Med*) become inflamed
inflar *vt* inflate; blow up (globo); (*fig, exagerar*) exaggerate
inflexi|ble *adj* inflexible. **~ón** *f* inflexion
influ|encia *f* influence (**en** on). **~ir** 17 *vt* influence. ● *vi*. **~ en** influence. **~jo** *m* influence. **~yente** *adj* influential
informa|ción *f* information; (*noticias*) news; (*en aeropuerto etc*) information desk; (*de teléfonos*) directory enquiries. **~dor** *m* informant
informal *adj* informal; (persona) unreliable
inform|ante *m & f* informant. **~ar** *vt/i* inform. **~arse** *vpr* find out. **~ática** *f* information technology, computing. **~ativo** *adj* informative; (programa) news. **~atizar** 10 *vt* computerize
informe *adj* shapeless. ● *m* report. **~s** *fpl* references, information
infracción *f* infringement. **~ de tráfico** traffic offence
infraestructura *f* infrastructure
infranqueable *adj* impassable; (*fig*) insuperable
infrarrojo *adj* infrared
infringir 14 *vt* infringe
infructuoso *adj* fruitless
ínfulas *fpl*. **darse ~** give o.s. airs. **tener ~ de** fancy o.s. as
infundado *adj* unfounded
infu|ndir *vt* instil. **~sión** *f* infusion
ingeni|ar *vt* invent. **~árselas para** find a way to
ingenier|ía *f* engineering. **~o** *m* engineer

ingenio *m* ingenuity; (*agudeza*) wit; (*LAm, de azúcar*) refinery. **~so** *adj* ingenious

ingenu|idad *f* naivety. **~o** *adj* naive

Inglaterra *f* England

ingl|és *adj* English. • *m* Englishman; (*lengua*) English. **~esa** *f* Englishwoman. **los ~eses** the English

ingrat|itud *f* ingratitude. **~o** *adj* ungrateful; (*desagradable*) thankless

ingrediente *m* ingredient

ingres|ar *vt* deposit. • *vi.* **~ar en** come in, enter; join (sociedad). **~o** *m* entrance; (*de dinero*) deposit; (*en sociedad, hospital*) admission. **~os** *mpl* income

inh|ábil *adj* unskilful; (*no apto*) unfit. **~abilidad** *f* unskilfulness; (*para cargo*) ineligibility

inhabitable *adj* uninhabitable

inhala|dor *m* inhaler. **~r** *vt* inhale

inherente *adj* inherent

inhibi|ción *f* inhibition. **~r** *vt* inhibit

inhóspito *adj* inhospitable

inhumano *adj* inhuman

inici|ación *f* beginning. **~al** *adj* & *f* initial. **~ar** *vt* initiate; (*comenzar*) begin, start. **~ativa** *f* initiative. **~o** *m* beginning

inigualado *adj* unequalled

ininterrumpido *adj* uninterrupted

injert|ar *vt* graft. **~to** *m* graft

injuri|a *f* insult. **~ar** *vt* insult. **~oso** *adj* insulting

injust|icia *f* injustice. **~o** *adj* unjust, unfair

inmaculado *adj* immaculate

inmaduro *adj* unripe; (persona) immature

inmediaciones *fpl.* **las ~** the vicinity, the surrounding area

inmediat|amente *adv* immediately. **~o** *adj* immediate; (*contiguo*) next. **de ~o** immediately

inmejorable *adj* excellent

inmemorable *adj* immemorial

inmens|idad *f* immensity. **~o** *adj* immense

inmersión *f* immersion

inmigra|ción *f* immigration. **~nte** *adj* & *m* & *f* immigrant. **~r** *vt* immigrate

inminen|cia *f* imminence. **~te** *adj* imminent

inmiscuirse 17 *vpr* interfere

inmobiliario *adj* property

inmolar *vt* sacrifice

inmoral *adj* immoral. **~idad** *f* immorality

inmortal *adj* immortal. **~izar** 10 *vt* immortalize

inmóvil *adj* immobile

inmovilizador *m* immobilizer

inmueble *adj.* **bienes ~s** property

inmund|icia *f* filth. **~o** *adj* filthy

inmun|e *adj* immune. **~idad** *f* immunity. **~ización** *f* immunization. **~izar** 10 *vt* immunize

inmuta|ble *adj* unchangeable. **~rse** *vpr* be perturbed. **sin ~rse** unperturbed

innato *adj* innate

innecesario *adj* unnecessary

innegable *adj* undeniable

innova|ción *f* innovation. **~r** *vi* innovate. • *vt* make innovations in

innumerable *adj* innumerable

inocen|cia *f* innocence. **~tada** *f* practical joke. **~te** *adj* innocent. **~tón** *adj* naïve

inocuo *adj* innocuous

inodoro *adj* odourless. • *m* toilet

inofensivo *adj* inoffensive

inolvidable *adj* unforgettable

inoperable *adj* inoperable

inoportuno *adj* untimely; (comentario) ill-timed

inoxidable *adj* stainless

inquiet|ar *vt* worry. **~arse** *vpr* get worried. **~o** *adj* worried; (*agitado*) restless. **~ud** *f* anxiety

inquilino *m* tenant

inquirir 4 *vt* enquire into, investigate

insaciable *adj* insatiable

insalubre *adj* unhealthy

insatisfecho *adj* unsatisfied; (*descontento*) dissatisfied

inscri|bir (*pp* **inscrito**) *vt* (*en registro*) register; (*en curso*) enrol; (*grabar*) inscribe. **~birse** *vpr* register. **~pción** *f* inscription; (*registro*) registration

insect|icida *m* insecticide. **~o** *m* insect

insegur|idad *f* insecurity. **~o** *adj* insecure; (ciudad) unsafe, dangerous

insemina|ción *f* insemination. **~r** *vt* inseminate

insensato *adj* foolish

insensible *adj* insensitive

inseparable *adj* inseparable

insertar *vt* insert

insidi|a *f* malice. **~oso** *adj* insidious

insigne *adj* famous

insignia *f* badge; (*bandera*) flag

insignificante *adj* insignificant

insinu|ación *f* insinuation. **~ante** *adj* insinuating. **~ar** 21 *vt* imply; insinuate (algo ofensivo). **~arse** *vpr.* **~ársele a** make a pass at

insípido *adj* insipid

insist|encia *f* insistence. **~ente** *adj* insistent. **~ir** *vi* insist; (*hacer hincapié*) stress

insolación *f* sunstroke

insolen|cia *f* rudeness, insolence. **~te** *adj* rude, insolent

insólito *adj* unusual

insolven|cia *f* insolvency. **~te** *adj & m & f* insolvent

insomn|e *adj* sleepless. • *m & f* insomniac. **~io** *m* insomnia

insondable *adj* unfathomable

insoportable *adj* unbearable

insospechado *adj* unexpected

insostenible *adj* untenable

inspec|ción *f* inspection. **~cionar** *vt* inspect. **~tor** *m* inspector

inspira|ción *f* inspiration. **~r** *vt* inspire. **~rse** *vpr* be inspired

instala|ción *f* installation. **~r** *vt* install. **~rse** *vpr* settle

instancia *f* request. **en última ~** as a last resort

instant|ánea *f* snapshot. **~áneo** *adj* instantaneous; (café etc) instant. **~e** *m* instant. **a cada ~e** constantly. **al ~e** immediately

instaura|ción *f* establishment. **~r** *vt* establish

instiga|ción *f* instigation. **~dor** *m* instigator. **~r** 12 *vt* instigate; (*incitar*) incite

instint|ivo *adj* instinctive. **~o** *m* instinct

institu|ción *f* institution. **~cional** *adj* institutional. **~ir** 17 *vt* establish. **~to** *m* institute; (*en enseñanza*) (secondary) school. **~triz** *f* governess

instru|cción *f* education; (*Mil*) training. **~cciones** *fpl* instruction. **~ctivo** *adj* instructive; (película etc) educational. **~ctor** *m* instructor. **~ir** 17 *vt* instruct, teach; (*Mil*) train

instrument|ación *f* instrumentation. **~al** *adj* instrumental. **~o** *m* instrument; (*herramienta*) tool

insubordina|ción *f* insubordination. **~r** *vt* stir up. **~rse** *vpr* rebel

insuficien|cia *f* insufficiency; (*inadecuación*) inadequacy. **~te** *adj* insufficient

insufrible *adj* insufferable

insular *adj* insular

insulina *f* insulin

insulso *adj* tasteless; (*fig*) insipid

insult|ar *vt* insult. **~o** *m* insult

insuperable *adj* insuperable; (*inmejorable*) unbeatable

insurgente *adj* insurgent

insurrec|ción *f* insurrection. **~to** *adj* insurgent

intachable *adj* irreproachable

intacto *adj* intact

intangible *adj* intangible

integra|ción *f* integration. **~l** *adj* integral; (*completo*) complete; (*incorporado*) built-in; (pan) wholemeal (*Brit*), wholewheat (*Amer*). **~r** *vt* make up

integridad *f* integrity; (*entereza*) wholeness

íntegro *adj* complete; (*fig*) upright

intelect|o *m* intellect. **~ual** *adj* & *m* & f intellectual

inteligen|cia *f* intelligence. **~te** *adj* intelligent

inteligible *adj* intelligible

intemperie *f*. **a la ~** in the open

intempestivo *adj* untimely

intenci|ón *f* intention. **con doble ~ón** implying sth else. **~onado** *adj* deliberate. **bien ~onado** well-meaning. **mal ~onado** malicious. **~onal** *adj* intentional

intens|idad *f* intensity. **~ificar** 7 *vt* intensify. **~ivo** *adj* intensive. **~o** *adj* intense

intent|ar *vt* try. **~o** *m* attempt; (*Mex, propósito*) intention

inter|calar *vt* insert. **~cambio** *m* exchange. **~ceder** *vt* intercede

interceptar *vt* intercept

interdicto *m* ban

inter|és *m* interest; (*egoísmo*) self-interest. **~esado** *adj* interested; (*parcial*) biassed; (*egoísta*) selfish. **~esante** *adj* interesting. **~esar** *vt* interest; (*afectar*) concern. • *vi* be of interest. **~esarse** *vpr* take an interest (**por** in)

interfaz *m* & *f* interface

interfer|encia *f* interference. **~ir** 4 *vi* interfere

interfono *m* intercom

interino *adj* temporary; (persona) acting. • *m* stand-in

interior *adj* interior; (comercio etc) domestic. • *m* inside. **Ministerio del I~** Interior Ministry

interjección *f* interjection

inter|locutor *m* speaker. **~mediario** *adj* & *m* intermediary. **~medio** *adj* intermediate. • *m* interval

interminable *adj* interminable

intermitente *adj* intermittent. • *m* indicator

internacional *adj* international

intern|ado *m* (*Escol*) boarding-school. **~ar** *vt* (*en manicomio*) commit; (*en hospital*) admit. **~arse** *vpr* penetrate

internauta *m* & *f* netsurfer

Internet *m* Internet

interno *adj* internal; (*en enseñanza*) boarding. • *m* boarder

interponer [34] *vt* interpose. **~se** *vpr* intervene

int|erpretación *f* interpretation. **~erpretar** *vt* interpret; (*Mús etc*) play. **~érprete** *m* interpreter; (*Mus*) performer

interroga|ción *f* interrogation; (*signo*) question mark. **~r** [12] *vt* question. **~tivo** *adj* interrogative

interru|mpir *vt* interrupt; cut off (suministro); cut short (viaje etc); block (tráfico). **~pción** *f* interruption. **~ptor** *m* switch

inter|sección *f* intersection. **~urbano** *adj* inter-city; (llamada) long-distance

intervalo *m* interval; (*espacio*) space. **a ~s** at intervals

interven|ir [53] *vt* control; (*Med*) operate on. ● *vi* intervene; (*participar*) take part. **~tor** *m* inspector; (*Com*) auditor

intestino *m* intestine

intim|ar *vi* become friendly. **~idad** *f* intimacy

intimidar *vt* intimidate

íntimo *adj* intimate; (amigo) close. ● *m* close friend

intolera|ble *adj* intolerable. **~nte** *adj* intolerant

intoxicar [7] *vt* poison

intranquilo *adj* worried

intransigente *adj* intransigent

intransitable *adj* impassable

intransitivo *adj* intransitive

intratable *adj* impossible

intrépido *adj* intrepid

intriga *f* intrigue. **~nte** *adj* intriguing. **~r** [12] *vt* intrigue

intrincado *adj* intricate

intrínseco *adj* intrinsic

introduc|ción *f* introduction. **~ir** [47] *vt* introduce; (*meter*) insert. **~irse** *vpr* get into

intromisión *f* interference

introvertido *adj* introverted. ● *m* introvert

intruso *m* intruder

intui|ción *f* intuition. **~r** [17] *vt* sense. **~tivo** *adj* intuitive

inunda|ción *f* flooding. **~r** *vt* flood

inusitado *adj* unusual

in|útil *adj* useless; (*vano*) futile. **~utilidad** *f* uselessness

invadir *vt* invade

inv|alidez *f* invalidity; (*Med*) disability. **~álido** *adj & m* invalid

invariable *adj* invariable

invas|ión *f* invasion. **~or** *adj* invading. ● *m* invader

invencible *adj* invincible

inven|ción *f* invention. **~tar** *vt* invent

inventario *m* inventory

invent|iva *f* inventiveness. **~ivo** *adj* inventive. **~or** *m* inventor

invernadero *m* greenhouse

invernal *adj* winter

inverosímil *adj* implausible

inver|sión *f* inversion; (*Com*) investment. **~sionista** *m & f* investor

inverso *adj* inverse; (*contrario*) opposite. **a la inversa** the other way round. **a la inversa de** contrary to

inversor *m* investor

invertir [4] *vt* reverse; (*Com*) invest; put in (tiempo)

investidura *f* investiture

investiga|ción *f* investigation; (*Univ*) research. **~dor** *m* investigator; (*Univ*) researcher. **~r** [12] *vt* investigate; (*Univ*) research

investir [5] *vt* invest

invicto *adj* unbeaten

invierno *m* winter
inviolable *adj* inviolate
invisible *adj* invisible
invita|ción *f* invitation. **~do** *m* guest. **~r** *vt* invite. **te invito a una copa** I'll buy you a drink
invocar 7 *vt* invoke
involuntario *adj* involuntary
invulnerable *adj* invulnerable
inyec|ción *f* injection. **~tar** *vt* inject

ir 49

- *verbo intransitivo*
- ....> to go. **fui a verla** I went to see her. **ir a pie** to go on foot. **ir en coche** to go by car. **vamos a casa** let's go home. **fue (a) por el pan** he went to get some bread

! Cuando la acción del verbo **ir** significa trasladarse hacia o con el interlocutor la traducción es *to come*, p.ej: **¡ya voy!** *I'm coming!* **yo voy contigo** *I'll come with you*

- ....> (*estar*) to be. **Iba con su novio** she was with her boyfriend. **¿cómo te va?** how are you?
- ....> (*sentar*) to suit. **ese color no le va** that colour doesn't suit her. **no me va ni me viene** I don't mind at all
- ....> (*Méx, apoyar*) **irle a** to support. **le va al equipo local** he supports the local team
- ....> (*en exclamaciones*) **¡vamos!** come on! **¡vaya!** what a surprise!; (*contrariedad*) oh, dear! **¡vaya noche!** what a night!
- **¡qué va!** nonsense!

Cuando el verbo intransitivo se emplea con expresiones como **ir de paseo, ir de compras, ir tirando** etc., ver bajo el respectivo nombre, verbo etc.

- *verbo auxiliar*
- ....> **ir a** + *infinitivo* (*para expresar futuro, propósito*) to be going to + *infinitive;* (*al prevenir*) **no te vayas a caer** be careful you don't fall. **no vaya a ser que llueva** in case it rains; (*en sugerencias*) **vamos a dormir** let's go to sleep. **vamos a ver** let's see
- ....> **ir** + *gerundio.* **ve arreglándote** start getting ready. **el tiempo va mejorando** the weather is gradually getting better.
- **irse** *verbo pronominal*
- ....> to go. **se ha ido a casa** he's gone home
- ....> (*marcharse*) to leave. **se fue sin despedirse** he left without saying goodbye. **se fue de casa** she left home

ira *f* anger. **~cundo** *adj* irascible
Irak *m* Iraq
Irán *m* Iran
iraní *adj & m & f* Iranian
iraquí *adj & m & f* Iraqi
iris *m* (*del ojo*) iris
Irlanda *f* Ireland
irland|és *adj* Irish. ● *m* Irishman; (*lengua*) Irish. **~esa** *f* Irishwoman. **los ~eses** the Irish
ir|onía *f* irony. **~ónico** *adj* ironic
irracional *adj* irrational

irradiar *vt* radiate
irreal *adj* unreal. **~idad** *f* unreality
irrealizable *adj* unattainable
irreconciliable *adj* irreconcilable
irreconocible *adj* unrecognizable
irrecuperable *adj* irretrievable
irreflexión *f* impetuosity
irregular *adj* irregular. **~idad** *f* irregularity
irreparable *adj* irreparable
irreprimible *adj* irrepressible
irreprochable *adj* irreproachable
irresistible *adj* irresistible
irrespetuoso *adj* disrespectful
irresponsable *adj* irresponsible
irriga|ción *f* irrigation. **~r** 12 *vt* irrigate
irrisorio *adj* derisory
irrita|ble *adj* irritable. **~ción** *f* irritation. **~r** *vt* irritate. **~rse** *vpr* get annoyed
irrumpir *vi* burst (**en** in)
isla *f* island. **las I~s Británicas** the British Isles
islámico *adj* Islamic
islandés *adj* Icelandic. • *m* Icelander; (*lengua*) Icelandic
Islandia *f* Iceland
isleño *adj* island. • *m* islander
Israel *m* Israel
israelí *adj* & *m* Israeli
Italia *f* Italy
italiano *adj* & *m* Italian
itinerario *adj* itinerary
IVA *abrev* (**impuesto sobre el valor agregado** (*LAm*), **impuesto sobre el valor añadido**) VAT
izar 10 *vt* hoist
izquierd|a *f*. **la ~a** the left hand; (*Pol*) left. **a la ~a** on the left; (*con movimiento*) to the left. **de ~a** left-wing. **~ista** *m* & *f* leftist. **~o** *adj* left

ja *int* ha!
jabalí *m* (*pl* **~es**) wild boar
jabalina *f* javelin
jab|ón *m* soap. **~onar** *vt* soap. **~onoso** *adj* soapy
jaca *f* pony
jacinto *m* hyacinth
jactarse *vpr* boast
jadea|nte *adj* panting. **~r** *vi* pant
jaguar *m* jaguar
jaiba *f* (*LAm*) crab
jalar *vt* (*LAm*) pull
jalea *f* jelly
jaleo *m* row, uproar. **armar un ~** kick up a fuss
jalón *m* (*LAm, tirón*) pull; (*Mex fam, trago*) drink; (*Mex, tramo*) stretch
jamás *adv* never. **nunca ~** never ever
jamelgo *m* nag
jamón *m* ham. **~ de York** boiled ham. **~ serrano** cured ham
Japón *m*. **el ~** Japan
japonés *adj* & *m* Japanese
jaque *m* check. **~ mate** checkmate
jaqueca *f* migraine
jarabe *m* syrup
jardín *m* garden. **~ de la infancia**, (*Mex*) **~ de niños** kindergarten, nursery school
jardiner|ía *f* gardening. **~o** *m* gardener

jarr|a *f* jug. **en ~as** with hands on hips. **~o** *m* jug. **caer como un ~o de agua fría** come as a shock. **~ón** *m* vase

jaula *f* cage

jauría *f* pack of hounds

jazmín *m* jasmine

jef|a *f* boss. **~atura** *f* leadership; (*sede*) headquarters. **~e** *m* boss; (*Pol etc*) leader. **~e de camareros** head waiter. **~e de estación** station-master. **~e de ventas** sales manager

jengibre *m* ginger

jer|arquía *f* hierarchy. **~árquico** *adj* hierarchical

jerez *m* sherry. **al ~** with sherry

jerez Sherry is produced in an area around Jerez de la Frontera near Cádiz. Sherries are drunk worldwide as an aperitif, and in Spain as an accompaniment to tapas. The main types are: the pale *fino* and *manzanilla* and the darker *oloroso* and *amontillado*. It is from *Jerez* that sherry takes its English name.

jerga *f* coarse cloth; (*argot*) jargon

jerigonza *f* jargon; (*galimatías*) gibberish

jeringa *f* syringe; (*LAm fam, molestia*) nuisance. **~r** 12 *vt* (*fig, fam, molestar*) annoy

jeroglífico *m* hieroglyph(ic)

jersey *m* (*pl* **~s**) jersey

Jesucristo *m* Jesus Christ. **antes de ~** BC, before Christ

jesuita *adj & m* Jesuit

Jesús *m* Jesus. • *int* good heavens!; (*al estornudar*) bless you!

jícara *f* (*Mex*) gourd

jilguero *m* goldfinch

jinete *m & f* rider

jipijapa *m* panama hat

jirafa *f* giraffe

jirón *m* shred, tatter

jitomate *m* (*Mex*) tomato

jorna|da *f* working day; (*viaje*) journey; (*etapa*) stage. **~l** *m* day's wage. **~lero** *m* day labourer

joroba *f* hump. **~do** *adj* hunch-backed. • *m* hunchback. **~r** *vt* 1 annoy

jota *f* letter J; (*danza*) jota, popular dance. **ni ~** nothing

joven (*pl* **jóvenes**) *adj* young. • *m* young man. • *f* young woman

jovial *adj* jovial

joy|a *f* jewel. **~as** *fpl* jewellery. **~ería** *f* jeweller's (shop). **~ero** *m* jeweller; (*estuche*) jewellery box

juanete *m* bunion

jubil|ación *f* retirement. **~ado** *adj* retired. **~ar** *vt* pension off. **~arse** *vpr* retire. **~eo** *m* jubilee

júbilo *m* joy

judaísmo *m* Judaism

judía *f* Jewish woman; (*alubia*) bean. **~ blanca** haricot bean. **~ escarlata** runner bean. **~ verde** French bean

judicial *adj* judicial

judío *adj* Jewish. • *m* Jewish man

judo *m* judo

juego *m* play; (*de mesa, niños*) game; (*de azar*) gambling; (*conjunto*) set. **estar en ~** be at stake. **estar fuera de ~** be offside. **hacer ~** match. **~s** *mpl* **malabares** juggling. **J~s** *mpl* **Olímpicos** Olympic Games. • *vb véase* JUGAR

juerga *f* spree

jueves *m invar* Thursday

juez *m* judge. **~ de instrucción** examining magistrate. **~ de línea**

linesman
juga|dor *m* player; (*habitual, por dinero*) gambler. **~r** [3] *vt* play. • *vi* play; (*apostar fuerte*) gamble. **~rse** *vpr* risk. **~r al fútbol**, (*LAm*) **~r fútbol** play football
juglar *m* minstrel
jugo *m* juice; (*de carne*) gravy; (*fig*) substance. **~so** *adj* juicy; (*fig*) substantial
juguet|e *m* toy. **~ear** *vi* play. **~ón** *adj* playful
juicio *m* judgement; (*opinión*) opinion; (*razón*) reason. **a mi ~** in my opinion. **~so** *adj* wise
juliana *f* vegetable soup
julio *m* July
junco *m* rush, reed
jungla *f* jungle
junio *m* June
junt|a *f* meeting; (*consejo*) board, committee; (*Pol*) junta; (*Tec*) joint. **~ar** *vt* join; (*reunir*) collect. **~arse** *vpr* join; (gente) meet. **~o** *adj* joined; (*en plural*) together. **~o a** next to. **~ura** *f* joint
jura|do *adj* sworn. • *m* jury; (*miembro de jurado*) juror. **~mento** *m* oath. **prestar ~mento** take an oath. **~r** *vt/i* swear. **~r en falso** commit perjury. **jurárselas a uno** have it in for s.o.
jurel *m* (type of) mackerel
jurídico *adj* legal
juris|dicción *f* jurisdiction. **~prudencia** *f* jurisprudence
justamente *adj* exactly; (*con justicia*) fairly
justicia *f* justice
justifica|ción *f* justification. **~r** [7] *vt* justify
justo *adj* fair, just; (*exacto*) exact; (ropa) tight. • *adv* just. **~ a tiempo** just in time
juven|il *adj* youthful. **~tud** *f* youth; (*gente joven*) young people
juzga|do *m* (*tribunal*) court. **~r** [12] *vt* judge. **a ~r por** judging by

Kk

kilo *m*, **kilogramo** *m* kilo, kilogram
kil|ometraje *m* distance in kilometres, mileage. **~ométrico** *adj* [I] endless. **~ómetro** *m* kilometre. **~ómetro cuadrado** square kilometre
kilovatio *m* kilowatt
kiosco *m* kiosk

Ll

la *artículo definido femenino* (*pl* **las**)
····> the. **la flor azul** the blue flower. **la casa de al lado** the house next door. **cerca de la iglesia** near the church *No se traduce en los siguientes casos:*
····> (*con nombre abstracto, genérico*) **la paciencia es una virtud** patience is a virtue. **odio la leche** I hate milk. **la madera es muy versátil** wood is very versatile
····> (*con algunas instituciones*)

termino la universidad mañana I finish university tomorrow. **no va nunca a la iglesia** he never goes to church. **está en la cárcel** he's in jail

....➤ (*con nombres propios*) **la Sra. Díaz** Mrs Díaz. **la doctora Lara** doctor Lara

....➤ (*con partes del cuerpo, artículos personales*) *se traduce por un posesivo.* **apretó la mano** he clenched his fist. **tienes la camisa desabrochada** your shirt is undone

....➤ **la + de. es la de Ana** it's Ana's. **la del sombrero** the one with the hat

....➤ **la + que** (*persona*) **la que me atendió** the one who served me. (*cosa*) **la que se rompió** the one that broke

....➤ **la + que** + *subjuntivo* (*quienquiera*) whoever. **la que gane pasará a la final** whoever wins will go to the final. (*cualquiera*) whichever. **compra la que sea más barata** buy whichever is cheaper

laberinto *m* labyrinth, maze

labia *f* gift of the gab

labio *m* lip

labor *f* work. **~es de aguja** needlework. **~es de ganchillo** crochet. **~es de punto** knitting. **~es domésticas** housework. **~able** *adj* working. **~ar** *vi* work

laboratorio *m* laboratory

laborioso *adj* laborious

laborista *adj* Labour. • *m & f* member of the Labour Party

labra|do *adj* worked; (madera) carved; (metal) wrought; (tierra) ploughed. **~dor** *m* farmer; (*obrero*) farm labourer. **~nza** *f* farming. **~r** *vt* work; carve (madera); cut (piedra); till (la tierra). **~rse** *vpr.* **~rse un porvenir** carve out a future for o.s.

labriego *m* peasant

laca *f* lacquer

lacayo *m* lackey

lacio *adj* straight; (*flojo*) limp

lacón *m* shoulder of pork

lacónico *adj* laconic

lacr|ar *vt* seal. **~e** *m* sealing wax

lactante *adj* (niño) still on milk

lácteo *adj* milky. **productos** *mpl* **~s** dairy products

ladear *vt* tilt. **~se** *vpr* lean

ladera *f* slope

ladino *adj* astute

lado *m* side. **al ~** near. **al ~ de** next to, beside. **de ~** sideways. **en todos ~s** everywhere. **los de al ~** the next door neighbours. **por otro ~** on the other hand. **por todos ~s** everywhere. **por un ~** on the one hand

ladr|ar *vi* bark. **~ido** *m* bark

ladrillo *m* brick

ladrón *m* thief, robber; (*de casas*) burglar

lagart|ija *f* (small) lizard. **~o** *m* lizard

lago *m* lake

lágrima *f* tear

lagrimoso *adj* tearful

laguna *f* small lake; (*fig, omisión*) gap

laico *adj* lay

lament|able *adj* deplorable; (*que da pena*) pitiful; (pérdida) sad. **~ar** *vt* be sorry about. **~arse** *vpr* lament; (*quejarse*) complain. **~o** *m* moan

l

lamer *vt* lick

lámina *f* sheet; (*ilustración*) plate; (*estampa*) picture card

lamina|do *adj* laminated. **~r** *vt* laminate

lámpara *f* lamp. **~ de pie** standard lamp

lamparón *m* stain

lampiño *adj* beardless; (cuerpo) hairless

lana *f* wool. **de ~** wool(len)

lanceta *f* lancet

lancha *f* boat. **~ motora** motor boat. **~ salvavidas** lifeboat

langost|a *f* (*de mar*) lobster; (*insecto*) locust. **~ino** *m* king prawn

languide|cer 11 *vi* languish. **~z** *f* languor

lánguido *adj* languid; (*decaído*) listless

lanilla *f* nap; (*tela fina*) flannel

lanudo *adj* woolly; (perro) shaggy

lanza *f* lance, spear

lanza|llamas *m invar* flame-thrower. **~miento** *m* throw; (*acción de lanzar*) throwing; (*de proyectil, de producto*) launch. **~miento de peso**, (*LAm*) **~miento de bala** shot put. **~r** 10 *vt* throw; (*de un avión*) drop; launch (proyectil, producto). **~rse** *vpr* throw o.s.

lapicero *m* (propelling) pencil

lápida *f* tombstone; (*placa conmemorativa*) memorial tablet

lapidar *vt* stone

lápiz *m* pencil. **~ de labios** lipstick. **a ~** in pencil

lapso *m* lapse

laptop *m* laptop

larg|a *f*. **a la ~a** in the long run. **dar ~as** put off. **~ar** 12 *vt* (*Naut*) let out; (*fam, dar*) give; Ⓘ deal (bofetada etc). **~arse** *vpr* Ⓘ beat it Ⓘ. **~o** *adj* long. • *m* length. **¡~o!** go away! **a lo ~o** lengthwise. **a lo ~o de** along. **tener 100 metros de ~o** be 100 metres long

laring|e *f* larynx. **~itis** *f* laryngitis

larva *f* larva

las *artículo definido fpl* the. *véase tb* **LA**. • *pron* them. **~ de** those, the ones. **~ de Vd** your ones, yours. **~ que** whoever, the ones

láser *m* laser

lástima *f* pity; (*queja*) complaint. **da ~ verlo así** it's sad to see him like that. **ella me da ~** I feel sorry for her. **¡qué ~!** what a pity!

lastim|ado *adj* hurt. **~ar** *vt* hurt. **~arse** *vpr* hurt o.s. **~ero** *adj* doleful. **~oso** *adj* pitiful

lastre *m* ballast; (*fig*) burden

lata *f* tinplate; (*envase*) tin (*esp Brit*), can; (*fam, molestia*) nuisance. **dar la ~** be a nuisance. **¡qué ~!** what a nuisance!

latente *adj* latent

lateral *adj* side, lateral

latido *m* beating; (*cada golpe*) beat

latifundio *m* large estate

latigazo *m* (*golpe*) lash; (*chasquido*) crack

látigo *m* whip

latín *m* Latin. **saber ~** Ⓘ know what's what Ⓘ

latino *adj* Latin. **L~américa** *f* Latin America. **~americano** *adj* & *m* Latin American

latir *vi* beat; (herida) throb

latitud *f* latitude

latón *m* brass

latoso *adj* annoying; (*pesado*) boring

laúd *m* lute

laureado *adj* honoured; (*premiado*) prize-winning

laurel *m* laurel; (*Culin*) bay

lava *f* lava

lava|ble *adj* washable. **~bo** *m* wash-basin; (*retrete*) toilet. **~dero** *m* sink. **~do** *m* washing. **~do de cerebro** brainwashing. **~do en seco** dry-cleaning. **~dora** *f* washing machine. **~ndería** *f* laundry. **~ndería automática** launderette, laundromat (*esp Amer*). **~platos** *m & f invar* dishwasher. ● *m* (*Mex, fregadero*) sink. **~r** *vt* wash. **~r en seco** dry-clean. **~rse** *vpr* have a wash. **~rse las manos** (*incl fig*) wash one's hands. **~tiva** *f* enema. **~vajillas** *m invar* dishwasher; (*detergente*) washing-up liquid (*Brit*), dishwashing liquid (*Amer*)

laxante *adj & m* laxative

lazada *f* bow

lazarillo *m* guide for a blind person

lazo *m* knot; (*lazada*) bow; (*fig, vínculo*) tie; (*con nudo corredizo*) lasso; (*Mex, cuerda*) rope

le *pron* (*acusativo, él*) him; (*acusativo, Vd*) you; (*dativo, él*) (to) him; (*dativo, ella*) (to) her; (*dativo, cosa*) (to) it; (*dativo, Vd*) (to) you

leal *adj* loyal; (*fiel*) faithful. **~tad** *f* loyalty; (*fidelidad*) faithfulness

lección *f* lesson

leche *f* milk; (*golpe*) bash. **~ condensada** condensed milk. **~ desnatada** skimmed milk. **~ en polvo** powdered milk. **~ sin desnatar** whole milk. **tener mala ~** be spiteful. **~ra** *f* (*vasija*) milk jug. **~ría** *f* dairy. **~ro** *adj* milk, dairy. ● *m* milkman

lecho *m* (*en literatura*) bed. **~ de río** river bed

lechoso *adj* milky

lechuga *f* lettuce

lechuza *f* owl

lect|or *m* reader; (*Univ*) language assistant. **~ura** *f* reading

leer 18 *vt/i* read

legación *f* legation

legado *m* legacy; (*enviado*) legate

legajo *m* bundle, file

legal *adj* legal. **~idad** *f* legality. **~izar** 10 *vt* legalize; (*certificar*) authenticate. **~mente** *adv* legally

legar 12 *vt* bequeath

legible *adj* legible

legi|ón *f* legion. **~onario** *m* legionary. **~onella** *f* legionnaire's disease

legisla|ción *f* legislation. **~dor** *m* legislator. **~r** *vi* legislate. **~tura** *f* term (of office); (*año parlamentario*) session; (*LAm, cuerpo*) legislature

leg|itimidad *f* legitimacy. **~ítimo** *adj* legitimate; (*verdadero*) real

lego *adj* lay; (*ignorante*) ignorant ● *m* layman

legua *f* league

legumbre *f* vegetable

lejan|ía *f* distance. **~o** *adj* distant

lejía *f* bleach

lejos *adv* far. **~ de** far from. **a lo ~** in the distance. **desde ~** from a distance, from afar

lema *m* motto

lencería *f* linen; (*de mujer*) lingerie

lengua *f* tongue; (*idioma*) language. **irse de la ~** talk too much. **morderse la ~** hold one's tongue

lenguas cooficiales The regional languages of Spain, *catalán*, *euskera* and *gallego*, which now have equal status with Castilian in the regions where they are spoken. Banned under Franco, they continued to be spoken privately. They are now widely used in public life, education, the media, cinema and literature.

lenguado *m* sole
lenguaje *m* language
lengüeta *f* (*de zapato*) tongue. **~da** *f*, **~zo** *m* lick
lente *f* lens. **~s** *mpl* glasses. **~s de contacto** contact lenses
lentej|a *f* lentil. **~uela** *f* sequin
lentilla *f* contact lens
lent|itud *f* slowness. **~o** *adj* slow
leñ|a *f* firewood. **~ador** *m* woodcutter. **~o** *m* log
Leo *m* Leo
le|ón *m* lion. **~ona** *f* lioness
leopardo *m* leopard
leotardo *m* thick tights
lepr|a *f* leprosy. **~oso** *m* leper
lerdo *adj* dim; (*torpe*) clumsy
les *pron* (*acusativo*) them; (*acusativo, Vds*) you; (*dativo*) (to) them; (*dativo, Vds*) (to) you
lesbiana *f* lesbian
lesi|ón *f* wound. **~onado** *adj* injured. **~onar** *vt* injure; (*dañar*) damage
letal *adj* lethal
let|árgico *adj* lethargic. **~argo** *m* lethargy
letr|a *f* letter; (*escritura*) handwriting; (*de una canción*) words, lyrics. **~a de cambio** bill of exchange. **~a de imprenta** print. **~ado** *adj* learned. **~ero** *m* notice; (*cartel*) poster
letrina *f* latrine
leucemia *f* leukaemia
levadura *f* yeast. **~ en polvo** baking powder
levanta|miento *m* lifting; (*sublevación*) uprising. **~r** *vt* raise, lift; (*construir*) build; (*recoger*) pick up. **~rse** *vpr* get up; (*ponerse de pie*) stand up; (*erguirse, sublevarse*) rise up
levante *m* east; (*viento*) east wind
levar *vt.* **~ anclas** weigh anchor
leve *adj* light; (sospecha etc) slight; (enfermedad) mild; (*de poca importancia*) trivial. **~dad** *f* lightness; (*fig*) slightness
léxico *m* vocabulary
lexicografía *f* lexicography
ley *f* law; (*parlamentaria*) act
leyenda *f* legend
liar 20 *vt* tie; (*envolver*) wrap up; roll (cigarrillo); (*fig, confundir*) confuse; (*fig, enredar*) involve. **~se** *vpr* get involved
libanés *adj* & *m* Lebanese
libelo *m* (*escrito*) libellous article; (*Jurid*) petition
libélula *f* dragonfly
libera|ción *f* liberation. **~dor** *adj* liberating. ● *m* liberator
liberal *adj* & *m* & *f* liberal. **~idad** *f* liberality
liber|ar *vt* free. **~tad** *f* freedom. **~tad de cultos** freedom of worship. **~tad de imprenta** freedom of the press. **~tad provisional** bail. **en ~tad** free. **~tador** *m* liberator. **~tar** *vt* free
libertino *m* libertine
libido *f* libido
libio *adj* & *m* Libyan

libra *f* pound. ~ **esterlina** pound sterling

Libra *m* Libra

libra|dor *m* (*Com*) drawer. **~r** *vt* free; (*de un peligro*) save. **~rse** *vpr* free o.s. **~rse de** get rid of

libre *adj* free. **estilo ~** (*en natación*) freestyle. **~ de impuestos** tax-free

librea *f* livery

libr|ería *f* bookshop (*Brit*), bookstore (*Amer*); (*mueble*) bookcase. **~ero** *m* bookseller; (*Mex, mueble*) bookcase. **~eta** *f* notebook. **~o** *m* book. **~o de bolsillo** paperback. **~o de ejercicios** exercise book. **~o de reclamaciones** complaints book

licencia *f* permission; (*documento*) licence. **~do** *m* graduate; (*Mex, abogado*) lawyer. **~ para manejar** (*Mex*) driving licence. **~r** *vt* (*Mil*) discharge; (*echar*) dismiss. **~tura** *f* degree

licencioso *adj* licentious

licitar *vt* bid for

lícito *adj* legal; (*permisible*) permissible

licor *m* liquor; (*dulce*) liqueur

licua|dora *f* blender. **~r** 21 liquefy; (*Culin*) blend

lid *f* fight. **en buena ~** by fair means. **~es** *fpl* matters

líder *m* leader

liderato *m*, **liderazgo** *m* leadership

lidia *f* bullfighting; (*lucha*) fight. **~r** *vt/i* fight

liebre *f* hare

lienzo *m* linen; (*del pintor*) canvas; (*muro, pared*) wall

liga *f* garter; (*alianza*) league; (*LAm, gomita*) rubber band. **~dura** *f* bond; (*Mus*) slur; (*Med*) ligature. **~mento** *m* ligament. **~r** 12 *vt* bind; (*atar*) tie; (*Mus*) slur. ● *vi* mix. **~r con** (*fig*) pick up. **~rse** *vpr* (*fig*) commit o.s.

liger|eza *f* lightness; (*agilidad*) agility; (*rapidez*) swiftness; (*de carácter*) fickleness. **~o** *adj* light; (*rápido*) quick; (*ágil*) agile; (*superficial*) superficial; (*de poca importancia*) slight. ● *adv* quickly. **a la ~a** lightly, superficially

liguero *m* suspender belt

lija *f* dogfish; (*papel de lija*) sandpaper. **~r** *vt* sand

lila *f* lilac. ● *m* (*color*) lilac

lima *f* file; (*fruta*) lime. **~duras** *fpl* filings. **~r** *vt* file (down)

limita|ción *f* limitation. **~do** *adj* limited. **~r** *vt* limit. **~r con** border on. **~tivo** *adj* limiting

límite *m* limit. **~ de velocidad** speed limit

limítrofe *adj* bordering

lim|ón *m* lemon; (*Mex*) lime. **~onada** *f* lemonade

limosn|a *f* alms. **pedir ~a** beg. **~ear** *vi* beg

limpia|botas *m invar* bootblack. **~parabrisas** *m invar* windscreen wiper (*Brit*), windshield wiper (*Amer*). **~pipas** *m invar* pipe-cleaner. **~r** *vt* clean; (*enjugar*) wipe. **~vidrios** *m invar* (*LAm*) window cleaner

limpi|eza *f* cleanliness; (*acción de limpiar*) cleaning. **~eza en seco** dry-cleaning. **~o** *adj* clean; (cielo) clear; (*fig, honrado*) honest; (*neto*) net. **pasar a ~o**, (*LAm*) **pasar en ~o** make a fair copy. ● *adv* fairly. **jugar ~o** play fair

linaje *m* lineage; (*fig, clase*) kind

lince *m* lynx

linchar *vt* lynch

lind|ar *vi* border (**con** on). **~e** *f*

boundary. **~ero** *m* border
lindo *adj* pretty, lovely. **de lo ~** ⓘ a lot
línea *f* line. **en ~** online. **en ~s generales** broadly speaking. **guardar la ~** watch one's figure
lingote *m* ingot
lingü|ista *m & f* linguist. **~ística** *f* linguistics. **~ístico** *adj* linguistic
lino *m* flax; (*tela*) linen
linterna *f* lantern; (*de bolsillo*) torch, flashlight (*Amer*)
lío *m* bundle; (*jaleo*) fuss; (*embrollo*) muddle; (*amorío*) affair
liquida|ción *f* liquidation; (*venta especial*) sale. **~r** *vt* liquify; (*Com*) liquidate; settle (cuenta)
líquido *adj* liquid; (*Com*) net. ● *m* liquid; (*Com*) cash
lira *f* lyre; (*moneda italiana*) lira
líric|a *f* lyric poetry. **~o** *adj* lyric(al)
lirio *m* iris
lirón *m* dormouse; (*fig*) sleepyhead. **dormir como un ~** sleep like a log
lisiado *adj* crippled
liso *adj* smooth; (pelo) straight; (tierra) flat; (*sencillo*) plain
lisonj|a *f* flattery. **~eador** *adj* flattering. ● *m* flatterer. **~ear** *vt* flatter. **~ero** *adj* flattering
lista *f* stripe; (*enumeración*) list. **~ de correos** poste restante. **a ~s** striped. **pasar ~** take the register. **~do** *adj* striped
listo *adj* clever; (*preparado*) ready
listón *m* strip; (*en saltos*) bar; (*Mex, cinta*) ribbon
litera *f* (*en barco, tren*) berth; (*en habitación*) bunk bed
literal *adj* literal
litera|rio *adj* literary. **~tura** *f* literature
litig|ar ⓬ *vi* dispute; (*Jurid*) litigate. **~io** *m* dispute; (*Jurid*) litigation
litografía *f* (*arte*) lithography; (*cuadro*) lithograph
litoral *adj* coastal. ● *m* coast
litro *m* litre
lituano *adj & m* Lithuanian
liturgia *f* liturgy
liviano *adj* fickle; (*LAm, de poco peso*) light
lívido *adj* livid
llaga *f* wound; (*úlcera*) ulcer
llama *f* flame; (*animal*) llama
llamada *f* call
llama|do *adj* called. ●*m* (*LAm*) call. **~miento** *m* call. **~r** *vt* call; (*por teléfono*) phone. ● *vi* call; (*golpear en la puerta*) knock; (*tocar el timbre*) ring. **~r por teléfono** phone, telephone. **~rse** *vpr* be called. **¿cómo te ~s?** what's your name?
llamarada *f* sudden blaze; (*fig, de pasión etc*) outburst
llamativo *adj* flashy; (color) loud; (persona) striking
llamear *vi* blaze
llano *adj* flat, level; (persona) natural; (*sencillo*) plain. ● *m* plain
llanta *f* (*Auto*) (wheel) rim; (*LAm, neumático*) tyre
llanto *m* crying
llanura *f* plain
llave *f* key; (*para tuercas*) spanner; (*LAm, del baño etc*) tap (*Brit*), faucet (*Amer*); (*Elec*) switch. **~ inglesa** monkey wrench. **cerrar con ~** lock. **echar la ~** lock up. **~ro** *m* key-ring
llega|da *f* arrival. **~r** ⓬ *vi* arrive, come; (*alcanzar*) reach; (*bastar*) be enough. **~r a** (*conseguir*) manage

to. ~**r a saber** find out. ~**r a ser** become. ~**r hasta** go as far as

llen|ar *vt* fill (up); (*rellenar*) fill in; (*cubrir*) cover (**de** with). ~**o** *adj* full. • *m* (*en el teatro etc*) full house. **de** ~ entirely

lleva|dero *adj* tolerable. ~**r** *vt* carry; (*inducir, conducir*) lead; (*acompañar*) take; wear (ropa). **¿cuánto tiempo** ~**s aquí?** how long have you been here? **llevo 3 años estudiando inglés** I've been studying English for 3 years. ~**rse** *vpr* take away; win (premio etc); (*comprar*) take. ~**rse bien** get on well together

llor|ar *vi* cry; (ojos) water. ~**iquear** *vi* whine. ~**iqueo** *m* whining. ~**o** *m* crying. ~**ón** *adj* whining. • *m* cry-baby. ~**oso** *adj* tearful

llov|er **2** *vi* rain. ~**izna** *f* drizzle. ~**iznar** *vi* drizzle

llueve *vb véase* **LLOVER**

lluvi|a *f* rain; (*fig*) shower. ~**oso** *adj* rainy; (clima) wet

lo *artículo definido neutro*. ~ **importante** what is important, the important thing. • *pron* (*él*) him; (*cosa*) it. ~ **que** what, that which

loa *f* praise. ~**ble** *adj* praiseworthy. ~**r** *vt* praise

lobo *m* wolf

lóbrego *adj* gloomy

lóbulo *m* lobe

local *adj* local. • *m* premises. ~**idad** *f* locality; (*de un espectáculo*) seat; (*entrada*) ticket. ~**izador** *m* pager; (*de reserva*) booking reference. ~**izar** **10** *vt* find, locate

loción *f* lotion

loco *adj* mad, crazy. • *m* lunatic. ~ **de alegría** mad with joy. **estar** ~ **por** be crazy about. **volverse** ~ go mad

locomo|ción *f* locomotion. ~**tora** *f* locomotive

locuaz *adj* talkative

locución *f* expression

locura *f* madness; (*acto*) crazy thing. **con** ~ madly

locutor *m* broadcaster

lod|azal *m* quagmire. ~**o** *m* mud

lógic|a *f* logic. ~**o** *adj* logical

logr|ar *vt* get; win (premio). ~ **hacer** manage to do. ~**o** *m* achievement; (*de premio*) winning; (*éxito*) success

loma *f* small hill

lombriz *f* worm

lomo *m* back; (*de libro*) spine. ~ **de cerdo** loin of pork

lona *f* canvas

loncha *f* slice; (*de tocino*) rasher

londinense *adj* from London. • *m* Londoner

Londres *m* London

loneta *f* thin canvas

longaniza *f* sausage

longev|idad *f* longevity. ~**o** *adj* long-lived

longitud *f* length; (*en geografía*) longitude

lonja *f* slice; (*de tocino*) rasher; (*Com*) market

loro *m* parrot

los *artículo definido mpl* the. *véase tb* **EL**. • *pron* them. ~ **de Antonio** Antonio's. ~ **que** whoever, the ones

losa *f* (*baldosa*) flagstone. ~ **sepulcral** tombstone

lote *m* share; (*de productos*) batch; (*terreno*) plot (*Brit*), lot (*Amer*)

lotería *f* lottery

loto *m* lotus

loza *f* crockery; (*fina*) china
lozano *adj* fresh; (vegetación) lush; (persona) healthy-looking
lubina *f* sea bass
lubrica|nte *adj* lubricating. ● *m* lubricant. **~r** 7 *vt* lubricate
lucero *m* bright star. **~ del alba** morning star
lucha *f* fight; (*fig*) struggle. **~dor** *m* fighter. **~r** *vi* fight; (*fig*) struggle
lucid|ez *f* lucidity. **~o** *adj* splendid
lúcido *adj* lucid
luciérnaga *f* glow-worm
lucimiento *m* brilliance
lucio *m* pike
lucir 11 *vt* (*fig*) show off. ● *vi* shine; (joya) sparkle; (*LAm, mostrarse*) look. **~se** *vpr* (*fig*) shine, excel; (*presumir*) show off
lucr|ativo *adj* lucrative. **~o** *m* gain
luego *adv* then; (*más tarde*) later (on); (*Mex, pronto*) soon. ● *conj* therefore. **~ que** as soon as. **desde ~** of course
lugar *m* place; (*espacio libre*) room. **~ común** cliché. **dar ~ a** give rise to. **en ~ de** instead of. **en primer ~** first. **hacer ~** make room. **tener ~** take place. **~eño** *adj* local, village
lugarteniente *m* deputy
lúgubre *adj* gloomy
lujo *m* luxury. **~so** *adj* luxurious. **de ~** luxury
lumbago *m* lumbago
lumbre *f* fire; (*luz*) light
luminoso *adj* luminous; (*fig*) bright; (letrero) illuminated
luna *f* moon; (*espejo*) mirror. **~ de miel** honeymoon. **claro de ~** moonlight. **estar en la ~** be miles away. **~r** *adj* lunar. ● *m* mole; (*en tela*) spot
lunes *m invar* Monday
lupa *f* magnifying glass
lustr|abotas *m invar* (*LAm*) bootblack. **~ar** *vt* shine, polish. **~e** *m* shine; (*fig, esplendor*) splendour. **dar ~e a, sacar ~e a** polish. **~oso** *adj* shining
luto *m* mourning. **estar de ~** be in mourning
luz *f* light; (*electricidad*) electricity. **luces altas** (*LAm*) headlights on full beam. **luces bajas** (*LAm*), **luces cortas** dipped headlights. **luces antiniebla** fog light. **luces largas** headlights on full beam. **a la ~ de** in the light of. **a todas luces** obviously. **dar a ~** give birth. **hacer la ~ sobre** shed light on. **sacar a la ~** bring to light

Mm

macabro *adj* macabre
macaco *m* macaque (monkey)
macanudo *adj* [I] great [I]
macarrones *mpl* macaroni
macerar *vt* macerate (fruta); marinade (carne etc)
maceta *f* mallet; (*tiesto*) flowerpot
machacar 7 *vt* crush. ● *vi* go on (**sobre** about)
machamartillo. **a ~** *adj* ardent; (*como adv*) firmly
machet|azo *m* blow with a machete; (*herida*) wound from a machete. **~e** *m* machete
mach|ista *m* male chauvinist. **~o** *adj* male; (*varonil*) macho

machu|car 7 *vt* bruise; (*aplastar*) crush. **~cón** *m* (*LAm*) bruise
macizo *adj* solid. • *m* mass; (*de plantas*) bed
madeja *f* skein
madera *m* (*vino*) Madeira. • *f* wood; (*naturaleza*) nature. **~ble** *adj* yielding timber. **~men** *m* woodwork
madero *m* log; (*de construcción*) timber
madona *f* Madonna
madr|astra *f* stepmother. **~e** *f* mother. **~eperla** *f* mother-of-pearl. **~eselva** *f* honeysuckle
madrigal *m* madrigal
madriguera *f* den; (*de conejo*) burrow
madrileño *adj* of Madrid. • *m* person from Madrid
madrina *f* godmother; (*en una boda*) matron of honour
madrug|ada *f* dawn. **de ~ada** at dawn. **~ador** *adj* who gets up early. • *m* early riser. **~ar** 12 *vi* get up early
madur|ación *f* maturing; (*de fruta*) ripening. **~ar** *vt/i* mature; (fruta) ripen. **~ez** *f* maturity; (*de fruta*) ripeness. **~o** *adj* mature; (fruta) ripe
maestr|ía *f* skill; (*Univ*) master's degree. **~o** *m* master; (*de escuela*) schoolteacher
mafia *f* mafia
magdalena *f* fairy cake (*Brit*), cup cake (*Amer*)
magia *f* magic
mágico *adj* magic; (*maravilloso*) magical
magist|erio *m* teaching (profession); (*conjunto de maestros*) teachers. **~rado** *m* magistrate; (*juez*) judge. **~ral** *adj* teaching; (*bien hecho*) masterly. **~ratura** *f* magistracy
magn|animidad *f* magnanimity. **~ánimo** *adj* magnanimous. **~ate** *m* magnate, tycoon
magnavoz *m* (*Mex*) megaphone
magnético *adj* magnetic
magneti|smo *m* magnetism. **~zar** 10 *vt* magnetize
magn|ificar *vt* extol; (*LAm*) magnify (objeto). **~ificencia** *f* magnificence. **~ífico** *adj* magnificent. **~itud** *f* magnitude
magnolia *f* magnolia
mago *m* magician; (*en cuentos*) wizard
magro *adj* lean; (tierra) poor
magulla|dura *f* bruise. **~r** *vt* bruise. **~rse** *vpr* bruise
mahometano *adj* Islamic
maíz *m* maize, corn (*Amer*)
majada *f* sheepfold; (*estiércol*) manure; (*LAm*) flock of sheep
majader|ía *f* silly thing. **~o** *m* idiot. • *adj* stupid
majest|ad *f* majesty. **~uoso** *adj* majestic
majo *adj* nice
mal *adv* badly; (*poco*) poorly; (*difícilmente*) hardly; (*equivocadamente*) wrongly; (*desagradablemente*) bad. • *adj*. **estar ~** be ill; (*anímicamente*) be in a bad way; (*incorrecto*) be wrong. **estar ~ de** (*escaso de*) be short of. *véase tb* MALO. • *m* evil; (*daño*) harm; (*enfermedad*) illness. **~ que bien** somehow (or other). **de ~ en peor** from bad to worse. **hacer ~ en** be wrong to. **¡menos ~!** thank goodness!
malabaris|mo *m* juggling. **~ta** *m & f* juggler
mala|consejado *adj* ill-advised.

m

~**costumbrado** *adj* spoilt. ~**crianza** (*LAm*) rudeness. ~**gradecido** *adj* ungrateful

malagueño *adj* of Málaga. • *m* person from Málaga

malaria *f* malaria

Malasia *f* Malaysia

malavenido *adj* incompatible

malaventura *adj* unfortunate

malayo *adj* Malay(an)

malbaratar *vt* sell off cheap; (*malgastar*) squander

malcarado *adj* nasty looking

malcriado *adj* (niño) spoilt

maldad *f* evil; (*acción*) wicked thing

maldecir 46 (*pero imperativo* **maldice**, *futuro y condicional regulares, pp* **maldecido** *o* **maldito**) *vt* curse. • *vi* curse; speak ill (**de** of)

m

maldi|ciente *adj* backbiting; (*que blasfema*) foul-mouthed. ~**ción** *f* curse. ~**to** *adj* damned. **¡~to sea!** damn (it)!

maleab|ilidad *f* malleability. ~**le** *adj* malleable

malea|nte *m* criminal. ~**r** *vt* damage; (*pervertir*) corrupt. ~**rse** *vpr* be spoilt; (*pervertirse*) be corrupted

malecón *m* breakwater; (*embarcadero*) jetty; (*Rail*) embankment; (*LAm, paseo marítimo*) seafront

maledicencia *f* slander

mal|eficio *m* curse. ~**éfico** *adj* evil

malestar *m* discomfort; (*fig*) uneasiness

malet|a *f* (suit)case. **hacer la ~a** pack (one's case). ~**ero** *m* porter; (*Auto*) boot, trunk (*Amer*). ~**ín** *m* small case; (*para documentos*) briefcase

mal|evolencia *f* malevolence. ~**évolo** *adj* malevolent

maleza *f* weeds; (*matorral*) undergrowth

mal|gastar *vt* waste. ~**hablado** *adj* foul-mouthed. ~**hechor** *m* criminal. ~**humorado** *adj* bad-tempered

malici|a *f* malice; (*picardía*) mischief. ~**arse** *vpr* suspect. ~**oso** *adj* malicious; (*pícaro*) mischievous

maligno *adj* malignant; (persona) evil

malintencionado *adj* malicious

malla *f* mesh; (*de armadura*) mail; (*de gimnasia*) leotard

Mallorca *f* Majorca

mallorquín *adj* & *m* Majorcan

malmirado *adj* (*con estar*) frowned upon

malo *adj* (*delante de nombre masculino en singular* **mal**) bad; (*enfermo*) ill. **~ de** difficult to. **estar de malas** (*malhumorado*) be in a bad mood; (*LAm, con mala suerte*) be out of luck. **lo ~ es que** the trouble is that. **por las malas** by force

malogr|ar *vt* waste; (*estropear*) spoil. ~**arse** *vpr* fall through

maloliente *adj* smelly

malpensado *adj* nasty, malicious

malsano *adj* unhealthy

malsonante *adj* ill-sounding; (*grosero*) offensive

malt|a *f* malt. ~**eada** *f* (*LAm*) milk shake. ~**ear** *vt* malt

maltr|atar *vt* ill-treat; (*pegar*) batter; mistreat (juguete etc). ~**echo** *adj* battered

malucho *adj* I under the weather

malva *f* mallow. **(color de) ~** *adj invar* mauve

malvado *adj* wicked
malvavisco *m* marshmallow
malversa|ción *f* embezzlement. **~dor** *adj* embezzling. • *m* embezzler. **~r** *vt* embezzle
Malvinas *fpl*. **las (islas) ~** the Falklands, the Falkland Islands
mama *f* mammary gland; (*de mujer*) breast
mamá *f* mum; (*usado por niños*) mummy
mama|da *f* sucking. **~r** *vt* suck; (*fig*) grow up with. • *vi* (bebé) feed; (animal) suckle. **dar de ~** breastfeed
mamario *adj* mammary
mamarracho *m* clown; (*cosa ridícula*) (ridiculous) sight; (*cosa mal hecha*) botch; (*cosa fea*) mess. **ir hecho un ~** look a sight
mameluco *m* (*LAm*) overalls; (*de niño*) rompers
mamífero *adj* mammalian. • *m* mammal
mamila *f* (*Mex*) feeding bottle
mamotreto *m* (*libro*) hefty volume; (*armatoste*) huge thing
mampara *f* screen
mampostería *f* masonry
mamut *m* mammoth
manada *f* herd; (*de lobos*) pack; (*de leones*) pride. **en ~** in crowds
mana|ntial *m* spring; (*fig*) source. **~r** *vi* flow; (*fig*) abound. • *vt* drip with
manaza *f* big hand
mancha *f* stain; (*en la piel*) blotch. **~do** *adj* stained; (*sucio*) dirty; (animal) spotted. **~r** *vt* stain; (*ensuciar*) dirty. **~rse** *vpr* get stained; (*ensuciarse*) get dirty
manchego *adj* of la Mancha. • *m* person from la Mancha
manchón *m* large stain
mancilla *f* blemish. **~r** *vt* stain
manco *adj* (*de una mano*) one-handed; (*de las dos manos*) handless; (*de un brazo*) one-armed; (*de los dos brazos*) armless
mancomun|adamente *adv* jointly. **~ar** *vt* unite; (*Jurid*) make jointly liable. **~arse** *vpr* unite. **~idad** *f* union
manda *f* (*Mex*) religious offering
manda|dero *m* messenger. **~do** *m* (*LAm*) shopping; (*diligencia*) errand. **hacer los ~dos** (*LAm*) do the shopping. **~miento** *m* order; (*Relig*) commandment. **~r** *vt* order; (*enviar*) send; (*gobernar*) rule. • *vi* be in command. **¿mande?** (*Mex*) pardon?
mandarin|a *f* (*naranja*) mandarin (orange). **~o** *m* mandarin tree
mandat|ario *m* attorney; (*Pol*) head of state. **~o** *m* mandate; (*Pol*) term of office
mandíbula *f* jaw
mando *m* command. **~ a distancia** remote control. **al ~ de** in charge of. **altos ~s** *mpl* high-ranking officers
mandolina *f* mandolin
mandón *adj* bossy
manducar **7** *vt* **I** stuff oneself with
manecilla *f* hand
manej|able *adj* manageable. **~ar** *vt* use; handle (asunto etc); (*fig*) manage; (*LAm, conducir*) drive. **~arse** *vpr* get by. **~o** *m* handling. **~os** *mpl* scheming
manera *f* way. **~s** *fpl* manners. **de alguna ~** somehow. **de ~ que** so (that). **de ninguna ~** by no means. **de otra ~** otherwise. **de todas ~s** anyway

manga *f* sleeve; (*tubo de goma*) hose; (*red*) net; (*para colar*) filter; (*LAm, de langostas*) swarm
mango *m* handle; (*fruta*) mango. **~near** *vt* boss about. • *vi* (*entrometerse*) interfere
manguera *f* hose(pipe)
manguito *m* muff
maní *m* (*pl* **~es**) (*LAm*) peanut
manía *f* mania; (*antipatía*) dislike. **tener la ~ de** have an obsession with
maniaco *adj*, **maníaco** *adj* maniac(al). • *m* maniac
maniatar *vt* tie s.o.'s hands
maniático *adj* maniac(al); (*obsesivo*) obsessive; (*loco*) crazy; (*delicado*) finicky
manicomio *m* lunatic asylum
m **manicura** *f* manicure; (*mujer*) manicurist
manido *adj* stale
manifesta|ción *f* manifestation, sign; (*Pol*) demonstration. **~nte** *m* demonstrator. **~r** 1 *vt* show; (*Pol*) state. **~rse** *vpr* show; (*Pol*) demonstrate
manifiesto *adj* clear; (error) obvious; (verdad) manifest. • *m* manifesto
manilargo *adj* light-fingered
manilla *f* (*de cajón etc*) handle; (*de reloj*) hand. **~r** *m* handlebar(s)
maniobra *f* manoeuvre. **~r** *vt* operate; (*Rail*) shunt. • *vt/i* manoeuvre. **~s** *fpl* (*Mil*) manoeuvres
manipula|ción *f* manipulation. **~r** *vt* manipulate
maniquí *m* dummy. • *m & f* model
mani|rroto *adj & m* spendthrift. **~ta** *f*, (*LAm*) **~to** *m* little hand
manivela *f* crank
manjar *m* delicacy
mano *f* hand; (*de animales*) front foot; (*de perros, gatos*) front paw. **~ de obra** work force. **¡~s arriba!** hands up! **a ~** by hand; (*próximo*) handy. **a ~ derecha** on the right. **de segunda ~** second hand. **echar una ~** lend a hand. **tener buena ~ para** be good at. • *m* (*LAm, fam*) mate (*Brit*), buddy (*Amer*)
manojo *m* bunch
manose|ar *vt* handle. **~o** *m* handling
manotada *f*, **manotazo** *m* slap
manote|ar *vi* gesticulate. **~o** *m* gesticulation
mansalva: **a ~** *adv* without risk
mansarda *f* attic
mansión *f* mansion. **~ señorial** stately home
manso *adj* gentle; (animal) tame
manta *f* blanket
mantec|a *f* fat. **~oso** *adj* greasy
mantel *m* tablecloth; (*del altar*) altar cloth. **~ería** *f* table linen
manten|er 40 *vt* support; (*conservar*) keep; (*sostener*) maintain. **~erse** *vpr* support o.s.; (*permanecer*) remain. **~se de/con** live off. **~imiento** *m* maintenance
mantequ|era *f* butter churn. **~illa** *f* butter
mant|illa *f* mantilla. **~o** *m* cloak. **~ón** *m* shawl
manual *adj & m* manual
manubrio *m* crank; (*LAm, de bicicleta*) handlebars
manufactura *f* manufacture. **~r** *vt* manufacture, make
manuscrito *adj* handwritten. • *m* manuscript
manutención *f* maintenance
manzana *f* apple; (*de edificios*)

block. **~r** *m* (*apple*) orchard. **~ de Adán** (*LAm*) Adam's apple

manzan|illa *f* camomile tea. ● *m* manzanilla, pale dry sherry. **~o** *m* apple tree

maña *f* skill. **~s** *fpl* cunning

mañan|a *f* morning. **~a por la ~a** tomorrow morning. **pasado ~a** the day after tomorrow. **en la ~a** (*LAm*), **por la ~a** in the morning. ● *m* future. ● *adv* tomorrow. **~ero** *adj* who gets up early. ● *m* early riser

mañoso *adj* clever; (*astuto*) crafty; (*LAm, caprichoso*) difficult

mapa *m* map

mapache *m* racoon

maqueta *f* scale model

maquiladora *f* (*Mex*) cross-border assembly plant

maquilla|je *m* make-up. **~r** *vt* make up. **~rse** *vpr* make up

máquina *f* machine; (*Rail*) engine. **~ de afeitar** shaver. **~ de escribir** typewriter. **~ fotográfica** camera

maquin|ación *f* machination. **~al** *adj* mechanical. **~aria** *f* machinery. **~ista** *m & f* operator; (*Rail*) engine driver

mar *m & f* sea. **alta ~** high seas. **la ~ de** [!] lots of

maraña *f* thicket; (*enredo*) tangle; (*embrollo*) muddle

maratón *m & f* marathon

maravill|a *f* wonder. **a las mil ~as**, **de ~as** marvellously. **contar/decir ~as de** speak wonderfully of. **hacer ~as** work wonders. **~ar** *vt* astonish. **~arse** *vpr* be astonished (**de** at). **~oso** *adj* marvellous, wonderful

marca *f* mark; (*de coches etc*) make; (*de alimentos, cosméticos*) brand; (*Deportes*) record. **~ de fábrica** trade mark. **de ~** brand name; (*fig*) excellent. **de ~ mayor** [!] absolute. **~do** *adj* marked. **~dor** *m* marker; (*Deportes*) scoreboard. **~r** [7] *vt* mark; (*señalar*) show; score (un gol); dial (número de teléfono). ● *vi* score

marcha *f* (*incl Mus*) march; (*Auto*) gear; (*desarrollo*) course; (*partida*) departure. **a toda ~** at full speed. **dar/hacer ~ atrás** put into reverse. **poner en ~** start; (*fig*) set in motion

marchante *m* (*f* **marchanta**) art dealer; (*Mex, en mercado*) stall holder

marchar *vi* go; (*funcionar*) work, go; (*Mil*) march. **~se** *vpr* leave

marchit|ar *vt* wither. **~arse** *vpr* wither. **~o** *adj* withered

marcial *adj* martial

marciano *adj & m* Martian

marco *m* frame; (*moneda alemana*) mark; (*deportes*) goal-posts

marea *f* tide. **~do** *adj* sick; (*en el mar*) seasick; (*aturdido*) dizzy; (*borracho*) drunk. **~r** *vt* make feel sick; (*aturdir*) make feel dizzy; (*confundir*) confuse. **~rse** *vpr* feel sick; (*en un barco*) get seasick; (*estar aturdido*) feel dizzy; (*irse la cabeza*) feel faint; (*emborracharse*) get slightly drunk; (*confundirse*) get confused

marejada *f* swell; (*fig*) wave

mareo *m* sickness; (*en el mar*) seasickness; (*aturdimiento*) dizziness; (*confusión*) muddle

marfil *m* ivory

margarina *f* margarine

margarita *f* daisy; (*cóctel*) margarita

marg|en *m* margin; (*de un ca-*

mino) side. ●*f* (*de un río*) bank. **~inado** *adj* excluded. ●*m* outcast. **al ~en** (*fig*) outside. **~inal** *adj* marginal. **~inar** *vt* (*excluir*) exclude; (*fijar márgenes*) set margins

mariachi *m* (*Mex*) (*música popular de Jalisco*) Mariachi music; (*conjunto*) Mariachi band; (*músico*) Mariachi musician

mariachi The word can mean the traditional Mexican musical ensemble, the musicians and the lively mestizo music they play. *Mariachis* wearing costumes based on those worn by *charros* can be seen in the Plaza Garibaldi, in Mexico City, where they are hired for parties, or to sing *mañanitas* or serenades.

m

maric|a *m* ⓘ sissy ⓘ. **~ón** *m* ⓘ homosexual, queer ⓘ; (*LAm, cobarde*) wimp

marido *m* husband

mariguana *f*, **marihuana** *f* marijuana

marimacho *f* mannish woman

marimba *f* (type of) drum (*LAm, especie de xilofón*) marimba

marin|a *f* navy; (*barcos*) fleet; (*cuadro*) seascape. **~a de guerra** navy. **~a mercante** merchant navy. **~ería** *f* seamanship; (*marineros*) sailors. **~ero** *adj* marine; (barco) seaworthy. ● *m* sailor. **a la ~era** in tomato and garlic sauce. **~o** *adj* marine

marioneta *f* puppet. **~s** *fpl* puppet show

maripos|a *f* butterfly. **~a nocturna** moth. **~ear** *vi* be fickle; (*galantear*) flirt. **~ón** *m* flirt

mariquita *f* ladybird (*Brit*), ladybug (*Amer*). ●*m* ⓘ sissy ⓘ

mariscador *m* shell-fisher

mariscal *m* marshal

maris|car *vt* fish for shellfish. **~co** *m* seafood, shellfish. **~quero** *m* (*pescador de mariscos*) seafood fisherman; (*vendedor de mariscos*) seafood seller

marital *adj* marital; (vida) married

marítimo *adj* maritime; (ciudad etc) coastal, seaside

marmita *f* cooking pot

mármol *m* marble

marmota *f* marmot

maroma *f* rope; (*Mex, voltereta*) somersault

marqu|és *m* marquess. **~esa** *f* marchioness.. **~esina** *f* glass canopy; (*en estadio*) roof

marran|a *f* sow. **~ada** *f* filthy thing; (*cochinada*) dirty trick. **~o** *adj* filthy. ● *m* hog

marrón *adj & m* brown

marroqu|í *adj & m & f* Moroccan. ● *m* (*leather*) morocco. **~inería** *f* leather goods

Marruecos *m* Morocco

marsopa *f* porpoise

marsupial *adj & m* marsupial

marta *f* marten

martajar *vt* (*Mex*) crush (maíz)

Marte *m* Mars

martes *m invar* Tuesday. **~ de carnaval** Shrove Tuesday

martill|ar *vt* hammer. **~azo** *m* blow with a hammer. **~ear** *vt* hammer. **~eo** *m* hammering. **~o** *m* hammer

martín *m* **pescador** kingfisher

martinete *m* (*del piano*) hammer; (*ave*) heron

martingala *f* (*ardid*) trick

mártir *m & f* martyr

martir|io *m* martyrdom; (*fig*) torment. **~izar** **10** *vt* martyr; (*fig*) torment, torture

marxis|mo *m* Marxism. **~ta** *adj & m & f* Marxist

marzo *m* March

más *adv & adj* (*comparativo*) more; (*superlativo*) most. **~ caro** dearer. **~ doloroso** more painful. **el ~ caro** the dearest; (*de dos*) the dearer. **el ~ curioso** the most curious; (*de dos*) the more curious. • *prep* plus. • *m* plus (sign). **~ bien** rather. **~ de** (*cantidad indeterminada*) more than. **~ o menos** more or less. **~ que** more than. **~ y ~** more and more. **a lo ~** at (the) most. **dos ~ dos** two plus two. **de ~** too many. **es ~** moreover. **nadie ~** nobody else. **no ~** no more

masa *f* mass; (*Culin*) dough. **en ~** en masse

masacre *f* massacre

masaj|e *m* massage. **~ear** *vt* massage. **~ista** *m* masseur. • *f* masseuse

mascada *f* (*Mex*) scarf

mascar **7** *vt* chew

máscara *f* mask

mascar|ada *f* masquerade. **~illa** *f* mask. **~ón** *m* (*Naut*) figurehead

mascota *f* mascot

masculin|idad *f* masculinity. **~o** *adj* masculine; (sexo) male. • *m* masculine

mascullar **3** *vt* mumble

masilla *f* putty

masivo *adj* massive, large-scale

mas|ón *m* Freemason. **~onería** *f* Freemasonry. **~ónico** *adj* Masonic

masoquis|mo *m* masochism. **~ta** *adj* masochistic. • *m & f* masochist

mastica|ción *f* chewing. **~r** **7** *vt* chew

mástil *m* (*Naut*) mast; (*de bandera*) flagpole; (*de guitarra, violín*) neck

mastín *m* mastiff

mastodonte *m* mastodon; (*fig*) giant

masturba|ción *f* masturbation. **~rse** *vpr* masturbate

mata *f* (*arbusto*) bush; (*LAm, planta*) plant

matad|ero *m* slaughterhouse. **~or** *adj* killing. • *m* (*torero*) matador

matamoscas *m invar* fly swatter

mata|nza *f* killing. **~r** *vt* kill (personas); slaughter (reses). **~rife** *m* butcher. **~rse** *vpr* kill o.s.; (*en un accidente*) be killed; (*Mex, para un examen*) cram. **~rse trabajando** work like mad

mata|polillas *m invar* moth killer. **~rratas** *m invar* rat poison

matasanos *m invar* quack

matasellos *m invar* postmark

mate *adj* matt. • *m* (*ajedrez*) (check)mate (*LAm, bebida*) maté

matemátic|as *fpl* mathematics, maths (*Brit*), math (*Amer*). **~o** *adj* mathematical. • *m* mathematician

materia *f* matter; (*material*) material; (*LAm, asignatura*) subject. **~ prima** raw material. **en ~ de** on the question of

material *adj & m* material. **~idad** *f* material nature. **~ismo** *m* materialism. **~ista** *adj* materialistic. • *m & f* materialist; (*Mex, constructor*) building contractor. **~izar** **10** *vt* materialize. **~izarse** *vpr* materialize. **~mente** *adv* materially; (*absolutamente*) absolutely

matern|al *adj* maternal; (amor) motherly. **~idad** *f* motherhood; (*hospital*) maternity hospital; (*sala*) maternity ward. **~o** *adj* motherly; (lengua) mother

matin|al *adj* morning. **~ée** *m* matinée

matiz *m* shade; (*fig*) nuance. **~ación** *f* combination of colours. **~ar** 10 *vt* blend (colores); (*introducir variedad*) vary; (*teñir*) tinge (**de** with)

mat|ón *m* bully; (*de barrio*) thug. **~onismo** *m* bullying; (*de barrio*) thuggery

matorral *m* scrub; (*conjunto de matas*) thicket

matraca *f* rattle. **dar ~** pester

matraz *m* flask

matriarca *f* matriarch. **~do** *m* matriarchy. **~l** *adj* matriarchal

matr|ícula *f* (*lista*) register, list; (*inscripción*) registration; (*Auto*) registration number; (*placa*) licence plate. **~icular** *vt* register. **~icularse** *vpr* enrol, register

m

matrimoni|al *adj* matrimonial. **~o** *m* marriage; (*pareja*) married couple

matriz *f* matrix; (*molde*) mould; (*útero*) womb, uterus

matrona *f* matron; (*partera*) midwife

matutino *adj* morning

maull|ar *vi* miaow. **~ido** *m* miaow

mausoleo *m* mausoleum

maxilar *adj* maxillary. ● *m* jaw(bone)

máxim|a *f* maxim. **~e** *adv* especially. **~o** *adj* maximum; (punto) highest. ● *m* maximum

maya *f* daisy. ● *adj* Mayan. ● *m & f* (*persona*) Maya

mayo *m* May

mayonesa *f* mayonnaise

mayor *adj* (*más grande, comparativo*) bigger; (*más grande, superlativo*) biggest; (*de edad, comparativo*) older; (*de edad, superlativo*) oldest; (*adulto*) grown-up; (*principal*) main, major; (*Mus*) major. ● *m & f* (*adulto*) adult. **al por ~** wholesale. **~al** *m* foreman. **~azgo** *m* entailed estate

mayordomo *m* butler

mayor|ía *f* majority. **~ista** *m & f* wholesaler. **~itario** *adj* majority; (socio) principal. **~mente** *adv* especially

mayúscul|a *f* capital (letter). **~o** *adj* capital; (*fig, grande*) big

mazacote *m* hard mass

mazapán *m* marzipan

mazmorra *f* dungeon

mazo *m* mallet; (*manojo*) bunch; (*LAm, de naipes*) pack (*Brit*), deck (*Amer*)

mazorca *f* cob. **~ de maíz** corncob

me *pron* (*acusativo*) me; (*dativo*) (to) me; (*reflexivo*) (to) myself

mecánic|a *f* mechanics. **~o** *adj* mechanical. ● *m* mechanic

mecani|smo *m* mechanism. **~zación** *f* mechanization. **~zar** 10 *vt* mechanize

mecanograf|ía *f* typing. **~iado** *adj* typed, typewritten. **~iar** 20 *vt* type

mecanógrafo *m* typist

mecate *m* (*Mex*) string; (*más grueso*) rope

mecedora *f* rocking chair

mecenas *m & f invar* patron

mecer 9 *vt* rock; swing (columpio). **~se** *vpr* rock; (*en un columpio*) swing

mecha *f* (*de vela*) wick; (*de explosivo*) fuse. **~s** *fpl* highlights

mechar *vt* stuff, lard
mechero *m* (cigarette) lighter
mechón *m* (*de pelo*) lock
medall|a *f* medal. **~ón** *m* medallion; (*relicario*) locket
media *f* stocking; (*promedio*) average. **a ~s** half each
mediación *f* mediation
mediado *adj* half full; (*a mitad de*) halfway through. **~s** *mpl.* **a ~s de marzo** in mid-March
mediador *m* mediator
medialuna *f* (*pl* **mediaslunas**) croissant
median|amente *adv* fairly. **~a** *f* (*Auto*) central reservation (*Brit*), median strip (*Amer*). **~era** *f* party wall. **~ero** *adj* (muro) party. **~o** *adj* medium; (*mediocre*) average, mediocre
medianoche *f* (*pl* **mediasnoches**) midnight; (*Culin*) type of roll
mediante *prep* through, by means of
mediar *vi* mediate; (*llegar a la mitad*) be halfway through; (*interceder*) intercede (**por** for)
medic|ación *f* medication. **~amento** *m* medicine. **~ina** *f* medicine. **~inal** *adj* medicinal
medición *f* measurement
médico *adj* medical. ● *m* doctor. **~ de cabecera** GP, general practitioner
medid|a *f* measurement; (*unidad*) measure; (*disposición*) measure, step; (*prudencia*) moderation. **a la ~a** made to measure. **a ~a que** as. **en cierta ~a** to a certain extent. **~or** *m* (*LAm*) meter
medieval *adj* medieval. **~ista** *m & f* medievalist
medio *adj* half (a); (*mediano*) average. **dos horas y media** two and a half hours. **~ litro** half a litre. **las dos y media** half past two. ● *m* middle; (*Math*) half; (*manera*) means; (*en deportes*) half(-back). **en ~** in the middle (**de** of). **por ~ de** through. **~ ambiente** *m* environment
medioambiental *adj* environmental
mediocr|e *adj* mediocre. **~idad** *f* mediocrity
mediodía *m* midday, noon; (*sur*) south
medioevo *m* Middle Ages
Medio Oriente *m* Middle East
medir **5** *vt* measure; weigh up (palabras etc). ● *vi* measure, be. **¿cuánto mide de alto?** how tall is it? **~se** *vpr* (*moderarse*) measure o.s.; (*Mex, probarse*) try on
medita|bundo *adj* thoughtful. **~ción** *f* meditation. **~r** *vt* think about. ● *vi* meditate
mediterráneo *adj* Mediterranean
Mediterráneo *m* Mediterranean
médium *m & f* medium
médula *f* marrow
medusa *f* jellyfish
megáfono *m* megaphone
megalómano *m* megalomaniac
mejicano *adj & m* Mexican
Méjico *m* Mexico
mejilla *f* cheek
mejillón *m* mussel
mejor *adj & adv* (*comparativo*) better; (*superlativo*) best. **~ dicho** rather. **a lo ~** perhaps. **tanto ~** so much the better. **~a** *f* improvement. **~able** *adj* improvable. **~amiento** *m* improvement
mejorana *f* marjoram
mejorar *vt* improve, better. ● *vi*

get better. **~se** *vpr* get better

mejunje *m* mixture

melanc|olía *f* melancholy. **~ólico** *adj* melancholic

melaza *f* molasses

melen|a *f* long hair; (*de león*) mane. **~udo** *adj* long-haired

melindr|es *mpl* affectation. **hacer ~es con la comida** be picky about food. **~oso** *adj* affected

mellizo *adj* & *m* twin

melocot|ón *m* peach. **~onero** *m* peach tree

mel|odía *f* melody. **~ódico** *adj* melodic. **~odioso** *adj* melodious

melodram|a *m* melodrama. **~ático** *adj* melodramatic

melómano *m* music lover

melón *m* melon

m **meloso** *adj* sickly-sweet; (canción) slushy

membran|a *f* membrane. **~oso** *adj* membranous

membrete *m* letterhead

membrill|ero *m* quince tree. **~o** *m* quince

memo *adj* stupid. • *m* idiot

memorable *adj* memorable

memorando *m*, **memorándum** *m* notebook; (*nota*) memorandum, memo

memori|a *f* memory; (*informe*) report; (*tesis*) thesis. **~as** *fpl* (*autobiografía*) memoirs. **de ~a** by heart; (citar) from memory. **~al** *m* memorial. **~ón** *m* good memory. **~zación** *f* memorizing. **~zar** 10 *vt* memorize

menaje *m* household goods. **~ de cocina** kitchenware

menci|ón *f* mention. **~onado** *adj* aforementioned. **~onar** *vt* mention

mendi|cidad *f* begging. **~gar** 12 *vt* beg for. • *vi* beg. **~go** *m* beggar

mendrugo *m* piece of stale bread

mene|ar *vt* wag (rabo); shake (cabeza); wiggle (caderas). **~arse** *vpr* move; (*con inquietud*) fidget; (*balancearse*) swing. **~o** *m* movement; (sacudida) shake

menester *m* occupation. **ser ~** be necessary. **~oso** *adj* needy

menestra *f* vegetable stew

mengano *m* so-and-so

mengua *f* decrease; (*falta*) lack. **~do** *adj* diminished. **~nte** *adj* (luna) waning; (marea) ebb. **~r** 15 *vt/i* decrease, diminish

meningitis *f* meningitis

menjurje *m* mixture

menopausia *f* menopause

menor *adj* (*más pequeño, comparativo*) smaller; (*más pequeño, superlativo*) smallest; (*más joven, comparativo*) younger; (*más joven, superlativo*) youngest; (*Mus*) minor. • *m* & *f* (*menor de edad*) minor. **al por ~** retail

menos *adj* (*comparativo*) less; (*comparativo, con plural*) fewer; (*superlativo*) least; (*superlativo, con plural*) fewest. • *adv* (*comparativo*) less; (*superlativo*) least. • *prep* except. **al ~** at least. **a ~ que** unless. **las dos ~ diez** ten to two. **ni mucho ~** far from it. **por lo ~** at least. **~cabar** *vt* lessen; (*fig, estropear*) damage. **~cabo** *m* lessening. **~preciable** *adj* contemptible. **~preciar** *vt* despise. **~precio** *m* contempt

mensaje *m* message. **~ro** *m* messenger

menso *adj* (*LAm, fam*) stupid

menstru|ación *f* menstruation. **~al** *adj* menstrual. **~ar** 21 *vi* menstruate

mensual *adj* monthly. **~idad** *f* monthly pay; (*cuota*) monthly payment

mensurable *adj* measurable

menta *f* mint

mental *adj* mental. **~idad** *f* mentality. **~mente** *adv* mentally

mentar 1 *vt* mention, name

mente *f* mind

mentecato *adj* stupid. • *m* idiot

mentir 4 *vi* lie. **~a** *f* lie. **~ijillas** *fpl*. **de ~ijillas** for a joke. **~oso** *adj* lying. • *m* liar

mentís *m invar* denial

mentor *m* mentor

menú *m* menu

menud|ear *vi* happen frequently; (*Mex, Com*) sell retail. **~encia** *f* trifle. **~encias** *fpl* (*LAm*) giblets. **~eo** *m* (*Mex*) retail trade. **~illos** *mpl* giblets. **~o** *adj* small; (lluvia) fine. **a ~o** often. **~os** *mpl* giblets

meñique *adj* (dedo) little. • *m* little finger

meollo *m* (*médula*) marrow; (*de tema etc*) heart

merca|chifle *m* hawker; (*fig*) profiteer. **~der** *m* merchant. **~dería** *f* (*LAm*) merchandise. **~do** *m* market. **M~do Común** Common Market. **~do negro** black market

mercan|cía(s) *f*(*pl*) goods, merchandise. **~te** *adj* merchant. • *m* merchant ship. **~til** *adj* mercantile, commercial. **~tilismo** *m* mercantilism

merced *f* favour. **su/vuestra ~** your honour

mercenario *adj & m* mercenary

mercer|ía *f* haberdashery (*Brit*), notions (*Amer*).

mercurial *adj* mercurial

mercurio *m* mercury

merec|edor *adj* worthy (**de** of). **~er** 11 *vt* deserve. **~erse** *vpr* deserve. **~idamente** *adv* deservedly. **~ido** *adj* well deserved. **~imiento** *m* (*mérito*) merit

merend|ar 1 *vt* have as an afternoon snack. • *vi* have an afternoon snack. **~ero** *m* snack bar; (*lugar*) picnic area

merengue *m* meringue

meridi|ano *adj* midday; (*fig*) dazzling. • *m* meridian. **~onal** *adj* southern. • *m* southerner

merienda *f* afternoon snack

merino *adj* merino

mérito *m* merit; (*valor*) worth

meritorio *adj* praiseworthy. • *m* unpaid trainee

merluza *f* hake

merma *f* decrease. **~r** *vt/i* decrease, reduce

mermelada *f* jam

mero *adj* mere; (*Mex, verdadero*) real. • *adv* (*Mex, precisamente*) exactly; (*Mex, casi*) nearly. • *m* grouper

merode|ador *m* prowler. **~ar** *vi* prowl

mes *m* month

mesa *f* table; (*para escribir o estudiar*) desk. **poner la ~** lay the table

mesarse *vpr* tear at one's hair

meser|a *f* (*LAm*) waitress. **~o** *m* (*LAm*) waiter

meseta *f* plateau; (*descansillo*) landing

Mesías *m* Messiah

mesilla *f*, **mesita** *f* small table. ~

de noche bedside table
mesón *m* inn
mesoner|a *f* landlady. **~o** *m* landlord
mestiz|aje *m* crossbreeding. **~o** *adj* (persona) half-caste; (animal) cross-bred. • *m* (*persona*) half-caste; (*animal*) cross-breed
mesura *f* moderation. **~do** *adj* moderate
meta *f* goal; (*de una carrera*) finish
metabolismo *m* metabolism
metafísic|a *f* metaphysics. **~o** *adj* metaphysical
met|áfora *f* metaphor. **~afórico** *adj* metaphorical
met|al *m* metal; (*de la voz*) timbre. **~ales** *mpl* (*instrumentos de latón*) brass. **~álico** *adj* (objeto) metal; (sonido) metallic
metal|urgia *f* metallurgy. **~úrgico** *adj* metallurgical
metamorfosis *f invar* metamorphosis
metedura de pata *f* blunder
mete|órico *adj* meteoric. **~orito** *m* meteorite. **~oro** *m* meteor. **~orología** *f* meteorology. **~orológico** *adj* meteorological. **~orólogo** *m* meteorologist
meter *vt* put; score (un gol); (*enredar*) involve; (*causar*) make. **~se** *vpr* get involved (**en** in); (*entrometerse*) meddle. **~se con uno** pick a quarrel with s.o.
meticulos|idad *f* meticulousness. **~o** *adj* meticulous
metida de pata *f* (*LAm*) blunder
metido *m* reprimand. • *adj*. **~ en años** getting on. **estar ~ en algo** be involved in sth. **estar muy ~ con uno** be well in with s.o.
metódico *adj* methodical
metodis|mo *m* Methodism. **~ta** *adj & m & f* Methodist
método *m* method
metodología *f* methodology
metraje *m* length. **de largo ~** (película) feature
metrall|a *f* shrapnel. **~eta** *f* sub-machine gun
métric|a *f* metrics. **~o** *adj* metric; (verso) metrical
metro *m* metre; (*tren*) underground (*Brit*), subway (*Amer*). **~ cuadrado** square metre
metrónomo *m* metronome
metr|ópoli *f* metropolis. **~opolitano** *adj* metropolitan. • *m* metropolitan; (*tren*) underground (*Brit*), subway (*Amer*)
mexicano *adj & m* Mexican
México *m* Mexico. **~ D. F.** Mexico City
mezcal *m* (*Mex*) mescal
mezc|la *f* (*acción*) mixing; (*substancia*) mixture; (*argamasa*) mortar. **~lador** *m* mixer. **~lar** *vt* mix; shuffle (los naipes). **~larse** *vpr* mix; (*intervenir*) interfere. **~olanza** *f* mixture
mezquin|dad *f* meanness. **~o** *adj* mean; (*escaso*) meagre. • *m* mean person
mezquita *f* mosque
mi *adj* my. • *m* (*Mus*) E; (*solfa*) mi
mí *pron* me
miau *m* miaow
mica *f* (*silicato*) mica
mico *m* (long-tailed) monkey
micro|bio *m* microbe. **~biología** *f* microbiology. **~cosmos** *m invar* microcosm. **~film(e)** *m* microfilm
micrófono *m* microphone
microonda *f* microwave. **~s** *m invar* microwave oven

microordenador *m* microcomputer

micros|cópico *adj* microscopic. **~copio** *m* microscope. **~urco** *m* long-playing record

miedo *m* fear (a for). **dar ~** frighten. **morirse de ~** be scared to death. **tener ~** be frightened. **~so** *adj* fearful

miel *f* honey

miembro *m* limb; (*persona*) member

mientras *conj* while. ● *adv* meanwhile. **~ que** whereas. **~ tanto** in the meantime

miércoles *m invar* Wednesday. **~ de ceniza** Ash Wednesday

mierda *f* (🅧) shit

mies *f* ripe, grain

miga *f* crumb; (*fig*, *meollo*) essence. **~jas** *fpl* crumbs; (*sobras*) scraps. **~r** 12 *vt* crumble

migra|ción *f* migration. **~torio** *adj* migratory

mijo *m* millet

mil *adj & m* a/one thousand. **~es de** thousands of. **~ novecientos noventa y nueve** nineteen ninety nine. **~ euros** a thousand euros

milagro *m* miracle. **~so** *adj* miraculous

milen|ario *adj* millenial. **~io** *m* millennium

milésimo *adj & m* thousandth

mili *f* 🅘 military service. **~cia** *f* soldiering; (*gente armada*) militia

mili|gramo *m* milligram. **~litro** *m* millilitre

milímetro *m* millimetre

militante *adj & m & f* activist

militar *adj* military. ● *m* soldier. **~ismo** *m* militarism. **~ista** *adj* militaristic. ● *m & f* militarist. **~izar** 10 *vt* militarize

milla *f* mile

millar *m* thousand. **a ~es** by the thousand

mill|ón *m* million. **un ~ón de libros** a million books. **~onada** *f* fortune. **~onario** *m* millionaire. **~onésimo** *adj & m* millionth

milonga *f* popular dance and music from the River Plate region

milpa *f* (*Mex*) maize field, cornfield (*Amer*)

milpies *m invar* woodlouse

mimar *vt* spoil

mimbre *m & f* wicker. **~arse** *vpr* sway. **~ra** *f* osier. **~ral** *m* osier-bed

mimetismo *m* mimicry

mímic|a *f* mime. **~o** *adj* mimic

mimo *m* mime; (*adj un niño*) spoiling; (*caricia*) cuddle

mimosa *f* mimosa

mina *f* mine. **~r** *vt* mine; (*fig*) undermine

minarete *m* minaret

mineral *m* mineral; (*mena*) ore. **~ogía** *f* mineralogy. **~ogista** *m & f* mineralogist

miner|ía *f* mining. **~o** *adj* mining. ● *m* miner

miniatura *f* miniature

minifundio *m* smallholding

minimizar 10 *vt* minimize

mínim|o *adj & m* minimum. **como ~** at least. **~um** *m* minimum

minino *m* 🅘 cat, puss 🅘

minist|erial *adj* ministerial; (*reunión*) cabinet. **~erio** *m* ministry. **~ro** *m* minister

minor|ía *f* minority. **~idad** *f* minority. **~ista** *m & f* retailer

minuci|a *f* trifle. **~osidad** *f* thoroughness. **~oso** *adj* thorough; (*de-*

m

tallado) detailed

minúscul|a *f* lower case letter. **~o** *adj* tiny

minuta *f* draft copy; (*de abogado*) bill

minut|ero *m* minute hand. **~o** *m* minute

mío *adj & pron* mine. **un amigo ~** a friend of mine

miop|e *adj* short-sighted. • *m & f* short-sighted person. **~ía** *f* short-sightedness

mira *f* sight; (*fig, intención*) aim. **a la ~** on the lookout. **con ~s a** with a view to. **~da** *f* look. **echar una ~da a** glance at. **~do** *adj* careful with money; (*comedido*) considerate. **bien ~do** highly regarded. **no estar bien ~do** be frowned upon. **~dor** *m* viewpoint. **~miento** *m* consideration. **~r** *vt* look at; (*observar*) watch; (*considerar*) consider. **~r fijamente a** stare at. • *vi* look (edificio etc). **~ hacia** face. **~rse** *vpr* (personas) look at each other

mirilla *f* peephole

miriñaque *m* crinoline

mirlo *m* blackbird

mirón *adj* nosey. • *m* nosey-parker; (*espectador*) onlooker

mirto *m* myrtle

misa *f* mass. **~l** *m* missal

misántropo *m* misanthropist

miscelánea *f* miscellany; (*Mex, tienda*) corner shop (*Brit*), small general store (*Amer*)

miser|able *adj* very poor; (*lastimoso*) miserable; (*tacaño*) mean. **~ia** *f* extreme poverty; (*suciedad*) squalor

misericordi|a *f* pity; (*piedad*) mercy. **~oso** *adj* merciful

mísero *adj* miserable; (*tacaño*) mean; (*malvado*) wicked

misil *m* missile

misi|ón *f* mission. **~onero** *m* missionary

misiva *f* missive

mism|ísimo *adj* very same. **~o** *adj* same; (*después de pronombre personal*) myself, yourself, himself, herself, itself, ourselves, yourselves, themselves; (enfático) very. • *adv.* **ahora ~** right now. **aquí ~** right here. **lo ~** the same

misterio *m* mystery. **~so** *adj* mysterious

místic|a *f* mysticism. **~o** *adj* mystical. • *m* mystic

mistifica|ción *f* mystification. **~r** 7 *vt* mystify

mitad *f* half; (*centro*) middle. **cortar algo por la ~** cut sth in half

mitigar 12 *vt* mitigate; quench (sed); relieve (dolor etc)

mitin *m*, **mitín** *m* meeting

mito *m* myth. **~logía** *f* mythology. **~lógico** *adj* mythological

mitón *m* mitten

mitote *m* (*Mex*) Aztec dance

mixt|o *adj* mixed. **educación mixta** coeducation

mobbing *m* harassment

mobiliario *m* furniture

moce|dad *f* youth. **~río** *m* young people. **~tón** *m* strapping lad. **~tona** *f* strapping girl

mochales *adj invar.* **estar ~** be round the bend

mochila *f* rucksack

mocho *adj* blunt. • *m* butt end

mochuelo *m* little owl

moción *f* motion

moco *m* mucus. **limpiarse los ~s** blow one's nose

moda *f* fashion. **estar de ~** be in

fashion. **~l** *adj* modal. **~les** *mpl* manners. **~lidad** *f* kind

model|ado *m* modelling. **~ador** *m* modeller. **~ar** *vt* model; (*fig, configurar*) form. **~o** *m & f* model

módem *m* modem

modera|ción *f* moderation. **~do** *adj* moderate. **~r** *vt* moderate; reduce (velocidad). **~rse** *vpr* control oneself

modern|idad *f* modernity. **~ismo** *m* modernism. **~ista** *m & f* modernist. **~izar** 10 *vt* modernize. **~o** *adj* modern; (*a la moda*) fashionable

modest|ia *f* modesty. **~o** *adj* modest

módico *adj* moderate

modifica|ción *f* modification. **~r** 7 *vt* modify

modismo *m* idiom

modist|a *f* dressmaker. **~o** *m* designer

modo *m* manner, way; (*Gram*) mood; (*Mus*) mode. **~ de ser** character. **de ~ que** so that. **de ningún ~** certainly not. **de todos ~s** anyhow. **ni ~** (*LAm*) no way

modorra *f* drowsiness

modula|ción *f* modulation. **~dor** *m* modulator. **~r** *vt* modulate

módulo *m* module

mofa *f* mockery. **~rse** *vpr*. **~rse de** make fun of

mofeta *f* skunk

moflet|e *m* chubby cheek. **~udo** *adj* with chubby cheeks

mohín *m* grimace. **hacer un ~** pull a face

moho *m* mould; (*óxido*) rust. **~so** *adj* mouldy; (metales) rusty

moisés *m* Moses basket

mojado *adj* wet

mojar *vt* wet; (*empapar*) soak; (*humedecer*) moisten, dampen

mojigat|ería *f* prudishness. **~o** *m* prude. • *adj* prudish

mojón *m* boundary post; (*señal*) signpost

molar *m* molar

mold|e *m* mould; (*aguja*) knitting needle. **~ear** *vt* mould, shape; (*fig*) form. **~ura** *f* moulding

mole *f* mass, bulk. • *m* (*Mex, salsa*) chili sauce with chocolate and sesame

mol|écula *f* molecule. **~ecular** *adj* molecular

mole|dor *adj* grinding. • *m* grinder. **~r** 2 grind

molest|ar *vt* annoy; (*incomodar*) bother. **¿le ~a que fume?** do you mind if I smoke? • *vi* be a nuisance. **no ~ar** do not disturb. **~arse** *vpr* bother; (*ofenderse*) take offence. **~ia** *f* bother, nuisance; (*inconveniente*) inconvenience; (*incomodidad*) discomfort. **~o** *adj* annoying; (*inconveniente*) inconvenient; (*ofendido*) offended

molicie *f* softness; (*excesiva comodidad*) easy life

molido *adj* ground; (*fig, muy cansado*) worn out

molienda *f* grinding

molin|ero *m* miller. **~ete** *m* toy windmill. **~illo** *m* mill; (*juguete*) toy windmill. **~o** *m* mill. **~ de agua** watermill. **~o de viento** windmill

molleja *f* gizzard

mollera *f* (*de la cabeza*) crown; (*fig, sesera*) brains

molusco *m* mollusc

moment|áneamente *adv* momentarily. **~áneo** *adj* (*breve*) momentary; (*pasajero*) temporary. **~o** *m* moment; (*ocasión*) time. **al ~o** at once. **de ~o** for the moment

momi|a *f* mummy. **~ficar** 7 *vt* mummify. **~ficarse** *vpr* become mummified

monacal *adj* monastic

monada *f* beautiful thing; (*niño bonito*) cute kid; (*acción tonta*) silliness

monaguillo *m* altar boy

mon|arca *m & f* monarch. **~arquía** *f* monarchy. **~árquico** *adj* monarchical

monasterio *m* monastery

mond|a *f* peeling; (*piel*) peel. **~adientes** *m invar* toothpick. **~adura** *f* peeling; (*piel*) peel. **~ar** *vt* peel (fruta etc). **~o** *adj* (*sin pelo*) bald

m

mondongo *m* innards

moned|a *f* coin; (*de un país*) currency. **~ero** *m* purse (*Brit*), change purse (*Amer*)

monetario *adj* monetary

mongolismo *m* Down's syndrome

monigote *m* weak character; (*muñeco*) rag doll; (*dibujo*) doodle

monitor *m* monitor

monj|a *f* nun. **~e** *m* monk. **~il** *adj* nun's; (*como de monja*) like a nun

mono *m* monkey; (*sobretodo*) overalls. • *adj* pretty

monocromo *adj & m* monochrome

monóculo *m* monocle

mon|ogamia *f* monogamy. **~ógamo** *adj* monogamous

monogra|fía *f* monograph. **~ma** *m* monogram

mon|ologar 12 *vi* soliloquize. **~ólogo** *m* monologue

monoplano *m* monoplane

monopoli|o *m* monopoly. **~zar** 10 *vt* monopolize

monos|ilábico *adj* monosyllabic. **~ílabo** *m* monosyllable

monoteís|mo *m* monotheism. **~ta** *adj* monotheistic. • *m & f* monotheist

mon|otonía *f* monotony. **~ótono** *adj* monotonous

monseñor *m* monsignor

monstruo *m* monster. **~sidad** *f* monstrosity; (*atrocidad*) atrocity. **~so** *adj* monstrous

monta *f* mounting; (*valor*) total value

montacargas *m invar* service lift (*Brit*), service elevator (*Amer*)

monta|dor *m* fitter. **~je** *m* assembly; (*Cine*) montage; (*teatro*) staging, production

montañ|a *f* mountain. **~a rusa** roller coaster. **~ero** *adj* mountaineer. **~és** *adj* mountain. • *m* highlander. **~ismo** *m* mountaineering. **~oso** *adj* mountainous

montaplatos *m invar* dumb waiter

montar *vt* ride; (*subirse a*) get on; (*ensamblar*) assemble; cock (arma); set up (una casa, un negocio). • *vi* ride; (*subirse*) mount. **~ a caballo** ride a horse

monte *m* (*montaña*) mountain; (*terreno inculto*) scrub; (*bosque*) woodland. **~ de piedad** pawnshop

montepío *m* charitable fund for dependents

montés *adj* wild

montevideano *adj & m* Montevidean

montículo *m* hillock

montón *m* heap, pile. **a montones** in abundance. **un ~ de**

loads of

montura *f* mount; (*silla*) saddle

monument|al *adj* monumental; (*fig, muy grande*) enormous. **~o** *m* monument

monzón *m & f* monsoon

moñ|a *f* ribbon. **~o** *m* bun; (*LAm, lazo*) bow

moque|o *m* runny nose. **~ro** *m* ⓘ handkerchief

moqueta *f* fitted carpet

moquillo *m* distemper

mora *f* mulberry; (*de zarzamora*) blackberry; (*Jurid*) default

morada *f* dwelling

morado *adj* purple

morador *m* inhabitant

moral *m* mulberry tree. ● *f* morals. ● *adj* moral. **~eja** *f* moral. **~idad** *f* morality. **~ista** *m & f* moralist. **~izador** *adj* moralizing. ● *m* moralist. **~izar** 10 *vt* moralize

morar *vi* live

moratoria *f* moratorium

mórbido *adj* soft; (*malsano*) morbid

morbo *m* illness. **~sidad** *f* morbidity. **~so** *adj* unhealthy

morcilla *f* black pudding

morda|cidad *f* sharpness. **~z** *adj* scathing

mordaza *f* gag

morde|dura *f* bite. **~r** 2 *vt* bite; (*Mex, exigir soborno a*) extract a bribe from. ● *vi* bite. **~rse** *vpr* bite o.s. **~rse las uñas** bite one's nails

mordi|da *f* (*Mex*) bribe. **~sco** *m* bite. **~squear** *vt* nibble (at)

moreno *adj* (*con ser*) dark; (*de pelo obscuro*) dark-haired; (*de raza negra*) dark-skinned; (*con estar*) brown, tanned

morera *f* white mulberry tree

moretón *m* bruise

morfema *m* morpheme

morfin|a *f* morphine. **~ómano** *m* morphine addict

morfol|ogía *f* morphology. **~ógico** *adj* morphological

moribundo *adj* dying

morir 6 (*pp* **muerto**) *vi* die; (*fig, extinguirse*) die away; (*fig, terminar*) end. **~ ahogado** drown. **~se** *vpr* die. **~se de hambre** starve to death; (*fig*) be starving. **se muere por una flauta** she's dying to have a flute

morisco *adj* Moorish. ● *m* Moor

morm|ón *m* Mormon. **~ónico** *adj* Mormon. **~onismo** *m* Mormonism

moro *adj* Moorish. ● *m* Moor

morral *m* (*mochila*) rucksack; (*de cazador*) gamebag; (*para caballos*) nosebag

morrillo *m* nape of the neck

morriña *f* homesickness

morro *m* snout

morrocotudo *adj* (ⓘ, *tremendo*) terrible; (*estupendo*) terrific ⓘ

morsa *f* walrus

mortaja *f* shroud

mortal *adj & m & f* mortal. **~idad** *f* mortality. **~mente** *adv* mortally

mortandad *f* loss of life; (*Mil*) carnage

mortecino *adj* failing; (color) pale

mortero *m* mortar

mortífero *adj* deadly

mortifica|ción *f* mortification. **~r** 7 *vt* (*atormentar*) torment. **~rse** *vpr* distress o.s.

mortuorio *adj* death

mosaico *m* mosaic; (*Mex, baldosa*) floor tile

mosca *f* fly. **~rda** *f* blowfly. **~rdón** *m* botfly; (*de cuerpo azul*)

m

bluebottle
moscatel *adj* muscatel
moscón *m* botfly; (*mosca de cuerpo azul*) bluebottle
moscovita *adj & m & f* Muscovite
mosque|arse *vpr* get cross. **~o** *m* resentment
mosquete *m* musket. **~ro** *m* musketeer
mosquit|ero *m* mosquito net. **~o** *m* mosquito
mostacho *m* moustache
mostaza *f* mustard
mosto *m* must, grape juice
mostrador *m* counter
mostrar **2** *vt* show. **~se** *vpr* (show oneself to) be. **se mostró muy amable** he was very kind
mota *f* spot, speck
mote *m* nickname
motea|do *adj* speckled. **~r** *vt* speckle
motejar *vt* call
motel *m* motel
motete *m* motet
motín *m* riot; (*de tropas, tripulación*) mutiny
motiv|ación *f* motivation. **~ar** *vt* motivate. **~o** *m* reason. **con ~o de** because of
motocicl|eta *f* motor cycle, motor bike **!**. **~ista** *m & f* motorcyclist
motoneta *f* (*LAm*) (motor) scooter
motor *adj* motor. • *m* motor, engine. **~ de arranque** starter motor. **~a** *f* motor boat. **~ismo** *m* motorcycling. **~ista** *m & f* motorist; (*de una moto*) motorcyclist. **~izar** **10** *vt* motorize
motriz *adj* motor
move|dizo *adj* movable; (*poco firme*) unstable; (persona) fickle. **~r** **2** *vt* move; shake (la cabeza); (*provocar*) cause. **~rse** *vpr* move; (*darse prisa*) hurry up
movi|ble *adj* movable. **~do** *adj* moved; (*Foto*) blurred
móvil *adj* mobile; (*Esp, teléfono*) mobile phone, cellphone. • *m* motive
movili|dad *f* mobility. **~zación** *f* mobilization. **~zar** **10** *vt* mobilize
movimiento *m* movement, motion; (*agitación*) bustle
moza *f* young girl. **~lbete** *m* lad
mozárabe *adj* Mozarabic. • *m & f* Mozarab
moz|o *m* young boy. **~uela** *f* young girl. **~uelo** *m* young boy/lad
mucam|a *f* (*LAm*) servant. **~o** *m* (*LAm*) servant
muchach|a *f* girl; (*sirvienta*) servant, maid. **~o** *m* boy, lad
muchedumbre *f* crowd
mucho *adj* a lot of; (*en negativas, preguntas*) much, a lot of. **~s** a lot of; (*en negativas, preguntas*) many, a lot of. • *pron* a lot; (*personas*) many (people). **como ~** at the most. **ni ~ menos** by no means. **por ~ que** however much. • *adv* a lot, very much; (*tiempo*) long, a long time
mucos|idad *f* mucus. **~o** *adj* mucous
muda *f* change of clothing; (*de animales*) shedding. **~ble** *adj* changeable; (personas) fickle. **~nza** *f* move, removal (*Brit*). **~r** *vt* change; shed (piel). **~rse** *vpr* (*de ropa*) change one's clothes; (*de casa*) move (house)
mudéjar *adj & m & f* Mudejar
mud|ez *f* dumbness. **~o** *adj*

dumb; (*callado*) silent
mueble *adj* movable. ● *m* piece of furniture. **~s** *mpl* furniture
mueca *f* grimace, face. **hacer una ~** pull a face
muela *f* back tooth, molar; (*piedra de afilar*) grindstone; (*piedra de molino*) millstone. **~ del juicio** wisdom tooth
muelle *adj* soft. ● *m* spring; (*Naut*) wharf; (*malecón*) jetty
muérdago *m* mistletoe
muero *vb véase* **MORIR**
muert|e *f* death; (*homicidio*) murder. **~o** *adj* dead. ● *m* dead person
muesca *f* nick; (*ranura*) slot
muestra *f* sample; (*prueba*) proof; (*modelo*) model; (*señal*) sign. **~rio** *m* collection of samples
muestro *vb véase* **MOSTRAR**
muevo *vb véase* **MOVER**
mugi|do *m* moo. **~r** 14 *vi* moo
mugr|e *m* dirt. **~iento** *adj* dirty, filthy
mugrón *m* sucker
mujer *f* woman; (*esposa*) wife. ● *int* my dear! **~iego** *adj* fond of the women. ● *m* womanizer. **~zuela** *f* prostitute
mula *f* mule. **~da** *f* drove of mules
mulato *adj* of mixed race (*black and white*). ● *m* person of mixed race
mulero *m* muleteer
muleta *f* crutch; (*toreo*) stick with a red flag
mulli|do *adj* soft. **~r** 22 *vt* soften
mulo *m* mule
multa *f* fine. **~r** *vt* fine
multi|color *adj* multicoloured. **~copista** *m* duplicator. **~cultural** *adj* multicultural. **~forme** *adj* multiform. **~lateral** *adj* multilateral. **~lingüe** *adj* multilingual. **~millonario** *m* multimillionaire
múltiple *adj* multiple
multiplic|ación *f* multiplication. **~ar** 7 *vt* multiply. **~arse** *vpr* multiply. **~idad** *f* multiplicity
múltiplo *m* multiple
multitud *f* multitude, crowd. **~inario** *adj* mass; (*concierto*) with mass audience
mund|ano *adj* wordly; (*de la sociedad elegante*) society. **~ial** *adj* world-wide. **la segunda guerra ~ial** the Second World War. **~illo** *m* world, circles. **~o** *m* world. **todo el ~o** everybody
munición *f* ammunition; (*provisiones*) supplies
municip|al *adj* municipal. **~alidad** *f* municipality. **~io** *m* municipality; (*ayuntamiento*) town council
muñe|ca *f* (*en anatomía*) wrist; (*juguete*) doll; (*maniquí*) dummy. **~co** *m* doll. **~quera** *f* wristband
muñón *m* stump
mura|l *adj* mural, wall. ● *m* mural. **~lla** *f* (city) wall. **~r** *vt* wall
murciélago *m* bat
murga *f* street band
murmullo *m* (*incl fig*) murmur
murmura|ción *f* gossip. **~dor** *adj* gossiping. ● *m* gossip. **~r** *vi* murmur; (*criticar*) gossip
muro *m* wall
murria *f* depression
mus *m* card game
musa *f* muse
musaraña *f* shrew
muscula|r *adj* muscular. **~tura** *f* muscles
músculo *m* muscle
musculoso *adj* muscular

muselina *f* muslin
museo *m* museum. **~ de arte** art gallery
musgo *m* moss. **~so** *adj* mossy
música *f* music
musical *adj & m* musical
músico *adj* musical. ● *m* musician
music|ología *f* musicology. **~ólogo** *m* musicologist
muslo *m* thigh
mustio *adj* (plantas) withered; (cosas) faded; (personas) gloomy; (*Mex, hipócrita*) two-faced
musulmán *adj & m* Muslim
muta|bilidad *f* mutability. **~ción** *f* mutation
mutila|ción *f* mutilation. **~do** *adj* crippled. ● *m* cripple. **~r** *vt* mutilate; maim (persona)
mutis *m* (*en el teatro*) exit. **~mo** *m* silence
mutu|alidad *f* mutuality; (*asociación*) friendly society. **~amente** *adv* mutually. **~o** *adj* mutual
muy *adv* very; (*demasiado*) too

Nn

nabo *m* turnip
nácar *m* mother-of-pearl
nac|er 11 *vi* be born; (pollito) hatch out; (planta) sprout. **~ido** *adj* born. **recien ~ido** newborn. **~iente** *adj* (sol) rising. **~imiento** *m* birth; (*de río*) source; (*belén*) crib. **lugar** *m* **de ~imiento** place of birth
naci|ón *f* nation. **~onal** *adj* national. **~onalidad** *f* nationality. **~onalismo** *m* nationalism. **~onalista** *m & f* nationalist. **~onalizar** 10 *vt* nationalize. **~onalizarse** *vpr* become naturalized
nada *pron* nothing, not anything. ● *adv* not at all. **¡~ de eso!** nothing of the sort! **antes que ~** first of all. **¡de ~!** (*después de 'gracias'*) don't mention it! **para ~** (not) at all. **por ~ del mundo** not for anything in the world
nada|dor *m* swimmer. **~r** *vi* swim. **~r de espalda(s)** do (the) backstroke
nadería *f* trifle
nadie *pron* no one, nobody
nado *m* (*Mex*) swimming. ● *adv* **a ~** swimming
naipe *m* (playing) card. **juegos** *mpl* **de ~s** card games
nalga *f* buttock. **~s** *fpl* bottom. **~da** *f* (*Mex*) smack on the bottom
nana *f* lullaby
naranj|a *f* orange. **~ada** *f* orangeade. **~al** *m* orange grove. **~ero** *m* orange tree
narcótico *adj & m* narcotic
nariz *f* nose. **¡narices!** rubbish!
narra|ción *f* narration. **~dor** *m* narrator. **~r** *vt* tell. **~tivo** *adj* narrative
nasal *adj* nasal
nata *f* cream
natación *f* swimming
natal *adj* native; (pueblo etc) home. **~idad** *f* birth rate
natillas *fpl* custard
nativo *adj & m* native
nato *adj* born
natural *adj* natural. ● *m* native. **~eza** *f* nature. **~eza muerta** still life. **~idad** *f* naturalness. **~ista** *m & f* naturalist. **~izar** 10 *vt* natural-

ize. **~izarse** *vpr* become naturalized. **~mente** *adv* naturally. ● *int* of course!

naufrag|ar 12 *vi* (barco) sink; (persona) be shipwrecked; (*fig*) fail. **~io** *m* shipwreck

náufrago *adj* shipwrecked. ● *m* shipwrecked person

náuseas *fpl* nausea. **dar ~s a uno** make s.o. feel sick. **sentir ~s** feel sick

náutico *adj* nautical

navaja *f* penknife; (*de afeitar*) razor. **~zo** *m* slash

naval *adj* naval

nave *f* ship; (*de iglesia*) nave. **~ espacial** spaceship. **quemar las ~s** burn one's boats

navega|ble *adj* navigable; (barco) seaworthy. **~ción** *f* navigation; (*tráfico*) shipping. **~dor** *m* (*Informática*) browser. **~nte** *m & f* navigator. **~r** 12 *vi* sail; (*Informática*) browse

Navid|ad *f* Christmas. **~eño** *adj* Christmas. **en ~ades** at Christmas. **¡feliz ~ad!** Happy Christmas! **por ~ad** at Christmas

nazi *adj & m & f* Nazi. **~smo** *m* Nazism

neblina *f* mist

nebuloso *adj* misty; (*fig*) vague

necedad *f* foolishness. **decir ~es** talk nonsense. **hacer una ~** do sth stupid

necesari|amente *adv* necessarily. **~o** *adj* necessary

necesi|dad *f* need; (*cosa esencial*) necessity; (*pobreza*) poverty. **~dades** *fpl* hardships. **no hay ~dad** there's no need. **por ~dad** (out) of necessity. **~tado** *adj* in need (**de** of). **~tar** *vt* need. ● *vi*. **~tar de** need

necio *adj* silly. ● *m* idiot

néctar *m* nectar

nectarina *f* nectarine

nefasto *adj* unfortunate; (consecuencia) disastrous; (influencia) harmful

nega|ción *f* denial; (*Gram*) negative. **~do** *adj* useless. **~r** 1 & 12 *vt* deny; (*rehusar*) refuse. **~rse** *vpr* refuse (**a** to). **~tiva** *f* (*acción*) denial; (*acción de rehusar*) refusal. **~tivo** *adj & m* negative

negligen|cia *f* negligence. **~te** *adj* negligent

negoci|able *adj* negotiable. **~ación** *f* negotiation. **~ante** *m & f* dealer. **~ar** *vt/i* negotiate. **~ar en** trade in. **~o** *m* business; (*Com, trato*) deal. **~os** *mpl* business. **hombre** *m* **de ~os** businessman

negr|a *f* black woman; (*Mus*) crotchet. **~o** *adj* black; (ojos) dark. ● *m* (*color*) black; (*persona*) black man. **~ura** *f* blackness. **~uzco** *adj* blackish

nen|a *f* little girl. **~o** *m* little boy

nenúfar *m* water lily

neocelandés *adj* from New Zealand. ● *m* New Zealander

neón *m* neon

nepotismo *m* nepotism

nervio *m* nerve; (*tendón*) sinew; (*en botánica*) vein. **~sidad** *f*, **~sismo** *m* nervousness; (*impaciencia*) impatience. **~so** *adj* nervous; (*de temperamento*) highly-strung. **ponerse ~so** get nervous

neto *adj* clear; (verdad) simple; (*Com*) net

neumático *adj* pneumatic. ● *m* tyre

neumonía *f* pneumonia

neur|algia *f* neuralgia. **~ología** *f* neurology. **~ólogo** *m* neurologist. **~osis** *f* neurosis. **~ótico** *adj* neurotic

neutr|al *adj* neutral. **~alidad** *f* neutrality. **~alizar** 10 *vt* neutralize. **~o** *adj* neutral; (*Gram*) neuter

neva|da *f* snowfall. **~r** 1 *vi* snow. **~sca** *f* blizzard

nevera *f* refrigerator, fridge (*Brit*)

nevisca *f* light snowfall

nexo *m* link

ni *conj*. **~... ~** neither... nor. **~ aunque** not even if. **~ siquiera** not even. **sin...~ ...** without ... or...

Nicaragua *f* Nicaragua

nicaragüense *adj & m & f* Nicaraguan

nicho *m* niche

nicotina *f* nicotine

nido *m* nest; (*de ladrones*) den

niebla *f* fog. **hay ~** it's foggy. **un día de ~** a foggy day

n

niet|a *f* granddaughter. **~o** *m* grandson. **~os** *mpl* grandchildren

nieve *f* snow; (*Mex, helado*) sorbet

niki *m* polo shirt

nimi|edad *f* triviality. **~o** *adj* insignificant

ninfa *f* nymph

ningún *véase* **NINGUNO**

ninguno *adj* (*delante de nombre masculino en singular* **ningún**) no; (*con otro negativo*) any. **de ninguna manera, de ningún modo** by no means. **en ninguna parte** nowhere. **sin ningún amigo** without any friends. ● *pron* (*de dos*) neither; (*de más de dos*) none; (*nadie*) no-one, nobody

niñ|a *f* (little) girl. **~era** *f* nanny. **~ería** *f* childish thing. **~ez** *f* childhood. **~o** *adj* childish. ● *m* (little) boy **de ~o** as a child. **desde ~o** from childhood

níquel *m* nickel

níspero *m* medlar

nitidez *f* clarity; (*de foto, imagen*) sharpness

nítido *adj* clear; (*foto, imagen*) sharp

nitrógeno *m* nitrogen

nivel *m* level; (*fig*) standard. **~ de vida** standard of living. **~ar** *vt* level. **~arse** *vpr* become level

no *adv* not; (*como respuesta*) no. **¿~?** isn't it? **¡a que ~!** I bet you don't! **¡cómo ~!** of course! **Felipe ~ tiene hijos** Felipe has no children. **¡que ~!** certainly not!

nob|iliario *adj* noble. **~le** *adj & m & f* noble. **~leza** *f* nobility

noche *f* night. **~ vieja** New Year's Eve. **de ~** at night. **hacerse de ~** get dark. **hacer ~** spend the night. **media ~** midnight. **en la ~** (*LAm*), **por la ~** at night

Nochevieja In Spain and other Spanish-speaking countries, where it is known as Año Nuevo, it is customary to see the New Year in by eating twelve grapes for good luck, one on each chime of the clock at midnight.

Nochebuena *f* Christmas Eve

noción *f* notion. **nociones** *fpl* rudiments

nocivo *adj* harmful

nocturno *adj* nocturnal; (clase) evening; (tren etc) night. ● *m* nocturne

nodriza *f* wet nurse

nogal *m* walnut tree; (*madera*) walnut

nómada *adj* nomadic. ● *m & f* nomad

nombr|ado *adj* famous; (*susodicho*) aforementioned. **~amiento** *m* appointment. **~ar** *vt* appoint; (*citar*) mention. **~e** *m* name; (*Gram*) noun; (*fama*) renown. **~e de pila** Christian name. **en ~e de** in the name of. **no tener ~e** be unspeakable. **poner de ~e** call

nomeolvides *m invar* forget-me-not

nómina *f* payroll

nomina|l *adj* nominal. **~tivo** *adj & m* nominative. **~tivo a** (cheque etc) made out to

non *adj* odd. • *m* odd number. **pares y ~es** odds and evens

nono *adj* ninth

nordeste *adj* (región) north-eastern; (viento) north-easterly. • *m* northeast

nórdico *adj* Nordic. • *m* Northern European

noria *f* water-wheel; (*en una feria*) big wheel (*Brit*), Ferris wheel (*Amer*)

norma *f* rule

normal *adj* normal. • *f* teachers' training college. **~idad** *f* normality (*Brit*), normalcy (*Amer*). **~izar** 10 *vt* normalize. **~mente** *adv* normally, usually

noroeste *adj* (región) north-western; (viento) north-westerly. • *m* northwest

norte *adj* (región) northern; (viento, lado) north. • *m* north; (*fig, meta*) aim

Norteamérica *f* (North) America

norteamericano *adj & m* (North) American

norteño *adj* northern. • *m* northerner

Noruega *f* Norway

noruego *adj & m* Norwegian

nos *pron* (*acusativo*) us; (*dativo*) (to) us; (*reflexivo*) (to) ourselves; (*recíproco*) (to) each other

nosotros *pron* we; (*con prep*) us

nost|algia *f* nostalgia; (*de casa, de patria*) homesickness. **~álgico** *adj* nostalgic

nota *f* note; (*de examen etc*) mark. **de ~** famous. **de mala ~** notorious. **digno de ~** notable. **~ble** *adj* notable. **~ción** *f* notation. **~r** *vt* notice. **es de ~r** it should be noted. **hacerse ~r** stand out

notario *m* notary

notici|a *f* (piece of) news. **~as** *fpl* news. **atrasado de ~as** behind with the news. **tener ~as de** hear from. **~ario**, (*LAm*) **~ero** *m* news

notifica|ción *f* notification. **~r** 7 *vt* notify

notori|edad *f* notoriety. **~o** *adj* well-known; (*evidente*) obvious; (*notable*) marked

novato *adj* inexperienced. • *m* novice

novecientos *adj & m* nine hundred

noved|ad *f* newness; (*cosa nueva*) innovation; (*cambio*) change; (*moda*) latest fashion. **llegar sin ~ad** arrive safely. **~oso** *adj* novel

novel|a *f* novel. **~ista** *m & f* novelist

noveno *adj* ninth

noventa *adj & m* ninety; (*nonagésimo*) ninetieth

novia *f* girlfriend; (*prometida*) fiancée; (*en boda*) bride. **~r** *vi* (*LAm*) go out together. **~zgo** *m* engagement

novicio *m* novice

noviembre *m* November

novill|a *f* heifer. **~o** *m* bullock. **hacer ~os** play truant

novio *m* boyfriend; (*prometido*) fiancé; (*en boda*) bridegroom. **los ~s** the bride and groom

nub|arrón *m* large dark cloud. **~e** *f* cloud; (*de insectos etc*) swarm. **~lado** *adj* cloudy, overcast. • *m* cloud. **~lar** *vt* cloud. **~larse** *vpr* become cloudy; (vista) cloud over. **~oso** *adj* cloudy

nuca *f* back of the neck

nuclear *adj* nuclear

núcleo *m* nucleus

nudillo *m* knuckle

nudis|mo *m* nudism. **~ta** *m & f* nudist

nudo *m* knot; (*de asunto etc*) crux. **tener un ~ en la garganta** have a lump in one's throat. **~so** *adj* knotty

nuera *f* daughter-in-law

nuestro *adj* our. • *pron* ours. **~ amigo** our friend. **un coche ~** a car of ours

nueva *f* (piece of) news. **~s** *fpl* news. **~mente** *adv* again

Nueva Zelanda *f*, (*LAm*) **Nueva Zelandia** *f* New Zealand

nueve *adj & m* nine

nuevo *adj* new. **de ~** again. **estar ~** be as good as new

nuez *f* walnut. **~ de Adán** Adam's apple. **~ moscada** nutmeg

nul|idad *f* nullity; (*fam, persona*) dead loss ⊡. **~o** *adj* useless; (*Jurid*) null and void

num|eración *f* numbering. **~eral** *adj & m* numeral. **~erar** *vt* number. **~érico** *adj* numerical

número *m* number; (*arábigo, romano*) numeral; (*de zapatos etc*) size; (*billete de lotería*) lottery ticket; (*de publicación*) issue. **sin ~** countless

numeroso *adj* numerous

nunca *adv* never. **~ (ja)más** never again. **casi ~** hardly ever. **como ~** like never before. **más que ~** more than ever

nupcial *adj* nuptial. **banquete ~** wedding breakfast

nutria *f* otter

nutri|ción *f* nutrition. **~do** *adj* nourished, fed; (*fig*) large; (aplausos) loud; (fuego) heavy. **~r** *vt* nourish, feed; (*fig*) feed. **~tivo** *adj* nutritious. **valor** *m* **~tivo** nutritional value

nylon *m* nylon

Ññ

ñapa *f* (*LAm*) extra goods given free

ñato *adj* (*LAm*) snub-nosed

ñoñ|ería *f*, **~ez** *f* insipidity. **~o** *adj* insipid; (*tímido*) bashful; (*quisquilloso*) prudish

Oo

o *conj* or. **~ bien** rather. **~... ~** either ... or

oasis *m invar* oasis

obed|ecer ⑪ *vt/i* obey. **~iencia** *f* obedience. **~iente** *adj* obedient

obes|idad *f* obesity. **~o** *adj* obese

obispo *m* bishop

obje|ción *f* objection. **~tar** *vt/i* object

objetivo *adj* objective. • *m* objective; (*foto etc*) lens

objeto *m* object. **~r** *m* objector. **~ de conciencia** conscientious objector

oblicuo *adj* oblique

obliga|ción *f* obligation; (*Com*) bond. **~do** *adj* obliged; (*forzoso*) obligatory; **~r** 12 *vt* force, oblige. **~rse** *vpr.* **~rse a** undertake to. **~torio** *adj* obligatory

oboe *m* oboe. • *m & f* (*músico*) oboist

obra *f* work; (*acción*) deed; (*de teatro*) play; (*construcción*) building work. **~ maestra** masterpiece. **en ~s** under construction. **por ~ de** thanks to. **~r** *vt* do

obrero *adj* labour; (clase) working. • *m* workman; (*de fábrica, construcción*) worker

obscen|idad *f* obscenity. **~o** *adj* obscene

obscu... *véase* **oscu...**

obsequi|ar *vt* lavish attention on. **~ar con** give, present with. **~o** *m* gift, present; (*agasajo*) attention. **~oso** *adj* obliging

observa|ción *f* observation. **hacer una ~ción** make a remark. **~dor** *m* observer. **~ncia** *f* observance. **~r** *vt* observe; (*notar*) notice. **~torio** *m* observatory

obses|ión *f* obsession. **~ionar** *vt* obsess. **~ivo** *adj* obsessive. **~o** *adj* obsessed

obst|aculizar 10 *vt* hinder; hold up (tráfico). **~áculo** *m* obstacle

obstante: **no ~** *adv* however, nevertheless; (*como prep*) in spite of

obstar *vi.* **eso no obsta para que vaya** that should not prevent him from going

obstina|do *adj* obstinate. **~rse** *vpr.* **~rse en** (+ *infinitivo*) insist on (+ *gerundio*)

obstru|cción *f* obstruction. **~ir** 17 *vt* obstruct

obtener 40 *vt* get, obtain

obtura|dor *m* (*Foto*) shutter. **~r** *vt* plug; fill (muela etc)

obvio *adj* obvious

oca *f* goose

ocasi|ón *f* occasion; (*oportunidad*) opportunity. **aprovechar la ~ón** take the opportunity. **con ~ón de** on the occasion of. **de ~ón** bargain; (*usado*) second-hand. **en ~ones** sometimes. **perder una ~ón** miss a chance. **~onal** *adj* chance. **~onar** *vt* cause

ocaso *m* sunset; (*fig*) decline

occident|al *adj* western. • *m & f* westerner. **~e** *m* west

océano *m* ocean

ochenta *adj & m* eighty

ocho *adj & m* eight. **~cientos** *adj & m* eight hundred

ocio *m* idleness; (*tiempo libre*) leisure time. **~sidad** *f* idleness. **~so** *adj* idle; (*inútil*) pointless

oct|agonal *adj* octagonal. **~ágono** *m* octagon

octano *m* octane

octav|a *f* octave. **~o** *adj & m* eighth

octogenario *adj & m* octogenarian

octubre *m* October

ocular *adj* eye

oculista *m & f* ophthalmologist, ophthalmic optician

ocult|ar *vt* hide. **~arse** *vpr* hide. **~o** *adj* hidden; (*secreto*) secret

ocupa|ción *f* occupation. **~do**

adj occupied; (persona) busy. **estar ~do** (asiento) be taken; (línea telefónica) be engaged (*Brit*), be busy (*Amer*). **~nte** *m & f* occupant. **~r** *vt* occupy, take up (espacio). **~rse** *vpr* look after

ocurr|encia *f* occurrence, event; (*idea*) idea; (*que tiene gracia*) witty remark. **~ir** *vi* happen. **¿qué ~e?** what's the matter? **~irse** *vpr* occur. **se me ~e que** it occurs to me that

oda *f* ode

odi|ar *vt* hate. **~o** *m* hatred. **~oso** *adj* hateful; (persona) horrible

oeste *adj* (región) western; (viento, lado) west. ● *m* west

ofen|der *vt* offend; (*insultar*) insult. **~derse** *vpr* take offence. **~sa** *f* offence. **~siva** *f* offensive. **~sivo** *adj* offensive

oferta *f* offer; (*en subasta*) bid. **~s de empleo** situations vacant. **en ~** on (special) offer

oficial *adj* official. ● *m* skilled worker; (*Mil*) officer

oficin|a *f* office. **~a de colocación** employment office. **~a de turismo** tourist office. **horas** *fpl* **de ~a** business hours. **~ista** *m & f* office worker

oficio *m* trade. **~so** *adj* (*no oficial*) unofficial

ofrec|er [11] *vt* offer; give (fiesta, banquete etc); (*prometer*) promise. **~erse** *vpr* (persona) volunteer. **~imiento** *m* offer

ofrenda *f* offering. **~r** *vt* offer

ofuscar [7] *vt* blind; (*confundir*) confuse. **~se** *vpr* get worked up

oí|ble *adj* audible. **~do** *m* ear; (*sentido*) hearing. **al ~do** in one's ear. **de ~das** by hearsay. **conocer de ~das** have heard of. **de ~do** by ear. **duro de ~do** hard of hearing

oigo *vb véase* oír

oír [50] *vt* hear. ¡oiga! listen!; (*al teléfono*) hello!

ojal *m* buttonhole

ojalá *int* I hope so! ● *conj* if only

ojea|da *f* glance. **dar una ~da a, echar una ~da a** have a quick glance at. **~r** *vt* have a look at

ojeras *fpl* rings under one's eyes

ojeriza *f* ill will. **tener ~ a** have a grudge against

ojo *m* eye; (*de cerradura*) keyhole; (*de un puente*) span. **¡~!** careful!

ola *f* wave

olé *int* bravo!

olea|da *f* wave. **~je** *m* swell

óleo *m* oil; (*cuadro*) oil painting

oleoducto *m* oil pipeline

oler [2] (*las formas que empiecen por* **ue** *se escriben* **hue**) *vt* smell. ● *vi* smell (a of). **me huele mal** (*fig*) it sounds fishy to me

olfat|ear *vt* sniff; scent (rastro). **~o** *m* (sense of) smell; (*fig*) intuition

olimpiada *f*, **olimpíada** *f* Olympic games, Olympics

olímpico *adj* Olympic; (*fig, fam*) total

oliv|a *f* olive. **~ar** *m* olive grove. **~o** *m* olive tree

olla *f* pot, casserole. **~ a/de presión, ~ exprés** pressure cooker

olmo *m* elm (tree)

olor *m* smell. **~oso** *adj* sweet-smelling

olvid|adizo *adj* forgetful. **~ar** *vt* forget. **~arse** *vpr* forget. **~arse de** forget. **se me ~ó** I forgot. **~o** *m* oblivion; (*acto*) omission

ombligo *m* navel

omi|sión *f* omission. **~tir** *vt* omit

ómnibus *adj* omnibus

omnipotente *adj* omnipotent

omóplato *m* shoulder blade

once *adj & m* eleven

ond|a *f* wave. **~a corta** short wave. **~a larga** long wave. **longitud** *f* **de ~a** wavelength. **~ear** *vi* wave; (agua) ripple. **~ulación** *f* undulation; (*del pelo*) wave. **~ular** *vi* wave

onomásti|co *adj* (índice) of names. ● *m* (*LAm*) saint's day

onomástica See ▶**SANTO** 

ONU *abrev* (**Organización de las Naciones Unidas**) UN

OPA *f* take-over bid

opac|ar **7** (*LAm*) make opaque; (*deslucir*) mar; (*anular*) overshadow. **~o** *adj* opaque; (*fig*) dull

opci|ón *f* option. **~onal** *adj* optional

open-jaw *m* open jaws ticket

ópera *f* opera

opera|ción *f* operation; (*Com*) transaction; **~ retorno** (*Esp*) *return to work* (*after the holidays*). **~dor** *m* operator; (*TV*) cameraman; (*Mex, obrero*) machinist. **~r** *vt* operate on; work (milagro etc); (*Mex*) operate (máquina). ● *vi* operate; (*Com*) deal. **~rio** *m* machinist. **~rse** *vpr* take place; (*Med*) have an operation. **~torio** *adj* operative

opereta *f* operetta

opin|ar *vi* express one's opinion. ● *vt* think. **~ que** think that. **¿qué opinas?** what do you think? **~ión** *f* opinion. **la ~ión pública** public opinion

opio *m* opium

opone|nte *adj* opposing. ● *m & f* opponent. **~r** *vt* oppose; offer (resistencia); raise (objeción). **~rse** *vpr* be opposed; (dos personas) oppose each other

oporto *m* port (wine)

oportun|idad *f* opportunity; (*cualidad de oportuno*) timeliness; (*LAm, ocasión*) occasion. **~ista** *m & f* opportunist. **~o** *adj* opportune; (*apropiado*) suitable

oposi|ción *f* opposition. **~ciones** *fpl* public examination. **~tor** *m* candidate; (*Pol*) opponent

opres|ión *f* oppression; (*ahogo*) difficulty in breathing. **~ivo** *adj* oppressive. **~or** *m* oppressor

oprimir *vt* squeeze; press (botón etc); (ropa) be too tight for; (*fig*) oppress

optar *vi* choose. **~ por** opt for

óptic|a *f* optics; (*tienda*) optician's (shop). **~o** *adj* optic(al). ● *m* optician

optimis|mo *m* optimism. **~ta** *adj* optimistic. ● *m & f* optimist

óptimo *adj* ideal; (condiciones) perfect

opuesto *adj* opposite; (opiniones) conflicting

opulen|cia *f* opulence. **~to** *adj* opulent

oración *f* prayer; (*Gram*) sentence

ora|dor *m* speaker. **~l** *adj* oral

órale *int* (*Mex*) come on!; (*de acuerdo*) OK!

orar *vi* pray (**por** for)

órbita *f* orbit

orden *f* order. **~ del día** agenda. **órdenes** *fpl* **sagradas** Holy Orders. **a sus órdenes** (*esp Mex*) can I help you? **~ de arresto** arrest warrant. **en ~** in order. **por ~** in turn.

~**ado** *adj* tidy

ordenador *m* computer

ordena|nza *f* ordinance. • *m* (*Mil*) orderly. ~**r** *vt* put in order; (*mandar*) order; (*Relig*) ordain; (*LAm, en restaurante*) order

ordeñar *vt* milk

ordinario *adj* ordinary; (*grosero*) common; (*de mala calidad*) poor-quality

orear *vt* air

orégano *m* oregano

oreja *f* ear

orfanato *m* orphanage

orfebre *m* goldsmith, silversmith

orfeón *m* choral society

orgánico *adj* organic

organillo *m* barrel-organ

organismo *m* organism

organista *m & f* organist

organiza|ción *f* organization. ~**dor** *m* organizer. ~**r** 10 *vt* organize. ~**rse** *vpr* get organized

O

órgano *m* organ

orgasmo *m* orgasm

orgía *f* orgy

orgullo *m* pride. ~**so** *adj* proud

orientación *f* orientation; (*guía*) guidance; (*Archit*) aspect

oriental *adj & m & f* oriental

orientar *vt* position; advise (persona). ~**se** *vpr* point; (persona) find one's bearings

oriente *m* east

orificio *m* hole

orig|en *m* origin. **dar** ~**en a** give rise to. ~**inal** *adj* original; (*excéntrico*) odd. ~**inalidad** *f* originality. ~**inar** *vt* give rise to. ~**inario** *adj* original; (*nativo*) native. **ser** ~**inario de** come from. ~**inarse** *vpr* originate; (incendio) start

orilla *f* (*del mar*) shore; (*de río*) bank; (*borde*) edge. **a** ~**s del mar** by the sea

orina *f* urine. ~**l** *m* chamber-pot. ~**r** *vi* urinate

oriundo *adj* native. **ser** ~ **de** (persona) come from; (especie etc) native to

ornamental *adj* ornamental

ornitología *f* ornithology

oro *m* gold. ~**s** *mpl* Spanish card suit. ~ **de ley** 9 carat gold. **hacerse de** ~ make a fortune. **prometer el** ~ **y el moro** promise the moon

orquesta *f* orchestra. ~**l** *adj* orchestral. ~**r** *vt* orchestrate

orquídea *f* orchid

ortiga *f* nettle

ortodoxo *adj* orthodox

ortografía *f* spelling

ortopédico *adj* orthopaedic

oruga *f* caterpillar

orzuelo *m* sty

os *pron* (*acusativo*) you; (*dativo*) (to) you; (*reflexivo*) (to) yourselves; (*recíproco*) (to) each other

osad|ía *f* boldness. ~**o** *adj* bold

oscila|ción *f* swinging; (*de precios*) fluctuation; (*Tec*) oscillation. ~**r** *vi* swing; (precio) fluctuate; (*Tec*) oscillate

oscur|ecer 11 *vi* get dark. • *vt* darken; (*fig*) obscure. ~**ecerse** *vpr* grow dark; (*nublarse*) cloud over. ~**idad** *f* darkness; (*fig*) obscurity. ~**o** *adj* dark; (*fig*) obscure. **a** ~**as** in the dark

óseo *adj* bone

oso *m* bear. ~ **de felpa**, ~ **de peluche** teddy bear

ostensible *adj* obvious

ostent|ación *f* ostentation. ~**ar**

vt show off; (*mostrar*) show. **~oso** *adj* ostentatious

osteópata *m & f* osteopath

ostión *m* (*esp Mex*) oyster

ostra *f* oyster

ostracismo *m* ostracism

Otan *abrev* (**Organización del Tratado del Atlántico Norte**) NATO, North Atlantic Treaty Organization

otitis *f* inflammation of the ear

otoño *m* autumn (*Brit*), fall (*Amer*)

otorga|miento *m* granting. **~r** 12 *vt* give; grant (préstamo); (*Jurid*) draw up (testamento)

otorrinolaringólogo *m* ear, nose and throat specialist

otro, otra

● *adjetivo*

····➤ another; (*con artículo, posesivo*) other. **come ~ pedazo** have another piece. **el ~ día** the other day. **mi ~ coche** my other car. **otra cosa** something else. **otra persona** somebody else. **otra vez** again

····➤ (*en plural*) other; (*con numeral*) another. **en otras ocasiones** on other occasions. **~s 3 vasos** another 3 glasses

····➤ (*siguiente*) next. **al ~ día** the next day. **me bajo en la otra estación** I get off at the next station

● *pronombre*

····➤ (*cosa*) another one. **lo cambié por ~** I changed it for another one

····➤ (*persona*) someone else. **invitó a ~** she invited someone else

····➤ (*en plural*) (some) others. **tengo ~s en casa** I have (some) others at home. **~s piensan lo contrario** others think the opposite

····➤ (*con artículo*) **el ~** the other one. **los ~s** the others. **uno detrás del ~** one after the other. **los ~s no vinieron** the others didn't come. **esta semana no, la otra** not this week, next week. **de un día para el ~** from one day to the next

➡ Para usos complementarios ver **uno, tanto**

ovación *f* ovation

oval *adj*, **ovalado** *adj* oval

óvalo *m* oval

ovario *m* ovary

oveja *f* sheep; (*hembra*) ewe

overol *m* (*LAm*) overalls

ovillo *m* ball. **hacerse un ~** curl up

OVNI *abrev* (**objeto volante no identificado**) UFO

ovulación *f* ovulation

oxida|ción *f* rusting. **~r** *vi* rust. **~rse** *vpr* go rusty

óxido *m* rust; (*en química*) oxide

oxígeno *m* oxygen

oye *vb véase* **OÍR**

oyente *adj* listening. ● *m & f* listener; (*Univ*) occasional student

ozono *m* ozone

Pp

pabellón *m* pavilion; (*en jardín*) summerhouse; (*en hospital*) block; (*de instrumento*) bell; (*bandera*) flag
pacer 11 *vi* graze
pachucho *adj* (fruta) overripe; (persona) poorly
pacien|cia *f* patience. **perder la ~cia** lose patience. **~te** *adj & m & f* patient
pacificar 7 *vt* pacify. **~se** *vpr* calm down
pacífico *adj* peaceful. **el (Océano) P~** the Pacific (Ocean)
pacifis|mo *m* pacifism. **~ta** *adj & m & f* pacifist
pact|ar *vi* agree, make a pact. **~o** *m* pact, agreement
padec|er 11 *vt/i* suffer (**de** from); (*soportar*) bear. **~er del corazón** have heart trouble. **~imiento** *m* suffering

P

padrastro *m* stepfather
padre *adj* ⊡ terrible; (*Mex, estupendo*) great. ● *m* father. **~s** *mpl* parents
padrino *m* godfather; (*en boda*) man who gives away the bride
padrón *m* register. **~ electoral** (*LAm*) electoral roll
paella *f* paella
paga *f* payment; (*sueldo*) pay. **~dero** *adj* payable
pagano *adj & m* pagan
pagar 12 *vt* pay; pay for (compras). ● *vi* pay. **~é** *m* IOU
página *f* page
pago *m* payment
país *m* country; (*ciudadanos*) nation. **~ natal** native land. **el P~ Vasco** the Basque Country. **los P~es Bajos** the Low Countries
paisaje *m* landscape, scenery
paisano *m* compatriot
paja *f* straw; (*en texto*) padding
pájaro *m* bird. **~ carpintero** woodpecker
paje *m* page
pala *f* shovel; (*para cavar*) spade; (*para basura*) dustpan; (*de pimpón*) bat
palabr|a *f* word; (*habla*) speech. **pedir la ~a** ask to speak. **tomar la ~a** take the floor. **~ota** *f* swear-word. **decir ~otas** swear
palacio *m* palace
paladar *m* palate
palanca *f* lever; (*fig*) influence. **~ de cambio (de velocidades)** gear lever (*Brit*), gear shift (*Amer*)
palangana *f* washbasin (*Brit*), washbowl (*Amer*)
palco *m* (*en el teatro*) box
palestino *adj & m* Palestinian
paleta *f* (*de pintor*) palette; (*de albañil*) trowel
paleto *m* yokel
paliativo *adj & m* palliative
palide|cer 11 *vi* turn pale. **~z** *f* paleness
pálido *adj* pale. **ponerse ~** turn pale
palillo *m* (*de dientes*) toothpick; (*para comer*) chopstick
paliza *f* beating
palma *f* (*de la mano*) palm; (*árbol*) palm (tree); (*de dátiles*) date palm. **dar ~s** clap. **~da** *f* pat; (*LAm*) slap. **~das** *fpl* applause
palmera *f* palm tree
palmo *m* span; (*fig*) few inches. **~ a ~** inch by inch

palmote|ar *vi* clap. **~o** *m* clapping, applause

palo *m* stick; (*de valla*) post; (*de golf*) club; (*golpe*) blow; (*de naipes*) suit; (*mástil*) mast

paloma *f* pigeon; (*blanca, símbolo*) dove

palomitas *fpl* popcorn

palpar *vt* feel

palpita|ción *f* palpitation. **~nte** *adj* throbbing. **~r** *vi* beat; (*latir con fuerza*) pound; (vena, sien) throb

palta *f* (*LAm*) avocado (pear)

paludismo *m* malaria

pamela *f* (*woman's*) *broad-brimmed dress hat*

pamp|a *f* pampas. **~ero** *adj* of the pampas

pan *m* bread; (*barra*) loaf. **~ integral** wholewheat bread, wholemeal bread (*Brit*). **~ tostado** toast. **~ rallado** breadcrumbs. **ganarse el ~** earn one's living

pana *f* corduroy

panader|ía *f* bakery; (*tienda*) baker's (shop). **~o** *m* baker

panal *m* honeycomb

panameño *adj & m* Panamanian

pancarta *f* banner, placard

panda *m* panda

pander|eta *f* (small) tambourine **~o** *m* tambourine

pandilla *f* gang

panecillo *m* (bread) roll

panel *m* panel

panfleto *m* pamphlet

pánico *m* panic. **tener ~** be terrified (a of)

panor|ama *m* panorama. **~ámico** *adj* panoramic

panque *m* (*Mex*) sponge cake

pantaletas *fpl* (*Mex*) panties, knickers (*Brit*)

pantalla *f* screen; (*de lámpara*) (lamp)shade

pantalón *m*, **pantalones** *mpl* trousers. **~ a la cadera** bumsters

pantano *m* marsh; (*embalse*) reservoir. **~so** *adj* marshy

pantera *f* panther

panti *m*, (*Mex*) **pantimedias** *fpl* tights (*Brit*), pantyhose (*Amer*)

pantomima *f* pantomime

pantorrilla *f* calf

pantufla *f* slipper

panz|a *f* belly. **~udo** *adj* potbellied

pañal *m* nappy (*Brit*), diaper (*Amer*)

paño *m* material; (*de lana*) woollen cloth; (*trapo*) cloth. **~ de cocina** dishcloth; (*para secar*) tea towel. **~ higiénico** sanitary towel. **en ~s menores** in one's underclothes

pañuelo *m* handkerchief; (*de cabeza*) scarf

papa *m* pope. ● *f* (*LAm*) potato. **~s fritas** (*LAm*) chips (*Brit*), French fries (*Amer*); (*de paquete*) crisps (*Brit*), chips (*Amer*)

papá *m* dad(dy). **~s** *mpl* parents. **P~ Noel** Father Christmas

papada *f* (*de persona*) double chin

papagayo *m* parrot

papalote *m* (*Mex*) kite

papanatas *m invar* simpleton

paparrucha *f* (*tontería*) silly thing

papaya *f* papaya, pawpaw

papel *m* paper; (*en el teatro etc*) role. **~ carbón** carbon paper. **~ de calcar** tracing paper. **~ de envolver** wrapping paper. **~ de plata** silver paper. **~ higiénico** toilet paper. ~ **pintado** wallpaper. ~ **secante** blotting paper. **~eo** *m* paperwork. **~era** *f* waste-paper basket. **~ería** *f* stationer's (shop). **~eta** *f* (*para votar*) (ballot) paper

paperas *fpl* mumps

paquete *m* packet; (*bulto*) parcel; (*LAm, de papas fritas*) bag; (*Mex, problema*) headache. ~ **postal** parcel

Paquistán *m* Pakistan

paquistaní *adj & m* Pakistani

par *adj* (número) even. ● *m* couple; (*dos cosas iguales*) pair. **a ~es** two by two. **de ~ en ~** wide open. **~es y nones** odds and evens. **sin ~** without equal. ● *f* par. **a la ~** (*Com*) at par. **a la ~ que** at the same time

para *preposición*

- ····➤ for. **es ~ ti** it's for you. **~ siempre** for ever. **¿~ qué?** what for? **~ mi cumpleaños** for my birthday
- ····➤ (*con infinitivo*) to. **es muy tarde ~ llamar** it's too late to call. **salió ~ divertirse** he went out to have fun. **lo hago ~ ahorrar** I do it (in order) to save money
- ····➤ (*dirección*) **iba ~ la oficina** he was going to the office. **empújalo ~ atrás** push it back. **¿vas ~ casa?** are you going home?
- ····➤ (*tiempo*) by. **debe estar listo ~ el 5** it must be ready by the 5th. **~ entonces** by then
- ····➤ (*LAm, hora*) to. **son 5 ~ la una** it's 5 to one
- ····➤ **~ que** so (that). **grité ~ que me oyera** I shouted so (that) he could hear me.

Note that **para que** is always followed by a verb in the subjunctive

parabienes *mpl* congratulations

parábola *f* (*narración*) parable

parabólica *f* satellite dish

para|brisas *m invar* windscreen (*Brit*), windshield (*Amer*). **~caídas** *m invar* parachute. **~caidista** *m & f* parachutist; (*Mil*) paratrooper. **~choques** *m invar* bumper (*Brit*), fender (*Amer*) (*Rail*) buffer

parad|a *f* (*acción*) stop; (*lugar*) bus stop; (*de taxis*) rank; (*Mil*) parade. **~ero** *m* whereabouts; (*LAm, lugar*) bus stop. **~o** *adj* stationary; (desempleado) unemployed. **estar ~** (*LAm, de pie*) be standing

paradoja *f* paradox

parador *m* state-owned hotel

i

parador (nacional de turismo) A national chain of hotels in Spain. They are often converted castles, palaces and monasteries. They provide a high standard of accommodation but are relatively inexpensive and often act as showcases for local craftsmanship and cooking.

parafina *f* paraffin

paraguas *m invar* umbrella

Paraguay *m* Paraguay

paraguayo *adj & m* Paraguayan

paraíso *m* paradise; (*en el teatro*) gallery

paralel|a *f* parallel (line). **~as** *fpl* parallel bars. **~o** *adj & m* parallel

par|álisis *f invar* paralysis. **~alítico** *adj* paralytic. **~alizar** 10 *vt*

paralyse
parámetro *m* parameter
paramilitar *adj* paramilitary
páramo *m* bleak upland
parangón *m* comparison.
paraninfo *m* main hall
paranoi|a *f* paranoia. **~co** *adj* paranoiac
parar *vt/i* stop. **sin ~** continuously. **~se** *vpr* stop; (*LAm, ponerse de pie*) stand
pararrayos *m invar* lightning conductor
parásito *adj* parasitic. ● *m* parasite
parcela *f* plot. **~r** *vt* divide into plots
parche *m* patch
parcial *adj* partial. **a tiempo ~** part-time. **~idad** *f* prejudice
parco *adj* laconic; (*sobrio*) frugal
parear *vt* put into pairs
parec|er *m* opinion. **al ~er** apparently. **a mi ~er** in my opinion. ● *vi* 11 seem; (*asemejarse*) look like; (*tener aspecto de*) look. **me ~e** I think. **~e fácil** it looks easy. **¿qué te ~e?** what do you think? **según ~e** apparently. **~erse** *vpr* look like. **~ido** *adj* similar. **bien ~ido** good-looking. ● *m* similarity
pared *f* wall. **~ por medio** next door. **~ón** *m* (*de fusilamiento*) wall. **llevar al ~ón** shoot
parej|a *f* pair; (*hombre y mujer*) couple; (*compañero*) partner. **~a de hecho** *legalised partnership of unmarried couple*. **~o** *adj* the same; (*LAm, sin desniveles*) even; (*LAm, liso*) smooth; (*Mex, equitativo*) equal. ● *adv* (*LAm*) evenly
parente|la *f* relations. **~sco** *m* relationship
paréntesis *m invar* parenthesis, bracket (*Brit*); (*intervalo*) break. **entre ~** in brackets (*Brit*), in parenthesis: (*fig*) by the way
paria *m & f* outcast
paridad *f* equality; (*Com*) parity
pariente *m & f* relation, relative
parir *vt* give birth to. ● *vi* give birth
parisiense *adj & m & f*, **parisino** *adj & m* Parisian
parking /'parkin/ *m* car park (*Brit*), parking lot (*Amer*)
parlament|ar *vi* talk. **~ario** *adj* parliamentary. ● *m* member of parliament (*Brit*), congressman (*Amer*). **~o** *m* parliament
parlanchín *adj* talkative. ● *m* chatterbox
parlante *m* (*LAm*) loudspeaker
paro *m* stoppage; (*desempleo*) unemployment; (*subsidio*) unemployment benefit; (*LAm, huelga*) strike. **~ cardíaco** cardiac arrest
parodia *f* parody
parpadear *vi* blink; (luz) flicker
párpado *m* eyelid
parque *m* park. **~ de atracciones** funfair. **~ eólico** wind farm. **~ infantil** playground. **~ zoológico** zoo, zoological gardens
parquímetro *m* parking meter
parra *f* grapevine
párrafo *m* paragraph
parrilla *f* grill; (*LAm, Auto*) luggage rack. **a la ~** grilled. **~da** *f* grill
párroco *m* parish priest
parroquia *f* parish; (*iglesia*) parish church. **~no** *m* parishioner
parte *m* (*informe*) report. **dar ~** report. **de mi ~** for me ● *f* part; (*porción*) share; (*Jurid*) party; (*Mex,*

repuesto) spare (part). **de ~ de** from. **¿de ~ de quién?** (*al teléfono*) who's speaking? **en cualquier ~** anywhere. **en gran ~** largely. **en ~** partly. **en todas ~s** everywhere. **la mayor ~** the majority. **la ~ superior** the top. **ninguna ~** nowhere. **por otra ~** on the other hand. **por todas ~s** everywhere

partera *f* midwife

partición *f* division; (*Pol*) partition

participa|ción *f* participation; (*noticia*) announcement; (*de lotería*) share. **~nte** *adj* participating. • *m & f* participant. **~r** *vt* announce. • *vi* take part

participio *m* participle

particular *adj* particular; (clase) private. **nada de ~** nothing special. • *m* private individual.

partida *f* departure; (*en registro*) entry; (*documento*) certificate; (*de mercancías*) consignment; (*juego*) game; (*de gente*) group

P

partidario *adj & m* partisan. **~ de** in favour of

parti|do *m* (*Pol*) party; (*encuentro*) match, game; (*LAm, de ajedrez*) game. **~r** *vt* cut; (*romper*) break; crack (nueces). • *vi* leave. **a ~r de** from. **~ de** start from. **~rse** *vpr* (*romperse*) break; (*dividirse*) split

partitura *f* (*Mus*) score

parto *m* labour. **estar de ~** be in labour

parvulario *m* kindergarten, nursery school (*Brit*)

pasa *f* raisin. **~ de Corinto** currant

pasa|da *f* passing; (*de puntos*) row. **de ~da** in passing. **~dero** *adj* passable. **~dizo** *m* passage. **~do** *adj* past; (día, mes etc) last; (*anticuado*) old-fashioned; (comida) bad, off. **~do mañana** the day after tomorrow. **~dos tres días** after three days. **~dor** *m* bolt; (*de pelo*) hair-slide

pasaje *m* passage; (*pasajeros*) passengers; (*LAm, de avión etc*) ticket. **~ro** *adj* passing. • *m* passenger

pasamano(s) *m* handrail; (*barandilla de escalera*) banister(s)

pasamontañas *m invar* balaclava

pasaporte *m* passport

pasar *vt* pass; (*atravesar*) go through; (*filtrar*) strain; spend (tiempo); show (película); (*tolerar*) tolerate; give (mensaje, enfermedad). • *vi* pass; (*suceder*) happen; (*ir*) go; (*venir*) come; (tiempo) go by. **~ de** have no interest in. **~lo bien** have a good time. **~ frío** be cold. **~ la aspiradora** vacuum. **~ por alto** leave out. **lo que pasa es que** the fact is that. **pase lo que pase** whatever happens. **¡pase Vd!** come in!, go in! **¡que lo pases bien!** have a good time! **¿qué pasa?** what's the matter?, what's happening? **~se** *vpr* pass; (dolor) go away; (flores) wither; (comida) go bad; spend (tiempo); (*excederse*) go too far

pasarela *f* footbridge; (*Naut*) gangway

pasatiempo *m* hobby, pastime

Pascua *f* (*fiesta de los hebreos*) Passover; (*de Resurrección*) Easter; (*Navidad*) Christmas. **~s** *fpl* Christmas

pase *m* pass

pase|ante *m & f* passer-by. **~ar** *vt* walk (perro); (*exhibir*) show off. • *vi* walk. **ir a ~ar, salir a ~ar** walk. **~arse** *vpr* walk. **~o** *m* walk; (*en coche etc*) ride; (*calle*) avenue. **~o**

marítimo promenade. **dar un ~o, ir de ~** go for a walk. **¡vete a ~o!** [I] get lost! [I]

pasillo *m* corridor; (*de cine, avión*) aisle

pasión *f* passion

pasivo *adj* passive

pasm|ar *vt* astonish. **~arse** *vpr* be astonished

paso *m* step; (*acción de pasar*) passing; (*camino*) way; (*entre montañas*) pass; (*estrecho*) strait(s). **~ a nivel** level crossing (*Brit*), grade crossing (*Amer*). **~ de cebra** zebra crossing. **~ de peatones** pedestrian crossing. **~ elevado** flyover (*Brit*), overpass (*Amer*). **a cada ~** at every turn. **a dos ~s** very near. **de ~** in passing. **de ~ por** just passing through. **oír ~s** hear footsteps. **prohibido el ~** no entry

pasota *m & f* drop-out

pasta *f* paste; (*masa*) dough; (*sl, dinero*) dough [x]. **~s** *fpl* pasta; (*pasteles*) pastries. **~ de dientes, ~ dentífrica** toothpaste

pastel *m* cake; (*empanada*) pie; (*lápiz*) pastel. **~ería** *f* cake shop

pasteurizado *adj* pasteurized

pastilla *f* pastille; (*de jabón*) bar; (*de chocolate*) piece

pasto *m* pasture; (*hierba*) grass; (*LAm, césped*) lawn. **~r** *m* shepherd; (*Relig*) minister. **~ra** *f* shepherdess

pata *f* leg; (*pie de perro, gato*) paw; (*de ave*) foot. **~s arriba** upside down. **a cuatro ~s** on all fours. **meter la ~** put one's foot in it. **tener mala ~** have bad luck. **~da** *f* kick. **~lear** *vi* stamp one's feet; (niño) kick

patata *f* potato. **~s fritas** chips (*Brit*), French fries (*Amer*); (*de bolsa*) (potato) crisps (*Brit*), (potato) chips (*Amer*)

patente *adj* obvious. • *f* licence

patern|al *adj* paternal; (cariño etc) fatherly. **~idad** *f* paternity. **~o** *adj* paternal; (cariño etc) fatherly

patético *adj* moving

patillas *fpl* sideburns

patín *m* skate; (*con ruedas*) roller skate. **patines en línea** Rollerblades (P)

patina|dor *m* skater. **~je** *m* skating. **~r** *vi* skate; (*resbalar*) slide; (coche) skid

patio *m* patio. **~ de butacas** stalls (*Brit*), orchestra (*Amer*)

pato *m* duck

patológico *adj* pathological

patoso *adj* clumsy

patraña *f* hoax

patria *f* homeland

patriarca *m* patriarch

patrimonio *m* patrimony; (*fig*) heritage

patri|ota *adj* patriotic. • *m & f* patriot. **~otismo** *m* patriotism

patrocin|ar *vt* sponsor. **~io** *m* sponsorship

patrón *m* (*jefe*) boss; (*de pensión etc*) landlord; (*en costura*) pattern

patrulla *f* patrol; (*fig, cuadrilla*) group. **~r** *vt/i* patrol

pausa *f* pause. **~do** *adj* slow

pauta *f* guideline

paviment|ar *vt* pave. **~o** *m* pavement

pavo *m* turkey. **~ real** peacock

pavor *m* terror

payas|ada *f* buffoonery. **~o** *m* clown

paz *f* peace

peaje *m* toll

peatón *m* pedestrian

peca *f* freckle

peca|do *m* sin; (*defecto*) fault. **~dor** *m* sinner. **~minoso** *adj* sinful. **~r** 7 *vi* sin

pech|o *m* chest; (*de mujer*) breast; (*fig, corazón*) heart. **dar el ~o a un niño** breast-feed a child. **tomar a ~o** take to heart. **~uga** *f* breast

pecoso *adj* freckled

peculiar *adj* peculiar, particular. **~idad** *f* peculiarity

pedal *m* pedal. **~ear** *vi* pedal

pedante *adj* pedantic

pedazo *m* piece, bit. **a ~s** in pieces. **hacer(se) ~s** smash

pediatra *m & f* paediatrician

pedicuro *m* chiropodist

pedi|do *m* order; (*LAm, solicitud*) request. **~r** 5 *vt* ask for; (*Com, en restaurante*) order. • *vi* ask. **~r prestado** borrow

pega|dizo *adj* catchy. **~joso** *adj* sticky

P

pega|mento *m* glue. **~r** 12 *vt* stick (on); (*coser*) sew on; give (enfermedad etc); (*juntar*) join; (*golpear*) hit; (*dar*) give. **~r fuego a** set fire to • *vi* stick. **~rse** *vpr* stick; (*pelearse*) hit each other. **~tina** *f* sticker

pein|ado *m* hairstyle. **~ar** *vt* comb. **~arse** *vpr* comb one's hair. **~e** *m* comb. **~eta** *f* ornamental comb

p.ej. *abrev* (**por ejemplo**) e.g.

pelado *adj* (fruta) peeled; (cabeza) bald; (terreno) bare

pela|je *m* (*de animal*) fur; (*fig, aspecto*) appearance. **~mbre** *m* (*de animal*) fur; (*de persona*) thick hair

pelar *vt* peel; shell (habas); skin (tomates); pluck (ave)

peldaño *m* step; (*de escalera de mano*) rung

pelea *f* fight; (*discusión*) quarrel. **~r** *vi* fight; (*discutir*) quarrel. **~rse** *vpr* fight; (*discutir*) quarrel

peletería *f* fur shop

peliagudo *adj* difficult, tricky

pelícano *m* pelican

película *f* film (*esp Brit*), movie (*esp Amer*). **~ de dibujos animados** cartoon (film)

peligro *m* danger; (*riesgo*) hazard, risk. **poner en ~** endanger. **~so** *adj* dangerous

pelirrojo *adj* red-haired

pellejo *m* skin

pellizc|ar 7 *vt* pinch. **~o** *m* pinch

pelma *m & f*, **pelmazo** *m* bore, nuisance

pelo *m* hair. **no tener ~s en la lengua** be outspoken. **tomar el ~ a uno** pull s.o.'s leg

pelota *f* ball. **~ vasca** pelota. **hacer la ~ a uno** suck up to s.o.

pelotera *f* squabble

peluca *f* wig

peludo *adj* hairy

peluquer|ía *f* hairdresser's. **~o** *m* hairdresser

pelusa *f* down

pena *f* sadness; (lástima) pity; (*LAm, vergüenza*) embarrassment; (*Jurid*) sentence. **~ de muerte** death penalty. **a duras ~s** with difficulty. **da ~ que** it's a pity that. **me da ~** it makes me sad. **merecer la ~** be worthwhile. **pasar ~s** suffer hardship. **¡qué ~!** what a pity! **valer la ~** be worthwhile

penal *adj* penal; (derecho) criminal. • *m* prison; (*LAm, penalty*)

penalty. **~idad** *f* suffering; (*Jurid*) penalty. **~ty** *m* penalty

pendiente *adj* hanging; (cuenta) outstanding; (asunto etc) pending. ● *m* earring. ● *f* slope

péndulo *m* pendulum

pene *m* penis

penetra|nte *adj* penetrating; (sonido) piercing; (viento) bitter. **~r** *vt* penetrate; (*fig*) pierce. ● *vi.* **~r en** penetrate; (*entrar*) go into

penicilina *f* penicillin

pen|ínsula *f* peninsula. **~insular** *adj* peninsular

penique *m* penny

penitencia *f* penitence; (*castigo*) penance

penoso *adj* painful; (*difícil*) difficult; (*LAm, tímido*) shy; (*LAm, embarazoso*) embarrassing

pensa|do *adj*. **bien ~do** all things considered. **menos ~do** least expected. **~dor** *m* thinker. **~miento** *m* thought. **~r** **1** *vt* think; (*considerar*) consider. **cuando menos se piensa** when least expected. **¡ni ~rlo!** no way! **pienso que sí** I think so. ● *vi* think. **~r en** think about. **~tivo** *adj* thoughtful

pensi|ón *f* pension; (*casa de huéspedes*) guest-house. **~ón completa** full board. **~onista** *m & f* pensioner; (*huésped*) lodger

penúltimo *adj & m* penultimate, last but one

penumbra *f* half-light

penuria *f* shortage. **pasar ~s** suffer hardship

peñ|a *f* rock; (*de amigos*) group; (*LAm, club*) folk club. **~ón** *m* rock. **el P~ón de Gibraltar** The Rock (of Gibraltar)

peón *m* labourer; (*en ajedrez*) pawn; (*en damas*) piece

peonza *f* (spinning) top

peor *adj* (*comparativo*) worse; (*superlativo*) worst. ● *adv* worse. **de mal en ~** from bad to worse. **lo ~** the worst thing. **tanto ~** so much the worse

pepin|illo *m* gherkin. **~o** *m* cucumber. **(no) me importa un ~o** I couldn't care less

pepita *f* pip; (*de oro*) nugget

pequeñ|ez *f* smallness; (*minucia*) trifle. **~o** *adj* small, little; (*de edad*) young; (*menor*) younger. ● *m* little one. **es el ~o** he's the youngest

pera *f* (*fruta*) pear. **~l** *m* pear (tree)

percance *m* mishap

percatarse *vpr.* **~ de** notice

perc|epción *f* perception. **~ibir** *vt* perceive; earn (dinero)

percha *f* hanger; (*de aves*) perch

percusión *f* percussion

perde|dor *adj* losing. ● *m* loser. **~r** **1** *vt* lose; (*malgastar*) waste; miss (tren etc). ● *vi* lose. **~rse** *vpr* get lost; (*desaparecer*) disappear; (*desperdiciarse*) be wasted; (*estropearse*) be spoilt. **echar(se) a ~r** spoil

pérdida *f* loss; (*de líquido*) leak; (*de tiempo*) waste

perdido *adj* lost

perdiz *f* partridge

perd|ón *m* pardon, forgiveness. **pedir ~ón** apologize. ● *int* sorry! **~onar** *vt* excuse, forgive; (*Jurid*) pardon. **¡~one (Vd)!** sorry!

perdura|ble *adj* lasting. **~r** *vi* last

perece|dero *adj* perishable. **~r** **11** *vi* perish

peregrin|ación *f* pilgrimage.

~o *adj* strange. • *m* pilgrim
perejil *m* parsley
perengano *m* so-and-so
perenne *adj* everlasting; (*planta*) perennial
perez|a *f* laziness. **~oso** *adj* lazy
perfec|ción *f* perfection. **a la ~ción** perfectly, to perfection. **~cionar** *vt* perfect; (*mejorar*) improve. **~cionista** *m & f* perfectionist. **~to** *adj* perfect; (*completo*) complete
perfil *m* profile; (*contorno*) outline. **~ado** *adj* well-shaped
perfora|ción *f* perforation. **~dora** *f* punch. **~r** *vt* pierce, perforate; punch (papel, tarjeta etc)
perfum|ar *vt* perfume. **~arse** *vpr* put perfume on. **~e** *m* perfume, scent. **~ería** *f* perfumery
pericia *f* skill
perif|eria *f* (*de ciudad*) outskirts. **~érico** *adj* (barrio) outlying. • *m* (*Mex, carretera*) ring road
perilla *f* (*barba*) goatee
perímetro *m* perimeter
periódico *adj* periodic(al). • *m* newspaper
periodis|mo *m* journalism. **~ta** *m & f* journalist
período *m*, **periodo** *m* period
periquito *m* budgerigar
periscopio *m* periscope
perito *adj & m* expert
perju|dicar 7 *vt* damage; (*desfavorecer*) not suit. **~dicial** *adj* damaging. **~icio** *m* damage. **en ~icio de** to the detriment of
perla *f* pearl. **de ~s** *adv* very well
permane|cer 11 *vi* remain. **~ncia** *f* permanence; (*estancia*) stay. **~nte** *adj* permanent. • *f* perm. • *m* (*Mex*) perm

permi|sivo *adj* permissive. **~so** *m* permission; (*documento*) licence; (*Mil etc*) leave. **~so de conducir** driving licence (*Brit*), driver's license (*Amer*). **con ~so** excuse me. **~tir** *vt* allow, permit. **¿me ~te?** may I? **~tirse** *vpr* allow s.o.
pernicioso *adj* pernicious; (persona) wicked
perno *m* bolt
pero *conj* but. • *m* fault; (*objeción*) objection
perogrullada *f* platitude
perpendicular *adj & f* perpendicular
perpetrar *vt* perpetrate
perpetu|ar 21 *vt* perpetuate. **~o** *adj* perpetual
perplejo *adj* perplexed
perr|a *f* (*animal*) bitch; (*moneda*) coin, penny (*Brit*), cent (*Amer*); (*rabieta*) tantrum. **estar sin una ~a** be broke. **~era** *f* dog pound; (*vehículo*) dog catcher's van. **~o** *adj* awful. • *m* dog. **~o galgo** greyhound. **de ~os** awful
persa *adj & m & f* Persian
perse|cución *f* pursuit; (*política etc*) persecution. **~guir** 5 & 13 *vt* pursue; (*por ideología etc*) persecute
persevera|nte *adj* persevering. **~r** *vi* persevere
persiana *f* blind; (*LAm, contraventana*) shutter
persignarse *vpr* cross o.s.
persist|ente *adj* persistent. **~ir** *vi* persist
person|a *f* person. **~as** *fpl* people. **~aje** *m* (*persona importante*) important figure; (*de obra literaria*) character. **~al** *adj* personal. • *m* staff. **~alidad** *f* personality. **~arse** *vpr* appear in person. **~ifi-**

P

car 7 *vt* personify
perspectiva *f* perspective
perspica|cia *f* shrewdness; (*de vista*) keen eyesight. **~z** *adj* shrewd; (vista) keen
persua|dir *vt* persuade. **~sión** *f* persuasion. **~sivo** *adj* persuasive
pertenecer 11 *vi* belong
pértiga *f* pole. **salto** *m* **con ~** pole vault
pertinente *adj* relevant
perturba|ción *f* disturbance. **~ción del orden público** breach of the peace. **~r** *vt* disturb; disrupt (orden)
Perú *m.* **el ~** Peru
peruano *adj & m* Peruvian
perver|so *adj* evil. • *m* evil person. **~tir** 4 *vt* pervert
pesa *f* weight. **~dez** *f* weight; (*de cabeza etc*) heaviness; (*lentitud*) sluggishness; (*cualidad de fastidioso*) tediousness; (*cosa fastidiosa*) bore, nuisance
pesadilla *f* nightmare
pesado *adj* heavy; (sueño) deep; (viaje) tiring; (*duro*) hard; (*aburrido*) boring, tedious
pésame *m* sympathy, condolences
pesar *vt* weigh. • *vi* be heavy. • *m* sorrow; (*remordimiento*) regret. **a ~ de (que)** in spite of. **pese a (que)** in spite of
pesca *f* fishing; (*peces*) fish; (*pescado*) catch. **Ir de ~** go fishing. **~da** *f* hake. **~dería** *f* fish shop. **~dilla** *f* whiting. **~do** *m* fish. **~dor** *adj* fishing. • *m* fisherman. **~r** 7 *vt* catch. • *vi* fish
pescuezo *m* neck
pesebre *m* manger
pesero *m* (*Mex*) minibus
peseta *f* peseta
pesimista *adj* pessimistic. • *m & f* pessimist
pésimo *adj* very bad, awful
peso *m* weight; (*moneda*) peso. **~ bruto** gross weight. **~ neto** net weight. **al ~** by weight. **de ~** influential
pesquero *adj* fishing
pestañ|a *f* eyelash. **~ear** *vi* blink
pest|e *f* plague; (*hedor*) stench. **~icida** *m* pesticide
pestillo *m* bolt; (*de cerradura*) latch
petaca *f* cigarette case; (*Mex, maleta*) suitcase
pétalo *m* petal
petardo *m* firecracker
petición *f* request; (*escrito*) petition
petirrojo *m* robin
petrificar 7 *vt* petrify
petr|óleo *m* oil. **~olero** *adj* oil. • *m* oil tanker
petulante *adj* smug
peyorativo *adj* pejorative
pez *f* fish; (*substancia negruzca*) pitch. **~ espada** swordfish
pezón *m* nipple
pezuña *f* hoof
piadoso *adj* compassionate; (*devoto*) devout
pian|ista *m & f* pianist. **~o** *m* piano. **~o de cola** grand piano
piar 20 *vi* chirp
picad|a *f.* **caer en ~a** (*LAm*) nosedive. **~o** *adj* perforated; (carne) minced (*Brit*), ground (*Amer*); (*ofendido*) offended; (mar) choppy; (diente) bad. • *m.* **caer en ~o** nosedive. **~ura** *f* bite, sting; (*de polilla*) moth hole
picaflor *m* (*LAm*) hummingbird

picante *adj* hot; (chiste etc) risqué

picaporte *m* door-handle; (*aldaba*) knocker

picar 7 *vt* (ave) peck; (insecto, pez) bite; (abeja, avispa) sting; (*comer poco*) pick at; mince (*Brit*), grind (*Amer*) (carne); chop (up) (cebolla etc); (*Mex, pinchar*) prick. ● *vi* itch; (ave) peck; (insecto, pez) bite; (sol) scorch; (comida) be hot

picardía *f* craftiness; (*travesura*) naughty thing

pícaro *adj* crafty; (niño) mischievous. ● *m* rogue

picazón *f* itch

pichón *m* pigeon; (*Mex, novato*) beginner

pico *m* beak; (*punta*) corner; (*herramienta*) pickaxe; (*cima*) peak. **y ~** (*con tiempo*) a little after; (*con cantidad*) a little more than. **~tear** *vt* peck; (*fam, comer*) pick at

picudo *adj* pointed

pido *vb véase* PEDIR

pie *m* foot; (*Bot, de vaso*) stem. **~ cuadrado** square foot. **a cuatro ~s** on all fours. **al ~ de la letra** literally. **a ~** on foot. **a ~(s) juntillas** (*fig*) firmly. **buscarle tres ~s al gato** split hairs. **de ~** standing (up). **de ~s a cabeza** from head to toe. **en ~** standing (up). **ponerse de ~** stand up

piedad *f* pity; (*Relig*) piety

piedra *f* stone; (*de mechero*) flint

piel *f* skin; (*cuero*) leather

pienso *vb véase* PENSAR

pierdo *vb véase* PERDER

pierna *f* leg

pieza *f* piece; (*parte*) part; (*obra teatral*) play; (*moneda*) coin; (*habitación*) room. **~ de recambio** spare part

P

pijama *m* pyjamas

pila *f* (*montón*) pile; (*recipiente*) basin; (*eléctrica*) battery. **~ bautismal** font. **~r** *m* pillar

píldora *f* pill

pilla|je *m* pillage. **~r** *vt* catch

pillo *adj* wicked. ● *m* rogue

pilot|ar *vt* pilot. **~o** *m* pilot

pim|entero *m* (*vasija*) pepperpot. **~entón** *m* paprika; (*LAm, fruto*) pepper. **~ienta** *f* pepper. **grano de ~ienta** peppercorn. **~iento** *m* pepper

pináculo *m* pinnacle

pinar *m* pine forest

pincel *m* paintbrush. **~ada** *f* brush-stroke. **la última ~ada** (*fig*) the finishing touch

pinch|ar *vt* pierce, prick; puncture (neumático); (*fig, incitar*) push; (*Med, fam*) give an injection to. **~azo** *m* prick; (*en neumático*) puncture. **~itos** *mpl* kebab(s); (*tapas*) savoury snacks. **~o** *m* point

ping-pong *m* table tennis, ping-pong

pingüino *m* penguin

pino *m* pine (tree)

pint|a *f* spot; (*fig, aspecto*) appearance. **tener ~a de** look like. **~ada** *f* graffiti. **~ar** *vt* paint. **no ~a nada** (*fig*) it doesn't count. **~arse** *vpr* put on make-up. **~or** *m* painter. **~oresco** *adj* picturesque. **~ura** *f* painting; (*material*) paint

pinza *f* (clothes-)peg (*Brit*), clothes-pin (*Amer*); (*de cangrejo etc*) claw. **~s** *fpl* tweezers

piñ|a *f* pine cone; (*fruta*) pineapple. **~ón** *m* (*semilla*) pine nut

pío *adj* pious. ● *m* chirp. **no decir ni ~** not say a word

piojo *m* louse

pionero *m* pioneer

pipa *f* pipe; (*semilla*) seed; (*de girasol*) sunflower seed

pique *m* resentment; (*rivalidad*) rivalry. **irse a ~** sink

piquete *m* picket; (*Mex*, *herida*) prick; (*Mex*, *de insecto*) sting

piragua *f* canoe

pirámide *f* pyramid

pirata *adj invar* pirate. • *m* & *f* pirate

Pirineos *mpl*. **los ~**the Pyrenees

piropo *m* flattering comment

pirueta *f* pirouette

pirulí *m* lollipop

pisa|da *f* footstep; (*huella*) footprint. **~papeles** *m invar* paperweight. **~r** *vt* tread on. • *vi* tread

piscina *f* swimming pool

Piscis *m* Pisces

piso *m* floor; (*vivienda*) flat (*Brit*), apartment (*Amer*); (*de autobús*) deck

pisotear *vt* trample (on)

pista *f* track; (*fig, indicio*) clue. **~ de aterrizaje** runway. **~ de baile** dance floor. **~ de carreras** racing track. **~ de hielo** ice-rink. **~ de tenis** tennis court

pistol|a *f* pistol. **~era** *f* holster. **~ero** *m* gunman

pistón *m* piston

pit|ar, (*LAm*) **~ear** *vt* whistle at; (conductor) hoot at; award (falta). • *vi* blow a whistle; (*Auto*) sound one's horn. **~ido** *m* whistle

pitill|era *f* cigarette case. **~o** *m* cigarette

pito *m* whistle; (*Auto*) horn

pitón *m* python

pitorre|arse *vpr*. **~arse de** make fun of. **~o** *m* teasing

pitorro *m* spout

piyama *m* (*LAm*) pyjamas

pizarr|a *f* slate; (*en aula*) blackboard. **~ón** *m* (*LAm*) blackboard

pizca *f* [I] tiny piece; (*de sal*) pinch. **ni ~** not at all

placa *f* plate; (*con inscripción*) plaque; (*distintivo*) badge. **~ de matrícula** number plate

place|ntero *adj* pleasant. **~r** [32] *vi*. **haz lo que te plazca** do as you please. **me ~ hacerlo** I'm pleased to do it. • *m* pleasure

plácido *adj* placid

plaga *f* (*also fig*) plague. **~do** *adj*. **~do de** filled with

plagio *m* plagiarism

plan *m* plan. **en ~ de** as

plana *f* page. **en primera ~** on the front page

plancha *f* iron; (*lámina*) sheet. **a la ~** grilled. **tirarse una ~** put one's foot in it. **~do** *m* ironing. **~r** *vt* iron. • *vi* do the ironing

planeador *m* glider

planear *vt* plan. • *vi* glide

planeta *m* planet

planicie *f* plain

planifica|ción *f* planning. **~r** [7] *vt* plan

planilla *f* (*LAm*) payroll; (*personal*) staff

plano *adj* flat. • *m* plane; (*de edificio*) plan; (*de ciudad*) street plan. **primer ~** foreground; (*Foto*) close-up

planta *f* (*del pie*) sole; (*en botánica, fábrica*) plant; (*plano*) ground plan; (*piso*) floor. **~ baja** ground floor (*Brit*), first floor (*Amer*)

planta|ción *f* plantation. **~r** *vt* plant; deal (golpe). **~r en la calle** throw out. **~rse** *vpr* stand; (*fig*) stand firm

plantear *vt* (*exponer*) expound; (*causar*) create; raise (cuestión)

plantilla *f* insole; (*nómina*) payroll; (*personal*) personnel

plaqué *m* plating. **de ~** plated

plástico *adj & m* plastic

plata *f* silver; (*fig, fam, dinero*) money. **~ de ley** hallmarked silver

plataforma *f* platform

plátano *m* plane (tree); (*fruta*) banana. **platanero** *m* banana tree

platea *f* stalls (*Brit*), orchestra (*Amer*)

plateado *adj* silver-plated; (*color de plata*) silver

pl|ática *f* talk. **~aticar** 7 *vi* (*Mex*) talk. ● *vt* (*Mex*) tell

platija *f* plaice

platillo *m* saucer; (*Mus*) cymbal. **~ volador** (*LAm*), **~ volante** flying saucer

platino *m* platinum. **~s** *mpl* (*Auto*) points

plato *m* plate; (*comida*) dish; (*parte de una comida*) course

P

platónico *adj* platonic

playa *f* beach; (*fig*) seaside

plaza *f* square; (*mercado*) market (place); (*sitio*) place; (*empleo*) job. **~ de toros** bullring

plazco *vb véase* PLACER

plazo *m* period; (*pago*) instalment; (*fecha*) date. **comprar a ~s** buy on hire purchase (*Brit*), buy on the installment plan (*Amer*)

plazuela *f* little square

pleamar *f* high tide

pleb|e *f* common people. **~eyo** *adj & m* plebeian. **~iscito** *m* plebiscite

plega|ble *adj* pliable; (silla) folding. **~r** 1 & 12 *vt* fold. **~rse** *vpr* bend; (*fig*) yield

pleito *m* (court) case; (*fig*) dispute

plenilunio *m* full moon

plen|itud *f* fullness; (*fig*) height. **~o** *adj* full. **en ~o día** in broad daylight. **en ~o verano** at the height of the summer

plieg|o *m* sheet. **~ue** *m* fold; (*en ropa*) pleat

plisar *vt* pleat

plom|ero *m* (*LAm*) plumber. **~o** *m* lead; (*Elec*) fuse. **con ~o** leaded. **sin ~o** unleaded

pluma *f* feather; (*para escribir*) pen. **~ atómica** (*Mex*) ballpoint pen. **~ estilográfica** fountain pen. **~je** *m* plumage

plum|ero *m* feather duster; (*para plumas, lápices etc*) pencil-case. **~ón** *m* down; (*edredón*) down-filled quilt

plural *adj & m* plural. **en ~** in the plural

pluri|empleo *m* having more than one job. **~partidismo** *m* multi-party system. **~étnico** *adj* multiethnic

plus *m* bonus

pluscuamperfecto *m* pluperfect

plusvalía *f* capital gain

pluvial *adj* rain

pobla|ción *f* population; (*ciudad*) city, town; (*pueblo*) village. **~do** *adj* populated. ● *m* village. **~r** 2 *vt* populate; (*habitar*) inhabit. **~rse** *vpr* get crowded

pobre *adj* poor. ● *m & f* poor person; (*fig*) poor thing. **¡~cito!** poor (little) thing! **¡~ de mí!** poor (old) me! **~za** *f* poverty

pocilga *f* pigsty

poción *f* potion

poco

● *adjetivo/pronombre*

····➤ **poco, poca** little, not much. **tiene poca paciencia** he has little patience. **¿cuánta leche queda? - poca** how much milk is there left? - not much

····➤ **pocos, pocas** few. **muy ~s días** very few days. **unos ~s dólares** a few dollars. **compré unos ~s** I bought a few. **aceptaron a muy ~s** very few (people) were accepted

····➤ **a ~ de llegar** soon after he arrived. **¡a ~ !** (*Mex*) really? **dentro de ~** soon. **~ a ~**, (*LAm*) **de a ~** gradually, little by little. **hace ~** recently, not long ago. **por ~** nearly. **un ~** (*cantidad*) a little; (*tiempo*) a while. **un ~ de** a (little) bit of, a little, some

● *adverbio*

····➤ (*con verbo*) not much. **lee muy ~** he doesn't read very much

····➤ (*con adjetivo*) **un lugar ~ conocido** a little known place. **es ~ inteligente** he's not very intelligent

! Cuando **poco** modifica a un adjetivo, muchas veces el inglés prefiere el uso del prefijo *un-*, p. ej. **poco amistoso** *unfriendly*. **poco agradecido** *ungrateful*

podar *vt* prune

poder 33 *verbo auxiliar* be able to. **no voy a ~ terminar** I won't be able to finish. **no pudo venir** he couldn't come. **¿puedo hacer algo?** can I do anything? **¿puedo pasar?** may I come in? **no ~ con** not be able to cope with; (*no aguantar*) not be able to stand. **no ~ más** be exhausted; (*estar harto de algo*) not be able to manage any more. **no ~ menos que** have no alternative but. **puede que** it is possible that. **puede ser** it is possible. **¿se puede ...?** may I...? ● *m* power. **en el ~** in power. **~es públicos** authorities. **~oso** *adj* powerful

podrido *adj* rotten

po|ema *m* poem. **~esía** *f* poetry; (*poema*) poem. **~eta** *m & f* poet. **~ético** *adj* poetic

polaco *adj* Polish. ● *m* Pole; (*lengua*) Polish

polar *adj* polar. **estrella ~** polestar

polea *f* pulley

pol|émica *f* controversy. **~emizar** 10 *vi* argue

polen *m* pollen

policía *f* police (force); (*persona*) policewoman. ● *m* policeman. **~co** *adj* police; (novela etc) detective

P

policromo *adj*, **polícromo** *adj* polychrome

polideportivo *m* sports centre

polietileno *m* polythene

poligamia *f* polygamy

polígono *m* polygon

polilla *f* moth

polio(mielitis) *f* polio(myelitis)

polític|a *f* politics; (*postura*) policy; (*mujer*) politician. **~ interior** domestic policy. **~o** *adj* political. **familia ~a** in-laws. ● *m* politician

póliza *f* (*de seguros*) policy

poll|o *m* chicken; (*gallo joven*) chick. **~uelo** *m* chick

polo *m* pole; (*helado*) ice lolly (*Brit*),

Popsicle (P) (*Amer*); (*juego*) polo. **P~ norte** North Pole

Polonia *f* Poland

poltrona *f* armchair

polución *f* pollution

polv|areda *f* dust cloud; (*fig, escándalo*) uproar. **~era** *f* compact. **~o** *m* powder; (*suciedad*) dust. **~os** *mpl* powder. **en ~o** powdered. **estar hecho ~o** be exhausted. **quitar el ~o** dust

pólvora *f* gunpowder; (*fuegos artificiales*) fireworks

polvoriento *adj* dusty

pomada *f* ointment

pomelo *m* grapefruit

pómez *adj*. **piedra** *f* **~** pumice stone

pomp|a *f* bubble; (*esplendor*) pomp. **~as fúnebres** funeral. **~oso** *adj* pompous; (*espléndido*) splendid

pómulo *m* cheekbone

ponchar *vt* (*Mex*) puncture

ponche *m* punch

poncho *m* poncho

P

ponderar *vt* (*alabar*) speak highly of

poner 34 *vt* put; put on (ropa, obra de teatro, TV etc); lay (la mesa, un huevo); set (examen, deberes); (*contribuir*) contribute; give (nombre); make (nervioso); pay (atención); show (película, interés); open (una tienda); equip (una casa). **~ con** (*al teléfono*) put through to. **~ por escrito** put into writing. **~ una multa** fine. **pongamos** let's suppose. • *vi* lay. **~se** *vpr* put o.s.; (*volverse*) get; put on (ropa); (sol) set. **~se a** start to. **~se a mal con uno** fall out with s.o.

pongo *vb véase* **PONER**

poniente *m* west; (*viento*) west wind

pont|ificar 7 *vi* pontificate. **~ífice** *m* pontiff

popa *f* stern

popote *m* (*Mex*) (drinking) straw

popul|acho *m* masses. **~ar** *adj* popular; (costumbre) traditional; (lenguaje) colloquial. **~aridad** *f* popularity. **~arizar** 10 *vt* popularize.

póquer *m* poker

poquito *m*. **un ~** a little bit. • *adv* a little

por *preposición*

····➤ for. **es ~ tu bien** it's for your own good. **lo compró por 5 dólares** he bought it for 5 dollars. **si no fuera por ti** if it weren't for you. **vino por una semana** he came for a week

➡ Para expresiones como **por la mañana, por la noche** etc., ver bajo el respectivo nombre

····➤ (*causa*) because of. **se retrasó ~ la lluvia** he was late because of the rain. **no hay trenes ~ la huelga** there aren't any trains because of the strike

····➤ (*medio, agente*) by. **lo envié ~ correo** I sent it by post. **fue destruida ~ las bombas** it was destroyed by the bombs

····➤ (*a través de*) through. **entró ~ la ventana** he got in through the window. **me enteré ~ un amigo** I found out through a friend. **~ todo el**

país throughout the country

····➤ (*a lo largo de*) along. **caminar ~ la playa** to walk along the beach. **cortar ~ la línea de puntos** cut along the dotted line

····➤ (*proporción*) per. **cobra 30 dólares ~ hora** he charges 30 dollars per hour. **uno ~ persona** one per person. **10 ~ ciento** 10 per cent

····➤ (*Mat*) times. **dos ~ dos (son) cuatro** two times two is four

····➤ (*modo*) in. **~ escrito** in writing. **pagar ~ adelantado** to pay in advance

➡ Para expresiones como **por dentro, por fuera** etc., ver bajo el respectivo adverbio

····➤ (*en locuciones*) **~ más que** no matter how much. **¿~ qué?** why? **~ si** in case. **~ supuesto** of course

porcelana *f* china

porcentaje *m* percentage

porcino *adj* pig

porción *f* portion; (*de chocolate*) piece

pordiosero *m* beggar

porfia|do *adj* stubborn. **~r** 20 *vi* insist

pormenor *m* detail

pornogr|afía *f* pornography. **~áfico** *adj* pornographic

poro *m* pore; (*Mex, puerro*) leek. **~so** *adj* porous

porque *conj* because; (*para que*) so that

porqué *m* reason

porquería *f* filth; (*basura*) rubbish; (*grosería*) dirty trick

porra *f* club

porrón *m* wine jug (with a long spout)

portaaviones *m invar* aircraft carrier

portada *f* (*de libro*) title page; (*de revista*) cover

portadocumentos *m invar* (*LAm*) briefcase

portador *m* bearer

portaequipaje(s) *m invar* boot (*Brit*), trunk (*Amer*); (*encima del coche*) roof-rack

portal *m* hall; (*puerta principal*) main entrance. **~es** *mpl* arcade

porta|ligas *m invar* suspender belt. **~monedas** *m invar* purse

portarse *vpr* behave

portátil *adj* portable. ● *m* portable computer, laptop

portavoz *m* spokesman. ● *f* spokeswoman

portazo *m* bang. **dar un ~** slam the door

porte *m* transport; (*precio*) carriage; (*LAm, tamaño*) size. **~ador** *m* carrier

portento *m* marvel

porteño *adj* from Buenos Aires

porter|ía *f* porter's lodge; (*en deportes*) goal. **~o** *m* caretaker, porter; (*en deportes*) goalkeeper. **~o automático** entryphone

pórtico *m* portico

portorriqueño *adj & m* Puerto Rican

Portugal *m* Portugal

portugués *adj & m* Portuguese

porvenir *m* future

posada *f* inn. **dar ~** give shelter

posar *vt* put. ● *vi* pose. **~se** *vpr*

(pájaro) perch; (avión) land
posdata *f* postscript
pose|edor *m* owner; (*de récord, billete, etc*) holder. **~er** 18 *vt* own; hold (récord); have (conocimientos). **~sión** *f* possession. **~sionarse** *vpr*. **~sionarse de** take possession of. **~sivo** *adj* possessive
posgraduado *adj & m* postgraduate
posguerra *f* post-war years
posib|ilidad *f* possibility. **~le** *adj* possible. **de ser ~le** if possible. **en lo ~le** as far as possible. **si es ~le** if possible
posición *f* position; (*en sociedad*) social standing
positivo *adj* positive
poso *m* sediment
posponer 34 *vt* put after; (*diferir*) postpone
posta *f.* **a ~** on purpose
postal *adj* postal. ● *f* postcard
poste *m* pole; (*de valla*) post
póster *m* (*pl* **~s**) poster
postergar 12 *vt* pass over; (*diferir*) postpone
posteri|dad *f* posterity. **~or** *adj* back; (años) later; (capítulos) subsequent. **~ormente** *adv* later
postigo *m* door; (*contraventana*) shutter
postizo *adj* false, artificial. ● *m* hairpiece
postrarse *vpr* prostrate o.s.
postre *m* dessert, pudding (*Brit*)
postular *vt* postulate; (*LAm*) nominate (candidato)
póstumo *adj* posthumous
postura *f* position, stance
potable *adj* drinkable; (agua) drinking
potaje *m* vegetable stew
potasio *m* potassium
pote *m* pot
poten|cia *f* power. **~cial** *adj & m* potential. **~te** *adj* powerful
potro *m* colt; (*en gimnasia*) horse
pozo *m* well; (*hoyo seco*) pit; (*de mina*) shaft; (*fondo común*) pool
práctica *f* practice. **en la ~** in practice
practica|nte *m & f* nurse. **~r** 7 *vt* practise; play (deportes); (*ejecutar*) carry out
práctico *adj* practical; (*conveniente, útil*) handy. ● *m* practitioner
prad|era *f* meadow; (*terreno grande*) prairie. **~o** *m* meadow
pragmático *adj* pragmatic
preámbulo *m* preamble
precario *adj* precarious; (medios) scarce
precaución *f* precaution; (*cautela*) caution. **con ~** cautiously
precaverse *vpr* take precautions
precede|ncia *f* precedence; (*prioridad*) priority. **~nte** *adj* preceding. ● *m* precedent. **~r** *vt/i* precede
precepto *m* precept. **~r** *m* tutor
precia|do *adj* valued; (don) valuable. **~rse** *vpr*. **~rse de** pride o.s. on
precio *m* price. **~ de venta al público** retail price. **al ~ de** at the cost of. **no tener ~** be priceless. **¿qué ~ tiene?** how much is it?
precios|idad *f* (*cosa preciosa*) beautiful thing. **¡es una ~idad!** it's beautiful! **~o** *adj* precious; (*bonito*) beautiful
precipicio *m* precipice
precipita|ción *f* precipitation; (*prisa*) rush. **~damente** *adv* hastily. **~do** *adj* hasty. **~r** *vt* (*apre-*

surar) hasten; (*arrojar*) hurl. **~rse** *vpr* throw o.s.; (*correr*) rush; (*actuar sin reflexionar*) act rashly

precis|amente *adj* exactly. **~ar** *vt* require; (*determinar*) determine. **~ión** *f* precision. **~o** *adj* precise; (*necesario*) necessary. **si es ~o** if necessary

preconcebido *adj* preconceived

precoz *adj* early; (niño) precocious

precursor *m* forerunner

predecesor *m* predecessor

predecir 46, (*pero imperativo* **predice**, *futuro y condicional regulares*) *vt* foretell

predestinado *adj* predestined

prédica *f* sermon

predicar 7 *vt/i* preach

predicción *f* prediction; (*del tiempo*) forecast

predilec|ción *f* predilection. **~to** *adj* favourite

predisponer 34 *vt* predispose

predomin|ante *adj* predominant. **~ar** *vi* predominate. **~io** *m* predominance

preeminente *adj* pre-eminent

prefabricado *adj* prefabricated

prefacio *m* preface

prefer|encia *f* preference; (*Auto*) right of way. **de ~encia** preferably. **~ente** *adj* preferential. **~ible** *adj* preferable. **~ido** *adj* favourite. **~ir** 4 *vt* prefer

prefijo *m* prefix; (*telefónico*) dialling code

pregonar *vt* announce

pregunta *f* question. **hacer una ~** ask a question. **~r** *vt/i* ask (**por** about). **~rse** *vpr* wonder

prehistórico *adj* prehistoric

preju|icio *m* prejudice. **~zgar** 12 *vt* prejudge

preliminar *adj & m* preliminary

preludio *m* prelude

premarital *adj*, **prematrimonial** *adj* premarital

prematuro *adj* premature

premedita|ción *f* premeditation. **~r** *vt* premeditate

premi|ar *vt* give a prize to; (*recompensar*) reward. **~o** *m* prize; (*recompensa*) reward. **~o gordo** jackpot

premonición *f* premonition

prenatal *adj* antenatal

prenda *f* garment; (*garantía*) surety; (*en juegos*) forfeit. **en ~ de** as a token of. **~r** *vt* captivate. **~rse** *vpr* fall in love (**de** with)

prende|dor *m* brooch. **~r** *vt* capture; (*sujetar*) fasten; light (cigarrillo); (*LAm*) turn on (gas, radio, etc). • *vi* catch; (*arraigar*) take root. **~rse** *vpr* (*encenderse*) catch fire

prensa *f* press. **~r** *vt* press

preñado *adj* pregnant; (*fig*) full

preocupa|ción *f* worry. **~do** *adj* worried. **~r** *vt* worry. **~rse** *vpr* worry. **~rse de** look after

prepara|ción *f* preparation. **~do** *adj* prepared. • *m* preparation. **~r** *vt* prepare. **~rse** *vpr* get ready. **~tivos** *mpl* preparations. **~torio** *adj* preparatory

preposición *f* preposition

prepotente *adj* arrogant; (actitud) high-handed

prerrogativa *f* prerogative

presa *f* (*cosa*) prey; (*embalse*) dam

presagi|ar *vt* presage. **~o** *m* omen

presb|iteriano *adj & m* Presbyterian. **~ítero** *m* priest

prescindir *vi*. **~ de** do without;

(*deshacerse de*) dispense with

prescri|bir (*pp* **prescrito**) *vt* prescribe. **~pción** *f* prescription

presencia *f* presence; (*aspecto*) appearance. **en ~ de** in the presence of. **~r** *vt* be present at; (*ver*) witness

presenta|ble *adj* presentable. **~ción** *f* presentation; (*de una persona a otra*) introduction. **~dor** *m* presenter. **~r** *vt* present; (*ofrecer*) offer; (*entregar*) hand in; (*hacer conocer*) introduce; show (película). **~rse** *vpr* present o.s.; (*hacerse conocer*) introduce o.s.; (*aparecer*) turn up

presente *adj* present; (*actual*) this. • *m* present. **los ~s** those present. **tener ~** remember

presenti|miento *m* premonition. **~r** **4** *vt* have a feeling (**que** that)

preserva|r *vt* preserve. **~tivo** *m* condom

presiden|cia *f* presidency; (*de asamblea*) chairmanship. **~cial** *adj* presidential. **~ta** *f* (woman) president. **~te** *m* president; (*de asamblea*) chairman. **~te del gobierno** prime minister

P

presidi|ario *m* convict. **~o** *m* prison

presidir *vt* be president of; preside over (tribunal); chair (reunión, comité)

presi|ón *f* pressure. **a ~ón** under pressure. **hacer ~ón** press. **~onar** *vt* press; (*fig*) put pressure on

preso *adj*. **estar ~** be in prison. **llevarse ~ a uno** take s.o. away under arrest. • *m* prisoner

presta|do *adj* (*de uno*) lent; (*a uno*) borrowed. **pedir ~do** borrow. **~mista** *m & f* moneylender

préstamo *m* loan; (*acción de pedir prestado*) borrowing; (*acción de prestar*) lending

prestar *vt* lend; give (ayuda etc); pay (atención). **~se** *vpr*. **~se a** be open to; (*ser apto*) be suitable (**para** for)

prestidigita|ción *f* conjuring. **~dor** *m* conjurer

prestigio *m* prestige. **~so** *adj* prestigious

presu|mido *adj* conceited. **~mir** *vi* show off; boast (**de** about). **~nción** *f* conceit; (*suposición*) presumption. **~nto** *adj* alleged. **~ntuoso** *adj* conceited

presup|oner **34** *vt* presuppose. **~uesto** *m* budget; (*precio estimado*) estimate

preten|cioso *adj* pretentious. **~der** *vt* try to; (*afirmar*) claim; (*solicitar*) apply for; (*cortejar*) court. **~diente** *m* pretender; (*a una mujer*) suitor. **~sión** *f* pretension; (*aspiración*) aspiration

pretérito *m* preterite, past

pretexto *m* pretext. **con el ~ de** on the pretext of

prevalecer **11** *vi* prevail (**sobre** over)

preven|ción *f* prevention; (*prejuicio*) prejudice. **~ido** *adj* ready; (*precavido*) cautious. **~ir** **53** *vt* prevent; (*advertir*) warn. **~tiva** *f* (*Mex*) amber light. **~tivo** *adj* preventive

prever **43** *vt* foresee; (*planear*) plan

previo *adj* previous

previs|ible *adj* predictable. **~ión** *f* forecast; (*prudencia*) precaution

prima *f* (*pariente*) cousin; (*cantidad*) bonus

primario *adj* primary

primavera *f* spring. **~l** *adj* spring

primer *adj véase* **PRIMERO**. **~a** *f* (*Auto*) first (gear); (*en tren etc*) first class. **~o** *adj* (*delante de nombre masculino en singular* **primer**) first; (*mejor*) best; (*principal*) leading. **la ~a fila** the front row. **lo ~o es** the most important thing is. **~a enseñanza** primary education. **a ~os de** at the beginning of. **de ~a** first-class. • *n* (the) first. • *adv* first

primitivo *adj* primitive

primo *m* cousin; ☐ fool. **hacer el ~** be taken for a ride

primogénito *adj & m* first-born, eldest

primor *m* delicacy; (*cosa*) beautiful thing

primordial *adj* fundamental; (interés) paramount

princesa *f* princess

principal *adj* main. **lo ~ es que** the main thing is that

príncipe *m* prince

principi|ante *m & f* beginner. **~o** *m* beginning; (*moral, idea*) principle; (*origen*) origin. **al ~o** at first. **a ~o(s) de** at the beginning of. **desde el ~o** from the start. **en ~o** in principle. **~os** *mpl* (*nociones*) rudiments

prión *m* prion

prioridad *f* priority

prisa *f* hurry, haste. **darse ~** hurry (up). **de ~** quickly. **tener ~** be in a hurry

prisi|ón *f* prison; (*encarcelamiento*) imprisonment. **~onero** *m* prisoner

prismáticos *mpl* binoculars

priva|ción *f* deprivation. **~da** *f* (*Mex*) private road. **~do** *adj* (*particular*) private. **~r** *vt* deprive (**de** of). **~tivo** *adj* exclusive (**de** to)

privilegi|ado *adj* privileged; (*muy bueno*) exceptional. **~o** *m* privilege

pro *prep.* **en ~ de** for, in favour of. • *m* advantage. **los ~s y los contras** the pros and cons

proa *f* bow

probab|ilidad *f* probability. **~le** *adj* probable, likely. **~lemente** *adv* probably

proba|dor *m* fitting-room. **~r** 2 *vt* try; try on (ropa); (*demostrar*) prove. • *vi* try. **~rse** *vpr* try on

probeta *f* test-tube

problema *m* problem. **hacerse ~as** (*LAm*) worry

procaz *adj* indecent

proced|encia *f* origin. **~ente** *adj* (*razonable*) reasonable. **~ente de** (coming) from. **~er** *m* conduct. • *vi* proceed. **~er contra** start legal proceedings against. **~er de** come from. **~imiento** *m* procedure; (*sistema*) process; (*Jurid*) proceedings

proces|ador *m.* **~ de textos** word processor. **~al** *adj* procedural. **costas ~ales** legal costs. **~amiento** *m* processing; (*Jurid*) prosecution. **~amiento de textos** word-processing.. **~ar** *vt* process; (*Jurid*) prosecute

procesión *f* procession

proceso *m* process; (*Jurid*) trial; (*transcurso*) course

proclamar *vt* proclaim

procrea|ción *f* procreation. **~r** *vt* procreate

procura|dor *m* attorney, solicitor; (*asistente*) clerk (*Brit*), paralegal (*Amer*). **~r** *vt* try; (*obtener*) obtain

prodigar 12 *vt* lavish

prodigio *m* prodigy; (*maravilla*) wonder; (*milagro*) miracle. **~so** *adj* prodigious

P

pródigo *adj* prodigal

produc|ción *f* production. **~ir** 47 *vt* produce; (*causar*) cause. **~irse** *vpr* (*suceder*) happen. **~tivo** *adj* productive. **~to** *m* product. **~tos agrícolas** farm produce. **~tos alimenticios** foodstuffs. **~tos de belleza** cosmetics. **~tos de consumo** consumer goods. **~tor** *m* producer.

proeza *f* exploit

profan|ación *f* desecration. **~ar** *vt* desecrate. **~o** *adj* profane

profecía *f* prophecy

proferir 4 *vt* utter; hurl (insultos etc)

profes|ión *f* profession. **~ional** *adj* professional. **~or** *m* teacher; (*en universidad*) lecturer. **~orado** *m* teaching profession; (*conjunto de profesores*) staff

prof|eta *m* prophet. **~etizar** 10 *vt/i* prophesize

prófugo *adj & m* fugitive

profund|idad *f* depth. **~o** *adj* deep; (*fig*) profound. **poco ~o** shallow

progenitor *m* ancestor

programa *m* programme; (*de estudios*) syllabus. **~ concurso** quiz show. **~ de entrevistas** chat show. **~ción** *f* programming; (*TV etc*) programmes; (*en periódico*) TV guide. **~r** *vt* programme. **~dor** *m* computer programmer

progres|ar *vi* (make) progress. **~ión** *f* progression. **~ista** *adj* progressive. **~ivo** *adj* progressive. **~o** *m* progress. **hacer ~os** make progress

prohibi|ción *f* prohibition. **~do** *adj* forbidden. **prohibido fumar** no smoking. **~r** *vt* forbid. **~tivo** *adj* prohibitive

prójimo *m* fellow man

prole *f* offspring

proletari|ado *m* proletariat. **~o** *adj & m* proletarian

prol|iferación *f* proliferation. **~iferar** *vi* proliferate. **~ífico** *adj* prolific

prolijo *adj* long-winded

prólogo *m* prologue

prolongar 12 *vt* prolong; (*alargar*) lengthen. **~se** *vpr* go on

promedio *m* average. **como ~** on average

prome|sa *f* promise. **~ter** *vt* promise. • *vi* show promise. **~terse** *vpr* (novios) get engaged. **~tida** *f* fiancée. **~tido** *adj* promised; (novios) engaged. • *m* fiancé

prominente *f* prominence

promiscu|idad *f* promiscuity. **~o** *adj* promiscuous

promo|ción *f* promotion. **~tor** *m* promoter. **~ver** 2 *vt* promote; (*causar*) cause

promulgar 12 *vt* promulgate

pronombre *m* pronoun

pron|osticar 7 *vt* predict; forecast (tiempo). **~óstico** *m* prediction; (*del tiempo*) forecast; (*Med*) prognosis

pront|itud *f* promptness. **~o** *adj* quick. • *adv* quickly; (*dentro de poco*) soon; (*temprano*) early. **de ~o** suddenly. **por lo ~o** for the time being. **tan ~o como** as soon as

pronuncia|ción *f* pronunciation. **~miento** *m* revolt. **~r** *vt* pronounce; deliver (discurso). **~rse** *vpr* (*declararse*) declare o.s.; (*sublevarse*) rise up

propagación *f* propagation

propaganda *f* propaganda;

(*anuncios*) advertising

propagar 12 *vt/i* propagate. **~se** *vpr* spread

propasarse *vpr* go too far

propens|ión *f* inclination. **~o** *adj* inclined

propici|ar *vt* favour; (*provocar*) bring about. **~o** *adj* favourable

propie|dad *f* property. **~tario** *m* owner

propina *f* tip

propio *adj* own; (*característico*) typical; (*natural*) natural; (*apropiado*) proper. **el ~ médico** the doctor himself

proponer 34 *vt* propose; put forward (persona). **~se** *vpr*. **~se hacer** intend to do

proporci|ón *f* proportion. **~onado** *adj* proportioned. **~onal** *adj* proportional. **~onar** *vt* provide

proposición *f* proposition

propósito *m* intention. **a ~** (*adrede*) on purpose; (*de paso*) by the way. **a ~ de** with regard to

propuesta *f* proposal

propuls|ar *vt* propel; (*fig*) promote. **~ión** *f* propulsion. **~ión a chorro** jet propulsion

prórroga *f* extension

prorrogar 12 *vt* extend

prosa *f* prose. **~ico** *adj* prosaic

proscri|bir (*pp* **proscrito**) *vt* exile; (*prohibir*) ban. **~to** *adj* banned. ● *m* exile; (*bandido*) outlaw

proseguir 5 & 13 *vt/i* continue

prospecto *m* prospectus; (*de fármaco*) directions for use

prosper|ar *vi* prosper; (persona) do well. **~idad** *f* prosperity

próspero *adj* prosperous. **¡P~ Año Nuevo!** Happy New Year!

prostit|ución *f* prostitution. **~uta** *f* prostitute

protagonista *m & f* protagonist

prote|cción *f* protection. **~ctor** *adj* protective. ● *m* protector; (*benefactor*) patron. **~ger** 14 *vt* protect. **~gida** *f* protegée. **~gido** *adj* protected. ● *m* protegé

proteína *f* protein

protesta *f* protest; (*manifestación*) demonstration; (*Mex, promesa*) promise; (*Mex, juramento*) oath

protestante *adj & m & f* Protestant

protestar *vt/i* protest

protocolo *m* protocol

provecho *m* benefit. **¡buen ~!** enjoy your meal! **de ~** useful. **en ~ de** to the benefit of. **sacar ~ de** benefit from

proveer 18 (*pp* **proveído** *y* **provisto**) *vt* supply, provide

provenir 53 *vi* come (**de** from)

proverbi|al *adj* proverbial. **~o** *m* proverb

provincia *f* province. **~l** *adj*, **~no** *adj* provincial

provisional *adj* provisional

provisto *adj* provided (**de** with)

provoca|ción *f* provocation. **~r** 7 *vt* provoke; (*causar*) cause. **~tivo** *adj* provocative

proximidad *f* proximity

próximo *adj* next; (*cerca*) near

proyec|ción *f* projection. **~tar** *vt* hurl; cast (luz); show (película). **~til** *m* missile. **~to** *m* plan. **~to de ley** bill. **en ~to** planned. **~tor** *m* projector

pruden|cia *f* prudence; (*cuidado*) caution. **~te** *adj* prudent, sensible

prueba *f* proof; (*examen*) test; (*de ropa*) fitting. **a ~** on trial. **a ~ de** proof against. **a ~ de agua** waterproof. **poner a ~** test

pruebo *vb véase* PROBAR

psicoan|álisis *f* psychoanalysis. **~alista** *m & f* psychoanalyst. **~alizar** 10 *vt* psychoanalyse

psic|ología *f* psychology. **~ológico** *adj* psychological. **~ólogo** *m* psychologist. **~ópata** *m & f* psychopath. **~osis** *f invar* psychosis

psiqu|e *f* psyche. **~iatra** *m & f* psychiatrist. **~iátrico** *adj* psychiatric

psíquico *adj* psychic

ptas, pts *abrev* (**pesetas**) pesetas

púa *f* sharp point; (*espina*) thorn; (*de erizo*) quill; (*de peine*) tooth; (*Mus*) plectrum

pubertad *f* puberty

publica|ción *f* publication. **~r** 7 *vt* publish

publici|dad *f* publicity; (*Com*) advertising. **~tario** *adj* advertising

P

público *adj* public. ● *m* public; (*de espectáculo etc*) audience

puchero *m* cooking pot; (*guisado*) stew. **hacer ~s** (*fig, fam*) pout

pude *vb véase* PODER

pudor *m* modesty. **~oso** *adj* modest

pudrir (*pp* **podrido**) *vt* rot; (*fig, molestar*) annoy. **~se** *vpr* rot

puebl|ecito *m* small village. **~erino** *m* country bumpkin. **~o** *m* town; (*aldea*) village; (*nación*) nation, people

puedo *vb véase* PODER

puente *m* bridge; (*fig, fam*) long weekend. **~ colgante** suspension bridge. **~ levadizo** drawbridge. **hacer ~** I have a long weekend

> **puente** *Puentes* are very important in Spain and Latin America. *Hacer Puente* means that when a working day falls between two public holidays, it too is taken as a holiday.

puerco *adj* filthy; (*grosero*) coarse. ● *m* pig. **~ espín** porcupine

puerro *m* leek

puerta *f* door; (*en deportes*) goal; (*de ciudad, en jardín*) gate. **~ principal** main entrance. **a ~ cerrada** behind closed doors

puerto *m* port; (*fig, refugio*) refuge; (*entre montañas*) pass. **~ franco** free port

puertorriqueño *adj & m* Puerto Rican

pues *adv* (*entonces*) then; (*bueno*) well. ● *conj* since

puest|a *f* setting; (*en juegos*) bet. **~a de sol** sunset. **~a en escena** staging. **~a en marcha** starting. **~o** *adj* put; (*vestido*) dressed. ● *m* place; (*empleo*) position, job; (*en mercado etc*) stall. ● *conj.* **~o que** since

pugna *f* struggle. **~r** *vi.* **~r por** strive to

puja *f* struggle (**por** to); (*en subasta*) bid. **~r** *vt* struggle; (*en subasta*) bid

pulcro *adj* neat

pulga *f* flea. **tener malas ~s** be bad-tempered

pulga|da *f* inch. **~r** *m* thumb; (*del pie*) big toe

puli|do *adj* polished; (modales) refined. **~r** *vt* polish; (*suavizar*) smooth

pulla *f* gibe

pulm|ón *m* lung. **~onar** *adj* pulmonary. **~onía** *f* pneumonia

pulpa *f* pulp
pulpería *f* (*LAm*) grocer's shop (*Brit*), grocery store (*Amer*)
púlpito *m* pulpit
pulpo *m* octopus
pulque *m* (*Mex*) pulque, alcoholic Mexican drink. **~ría** *f* bar
pulsa|ción *f* pulsation. **~dor** *m* button. **~r** *vt* press; (*Mus*) pluck
pulsera *f* bracelet
pulso *m* pulse; (*firmeza*) steady hand. **echar un ~** arm wrestle. **tomar el ~ a uno** take s.o.'s pulse
pulular *vi* teem with
puma *m* puma
puna *f* puna, high plateau
punitivo *adj* punitive
punta *f* point; (*extremo*) tip. **estar de ~** be in a bad mood. **ponerse de ~ con uno** fall out with s.o. **sacar ~ a** sharpen
puntada *f* stitch
puntaje *m* (*LAm*) score
puntal *m* prop, support
puntapié *m* kick
puntear *vt* mark; (*Mus*) pluck; (*LAm, en deportes*) lead
puntería *f* aim; (*destreza*) markmanship
puntiagudo *adj* pointed; (*afilado*) sharp
puntilla *f* (*encaje*) lace. **en ~s** (*LAm*), **de ~s** on tiptoe
punto *m* point; (*señal, trazo*) dot; (*de examen*) mark; (*lugar*) spot, place; (*de taxis*) stand; (*momento*) moment; (*punto final*) full stop (*Brit*), period (*Amer*); (*puntada*) stitch. **~ de vista** point of view. **~ com** dot-com. **~ final** full stop (*Brit*), period (*Amer*). **~ muerto** (*Auto*) neutral (gear). **~ y aparte** full stop, new paragraph (*Brit*), period, new paragraph (*Amer*). **~ y coma** semicolon. **a ~** on time; (*listo*) ready. **a ~ de** on the point of. **de ~** knitted. **dos ~s** colon. **en ~** exactly. **hacer ~** knit. **hasta cierto ~** to a certain extent
puntuación *f* punctuation; (*en deportes, acción*) scoring; (*en deportes, número de puntos*) score
puntual *adj* punctual; (*exacto*) accurate. **~idad** *f* punctuality; (*exactitud*) accuracy
puntuar **21** *vt* punctuate; mark (*Brit*), grade (*Amer*) (examen). ● *vi* score (points)
punza|da *f* sharp pain; (*fig*) pang. **~nte** *adj* sharp. **~r** **10** *vt* prick
puñado *m* handful. **a ~s** by the handful
puñal *m* dagger. **~ada** *f* stab
puñ|etazo *m* punch. **~o** *m* fist; (*de ropa*) cuff; (*mango*) handle. **de su ~o (y letra)** in his own handwriting
pupa *f* (*fam, en los labios*) cold sore
pupila *f* pupil
pupitre *m* desk
puré *m* purée; (*sopa*) thick soup. **~ de papas** (*LAm*), **~ de patatas** mashed potatoes
pureza *f* purity
purga *f* purge. **~torio** *m* purgatory
puri|ficación *f* purification. **~ficar** **7** *vt* purify. **~sta** *m & f* purlst. **~tano** *adj* puritanical. ● *m* puritan
puro *adj* pure; (cielo) clear. **de pura casualidad** by sheer chance. **de ~ tonto** out of sheer stupidity. ● *m* cigar
púrpura *f* purple
pus *m* pus
puse *vb véase* **PONER**

P

pusilánime *adj* fainthearted

puta *f* (*vulg*) whore

Qq

que *pron rel* (*personas, sujeto*) who; (*personas, complemento*) whom; (*cosas*) which, that. • *conj* that. **¡~ tengan Vds buen viaje!** have a good journey! **¡~ venga!** let him come! **~ venga o no venga** whether he comes or not. **creo ~ tiene razón** I think (that) he is right. **más ~** more than. **lo ~** what. **yo ~ tú** if I were you

qué *adj* (*con sustantivo*) what; (*con a o adv*) how. • *pron* what. **¡~ bonito!** how nice!. **¿en ~ piensas?** what are you thinking about?

quebra|da *f* gorge; (*paso*) pass. **~dizo** *adj* fragile. **~do** *adj* broken; (*Com*) bankrupt. • *m* (*Math*) fraction. **~ntar** *vt* break; disturb (paz). **~nto** *m* (*pérdida*) loss; (*daño*) damage. **~r** 1 *vt* break. • *vi* break; (*Com*) go bankrupt. **~rse** *vpr* break

quechua *adj* Quechua. • *m & f* Quechuan. • *m* (*lengua*) Quechua

quedar *vi* stay, remain; (*estar*) be; (*haber todavía*) be left. **~ bien** come off well. **~se** *vpr* stay. **~ con** arrange to meet. **~ en** agree to. **~ en nada** come to nothing. **~ por** (+ *infinitivo*) remain to be (+ *pp*)

quehacer *m* work. **~es domésticos** household chores

quej|a *f* complaint; (*de dolor*) moan. **~arse** *vpr* complain (**de** about); (*gemir*) moan. **~ido** *m* moan

quema|do *adj* burnt; (*LAm, bronceado*) tanned; (*fig*) annoyed. **~dor** *m* burner. **~dura** *f* burn. **~r** *vt/i* burn. **~rse** *vpr* burn o.s.; (*consumirse*) burn up; (*con el sol*) get sunburnt. **~rropa** *adv.* **a ~rropa** point-blank

quena *f* Indian flute

quepo *vb véase* CABER

querella *f* (*riña*) quarrel, dispute; (*Jurid*) criminal action

quer|er 35 *vt* want; (*amar*) love; (*necesitar*) need. **~er decir** mean. • *m* love; (*amante*) lover. **como quiera que** however. **cuando quiera que** whenever. **donde quiera** wherever. **¿quieres darme ese libro?** would you pass me that book? **¿quieres un helado?** would you like an ice-cream? **quisiera ir a la playa** I'd like to go to the beach. **sin ~er** without meaning to. **~ido** *adj* dear; (*amado*) loved

querosén *m*, **queroseno** *m* kerosene

querubín *m* cherub

ques|adilla *f* (*Mex*) tortilla filled with cheese. **~o** *m* cheese

quetzal *m* (*unidad monetaria ecuatoriana*) quetzal

quicio *m* frame. **sacar de ~ a uno** infuriate s.o.

quiebra *f* (*Com*) bankruptcy

quien *pron rel* (*sujeto*) who; (*complemento*) whom

quién *pron interrogativo* (*sujeto*) who; (*tras preposición*) **¿con ~?** who with?, to whom?. **¿de ~ son estos libros?** whose are these books?

quienquiera *pron* whoever

quiero *vb véase* QUERER

quiet|o *adj* still; (*inmóvil*) motionless; (carácter etc) calm. **~ud** *f* stillness

quijada *f* jaw

quilate *m* carat

quilla *f* keel

quimera *f* (*fig*) illusion

químic|a *f* chemistry. **~o** *adj* chemical. • *m* chemist

quince *adj & m* fifteen. **~ días** a fortnight. **~na** *f* fortnight. **~nal** *adj* fortnightly

quincuagésimo *adj* fiftieth

quiniela *f* pools coupon. **~s** *fpl* (football) pools

quinientos *adj & m* five hundred

quinquenio *m* (period of) five years

quinta *f* (*casa*) villa

quintal *m* a hundred kilograms

quinteto *m* quintet

quinto *adj & m* fifth

quiosco *m* kiosk; (*en jardín*) summerhouse; (*en parque etc*) bandstand

quirúrgico *adj* surgical

quise *vb véase* QUERER

quisquill|a *f* trifle; (*camarón*) shrimp. **~oso** *adj* irritable; (*exigente*) fussy

quita|esmalte *m* nail polish remover. **~manchas** *m invar* stain remover. **~nieves** *m invar* snow plough. **~r** *vt* remove, take away; take off (ropa); (*robar*) steal. **~ndo** (*fam, a excepción de*) apart from. **~rse** *vpr* get rid of (dolor); take off (ropa). **~rse de** (*no hacerlo más*) stop. **~rse de en medio** get out of the way. **~sol** *m* sunshade

quizá(s) *adv* perhaps

quórum *m* quorum

Rr

rábano *m* radish. **~ picante** horseradish. **me importa un ~** I couldn't care less

rabi|a *f* rabies; (*fig*) rage. **~ar** *vi* (*de dolor*) be in great pain; (*estar enfadado*) be furious. **dar ~a** infuriate. **~eta** *f* tantrum

rabino *m* rabbi

rabioso *adj* rabid; (*furioso*) furious

rabo *m* tail

racha *f* gust of wind; (*fig*) spate. **pasar por una mala ~** go through a bad patch

racial *adj* racial

racimo *m* bunch

ración *f* share, ration; (*de comida*) portion

raciona|l *adj* rational. **~lizar** 10 *vt* rationalize. **~r** *vt* (*limitar*) ration; (*repartir*) ration out

racis|mo *m* racism. **~ta** *adj* racist

radar *m* radar

radiación *f* radiation

radiactiv|idad *f* radioactivity. **~o** *adj* radioactive

radiador *m* radiator

radiante *adj* radiant; (*brillante*) brilliant

radical *adj & m & f* radical

radicar 7 *vi* lie (**en** in). **~se** *vpr* settle

radio *m* radius; (*de rueda*) spoke; (*LAm*) radio. • *f* radio. **~actividad** *f* radioactivity. **~activo** *adj* radioactive. **~difusión** *f* broadcasting. **~emisora** *f* radio station. **~escucha** *m & f* listener. **~grafía** *f* radiography

radi|ólogo *m* radiologist. **~oterapia** *f* radiotherapy
radioyente *m & f* listener
raer 36 *vt* scrape; (*quitar*) scrape off
ráfaga *f* (*de viento*) gust; (*de ametralladora*) burst
rafia *f* raffia
raído *adj* threadbare
raíz *f* root. **a ~ de** as a result of. **echar raíces** (*fig*) settle
raja *f* split; (*Culin*) slice. **~r** *vt* split. **~rse** *vpr* split; (*fig*) back out
rajatabla. **a ~** rigorously
ralea *f* sort
ralla|dor *m* grater. **~r** *vt* grate
ralo *adj* (pelo) thin
rama *f* branch. **~je** *m* branches. **~l** *m* branch
rambla *f* watercourse; (*avenida*) avenue
ramera *f* prostitute
ramifica|ción *f* ramification. **~rse** 7 *vpr* branch out
ram|illete *m* bunch. **~o** *m* branch; (*de flores*) bunch, bouquet
rampa *f* ramp, slope
rana *f* frog
r **ranch|era** *f* (*Mex*) folk song. **~ero** *m* cook; (*Mex, hacendado*) rancher. **~o** *m* (*LAm, choza*) hut; (*LAm, casucha*) shanty; (*Mex, hacienda*) ranch
rancio *adj* rancid; (vino) old; (*fig*) ancient
rango *m* rank
ranúnculo *m* buttercup
ranura *f* groove; (*para moneda*) slot
rapar *vt* shave; crop (pelo)
rapaz *adj* rapacious; (ave) of prey
rape *m* monkfish
rapidez *f* speed
rápido *adj* fast, quick. • *adv* quickly. • *m* (*tren*) express. **~s** *mpl* rapids
rapiña *f* robbery. **ave** *f* **de ~** bird of prey
rapsodia *f* rhapsody
rapt|ar *vt* kidnap. **~o** *m* kidnapping; (*de ira etc*) fit
raqueta *f* racquet
rar|eza *f* rarity; (*cosa rara*) oddity. **~o** *adj* rare; (*extraño*) odd. **es ~o que** it is strange that. **¡qué ~o!** how strange!
ras. **a ~ de** level with
rasca|cielos *m invar* skyscraper. **~r** 7 *vt* scratch; (*raspar*) scrape
rasgar 12 *vt* tear
rasgo *m* characteristic; (*gesto*) gesture; (*de pincel*) stroke. **~s** *mpl* (*facciones*) features
rasguear *vt* strum
rasguñ|ar *vt* scratch. **~o** *m* scratch
raso *adj* (cucharada etc) level; (vuelo etc) low. **al ~** in the open air. • *m* satin
raspa|dura *f* scratch; (*acción*) scratching. **~r** *vt* scratch; (*rozar*) scrape
rastr|a. **a ~as** dragging. **~ear** *vt* track. **~ero** *adj* creeping. **~illar** *vt* rake. **~illo** *m* rake. **~o** *m* track; (*señal*) sign. **ni ~o** not a trace
rata *f* rat
ratero *m* petty thief
ratifica|ción *f* ratification. **~r** 7 *vt* ratify
rato *m* moment, short time. **~s libres** spare time. **a ~s** at times. **a cada ~** (*LAm*) always. **hace un ~** a moment ago. **pasar un mal ~** have a rough time
rat|ón *m* mouse. **~onera** *f*

mousetrap; (*madriguera*) mouse hole

raudal *m* torrent. **a ~les** in abundance

raya *f* line; (*lista*) stripe; (*de pelo*) parting. **a ~s** striped. **pasarse de la ~** go too far. **~r** *vt* scratch. **~r en** border on

rayo *m* ray; (*descarga eléctrica*) lightning. **~ de luna** moonbeam. **~ láser** laser beam. **~s X** X-rays

raza *f* race; (*de animal*) breed. **de ~** (caballo) thoroughbred; (perro) pedigree

raz|ón *f* reason. **a ~ón de** at the rate of. **tener ~ón** be right. **~onable** *adj* reasonable. **~onar** *vt* reason out. • *vi* reason

RDSI *abrev* (**Red Digital de Servicios Integrados**) ISDN

re *m* D; (*solfa*) re

reac|ción *f* reaction; (*LAm, Pol*) right wing. **~ción en cadena** chain reaction. **~cionario** *adj & m* reactionary. **~tor** *m* reactor; (*avión*) jet

real *adj* real; (*de rey etc*) royal; (hecho) true. • *m* real, old Spanish coin

realidad *f* reality; (*verdad*) truth. **en ~** in fact. **hacerse ~** come true

realis|mo *m* realism. **~ta** *adj* realistic. • *m & f* realist

realiza|ción *f* fulfilment. **~r** 10 *vt* carry out; make (viaje); fulfil (ilusión); (*vender*) sell. **~rse** *vpr* (sueño, predicción etc) come true; (persona) fulfil o.s.

realzar 10 *vt* (*fig*) enhance

reanimar *vt* revive. **~se** *vpr* revive

reanudar *vt* resume; renew (amistad)

reavivar *vt* revive

rebaja *f* reduction. **en ~s** in the sale. **~do** *adj* (precio) reduced. **~r** *vt* lower; lose (peso)

rebanada *f* slice

rebaño *m* herd; (*de ovejas*) flock

rebasar *vt* exceed; (*dejar atrás*) leave behind; (*Mex, Auto*) overtake

rebatir *vt* refute

rebel|arse *vpr* rebel. **~de** *adj* rebellious; (grupo) rebel. • *m* rebel. **~día** *f* rebelliousness. **~ión** *f* rebellion

rebosa|nte *adj* brimming (**de** with). **~r** *vi* overflow; (*abundar*) abound

rebot|ar *vt* bounce; (*rechazar*) repel. • *vi* bounce; (bala) ricochet. **~e** *m* bounce, rebound. **de ~e** on the rebound

reboz|ar 10 *vt* wrap up; (*Culin*) coat in batter. **~o** *m* (*LAm*) shawl

rebusca|do *adj* affected; (*complicado*) over-elaborate. **~r** 7 *vt* search through

rebuznar *vi* bray

recado *m* errand; (*mensaje*) message

reca|er 29 *vi* fall back; (*Med*) relapse; (*fig*) fall. **~ída** *f* relapse

recalcar 7 *vt* stress

recalcitrante *adj* recalcitrant

recalentar 1 *vt* reheat; (*demasiado*) overheat

recámara *f* small room; (*de arma de fuego*) chamber; (*Mex, dormitorio*) bedroom

recambio *m* (*Mec*) spare (part); (*de pluma etc*) refill. **de ~** spare

recapitular *vt* sum up

recarg|ar 12 *vt* overload; (*aumentar*) increase; recharge (batería); top up (movíl). **~o** *m* increase

recat|ado *adj* modest. **~o** *m* prudence; (*modestia*) modesty. **sin ~o** openly

recauda|ción *f* (*cantidad*) takings. **~dor** *m* tax collector. **~r** *vt* collect

recel|ar *vt* suspect. • *vi* be suspicious (**de** of). **~o** *m* distrust; (*temor*) fear. **~oso** *adj* suspicious

recepci|ón *f* reception. **~onista** *m & f* receptionist

receptáculo *m* receptacle

receptor *m* receiver

recesión *f* recession

receta *f* recipe; (*Med*) prescription

rechaz|ar 10 *vt* reject; defeat (moción); repel (ataque); (*no aceptar*) turn down. **~o** *m* rejection

rechifla *f* booing

rechinar *vi* squeak. **le rechinan los dientes** he grinds his teeth

rechoncho *adj* stout

recib|imiento *m* (*acogida*) welcome. **~ir** *vt* receive; (*acoger*) welcome • *vi* entertain. **~irse** *vpr* graduate. **~o** *m* receipt. **acusar ~o** acknowledge receipt

reci|én *adv* recently; (*LAm, hace poco*) just. **~ casado** newly married. **~ nacido** newborn. **~ente** *adj* recent; (*Culin*) fresh

recinto *m* enclosure; (*local*) premises

recio *adj* strong; (voz) loud. • *adv* hard; (*en voz alta*) loudly

recipiente *m* receptacle. • *m & f* recipient

recíproco *adj* reciprocal; (sentimiento) mutual

recita|l *m* recital; (*de poesías*) reading. **~r** *vt* recite

reclama|ción *f* claim; (*queja*) complaint. **~r** *vt* claim. • *vi* appeal

réclame *m* (*LAm*) advertisement

reclamo *m* (*LAm*) complaint

reclinar *vi* lean. **~se** *vpr* lean

reclus|ión *f* imprisonment. **~o** *m* prisoner

recluta *m & f* recruit. **~miento** *m* recruitment. **~r** *vt* recruit

recobrar *vt* recover. **~se** *vpr* recover

recodo *m* bend

recog|er 14 *vt* collect; pick up (cosa caída); (*cosechar*) harvest. **~erse** *vpr* withdraw; (*ir a casa*) go home; (*acostarse*) go to bed. **~ida** *f* collection; (*cosecha*) harvest

recomenda|ción *f* recommendation. **~r** 1 *vt* recommend; (*encomendar*) entrust

recomenzar 1 & 10 *vt/i* start again

recompensa *f* reward. **~r** *vt* reward

reconcilia|ción *f* reconciliation. **~r** *vt* reconcile. **~rse** *vpr* be reconciled

reconoc|er 11 *vt* recognize; (*admitir*) acknowledge; (*examinar*) examine. **~imiento** *m* recognition; (*admisión*) acknowledgement; (*agradecimiento*) gratitude; (*examen*) examination

reconozco *vb véase* **RECONOCER**

reconquista *f* reconquest. **~r** *vt* reconquer; (*fig*) win back

Reconquista The period in Spain's history during which the Christian kingdoms slowly recovered the territories occupied by the Moslem Moors of North Africa. The Moorish invasion began in 711 AD and was halted in 718. The expulsion of

r

the last Moorish ruler of Granada in 1492 completed the *Reconquista*.

reconsiderar *vt* reconsider

reconstruir 17 *vt* reconstruct

récord /ˈrekor/ *m* (*pl* **~s**) record

recordar 2 *vt* remember; (*hacer acordar*) remind. • *vi* remember. **que yo recuerde** as far as I remember. **si mal no recuerdo** if I remember rightly

recorr|er *vt* tour (país); go round (zona, museo); cover (distancia). **~ mundo** travel all around the world. **~ido** *m* journey; (*trayecto*) route

recort|ar *vt* cut (out). **~e** *m* cutting (out); (*de periódico etc*) cutting

recostar 2 *vt* lean. **~se** *vpr* lie down

recoveco *m* bend; (*rincón*) nook

recre|ación *f* recreation. **~ar** *vt* recreate; (*divertir*) entertain. **~arse** *vpr* amuse o.s. **~ativo** *adj* recreational. **~o** *m* recreation; (*en escuela*) break

recrudecer 11 *vi* intensify

recta *f* straight line. **~ final** home stretch

rect|angular *adj* rectangular. **~ángulo** *adj* rectangular; (triángulo) right-angled. • *m* rectangle

rectifica|ción *f* rectification. **~r** 7 *vt* rectify

rect|itud *f* straightness; (*fig*) honesty. **~o** *adj* straight; (*fig, justo*) fair; (*fig, honrado*) honest. **todo ~o** straight on. • *m* rectum

rector *adj* governing. • *m* rector

recubrir (*pp* **recubierto**) *vt* cover (**con, de** with)

recuerdo *m* memory; (*regalo*) souvenir. **~s** *mpl* (*saludos*) regards. • *vb véase* RECORDAR

recupera|ción *f* recovery. **~r** *vt* recover. **~r el tiempo perdido** make up for lost time. **~rse** *vpr* recover

recur|rir *vi*. **~rir a** resort to (cosa); turn to (persona). **~so** *m* resort; (*medio*) resource; (*Jurid*) appeal. **~sos** *mpl* resources

red *f* network; (*malla*) net; (*para equipaje*) luggage rack; (*Com*) chain; (*Elec, gas*) mains. **la R~** the Net

redac|ción *f* writing; (*lenguaje*) wording; (*conjunto de redactores*) editorial staff; (*oficina*) editorial office; (*Escol, Univ*) essay. **~tar** *vt* write. **~tor** *m* writer; (*de periódico*) editor

redada *f* catch; (*de policía*) raid

redecilla *f* small net; (*para el pelo*) hairnet

redentor *adj* redeeming

redimir *vt* redeem

redoblar *vt* redouble; step up (vigilancia)

redomado *adj* utter

redond|a *f* (*de imprenta*) roman (type); (*Mus*) semibreve (*Brit*), whole note (*Amer*). **a la ~a** around. **~ear** *vt* round off. **~el** *m* circle; (*de plaza de toros*) arena. **~o** *adj* round; (*completo*) complete; (*Mex, boleto*) return, round-trip (*Amer*). **en ~o** round; (*categóricamente*) flatly

reduc|ción *f* reduction. **~ido** *adj* reduced; (*limitado*) limited; (*pequeño*) small; (precio) low. **~ir** 47 *vt* reduce. **~irse** *vpr* be reduced; (*fig*) amount

reduje *vb véase* REDUCIR

redundan|cia *f* redundancy. **~te** *adj* redundant

reduzco *vb véase* REDUCIR

reembols|ar *vt* reimburse. **~o** *m* repayment. **contra ~o** cash on delivery
reemplaz|ar 10 *vt* replace. **~o** *m* replacement
refacci|ón *f* (*LAm*) refurbishment; (*Mex, Mec*) spare part. **~onar** *vt* (*LAm*) refurbish. **~onaria** *f* (*Mex*) repair shop
referencia *f* reference; (*información*) report. **con ~ a** with reference to. **hacer ~ a** refer to
referéndum *m* (*pl* **~s**) referendum
referir 4 *vt* tell; (*remitir*) refer. **~se** *vpr* refer. **por lo que se refiere a** as regards
refiero *vb véase* REFERIR
refilón. de ~ obliquely
refin|amiento *m* refinement. **~ar** *vt* refine. **~ería** *f* refinery
reflector *m* reflector; (*proyector*) searchlight
reflej|ar *vt* reflect. **~o** *adj* reflex. • *m* reflection; (*Med*) reflex; (*en el pelo*) highlights
reflexi|ón *f* reflection. **sin ~ón** without thinking. **~onar** *vi* reflect. **~vo** *adj* (persona) thoughtful; (*Gram*) reflexive
reforma *f* reform. **~s** *fpl* (*reparaciones*) repairs. **~r** *vt* reform. **~rse** *vpr* reform
reforzar 2 & 10 *vt* reinforce
refrac|ción *f* refraction. **~tario** *adj* heat-resistant
refrán *m* saying
refregar 1 & 12 *vt* scrub
refresc|ar 7 *vt* refresh; (*enfriar*) cool. • *vi* get cooler. **~arse** *vpr* refresh o.s. **~o** *m* cold drink. **~os** *mpl* refreshments
refrigera|ción *f* refrigeration; (*aire acondicionado*) air-conditioning; (*de motor*) cooling. **~r** *vt* refrigerate; air-condition (lugar); cool (motor). **~dor** *m* refrigerator
refuerzo *m* reinforcement
refugi|ado *m* refugee. **~arse** *vpr* take refuge. **~o** *m* refuge, shelter
refunfuñar *vi* grumble
refutar *vt* refute
regadera *f* watering-can; (*Mex, ducha*) shower
regala|do *adj* as a present, free; (*cómodo*) comfortable. **~r** *vt* give
regalo *m* present, gift
regañ|adientes. a ~adientes reluctantly. **~ar** *vt* scold. • *vi* moan; (*dos personas*) quarrel. **~o** *m* (*reprensión*) scolding
regar 1 & 12 *vt* water
regata *f* boat race; (*serie*) regatta
regate|ar *vt* haggle over; (*economizar*) economize on. • *vi* haggle; (*en deportes*) dribble. **~o** *m* haggling; (*en deportes*) dribbling
regazo *m* lap
regenerar *vt* regenerate
régimen *m* (*pl* **regímenes**) regime; (*Med*) diet; (*de lluvias*) pattern
regimiento *m* regiment
regi|ón *f* region. **~onal** *adj* regional
regir 5 & 14 *vt* govern. • *vi* apply, be in force
registr|ado *adj* registered. **~ar** *vt* register; (*Mex*) check in (equipaje); (*grabar*) record; (*examinar*) search. **~arse** *vpr* register; (*darse*) be reported. **~o** *m* (*acción de registrar*) registration; (*libro*) register; (*cosa anotada*) entry; (*inspección*) search. **~o civil** (*oficina*) registry office
regla *f* ruler; (*norma*) rule; (*mens-*

truación) period. **en ~** in order. **por ~ general** as a rule. **~mentación** *f* regulation. **~mentar** *vt* regulate. **~mentario** *adj* regulation; (horario) set. **~mento** *m* regulations

regocij|arse *vpr* be delighted. **~o** *m* delight

regode|arse *vpr* (+ *gerundio*) delight in (+ *gerund*). **~o** *m* delight

regordete *adj* chubby

regres|ar *vi* return; (*LAm*) send back (persona). **~arse** *vpr* (*LAm*) return. **~ivo** *adj* backward. **~o** *m* return

regula|ble *adj* adjustable. **~dor** *m* control. **~r** *adj* regular; (*mediano*) average; (*no bueno*) so-so. ● *vt* regulate; adjust (volumen etc). **~ridad** *f* regularity. **con ~ridad** regularly

rehabilita|ción *f* rehabilitation; (*en empleo etc*) reinstatement. **~r** *vt* rehabilitate; (*en cargo*) reinstate

rehacer 31 *vt* redo; (*repetir*) repeat; rebuild (vida). **~se** *vpr* recover

rehén *m* hostage

rehogar 12 *vt* sauté

rehuir 17 *vt* avoid

rehusar *vt/i* refuse

reimpr|esión *f* reprinting. **~imir** (*pp* **reimpreso**) *vt* reprint

reina *f* queen. **~do** *m* reign. **~nte** *adj* ruling; (*fig*) prevailing. **~r** *vi* reign; (*fig*) prevail

reincidir *vi* (*Jurid*) reoffend

reino *m* kingdom. **R~ Unido** United Kingdom

reintegr|ar *vt* reinstate (persona); refund (cantidad). **~arse** *vpr* return. **~o** *m* refund

reír 51 *vi* laugh. **~se** *vpr* laugh. **~se de** laugh at. **echarse a ~** burst out laughing

reivindica|ción *f* claim. **~r** 7 *vt* claim; (*rehabilitar*) restore

rej|a *f* grille; (*verja*) railing. **entre ~as** behind bars. **~illa** *f* grille, grating; (*red*) luggage rack

rejuvenecer 11 *vt/i* rejuvenate. **~se** *vpr* be rejuvenated

relaci|ón *f* connection; (*trato*) relation(ship); (*relato*) account; (*lista*) list. **con ~ón a, en ~ón a** in relation to. **~onado** *adj* related. **bien ~onado** well-connected. **~onar** *vt* relate (**con** to). **~onarse** *vpr* be connected; (*tratar*) mix (**con** with)

relaja|ción *f* relaxation; (*aflojamiento*) slackening. **~do** *adj* relaxed. **~r** *vt* relax; (*aflojar*) slacken. **~rse** *vpr* relax

relamerse *vpr* lick one's lips

relámpago *m* (flash of) lightning

relatar *vt* tell, relate

relativ|idad *f* relativity. **~o** *adj* relative

relato *m* tale; (*relación*) account

relegar 12 *vt* relegate. **~ al olvido** consign to oblivion

relev|ante *adj* outstanding. **~ar** *vt* relieve; (*substituir*) replace. **~o** *m* relief. **carrera** *f* **de ~os** relay race

relieve *m* relief; (*fig*) importance. **de ~** important. **poner de ~** emphasize

religi|ón *f* religion. **~osa** *f* nun. **~oso** *adj* religious. ● *m* monk

relinch|ar *vi* neigh. **~o** *m* neigh

reliquia *f* relic

rellano *m* landing

rellen|ar *vt* refill; (*Culin*) stuff; fill in (formulario). **~o** *adj* full up; (*Culin*) stuffed. ● *m* filling; (*Culin*) stuffing

reloj *m* clock; (*de bolsillo o pulsera*)

watch. ~ **de caja** grandfather clock. ~ **de pulsera** wrist-watch. ~ **de sol** sundial. ~ **despertador** alarm clock. ~**ería** *f* watchmaker's (shop). ~**ero** *m* watchmaker

reluci|ente *adj* shining. ~**r** 11 *vi* shine; (*destellar*) sparkle

relumbrar *vi* shine

remach|ar *vt* rivet. ~**e** *m* rivet

remangar 12 *vt* roll up

remar *vi* row

remat|ado *adj* (*total*) complete. ~**ar** *vt* finish off; (*agotar*) use up; (*Com*) sell off cheap; (*LAm, subasta*) auction; (*en tenis*) smash. ~**e** *m* end; (*fig*) finishing touch; (*LAm, subastar*) auction; (*en tenis*) smash. **de** ~**e** completely

remedar *vt* imitate

remedi|ar *vt* remedy; repair (daño); (*fig, resolver*) solve. **no lo pude** ~**ar** I couldn't help it. ~**o** *m* remedy; (*fig*) solution; (*LAm, medicamento*) medicine. **como último** ~**o** as a last resort. **no hay más** ~**o** there's no other way. **no tener más** ~**o** have no choice

remedo *m* poor imitation

rem|endar 1 *vt* repair. ~**iendo** *m* patch

r

remilg|ado *adj* fussy; (*afectado*) affected. ~**o** *m* fussiness; (*afectación*) affectation. ~**oso** *adj* (*Mex*) fussy

reminiscencia *f* reminiscence

remisión *f* remission; (*envío*) sending; (*referencia*) reference

remit|e *m* sender's name and address. ~**ente** *m* sender. ~**ir** *vt* send; (*referir*) refer • *vi* diminish

remo *m* oar

remoj|ar *vt* soak; (*fig, fam*) celebrate. ~**o** *m* soaking. **poner a** ~**o** soak

remolacha *f* beetroot. ~ **azucarera** sugar beet

remolcar 7 *vt* tow

remolino *m* swirl; (*de aire etc*) whirl

remolque *m* towing; (*cabo*) towrope; (*vehículo*) trailer. **a** ~ on tow. **dar** ~ **a** tow

remontar *vt* overcome. ~ **el vuelo** soar up; (avión) gain height. ~**se** *vpr* soar up; (*en el tiempo*) go back to

remord|er 2 *vi*. **eso le remuerde** he feels guilty for it. **me remuerde la conciencia** I have a guilty conscience. ~**imiento** *m* remorse. **tener** ~**imientos** feel remorse

remoto *adj* remote; (época) distant

remover 2 *vt* stir (líquido); turn over (tierra); (*quitar*) remove; (*fig, activar*) revive

remunera|ción *f* remuneration. ~**r** *vt* remunerate

renac|er 11 *vi* be reborn; (*fig*) revive. ~**imiento** *m* rebirth. **R**~**imiento** Renaissance

renacuajo *m* tadpole; (*fig*) tiddler

rencilla *f* quarrel

rencor *m* bitterness. **guardar** ~ **a** have a grudge against. ~**oso** *adj* resentful

rendi|ción *f* surrender. ~**do** *adj* submissive; (*agotado*) exhausted

rendija *f* crack

rendi|miento *m* performance; (*Com*) yield. ~**r** 5 *vt* yield; (*agotar*) exhaust; pay (homenaje); present (informe). • *vi* pay; (*producir*) produce. ~**rse** *vpr* surrender

renegar 1 & 12 *vt* deny. • *vi* grumble. ~ **de** renounce (fe etc); disown (personas)

renglón *m* line; (*Com*) item. **a ~ seguido** straight away

reno *m* reindeer

renombr|ado *adj* renowned. **~e** *m* renown

renova|ción *f* renewal; (*de edificio*) renovation; (*de mobiliario*) complete change. **~r** *vt* renew; renovate (edificio); change (mobiliario)

rent|a *f* income; (*Mex, alquiler*) rent. **~a vitalicia** (life) annuity. **~able** *adj* profitable. **~ar** *vt* yield; (*Mex, alquilar*) rent, hire. **~ista** *m & f* person of independent means

renuncia *f* renunciation; (*dimisión*) resignation. **~r** *vi.* **~r a** renounce, give up; (*dimitir*) resign

reñi|do *adj* hard-fought. **estar ~do con** be incompatible with (cosa); be on bad terms with (persona). **~r** [5] & [22] *vt* scold. ● *vi* quarrel

reo *m & f* (*Jurid*) accused; (*condenado*) convicted offender; (*pez*) sea trout

reojo. mirar de ~ look out of the corner of one's eye at

reorganizar [10] *vt* reorganize

repar|ación *f* repair; (*acción*) repairing (*fig, compensación*) reparation. **~ar** *vt* repair; (*fig*) make amends for; (*notar*) notice. ● *vi.* **~ar en** notice; (*hacer caso de*) pay attention to. **~o** *m* fault; (*objeción*) objection. **poner ~os** raise objections

repart|ición *f* distribution. **~idor** *m* delivery man. **~imiento** *m* distribution. **~ir** *vt* distribute, share out; deliver (cartas, leche etc); hand out (folleto, premio). **~o** *m* distribution; (*de cartas, leche etc*) delivery; (*actores*) cast

repas|ar *vt* go over; check (cuenta); revise (texto); (*leer a la ligera*) glance through; (*coser*) mend. ● *vi* revise. **~o** *m* revision; (*de ropa*) mending. **dar un ~o** look through

repatria|ción *f* repatriation. **~r** *vt* repatriate

repele|nte *adj* repulsive. ● *m* insect repellent. **~r** *vt* repel

repent|e. de ~ suddenly. **~ino** *adj* sudden

repercu|sión *f* repercussion. **~tir** *vi* reverberate; (*fig*) have repercussions (**en** on)

repertorio *m* repertoire

repeti|ción *f* repetition; (*de programa*) repeat. **~damente** *adv* repeatedly. **~r** [5] *vt* repeat; have a second helping of (plato); (*imitar*) copy. ● *vi* have a second helping of

repi|car [7] *vt* ring (campanas). **~que** *m* peal

repisa *f* shelf. **~ de chimenea** mantlepiece

repito *vb véase* REPETIR

replegarse [1] & [12] *vpr* withdraw

repleto *adj* full up. **~ de gente** packed with people

réplica *adj* reply; (*copia*) replica

replicar [7] *vi* reply

repollo *m* cabbage

reponer [34] *vt* replace; revive (obra de teatro); (*contestar*) reply. **~se** *vpr* recover

report|aje *m* report; (*LAm, entrevista*) interview. **~ar** *vt* yield; (*LAm, denunciar*) report. **~e** *m* (*Mex, informe*) report; (*Mex, queja*) complaint. **~ero** *m* reporter

repos|ado *adj* quiet; (*sin prisa*) unhurried. **~ar** *vi* rest; (líquido) settle. **~o** *m* rest

repost|ar *vt* replenish. ● *vi* (avión)

refuel; (*Auto*) fill up. **~ería** *f* pastrymaking

reprender *vt* reprimand

represalia *f* reprisal. **tomar ~s** retaliate

representa|ción *f* representation; (*en el teatro*) performance. **en ~ción de** representing. **~nte** *m* representative. **~r** *vt* represent; perform (obra de teatro); play (papel); (*aparentar*) look. **~rse** *vpr* imagine. **~tivo** *adj* representative

represi|ón *f* repression. **~vo** *adj* repressive

reprimenda *f* reprimand

reprimir *vt* supress. **~se** *vpr* control o.s.

reprobar **2** *vt* condemn; (*LAm, Univ, etc*) fail

reproch|ar *vt* reproach. **~e** *m* reproach

reproduc|ción *f* reproduction. **~ir** **47** *vt* reproduce. **~tor** *adj* reproductive; (animal) breeding

reptil *m* reptile

rep|ública *f* republic. **~ublicano** *adj & m* republican

repudiar *vt* condemn; (*Jurid*) repudiate

r

repuesto *m* (*Mec*) spare (part). **de ~** spare

repugna|ncia *f* disgust. **~nte** *adj* repugnant; (olor) disgusting. **~r** *vt* disgust

repuls|a *f* rebuff. **~ión** *f* repulsion. **~ivo** *adj* repulsive

reputa|ción *f* reputation. **~do** *adj* reputable. **~r** *vt* consider

requeri|miento *m* request; (*necesidad*) requirement. **~r** **4** *vt* require; summons (persona)

requesón *m* curd cheese

requete... *prefijo* (*fam*) extremely

requis|a *f* requisition; (*confiscación*) seizure; (*inspección*) inspection; (*Mil*) requisition. **~ar** *vt* requisition; (*confiscar*) seize; (*inspeccionar*) inspect. **~ito** *m* requirement

res *f* animal. **~ lanar** sheep. **~ vacuna** (*vaca*) cow; (*toro*) bull; (*buey*) ox. **carne de ~** (*Mex*) beef

resabido *adj* well-known; (persona) pedantic

resaca *f* undercurrent; (*después de beber*) hangover

resaltar *vi* stand out. **hacer ~** emphasize

resarcir **9** *vt* repay; (*compensar*) compensate. **~se** *vpr* make up for

resbal|adilla *f* (*Mex*) slide. **~adizo** *adj* slippery. **~ar** *vi* slip; (*Auto*) skid; (líquido) trickle. **~arse** *vpr* slip; (*Auto*) skid; (líquido) trickle. **~ón** *m* slip; (*de vehículo*) skid. **~oso** *adj* (*LAm*) slippery

rescat|ar *vt* rescue; (*fig*) recover. **~e** *m* ransom; (*recuperación*) recovery; (*salvamento*) rescue

rescoldo *m* embers

resecar **7** *vt* dry up. **~se** *vpr* dry up

resenti|do *adj* resentful. **~miento** *m* resentment. **~rse** *vpr* feel the effects; (*debilitarse*) be weakened; (*ofenderse*) take offence (**de** at)

reseña *f* summary; (*de persona*) description; (*en periódico*) report, review. **~r** *vt* describe; (*en periódico*) report on, review

reserva *f* reservation; (*provisión*) reserve(s). **de ~** in reserve. **~ción** *f* (*LAm*) reservation. **~do** *adj* reserved. **~r** *vt* reserve; (*guardar*) keep, save. **~rse** *vpr* save o.s.

resfria|do *m* cold. **~rse** *vpr* catch

a cold

resguard|ar *vt* protect. **~arse** *vpr* protect o.s.; (*fig*) take care. **~o** *m* protection; (*garantía*) guarantee; (*recibo*) receipt

resid|encia *f* residence; (*Univ*) hall of residence (*Brit*), dormitory (*Amer*); (*de ancianos etc*) home. **~encial** *adj* residential. **~ente** *adj* & *m* & *f* resident. **~ir** *vi* reside; (*fig*) lie (**en** in)

residu|al *adj* residual. **~o** *m* residue. **~os** *mpl* waste

resigna|ción *f* resignation. **~rse** *vpr* resign o.s. (**a** to)

resist|encia *f* resistence. **~ente** *adj* resistent. **~ir** *vt* resist; (*soportar*) bear. • *vi* resist. **ya no resisto más** I can't take it any more

resol|ución *f* resolution; (*solución*) solution; (*decisión*) decision. **~ver** 2 (*pp* **resuelto**) resolve; solve (problema etc). **~verse** *vpr* resolve itself; (*resultar bien*) work out; (*decidir*) decide

resona|ncia *f* resonance. **tener ~ncia** cause a stir. **~nte** *adj* resonant; (*fig*) resounding. **~r** 2 *vi* resound

resorte *m* spring; (*Mex, elástico*) elastic. **tocar (todos los) ~s** (*fig*) pull strings

respald|ar *vt* back; (*escribir*) endorse. **~arse** *vpr* lean back. **~o** *m* backing; (*de asiento*) back

respect|ar *vi.* **en lo que ~a a** with regard to. **en lo que a mí ~a** as far as I'm concerned. **~ivo** *adj* respective. **~o** *m* respect. **al ~o** on this matter. **(con) ~o a** with regard to

respet|able *adj* respectable. • *m* audience. **~ar** *vt* respect. **~o** *m* respect. **faltar al ~o a** be disrespectful to. **~uoso** *adj* respectful

respir|ación *f* breathing; (*ventilación*) ventilation. **~ar** *vi* breathe; (*fig*) breathe a sigh of relief. **~o** *m* breathing; (*fig*) rest

resplandecer 11 *vi* shine. **~eciente** *adj* shining. **~or** *m* brilliance; (*de llamas*) glow

responder *vi* answer; (*replicar*) answer back; (*reaccionar*) respond. **~ de** be responsible for. **~ por uno** vouch for s.o.

responsab|ilidad *f* responsibility. **~le** *adj* responsible

respuesta *f* reply, answer

resquebrajar *vt* crack. **~se** *vpr* crack

resquemor *m* (*fig*) uneasiness

resquicio *m* crack; (*fig*) possibility

resta *f* subtraction

restablecer 11 *vt* restore. **~se** *vpr* recover

rest|ante *adj* remaining. **lo ~nte** the rest. **~ar** *vt* take away; (*substraer*) subtract. • *vi* be left

restaura|ción *f* restoration. **~nte** *m* restaurant. **~r** *vt* restore

restitu|ción *f* restitution. **~ir** 17 *vt* return; (*restaurar*) restore

resto *m* rest, remainder; (*en matemática*) remainder. **~s** *mpl* remains; (*de comida*) leftovers

restorán *m* restaurant

restregar 1 & 12 *vt* rub

restri|cción *f* restriction. **~ngir** 14 *vt* restrict, limit

resucitar *vt* resuscitate; (*fig*) revive. • *vi* return to life

resuello *m* breath; (*respiración*) heavy breathing

resuelto *adj* resolute

resulta|do *m* result (**en** in). **~r** *vi* result; (*salir*) turn out; (*dar resul-*

tado) work; (*ser*) be; (*costar*) come to

resum|en *m* summary. en **~en** in short. **~ir** *vt* summarize; (*recapitular*) sum up

resur|gir 14 *vi* reemerge; (*fig*) revive. **~gimiento** *m* resurgence. **~rección** *f* resurrection

retaguardia *f* (*Mil*) rearguard

retahíla *f* string

retar *vt* challenge

retardar *vt* slow down; (*demorar*) delay

retazo *m* remnant; (*fig*) piece, bit

reten|ción *f* retention. **~er** 40 *vt* keep; (*en la memoria*) retain; (*no dar*) withhold

reticencia *f* insinuation; (*reserva*) reluctance

retina *f* retina

retir|ada *f* withdrawal. **~ado** *adj* remote; (vida) secluded; (*jubilado*) retired. **~ar** *vt* move away; (*quitar*) remove; withdraw (dinero); (*jubilar*) pension off. **~arse** *vpr* draw back; (*Mil*) withdraw; (*jubilarse*) retire; (*acostarse*) go to bed. **~o** *m* retirement; (*pensión*) pension; (*lugar apartado*) retreat; (*LAm, de apoyo, fondos*) withdrawal

reto *m* challenge

retocar 7 *vt* retouch

retoño *m* shoot; (*fig*) kid

retoque *m* (*acción*) retouching; (*efecto*) finishing touch

retorc|er 2 & 9 *vt* twist; wring (ropa). **~erse** *vpr* get twisted up; (*de dolor*) writhe. **~ijón** *m* (*LAm*) stomach cramp

retóric|a *f* rhetoric; (*grandilocuencia*) grandiloquence. **~o** *m* rhetorical

retorn|ar *vt/i* return. **~o** *m* return

retortijón *m* twist; (*de tripas*) stomach cramp

retractarse *vpr* retract. **~ de lo dicho** withdraw what one said

retransmitir *vt* repeat; (*radio, TV*) broadcast. **~ en directo** broadcast live

retras|ado *adj* (*con ser*) mentally handicapped; (*con estar*) behind; (reloj) slow; (*poco desarrollado*) backward; (*anticuado*) old-fashioned. **~ar** *vt* delay; put back (reloj); (*retardar*) slow down; (*posponer*) postpone. • *vi* (reloj) be slow. **~arse** *vpr* be late; (reloj) be slow. **~o** *m* delay; (*poco desarrollo*) backwardness; (*de reloj*) slowness. **traer ~o** be late. **~os** *mpl* arrears

retrato *m* portrait; (*fig, descripción*) description. **ser el vivo ~ de** be the living image of

retrete *m* toilet

retribu|ción *f* payment; (*recompensa*) reward. **~ir** 17 *vt* pay; (*recompensar*) reward; (*LAm*) return (favor)

retroce|der *vi* move back; (*fig*) back down. **~so** *m* backward movement; (*de arma de fuego*) recoil; (*Med*) relapse

retrógrado *adj* & *m* (*Pol*) reactionary

retrospectivo *adj* retrospective

retrovisor *m* rear-view mirror

retumbar *vt* echo; (trueno etc) boom

reum|a *m*, **reúma** *m* rheumatism. **~ático** *adj* rheumatic. **~atismo** *m* rheumatism

reuni|ón *f* meeting; (*entre amigos*) reunion. **~r** 23 *vt* join together; (*recoger*) gather (together); raise (fondos). **~rse** *vpr* meet; (amigos etc) get together

revalidar *vt* confirm; (*Mex, estudios*) validate

revalorizar 10 *vt*, (*LAm*) **revaluar** 21 *vt* revalue; increase (pensiones). **~se** *vpr* appreciate

revancha *f* revenge; (*en deportes*) return match. **tomar la ~** get one's own back

revela|ción *f* revelation. **~do** *m* developing. **~dor** *adj* revealing. **~r** *vt* reveal; (*Foto*) develop

revent|ar 1 *vi* burst; (*tener ganas*) be dying to. **~arse** *vpr* burst. **~ón** *m* burst; (*Auto*) blow out; (*Mex, fiesta*) party

reveren|cia *f* reverence; (*de hombre, niño*) bow; (*de mujer*) curtsy. **~ciar** *vt* revere. **~do** *adj* (*Relig*) reverend. **~te** *adj* reverent

revers|ible *adj* reversible. **~o** *m* reverse; (*de papel*) back

revertir 4 *vi* revert (a to)

revés *m* wrong side; (*de prenda*) inside; (*contratiempo*) setback; (*en deportes*) backhand. **al ~** the other way round; (*con lo de arriba abajo*) upside down; (*con lo de dentro fuera*) inside out

revesti|miento *m* coating. **~r** 5 *vt* cover

revis|ar *vt* check; overhaul (mecanismo); service (coche etc); (*LAm, equipaje*) search. **~ión** *f* check(ing)); (*Med*) checkup; (*de coche etc*) service; (*LAm, de equipaje*) inspection. **~or** *m* inspector

revista *f* magazine; (*inspección*) inspection; (*artículo*) review; (*espectáculo*) revue. **pasar ~ a** inspect

revivir *vi* revive

revolcar 2 & 7 *vt* knock over. **~se** *vpr* roll around

revolotear *vi* flutter

revoltijo *m*, **revoltillo** *m* mess

revoltoso *adj* rebellious; (niño) naughty

revoluci|ón *f* revolution. **~onar** *vt* revolutionize. **~onario** *adj & m* revolutionary

revolver 2 (*pp* **revuelto**) *vt* mix; stir (líquido); (*desordenar*) mess up

revólver *m* revolver

revuelo *m* fluttering; (*fig*) stir

revuelt|a *f* revolt; (*conmoción*) disturbance. **~o** *adj* mixed up; (líquido) cloudy; (mar) rough; (tiempo) unsettled; (huevos) scrambled

rey *m* king. **los ~es** the king and queen. **los R~es Magos** the Three Wise Men

reyerta *f* brawl

rezagarse 12 *vpr* fall behind

rez|ar 10 *vt* say. • *vi* pray; (*decir*) say. **~o** *m* praying; (*oración*) prayer

rezongar 12 *vi* grumble

ría *f* estuary

riachuelo *m* stream

riada *f* flood

ribera *f* bank

ribete *m* border; (*fig*) embellishment

rico *adj* rich; (*Culin, fam*) good, nice. • *m* rich person

rid|ículo *adj* ridiculous. **~iculizar** 10 *vt* ridicule

riego *m* watering; (*irrigación*) irrigation

riel *m* rail

rienda *f* rein

riesgo *m* risk. **correr (el) ~ de** run the risk of

rifa *f* raffle. **~r** *vt* raffle

rifle *m* rifle

rigidez *f* rigidity; (*fig*) inflexibility

rígido *adj* rigid; (*fig*) inflexible

r

rig|or *m* strictness; (*exactitud*) exactness; (*de clima*) severity. **de ~or** compulsory. **en ~or** strictly speaking. **~uroso** *adj* rigorous

rima *f* rhyme. **~r** *vt/i* rhyme

rimbombante *adj* resounding; (lenguaje) pompous; (*fig, ostentoso*) showy

rímel *m* mascara

rin *m* (*Mex*) rim

rincón *m* corner

rinoceronte *m* rhinoceros

riña *f* quarrel; (*pelea*) fight

riñón *m* kidney

río *m* river; (*fig*) stream. **~ abajo** downstream. **~ arriba** upstream. • *vb véase* **REÍR**

riqueza *f* wealth; (*fig*) richness. **~s** *fpl* riches

ris|a *f* laugh. **desternillarse de ~a** split one's sides laughing. **la ~a** laughter. **~otada** *f* guffaw. **~ueño** *adj* smiling; (*fig*) cheerful

rítmico *adj* rhythmic(al)

ritmo *m* rhythm; (*fig*) rate

rit|o *m* rite; (*fig*) ritual. **~ual** *adj & m* ritual

rival *adj & m & f* rival. **~idad** *f* rivalry. **~izar** 10 *vi* rival

r

riz|ado *adj* curly. **~ar** 10 *vt* curl; ripple (agua). **~o** *m* curl; (*en agua*) ripple

róbalo *m* bass

robar *vt* steal (cosa); rob (banco); (*raptar*) kidnap

roble *m* oak (tree)

robo *m* theft; (*de banco, museo*) robbery; (*en vivienda*) burglary

robusto *adj* robust

roca *f* rock

roce *m* rubbing; (*señal*) mark; (*fig, entre personas*) regular contact; (*Pol*) friction. **tener un ~ con uno** have a brush with s.o.

rociar 20 *vt* spray

rocín *m* nag

rocío *m* dew

rodaballo *m* turbot

rodaja *f* slice. **en ~s** sliced

roda|je *m* (*de película*) shooting; (*de coche*) running in. **~r** 2 *vt* shoot (película); run in (coche). • *vi* roll; (coche) run; (*hacer una película*) shoot

rode|ar *vt* surround; (*LAm*) round up (ganado). **~arse** *vpr* surround o.s. (**de** with). **~o** *m* detour; (*de ganado*) round-up. **andar con ~os** beat about the bush. **sin ~os** plainly

rodill|a *f* knee. **ponerse de ~as** kneel down. **~era** *f* knee-pad

rodillo *m* roller; (*Culin*) rolling-pin

roe|dor *m* rodent. **~r** 37 *vt* gnaw

rogar 2 & 12 *vt/i* beg; (*Relig*) pray; **se ruega a los Sres. pasajeros...** passengers are requested.... **se ruega no fumar** please do not smoke

roj|izo *adj* reddish. **~o** *adj & m* red. **ponerse ~o** blush

roll|izo *adj* plump; (bebé) chubby. **~o** *m* roll; (*de cuerda*) coil; (*Culin, rodillo*) rolling-pin; (*fig, fam, pesadez*) bore

romance *adj* Romance. • *m* (*idilio*) romance; (*poema*) ballad

roman|o *adj & m* Roman. **a la ~a** (*Culin*) (deep-)fried in batter

rom|anticismo *m* romanticism. **~ántico** *adj* romantic

romería *f* pilgrimage; (*LAm, multitud*) mass

romero *m* rosemary

romo *adj* blunt; (nariz) snub

rompe|cabezas *m invar* puzzle;

(*de piezas*) jigsaw (puzzle). **~olas** *m invar* breakwater

romp|er (*pp* **roto**) *vt* break; tear (hoja, camisa etc); break off (relaciones etc). • *vi* break; (novios) break up. **~er a** burst out. **~erse** *vpr* break

ron *m* rum

ronc|ar 7 *vi* snore. **~o** *adj* hoarse

roncha *f* lump; (*por alergia*) rash

ronda *f* round; (*patrulla*) patrol; (*serenata*) serenade. **~r** *vt* patrol. • *vi* be on patrol; (*merodear*) hang around

ronqu|era *f* hoarseness. **~ido** *m* snore

ronronear *vi* purr

roñ|a *f* (*suciedad*) grime. **~oso** *adj* dirty; (*oxidado*) rusty; (*tacaño*) mean

rop|a *f* clothes, clothing. **~a blanca** linen, underwear. **~a de cama** bedclothes. **~a interior** underwear. **~aje** *m* robes; (*excesivo*) heavy clothing. **~ero** *m* wardrobe

ros|a *adj invar* pink. • *f* rose. • *m* pink. **~áceo** *adj* pinkish. **~ado** *adj* pink; (mejillas) rosy. • *m* (*vino*) rosé. **~al** *m* rose-bush

rosario *m* rosary; (*fig*) series

ros|ca *f* (*de tornillo*) thread; (*de pan*) roll; (*bollo*) type of doughnut. **~co** *m* roll. **~quilla** *f* type of doughnut

rostro *m* face

rota|ción *f* rotation. **~r** *vt/i* rotate. **~rse** *vpr* take turns. **~tivo** *adj* rotary

roto *adj* broken

rótula *f* kneecap

rotulador *m* felt-tip pen

rótulo *m* sign; (*etiqueta*) label; (*logotipo*) logo

rotundo *adj* categorical

rotura *f* tear; (*grieta*) crack

rozadura *f* scratch

rozagante *adj* (*LAm*) healthy

rozar 10 *vt* rub against; (*ligeramente*) brush against; (*raspar*) graze. **~se** *vpr* rub; (*con otras personas*) mix

Rte. *abrev* (**Remite(nte)**) sender

rubéola *f* German measles

rubí *m* ruby

rubicundo *adj* ruddy

rubio *adj* (pelo) fair; (persona) fair-haired; (tabaco) Virginia

rubor *m* blush; (*Mex*, *cosmético*) blusher. **~izarse** 10 *vpr* blush

rúbrica *f* (*de firma*) flourish; (*firma*) signature; (*título*) heading

rudeza *f* roughness

rudiment|ario *adj* rudimentary. **~os** *mpl* rudiments

rueca *f* distaff

rueda *f* wheel; (*de mueble*) castor; (*de personas*) ring; (*Culin*) slice. **~ de prensa** press conference

ruedo *m* edge; (*redondel*) bullring

ruego *m* request; (*súplica*) entreaty. • *vb véase* ROGAR

rufián *m* pimp; (*granuja*) rogue

rugby *m* rugby

rugi|do *m* roar. **~r** 14 *vi* roar

ruibarbo *m* rhubarb

ruido *m* noise. **~so** *adj* noisy; (*fig*) sensational

ruin *adj* despicable; (*tacaño*) mean

ruin|a *f* ruin; (*colapso*) collapse. **~oso** *adj* ruinous

ruiseñor *m* nightingale

ruleta *f* roulette

rulo *m* curler

rumano *adj* & *m* Romanian

rumbo *m* direction; (*fig*) course;

(*fig, esplendidez*) lavishness. **con ~ a** in the direction of. **~so** *adj* lavish

rumia|nte *adj & m* ruminant. **~r** *vt* chew; (*fig*) brood over. • *vi* ruminate

rumor *m* rumour; (*ruido*) murmur. **~earse** *vpr* **se ~ea que** rumour has it that. **~oso** *adj* murmuring

runrún *m* (*de voces*) murmur; (*de motor*) whirr

ruptura *f* breakup; (*de relaciones etc*) breaking off; (*de contrato*) breach

rural *adj* rural

ruso *adj & m* Russian

rústico *adj* rural; (*de carácter*) coarse. **en rústica** paperback

ruta *f* route; (*fig*) course

rutina *f* routine. **~rio** *adj* routine; (trabajo) monotonous

Ss

S.A. *abrev* (**Sociedad Anónima**) Ltd, plc, Inc (*Amer*)

sábado *m* Saturday

sábana *f* sheet

sabañón *m* chilblain

sabático *adj* sabbatical

sab|elotodo *m & f invar* know-all [I]. **~er** [38] *vt* know; (*ser capaz de*) be able to, know how to; (*enterarse de*) find out. • *vi* know. **~er a** taste of. **hacer ~er** let know. **¡qué sé yo!** how should I know? **que yo sepa** as far as I know. **¿~es nadar?** can you swim? **un no sé qué** a certain sth. **¡yo qué sé!** how should I know? **¡vete a ~er!** who knows? **~er** *m* knowledge. **~ido** *adj* well-known. **~iduría** *f* wisdom; (*conocimientos*) knowledge

sabi|endas. a ~ knowingly; (*a propósito*) on purpose. **~hondo** *m* know-all. **~o** *adj* learned; (*prudente*) wise

sabor *m* taste, flavour; (*fig*) flavour. **~ear** *vt* taste; (*fig*) savour

sabot|aje *m* sabotage. **~eador** *m* saboteur. **~ear** *vt* sabotage

sabroso *adj* tasty; (chisme) juicy; (*LAm, agradable*) pleasant

sabueso *m* (*perro*) bloodhound; (*fig, detective*) detective

saca|corchos *m invar* corkscrew. **~puntas** *m invar* pencil-sharpener

sacar [7] *vt* take out; put out (parte del cuerpo); (*quitar*) remove; take (foto); win (premio); get (billete, entrada); withdraw (dinero); reach (solución); draw (conclusión); make (copia). **~ adelante** bring up (niño); carry on (negocio)

sacarina *f* saccharin

sacerdo|cio *m* priesthood. **~te** *m* priest

saciar *vt* satisfy; quench (sed)

saco *m* sack; (*LAm, chaqueta*) jacket. **~ de dormir** sleeping-bag

sacramento *m* sacrament

sacrific|ar [7] *vt* sacrifice; slaughter (res); put to sleep (perro, gato). **~arse** *vpr* sacrifice o.s. **~io** *m* sacrifice; (*de res*) slaughter

sacr|ilegio *m* sacrilege. **~ílego** *adj* sacrilegious

sacudi|da *f* shake; (*movimiento brusco*) jolt, jerk; (*fig*) shock. **~da eléctrica** electric shock. **~r** *vt* shake; (*golpear*) beat. **~rse** *vpr* shake off; (*fig*) get rid of

sádico *adj* sadistic. • *m* sadist

sadismo *m* sadism

safari *m* safari

sagaz *adj* shrewd

Sagitario *m* Sagittarius

sagrado *adj* (lugar) holy, sacred; (altar, escrituras) holy; (*fig*) sacred

sal *f* salt. ● *vb véase* SALIR

sala *f* room; (*en casa*) living room; (*en hospital*) ward; (*para reuniones etc*) hall; (*en teatro*) house; (*Jurid*) courtroom. ~ **de embarque** departure lounge. ~ **de espera** waiting room. ~ **de estar** living room. ~ **de fiestas** nightclub

salado *adj* salty; (agua del mar) salt; (*no dulce*) savoury; (*fig*) witty

salario *m* wage

salchich|a *f* (pork) sausage. **~ón** *m* salami

sald|ar *vt* settle (cuenta); (*vender*) sell off. **~o** *m* balance. **~os** *mpl* sales. **venta de ~os** clearance sale

salero *m* salt-cellar

salgo *vb véase* SALIR

sali|da *f* departure; (*puerta*) exit, way out; (*de gas, de líquido*) leak; (*de astro*) rising; (*Com, venta*) sale; (*chiste*) witty remark; (*fig*) way out; **~da de emergencia** emergency exit. **~ente** *adj* (*Archit*) projecting; (pómulo etc) prominent. **~r** 52 *vi* leave; (*ir afuera*) go out; (*Informática*) exit; (revista etc) be published; (*resultar*) turn out; (astro) rise; (*aparecer*) appear. **~r adelante** get by. **~rse** *vpr* leave; (recipiente, líquido etc) leak. **~rse con la suya** get one's own way

saliva *f* saliva

salmo *m* psalm

salm|ón *m* salmon. **~onete** *m* red mullet

salón *m* living-room, lounge. ~ **de actos** assembly hall. ~ **de clases** classroom. ~ **de fiestas** dancehall

salpica|dera *f* (*Mex*) mudguard. **~dero** *m* (*Auto*) dashboard. **~dura** *f* splash; (*acción*) splashing. **~r** 7 *vt* splash; (*fig*) sprinkle

sals|a *f* sauce; (*para carne asada*) gravy; (*Mus*) salsa. **~a verde** parsley sauce. **~era** *f* sauce-boat

salt|amontes *m invar* grasshopper. **~ar** *vt* jump (over); (*fig*) miss out. ● *vi* jump; (*romperse*) break; (líquido) spurt out; (*desprenderse*) come off; (pelota) bounce; (*estallar*) explode. **~eador** *m* highwayman. **~ear** *vt* (*Culin*) sauté

salt|o *m* jump; (*al agua*) dive. **~o de agua** waterfall. ~ **mortal** somersault. **de un ~o** with one jump. **~ón** *adj* (ojos) bulging

salud *f* health. ● *int* cheers!; (*LAm, al estornudar*) bless you! **~able** *adj* healthy

salud|ar *vt* greet, say hello to; (*Mil*) salute. **lo ~a atentamente** (*en cartas*) yours faithfully. ~ **con la mano** wave. **~o** *m* greeting; (*Mil*) salute. **~os** *mpl* best wishes

salva *f* salvo. **una ~ de aplausos** a burst of applause

salvación *f* salvation

salvado *m* bran

salvaguardia *f* safeguard

salvaje *adj* (*planta, animal*) wild; (*primitivo*) savage. ● *m & f* savage

salva|mento *m* rescue. **~r** *vt* save, rescue; (*atravesar*); cross (*recorrer*); travel (*fig*) overcome. **~rse** *vpr* save o.s. **~vidas** *m & f invar* lifeguard. ● *m* lifebelt. **chaleco** *m* **~vidas** life-jacket

salvo *adj* safe. ● *adv & prep* except (for). **a ~** out of danger. **poner a ~** put in a safe place. ~ **que** unless. **~conducto** *m* safe-conduct.

San *adj* Saint, St. **~ Miguel** St Michael

sana|r *vt* cure. ● *vi* recover; heal (herida). **~torio** *m* sanatorium

sanci|ón *f* sanction. **~onar** *vt* sanction

sandalia *f* sandal

sandía *f* watermelon

sándwich /'saŋgwitʃ/ *m* (*pl* **~s, ~es**) sandwich

sangr|ante *adj* bleeding; (*fig*) flagrant. **~ar** *vt/i* bleed. **~e** *f* blood. **a ~e fría** in cold blood

sangría *f* (*bebida*) sangria

sangriento *adj* bloody

sangu|ijuela *f* leech. **~íneo** *adj* blood

san|idad *f* health. **~itario** *adj* sanitary. ● *m* (*Mex*) toilet. **~o** *adj* healthy; (mente) sound. **~o y salvo** safe and sound. **cortar por lo ~o** settle things once and for all

santiamén *m*. **en un ~** in an instant

sant|idad *f* sanctity. **~ificar** 7 *vt* sanctify. **~iguarse** 15 *vpr* cross o.s. **~o** *adj* holy; (*delante de nombre*) Saint, St. ● *m* saint; (*día*) saint's day, name day. **~uario** *m* sanctuary. **~urrón** *adj* sanctimonious

S

> *i*
>
> **santo** Most first names in Spanish-speaking countries are those of saints. A person's *santo* (also known as *onomástico* in Latin America and *onomástica* in Spain) is the saint's day of the saint they are named after. As well as celebrating their calendar birthday many people also celebrate their *santo*.

saña *f* viciousness. **con ~** viciously

sapo *m* toad

saque *m* (*en tenis*) service; (*inicial en fútbol*) kick-off. **~ de banda** throw-in; (*en rugby*) line-out. **~ de esquina** corner (kick)

saque|ar *vt* loot. **~o** *m* looting

sarampión *m* measles

sarape *m* (*Mex*) colourful blanket

sarc|asmo *m* sarcasm. **~ástico** *adj* sarcastic

sardina *f* sardine

sargento *m* sergeant

sarpullido *m* rash

sartén *f or m* frying-pan (*Brit*), frypan (*Amer*)

sastre *m* tailor. **~ría** *f* tailoring; (*tienda*) tailor's (shop)

Sat|anás *m* Satan. **~ánico** *adj* satanic

satélite *m* satellite

satinado *adj* shiny

sátira *f* satire

satírico *adj* satirical. ● *m* satirist

satisf|acción *f* satisfaction. **~acer** 31 *vt* satisfy; (*pagar*) pay; (*gustar*) please; meet (gastos, requisitos). **~acerse** *vpr* satisfy o.s.; (*vengarse*) take revenge. **~actorio** *adj* satisfactory. **~echo** *adj* satisfied. **~echo de sí mismo** smug

satura|ción *f* saturation. **~r** *vt* saturate

Saturno *m* Saturn

sauce *m* willow. **~ llorón** weeping willow

sauna *f*, (*LAm*) **sauna** *m* sauna

saxofón *m*, **saxófono** *m* saxophone

sazona|do *adj* ripe; (*Culin*) seasoned. **~r** *vt* ripen; (*Culin*) season

se *pronombre*

● (*en lugar de le, les*) **se lo di** (*a él*) I gave it to him; (*a ella*) I gave it to her; (*a usted, ustedes*) I gave it to you; (*a ellos, ellas*) I gave it to them. **se lo compré** I bought it for him (*or* her *etc*). **se lo quité** I took it away from him (*or* her *etc*). **se lo dije** I told him (*or* her *etc*)

····➤ (*reflexivo*) **se secó** (*él*) he dried himself; (*ella*) she dried herself; (*usted*) you dried yourself. (*sujeto no humano*) it dried itself. **se secaron** (*ellos, ellas*) they dried themselves. (*ustedes*) you dried yourselves. (*con partes del cuerpo*) **se lavó la cara** (*él*) he washed his face; (*con efectos personales*) **se limpian los zapatos** they clean their shoes

····➤ (*recíproco*) each other, one another. **se ayudan mucho** they help each other a lot. **no se hablan** they don't speak to each other

····➤ (*cuando otro hace la acción*) **va a operarse** she's going to have an operation. **se cortó el pelo** he had his hair cut

····➤ (*enfático*) **se bebió el café** he drank his coffee. **se subió al tren** he got on the train

➡ **se** also forms part of certain pronominal verbs such as **equivocarse, arrepentirse, caerse** etc., which are treated under the respective entries

····➤ (*voz pasiva*) **se construyeron muchas casas** many houses were built. **se vendió rápidamente** it was sold very quickly

····➤ (*impersonal*) **antes se escuchaba más radio** people used to listen to the radio more in the past. **no se puede entrar** you can't get in. **se está bien aquí** it's very nice here

····➤ (*en instrucciones*) **sírvase frío** serve cold

sé *vb véase* **SABER** *y* **SER**

sea *vb véase* **SER**

seca|dor *m* drier; (*de pelo*) hair-drier. **~nte** *adj* drying. ● *m* blotting-paper. **~r** **7** *vt* dry. **~rse** *vpr* dry; (río etc) dry up; (persona) dry o.s.

sección *f* section

seco *adj* dry; (frutos, flores) dried; (*flaco*) thin; (respuesta) curt. **a secas** just. **en ~** (*bruscamente*) suddenly. **lavar en ~** dry-clean

secretar|ía *f* secretariat; (*Mex, ministerio*) ministry. **~io** *m* secretary; (*Mex, Pol*) minister

secreto *adj & m* secret

secta *f* sect. **~rio** *adj* sectarian

sector *m* sector

secuela *f* consequence

secuencia *f* sequence

secuestr|ar *vt* confiscate; kidnap (persona); hijack (avión). **~o** *m* seizure; (*de persona*) kidnapping; (*de avión*) hijack(ing)

secundar *vt* second, help. **~io** *adj* secondary

sed *f* thirst. ● *vb véase* **SER**. **tener ~** be thirsty. **tener ~ de** (*fig*) be hungry for

seda *f* silk. **~ dental** dental floss

sedante *adj & m* sedative

sede *f* seat; (*Relig*) see; (*de organismo*) headquarters; (*de congreso,*

S

juegos etc) venue
sedentario *adj* sedentary
sedici|ón *f* sedition. **~oso** *adj* seditious
sediento *adj* thirsty
seduc|ción *f* seduction. **~ir** 47 *vt* seduce; (*atraer*) attract. **~tor** *adj* seductive. • *m* seducer
seglar *adj* secular. • *m* layman
segrega|ción *f* segregation. **~r** 12 *vt* segregate
segui|da *f*. en **~da** immediately. **~do** *adj* continuous; (*en plural*) consecutive. **~ de** followed by. • *adv* straight; (*LAm, a menudo*) often. **todo ~do** straight ahead. **~dor** *m* follower; (*en deportes*) supporter. **~r** 5 & 13 *vt* follow. • *vi* (*continuar*) continue; (*por un camino*) go on. **~r adelante** carry on
según *prep* according to. • *adv* it depends; (*a medida que*) as
segund|a *f* (*Auto*) second gear; (*en tren, avión etc*) second class. **~o** *adj & m* second
segur|amente *adv* certainly; (*muy probablemente*) surely. **~idad** *f* security; (*ausencia de peligro*) safety; (*certeza*) certainty; (*aplomo*) confidence. **~idad en sí mismo** self-confidence. **~idad social** social security. **~o** *adj* safe; (*cierto*) certain, sure; (*estable*) secure; (*de fiar*) reliable. • *adv* for certain. • *m* insurance; (*dispositivo de seguridad*) safety device. **~o de sí mismo** self-confident. **~o contra terceros** third-party insurance
seis *adj & m* six. **~cientos** *adj & m* six hundred
seísmo *m* earthquake
selec|ción *f* selection. **~cionar** *vt* select, choose. **~tivo** *adj* selective. **~to** *adj* selected; (*fig*) choice
sell|ar *vt* stamp; (*cerrar*) seal. **~o** *m* stamp; (*precinto*) seal; (*fig, distintivo*) hallmark; (*LAm, en moneda*) reverse
selva *f* forest; (*jungla*) jungle
semáforo *m* (*Auto*) traffic lights; (*Rail*) signal; (*Naut*) semaphore
semana *f* week. **S~ Santa** Holy Week. **~l** *adj* weekly. **~rio** *adj & m* weekly

> **Semana Santa** The most famous Holy Week celebrations in the Spanish-speaking world are held in Sevilla between Palm Sunday and Easter Sunday. Lay brotherhoods, *cofradías*, process through the city in huge parades. During the processions they sing *saetas*, flamenco verses mourning Christ's passion.

semántic|a *f* semantics. **~o** *adj* semantic
semblante *m* face; (*fig*) look
sembrar 1 *vt* sow; (*fig*) scatter
semeja|nte *adj* similar; (*tal*) such. • *m* fellow man. **~nza** *f* similarity. **a ~nza de** like. **~r** *vi*. **~r a** resemble
semen *m* semen. **~tal** *adj* stud. • *m* stud animal
semestr|al *adj* half-yearly. **~e** *m* six months
semi|circular *adj* semicircular. **~círculo** *m* semicircle. **~final** *f* semifinal
semill|a *f* seed. **~ero** *m* seedbed; (*fig*) hotbed
seminario *m* (*Univ*) seminar; (*Relig*) seminary
sémola *f* semolina
senado *m* senate. **~r** *m* senator

sencill|ez *f* simplicity. **~o** *adj* simple; (*para viajar*) single ticket; (*disco*) single; (*LAm, dinero suelto*) change

senda *f,* **sendero** *m* path

sendos *adj pl* each

seno *m* bosom. **~ materno** womb

sensaci|ón *f* sensation; (*percepción, impresión*) feeling. **~onal** *adj* sensational

sensat|ez *f* good sense. **~o** *adj* sensible

sensi|bilidad *f* sensibility. **~ble** *adj* sensitive; (*notable*) notable; (*lamentable*) lamentable. **~tivo** *adj* (órgano) sense

sensual *adj* sensual. **~idad** *f* sensuality

senta|do *adj* sitting (down); **dar algo por ~do** take something for granted. **~dor** *adj* (*LAm*) flattering. **~r** **1** *vt* sit; (*establecer*) establish. • *vi* suit; (*de medidas*) fit; (comida) agree with. **~rse** *vpr* sit (down)

sentencia *f* (*Jurid*) sentence. **~r** *vt* sentence (**a** to)

sentido *adj* heartfelt; (*sensible*) sensitive. • *m* sense; (*dirección*) direction; (*conocimiento*) consciousness. **~ común** common sense. **~ del humor** sense of humour. **~ único** one-way. **doble ~** double meaning. **no tener ~** not make sense. **perder el ~** faint. **sin ~** senseless

sentim|ental *adj* sentimental. **~iento** *m* feeling; (*sentido*) sense; (*pesar*) regret

sentir **4** *vt* feel; (oír) hear; (*lamentar*) be sorry for. **lo siento mucho** I'm really sorry. • *m* (*opinión*) opinion. **~se** *vpr* feel; (*Mex, ofenderse*) be offended

seña *f* sign. **~s** *fpl* (*dirección*) address; (*descripción*) description. **dar ~s de** show signs of

señal *f* signal; (*letrero, aviso*) sign; (*telefónica*) tone; (*Com*) deposit. **dar ~es de** show signs of. **en ~ de** as a token of. **~ado** *adj* (hora, día) appointed. **~ar** *vt* signal; (*poner señales en*) mark; (*apuntar*) point out; (manecilla, aguja) point to; (*determinar*) fix. **~arse** *vpr* stand out

señor *m* man, gentleman; (*delante de nombre propio*) Mr; (*tratamiento directo*) sir. **~a** *f* lady, woman; (*delante de nombre propio*) Mrs; (*esposa*) wife; (*tratamiento directo*) madam. **el ~** Mr. **muy ~ mío** Dear Sir. **¡no ~!** certainly not!. **~ial** *adj* (casa) stately. **~ita** *f* young lady; (*delante de nombre propio*) Miss; (*tratamiento directo*) miss. **~ito** *m* young gentleman

señuelo *m* lure

sepa *vb véase* SABER

separa|ción *f* separation. **~do** *adj* separate. **por ~do** separately. **~r** *vt* separate; (*de empleo*) dismiss. **~rse** *vpr* separate; (amigos) part. **~tista** *adj & m & f* separatist

septentrional *adj* north(ern)

septiembre *m* September

séptimo *adj* seventh

sepulcro *m* sepulchre

sepult|ar *vt* bury. **~ura** *f* burial; (*tumba*) grave. **~urero** *m* gravedigger

sequ|edad *f* dryness. **~ía** *f* drought

séquito *m* entourage; (*fig*) train

ser **39**

• verbo intransitivo

····> to be. **es bajo** he's short. **es abogado** he's a lawyer.

S

ábreme, soy yo open up, it's me. **¿cómo es?** (*como persona*) what's he like?; (*físicamente*) what does he look like? **era invierno** it was winter

····➤ **ser de** (*indicando composición*) to be made of. **es de hierro** it's made of iron. (*provenir de*) to be from. **es de México** he's from Mexico. (*pertenecer a*) to belong to. **el coche es de Juan** the car belongs to Juan, it's Juan's car

····➤ (*sumar*) **¿cuánto es todo?** how much is that altogether? **son 40 dólares** that's 40 dollars. **somos 10** there are 10 of us

····➤ (*con la hora*) **son las 3** it's 3 o'clock. **~ía la una** it must have been one o'clock

····➤ (*tener lugar*) to be held. **~á en la iglesia** it will be held in the church

····➤ (*ocurrir*) to happen **¿dónde fue el accidente?** where did the accident happen? **me contó cómo fue** he told me how it happened

····➤ (*en locuciones*) **a no ~ que** unless. **como sea** no matter what. **cuando sea** whenever. **donde sea** wherever. **¡eso es!** that's it! **es que** the thing is. **lo que sea** anything. **no sea que, no vaya a ~ que** in case. **o sea** in other words. **sea ... sea ...** either ... or ... **sea como sea** at all costs

● *nombre masculino* being; (*persona*) person. **el ~ humano** the human being. **un ~ amargado** a bitter person. **los ~es queridos** the loved ones

S

seren|ar *vt* calm down. **~arse** *vpr* calm down. **~ata** *f* serenade. **~idad** *f* serenity. **~o** *adj* serene; (cielo) clear; (mar) calm

seri|al *m* serial. **~e** *f* series. **fuera de ~e** (*fig*) out of this world. **producción** *f* **en ~e** mass production

seri|edad *f* seriousness. **~o** *adj* serious; (*confiable*) reliable; **en ~o** seriously. **poco ~o** frivolous

sermón *m* sermon; (*fig*) lecture

serp|enteante *adj* winding. **~entear** *vi* wind. **~iente** *f* snake. **~iente de cascabel** rattlesnake

serr|ar **1** *vt* saw. **~ín** *m* sawdust. **~uchar** *vt* (*LAm*) saw. **~ucho** *m* (hand)saw

servi|cial *adj* helpful. **~cio** *m* service; (*conjunto*) set; (*aseo*) toilet; **~cio a domicilio** delivery service. **~dor** *m* servant. **su (seguro) ~dor** (*en cartas*) yours faithfully. **~dumbre** *f* servitude; (*criados*) servants, staff. **~l** *adj* servile

servidor *m* server; (*criado*) servant

servilleta *f* napkin, serviette

servir **5** *vt* serve; (*en restaurante*) wait on. ● *vi* serve; (*ser útil*) be of use. **~se** *vpr* help o.s.. **~se de** use. **no ~ de nada** be useless. **para ~le** at your service. **sírvase sentarse** please sit down

sesent|a *adj & m* sixty. **~ón** *adj & m* sixty-year-old

seseo *m* pronunciation of the Spanish *c* as an *s*

sesión *f* session; (*en el cine, teatro*) performance

seso *m* brain

seta *f* mushroom

sete|cientos *adj & m* seven hundred. **~nta** *adj & m* seventy. **~ntón** *adj & m* seventy-year-old

setiembre *m* September

seto *m* fence; (*de plantas*) hedge. **~ vivo** hedge

seudónimo *m* pseudonym

sever|idad *f* severity; (*de profesor etc*) strictness. **~o** *adj* severe; (profesor etc) strict

sevillan|as *fpl* popular dance from Seville. **~o** *m* person from Seville

sexo *m* sex

sext|eto *m* sextet. **~o** *adj* sixth

sexual *adj* sexual. **~idad** *f* sexuality

si *m* (*Mus*) B; (*solfa*) te. ● *conj* if; (*dubitativo*) whether; **~ no** otherwise. **por ~ (acaso)** in case

sí[1] *pron reflexivo* (*él*) himself; (*ella*) herself; (*de cosa*) itself; (*uno*) oneself; (*Vd*) yourself; (*ellos, ellas*) themselves; (*Vds*) yourselves; (*recíproco*) each other

sí[2] *adv* yes. ● *m* consent

sida *m* Aids

sidra *f* cider

siembra *f* sowing; (*época*) sowing time

siempre *adv* always; (*LAm, todavía*) still; (*Mex, por fin*) after all. **~ que** if; (*cada vez*) whenever. **como ~** as usual. **de ~** (*acostumbrado*) usual. **lo de ~** the usual thing. **para ~** for ever

sien *f* temple

siento *vb véase* SENTAR *y* SENTIR

sierra *f* saw; (*cordillera*) mountain range

siesta *f* nap, siesta

siete *adj & m* seven

sífilis *f* syphilis

sifón *m* U-bend; (*de soda*) syphon

sigilo *m* stealth; (*fig*) secrecy

sigla *f* abbreviation

siglo *m* century; (*época*) age. **hace ~s que no escribe** he hasn't written for ages

significa|ción *f* significance. **~do** *adj* (*conocido*) well-known. ● *m* meaning; (*importancia*) significance. **~r** [7] *vt* mean; (*expresar*) express. **~tivo** *adj* meaningful; (*importante*) significant

signo *m* sign. **~ de admiración** exclamation mark. **~ de interrogación** question mark

sigo *vb véase* SEGUIR

siguiente *adj* following, next. **lo ~** the following

sílaba *f* syllable

silb|ar *vt/i* whistle. **~ato** *m*, **~ido** *m* whistle

silenci|ador *m* silencer. **~ar** *vt* hush up. **~o** *m* silence. **~oso** *adj* silent

sill|a *f* chair; (*de montar*) saddle (*Relig*) see **~a de ruedas** wheelchair. **~ín** *m* saddle. **~ón** *m* armchair

silueta *f* silhouette; (*dibujo*) outline

silvestre *adj* wild

simb|ólico *adj* symbolic(al). **~olismo** *m* symbolism. **~olizar** [10] *vt* symbolize

símbolo *m* symbol

sim|etría *f* symmetry. **~étrico** *adj* symmetric(al)

similar *adj* similar (**a** to)

simp|atía *f* friendliness; (*cariño*) affection. **~ático** *adj* nice, likeable; (ambiente) pleasant. **~atizante** *m & f* sympathizer. **~atizar** [10] *vi* get on (well together)

S

simpl|e *adj* simple; (*mero*) mere. **~eza** *f* simplicity; (*tontería*) stupid thing; (*insignificancia*) trifle. **~icidad** *f* simplicity. **~ificar** 7 *vt* simplify. **~ista** *adj* simplistic. **~ón** *m* simpleton

simula|ción *f* simulation. **~r** *vt* simulate; (*fingir*) feign

simultáneo *adj* simultaneous

sin *prep* without. **~ saber** without knowing. **~ querer** accidentally

sinagoga *f* synagogue

sincer|idad *f* sincerity. **~o** *adj* sincere

sincronizar 10 *vt* synchronize

sindica|l *adj* (trade-)union. **~lista** *m & f* trade-unionist. **~to** *m* trade union

síndrome *m* syndrome

sinfín *m* endless number (**de** of)

sinfonía *f* symphony

singular *adj* singular; (*excepcional*) exceptional. **~izarse** *vpr* stand out

siniestro *adj* sinister. • *m* disaster; (*accidente*) accident

sinnúmero *m* endless number (**de** of)

sino *m* fate. • *conj* but

sinónimo *adj* synonymous. • *m* synonym (**de** for)

sintaxis *f* syntax

síntesis *f invar* synthesis; (*resumen*) summary

sint|ético *adj* synthetic. **~etizar** 10 *vt* synthesize; (*resumir*) summarize

síntoma *f* symptom

sintomático *adj* symptomatic

sinton|ía *f* tuning; (*Mus*) signature tune. **~izar** 10 *vt* (*con la radio*) tune (in) to

sinvergüenza *m & f* crook

siquiera *conj* even if. • *adv* at least. **ni ~** not even

sirena *f* siren; (*en cuentos*) mermaid

sirio *adj & m* Syrian

sirvient|a *f* maid. **~e** *m* servant

sirvo *vb véase* SERVIR

sísmico *adj* seismic

sismo *m* earthquake

sistem|a *m* system. **por ~a** as a rule. **~ático** *adj* systematic

sitiar *vt* besiege; (*fig*) surround

sitio *m* place; (*espacio*) space; (*Mil*) siege; (*Mex, parada de taxi*) taxi rank. **en cualquier ~** anywhere. **~ web** website

situa|ción *f* situation; (*estado, condición*) position. **~r** 21 *vt* place, put; locate (edificio). **~rse** *vpr* be successful, establish o.s.

slip /es'lip/ *m* (*pl* **~s**) underpants, briefs

smoking /es'mokin/ *m* (*pl* **~s**) dinner jacket (*Brit*), tuxedo (*Amer*)

sobaco *m* armpit

sobar *vt* handle; knead (masa)

soberan|ía *f* sovereignty. **~o** *adj* sovereign; (*fig*) supreme. • *m* sovereign

soberbi|a *f* pride; (*altanería*) arrogance. **~o** *adj* proud; (*altivo*) arrogant

soborn|ar *vt* bribe. **~o** *m* bribe

sobra *f* surplus. **de ~** more than enough. **~s** *fpl* leftovers. **~do** *adj* more than enough. **~nte** *adj* surplus. **~r** *vi* be left over; (*estorbar*) be in the way

sobre *prep* on; (*encima de*) on top of; (*más o menos*) about; (*por encima de*) above; (*sin tocar*) over. **~ todo** above all, especially. • *m* envelope. **~cargar** 12 *vt* overload. **~coger** 14 *vt* startle; (*conmover*) move. **~cubierta** *f* dustcover. **~dosis** *f invar* overdose. **~entender** **1** *vt* understand, infer. **~girar** *vt* (*LAm*) overdraw. **~giro** *m* (*LAm*) overdraft. **~humano** *adj* superhuman. **~llevar** *vt* bear. **~mesa** *f.* **de ~mesa** after-dinner. **~natural** *adj* supernatural. **~nombre** *m* nickname. **~pasar** *vt* exceed. **~peso** *m* (*LAm*) excess baggage. **~poner** **34** *vt* superimpose. **~ponerse** *vpr* overcome. **~saliente** *adj* (*fig*) outstanding. • *m* excellent mark. **~salir** **52** *vi* stick out; (*fig*) stand out. **~saltar** *vt* startle. **~salto** *m* fright. **~sueldo** *m* bonus. **~todo** *m* overcoat. **~venir** **53** *vi* happen. **~viviente** *adj* surviving. • *m & f* survivor. **~vivir** *vi* survive. **~volar** *vt* fly over

sobriedad *f* moderation; (*de estilo*) simplicity

sobrin|a *f* niece. **~o** *m* nephew. **~os** (*varones*) nephews; (*varones y mujeres*) nieces and nephews

sobrio *adj* moderate, sober

socavar *vt* undermine

soci|able *adj* sociable. **~al** *adj* social. **~aldemócrata** *m & f* social democrat. **~alismo** *m* socialism. **~alista** *adj & m & f* socialist. **~edad** *f* society; (*Com*) company. **~edad anónima** limited company. **~o** *m* member; (*Com*) partner. **~ología** *f* sociology. **~ólogo** *m* sociologist

socorr|er *vt* help. **~o** *m* help

soda *f* (*bebida*) soda (water)

sodio *m* sodium

sofá *m* sofa, settee

sofistica|ción *f* sophistication. **~do** *adj* sophisticated

sofo|cante *adj* suffocating; (*fig*) stifling. **~car** **7** *vt* smother (fuego); (*fig*) stifle. **~carse** *vpr* get upset

soga *f* rope

soja *f* soya (bean)

sojuzgar **12** *vt* subdue

sol *m* sun; (*luz*) sunlight; (*Mus*) G; (*solfa*) soh. **al ~** in the sun. **día** *m* **de ~** sunny day. **hace ~, hay ~** it is sunny. **tomar el ~** sunbathe

solamente *adv* only

solapa *f* lapel; (*de bolsillo etc*) flap. **~do** *adj* sly

solar *adj* solar. • *m* plot

solariego *adj* (casa) ancestral

soldado *m* soldier. **~ raso** private

solda|dor *m* welder; (*utensilio*) soldering iron. **~r** **2** *vt* weld, solder

soleado *adj* sunny

soledad *f* solitude; (*aislamiento*) loneliness

solemn|e *adj* solemn. **~idad** *f* solemnity

soler **2** *vi* be in the habit of. **suele despertarse a las 6** he usually wakes up at 6 o'clock

sol|icitante *m* applicant. **~ de asilo** asylum seeker. **~icitar** *vt* request, ask for; apply for (empleo). **~ícito** *adj* solicitous. **~icitud** *f* request; (*para un puesto*) application; (*formulario*) application form; (*preocupación*) concern

solidaridad *f* solidarity

solid|ez *f* solidity; (*de argumento etc*) soundness. **~ificarse** **7** *vpr* solidify

sólido *adj* solid; (argumento etc) sound. • *m* solid

soliloquio *m* soliloquy

solista *m & f* soloist

solitario *adj* solitary; (*aislado*) lonely. • *m* loner; (*juego, diamante*) solitaire

solloz|ar 10 *vi* sob. **~o** *m* sob

solo *adj* (*sin compañía*) alone; (*aislado*) lonely; (*sin ayuda*) by oneself; (*único*) only; (*Mus*) solo; (café) black. • *m* solo; (*juego*) solitaire. **a solas** alone

sólo *adv* only. **~ que** except that. **no ~... sino también** not only... but also.... **tan ~** only

solomillo *m* sirloin

soltar 2 *vt* let go of; (*dejar ir*) release; (*dejar caer*) drop; (*dejar salir, decir*) let out; give (golpe etc). **~se** *vpr* come undone; (*librarse*) break loose

solter|a *f* single woman. **~o** *adj* single. • *m* bachelor

soltura *f* looseness; (*fig*) ease, fluency

solu|ble *adj* soluble. **~ción** *f* solution. **~cionar** *vt* solve; settle (huelga, asunto)

solvente *adj & m* solvent

sombr|a *f* shadow; (*lugar sin sol*) shade. **a la ~a** in the shade. **~eado** *adj* shady

sombrero *m* hat. **~ hongo** bowler hat

sombrío *adj* sombre

somero *adj* superficial

someter *vt* subdue; subject (persona); (*presentar*) submit. **~se** *vpr* give in

somn|oliento *adj* sleepy. **~ífero** *m* sleeping-pill

somos *vb véase* **SER**

son *m* sound. • *vb véase* **SER**

sonámbulo *m* sleepwalker. **ser ~** walk in one's sleep

sonar 2 *vt* blow; ring (timbre). • *vi* sound; (timbre, teléfono etc) ring; (despertador) go off; (*Mus*) play; (*fig, ser conocido*) be familiar. **~ a** sound like. **~se** *vpr* blow one's nose

sonde|ar *vt* sound out; explore (espacio); (*Naut*) sound. **~o** *m* poll; (*Naut*) sounding

soneto *m* sonnet

sonido *m* sound

sonoro *adj* sonorous; (*ruidoso*) loud

sonr|eír 51 *vi* smile. **~eírse** *vpr* smile. **~isa** *f* smile

sonroj|arse *vpr* blush. **~o** *m* blush

sonrosado *adj* rosy, pink

sonsacar 7 *vt* wheedle out

soñ|ado *adj* dream. **~ador** *m* dreamer. **~ar** 2 *vi* dream (**con** of). **¡ni ~arlo!** not likely!

sopa *f* soup

sopesar *vt* (*fig*) weigh up

sopl|ar *vt* blow; blow out (vela); blow off (polvo); (*inflar*) blow up. • *vi* blow. **~ete** *m* blowlamp. **~o** *m* puff

soport|al *m* porch. **~ales** *mpl* arcade. **~ar** *vt* support; (*fig*) bear, put up with. **~e** *m* support

soprano *f* soprano

sor *f* sister

sorb|er *vt* sip; (*con ruido*) slurp; (*absorber*) absorb. **~ por la nariz** sniff. **~ete** *m* sorbet, water-ice. **~o** *m* (*pequeña cantidad*) sip; (*trago grande*) gulp

sordera *f* deafness

sórdido *adj* squalid; (asunto) sordid

sordo *adj* deaf; (ruido etc) dull. • *m* deaf person. **hacerse el ~** turn a deaf ear. **~mudo** *adj* deaf and dumb

soroche *m* (*LAm*) mountain sickness

sorpre|ndente *adj* surprising.

~nder *vt* surprise. **~nderse** *vpr* be surprised. **~sa** *f* surprise

sorte|ar *vt* draw lots for; (*fig*) avoid. **~o** *m* draw. **por ~o** by drawing lots

sortija *f* ring; (*de pelo*) ringlet

sortilegio *m* sorcery; (*embrujo*) spell

sos|egar 1 & 12 *vt* calm. **~iego** *m* calmness

soslayo. **de ~** sideways

soso *adj* tasteless; (*fig*) dull

sospech|a *f* suspicion. **~ar** *vt* suspect. • *vi*. **~ de** suspect. **~oso** *adj* suspicious. • *m* suspect

sost|én *m* support; (*prenda femenina*) bra [I], brassière. **~ener** 40 *vt* support; bear (peso); (*sujetar*) hold; (*sustentar*) maintain; (*alimentar*) sustain. **~enerse** *vpr* support o.s.; (*continuar*) remain. **~enido** *adj* sustained; (*Mus*) sharp. • *m* (*Mus*) sharp

sota *f* (*de naipes*) jack

sótano *m* basement

soviético *adj* (*Historia*) Soviet

soy *vb véase* **SER**

Sr. *abrev* (**Señor**) Mr. **~a.** *abrev* (**Señora**) Mrs. **~ta.** *abrev* (**Señorita**) Miss

su *adj* (*de él*) his; (*de ella*) her; (*de animal, objeto*) its; (*de uno*) one's; (*de Vd*) your; (*de ellos, de ellas*) their; (*de Vds*) your

suav|e *adj* smooth; (*fig*) gentle; (color, sonido) soft; (tabaco, sedante) mild. **~idad** *f* smoothness, softness. **~izante** *m* conditioner; (*para ropa*) softener. **~izar** 10 *vt* smooth, soften

subalimentado *adj* underfed

subarrendar 1 *vt* sublet

subasta *f* auction. **~r** *vt* auction

sub|campeón *m* runner-up. **~consciencia** *f* subconscious. **~consciente** *adj* & *m* subconscious. **~continente** *m* subcontinent. **~desarrollado** *adj* underdeveloped. **~director** *m* assistant manager

súbdito *m* subject

sub|dividir *vt* subdivide. **~estimar** *vt* underestimate

subi|da *f* rise; (*a montaña*) ascent; (*pendiente*) slope. **~do** *adj* (color) intense. **~r** *vt* go up; climb (mountain); (*llevar*) take up; (*aumentar*) raise; turn up (radio, calefacción). • *vi* go up. **~r a** get into (coche); get on (autobús, avión, barco, tren); (*aumentar*) rise. **~ a pie** walk up. **~rse** *vpr* climb up. **~rse a** get on (tren etc)

súbito *adj* sudden. **de ~** suddenly

subjetivo *adj* subjective

subjuntivo *adj* & *m* subjunctive

subleva|ción *f* uprising. **~rse** *vpr* rebel

sublim|ar *vt* sublimate. **~e** *adj* sublime

submarino *adj* underwater. • *m* submarine

subordinado *adj* & *m* subordinate

subrayar *vt* underline

subsanar *vt* rectify; overcome (dificultad); make up for (carencia)

subscri|bir *vt* (*pp* **subscrito**) sign. **~birse** *vpr* subscribe (**a** to). **~pción** *f* subscription

subsidi|ario *adj* subsidiary. **~o** *m* subsidy. **~o de desempleo, ~ de paro** unemployment benefit

subsiguiente *adj* subsequent

subsist|encia *f* subsistence. **~ir** *vi* subsist; (*perdurar*) survive

substraer 41 *vt* take away

S

subterráneo *adj* underground
subtítulo *m* subtitle
suburb|ano *adj* suburban. **~io** *m* suburb; (*barrio pobre*) depressed area
subvenci|ón *f* subsidy. **~onar** *vt* subsidize
subver|sión *f* subversion. **~sivo** *adj* subversive. **~tir** 4 *vt* subvert
succi|ón *f* suction. **~onar** *vt* suck
suce|der *vi* happen; (*seguir*) **~ a** follow. ● *vt* (*substituir*) succeed. **lo que ~de es que** the trouble is that. **¿qué ~de?** what's the matter? **~sión** *f* succession. **~sivo** *adj* successive; (*consecutivo*) consecutive. **en lo ~sivo** in future. **~so** *m* event; (*incidente*) incident. **~sor** *m* successor
suciedad *f* dirt; (*estado*) dirtiness
sucinto *adj* concise; (prenda) scanty
sucio *adj* dirty; (conciencia) guilty. **en ~** in rough
sucre *m* (*unidad monetaria del Ecuador*) sucre
suculento *adj* succulent
sucumbir *vi* succumb (a to)
sucursal *f* branch (office)
Sudáfrica *f* South Africa
sudafricano *adj & m* South African
Sudamérica *f* South America
sudamericano *adj & m* South American
sudar *vi* sweat
sud|este *m* south-east. **~oeste** *m* south-west
sudor *m* sweat
Suecia *f* Sweden
sueco *adj* Swedish. ● *m* (*persona*) Swede; (*lengua*) Swedish. **hacerse el ~** pretend not to hear
suegr|a *f* mother-in-law. **~o** *m* father-in-law. **mis ~os** my in-laws
suela *f* sole
sueldo *m* salary
suelo *m* ground; (*dentro de edificio*) floor; (*territorio*) soil; (*en la calle etc*) road surface. ● *vb véase* SOLER
suelto *adj* loose; (cordones) undone; (*sin pareja*) odd; (lenguaje) fluent. **con el pelo ~** with one's hair down. ● *m* change
sueño *m* sleep; (*lo soñado, ilusión*) dream. **tener ~** be sleepy
suerte *f* luck; (*destino*) fate; (*azar*) chance. **de otra ~** otherwise. **de ~ que** so. **echar ~s** draw lots. **por ~** fortunately. **tener ~** be lucky
suéter *m* sweater, jersey
suficien|cia *f* (*aptitud*) aptitude; (*presunción*) smugness. **~te** *adj* enough, sufficient; (*presumido*) smug. **~temente** *adv* sufficiently
sufijo *m* suffix
sufragio *m* (*voto*) vote
sufri|miento *m* suffering. **~r** *vt* suffer; undergo (cambio); have (accident). ● *vi* suffer
suge|rencia *f* suggestion. **~rir** 4 *vt* suggest. **~stión** *f* (*en psicología*) suggestion. **es pura ~stión** it's all in one's mind. **~stionable** *adj* impressionable. **~stionar** *vt* influence. **~stivo** *adj* (*estimulante*) stimulating; (*atractivo*) sexy
suicid|a *adj* suicidal. ● *m & f* suicide victim; (*fig*) maniac. **~arse** *vpr* commit suicide. **~io** *m* suicide
Suiza *f* Switzerland
suizo *adj & m* Swiss
suje|ción *f* subjection. **con ~ a** in accordance with. **~tador** *m* bra I, brassière. **~tapapeles** *m invar* paper-clip. **~tar** *vt* fasten; (*agarrar*)

hold. **~tarse** *vpr.* **~se a** hold on to; (*someterse*) abide by. **~to** *adj* fastened; (*susceptible*) subject (a to). • *m* individual; (*Gram*) subject.

suma *f* sum; (*Math*) addition; (*combinación*) combination. **en ~** in short. **~mente** *adv* extremely. **~r** *vt* add (up); (*totalizar*) add up to. • *vi* add up. **~rse** *vpr.* **~rse a** join in

sumario *adj* brief; (*Jurid*) summary. • *m* table of contents; (*Jurid*) pre-trial proceedings

sumergi|ble *adj* submersible. **~r** **14** *vt* submerge

suministr|ar *vt* supply. **~o** *m* supply; (*acción*) supplying

sumir *vt* sink; (*fig*) plunge

sumis|ión *f* submission. **~o** *adj* submissive

sumo *adj* great; (*supremo*) supreme. **a lo ~** at the most

suntuoso *adj* sumptuous

supe *vb véase* **SABER**

superar *vt* surpass; (*vencer*) overcome; beat (marca); (*dejar atrás*) get over. **~se** *vpr* better o.s.

supercheria *f* swindle

superfici|al *adj* superficial. **~e** *f* surface; (*extensión*) area. **de ~e** surface

superfluo *adj* superfluous

superior *adj* superior; (*más alto*) higher; (*mejor*) better; (piso) upper. • *m* superior. **~idad** *f* superiority

superlativo *adj & m* superlative

supermercado *m* supermarket

supersticí|ón *f* superstition. **~oso** *adj* superstitious

supervis|ar *vt* supervise. **~ión** *f* supervision. **~or** *m* supervisor

superviv|encia *f* survival. **~iente** *adj* surviving. • *m & f* survivor

suplantar *vt* supplant

suplement|ario *adj* supplementary. **~o** *m* supplement

suplente *adj & m & f* substitute

súplica *f* entreaty; (*Jurid*) request

suplicar **7** *vt* beg

suplicio *m* torture

suplir *vt* make up for; (*reemplazar*) replace

supo|ner **34** *vt* suppose; (*significar*) mean; involve (gasto, trabajo). **~sición** *f* supposition

suprem|acía *f* supremacy. **~o** *adj* supreme

supr|esión *f* suppression; (*de impuesto*) abolition; (*de restricción*) lifting. **~imir** *vt* suppress; abolish (impuesto); lift (restricción); delete (párrafo)

supuesto *adj* supposed; (falso) false; (*denominado*) so-called. • *m* assumption. **¡por ~!** of course!

sur *m* south; (*viento*) south wind

surc|ar **7** *vt* plough; cut through (agua). **~o** *m* furrow; (*de rueda*) rut

surfear *vi* (*Informática*) surf

surgir **14** *vi* spring up; (*elevarse*) loom up; (*aparecer*) appear; (dificultad, oportunidad) arise

surrealis|mo *m* surrealism. **~ta** *adj & m & f* surrealist

surti|do *adj* well-stocked; (*variado*) assorted. • *m* assortment, selection. **~dor** *m* (*de gasolina*) petrol pump (*Brit*), gas pump (*Amer*). **~r** *vt* supply; have (efecto). **~rse** *vpr* provide o.s. (**de** with)

susceptib|ilidad *f* sensitivity. **~le** *adj* susceptible; (*sensible*) sensitive

suscitar *vt* provoke; arouse

(curiosidad, interés)

suscr... *véase* **SUBSCR...**

susodicho *adj* aforementioned

suspen|der *vt* suspend; stop (tratamiento); call off (viaje); (*en examen*) fail; (*colgar*) hang (**de** from). **~se** *m* suspense. **novela de ~se** thriller. **~sión** *f* suspension. **~so** *m* fail; (*LAm, en libro, película*) suspense. **en ~so** suspended

suspir|ar *vi* sigh. **~o** *m* sigh

sust... *véase* **SUBST...**

sustanci|a *f* substance. **~al** *adj* substantial. **~oso** *adj* substantial

sustantivo *m* noun

sustent|ación *f* support. **~ar** *vt* support; (*alimentar*) sustain; (*mantener*) maintain. **~o** *m* support; (*alimento*) sustenance

sustitu|ción *f* substitution; (*permanente*) replacement. **~ir** 17 *vt* substitute, replace. **~to** *m* substitute; (*permanente*) replacement

susto *m* fright

susurr|ar *vi* (persona) whisper; (agua) murmur; (hojas) rustle

sutil *adj* fine; (*fig*) subtle. **~eza** *f* subtlety

suyo *adj & pron* (*de él*) his; (*de ella*) hers; (*de animal*) its; (*de Vd*) yours; (*de ellos, de ellas*) theirs; (*de Vds*) yours. **un amigo ~** a friend of his, a friend of theirs, etc

s

t

Tt

tabac|alera *f* (state) tobacco monopoly. **~o** *m* tobacco; (*cigarrillos*) cigarettes

tabern|a *f* bar. **~ero** *m* barman; (*dueño*) landlord

tabique *m* partition wall; (*Mex, ladrillo*) brick

tabl|a *f* plank; (*del suelo*) floorboard; (*de vestido*) pleat; (*índice*) index; (*gráfico, en matemática etc*) table. **hacer ~as** (*en ajedrez*) draw. **~a de surf** surfboard. **~ado** *m* platform; (*en el teatro*) stage. **~ao** *m* place where flamenco shows are held. **~ero** *m* board. **~ero de mandos** dashboard

tableta *f* tablet; (*de chocolate*) bar

tabl|illa *f* splint; (*Mex, de chocolate*) bar. **~ón** *m* plank. **~ón de anuncios** notice board (*esp Brit*), bulletin board (*Amer*)

tabú *m* (*pl* **~es**, **~s**) taboo

tabular *vt* tabulate

taburete *m* stool

tacaño *adj* mean

tacha *f* stain, blemish. **sin ~** unblemished; (conducta) irreproachable. **~r** *vt* (*con raya*) cross out; (*Jurid*) impeach. **~ de** accuse of

tácito *adj* tacit

taciturno *adj* taciturn; (*triste*) glum

taco *m* plug; (*LAm, tacón*) heel; (*de billar*) cue; (*de billetes*) book; (*fig, fam, lío*) mess; (*palabrota*) swearword; (*Mex, Culin*) taco, filled tortilla

tacón *m* heel

táctic|a *f* tactics. **~o** *adj* tactical

táctil *adj* tactile
tacto *m* touch; (*fig*) tact
tahúr *m* card-sharp
tailandés *adj & m* Thai
Tailandia *f* Thailand
taimado *adj* sly
taj|ada *f* slice. **sacar ~ada** profit. **~ante** *adj* categorical; (tono) sharp. **~ear** *vt* (*LAm*) slash. **~o** *m* cut; (*en mina*) face
tal *adj* such. **de ~ manera** in such a way. **un ~** someone called. ● *pron.* **como ~** as such. **y ~** and things like that. ● *adv.* **con ~ de que** as long as. **~ como** the way. **~ para cual** 🅸 two of a kind. **~ vez** maybe. **¿qué ~?** how are you? **¿qué ~ es ella?** what's she like?
taladr|ar *vt* drill. **~o** *m* drill
talante *m* mood. **de buen ~** (estar) in a good mood; (ayudar) willingly
talar *vt* fell
talco *m* talcum powder
talega *f*, **talego** *m* sack
talento *m* talent; (*fig*) talented person
talismán *m* talisman
talla *f* carving; (*de diamante etc*) cutting; (*estatura*) height; (*tamaño*) size. **~do** *m* carving; (*de diamante etc*) cutting. **~dor** *m* carver; (*cortador*) cutter; (*LAm*, *de naipes*) dealer. **~r** *vt* carve; sculpt (escultura); cut (diamante); (*Mex*, *restregar*) scrub. **~rse** *vpr* (*Mex*) rub o.s.
tallarín *m* noodle
talle *m* waist; (*figura*) figure
taller *m* workshop; (*de pintor etc*) studio; (*Auto*) garage
tallo *m* stem, stalk
tal|ón *m* heel; (*recibo*) counterfoil; (*cheque*) cheque. **~onario** *m* receipt book; (*de cheques*) cheque book
tamal *m* (*LAm*) tamale
tamaño *adj* such a. ● *m* size. **de ~ natural** life-size
tambalearse *vpr* (*persona*) stagger; (cosa) wobble
también *adv* also, too
tambor *m* drum. **~ del freno** brake drum. **~ilear** *vi* drum
tamiz *m* sieve. **~ar** 10 *vt* sieve
tampoco *adv* neither, nor, not either. **yo ~ fui** I didn't go either
tampón *m* tampon; (*para entintar*) ink-pad
tan *adv* so. **~... como** as... as. **¿qué ~...?** (*LAm*) how...?
tanda *f* group; (*de obreros*) shift
tang|ente *adj & f* tangent. **~ible** *adj* tangible
tango *m* tango
tanque *m* tank
tante|ar *vt* estimate; sound up (persona); (*ensayar*) test; (*fig*) weigh up; (*LAm*, *palpar*) feel. ● *vi* (*LAm*) feel one's way. **~o** *m* estimate; (*prueba*) test; (*en deportes*) score
tanto *adj* (*en singular*) so much; (*en plural*) so many; (*comparación en singular*) as much; (*comparación en plural*) as many. ● *pron* so much; (*en plural*) so many. ● *adv* so; (*con verbo*) so much. **hace ~ tiempo** it's been so long. **~... como** both ...and. **¿qué ~...?** (*LAm*) how much...? **~ como** as well as; (*cantidad*) as much as. **~ más... cuanto que** all the more ... because. **~ si... como si** whether ... or. **a ~s de** sometime in. **en ~, entre ~** meanwhile. **en ~ que** while. **entre ~** meanwhile. **hasta**

~ **que** until. **no es para** ~ it's not as bad as all that. **otro** ~ the same; (*el doble*) as much again. **por (lo)** ~ therefore. ● *m* certain amount; (*punto*) point; (*gol*) goal. **estar al** ~ **de** be up to date with

tañer 22 *vi* peal

tapa *f* lid; (*de botella*) top; (*de libro*) cover. ~**s** *fpl* savoury snacks. ~**dera** *f* cover, lid; (*fig*) cover. ~**r** *vt* cover; (*abrigar*) wrap up; (*obturar*) plug. ~**rrabo(s)** *m invar* loincloth

> **tapas** In Spain these are small portions of food served in bars and cafés with a drink. There is a wide variety, including Spanish omelette, seafood, different kinds of cooked potatoes, cheese, ham, chorizo etc. The practice of going out for a drink and *tapas* is known as *tapeo*.

tapete *m* (*de mesa*) table cover; (*Mex, alfombra*) rug

tapia *f* wall. ~**r** *vt* enclose

tapi|cería *f* tapestry; (*de muebles*) upholstery. ~**z** *m* tapestry. ~**zar** 10 *vt* upholster (muebles)

tapón *m* stopper; (*Tec*) plug

taqu|igrafía *f* shorthand

taquill|a *f* ticket office; (*fig, dinero*) takings. ~**ero** *adj* box-office

tara *f* (*peso*) tare; (*defecto*) defect

tarántula *f* tarantula

tararear *vt/i* hum

tarda|nza *f* delay. ~**r** *vt* take. ● *vi* (*retrasarse*) be late; (*emplear mucho tiempo*) take a long time. **a más** ~**r** at the latest. **sin** ~**r** without delay

tard|e *adv* late. ● *f* (*antes del atardecer*) afternoon; (*después del atardecer*) evening. **en la** ~**e** (*LAm*), **por la** ~**e** in the afternoon. ~**ío** *adj* late

tarea *f* task, job

tarifa *f* rate; (*en transporte*) fare; (*lista de precios*) tariff

tarima *f* dais

tarjeta *f* card. ~ **de crédito** credit card. ~ **de fidelidad** loyalty card. ~ **postal** postcard. **T**~ **Sanitaria Europea** European Health Insurance Card. **t**~ **SIM** SIM card. ~ **telefónica** telephone card

tarro *m* jar; (*Mex, taza*) mug

tarta *f* cake; (*con base de masa*) tart. ~ **helada** ice-cream gateau

tartamud|ear *vi* stammer. ~**o** *adj*. **es** ~**o** he stammers

tasa *f* valuation; (*impuesto*) tax; (*índice*) rate. ~**r** *vt* value; (*limitar*) ration

tasca *f* bar

tatarabuel|a *f* great-great-grandmother. ~**o** *m* great-great-grandfather. ~**os** *mpl* great-great-grandparents

tatua|je *m* (*acción*) tattooing; (*dibujo*) tattoo. ~**r** 21 *vt* tattoo

taurino *adj* bullfighting

Tauro *m* Taurus

tauromaquia *f* bullfighting

taxi *m* taxi. ~**ista** *m & f* taxi-driver

taz|a *f* cup. ~**ón** *m* bowl

te *pron* (*acusativo*) you; (*dativo*) (to) you; (*reflexivo*) (to) yourself

té *m* tea; (*LAm, reunión*) tea party

teatr|al *adj* theatre; (*exagerado*) theatrical. ~**o** *m* theatre; (*literatura*) drama

tebeo *m* comic

tech|ado *m* roof. ~**ar** *vt* roof. ~**o** *m* (*interior*) ceiling; (*LAm, tejado*) roof. ~**umbre** *f* roof

tecl|a *f* key. **~ado** *m* keyboard. **~ear** *vt* key in

técnica *f* technique

tecnicismo *m* technical nature; (*palabra*) technical term

técnico *adj* technical. • *m* technician; (*en deportes*) trainer

tecnol|ogía *f* technology. **~ógico** *adj* technological

tecolote *m* (*Mex*) owl

teja *f* tile. **~s de pizarra** slates. **~do** *m* roof. **a toca ~** cash

teje|dor *m* weaver. **~r** *vt* weave; (*hacer punto*) knit

tejemaneje *m* [I] intrigue. **~s** *mpl* scheming

tejido *m* material; (*Anat, fig*) tissue. **~s** *mpl* textiles

tejón *m* badger

tela *f* material, fabric; (*de araña*) web; (*en líquido*) skin

telar *m* loom. **~es** *mpl* textile mill

telaraña *f* spider's web, cobweb

tele *f* [I] TV, telly

tele|banca *f* telephone banking. **~comunicación** *f* telecommunication. **~diario** *m* television news. **~dirigido** *adj* remote-controlled; (misil) guided. **~férico** *m* cable-car

tel|efonear *vt/i* telephone. **~efónico** *adj* telephone. **~efonista** *m & f* telephonist.

teléfono *m* telephone. **~ celular** (*LAm*) mobile phone, cellular phone. **~ móvil** (*Esp*) mobile phone, cellular phone. **~ satélite** satphone

tel|egrafía *f* telegraphy. **~égrafo** *m* telegraph. **~egrama** *m* telegram

telenovela *f* television soap opera

teleobjetivo *m* telephoto lens

telep|atía *f* telepathy. **~ático** *adj* telepathic

telesc|ópico *adj* telescopic. **~opio** *m* telescope

telesilla *m & f* chair-lift

telespectador *m* viewer

telesquí *m* ski-lift

televi|dente *m & f* viewer. **~sar** *vt* televise. **~sión** *f* television. **~sor** *m* television (set)

télex *m invar* telex

telón *m* curtain

tema *m* subject; (*Mus*) theme

tembl|ar [1] *vi* shake; (*de miedo*) tremble; (*de frío*) shiver. **~or** *m* shaking; (*de miedo*) trembling; (*de frío*) shivering; **~or de tierra** earth tremor. **~oroso** *adj* trembling

tem|er *vt* be afraid (of). • *vi* be afraid. **~erse** *vpr* be afraid. **~erario** *adj* reckless. **~eroso** *adj* frightened. **~ible** *adj* fearsome. **~or** *m* fear

témpano *m* floe

temperamento *m* temperament

temperatura *f* temperature

tempest|ad *f* storm. **~uoso** *adj* stormy

templ|ado *adj* (*tibio*) warm; (clima, tiempo) mild; (*valiente*) courageous. **~anza** *f* mildness. **~ar** *vt* temper; (*calentar*) warm up. **~e** *m* tempering; (coraje) courage; (*humor*) mood

templo *m* temple

tempora|da *f* season. **~l** *adj* temporary. • *m* storm

tempran|ero *adj* (frutos) early. **ser ~ero** be an early riser. **~o** *adj & adv* early

tenacidad *f* tenacity

tenacillas *fpl* tongs

tenaz *adj* tenacious

tenaza *f*, **tenazas** *fpl* pliers; (*de chimenea, Culin*) tongs; (*de cangrejo*) pincer

tende|ncia *f* tendency. **~nte** *adj*. **~nte a** aimed at. **~r** 1 *vt* spread (out); hang out (ropa a secar); (*colocar*) lay. ● *vi* tend (**a** to). **~rse** *vpr* lie down

tender|ete *m* stall. **~o** *m* shopkeeper

tendido *adj* spread out; (ropa) hung out; (persona) lying down. ● *m* (*en plaza de toros*) front rows

tendón *m* tendon

tenebroso *adj* gloomy; (asunto) sinister

tenedor *m* fork; (*poseedor*) holder

tener 40

● *verbo transitivo*

! El presente del verbo **tener** admite dos traducciones: *to have* y *to have got*, este último de uso más extendido en el inglés británico

····➤to have. **¿tienen hijos?** do you have any children?, have you got any children? **no tenemos coche** we don't have a car, we haven't got a car. **tiene gripe** he has (the) flu, he's got (the) flu

····➤to be. (dimensiones, edad) **tiene 1 metro de largo** it's 1 meter long. **tengo 20 años** I'm 20 (years old)

····➤(*sentir*) **tener** + *nombre* to be + *adjective*. **~ celos** to be jealous. **~ frío** to be cold

····➤(*sujetar, sostener*) to hold. **tenme la escalera** hold the ladder for me

····➤(*indicando estado*) **tiene las manos sucias** his hands are dirty. **me tiene preocupada** I'm worried about him. **me tuvo esperando** he kept me waiting

····➤(*llevar puesto*) to be wearing, to have on. **¡qué zapatos más elegantes tienes!** those are very smart shoes you're wearing! **tienes el suéter al revés** you have your sweater on inside out

····➤(*considerar*) **~ a uno por algo** to think s.o. is sth. **lo tenía por tímido** I thought he was shy

● *verbo auxiliar*

····➤**~ que hacer algo** to have to do sth. **tengo que irme** I have to go

····➤**tener** + *participio pasado*. **tengo pensado comprarlo** I'm thinking of buying it. **tenía entendido otra cosa** I understood something else

····➤(*LAm, con expresiones temporales*) **tienen 2 años de estar aquí** they've been here for 2 months. **tiene mucho tiempo sin verlo** she hasn't seen him for a long time

····➤(*en locuciones*) **aquí tiene** here you are. **¿qué tienes?** what's the matter with you? **¿y eso qué tiene?** (*LAm*) and what's wrong with that?

● **tenerse** *verbo pronominal*

····➤(*sostenerse*) **no podía ~se en pie** (*de cansancio*) he was dead on his feet; (*de borracho*) he could hardly stand

t

····➤ (*considerarse*) to consider o.s. **se tiene por afortunado** he considers himself lucky

tengo *vb véase* **TENER**
teniente *m* lieutenant
tenis *m* tennis. **~ de mesa** table tennis. **~ta** *m & f* tennis player
tenor *m* sense; (*Mus*) tenor. **a ~ de** according to
tens|ión *f* tension; (*arterial*) blood pressure; (*Elec*) voltage; (*estrés*) strain. **~o** *adj* tense
tentación *f* temptation
tentáculo *m* tentacle
tenta|dor *adj* tempting. **~r** **1** *vt* tempt; (*palpar*) feel
tentativa *f* attempt
tenue *adj* thin; (luz, voz) faint; (color) subdued
teñi|r **5** & **22** *vt* dye; (*fig*) tinge (**de** with). **~rse** *vpr* dye one's hair
teología *f* theology
te|oría *f* theory. **~órico** *adj* theoretical
tequila *f* tequila
terap|euta *m & f* therapist. **~éutico** *adj* therapeutic. **~ia** *f* therapy
terc|er *adj véase* **TERCERO**. **~era** *f* (*Auto*) third (gear). **~ero** *adj* (*delante de nombre masculino en singular* **tercer**) third. ● *m* third party. **~io** *m* third
terciopelo *m* velvet
terco *adj* obstinate
tergiversar *vt* distort
termal *adj* thermal
térmico *adj* thermal
termina|ción *f* ending; (*conclusión*) conclusion. **~l** *adj & m* terminal. **~nte** *adj* categorical. **~r** *vt* finish, end. **~r por** end up. **~rse** *vpr* come to an end
término *m* end; (*palabra*) term; (*plazo*) period. **~ medio** average. **dar ~ a** finish off. **en primer ~** first of all. **en último ~** as a last resort. **estar en buenos ~s con** be on good terms with. **llevar a ~** carry out
terminología *f* terminology
termita *f* termite
termo *m* Thermos (P) flask, flask
termómetro *m* thermometer
termo|nuclear *adj* thermonuclear. **~stato** *m* thermostat
terner|a *f* (*carne*) veal. **~o** *m* calf
ternura *f* tenderness
terquedad *f* stubbornness
terrado *m* flat roof
terraplén *m* embankment
terrateniente *m & f* landowner
terraza *f* terrace; (*balcón*) balcony; (*terrado*) flat roof
terremoto *m* earthquake
terre|no *adj* earthly. ● *m* land; (*solar*) plot (*fig*) field. **~stre** *adj* land; (*Mil*) ground
terrible *adj* terrible. **~mente** *adv* awfully
territori|al *adj* territorial. **~o** *m* territory
terrón *m* (*de tierra*) clod; (*Culin*) lump
terror *m* terror. **~ífico** *adj* terrifying. **~ismo** *m* terrorism. **~ista** *m & f* terrorist
terso *adj* smooth
tertulia *f* gathering
tesina *f* dissertation
tesón *m* tenacity
tesor|ería *f* treasury. **~ero** *m* treasurer. **~o** *m* treasure; (*tesorería*) treasury; (*libro*) thesaurus
testaferro *m* figurehead
testa|mento *m* will. **T~mento** (*Relig*) Testament. **~r** *vi* make a will

testarudo *adj* stubborn
testículo *m* testicle
testi|ficar [7] *vt/i* testify. **~go** *m* witness. **~go ocular, ~go presencial** eyewitness. **ser ~go de** witness. **~monio** *m* testimony
teta *f* tit (*fam o vulg*); (*de biberón*) teat
tétanos *m* tetanus
tetera *f* (*para el té*) teapot
tetilla *f* nipple; (*de biberón*) teat
tétrico *adj* gloomy
textil *adj & m* textile
text|o *m* text. **~ual** *adj* textual; (traducción) literal; (palabras) exact
textura *f* texture
tez *f* complexion
ti *pron* you
tía *f* aunt; [!] woman
tiara *f* tiara
tibio *adj* lukewarm
tiburón *m* shark
tiempo *m* time; (*atmosférico*) weather; (*Mus*) tempo; (*Gram*) tense; (*en partido*) half. **a su ~** in due course. **a ~** in time. **¿cuánto ~?** how long? **hace buen ~** the weather is fine. **hace ~** some time ago. **mucho ~** a long time. **perder el ~** waste time
tienda *f* shop (*esp Brit*), store (*esp Amer*); (*de campaña*) tent. **~ de comestibles, ~ de ultramarinos** grocer's (shop) (*Brit*), grocery store (*Amer*)
tiene *vb véase* **TENER**
tienta. **andar a ~s** feel one's way
tierno *adj* tender; (*joven*) young
tierra *f* land; (*planeta, Elec*) earth; (*suelo*) ground; (*en geología*) soil, earth; (*LAm, polvo*) dust. **por ~** overland, by land
tieso *adj* stiff; (*engreído*) conceited
tiesto *m* flowerpot
tifón *m* typhoon
tifus *m* typhus; (*fiebre tifoidea*) typhoid (fever)
tigre *m* tiger. **~sa** *f* tigress
tijera *f*, **tijeras** *fpl* scissors; (*de jardín*) shears
tijeretear *vt* snip
tila *f* (*infusión*) lime tea
tild|ar *vt*. **~ar de** (*fig*) brand as. **~e** *f* tilde
tilo *m* lime(-tree)
timar *vt* swindle
timbal *m* kettledrum; (*Culin*) timbale, meat pie. **~es** *mpl* (*Mus*) timpani
timbr|ar *vt* stamp. **~e** *m* (*sello*) fiscal stamp; (*Mex*) postage stamp; (*Elec*) bell; (*sonido*) timbre
timidez *f* shyness
tímido *adj* shy
timo *m* swindle
timón *m* rudder; (*rueda*) wheel; (*fig*) helm
tímpano *m* eardrum
tina *f* tub. **~co** *m* (*Mex*) water tank. **~ja** *f* large earthenware jar
tinglado *m* mess; (*asunto*) racket
tinieblas *fpl* darkness; (*fig*) confusion
tino *f* good sense; (*tacto*) tact
tint|a *f* ink. **de buena ~a** on good authority. **~e** *m* dyeing; (*color*) dye; (*fig*) tinge. **~ero** *m* ink-well
tintinear *vi* tinkle; (vasos) chink, clink
tinto *adj* (vino) red
tintorería *f* dry cleaner's
tintura *f* dyeing; (*color*) dye
tío *m* uncle; [!] man. **~s** *mpl* uncle and aunt
tiovivo *m* merry-go-round

típico *adj* typical

tipo *m* type; (*fam, persona*) person; (*figura de mujer*) figure; (*figura de hombre*) build; (*Com*) rate

tip|ografía *f* typography. **~ográfico** *adj* typographic(al)

tira *f* strip. **la ~ de** lots of

tirabuzón *m* corkscrew; (*de pelo*) ringlet

tirad|a *f* distance; (*serie*) series; (*de periódico etc*) print-run. **de una ~a** in one go. **~o** *adj* (*barato*) very cheap; (*fam, fácil*) very easy. **~or** *m* (*asa*) handle

tiran|ía *f* tyranny. **~izar** 10 *vt* tyrannize. **~o** *adj* tyrannical. ● *m* tyrant

tirante *adj* tight; (*fig*) tense; (relaciones) strained. ● *m* strap. **~s** *mpl* braces (*esp Brit*), suspenders (*Amer*)

tirar *vt* throw; (*desechar*) throw away; (*derribar*) knock over; drop (bomba); fire (cohete); (*imprimir*) print. ● *vi* (*disparar*) shoot. **~ a** tend to (be); (*parecerse a*) resemble. **~ abajo** knock down. **~ de** pull. **a todo ~** at the most. **ir tirando** get by. **~se** *vpr* throw o.s.; (*tumbarse*) lie down

tirita *f* (sticking) plaster

tiritar *vi* shiver (**de** with)

tiro *m* throw; (*disparo*) shot. **~ libre** free kick. **a ~** within range. **errar el ~** miss. **pegarse un ~** shoot o.s.

tiroides *m* thyroid (gland)

tirón *m* tug. **de un ~** in one go

tirote|ar *vt* shoot at. **~o** *m* shooting

tisana *f* herb tea

tisú *m* (*pl* **~s**, **~es**) tissue

títere *m* puppet. **~s** *mpl* puppet show

titilar *vi* (estrella) twinkle

titiritero *m* puppeteer; (*acróbata*) acrobat

titube|ante *adj* faltering; (*fig*) hesitant. **~ar** *vi* falter. **~o** *m* hesitation

titula|do *adj* (libro) entitled; (persona) qualified. **~r** *m* headline; (*persona*) holder. ● *vt* call. **~rse** *vpr* be called; (persona) graduate

título *m* title; (*académico*) qualification; (*Univ*) degree. **a ~ de** as, by way of

tiza *f* chalk

tiz|nar *vt* dirty. **~ne** *m* soot

toall|a *f* towel. **~ero** *m* towel-rail

tobillo *m* ankle

tobogán *m* slide; (*para la nieve*) toboggan

tocadiscos *m invar* record-player

toca|do *adj* touched !. ● *m* headdress. **~dor** *m* dressing-table. **~nte** *adj*. **en lo ~nte a** with regard to. **~r** 7 *vt* touch; (*palpar*) feel; (*Mus*) play; ring (timbre); (*mencionar*) touch on; (barco) stop at. ● *vi* ring; (*corresponder a uno*). **te ~ a ti** it's your turn. **en lo que ~ a** as for. **~rse** *vpr* touch; (personas); touch each other

tocayo *m* namesake

tocino *m* bacon

tocólogo *m* obstetrician

todavía *adv* still; (*con negativos*) yet. **~ no** not yet

todo, **toda**

● *adjetivo*

····➤ (*la totalidad*) all. **~ el vino** all the wine. **~s los edificios** all the buildings. **~ ese dinero** all that money. **~ el mundo** everyone. (*como adv*) **está toda sucia** it's all dirty

....➤ (*entero*) whole. **~ el día** the whole day, all day. **toda su familia** his whole family. **~ el tiempo** the whole time, all the time

....➤ (*cada, cualquiera*) every. **~ tipo de coche** every type of car. **~s los días** every day

....➤ (*enfático*) **a toda velocidad** at top speed. **es ~ un caballero** he's a real gentleman

....➤ (*en locuciones*) **ante ~** above all. **a ~ esto** meanwhile. **con ~** even so. **del ~** totally. **~ lo contrario** quite the opposite

➡ Para expresiones como **todo recto, todo seguido** etc., ver bajo el respectivo adjetivo

● *pronombre*

....➤ all; (*todas las cosas*) everything. **eso es ~** that's all. **lo perdieron ~** they lost everything. **quiere comprar ~** he wants to buy everything

....➤ **todos, todas** all; (*todo el mundo*) everyone. **los compró ~s** he bought them all, he bought all of them. **~s queríamos ir** we all wanted to go. **vinieron ~s** everyone came

● *nombre masculino* **el/un ~** the/a whole

toldo *m* awning

tolera|ncia *f* tolerance. **~nte** *adj* tolerant. **~r** *vt* tolerate

toma *f* taking; (*de universidad etc*) occupation; (*Med*) dose; (*de agua*) intake; (*Elec*) socket; (*LAm, acequia*) irrigation channel. ● *int* well!, fancy that! **~ de corriente** power point. **~dura** *f*. **~dura de pelo** hoax. **~r** *vt* take; catch (autobús, tren); occupy (universidad etc); (*beber*) drink, have; (*comer*) eat, have. ● *vi* take; (*esp LAm, beber*) drink; (*LAm, dirigirse*) go. **~r a bien** take well. **~r a mal** take badly. **~r en serio** take seriously. **~rla con uno** pick on s.o. **~r por** take for. **~ y daca** give and take. **¿qué va a ~r?** what would you like? **~rse** *vpr* take; (*beber*) drink, have; (*comer*) eat, have

tomate *m* tomato

tomillo *m* thyme

tomo *m* volume

ton: **sin ~ ni son** without rhyme or reason

tonad|a *f* tune; (*canción*) popular song; (*LAm, acento*) accent. **~illa** *f* tune

tonel *m* barrel. **~ada** *f* ton. **~aje** *m* tonnage

tónic|a *f* trend; (*bebida*) tonic water. **~o** *adj* tonic; (sílaba) stressed. ● *m* tonic

tonificar 7 *vt* invigorate

tono *m* tone; (*Mus, modo*) key; (*color*) shade

tont|ería *f* silliness; (*cosa*) silly thing; (*dicho*) silly remark. **dejarse de ~erías** stop fooling around. **~o** *adj* silly. ● *m* fool, idiot; (*payaso*) clown. **hacer el ~o** act the fool. **hacerse el ~o** act dumb

topacio *m* topaz

topar *vi*. **~ con** run into

tope *adj* maximum. ● *m* end; (*de tren*) buffer; (*Mex, Auto*) speed bump. **hasta los ~s** crammed full. **ir a ~** go flat out

tópico *adj* trite. **de uso ~** (*Med*) for external use only. ● *m* cliché

t

topo *m* mole

topogr|afía *f* topography. **~áfico** *adj* topographical

toque *m* touch; (*sonido*) sound; (*de campana*) peal; (*de reloj*) stroke. **~ de queda** curfew. **dar los últimos ~s** put the finishing touches. **~tear** *vt* fiddle with

toquilla *f* shawl

tórax *m invar* thorax

torcer 2 & 9 *vt* twist; (*doblar*) bend; wring out (ropa). ● *vi* turn. **~se** *vpr* twist

tordo *adj* dapple grey. ● *m* thrush

tore|ar *vt* fight; (*evitar*) dodge. ● *vi* fight (bulls). **~o** *m* bullfighting. **~ro** *m* bullfighter

torment|a *f* storm. **~o** *m* torture. **~oso** *adj* stormy

tornado *m* tornado

tornasolado *adj* irridescent

torneo *m* tournament

tornillo *m* screw

torniquete *m* (*Med*) tourniquet; (*entrada*) turnstile

torno *m* lathe; (*de alfarero*) wheel. **en ~ a** around

toro *m* bull. **~s** *mpl* bullfighting. **ir a los ~s** go to a bullfight

(la fiesta de) los toros
Bullfighting is popular in Spain and some Latin American countries. The season runs from March to October in Spain, from November to March in Latin America. The bullfighters who take part in a corrida gather in *cuadrillas*. The principal bullfighter or *matador* is assisted by *peones*.

toronja *f* (*LAm*) grapefruit

torpe *adj* clumsy; (*estúpido*) stupid

torpedo *m* torpedo

torpeza *f* clumsiness; (*de inteligencia*) slowness. **una ~** a blunder

torre *f* tower; (*en ajedrez*) castle, rook; (*Elec*) pylon; (*edificio*) tower block (*Brit*), apartment block (*Amer*)

torren|cial *adj* torrential. **~te** *m* torrent; (*circulatorio*) bloodstream; (*fig*) flood

tórrido *adj* torrid

torsión *f* twisting

torso *m* torso

torta *f* tart; (*LAm, de verduras*) pie; (*golpe*) slap, punch; (*Mex, bocadillo*) filled roll. **no entender ni ~** not understand a thing. **~zo** *m* slap, punch. **pegarse un ~zo** have a bad accident

tortícolis *f* stiff neck

tortilla *f* omelette; (*Mex, de maíz*) tortilla. **~ española** potato omelette. **~ francesa** plain omelette

tórtola *f* turtle-dove

tortuoso *adj* winding; (*fig*) devious

tortura *f* torture. **~r** *vt* torture

tos *f* cough. **~ ferina** whooping cough

tosco *adj* crude; (persona) coarse

toser *vi* cough

tost|ada *f* piece of toast. **~adas** *fpl* toast; (*Mex, de tortilla*) fried tortillas. **~ado** *adj* (pan) toasted; (café) roasted; (persona, color) tanned. **~ar** *vt* toast (pan); roast (café); tan (piel)

total *adj* total. ● *adv* after all. **~ que** so, to cut a long story short. ● *m* total; (*totalidad*) whole. **~idad** *f* whole. **~itario** *adj* totalitarian. **~izar** 10 *vt* total

tóxico *adj* toxic

toxi|cómano *m* drug addict. **~na** *f* toxin

t

tozudo *adj* stubborn

traba *f* catch; (*fig, obstáculo*) obstacle. **poner ~s a** hinder

trabaj|ador *adj* hard-working. ● *m* worker. **~ar** *vt* work; knead (masa). ● *vi* work (**de** as); (actor) act. **¿en qué ~as?** what do you do? **~o** *m* work. **costar ~o** be difficult. **~oso** *adj* hard

trabalenguas *m invar* tongue-twister

traba|r *vt* (*sujetar*) fasten; (*unir*) join; (*entablar*) strike up. **~rse** *vpr* get stuck. **trabársele la lengua** get tongue-tied

trácala *m* (*Mex*) cheat. ● *f* (*Mex*) trick

tracción *f* traction

tractor *m* tractor

tradici|ón *f* tradition. **~onal** *adj* traditional

traduc|ción *f* translation. **~ir** 47 *vt* translate (**a** into). **~tor** *m* translator

traer 41 *vt* bring; (*llevar*) carry; (*causar*) cause. **traérselas** be difficult

trafica|nte *m & f* dealer. **~r** 7 *vi* deal

tráfico *m* traffic; (*Com*) trade

traga|luz *m* skylight. **~perras** *f invar* slot-machine. **~r** 12 *vt* swallow; (*comer mucho*) devour; (*soportar*) put up with. **no lo trago** I can't stand him. **~rse** *vpr* swallow; (*fig*) swallow up

t

tragedia *f* tragedy

trágico *adj* tragic. ● *m* tragedian

trag|o *m* swallow, gulp; (*pequeña porción*) sip; (*fig, disgusto*) blow; (*LAm, bebida alcohólica*) drink. **echar(se) un ~o** have a drink. **~ón** *adj* greedy. ● *m* glutton.

trai|ción *f* treachery; (*Pol*) treason. **~cionar** *vt* betray. **~cionero** *adj* treacherous. **~dor** *adj* treacherous. ● *m* traitor

traigo *vb véase* TRAER

traje *m* dress; (*de hombre*) suit. **~ de baño** swimming-costume. **~ de etiqueta**, **~ de noche** evening dress. ● *vb véase* TRAER

traj|ín *m* coming and going; (*ajetreo*) hustle and bustle. **~inar** *vi* bustle about

trama *f* weft; (*fig, argumento*) plot. **~r** *vt* weave; (*fig*) plot

tramitar *vt* negotiate

trámite *m* step. **~s** *mpl* procedure

tramo *m* (*parte*) section; (*de escalera*) flight

tramp|a *f* trap; (*fig*) trick. **hacer ~a** cheat. **~illa** *f* trapdoor

trampolín *m* trampoline; (*de piscina*) springboard; (*rígido*) diving board

tramposo *adj* cheating. ● *m* cheat

tranca *f* bar. **~r** *vt* bar

trance *m* moment; (*hipnótico etc*) trance

tranco *m* stride

tranquil|idad *f* peace; (*de espíritu*) peace of mind. **con ~** calmly. **~izar** 10 *vt* calm down; (*reconfortar*) reassure. **~o** *adj* calm; (lugar) quiet; (conciencia) clear. **estáte ~o** don't worry

transa|cción *f* transaction; (*acuerdo*) settlement. **~r** *vi* (*LAm*) compromise

transatlántico *adj* transatlantic. ● *m* (ocean) liner

transbord|ador *m* ferry. **~ar** *vt* transfer. **~o** *m* transfer. **hacer ~o** change (**en** at)

transcri|bir (*pp* **transcrito**) *vt* transcribe. **~pción** *f* transcription

transcur|rir *vi* pass. **~so** *m* course
transeúnte *m & f* passer-by
transfer|encia *f* transfer. **~ir** [4] *vt* transfer
transforma|ción *f* transformation. **~dor** *m* transformer. **~r** *vt* transform
transfusión *f* transfusion
transgre|dir *vt* transgress. **~sión** *f* transgression
transición *f* transition
transigir [14] *vi* give in, compromise
transistor *m* transistor
transita|ble *adj* passable. **~r** *vi* go
transitivo *adj* transitive
tránsito *m* transit; (*tráfico*) traffic
transitorio *adj* transitory
transmi|sión *f* transmission; (*radio, TV*) broadcast **~sor** *m* transmitter. **~sora** *f* broadcasting station. **~tir** *vt* transmit; (*radio, TV*) broadcast; (*fig*) pass on
transparen|cia *f* transparency. **~tar** *vt* show. **~te** *adj* transparent
transpira|ción *f* perspiration. **~r** *vi* transpire; (*sudar*) sweat
transport|ar *vt* transport. **~e** *m* transport. **empresa** *f* **de ~es** removals company
transversal *adj* transverse. **una calle ~ a la Gran Vía** a street which crosses the Gran Vía
tranvía *m* tram
trapear *vt* (*LAm*) mop
trapecio *m* trapeze; (*Math*) trapezium
trapo *m* cloth. **~s** *mpl* rags; ([!], *ropa*) clothes **a todo ~** out of control
tráquea *f* windpipe, trachea
traquete|ar *vt* bang, rattle; (*persona*) rush around. **~o** *m* banging, rattle
tras *prep* after; (*detrás*) behind
trascende|ncia *f* significance; (*alcance*) implication. **~ntal** *adj* transcendental; (*importante*) important. **~r** [1] *vi* (*saberse*) become known; (*extenderse*) spread
trasero *adj* back, rear. • *m* (*de persona*) bottom
trasfondo *m* background
traslad|ar *vt* move; transfer (empleado etc); (*aplazar*) postpone. **~o** *m* transfer; (*copia*) copy. (*mudanza*) removal. **dar ~o** notify
trasl|úcido *adj* translucent. **~ucirse** [11] *vpr* be translucent; (*dejarse ver*) show through; (*fig, revelarse*) be revealed. **~uz** *m*. **al ~uz** against the light
trasmano. **a ~** out of the way
trasnochar *vt* (*acostarse tarde*) go to bed late; (*no acostarse*) stay up all night; (*no dormir*) be unable to sleep
traspas|ar *vt* go through; (*transferir*) transfer; go beyond (límite). **se ~a** for sale. **~o** *m* transfer
traspié *m* trip; (*fig*) slip. **dar un ~** stumble; (*fig*) slip up
trasplant|ar *vt* transplant. **~e** *m* transplant
trastada *f* prank; (*jugada*) dirty trick
traste *m* fret. **dar al ~ con** ruin. **ir al ~** fall through. **~s** *mpl* (*Mex*) junk
trastero *m* storeroom
trasto *m* piece of junk. • **~s** *mpl* junk
trastorn|ado *adj* mad. **~ar** *vt* upset; (*volver loco*) drive mad; (*fig, fam, gustar mucho*) delight. **~arse**

vpr get upset; (*volverse loco*) go mad. **~o** *m* (*incl Med*) upset; (*Pol*) disturbance; (*fig*) confusion

trat|able *adj* friendly; (*Med*) treatable. **~ado** *m* treatise; (*acuerdo*) treaty. **~amiento** *m* treatment; (*título*) title. **~ante** *m & f* dealer. **~ar** *vt* (*incl Med*) treat; deal with (asunto etc); (*manejar*) handle; (*de tú, de Vd*) address (**de** as). ● *vi* deal (with). **~ar con** have to do with; (*Com*) deal in. **~ar de** be about; (*intentar*) try. **¿de qué se ~a?** what's it about? **~o** *m* treatment; (*acuerdo*) agreement; (*título*) title; (*relación*) relationship. **¡~o hecho!** agreed! **~os** *mpl* dealings

traum|a *m* trauma. **~ático** *adj* traumatic

través: **a ~ de** through; (*de lado a lado*) crossways

travesaño *m* crossbeam; (*de portería*) crossbar

travesía *f* crossing; (*calle*) side-street

trav|esura *f* prank. **~ieso** *adj* (niño) mischievous, naughty

trayecto *m* (*tramo*) stretch; (*ruta*) route; (*viaje*) journey. **~ria** *f* trajectory; (*fig*) course

traz|a *f* (*aspecto*) appearance. **~as** *fpl* signs. **~ado** *m* plan. **~ar** [10] *vt* draw; (*bosquejar*) sketch. **~o** *m* stroke; (*línea*) line

trébol *m* clover. **~es** *mpl* (*en naipes*) clubs

trece *adj & m* thirteen

trecho *m* stretch; (*distancia*) distance; (*tiempo*) while. **a ~s** here and there. **de ~ en ~** at intervals

tregua *f* truce; (*fig*) respite

treinta *adj & m* thirty

tremendo *adj* terrible; (*extraordinario*) terrific

tren *m* train. **~ de aterrizaje** landing gear. **~ de vida** lifestyle

tren|cilla *f* braid. **~za** *f* braid; (*de pelo*) plait. **~zar** [10] *vt* plait

trepa|dor *adj* climbing. **~dora** *f* climber. **~r** *vt/i* climb. **~rse** *vpr*. **~rse a** climb (árbol); climb onto (silla etc)

tres *adj & m* three. **~cientos** *adj & m* three hundred. **~illo** *m* three-piece suite; (*Mus*) triplet

treta *f* trick

tri|angular *adj.* triangular. **~ángulo** *m* triangle

trib|al *adj* tribal. **~u** *f* tribe

tribuna *f* platform; (*de espectadores*) stand. **~l** *m* court; (*de examen etc*) board; (*fig*) tribunal

tribut|ar *vt* pay. **~o** *m* tribute; (*impuesto*) tax

triciclo *m* tricycle

tricolor *adj* three-coloured

tricotar *vt/i* knit

tridimensional *adj* three-dimensional

trig|al *m* wheat field. **~o** *m* wheat

trigésimo *adj* thirtieth

trigueño *adj* olive-skinned; (pelo) dark blonde

trilla|do *adj* (*fig, manoseado*) trite; (*fig, conocido*) well-known. **~r** *vt* thresh

trilogía *f* trilogy

trimestr|al *adj* quarterly. **~e** *m* quarter; (*en enseñanza*) term

trin|ar *vi* warble. **estar que trina** be furious

trinchar *vt* carve

trinchera *f* ditch; (*Mil*) trench; (*abrigo*) trench coat

trineo *m* sledge

trinidad *f* trinity

trino *m* warble

trío *m* trio

tripa *f* intestine; (*fig, vientre*) tummy, belly. **~s** *fpl* (*de máquina etc*) parts, workings. **revolver las ~s** turn one's stomach

tripl|e *adj* triple. • *m*. **el ~e (de)** three times as much (as). **~icado** *adj*. **por ~icado** in triplicate. **~icar** 7 *vt* treble

tripula|ción *f* crew. **~nte** *m & f* member of the crew. **~r** *vt* man

tris *m*. **estar en un ~** be on the point of

triste *adj* sad; (paisaje, tiempo etc) gloomy; (*fig, insignificante*) miserable. **~za** *f* sadness

triturar *vt* crush

triunf|al *adj* triumphal. **~ante** *adj* triumphant. **~ar** *vi* triumph (**de, sobre** over). **~o** *m* triumph

trivial *adj* trivial. **~idad** *f* triviality

trizas. **hacer algo ~** smash sth to pieces. **hacerse ~** smash

trocear *vt* cut up, chop

trocha *f* narrow path; (*LAm, rail*) gauge

trofeo *m* trophy

tromba *f* whirlwind; (*marina*) waterspout. **~ de agua** heavy downpour

trombón *m* trombone

trombosis *f invar* thrombosis

trompa *f* horn; (*de orquesta*) French horn; (*de elefante*) trunk; (*hocico*) snout; (*en anatomía*) tube. **coger una ~** I get drunk. **~zo** *m* bump

trompet|a *f* trumpet; (*músico*) trumpet player; (*Mil*) trumpeter. **~illa** *f* ear-trumpet

trompo *m* (*juguete*) (spinning) top

tronar *vt* (*Mex*) shoot. • *vi* thunder

tronchar *vt* bring down; (*fig*) cut short. **~se de risa** laugh a lot

tronco *m* trunk. **dormir como un ~** sleep like a log

trono *m* throne

trop|a *f* troops. **~el** *m* mob

tropez|ar 1 & 10 *vi* trip; (*fig*) slip up. **~ar con** run into. **~ón** *m* stumble; (*fig*) slip

tropical *adj* tropical

trópico *adj* tropical. • *m* tropic

tropiezo *m* slip; (*desgracia*) hitch

trot|ar *vi* trot. **~e** *m* trot; (*fig*) toing and froing. **al ~e** at a trot; (*de prisa*) in a rush. **de mucho ~e** hard-wearing

trozo *m* piece, bit. **a ~s** in bits

trucha *f* trout

truco *m* trick. **coger el ~** get the knack

trueno *m* thunder; (*estampido*) bang

trueque *m* exchange; (*Com*) barter

trufa *f* truffle

truhán *m* rogue

truncar 7 *vt* truncate; (*fig*) cut short

tu *adj* your

tú *pron* you

tuba *f* tuba

tubérculo *m* tuber

tuberculosis *f* tuberculosis

tub|ería *f* pipes; (*oleoducto etc*) pipeline. **~o** *m* tube. **~o de ensayo** test tube. **~o de escape** (*Auto*) exhaust (pipe). **~ular** *adj* tubular

tuerca *f* nut

tuerto *adj* one-eyed, blind in one eye. • *m* one-eyed person

tuétano *m* marrow; (*fig*) heart. **hasta los ~s** completely

tufo *m* stench
tugurio *m* hovel
tul *m* tulle
tulipán *m* tulip
tulli|do *adj* paralysed. **~r** 22 *vt* cripple
tumba *f* grave, tomb
tumb|ar *vt* knock over, knock down (estructura); (*fig, fam, en examen*) fail. **~arse** *vpr* lie down. **~o** *m* jolt. **dar un ~o** tumble. **~ona** *f* sun lounger
tumor *m* tumour
tumulto *m* turmoil; (*Pol*) riot
tuna *f* prickly pear; (*de estudiantes*) student band
tunante *m & f* rogue
túnel *m* tunnel
túnica *f* tunic
tupé *m* toupee; (*fig*) nerve
tupido *adj* thick
turba *f* peat; (*muchedumbre*) mob
turbado *adj* upset
turbante *m* turban
turbar *vt* upset; (*molestar*) disturb. **~se** *vpr* be upset
turbina *f* turbine
turbi|o *adj* cloudy; (vista) blurred; (asunto etc) shady. **~ón** *m* squall
turbulen|cia *f* turbulence; (*disturbio*) disturbance. **~te** *adj* turbulent
turco *adj* Turkish. ● *m* Turk; (*lengua*) Turkish
tur|ismo *m* tourism; (*coche*) car. **hacer ~** travel around. **~ cultural** heritage tourism. **~ patrimonial** (*LAm*) heritage tourism. **~ista** *m & f* tourist. **~ístico** *adj* tourist
turn|arse *vpr* take turns (**para** to). **~o** *m* turn; (*de trabajo*) shift. **de ~** on duty
turquesa *f* turquoise
Turquía *f* Turkey
turrón *m* nougat
tutear *vt* address as *tú*. **~se** *vpr* be on familiar terms
tutela *f* (*Jurid*) guardianship; (*fig*) protection
tutor *m* guardian; (*en enseñanza*) form master
tuve *vb véase* **TENER**
tuyo *adj & pron* yours. **un amigo ~** a friend of yours

Uu

u *conj* or
ubic|ar *vt* (*LAm*) place; (*localizar*) find. **~arse** *vpr* (*LAm*) be situated; (*orientarse*) find one's way around
ubre *f* udder
Ud. *abrev* (**Usted**) you
UE *abrev* (**Unión Europea**) EU
uf *int* phew!; (*de repugnancia*) ugh!
ufan|arse *vpr* be proud (**con, de** of); (*jactarse*) boast (**con, de** about). **~o** *adj* proud
úlcera *f* ulcer
últimamente *adv* (*recientemente*) recently; (*finalmente*) finally
ultim|ar *vt* complete; (*LAm, matar*) kill. **~átum** *m* ultimatum
último *adj* last; (*más reciente*) latest; (*más lejano*) furthest; (*más alto*) top; (*más bajo*) bottom; (*definitivo*) final. ● *m* last one. **estar en las últimas** be on one's last legs; (*sin dinero*) be down to one's last penny. **por ~** finally. **vestido a la última** dressed in the latest fashion

ultra *adj* ultra, extreme

ultraj|ante *adj* offensive. **~e** *m* insult, outrage

ultramar *m*. **de ~** overseas; (productos) foreign. **~inos** *mpl* groceries. **tienda de ~s** grocer's (shop) (*Brit*), grocery store (*Amer*)

ultranza. **a ~** (*con decisión*) decisively; (*extremo*) out-and-out

ultravioleta *adj invar* ultraviolet

umbilical *adj* umbilical

umbral *m* threshold

un, **una** *artículo indefinido*

! The masculine article **un** is also used before feminine nouns which begin with stressed **a** or **ha**, e.g. **un alma piadosa, un hada madrina**

- (*en sing*) a; (*antes de sonido vocálico*) an. **un perro** a dog. **una hora** an hour
- **unos, unas** (*cantidad incierta*) some. **compré ~os libros** I bought some books. (*cantidad cierta*) **tiene ~os ojos preciosos** she has beautiful eyes. **tiene ~os hijos muy buenos** her children are very good. (*en aproximaciones*) about. **en ~as 3 horas** in about 3 hours

For further information see **uno**

un|ánime *adj* unanimous. **~animidad** *f* unanimity

undécimo *adj* eleventh

ungüento *m* ointment

únic|amente *adv* only. **~o** *adj* only; (*fig, incomparable*) unique

unicornio *m* unicorn

unid|ad *f* unit; (*cualidad*) unity. **~ad de disco** disk drive. **~o** *adj* united

unifica|ción *f* unification. **~r** 7 *vt* unite, unify

uniform|ar *vt* standardize. **~e** *adj & m* uniform. **~idad** *f* uniformity

unilateral *adj* unilateral

uni|ón *f* union; (*cualidad*) unity; (*Tec*) joint. **~r** *vt* join; mix (líquidos). **~rse** *vpr* join together; (caminos) converge; (compañías) merge

unísono *m* unison. **al ~** in unison

univers|al *adj* universal. **~idad** *f* university. **~itario** *adj* university. **~o** *m* universe

uno, **una**

● *adjetivo*

Note that **uno** becomes **un** before masculine nouns

one. **una peseta** one peseta. **un dólar** one dollar. **ni una persona** not one person, not a single person. **treinta y un años** thirty one years

● *pronombre*

- one. **~ es mío** one (of them) is mine. **es la una** it's one o'clock. **se ayudan el ~ al otro** they help one another, they help each other. **lo que sienten el ~ por el otro** what they feel for each other
- (*fam, alguien*) someone. **le pregunté a ~** I asked someone
- **unos, unas** some. **no tenía vasos así es que le presté ~s** she didn't have any glasses so I lent her some. **a ~s les**

gusta, a otros no some like it, others don't. los ~s a los otros one another, each other ....➤ (*impersonal*) you. ~ no sabe qué decir you don't know what to say

untar *vt* grease; (*cubrir*) spread; (*fig, fam, sobornar*) bribe

uña *f* nail; (*de animal*) claw; (*casco*) hoof

uranio *m* uranium

Urano *m* Uranus

urban|idad *f* politeness. **~ismo** *m* town planning. **~ización** *f* development. **~izar** 10 *vt* develop. **~o** *adj* urban

urbe *f* big city

urdir *vt* (*fig*) plot

urg|encia *f* urgency; (*emergencia*) emergency. **~encias** A & E, (*Amer*) emergency room. **~ente** *adj* urgent; (carta) express. **~ir** 14 *vi* be urgent.

urinario *m* urinal

urna *f* urn; (*Pol*) ballot box

urraca *f* magpie

URSS *abrev* (*Historia*) USSR

Uruguay *m*. **el ~** Uruguay

uruguayo *adj & m* Uruguayan

us|ado *adj* (*con estar*) used; (ropa etc) worn; (*con ser*) secondhand. **~ar** *vt* use; (*llevar*) wear. **~arse** *vpr* (*LAm*) be in fashion. **~o** *m* use; (*costumbre*) custom. **al ~o de** in the style of

usted *pron* you. **~es** you

usual *adj* usual

usuario *adj* user

usur|a *f* usury. **~ero** *m* usurer

usurpar *vt* usurp

utensilio *m* utensil; (*herramienta*) tool

útero *m* womb, uterus

útil *adj* useful. **~es** *mpl* implements; (*equipo*) equipment

utili|dad *f* usefulness. **~dades** *fpl* (*LAm*) profits. **~zación** *f* use, utilization. **~zar** 10 *vt* use, utilize

utopía *f* Utopia

uva *f* grape. **~ pasa** raisin. **mala ~** bad mood

vaca *f* cow. **carne de ~** beef

vacaciones *fpl* holiday(s), vacation(s) (*Amer*). **de ~** on holiday, on vacation (*Amer*)

vacante *adj* vacant. ● *f* vacancy

vaciar 20 *vt* empty; (*ahuecar*) hollow out; (*en molde*) cast

vacila|ción *f* hesitation. **~nte** *adj* unsteady; (*fig*) hesitant. **~r** *vi* hesitate (Ⓘ, *bromear*) tease; (*LAm, divertirse*) have fun

vacío *adj* empty; (*frívolo*) frivolous. ● *m* empty space; (*estado*) emptiness; (*en física*) vacuum; (*fig*) void

vacuna *f* vaccine. **~ción** *f* vaccination. **~r** *vt* vaccinate

vacuno *adj* bovine

vad|ear *vt* ford. **~o** *m* ford

vaga|bundear *vi* wander. **~bundo** *adj* vagrant; (perro) stray. **niño ~** street urchin. ● *m* tramp, vagrant. **~ncia** *f* vagrancy; (*fig*) laziness. **~r** 12 *vi* wander (about)

vagina *f* vagina

vago *adj* vague; (*holgazán*) lazy. ● *m* layabout

vag|ón *m* coach, carriage; (*de mer-*

u v

cancías) wagon. **~ón restaurante** dining-car. **~oneta** *f* small freight wagon; (*Mex, para pasajeros*) van

vaho *m* breath; (*vapor*) steam. **~s** *mpl* inhalation

vain|a *f* sheath; (*de semillas*) pod. **~illa** *f* vanilla

vaiv|én *m* swinging; (*de tren etc*) rocking. **~enes** *mpl* (*fig, de suerte*) swings

vajilla *f* dishes, crockery

vale *m* voucher; (*pagaré*) IOU. **~dero** *adj* valid

valenciano *adj* from Valencia

valentía *f* bravery, courage

valer 42 *vt* be worth; (*costar*) cost; (*fig, significar*) mean. ● *vi* be worth; (*costar*) cost; (*servir*) be of use; (*ser valedero*) be valid; (*estar permitido*) be allowed. **~ la pena** be worthwhile, be worth it. **¿cuánto vale?** how much is it? **no ~ para nada** be useless. **eso no me vale** (*Mex, fam*) I don't give a damn about that. **¡vale!** all right!, OK! !

valeroso *adj* courageous

valgo *vb véase* **VALER**

valía *f* worth

validez *f* validity. **dar ~ a** validate

válido *adj* valid

valiente *adj* brave; (*en sentido irónico*) fine. ● *m* brave person

valija *f* suitcase. **~ diplomática** diplomatic bag

valioso *adj* valuable

valla *f* fence; (*en atletismo*) hurdle

valle *m* valley

val|or *m* value, worth; (*coraje*) courage. **objetos** *mpl* **de ~or** valuables. **sin ~or** worthless. **~ores** *mpl* securities. **~oración** *f* valuation. **~orar** *vt* value

vals *m invar* waltz

válvula *f* valve

vampiro *m* vampire

vanagloriarse *vpr* boast

vandalismo *m* vandalism

vándalo *m & f* vandal

vanguardia *f* vanguard. **de ~** (*en arte, música etc*) avant-garde

van|idad *f* vanity. **~idoso** *adj* vain. **~o** *adj* vain; (*inútil*) futile; (palabras) empty. **en ~** in vain

vapor *m* steam, vapour; (*Naut*) steamer. **al ~** (*Culin*) steamed. **~izador** *m* vaporizer. **~izar** 10 vaporize

vaquer|o *m* cowherd, cowboy. **~os** *mpl* jeans

vara *f* stick; (*de autoridad*) staff (*medida*) yard

varar *vi* run aground

varia|ble *adj & f* variable. **~ción** *f* variation. **~do** *adj* varied. **~nte** *f* variant; (*Auto*) by-pass. **~ntes** *fpl* hors d'oeuvres. **~r** 20 *vt* change; (*dar variedad a*) vary. ● *vi* vary; (*cambiar*) change

varicela *f* chickenpox

variedad *f* variety

varilla *f* stick; (*de metal*) rod

varios *adj* several

varita *f* wand

variz *f* (*pl* **varices**, (*LAm*) **várices**) varicose vein

var|ón *adj* male. ● *m* man; (*niño*) boy. **~onil** *adj* manly

vasco *adj & m* Basque

vaselina *f* Vaseline (P), petroleum jelly

vasija *f* vessel, pot

vaso *m* glass; (*en anatomía*) vessel

vástago *m* shoot; (*descendiente*) descendant

vasto *adj* vast
vaticin|ar *vt* forecast. **~io** *m* prediction, forecast
vatio *m* watt
vaya *vb véase* IR
Vd. *abrev* (**Usted**) you
vecin|al *adj* local. **~dad** *f* neighbourhood; (*vecinos*) residents; (*Mex, edificio*) tenement house. **~dario** *m* neighbourhood; (*vecinos*) residents. **~o** *adj* neighbouring. ● *m* neighbour; (*de barrio, edificio*) resident
ve|da *f* close season. **~do** *m* reserve. **~do de caza** game reserve. **~r** *vt* prohibit
vega *f* fertile plain
vegeta|ción *f* vegetation. **~l** *adj & m* plant, vegetable. **~r** *vi* grow; (persona) vegetate. **~riano** *adj & m* vegetarian
vehemente *adj* vehement
vehículo *m* vehicle
veinte *adj & m* twenty
veinti|cinco *adj & m* twenty-five. **~cuatro** *adj & m* twenty-four. **~dós** *adj & m* twenty-two. **~nueve** *adj & m* twenty-nine; **~ocho** *adj & m* twenty-eight. **~séis** *adj & m* twenty-six. **~siete** *adj & m* twenty-seven. **~trés** *adj & m* twenty-three. **~uno** *adj & m* (*delante de nombre masculino* **veintiún**) twenty-one
vejación *f* humiliation
vejar *vt* ill-treat
veje|storio *m* old crock; (*LAm, cosa*) old relic. **~z** *f* old age
vejiga *f* bladder
vela *f* (*Naut*) sail; (*de cera*) candle; (*vigilia*) vigil. **pasar la noche en ~** have a sleepless night
velada *f* evening
vela|do *adj* veiled; (*Foto*) exposed. **~r** *vt* watch over; hold a wake over (difunto); (*encubrir*) veil; (*Foto*) expose. ● *vi* stay awake. **~r por** look after. **~rse** *vpr* (*Foto*) get exposed
velero *m* sailing-ship
veleta *f* weather vane
vell|o *m* hair; (*pelusa*) down. **~ón** *m* fleece
velo *m* veil
veloc|idad *f* speed; (*Auto, Mec*) gear. **a toda ~idad** at full speed. **~ímetro** *m* speedometer. **~ista** *m & f* sprinter
velódromo *m* cycle-track
veloz *adj* fast, quick
vena *f* vein; (*en madera*) grain. **estar de/en ~** be in the mood
venado *m* deer; (*Culin*) venison
vencedor *adj* winning. ● *m* winner
venc|er **9** *vt* defeat; (*superar*) overcome. ● *vi* win; (pasaporte) expire. **~erse** *vpr* collapse; (*LAm, pasaporte*) expire. **~ido** *adj* beaten; (pasaporte) expired; (*Com, atrasado*) in arrears. **darse por ~ido** give up. **~imiento** *m* due date; (*de pasaporte*) expiry date
venda *f* bandage. **~je** *m* dressing. **~r** *vt* bandage
vendaval *m* gale
vende|dor *adj* selling. ● *m* seller; (*en tienda*) salesperson. **~dor ambulante** pedlar. **~r** *vt* sell. **se ~** for sale. **~rse** *vpr* (persona) sell out
vendimia *f* grape harvest
veneciano *adj* Venetian
veneno *m* poison; (*malevolencia*) venom. **~so** *adj* poisonous
venera|ble *adj* venerable. **~ción** *f* reverence. **~r** *vt* revere
venéreo *adj* venereal

venezolano *adj & m* Venezuelan

Venezuela *f* Venezuela

venga|nza *f* revenge. **~r** 12 *vt* avenge. **~rse** *vpr* take revenge (**de, por** for) (**en** on). **~tivo** *adj* vindictive

vengo *vb véase* **VENIR**

venia *f* (*permiso*) permission. **~l** *adj* venial

veni|da *f* arrival; (*vuelta*) return. **~dero** *adj* coming. **~r** 53 *vi* come. **~r bien** suit. **la semana que viene** next week. **¡venga!** come on!

venta *f* sale; (*posada*) inn. **en ~** for sale

ventaj|a *f* advantage. **~oso** *adj* advantageous

ventan|a *f* (*inc informática*) window; (*de la nariz*) nostril. **~illa** *f* window

ventarrón *m* ! strong wind

ventila|ción *f* ventilation. **~dor** *m* fan. **~r** *vt* air

vent|isca *f* blizzard. **~olera** *f* gust of wind. **~osa** *f* sucker. **~osidad** *f* wind, flatulence. **~oso** *adj* windy

ventrílocuo *m* ventriloquist

ventur|a *f* happiness; (*suerte*) luck. **a la ~a** with no fixed plan. **echar la buena ~a a uno** tell s.o.'s fortune. **por ~a** fortunately; (*acaso*) perhaps. **~oso** *adj* happy, lucky

Venus *m* Venus

ver 43 *vt* see; watch (televisión). • *vi* see. **a mi modo de ~** in my view. **a ~** let's see. **dejarse ~** show. **no lo puedo ~** I can't stand him. **no tener nada que ~ con** have nothing to do with. **vamos a ~** let's see. **ya lo veo** that's obvious. **ya ~emos** we'll see. **~se** *vpr* see o.s.; (*encontrarse*) find o.s.; (dos personas) meet; (*LAm, parecer*) look

veran|eante *m & f* holidaymaker, vacationer (*Amer*). **~ear** *vi* spend one's summer holiday. **~eo** *m*. **ir de ~eo** spend one's summer holiday. **lugar** *m* **de ~eo** summer resort. **~iego** *adj* summer. **~o** *m* summer

vera|s. de ~ really; (*verdadero*) real. **~z** *adj* truthful

verbal *adj* verbal

verbena *f* (*fiesta*) fair; (*baile*) dance

verbo *m* verb. **~so** *adj* verbose

verdad *f* truth. **¿~?** isn't it?, aren't they?, won't it? etc. **a decir ~** to tell the truth. **de ~** really. **~eramente** *adv* really. **~ero** *adj* true; (*fig*) real

verd|e *adj* green; (fruta) unripe; (chiste) dirty. • *m* green; (*hierba*) grass. **~or** *m* greenness

verdugo *m* executioner; (*fig*) tyrant

verdu|lería *f* greengrocer's (shop). **~lero** *m* greengrocer

vereda *f* path; (*LAm, acera*) pavement (*Brit*), sidewalk (*Amer*)

veredicto *m* verdict

verg|onzoso *adj* shameful; (*tímido*) shy. **~üenza** *f* shame; (*bochorno*) embarrassment. **¡es una ~üenza!** it's a disgrace! **me da ~üenza** I'm ashamed/embarrassed. **tener ~üenza** be ashamed/embarrassed

verídico *adj* true

verifica|ción *f* verification. **~r** 7 *vt* check. **~rse** *vpr* take place; (*resultar verdad*) come true

verja *f* (*cerca*) railings; (*puerta*) iron gate

vermú *m*, **vermut** *m* vermouth

verosímil *adj* likely; (relato) credible

verruga *f* wart

versa|do *adj* versed. **~r** *vi*. **~ sobre** deal with

versátil *adj* versatile; (*fig*) fickle

versión *f* version; (*traducción*) translation

verso *m* verse; (*poema*) poem

vértebra *f* vertebra

verte|dero *m* dump; (*desagüe*) drain **~r** 1 *vt* pour; (*derramar*) spill ● *vi* flow

vertical *adj* & *f* vertical

vértice *f* vertex

vertiente *f* slope

vertiginoso *adj* dizzy

vértigo *m* (*Med*) vertigo. **dar ~** make dizzy

vesícula *f* vesicle. **~ biliar** gall bladder

vespertino *adj* evening

vestíbulo *m* hall; (*de hotel, teatro*) foyer

vestido *m* dress

vestigio *m* trace. **~s** *mpl* remains

vest|imenta *f* clothes. **~ir** 5 *vt* (*llevar*) wear; dress (niño etc). ● *vi* dress. **~ir de** wear. **~irse** *vpr* get dressed. **~irse de** wear; (*disfrazarse*) dress up as. **~uario** *m* wardrobe; (*en gimnasio etc*) changing room (*Brit*), locker room (*Amer*)

vetar *vt* veto

veterano *adj* veteran

veterinari|a *f* veterinary science. **~o** *adj* veterinary. ● *m* vet [T], veterinary surgeon (*Brit*), veterinarian (*Amer*)

veto *m* veto

vez *f* time; (*turno*) turn. **a la ~** at the same time. **alguna ~** sometimes; (*en preguntas*) ever. **algunas veces** sometimes. **a su ~** in turn. **a veces** sometimes. **cada ~** each time. **cada ~ más** more and more. **de una ~** in one go. **de una ~ para siempre** once and for all. **de ~ en cuando** from time to time. **dos veces** twice. **en ~ de** instead of. **érase una ~, había una ~** once upon a time there was. **otra ~** again. **pocas veces, rara ~** seldom. **una ~ (que)** once

vía *f* road; (*Rail*) line; (*en anatomía*) tract; (*fig*) way. **~ férrea** railway (*Brit*), railroad (*Amer*). **~ rápida** fast lane. **estar en ~s de** be in the process of. ● *prep* via. **~ aérea** by air. **~ de comunicación** means of communication.

viab|ilidad *f* viability. **~le** *adj* viable

viaducto *m* viaduct

viaj|ante *m* & *f* commercial traveller. **~ar** *vi* travel. **~e** *m* journey; (*corto*) trip. **~e de novios** honeymoon. **¡buen ~e!** have a good journey!. **estar de ~** be away. **salir de ~** go on a trip. **~ero** *m* traveller; (*pasajero*) passenger

víbora *f* viper

vibra|ción *f* vibration. **~nte** *adj* vibrant. **~r** *vt/i* vibrate

vicario *m* vicar

viceversa *adv* vice versa

vici|ado *adj* (texto) corrupt; (aire) stale. **~ar** *vt* corrupt; (*estropear*) spoil. **~o** *m* vice; (*mala costumbre*) bad habit. **~oso** *adj* dissolute; (*círculo*) vicious

víctima *f* victim; (*de un accidente*) casualty

victori|a *f* victory. **~oso** *adj* victorious

vid *f* vine

V

vida *f* life; (*duración*) lifetime. **¡~ mía!** my darling! **de por ~** for life. **en mi ~** never (in my life). **estar con ~** be still alive

vídeo *m*, (*LAm*) **video** *m* video; (*cinta*) videotape; (*aparato*) video recorder

videojuego *m* video game

vidri|era *f* stained glass window; (*puerta*) glass door; (*LAm, escaparate*) shop window. **~ería** *f* glass works. **~ero** *m* glazier. **~o** *m* glass; (*LAm, en ventana*) window pane. **limpiar los ~os** clean the windows. **~oso** *adj* glassy

vieira *f* scallop

viejo *adj* old. • *m* old person

viene *vb véase* **VENIR**

viento *m* wind. **hacer ~** be windy

vientre *m* stomach; (*cavidad*) abdomen; (*matriz*) womb; (*intestino*) bowels; (*de vasija etc*) belly

viernes *m invar* Friday. **V~ Santo** Good Friday

viga *f* beam; (*de metal*) girder

vigen|cia *f* validity. **~te** *adj* valid; (ley) in force. **entrar en ~cia** come into force

vigésimo *adj* twentieth

vigía *f* watch-tower. • *m & f* (*persona*) lookout

vigil|ancia *f* vigilance. **~ante** *adj* vigilant. • *m & f* security guard; (*nocturno*) watchman. **~ar** *vt* keep an eye on. • *vi* be vigilant; (vigía) keep watch. **~ia** *f* vigil; (*Relig*) fasting

vigor *m* vigour; (*vigencia*) force. **entrar en ~** come into force. **~oso** *adj* vigorous

vil *adj* vile. **~eza** *f* vileness; (*acción*) vile deed

villa *f* (*casa*) villa; (*Historia*) town. **la V~** Madrid

villancico *m* (Christmas) carol

villano *adj* villanous; (*Historia*) peasant

vilo. **en ~** in the air

vinagre *m* vinegar. **~ra** *f* vinegar bottle. **~ras** *fpl* cruet. **~ta** *f* vinaigrette

vincular *vt* bind

vínculo *m* tie, bond

vindicar **7** *vt* (*rehabilitar*) vindicate

vine *vb véase* **VENIR**

vinicult|or *m* wine-grower. **~ura** *f* wine growing

vino *m* wine. **~ de la casa** house wine. **~ de mesa** table wine. **~ tinto** red wine

viñ|a *f* vineyard. **~atero** *m* (*LAm*) wine-grower. **~edo** *m* vineyard

viola *f* viola

viola|ción *f* violation; (*de una mujer*) rape. **~r** *vt* violate; break (ley); rape (mujer)

violen|cia *f* violence; (*fuerza*) force. **~tarse** *vpr* get embarrassed. **~to** *adj* violent; (*fig*) awkward

violeta *adj invar & f* violet

viol|ín *m* violin. • *m & f* (*músico*) violinist. **~inista** *m & f* violinist. **~ón** *m* double bass. **~onc(h)elista** *m & f* cellist. **~onc(h)elo** *m* cello

vira|je *m* turn. **~r** *vt* turn. • *vi* turn; (*fig*) change direction. **~r bruscamente** swerve

virg|en *adj*. **ser ~en** be a virgin. • *f* virgin. **~inal** *adj* virginal. **~inidad** *f* virginity

Virgo *m* Virgo

viril *adj* virile. **~idad** *f* virility

virtu|al *adj* virtual. **~d** *f* virtue; (*capacidad*) power. **en ~ de** by virtue of. **~oso** *adj* virtuous. • *m* virtuoso

viruela *f* smallpox

virulento *adj* virulent

virus *m invar* virus

visa *f* (*LAm*) visa. **~ado** *m* visa. **~r** *vt* endorse

vísceras *fpl* entrails

viscoso *adj* viscous

visera *f* visor; (*de gorra*) peak

visib|ilidad *f* visibility. **~le** *adj* visible

visillo *m* (*cortina*) net curtain

visi|ón *f* vision; (*vista*) sight. **~onario** *adj & m* visionary

visita *f* visit; (*visitante*) visitor; (*invitado*) guest; (*Internet*) hit. **~nte** *m & f* visitor. **~r** *vt* visit

vislumbrar *vt* glimpse

viso *m* sheen; (*aspecto*) appearance

visón *m* mink

visor *m* viewfinder

víspera *f* day before, eve

vista *f* sight, vision; (*aspecto, mirada*) look; (*panorama*) view. **apartar la ~** look away. **a primera ~, a simple ~** at first sight. **con ~s a** with a view to. **en ~ de** in view of. **estar a la ~** be obvious. **hacer la ~ gorda** turn a blind eye. **perder la ~** lose one's sight. **tener a la ~** have in front of one. **volver la ~ atrás** look back. **~zo** *m* glance. **dar/echar un ~zo a** glance at

visto *adj* seen; (*poco original*) common (*considerado*) considered. **~ que** since. **bien ~** acceptable. **está ~ que** it's obvious that. **mal ~** unacceptable. **por lo ~** apparently. ● *vb véase* VESTIR. **~ bueno** *m* approval. **~so** *adj* colourful, bright

visual *adj* visual. **campo ~** field of vision

vital *adj* vital. **~icio** *adj* life; (*cargo*) held for life. **~idad** *f* vitality

vitamina *f* vitamin

viticult|or *m* wine-grower. **~ura** *f* wine growing

vitorear *vt* cheer

vítreo *adj* vitreous

vitrina *f* showcase; (*en casa*) glass cabinet; (*LAm, escaparate*) shop window

viud|a *f* widow. **~ez** *f* widowhood. **~o** *adj* widowed. ● *m* widower

viva *m* cheer. **~cidad** *f* liveliness. **~mente** *adv* vividly. **~z** *adj* lively

víveres *mpl* supplies

vivero *m* nursery; (*de peces*) hatchery; (*de moluscos*) bed

viveza *f* vividness; (*de inteligencia*) sharpness; (*de carácter*) liveliness

vívido *adj* vivid

vividor *m* pleasure seeker

vivienda *f* housing; (*casa*) house; (*piso*) flat (*Brit*), apartment (*esp Amer*). **sin ~** homeless

viviente *adj* living

vivificar **7** *vt* (*animar*) enliven

vivir *vt* live through. ● *vi* live; (*estar vivo*) be alive. **¡viva!** hurray! **¡viva el rey!** long live the king! ● *m* life. **~ de** live on. **de mal ~** dissolute

vivisección *f* vivisection

vivo *adj* alive; (*viviente*) living; (*color*) bright; (*listo*) clever; (*fig*) lively. ● *m* sharp operator

vocab|lo *m* word. **~ulario** *m* vocabulary

vocación *f* vocation

vocal *adj* vocal. ● *f* vowel. ● *m & f* member. **~ista** *m & f* vocalist

voce|ar *vt* call (mercancías); (*fig*)

proclaim; (*Mex*) page (persona). ● *vi* shout. **~río** *m* shouting. **~ro** (*LAm*) spokeperson

vociferar *vi* shout

vola|dor *adj* flying. ● *m* rocket. **~ndas**. **en ~ndas** in the air. **~nte** *adj* flying. ● *m* (*Auto*) steering-wheel; (*nota*) note; (*rehilete*) shuttlecock. **~r** **2** *vt* blow up. ● *vi* fly; (*fam, desaparecer*) disappear

volátil *adj* volatile

volcán *m* volcano. **~ico** *adj* volcanic

volcar **2** & **7** *vt* knock over; (*vaciar*) empty out; turn over (molde). ● *vi* overturn. **~se** *vpr* fall over; (vehículo) overturn; (*fig*) do one's utmost. **~se en** throw o.s. into

vóleibol *m*, (*Mex*) **volibol** *m* volleyball

voltaje *m* voltage

volte|ar *vt* turn over; (*en el aire*) toss; ring (campanas); (*LAm*) turn over (colchón etc). **~arse** *vpr* (*LAm*) turn around; (carro) overturn. **~reta** *f* somersault

voltio *m* volt

voluble *adj* (*fig*) fickle

volum|en *m* volume. **~inoso** *adj* voluminous

voluntad *f* will; (*fuerza de voluntad*) willpower; (*deseo*) wish; (*intención*) intention. **buena ~** goodwill. **mala ~** ill will

voluntario *adj* voluntary. ● *m* volunteer

voluptuoso *adj* voluptuous

volver **2** (*pp* **vuelto**) *vt* turn; (*de arriba a abajo*) turn over; (*devolver*) restore. ● *vi* return; (*fig*) revert. **~ a hacer algo** do sth again. **~ en sí** come round. **~se** *vpr* turn round; (*hacerse*) become

vomit|ar *vt* bring up. ● *vi* be sick, vomit. **~ivo** *adj* disgusting

vómito *m* vomit; (*acción*) vomiting

voraz *adj* voracious

vos *pron* (*LAm*) you. **~otros** *pron* you; (*reflexivo*) yourselves

vot|ación *f* voting; (*voto*) vote. **~ante** *m* & *f* voter. **~ar** *vt* vote for. ● *vi* vote (**por** for). **~o** *m* vote; (*Relig*) vow

voy *vb véase* **IR**

voz *f* voice; (*rumor*) rumour; (*palabra*) word. **~ pública** public opinion. **a media ~** softly. **a una ~** unanimously. **dar voces** shout. **en ~ alta** loudly

vuelco *m* upset. **el corazón me dio un ~** my heart missed a beat

vuelo *m* flight; (*acción*) flying; (*de ropa*) flare. **al ~** in flight; (*fig*) in passing

vuelta *f* turn; (*curva*) bend; (*paseo*) walk; (*revolución*) revolution; (*regreso*) return; (*dinero*) change. **a la ~** on one's return. **a la ~ de la esquina** round the corner. **dar la ~ al mundo** go round the world. **dar una ~** go for a walk. **estar de ~** be back

vuelvo *vb véase* **VOLVER**

vuestro *adj* your. ● *pron* yours. **un amigo ~** a friend of yours

vulg|ar *adj* vulgar; (persona) common. **~aridad** *f* vulgarity. **~arizar** **10** *vt* popularize. **~o** *m* common people

vulnerable *adj* vulnerable

Ww

wáter /'(g)water/ *m* toilet
Web *m* /'(g)web/. **el ~** the Web
whisky /'(g)wiski/ *m* whisky

xenofobia *f* xenophobia
xilófono *m* xylophone

y *conj* and
ya *adv* already; (*ahora*) now; (*con negativos*) any more; (*para afirmar*) yes, sure; (*en seguida*) immediately; (*pronto*) soon. **~ mismo** (*LAm*) right away. ● *int* of course! **~ no** no longer. **~ que** since. **¡~, ~!** oh sure!
yacaré *m* (*LAm*) alligator
yac|er 44 *vi* lie. **~imiento** *m* deposit; (*de petróleo*) oilfield
yanqui *m & f* American, Yank(ee)
yate *m* yacht
yegua *f* mare
yelmo *m* helmet
yema *f* (*en botánica*) bud; (*de huevo*) yolk; (*golosina*) sweet. **~ del dedo** fingertip
yerba *f* (*LAm*) grass; (*Med*) herb
yergo *vb véase* ERGUIR
yermo *adj* uninhabited; (*no cultivable*) barren. ● *m* wasteland
yerno *m* son-in-law
yerro *m* mistake. ● *vb véase* ERRAR
yeso *m* plaster; (*mineral*) gypsum
yo *pron* I. **~ mismo** myself. **¿quién, ~?** who, me? **soy ~** it's me
yodo *m* iodine
yoga *m* yoga
yogur *m* yog(h)urt
yuca *f* yucca
yugo *m* yoke
Yugoslavia *f* Yugoslavia
yugoslavo *adj & m* Yugoslav
yunque *m* anvil
yunta *f* yoke

Zz

zafarrancho *m* (*confusión*) mess; (*riña*) quarrel
zafarse *vpr* escape; get out of (obligación etc); (*Mex, dislocarse*) dislocate
zafiro *m* sapphire
zaga *f* rear; (*en deportes*) defence. **a la ~** behind
zaguán *m* hall
zaherir 4 *vt* hurt
zahorí *m* dowser
zaino *adj* (caballo) chestnut; (vaca) black
zalamer|ía *f* flattery. **~o** *adj* flattering. ● *m* flatterer
zamarra *f* (*piel*) sheepskin; (*prenda*) sheepskin jacket

zamarrear *vt* shake

zamba *f* South American dance

zambulli|da *f* dive; (*baño*) dip. **~rse** *vpr* dive

zamparse *vpr* gobble up

zanahoria *f* carrot

zancad|a *f* stride. **~illa** *f* trip. **hacer una ~illa a uno** trip s.o. up

zanc|o *m* stilt. **~udo** *adj* long-legged; (ave) wading. ● *m* (*LAm*) mosquito

zanganear *vi* idle

zángano *m* drone. ●*m & f* (*persona*) idler

zangolotear *vt* shake. ● *vi* rattle; (persona) fidget

zanja *f* ditch; (*para tuberías etc*) trench. **~r** *vt* (*fig*) settle

zapat|ear *vi* tap with one's feet. **~ería** *f* shoe shop; (*arte*) shoemaking. **~ero** *m* shoemaker; (*el que remienda zapatos*) cobbler. **~illa** *f* slipper; (*de deportes*) trainer. **~illa de ballet** ballet shoe. **~o** *m* shoe

zarand|a *f* sieve. **~ear** *vt* (*sacudir*) shake

zarcillo *m* earring

zarpa *f* paw

zarpar *vi* set sail, weigh anchor

zarza *f* bramble. **~mora** *f* blackberry

zarzuela *f* Spanish operetta

> **i** **zarzuela** A musical drama consisting of alternating passages of dialogue, songs, choruses, and dancing that originated in Spain in the seventeenth century. Also popular in Latin America, its name derives from the Palacio de la Zarzuela, the Madrid palace where the Royal family now lives.

zigzag *m* zigzag. **~uear** *vi* zigzag

zinc *m* zinc

zócalo *m* skirting-board; (*pedestal*) plinth; (*Mex*, *plaza*) main square

zodiaco *m*, **zodíaco** *m* zodiac

zona *f* zone; (*área*) area

zoo *m* zoo. **~logía** *f* zoology. **~lógico** *adj* zoological

zoólogo *m* zoologist

zopenco *adj* stupid. ● *m* idiot

zoquete *m* blockhead

zorr|a *f* vixen **~illo** *m* (*LAm*) skunk.. **~o** *m* fox

zorzal *m* thrush

zozobra *f* (*fig*) anxiety. **~r** *vi* founder

zueco *m* clog

zumb|ar *vt* **I** give (golpe etc). ● *vi* buzz. **~ido** *m* buzzing

zumo *m* juice

zurci|do *m* darning. **~r** **9** *vt* darn

zurdo *adj* left-handed; (mano) left

zurrar *vt* (*fig, fam, dar golpes*) beat (up)

zutano *m* so-and-so

Phrasefinder/Frases útiles

Useful phrases / Expresiones útiles

yes, please/no, thank you	sí, por favor/no, gracias
sorry	perdone
excuse me	disculpe
I'm sorry, I don't understand	perdone, pero no le entiendo
you're welcome!	¡de nada!, ¡no hay de qué!

Meeting people / Saludos

hello/goodbye	hola/adiós
how are you?	¿cómo está usted?
nice to meet you	mucho gusto

Asking questions	Preguntas
do you speak English/Spanish?	¿habla usted inglés/español?
what's your name?	¿cómo se llama?
where are you from?	¿de dónde es?
how much is it?	¿cuánto es?
where is...?	¿dónde está...?
can I have...?	¿me da...?
would you like...?	¿quiere usted...?

About you	Información personal
my name is...	me llamo...
I'm American/I'm Mexican	soy americano/-a/mexicano/-a
I don't speak Spanish/English	no hablo español/inglés
I live near Seville/Chester	vivo cerca de Sevilla/Chester
I'm a student	soy estudiante
I work in an office	trabajo en una oficina

Emergencies	Emergencias
can you help me, please?	¿me ayuda, por favor?
I'm lost	me he perdido
I'm ill	no me encuentro bien
call an ambulance	llamen a una ambulancia

Reading signs	Carteles y señales
no entry	prohibido el paso
no smoking	prohibido fumar
fire exit	salida de emergencia
for sale	en venta
push	empujar
pull	tirar, (*LAm*) jalar
press	apretar, pulsar

Going Places/Viajes

By rail and underground — En tren y en metro

By rail and underground	En tren y en metro
where can I buy a ticket?	¿dónde se sacan los billetes, (*LAm*) boletos?
what time is the next train to Barcelona/New York?	¿a qué hora sale el próximo tren para Barcelona/Nueva York?
do I have to change?	¿tengo que hacer algún transbordo?
can I take my bike on the train?	¿puedo llevar la bicicleta en el tren?
which platform for the train to San Sebastian/Bath?	¿de qué andén sale el tren para San Sebastián/Bath?
a single/return, (*Amer*) round trip to Baltimore/Valencia, please	un billete, (*LAm*) boleto de ida/ida y vuelta para Baltimore/Valencia, por favor
I'd like an all-day ticket	quiero un billete, (*LAm*) boleto que valga para todo el día
I'd like to reserve a seat	quisiera reservar una plaza
is there a student/senior citizen discount?	¿hacen descuentos para estudiantes/jubilados?
is this the train for Seville/Manchester?	¿éste es el tren para Sevilla/Manchester?
what time does the train arrive in Madrid/Washington?	¿a qué hora llega el tren a Madrid/Washington?
have I missed the train?	¿he perdido el tren?
which line do I need to take for the Prado/London Eye?	¿qué línea se coge, (*LAm*) toma para ir al Prado/London Eye?

YOU WILL HEAR:	OIRÁS:
el tren va a llegar al andén número 2	the train is arriving at platform 2
hay un tren que sale para Madrid a las 10	there's a train to Madrid at 10 o'clock
el tren llegará con retraso/puntual	the train is delayed/on time
la próxima parada es..., (*LAm*) el próximo paradero es...	the next stop is...
su billete, (*LAm*) boleto no es válido	your ticket isn't valid

MORE USEFUL WORDS:	MÁS PALABRAS ÚTILES:
underground station, (*Amer*) subway station	estación de metro
timetable	horario
connection	transbordo
seat reservation	reserva de plaza/asiento
express train	tren expreso
local train	tren de cercanías
high-speed train	tren de alta velocidad

DID YOU KNOW...?	¿SABÍAS QUE...?
In some of the larger Spanish train stations, you will need to take a ticket and wait for your number to be called before you can speak to a clerk.	En Inglaterra se puede ir del aeropuerto de Heathrow al centro de Londres en menos de veinte minutos gracias a un tren que se llama Heathrow Express.

At the airport En el aeropuerto

when's the next flight to Paris/ Rome?	¿cuándo sale el próximo vuelo para París/Roma?
what time do I have to check in?	¿a qué hora tengo que facturar, (*LAm*) chequear, (*Mex*) registrar el equipaje?
where do I check in?	¿dónde puedo facturar, (*LAm*) chequear, (*Mex*) registrar el equipaje?
I'd like to confirm my flight	quisiera confirmar mi vuelo
I'd like a window seat/an aisle seat	quisiera un asiento de ventanilla/ pasillo
I want to change/cancel my reservation	quiero cambiar/cancelar mi reserva
can I carry this in my hand, (*Amer*) carry-on luggage?	¿puedo llevar ésto como equipaje de mano?
my luggage hasn't arrived	mi equipaje no ha llegado

YOU WILL HEAR:	OIRÁS:
el vuelo BA7057 saldrá con retraso/ha sido cancelado	flight BA7057 is delayed/cancelled
vaya a la puerta (de embarque), (*Mex*) sala de abordar 29	please go to gate 29
su tarjeta de embarque, (*Mex*) pase de abordar, por favor	your boarding card, please

MORE USEFUL WORDS:	MÁS PALABRAS ÚTILES:
arrivals	llegadas
departures	salidas
baggage claim	recogida de equipajes

Asking how to get there | Cómo llegar a los sitios

how do I get to the airport?	¿cómo se llega al aeropuerto?
how long will it take to get there?	¿cuánto tiempo se tarda en llegar?
how far is it from here?	¿a qué distancia está?
which bus do I take for the cathedral?	¿qué autobús debo coger, (*LAm*) tomar, para ir a la catedral?
where does this bus go?	¿a dónde va este autobús?
does this bus/train go to...?	¿éste autobús/tren va a ...?
where should I get off?	¿dónde me tengo que bajar?
how much is it to the town centre?	¿cuánto cuesta ir al centro de la ciudad?
what time is the last bus?	¿a qué hora sale el último autobús?
where's the nearest underground station, (*Amer*) subway station?	¿dónde está la estación de metro más cercana?
is this the turning for...?	¿es ésta la calle para...?
can you call me a taxi?	¿me puede pedir un taxi?

YOU WILL HEAR:	OIRÁS:
tome la primera (calle) a la derecha	take the first turning, (*Amer*) turn on the right
al llegar al semáforo/después de pasar la iglesia, gire a la izquierda	turn left at the traffic lights/ just past the church

Disabled travellers | Viajeros discapacitados

I'm disabled	soy minusválido
is there wheelchair access?	¿hay un acceso para sillas de ruedas?
are guide dogs permitted?	¿se permite la entrada de perros lazarillo?

On the road Por carretera

where's the nearest petrol station, (*Amer*) gas station?	¿dónde está la gasolinera más cercana?
what's the best way to get there?	¿cuál es la mejor forma de llegar?
I've got a puncture, (*Amer*) flat tire	he tenido un pinchazo, (*Mex*) se nos ponchó una llanta
I'd like to hire, (*Amer*) rent a bike/car	quisiera alquilar, (*Mex*) rentar una bicicleta/un coche
where can I park around here?	¿dónde puedo aparcar por aquí?
there's been an accident	ha habido un accidente
my car's broken down	se me ha estropeado el coche, (*LAm*) se me descompuso el carro
the car won't start	el coche, (*LAm*) carro no arranca
where's the nearest garage?	¿dónde está el taller más cercano?
pump number six, please	surtidor, (*Andes*, *Ven*) bomba número seis, por favor
fill it up, please	llénelo, por favor
can I wash my car here?	¿tienen túnel de lavado?
can I park here?	¿aquí se puede aparcar, (*LAm*) estacionar, (*Col*) parquear?
there's a problem with the brakes/lights	les pasa algo a los frenos/los faros
the clutch/gearstick isn't working	no funciona el embrague/cambio de marchas, (*LAm*) la palanca de cambios, (*Mex*) de velocidades
take the third exit off the roundabout, (*Amer*) traffic circle	en la rotonda, vaya por la tercera salida
turn right at the next junction	gire a la derecha en el próximo cruce
slow down	vaya más despacio
I can't drink – I'm driving	tengo que conducir, (*LAm*) manejar así que no puedo beber, (*LAm*) tomar
can I buy a road map here?	¿venden mapas de carreteras?

YOU WILL HEAR:	OIRÁS:
enséñeme su carnet de conducir, (*LAm*) licencia, (*Col*) pase, (*Chi*) carné, (*Ur*) libreta de manejar, (*Per*) su brevete, (*Arg*) registro	can I see your driving licence?
tiene que rellenar un parte de accidente	you need to fill out an accident report
esta carretera es de un solo sentido	this road is one-way
está prohibido aparcar, (*LAm*) estacionar aquí	you can't park here

MORE USEFUL WORDS:	MÁS PALABRAS ÚTILES:
diesel	diésel
unleaded	sin plomo
motorway, (*Amer*) expressway	autopista
toll	peaje, (*Mex*) cuota
satnav, (*Amer*) GPS	navegación vía satélite
speed camera	radar de tráfico, (*Chi*) fotorradar
roundabout	rotonda, glorieta
crossroads	cruce
dual carriageway, (*Amer*) divided highway	vía de doble sentido
exit	salida
traffic lights	semáforo
driver	conductor, -ora, chofer (*or esp Spain*) chófer

DID YOU KNOW...?	¿SABÍAS QUE...?
The speed limits on Spanish roads are as follows: motorway 120 km/h (74 mph), open roads 90-100 km/h (56-62 mph), towns and villages 50 km/h (31 mph).	Para entrar en coche hasta el centro de Londres hay que pagar una tasa de circulación especial; hay un sistema electrónico para detectar a los infractores.

COMMON SPANISH ROAD SIGNS

Aparcamiento, (*LAm*) estacionamiento, (*Col*) parqueadero	Parking
Atención: Paso a nivel de tren	Beware: level crossing
Autopista	Motorway, (*Amer*) Expressway
Autovía	Dual carriageway, (*Amer*) Divided highway
Cambio de sentido, (*Mex*) retorno	Change of direction
Casco urbano	Urban area
Ceda el Paso	Give Way, (*Amer*) Yield
(*LAm*) Cuidado: Cruce de ferrocarril/vía férrea	Beware: level crossing
Desvío	Detour
Dirección Única, (*LAm*) calle de sentido único	One-way street
Obras	Roadworks, (*Amer*) Men working
Peligro	Danger
Vado permanente	No parking (at any time)
Zona de residentes	Parking only for people with resident cards
Zona peatonal	Pedestrian area

SEÑALES DE TRÁFICO CORRIENTES EN PAÍSES DE HABLA INGLESA

Cattle	Ganado
Contraflow	Carril en sentido contrario
Ford	Vado, (*LAm*) Acceso
Get in lane	Incorpórese al carril
Give way	Ceda el Paso
Keep clear	No estacionar
No overtaking, (*Amer*) Do not pass	Prohibido adelantar, (*Mex*) rebasar
Pedestrians crossing	Peatones cruzando
Red route – no stopping	Prohibido parar
Reduce speed now	Reduzca su velocidad
Stop	Stop, (*LAm*) pare

Keeping in touch/Comunicación

On the phone	Por teléfono
where can I buy a phone card?	¿dónde puedo comprar una tarjeta telefónica?
may I use your phone?	¿podría usar su teléfono?
do you have a mobile, (*Amer*) cell phone?	¿tiene usted un móvil, (*LAm*) un celular?
what is your phone number?	¿cuál es su número (de teléfono)?
what is the area code for Santiago/ Cardiff?	¿cuál es el prefijo, (*LAm*) código de Santiago/Cardiff?
I want to make a phone call	quiero hacer una llamada
I'd like to reverse the charges, (*Amer*) call collect	quisiera hacer una llamada a cobro revertido, (*LAm*) una llamada por cobrar
the line's engaged/busy	está comunicando, (*LAm*) está ocupado
there's no answer	no contestan
hello, this is Natalia	hola, soy, (*esp LAm*) habla Natalia
is Juan there, please?	¿está Juan, por favor?
who's calling?	¿de parte de quién?
sorry, wrong number	perdone, se ha confundido
just a moment, please	un momentito, por favor
would you like to hold?	¿le importa esperar?
it's a business/personal call	es una llamada personal/de negocios
I'll put you through to him/her	le pongo (*or* le paso, comunico) con él/ella
s/he cannot come to the phone at the moment	en este momento está ocupado/-a
please tell him/her I called	dígale que he llamado, (*LAm*) que llamé, por favor
I'd like to leave a message for him/her	quisiera dejarle un mensaje

I'll try again later	volveré a llamar más tarde
please tell him/her that María called	dígale que ha llamado, (*LAm*) que llamó María, por favor
can he/she call me back?	¿le puede decir que me llame?
my home number is...	mi número de casa es...
my business number is...	mi número del trabajo es...
my fax number is...	mi número de fax es...
we were cut off	se ha cortado, (*LAm*) se cortó
I'll call you later	te llamaré más tarde
I need to top up my phone	tengo que recargar el saldo
the battery's run out	me he quedado sin batería
I'm running low on credit	se me está gastando el saldo
send me a text	mándame un mensaje
there's no signal here	aquí no hay cobertura
you're breaking up	te oigo fatal, (*LAm*) te escucho muy mal
could you speak a little louder?	¿podría hablar un poco más alto?

YOU WILL HEAR:	OIRÁS:
sí, diga, dígame, (*LAm*) aló, (*Mex*) bueno	hello
llámame al móvil, (*LAm*) al celular	call me on my mobile, (*Amer*) cell phone
¿quiere dejar un mensaje/recado?	would you like to leave a message?

MORE USEFUL WORDS:	MÁS PALABRAS ÚTILES:
text message	mensaje (de texto)/SMS
top-up card	tarjeta de saldo, (*LAm*) de prepago
phone box, (*Amer*) phone booth	cabina de teléfono
dial	marcar, (*LAm*) discar
directory enquiries	información de direcciones/guía

Writing | Por carta

what's your address?	¿cuál es su dirección?
where is the nearest post office?	¿dónde está la oficina de correos más cercana?, (*LAm*) ¿dónde está el correo más cercano?
could I have a stamp for Argentina/Italy, please?	¿me da un sello, (*LAm*) una estampilla, (*Mex*) un timbre para Argentina/Italia, por favor?
I'd like to send a parcel	quisiera mandar un paquete
where is the nearest postbox, (*Amer*) mailbox?	¿dónde está el buzón más cercano?
dear Isabel/Fred	querida/querido Isabel/Fred
dear Sir or Madam	muy señor mío
yours sincerely	atentamente
yours faithfully	le envía un cordial saludo
best wishes	un abrazo

YOU WILL HEAR:	OIRÁS:
¿Quiere mandarlo por envío urgente?	Would you like to send it first class?
¿Contiene objetos de valor?	Is it valuable?

MORE USEFUL WORDS:	MÁS PALABRAS ÚTILES:
letter	carta
postcode, (*Amer*) ZIP code	código postal
airmail	correo aéreo
postcard	postal
fragile	frágil
urgent	urgente
registered post, (*Amer*) mail	correo certificado

On line En línea

are you on the Internet?	¿está conectado/-a a Internet?
what's your e-mail address?	¿cuál es su dirección de correo electrónico?
I'll e-mail it to you on Tuesday	se lo mandaré por correo electrónico el martes
I looked it up on the Internet	lo he buscado, (*LAm*) lo busqué en Internet
the information is on their website	la información está en su sitio web
my e-mail address is jane dot smith at new99 dot com	mi correo electrónico es jane punto smith arroba new99 punto com
can I check my e-mail here?	¿puedo mirar el correo (electrónico)?
I have broadband/dial-up	tengo banda ancha/ conexión por módem
do you have wireless internet access?	¿tienen wi-fi?
I'll send you the file as an attachment	le mandaré el archivo como (archivo) adjunto, (*LAm also*) anexo

YOU WILL SEE:	VERÁS:
buscar	search
hacer doble clic en el icono	double-click on the icon
abrir la aplicación	open (up) the application
descargar archivo	download file

MORE USEFUL WORDS:	MÁS PALABRAS ÚTILES:
subject (of an email)	asunto (de un email)
password	contraseña
social networking site	red de contacto en línea
search engine	buscador
mouse	ratón, (*LAm also*) mouse
keyboard	teclado

Meeting up Citas, encuentros

what shall we do this evening?	¿qué hacemos esta tarde?
do you want to go out tonight?	¿quieres que salgamos esta noche?
where shall we meet?	¿dónde quedamos, (*LAm*) nos encontramos?
I'll see you outside the café at 6 o'clock	nos vemos a las 6 a la puerta de la cafetería
see you later	hasta luego
I can't today, I'm busy	hoy no puedo, estoy ocupado/-a
I'm sorry, I've got something planned	lo siento, tengo otros planes
let's meet for a coffee in town	¿nos tomamos un café por ahí?
would you like to see a show/film (*Amer*) movie?	¿quieres que vayamos al teatro/ cine?
what about next week instead?	¿qué tal si lo dejamos para la semana que viene?
shall we go for something to eat?	¿vamos a tomar, (*LAm*) comer algo?

YOU WILL HEAR:	OIRÁS:
encantado/-a	nice to meet you
¿te invito a una copa?	can I buy you a drink?

MORE USEFUL WORDS:	MÁS PALABRAS ÚTILES:
bar	bar
bar (*serving counter in a bar/pub*)	barra
meal	comida
snack	algo para picar
date	cita
cigarette	pitillo

Food and Drink/Comer y beber

Booking a restaurant	Reservar mesa en un restaurante
can you recommend a good restaurant?	¿me puede recomendar un buen restaurante?
I'd like to reserve a table for four	quisiera reservar una mesa para cuatro
a reservation for tomorrow evening at eight o'clock	una reserva para mañana a las ocho de la tarde

Ordering	Pedir la comida
could we see the menu/wine list, please?	¿nos enseña el menú/la carta de vinos, por favor?
do you have a vegetarian/children's menu?	¿tienen un menú especial para vegetarianos/niños?
as a starter... and to follow...	de primero.. y de segundo...
could we have some more bread?	¿nos puede traer más pan?
what would you recommend?	¿qué recomienda?
I'd like a white coffee ...black coffee ...a decaffeinated coffee	quisiera un café con leche ...café solo, (*LAm*) café negro ...un café descafeinado
could I have the bill, (*Amer*) check?	¿me trae la cuenta, por favor?

YOU WILL HEAR	OIRÁS
¿Ya han decidido lo que van a pedir?	Are you ready to order?
¿Quieren entrada/un aperitivo?	Would you like a starter/aperitif?
¿Qué van a pedir de segundo plato?	What will you have as main course?
¿Quieren postre/café?	Would you like a dessert/coffee?
¿Algo más?	Anything else?
¡Buen provecho!	Enjoy your meal!
El servicio (no) está incluido.	Service is (not) included.

The menu La carta/El menú

starters	de primero
hors d'oeuvres	entremeses, (*Mex*) botanas
omelette	omelette, tortilla
soup	sopa
fish	**pescado**
bass	lubina
cod	bacalao
eel	anguila
hake	merluza
herring	arenque
monkfish	rape
mullet	mújol, (*LAm*) lisa
mussels	mejillones
oyster	ostra, (*Mex*) ostión
prawns	gambas
salmon	salmón
sardines	sardinas
shrimps	gambas
sole	lenguado
squid	calamares
trout	trucha
tuna	atún
turbot	rodaballo
meat	**carne**
beef	carne de vaca
chicken	pollo
duck	pato

de primero	starters
entremeses, botanas (*Mex*)	hors d'oeuvres
omelette, tortilla	omelette
sopa	soup
pescado	**fish**
anguila	eel
arenque	herring
atún	tuna
bacalao	cod
calamares	squid
camarones (*LAm*)	prawns, shrimps
gambas	prawns, shrimps
lenguado	sole
lisa (*LAm*)	mullet
lubina	bass
mejillones	mussels
merluza	hake
mújol	mullet
ostra, (*Mex*) ostión	oyster
rape	monkfish
róbalo	bass
rodaballo	turbot
trucha	trout
carne	**meat**
bistec, filete	steak
carne de vaca, de res (*Mex*)	beef

goose	ganso
hare	liebre
ham	jamón
kidneys	riñones
lamb	cordero
liver	hígado
pork	cerdo
quail	codorniz
rabbit	conejo
steak	bistec, filete
tenderloin	lomo
turkey	pavo
veal	ternera
venison	venado
white meat	carne blanca

vegetables	**verduras**
artichoke	alcachofa
asparagus	ésparragos
aubergine	berenjena
beans	frijoles
carrots	zanahorias
cabbage	col, repollo
celery	apio
endive	endivia
lettuce	lechuga
mushrooms	champiñones
peas	guisantes, (*LAm*) arvejas
pepper	pimiento
potatoes	patatas, (*LAm*) papas
runner bean	habichuela

cerdo	pork
codorniz	quail
conejo	rabbit
cordero	lamb
ganso	goose
hígado	liver
jamón	ham
liebre	hare
pato	duck
pollo	chicken
puerco (*Mex*)	pork
riñones	kidneys
solomillo (*Esp*)	sirloin steak
ternera	veal
venado	venison

verduras	**vegetables**
alcachofa	artichoke
arvejas (*LAm*)	peas
apio	celery
batata	sweet potato
berenjena	aubergine
camote (*LAm*)	sweet potato
cebollas	onions
champiñones	mushrooms
chícharos (*Mex*)	peas
col, repollo	cabbage
coliflor	cauliflower
ésparragos	asparagus
frijoles	beans
guisantes	peas
haba	broad bean

tomato	tomate, (*Mex*) jitomate	jitomate (*Mex*)	tomato
sweet potato	batata, camote (*LAm*)	papas	potatoes
zucchini	calabacines	patatas	potatoes
		pimiento	pepper
		zanahorias	carrots

the way it's cooked	**cómo se prepara**	**cómo se prepara**	**the way it's cooked**
boiled	cocido -da	a la parilla	grilled
roast	asado -da	a la plancha	griddled
fried	frito -ta	asado -da	roast
pureed	puré de	bien cocido	well done
grilled	a la parilla	bien hecho	well done
griddled	a la plancha	cocido -da	boiled
stewed	estofado -da, guisado -da	estofado -da	stewed
		guisado -da	stewed
rare	poco hecho	frito -ta	fried
well done	bien hecho	poco hecho	rare

deserts	**postres**	**postres**	**deserts**
ice cream	helados	fruta	fruit
fruits	fruta	helados	ice cream
pie	tarta, (*LAm*) pay	pastel, (*LAm*) pay	pie
tart	tarta	tarta	tart

other		**otros**	
bread	pan	aceite de oliva	olive oil
butter	mantequilla	ajo	garlic
cheese	queso	arroz	rice
cheeseboard	tabla de quesos	condimento	seasoning
garlic	ajo	mantequilla	butter
mayonnaise	mayonesa	mayonesa	mayonnaise
mustard	mostaza	mostaza	mustard
olive oil	aceite de oliva	pan	bread

pepper	pimienta
rice	arroz
salt	sal
sauce	salsa
seasoning	condimento
vinegar	vinagre

pimienta	pepper
queso	cheese
sal	salt
salsa	sauce
tabla de quesos	cheeseboard
vinagre	vinegar

drinks bebidas

beer	cerveza
bottle	botella
carbonated	con gas
half-bottle	media botella
liqueur	licor
mineral water	agua mineral
red wine	vino tinto
rosé	vino rosado
soft drink	bebida no alcohólica
still	sin gas
house wine	vino de la casa
table wine	vino de mesa
white wine	vino blanco
wine	vino

bebidas drinks

agua mineral	mineral water
bebida no alcohólica	soft drink
botella	botella
cerveza	beer
con gas	carbonated
licor	liqueur
media botella	half-bottle
sin gas	still
vino	wine
vino blanco	white wine
vino de la casa	house wine
vino de mesa	table wine
vino rosado	rosé
vino tinto	red wine

Places to stay/Alojamiento

Camping — Campings

can we pitch our tent here?	¿podemos montar la tienda (de campaña) aquí?
can we park our caravan here?	¿podemos aparcar la caravana aquí?, (*LAm*) ¿podemos estacionar el tráiler aquí?
what are the facilities like?	¿cómo son las instalaciones?
how much is it per night?	¿cuánto cobran por (pasar la) noche?
where do we park the car?	¿dónde podemos aparcar, (esp *LAm*) estacionar?
we're looking for a campsite	estamos buscando un camping

At the hotel — Hoteles

I'd like a double/ single room with bath	quisiera una habitación individual/ doble con baño
we have a reservation in the name of Morris	tenemos una reserva a nombre de Morris
we'll be staying three nights, from Friday to Sunday	nos quedaremos tres noches, de viernes a domingo
how much does the room cost?	¿cuánto cuesta la habitación?
I'd like to see the room	quisiera ver la habitación
what time is breakfast?	¿a qué hora se sirve el desayuno?
can I leave this in your safe?	¿puedo dejar esto en la caja fuerte?
bed and breakfast	(lugar donde dan) alojamiento y desayuno
we'd like to stay another night	nos gustaría quedarnos una noche más
please call me at 7:30	¿me podría despertar a las 7:30, por favor?
are there any messages for me?	¿hay algún mensaje para mí?

Hostels — Albergues

could you tell me where the youth hostel is?	¿me podría indicar dónde está el albergue?
what time does the hostel close?	¿a qué hora cierra el albergue?
I'll be staying in a hostel	me alojaré en un albergue
the hostel we're staying in is great value	el albergue donde nos alojamos ofrece una buena relación calidad-precio
I know a really good hostel in Dublin	conozco un albergue estupendo en Dublín
I'd like to go backpacking in Australia	me gustaría irme a Australia con la mochila al hombro

Rooms to rent — Alquiler de habitaciones

I'm looking for a room with a reasonable rent	quiero alquilar, (*Mex*) rentar una habitación que tenga un precio razonable
I'd like to rent an apartment for a few weeks	me gustaría alquilar, (*Mex*) rentar un apartamento para unas cuantas semanas
where do I find out about rooms to rent?	¿dónde me puedo informar sobre alquileres, (*Mex*) rentas de habitaciones?
what's the weekly rent?	¿cuánto cuesta el alquiler, (*Mex*) la renta semanal?
I'm staying with friends at the moment	en este momento estoy alojado en casa de unos amigos
I rent an apartment on the outskirts of town	vivo en un apartamento alquilado, (*Mex*) rentado en las afueras
the room's fine – I'll take it	la habitación está muy bien, me la quedo
the deposit is one month's rent in advance	como depósito, se paga un mes de alquiler, (*Mex*) renta por adelantado

Shopping/Las compras

At the bank | En el banco

I'd like to change some money	quisiera cambiar dinero
I want to change some dollars into euros	quisiera cambiar dólares a euros
do you take Eurocheques?	¿aceptan Eurocheques?
what's the exchange rate today?	¿a cuánto está hoy el cambio?
I prefer traveller's cheques, (*Amer*) traveler's checks to cash	prefiero cheques de viaje que dinero en metálico, (*esp LAm*) en efectivo
I'd like to transfer some money from my account	quisiera hacer una transferencia desde mi cuenta corriente
I'll get some money from the cash machine	sacaré dinero del cajero (automático)
I'm with another bank	no soy cliente/-a de este banco

Finding the right shop | Dar con la tienda adecuada

where's the main shopping district?	¿dónde está la zona de tiendas?
where can I buy batteries/ postcards?	¿dónde puedo comprar unas pilas/ postales?
where's the nearest pharmacy/ bookshop?	¿dónde está la farmacia/librería más cercana?
is there a good food shop around here?	¿hay una buena tienda de comestibles por aquí?
what time do the shops open/close?	¿a qué hora abren/cierran las tiendas?
where did you get those?	¿dónde los/las ha comprado?
I'm looking for presents for my family	estoy buscando regalos para mi familia
we'll do our shopping on Saturday	(nosotros) haremos las compras el sábado
I love shopping	me encanta ir de compras

Are you being served? ¿Lo/La atienden?

how much does that cost?	¿cuánto cuesta?
can I try it on?	¿me lo puedo probar?
could you wrap it for me, please?	¿me lo envuelve, por favor?
can I pay by credit card/cheque, (*Amer*) check?	¿puedo pagar con tarjeta/cheque?
do you have this in another colour, (*Amer*) color?	¿tiene éste/-a en otro color?
could I have a bag, please?	¿me da una bolsa, por favor?
I'm just looking	sólo estoy mirando
I'll think about it	me lo voy a pensar
I'd like a receipt, please	¿me da el recibo, por favor?
I need a bigger/smaller size	necesito una talla más grande/más pequeña
I take a size 10/a medium	uso la talla 38/mediana
it doesn't suit me	no me queda bien
I'm sorry, I don't have any change/ anything smaller	perdone, pero no tengo cambio/ billetes más pequeños
that's all, thank you	nada más, gracias

Changing things Devoluciones

can I have a refund?	¿me podría devolver el dinero?
can you mend it for me?	¿me lo/la podrían arreglar?
can I speak to the manager?	quisiera hablar con el encargado/ la encargada
it doesn't work	no funciona
I'd like to change it, please	quisiera cambiarlo/-a, por favor
I bought this here yesterday	compré esto ayer

Currency Convertor Convertidor de divisas

€/$	£/$	£/$	€/$
0.25		0.25	
0.5		0.5	
0.75		0.75	
1		1	
1.5		1.5	
2		2	
3		3	
5		5	
10		10	
20		20	
30		30	
40		40	
50		50	
100		100	
200		200	
1000		1000	

Sports and leisure/Deportes y ocio

Keeping fit | Mantenerse en forma

where can we play tennis/squash?	¿dónde se puede jugar al tenis/ squash, (*LAm*) jugar tenis/squash?
where is the local sports centre, (*Amer*) center?	¿hay por aquí cerca un polideportivo?
what's the charge per day?	¿cuánto cobran (al día)?
is there a reduction for children/ a student discount?	¿hacen descuentos a niños/ estudiantes?
I'm looking for a swimming pool/ tennis court	estoy buscando una piscina, (*Mex*) alberca/un club de tenis
are there any yoga/pilates classes here?	¿hay clases de yoga/pilates?
I want to do aerobics	quiero hacer aerobic
is there a hotel gym?	¿hay gimnasio en este hotel?
you have to be a member	(para entrar) hace falta ser socio
I would like to go fishing/riding	me gustaría ir a pescar/montar a caballo
I love swimming	me encanta nadar

Watching sport | Ver espectáculos deportivos

is there a match, (*Amer*) game on Saturday?	¿hay un partido el sábado?
which teams are playing?	¿quién está jugando?
where can I get tickets?	¿dónde se compran las entradas?
I'd like to see a match	me gustaría ver un partido
my favourite, (*Amer*) favorite team is...	mi equipo favorito es el...
let's watch the match, (*Amer*) game on TV	veamos el partido por la tele
who's winning?	¿quién gana?
the reds are winning 3-1	los rojos van ganando 3 a 1

SPORTS AND PASTIMES

American football/football	fútbol americano
badminton	bádminton
basketball	baloncesto, (*LAm*) básquetbol
cycling	ciclismo
football/soccer	fútbol
golf	golf
hiking	montañismo
horse-riding	equitación
paddle tennis	pádel, (*LAm*) paddle
pelota	pelota
roller-blading	patinaje
running	correr
sailing	vela
surfing	surf
swimming	natación

DEPORTES Y PASATIEMPOS

bádminton	badminton
baloncesto, (*LAm*) básquetbol	basketball
ciclismo	cycling
correr	running
equitación	horse-riding
fútbol americano	American football/football
fútbol	football/soccer
golf	golf
montañismo	hiking
natación	swimming
pádel, (*LAm*) paddle	paddle tennis
patinaje	roller-blading
pelota	pelota
surf	surfing
vela	sailing

Movies/theatres/clubs — Cine/Teatro/Discotecas

what's on?	¿qué ponen, (*esp LAm*) dan (en el cine/teatro)?
when does the box office open/ close?	¿a qué hora abren/cierran la taquilla, (*LAm*) boletería?
what time does the concert/ performance start?	¿a qué hora empieza el concierto/ la representación?
when does it finish?	¿a qué hora termina?
are there any seats left for tonight?	¿quedan entradas para esta noche?
how much are the tickets?	¿cuánto cuestan las entradas?
where can I get a programme, (*Amer*) program?	¿dónde puedo conseguir un programa?
I want to book tickets for tonight's performance	quiero reservar entradas para esta noche
I'll book seats in the circle	reservaré entradas de platea
I'd rather have seats in the stalls, (*Amer*) orchestra	prefiero el patio de butacas
somewhere in the middle, but not too far back	que sean centrales, pero no demasiado atrás
four, please	cuatro, por favor
for Saturday	para el sábado
we'd like to go to a club	nos gustaría ir a una discoteca

Hobbies — Aficiones y hobbies

what do you do at, (*Amer*) on weekends?	¿qué hace los fines de semana?
I like reading/listening to music/ going out	me gusta leer/escuchar música/ salir
do you like watching TV/ shopping/travelling?	¿te gusta ver la tele/ir de compras/ viajar?
I read a lot	leo mucho
I collect musical instruments	colecciono instrumentos musicales

Good timing/A tiempo

Telling the time / La hora

what time is it?	¿qué hora es?
it's 2 o'clock	son las 2
at about 8 o'clock	hacia las 8
from 10 o'clock onwards	a partir de las 10
at 5 o'clock in the morning/ afternoon	a las cinco de la mañana/tarde
it's five past/quarter past/half past one	es la una y cinco/y cuarto/y media
it's twenty-five to/quarter to one	es la una menos veinticinco/menos cuarto/(*LAm*) son veinticinco/un cuarto para la una
a quarter/three quarters of an hour	un cuarto/tres cuartos de hora

Days and dates / Días y fechas

Sunday, Monday, Tuesday, Wednesday, Thursday, Friday, Saturday	domingo, lunes, martes, miércoles, jueves, viernes, sábado
January, February, March, April, May, June, July, August, September, October, November, December	enero, febrero, marzo, abril, mayo, junio, julio, agosto, septiembre, octubre, noviembre, diciembre
what's the date?	¿qué fecha es hoy?
it's the second of June	(es el) dos de junio
we meet up every Monday	nos vemos todos los lunes
we're going away in August	nos vamos fuera en agosto
on November 8th	el 8 de noviembre

Public holidays and special days / Fiestas y celebraciones especiales

Public holidays and special days	Fiestas y celebraciones especiales
Bank holiday	día festivo en el Reino Unido
Bank holiday Monday	lunes de puente
New Year's Day (Jan 1)	Año Nuevo (1 de enero)
Epiphany (Jan 6)	Reyes (6 de enero)
St Valentine's Day (Feb 14)	San Valentín (14 de febrero)
Shrove Tuesday/Pancake Day	Martes de Carnaval
Ash Wednesday	Miércoles de Ceniza
Holy Week	Semana Santa
Good Friday	Viernes Santo
Easter	Pascua (de Resurrección)
Easter Monday	lunes de Pascua
May Day (May 1)	1 de mayo, día del trabajador
Independence Day	4 de julio, fiesta de la independencia de los EEUU
Thanksgiving	día de Acción de Gracias, fiesta típica de EEUU y Canadá
Halloween (Oct 31)	Halloween (fiesta de fantasmas y brujas que se celebra la víspera de Todos los Santos)
All Saints' Day	Todos los Santos
Guy Fawkes Day/ Bonfire Night (Nov 5)	fiesta de Guy Fawkes (5 de noviembre: se celebra que el católico Guy Fawkes fracasó en su intento de incendiar el parlamento)
Remembrance Sunday	fiesta en recuerdo a los caídos en las dos guerras mundiales
St Nicholas' Day (Dec 6)	San Nicolás (6 de diciembre)
Christmas Eve (Dec 24)	Nochebuena (24 de diciembre)
Christmas Day (Dec 25)	Navidad (25 de diciembre)
Boxing Day (Dec 26)	día de fiesta que sigue al día de Navidad
New Year's Eve (Dec 31)	Nochevieja (31 de diciembre)

Health and Beauty/Salud y belleza

At the doctor's — En el médico

can I see a doctor?	¿podría verme un médico?
I don't feel well	no me encuentro, (*LAm*) no me siento bien
it hurts here	me duele aquí
I have a migraine/stomach ache	tengo migrañas/dolor de tripa, (*LAm*) de estómago
are there any side effects?	¿tiene efectos secundarios?
I have a sore ankle/wrist/knee	me he hecho daño, (*LAm*) me hice daño en el tobillo/la muñeca/ la rodilla

YOU WILL HEAR:	OIRÁS:
necesita pedir cita (*or* pedir hora)	you need to make an appointment
siéntese, por favor	please take a seat
¿tiene una Tarjeta Sanitaria Europea (TSE)?	do you have a European Health Insurance Card (EHIC)?
¿tiene seguro médico?	do you have Health Insurance?
tengo que tomarle la tensión, (*LAm*) presión	I need to take your blood pressure

MORE USEFUL WORDS:	MÁS PALABRAS ÚTILES:
nurse	enfermera/-o
antibiotics	antibióticos
medicine	medicina
infection	infección
treatment	tratamiento
rest	reposo

At the pharmacy | En la farmacia

can I have some painkillers?	¿me puede dar un analgésico?
I have asthma/hay fever/eczema	tengo asma/alergia al polen/eccema
I've been stung by a wasp/bee	me ha picado una avispa/abeja
I've got a cold/cough/the flu	tengo catarro/tos/gripe
I need something for diarrhoea/ stomachache	necesito algo para la diarrea/ el dolor de estómago
I'm pregnant	estoy embarazada

YOU WILL HEAR:	OIRÁS:
¿lo ha tomado alguna vez?/ ¿ha tomado alguna vez este medicamento?	have you taken this/these before?/ have you taken this medicine before?
su receta estará lista en diez minutos	your prescription will be ready in ten minutes
tómese con las comidas/ tres veces al día	take at mealtimes/ three times a day
¿tiene alguna alergia?	are you allergic to anything?
¿está tomando otros medicamentos?	are you taking any other medication?

MORE USEFUL WORDS:	MÁS PALABRAS ÚTILES:
plasters, (*Amer*) Band-Aid™	tiritas, (*LAm*) curitas
insect repellent	repelente contra insectos
contraception	anticonceptivos
sun cream	crema de sol
aftersun	loción aftersun, (*LAm*) para después de asolearse
dosage	dosis

At the hairdresser's/salon — En la peluquería

I'd like a cut and blow dry	¿me puede cortar y secar?
just a trim please	corte nada más que las puntas, por favor
a grade 3 back and sides	lo quiero al 3 por detrás y por los lados
I'd like my hair washed first please	lavar y cortar, por favor
can I have a manicure/pedicure/ facial?	¿hacen la manicura/la pedicura/ tratamiento facial?
how much is a head/back massage?	¿cuánto cuesta el masaje de cabeza/espalda?
can I see a price list?	¿puedo ver la lista de precios?
do you offer reflexology/ aromatherapy treatments?	¿hacen reflexología/aromaterapia?

YOU WILL HEAR:	OIRÁS:
¿quiere que le seque el pelo?	would you like your hair blow-dried?
¿dónde quiere la raya, (*Col*, *Ven*) la carrera, (*Chi*) la partidura?	where is your parting, (*Amer*) part?
¿quiere que le corte a (*LAm*) en capas?	would you like your hair layered?

MORE USEFUL WORDS:	MÁS PALABRAS ÚTILES:
dry/greasy/fine/flyaway/frizzy	seco/graso/fino/lacio/crespo
highlights	mechas, (*Mex*) luces, (*Chi*, *Mex*) rayitos, (*Col*) mechones, (*RPl*) claritos
extensions	extensiones
sunbed	solarium, (*LAm also*) cama solar
leg/arm/bikini wax	depilación a la cera en las piernas/ los brazos/las ingles

At the dentist's | En el dentista

I have toothache	me duele un diente
I'd like an emergency appointment	necesito una cita de urgencia
I have cracked a tooth	se me ha roto, (*LAm*) se me rompió un diente
my gums are bleeding	me sangran las encías

YOU WILL HEAR:	OIRÁS:
abra la boca	open your mouth
necesita un empaste, (*Chi*, *Mex*) una tapadura, (*RPl*) una emplomadura, (*Col*) una calza	you need a filling
tenemos que hacer una radiografía	we need to take an X-ray
enjuáguese, por favor	please rinse

MORE USEFUL WORDS:	MÁS PALABRAS ÚTILES:
anaesthetic	anestesia
root canal treatment	endodoncia
injection	inyección
floss	hilo dental

DID YOU KNOW...?	¿SABÍAS QUE...?
Spanish hairdressers will normally wash your hair before your haircut. If you don't want them to do so, you should tell them beforehand.	Antiguamente, las peluquerías se anunciaban con un poste pintado con bandas rojas y blancas en espiral.

Weights & measures/Pesos y medidas

Length/Longitud

inches/pulgadas	0.39	3.9	7.8	11.7	15.6	19.7	39
cm/centímetros	1	10	20	30	40	50	100

Distance/Distancia

miles/millas	0.62	6.2	12.4	18.6	24.9	31	62
km/km	1	10	20	30	40	50	100

Weight/Peso

pounds/libras	2.2	22	44	66	88	110	220
kg/kilos	1	10	20	30	40	50	100

Capacity/Capacidad

gallons/galones	0.22	2.2	4.4	6.6	8.8	11	22
litres/litros	1	10	20	30	40	50	100

Temperature/Temperatura

°C	0	5	10	15	20	25	30	37	38	40
°F	32	41	50	59	68	77	86	98.4	100	104

Clothing and shoe sizes/Tallas de ropa y calzado

Women's clothing sizes/Ropa de señora

UK	8	10	12	14	16	18
US	6	8	10	12	14	16
Continent	36	38	40	42	44	46

Men's clothing sizes/Ropa de caballero

UK/US	36	38	40	42	44	46
Continent	46	48	50	52	54	56

Men's and women's shoes/Calzado de señora y caballero

UK women	4	5	6	7	7.5	8			
UK men			6	7	8	9	10	11	
US	6.5	7.5	8.5	9.5	10.5	11.5	12.5	13.5	14.5
Continent	37	38	39	40	41	42	43	44	45

Aa

a /ə/, *stressed form* /eɪ/

before vowel sound or silent 'h' **an**

indefinite article

····➤un (*m*), una (*f*). **a problem** un problema. **an apple** una manzana. **have you got a pencil?** ¿tienes un lápiz?

! Feminine singular nouns beginning with stressed or accented *a* or *ha* take the article *un* instead of *una*, e.g. *un águila, un hada*

····➤(*when talking about prices and quantities*) por. **30 miles an hour** 30 millas por hora. **twice a week** dos veces por semana, dos veces a la semana

! There are many cases in which **a** is not translated, such as when talking about people's professions, in exclamations, etc: **she's a lawyer** *es abogada.* **what a beautiful day!** *¡qué día más precioso!.* **have you got a car?** *¿tienes coche?* **half a cup** *media taza*

A & E /eɪənd'i:/ *n* urgencias *fpl*

aback /ə'bæk/ *adv.* **be taken ~** quedar desconcertado

abandon /ə'bændən/ *vt* abandonar. ●*n* abandono *m*, desenfado *m*. **~ed** *a* abandonado

abashed /ə'bæʃt/ *adj* confuso

abate /ə'beɪt/ *vi* disminuir; (storm etc) calmarse

abattoir /'æbətwɑ:(r)/ *n* matadero *m*

abbess /'æbɪs/ *n* abadesa *f*

abbey /'æbɪ/ *n* abadía *f*

abbot /'æbət/ *n* abad *m*

abbreviat|e /ə'bri:vɪeɪt/ *vt* abreviar. **~ion** /-'eɪʃn/ *n* abreviatura *f*; (*act*) abreviación *f*

abdicat|e /'æbdɪkeɪt/ *vt/i* abdicar. **~ion** /-'eɪʃn/ *n* abdicación *f*

abdom|en /'æbdəmən/ *n* abdomen *m*. **~inal** /-'dɒmɪnl/ *adj* abdominal

abduct /æb'dʌkt/ *vt* secuestrar. **~ion** /-ʃn/ *n* secuestro *m*

abhor /əb'hɔ:(r)/ *vt* (*pt* **abhorred**) aborrecer. **~rence** /-'hɒrəns/ *n* aborrecimiento *m*. **~rent** /-'hɒrənt/ *adj* aborrecible

abide /ə'baɪd/ *vt* (*pt* **abided**) soportar. ●*vi* (*old use, pt* **abode**) morar. □ **~ by** *vt* atenerse a; cumplir (promise)

ability /ə'bɪlətɪ/ *n* capacidad *f*; (*cleverness*) habilidad *f*

abject /'æbdʒekt/ *adj* (*wretched*) miserable

ablaze /ə'bleɪz/ *adj* en llamas

able /'eɪbl/ *adj* (**-er**, **-est**) capaz. **be ~** poder; (*know how to*) saber. **~-bodied** /-'bɒdɪd/ *adj* sano, no discapacitado

ably /'eɪblɪ/ *adv* hábilmente

abnormal /æb'nɔ:ml/ *adj* anormal. **~ity** /-'mælətɪ/ *n* anormalidad *f*

aboard /əˈbɔːd/ *adv* a bordo. ● *prep* a bordo de

abode /əˈbəʊd/ *see* ABIDE. ● *n* (*old use*) domicilio *m*

aboli|sh /əˈbɒlɪʃ/ *vt* abolir. **~tion** /æbəˈlɪʃn/ *n* abolición *f*

abominable /əˈbɒmɪnəbl/ *adj* abominable

aborigin|al /æbəˈrɪdʒənl/ *adj & n* aborigen (*m & f*), indígena (*m & f*). **~es** /-iːz/ *npl* aborígenes *mpl*

abort /əˈbɔːt/ *vt* hacer abortar. **~ion** /-ʃn/ *n* aborto *m* provocado; (*fig*) aborto *m*. **have an ~ion** hacerse un aborto. **~ive** *adj* fracasado

abound /əˈbaʊnd/ *vi* abundar (**in** en)

about /əˈbaʊt/ *adv* (*approximately*) alrededor de; (*here and there*) por todas partes; (*in existence*) por aquí. **~ here** por aquí. **be ~ to** estar a punto de. ● *prep* sobre; (*around*) alrededor de; (*somewhere in*) en. **talk ~** hablar de. **~-face**, **~-turn** *n* (*fig*) cambio *m* rotundo

above /əˈbʌv/ *adv* arriba. ● *prep* encima de; (*more than*) más de. **~ all** sobre todo. **~ board** *adj* legítimo. ● *adv* abiertamente. **~-mentioned** *adj* susodicho

abrasi|on /əˈbreɪʒn/ *n* abrasión *f*. **~ve** /-sɪv/ *adj* abrasivo

abreast /əˈbrest/ *adv*. **march four ~** marchar en columna de cuatro en fondo. **keep ~ of** mantenerse al corriente de

abroad /əˈbrɔːd/ *adv* (*be*) en el extranjero; (*go*) al extranjero; (*far and wide*) por todas partes

abrupt /əˈbrʌpt/ *adj* brusco. **~ly** *adv* (*suddenly*) repentinamente; (*curtly*) bruscamente

abscess /ˈæbsɪs/ *n* absceso *m*

abscond /əbˈskɒnd/ *vi* fugarse

absen|ce /ˈæbsəns/ *n* ausencia *f*; (*lack*) falta *f*. **~t** /ˈæbsənt/ *adj* ausente. **~t-minded** /-ˈmaɪndɪd/ *adj* distraído. **~t-mindedness** *n* distracción *f*, despiste *m*. **~tee** /-ˈtiː/ *n* ausente *m & f*. **~teeism** *n* absentismo *m*, ausentismo *m* (*LAm*)

absolute /ˈæbsəluːt/ *adj* absoluto. **~ly** *adv* absolutamente

absolve /əbˈzɒlv/ *vt* (*from sin*) absolver; (*from obligation*) liberar

absor|b /əbˈzɔːb/ *vt* absorber. **~bent** /-bent/ *adj* absorbente. **~bent cotton** *n* (*Amer*) algodón *m* hidrófilo. **~ption** /əbˈzɔːpʃən/ *n* absorción *f*

abstain /əbˈsteɪn/ *vi* abstenerse (**from** de)

abstemious /əbˈstiːmɪəs/ *adj* abstemio

abstention /əbˈstenʃn/ *n* abstención *f*

abstract /ˈæbstrækt/ *adj* abstracto. ● *n* (*summary*) resumen *m*; (*painting*) cuadro *m* abstracto. ● /əbˈstrækt/ *vt* extraer; (*summarize*) resumir. **~ion** /-ʃn/ *n* abstracción *f*

absurd /əbˈsɜːd/ *adj* absurdo. **~ity** *n* absurdo *m*, disparate *m*

abundan|ce /əˈbʌndəns/ *n* abundancia *f*. **~t** *adj* abundante

abus|e /əˈbjuːz/ *vt* (*misuse*) abusar de; (*ill-treat*) maltratar; (*insult*) insultar. ● /əˈbjuːs/ *n* abuso *m*; (*insults*) insultos *mpl*. **~ive** /əˈbjuːsɪv/ *adj* injurioso

abysmal /əˈbɪzməl/ *adj* [I] pésimo

abyss /əˈbɪs/ *n* abismo *m*

academic /ækəˈdemɪk/ *adj* académico; (*pej*) teórico. ● *n* universitario *m*, catedrático *m*

academy /əˈkædəmɪ/ *n* academia *f*.

accelerat|e /əkˈseləreɪt/ *vt* acelerar. ● *vi* acelerar; (*Auto*) apretar el acelerador. **~ion** /-ˈreɪʃn/ *n* aceleración *f*. **~or** *n* acelerador *m*

accent /ˈæksənt/ *n* acento *m*

accept /əkˈsept/ *vt* aceptar. **~able** *adj* aceptable. **~ance** *n* aceptación *f*; (*approval*) aprobación *f*

access /ˈækses/ *n* acceso *m*. **~ible** /əkˈsesəbl/ *adj* accesible; (person) tratable

accession /ækˈseʃn/ *n* (*to power, throne etc*) ascenso *m*; (*thing added*) adquisición *f*

accessory /əkˈsesərɪ/ *adj* accesorio. ● *n* accesorio *m*, complemento *m*; (*Jurid*) cómplice *m & f*

accident /ˈæksɪdənt/ *n* accidente *m*; (*chance*) casualidad *f*. **by ~** sin querer; (*by chance*) por casualidad. **~al** /-ˈdentl/ *adj* accidental, fortuito. **~ally** /-ˈdentəlɪ/ *adv* sin querer; (*by chance*) por casualidad. **~-prone** *adj* propenso a los accidentes

acclaim /əˈkleɪm/ *vt* aclamar. ● *n* aclamación *f*

accolade /ˈækəleɪd/ *n* (*praise*) encomio *m*

accommodat|e /əˈkɒmədeɪt/ *vt* (*give hospitality to*) alojar; (*adapt*) acomodar; (*oblige*) complacer. **~ing** *adj* complaciente. **~ion** /-ˈdeɪʃn/ *n*, **~ions** *npl* (*Amer*) alojamiento *m*

accompan|iment /əˈkʌmpənɪmənt/ *n* acompañamiento *m*. **~ist** *n* acompañante *m & f*. **~y** /əˈkʌmpənɪ/ *vt* acompañar

accomplice /əˈkʌmplɪs/ *n* cómplice *m & f*

accomplish /əˈkʌmplɪʃ/ *vt* (*complete*) acabar; (*achieve*) realizar; (*carry out*) llevar a cabo. **~ed** *adj* consumado. **~ment** *n* realización *f*; (*ability*) talento *m*; (*thing achieved*) triunfo *m*, logro *m*

accord /əˈkɔːd/ *vi* concordar. ● *vt* conceder. ● *n* acuerdo *m*; (*harmony*) armonía *f*. **of one's own ~** espontáneamente. **~ance** *n*. **in ~ance with** de acuerdo con. **~ing** *adv*. **~ing to** según. **~ingly** *adv* en conformidad; (*therefore*) por consiguiente

accordion /əˈkɔːdɪən/ *n* acordeón *m*

accost /əˈkɒst/ *vt* abordar

account /əˈkaʊnt/ *n* cuenta *f*; (*description*) relato *m*. **~s** *npl* (*in business*) contabilidad *f*. **on ~ of** a causa de. **on no ~** de ninguna manera. **on this ~** por eso. **take into ~** tener en cuenta. ● *vt* considerar. □ **~ for** *vt* dar cuenta de, explicar

accountan|cy /əˈkaʊntənsɪ/ *n* contabilidad *f*. **~t** *n* contable *m & f*, contador *m* (*LAm*)

accumulat|e /əˈkjuːmjʊleɪt/ *vt* acumular. ● *vi* acumularse. **~ion** /-ˈleɪʃn/ *n* acumulación *f*

accura|cy /ˈækjərəsɪ/ *n* exactitud *f*, precisión *f*. **~te** /-ət/ *adj* exacto, preciso

accus|ation /ækjuːˈzeɪʃn/ *n* acusación *f*. **~e** /əˈkjuːz/ *vt* acusar

accustom /əˈkʌstəm/ *vt* acostumbrar. **~ed** *adj*. **be ~ed (to)** estar acostumbrado (a). **get ~ed (to)** acostumbrarse (a)

ace /eɪs/ *n* as *m*

ache /eɪk/ *n* dolor *m*. ● *vi* doler. **my leg ~s** me duele la pierna

achieve /əˈtʃiːv/ *vt* realizar; lograr

(success). **~ment** *n* realización *f*; (*feat*) proeza *f*; (*thing achieved*) logro *m*

acid /ˈæsɪd/ *adj & n* ácido (*m*). **~ic** *adj* /əˈsɪdɪk/ *adj* ácido. **~ rain** *n* lluvia *f* ácida

acknowledge /əkˈnɒlɪdʒ/ *vt* reconocer. **~ receipt of** acusar recibo de. **~ment** *n* reconocimiento *m*; (*Com*) acuse *m* de recibo

acne /ˈæknɪ/ *n* acné *m*

acorn /ˈeɪkɔːn/ *n* bellota *f*

acoustic /əˈkuːstɪk/ *adj* acústico. **~s** *npl* acústica *f*

acquaint /əˈkweɪnt/ *vt*. **~ s.o. with** poner a uno al corriente de. **be ~ed with** conocer (person); saber (fact). **~ance** *n* conocimiento *m*; (*person*) conocido *m*

acquiesce /ækwɪˈes/ *vi* consentir (**in** en). **~nce** *n* aquiescencia *f*, consentimiento *m*

acqui|re /əˈkwaɪə(r)/ *vt* adquirir; aprender (language). **~re a taste for** tomar gusto a. **~sition** /ækwɪˈzɪʃn/ *n* adquisición *f*. **~sitive** /əˈkwɪzətɪv/ *adj* codicioso

acquit /əˈkwɪt/ *vt* (*pt* **acquitted**) absolver. **~tal** *n* absolución *f*

acre /ˈeɪkə(r)/ *n* acre *m*

acrid /ˈækrɪd/ *adj* acre

acrimonious /ækrɪˈməʊnɪəs/ *adj* cáustico, mordaz

acrobat /ˈækrəbæt/ *n* acróbata *m & f*. **~ic** /-ˈbætɪk/ *adj* acrobático. **~ics** *npl* acrobacia *f*

acronym /ˈækrənɪm/ *n* acrónimo *m*, siglas *fpl*

across /əˈkrɒs/ *adv & prep* (*side to side*) de un lado al otro; (*on other side*) al otro lado de; (*crosswise*) a través. **it is 20 metres ~** tiene 20 metros de ancho. **go** *or* **walk ~** atravesar, cruzar

act /ækt/ *n* acto *m*; (*action*) acción *f*; (*in variety show*) número *m*; (*decree*) decreto *m*. ● *vt* hacer (part, role). ● *vi* actuar; (*pretend*) fingir. **~ as** actuar de; (object) servir de. **~ for** representar. **~ing** *adj* interino. ● *n* (*of play*) representación *f*; (*by actor*) interpretación *f*; (*profession*) profesión *f* de actor

action /ˈækʃn/ *n* acción *f*; (*Jurid*) demanda *f*; (*plot*) argumento *m*. **out of ~** (*on sign*) no funciona. **put out of ~** inutilizar. **take ~** tomar medidas **~ replay** *n* repetición *f* de la jugada

activate /ˈæktɪveɪt/ *vt* activar

activ|e /ˈæktɪv/ *adj* activo; (*energetic*) lleno de energía; (volcano) en actividad. **~ist** *n* activista *m & f*. **~ity** /-ˈtɪvətɪ/ *n* actividad *f*

act|or /ˈæktə(r)/ *n* actor *m*. **~ress** /-trɪs/ *n* actriz *f*

actual /ˈæktʃʊəl/ *adj* verdadero. **~ly** *adv* en realidad, efectivamente; (*even*) incluso

acute /əˈkjuːt/ *adj* agudo. **~ly** *adv* agudamente

ad /æd/ *n* ⊞ anuncio *m*, aviso *m* (*LAm*)

AD /eɪˈdiː/ *abbr* (= **Anno Domini**) d. de J.C.

Adam's apple /ædəmzˈæpl/ *n* nuez *f* (de Adán)

adapt /əˈdæpt/ *vt* adaptar. ● *vi* adaptarse. **~ability** /-əˈbɪlətɪ/ *n* adaptabilidad *f*. **~able** /-əbl/ *adj* adaptable. **~ation** /ædæpˈteɪʃn/ *n* adaptación *f*; (*of book etc*) versión *f*. **~or** /əˈdæptə(r)/ *n* (*Elec, with several sockets*) enchufe *m* múltiple; (*Elec, for different sockets*) adaptador *m*

add /æd/ *vt* añadir. ● *vi* sumar. □ **~ up** *vt* sumar; (*fig*) tener sentido. **~**

up to equivaler a
adder /ˈædə(r)/ *n* víbora *f*
addict /ˈædɪkt/ *n* adicto *m*; (*fig*) entusiasta *m & f*. **~ed** /əˈdɪktɪd/ *adj*. **~ed to** adicto a; (*fig*) fanático de. **~ion** /əˈdɪkʃn/ *n* (*Med*) dependencia *f*; (*fig*) afición *f*. **~ive** /əˈdɪktɪv/ *adj* que crea adicción; (*fig*) que crea hábito
addition /əˈdɪʃn/ *n* suma *f*. **in ~** además. **~al** *adj* suplementario
address /əˈdres/ *n* dirección *f*; (*on form*) domicilio *m*; (*speech*) discurso *m*. ●*vt* poner la dirección en; (*speak to*) dirigirse a. **~ book** *n* libreta *f* de direcciones. **~ee** /ædreˈsiː/ *n* destinatario *m*
adept /ˈædept/ *adj & n* experto (*m*)
adequa|cy /ˈædɪkwəsɪ/ *n* suficiencia *f*. **~te** /-ət/ *adj* suficiente, adecuado. **~tely** *adv* suficientemente, adecuadamente
adhere /ədˈhɪə(r)/ *vi* adherirse (**to** a); observar (rule). **~nce** /-rəns/ *n* adhesión *f*; (*to rules*) observancia *f*
adhesi|on /ədˈhiːʒn/ *n* adherencia *f*. **~ve** /-sɪv/ *adj & n* adhesivo (*m*)
adjacent /əˈdʒeɪsnt/ *adj* contiguo
adjective /ˈædʒɪktɪv/ *n* adjetivo *m*
adjourn /əˈdʒɜːn/ *vt* aplazar; suspender (meeting etc). ●*vi* suspenderse
adjust /əˈdʒʌst/ *vt* ajustar (machine); (*arrange*) arreglar. ●*vi*. **~ (to)** adaptarse (a). **~able** *adj* ajustable. **~ment** *n* adaptación *f*; (*Tec*) ajuste *m*
administer /ədˈmɪnɪstə(r)/ *vt* administrar
administrat|ion /ədmɪnɪˈstreɪʃn/ *n* administración *f*. **~ive** /ədˈmɪnɪstrətɪv/ *adj* administrativo. **~or** /ədˈmɪnɪstreɪtə(r)/ *n* administrador *m*
admirable /ˈædmərəbl/ *adj* admirable
admiral /ˈædmərəl/ *n* almirante *m*
admir|ation /ædməˈreɪʃn/ *n* admiración *f*. **~e** /ədˈmaɪə(r)/ *vt* admirar. **~er** /ədˈmaɪərə(r)/ *n* admirador *m*
admission /ədˈmɪʃn/ *n* admisión *f*; (*entry*) entrada *f*
admit /ədˈmɪt/ *vt* (*pt* **admitted**) dejar entrar; (*acknowledge*) admitir, reconocer. **~ to** confesar. **be ~ted** (*to hospital etc*) ingresar. **~tance** *n* entrada *f*. **~tedly** *adv* es verdad que
admonish /ədˈmɒnɪʃ/ *vt* reprender; (*advise*) aconsejar
ado /əˈduː/ *n* alboroto m; (*trouble*) dificultad *f*. **without more** *or* **further ~** en seguida, sin más
adolescen|ce /ædəˈlesns/ *n* adolescencia *f*. **~t** *adj & n* adolescente (*m & f*)
adopt /əˈdɒpt/ *vt* adoptar. **~ed** *adj* (child) adoptivo. **~ion** /-ʃn/ *n* adopción *f*
ador|able /əˈdɔːrəbl/ *adj* adorable. **~ation** /ædəˈreɪʃn/ *n* adoración *f*. **~e** /əˈdɔː(r)/ *vt* adorar
adorn /əˈdɔːn/ *vt* adornar. **~ment** *n* adorno *m*
adrift /əˈdrɪft/ *adj & adv* a la deriva
adult /ˈædʌlt/ *adj & n* adulto (*m*)
adulter|er /əˈdʌltərə(r)/ *n* adúltero *m*. **~ess** /-ɪs/ *n* adúltera *f*. **~y** *n* adulterio *m*
advance /ədˈvɑːns/ *vt* adelantar. ●*vi* adelantarse. ●*n* adelanto *m*. **in ~** con anticipación, por adelantado. **~d** *adj* avanzado; (studies) superior
advantage /ədˈvɑːntɪdʒ/ *n* ventaja *f*. **take ~ of** aprovecharse de; abusar de (person). **~ous** /ædvən

a

'teɪdʒəs/ *adj* ventajoso

advent /'ædvənt/ *n* venida *f*. **A~** *n* adviento *m*

adventur|e /əd'ventʃə(r)/ *n* aventura *f*. **~er** *n* aventurero *m*. **~ous** *adj* (person) aventurero; (thing) arriesgado; (*fig, bold*) audaz

adverb /'ædvɜːb/ *n* adverbio *m*

adversary /'ædvəsərɪ/ *n* adversario *m*

advers|e /'ædvɜːs/ *adj* adverso, contrario, desfavorable. **~ity** /əd'vɜːsətɪ/ *n* infortunio *m*

advert /'ædvɜːt/ *n* ⓘ anuncio *m*, aviso *m* (*LAm*). **~ise** /'ædvətaɪz/ *vt* anunciar. ● *vi* hacer publicidad; (*seek, sell*) poner un anuncio. **~isement** /əd'vɜːtɪsmənt/ *n* anuncio *m*, aviso *m* (*LAm*). **~iser** /'ædvətaɪzə(r)/ *n* anunciante *m & f*

advice /əd'vaɪs/ *n* consejo *m*; (*report*) informe *m*

advis|able /əd'vaɪzəbl/ *adj* aconsejable. **~e** /əd'vaɪz/ *vt* aconsejar; (*inform*) avisar. **~e against** aconsejar en contra de. **~er** *n* consejero *m*; (*consultant*) asesor *m*. **~ory** *adj* consultivo

advocate /'ædvəkət/ *n* defensor *m*; (*Jurid*) abogado *m*. ● /'ædvəkeɪt/ *vt* recomendar

aerial /'eərɪəl/ *adj* aéreo. ● *n* antena *f*

aerobics /eə'rəʊbɪks/ *npl* aeróbica *f*

aerodrome /'eərədrəʊm/ *n* aeródromo *m*

aerodynamic /eərəʊdaɪ'næmɪk/ *adj* aerodinámico

aeroplane /'eərəpleɪn/ *n* avión *m*

aerosol /'eərəsɒl/ *n* aerosol *m*

aesthetic /iːs'θetɪk/ *adj* estético

afar /ə'fɑː(r)/ *adv* lejos

affable /'æfəbl/ *adj* afable

affair /ə'feə(r)/ *n* asunto *m*. **(love) ~** aventura *f*, amorío *m*. **~s** *npl* (*business*) negocios *mpl*

affect /ə'fekt/ *vt* afectar; (*pretend*) fingir. **~ation** /æfek'teɪʃn/ *n* afectación *f*. **~ed** *adj* afectado, amanerado

affection /ə'fekʃn/ *n* cariño *m*. **~ate** /-ət/ *adj* cariñoso

affiliate /ə'fɪlɪeɪt/ *vt* afiliar

affirm /ə'fɜːm/ *vt* afirmar. **~ative** /-ətɪv/ *adj* afirmativo. ● *n* respuesta *f* afirmativa

afflict /ə'flɪkt/ *vt* afligir. **~ion** /-ʃn/ *n* aflicción *f*, pena *f*

affluen|ce /'æflʊəns/ *n* riqueza *f*. **~t** *adj* rico.

afford /ə'fɔːd/ *vt* permitirse; (*provide*) dar. **he can't ~ a car** no le alcanza el dinero para comprar un coche

affront /ə'frʌnt/ *n* afrenta *f*, ofensa *f*. ● *vt* afrentar, ofender

afield /ə'fiːld/ *adv*. **far ~** muy lejos

afloat /ə'fləʊt/ *adv* a flote

afraid /ə'freɪd/ *adj*. **be ~** tener miedo (**of** a); (*be sorry*) sentir, lamentar

afresh /ə'freʃ/ *adv* de nuevo

Africa /'æfrɪkə/ *n* África *f*. **~n** *adj & n* africano (*m*). **~n-American** *adj & n* norteamericano (*m*) de origen africano

after /'ɑːftə(r)/ *adv* después; (*behind*) detrás. ● *prep* después de; (*behind*) detrás de. **it's twenty ~ four** (*Amer*) son las cuatro y veinte. **be ~** (*seek*) andar en busca de. ● *conj* después de que. ● *adj* posterior. **~-effect** *n* consecuencia *f*, efecto *m* secundario. **~math** /'ɑːftəmæθ/ *n* secuelas *fpl*. **~noon** /-'nuːn/ *n* tarde *f*. **~shave** *n* loción *f* para después de afeitarse. **~thought** *n* ocurrencia *f* tardía. **~wards** /-wədz/ *adv* después

again /ə'gen/ *adv* otra vez; (*besides*) además. **do ~** volver a hacer, hacer otra vez. **~ and ~** una y otra vez

against /ə'genst/ *prep* contra; (*in opposition to*) en contra de, contra

age /eɪdʒ/ *n* edad *f*. **at four years of ~** a los cuatro años. **under ~** menor de edad. **~s** *npl* ⓘ siglos *mpl*. ● *vt/i* (*pres p* **ageing**) envejecer. **~d** /'eɪdʒd/ *adj* de ... años. **~d 10** de 10 años. **~d** /'eɪdʒɪd/ *adj* viejo, anciano

agency /'eɪdʒənsɪ/ *n* agencia *f*; (*department*) organismo *m*

agenda /ə'dʒendə/ *n* orden *m* del día

agent /'eɪdʒənt/ *n* agente *m & f*; (*representative*) representante *m & f*

aggravat|e /'ægrəveɪt/ *vt* agravar; (*fam, irritate*) irritar. **~ion** /-'veɪʃn/ *n* agravación *f*; (*fam, irritation*) irritación *f*

aggress|ion /ə'greʃn/ *n* agresión *f*. **~ive** *adj* agresivo. **~iveness** *n* agresividad *f*. **~or** *n* agresor *m*

aggrieved /ə'gri:vd/ *adj* apenado, ofendido

aghast /ə'gɑ:st/ *adj* horrorizado

agil|e /'ædʒaɪl/ *adj* ágil. **~ity** /ə'dʒɪlətɪ/ *n* agilidad *f*

aging /'eɪdʒɪŋ/ *adj* envejecido. ● *n* envejecimiento *m*

agitat|e /'ædʒɪteɪt/ *vt* agitar. **~ed** *adj* nervioso. **~ion** /-'teɪʃn/ *n* agitación *f*, excitación *f*. **~or** *n* agitador *m*

ago /ə'gəʊ/ *adv*. **a long time ~** hace mucho tiempo. **3 days ~** hace 3 días

agon|ize /'ægənaɪz/ *vi* atormentarse. **~izing** *adj* (pain) atroz; (experience) angustioso. **~y** *n* dolor *m* (agudo); (*mental*) angustia *f*

agree /ə'gri:/ *vt* acordar. ● *vi* estar de acuerdo; (*of figures*) concordar; (*get on*) entenderse. □ **~ on** *vt* acordar (date, details). □ **~ with** *vt* (*of food etc*) sentarle bien a. **~able** /ə'gri:əbl/ *adj* agradable. **be ~able** (*willing*) estar de acuerdo. **~d** *adj* (time, place) convenido. **~ment** /-mənt/ *n* acuerdo *m*. **in ~ment** de acuerdo

agricultur|al /ægrɪ'kʌltʃərəl/ *adj* agrícola. **~e** /'ægrɪkʌltʃə(r)/ *n* agricultura *f*

aground /ə'graʊnd/ *adv*. **run ~** (*of ship*) varar, encallar

ahead /ə'hed/ *adv* delante; (*in time*) antes de. **be ~** ir delante

aid /eɪd/ *vt* ayudar. ● *n* ayuda *f*. **in ~ of** a beneficio de

AIDS /eɪdz/ *n* sida *m*

ailment /'eɪlmənt/ *n* enfermedad *f*

aim /eɪm/ *vt* apuntar; (*fig*) dirigir. ● *vi* apuntar; (*fig*) pretender. ● *n* puntería *f*; (*fig*) objetivo *m*. **~less** *adj*, **~lessly** *adv* sin objeto, sin rumbo

air /eə(r)/ *n* aire *m*. **be on the ~** (*Radio, TV*) estar en el aire. **put on ~s** darse aires. ● *vt* airear. **~ bag** *n* (*Auto*) bolsa *f* de aire. **~ base** *n* base *f* aérea. **~borne** *adj* en el aire; (*Mil*) aerotransportado. **~-conditioned** *adj* climatizado, con aire acondicionado. **~ conditioning** *n* aire *m* acondicionado. **~craft** *n* (*pl invar*) avión *m*. **~craft carrier** *n* portaaviones *m*. **~field** *n* aeródromo *m*. **A~ Force** *n* fuerzas *fpl* aéreas. **~ freshener** *n* ambientador *m*. **~gun** *n* escopeta *f* de aire comprimido. **~ hostess** *n* azafata *f*, aeromoza *f* (*LAm*). **~line** *n* línea *f* aérea. **~ mail** *n* correo *m* aéreo. **~plane** *n* (*Amer*) avión *m*. **~port** *n* aeropuerto *m*. **~sick** *adj* mareado (en un avión). **~tight** *adj* hermético. **~ traffic controller** *n* controlador *m* aéreo. **~y** *adj* (**-ier**, **-iest**) aireado; (manner) desenfadado

aisle /aɪl/ *n* nave *f* lateral; (*gangway*) pasillo *m*

ajar /əˈdʒɑː(r)/ *adj* entreabierto

alarm /əˈlɑːm/ *n* alarma *f*. ●*vt* asustar. **~ clock** *n* despertador *m*. **~ist** *n* alarmista *m & f*

Albania /ælˈbeɪnɪə/ *n* Albania *f*. **~n** *adj & n* albanés (*m*)

albatross /ˈælbətrɒs/ *n* albatros *m*

album /ˈælbəm/ *n* álbum *m*

alcohol /ˈælkəhɒl/ *n* alcohol *m*. **~ic** /-ˈhɒlɪk/ *adj & n* alcohólico (*m*)

alcove /ˈælkəʊv/ *n* nicho *m*

ale /eɪl/ *n* cerveza *f*

alert /əˈlɜːt/ *adj* vivo; (*watchful*) vigilante. ●*n* alerta *f*. **on the ~** alerta. ●*vt* avisar

algebra /ˈældʒɪbrə/ *n* álgebra *f*

Algeria /ælˈdʒɪərɪə/ *n* Argelia *f*. **~n** *adj & n* argelino (*m*)

alias /ˈeɪlɪəs/ *n* (*pl* **-ases**) alias *m*. ●*adv* alias

alibi /ˈælɪbaɪ/ *n* (*pl* **-is**) coartada *f*

alien /ˈeɪlɪən/ *n* extranjero *m*. ●*adj* ajeno. **~ate** /-eɪt/ *vt* enajenar. **~ation** /-ˈneɪʃn/ *n* enajenación *f*

alienat|e /ˈeɪlɪəneɪt/ *vt* enajenar. **~ion** /-ˈneɪʃn/ *n* enajenación *f*

alight /əˈlaɪt/ *adj* ardiendo; (light) encendido

align /əˈlaɪn/ *vt* alinear. **~ment** *n* alineación *f*

alike /əˈlaɪk/ *adj* parecido, semejante. **look** *or* **be ~** parecerse. ●*adv* de la misma manera

alive /əˈlaɪv/ *adj* vivo. **~ with** lleno de

alkali /ˈælkəlaɪ/ *n* (*pl* **-is**) álcali *m*. **~ne** *adj* alcalino

all /ɔːl/

●*adjective* todo, -da; (*pl*) todos, -das. **~ day** todo el día. **~ the windows** todas las ventanas. **~ four of us went** fuimos los cuatro

●*pronoun*

····➤(*everything*) todo. **that's ~** eso es todo. **I did ~ I could to persuade her** hice todo lo que pude para convencerla

····➤(*after pronoun*) todo, -da; (*pl*) todos, -das. **he helped us ~** nos ayudó a todos

····➤**all of** todo, -da, (*pl*) todos, -das. **~ of the paintings** todos los cuadros. **~ of the milk** toda la leche

····➤(*in phrases*) **all in all** en general. **not at all** (*in no way*) de ninguna manera; (*after thanks*) de nada, no hay de qué. **it's not at ~ bad** no está nada mal. **I don't like it at ~** no me gusta nada

●*adverb*

····➤(*completely*) completamente. **she was ~ alone** estaba completamente sola. **I got ~ dirty** me ensucié todo/toda. **I don't know him ~ that well** no lo conozco tan bien

····➤(*in scores*) **the score was one ~** iban empatados uno a uno

····➤(*in phrases*) **to be all for sth**

estar completamente a favor de algo. **to be all in** 🄸 estar rendido

all-around /ɔ:lə'raʊnd/ *adj* (*Amer*) completo

allay /ə'leɪ/ *vt* aliviar (pain); aquietar (fears etc)

all-clear /ɔ:l'klɪə(r)/ *n* fin *m* de (la) alarma; (*permission*) visto *m* bueno

alleg|ation /ælɪ'geɪʃn/ *n* alegato *m*. **~e** /ə'ledʒ/ *vt* alegar. **~ed** *adj* presunto. **~edly** /-ɪdlɪ/ *adv* según se dice, supuestamente

allegiance /ə'li:dʒəns/ *n* lealtad *f*

allegory /'ælɪgərɪ/ *n* alegoría *f*

allerg|ic /ə'lɜ:dʒɪk/ *adj* alérgico (**to** a). **~y** /'ælədʒɪ/ *n* alergia *f*

alleviate /ə'li:vɪeɪt/ *vt* aliviar

alley /'ælɪ/ (*pl* **-eys**) *n* callejuela *f*

alliance /ə'laɪəns/ *n* alianza *f*

alligator /'ælɪgeɪtə(r)/ *n* caimán *m*

allocat|e /'æləkeɪt/ *vt* asignar; (*share out*) repartir. **~ion** /-'keɪʃn/ *n* asignación *f*; (*distribution*) reparto *m*

allot /ə'lɒt/ *vt* (*pt* **allotted**) asignar. **~ment** *n* asignación *f*; (*land*) parcela *f*

allow /ə'laʊ/ *vt* permitir; (*grant*) conceder; (*reckon on*) prever; (*agree*) admitir. □ **~ for** *vt* tener en cuenta. **~ance** /ə'laʊəns/ *n* concesión *f*; (*pension*) pensión *f*; (*Com*) rebaja *f*. **make ~ances for** ser indulgente con (person); (*take into account*) tener en cuenta

alloy /'ælɔɪ/ *n* aleación *f*

all: ~ right *adj & adv* bien. ●*int* ¡vale!, ¡okey! (*esp LAm*), ¡órale! (*Mex*). **~-round** *adj* completo

allusion /ə'lu:ʒn/ *n* alusión *f*

ally /'ælaɪ/ *n* aliado *m*. ●/ə'laɪ/ *vt*. **~ o.s.** aliarse (**with** con)

almighty /ɔ:l'maɪtɪ/ *adj* todopoderoso

almond /'ɑ:mənd/ *n* almendra *f*

almost /'ɔ:lməʊst/ *adv* casi

alone /ə'ləʊn/ *adj* solo. ●*adv* sólo, solamente

along /ə'lɒŋ/ *prep* por, a lo largo de. ●*adv*. **~ with** junto con. **all ~** todo el tiempo. **come ~** venga. **~side** /-'saɪd/ *adv* (*Naut*) al costado. ●*prep* al lado de

aloof /ə'lu:f/ *adv* apartado. ●*adj* reservado

aloud /ə'laʊd/ *adv* en voz alta

alphabet /'ælfəbet/ *n* alfabeto *m*. **~ical** /-'betɪkl/ *adj* alfabético

Alps /ælps/ *npl*. **the ~** los Alpes

already /ɔ:l'redɪ/ *adv* ya

Alsatian /æl'seɪʃn/ *n* pastor *m* alemán

also /'ɔ:lsəʊ/ *adv* también; (*moreover*) además

altar /'ɔ:ltə(r)/ *n* altar *m*

alter /'ɔ:ltə(r)/ *vt* cambiar. ●*vi* cambiarse. **~ation** /-'reɪʃn/ *n* modificación *f*; (*to garment*) arreglo *m*

alternate /ɔ:l'tɜ:nət/ *adj* alterno; (*Amer*) *see* ALTERNATIVE. ●/'ɔ:ltəneɪt/ *vt/i* alternar. **~ly** /ɔ:l'tɜ:nətlɪ/ *adv* alternativamente

alternative /ɔ:l'tɜ:nətɪv/ *adj* alternativo. ●*n* alternativa *f*. **~ly** *adv* en cambio, por otra parte

although /ɔ:l'ðəʊ/ *conj* aunque

altitude /'æltɪtju:d/ *n* altitud *f*

altogether /ɔ:ltə'geðə(r)/ *adv* completamente; (*on the whole*) en total

aluminium /æljʊ'mɪnɪəm/, **aluminum** /ə'lu:mɪnəm/ (*Amer*) *n* aluminio *m*

a

always /'ɔ:lweɪz/ *adv* siempre

am /æm/ *see* **BE**

a.m. *abbr* (= **ante meridiem**) de la mañana

amalgamate /ə'mælgəmeɪt/ *vt* amalgamar. ● *vi* amalgamarse

amass /ə'mæs/ *vt* acumular

amateur /'æmətə(r)/ *adj & n* amateur (*m & f*). **~ish** *adj* (*pej*) torpe, chapucero

amaz|e /ə'meɪz/ *vt* asombrar. **~ed** *adj* asombrado, estupefacto. **be ~ed at** quedarse asombrado de, asombrarse de. **~ement** *n* asombro *m*. **~ing** *adj* increíble

ambassador /æm'bæsədə(r)/ *n* embajador *m*

ambigu|ity /æmbɪ'gju:ətɪ/ *n* ambigüedad *f*. **~ous** /æm'bɪgjʊəs/ *adj* ambiguo

ambiti|on /æm'bɪʃn/ *n* ambición *f*. **~ous** /-ʃəs/ *adj* ambicioso

ambivalent /æm'bɪvələnt/ *adj* ambivalente

amble /'æmbl/ *vi* andar despacio, andar sin prisa

ambulance /'æmbjʊləns/ *n* ambulancia *f*

ambush /'æmbʊʃ/ *n* emboscada *f*. ● *vt* tender una emboscada a

amen /ɑ:'men/ *int* amén

amend /ə'mend/ *vt* enmendar. **~ment** *n* enmienda *f*. **~s** *npl*. **make ~s** reparar

amenities /ə'mi:nətɪz/ *npl* servicios *mpl*; (*of hotel, club*) instalaciones *fpl*

America /ə'merɪkə/ *n* (*continent*) América; (*North America*) Estados *mpl* Unidos, Norteamérica *f*. **~n** *adj & n* americano (*m*); (*North American*) estadounidense (*m & f*), norteamericano (*m*). **~nism** *n* americanismo *m*

American dream El sueño americano se basa en la idea de que cualquier persona en los Estados Unidos puede prosperar mediante el trabajo duro. Para los inmigrantes y las minorías, el concepto abarca la libertad y la igualdad de derechos.

amiable /'eɪmɪəbl/ *adj* simpático

amicable /'æmɪkəbl/ *adj* amistoso

amid(st) /ə'mɪd(st)/ *prep* entre, en medio de

ammonia /ə'məʊnɪə/ *n* amoníaco *m*, amoniaco *m*

ammunition /æmjʊ'nɪʃn/ *n* municiones *fpl*

amnesty /'æmnəstɪ/ *n* amnistía *f*

amok /ə'mɒk/ *adv*. **run ~** volverse loco

among(st) /ə'mʌŋ(st)/ *prep* entre

amount /ə'maʊnt/ *n* cantidad *f*; (*total*) total *m*, suma *f*. □ **~ to** *vt* sumar; (*fig*) equivaler a, significar

amp(ere) /'amp(eə(r))/ *n* amperio *m*

amphibi|an /æm'fɪbɪən/ *n* anfibio *m*. **~ous** /-əs/ *adj* anfibio

amphitheatre /'æmfɪθɪətə(r)/ *n* anfiteatro *m*

ampl|e /'æmpl/ *adj* (**-er**, **-est**) amplio; (*enough*) suficiente; (*plentiful*) abundante. **~y** *adv* ampliamente, bastante

amplif|ier /'æmplɪfaɪə(r)/ *n* amplificador *m*. **~y** /'æmplɪfaɪ/ *vt* amplificar

amputat|e /'æmpjʊteɪt/ *vt* amputar. **~ion** /-'teɪʃn/ *n* amputación *f*

amus|e /ə'mju:z/ *vt* divertir. **~ed** *adj* (expression) divertido. **keep s.o. ~ed** entretener a uno. **~ement** *n* diversión *f*. **~ing** *adj* divertido

an /ən, æn/ *see* **A**

anaemi|a /ə'ni:mɪə/ *n* anemia *f*. **~c** *adj* anémico

anaesthe|tic /ænɪs'θetɪk/ *n* anestésico *m*. **~tist** /ə'ni:sθɪtɪst/ *n* anestesista *m & f*

anagram /'ænəgræm/ *n* anagrama *m*

analogy /ə'nælədʒɪ/ *n* analogía *f*

analy|se /'ænəlaɪz/ *vt* analizar. **~sis** /ə'næləsɪs/ *n* (*pl* **-ses** /-si:z/) *n* análisis *m*. **~st** /'ænəlɪst/ *n* analista *m & f*. **~tic(al)** /ænə'lɪtɪk(əl)/ *adj* analítico

anarch|ist /'ænəkɪst/ *n* anarquista *m & f*. **~y** *n* anarquía *f*

anatom|ical /ænə'tɒmɪkl/ *adj* anatómico. **~y** /ə'nætəmɪ/ *n* anatomía *f*

ancest|or /'ænsestə(r)/ *n* antepasado *m*. **~ral** /-'sestrəl/ *adj* ancestral. **~ry** /'ænsestrɪ/ *n* ascendencia *f*

anchor /'æŋkə(r)/ *n* ancla *f*. ● *vt* anclar; (*fig*) sujetar. ● *vi* anclar. **~man** *n* (*on TV*) presentador *m*. **~woman** *n* (*on TV*) presentadora *f*.

ancient /'eɪnʃənt/ *adj* antiguo, viejo

ancillary /æn'sɪlərɪ/ *adj* auxiliar

and /ənd, ænd/ *conj* y; (*before* **i-** *and* **hi-**) e. **bread ~ butter** pan *m* con mantequilla. **go ~ see him** ve a verlo. **more ~ more** cada vez más. **try ~ come** trata de venir

anecdot|al /ænɪk'dəʊtl/ *adj* anecdótico. **~e** /'ænɪkdəʊt/ *n* anécdota *f*

anew /ə'nju:/ *adv* de nuevo

angel /'eɪndʒl/ *n* ángel *m*. **~ic** /æn'dʒelɪk/ *adj* angélico

anger /'æŋgə(r)/ *n* ira *f*. ● *vt* enfadar, (*esp LAm*) enojar

angle /'æŋgl/ *n* ángulo *m*; (*fig*) punto *m* de vista. **~r** /'æŋglə(r)/ *n* pescador *m*

Anglican /'æŋglɪkən/ *adj & n* anglicano (*m*)

angr|ily /'æŋgrɪlɪ/ *adv* con enfado, (*esp LAm*) con enojo. **~y** /'æŋgrɪ/ *adj* (**-ier**, **-iest**) enfadado, (*esp LAm*) enojado. **get ~y** enfadarse, enojarse (*esp LAm*)

anguish /'æŋgwɪʃ/ *n* angustia *f*

animal /'ænɪməl/ *adj & n* animal (*m*)

animat|e /'ænɪmeɪt/ *vt* animar. **~ion** /-'meɪʃn/ *n* animación *f*

animosity /ænɪ'mɒsətɪ/ *n* animosidad *f*

ankle /'æŋkl/ *n* tobillo *m*. **~ boot** botín *m*. **~ sock** calcetín *m* corto

annexe /'æneks/ *n* anexo *m*

annihilat|e /ə'naɪəleɪt/ *vt* aniquilar. **~ion** /-'leɪʃn/ *n* aniquilación *f*

anniversary /ænɪ'vɜ:sərɪ/ *n* aniversario *m*

announce /ə'naʊns/ *vt* anunciar, comunicar. **~ment** *n* anuncio *m*; (*official*) comunicado *m*. **~r** *n* (*Radio, TV*) locutor *m*

annoy /ə'nɔɪ/ *vt* molestar. **~ance** *n* molestia *m*. **~ed** *adj* enfadado, enojado (*LAm*). **~ing** *adj* molesto

annual /'ænjʊəl/ *adj* anual. ● *n* anuario *m*. **~ly** *adv* cada año

annul /ə'nʌl/ *vt* (*pt* **annulled**) anular. **~ment** *n* anulación *f*

anonymous /ə'nɒnɪməs/ *adj* anónimo

anorak /'ænəræk/ *n* anorac *m*

another /ə'nʌðə(r)/ *adj & pron* otro. **~ 10 minutes** 10 minutos más. **in ~ way** de otra manera. **one ~** el uno al otro; (*pl*) unos a otros

a

answer /'ɑːnsə(r)/ *n* respuesta *f*; (*solution*) solución *f*. ●*vt* contestar; escuchar, oír (prayer). **~ the door** abrir la puerta. ●*vi* contestar. □ **~ back** *vi* contestar. □ **~ for** *vt* ser responsable de. **~able** *adj* responsable. **~ing machine** *n* contestador *m* automático

ant /ænt/ *n* hormiga *f*

antagoni|sm /æn'tægənɪzəm/ *n* antagonismo *m*. **~stic** /-'nɪstɪk/ *adj* antagónico, opuesto. **~ze** /æn 'tægənaɪz/ *vt* provocar la enemistad de

Antarctic /æn'tɑːktɪk/ *adj* antártico. ●*n* **the ~** la región antártica

antelope /'æntɪləʊp/ *n* antílope *m*

antenatal /'æntɪneɪtl/ *adj* prenatal

antenna /æn'tenə/ (*pl* **-nae** /-niː/) (*of insect etc*) *n* antena *f*; (*pl* **-nas**) (*of radio, TV*) antena *f*

anthem /'ænθəm/ *n* himno *m*

anthology /æn'θɒlədʒɪ/ *n* antología *f*

anthrax /'ænθræks/ *n* ántrax *m*

anthropolog|ist /ænθrə 'pɒlədʒɪst/ *n* antropológo *m*. **~y** *n* antropología *f*

anti-... /æntɪ/ *pref* anti... **~aircraft** /-'eəkrɑːft/ *adj* antiaéreo

antibiotic /æntɪbaɪ'ɒtɪk/ *adj & n* antibiótico (*m*)

anticipat|e /æn'tɪsɪpeɪt/ *vt* anticiparse a; (*foresee*) prever; (*forestall*) prevenir. **~ion** /-'peɪʃn/ *n* (*foresight*) previsión *f*; (*expectation*) expectativa *f*

anti: ~climax /-'klaɪmæks/ *n* decepción *f*. **~clockwise** /-'klɒkwaɪz/ *adv & adj* en sentido contrario al de las agujas del reloj

antidote /'æntɪdəʊt/ *m* antídoto *m*

antifreeze /'æntɪfriːz/ *n* anticongelante *m*

antiperspirant /æntɪ 'pɜːspɪrənt/ *n* antitranspirante *m*

antiquated /'æntɪkweɪtɪd/ *adj* anticuado

antique /æn'tiːk/ *adj* antiguo. ●*n* antigüedad *f*. **~ dealer** anticuario *m*. **~ shop** tienda *f* de antigüedades

antiquity /æn'tɪkwətɪ/ *n* antigüedad *f*

anti: ~septic /-'septɪk/ *adj & n* antiséptico (*m*). **~social** /-'səʊʃl/ *adj* antisocial

antlers /'æntləz/ *npl* cornamenta *f*

anus /'eɪnəs/ *n* ano *m*

anvil /'ænvɪl/ *n* yunque *m*

anxi|ety /æŋ'zaɪətɪ/ *n* ansiedad *f*; (*worry*) inquietud *f*; (*eagerness*) anhelo *m*. **~ous** /'æŋkʃəs/ *adj* inquieto; (*eager*) deseoso. **~ously** *adv* con inquietud; (*eagerly*) con impaciencia

any /'enɪ/ *adj* algún; (*negative*) ningún *m*; (*whatever*) cualquier; (*every*) todo. **at ~ moment** en cualquier momento. **have you ~ wine?** ¿tienes vino? ●*pron* alguno; (*negative*) ninguno. **have we ~?** ¿tenemos algunos? **not ~** ninguno. ●*adv* (*a little*) un poco, algo. **is it ~ better?** ¿está algo mejor?

anybody /'enɪbɒdɪ/ *pron* alguien; (*after negative*) nadie. **~ can do it** cualquiera puede hacerlo

anyhow /'enɪhaʊ/ *adv* de todas formas; (*in spite of all*) a pesar de todo; (*badly*) de cualquier manera

anyone /'enɪwʌn/ *pron see* **ANYBODY**

anything /'enɪθɪŋ/ *pron* algo; (*whatever*) cualquier cosa; (*after negative*) nada. **~ but** todo menos

anyway /ˈenɪweɪ/ *adv* de todas formas

anywhere /ˈenɪweə(r)/ *adv* en cualquier parte; (*after negative*) en ningún sitio. ~ **else** en cualquier otro lugar. ~ **you go** dondequiera que vayas

apart /əˈpɑːt/ *adv* aparte; (*separated*) separado. ~ **from** aparte de. **come** ~ romperse. **take** ~ desmontar

apartheid /əˈpɑːtheɪt/ *n* apartheid *m*

apartment /əˈpɑːtmənt/ *n* (*Amer*) apartamento *m*, piso *m*. ~ **building** *n* (*Amer*) edificio *m* de apartamentos, casa *f* de pisos

apath|etic /æpəˈθetɪk/ *adj* apático. ~**y** /ˈæpəθɪ/ *n* apatía *f*

ape /eɪp/ *n* mono *m*. ● *vt* imitar

aperitif /əˈperətɪf/ *n* aperitivo *m*

aperture /ˈæpətʃuə(r)/ *n* abertura *f*

apex /ˈeɪpeks/ *n* ápice *m*

aphrodisiac /æfrəˈdɪzɪæk/ *adj* & *n* afrodisíaco (*m*), afrodisiaco (*m*)

apolog|etic /əpɒləˈdʒetɪk/ *adj* lleno de disculpas. **be** ~**etic** disculparse. ~**ize** /əˈpɒlədʒaɪz/ *vi* disculparse (**for** de). ~**y** /əˈpɒlədʒɪ/ *n* disculpa *f*

apostle /əˈpɒsl/ *n* apóstol *m*

apostrophe /əˈpɒstrəfɪ/ *n* apóstrofo *m*

appal /əˈpɔːl/ *vt* (*pt* **appalled**) horrorizar. ~**ling** *adj* espantoso

apparatus /æpəˈreɪtəs/ *n* aparato *m*

apparel /əˈpærəl/ *n* (*Amer*) ropa *f*

apparent /əˈpærənt/ *adj* aparente; (*clear*) evidente. ~**ly** *adv* por lo visto

apparition /æpəˈrɪʃn/ *n* aparición *f*

appeal /əˈpiːl/ *vi* apelar; (*attract*) atraer. ● *n* llamamiento *m*; (*attraction*) atractivo *m*; (*Jurid*) apelación *f*. ~**ing** *adj* atrayente

appear /əˈpɪə(r)/ *vi* aparecer; (*seem*) parecer; (*in court*) comparecer. ~**ance** *n* aparición *f*; (*aspect*) aspecto *m*; (*in court*) comparecencia *f*

appease /əˈpiːz/ *vt* aplacar; (*pacify*) apaciguar

append /əˈpend/ *vt* adjuntar

appendicitis /əpendɪˈsaɪtɪs/ *n* apendicitis *f*

appendix /əˈpendɪks/ *n* (*pl* **-ices** /-ɪsiːz/) (*of book*) apéndice *m*. (*pl* **-ixes**) (*organ*) apéndice *m*

appetite /ˈæpɪtaɪt/ *n* apetito *m*

applau|d /əˈplɔːd/ *vt/i* aplaudir. ~**se** /əˈplɔːz/ *n* aplausos *mpl*. **round of** ~**se** aplauso *m*

apple /ˈæpl/ *n* manzana *f*. ~ **tree** *n* manzano *m*

appliance /əˈplaɪəns/ *n* aparato *m*. **electrical** ~ electrodoméstico *m*

applic|able /ˈæplɪkəbl/ *adj* aplicable; (*relevant*) pertinente. ~**ant** /ˈæplɪkənt/ *n* candidato *m*, solicitante *m* & *f*. ~**ation** /æplɪˈkeɪʃn/ *n* aplicación *f*; (*request*) solicitud *f*. ~**ation form** formulario *m* (de solicitud)

appl|ied /əˈplaɪd/ *adj* aplicado. ~**y** /əˈplaɪ/ *vt* aplicar. ● *vi* aplicarse; (*ask*) presentar una solicitud. ~**y for** solicitar (job etc)

appoint /əˈpɔɪnt/ *vt* nombrar; (*fix*) señalar. ~**ment** *n* cita *f*

apprais|al /əˈpreɪzl/ *n* evaluación *f*. ~**e** /əˈpreɪz/ *vt* evaluar

appreciable /əˈpriːʃəbl/ *adj* (*considerable*) considerable

appreciat|e /əˈpriːʃɪeɪt/ *vt* (*value*)

apreciar; (*understand*) comprender; (*be grateful for*) agradecer. **~ion** /-'eɪʃn/ *n* aprecio *m*; (*gratitude*) agradecimiento *m*. **~ive** /ə'priːʃɪətɪv/ *adj* agradecido

apprehen|sion /æprɪ'henʃn/ *n* (*fear*) recelo *f*. **~sive** *adj* aprensivo

apprentice /ə'prentɪs/ *n* aprendiz *m*. ● *vt*. **be ~d to s.o.** estar de aprendiz con uno. **~ship** *n* aprendizaje *m*

approach /ə'prəʊtʃ/ *vt* acercarse a. ● *vi* acercarse. ● *n* acercamiento *m*; (*to problem*) enfoque *m*; (*access*) acceso *m*

appropriate /ə'prəʊprɪət/ *adj* apropiado. ● /ə'prəʊprɪeɪt/ *vt* apropiarse de. **~ly** /-ətli/ *adv* apropiadamente

approv|al /ə'pruːvl/ *n* aprobación *f*. **on ~al** a prueba. **~e** /ə'pruːv/ *vt/i* aprobar. **~ingly** *adv* con aprobación

approximat|e /ə'prɒksɪmət/ *adj* aproximado. ● /ə'prɒksɪmeɪt/ *vt* aproximarse a. **~ely** /-ətlɪ/ *adv* aproximadamente. **~ion** /-'meɪʃn/ *n* aproximación *f*

apricot /'eɪprɪkɒt/ *n* albaricoque *m*, chabacano *m* (*Mex*)

April /'eɪprəl/ *n* abril *m*. **~ fool!** ¡inocentón!

apron /'eɪprən/ *n* delantal *m*

apt /æpt/ *adj* apropiado. **be ~ to** tener tendencia a. **~itude** /'æptɪtjuːd/ *n* aptitud *f*. **~ly** *adv* acertadamente

aquarium /ə'kweərɪəm/ *n* (*pl* **-ums**) acuario *m*

Aquarius /ə'kweərɪəs/ *n* Acuario *m*

aquatic /ə'kwætɪk/ *adj* acuático

aqueduct /'ækwɪdʌkt/ *n* acueducto *m*

Arab /'ærəb/ *adj & n* árabe (*m & f*). **~ian** /ə'reɪbɪən/ *adj* árabe. **~ic** /'ærəbɪk/ *adj & n* árabe (*m*). **~ic numerals** números *mpl* arábigos

arable /'ærəbl/ *adj* cultivable

arbitrary /'ɑːbɪtrərɪ/ *adj* arbitrario

arbitrat|e /'ɑːbɪtreɪt/ *vi* arbitrar. **~ion** /-'treɪʃn/ *n* arbitraje *m*. **~or** *n* árbitro *m*

arc /ɑːk/ *n* arco *m*

arcade /ɑː'keɪd/ *n* arcada *f*; (*around square*) soportales *mpl*; (*shops*) galería *f*

arch /ɑːtʃ/ *n* arco *m*. ● *vt* arquear. ● *vi* arquearse

archaeolog|ical /ɑːkɪə'lɒdʒɪkl/ *adj* arqueológico. **~ist** /ɑːkɪ'ɒlədʒɪst/ *n* arqueólogo *m*. **~y** /ɑːkɪ'ɒlədʒɪ/ *n* arqueología *f*

archaic /ɑː'keɪɪk/ *adj* arcaico

archbishop /ɑːtʃ'bɪʃəp/ *n* arzobispo *m*

archer /'ɑːtʃə(r)/ *n* arquero *m*. **~y** *n* tiro *m* con arco

architect /'ɑːkɪtekt/ *n* arquitecto *m*. **~ure** /-tʃə(r)/ *n* arquitectura *f*. **~ural** /-'tektʃərəl/ *adj* arquitectónico

archives /'ɑːkaɪvz/ *npl* archivo *m*

archway /'ɑːtʃweɪ/ *n* arco *m*

Arctic /'ɑːktɪk/ *adj* ártico. ● *n*. **the ~** el Ártico

ard|ent /'ɑːdənt/ *adj* fervoroso; (supporter, lover) apasionado. **~our** /'ɑːdə(r)/ *n* fervor *m*; (*love*) pasión *f*

arduous /'ɑːdjʊəs/ *adj* arduo

are /ɑː(r)/ *see* **BE**

area /'eərɪə/ *n* (*Math*) superficie *f*; (*of country*) zona *f*; (*of city*) barrio *m*

arena /ə'riːnə/ *n* arena *f*; (*scene of activity*) ruedo *m*

aren't /ɑːnt/ = **are not**

Argentin|a /ɑːdʒən'tiːnə/ *n* Argentina *f*. **~ian** /-'tɪnɪən/ *adj & n* argentino (*m*)

argu|able /'ɑːgjʊəbl/ *adj* discutible. **~e** /'ɑːgjuː/ *vi* discutir; (*reason*) razonar. **~ment** /'ɑːgjʊmənt/ *n* disputa *f*; (*reasoning*) argumento *m*. **~mentative** /ɑːgjʊ'mentətɪv/ *adj* discutidor

arid /'ærɪd/ *adj* árido

Aries /'eəriːz/ *n* Aries *m*

arise /ə'raɪz/ *vi* (*pt* **arose**, *pp* **arisen**) surgir (**from** de)

aristocra|cy /ærɪ'stɒkrəsɪ/ *n* aristocracia *f*. **~t** /'ærɪstəkræt/ *n* aristócrata *m & f*. **~tic** /-'krætɪk/ *adj* aristocrático

arithmetic /ə'rɪθmətɪk/ *n* aritmética *f*

ark /ɑːk/ *n* (*Relig*) arca *f*

arm /ɑːm/ *n* brazo *m*; (*of garment*) manga *f*. **~s** *npl* armas *fpl*. ● *vt* armar

armament /'ɑːməmənt/ *n* armamento *m*

arm: ~band *n* brazalete *m*. **~chair** *n* sillón *m*

armed /ɑːmd/ *adj* armado. **~ robbery** *n* robo *m* a mano armada

armful /'ɑːmfʊl/ *n* brazada *f*

armour /'ɑːmə(r)/ *n* armadura *f*. **~ed** /'ɑːməd/ *adj* blindado. **~y** /'ɑːmərɪ/ *n* arsenal *m*

armpit /'ɑːmpɪt/ *n* sobaco *m*, axila *f*

army /'ɑːmɪ/ *n* ejército *m*

aroma /ə'rəʊmə/ *n* aroma *m*

arose /ə'rəʊz/ *see* ARISE

around /ə'raʊnd/ *adv* alrededor; (*near*) cerca. **all ~** por todas partes. ● *prep* alrededor de; (*with time*) a eso de

arouse /ə'raʊz/ *vt* despertar

arrange /ə'reɪndʒ/ *vt* arreglar; (*fix*) fijar. **~ment** *n* arreglo *m*; (*agreement*) acuerdo *m*. **~ments** *npl* (*plans*) preparativos *mpl*

arrears /ə'rɪəz/ *npl* atrasos *mpl*. **in ~** atrasado en el pago (**with** de)

arrest /ə'rest/ *vt* detener. ● *n* detención *f*. **under ~** detenido

arriv|al /ə'raɪvl/ *n* llegada *f*. **new ~al** recién llegado *m*. **~e** /ə'raɪv/ *vi* llegar

arrogan|ce /'ærəgəns/ *n* arrogancia *f*. **~t** *adj* arrogante. **~tly** *adv* con arrogancia

arrow /'ærəʊ/ *n* flecha *f*

arse /ɑːs/ *n* (*vulgar*) culo *m*

arsenal /'ɑːsənl/ *n* arsenal *m*

arsenic /'ɑːsnɪk/ *n* arsénico *m*

arson /'ɑːsn/ *n* incendio *m* provocado. **~ist** *n* incendiario *m*

art[1] /ɑːt/ *n* arte *m*. **A~s** *npl* (*Univ*) Filosofía y Letras *fpl*. **fine ~s** bellas artes *fpl*

art[2] /ɑːt/ (*old use, with* **thou**) *see* ARE

artery /'ɑːtərɪ/ *n* arteria *f*

art gallery *n* museo *m* de arte, pinacoteca *f*; (commercial) galería *f* de arte

arthritis /ɑː'θraɪtɪs/ *n* artritis *f*

article /'ɑːtɪkl/ *n* artículo *m*. **~ of clothing** prenda *f* de vestir

articulat|e /ɑː'tɪkjʊlət/ *adj* (utterance) articulado; (person) que sabe expresarse. ● /ɑː'tɪkjʊleɪt/ *vt/i* articular. **~ed lorry** *n* camión *m* articulado. **~ion** /-'leɪʃn/ *n* articulación *f*

artificial /ɑːtɪ'fɪʃl/ *adj* artificial. **~ respiration** respiración *f* artificial

artillery /ɑː'tɪlərɪ/ *n* artillería *f*

artist /'ɑːtɪst/ *n* artista *m & f*. **~tic** /ɑː'tɪstɪk/ *adj* artístico. **~ry** /'ɑːtɪstrɪ/ *n* arte *m*, habilidad *f*

as /æz, əz/ *adv & conj* como; (*since*) ya que; (*while*) mientras. **~ big ~**

tan grande como. ~ **far** ~ (*distance*) hasta; (*qualitative*) en cuanto a. ~ **far** ~ **I know** que yo sepa. ~ **if** como si. ~ **long** ~ mientras. ~ **much** ~ tanto como. ~ **soon** ~ tan pronto como. ~ **well** también

asbestos /æz'bestɒs/ *n* amianto *m*, asbesto *m*

ascen|d /ə'send/ *vt/i* subir. **A~sion** /ə'senʃn/ *n*. **the A~sion** la Ascensión. **~t** /ə'sent/ *n* subida *f*

ascertain /æsə'teɪn/ *vt* averiguar

ash /æʃ/ *n* ceniza *f*. ●*n*. ~ **(tree)** fresno *m*

ashamed /ə'ʃeɪmd/ *adj* avergonzado (**of** de). **be** ~ **of s.o.** avergonzarse de uno

ashore /ə'ʃɔ:(r)/ *adv* a tierra. **go** ~ desembarcar

ash: ~tray *n* cenicero *m*. **A~ Wednesday** *n* Miércoles *m* de Ceniza

Asia /'eɪʃə/ *n* Asia *f*. **~n** *adj & n* asiático (*m*). **~tic** /-ɪ'ætɪk/ *adj* asiático

aside /ə'saɪd/ *adv* a un lado. ●*n* (*in theatre*) aparte *m*

ask /ɑ:sk/ *vt* pedir; hacer (question); (*invite*) invitar. ~ **about** enterarse de. ~ **s.o. to do something** pedirle a uno que haga algo. □~ **after** *vt* preguntar por. □~ **for** *vt*. ~ **for help** pedir ayuda. ~ **for trouble** buscarse problemas. □~ **in** *vt*. ~ **s.o. in** invitar a uno a pasar

askew /ə'skju:/ *adv & adj* torcido

asleep /ə'sli:p/ *adv & adj* dormido. **fall** ~ dormirse

asparagus /ə'spærəgəs/ *n* espárrago *m*

aspect /'æspekt/ *n* aspecto *m*

asphalt /'æsfælt/ *n* asfalto *m*. ●*vt* asfaltar

aspir|ation /æspə'reɪʃn/ *n* aspiración *f*. **~e** /əs'paɪə(r)/ *vi* aspirar

aspirin /'æsprɪn/ *n* aspirina *f*

ass /æs/ *n* asno *m*; (*fig, fam*) imbécil *m*; (*Amer vulgar*) culo *m*

assassin /ə'sæsɪn/ *n* asesino *m*. **~ate** /-eɪt/ *vt* asesinar. **~ation** /-'eɪʃn/ *n* asesinato *m*

assault /ə'sɔ:lt/ *n* (*Mil*) ataque *m*; (*Jurid*) atentado *m*. ●*vt* asaltar

assembl|e /ə'sembl/ *vt* reunir; (*Mec*) montar. ●*vi* reunirse. **~y** *n* reunión *f*; (*Pol etc*) asamblea *f*. **~y line** *n* línea *f* de montaje

assent /ə'sent/ *n* asentimiento *m*. ●*vi* asentir

assert /ə'sɜ:t/ *vt* afirmar; hacer valer (one's rights). **~ion** /-ʃn/ *n* afirmación *f*. **~ive** *adj* positivo, firme

assess /ə'ses/ *vt* evaluar; (*determine*) determinar; fijar (tax etc). **~ment** *n* evaluación *f*

asset /'æset/ *n* (*advantage*) ventaja *f*. **~s** *npl* (*Com*) bienes *mpl*

assign /ə'saɪn/ *vt* asignar; (*appoint*) nombrar. **~ment** *n* asignación *f*; (*mission*) misión *f*; (*task*) función *f*; (*for school*) trabajo *m*

assimilate /ə'sɪmɪleɪt/ *vt* asimilar. ●*vi* asimilarse

assist /ə'sɪst/ *vt/i* ayudar. **~ance** *n* ayuda *f*. **~ant** *n* ayudante *m & f*; (*shop*) dependienta *f*, dependiente *m*. ●*adj* auxiliar, adjunto

associat|e /ə'səʊʃɪeɪt/ *vt* asociar. ●*vi* asociarse. ●/ə'səʊʃɪət/ *adj* asociado. ●*n* colega *m & f*; (*Com*) socio *m*. **~ion** /-'eɪʃn/ *n* asociación *f*.

assort|ed /ə'sɔ:tɪd/ *adj* surtido. **~ment** *n* surtido *m*

assum|e /ə'sju:m/ *vt* suponer; tomar (power, attitude); asumir (role, burden). **~ption** /ə'sʌmpʃn/ *n* suposición *f*

assur|ance /ə'ʃʊərəns/ *n* seguridad *f*; (*insurance*) seguro *m*. **~e** /ə'ʃʊə(r)/ *vt* asegurar. **~ed** *adj* seguro

asterisk /'æstərɪsk/ *n* asterisco *m*

asthma /'æsmə/ *n* asma *f*. **~tic** /-'mætɪk/ *adj & n* asmático (*m*)

astonish /ə'stɒnɪʃ/ *vt* asombrar. **~ed** *adj* asombrado. **~ing** *adj* asombroso. **~ment** *n* asombro *m*

astound /ə'staʊnd/ *vt* asombrar. **~ed** *adj* atónito. **~ing** *adj* increíble

astray /ə'streɪ/ *adv*. **go ~** extraviarse. **lead ~** llevar por mal camino

astrology /ə'strɒlədʒɪ/ *n* astrología *f*

astronaut /'æstrənɔ:t/ *n* astronauta *m & f*

astronom|er /ə'strɒnəmə(r)/ *n* astrónomo *m*. **~ical** /æstrə'nɒmɪkl/ *adj* astronómico. **~y** /ə'strɒnəmɪ/ *n* astronomía *f*

astute /ə'stju:t/ *adj* astuto

asylum /ə'saɪləm/ *n* asilo *m*. **lunatic ~** manicomio *m*. **~ seeker** *n* solicitante *m & f* de asilo

at /æt/ *preposition*

····➤(*location*) en. **she's at the office** está en la oficina. **at home** en casa. **call me at the office** llámame a la oficina

> For translations of phrases such as **at the top, at the front of, at the back of** see entries **top, front** etc

····➤(*at the house of*) en casa de. **I'll be at Rachel's** estaré en casa de Rachel

····➤(*Comput*: @) arroba *f*

····➤(*talking about time*) **at 7 o'clock** a las siete. **at night** por la noche, de noche, en la noche (*LAm*). **at Christmas** en Navidad

····➤(*talking about age*) a. **at six (years of age)** a los seis años

····➤(*with measurements, numbers etc*) a. **at 60 miles an hour** a 60 millas por hora. **at a depth of** a una profundidad de. **three at a time** de tres en tres

> For translations of phrasal verbs with **at**, such as **look at**, see entries for those verbs

ate /et/ *see* EAT

atheis|m /'eɪθɪɪzəm/ *n* ateísmo *m*. **~t** *n* ateo *m*

athlet|e /'æθli:t/ *n* atleta *m & f*. **~ic** /-'letɪk/ *adj* atlético. **~ics** *npl* atletismo *m*; (*Amer, Sport*) deportes *mpl*

Atlantic /ət'læntɪk/ *adj* atlántico. ●*n*. **the ~ (Ocean)** el (Océano) Atlántico

atlas /'ætləs/ *n* atlas *m*

ATM *abbr* (= **automated teller machine**) cajero *m* automático

atmospher|e /'ætməsfɪə(r)/ *n* atmósfera *f*; (*fig*) ambiente *m*. **~ic** /-'ferɪk/ *adj* atmosférico

atom /'ætəm/ *n* átomo *m*. **~ic** /ə'tɒmɪk/ *adj* atómico

atroci|ous /ə'trəʊʃəs/ *adj* atroz. **~ty** /ə'trɒsətɪ/ *n* atrocidad *f*

attach /ə'tætʃ/ *vt* sujetar; adjuntar (document etc). **be ~ed to** (*be fond of*) tener cariño a. **~ment** *n* (*affection*) cariño *m*; (*tool*) accesorio *m*; (*to email*) archivo *m* adjunto

attack /ə'tæk/ *n* ataque *m*. ● *vt/i* atacar. **~er** *n* agresor *m*

attain /ə'teɪn/ *vt* conseguir. **~able** *adj* alcanzable

attempt /ə'tempt/ *vt* intentar. ● *n* tentativa *f*; (*attack*) atentado *m*

attend /ə'tend/ *vt* asistir a; (*escort*) acompañar. ● *vi* prestar atención. □ **~ to** *vt* (*look after*) ocuparse de. **~ance** *n* asistencia *f*; (*people present*) concurrencia *f*.

atten|tion /ə'tenʃn/ *n* atención *f*. **~tion!** (*Mil*) ¡firmes! **pay ~tion** prestar atención. **~tive** *adj* atento

attic /'ætɪk/ *n* desván *m*

attire /ə'taɪə(r)/ *n* atavío *m*

attitude /'ætɪtjuːd/ *n* postura *f*

attorney /ə'tɜːnɪ/ *n* (*pl* **-eys**) (*Amer*) abogado *m*

attract /ə'trækt/ *vt* atraer. **~ion** /-ʃn/ *n* atracción *f*; (*charm*) atractivo *m*. **~ive** *adj* atractivo; (*interesting*) atrayente

attribute /ə'trɪbjuːt/ *vt* atribuir. ● /'ætrɪbjuːt/ *n* atributo *m*

aubergine /'əʊbəʒiːn/ *n* berenjena *f*

auction /'ɔːkʃn/ *n* subasta *f*. ● *vt* subastar. **~eer** /-ə'nɪə(r)/ *n* subastador *m*

audaci|ous /ɔː'deɪʃəs/ *adj* audaz. **~ty** /ɔː'dæsətɪ/ *n* audacia *f*

audible /'ɔːdəbl/ *adj* audible

audience /'ɔːdɪəns/ *n* (*at play, film*) público *m*; (*TV*) audiencia *f*; (*interview*) audiencia *f*

audiovisual /ɔːdɪəʊ'vɪʒʊəl/ *adj* audiovisual

audit /'ɔːdɪt/ *n* revisión *f* de cuentas. ● *vt* revisar

audition /ɔː'dɪʃn/ *n* audición *f*. ● *vt* hacerle una audición a. ● *vi* dar una audición (**for** para)

auditor /'ɔːdɪtə(r)/ *n* interventor *m* de cuentas

auditorium /ɔːdɪ'tɔːrɪəm/ (*pl* **-riums** *or* **-ria** /-rɪə/) *n* sala *f*, auditorio *m*

augment /ɔːg'ment/ *vt* aumentar

augur /'ɔːgə(r)/ *vt* augurar. **it ~s well** es de buen agüero

August /'ɔːgəst/ *n* agosto *m*

aunt /ɑːnt/ *n* tía *f*

au pair /əʊ'peə(r)/ *n* chica *f* au pair

aura /'ɔːrə/ *n* aura *f*, halo *m*

auster|e /ɔː'stɪə(r)/ *adj* austero. **~ity** /ɔː'sterətɪ/ *n* austeridad *f*

Australia /ɒ'streɪlɪə/ *n* Australia *f*. **~n** *adj* & *n* australiano (*m*)

Austria /'ɒstrɪə/ *n* Austria *f*. **~n** *adj* & *n* austríaco (*m*)

authentic /ɔː'θentɪk/ *adj* auténtico. **~ate** /-keɪt/ *vt* autenticar. **~ity** /-ən'tɪsətɪ/ *n* autenticidad *f*

author /'ɔːθə(r)/ *n* autor *m*. **~ess** /-ɪs/ *n* autora *f*

authoritative /ɔː'θɒrɪtətɪv/ *adj* autorizado; (*manner*) autoritario

authority /ɔː'θɒrətɪ/ *n* autoridad *f*; (*permission*) autorización *f*

authoriz|ation /ɔːθəraɪ'zeɪʃn/ *n* autorización *f*. **~e** /'ɔːθəraɪz/ *vt* autorizar

autobiography /ɔːtəʊbaɪ'ɒgrəfɪ/ *n* autobiografía *f*

autograph /'ɔːtəgrɑːf/ *n* autógrafo *m*. ● *vt* firmar, autografiar

automat|e /'ɔːtəmeɪt/ *vt* automatizar. **~ic** /-'mætɪk/ *adj* automático. **~ion** /-'meɪʃn/ *n* automatización *f*. **~on** /ɔː'tɒmətən/ *n* (*pl* **-tons** *or* **-ta** /-tə/) autómata *m*

automobile /'ɔːtəməbiːl/ *n*

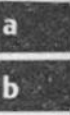

(*Amer*) coche *m*, carro *m* (*LAm*), automóvil *m*

autonom|ous /ɔ:'tɒnəməs/ *adj* autónomo. **~y** *n* autonomía *f*

autopsy /'ɔ:tɒpsɪ/ *n* autopsia *f*

autumn /'ɔ:təm/ *n* otoño *m*. **~al** /ɔ:'tʌmnəl/ *adj* otoñal

auxiliary /ɔ:g'zɪlɪərɪ/ *adj & n* auxiliar (*m & f*)

avail /ə'veɪl/ *n*. **to no ~** inútil

availab|ility /əveɪlə'bɪlətɪ/ *n* disponibilidad *f*. **~le** /ə'veɪləbl/ *adj* disponible

avalanche /'ævəlɑ:nʃ/ *n* avalancha *f*

avaric|e /'ævərɪs/ *n* avaricia *f*. **~ious** /-'rɪʃəs/ *adj* avaro

avenue /'ævənju:/ *n* avenida *f*; (*fig*) vía *f*

average /'ævərɪdʒ/ *n* promedio *m*. **on ~** por término medio. ● *adj* medio

avers|e /ə'vɜ:s/ *adj*. **be ~e to** ser reacio a. **~ion** /-ʃn/ *n* repugnancia *f*

avert /ə'vɜ:t/ *vt* (*turn away*) apartar; (*ward off*) desviar

aviation /eɪvɪ'eɪʃn/ *n* aviación *f*

avid /'ævɪd/ *adj* ávido

avocado /ævə'kɑ:dəʊ/ *n* (*pl* **-os**) aguacate *m*

avoid /ə'vɔɪd/ *vt* evitar. **~able** *adj* evitable. **~ance** *n* el evitar

await /ə'weɪt/ *vt* esperar

awake /ə'weɪk/ *vt/i* (*pt* **awoke**, *pp* **awoken**) despertar. ● *adj* despierto. **wide ~** completamente despierto; (*fig*) despabilado. **~n** /ə'weɪkən/ *vt/i* despertar. **~ning** *n* el despertar

award /ə'wɔ:d/ *vt* otorgar; (*Jurid*) adjudicar. ● *n* premio *m*; (*Jurid*) adjudicación *f*; (*scholarship*) beca *f*

aware /ə'weə(r)/ *adj*. **be ~ of sth** ser consciente de algo, darse cuenta de algo. **~ness** *n* conciencia *f*

awash /ə'wɒʃ/ *adj* inundado

away /ə'weɪ/ *adv* (*absent*) fuera. **far ~** muy lejos. ● *adj* **~ match** partido *m* fuera de casa

awe /ɔ:/ *n* temor *m*. **~-inspiring** *adj* impresionante. **~some** /-səm/ *adj* imponente

awful /'ɔ:fʊl/ *adj* terrible, malísimo. **feel ~** sentirse muy mal

awkward /'ɔ:kwəd/ *adj* difícil; (*inconvenient*) inoportuno; (*clumsy*) desmañado; (*embarrassed*) incómodo. **~ness** *n* dificultad *f*; (*discomfort*) molestia *f*; (*clumsiness*) torpeza *f*

awning /'ɔ:nɪŋ/ *n* toldo *m*

awoke/ə'wəʊk/, **awoken** /ə'wəʊkən/ *see* **AWAKE**

axe /æks/ *n* hacha *f*. ● *vt* (*pres p* **axing**) cortar con hacha; (*fig*) recortar

axis /'æksɪs/ *n* (*pl* **axes**/-i:z/) eje *m*

axle /'æksl/ *n* eje *m*

Bb

BA /bi:'eɪ/ *abbr see* **BACHELOR**

babble /'bæbl/ *vi* balbucir; (*chatter*) parlotear; (stream) murmullar.

baboon /bə'bu:n/ *n* mandril *m*

baby /'beɪbɪ/ *n* niño *m*, bebé *m*. **~ buggy**, **~ carriage** *n* (*Amer*) cochecito *m*. **~ish** *adj* /'beɪbɪɪʃ/ infantil. **~-sit** *vi* cuidar a los niños, hacer de canguro. **~-sitter** *n* baby

b

sitter *m & f*, canguro *m & f*

bachelor /'bætʃələ(r)/ *n* soltero *m*. **B~ of Arts (BA)** licenciado *m* en filosofía y letras. **B~ of Science (BSc)** licenciado *m* en ciencias

back /bæk/ *n* espalda *f*; (*of car*) parte *f* trasera; (*of chair*) respaldo *m*; (*of cloth*) revés *m*; (*of house*) parte *f* de atrás; (*of animal, book*) lomo *m*; (*of hand, document*) dorso *m*; (*football*) defensa *m & f*. **in the ~ of beyond** en el quinto infierno. ●*adj* trasero. **the ~ door** la puerta trasera. ●*adv* atrás; (*returned*) de vuelta. ●*vt* apoyar; (*betting*) apostar a; dar marcha atrás a (car). ●*vi* retroceder; (car) dar marcha atrás. □ **~ down** *vi* volverse atrás. □ **~ out** *vi* retirarse. □ **~ up** *vt* apoyar; (*Comp*) hacer una copia de seguridad de. **~ache** *n* dolor *m* de espalda. **~bone** *n* columna *f* vertebral; (*fig*) pilar *m*. **~date** /-'deɪt/ *vt* antedatar. **~er** *n* partidario *m*; (*Com*) financiador *m*. **~fire** /-'faɪə(r)/ *vi* (*Auto*) petardear; (*fig*) fallar. **his plan ~fired on him** le salió el tiro por la culata. **~ground** *n* fondo *m*; (*environment*) antecedentes *mpl*. **~hand** *n* (*Sport*) revés *m*. **~ing** *n* apoyo *m*. **~lash** *n* reacción *f*. **~log** *n* atrasos *mpl*. **~side** /-'saɪd/ *n* 🅸 trasero *m*. **~stage** /-'steɪdʒ/ *adj* de bastidores. ●*adv* entre bastidores. **~stroke** *n* (*tennis etc*) revés *m*; (*swimming*) estilo *m* espalda, estilo *m* dorso (*Mex*). **~-up** *n* apoyo *m*; (*Comp*) copia *f* de seguridad. **~ward** /-wəd/ *adj* (step etc) hacia atrás; (*retarded*) retrasado; (*undeveloped*) atrasado. ●*adv* (*Amer*) *see* **BACKWARDS**. **~wards** *adv* hacia atrás; (*fall*) de espaldas; (*back to front*) al revés. **go ~wards and forwards** ir de acá para allá. **~water** *n* agua *f* estancada; (*fig*) lugar *m* apartado

bacon /'beɪkən/ *n* tocino *m*

bacteria /bæk'tɪərɪə/ *npl* bacterias *fpl*

bad /bæd/ *adj* (**worse**, **worst**) malo, (*before masculine singular noun*) mal; (*serious*) grave; (*harmful*) nocivo; (language) indecente. **feel ~** sentirse mal

bade /beɪd/ *see* **BID**

badge /bædʒ/ *n* distintivo *m*, chapa *f*

badger /'bædʒə(r)/ *n* tejón *m*. ●*vt* acosar

bad: ~ly *adv* mal. **want ~ly** desear muchísimo. **~ly injured** gravemente herido. **~ly off** mal de dinero. **~-mannered** /-'mænəd/ *adj* mal educado

badminton /'bædmɪntən/ *n* bádminton *m*

bad-tempered /bæd'tempəd/ *adj* (*always*) de mal carácter; (*temporarily*) de mal humor

baffle /'bæfl/ *vt* desconcertar. **~d** *adj* perplejo

bag /bæg/ *n* bolsa *f*; (*handbag*) bolso *m*. ●*vt* (*pt* **bagged**) ensacar; (*take*) coger (*esp Spain*), agarrar (*LAm*). **~s** *npl* (*luggage*) equipaje *m*

baggage /'bægɪdʒ/ *n* equipaje *m*. **~ room** *n* (*Amer*) consigna *f*

baggy /'bægɪ/ *adj* (clothes) holgado

bagpipes /'bægpaɪps/ *npl* gaita *f*

baguette /bæ'get/ *n* baguette *f*

bail[1] /beɪl/ *n* fianza *f*. ●*vt* poner en libertad bajo fianza. **~ s.o. out** pagar la fianza a uno

bail[2] *vt*. **~ out** (*Naut*) achicar

bait /beɪt/ *n* cebo *m*

bak|e /beɪk/ *vt* cocer al horno. ●*vi* cocerse. **~er** *n* panadero *m*. **~ery**

n panadería *f*

balance /ˈbæləns/ *n* equilibrio *m*; (*Com*) balance *m*; (*sum*) saldo *m*; (*scales*) balanza *f*; (*remainder*) resto *m*. •*vt* equilibrar (load); mantener en equilibrio (object); nivelar (budget). •*vi* equilibrarse; (*Com*) cuadrar. **~d** *adj* equilibrado

balcony /ˈbælkənɪ/ *n* balcón *m*

bald /bɔːld/ *adj* (**-er**, **-est**) calvo, pelón (*Mex*)

bale /beɪl/ *n* bala *f*, fardo *m*. •*vi*. **~ out** lanzarse en paracaídas

Balearic /bælɪˈærɪk/ *adj*. **the ~ Islands** las Islas *fpl* Baleares

ball /bɔːl/ *n* bola *f*; (*tennis etc*) pelota *f*; (*football etc*) balón *m*, pelota *f* (*esp LAm*); (*of yarn*) ovillo *m*; (*dance*) baile *m*

ballad /ˈbæləd/ *n* balada *f*

ballast /ˈbæləst/ *n* lastre *m*

ball bearing *n* cojinete *m* de bolas

ballerina /bæləˈriːnə/ *f* bailarina *f*

ballet /ˈbæleɪ/ *n* ballet *m*. **~ dancer** *n* bailarín *m* de ballet, bailarina *f* de ballet

balloon /bəˈluːn/ *n* globo *m*

ballot /ˈbælət/ *n* votación *f*. **~ box** *n* urna *f*. **~ paper** *n* papeleta *f*.

ball: ~point *n*. **~point (pen)** bolígrafo *m*, pluma *f* atómica (*Mex*). **~room** *n* salón *m* de baile

bamboo /bæmˈbuː/ *n* bambú *m*

ban /bæn/ *vt* (*pt* **banned**) prohibir. **~ s.o. from sth** prohibir algo a uno. •*n* prohibición *f*

banal /bəˈnɑːl/ *adj* banal. **~ity** /bəˈnælətɪ/ *n* banalidad *f*

banana /bəˈnɑːnə/ *n* plátano *m*

band /bænd/ *n* (*strip*) banda *f*. •*n* (*Mus*) orquesta *f*; (*military, brass*) banda *f*. □ **~ together** *vi* juntarse

bandage /ˈbændɪdʒ/ *n* venda *f*. •*vt* vendar

Band-Aid /ˈbændeɪd/ *n* (*Amer*, ®) tirita *f*, curita *f* (*LAm*)

B & B /ˈbiːənbiː/ *abbr* (= **bed and breakfast**) cama *f* y desayuno; (*place*) pensión *f*

bandit /ˈbændɪt/ *n* bandido *m*

band: ~stand *n* quiosco *m* de música. **~wagon** *n*. **jump on the ~wagon** (*fig*) subirse al carro

bandy /ˈbændɪ/ *adj* (**-ier**, **-iest**) patizambo

bang /bæŋ/ *n* (*noise*) ruido *m*; (*blow*) golpe *m*; (*of gun*) estampido *m*; (*of door*) golpe *m*. •*vt* (*strike*) golpear. **~ the door** dar un portazo. •*adv* exactamente. •*int* ¡pum! **~s** *npl* (*Amer*) flequillo *m*, cerquillo *m* (*LAm*), fleco *m* (*Mex*)

banger /ˈbæŋə(r)/ *n* petardo *m*; (🄸, *Culin*) salchicha *f*

bangle /ˈbæŋgl/ *n* brazalete *m*

banish /ˈbænɪʃ/ *vt* desterrar

banisters /ˈbænɪstəz/ *npl* pasamanos *m*

banjo /ˈbændʒəʊ/ *n* (*pl* **-os**) banjo *m*

bank /bæŋk/ *n* (*Com*) banco *m*; (*of river*) orilla *f*. •*vt* depositar. •*vi* (*in flying*) ladearse. □ **~ on** *vt* contar con. □ **~ with** *vi* tener una cuenta con. **~ card** *n* tarjeta *f* bancaria; (*Amer*) tarjeta *f* de crédito (*expedida por un banco*). **~er** *n* banquero *m*. **~ holiday** *n* día *m* festivo, día *m* feriado (*LAm*). **~ing** *n* (*Com*) banca *f*. **~note** *n* billete *m* de banco

bankrupt /ˈbæŋkrʌpt/ *adj* & *n* quebrado (*m*). **go ~** quebrar. •*vt* hacer quebrar. **~cy** /-rʌpsɪ/ *n* bancarrota *f*, quiebra *f*

bank statement *n* estado *m*

de cuenta

banner /ˈbænə(r)/ *n* bandera *f*; (*in demonstration*) pancarta *f*

banquet /ˈbæŋkwɪt/ *n* banquete *m*

banter /ˈbæntə(r)/ *n* chanza *f*

bap /bæp/ *n* panecillo *m* blando

baptism /ˈbæptɪzəm/ *n* bautismo *m*; (*act*) bautizo *m*

Baptist /ˈbæptɪst/ *n* bautista *m & f*

baptize /bæpˈtaɪz/ *vt* bautizar

bar /bɑ:(r)/ *n* barra *f*; (*on window*) reja *f*; (*of chocolate*) tableta *f*; (*of soap*) pastilla *f*; (*pub*) bar *m*; (*Mus*) compás *m*; (*Jurid*) abogacia *f*; (*fig*) obstáculo *m*. ● *vt* (*pt* **barred**) atrancar (door); (*exclude*) excluir; (*prohibit*) prohibir. ● *prep* excepto

barbar|ian /bɑ:ˈbeərɪən/ *adj & n* bárbaro (*m*). **~ic** /bɑ:ˈbærɪk/ *adj* bárbaro

barbecue /ˈbɑ:bɪkju:/ *n* barbacoa *f*. ● *vt* asar a la parilla

barbed wire /bɑ:bd ˈwaɪə(r)/ *n* alambre *m* de púas

barber /ˈbɑ:bə(r)/ *n* peluquero *m*, barbero *m*

barbwire /ˈbɑ:bˈwaɪə(r)/ *n* (*Amer*) *see* **BARBED WIRE**

bare /beə(r)/ *adj* (-er, -est) desnudo; (*room*) con pocos muebles; (*mere*) simple; (*empty*) vacío. ● *vt* desnudar; (*uncover*) descubrir. **~ one's teeth** mostrar los dientes. **~back** *adv* a pelo. **~faced** *adj* descarado. **~foot** *adj* descalzo. **~headed** /-ˈhedɪd/ *adj* descubierto. **~ly** *adv* apenas.

bargain /ˈbɑ:gɪn/ *n* (*agreement*) pacto *m*; (*good buy*) ganga *f*. ● *vi* negociar; (*haggle*) regatear. □ **~ for** *vt* esperar, contar con

barge /bɑ:dʒ/ *n* barcaza *f*. ● *vi*. **~ in** irrumpir

baritone /ˈbærɪtəʊn/ *n* barítono *m*

bark /bɑ:k/ *n* (*of dog*) ladrido *m*; (*of tree*) corteza *f*. ● *vi* ladrar

barley /ˈbɑ:lɪ/ *n* cebada *f*

bar: ~maid *n* camarera *f*. **~man** /-mən/ *n* camarero *m*, barman *m*

barmy /ˈbɑ:mɪ/ *adj* ▣ chiflado

barn /bɑ:n/ *n* granero *m*

barometer /bəˈrɒmɪtə(r)/ *n* barómetro *m*

baron /ˈbærən/ *n* barón *m*. **~ess** /-ɪs/ *n* baronesa *f*

barracks /ˈbærəks/ *npl* cuartel *m*

barrage /ˈbærɑ:ʒ/ *n* (*Mil*) barrera *f*; (*dam*) presa *f*. **a ~ of questions** un aluvión de preguntas

barrel /ˈbærəl/ *n* barril *m*; (*of gun*) cañón *m*

barren /ˈbærən/ *adj* estéril

barrette /bəˈret/ *n* (*Amer*) pasador *m*

barricade /bærɪˈkeɪd/ *n* barricada *f*. ● *vt* cerrar con barricadas

barrier /ˈbærɪə(r)/ *n* barrera *f*

barrister /ˈbærɪstə(r)/ *n* abogado *m*

bartender /ˈbɑ:tendə(r)/ *n* (*Amer*) (*male*) camarero *m*, barman *m*; (*female*) camarera *f*

barter /ˈbɑ:tə(r)/ *n* trueque *m*. ● *vt* trocar

base /beɪs/ *n* base *f*. ● *vt* basar. **~ball** *n* béisbol *m*, beisbol *m* (*Mex*)

basement /ˈbeɪsmənt/ *n* sótano *m*

bash /bæʃ/ *vt* golpear. ● *n* golpe *m*. **have a ~** ▣ probar

bashful /ˈbæʃfl/ *adj* tímido

basic /ˈbeɪsɪk/ *adj* básico, fundamental. **~ally** *adv* fundamentalmente

basin /'beɪsn/ *n* (*for washing*) palangana *f*; (*for food*) cuenco *m*; (*of river*) cuenca *f*

basis /'beɪsɪs/ *n* (*pl* **bases**/-si:z/) base *f*

bask /bɑ:sk/ *vi* asolearse; (*fig*) gozar (**in** de)

basket /'bɑ:skɪt/ *n* cesta *f*; (*big*) cesto *m*. **~ball** *n* baloncesto *m*, básquetbol *m* (*LAm*)

bass[1] /beɪs/ *adj* bajo. ● *n* (*Mus*) bajo *m*

bass[2] /bæs/ *n* (*fish*) lubina *f*

bassoon /bə'su:n/ *n* fagot *m*

bastard /'bɑ:stəd/ *n* bastardo *m*. **you ~!** (*vulgar*) ¡cabrón! (*vulgar*)

bat /bæt/ *n* (*for baseball, cricket*) bate *m*; (*for table tennis*) raqueta *f*; (*mammal*) murciélago *m*. **off one's own ~** por sí solo. ● *vt* (*pt* **batted**) golpear. **without ~ting an eyelid** sin pestañear. ● *vi* batear

batch /bætʃ/ *n* (*of people*) grupo *m*; (*of papers*) pila *f*; (*of goods*) remesa *f*; (*of bread*) hornada *f*; (*Comp*) lote *m*

bated /'beɪtɪd/ *adj*. **with ~ breath** con aliento entrecortado

bath /bɑ:θ/ *n* (*pl* **-s** /bɑ:ðz/) baño *m*; (*tub*) bañera *f*, tina *f* (*LAm*). **~s** *npl* (*swimming pool*) piscina *f*, alberca *f* (*Mex*). **have a ~, take a ~** (*Amer*) bañarse. ● *vt* bañar. ● *vi* bañarse

bathe /beɪð/ *vt* bañar. ● *vi* bañarse. ● *n* baño *m*. **~r** *n* bañista *m & f*

bathing /'beɪðɪŋ/ *n* baños *mpl*. **~ costume, ~ suit** *n* traje *m* de baño

bathroom /'bɑ:θrʊm/ *n* cuarto *m* de baño; (*Amer, toilet*) servicio *m*, baño *m* (*LAm*)

batsman /'bætsmən/ *n* (*pl* **-men**) bateador *m*

battalion /bə'tælɪən/ *n* batallón *m*

batter /'bætə(r)/ *vt* (*beat*) apalear; (*cover with batter*) rebozar. ● *n* batido *m* para rebozar; (*Amer, for cake*) masa *f*. **~ed** /'bætəd/ *adj* (car etc) estropeado; (wife etc) maltratado

battery /'bætərɪ/ *n* (*Mil, Auto*) batería *f*; (*of torch, radio*) pila *f*

battle /'bætl/ *n* batalla *f*; (*fig*) lucha *f*. ● *vi* luchar. **~field** *n* campo *m* de batalla. **~ship** *n* acorazado *m*

bawl /bɔ:l/ *vt/i* gritar

bay /beɪ/ *n* (*on coast*) bahía *f*. **keep at ~** mantener a raya

bayonet /'beɪənet/ *n* bayoneta *f*

bay window /beɪ 'wɪndəʊ/ *n* ventana *f* salediza

bazaar /bə'zɑ:(r)/ *n* bazar *m*

BC *abbr* (= **before Christ**) a. de C., antes de Cristo

be /bi:/

present **am, are, is;** past **was, were;** past participle **been**

● *intransitive verb*

! Spanish has two verbs meaning **be**, *ser* and *estar*. See those entries for further information about the differences between them.

····➤ (*position, changed condition or state*) estar. **where is the library?** ¿dónde está la biblioteca? **she's tired** está cansada. **how are you?** ¿cómo estás?

····➤ (*identity, nature or permanent characteristics*) ser.**she's tall** es alta. **he's Scottish** es

b

escocés. **I'm a journalist** soy periodista. **he's very kind** es muy bondadoso

····▸ (*feel*) **to be** + *adjective* tener + *sustantivo*. **to be cold/hot** tener frío/calor. **he's hungry/thirsty** tiene hambre/sed

····▸ (*age*) **he's thirty** tiene treinta años

····▸ (*weather*) **it's cold/hot** hace frío/calor. **it was 40 degrees** hacía 40 grados

● *auxiliary verb*

····▸ (*in tenses*) estar. **I'm working** estoy trabajando. **they were singing** estaban cantando, cantaban

····▸ (*in tag questions*) **it's a beautiful house, isn't it?** es una casa preciosa, ¿verdad? *or* ¿no? *or* ¿no es cierto?

····▸ (*in short answers*) **are you disappointed? - yes, I am** ¿estás desilusionado? - sí (,lo estoy). **I'm surprised, aren't you?** estoy sorprendido, ¿tú no?

····▸ (*in passive sentences*) **it was built in 1834** fue construido en 1834, se construyó en 1834. **she was told that ...** le dijeron que..., se le dijo que ...

! Note that passive sentences in English are often translated using the pronoun *se* or using the third person plural.

beach /biːtʃ/ *n* playa *f*

beacon /ˈbiːkən/ *n* faro *m*

bead /biːd/ *n* cuenta *f*; (*of glass*) abalorio *m*

beak /biːk/ *n* pico *m*

beaker /ˈbiːkə(r)/ *n* taza *f* (*alta y sin asa*)

beam /biːm/ *n* (*of wood*) viga *f*; (*of light*) rayo *m*; (*Naut*) bao *m*. ● *vt* emitir. ● *vi* irradiar; (*smile*) sonreír

bean /biːn/ *n* alubia *f*, frijol *m* (*LAm*); (*broad bean*) haba *f*; (*of coffee*) grano *m*

bear /beə(r)/ *vt* (*pt* **bore**, *pp* **borne**) llevar; parir (niño); (*endure*) soportar. ~ **right** torcer a la derecha. ~ **in mind** tener en cuenta. □ ~ **with** *vt* tener paciencia con. ● *n* oso *m*. ~**able** *adj* soportable

beard /bɪəd/ *n* barba *f*. ~**ed** *adj* barbudo

bearer /ˈbeərə(r)/ *n* portador *m*; (*of passport*) titular *m & f*

bearing /ˈbeərɪŋ/ *n* comportamiento *m*; (*relevance*) relación *f*; (*Mec*) cojinete *m*. **get one's ~s** orientarse. **lose one's ~s** desorientarse

beast /biːst/ *n* bestia *f*; (*person*) bruto *m*. ~**ly** *adj* (**-ier**, **-iest**) bestial; ⓘ horrible

beat /biːt/ *vt* (*pt* **beat**, *pp* **beaten**) (*hit*) pegar; (*Culin*) batir; (*defeat*) derrotar; (*better*) sobrepasar; batir (record); (*baffle*) dejar perplejo. ~ **it** ⊠ largarse. ● *vi* (heart) latir. ● *n* latido *m*; (*Mus*) ritmo *m*; (*of policeman*) ronda *f*. □ ~ **up** *vt* darle una paliza a; (*Culin*) batir. ~ **up on** (*Amer, fam*) darle una paliza a. ~**er** *n* batidor *m*. ~**ing** *n* paliza *f*

beautician /bjuːˈtɪʃn/ *n* esteticista *m & f*

beautiful /ˈbjuːtɪfl/ *adj* hermoso. ~**ly** *adv* maravillosamente

beauty /ˈbjuːtɪ/ *n* belleza *f*. ~ **salon**, ~ **shop** (*Amer*) *n* salón *m* de belleza. ~ **spot** *n* (*on face*) lunar *m*; (*site*) lugar *m* pintoresco

beaver /ˈbiːvə(r)/ *n* castor *m*

became /bɪˈkeɪm/ *see* BECOME

because /bɪˈkɒz/ *conj* porque. ●*adv.* ~ **of** por, a causa de

beckon /ˈbekən/ *vt/i.* ~ **(to)** hacer señas (a)

become /bɪˈkʌm/ *vi* (*pt* **became**, *pp* **become**) hacerse, llegar a ser, volverse, convertirse en. **what has ~ of her?** ¿qué es de ella?

bed /bed/ *n* cama *f*; (*layer*) estrato *m*; (*of sea, river*) fondo *m*; (*of flowers*) macizo *m*. **go to ~** acostarse. ●*vi* (*pt* **bedded**). **~ and breakfast (B & B)** cama y desayuno; (*place*) pensión *f*. **~bug** *n* chinche *f*. **~clothes** *npl*, **~ding** *n* ropa *f* de cama, cobijas *fpl* (*LAm*)

Bed and breakfast Los bed & breakfast o B&B son casas privadas o pequeños hoteles que ofrecen alojamiento y desayuno a precios generalmente módicos.

bed: ~room *n* dormitorio *m*, cuarto *m*, habitación *f*, recámara *f* (*Mex*). **~-sitter** /-ˈsɪtə(r)/ *n* habitación *f* con cama y uso de cocina y baño compartidos, estudio *m*. **~spread** *n* colcha *f*. **~time** *n* hora *f* de acostarse

bee /biː/ *n* abeja *f*; (*Amer, social gathering*) círculo *m*

beech /biːtʃ/ *n* haya *f*

beef /biːf/ *n* carne *f* de vaca, carne *f* de res (*Mex*). ●*vi* ⊠ quejarse. **~burger** *n* hamburguesa *f*. **~y** *adj* (**-ier, -iest**) musculoso

bee: ~hive *n* colmena *f*. **~line** *n*. **make a ~line for** ir en línea recta hacia

been /biːn/ *see* BE

beer /bɪə(r)/ *n* cerveza *f*

beet /biːt/ *n* (*Amer*) remolacha *f*, betabel *f* (*Mex*)

beetle /ˈbiːtl/ *n* escarabajo *m*

beetroot /ˈbiːtruːt/ *n invar* remolacha *f*, betabel *f* (*Mex*)

befall /bɪˈfɔːl/ *vt* (*pt* **befell**, *pp* **befallen**) ocurrirle a. ●*vi* ocurrir

before /bɪˈfɔː(r)/ *prep* (*time*) antes de; (*place*) delante de. **~ leaving** antes de marcharse. ●*adv* (*place*) delante; (*time*) antes. **a week ~** una semana antes. **the week ~** la semana anterior. ●*conj* (*time*) antes de que. **~ he leaves** antes de que se vaya. **~hand** *adv* de antemano

befriend /bɪˈfrend/ *vt* hacerse amigo de

beg /beg/ *vt/i* (*pt* **begged**) mendigar; (*entreat*) suplicar; (*ask*) pedir. **~ s.o.'s pardon** pedir perdón a uno. **I ~ your pardon!** ¡perdone Vd! **I ~ your pardon?** ¿cómo?

began /bɪˈgæn/ *see* BEGIN

beggar /ˈbegə(r)/ *n* mendigo *m*

begin /bɪˈgɪn/ *vt/i* (*pt* **began**, *pp* **begun**, *pres p* **beginning**) comenzar, empezar. **~ner** *n* principiante *m & f*. **~ning** *n* principio *m*

begrudge /bɪˈgrʌdʒ/ *vt* envidiar; (*give*) dar de mala gana

begun /bɪˈgʌn/ *see* BEGIN

behalf /bɪˈhɑːf/ *n*. **on ~ of, in ~ of** (*Amer*) de parte de, en nombre de

behav|e /bɪˈheɪv/ *vi* comportarse, portarse. **~e (o.s.)** portarse bien. **~iour** /bɪˈheɪvjə(r)/ *n* comportamiento *m*

behead /bɪˈhed/ *vt* decapitar

behind /bɪˈhaɪnd/ *prep* detrás de, atrás de (*LAm*). ●*adv* detrás; (*late*) atrasado. ●*n* ⊡ trasero *m*

beige /beɪʒ/ *adj & n* beige (*m*)

being /ˈbiːɪŋ/ *n* ser *m*. **come into ~** nacer

b

belated /bɪˈleɪtɪd/ *adj* tardío
belch /beltʃ/ *vi* eructar. ▫ ~ **out** *vt* arrojar (smoke)
belfry /ˈbelfrɪ/ *n* campanario *m*
Belgi|an /ˈbeldʒən/ *adj & n* belga (*m & f*). ~**um** /ˈbeldʒəm/ *n* Bélgica *f*
belie|f /bɪˈliːf/ *n* (*trust*) fe *f*; (*opinion*) creencia *f*. ~**ve** /bɪˈliːv/ *vt/i* creer. ~**ve in** creer en. **make** ~**ve** fingir
belittle /bɪˈlɪtl/ *vt* menospreciar (achievements); denigrar (person)
bell /bel/ *n* campana *f*; (*on door, bicycle*) timbre *m*
belligerent /bɪˈlɪdʒərənt/ *adj* beligerante
bellow /ˈbeləʊ/ *vt* gritar. • *vi* bramar. ~**s** *npl* fuelle *m*
bell pepper *n* (*Amer*) pimiento *m*
belly /ˈbelɪ/ *n* barriga *f*
belong /bɪˈlɒŋ/ *vi* pertenecer (**to** a); (*club*) ser socio (**to** de); (*have as usual place*) ir. ~**ings** /bɪˈlɒŋɪŋz/ *npl* pertenencias *fpl*. **personal** ~**ings** efectos *mpl* personales
beloved /bɪˈlʌvɪd/ *adj* querido
below /bɪˈləʊ/ *prep* debajo de, abajo de (*LAm*); (*fig*) inferior a. • *adv* abajo
belt /belt/ *n* cinturón *m*; (*area*) zona *f*. • *vt* (*fig*) rodear; ⊠ darle una paliza a. ~**way** *n* (*Amer*) carretera *f* de circunvalación
bench /bentʃ/ *n* banco *m*
bend /bend/ *n* curva *f*. • *vt* (*pt & pp* **bent**) doblar; torcer (arm, leg). • *vi* doblarse; (road) torcerse. ▫ ~ **down** *vi* inclinarse ▫ ~ **over** *vi* agacharse
beneath /bɪˈniːθ/ *prep* debajo de; (*fig*) inferior a. • *adv* abajo
beneficial /benɪˈfɪʃl/ *adj* provechoso
beneficiary /benɪˈfɪʃərɪ/ *n* beneficiario *m*
benefit /ˈbenɪfɪt/ *n* provecho *m*, ventaja *f*; (*allowance*) prestación *f*; (*for unemployed*) subsidio *m*; (*perk*) beneficio *m*. • *vt* (*pt* **benefited**, *pres p* **benefiting**) beneficiar. • *vi* beneficiarse
benevolent /bəˈnevələnt/ *adj* benévolo
benign /bɪˈnaɪn/ *adj* benigno
bent /bent/ *see* BEND. • *n* inclinación *f*. • *adj* torcido; (⊠, *corrupt*) corrompido
bereave|d /bɪˈriːvd/ *n*. **the** ~**d** la familia del difunto. ~**ment** *n* pérdida *f*; (*mourning*) luto *m*
beret /ˈbereɪ/ *n* boina *f*
berry /ˈberɪ/ *n* baya *f*
berserk /bəˈsɜːk/ *adj*. **go** ~ volverse loco
berth /bɜːθ/ *n* litera *f*; (*anchorage*) amarradero *m*. **give a wide** ~ **to** evitar. • *vt/i* atracar
beside /bɪˈsaɪd/ *prep* al lado de. **be** ~ **o.s.** estar fuera de sí
besides /bɪˈsaɪdz/ *prep* además de; (*except*) excepto. • *adv* además
besiege /bɪˈsiːdʒ/ *vt* sitiar, asediar; (*fig*) acosar
best /best/ *adj* (el) mejor. **the** ~ **thing is to...** lo mejor es... • *adv* mejor. **like** ~ preferir. • *n* lo mejor. **at** ~ a lo más. **do one's** ~ hacer todo lo posible. **make the** ~ **of** contentarse con. ~ **man** *n* padrino *m* (de boda)
bestow /bɪˈstəʊ/ *vt* conceder
bestseller /bestˈselə(r)/ *n* éxito *m* de librería, bestseller *m*
bet /bet/ *n* apuesta *f*. • *vt/i* (*pt* **bet** *or* **betted**) apostar
betray /bɪˈtreɪ/ *vt* traicionar. ~**al** *n* traición *f*

better /ˈbetə(r)/ *adj & adv* mejor. ~ **off** en mejores condiciones; (*richer*) más rico. **get** ~ mejorar. **all the** ~ tanto mejor. **I'd** ~ **be off** me tengo que ir. **the** ~ **part of** la mayor parte de. • *vt* mejorar; (*beat*) sobrepasar. ~ **o.s.** superarse. • *n* superior *m*. **get the** ~ **of** vencer a. **my** ~**s** mis superiores *mpl*

between /bɪˈtwi:n/ *prep* entre. • *adv* en medio

beverage /ˈbevərɪdʒ/ *n* bebida *f*

beware /bɪˈweə(r)/ *vi* tener cuidado. • *int* ¡cuidado!

bewilder /bɪˈwɪldə(r)/ *vt* desconcertar. ~**ment** *n* aturdimiento *m*

bewitch /bɪˈwɪtʃ/ *vt* hechizar; (*delight*) cautivar

beyond /bɪˈjɒnd/ *prep* más allá de; (*fig*) fuera de. ~ **doubt** sin lugar a duda. • *adv* más allá

bias /ˈbaɪəs/ *n* tendencia *f*; (*prejudice*) prejuicio *m*. • *vt* (*pt* **biased**) influir en. ~**ed** *adj* parcial

bib /bɪb/ *n* babero *m*

Bible /ˈbaɪbl/ *n* Biblia *f*

biblical /ˈbɪblɪkl/ *adj* bíblico

bibliography /bɪblɪˈɒgrəfɪ/ *n* bibliografía *f*

biceps /ˈbaɪseps/ *n invar* bíceps *m*

bicker /ˈbɪkə(r)/ *vi* altercar

bicycle /ˈbaɪsɪkl/ *n* bicicleta *f*

bid /bɪd/ *n* (*offer*) oferta *f*; (*attempt*) tentativa *f*. • *vi* hacer una oferta. • *vt* (*pt & pp* **bid**, *pres p* **bidding**) ofrecer; (*pt* **bid**, *pp* **bidden**, *pres p* **bidding**) mandar; dar (welcome, good day etc). ~**der** *n* postor *m*. ~**ding** *n* (*at auction*) ofertas *fpl*; (*order*) mandato *m*

bide /baɪd/ *vt*. ~ **one's time** esperar el momento oportuno

bifocals /baɪˈfəʊklz/ *npl* gafas *fpl* bifocales, anteojos *mpl* bifocales (*LAm*)

big /bɪg/ *adj* (**bigger**, **biggest**) grande, (*before singular noun*) gran. • *adv*. **talk** ~ fanfarronear

bigam|ist /ˈbɪgəmɪst/ *n* bígamo *m*. ~**ous** /ˈbɪgəməs/ *adj* bígamo. ~**y** *n* bigamia *f*

big-headed /-ˈhedɪd/ *adj* engreído

bigot /ˈbɪgət/ *n* fanático *m*. ~**ed** *adj* fanático

bike /baɪk/ *n* [I] bici *f* [I]

bikini /bɪˈki:nɪ/ *n* (*pl* **-is**) bikini *m*

bile /baɪl/ *n* bilis *f*

bilingual /baɪˈlɪŋgwəl/ *adj* bilingüe

bill /bɪl/ *n* cuenta *f*; (*invoice*) factura *f*; (*notice*) cartel *m*; (*Amer, banknote*) billete *m*; (*Pol*) proyecto *m* de ley; (*of bird*) pico *m*

billet /ˈbɪlɪt/ *n* (*Mil*) alojamiento *m*. • *vt* alojar

billfold /ˈbɪlfəʊld/ *n* (*Amer*) cartera *f*, billetera *f*

billiards /ˈbɪlɪədz/ *n* billar *m*

billion /ˈbɪlɪən/ *n* billón *m*; (*Amer*) mil millones *mpl*

bin /bɪn/ *n* recipiente *m*; (*for rubbish*) cubo *m* de basura, bote *m* de basura (*Mex*); (*for waste paper*) papelera *f*

bind /baɪnd/ *vt* (*pt* **bound**) atar; encuadernar (book); (*Jurid*) obligar. • *n* [I] lata *f*. ~**ing** *n* (*of books*) encuadernación *f*; (*braid*) ribete *m*

binge /bɪndʒ/ *n* [※], (*of food*) comilona *f*; (*of drink*) borrachera *f*. **go on a** ~ ir de juerga

bingo /ˈbɪŋgəʊ/ *n* bingo *m*

binoculars /bɪˈnɒkjʊləz/ *npl* gemelos *mpl*

biofuel /ˈbaɪəʊfju:əl/ *n* biocarburante *m*

biograph|er /baɪˈɒgrəfə(r)/ *n*

biógrafo *m*. **~y** *n* biografía *f*

biolog|ical /baɪə'lɒdʒɪkl/ *adj* biológico. **~ist** /baɪ'ɒlədʒɪst/ *n* biólogo *m*. **~y** /baɪ'ɒlədʒɪ/ *n* biología *f*

bioterrorism /baɪəʊ'terərɪzm/ *n* bioterrorismo *m*

birch /bɜ:tʃ/ *n* (*tree*) abedul *m*

bird /bɜ:d/ *n* ave *f*; (*small*) pájaro *m*; (*sl*, *girl*) chica *f*

Biro /'baɪərəʊ/ *n* (*pl* **-os**) (®) bolígrafo *m*

birth /bɜ:θ/ *n* nacimiento *m*. **give ~** dar a luz. **~ certificate** *n* partida *f* de nacimiento. **~ control** *n* control *m* de la natalidad. **~day** *n* cumpleaños *m*. **~mark** *n* marca *f* de nacimiento. **~place** *n* lugar *m* de nacimiento. **~ rate** *n* natalidad *f*

biscuit /'bɪskɪt/ *n* galleta *f*

bisect /baɪ'sekt/ *vt* bisecar

bishop /'bɪʃəp/ *n* obispo *m*; (*Chess*) alfil *m*

bit /bɪt/ *see* BITE. •*n* trozo *m*; (*quantity*) poco *m*; (*of horse*) bocado *m*; (*Mec*) broca *f*; (*Comp*) bit *m*

bitch /bɪtʃ/ *n* perra *f*; (*fam, woman*) bruja *f* ⊡

bit|e /baɪt/ *vt/i* (*pt* **bit**, *pp* **bitten**) morder; (*insect*) picar. **~e one's nails** morderse las uñas. •*n* mordisco *m*; (*mouthful*) bocado *m*; (*of insect etc*) picadura *f*. **~ing** /'baɪtɪŋ/ *adj* mordaz

bitter /'bɪtə(r)/ *adj* amargo; (*of weather*) glacial. •*n* cerveza *f* amarga. **~ly** *adv* amargamente. **it's ~ly cold** hace un frío glacial. **~ness** *n* amargor *m*; (*resentment*) amargura *f*

bizarre /bɪ'zɑ:(r)/ *adj* extraño

black /blæk/ *adj* (**-er**, **-est**) negro. **~ and blue** amoratado. •*n* negro *m*; (*coffee*) solo, negro (*LAm*). •*vt* ennegrecer; limpiar (shoes). **~ out** *vi* desmayarse. **~ and white** *n* blanco y negro *m*. **~-and-white** *adj* en blanco y negro. **~berry** /-bərɪ/ *n* zarzamora *f*. **~bird** *n* mirlo *m*. **~board** *n* pizarra *f*. **~currant** /-'kʌrənt/ *n* grosella *f* negra. **~en** *vt* ennegrecer. **~ eye** *n* ojo *m* morado. **~list** *vt* poner en la lista negra. **~mail** *n* chantaje *m*. •*vt* chantajear. **~mailer** *n* chantajista *m & f*. **~out** *n* apagón *m*; (*Med*) desmayo *m*; (*of news*) censura *f*. **~smith** *n* herrero *m*

bladder /'blædə(r)/ *n* vejiga *f*

blade /bleɪd/ *n* (*of knife, sword*) hoja *f*. **~ of grass** brizna *f* de hierba

blame /bleɪm/ *vt* echar la culpa a. **be to ~** tener la culpa. •*n* culpa *f*. **~less** *adj* inocente

bland /blænd/ *adj* (**-er**, **-est**) suave

blank /blæŋk/ *adj* (page, space) en blanco; (cassette) virgen; (cartridge) sin bala; (*fig*) vacío. •*n* blanco *m*

blanket /'blæŋkɪt/ *n* manta *f*, cobija *f* (*LAm*), frazada (*LAm*); (*fig*) capa *f*. •*vt* (*pt* **blanketed**) (*fig*) cubrir (**in**, **with** de)

blare /bleə(r)/ *vi* sonar muy fuerte. •*n* estrépito *m*

blasphem|e /blæs'fi:m/ *vt/i* blasfemar. **~ous** /'blæsfəməs/ *adj* blasfemo. **~y** /'blæsfəmɪ/ *n* blasfemia *f*

blast /blɑ:st/ *n* explosión *f*; (*gust*) ráfaga *f*; (*sound*) toque *m*. •*vt* volar. **~ed** *adj* maldito. **~-off** *n* (*of missile*) despegue *m*

blatant /'bleɪtnt/ *adj* patente; (*shameless*) descarado

blaze /'bleɪz/ *n* llamarada *f*; (*of light*) resplandor *m*; (*fig*) arranque *m*. •*vi* arder en llamas; (*fig*) brillar

blazer /ˈbleɪzə(r)/ *n* chaqueta *f*

bleach /bliːtʃ/ *n* lejía *f*, cloro *m* (*LAm*), blanqueador *m* (*LAm*). •*vt* blanquear; decolorar (hair).

bleak /bliːk/ *adj* (**-er**, **-est**) desolado; (*fig*) sombrío

bleat /bliːt/ *n* balido *m*. •*vi* balar

bleed /bliːd/ *vt/i* (*pt* **bled** /bled/) sangrar

bleep /bliːp/ *n* pitido *m*

blemish /ˈblemɪʃ/ *n* mancha *f*

blend /blend/ *n* mezcla *f*. •*vt* mezclar. •*vi* combinarse. **~er** *n* licuadora *f*

bless /bles/ *vt* bendecir. **~ you!** (*on sneezing*) ¡Jesús!, ¡salud! (*Mex*). **~ed** /ˈblesɪd/ *adj* bendito. **~ing** *n* bendición *f*; (*advantage*) ventaja *f*

blew /bluː/ *see* BLOW

blight /blaɪt/ *n* añublo *m*, tizón *m*; (*fig*) plaga *f*. •*vt* añublar, atizonar; (*fig*) destrozar

blind /blaɪnd/ *adj* ciego. **~ alley** callejón *m* sin salida. •*n* persiana *f*; (*fig*) pretexto *m*. •*vt* dejar ciego; (*dazzle*) deslumbrar. **~fold** *adj & adv* con los ojos vendados. •*n* venda *f*. •*vt* vendar los ojos a. **~ly** *adv* a ciegas. **~ness** *n* ceguera *f*

blink /blɪŋk/ *vi* parpadear; (light) centellear. **~ers** *npl* (*on horse*) anteojeras *fpl*

bliss /blɪs/ *n* felicidad *f*. **~ful** *adj* feliz

blister /ˈblɪstə(r)/ *n* ampolla *f*

blizzard /ˈblɪzəd/ *n* ventisca *f*

bloated /ˈbləʊtɪd/ *adj* hinchado (**with** de)

blob /blɒb/ *n* (*drip*) gota *f*; (*stain*) mancha *f*

bloc /blɒk/ *n* (*Pol*) bloque *m*

block /blɒk/ *n* bloque *m*; (*of wood*) zoquete *m*; (*of buildings*) manzana *f*, cuadra *f* (*LAm*). **in ~ letters** en letra de imprenta. **~ of flats** edificio *m* de apartamentos, casa *f* de pisos. •*vt* bloquear. **~ade** /blɒˈkeɪd/ *n* bloqueo *m*. •*vt* bloquear. **~age** /-ɪdʒ/ *n* obstrucción *f*. **~head** *n* 🄸 zopenco *m*

bloke /bləʊk/ *n* 🄸 tipo *m*, tío *m* 🄸

blond /blɒnd/ *adj & n* rubio (*m*), güero (*m*) (*Mex fam*). **~e** *adj & n* rubia (*f*), güera (*f*) (*Mex fam*)

blood /blʌd/ *n* sangre *f*. **~bath** *n* masacre *m*. **~-curdling** /-kɜːdlɪŋ/ *adj* horripilante. **~hound** *n* sabueso *m*. **~ pressure** *n* tensión *f* arterial. **high ~ pressure** hipertensión *f*. **~shed** *n* derramamiento *m* de sangre. **~shot** *adj* sanguinolento; (eye) inyectado de sangre. **~stream** *n* torrente *m* sanguíneo. **~thirsty** *adj* sanguinario. **~y** *adj* (**-ier**, **-iest**) sangriento; (*stained*) ensangrentado; 🅇 maldito

bloom /bluːm/ *n* flor *f*. •*vi* florecer

blossom /ˈblɒsəm/ *n* flor *f*. •*vi* florecer. **~ (out) into** (*fig*) llegar a ser

blot /blɒt/ *n* borrón *m*. •*vt* (*pt* **blotted**) manchar; (*dry*) secar. □ **~ out** *vt* oscurecer

blotch /blɒtʃ/ *n* mancha *f*. **~y** *adj* lleno de manchas

blotting-paper /ˈblɒtɪŋ/ *n* papel *m* secante

blouse /blaʊz/ *n* blusa *f*

blow /bləʊ/ *vt* (*pt* **blew**, *pp* **blown**) soplar; fundir (fuse); tocar (trumpet). •*vi* soplar; (fuse) fundirse; (*sound*) sonar. •*n* golpe *m*. □ **~ down** *vt* derribar. □ **~ out** *vi* apagar (candle). □ **~ over** *vi* pasar. □ **~ up** *vt* inflar; (*explode*) volar;

(*Photo*) ampliar. *vi* (*explode*) estallar; (*burst*) reventar. **~-dry** *vt* secar con secador. **~lamp** *n* soplete *m*. **~out** *n* (*of tyre*) reventón *m*. **~ torch** *n* soplete *m*

blue /blu:/ *adj* (**-er**, **-est**) azul; (joke) verde. • *n* azul *m*. **out of the ~** totalmente inesperado. **~s** *npl*. **have the ~s** tener tristeza. **~bell** *n* campanilla *f*. **~berry** *n* arándano *m*. **~bottle** *n* moscarda *f*. **~print** *n* plano *m*; (*fig, plan*) programa *m*

bluff /blʌf/ *n* (*poker*) farol *m*, bluff *m* (*LAm*), blof *m* (*Mex*). • *vt* engañar. • *vi* tirarse un farol, hacer un bluf (*LAm*), blofear (*Mex*)

blunder /'blʌndə(r)/ *vi* cometer un error. • *n* metedura *f* de pata

blunt /blʌnt/ *adj* desafilado; (person) directo, abrupto. • *vt* desafilar. **~ly** *adv* francamente

blur /blɜ:(r)/ *n* impresión *f* indistinta. • *vt* (*pt* **blurred**) hacer borroso

blurb /blɜ:b/ *n* resumen *m* publicitario

blurt /blɜ:t/ *vt*. **~ out** dejar escapar

blush /blʌʃ/ *vi* ruborizarse. • *n* rubor *m*

boar /bɔ:(r)/ *n* verraco *m*. **wild ~** jabalí *m*

board /bɔ:d/ *n* tabla *f*, tablero *m*; (*for notices*) tablón *m* de anuncios, tablero *m* de anuncios (*LAm*); (*blackboard*) pizarra *f*; (*food*) pensión *f*; (*of company*) junta *f*. **~ and lodging** casa y comida. **full ~** pensión *f* completa. **go by the ~** ser abandonado. • *vt* alojar; **~ a ship** embarcarse. • *vi* alojarse (**with** en casa de); (*at school*) ser interno. **~er** *n* huésped *m* & *f*; (*school*) interno *m*. **~ing card** *n* tarjeta *f* de embarque. **~ing house** *n* casa *f* de huéspedes, pensión *f*. **~ing pass** *n see* **~ING CARD**. **~ing school** *n* internado *m*

boast /bəʊst/ *vt* enorgullecerse de. • *vi* jactarse. • *n* jactancia *f*. **~ful** *adj* jactancioso

boat /bəʊt/ *n* barco *m*; (*small*) bote *m*, barca *f*

bob /bɒb/ *vi* (*pt* **bobbed**) menearse, subir y bajar. □ **~ up** *vi* presentarse súbitamente

bobbin /'bɒbɪn/ *n* carrete *m*; (*in sewing machine*) canilla *f*, bobina *f*

bobby pin /'bɒbɪ/ *n* (*Amer*) horquilla *f*, pasador *m* (*Mex*). **~ sox** /sɒks/ *npl* (*Amer*) calcetines *mpl* cortos

bobsleigh /'bɒbsleɪ/ *n* bob (sleigh) *m*

bode /bəʊd/ *vi*. **~ well/ill** ser de buen/mal agüero

bodice /'bɒdɪs/ *n* corpiño *m*

bodily /'bɒdɪlɪ/ *adj* físico, corporal. • *adv* físicamente

body /'bɒdɪ/ *n* cuerpo *m*; (*dead*) cadáver *m*. **~guard** *n* guardaespaldas *m*. **~ part** *n* pedazo *m* de cuerpo. **~work** *n* carrocería *f*

bog /bɒg/ *n* ciénaga *f*. □ **~ down** *vt* (*pt* **bogged**). **get ~ged down** empantanarse

boggle /'bɒgl/ *vi* sobresaltarse. **the mind ~s** uno se queda atónito

bogus /'bəʊgəs/ *adj* falso

boil /bɔɪl/ *vt/i* hervir. **be ~ing hot** estar ardiendo; (weather) hacer mucho calor. • *n* furúnculo *m*. □ **~ away** *vi* evaporarse. □ **~ down to** *vt* reducirse a. □ **~ over** *vi* rebosar. **~ed** *adj* hervido; (egg) pasado por agua. **~er** *n* caldera *f*. **~er suit** *n* mono *m*, overol *m* (*LAm*)

boisterous /'bɔɪstərəs/ *adj* ruidoso, bullicioso

bold /bəʊld/ *adj* (**-er**, **-est**) audaz. **~ly** *adv* con audacia, audazmente

Bolivia /bəˈlɪvɪə/ *n* Bolivia *f*. **~n** *adj & n* boliviano (*m*)

bolster /ˈbəʊlstə(r)/ □ **~ up** *vt* sostener

bolt /bəʊlt/ *n* (*on door*) cerrojo *m*; (*for nut*) perno *m*; (*lightning*) rayo *m*; (*leap*) fuga *f*. ● *vt* echar el cerrojo a (door); engullir (food). ● *vi* fugarse. ● *adv*. **~ upright** rígido

bomb /bɒm/ *n* bomba *f*. ● *vt* bombardear. **~ard** /bɒmˈbɑːd/ *vt* bombardear **~er** /ˈbɒmə(r)/ *n* (*plane*) bombardero *m*; (*terrorist*) terrorista *m & f*. **~ing** /ˈbɒmɪŋ/ *n* bombardeo *m*. **~shell** *n* bomba *f*

bond /bɒnd/ *n* (*agreement*) obligación *f*; (*link*) lazo *m*; (*Com*) bono *m*. ● *vi* (*stick*) adherirse. **~age** /-ɪdʒ/ *n* esclavitud *f*

bone /bəʊn/ *n* hueso *m*; (*of fish*) espina *f*. ● *vt* deshuesar; quitar las espinas a (fish). **~-dry** *adj* completamente seco. **~ idle** *adj* holgazán

bonfire /ˈbɒnfaɪə(r)/ *n* hoguera *f*, fogata *f*

bonnet /ˈbɒnɪt/ *n* gorra *f*; (*Auto*) capó *m*, capote *m* (*Mex*)

bonus /ˈbəʊnəs/ *n* (*payment*) bonificación *f*; (*fig*) ventaja *f*

bony /ˈbəʊnɪ/ *adj* (**-ier**, **-iest**) huesudo; (fish) lleno de espinas

boo /buː/ *int* ¡bu! ● *vt/i* abuchear

boob /buːb/ *n* (*fam, mistake*) metedura *f* de pata. ● *vi* ⊡ meter la pata

book /bʊk/ *n* libro *m*; (*of cheques etc*) talonario *m*, chequera *f*; (*notebook*) libreta *f*; (*exercise book*) cuaderno *m*. **~s** (*mpl*) (*Com*) cuentas *fpl*. ● *vt* (*enter*) registrar; (*reserve*) reservar. ● *vi* reservar. **~case** *n* biblioteca *f*, librería *f*, librero *m* (*Mex*). **~ing** *n* reserva *f*, reservación *f* (*LAm*). **~ing office** *n* (*in theatre*) taquilla *f*, boletría *f* (*LAm*). **~keeping** *n* contabilidad *f*. **~let** /ˈbʊklɪt/ *n* folleto *m*. **~maker** *n* corredor *m* de apuestas. **~mark** *n* señal *f*. **~seller** *n* librero *m*. **~shop**, (*Amer*) **~store** *n* librería *f*. **~worm** *n* (*fig*) ratón *m* de biblioteca

boom /buːm/ *vi* retumbar; (*fig*) prosperar. ● *n* estampido *m*; (*Com*) boom *m*

boost /buːst/ *vt* estimular; reforzar (morale). ● *n* empuje *m*. **~er** *n* (*Med*) revacunación *f*. **~er cable** *n* (*Amer*) cable *m* de arranque

boot /buːt/ *n* bota *f*; (*Auto*) maletero *m*, cajuela *f* (*Mex*). □ **~ up** *vt* (*Comp*) cargar

booth /buːð/ *n* cabina *f*; (*at fair*) puesto *m*

booze /buːz/ *vi* ⊡ beber mucho. ● *n* ⊡ alcohol *m*

border /ˈbɔːdə(r)/ *n* borde *m*; (*frontier*) frontera *f*; (*in garden*) arriate *m*. □ **~ on** *vt* lindar con. **~line** *n* línea *f* divisoria. **~line case** *n* caso *m* dudoso

bor|e /bɔː(r)/ *see* BEAR. ● *vt* (*annoy*) aburrir; (*Tec*) taladrar. ● *vi* taladrar. ● *n* (*person*) pelmazo *m*; (*thing*) lata *f*. **~ed** *adj* aburrido. **be ~ed** estar aburrido. **get ~ed** aburrirse. **~edom** /ˈbɔːdəm/ *n* aburrimiento *m*. **~ing** *adj* aburrido, pesado

born /bɔːn/ *adj* nato. **be ~** nacer

borne /bɔːn/ *see* BEAR

borough /ˈbʌrə/ *n* municipio *m*

borrow /ˈbɒrəʊ/ *vt* pedir prestado

boss /bɒs/ *n* ⊡ jefe *m*. ● *vt*. **~ (about)** ⊡ dar órdenes a. **~y** *adj* mandón

b

b

botan|ical /bə'tænɪkl/ *adj* botánico. **~ist** /'bɒtənɪst/ *n* botánico *m*. **~y** /'bɒtənɪ/ *n* botánica *f*

both /bəʊθ/ *adj & pron* ambos (*mpl*), los dos (*mpl*). ● *adv* al mismo tiempo, a la vez. **~ Ann and Brian came** tanto Ann como Bob vinieron.

bother /'bɒðə(r)/ *vt* (*inconvenience*) molestar; (*worry*) preocupar. **~ it!** ¡caramba! ● *vi* molestarse. **~ about** preocuparse de. **~ doing** tomarse la molestia de hacer. ● *n* molestia *f*

bottle /'bɒtl/ *n* botella, mamila *f* (*Mex*); (*for baby*) biberón *m*. ● *vt* embotellar. □ **~ up** *vt* (*fig*) reprimir. **~neck** *n* (*traffic jam*) embotellamiento *m*. **~ opener** *n* abrebotellas *m*, destapador *m* (*LAm*)

bottom /'bɒtəm/ *n* fondo *m*; (*of hill*) pie *m*; (*buttocks*) trasero *m*. ● *adj* de más abajo; (price) más bajo; (lip, edge) inferior. **~less** *adj* sin fondo

bough /baʊ/ *n* rama *f*

bought /bɔ:t/ *see* BUY

boulder /'bəʊldə(r)/ *n* canto *m*

bounce /baʊns/ *vt* hacer rebotar. ● *vi* rebotar; (person) saltar; [!] (cheque) ser rechazado. ● *n* rebote *m*

bound /baʊnd/ *see* BIND. ● *vi* saltar. ● *n* (*jump*) salto *m*. **~s** *npl* (*limits*) límites *mpl*. **out of ~s** zona *f* prohibida. ● *adj*. **be ~ for** dirigirse a. **~ to** obligado a; (*certain*) seguro de

boundary /'baʊndərɪ/ *n* límite *m*

bouquet /bʊ'keɪ/ *n* ramo *m*; (*of wine*) buqué *m*, aroma *m*

bout /baʊt/ *n* período *m*; (*Med*) ataque *m*; (*Sport*) encuentro *m*

bow¹ /bəʊ/ *n* (*weapon, Mus*) arco *m*; (*knot*) lazo *m*, moño *m* (*LAm*)

bow² /baʊ/ *n* reverencia *f*; (*Naut*) proa *f*; ● *vi* inclinarse. ● *vt* inclinar

bowels /'baʊəlz/ *npl* intestinos *mpl*; (*fig*) entrañas *fpl*

bowl /bəʊl/ *n* (*container*) cuenco *m*; (*for washing*) palangana *f*; (*ball*) bola *f*. ● *vt* (*cricket*) arrojar. ● *vi* (*cricket*) arrojar la pelota. □ **~ over** *vt* derribar

bowl: ~er *n* (*cricket*) lanzador *m*. **~er (hat)** sombrero *m* de hongo, bombín *m*. **~ing** *n* bolos *mpl*. **~ing alley** *n* bolera *f*

bow tie /bəʊ 'taɪ/ *n* corbata *f* de lazo, pajarita *f*

box /bɒks/ *n* caja *f*; (*for jewels etc*) estuche *m*; (*in theatre*) palco *m*. ● *vt* boxear contra. **~ s.o.'s ears** dar una manotada a uno. ● *vi* boxear. **~er** *n* boxeador *m*. **~ing** *n* boxeo *m*. **B~ing Day** *n* el 26 de diciembre. **~ office** *n* taquilla *f*, boletería *f* (*LAm*). **~ room** *n* trastero *m*

boy /bɔɪ/ *n* chico *m*, muchacho *m*; (*young*) niño *m*

boy: ~ band *n* grupo *m* pop de chicos. **~friend** *n* novio *m*. **~hood** *n* niñez *f*. **~ish** *adj* de muchacho; (*childish*) infantil

boycott /'bɔɪkɒt/ *vt* boicotear. ● *n* boicoteo *m*

bra /brɑ:/ *n* sostén *m*, sujetador *m*, brasier *m* (*Mex*)

brace /breɪs/ *n* abrazadera *f*. ● *vt* asegurar. **~ o.s.** prepararse. **~s** *npl* tirantes *mpl*; (*Amer, dental*) aparato(s) *m(pl)*

bracelet /'breɪslɪt/ *n* pulsera *f*

bracken /'brækən/ *n* helecho *m*

bracket /'brækɪt/ *n* soporte *m*; (*group*) categoría *f*; (*parenthesis*) paréntesis *m*. **square ~s** corchetes *mpl*. ● *vt* poner entre paréntesis;

(*join together*) agrupar

brag /bræg/ *vi* (*pt* **bragged**) jactarse (**about** de)

braid /breɪd/ *n* galón *m*; (*Amer, in hair*) trenza *f*

brain /breɪn/ *n* cerebro *m*. ●*vt* romper la cabeza a. **~child** *n* invento *m*. **~ drain** *n* 🅸 fuga *f* de cerebros. **~storm** *n* ataque *m* de locura; (*Amer, brainwave*) idea *f* genial. **~wash** *vt* lavar el cerebro. **~wave** *n* idea *f* genial. **~y** *adj* (**-ier**, **-iest**) inteligente

brake /breɪk/ *n* freno *m*. ●*vt/i* frenar. **~ fluid** *n* líquido *m* de freno. **~ lights** *npl* luces *fpl* de freno

bramble /ˈbræmbl/ *n* zarza *f*

bran /bræn/ *n* salvado *m*

branch /brɑːntʃ/ *n* rama *f*; (*of road*) bifurcación *f*; (*Com*) sucursal *m*; (*fig*) ramo *m*. □ **~ off** *vi* bifurcarse. □ **~ out** *vi* ramificarse

brand /brænd/ *n* marca *f*. ●*vt* marcar; (*label*) tildar de

brandish /ˈbrændɪʃ/ *vt* blandir

brand: ~ name: *n* marca *f*. **~-new** /-ˈnjuː/ *adj* flamante

brandy /ˈbrændɪ/ *n* coñac *m*

brash /bræʃ/ *adj* descarado

brass /brɑːs/ *n* latón *m*. **get down to ~ tacks** (*fig*) ir al grano. **~ band** *n* banda *f* de música

brassière /ˈbræsjeə(r)/ *n see* **BRA**

brat /bræt/ *n* (*pej*) mocoso *m*

bravado /brəˈvɑːdəʊ/ *n* bravata *f*

brave /breɪv/ *adj* (**-er**, **-est**) valiente. ●*n* (*North American Indian*) guerrero *m* indio. **the ~** *npl* los valientes. ●*vt* afrontar. **~ry** /-ərɪ/ *n* valentía *f*, valor *m*

brawl /brɔːl/ *n* alboroto *m*. ●*vi* pelearse

brazen /ˈbreɪzn/ *adj* descarado

Brazil /brəˈzɪl/ *n* Brasil *m*. **~ian** /-jən/ *adj & n* brasileño (*m*)

breach /briːtʃ/ *n* infracción *f*, violación *f*; (*of contract*) incumplimiento *m*; (*gap*) brecha *f*. **~ of the peace** alteración *f* del orden público. ●*vt* abrir una brecha en

bread /bred/ *n* pan *m*. **a loaf of ~** un pan. **~crumbs** *npl* migajas *fpl*; (*Culin*) pan *m* rallado, pan *m* molido (*Mex*)

breadth /bredθ/ *n* anchura *f*

breadwinner /ˈbredwɪnə(r)/ *n* sostén *m* de la familia

break /breɪk/ *vt* (*pt* **broke**, *pp* **broken**) romper; infringir, violar (law); batir (record); comunicar (news); interrumpir (journey). ●*vi* romperse; (news) divulgarse. ●*n* ruptura *f*; (*interval*) intervalo *m*; (*fam, chance*) oportunidad *f*; (*in weather*) cambio *m*. □ **~ away** *vi* escapar. □ **~ down** *vt* derribar; analizar (figures). *vi* estropearse, descomponerse (*LAm*); (*Auto*) averiarse; (*cry*) deshacerse en lágrimas. □ **~ in** *vi* (intruder) entrar (*para robar*). □ **~ into** *vt* entrar en (*para robar*) (house etc); (*start doing*) ponerse a. □ **~ off** *vi* interrumpirse. □ **~ out** *vi* (war, disease) estallar; (*run away*) escaparse. □ **~ up** *vi* romperse; (band, lovers) separarse; (schools) terminar. **~able** *adj* frágil. **~age** /-ɪdʒ/ *n* rotura *f*. **~down** *n* (*Tec*) falla *f*; (*Med*) colapso *m*, crisis *f* nerviosa; (*of figures*) análisis *f*. **~er** *n* (*wave*) ola *f* grande

breakfast /ˈbrekfəst/ *n* desayuno *m*. **have ~** desayunar

break: ~through *n* adelanto *m*. **~water** *n* rompeolas *m*

breast /brest/ *n* pecho *m*; (*of chicken etc*) pechuga *f*. (estilo *m*)

~stroke *n* braza *f*, (estilo *m*) pecho *m* (*LAm*)

b

breath /breθ/ *n* aliento *m*, respiración *f*. **be out of ~** estar sin aliento. **hold one's ~** aguantar la respiración. **under one's ~** a media voz

breath|e /bri:ð/ *vt/i* respirar. **~er** *n* descanso *m*, pausa *f*. **~ing** *n* respiración *f*

breathtaking /'breθteɪkɪŋ/ *adj* impresionante

bred /bred/ *see* BREED

breed /bri:d/ *vt* (*pt* **bred**) criar; (*fig*) engendrar. ● *vi* reproducirse. ● *n* raza *f*

breez|e /bri:z/ *n* brisa *f*. **~y** *adj* de mucho viento

brew /bru:/ *vt* hacer (beer); preparar (tea). ● *vi* hacer cerveza; (tea) reposar; (*fig*) prepararse. ● *n* infusión *f*. **~er** *n* cervecero *m*. **~ery** *n* cervecería *f*, fábrica *f* de cerveza

bribe /braɪb/ *n* soborno *m*. ● *vt* sobornar. **~ry** /braɪbərɪ/ *n* soborno *m*

brick /brɪk/ *n* ladrillo *m*. **~layer** *n* albañil *m*

bridal /'braɪdl/ *adj* nupcial

bride /braɪd/ *m* novia *f*. **~groom** *n* novio *m*. **~smaid** /'braɪdzmeɪd/ *n* dama *f* de honor

bridge /brɪdʒ/ *n* puente *m*; (*of nose*) caballete *m*; (*Cards*) bridge *m*. ● *vt* tender un puente sobre. **~ a gap** llenar un vacío

bridle /'braɪdl/ *n* brida *f*. **~ path** *n* camino *m* de herradura

brief /bri:f/ *adj* (-er, -est) breve. ● *n* (*Jurid*) escrito *m*. ● *vt* dar instrucciones a. **~case** *n* maletín *m*, portafolio(s) *m* (*LAm*). **~ly** *adv* brevemente. **~s** *npl* (*man's*) calzoncillos *mpl*; (*woman's*) bragas *fpl*, calzones *mpl* (*LAm*), pantaletas *fpl* (*Mex*)

brigade /brɪ'geɪd/ *n* brigada *f*

bright /braɪt/ *adj* (-er, -est) brillante, claro; (*clever*) listo; (*cheerful*) alegre. **~en** *vt* aclarar; hacer más alegre (house etc). ● *vi* (*weather*) aclararse; (face) illuminarse

brillian|ce /'brɪljəns/ *n* brillantez *f*, brillo *m*. **~t** *adj* brillante

brim /brɪm/ *n* borde *m*; (*of hat*) ala *f*. □ **~ over** *vi* (*pt* **brimmed**) desbordarse

brine /braɪn/ *n* salmuera *f*

bring /brɪŋ/ *vt* (*pt* **brought**) traer; (*lead*) llevar. □ **~ about** *vt* causar. □ **~ back** *vt* devolver. □ **~ down** *vt* derribar. □ **~ off** *vt* lograr. □ **~ on** *vt* causar. □ **~ out** *vt* sacar; lanzar (product); publicar (book). □ **~ round/to** *vt* hacer volver en sí. □ **~ up** *vt* (*Med*) vomitar; educar (children); plantear (question)

brink /brɪŋk/ *n* borde *m*

brisk /brɪsk/ *adj* (-er, -est) enérgico, vivo

bristle /'brɪsl/ *n* cerda *f*. ● *vi* erizarse

Brit|ain /'brɪtən/ *n* Gran Bretaña *f*. **~ish** /'brɪtɪʃ/ *adj* británico. ● *npl* **the ~ish** los británicos. **~on** /'brɪtən/ *n* británico *m*

Brittany /'brɪtənɪ/ *n* Bretaña *f*

brittle /'brɪtl/ *adj* quebradizo

broach /brəʊtʃ/ *vt* abordar

broad /brɔ:d/ *adj* (-er, -est) ancho. **in ~ daylight** a plena luz del día. **~band** *n* banda *f* ancha. **~ bean** *n* haba *f* **~cast** *n* emisión *f*. ● *vt* (*pt* **broadcast**) emitir. ● *vi* hablar por la radio. **~caster** *n* locutor *m*. **~casting** *n* radio-difusión *f*. **~en** *vt* ensanchar. ● *vi* ensancharse. **~ly** *adv* en general. **~-minded** /-'maɪndɪd/ *adj* de miras amplias, tolerante

broccoli /ˈbrɒkəlɪ/ *n invar* brécol *m*

brochure /ˈbrəʊʃə(r)/ *n* folleto *m*

broil /brɔɪl/ *vt* (*Amer*) asar a la parrilla. **~er** *n* (*Amer*) parrilla *f*

broke /brəʊk/ *see* BREAK. ● *adj* [I] sin blanca, en la ruina

broken /ˈbrəʊkən/ *see* BREAK. ● *adj* roto

broker /ˈbrəʊkə(r)/ *n* corredor *m*

brolly /ˈbrɒlɪ/ *n* [I] paraguas *m*

bronchitis /brɒŋˈkaɪtɪs/ *n* bronquitis *f*

bronze /brɒnz/ *n* bronce *m*. ● *adj* de bronce

brooch /brəʊtʃ/ *n* broche *m*

brood /bru:d/ *n* cría *f*; (*humorous*) prole *m*. ● *vi* empollar; (*fig*) meditar

brook /brʊk/ *n* arroyo *m*. ● *vt* soportar

broom /bru:m/ *n* escoba *f*. **~stick** *n* palo *m* de escoba

broth /brɒθ/ *n* caldo *m*

brothel /ˈbrɒθl/ *n* burdel *m*

brother /ˈbrʌðə(r)/ *n* hermano *m*. **~hood** *n* fraternidad *f*. **~-in-law** (*pl* **~s-in-law**) *n* cuñado *m*. **~ly** *adj* fraternal

brought /brɔ:t/ *see* BRING

brow /braʊ/ *n* frente *f*; (*of hill*) cima *f*. **~beat** *vt* (*pt* **-beaten**, *pp* **-beat**) intimidar

brown /braʊn/ *adj* (**-er**, **-est**) marrón, café (*Mex*); (hair) castaño; (skin) moreno; (*tanned*) bronceado. ● *n* marrón *m*, café *m* (*Mex*). ● *vt* poner moreno; (*Culin*) dorar. **~ bread** *n* pan *m* integral. **~ sugar** /braʊn ˈʃʊgə(r)/ *n* azúcar *m* moreno, azúcar *f* morena

browse /braʊz/ *vi* (*in a shop*) curiosear; (animal) pacer; (*Comp*) navegar. **~r** (*Comp*) browser *m*, navegador *m*

bruise /bru:z/ *n* magulladura *f*. ● *vt* magullar; machucar (fruit)

brunch /brʌntʃ/ *n* [I] desayuno *m* tardío

brunette /bru:ˈnet/ *n* morena *f*

brunt /brʌnt/ *n*. **bear** *o* **take the ~ of sth** sufrir algo

brush /brʌʃ/ *n* cepillo *m*; (*large*) escoba; (*for decorating*) brocha *f*; (*artist's*) pincel; (*skirmish*) escaramuza *f*. ● *vt* cepillar. □ **~ against** *vt* rozar. □ **~ aside** *vt* rechazar. □ **~ off** *vt* (*rebuff*) desairar. □ **~ up (on)** *vt* refrescar

brusque /bru:sk/ *adj* brusco. **~ly** *adv* bruscamente

Brussels /ˈbrʌslz/ *n* Bruselas *f*. **~ sprout** *n* col *f* de Bruselas

brutal /ˈbru:tl/ *adj* brutal. **~ity** /-ˈtælətɪ/ *n* brutalidad *f*. **~ly** *adv* brutalmente

brute /bru:t/ *n* bestia *f*. **~ force** fuerza *f* bruta

BSc *abbr see* BACHELOR

BSE *abbr* (**bovine spongiform encephalopathy**) EBE *f*

bubbl|e /ˈbʌbl/ *n* burbuja *f*. ● *vi* burbujear. □ **~ over** *vi* desbordarse. **~ly** *adj* burbujeante

buck /bʌk/ *adj* macho. ● *n* (*deer*) ciervo *m*; (*Amer fam*) dólar *m*. **pass the ~** pasar la pelota

bucket /ˈbʌkɪt/ *n* balde *m*, cubo *m*, cubeta *f* (*Mex*)

buckle /ˈbʌkl/ *n* hebilla *f*. ● *vt* abrochar. ● *vi* torcerse

bud /bʌd/ *n* brote *m*. ● *vi* (*pt* **budded**) brotar.

Buddhis|m /ˈbʊdɪzəm/ *n* budismo *m*. **~t** *adj* & *n* budista (*m* & *f*)

budding /ˈbʌdɪŋ/ *adj* (*fig*) en ciernes

b

buddy /ˈbʌdɪ/ *n* [!] amigo *m*, cuate *m* (*Mex*)

budge /bʌdʒ/ *vt* mover. ●*vi* moverse

budgerigar /ˈbʌdʒərɪgɑ:(r)/ *n* periquito *m*

budget /ˈbʌdʒɪt/ *n* presupuesto *m*

buffalo /ˈbʌfələʊ/ *n* (*pl* **-oes** *or* **-o**) búfalo *m*

buffer /ˈbʌfə(r)/ *n* parachoques *m*

buffet[1] /ˈbʊfeɪ/ *n* (*meal*) buffet *m*; (*in train*) bar *m*

buffet[2] /ˈbʌfɪt/ *n* golpe *m*

bug /bʌg/ *n* bicho *m*; [!] (*germ*) microbio *m*; (*fam*, *device*) micrófono *m* oculto. ●*vt* (*pt* **bugged**) [!] ocultar un micrófono en; (*bother*) molestar

buggy /ˈbʌgɪ/ *n*. **baby** ~ sillita *f* de paseo (*plegable*); (*Amer*) cochecito *m*

bugle /ˈbju:gl/ *n* corneta *f*

build /bɪld/ *vt*/*i* (*pt* **built**) construir. ●*n* (*of person*) figura *f*, tipo *m*. □ ~ **up** *vt*/*i* fortalecer; (*increase*) aumentar. ~**er** *n* (*contractor*) contratista *m* & *f*; (*labourer*) albañil *m*. ~**ing** *n* edificio *m*; (*construction*) construcción *f*. ~**up** *n* aumento *m*; (*of gas etc*) acumulación *f*

built /bɪlt/ *see* **BUILD**. ~**-in** *adj* empotrado. ~**-up area** *n* zona *f* urbanizada

bulb /bʌlb/ *n* bulbo *m*; (*Elec*) bombilla *f*, foco *m* (*Mex*)

Bulgaria /bʌlˈgeərɪə/ *n* Bulgaria *f*. ~**n** *adj* & *n* búlgaro (*m*)

bulg|e /bʌldʒ/ *n* protuberancia *f*. ●*vi* pandearse. ~**ing** *adj* abultado; (eyes) saltón

bulk /bʌlk/ *n* bulto *m*, volumen *m*. **in** ~ a granel; (*loose*) suelto. **the** ~ **of** la mayor parte de. ~**y** *adj* voluminoso

bull /bʊl/ *n* toro *m*. ~**dog** *n* buldog *m*. ~**dozer** /-dəʊzə(r)/ *n* bulldozer *m*

bullet /ˈbʊlɪt/ *n* bala *f*

bulletin /ˈbʊlətɪn/ *n* anuncio *m*; (*journal*) boletín *m*. ~ **board** *n* (*Amer*) tablón *m* de anuncios, tablero *m* de anuncios (*LAm*)

bulletproof /ˈbʊlɪtpru:f/ *adj* a prueba de balas

bullfight /ˈbʊlfaɪt/ *n* corrida *f* (de toros). ~**er** *n* torero *m*. ~**ing** *n* (deporte *m* de) los toros

bull: ~**ring** *n* plaza *f* de toros. ~**'s-eye** *n* diana *f*. ~**shit** *n* (*vulgar*) sandeces *fpl* [!], gilipolleces *fpl* [✖]

bully /ˈbʊlɪ/ *n* matón *m*. ●*vt* intimidar. ~**ing** *n* intimidación *f*

bum /bʌm/ *n* (*fam*, *backside*) trasero *m*; (*Amer fam*, *tramp*) holgazán *m*

bumblebee /ˈbʌmblbi:/ *n* abejorro *m*

bump /bʌmp/ *vt* chocar contra. ●*vi* dar sacudidas. ●*n* (*blow*) golpe *m*; (*jolt*) sacudida *f*. □ ~ **into** *vt* chocar contra; (*meet*) encontrar.

bumper /ˈbʌmpə(r)/ *n* parachoques *m*. ●*adj* récord. ~ **edition** *n* edición *f* especial

bun /bʌn/ *n* bollo *m*; (*bread roll*) panecillo *m*, bolillo *m* (*Mex*); (*hair*) moño *m*, chongo *m* (*Mex*)

bunch /bʌntʃ/ *n* (*of people*) grupo *m*; (*of bananas*, *grapes*) racimo *m*; (*of flowers*) ramo *m*

bundle /ˈbʌndl/ *n* bulto *m*; (*of papers*) legajo *m*. □ ~ **up** *vt* atar

bungalow /ˈbʌŋgələʊ/ *n* casa *f* de un solo piso

bungle /ˈbʌŋgl/ *vt* echar a perder

bunk /bʌŋk/ *n* litera *f*

bunker /ˈbʌŋkə(r)/ *n* carbonera *f*;

(*Golf, Mil*) búnker *m*
bunny /'bʌnɪ/ *n* conejito *m*
buoy /bɔɪ/ *n* boya *f*. □ **~ up** *vt* hacer flotar; (*fig*) animar
buoyant /'bɔɪənt/ *adj* flotante; (*fig*) optimista
burden /'bɜ:dn/ *n* carga *f*. ●*vt* cargar (**with** de)
bureau /'bjʊərəʊ/ *n* (*pl* **-eaux** /-əʊz/) agencia *f*; (*desk*) escritorio *m*; (*Amer, chest of drawers*) cómoda *f*
bureaucra|cy /bjʊə'rɒkrəsɪ/ *n* burocracia *f*. **~t** /'bjʊərəkræt/ *n* burócrata *m & f*. **~tic** /-'krætɪk/ *adj* burocrático
burger /'bɜ:gə(r)/ *n* 🅸 hamburguesa *f*
burgl|ar /'bɜ:glə(r)/ *n* ladrón *m*. **~ar alarm** *n* alarma *f* antirrobo. **~ary** *n* robo *m* (*en casa o edificio*). **~e** /'bɜ:gl/ *vt* entrar a robar en. **we were ~ed** nos entraron a robar
burial /'berɪəl/ *n* entierro *m*
burly /'bɜ:lɪ/ *adj* (**-ier**, **-iest**) corpulento
burn /bɜ:n/ *vt* (*pt* **burned** *or* **burnt**) quemar. ●*vi* quemarse. ●*n* quemadura *f*. **~er** *n* quemador *m*. □ **~ down** *vt* incendiar. *vi* incendiarse
burnt /bɜ:nt/ *see* BURN
burp /bɜ:p/ *n* 🅸 eructo *m*. ●*vi* 🅸 eructar
burrow /'bʌrəʊ/ *n* madriguera *f*. ●*vt* excavar
burst /bɜ:st/ *vt* (*pt* **burst**) reventar. ●*vi* reventarse. **~ into tears** echarse a llorar. **~ out laughing** echarse a reír. ●*n* (*Mil*) ráfaga *f*; (*of activity*) arrebato; (*of applause*) salva *f*
bury /'berɪ/ *vt* enterrar; (*hide*) ocultar
bus /bʌs/ *n* (*pl* **buses**) autobús *m*, camión *m* (*Mex*)
bush /bʊʃ/ *n* arbusto *m*; (*land*) monte *m*. **~y** *adj* espeso
business /'bɪznɪs/ *n* negocio *m*; (*Com*) negocios *mpl*; (*profession*) ocupación *f*; (*fig*) asunto *m*. **mind one's own ~** ocuparse de sus propios asuntos. **~like** *adj* práctico, serio. **~man** /-mən/ *n* hombre *m* de negocios. **~woman** *n* mujer *f* de negocios
busker /'bʌskə(r)/ *n* músico *m* ambulante
bus stop *n* parada *f* de autobús, paradero *m* de autobús (*LAm*)
bust /bʌst/ *n* busto *m*; (*chest*) pecho *m*. ●*vt* (*pt* **busted** *or* **bust**) 🅸 romper. ●*vi* romperse. ●*adj* roto. **go ~** 🅸 quebrar
bust-up /'bʌstʌp/ *n* 🅸 riña *f*
busy /'bɪzɪ/ *adj* (**-ier**, **-iest**) ocupado; (street) concurrido. **be ~** (*Amer*) (phone) estar comunicando, estar ocupado (*LAm*). ●*vt*. **~ o.s. with** ocuparse de. **~body** *n* entrometido *m*
but /bʌt/ *conj* pero; (*after negative*) sino. ●*prep* menos. **~ for** si no fuera por. **last ~ one** penúltimo
butcher /'bʊtʃə(r)/ *n* carnicero *m*. ●*vt* matar; (*fig*) hacer una carnicería con
butler /'bʌtlə(r)/ *n* mayordomo *m*
butt /bʌt/ *n* (*of gun*) culata *f*; (*of cigarette*) colilla *f*; (*target*) blanco *m*; (*Amer fam, backside*) trasero *m*. ●*vi* topar. □ **~ in** *vi* interrumpir
butter /'bʌtə(r)/ *n* mantequilla *f*. ●*vt* untar con mantequilla. **~cup** *n* ranúnculo *m*. **~fingers** *n* manazas *m*, torpe *m*. **~fly** *n* mariposa *f*; (*swimming*) estilo *m* mariposa
buttock /'bʌtək/ *n* nalga *f*

b c

button /ˈbʌtn/ *n* botón *m*. • *vt* abotonar. • *vi* abotonarse. **~hole** *n* ojal *m*. • *vt* (*fig*) detener

buy /baɪ/ *vt/i* (*pt* **bought**) comprar. • *n* compra *f*. **~er** *n* comprador *m*

buzz /bʌz/ *n* zumbido *m*. • *vi* zumbar. □ **~ off** *vi* ☒ largarse. **~er** *n* timbre *m*

by /baɪ/ *prep* por; (*near*) cerca de; (*before*) antes de; (*according to*) según. **~ and large** en conjunto, en general. **~ car** en coche. **~ oneself** por sí solo

bye/baɪ/, **bye-bye** /ˈbaɪbaɪ/ *int* 🅸 ¡adiós!

by: ~-election *n* elección *f* parcial. **~-law** *n* reglamento *m* (local). **~pass** *n* carretera *f* de circunvalación. • *vt* eludir; (road) circunvalar. **~-product** *n* subproducto *m*. **~stander** /-stændə(r)/ *n* espectador *m*

byte /baɪt/ *n* (*Comp*) byte *m*, octeto *m*

Cc

cab /kæb/ *n* taxi *m*; (*of lorry, train*) cabina *f*

cabaret /ˈkæbəreɪ/ *n* cabaret *m*

cabbage /ˈkæbɪdʒ/ *n* col *f*, repollo *m*

cabin /ˈkæbɪn/ *n* (*house*) cabaña *f*; (*in ship*) camarote *m*; (*in plane*) cabina *f*

cabinet /ˈkæbɪnɪt/ *n* (*cupboard*) armario *m*; (*for display*) vitrina *f*. **C~** (*Pol*) gabinete *m*

cable /ˈkeɪbl/ *n* cable *m*. **~ car** *n* teleférico *m*. **~ TV** *n* televisión *f* por cable, cablevisión *f* (*LAm*)

cackle /ˈkækl/ *n* (*of hen*) cacareo *m*; (*laugh*) risotada *f*. • *vi* cacarear; (*laugh*) reírse a carcajadas

cactus /ˈkæktəs/ *n* (*pl* **-ti** /-taɪ/ *or* **-tuses**) cacto *m*

caddie, caddy /ˈkædɪ/ *n* (*golf*) portador *m* de palos

cadet /kəˈdet/ *n* cadete *m*

cadge /kædʒ/ *vt/i* gorronear

café /ˈkæfeɪ/ *n* cafetería *f*

cafeteria /kæfɪˈtɪərɪə/ *n* restaurante *m* autoservicio

caffeine /ˈkæfiːn/ *n* cafeína *f*

cage /keɪdʒ/ *n* jaula *f*. • *vt* enjaular

cake /keɪk/ *n* pastel *m*, tarta *f*; (*sponge*) bizcocho *m*. **~ of soap** pastilla *f* de jabón

calamity /kəˈlæmətɪ/ *n* calamidad *f*

calcium /ˈkælsɪəm/ *n* calcio *m*

calculat|e /ˈkælkjʊleɪt/ *vt/i* calcular. **~ion** /-ˈleɪʃn/ *n* cálculo *m*. **~or** *n* calculadora *f*

calculus /ˈkælkjʊləs/ *n* (*Math*) cálculo *m*

calendar /ˈkælɪndə(r)/ *n* calendario *m*

calf /kɑːf/ *n* (*pl* **calves**) (*animal*) ternero *m*; (*of leg*) pantorrilla *f*

calibre /ˈkælɪbə(r)/ *n* calibre *m*

call /kɔːl/ *vt/i* llamar. • *n* llamada *f*; (*shout*) grito *m*; (*visit*) visita *f*. **be on ~** estar de guardia. **long-distance ~** llamada *f* de larga distancia, conferencia *f*. □ **~ back** *vt* hacer volver; (*on phone*) volver a llamar. *vi* volver; (*on phone*) volver a llamar. □ **~ for** *vt* pedir; (*fetch*) ir a buscar. □ **~ off** *vt* suspender. □ **~ on** *vt* pasar a visitar. □ **~ out** *vi* dar voces. □ **~ together** *vt* convocar. □ **~ up** *vt* (*Mil*) llamar al servicio militar; (*phone*) llamar. **~**

box *n* cabina *f* telefónica. ~ **centre** *n* centro *m* de llamadas. **~er** *n* visita *f*; (*phone*) persona que llama *m*. **~ing** *n* vocación *f*

callous /'kæləs/ *adj* insensible, cruel

calm /kɑːm/ *adj* (**-er**, **-est**) tranquilo; (sea) en calma. ● *n* tranquilidad *f*, calma *f*. ● *vt* calmar. ● *vi* calmarse. ~ **down** *vi* tranquilizarse. *vt* calmar. **~ly** *adv* con calma

calorie /'kælərɪ/ *n* caloría *f*

calves /kɑːvz/ *npl see* **CALF**

camcorder /'kæmkɔːdə(r)/ *n* videocámara *f*, camcórder *m*

came /keɪm/ *see* **COME**

camel /'kæml/ *n* camello *m*

camera /'kæmərə/ *n* cámara *f*, máquina *f* fotográfica **~man** /-mən/ *n* camarógrafo *m*, cámara *m*

camouflage /'kæməflɑːʒ/ *n* camuflaje *m*. ● *vt* camuflar

camp /kæmp/ *n* campamento *m*. ● *vi* acampar. **go ~ing** hacer camping

campaign /kæm'peɪn/ *n* campaña *f*. ● *vi* hacer campaña

camp: ~bed *n* catre *m* de tijera. **~er** *n* campista *m & f*; (*vehicle*) cámper *m*. **~ground** *n* (*Amer*) *see* **~SITE**. **~ing** *n* camping *m*. **~site** *n* camping *m*

campus /'kæmpəs/ *n* (*pl* **-puses**) campus *m*, ciudad *f* universitaria

can[1] /kæn//kən/

negative **can't, cannot** (formal); past **could**

auxiliary verb

····▸(*be able to*) poder. **I ~'t lift it** no lo puedo levantar. **she says she ~ come** dice que puede venir

····▸(*be allowed to*) poder. **~ I smoke?** ¿puedo fumar?

····▸(*know how to*) saber. **~ you swim?** ¿sabes nadar?

····▸(*with verbs of perception*) *not translated*. **I ~'t see you** no te veo. **I ~ hear you better now** ahora te oigo mejor

····▸(*in requests*) **~ I have a glass of water, please?** ¿me trae un vaso de agua, por favor?. **~ I have a kilo of cheese, please?** ¿me da un kilo de queso, por favor?

····▸(*in offers*) **~ I help you?** ¿te ayudo?; (*in shop*) ¿lo/la atienden?

can[2] /kæn/ *n* lata *f*, bote *m*. ● *vt* (*pt* **canned**) enlatar. **~ned music** música *f* grabada

Canad|a /'kænədə/ *n* (el) Canadá *m*. **~ian** /kə'neɪdɪən/ *adj & n* canadiense (*m & f*)

canal /kə'næl/ *n* canal *m*

Canaries /kə'neərɪz/ *npl* = **CANARY ISLANDS**

canary /kə'neərɪ/ *n* canario *m*. **C~ Islands** *npl*. **the C~ Islands** las Islas Canarias

cancel /'kænsl/ *vt* (*pt* **cancelled**) cancelar; anular (command, cheque); (*delete*) tachar. **~lation** /-'leɪʃn/ *n* cancelación *f*

cancer /'kænsə(r)/ *n* cáncer *m*. **C~** *n* (*in astrology*) Cáncer *m*. **~ous** *adj* canceroso

candid /'kændɪd/ *adj* franco

candidate /'kændɪdeɪt/ *n* candidato *m*

candle /'kændl/ *n* vela *f*. **~stick** *n* candelero *m*

candour /ˈkændə(r)/ *n* franqueza *f*

candy /ˈkændɪ/ *n* (*Amer*) caramelo *m*, dulce *f* (*LAm*). **~floss** /-flɒs/ *n* algodón *m* de azúcar

cane /keɪn/ *n* caña *f*; (*for baskets*) mimbre *m*; (*stick*) bastón *m*; (*for punishment*) palmeta *f*. ● *vt* castigar con palmeta

canister /ˈkænɪstə(r)/ *n* bote *m*

cannabis /ˈkænəbɪs/ *n* cáñamo *m* índico, hachís *m*, cannabis *m*

cannibal /ˈkænɪbl/ *n* caníbal *m*. **~ism** *n* canibalismo *m*

cannon /ˈkænən/ *n invar* cañón *m*. **~ ball** *n* bala *f* de cañón

cannot /ˈkænət/ *see* CAN[1]

canoe /kəˈnuː/ *n* canoa *f*, piragua *f*. ● *vi* ir en canoa

canon /ˈkænən/ *n* canon *m*; (*person*) canónigo *m*. **~ize** *vt* canonizar

can opener *n* abrelatas *m*

canopy /ˈkænəpɪ/ *n* dosel *m*

can't /kɑːnt/ *see* CAN[1]

cantankerous /kænˈtæŋkərəs/ *adj* mal humorado

canteen /kænˈtiːn/ *n* cantina *f*; (*of cutlery*) juego *m* de cubiertos

canter /ˈkæntə(r)/ *n* medio galope *m*. ● *vi* ir a medio galope

canvas /ˈkænvəs/ *n* lona *f*; (*artist's*) lienzo *m*

canvass /ˈkænvəs/ *vi* hacer campaña, solicitar votos. **~ing** *n* solicitación *f* (de votos)

canyon /ˈkænjən/ *n* cañón *m*

cap /kæp/ *n* gorra *f*; (*lid*) tapa *f*; (*of cartridge*) cápsula *f*; (*of pen*) capuchón *m*. ● *vt* (*pt* **capped**) tapar, poner cápsula a; (*outdo*) superar

capab|ility /keɪpəˈbɪlətɪ/ *n* capacidad *f*. **~le** /ˈkeɪpəbl/ *adj* capaz

capacity /kəˈpæsətɪ/ *n* capacidad *f*; (*function*) calidad *f*

cape /keɪp/ *n* (*cloak*) capa *f*; (*headland*) cabo *m*

capital /ˈkæpɪtl/ *adj* capital. **~ letter** mayúscula *f*. ● *n* (*town*) capital *f*; (*money*) capital *m*. **~ism** *n* capitalismo *m*. **~ist** *adj & n* capitalista (*m & f.*) **~ize** *vt* capitalizar; escribir con mayúsculas (word). ● *vi*. **~ize on** aprovechar

capitulat|e /kəˈpɪtʃʊleɪt/ *vi* capitular. **~ion** /-ˈleɪʃn/ *n* capitulación *f*

> **Capitol** El Capitolio o sede del Congreso (*Congress*) de EE.UU., en Washington DC. Situado en *Capitol Hill*, a menudo la prensa emplea este nombre para hacer referencia al Congreso de EE.UU.

Capricorn /ˈkæprɪkɔːn/ *n* Capricornio *m*

capsize /kæpˈsaɪz/ *vt* hacer volcar. ● *vi* volcarse

capsule /ˈkæpsjuːl/ *n* cápsula *f*

captain /ˈkæptɪn/ *n* capitán *m*; (*of plane*) comandante *m & f*. ● *vt* capitanear

caption /ˈkæpʃn/ *n* (*heading*) título *m*; (*of cartoon etc*) leyenda *f*

captivate /ˈkæptɪveɪt/ *vt* encantar

captiv|e /ˈkæptɪv/ *adj & n* cautivo (*m*). **~ity** /-ˈtɪvətɪ/ *n* cautiverio *m*, cautividad *f*

capture /ˈkæptʃə(r)/ *vt* capturar; atraer (attention); (*Mil*) tomar. ● *n* apresamiento *m*; (*Mil*) toma *f*

car /kɑː(r)/ *n* coche *m*, carro *m* (*LAm*); (*Amer, of train*) vagón *m*

caramel /ˈkærəmel/ *n* azúcar *m* quemado; (*sweet*) caramelo *m*, dulce *m* (*LAm*)

caravan /ˈkærəvæn/ *n* caravana *f*

carbohydrate /kɑ:bəʊˈhaɪdreɪt/ *n* hidrato *m* de carbono

carbon /ˈkɑ:bən/ *n* carbono *m*; (*paper*) carbón *m*. **~ copy** *n* copia *f* al carbón. **~ dioxide** /daɪˈɒksaɪd/ *n* anhídrido *m* carbónico. **~ footprint** *n* huella *f* de carbono. **~ monoxide** /məˈnɒksaɪd/ *n* monóxido de carbono

carburettor /kɑ:bjʊˈretə(r)/ *n* carburador *m*

carcass /ˈkɑ:kəs/ *n* cuerpo *m* de animal muerto; (*for meat*) res *f* muerta

card /kɑ:d/ *n* tarjeta *f*; (*for games*) carta *f*; (*membership*) carnet *m*; (*records*) ficha *f*. **~board** *n* cartón *m*

cardigan /ˈkɑ:dɪgən/ *n* chaqueta *f* de punto, rebeca *f*

cardinal /ˈkɑ:dɪnəl/ *adj* cardinal. ● *n* cardenal *m*

care /keə(r)/ *n* cuidado *m*; (*worry*) preocupación *f*; (*protection*) cargo *m*. **~ of** a cuidado de, en casa de. **take ~** tener cuidado. **take ~ of** cuidar de (person); ocuparse de (matter). ● *vi* interesarse. **I don't ~** me da igual. □ **~ about** *vt* preocuparse por. □ **~ for** *vt* cuidar de; (*like*) querer

career /kəˈrɪə(r)/ *n* carrera *f*. ● *vi* correr a toda velocidad

care: **~free** *adj* despreocupado. **~ful** *adj* cuidadoso; (*cautious*) prudente. **be ~ful** tener cuidado. **~fully** *adv* con cuidado. **~less** *adj* negligente; (*not worried*) indiferente. **~lessly** *adv* descuidadamente. **~lessness** *n* descuido *m* **~r** *n persona que cuida de un discapacitado*

caress /kəˈres/ *n* caricia *f*. ● *vt* acariciar

caretaker /ˈkeəteɪkə(r)/ *n* vigilante *m*; (*of flats etc*) portero *m*

car ferry *n* transbordador *m* de coches

cargo /ˈkɑ:gəʊ/ *n* (*pl* **-oes**) carga *f*

Caribbean /kærɪˈbi:ən/ *adj* caribeño. **the ~ (Sea)** *n* el mar Caribe

caricature /ˈkærɪkətʃʊə(r)/ *n* caricatura *f*. ● *vt* caricaturizar

carnage /ˈkɑ:nɪdʒ/ *n* carnicería *f*, matanza *f*

carnation /kɑ:ˈneɪʃn/ *n* clavel *m*

carnival /ˈkɑ:nɪvl/ *n* carnaval *m*

carol /ˈkærəl/ *n* villancico *m*

carousel /kærəˈsel/ *n* tiovivo *m*, carrusel *m* (*LAm*); (*for baggage*) cinta *f* transportadora

carp /kɑ:p/ *n invar* carpa *f*. □ **~ at** *vi* quejarse de

car park *n* aparcamiento *m*, estacionamiento *m*

carpent|er /ˈkɑ:pɪntə(r)/ *n* carpintero *m*. **~ry** /-trɪ/ *n* carpintería *f*

carpet /ˈkɑ:pɪt/ *n* alfombra *f*. **~ sweeper** *n* cepillo *m* mecánico

carriage /ˈkærɪdʒ/ *n* coche *m*; (*Mec*) carro *m*; (*transport*) transporte *m*; (*cost, bearing*) porte *m*; (*of train*) vagón *m*. **~way** *n* calzada *f*

carrier /ˈkærɪə(r)/ *n* transportista *m & f*; (*company*) empresa *f* de transportes; (*Med*) portador *m*. **~ bag** *n* bolsa *f*

carrot /ˈkærət/ *n* zanahoria *f*

carry /ˈkærɪ/ *vt* llevar; transportar (goods); (*involve*) llevar consigo, implicar. ● *vi* (sounds) llegar, oírse. □ **~ off** *vt* llevarse. □ **~ on** *vi* seguir, continuar. □ **~ out** *vt* realizar; cumplir (promise, threat). **~ cot** *n* cuna *f* portátil

carsick /ˈkɑ:sɪk/ *adj* mareado (*por viajar en coche*)

C

cart /kɑːt/ *n* carro *m*; (*Amer, in supermarket, airport*) carrito *m*. ● *vt* acarrear; (*fam, carry*) llevar

carton /ˈkɑːtən/ *n* caja *f* de cartón

cartoon /kɑːˈtuːn/ *n* caricatura *f*, chiste *m*; (*strip*) historieta *f*; (*film*) dibujos *mpl* animados

cartridge /ˈkɑːtrɪdʒ/ *n* cartucho *m*

carve /kɑːv/ *vt* tallar; trinchar (meat)

cascade /kæsˈkeɪd/ *n* cascada *f*. ● *vi* caer en cascadas

case /keɪs/ *n* caso *m*; (*Jurid*) proceso *m*; (*crate*) cajón *m*; (*box*) caja *f*; (*suitcase*) maleta *f*, petaca *f* (*Mex*). **in any ~** en todo caso. **in ~ he comes** por si viene. **in ~ of** en caso de

cash /kæʃ/ *n* dinero *m* efectivo. **pay (in) ~** pagar al contado. ● *vt* cobrar. **~ in (on)** aprovecharse de. **~ desk** *n* caja *f*. **~ dispenser** *n* cajero *m* automático

cashier /kæˈʃɪə(r)/ *n* cajero *m*

cashpoint /ˈkæʃpɔɪnt/ *n* cajero *m* automático

casino /kəˈsiːnəʊ/ *n* (*pl* **-os**) casino *m*

cask /kɑːsk/ *n* barril *m*

casket /ˈkɑːskɪt/ *n* cajita *f*; (*Amer*) ataúd *m*, cajón *m* (*LAm*)

casserole /ˈkæsərəʊl/ *n* cacerola *f*; (*stew*) guiso *m*, guisado *m* (*Mex*)

cassette /kəˈset/ *n* cassette *m* & *f*

cast /kɑːst/ *vt* (*pt* **cast**) arrojar; fundir (metal); emitir (vote). ● *n* lanzamiento *m*; (*in play*) reparto *m*; (*mould*) molde *m*

castanets /kæstəˈnets/ *npl* castañuelas *fpl*

castaway /ˈkɑːstəweɪ/ *n* náufrago *m*

caster /ˈkɑːstə(r)/ *n* ruedecita *f*. **~ sugar** *n* azúcar *m* extrafino

Castil|e /kæˈstiːl/ *n* Castilla *f*. **~ian** /kæˈstɪlɪən/ *adj* & *n* castellano (*m*)

cast: ~ iron *n* hierro *m* fundido. **~-iron** *adj* (*fig*) sólido

castle /ˈkɑːsl/ *n* castillo *m*; (*Chess*) torre *f*

cast-offs /ˈkɑːstɒfs/ *npl* desechos *mpl*

castrat|e /kæˈstreɪt/ *vt* castrar. **~ion** /-ʃn/ *n* castración *f*

casual /ˈkæʒʊəl/ *adj* casual; (meeting) fortuito; (work) ocasional; (attitude) despreocupado; (clothes) informal, de sport. **~ly** *adv* de paso

casualt|y /ˈkæʒʊəltɪ/ *n* (*injured*) herido *m*; (*dead*) víctima *f*; (*in hospital*) urgencias *fpl*. **~ies** *npl* (*Mil*) bajas *fpl*

cat /kæt/ *n* gato *m*

Catalan /ˈkætəlæn/ *adj* & *n* catalán (*m*)

catalogue /ˈkætəlɒg/ *n* catálogo *m*. ● *vt* catalogar

Catalonia /kætəˈləʊnɪə/ *n* Cataluña *f*

catalyst /ˈkætəlɪst/ *n* catalizador *m*

catamaran /kætəməˈræn/ *n* catamarán *m*

catapult /ˈkætəpʌlt/ *n* catapulta *f*; (*child's*) tirachinas *f*, resortera *f* (*Mex*)

catarrh /kəˈtɑː(r)/ *n* catarro *m*

catastroph|e /kəˈtæstrəfɪ/ *n* catástrofe *m*. **~ic** /kætəˈstrɒfɪk/ *adj* catastrófico

catch /kætʃ/ *vt* (*pt* **caught**) coger (*esp Spain*), agarrar; tomar (train, bus); (*unawares*) sorprender, pillar; (*understand*) entender; contagiarse de (disease). **~ a cold** resfriarse.

~ **sight of** avistar. • *vi* (*get stuck*) engancharse; (fire) prenderse. • *n* (*by goalkeeper*) parada *f*; (*of fish*) pesca *f*; (*on door*) pestillo *m*; (*on window*) cerradura *f*. □ ~ **on** *vi* [I] hacerse popular. □ ~ **up** *vi* poner al día. ~ **up with** alcanzar; ponerse al corriente de (news etc). ~**ing** *adj* contagioso. ~**phrase** *n* eslogan *m*. ~**y** *adj* pegadizo

categor|ical /kætɪ'gɒrɪkl/ *adj* categórico. ~**y** /'kætɪgərɪ/ *n* categoría *f*

cater /'keɪtə(r)/ *vi* encargarse del servicio de comida. ~ **for** proveer a (needs). ~**er** *n* proveedor *m*

caterpillar /'kætəpɪlə(r)/ *n* oruga *f*, azotador *m* (*Mex*)

cathedral /kə'θi:drəl/ *n* catedral *f*

catholic /'kæθəlɪk/ *adj* universal. **C~** *adj & n* católico (*m*). **C~ism** /kə 'θɒlɪsɪzəm/ *n* catolicismo *m*

cat: ~nap *n* sueñecito *m*. **C~seyes** *npl* (®) catafaros *mpl*

cattle /'kætl/ *npl* ganado *m*

catwalk *n* pasarela *f*

Caucasian /kɔ:'keɪʒən/ *n*. **a male ~** (*Amer*) un hombre de raza blanca

caught /kɔ:t/ *see* CATCH

cauliflower /'kɒlɪflaʊə(r)/ *n* coliflor *f*

cause /kɔ:z/ *n* causa *f*, motivo *m*. • *vt* causar

cautio|n /'kɔ:ʃn/ *n* cautela *f*; (*warning*) advertencia *f*. • *vt* advertir; (*Jurid*) amonestar. ~**us** /-ʃəs/ *adj* cauteloso, prudente

cavalry /'kævəlrɪ/ *n* caballería *f*

cave /keɪv/ *n* cueva *f*. □ ~ **in** *vi* hundirse. ~**man** *n* troglodita *m*

cavern /'kævən/ *n* caverna *f*

caviare /'kævɪɑ:(r)/ *n* caviar *m*

cavity /'kævətɪ/ *n* cavidad *f*; (*in tooth*) caries *f*

CCTV *abbr* (**closed circuit television**) CCTV *m*

CD *abbr* (= **compact disc**) CD *m*. ~ **player** (reproductor *m* de) compact-disc *m*. ~**-ROM** *n* CD-ROM *m*

cease /si:s/ *vt/i* cesar. ~**fire** *n* alto *m* el fuego

cedar /'si:də(r)/ *n* cedro *m*

ceiling /'si:lɪŋ/ *n* techo *m*

celebrat|e /'selɪbreɪt/ *vt* celebrar. • *vi* divertirse. ~**ed** *adj* célebre. ~**ion** /-'breɪʃn/ *n* celebración *f*; (*party*) fiesta *f*

celebrity /sɪ'lebrətɪ/ *n* celebridad *f*

celery /'selərɪ/ *n* apio *m*

cell /sel/ *n* celda *f*; (*in plants, electricity*) célula *f*

cellar /'selə(r)/ *n* sótano *m*; (*for wine*) bodega *f*

cello /'tʃeləʊ/ *n* (*pl* **-os**) violonc(h)elo *m*, chelo *m*

Cellophane /'seləfeɪn/ *n* (®) celofán *m* (®)

cellphone /'selfəʊn/ *n* celular *m* (*LAm*), móvil *m* (*Esp*)

cellul|ar /'seljʊlə(r)/ *adj* celular. ~ **phone** *n* teléfono celular *m* (*LAm*), teléfono móvil *m* (*Esp*). ~**oid** *n* celuloide *m*

Celsius /'selsɪəs/ *adj*. **20 degrees ~** 20 grados centígrados *or* Celsio(s)

cement /sɪ'ment/ *n* cemento *m*. • *vt* cementar

cemetery /'semətrɪ/ *n* cementerio *m*

cens|or /'sensə(r)/ *n* censor *m*. • *vt* censurar. ~**ship** *n* censura *f*. ~**ure** /'senʃə(r)/ *vt* censurar

census /'sensəs/ *n* censo *m*

cent /sent/ *n* ($) centavo *m*; (€) céntimo *m*

centenary /sen'ti:nərɪ/ *n* centenario *m*

centi|grade /'sentɪgreɪd/ *adj* centígrado. **~litre** *n* centilitro *m*. **~metre** *n* centímetro *m*. **~pede** /-pi:d/ *n* ciempiés *m*

central /'sentrəl/ *adj* central; (*of town*) céntrico. **~ heating** *n* calefacción *f* central. **~ize** *vt* centralizar

centre /'sentə(r)/ *n* centro *m*. ● *vt* (*pt* **centred**) centrar. ● *vi* centrarse (**on** en)

century /'sentʃərɪ/ *n* siglo *m*

cereal /'sɪərɪəl/ *n* cereal *m*

ceremon|ial /serɪ'məʊnɪəl/ *adj* & *n* ceremonial (*m*). **~y** /'serɪmənɪ/ *n* ceremonia *f*

certain /'sɜ:tn/ *adj* cierto. **for ~** seguro. **make ~ of** asegurarse de. **~ly** *adv* desde luego

certificate /sə'tɪfɪkət/ *n* certificado *m*; (*of birth, death etc*) partida *f*

certify /'sɜ:tɪfaɪ/ *vt* certificar

chafe /tʃeɪf/ *vt* rozar. ● *vi* rozarse

chaffinch /'tʃæfɪntʃ/ *n* pinzón *m*

chagrin /'ʃægrɪn/ *n* disgusto *m*

chain /tʃeɪn/ *n* cadena *f*. ● *vt* encadenar. **~ reaction** *n* reacción *f* en cadena. **~-smoker** *n* fumador *m* que siempre tiene un cigarrillo encendido. **~ store** *n* tienda *f* de una cadena

chair /tʃeə(r)/ *n* silla *f*; (*Univ*) cátedra *f*. ● *vt* presidir. **~lift** *n* telesquí *m*, telesilla *m* (*LAm*). **~man** /-mən/ *n* presidente *m*

chalet /'ʃæleɪ/ *n* chalé *m*

chalk /tʃɔ:k/ *n* (*in geology*) creta *f*; (*stick*) tiza *f*, gis *m* (*Mex*)

challeng|e /'tʃælɪndʒ/ *n* desafío *m*; (*fig*) reto *m*. ● *vt* desafiar; (*question*) poner en duda. **~ing** *adj* estimulante

chamber /'tʃeɪmbə(r)/ *n* (*old use*) cámara *f*. **~maid** *n* camarera *f*. **~ pot** *n* orinal *m*

champagne /ʃæm'peɪn/ *n* champaña *m*, champán *m*

champion /'tʃæmpɪən/ *n* campeón *m*. ● *vt* defender. **~ship** *n* campeonato *m*

chance /tʃɑ:ns/ *n* casualidad *f*; (*likelihood*) posibilidad *f*; (*opportunity*) oportunidad *f*; (*risk*) riesgo *m*. **by ~** por casualidad. ● *adj* fortuito

chancellor /'tʃɑ:nsələ(r)/ *n* canciller *m*; (*Univ*) rector *m*. **C~ of the Exchequer** Ministro *m* de Hacienda

chandelier /ʃændə'lɪə(r)/ *n* araña *f* (de luces)

chang|e /tʃeɪndʒ/ *vt* cambiar; (*substitute*) reemplazar. **~ one's mind** cambiar de idea. ● *vi* cambiarse. ● *n* cambio *m*; (*coins*) cambio *m*, sencillo *m* (*LAm*), feria *f* (*Mex*); (*money returned*) cambio *m*, vuelta *f*, vuelto *m* (*LAm*). **~eable** *adj* cambiable; (weather) variable. **~ing room** *n* (*Sport*) vestuario *m*, vestidor *m* (*Mex*); (*in shop*) probador *m*

channel /'tʃænl/ *n* canal *m*; (*fig*) medio *m*. ● *vt* (*pt* **channelled**) acanalar; (*fig*) encauzar. **the (English) C~** el Canal de la Mancha. **C~ Islands** *npl*. **the C~ Islands** las islas Anglonormandas. **C~ Tunnel** *n*. **the C~ Tunnel** el Eurotúnel

chant /tʃɑ:nt/ *n* canto *m*. ● *vt/i* cantar

chao|s /'keɪɒs/ *n* caos *m*. **~tic** /-'ɒtɪk/ *adj* caótico

chap /tʃæp/ *n* [!] tipo *m*, tío *m* [!]. ● *vt* (*pt* **chapped**) agrietar. ● *vi* agrietarse

chapel /'tʃæpl/ *n* capilla *f*
chaperon /'ʃæpərəʊn/ *n* acompañante *f*
chapter /'tʃæptə(r)/ *n* capítulo *m*
char /tʃɑː(r)/ *vt* (*pt* **charred**) carbonizar
character /'kærəktə(r)/ *n* carácter *m*; (*in book, play*) personaje *m*. **in ~** característico. **~istic** /-'rɪstɪk/ *adj* típico. ●*n* característica *f*. **~ize** *vt* caracterizar
charade /ʃə'rɑːd/ *n* farsa *f*. **~s** *npl* (*game*) charada *f*
charcoal /'tʃɑːkəʊl/ *n* carbón *m* vegetal; (*for drawing*) carboncillo *m*
charge /tʃɑːdʒ/ *n* precio *m*; (*Elec, Mil*) carga *f*; (*Jurid*) acusación *f*; (*task, custody*) encargo *m*; (*responsibility*) responsabilidad *f*. **in ~ of** responsable de, encargado de. **the person in ~** la persona responsable. **take ~ of** encargarse de. ●*vt* pedir; (*Elec, Mil*) cargar; (*Jurid*) acusar. ●*vi* cargar; (animal) embestir (**at** contra)
charit|able /'tʃærɪtəbl/ *adj* caritativo. **~y** /'tʃærɪtɪ/ *n* caridad *f*; (*society*) institución *f* benéfica
charm /tʃɑːm/ *n* encanto *m*; (*spell*) hechizo *m*; (*on bracelet*) dije *m*, amuleto *m*. ●*vt* encantar. **~ing** *adj* encantador
chart /tʃɑːt/ *n* (*for navigation*) carta *f* de navegación; (*table*) tabla *f*
charter /'tʃɑːtə(r)/ *n* carta *f*. ●*vt* alquilar (bus, train); fletar (plane, ship). **~ flight** *n* vuelo *m* chárter
chase /tʃeɪs/ *vt* perseguir. ●*vi* correr (**after** tras). ●*n* persecución *f*. □ **~ away**, **~ off** *vt* ahuyentar
chassis /'ʃæsɪ/ *n* chasis *m*
chastise /tʃæs'taɪz/ *vt* castigar
chastity /'tʃæstətɪ/ *n* castidad *f*
chat /tʃæt/ *n* charla *f*, conversación *f* (*LAm*), plática *f* (*Mex*). ●*vi* (*pt* **chatted**) charlar, conversar (*LAm*), platicar (*Mex*)
chatter /'tʃætə(r)/ *n* charla *f*. ●*vi* charlar. **his teeth are ~ing** le castañetean los dientes. **~box** *n* parlanchín *m*
chauffeur /'ʃəʊfə(r)/ *n* chófer *m*
chauvinis|m /'ʃəʊvɪnɪzəm/ *n* patriotería *f*; (*male*) machismo *m*. **~t** *n* patriotero *m*; (*male*) machista *m*
cheap /tʃiːp/ *adj* (**-er**, **-est**) barato; (*poor quality*) de baja calidad; (rate) económico. **~(ly)** *adv* barato, a bajo precio
cheat /'tʃiːt/ *vt* defraudar; (*deceive*) engañar. ●*vi* (*at cards*) hacer trampas. ●*n* trampa *f*; (*person*) tramposo *m*
check /tʃek/ *vt* comprobar; (*examine*) inspeccionar; (*curb*) frenar. ●*vi* comprobar. ●*n* comprobación *f*; (*of tickets*) control *m*; (*curb*) freno *m*; (*Chess*) jaque *m*; (*pattern*) cuadro *m*; (*Amer, bill*) cuenta *f*; (*Amer, cheque*) cheque *m*. □ **~ in** *vi* registrarse; (*at airport*) facturar el equipaje, chequear el equipaje (*LAm*), registrar el equipaje (*Mex*). □ **~ out** *vi* pagar la cuenta y marcharse. □ **~ up** *vi* confirmar. □ **~ up on** *vt* investigar. **~book** *n* (*Amer*) see **CHEQUEBOOK**. **~ered** /'tʃekəd/ *adj* (*Amer*) see **CHEQUERED**
checkers /'tʃekəz/ *n* (*Amer*) damas *fpl*
check: ~mate *n* jaque *m* mate. ●*vt* dar mate a. **~out** *n* caja *f*. **~point** control *m*. **~up** *n* chequeo *m*, revisión
cheek /tʃiːk/ *n* mejilla *f*; (*fig*) descaro *m*. **~bone** *n* pómulo *m*. **~y** *adj* descarado
cheep /tʃiːp/ *vi* piar

C

cheer /tʃɪə(r)/ *n* alegría *f*; (*applause*) viva *m*. **~s!** ¡salud!. ● *vt* alegrar; (*applaud*) aplaudir. ● *vi* alegrarse; (*applaud*) aplaudir. **~ up!** ¡anímate! **~ful** *adj* alegre

cheerio /tʃɪərɪ'əʊ/ *int* Ⓘ ¡adiós!, ¡hasta luego!

cheerless /'tʃɪəlɪs/ *adj* triste

cheese /tʃi:z/ *n* queso *m*

cheetah /'tʃi:tə/ *n* guepardo *m*

chef /ʃef/ *n* jefe *m* de cocina

chemical /'kemɪkl/ *adj* químico. ● *n* producto *m* químico

chemist /'kemɪst/ *n* farmacéutico *m*; (*scientist*) químico *m*. **~ry** *n* química *f*. **~'s (shop)** *n* farmacia *f*

cheque /tʃek/ *n* cheque *m*, talón *m*. **~book** *n* chequera *f*, talonario *m*

cherish /'tʃerɪʃ/ *vt* cuidar; (*love*) querer; abrigar (hope)

cherry /'tʃerɪ/ *n* cereza *f*. **~ tree** *n* cerezo *m*

chess /tʃes/ *n* ajedrez *m*. **~board** *n* tablero *m* de ajedrez

chest /tʃest/ *n* pecho *m*; (*box*) cofre *m*, cajón *m*

chestnut /'tʃesnʌt/ *n* castaña *f*. ● *adj* castaño. **~ tree** *n* castaño *m*

chest of drawers *n* cómoda *f*

chew /tʃu:/ *vt* masticar. **~ing gum** *n* chicle *m*

chic /ʃi:k/ *adj* elegante

chick /tʃɪk/ *n* polluelo *m*. **~en** /'tʃɪkɪn/ *n* pollo *m*. ● *adj* Ⓘ cobarde. ▫ **~en out** *vi* Ⓘ acobardarse. **~enpox** /'tʃɪkɪnpɒks/ *n* varicela *f*. **~pea** *n* garbanzo *m*

chicory /'tʃɪkərɪ/ *n* (*in coffee*) achicoria *f*; (*in salad*) escarola *f*

chief /tʃi:f/ *n* jefe *m*. ● *adj* principal. **~ly** *adv* principalmente

chilblain /'tʃɪlbleɪn/ *n* sabañón *m*

child /tʃaɪld/ *n* (*pl* **children** /'tʃɪldrən/) niño *m*; (*offspring*) hijo *m*. **~birth** *n* parto *m*. **~hood** *n* niñez *f*. **~ish** *adj* infantil. **~less** *adj* sin hijos. **~like** *adj* ingenuo, de niño

Chile /'tʃɪlɪ/ *n* Chile *m*. **~an** *adj & n* chileno (*m*)

chill /tʃɪl/ *n* frío *m*; (*illness*) resfriado *m*. ● *adj* frío. ● *vt* enfriar; refrigerar (food)

chilli /'tʃɪlɪ/ *n* (*pl* **-ies**) chile *m*

chilly /'tʃɪlɪ/ *adj* frío

chime /tʃaɪm/ *n* carillón *m*. ● *vt* tocar (bells); dar (hours). ● *vi* repicar

chimney /'tʃɪmnɪ/ *n* (*pl* **-eys**) chimenea *f*. **~ sweep** *n* deshollinador *m*

chimpanzee /tʃɪmpæn'zi:/ *n* chimpancé *m*

chin /tʃɪn/ *n* barbilla *f*

china /'tʃaɪnə/ *n* porcelana *f*

Chin|a /'tʃaɪnə/ *n* China *f*. **~ese** /-'ni:z/ *adj & n* chino (*m*)

chink /tʃɪŋk/ *n* (*crack*) grieta *f*; (*sound*) tintín *m*. ● *vi* tintinear

chip /tʃɪp/ *n* pedacito *m*; (*splinter*) astilla *f*; (*Culin*) patata *f* frita, papa *f* frita (*LAm*); (*in gambling*) ficha *f*; (*Comp*) chip *m*. **have a ~ on one's shoulder** guardar rencor. ● *vt* (*pt* **chipped**) desportillar. ▫ **~ in** *vi* Ⓘ interrumpir; (*with money*) contribuir

chiropodist /kɪ'rɒpədɪst/ *n* callista *m & f*, pedicuro *m*

chirp /tʃɜ:p/ *n* pío *m*. ● *vi* piar. **~y** *adj* alegre

chisel /'tʃɪzl/ *n* formón *m*. ● *vt* (*pt* **chiselled**) cincelar

chivalr|ous /'ʃɪvəlrəs/ *adj* caballeroso. **~y** /-rɪ/ *n* caballerosidad *f*

chlorine /'klɔ:ri:n/ *n* cloro *m*

chock /tʃɒk/ *n* cuña *f*. **~-a-block** *adj*. **~-full** *adj* atestado

chocolate /ˈtʃɒklət/ *n* chocolate *m*; (*individual sweet*) bombón *m*, chocolate *m* (*LAm*)

choice /tʃɔɪs/ *n* elección *f*; (*preference*) preferencia *f*. ● *adj* escogido

choir /ˈkwaɪə(r)/ *n* coro *m*

choke /tʃəʊk/ *vt* sofocar. ● *vi* sofocarse. ● *n* (*Auto*) choke *m*, estárter *m*, ahogador *m* (*Mex*)

cholera /ˈkɒlərə/ *n* cólera *m*

cholesterol /kəˈlestərɒl/ *n* colesterol *m*

choose /tʃu:z/ *vt/i* (*pt* **chose**, *pp* **chosen**) elegir, escoger. **~y** *adj* [!] exigente

chop /tʃɒp/ *vt* (*pt* **chopped**) cortar. ● *n* (*Culin*) chuleta *f*. □ **~ down** *vt* talar. □ **~ off** *vt* cortar. **~per** *n* hacha *f*; (*butcher's*) cuchilla *f*. **~py** *adj* picado

chord /kɔ:d/ *n* (*Mus*) acorde *m*

chore /tʃɔ:(r)/ *n* tarea *f*, faena *f*. **household ~s** *npl* quehaceres *mpl* domésticos

chorus /ˈkɔ:rəs/ *n* coro *m*; (*of song*) estribillo *m*

chose/tʃəʊz/, **chosen** /ˈtʃəʊzn/ *see* **CHOOSE**

Christ /kraɪst/ *n* Cristo *m*

christen /ˈkrɪsn/ *vt* bautizar. **~ing** *n* bautizo *m*

Christian /ˈkrɪstjən/ *adj & n* cristiano (*m*). **~ity** /krɪstɪˈænətɪ/ *n* cristianismo *m*. **~ name** *n* nombre *m* de pila

Christmas /ˈkrɪsməs/ *n* Navidad *f*. **Merry ~!** ¡Feliz Navidad!, ¡Felices Pascuas! **Father ~** Papá *m* Noel. ● *adj* de Navidad, navideño. **~ card** *n* tarjeta *f* de Navidad *f*. **~ day** *n* día *m* de Navidad. **~ Eve** *n* Nochebuena *f*. **~ tree** *n* árbol *m* de Navidad

chrom|e /krəʊm/ *n* cromo *m*. **~ium** /ˈkrəʊmɪəm/ *n* cromo *m*

chromosome /ˈkrəʊməsəʊm/ *n* cromosoma *m*

chronic /ˈkrɒnɪk/ *adj* crónico; (*fam, bad*) terrible

chronicle /ˈkrɒnɪkl/ *n* crónica *f*. ● *vt* historiar

chronological /krɒnəˈlɒdʒɪkl/ *adj* cronológico

chubby /ˈtʃʌbɪ/ *adj* (**-ier**, **-iest**) regordete; (person) gordinflón [!]

chuck /tʃʌk/ *vt* [!] tirar. □ **~ out** *vt* tirar

chuckle /ˈtʃʌkl/ *n* risa *f* ahogada. ● *vi* reírse entre dientes

chug /tʃʌg/ *vi* (*pt* **chugged**) (*of motor*) traquetear

chum /tʃʌm/ *n* amigo *m*, compinche *m*, cuate *m* (*Mex*)

chunk /tʃʌŋk/ *n* trozo *m* grueso. **~y** *adj* macizo

church /ˈtʃɜ:tʃ/ *n* iglesia *f*. **~yard** *n* cementerio *m*

churn /ˈtʃɜ:n/ *n* (*for milk*) lechera *f*, cántara *f*; (*for making butter*) mantequera *f*. ● *vt* agitar. □ **~ out** *vt* producir en profusión

chute /ʃu:t/ *n* tobogán *m*

cider /ˈsaɪdə(r)/ *n* sidra *f*

cigar /sɪˈgɑ:(r)/ *n* puro *m*

cigarette /sɪgəˈret/ *n* cigarrillo *m*. **~ end** *n* colilla *f*. **~ holder** *n* boquilla *f*. **~ lighter** *n* mechero *m*, encendedor *m*

cinecamera /ˈsɪnɪkæmərə/ *n* tomavistas *m*, filmadora *f* (*LAm*)

cinema /ˈsɪnəmə/ *n* cine *m*

cipher /ˈsaɪfə(r)/ *n* (*Math*, *fig*) cero *m*; (*code*) clave *f*

circle /ˈsɜ:kl/ *n* círculo *m*; (*in theatre*) anfiteatro *m*. ● *vt* girar alrede-

C

dor de. • *vi* dar vueltas

circuit /'sɜːkɪt/ *n* circuito *m*

circular /'sɜːkjʊlə(r)/ *adj & n* circular (*f*)

circulat|e /'sɜːkjʊleɪt/ *vt* hacer circular. • *vi* circular. **~ion** /-'leɪʃn/ *n* circulación *f*; (*number of copies*) tirada *f*

circumcise /'sɜːkəmsaɪz/ *vt* circuncidar

circumference /sə'kʌmfərəns/ *n* circunferencia *f*

circumstance /'sɜːkəmstəns/ *n* circunstancia *f*. **~s** (*means*) *npl* situación *f* económica

circus /'sɜːkəs/ *n* circo *m*

cistern /'sɪstən/ *n* cisterna *f*

cite /saɪt/ *vt* citar

citizen /'sɪtɪzn/ *n* ciudadano *m*; (*inhabitant*) habitante *m & f*

citrus /'sɪtrəs/ *n*. **~ fruits** cítricos *mpl*

city /'sɪtɪ/ *n* ciudad *f*; **the C~** el centro *m* financiero de Londres

> i
>
> **City - the** Área ubicada dentro de los límites de la antigua ciudad de Londres. Actualmente es el centro financiero de la capital donde tienen sus sedes centrales muchas instituciones financieras. A menudo, cuando se habla de *The City*, se está refiriendo a ésas y no a la zona propiamente dicha.

civic /'sɪvɪk/ *adj* cívico

civil /'sɪvl/ *adj* civil; (*polite*) cortés

civilian /sɪ'vɪlɪən/ *adj & n* civil (*m & f*)

civiliz|ation /sɪvɪlaɪ'zeɪʃn/ *n* civilización *f*. **~ed** /'sɪvəlaɪzd/ *adj* civilizado.

civil: ~ partnership *n* matrimonio *m* de homosexuales. **~ servant** *n* funcionario *m* (del Estado), burócrata *m & f* (*Mex*). **~ service** *n* administración *f* pública. **~ war** *n* guerra *f* civil

clad /klæd/ see **CLOTHE**

claim /kleɪm/ *vt* reclamar; (*assert*) pretender. • *n* reclamación *f*; (*right*) derecho *m*; (*Jurid*) demanda *f*

clairvoyant /kleə'vɔɪənt/ *n* clarividente *m & f*

clam /klæm/ *n* almeja *f*. • *vi* (*pt* **clammed**). **~ up** [I] ponerse muy poco comunicativo

clamber /'klæmbə(r)/ *vi* trepar a gatas

clammy /'klæmɪ/ *adj* (**-ier**, **-iest**) húmedo

clamour /'klæmə(r)/ *n* clamor *m*. • *vi*. **~ for** pedir a gritos

clamp /klæmp/ *n* abrazadera *f*; (*Auto*) cepo *m*. • *vt* sujetar con abrazadera; poner cepo a (car). □ **~ down on** *vt* reprimir

clan /klæn/ *n* clan *m*

clang /klæŋ/ *n* sonido *m* metálico

clap /klæp/ *vt* (*pt* **clapped**) aplaudir; batir (hands). • *vi* aplaudir. • *n* palmada *f*; (*of thunder*) trueno *m*

clarif|ication /klærɪfɪ'keɪʃn/ *n* aclaración *f*. **~y** /'klærɪfaɪ/ *vt* aclarar. • *vi* aclararse

clarinet /klærɪ'net/ *n* clarinete *m*

clarity /'klærətɪ/ *n* claridad *f*

clash /klæʃ/ *n* choque *m*; (*noise*) estruendo *m*; (*contrast*) contraste *m*; (*fig*) conflicto *m*. • *vt* golpear. • *vi* encontrarse; (colours) desentonar

clasp /klɑːsp/ *n* cierre *m*. • *vt* agarrar; apretar (hand)

class /klɑːs/ *n* clase *f*. **evening ~** *n* clase nocturna. • *vt* clasificar

classic /'klæsɪk/ *adj & n* clásico (*m*). **~al** *adj* clásico. **~s** *npl* estudios *mpl* clásicos

classif|ication /klæsɪfɪ'keɪʃn/ *n* clasificación *f*. **~y** /'klæsɪfaɪ/ *vt* clasificar

class: ~room *n* aula *f*, clase *f*. **~y** *adj* [I] elegante

clatter /'klætə(r)/ *n* ruido *m*; (*of train*) traqueteo *m*. ● *vi* hacer ruido

clause /klɔːz/ *n* cláusula *f*; (*Gram*) oración *f*

claustrophobia /klɔːstrə'fəʊbɪə/ *n* claustrofobia *f*

claw /klɔː/ *n* garra *f*; (*of cat*) uña *f*; (*of crab*) pinza *f*. ● *vt* arañar

clay /kleɪ/ *n* arcilla *f*

clean /kliːn/ *adj* (**-er**, **-est**) limpio; (stroke) bien definido. ● *adv* completamente. ● *vt* limpiar. ● *vi* limpiar. □ **~ up** *vt* hacer la limpieza. **~er** *n* persona *f* que hace la limpieza. **~liness** /'klenlɪnɪs/ *n* limpieza *f*

cleans|e /klenz/ *vt* limpiar. **~er** *n* producto *m* de limpieza; (*for skin*) crema *f* de limpieza. **~ing cream** *n* crema *f* de limpieza

clear /klɪə(r)/ *adj* (**-er**, **-est**) claro; (*transparent*) transparente; (*without obstacles*) libre; (profit) neto; (sky) despejado. **keep ~ of** evitar. ● *adv* claramente. ● *vt* despejar; liquidar (goods); (*Jurid*) absolver; (*jump over*) saltar por encima de; quitar, levantar (*LAm*) (table). □ **~ off** *vi* [x], **~ out** *vi* ([I], *go away*) largarse. □ **~ up** *vt* (*tidy*) ordenar; aclarar (mystery). *vi* (weather) despejarse. **~ance** *n* (*removal of obstructions*) despeje *m*; (*authorization*) permiso *m*; (*by security*) acreditación *f*. **~ing** *n* claro *m*. **~ly** *adv* evidentemente. **~way** *n* carretera *f* en la que no se permite parar

cleavage /'kliːvɪdʒ/ *n* escote *m*

clef /klef/ *n* (*Mus*) clave *f*

clench /klentʃ/ *vt* apretar

clergy /'klɜːdʒɪ/ *n* clero *m*. **~man** /-mən/ *n* clérigo *m*

cleric /'klerɪk/ *n* clérigo *m*. **~al** *adj* clerical; (*of clerks*) de oficina

clerk /klɑːk/ *n* empleado *m*; (*Amer, salesclerk*) vendedor *m*

clever /'klevə(r)/ *adj* (**-er**, **-est**) inteligente; (*skilful*) hábil. **~ly** *adv* inteligentemente; (*with skill*) hábilmente. **~ness** *n* inteligencia *f*

cliché /'kliːʃeɪ/ *n* lugar *m* común *m*, cliché *m*

click /klɪk/ *n* golpecito *m*. ● *vi* chascar; [I] llevarse bien. **~ on sth** hacer clic en algo. ● *vt* chasquear

client /'klaɪənt/ *n* cliente *m*

cliff /klɪf/ *n* acantilado *m*

climat|e /'klaɪmət/ *n* clima *m*. **~e change** *n* cambio *m* climático. **~ic** /-'mætɪk/ *adj* climático

climax /'klaɪmæks/ *n* clímax *m*; (*orgasm*) orgasmo *m*

climb /klaɪm/ *vt* subir (stairs); trepar (tree); escalar (mountain). ● *vi* subir. ● *n* subida *f*. □ **~ down** *vi* bajar; (*fig*) ceder. **~er** *n* (*Sport*) alpinista *m & f*, andinista *m & f* (*LAm*); (*plant*) trepadora *f*

clinch /klɪntʃ/ *vt* cerrar (deal)

cling /klɪŋ/ *vi* (*pt* **clung**) agarrarse; (*stick*) pegarse

clinic /'klɪnɪk/ *n* centro *m* médico; (*private hospital*) clínica *f*. **~al** *adj* clínico

clink /klɪŋk/ *n* tintineo *m*. ● *vt* hacer tintinear. ● *vi* tintinear

clip /klɪp/ *n* (fastener) clip *m*; (*for paper*) sujetapapeles *m*; (*for hair*) horquilla *f*. ● *vt* (*pt* **clipped**) (*cut*) cortar; (*join*) sujetar. **~pers** /'klɪpəz/ *npl* (*for hair*) maquinilla *f* para cortar el pelo; (*for nails*) cortauñas *m.* ~**ping** *n* recorte *m*

cloak /kləʊk/ *n* capa *f.* ~**room** *n* guardarropa *m*; (*toilet*) lavabo *m*, baño *m* (*LAm*)

clock /klɒk/ *n* reloj *m.* ~**wise** *a/adv* en el sentido de las agujas del reloj. ~**work** *n* mecanismo *m* de relojería. **like** ~**work** con precisión

clog /klɒg/ *n* zueco *m.* ● *vt* (*pt* **clogged**) atascar

cloister /'klɔɪstə(r)/ *n* claustro *m*

clone /kləʊn/ *n* clon *m*

close[1] /kləʊs/ *adj* (**-er**, **-est**) cercano; (*together*) apretado; (friend) íntimo; (weather) bochornoso; (link etc) estrecho; (game, battle) reñido. **have a** ~ **shave** (*fig*) escaparse de milagro. ● *adv* cerca

close[2] /kləʊz/ *vt* cerrar. ● *vi* cerrarse; (*end*) terminar. ~ **down** *vt/i* cerrar. ● *n* fin *m.* ~**d** *adj* cerrado

closely /'kləʊslɪ/ *adv* estrechamente; (*at a short distance*) de cerca; (*with attention*) detenidamente; (*precisely*) rigurosamente

closet /'klɒzɪt/ *n* (*Amer*) armario *m*; (*for clothes*) armario *m*, closet *m* (*LAm*)

close-up /'kləʊsʌp/ *n* (*Cinema etc*) primer plano *m*

closure /'kləʊʒə(r)/ *n* cierre *m*

clot /klɒt/ *n* (*Med*) coágulo *m*; [!] tonto *m.* ● *vi* (*pt* **clotted**) cuajarse; (blood) coagularse

cloth /klɒθ/ *n* tela *f*; (*duster*) trapo *m*; (*tablecloth*) mantel *m*

cloth|e /kləʊð/ *vt* (*pt* **clothed** *or* **clad**) vestir. ~**es** /kləʊðz/ *npl* ropa. ~**espin**, ~**espeg** (*Amer*) *n* pinza *f* (para tender la ropa). ~**ing** *n* ropa *f*

cloud /klaʊd/ *n* nube *f.* ● ~ **over** *vi* nublarse. ~**y** *adj* (**-ier**, **-iest**) nublado; (liquid) turbio

clout /klaʊt/ *n* bofetada *f.* ● *vt* abofetear

clove /kləʊv/ *n* clavo *m.* ~ **of garlic** *n* diente *m* de ajo

clover /'kləʊvə(r)/ *n* trébol *m*

clown /klaʊn/ *n* payaso *m.* ● *vi* hacer el payaso

club /klʌb/ *n* club *m*; (*weapon*) porra *f*; (*golf club*) palo *m* de golf; (*at cards*) trébol *m.* ● *vt* (*pt* **clubbed**) aporrear. □ ~ **together** *vi* contribuir con dinero (**to** para)

cluck /klʌk/ *vi* cloquear

clue /klu:/ *n* pista *f*; (*in crosswords*) indicación *f.* **not to have a** ~ no tener la menor idea

clump /klʌmp/ *n* grupo *m.* ● *vt* agrupar

clums|iness /'klʌmzɪnɪs/ *n* torpeza *f.* ~**y** /'klʌmzɪ/ *adj* (**-ier**, **-iest**) torpe

clung /klʌŋ/ *see* CLING

cluster /'klʌstə(r)/ *n* grupo *m.* ● *vi* agruparse

clutch /klʌtʃ/ *vt* agarrar. ● *n* (*Auto*) embrague *m*

clutter /'klʌtə(r)/ *n* desorden *m.* ● *vt.* ~ **(up)** abarrotar. ~**ed** /'klʌtəd/ *adj* abarratado de cosas

coach /kəʊtʃ/ *n* autocar *m*, autobús *m*; (*of train*) vagón *m*; (*horse-drawn*) coche *m*; (*Sport*) entrenador *m.* ● *vt* (*Sport*) entrenar

coal /kəʊl/ *n* carbón *m*

coalition /kəʊə'lɪʃn/ *n* coalición *f*

coarse /kɔ:s/ *adj* (**-er**, **-est**) grueso; (material) basto; (*person, language*) ordinario

coast /kəʊst/ *n* costa *f.* ● *vi* (*with cycle*) deslizarse sin pedalear; (*with car*) ir en punto muerto. ~**al** *adj* costero. ~**guard** *n* guardacostas *m.* ~**line** *n* litoral *m*

C

coat /kəʊt/ *n* abrigo *m*; (*jacket*) chaqueta *f*; (*of animal*) pelo *m*; (*of paint*) mano *f*. ● *vt* cubrir, revestir. **~hanger** *n* percha *f*, gancho *m* (*LAm*). **~ing** *n* capa *f*. **~ of arms** *n* escudo *m* de armas

coax /kəʊks/ *vt* engatusar

cobbler /'kɒblə(r)/ *n* zapatero *m* (remendón)

cobblestone /'kɒbəlstəʊn/ *n* adoquín *m*

cobweb /'kɒbweb/ *n* telaraña *f*

cocaine /kə'keɪn/ *n* cocaína *f*

cock /kɒk/ *n* (*cockerel*) gallo *m*; (*male bird*) macho *m*. ● *vt* amartillar (gun); aguzar (ears). **~erel** /'kɒkərəl/ *n* gallo *m*. **~-eyed** /-aɪd/ *adj* 🄸 torcido

cockney /'kɒknɪ/ *adj & n* (*pl* **-eys**) londinense (*m & f*) (del este de Londres)

cockpit /'kɒkpɪt/ *n* (*in aircraft*) cabina *f* del piloto

cockroach /'kɒkrəʊtʃ/ *n* cucaracha *f*

cocktail /'kɒkteɪl/ *n* cóctel *m*

cock-up /'kɒkʌp/ *n* 🅇 lío *m*

cocky /'kɒkɪ/ *adj* (**-ier**, **-iest**) engreído

cocoa /'kəʊkəʊ/ *n* cacao *m*; (*drink*) chocolate *m*, cocoa *f* (*LAm*)

coconut /'kəʊkənʌt/ *n* coco *m*

cocoon /kə'ku:n/ *n* capullo *m*

cod /kɒd/ *n invar* bacalao *m*

code /kəʊd/ *n* código *m*; (*secret*) clave *f*; **in ~** en clave

coeducational /kəʊedʒʊ'keɪʃənl/ *adj* mixto

coerc|e /kəʊ'ɜ:s/ *vt* coaccionar. **~ion** /-ʃn/ *n* coacción *f*

coffee /'kɒfɪ/ *n* café *m*. **~ bean** *n* grano *m* de café. **~ maker** *n* cafetera *f*. **~pot** *n* cafetera *f*

coffin /'kɒfɪn/ *n* ataúd *m*, cajón *m* (*LAm*)

cog /kɒg/ *n* diente *m*; (*fig*) pieza *f*

coherent /kəʊ'hɪərənt/ *adj* coherente

coil /kɔɪl/ *vt* enrollar. ● *n* rollo *m*; (*one ring*) vuelta *f*

coin /kɔɪn/ *n* moneda *f*. ● *vt* acuñar

coincide /kəʊɪn'saɪd/ *vi* coincidir. **~nce** /kəʊ'ɪnsɪdəns/ *n* casualidad *f*. **~ntal** /kəʊɪnsɪ'dentl/ *adj* casual

coke /kəʊk/ *n* (*coal*) coque *m*. **C~** (®) Coca-Cola *f* (®)

colander /'kʌləndə(r)/ *n* colador *m*

cold /kəʊld/ *adj* (**-er**, **-est**) frío. **be ~** (person) tener frío. **it is ~** (*weather*) hace frío. ● *n* frío *m*; (*Med*) resfriado *m*. **have a ~** estar resfriado. **~-blooded** /-'blʌdɪd/ *adj* (animal) de sangre fría; (murder) a sangre fría. **~-shoulder** /-'ʃəʊldə(r)/ *vt* tratar con frialdad. **~ sore** *n* herpes *m* labial. **~ storage** *n* conservación *f* en frigorífico

coleslaw /'kəʊlslɔ:/ *n* ensalada *f* de col

collaborat|e /kə'læbəreɪt/ *vi* colaborar. **~ion** /-'reɪʃn/ *n* colaboración *f*. **~or** *n* colaborador *m*

collaps|e /kə'læps/ *vi* derrumbarse; (*Med*) sufrir un colapso. ● *n* derrumbamiento *m*; (*Med*) colapso *m*. **~ible** /-əbl/ *adj* plegable

collar /'kɒlə(r)/ *n* cuello *m*; (*for animals*) collar *m*. ● *vt* 🄸 hurtar. **~bone** *n* clavícula *f*

colleague /'kɒli:g/ *n* colega *m & f*

collect /kə'lekt/ *vt* reunir; (*hobby*) coleccionar, juntar (*LAm*); (*pick up*) recoger; cobrar (rent). ● *vi* (people) reunirse; (things) acumularse. **~ion** /-ʃn/ *n* colección *f*; (*in church*) colecta *f*; (*of post*) recogida

f. **~or** *n* coleccionista *m & f*
college /ˈkɒlɪdʒ/ *n* colegio *m*; (*of art, music etc*) escuela *f*; (*Amer*) universidad *f*
colli|de /kəˈlaɪd/ *vi* chocar. **~sion** /-ˈlɪʒn/ *n* choque *m*
colloquial /kəˈləʊkwɪəl/ *adj* coloquial
Colombia /kəˈlʌmbɪə/ *n* Colombia *f*. **~n** *adj & n* colombiano (*m*)
colon /ˈkəʊlən/ *n* (*Gram*) dos puntos *mpl*; (*Med*) colon *m*
colonel /ˈkɜːnl/ *n* coronel *m*
colon|ial /kəˈləʊnɪəl/ *adj* colonial. **~ize** /ˈkɒlənaɪz/ *vt* colonizar. **~y** /ˈkɒlənɪ/ *n* colonia *f*
colossal /kəˈlɒsl/ *adj* colosal
colour /ˈkʌlə(r)/ *n* color *m*. **off ~** (*fig*) indispuesto. ● *adj* de color(es), en color(es) ● *vt* colorear; (*dye*) teñir. **~-blind** *adj* daltónico. **~ed** /ˈkʌləd/ *adj* de color. **~ful** *adj* lleno de color; (*fig*) pintoresco. **~ing** *n* color; (*food colouring*) colorante *m*. **~less** *adj* incoloro
column /ˈkɒləm/ *n* columna *f*. **~ist** *n* columnista *m & f*
coma /ˈkəʊmə/ *n* coma *m*
comb /kəʊm/ *n* peine *m*. ● *vt* (*search*) registrar. **~ one's hair** peinarse
combat /ˈkɒmbæt/ *n* combate *m*. ● *vt* (*pt* **combated**) combatir
combination /kɒmbɪˈneɪʃn/ *n* combinación *f*
combine /kəmˈbaɪn/ *vt* combinar. ● *vi* combinarse. ● /ˈkɒmbaɪn/ *n* asociación *f*. **~ harvester** *n* cosechadora *f*
combustion /kəmˈbʌstʃən/ *n* combustión *f*
come /kʌm/ *vi* (*pt* **came**, *pp* **come**) venir; (*occur*) pasar. □ **~ across** *vt* encontrarse con (person); encontrar (object). □ **~ apart** *vi* deshacerse. □ **~ away** *vi* (*leave*) salir; (*become detached*) salirse. □ **~ back** *vi* volver. □ **~ by** *vt* obtener. □ **~ down** *vi* bajar. □ **~ in** *vi* entrar; (*arrive*) llegar. □ **~ into** *vt* entrar en; heredar (money). □ **~ off** *vi* desprenderse; (*succeed*) tener éxito. *vt*. **~ off it!** 🅸 ¡no me vengas con eso! □ **~ on** *vi* (*start to work*) encenderse. **~ on, hurry up!** ¡vamos, date prisa! □ **~ out** *vi* salir. □ **~ round** *vi* (*after fainting*) volver en sí; (*be converted*) cambiar de idea; (*visit*) venir. □ **~ to** *vt* llegar a (decision etc). □ **~ up** *vi* subir; (*fig*) surgir. □ **~ up with** *vt* proponer (idea). **~back** *n* retorno *m*; (*retort*) réplica *f*
comedian /kəˈmiːdɪən/ *n* cómico *m*
comedy /ˈkɒmədɪ/ *n* comedia *f*
comet /ˈkɒmɪt/ *n* cometa *m*
comfort /ˈkʌmfət/ *n* comodidad *f*; (*consolation*) consuelo *m*. ● *vt* consolar. **~able** *adj* cómodo. **~er** *n* (*for baby*) chupete *m*, chupón *m* (*LAm*); (*Amer, for bed*) edredón *m*
comic /ˈkɒmɪk/ *adj* cómico. ● *n* cómico *m*; (*periodical*) revista *f* de historietas, tebeo *m*. **~al** *adj* cómico. **~ strip** *n* tira *f* cómica
coming /ˈkʌmɪŋ/ *n* llegada *f*. **~s and goings** idas *fpl* y venidas. ● *adj* próximo; (week, month etc) que viene
comma /ˈkɒmə/ *n* coma *f*
command /kəˈmɑːnd/ *n* orden *f*; (*mastery*) dominio *m*. ● *vt* ordenar; imponer (respect)
commandeer /kɒmənˈdɪə(r)/ *vt* requisar
command: ~er *n* comandante *m*. **~ing** *adj* imponente. **~ment** *n* mandamiento *m*

commando /kəˈmɑːndəʊ/ *n* (*pl* **-os**) comando *m*
commemorat|e /kəˈmeməreɪt/ *vt* conmemorar. **~ion** /-ˈreɪʃn/ *n* conmemoración *f*. **~ive** /-ətɪv/ *adj* conmemorativo
commence /kəˈmens/ *vt* dar comienzo a. ●*vi* iniciarse
commend /kəˈmend/ *vt* alabar. **~able** *adj* loable. **~ation** /kɒmenˈdeɪʃn/ *n* elogio *m*
comment /ˈkɒment/ *n* observación *f*. ●*vi* hacer observaciones (**on** sobre)
commentary /ˈkɒməntrɪ/ *n* comentario *m*; (*Radio, TV*) reportaje *m*
commentat|e /ˈkɒmənteɪt/ *vi* narrar. **~or** *n* (*Radio, TV*) locutor *m*
commerc|e /ˈkɒmɜːs/ *n* comercio *m*. **~ial** /kəˈmɜːʃl/ *adj* comercial. ●*n* anuncio *m*; aviso *m* (*LAm*). **~ialize** *vt* comercializar
commiserat|e /kəˈmɪzəreɪt/ *vi* compadecerse (**with** de). **~ion** /-ˈreɪʃn/ *n* conmiseración *f*
commission /kəˈmɪʃn/ *n* comisión *f*. **out of ~** fuera de servicio. ●*vt* encargar; (*Mil*) nombrar oficial
commissionaire /kəmɪʃəˈneə(r)/ *n* portero *m*
commit /kəˈmɪt/ *vt* (*pt* **committed**) cometer; (*entrust*) confiar. **~ o.s.** comprometerse. **~ment** *n* compromiso *m*
committee /kəˈmɪtɪ/ *n* comité *m*
commodity /kəˈmɒdətɪ/ *n* producto *m*, artículo *m*
common /ˈkɒmən/ *adj* (**-er**, **-est**) común; (*usual*) corriente; (*vulgar*) ordinario. ●*n*. **in ~** en común. **~er** *n* plebeyo *m*. **~ law** *n* derecho *m* consuetudinario. **~ly** *adv* comúnmente. **C~ Market** *n* Mercado *m* Común. **~place** *adj* banal. ●*n* banalidad *f*. **~ room** *n* sala *f* común, salón *m* común. **C~s** *n*. **the (House of) C~s** la Cámara de los Comunes. **~ sense** *n* sentido *m* común. **C~wealth** *n*. **the C~wealth** la Mancomunidad *f* Británica

c

commotion /kəˈməʊʃn/ *n* confusión *f*

> **Commonwealth** *La Commonwealth* es una asociación de las antiguas colonias y territorios que conformaban el Imperio Británico. Cada dos años se celebra una reunión de sus jefes de gobierno. Entre los países miembros existen muchos vínculos culturales, educativos y deportivos. En EE.UU., es el término oficial para referirse a cuatro estados: Kentucky, Massachussets, Pensilvania y Virginia.

commune /ˈkɒmjuːn/ *n* comuna *f*
communicat|e /kəˈmjuːnɪkeɪt/ *vt* comunicar. ●*vi* comunicarse. **~ion** /-ˈkeɪʃn/ *n* comunicación *f*. **~ive** /-ətɪv/ *adj* comunicativo
communion /kəˈmjuːnɪən/ *n* comunión *f*
communis|m /ˈkɒmjʊnɪsəm/ *n* comunismo *m*. **~t** *n* comunista *m* & *f*
community /kəˈmjuːnətɪ/ *n* comunidad *f*. **~ centre** *n* centro *m* social
commute /kəˈmjuːt/ *vi* viajar diariamente (*entre el lugar de residencia y el trabajo*). ●*vt* (*Jurid*) conmutar. **~r** *n* viajero *m* diario
compact /kəmˈpækt/ *adj* compacto. ●/ˈkɒmpækt/ *n* (*for powder*) polvera *f*. **~ disc**, **~ disk** /ˈkɒmpækt/ *n* disco *m* compacto,

compact-disc *m.* ~ **disc player** *n* (reproductor *m* de) compact-disc

companion /kəm'pænɪən/ *n* compañero *m.* ~**ship** *n* compañía *f*

company /'kʌmpənɪ/ *n* compañía *f*; (*guests*) visita *f*; (*Com*) sociedad *f*

compar|able /'kɒmpərəbl/ *adj* comparable. ~**ative** /kəm'pærətɪv/ *adj* comparativo; (*fig*) relativo. ● *n* (*Gram*) comparativo *m.* ~**e** /kəm'peə(r)/ *vt* comparar. ~**ison** /kəm'pærɪsn/ *n* comparación *f*

compartment /kəm'pɑ:tmənt/ *n* compartim(i)ento *m*

compass /'kʌmpəs/ *n* brújula *f.* ~**es** *npl* compás *m*

compassion /kəm'pæʃn/ *n* compasión *f.* ~**ate** /-ət/ *adj* compasivo

compatible /kəm'pætəbl/ *adj* compatible

compel /kəm'pel/ *vt* (*pt* **compelled**) obligar. ~**ling** *adj* irresistible

compensat|e /'kɒmpənseɪt/ *vt* compensar; (*for loss*) indemnizar. ● *vi.* ~**e for sth** compensar algo. ~**ion** /-'seɪʃn/ *n* compensación *f*; (*financial*) indemnización *f*

compère /'kɒmpeə(r)/ *n* presentador *m.* ● *vt* presentar

compete /kəm'pi:t/ *vi* competir

competen|ce /'kɒmpətəns/ *n* competencia *f.* ~**t** *adj* competente

competit|ion /kɒmpə'tɪʃn/ *n* (*contest*) concurso *m*; (*Sport*) competición *f*, competencia *f* (*LAm*); (*Com*) competencia *f.* ~**ive** /kəm'petətɪv/ *adj* competidor; (price) competitivo. ~**or** /kəm'petɪtə(r)/ *n* competidor *m*; (*in contest*) concursante *m & f*

compile /kəm'paɪl/ *vt* compilar

complacen|cy /kəm'pleɪsənsɪ/ *n* autosuficiencia *f.* ~**t** *adj* satisfecho de sí mismo

complain /kəm'pleɪn/ *vi.* ~ **(about)** quejarse (de). ● *vt.* ~ **that** quejarse de que. ~**t** *n* queja *f*; (*Med*) enfermedad *f*

complement /'kɒmplɪmənt/ *n* complemento *m.* ● *vt* complementar. ~**ary** /-'mentrɪ/ *adj* complementario

complet|e /kəm'pli:t/ *adj* completo; (*finished*) acabado; (*downright*) total. ● *vt* acabar; llenar (a form). ~**ely** *adv* completamente. ~**ion** /-ʃn/ *n* finalización *f*

complex /'kɒmpleks/ *adj* complejo. ● *n* complejo *m*

complexion /kəm'plekʃn/ *n* tez *f*; (*fig*) aspecto *m*

complexity /kəm'pleksətɪ/ *n* complejidad *f*

complicat|e /'kɒmplɪkeɪt/ *vt* complicar. ~**ed** *adj* complicado. ~**ion** /-'keɪʃn/ *n* complicación *f*

compliment /'kɒmplɪmənt/ *n* cumplido *m*; (*amorous*) piropo *m.* ● *vt* felicitar. ~**ary** /-'mentrɪ/ *adj* halagador; (*given free*) de regalo. ~**s** *npl* saludos *mpl*

comply /kəm'plaɪ/ *vi.* ~ **with** conformarse con

component /kəm'pəʊnənt/ *adj & n* componente (*m*)

compos|e /kəm'pəʊz/ *vt* componer. **be** ~**ed of** estar compuesto de. ~**er** *n* compositor *m.* ~**ition** /kɒmpə'zɪʃn/ *n* composición *f*

compost /'kɒmpɒst/ *n* abono *m*

composure /kəm'pəʊʒə(r)/ *n* serenidad *f*

compound /'kɒmpaʊnd/ *n* compuesto *m*; (*enclosure*) recinto *m.* ● *adj* compuesto; (fracture) complicado

comprehen|d /kɒmprɪ'hend/ *vt* comprender. **~sion** /kɒmprɪ'henʃn/ *n* comprensión *f.* **~sive** /kɒmprɪ'hensɪv/ *adj* extenso; (insurance) contra todo riesgo. **~sive (school)** *n* instituto *m* de enseñanza secundaria

compress /'kɒmpres/ *n* (*Med*) compresa *f.* ● /kəm'pres/ *vt* comprimir. **~ion** /-'preʃn/ *n* compresión *f*

comprise /kəm'praɪz/ *vt* comprender

compromis|e /'kɒmprəmaɪz/ *n* acuerdo *m*, compromiso *m*, arreglo *m.* ● *vt* comprometer. ● *vi* llegar a un acuerdo. **~ing** *adj* (situation) comprometido

compuls|ion /kəm'pʌlʃn/ *n* (*force*) coacción *f*; (*obsession*) compulsión *f.* **~ive** /kəm'pʌlsɪv/ *adj* compulsivo. **~ory** /kəm'pʌlsərɪ/ *adj* obligatorio

comput|e /kəm'pju:t/ *vb* calcular. **comput|er** *n* ordenador *m*, computadora *f* (*LAm*). **~erize** *vt* computarizar, computerizar. **~er studies** *n*, **~ing** *n* informática *f*, computación *f*

comrade /'kɒmreɪd/ *n* camarada *m & f*

con /kɒn/ *vt* (*pt* **conned**) [I] estafar. ● *n* (*fraud*) estafa *f*; (*objection*) *see* **PRO**

concave /'kɒŋkeɪv/ *adj* cóncavo

conceal /kən'si:l/ *vt* ocultar

concede /kən'si:d/ *vt* conceder

conceit /kən'si:t/ *n* vanidad *f.* **~ed** *adj* engreído

conceiv|able /kən'si:vəbl/ *adj* concebible. **~e** /kən'si:v/ *vt/i* concebir

concentrat|e /'kɒnsəntreɪt/ *vt* concentrar. ● *vi* concentrarse (**on** en). **~ion** /-'treɪʃn/ *n* concentración *f*

concept /'kɒnsept/ *n* concepto *m*

conception /kən'sepʃn/ *n* concepción *f*

concern /kən'sɜ:n/ *n* asunto *m*; (*worry*) preocupación *f*; (*Com*) empresa *f.* ● *vt* tener que ver con; (*deal with*) tratar de. **as far as I'm ~ed** en cuanto a mí. **be ~ed about** preocuparse por. **~ing** *prep* acerca de

concert /'kɒnsət/ *n* concierto *m*. **~ed** /kən'sɜ:tɪd/ *adj* concertado

concertina /kɒnsə'ti:nə/ *n* concertina *f*

concerto /kən'tʃɜ:təʊ/ *n* (*pl* **-os** *or* **-ti** /-tɪ/) concierto *m*

concession /kən'seʃn/ *n* concesión *f*

concise /kən'saɪs/ *adj* conciso

conclu|de /kən'klu:d/ *vt/i* concluir. **~ding** *adj* final. **~sion** /-ʃn/ *n* conclusión *f.*. **~sive** /-sɪv/ *adj* decisivo. **~sively** *adv* concluyentemente

concoct /kən'kɒkt/ *vt* confeccionar; (*fig*) inventar. **~ion** /-ʃn/ *n* mezcla *f*; (*drink*) brebaje *m*

concrete /'kɒŋkri:t/ *n* hormigón *m*, concreto *m* (*LAm*). ● *adj* concreto

concussion /kən'kʌʃn/ *n* conmoción *f* cerebral

condemn /kən'dem/ *vt* condenar. **~ation** /kɒndem'neɪʃn/ *n* condena *f*

condens|ation /kɒnden'seɪʃn/ *n* condensación *f.* **~e** /kən'dens/ *vt* condensar. ● *vi* condensarse

condescend /kɒndɪ'send/ *vi* dignarse (**to** a). **~ing** *adj* superior

condition /kən'dɪʃn/ *n* condición

f. **on ~ that** a condición de que. ●*vt* condicionar. **~al** *adj* condicional. **~er** *n* (*for hair*) suavizante *m*, enjuague *m* (*LAm*)

c

condo /ˈkɒndəʊ/ *n* (*pl* **-os**) (*Amer fam*) *see* **CONDOMINIUM**

condolences /kənˈdəʊlənsɪz/ *npl* pésame *m*

condom /ˈkɒndɒm/ *n* condón *m*

condominium /kɒndəˈmɪnɪəm/ *n* (*Amer*) apartamento *m*, piso *m* (en régimen de propiedad horizontal)

condone /kənˈdəʊn/ *vt* condonar

conduct /kənˈdʌkt/ *vt* llevar a cabo (business, experiment); conducir (electricity); dirigir (orchestra). ●/ˈkɒndʌkt/ *n* conducta *f*. **~or** /kənˈdʌktə(r)/ *n* director *m*; (*of bus*) cobrador *m*. **~ress** /kənˈdʌktrɪs/ *n* cobradora *f*

cone /kəʊn/ *n* cono *m*; (*for ice cream*) cucurucho *m*, barquillo *m* (*Mex*)

confectionery /kənˈfekʃənrɪ/ *n* productos *mpl* de confitería

confederation /kənfedəˈreɪʃn/ *n* confederación *f*

conference /ˈkɒnfərəns/ *n* congreso *m*; **an international ~ on ...** un congreso internacional sobre ...

confess /kənˈfes/ *vt* confesar. ●*vi* confesarse. **~ion** /-ʃn/ *n* confesión *f*

confetti /kənˈfetɪ/ *n* confeti *m*

confide /kənˈfaɪd/ *vt/i* confiar

confiden|ce /ˈkɒnfɪdəns/ *n* confianza *f*; (*self-confidence*) confianza *f* en sí mismo; (*secret*) confidencia *f*. **~ce trick** *n* estafa *f*, timo *m*. **~t** /ˈkɒnfɪdənt/ *adj* seguro de sí mismo. **be ~t of** confiar en

confidential /kɒnfɪˈdenʃl/ *adj* confidencial. **~ity** /-denʃɪˈælətɪ/ *n* confidencialidad *f*

configur|ation /kənfɪgəˈreɪʃn/ *n* configuración *f*. **~e** /kənˈfɪgə(r)/ *vt* configurar

confine /kənˈfaɪn/ *vt* confinar; (*limit*) limitar. **~ment** *n* (*imprisonment*) prisión *f*

confirm /kənˈfɜːm/ *vt* confirmar. **~ation** /kɒnfəˈmeɪʃn/ *n* confirmación *f*. **~ed** *adj* inveterado

confiscat|e /ˈkɒnfɪskeɪt/ *vt* confiscar. **~ion** /-ˈkeɪʃn/ *n* confiscación *f*

conflict /ˈkɒnflɪkt/ *n* conflicto *m*. ●/kənˈflɪkt/ *vi* chocar. **~ing** /kənˈflɪktɪŋ/ *adj* contradictorio

conform /kənˈfɔːm/ *vi* conformarse. **~ist** *n* conformista *m & f*

confound /kənˈfaʊnd/ *vt* confundir. **~ed** *adj* 🅸 maldito

confront /kənˈfrʌnt/ *vt* hacer frente a; (*face*) enfrentarse con. **~ation** /kɒnfrʌnˈteɪʃn/ *n* confrontación *f*

confus|e /kənˈfjuːz/ *vt* confundir. **~ed** *adj* confundido. **get ~ed** confundirse. **~ing** *adj* confuso. **~ion** /-ʒn/ *n* confusión *f*

congeal /kənˈdʒiːl/ *vi* coagularse

congest|ed /kənˈdʒestɪd/ *adj* congestionado. **~ion** /-tʃən/ *n* congestión *f*

congratulat|e /kənˈgrætjʊleɪt/ *vt* felicitar. **~ions** /-ˈleɪʃnz/ *npl* enhorabuena *f*, felicitaciones *fpl* (*LAm*)

congregat|e /ˈkɒŋgrɪgeɪt/ *vi* congregarse. **~ion** /-ˈgeɪʃn/ *n* asamblea *f*; (*Relig*) fieles *mpl*, feligreses *mpl*

congress /ˈkɒŋgres/ *n* congreso *m*. **C~** (*Amer*) el Congreso. **~man** /-mən/ *n* (*Amer*) miembro *m* del Congreso. **~woman** *n* (*Amer*) miembro *f* del Congreso.

Congress El Congreso es el organismo legislativo de EE.UU. Se reúne en el Capitolio (*Capitol*) y está compuesto por dos cámaras: El Senado y la Cámara de Representantes. Se renueva cada dos años y su función es elaborar leyes que deben ser aprobadas, primero, por las dos cámaras y posteriormente por el Presidente.

conifer /'kɒnɪfə(r)/ *n* conífera *f*

conjugat|e /'kɒndʒʊgeɪt/ *vt* conjugar. **~ion** /-'geɪʃn/ *n* conjugación *f*

conjunction /kən'dʒʌŋkʃn/ *n* conjunción *f*

conjur|e /'kʌndʒə(r)/ *vi* hacer juegos de manos. ● *vt*. □ **~e up** *vt* evocar. **~er**, **~or** *n* prestidigitador *m*

conk /kɒŋk/ *vi*. **~ out** [!] fallar; (person) desmayarse

conker /'kɒŋkə(r)/ *n* [!] castaña *f* de Indias

conman /'kɒnmæn/ *n* (*pl* **-men**) [!] estafador *m*, timador *m*

connect /kə'nekt/ *vt* conectar; (*associate*) relacionar. ● *vi* (*be fitted*) estar conectado (**to** a). □ **~ with** *vt* (train) enlazar con. **~ed** *adj* unido; (*related*) relacionado. **be ~ed with** tener que ver con, estar emparentado con. **~ion** /-ʃn/ *n* conexión *f*; (*Rail*) enlace *m*; (*fig*) relación *f*. **in ~ion with** a propósito de, con respecto a

connive /kə'naɪv/ *vi*. **~e at** ser cómplice en

connoisseur /kɒnə'sɜ:(r)/ *n* experto *m*

connotation /kɒnə'teɪʃn/ *n* connotación *f*

conquer /'kɒŋkə(r)/ *vt* conquistar; (*fig*) vencer. **~or** *n* conquistador *m*

conquest /'kɒŋkwest/ *n* conquista *f*

conscience /'kɒnʃəns/ *n* conciencia *f*

conscientious /kɒnʃɪ'enʃəs/ *adj* concienzudo

conscious /'kɒnʃəs/ *adj* consciente; (*deliberate*) intencional. **~ly** *adv* a sabiendas. **~ness** *n* consciencia *f*; (*Med*) conocimiento *m*

conscript /'kɒnskrɪpt/ *n* recluta *m & f*, conscripto *m* (*LAm*). ● /kən'skrɪpt/ *vt* reclutar. **~ion** /kən'skrɪpʃn/ *n* reclutamiento *m*, conscripción *f* (*LAm*)

consecrate /'kɒnsɪkreɪt/ *vt* consagrar

consecutive /kən'sekjʊtɪv/ *adj* sucesivo

consensus /kən'sensəs/ *n* consenso *m*

consent /kən'sent/ *vi* consentir. ● *n* consentimiento *m*

consequen|ce /'kɒnsɪkwəns/ *n* consecuencia *f*. **~t** *adj* consiguiente. **~tly** *adv* por consiguiente

conservation /kɒnsə'veɪʃn/ *n* conservación *f*, preservación *f*. **~ist** *n* conservacionista *m & f*

conservative /kən'sɜ:vətɪv/ *adj* conservador; (*modest*) prudente, moderado. **C~** *adj & n* conservador (*m*)

conservatory /kən'sɜ:vətrɪ/ *n* invernadero *m*

conserve /kən'sɜ:v/ *vt* conservar

consider /kən'sɪdə(r)/ *vt* considerar; (*take into account*) tomar en cuenta. **~able** *adj* considerable. **~ably** *adv* considerablemente

considerat|e /kən'sɪdərət/ *adj*

considerado. **~ion** /-'reɪʃn/ *n* consideración *f*. **take sth into ~ion** tomar algo en cuenta

considering /kən'sɪdərɪŋ/ *prep* teniendo en cuenta. ● *conj*. **~ (that)** teniendo en cuenta que

consign /kən'saɪn/ *vt* consignar; (*send*) enviar. **~ment** *n* envío *m*

consist /kən'sɪst/ *vi*. **~ of** consistir en. **~ency** *n* consistencia *f*; (*fig*) coherencia *f*. **~ent** *adj* coherente; (*unchanging*) constante. **~ent with** compatible con. **~ently** *adv* constantemente

consolation /kɒnsə'leɪʃn/ *n* consuelo *m*

console /kən'səʊl/ *vt* consolar. ● /'kɒnsəʊl/ *n* consola *f*

consolidate /kən'sɒlɪdeɪt/ *vt* consolidar

consonant /'kɒnsənənt/ *n* consonante *f*

conspicuous /kən'spɪkjʊəs/ *adj* (*easily seen*) visible; (*showy*) llamativo; (*noteworthy*) notable

conspir|acy /kən'spɪrəsɪ/ *n* conspiración *f*. **~ator** /kən'spɪrətə(r)/ *n* conspirador *m*. **~e** /kən'spaɪə(r)/ *vi* conspirar

constable /'kʌnstəbl/ *n* agente *m* & *f* de policía

constant /'kɒnstənt/ *adj* constante. **~ly** *adv* constantemente

constellation /kɒnstə'leɪʃn/ *n* constelación *f*

consternation /kɒnstə'neɪʃn/ *n* consternación *f*

constipat|ed /'kɒnstɪpeɪtɪd/ *adj* estreñido. **~ion** /-'peɪʃn/ *n* estreñimiento *m*

constituen|cy /kən'stɪtjʊənsɪ/ *n* distrito *m* electoral. **~t** *n* (*Pol*) elector *m*. ● *adj* constituyente, constitutivo

constitut|e /'kɒnstɪtju:t/ *vt* constituir. **~ion** /-'tju:ʃn/ *n* constitución *f*. **~ional** /-'tju:ʃənl/ *adj* constitucional. ● *n* paseo *m*

constrict /kən'strɪkt/ *vt* apretar. **~ion** /-ʃn/ *n* constricción *f*

construct /kən'strʌkt/ *vt* construir. **~ion** /-ʃn/ *n* construcción *f*. **~ive** *adj* constructivo

consul /'kɒnsl/ *n* cónsul *m* & *f*. **~ate** /'kɒnsjʊlət/ *n* consulado *m*

consult /kən'sʌlt/ *vt/i* consultar. **~ancy** *n* asesoría. **~ant** *n* asesor *m*; (*Med*) especialista *m* & *f*; (*Tec*) consejero *m* técnico. **~ation** /kɒnsəl'teɪʃn/ *n* consulta *f*

consume /kən'sju:m/ *vt* consumir. **~r** *n* consumidor *m*. ● *adj* de consumo

consummate /'kɒnsəmət/ *adj* consumado. ● /'kɒnsəmeɪt/ *vt* consumar

consumption /kən'sʌmpʃn/ *n* consumo *m*

contact /'kɒntækt/ *n* contacto *m*. ● *vt* ponerse en contacto con. **~ lens** *n* lentilla *f*, lente *f* de contacto (*LAm*)

contagious /kən'teɪdʒəs/ *adj* contagioso

contain /kən'teɪn/ *vt* contener. **~ o.s.** contenerse. **~er** *n* recipiente *m*; (*Com*) contenedor *m*

contaminat|e /kən'tæmɪneɪt/ *vt* contaminar. **~ion** /-'neɪʃn/ *n* contaminación *f*

contemplate /'kɒntəmpleɪt/ *vt* contemplar; (*consider*) considerar

contemporary /kən'tempərərɪ/ *adj* & *n* contemporáneo (*m*)

contempt /kən'tempt/ *n* desprecio *m*. **~ible** *adj* despreciable. **~uous** /-tjʊəs/ *adj* desdeñoso

contend /kən'tend/ *vt* competir.

~er *n* aspirante *m & f* (for a)

content /kən'tent/ *adj* satisfecho. ● /'kɒntent/ *n* contenido *m*. ● /kən 'tent/ *vt* contentar. **~ed** /kən 'tentɪd/ *adj* satisfecho. **~ment** /kən'tentmənt/ *n* satisfacción *f*. **~s** /'kɒntents/ *n* contenido *m*; (*of book*) índice *m* de materias

contest /'kɒntest/ *n* (*competition*) concurso *m*; (*Sport*) competición *f*, competencia *f* (*LAm*). ● /kən'test/ *vt* disputar. **~ant** /kən'testənt/ *n* concursante *m & f*

context /'kɒntekst/ *n* contexto *m*

continent /'kɒntɪnənt/ *n* continente *m*. **the C~** Europa *f*. **~al** /-'nentl/ *adj* continental. **~al quilt** *n* edredón *m*

contingen|cy /kən'tɪndʒənsɪ/ *n* contingencia *f*. **~t** *adj & n* contingente (*m*)

continu|al /kən'tɪnjʊəl/ *adj* continuo. **~ally** *adv* continuamente. **~ation** /-'eɪʃn/ *n* continuación *f*. **~e** /kən'tɪnju:/ *vt/i* continuar, seguir. **~ed** *adj* continuo. **~ity** /kɒntɪ'nju:ətɪ/ *n* continuidad *f*. **~ous** /kən'tɪnjʊəs/ *adj* continuo. **~ously** *adv* continuamente

contort /kən'tɔ:t/ *vt* retorcer. **~ion** /-ʃn/ *n* contorsión *f*. **~ionist** /-ʃənɪst/ *n* contorsionista *m & f*

contour /'kɒntʊə(r)/ *n* contorno *m*

contraband /'kɒntrəbænd/ *n* contrabando *m*

contracepti|on /kɒntrə'sepʃn/ *n* anticoncepción *f*. **~ve** /-tɪv/ *adj & n* anticonceptivo (*m*)

contract /'kɒntrækt/ *n* contrato *m*. ● /kən'trækt/ *vt* contraer. ● *vi* contraerse. **~ion** /kən'trækʃn/ *n* contracción *f*. **~or** /kən'træktə(r)/ *n* contratista *m & f*

contradict /kɒntrə'dɪkt/ *vt* contradecir. **~ion** /-ʃn/ *n* contradicción *f*. **~ory** *adj* contradictorio

contraption /kən'træpʃn/ *n* [!] artilugio *m*

contrary /'kɒntrərɪ/ *adj* contrario. **the ~** lo contrario. **on the ~** al contrario. ● *adv*. **~ to** contrariamente a. ● /kən'treərɪ/ *adj* (*obstinate*) terco

contrast /'kɒntrɑ:st/ *n* contraste *m*. ● /kən'trɑ:st/ *vt/i* contrastar. **~ing** *adj* contrastante

contravene /kɒntrə'vi:n/ *vt* contravenir

contribut|e /kən'trɪbju:t/ *vt* contribuir con. ● *vi* contribuir. **~e to** escribir para (newspaper). **~ion** /kɒntrɪ'bju:ʃn/ *n* contribución *f*. **~or** *n* contribuyente *m & f*; (*to newspaper*) colaborador *m*

contrite /'kɒntraɪt/ *adj* arrepentido, pesaroso

contriv|e /kən'traɪv/ *vt* idear. **~e to** conseguir. **~ed** *adj* artificioso

control /kən'trəʊl/ *vt* (*pt* **controlled**) controlar. ● *n* control *m*. **~ler** *n* director *m*. **~s** *npl* (*Mec*) mandos *mpl*

controvers|ial /kɒntrə'vɜ:ʃl/ controvertido. **~y** /'kɒntrəvɜ:sɪ/ *n* controversia *f*

conundrum /kə'nʌndrəm/ *n* adivinanza *f*

convalesce /kɒnvə'les/ *vi* convalecer. **~nce** *n* convalecencia *f*

convector /kən'vektə(r)/ *n* estufa *f* de convección

convene /kən'vi:n/ *vt* convocar. ● *vi* reunirse

convenien|ce /kən'vi:nɪəns/ *n* conveniencia *f*, comodidad *f*. **all modern ~ces** todas las comodidades. **at your ~ce** según le con-

C

venga. **~ces** *npl* servicios *mpl*, baños *mpl* (*LAm*). **~t** *adj* conveniente; (place) bien situado; (time) oportuno. **be ~t** convenir. **~tly** *adv* convenientemente

convent /ˈkɒnvənt/ *n* convento *m*

convention /kənˈvenʃn/ *n* convención *f*. **~al** *adj* convencional

converge /kənˈvɜːdʒ/ *vi* converger

conversation /kɒnvəˈseɪʃn/ *n* conversación *f*. **~al** *adj* familiar, coloquial.

converse /kənˈvɜːs/ *vi* conversar. ● /ˈkɒnvɜːs/ *adj* inverso. ● *n* lo contrario. **~ly** *adv* a la inversa

conver|sion /kənˈvɜːʃn/ *n* conversión *f*. **~t** /kənˈvɜːt/ *vt* convertir. ● /ˈkɒnvɜːt/ *n* converso *m*. **~tible** /kənˈvɜːtɪbl/ *adj* convertible. ● *n* (*Auto*) descapotable *m*, convertible *m* (*LAm*)

convex /ˈkɒnveks/ *adj* convexo

convey /kənˈveɪ/ *vt* transportar (goods, people); comunicar (idea, feeling). **~or belt** *n* cinta *f* transportadora, banda *f* transportadora (*LAm*)

convict /kənˈvɪkt/ *vt* condenar. ● /ˈkɒnvɪkt/ *n* presidiario *m*. **~ion** /kənˈvɪkʃn/ *n* condena *f*; (*belief*) creencia *f*

convinc|e /kənˈvɪns/ *vt* convencer. **~ing** *adj* convincente

convoluted /ˈkɒnvəluːtɪd/ *adj* (argument) intrincado

convoy /ˈkɒnvɔɪ/ *n* convoy *m*

convuls|e /kənˈvʌls/ *vt* convulsionar. **be ~ed with laughter** desternillarse de risa. **~ion** /-ʃn/ *n* convulsión *f*

coo /kuː/ *vi* arrullar

cook /kʊk/ *vt* hacer, preparar. ● *vi* cocinar; (food) hacerse. ● *n* cocinero *m*. □ **~ up** *vt* Ⓘ inventar. **~book** *n* libro *m* de cocina. **~er** *n* cocina *f*, estufa *f* (*Mex*). **~ery** *n* cocina *f*

cookie /ˈkʊkɪ/ *n* (*Amer*) galleta *f*

cool /kuːl/ *adj* (**-er**, **-est**) fresco; (*calm*) tranquilo; (*unfriendly*) frío. ● *n* fresco *m*; ☒ calma *f*. ● *vt* enfriar. ● *vi* enfriarse. □ **~ down** *vi* (person) calmarse. **~ly** *adv* tranquilamente

coop /kuːp/ *n* gallinero *m*. □ **~ up** *vt* encerrar

co-op /ˈkəʊɒp/ *n* cooperativa *f*

cooperat|e /kəʊˈɒpəreɪt/ *vi* cooperar. **~ion** /-ˈreɪʃn/ *n* cooperación *f*. **~ive** /kəʊˈɒpərətɪv/ *adj* cooperativo. ● *n* cooperativa *f*

co-opt /kəʊˈɒpt/ *vt* cooptar

co-ordinat|e /kəʊˈɔːdɪneɪt/ *vt* coordinar. ● /kəʊˈɔːdɪnət/ *n* (*Math*) coordenada *f*. **~es** *npl* prendas *fpl* para combinar. **~ion** /kəʊɔːdɪˈneɪʃn/ *n* coordinación *f*

cop /kɒp/ *n* Ⓘ poli *m & f* Ⓘ, tira *m & f* (*Mex, fam*)

cope /kəʊp/ *vi* arreglárselas. **~ with** hacer frente a

copious /ˈkəʊpɪəs/ *adj* abundante

copper /ˈkɒpə(r)/ *n* cobre *m*; (*coin*) perra *f*; Ⓘ poli *m & f* Ⓘ, tira *m & f* (*Mex, fam*). ● *adj* de cobre

copy /ˈkɒpɪ/ *n* copia *f*; (*of book, newspaper*) ejemplar *m*. ● *vt* copiar. **~right** *n* derechos *mpl* de reproducción

coral /ˈkɒrəl/ *n* coral *m*

cord /kɔːd/ *n* cuerda *f*; (*fabric*) pana *f*; (*Amer, Elec*) cordón *m*, cable *m*

cordial /ˈkɔːdɪəl/ *adj* cordial. ● *n* refresco *m* (concentrado)

cordon /ˈkɔːdn/ *n* cordón *m*. □ **~ off** *vt* acordonar

core /kɔ:(r)/ *n* (*of apple*) corazón *m*; (*of Earth*) centro *m*; (*of problem*) meollo *m*

cork /kɔ:k/ *n* corcho *m*. **~screw** *n* sacacorchos *m*

corn /kɔ:n/ *n* (*wheat*) trigo *m*; (*Amer*) maíz *m*; (*hard skin*) callo *m*

corned beef /kɔ:nd 'bi:f/ *n* carne *f* de vaca en lata

corner /'kɔ:nə(r)/ *n* ángulo *m*; (*inside*) rincón *m*; (*outside*) esquina *f*; (*football*) córner *m*. ● *vt* arrinconar; (*Com*) acaparar

cornet /'kɔ:nɪt/ *n* (*Mus*) corneta *f*; (*for ice cream*) cucurucho *m*, barquillo *m* (*Mex*)

corn: ~flakes *npl* copos *mpl* de maíz. **~flour** *n* maizena *f* (®)

Cornish /'kɔ:nɪʃ/ *adj* de Cornualles

cornstarch /'kɔ:nstɑ:tʃ/ *n* (*Amer*) maizena *f* (®)

corny /'kɔ:nɪ/ *adj* (*fam, trite*) gastado

coronation /kɒrə'neɪʃn/ *n* coronación *f*

coroner /'kɒrənə(r)/ *n* juez *m* de primera instancia

corporal /'kɔ:pərəl/ *n* cabo *m*. ● *adj* corporal

corporate /'kɔ:pərət/ *adj* corporativo

corporation /kɔ:pə'reɪʃn/ *n* corporación *f*; (*Amer*) sociedad *f* anónima

corps /kɔ:(r)/ *n* (*pl* **corps**/kɔ:z/) cuerpo *m*

corpse /kɔ:ps/ *n* cadáver *m*

corpulent /'kɔ:pjʊlənt/ *adj* corpulento

corral /kə'rɑ:l/ *n* (*Amer*) corral *m*

correct /kə'rekt/ *adj* correcto; (time) exacto. ● *vt* corregir. **~ion** /-ʃn/ *n* corrección *f*

correspond /kɒrɪ'spɒnd/ *vi* corresponder; (*write*) escribirse. **~ence** *n* correspondencia *f*. **~ent** *n* corresponsal *m & f*

corridor /'kɒrɪdɔ:(r)/ *n* pasillo *m*

corro|de /kə'rəʊd/ *vt* corroer. ● *vi* corroerse. **~sion** /-ʒn/ *n* corrosión *f*. **~sive** /-sɪv/ *adj* corrosivo

corrugated /'kɒrəgeɪtɪd/ *adj* ondulado. **~ iron** *n* chapa *f* de zinc

corrupt /kə'rʌpt/ *adj* corrompido. ● *vt* corromper. **~ion** /-ʃn/ *n* corrupción *f*

corset /'kɔ:sɪt/ *n* corsé *m*

cosmetic /kɒz'metɪk/ *adj & n* cosmético (*m*)

cosmic /'kɒzmɪk/ *adj* cósmico

cosmopolitan /kɒzmə'pɒlɪtən/ *adj & n* cosmopolita (*m & f*)

cosmos /'kɒzmɒs/ *n* cosmos *m*

cosset /'kɒsɪt/ *vt* (*pt* **cosseted**) mimar

cost /kɒst/ *vt* (*pt* **cost**) costar; (*pt* **costed**) calcular el coste de, calcular el costo de (*LAm*). ● *n* coste *m*, costo *m* (*LAm*). **at all ~s** cueste lo que cueste. **to one's ~** a sus expensas. **~s** *npl* (*Jurid*) costas *fpl*

Costa Rica /kɒstə'ri:kə/ *n* Costa *f* Rica. **~n** *adj & n* costarricense (*m & f*), costarriqueño (*m & f*)

cost: ~-effective *adj* rentable. **~ly** *adj* (**-ier**, **-iest**) costoso

costume /'kɒstju:m/ *n* traje *m*; (*for party, disguise*) disfraz *m*

cosy /'kəʊzɪ/ *adj* (**-ier**, **-iest**) acogedor. ● *n* cubreteras *m*

cot /kɒt/ *n* cuna *f*

cottage /'kɒtɪdʒ/ *n* casita *f*. **~ cheese** *n* requesón *m*. **~ pie** *n* pastel *m* de carne cubierta con puré

cotton /'kɒtn/ *n* algodón *m*; (*thread*) hilo *m*; (*Amer*) *see* ~

wool. □ ~ on *vi* 🅸 comprender. ~ **bud** *n* bastoncillo *m*, cotonete *m* (*Mex*). ~ **candy** *n* (*Amer*) algodón *m* de azúcar. ~ **swab** *n* (*Amer*) *see* ~ **BUD**. ~ **wool** *n* algodón *m* hidrófilo

couch /kaʊtʃ/ *n* sofá *m*

cough /kɒf/ *vi* toser. ●*n* tos *f*. □ ~ **up** *vt* 🅸 pagar. ~ **mixture** *n* jarabe *m* para la tos

could /kʊd/ *pt of* **CAN**[1]

couldn't /'kʊdnt/ = **could not**

council /'kaʊnsl/ *n* consejo *m*; (*of town*) ayuntamiento *m*. ~ **house** *n* vivienda *f* subvencionada. ~**lor** *n* concejal *m*

counsel /'kaʊnsl/ *n* consejo *m*; (*pl invar*) (*Jurid*) abogado *m*. ●*vt* (*pt* **counselled**) aconsejar. ~**ling** *n* terapia *f* de apoyo. ~**lor** *n* consejero *m*

count /kaʊnt/ *n* recuento *m*; (*nobleman*) conde *m*. ●*vt/i* contar. □ ~ **on** *vt* contar. ~**down** *n* cuenta *f* atrás

counter /'kaʊntə(r)/ *n* (*in shop*) mostrador *m*; (*in bank, post office*) ventanilla *f*; (*token*) ficha *f*. ●*adv*. ~ **to** en contra de. ●*adj* opuesto. ●*vt* oponerse a; parar (blow)

counter... /'kaʊntə(r)/ *pref* contra.... ~**act** /-'ækt/ *vt* contrarrestar. ~**-attack** *n* contraataque *m*. ●*vt/i* contraatacar. ~**balance** *n* contrapeso *m*. ●*vt/i* contrapesar. ~**clockwise** /-'klɒkwaɪz/ *a/adv* (*Amer*) en sentido contrario al de las agujas del reloj

counterfeit /'kaʊntəfɪt/ *adj* falsificado. ●*n* falsificación *f*. ●*vt* falsificar

counterfoil /'kaʊntəfɔɪl/ *n* matriz *f*, talón *m* (*LAm*)

counter-productive /kaʊntəprə'dʌktɪv/ *adj* contraproducente

countess /'kaʊntɪs/ *n* condesa *f*

countless /'kaʊntlɪs/ *adj* innumerable

country /'kʌntrɪ/ *n* (*native land*) país *m*; (*countryside*) campo *m*; (*Mus*) (música *f*) country *m*. ~**-and-western** /-en'westən/ (música *f*) country *m*. ~**man** /-mən/ *n* (*of one's own country*) compatriota *m*. ~**side** *n* campo *m*; (*landscape*) paisaje *m*

county /'kaʊntɪ/ *n* condado *m*

coup /ku:/ *n* golpe *m*

couple /'kʌpl/ *n* (*of things*) par *m*; (*of people*) pareja *f*; (*married*) matrimonio *m*. **a** ~ **of** un par de

coupon /'ku:pɒn/ *n* cupón *m*

courage /'kʌrɪdʒ/ *n* valor *m*. ~**ous** /kə'reɪdʒəs/ *adj* valiente

courgette /kʊə'ʒet/ *n* calabacín *m*

courier /'kʊrɪə(r)/ *n* mensajero *m*; (*for tourists*) guía *m* & *f*

course /kɔ:s/ *n* curso *m*; (*behaviour*) conducta *f*; (*in navigation*) rumbo *m*; (*Culin*) plato *m*; (*for golf*) campo *m*. **in due** ~ a su debido tiempo. **in the** ~ **of** en el transcurso de, durante. **of** ~ claro, por supuesto. **of** ~ **not** claro que no, por supuesto que no

court /kɔ:t/ *n* corte *f*; (*tennis*) pista *f*; cancha *f* (*LAm*); (*Jurid*) tribunal *m*. ●*vt* cortejar; buscar (danger)

courteous /'kɜ:tɪəs/ *adj* cortés

courtesy /'kɜ:təsɪ/ *n* cortesía *f*

courtier /'kɔ:tɪə(r)/ *n* (*old use*) cortesano *m*

court: ~ **martial** *n* (*pl* ~**s martial**) consejo *m* de guerra. **-martial** *vt* (*pt* ~**-martialled**) juzgar en consejo de guerra. ~**ship** *n* cortejo *m*. ~**yard** *n*

patio *m*
cousin /'kʌzn/ *n* primo *m*. **first ~** primo carnal. **second ~** primo segundo
cove /kəʊv/ *n* ensenada *f*, cala *f*
Coventry /'kɒvntrɪ/ *n*. **send s.o. to ~** hacer el vacío a uno
cover /'kʌvə(r)/ *vt* cubrir. ● *n* cubierta *f*; (*shelter*) abrigo *m*; (*lid*) tapa *f*; (*for furniture*) funda *f*; (*pretext*) pretexto *m*; (*of magazine*) portada *f*. □ **~ up** *vt* cubrir; (*fig*) ocultar. **~age** *n* cobertura *f*. **~ charge** *n* precio *m* del cubierto. **~ing** *n* cubierta *f*. **~ing letter** *n* carta *f* adjunta
covet /'kʌvɪt/ *vt* codiciar
cow /kaʊ/ *n* vaca *f*
coward /'kaʊəd/ *n* cobarde *m*. **~ice** /'kaʊədɪs/ *n* cobardía *f*. **~ly** *adj* cobarde.
cowboy /'kaʊbɔɪ/ *n* vaquero *m*
cower /'kaʊə(r)/ *vi* encogerse, acobardarse
coxswain /'kɒksn/ *n* timonel *m*
coy /kɔɪ/ *adj* (**-er**, **-est**) (*shy*) tímido; (*evasive*) evasivo
crab /kræb/ *n* cangrejo *m*, jaiba *f* (*LAm*)
crack /kræk/ *n* grieta *f*; (*noise*) crujido *m*; (*of whip*) chasquido *m*; (*drug*) crack *m*. ● *adj* [!] de primera. ● *vt* agrietar; chasquear (whip, fingers); cascar (nut); gastar (joke); resolver (problem). ● *vi* agrietarse. **get ~ing** [!] darse prisa. □ **~ down on** *vt* [!] tomar medidas enérgicas contra
cracker /'krækə(r)/ *n* (*Culin*) cracker *f*, galleta *f* (*salada*); (*Christmas cracker*) sorpresa *f* (que estalla al abrirla)
crackle /'krækl/ *vi* crepitar. ● *n* crepitación *f*, crujido *m*
crackpot /'krækpɒt/ *n* [!] chiflado *m*
cradle /'kreɪdl/ *n* cuna *f*. ● *vt* acunar
craft /krɑːft/ *n* destreza *f*; (*technique*) arte *f*; (*cunning*) astucia *f*. ● *n invar* (*boat*) barco *m*
craftsman /'krɑːftsmən/ *n* (*pl* **-men**) artesano *m*. **~ship** *n* artesanía *f*
crafty /'krɑːftɪ/ *adj* (**-ier**, **-iest**) astuto
cram /kræm/ *vt* (*pt* **crammed**) rellenar. **~ with** llenar de. ● *vi* (*for exams*) memorizar, empollar [✖], zambutir (*Mex*)
cramp /kræmp/ *n* calambre *m*
cramped /kræmpt/ *adj* apretado
crane /kreɪn/ *n* grúa *f*. ● *vt* estirar (neck)
crank /krænk/ *n* manivela *f*; (*person*) excéntrico *m*. **~y** *adj* excéntrico
cranny /'krænɪ/ *n* grieta *f*
crash /kræʃ/ *n* accidente *m*; (*noise*) estruendo *m*; (*collision*) choque *m*; (*Com*) quiebra *f*. ● *vt* estrellar. ● *vi* quebrar con estrépito; (*have accident*) tener un accidente; (car etc) estrellarse, chocar; (*fail*) fracasar. **~ course** *n* curso *m* intensivo. **~ helmet** *n* casco *m* protector. **~-land** *vi* hacer un aterrizaje forzoso
crass /kræs/ *adj* craso, burdo
crate /kreɪt/ *n* cajón *m*. ● *vt* embalar
crater /'kreɪtə(r)/ *n* cráter *m*
crav|e /kreɪv/ *vt* ansiar. **~ing** *n* ansia *f*
crawl /krɔːl/ *vi* (baby) gatear; (*move slowly*) avanzar lentamente; (*drag o.s.*) arrastrarse. **~ to** humillarse ante. **~ with** hervir de. ● *n*

(*swimming*) crol *m*. **at a ~** a paso lento

crayon /ˈkreɪən/ *n* lápiz *m* de color; (*made of wax*) lápiz *m* de cera, crayola *f* (®), crayón *m* (*Mex*)

craz|e /kreɪz/ *n* manía *f*. **~y** /ˈkreɪzɪ/ *adj* (**-ier**, **-iest**) loco. **be ~y about** estar loco por

creak /kriːk/ *n* crujido *m*; (*of hinge*) chirrido *m*. ●*vi* crujir; (hinge) chirriar

cream /kriːm/ *n* crema *f*; (*fresh*) nata *f*, crema *f* (*LAm*). ●*adj* (*colour*) color crema. ●*vt* (*beat*) batir. **~ cheese** *n* queso *m* para untar, queso *m* crema (*LAm*). **~y** *adj* cremoso

crease /kriːs/ *n* raya *f*, pliegue *m* (*Mex*); (*crumple*) arruga *f*. ●*vt* plegar; (*wrinkle*) arrugar. ●*vi* arrugarse

creat|e /kriːˈeɪt/ *vt* crear. **~ion** /-ʃn/ *n* creación *f*. **~ive** *adj* creativo. **~or** *n* creador *m*

creature /ˈkriːtʃə(r)/ *n* criatura *f*

crèche /kreʃ/ *n* guardería *f* (infantil)

credib|ility /kredəˈbɪlətɪ/ *n* credibilidad *f*. **~le** /ˈkredəbl/ *adj* creíble

credit /ˈkredɪt/ *n* crédito *m*; (*honour*) mérito *m*. **take the ~ for** atribuirse el mérito de. ●*vt* (*pt* **credited**) acreditar; (*believe*) creer. **~ s.o. with** atribuir a uno. **~ card** *n* tarjeta *f* de crédito. **~or** *n* acreedor *m*

creed /kriːd/ *n* credo *m*

creek /kriːk/ *n* ensenada *f*. **up the ~** ☒ en apuros

creep /kriːp/ *vi* (*pt* **crept**) arrastrarse; (*plant*) trepar. ●*n* ⓘ adulador. **~s** /kriːps/ *npl*. **give s.o. the ~s** poner los pelos de punta a uno. **~er** *n* enredadera *f*

cremat|e /krɪˈmeɪt/ *vt* incinerar. **~ion** /-ʃn/ *n* cremación *f*. **~orium** /kreməˈtɔːrɪəm/ *n* (*pl* **-ia** /-ɪə/) crematorio *m*

crept /krept/ *see* CREEP

crescendo /krɪˈʃendəʊ/ *n* (*pl* **-os**) crescendo *m*

crescent /ˈkresnt/ *n* media luna *f*; (*street*) calle *f* en forma de media luna

crest /krest/ *n* cresta *f*; (*on coat of arms*) emblema *m*

crevice /ˈkrevɪs/ *n* grieta *f*

crew /kruː/ *n* tripulación *f*; (*gang*) pandilla *f*. **~ cut** *n* corte *m* al rape

crib /krɪb/ *n* (*Amer*) cuna *f*; (*Relig*) belén *m*. ●*vt/i* (*pt* **cribbed**) copiar

crick /krɪk/ *n* calambre *m*; (*in neck*) tortícolis *f*

cricket /ˈkrɪkɪt/ *n* (*Sport*) críquet *m*; (*insect*) grillo *m*

crim|e /kraɪm/ *n* delito *m*; (*murder*) crimen *m*; (*acts*) delincuencia *f*. **~inal** /ˈkrɪmɪnl/ *adj* & *n* criminal (*m* & *f*)

crimson /ˈkrɪmzn/ *adj* & *n* carmesí (*m*)

cringe /krɪndʒ/ *vi* encogerse; (*fig*) humillarse

crinkle /ˈkrɪŋkl/ *vt* arrugar. ●*vi* arrugarse. ●*n* arruga *f*

cripple /ˈkrɪpl/ *n* lisiado *m*. ●*vt* lisiar; (*fig*) paralizar

crisis /ˈkraɪsɪs/ *n* (*pl* **crises** /-siːz/) crisis *f*

crisp /krɪsp/ *adj* (**-er**, **-est**) (*Culin*) crujiente; (air) vigorizador. **~s** *npl* patatas *fpl* fritas, papas *fpl* fritas (*LAm*) (*de bolsa*)

crisscross /ˈkrɪskrɒs/ *adj* entrecruzado. ●*vt* entrecruzar. ●*vi* entrecruzarse

criterion /kraɪˈtɪərɪən/ *n* (*pl* **-ia** /-ɪə/) criterio *m*

critic /ˈkrɪtɪk/ *n* crítico *m*. **~al** *adj* crítico. **~ally** *adv* críticamente; (*ill*) gravemente

critici|sm /ˈkrɪtɪsɪzəm/ *n* crítica *f*. **~ze** /ˈkrɪtɪsaɪz/ *vt/i* criticar

croak /krəʊk/ *n* (*of person*) gruñido *m*; (*of frog*) canto *m*. •*vi* gruñir; (frog) croar

Croat /ˈkrəʊæt/ *n* croata *m & f*. **~ia** /krəʊˈeɪʃə/ *n* Croacia *f*. **~ian** *adj* croata

crochet /ˈkrəʊʃeɪ/ *n* crochet *m*, ganchillo *m*. •*vt* tejer a crochet *or* a ganchillo

crockery /ˈkrɒkərɪ/ *n* loza *f*

crocodile /ˈkrɒkədaɪl/ *n* cocodrilo *m*. **~ tears** *npl* lágrimas *fpl* de cocodrilo

crocus /ˈkrəʊkəs/ *n* (*pl* **-es**) azafrán *m* de primavera

crook /krʊk/ *n* 🅸 sinvergüenza *m & f*. **~ed** /ˈkrʊkɪd/ *adj* torcido, chueco (*LAm*); (*winding*) tortuoso; (*dishonest*) deshonesto

crop /krɒp/ *n* cosecha *f*; (*haircut*) corte *m* de pelo muy corto. •*vt* (*pt* **cropped**) cortar. □ **~ up** *vi* surgir

croquet /ˈkrəʊkeɪ/ *n* croquet *m*

cross /krɒs/ *n* cruz *f*; (*of animals*) cruce *m*. •*vt* cruzar; (*oppose*) contrariar. **~ s.o.'s mind** ocurrírsele a uno. •*vi* cruzar. **~ o.s.** santiguarse. •*adj* enfadado, enojado (*esp LAm*). □ **~ out** *vt* tachar. **~bar** *n* travesaño *m*. **~-examine** /-ɪɡˈzæmɪn/ *vt* interrogar. **~-eyed** *adj* bizco. **~fire** *n* fuego *m* cruzado. **~ing** *n* (*by boat*) travesía *f*; (*on road*) cruce *m* peatonal. **~ly** *adv* con enfado, con enojo (*esp LAm*). **~-purposes** /-ˈpɜːpəsɪz/ *npl*. **talk at ~-purposes** hablar sin entenderse. **~-reference** /-ˈrefrəns/ *n* remisión *f*. **~roads** *n invar* cruce *m*. **~-section** /-ˈsekʃn/ *n* sección *f* transversal; (*fig*) muestra *f* representativa. **~walk** *n* (*Amer*) paso de peatones. **~word** *n* **~word (puzzle)** crucigrama *m*

crotch /krɒtʃ/ *n* entrepiernas *fpl*

crouch /kraʊtʃ/ *vi* agacharse

crow /krəʊ/ *n* cuervo *m*. **as the ~ flies** en línea recta. •*vi* cacarear. **~bar** *n* palanca *f*

crowd /kraʊd/ *n* muchedumbre *f*. •*vt* amontonar; (*fill*) llenar. •*vi* amontonarse; (*gather*) reunirse. **~ed** *adj* atestado

crown /kraʊn/ *n* corona *f*; (*of hill*) cumbre *f*; (*of head*) coronilla *f*. •*vt* coronar

crucial /ˈkruːʃl/ *adj* crucial

crucifix /ˈkruːsɪfɪks/ *n* crucifijo *m*. **~ion** /-ˈfɪkʃn/ *n* crucifixión *f*

crucify /ˈkruːsɪfaɪ/ *vt* crucificar

crude /kruːd/ *adj* (**-er**, **-est**) (*raw*) crudo; (*rough*) tosco; (*vulgar*) ordinario

cruel /ˈkrʊəl/ *adj* (**crueller**, **cruellest**) cruel. **~ty** *n* crueldad *f*

cruet /ˈkruːɪt/ *n* vinagrera *f*

cruise /kruːz/ *n* crucero *m*. •*vi* hacer un crucero; (*of car*) circular lentamente. **~r** *n* crucero *m*

crumb /krʌm/ *n* miga *f*

crumble /ˈkrʌmbl/ *vt* desmenuzar. •*vi* desmenuzarse; (*collapse*) derrumbarse

crummy /ˈkrʌmɪ/ *adj* (**-ier**, **-iest**) 🆇 miserable

crumpet /ˈkrʌmpɪt/ *n* bollo *m* blando

crumple /ˈkrʌmpl/ *vt* arrugar. •*vi* arrugarse

crunch /krʌntʃ/ *vt* hacer crujir; (*bite*) masticar. **~y** *adj* crujiente

crusade /kruːˈseɪd/ *n* cruzada *f*.

~r *n* cruzado *m*
crush /krʌʃ/ *vt* aplastar; arrugar (clothes). ● *n* (*crowd*) aglomeración *f*. **have a ~ on** 🅸 estar chiflado por
crust /krʌst/ *n* corteza *f*. **~y** *adj* (bread) de corteza dura
crutch /krʌtʃ/ *n* muleta *f*; (*between legs*) entrepiernas *fpl*
crux /krʌks/ *n* (*pl* **cruxes**). **the ~ (of the matter)** el quid (de la cuestión)
cry /kraɪ/ *n* grito *m*. **be a far ~ from** (*fig*) distar mucho de. ● *vi* llorar; (*call out*) gritar. □ **~ off** *vi* echarse atrás, rajarse. **~baby** *n* llorón *m*
crypt /krɪpt/ *n* cripta *f*
cryptic /'krɪptɪk/ *adj* enigmático
crystal /'krɪstl/ *n* cristal *m*. **~lize** *vi* cristalizarse
cub /kʌb/ *n* cachorro *m*. **C~ (Scout)** *n* lobato *m*
Cuba /'kju:bə/ *n* Cuba *f*. **~n** *adj & n* cubano (*m*)
cubbyhole /'kʌbɪhəʊl/ *n* cuchitril *m*
cub|e /kju:b/ *n* cubo *m*. **~ic** *adj* cúbico
cubicle /'kju:bɪkl/ *n* cubículo *m*; (*changing room*) probador *m*
cuckoo /'kʊku:/ *n* cuco *m*, cuclillo *m*
cucumber /'kju:kʌmbə(r)/ *n* pepino *m*
cuddl|e /'kʌdl/ *vt* abrazar. ● *vi* abrazarse. ● *n* abrazo *m*. **~y** *adj* adorable
cue /kju:/ *n* (*Mus*) entrada *f*; (*in theatre*) pie *m*; (*in snooker*) taco *m*
cuff /kʌf/ *n* puño *m*; (*Amer, of trousers*) vuelta *f*, dobladillo *m*; (*blow*) bofetada *f*. **speak off the ~** hablar de improviso. ● *vt* abofetear. **~link** *n* gemelo *m*, mancuerna *f* (*Mex*)
cul-de-sac /'kʌldəsæk/ *n* callejón *m* sin salida
culinary /'kʌlɪnərɪ/ *adj* culinario
cull /kʌl/ *vt* sacrificar en forma selectiva (animals)
culminat|e /'kʌlmɪneɪt/ *vi* culminar. **~ion** /-'neɪʃn/ *n* culminación *f*
culprit /'kʌlprɪt/ *n* culpable *m & f*
cult /kʌlt/ *n* culto *m*
cultivat|e /'kʌltɪveɪt/ *vt* cultivar. **~ion** /-'veɪʃn/ *n* cultivo *m*
cultur|al /'kʌltʃərəl/ *adj* cultural. **~e** /'kʌltʃə(r)/ *n* cultura *f*; (*Bot etc*) cultivo *m*. **~ed** *adj* cultivado; (person) culto
cumbersome /'kʌmbəsəm/ *adj* incómodo; (*heavy*) pesado
cunning /'kʌnɪŋ/ *adj* astuto. ● *n* astucia *f*
cup /kʌp/ *n* taza *f*; (*trophy*) copa *f*
cupboard /'kʌbəd/ *n* armario *m*
curator /kjʊə'reɪtə(r)/ *n* (*of museum*) conservador *m*
curb /kɜ:b/ *n* freno *m*; (*Amer*) bordillo *m* (de la acera), borde *m* de la banqueta (*Mex*). ● *vt* refrenar
curdle /'kɜ:dl/ *vt* cuajar. ● *vi* cuajarse; (*go bad*) cortarse
cure /kjʊə(r)/ *vt* curar. ● *n* cura *f*
curfew /'kɜ:fju:/ *n* toque *m* de queda
curio|sity /kjʊərɪ'ɒsətɪ/ *n* curiosidad *f*. **~us** /'kjʊərɪəs/ *adj* curioso
curl /kɜ:l/ *vt* rizar, enchinar (*Mex*). **~ o.s. up** acurrucarse. ● *vi* (hair) rizarse, enchinarse (*Mex*); (paper) ondularse. ● *n* rizo *m*, chino *m* (*Mex*). **~er** *n* rulo *m*, chino *m* (*Mex*). **~y** *adj* (**-ier, -iest**) rizado, chino (*Mex*)
currant /'kʌrənt/ *n* pasa *f* de Corinto

currency /'kʌrənsɪ/ *n* moneda *f*

current /'kʌrənt/ *adj & n* corriente (*f*); (*existing*) actual. ~ **affairs** *npl* sucesos de actualidad. ~**ly** *adv* actualmente

curriculum /kə'rɪkjʊləm/ *n* (*pl* **-la**) programa *m* de estudios. ~ **vitae** *n* currículum *m* vitae

curry /'kʌrɪ/ *n* curry *m*. ● *vt* preparar al curry

curse /kɜ:s/ *n* maldición *f*; (*oath*) palabrota *f*. ● *vt* maldecir. ● *vi* decir palabrotas

cursory /'kɜ:sərɪ/ *adj* superficial

curt /kɜ:t/ *adj* brusco

curtain /'kɜ:tn/ *n* cortina *f*; (*in theatre*) telón *m*

curtsey, **curtsy** /'kɜ:tsɪ/ *n* reverencia *f*. ● *vi* hacer una reverencia

curve /kɜ:v/ *n* curva *f*. ● *vi* estar curvado; (road) torcerse

cushion /'kʊʃn/ *n* cojín *m*, almohadón *m*

cushy /'kʊʃɪ/ *adj* (**-ier**, **-iest**) 🅸 fácil

custard /'kʌstəd/ *n* natillas *fpl*

custody /'kʌstədɪ/ *n* custodia *f*; **be in** ~ *Jurid* estar detenido

custom /'kʌstəm/ *n* costumbre *f*; (*Com*) clientela *f*. ~**ary** /-ərɪ/ *adj* acostumbrado. ~**er** *n* cliente *m*. ~**s** *npl* aduana *f*. ~**s officer** *n* aduanero *m*

cut /kʌt/ *vt/i* (*pt* **cut**, *pres p* **cutting**) cortar; reducir (prices). ● *n* corte *m*; (*reduction*) reducción *f*. □ ~ **across** *vt* cortar camino por. □ ~ **back**, ~ **down** *vt* reducir. □ ~ **in** *vi* interrumpir. □ ~ **off** *vt* cortar; (*phone*) desconectar; (*fig*) aislar. □ ~ **out** *vt* recortar; (*omit*) suprimir. □ ~ **through** *vt* cortar camino por. □ ~ **up** *vt* cortar en pedazos

cute /kju:t/ *adj* (**-er**, **-est**) 🅸 mono, amoroso (*LAm*); (*Amer, attractive*) guapo, buen mozo (*LAm*)

cutlery /'kʌtlərɪ/ *n* cubiertos *mpl*

cutlet /'kʌtlɪt/ *n* chuleta *f*

cut: ~**-price**, (*Amer*) ~**-rate** *adj* a precio reducido. ~**-throat** *adj* despiadado. ~**ting** *adj* cortante; (remark) mordaz. ● *n* (*from newspaper*) recorte *m*; (*of plant*) esqueje *m*

CV *n* (= **curriculum vitae**) currículum *m* (vitae)

cyberspace /'saɪbəspeɪs/ ciberespacio *m*

cycl|e /'saɪkl/ *n* ciclo *m*; (*bicycle*) bicicleta *f*. ● *vi* ir en bicicleta. ~**ing** *n* ciclismo *m*. ~**ist** *n* ciclista *m & f*

cylind|er /'sɪlɪndə(r)/ *n* cilindro *m*. ~**er head** (*Auto*) *n* culata *f*. ~**rical** /-'lɪndrɪkl/ *adj* cilíndrico

cymbal /'sɪmbl/ *n* címbalo *m*

cynic /'sɪnɪk/ *n* cínico *m*. ~**al** *adj* cínico. ~**ism** /-sɪzəm/ *n* cinismo *m*

Czech /tʃek/ *adj & n* checo (*m*). ~**oslovakia** /-əslə'vækɪə/ *n* (*History*) Checoslovaquia *f*. ~ **Republic** *n*. **the** ~ **Republic** *n* la República Checa

Dd

dab /dæb/ *vt* (*pt* **dabbed**) tocar ligeramente. ● *n* toque *m* suave. a ~ of un poquito de

dad /dæd/ *n* 🅸 papá *m*. ~**dy** *n* papi *m*. ~**dy-long-legs** *n invar* (*cranefly*) típula *f*; (*Amer, harvestman*) segador *m*, falangio *m*

daffodil /'dæfədɪl/ *n* narciso *m*

daft /dɑ:ft/ *adj* (**-er**, **-est**) [I] tonto

dagger /ˈdægə(r)/ *n* daga *f*, puñal *m*

daily /ˈdeɪlɪ/ *adj* diario. ●*adv* diariamente, cada día

> **Dáil Éireann** Es el nombre de la cámara baja del Parlamento de la República de Irlanda. Se pronuncia /dɔɪl/ y consta de 166 representantes o diputados, comúnmente llamados *TDs*, que representan 41 circunscripciones. Se eligen por medio del sistema de representación proporcional. Según la Constitución debe haber un diputado por cada 20.000 a 30.000 personas.

dainty /ˈdeɪntɪ/ *adj* (**-ier**, **-iest**) delicado

dairy /ˈdeərɪ/ *n* vaquería *f*; (*shop*) lechería *f*

daisy /ˈdeɪzɪ/ *n* margarita *f*

dam /dæm/ *n* presa *f*, represa *f* (*LAm*)

damag|e /ˈdæmɪdʒ/ *n* daño *m*; **~s** (*npl*, *Jurid*) daños *mpl* y perjuicios *mpl*. ●*vt* (*fig*) dañar, estropear. **~ing** *adj* perjudicial

dame /deɪm/ *n* (*old use*) dama *f*; (*Amer*, *sl*) chica *f*

damn /dæm/ *vt* condenar; (*curse*) maldecir. ●*int* [I] ¡caray! [I]. ●*adj* maldito. ●*n* **I don't give a ~** (no) me importa un comino

damp /dæmp/ *n* humedad *f*. ●*adj* (**-er**, **-est**) húmedo. ●*vt* mojar. **~ness** *n* humedad *f*

danc|e /dɑ:ns/ *vt/i* bailar. ●*n* baile *m*. **~e hall** *n* salón *m* de baile. **~er** *n* bailador *m*; (*professional*) bailarín *m*. **~ing** *n* baile *m*

dandelion /ˈdændɪlaɪən/ *n* diente *m* de león

dandruff /ˈdændrʌf/ *n* caspa *f*

dandy /ˈdændɪ/ *n* petimetre *m*

Dane /deɪn/ *n* danés *m*

danger /ˈdeɪndʒə(r)/ *n* peligro *m*; (*risk*) riesgo *m*. **~ous** *adj* peligroso

dangle /ˈdæŋgl/ *vt* balancear. ●*vi* suspender, colgar

Danish /ˈdeɪnɪʃ/ *adj* danés. ●*m* (*language*) danés *m*

dar|e /deə(r)/ *vt* desafiar. ●*vi* atreverse a. **I ~ say** probablemente. ●*n* desafío *m*. **~edevil** *n* atrevido *m*. **~ing** *adj* atrevido

dark /dɑ:k/ *adj* (**-er**, **-est**) oscuro; (skin, hair) moreno. ●*n* oscuridad *f*; (*nightfall*) atardecer. **in the ~** a oscuras. **~en** *vt* oscurecer. ●*vi* oscurecerse. **~ness** *n* oscuridad *f*. **~room** *n* cámara *f* oscura

darling /ˈdɑ:lɪŋ/ *adj* querido. ●*n* cariño *m*

darn /dɑ:n/ *vt* zurcir

dart /dɑ:t/ *n* dardo *m*. ●*vi* lanzarse; (*run*) precipitarse. **~board** *n* diana *f*. **~s** *npl* los dardos *mpl*

dash /dæʃ/ *vi* precipitarse. ●*vt* tirar; (*break*) romper; defraudar (hopes). ●*n* (*small amount*) poquito *m*; (*punctuation mark*) guión *m*. □ **~ off** *vi* marcharse apresuradamente. **~ out** *vi* salir corriendo. **~board** *n* tablero *m* de mandos

data /ˈdeɪtə/ *npl* datos *mpl*. **~base** *n* base *f* de datos. **~ processing** *n* proceso *m* de datos

date /deɪt/ *n* fecha *f*; (*appointment*) cita *f*; (*fruit*) dátil *m*. **to ~** hasta la fecha. ●*vt* fechar. ●*vi* datar; datar (remains); (*be old-fashioned*) quedar anticuado. **~d** *adj* pasado de moda

daub /dɔ:b/ *vt* embadurnar

daughter /ˈdɔːtə(r)/ *n* hija *f*. **~-in-law** *n* nuera *f*

dawdle /ˈdɔːdl/ *vi* andar despacio; (*waste time*) perder el tiempo

dawn /dɔːn/ *n* amanecer *m*. ● *vi* amanecer; (*fig*) nacer. **it ~ed on me that** caí en la cuenta de que

day /deɪ/ *n* día *m*; (*whole day*) jornada *f*; (*period*) época *f*. **~break** *n* amanecer *m*. **~ care center** *n* (*Amer*) guardería *f* infantil. **~dream** *n* ensueño *m*. ● *vi* soñar despierto. **~light** *n* luz *f* del día. **~time** *n* día *m*

daze /deɪz/ *vt* aturdir. ● *n* aturdimiento *m*. **in a ~** aturdido. **~d** *adj* aturdido

dazzle /ˈdæzl/ *vt* deslumbrar

dead /ded/ *adj* muerto; (*numb*) dormido. ● *adv* justo; (🅸, *completely*) completamente. **~ beat** rendido. **~ slow** muy lento. **stop ~** parar en seco. **~en** *vt* amortiguar (sound, blow); calmar (pain). **~ end** *n* callejón *m* sin salida. **~line** *n* fecha *f* tope, plazo *m* de entrega. **~lock** *n* punto *m* muerto. **~ly** *adj* (**-ier**, **-iest**) mortal

deaf /def/ *adj* (**-er**, **-est**) sordo. **~en** *vt* ensordecer. **~ness** *n* sordera *f*

deal /diːl/ *n* (*agreement*) acuerdo *m*; (*treatment*) trato *m*. **a good ~** bastante. **a great ~ (of)** muchísimo. ● *vt* (*pt* **dealt**) dar (a blow, cards). ● *vi* (*cards*) dar, repartir. □ **~ in** *vt* comerciar en. □ **~ out** *vt* repartir, distribuir. □ **~ with** *vt* tratar con (person); tratar de (subject); ocuparse de (problem). **~er** *n* comerciante *m*. **drug ~er** traficante *m* & *f* de drogas

dean /diːn/ *n* deán *m*; (*Univ*) decano *m*

dear /dɪə(r)/ *adj* (**-er**, **-est**) querido; (*expensive*) caro. ● *n* querido *m*. ● *adv* caro. ● *int*. **oh ~!** ¡ay por Dios! **~ me!** ¡Dios mío! **~ly** *adv* (*pay*) caro; (*very much*) muchísimo

death /deθ/ *n* muerte *f*. **~ sentence** *n* pena *f* de muerte. **~ trap** *n* lugar *m* peligroso.

debat|able /dɪˈbeɪtəbl/ *adj* discutible. **~e** /dɪˈbeɪt/ *n* debate *m*. ● *vt* debatir, discutir

debauchery /dɪˈbɔːtʃərɪ/ *vt* libertinaje *m*

debit /ˈdebɪt/ *n* débito *m*. ● *vt* debitar, cargar. **~ card** *n* tarjeta *f* de cobro automático

debris /ˈdebriː/ *n* escombros *mpl*

debt /det/ *n* deuda *f*. **be in ~** tener deudas. **~or** *n* deudor *m*

debut /ˈdebjuː/ debut *m*

decade /ˈdekeɪd/ *n* década *f*

decaden|ce /ˈdekədəns/ *n* decadencia *f*. **~t** *adj* decadente

decay /dɪˈkeɪ/ *vi* descomponerse; (tooth) cariarse. ● *n* descomposición *f*; (*of tooth*) caries *f*

deceased /dɪˈsiːst/ *adj* difunto

deceit /dɪˈsiːt/ *n* engaño *m*. **~ful** *adj* falso. **~fully** *adv* falsamente

deceive /dɪˈsiːv/ *vt* engañar

December /dɪˈsembə(r)/ *n* diciembre *m*

decen|cy /ˈdiːsənsɪ/ *n* decencia *f*. **~t** *adj* decente; (*fam, good*) bueno; (*fam, kind*) amable. **~tly** *adv* decentemente

decepti|on /dɪˈsepʃn/ *n* engaño *m*. **~ve** /-tɪv/ *adj* engañoso

decibel /ˈdesɪbel/ *n* decibel(io) *m*

decide /dɪˈsaɪd/ *vt/i* decidir. **~d** *adj* resuelto; (*unquestionable*) indudable

decimal /ˈdesɪml/ *adj* & *n* decimal (*m*). **~ point** *n* coma *f* (decimal),

d

punto *m* decimal

decipher /dɪˈsaɪfə(r)/ *vt* descifrar

decis|ion /dɪˈsɪʒn/ *n* decisión *f*. **~ive** /dɪˈsaɪsɪv/ *adj* decisivo; (*manner*) decidido

deck /dek/ *n* (*Naut*) cubierta *f*; (*Amer, of cards*) baraja *f*; (*of bus*) piso *m*. ● *vt* adornar. **~chair** *n* tumbona *f*, silla *f* de playa

declar|ation /dekləˈreɪʃn/ *n* declaración *f*. **~e** /dɪˈkleə(r)/ *vt* declarar

decline /dɪˈklaɪn/ *vt* rehusar; (*Gram*) declinar. ● *vi* disminuir; (*deteriorate*) deteriorarse. ● *n* decadencia *f*; (*decrease*) disminución *f*

decode /diːˈkəʊd/ *vt* descifrar

decompose /diːkəmˈpəʊz/ *vi* descomponerse

décor /ˈdeɪkɔː(r)/ *n* decoración *f*

decorat|e /ˈdekəreɪt/ *vt* adornar, decorar (*LAm*); empapelar y pintar (room). **~ion** /-ˈreɪʃn/ *n* (*act*) decoración *f*; (*ornament*) adorno *m*. **~ive** /-ətɪv/ *adj* decorativo. **~or** *n* pintor *m* decorador

decoy /ˈdiːkɔɪ/ *n* señuelo *m*. ● /dɪˈkɔɪ/ *vt* atraer con señuelo

decrease /dɪˈkriːs/ *vt/i* disminuir. ● /ˈdiːkriːs/ *n* disminución *f*

decree /dɪˈkriː/ *n* decreto *m*. ● *vt* decretar

decrepit /dɪˈkrepɪt/ *adj* decrépito

decriminalize /diːˈkrɪmɪnəlaɪz/ *vt* despenalizar

dedicat|e /ˈdedɪkeɪt/ *vt* dedicar. **~ion** /-ˈkeɪʃn/ *n* dedicación *f*

deduce /dɪˈdjuːs/ *vt* deducir

deduct /dɪˈdʌkt/ *vt* deducir. **~ion** /-ʃn/ *n* deducción *f*

deed /diːd/ *n* hecho *m*; (*Jurid*) escritura *f*

deem /diːm/ *vt* juzgar, considerar

deep /diːp/ *adj* (**-er**, **-est**) *adv* profundo. ● *adv* profundamente. **be ~ in thought** estar absorto en sus pensamientos. **~en** *vt* hacer más profundo. ● *vi* hacerse más profundo. **~freeze** *n* congelador *m*, freezer *m* (*LAm*). **~ly** *adv* profundamente

deer /dɪə(r)/ *n invar* ciervo *m*

deface /dɪˈfeɪs/ *vt* desfigurar

default /dɪˈfɔːlt/ *vi* faltar. ● *n* opción por defecto. **by ~** en rebeldía

defeat /dɪˈfiːt/ *vt* vencer; (*frustrate*) frustrar. ● *n* derrota *f*. **~ism** *n* derrotismo *m*. **~ist** *n* derrotista *a* & (*m* & *f*)

defect /ˈdiːfekt/ *n* defecto *m*. ● /dɪˈfekt/ *vi* desertar. **~ to** pasar a. **~ion** /dɪˈfekʃn/ *n* (*Pol*) defección *f*. **~ive** /dɪˈfektɪv/ *adj* defectuoso

defence /dɪˈfens/ *n* defensa *f*. **~less** *adj* indefenso

defen|d /dɪˈfend/ *vt* defender. **~dant** *n* (*Jurid*) acusado *m*. **~sive** /-sɪv/ *adj* defensivo. ● *n* defensiva *f*

defer /dɪˈfɜː(r)/ *vt* (*pt* **deferred**) aplazar. **~ence** /ˈdefərəns/ *n* deferencia *f*. **~ential** /defəˈrenʃl/ *adj* deferente

defian|ce /dɪˈfaɪəns/ *n* desafío *m*. **in ~ce of** a despecho de. **~t** *adj* desafiante. **~tly** *adv* con actitud desafiante

deficien|cy /dɪˈfɪʃənsɪ/ *n* falta *f*. **~t** *adj* deficiente. **be ~t in** carecer de

deficit /ˈdefɪsɪt/ *n* déficit *m*

define /dɪˈfaɪn/ *vt* definir

definite /ˈdefɪnɪt/ *adj* (*final*) definitivo; (*certain*) seguro; (*clear*) claro; (*firm*) firme. **~ly** *adv* seguramente; (*definitively*) definitivamente

definition /defɪˈnɪʃn/ *n* definición *f*

definitive /dɪ'fɪnətɪv/ *adj* definitivo

deflate /dɪ'fleɪt/ *vt* desinflar. ● *vi* desinflarse

deflect /dɪ'flekt/ *vt* desviar

deform /dɪ'fɔ:m/ *vt* deformar. **~ed** *adj* deforme. **~ity** *n* deformidad *f*

defrost /di:'frɒst/ *vt* descongelar. ● *vi* descongelarse

deft /deft/ *adj* (**-er**, **-est**) hábil. **~ly** *adv* hábilmente *f*

defuse /di:'fju:z/ *vt* desactivar (bomb); (*fig*) calmar

defy /dɪ'faɪ/ *vt* desafiar

degenerate /dɪ'dʒenəreɪt/ *vi* degenerar. ● /dɪ'dʒenərət/ *adj & n* degenerado (*m*)

degrad|ation /degrə'deɪʃn/ *n* degradación *f*. **~e** /dɪ'greɪd/ *vt* degradar

degree /dɪ'gri:/ *n* grado *m*; (*Univ*) licenciatura *f*; (*rank*) rango *m*. **to a certain ~** hasta cierto punto

deign /deɪn/ *vi*. **~ to** dignarse

deity /'di:ɪtɪ/ *n* deidad *f*

deject|ed /dɪ'dʒektɪd/ *adj* desanimado. **~ion** /-ʃn/ *n* abatimiento *m*

delay /dɪ'leɪ/ *vt* retrasar, demorar (*LAm*). ● *vi* tardar, demorar (*LAm*). ● *n* retraso *m*, demora *f* (*LAm*)

delegat|e /'delɪgeɪt/ *vt/i* delegar. ● /'delɪgət/ *n* delegado *m*. **~ion** /-'geɪʃn/ *n* delegación *f*

delet|e /dɪ'li:t/ *vt* tachar. **~ion** /-ʃn/ *n* supresión *f*

deliberat|e /dɪ'lɪbəreɪt/ *vt/i* deliberar. ● /dɪ'lɪbərət/ *adj* intencionado; (steps etc) pausado. **~ely** *adv* a propósito. **~ion** /-'reɪʃn/ *n* deliberación *f*

delica|cy /'delɪkəsɪ/ *n* delicadeza *f*; (*food*) manjar *m*. **~te** /'delɪkət/ *adj* delicado

delicatessen /delɪkə'tesn/ *n* charcutería *f*, salchichonería *f* (*Mex*)

delicious /dɪ'lɪʃəs/ *adj* delicioso

delight /dɪ'laɪt/ *n* placer *m*. ● *vt* encantar. ● *vi* deleitarse. **~ed** *adj* encantado. **~ful** *adj* delicioso

deliri|ous /dɪ'lɪrɪəs/ *adj* delirante. **~um** /-əm/ *n* delirio *m*

deliver /dɪ'lɪvə(r)/ *vt* entregar; (*distribute*) repartir; (*aim*) lanzar; (*Med*) **he ~ed the baby** la asistió en el parto. **~ance** *n* liberación *f*. **~y** *n* entrega *f*; (*of post*) reparto *m*; (*Med*) parto *m*

delta /'deltə/ *n* (*of river*) delta *m*

delude /dɪ'lu:d/ *vt* engañar. **~ o.s.** engañarse

deluge /'delju:dʒ/ *n* diluvio *m*

delusion /dɪ'lu:ʒn/ *n* ilusión *f*

deluxe /dɪ'lʌks/ *adj* de lujo

delve /delv/ *vi* hurgar. **~ into** (*investigate*) ahondar en

demand /dɪ'mɑ:nd/ *vt* exigir. ● *n* petición *f*, pedido *m* (*LAm*); (*claim*) exigencia *f*; (*Com*) demanda *f*. **in ~** muy popular, muy solicitado. **on ~** a solicitud. **~ing** *adj* exigente. **~s** *npl* exigencias *fpl*

demented /dɪ'mentɪd/ *adj* demente

demo /'deməʊ/ *n* (*pl* **-os**) ⊞ manifestación *f*

democra|cy /dɪ'mɒkrəsɪ/ *n* democracia *f*. **~t** /'deməkræt/ *n* demócrata *m & f*. **D~t** *a & n* (*in US*) demócrata (*m & f*). **~tic** /demə'krætɪk/ *adj* democrático

demoli|sh /dɪ'mɒlɪʃ/ *vt* derribar. **~tion** /demə'lɪʃn/ *n* demolición *f*

demon /'di:mən/ *n* demonio *m*

demonstrat|e /'demənstreɪt/ *vt* demostrar. ● *vi* manifestarse, hacer una manifestación. **~ion** /-'streɪʃn/ *n* demostración *f*; (*Pol*) manifestación *f*. **~or** /'demənstreɪtə(r)/*n* (*Pol*) manifestante *m & f*; (*marketing*) demostrador *m*

demoralize /dɪ'mɒrəlaɪz/ *vt* desmoralizar

demote /dɪ'məʊt/ *vt* bajar de categoría

demure /dɪ'mjʊə(r)/ *adj* recatado

den /den/ *n* (*of animal*) guarida *f*, madriguera *f*

denial /dɪ'naɪəl/ *n* denegación *f*; (*statement*) desmentimiento *m*

denim /'denɪm/ *n* tela *f* vaquera *or* de jeans, mezclilla (*Mex*) *f*. **~s** *npl* vaqueros *mpl*, jeans *mpl*, tejanos *mpl*, pantalones *mpl* de mezclilla (*Mex*)

Denmark /'denmɑːk/ *n* Dinamarca *f*

denote /dɪ'nəʊt/ *vt* denotar

denounce /dɪ'naʊns/ *vt* denunciar

dens|e /dens/ *adj* (**-er**, **-est**) espeso; (person) torpe. **~ely** *adv* densamente. **~ity** *n* densidad *f*

dent /dent/ *n* abolladura *f*. ●*vt* abollar

dental /'dentl/ *adj* dental. **~ floss** /flɒs/ *n* hilo *m or* seda *f* dental. **~ surgeon** *n* dentista *m & f*

dentist /'dentɪst/ *n* dentista *m & f*. **~ry** *n* odontología *f*

dentures /'dentʃəz/ *npl* dentadura *f* postiza

deny /dɪ'naɪ/ *vt* negar; desmentir (rumour); denegar (request)

deodorant /dɪ'əʊdərənt/ *adj & n* desodorante (*m*)

depart /dɪ'pɑːt/ *vi* partir, salir. **~ from** (*deviate from*) apartarse de

department /dɪ'pɑːtmənt/ *n* departamento *m*; (*Pol*) ministerio *m*, secretaría *f* (*Mex*). **~ store** *n* grandes almacenes *mpl*, tienda *f* de departamentos (*Mex*)

departure /dɪ'pɑːtʃə(r)/ *n* partida *f*; (*of train etc*) salida *f*

depend /dɪ'pend/ *vi* depender. **~ on** depender de. **~able** *adj* digno de confianza. **~ant** /dɪ'pendənt/ *n* familiar *m & f* dependiente. **~ence** *n* dependencia *f*. **~ent** *adj* dependiente. **be ~ent on** depender de

depict /dɪ'pɪkt/ *vt* representar; (*in words*) describir

deplete /dɪ'pliːt/ *vt* agotar

deplor|able /dɪ'plɔːrəbl/ *adj* deplorable. **~e** /dɪ'plɔː(r)/ *vt* deplorar

deploy /dɪ'plɔɪ/ *vt* desplegar

deport /dɪ'pɔːt/ *vt* deportar. **~ation** /-'teɪʃn/ *n* deportación *f*

depose /dɪ'pəʊz/ *vt* deponer

deposit /dɪ'pɒzɪt/ *vt* (*pt* **deposited**) depositar. ●*n* depósito *m*

depot /'depəʊ/ *n* depósito *m*; (*Amer*) estación *f* de autobuses

deprav|ed /dɪ'preɪvd/ *adj* depravado. **~ity** /dɪ'prævətɪ/ *n* depravación *f*

depress /dɪ'pres/ *vt* deprimir; (*press down*) apretar. **~ed** *adj* deprimido. **~ing** *adj* deprimente. **~ion** /-ʃn/ *n* depresión *f*

depriv|ation /deprɪ'veɪʃn/ *n* privación *f*. **~e** /dɪ'praɪv/ *vt*. **~e of** privar de. **~d** *adj* carenciado

depth /depθ/ *n* profundidad *f*. **be out of one's ~** perder pie; (*fig*) meterse en honduras. **in ~** a fondo

deput|ize /'depjʊtaɪz/ *vi*. **~ize for** sustituir a. **~y** /'depjʊtɪ/ *n* sustituto *m*. **~y chairman** *n* vicepresidente *m*

derail /dɪ'reɪl/ *vt* hacer descarrilar. **~ment** *n* descarrilamiento *m*

derelict /'derəlɪkt/ *adj* abandonado y en ruinas

deri|de /dɪ'raɪd/ *vt* mofarse de.

~sion /dɪ'rɪʒn/ *n* mofa *f*. **~sive** /dɪ'raɪsɪv/ *adj* burlón. **~sory** /dɪ'raɪsərɪ/ *adj* (offer etc) irrisorio

deriv|ation /derɪ'veɪʃn/ *n* derivación *f*. **~ative** /dɪ'rɪvətɪv/ *n* derivado *m*. **~e** /dɪ'raɪv/ *vt/i* derivar

derogatory /dɪ'rɒgətrɪ/ *adj* despectivo

descen|d /dɪ'send/ *vt/i* descender, bajar. **~dant** *n* descendiente *m* & *f*. **~t** *n* descenso *m*, bajada *f*; (*lineage*) ascendencia *f*

descri|be /dɪs'kraɪb/ *vt* describir. **~ption** /-'krɪpʃn/ *n* descripción *f*. **~ptive** /-'krɪptɪv/ *adj* descriptivo

desecrate /'desɪkreɪt/ *vt* profanar

desert[1] /dɪ'zɜːt/ *vt* abandonar. ●*vi* (*Mil*) desertar. **~er** /dɪ'zɜːtə(r)/ *n* desertor *m*

desert[2] /'dezət/ *adj* & *n* desierto (*m*)

deserts /dɪ'zɜːts/ *npl* lo merecido. **get one's just ~** llevarse su merecido

deserv|e /dɪ'zɜːv/ *vt* merecer. **~ing** *adj* (cause) meritorio

design /dɪ'zaɪn/ *n* diseño *m*; (*plan*) plan *m*. **~s** (*intentions*) propósitos *mpl*. ●*vt* diseñar; (*plan*) planear

designate /'dezɪgneɪt/ *vt* designar

designer /dɪ'zaɪnə(r)/ *n* diseñador *m*; (*fashion* **~**) diseñador *m* de modas. ●*adj* (clothes) de diseño exclusivo

desirable /dɪ'zaɪərəbl/ *adj* deseable

desire /dɪ'zaɪə(r)/ *n* deseo *m*. ●*vt* desear

desk /desk/ *n* escritorio *m*; (*at school*) pupitre *m*; (*in hotel*) recepción *f*; (*Com*) caja *f*. **~top publishing** *n* autoedición *f*, edición *f* electrónica

desolat|e /'desələt/ *adj* desolado; (*uninhabited*) deshabitado. **~ion** /-'leɪʃn/ *n* desolación *f*

despair /dɪ'speə(r)/ *n* desesperación *f*. **be in ~** estar desesperado. ●*vi*. **~ of** desesperarse de

despatch /dɪ'spætʃ/ *vt, n see* DISPATCH

desperat|e /'despərət/ *adj* desesperado. **~ely** *adv* desesperadamente. **~ion** /-'reɪʃn/ *n* desesperación *f*

despicable /dɪ'spɪkəbl/ *adj* despreciable

despise /dɪ'spaɪz/ *vt* despreciar

despite /dɪ'spaɪt/ *prep* a pesar de

despondent /dɪ'spɒndənt/ *adj* abatido

despot /'despɒt/ *n* déspota *m*

dessert /dɪ'zɜːt/ *n* postre *m*. **~spoon** *n* cuchara *f* de postre

destination /destɪ'neɪʃn/ *n* destino *m*

destiny /'destɪnɪ/ *n* destino *m*

destitute /'destɪtjuːt/ *adj* indigente

destroy /dɪ'strɔɪ/ *vt* destruir. **~er** *n* destructor *m*

destructi|on /dɪ'strʌkʃn/ *n* destrucción *f*. **~ve** /-ɪv/ *adj* destructivo

desultory /'desəltrɪ/ *adj* desganado

detach /dɪ'tætʃ/ *vt* separar. **~able** *adj* separable. **~ed** *adj* (*aloof*) distante; (*house*) no adosado. **~ment** *n* desprendimiento *m*; (*Mil*) destacamento *m*; (*aloofness*) indiferencia *f*

detail /'diːteɪl/ *n* detalle *m*. **explain sth in ~** explicar algo detalladamente. ●*vt* detallar; (*Mil*) destacar. **~ed** *adj* detallado

detain /dɪ'teɪn/ *vt* detener; (*delay*) retener. **~ee** /diːteɪ'niː/ *n* detenido *m*

d

d

detect /dɪ'tekt/ *vt* percibir; (*discover*) descubrir. **~ive** *n* (*private*) detective *m*; (*in police*) agente *m* & *f*. **~or** *n* detector *m*

detention /dɪ'tenʃn/ *n* detención *f*

deter /dɪ'tɜ:(r)/ *vt* (*pt* **deterred**) disuadir; (*prevent*) impedir

detergent /dɪ'tɜ:dʒənt/ *adj & n* detergente (*m*)

deteriorat|e /dɪ'tɪərɪəreɪt/ *vi* deteriorarse. **~ion** /-'reɪʃn/ *n* deterioro *m*

determin|ation /dɪtɜ:mɪ'neɪʃn/ *n* determinación *f*. **~e** /dɪ'tɜ:mɪn/ *vt* determinar; (*decide*) decidir. **~ed** *adj* determinado; (*resolute*) decidido

deterrent /dɪ'terənt/ *n* elemento *m* de disuasión

detest /dɪ'test/ *vt* aborrecer. **~able** *adj* odioso

detonat|e /'detəneɪt/ *vt* hacer detonar. • *vi* detonar. **~ion** /-'neɪʃn/ *n* detonación *f*. **~or** *n* detonador *m*

detour /'di:tʊə(r)/ *n* rodeo *m*; (*Amer, of transport*) desvío *m*, desviación *f*. • *vt* (*Amer*) desviar

detract /dɪ'trækt/ *vi*. **~ from** disminuir

detriment /'detrɪmənt/ *n*. **to the ~ of** en perjuicio de. **~al** /-'mentl/ *adj* perjudicial

devalue /di:'vælju:/ *vt* desvalorizar

devastat|e /'devəsteɪt/ *vt* devastar. **~ing** *adj* devastador; (*fig*) arrollador. **~ion** /-'steɪʃn/ *n* devastación *f*

develop /dɪ'veləp/ *vt* desarrollar; contraer (illness); urbanizar (land). • *vi* desarrollarse; (*appear*) surgir. **~ing** *adj* (country) en vías de desarrollo. **~ment** *n* desarrollo *m*. **(new) ~ment** novedad *f*

deviant /'di:vɪənt/ *adj* desviado

deviat|e /'di:vɪeɪt/ *vi* desviarse. **~ion** /-'eɪʃn/ *n* desviación *f*

device /dɪ'vaɪs/ *n* dispositivo *m*; (*scheme*) estratagema *f*

devil /'devl/ *n* diablo *m*

devious /'di:vɪəs/ *adj* taimado

devise /dɪ'vaɪz/ *vt* idear

devoid /dɪ'vɔɪd/ *adj*. **be ~ of** carecer de

devolution /di:və'lu:ʃn/ *n* descentralización *f*; (*of power*) delegación *f*

devot|e /dɪ'vəʊt/ *vt* dedicar. **~ed** *adj* (couple) unido; (service) leal. **~ee** /devə'ti:/ *n* partidario *m*. **~ion** /-ʃn/ *n* devoción *f*

devour /dɪ'vaʊə(r)/ *vt* devorar

devout /dɪ'vaʊt/ *adj* devoto

dew /dju:/ *n* rocío *m*

dexterity /dek'sterətɪ/ *n* destreza *f*

diabet|es /daɪə'bi:ti:z/ *n* diabetes *f*. **~ic** /-'betɪk/ *adj & n* diabético (*m*)

diabolical /daɪə'bɒlɪkl/ *adj* diabólico

diagnos|e /'daɪəgnəʊz/ *vt* diagnosticar. **~is** /-'nəʊsɪs/ *n* (*pl* **-oses**/-si:z/) diagnóstico *m*

diagonal /daɪ'ægənl/ *adj & n* diagonal (*f*)

diagram /'daɪəgræm/ *n* diagrama *m*

dial /'daɪəl/ *n* cuadrante *m*; (*on clock, watch*) esfera *f*; (*on phone*) disco *m*. • *vt* (*pt* **dialled**) marcar, discar (*LAm*)

dialect /'daɪəlekt/ *n* dialecto *m*

dialling:: **~ code** *n* prefijo *m*, código *m* de la zona (*LAm*). **~ tone** *n* tono *m* de marcar, tono *m* de discado (*LAm*)

dialogue /'daɪəlɒg/ *n* diálogo *m*

dial tone *n* (*Amer*) see **DIALLING TONE**

diameter /daɪˈæmɪtə(r)/ *n* diámetro *m*

diamond /ˈdaɪəmənd/ *n* diamante *m*; (*shape*) rombo *m*. **~s** *npl* (*Cards*) diamantes *mpl*

diaper /ˈdaɪəpə(r)/ *n* (*Amer*) pañal *m*

diaphragm /ˈdaɪəfræm/ *n* diafragma *m*

diarrhoea /daɪəˈrɪə/ *n* diarrea *f*

diary /ˈdaɪərɪ/ *n* diario *m*; (*book*) agenda *f*

dice /daɪs/ *n invar* dado *m*. ● *vt* (*Culin*) cortar en cubitos

dictat|e /dɪkˈteɪt/ *vt/i* dictar. **~ion** /dɪkˈteɪʃn/ *n* dictado *m*. **~or** *n* dictador *m*. **~orship** *n* dictadura *f*

dictionary /ˈdɪkʃənərɪ/ *n* diccionario *m*

did /dɪd/ see **DO**

didn't /ˈdɪdnt/ = **did not**

die /daɪ/ *vi* (*pres p* **dying**) morir. **be dying to** morirse por. □ **~ down** *vi* irse apagando. □ **~ out** *vi* extinguirse

diesel /ˈdiːzl/ *n* (*fuel*) gasóleo *m*. **~ engine** *n* motor *m* diesel

diet /ˈdaɪət/ *n* alimentación *f*; (*restricted*) régimen *m*. **be on a ~** estar a régimen. ● *vi* estar a régimen

differ /ˈdɪfə(r)/ *vi* ser distinto; (*disagree*) no estar de acuerdo. **~ence** /ˈdɪfrəns/ *n* diferencia *f*; (*disagreement*) desacuerdo *m*. **~ent** /ˈdɪfrənt/ *adj* distinto, diferente. **~ently** *adv* de otra manera

difficult /ˈdɪfɪkəlt/ *adj* difícil. **~y** *n* dificultad *f*

diffus|e /dɪˈfjuːs/ *adj* difuso. ● /dɪˈfjuːz/ *vt* difundir. ● *vi* difundirse. **~ion** /-ʒn/ *n* difusión *f*

dig /dɪg/ *n* (*poke*) empujón *m*; (*poke with elbow*) codazo *m*; (*remark*) indirecta *f*. **~s** *npl* 🅸 alojamiento *m* ● *vt* (*pt* **dug**, *pres p* **digging**) cavar; (*thrust*) empujar. ● *vi* cavar. □ **~ out** *vt* extraer. □ **~ up** *vt* desenterrar

digest /ˈdaɪdʒest/ *n* resumen *m*. ● /daɪˈdʒest/ *vt* digerir. **~ion** /-ˈdʒestʃn/ *n* digestión *f*. **~ive** /-ˈdʒestɪv/ *adj* digestivo

digger /ˈdɪgə(r)/ *n* (*Mec*) excavadora *f*

digit /ˈdɪdʒɪt/ *n* dígito *m*; (*finger*) dedo *m*. **~al** /ˈdɪdʒɪtl/ *adj* digital

dignified /ˈdɪgnɪfaɪd/ *adj* solemne

dignitary /ˈdɪgnɪtərɪ/ *n* dignatario *m*

dignity /ˈdɪgnətɪ/ *n* dignidad *f*

digress /daɪˈgres/ *vi* divagar. **~ from** apartarse de. **~ion** /-ʃn/ *n* digresión *f*

dike /daɪk/ *n* dique *m*

dilapidated /dɪˈlæpɪdeɪtɪd/ *adj* ruinoso

dilate /daɪˈleɪt/ *vt* dilatar. ● *vi* dilatarse

dilemma /daɪˈlemə/ *n* dilema *m*

diligent /ˈdɪlɪdʒənt/ *adj* diligente

dilute /daɪˈljuːt/ *vt* diluir

dim /dɪm/ *adj* (**dimmer**, **dimmest**) (light) débil; (room) oscuro; (*fam, stupid*) torpe. ● *vt* (*pt* **dimmed**) atenuar. **~ one's headlights** (*Amer*) poner las (luces) cortas *or* de cruce, poner las (luces) bajas (*LAm*). ● *vi* (light) irse atenuando

dime /daɪm/ *n* (*Amer*) *moneda de diez centavos*

dimension /daɪˈmenʃn/ *n* dimensión *f*

diminish /dɪˈmɪnɪʃ/ *vt/i* disminuir

dimple /ˈdɪmpl/ *n* hoyuelo *m*

d

din /dɪn/ *n* jaleo *m*

dine /daɪn/ *vi* cenar. **~r** *n* comensal *m & f*; (*Amer, restaurant*) cafetería *f*

dinghy /ˈdɪŋgɪ/ *n* bote *m*; (*inflatable*) bote *m* neumático

dingy /ˈdɪndʒɪ/ *adj* (**-ier**, **-iest**) miserable, sucio

dinner /ˈdɪnə(r)/ *n* cena *f*, comida *f* (*LAm*). **have ~** cenar, comer (*LAm*). **~ party** *n* cena *f*, comida *f* (*LAm*)

dinosaur /ˈdaɪnəsɔː(r)/ *n* dinosaurio *m*

dint /dɪnt/ *n*. **by ~ of** a fuerza de

dip /dɪp/ *vt* (*pt* **dipped**) meter; (*in liquid*) mojar. **~ one's headlights** poner las (luces) cortas *or* de cruce, poner las (luces) bajas (*LAm*). ● *vi* bajar. ● *n* (*slope*) inclinación *f*; (*in sea*) baño *m*. □ **~ into** *vt* hojear (book)

diphthong /ˈdɪfθɒŋ/ *n* diptongo *m*

diploma /dɪˈpləʊmə/ *n* diploma *m*

diploma|cy /dɪˈpləʊməsɪ/ *n* diplomacia *f*. **~t** /ˈdɪpləmæt/ *n* diplomático *m*. **~tic** /-ˈmætɪk/ *adj* diplomático

dipstick /ˈdɪpstɪk/ *n* (*Auto*) varilla *f* del nivel de aceite

dire /daɪə(r)/ *adj* (**-er**, **-est**) terrible; (need, poverty) extremo

direct /dɪˈrekt/ *adj* directo. ● *adv* directamente. ● *vt* dirigir; (*show the way*) indicar. **~ion** /-ʃn/ *n* dirección *f*. **~ions** *npl* instrucciones *fpl*. **~ly** *adv* directamente; (*at once*) en seguida. ● *conj* [!] en cuanto. **~or** *n* director *m*; (*of company*) directivo *m*

directory /dɪˈrektərɪ/ *n* guía *f*; (*Comp*) directorio *m*

dirt /dɜːt/ *n* suciedad *f*. **~y** *adj* (**-ier**, **-iest**) sucio. ● *vt* ensuciar

disab|ility /dɪsəˈbɪlətɪ/ *n* invalidez *f*. **~le** /dɪsˈeɪbl/ *vt* incapacitar. **~led** *adj* minusválido

disadvantage /dɪsədˈvɑːntɪdʒ/ *n* desventaja *f*. **~d** *adj* desfavorecido

disagree /dɪsəˈgriː/ *vi* no estar de acuerdo (**with** con). **~ with** (food, climate) sentarle mal a. **~able** *adj* desagradable. **~ment** *n* desacuerdo *m*; (*quarrel*) riña *f*

disappear /dɪsəˈpɪə(r)/ *vi* desaparecer. **~ance** *n* desaparición *f*

disappoint /dɪsəˈpɔɪnt/ *vt* decepcionar. **~ing** *adj* decepcionante. **~ment** *n* decepción *f*

disapprov|al /dɪsəˈpruːvl/ *n* desaprobación *f*. **~e** /dɪsəˈpruːv/ *vi*. **~e of** desaprobar. **~ing** *adj* de reproche

disarm /dɪsˈɑːm/ *vt* desarmar. ● *vi* desarmarse. **~ament** *n* desarme *m*

disarray /dɪsəˈreɪ/ *n* desorden *m*

disast|er /dɪˈzɑːstə(r)/ *n* desastre *m*. **~rous** /-strəs/ *adj* catastrófico

disband /dɪsˈbænd/ *vt* disolver. ● *vi* disolverse

disbelief /dɪsbɪˈliːf/ *n* incredulidad *f*

disc /dɪsk/ *n* disco *m*

discard /dɪsˈkɑːd/ *vt* descartar; abandonar (beliefs etc)

discern /dɪˈsɜːn/ *vt* percibir. **~ing** *adj* exigente; (ear, eye) educado

discharge /dɪsˈtʃɑːdʒ/ *vt* descargar; cumplir (duty); (*Mil*) licenciar. ● /ˈdɪstʃɑːdʒ/ *n* descarga *f*; (*Med*) secreción *f*; (*Mil*) licenciamiento *m*

disciple /dɪˈsaɪpl/ *n* discípulo *m*

disciplin|ary /dɪsəˈplɪnərɪ/ *adj* disciplinario. **~e** /ˈdɪsɪplɪn/ *n* disciplina *f*. ● *vt* disciplinar; (*punish*) sancionar

disc jockey /ˈdɪskdʒɒkɪ/ *n* pinchadiscos *m & f*

disclaim /dɪs'kleɪm/ *vt* desconocer. **~er** *n* (*Jurid*) descargo *m* de responsabilidad

disclos|e /dɪs'kləʊz/ *vt* revelar. **~ure** /-ʒə(r)/ *n* revelación *f*

disco /'dɪskəʊ/ *n* (*pl* **-os**) [!] discoteca *f*

discolour /dɪs'kʌlə(r)/ *vt* decolorar. ● *vi* decolorarse

discomfort /dɪs'kʌmfət/ *n* malestar *m*; (*lack of comfort*) incomodidad *f*

disconcert /dɪskən'sɜːt/ *vt* desconcertar

disconnect /dɪskə'nekt/ *vt* separar; (*Elec*) desconectar

disconsolate /dɪs'kɒnsələt/ *adj* desconsolado

discontent /dɪskən'tent/ *n* descontento *m*. **~ed** *adj* descontento

discontinue /dɪskən'tɪnjuː/ *vt* interrumpir

discord /'dɪskɔːd/ *n* discordia *f*; (*Mus*) disonancia *f*. **~ant** /-'skɔːdənt/ *adj* discorde; (*Mus*) disonante

discotheque /'dɪskətek/ *n* discoteca *f*

discount /'dɪskaʊnt/ *n* descuento *m*. ● /dɪs'kaʊnt/ *vt* hacer caso omiso de; (*Com*) descontar

discourag|e /dɪs'kʌrɪdʒ/ *vt* desanimar; (*dissuade*) disuadir. **~ing** *adj* desalentador

discourteous /dɪs'kɜːtɪəs/ *adj* descortés

discover /dɪs'kʌvə(r)/ *vt* descubrir. **~y** *n* descubrimiento *m*

discredit /dɪs'kredɪt/ *vt* (*pt* **discredited**) desacreditar. ● *n* descrédito *m*

discreet /dɪs'kriːt/ *adj* discreto. **~ly** *adv* discretamente

discrepancy /dɪ'skrepənsɪ/ *n* discrepancia *f*

discretion /dɪ'skreʃn/ *n* discreción *f*

discriminat|e /dɪs'krɪmɪneɪt/ *vt* discriminar. **~e between** distinguir entre. **~ing** *adj* perspicaz. **~ion** /-'neɪʃn/ *n* discernimiento *m*; (*bias*) discriminación *f*

discus /'dɪskəs/ *n* disco *m*

discuss /dɪ'skʌs/ *vt* discutir. **~ion** /-ʃn/ *n* discusión *f*

disdain /dɪs'deɪn/ *n* desdén *m*. **~ful** *adj* desdeñoso

disease /dɪ'ziːz/ *n* enfermedad *f*

disembark /dɪsɪm'bɑːk/ *vi* desembarcar

disenchant|ed /dɪsɪn'tʃɑːntɪd/ *adj* desilusionado. **~ment** *n* desencanto *m*

disentangle /dɪsɪn'tæŋgl/ *vt* desenredar

disfigure /dɪs'fɪgə(r)/ *vt* desfigurar

disgrace /dɪs'greɪs/ *n* vergüenza *f*. ● *vt* deshonrar. **~ful** *adj* vergonzoso

disgruntled /dɪs'grʌntld/ *adj* descontento

disguise /dɪs'gaɪz/ *vt* disfrazar. ● *n* disfraz *m*. **in ~** disfrazado

disgust /dɪs'gʌst/ *n* repugnancia *f*, asco *m*. ● *vt* dar asco a. **~ed** *adj* indignado; (*stronger*) asqueado. **~ing** *adj* repugnante, asqueroso

dish /dɪʃ/ *n* plato *m*. **wash** *or* **do the ~es** fregar los platos, lavar los trastes (*Mex*). □ **~ up** *vt/i* servir. **~cloth** *n* bayeta *f*

disheartening /dɪs'hɑːtnɪŋ/ *adj* desalentador

dishonest /dɪs'ɒnɪst/ *adj* deshonesto. **~y** *n* falta *f* de honradez

dishonour /dɪs'ɒnə(r)/ *n* deshonra *f*

d

dish: ~ **soap** *n* (*Amer*) lavavajillas *m*. ~ **towel** *n* paño *m* de cocina. ~**washer** *n* lavaplatos *m*, lavavajillas *m*. ~**washing liquid** *n* (*Amer*) *see* ~ SOAP
disillusion /dɪsɪ'lu:ʒn/ *vt* desilusionar. ~**ment** *n* desilusión *f*
disinfect /dɪsɪn'fekt/ *vt* desinfectar. ~**ant** *n* desinfectante *m*
disintegrate /dɪs'ɪntɪgreɪt/ *vt* desintegrar. ● *vi* desintegrarse
disinterested /dɪs'ɪntrəstɪd/ *adj* desinteresado
disjointed /dɪs'dʒɔɪntɪd/ *adj* inconexo
disk /dɪsk/ *n* disco *m*. ~ **drive** (*Comp*) unidad *f* de discos. ~**ette** /dɪs'ket/ *n* disquete *m*
dislike /dɪs'laɪk/ *n* aversión *f*. ● *vt*. I ~ **dogs** no me gustan los perros
dislocate /'dɪsləkeɪt/ *vt* dislocar(se) (limb)
dislodge /dɪs'lɒdʒ/ *vt* sacar
disloyal /dɪs'lɔɪəl/ *adj* desleal. ~**ty** *n* deslealtad *f*
dismal /'dɪzməl/ *adj* triste; (*bad*) fatal
dismantle /dɪs'mæntl/ *vt* desmontar
dismay /dɪs'meɪ/ *n* consternación *f*. ● *vt* consternar
dismiss /dɪs'mɪs/ *vt* despedir; (*reject*) rechazar. ~**al** *n* despido *m*; (*of idea*) rechazo *m*
dismount /dɪs'maʊnt/ *vi* desmontar
disobe|dience /dɪsə'bi:dɪəns/ *n* desobediencia *f*. ~**dient** *adj* desobediente. ~**y** /dɪsə'beɪ/ *vt/i* desobedecer
disorder /dɪs'ɔ:də(r)/ *n* desorden *m*; (*ailment*) afección *f*. ~**ly** *adj* desordenado
disorganized /dɪs'ɔ:gənaɪzd/ *adj* desorganizado
disorientate /dɪs'ɔ:rɪənteɪt/ *vt* desorientar
disown /dɪs'əʊn/ *vt* repudiar
disparaging /dɪs'pærɪdʒɪŋ/ *adj* despreciativo
dispatch /dɪs'pætʃ/ *vt* despachar. ● *n* despacho *m*. ~ **rider** *n* mensajero *m*
dispel /dɪs'pel/ *vt* (*pt* **dispelled**) disipar
dispens|able /dɪs'pensəbl/ *adj* prescindible. ~**e** *vt* distribuir; (*Med*) preparar. □ ~ **with** *vt* prescindir de
dispers|al /dɪ'spɜ:sl/ *n* dispersión *f*. ~**e** /dɪ'spɜ:s/ *vt* dispersar. ● *vi* dispersarse
dispirited /dɪs'pɪrɪtɪd/ *adj* desanimado
display /dɪs'pleɪ/ *vt* exponer (goods); demostrar (feelings). ● *n* exposición *f*; (*of feelings*) demostración *f*
displeas|e /dɪs'pli:z/ *vt* desagradar. **be** ~**ed with** estar disgustado con. ~**ure** /-'pleʒə(r)/ *n* desagrado *m*
dispos|able /dɪs'pəʊzəbl/ *adj* desechable. ~**al** /dɪs'pəʊzl/ *n* (*of waste*) eliminación *f*. **at s.o.'s** ~**al** a la disposición de uno. ~**e of** /dɪs'pəʊz/ *vt* deshacerse de
disproportionate /dɪsprə'pɔ:ʃənət/ *adj* desproporcionado
disprove /dɪs'pru:v/ *vt* desmentir (claim); refutar (theory)
dispute /dɪs'pju:t/ *vt* discutir. ● *n* disputa *f*. **in** ~ disputado
disqualif|ication /dɪskwɒlɪfɪ'keɪʃn/ *n* descalificación *f*. ~**y** /dɪs'kwɒlɪfaɪ/ *vt* incapacitar; (*Sport*) descalificar
disregard /dɪsrɪ'gɑ:d/ *vt* no hacer caso de. ● *n* indiferencia *f* (**for** a)

disreputable /dɪs'repjʊtəbl/ *adj* de mala fama

disrespect /dɪsrɪ'spekt/ *n* falta *f* de respeto

disrupt /dɪs'rʌpt/ *vt* interrumpir; trastornar (plans). **~ion** /-ʃn/ *n* trastorno *m*. **~ive** *adj* (influence) perjudicial, negativo

dissatis|faction /dɪsætɪs 'fækʃn/ *n* descontento *m*. **~fied** /dɪ'sætɪsfaɪd/ *adj* descontento

dissect /dɪ'sekt/ *vt* disecar

dissent /dɪ'sent/ *vi* disentir. • *n* disentimiento *m*

dissertation /dɪsə'teɪʃn/ *n* (*Univ*) tesis *f*

dissident /'dɪsɪdənt/ *adj & n* disidente (*m & f*)

dissimilar /dɪ'sɪmɪlə(r)/ *adj* distinto

dissolute /'dɪsəlu:t/ *adj* disoluto

dissolve /dɪ'zɒlv/ *vt* disolver. • *vi* disolverse

dissuade /dɪ'sweɪd/ *vt* disuadir

distan|ce /'dɪstəns/ *n* distancia *f*. **from a ~ce** desde lejos. **in the ~ce** a lo lejos. **~t** *adj* distante, lejano; (*aloof*) distante

distaste /dɪs'teɪst/ *n* desagrado *m*. **~ful** *adj* desagradable

distil /dɪs'tɪl/ *vt* (*pt* **distilled**) destilar. **~lery** /dɪs'tɪlərɪ/ *n* destilería *f*

distinct /dɪs'tɪŋkt/ *adj* distinto; (*clear*) claro; (*marked*) marcado. **~ion** /-ʃn/ *n* distinción *f*; (*in exam*) sobresaliente *m*. **~ive** *adj* distintivo

distinguish /dɪs'tɪŋgwɪʃ/ *vt/i* distinguir. **~ed** *adj* distinguido

distort /dɪs'tɔ:t/ *vt* torcer. **~ion** /-ʃn/ *n* deformación *f*

distract /dɪs'trækt/ *vt* distraer. **~ed** *adj* distraído. **~ion** /-ʃn/ *n* distracción *f*; (*confusion*) aturdimiento *m*

distraught /dɪs'trɔ:t/ *adj* consternado, angustiado

distress /dɪs'tres/ *n* angustia *f*. • *vt* afligir. **~ed** *adj* afligido. **~ing** *adj* penoso

distribut|e /dɪ'strɪbju:t/ *vt* repartir, distribuir. **~ion** /-'bju:ʃn/ *n* distribución *f*. **~or** *n* distribuidor *m*; (*Auto*) distribuidor *m* (del encendido)

district /'dɪstrɪkt/ *n* zona *f*, región *f*; (*of town*) barrio *m*

distrust /dɪs'trʌst/ *n* desconfianza *f*. • *vt* desconfiar de

disturb /dɪs'tɜ:b/ *vt* molestar; (*perturb*) inquietar; (*move*) desordenar; (*interrupt*) interrumpir. **~ance** *n* disturbio *m*; (*tumult*) alboroto *m*. **~ed** *adj* trastornado. **~ing** *adj* inquietante

disused /dɪs'ju:zd/ *adj* fuera de uso

ditch /dɪtʃ/ *n* zanja *f*; (*for irrigation*) acequia *f*. • *vt* [!] abandonar

dither /'dɪðə(r)/ *vi* vacilar

ditto /'dɪtəʊ/ *adv* ídem

divan /dɪ'væn/ *n* diván *m*

dive /daɪv/ *vi* tirarse (al agua), zambullirse; (*rush*) meterse (precipitadamente). • *n* (*into water*) zambullida *f*; (*Sport*) salto *m* (de trampolín); (*of plane*) descenso *m* en picado, descenso *m* en picada (*LAm*); ([!], *place*) antro *m*. **~r** *n* saltador *m*; (*underwater*) buzo *m*

diverge /daɪ'vɜ:dʒ/ *vi* divergir. **~nt** *adj* divergente

divers|e /daɪ'vɜ:s/ *adj* diverso. **~ify** *vt* diversificar. **~ity** *n* diversidad *f*

diver|sion /daɪ'vɜ:ʃn/ *n* desvío *m*; desviación *f*; (*distraction*) diversión *f*. **~t** /daɪ'vɜ:t/ *vt* desviar; (*entertain*) divertir

d

divide /dɪ'vaɪd/ *vt* dividir. ●*vi* dividirse. **~d highway** *n* (*Amer*) autovía *f*, carretera *f* de doble pista

dividend /'dɪvɪdend/ *n* dividendo *m*

d

divine /dɪ'vaɪn/ *adj* divino

division /dɪ'vɪʒn/ *n* división *f*

divorce /dɪ'vɔ:s/ *n* divorcio *m*. ●*vt* divorciarse de. **get ~d** divorciarse. ●*vi* divorciarse. **~e** /dɪvɔ:'si:/ *n* divorciado *m*

divulge /daɪ'vʌldʒ/ *vt* divulgar

DIY *abbr see* **DO-IT-YOURSELF**

dizz|iness /'dɪzɪnɪs/ *n* vértigo *m*. **~y** *adj* (**-ier**, **-iest**) mareado. **be** *or* **feel ~y** marearse

DJ *abbr see* **DISC JOCKEY**

do /du://dʊ, də/

3rd person singular present **does;** past **did;** past participle **done**

●*transitive verb*

····➤hacer. **he does what he wants** hace lo que quiere. **to do one's homework** hacer los deberes. **to do the cooking** preparar la comida, cocinar. **well done!** ¡muy bien!

····➤(*clean*) lavar (dishes). limpiar (windows)

····➤(*as job*) **what does he do?** ¿en qué trabaja?

····➤(*swindle*) estafar. **I've been done!** ¡me han estafado!

····➤(*achieve*) **she's done it!** ¡lo ha logrado!

●*intransitive verb*

····➤hacer. **do as you're told!** ¡haz lo que se te dice!

····➤(*fare*) **how are you doing?** (*with a task*) ¿qué tal te va? **how do you do?**, (*as greeting*) mucho gusto, encantado

····➤(*perform*) **she did well/badly** le fue bien/mal

····➤(*be suitable*) **will this do?** ¿esto sirve?

····➤(*be enough*) ser suficiente, bastar. **one box will do** con una caja basta, con una caja es suficiente

●*auxiliary verb*

····➤(*to form interrogative and negative*) **do you speak Spanish?** ¿hablas español?. **I don't want to** no quiero. **don't shut the door** no cierres la puerta

····➤(*in tag questions*) **you eat meat, don't you?** ¿comes carne, ¿verdad? *or* ¿no? **he lives in London, doesn't he?** vive en Londres, ¿no? *or* ¿verdad? *or* ¿no es cierto?

····➤(*in short answers*) **do you like it? - yes, I do** ¿te gusta? - sí. **who wrote it? - I did** ¿quién lo escribió? - yo

····➤(*emphasizing*) **do come in!** ¡pase Ud!. **you do exaggerate!** ¡cómo exageras! ▫ **do away with** *vt* abolir. ▫ **do in** *vt* (*sl, kill*) eliminar. ▫ **do up** *vt* abrochar (coat etc); arreglar (house). ▫ **do with** *vt* (*need*) (*with can, could*) necesitar; (*expressing connection*) **it has nothing to do with that** no tiene nada que ver con eso. ▫ **do without** *vt* prescindir de

docile /'dəʊsaɪl/ *adj* dócil

dock /dɒk/ *n* (*Naut*) dársena *f*; (*wharf, quay*) muelle *m*; (*Jurid*) banquillo *m* de los acusados. **~s** *npl* (*port*) puerto *m*. ●*vt* cortar (tail);

atracar (ship). •*vi* (ship) atracar. **~er** *n* estibador *m*. **~yard** *n* astillero *m*

doctor /'dɒktə(r)/ *n* médico *m*, doctor *m*

doctrine /'dɒktrɪn/ *n* doctrina *f*

document /'dɒkjʊmənt/ *n* documento *m*. **~ary** /-'mentrɪ/ *adj & n* documental (*m*)

dodg|e /dɒdʒ/ *vt* esquivar. •*vi* esquivarse. •*n* treta *f*. **~ems** /'dɒdʒəmz/ *npl* autos *mpl* de choque. **~y** *adj* (**-ier**, **-iest**) (*awkward*) difícil

doe /dəʊ/ *n* (*rabbit*) coneja *f*; (*hare*) liebre *f* hembra; (*deer*) cierva *f*

does /dʌz/ *see* DO

doesn't /'dʌznt/ = **does not**

dog /dɒg/ *n* perro *m*. •*vt* (*pt* **dogged**) perseguir

dogged /'dɒgɪd/ *adj* obstinado

doghouse /'dɒghaʊs/ *n* (*Amer*) casa *f* del perro. **in the ~** 🄸 en desgracia

dogma /'dɒgmə/ *n* dogma *m*. **~tic** /-'mætɪk/ *adj* dogmático

do|ings *npl* actividades *fpl*. **~-it-yourself** /du:ɪtjɔ:'self/ *n* bricolaje *m*

dole /dəʊl/ *n* 🄸 subsidio *m* de paro, subsidio *m* de desempleo. **on the ~** 🄸 parado, desempleado. □ **~ out** *vt* distribuir

doleful /'dəʊlfl/ *adj* triste

doll /dɒl/ *n* muñeca *f*

dollar /'dɒlə(r)/ *n* dólar *m*

dollarization /dɒlərаɪ'zeɪʃn/ *n* dolarización *f*

dollop /'dɒləp/ *n* 🄸 porción *f*

dolphin /'dɒlfɪn/ *n* delfín *m*

domain /dəʊ'meɪn/ *n* dominio *m*

dome /dəʊm/ *n* cúpula *f*

domestic /də'mestɪk/ *adj* doméstico; (trade, flights, etc) nacional. **~ated** /də'mestɪkeɪtɪd/ *adj* (animal) domesticado. **~ science** *n* economía *f* doméstica

domin|ance /'dɒmɪnəns/ *n* dominio *m*. **~ant** *adj* dominante. **~ate** /-eɪt/ *vt/i* dominar. **~ation** /-'neɪʃn/ *n* dominación *f*. **~eering** *adj* dominante

Dominican Republic /də'mɪnɪkən/ *n* República *f* Dominicana

dominion /də'mɪnjən/ *n* dominio *m*

domino /'dɒmɪnəʊ/ *n* (*pl* **-oes**) ficha *f* de dominó. **~es** *npl* (*game*) dominó *m*

donat|e /dəʊ'neɪt/ *vt* donar. **~ion** /-ʃn/ *n* donativo *m*, donación *f*

done /dʌn/ *see* DO

donkey /'dɒŋkɪ/ *n* burro *m*, asno *m*. **~'s years** 🄸 siglos *mpl*

donor /'dəʊnə(r)/ *n* donante *m & f*

don't /dəʊnt/ = **do not**

doodle /'du:dl/ *vi/t* garrapatear

doom /du:m/ *n* destino *m*; (*death*) muerte *f*. •*vt*. **be ~ed to** estar condenado a

door /dɔ:(r)/ *n* puerta *f*. **~bell** *n* timbre *m*. **~ knob** *n* pomo *m* (de la puerta). **~mat** *n* felpudo *m*. **~step** *n* peldaño *m*. **~way** *n* entrada *f*

dope /dəʊp/ *n* 🄸 droga *f*; (*sl, idiot*) imbécil *m*. •*vt* 🄸 drogar

dormant /'dɔ:mənt/ *adj* aletargado, (volcano) inactivo

dormice /'dɔ:maɪs/ *see* DORMOUSE

dormitory /'dɔ:mɪtrɪ/ *n* dormitorio *m*

dormouse /'dɔ:maʊs/ *n* (*pl* **-mice**) lirón *m*

DOS /dɒs/ *abbr* (= **disc-operating system**) DOS *m*

d

dos|age /'dəʊsɪdʒ/ *n* dosis *f.* **~e** /dəʊs/ *n* dosis *f*

dot /dɒt/ *n* punto *m.* **on the ~** en punto. **~-com** *n* punto *m* com. **~-com company** empresa *f* puntocom

dote /dəʊt/ *vi.* **~ on** adorar

dotty /'dɒtɪ/ *adj* (**-ier, -iest**) 🅸 chiflado

double /'dʌbl/ *adj* doble. ● *adv* el doble. ● *n* doble *m*; (*person*) doble *m & f.* **at the ~** corriendo. ● *vt* doblar; redoblar (efforts etc). ● *vi* doblarse. **~ bass** /beɪs/ *n* contrabajo *m.* **~ bed** *n* cama *f* de matrimonio, cama *f* de doa plazas (*LAm*). **~ chin** *n* papada *f.* **~ click** *vt* hacer doble clic en. **~-cross** /-'krɒs/ *vt* traicionar. **~-decker** /-'dekə(r)/ *n* autobús *m* de dos pisos. **~ Dutch** *n* 🅸 chino *m.* **~ glazing** /-'gleɪzɪŋ/ *n* doble ventana *f.* **~s** *npl* (*tennis*) dobles *mpl*

doubly /'dʌblɪ/ *adv* doblemente

doubt /daʊt/ *n* duda *f.* ● *vt* dudar; (*distrust*) dudar de. **~ful** *adj* dudoso. **~less** *adv* sin duda

dough /dəʊ/ *n* masa *f*; (*sl, money*) pasta *f* 🅿, lana *f* (*LAm fam*). **~nut** *n* donut *m*, dona *f* (*Mex*)

dove /dʌv/ *n* paloma *f*

down /daʊn/ *adv* abajo. **~ with** abajo. **come ~** bajar. **go ~** bajar; (sun) ponerse. ● *prep* abajo. ● *adj* 🅸 deprimido. ● *vt* derribar; (*fam, drink*) beber. ● *n* (*feathers*) plumón *m.* **~ and out** *adj* en la miseria. **~cast** *adj* abatido. **~fall** *n* perdición *f*; (*of king, dictator*) caída *f.* **~-hearted** /-'hɑːtɪd/ *adj* abatido. **~hill** /-'hɪl/ *adv* cuesta abajo. **~load** /-'ləʊd/ *vt* (*Comp*) bajar. **~market** /-'mɑːkɪt/ *adj* (newspaper) popular; (store) barato. **~ payment** *n* depósito *m.* **~pour** *n* aguacero *m.* **~right** *adj* completo. ● *adv* completamente. **~s** *npl* colinas *fpl.* **~stairs** /-'steəz/ *adv* abajo. ● /-steəz/ *adj* de abajo. **~stream** *adv* río abajo. **~-to-earth** /-tʊ'ɜːθ/ *adj* práctico. **~town** /-'taʊn/ *n* centro *m* (de la ciudad). ● *adv.* **go ~town** ir al centro. **~ under** *adv* en las antípodas; (*in Australia*) en Australia. **~ward** /-wəd/ *adj & adv*, **~wards** *adv* hacia abajo

dowry /'daʊərɪ/ *n* dote *f*

> *i* **Downing Street** Es una calle en el barrio londinense de Westminster. El número 10 es la residencia oficial del Primer Ministro y el 11, la del *Chancellor of the Exchequer* (Ministro de Economía y Hacienda). Los periodistas suelen utilizar las expresiones *Downing Street* o *Number 10* para referirse al Primer Ministro y al Gobierno.

doze /dəʊz/ *vi* dormitar

dozen /'dʌzn/ *n* docena *f.* **a ~ eggs** una docena de huevos. **~s of** 🅸 miles de, muchos

Dr /'dɒktə(r)/ *abbr* (**Doctor**)

drab /dræb/ *adj* monótono

draft /drɑːft/ *n* borrador *m*; (*Com*) letra *f* de cambio; (*Amer, Mil*) reclutamiento *m*; (*Amer, of air*) corriente *f* de aire. ● *vt* redactar el borrador de; (*Amer, conscript*) reclutar

drag /dræg/ *vt* (*pt* **dragged**) arrastrar. ● *n* 🅸 lata *f*

dragon /'drægən/ *n* dragón *m.* **~fly** *n* libélula *f*

drain /dreɪn/ *vt* vaciar (tank, glass); drenar (land); (*fig*) agotar. ● *vi* escurrirse. ● *n* (*pipe*) sumidero *m*, resumidero *m* (*LAm*); (*plughole*) desagüe *m.* **~board** (*Amer*), **~ing**

board *n* escurridero *m*

drama /ˈdrɑːmə/ *n* drama *m*; (*art*) arte *m* teatral. **~tic** /drəˈmætɪk/ *adj* dramático. **~tist** /ˈdræmətɪst/ *n* dramaturgo *m*. **~tize** /ˈdræmətaɪz/ *vt* adaptar al teatro; (*fig*) dramatizar

drank /dræŋk/ *see* DRINK

drape /dreɪp/ *vt* cubrir; (*hang*) colgar. **~s** *npl* (*Amer*) cortinas *fpl*

drastic /ˈdræstɪk/ *adj* drástico

draught /drɑːft/ *n* corriente *f* de aire. **~ beer** *n* cerveza *f* de barril. **~s** *npl* (*game*) juego *m* de damas *fpl*. **~y** *adj* lleno de corrientes de aire

draw /drɔː/ *vt* (*pt* **drew**, *pp* **drawn**) tirar; (*attract*) atraer; dibujar (picture); trazar (line). **~ the line** trazar el límite. ● *vi* (*Art*) dibujar; (*Sport*) empatar; **~ near** acercarse. ● *n* (*Sport*) empate *m*; (*in lottery*) sorteo *m*. □ **~ in** *vi* (days) acortarse. □ **~ out** *vt* sacar (money). □ **~ up** *vi* pararse. *vt* redactar (document); acercar (chair). **~back** *n* desventaja *f*. **~bridge** *n* puente *m* levadizo

drawer /drɔː(r)/ *n* cajón *m*, gaveta *f* (*Mex*). **~s** *npl* calzones *mpl*

drawing /ˈdrɔːɪŋ/ *n* dibujo *m*. **~ pin** *n* tachuela *f*, chincheta *f*, chinche *f*. **~ room** *n* salón *m*

drawl /drɔːl/ *n* habla *f* lenta

drawn /drɔːn/ *see* DRAW

dread /dred/ *n* terror *m*. ● *vt* temer. **~ful** *adj* terrible. **~fully** *adv* terriblemente

dream /driːm/ *n* sueño *m*. ● *vt/i* (*pt* **dreamed** *or* **dreamt** /dremt/) soñar. □ **~ up** *vt* idear. *adj* ideal. **~er** *n* soñador *m*

dreary /ˈdrɪərɪ/ *adj* (**-ier, -iest**) triste; (*boring*) monótono

dredge /dredʒ/ *n* draga *f*. ● *vt* dragar. **~r** *n* draga *f*

dregs /dregz/ *npl* posos *mpl*, heces *fpl*; (*fig*) hez *f*

drench /drentʃ/ *vt* empapar

dress /dres/ *n* vestido *m*; (*clothing*) ropa *f*. ● *vt* vestir; (*decorate*) adornar; (*Med*) vendar. ● *vi* vestirse. □ **~ up** *vi* ponerse elegante. **~ up as** disfrazarse de. **~ circle** *n* primer palco *m*

d

dressing /ˈdresɪŋ/ *n* (*sauce*) aliño *m*; (*bandage*) vendaje *m*. **~-down** /-ˈdaʊn/ *n* rapapolvo *m*, reprensión *f*. **~ gown** *n* bata *f*. **~ room** *n* vestidor *m*; (*in theatre*) camarín *m*. **~ table** *n* tocador *m*

dress: ~maker *n* modista *m & f*. **~making** *n* costura *f*. **~ rehearsal** *n* ensayo *m* general

drew /druː/ *see* DRAW

dribble /ˈdrɪbl/ *vi* (baby) babear; (*in football*) driblar, driblear

drie|d /draɪd/ *adj* (food) seco; (milk) en polvo. **~r** /ˈdraɪə(r)/ *n* secador *m*

drift /drɪft/ *vi* ir a la deriva; (snow) amontonarse. ● *n* (*movement*) dirección *f*; (*of snow*) montón *m*

drill /drɪl/ *n* (*tool*) taladro *m*; (*of dentist*) torno *m*; (*training*) ejercicio *m*. ● *vt* taladrar, perforar; (*train*) entrenar. ● *vi* entrenarse

drink /drɪŋk/ *vt/i* (*pt* **drank**, *pp* **drunk**) beber, tomar (*LAm*). ● *n* bebida *f*. **~able** *adj* bebible; (water) potable. **~er** *n* bebedor *m*. **~ing water** *n* agua *f* potable

drip /drɪp/ *vi* (*pt* **dripped**) gotear. ● *n* gota *f*; (*Med*) goteo *m* intravenoso; (*fam, person*) soso *m*. **~-dry** /-ˈdraɪ/ *adj* de lava y pon. **~ping** *adj*. **be ~ping wet** estar chorreando

drive /draɪv/ *vt* (*pt* **drove**, *pp*

d

driven) conducir, manejar (*LAm*) (car etc). ~ **s.o. mad** volver loco a uno. ~ **s.o. to do sth** llevar a uno a hacer algo. ●*vi* conducir, manejar (*LAm*). ~ **at** querer decir. ~ **in** (*in car*) entrar en coche. ●*n* paseo *m*; (*road*) calle *f*; (*private road*) camino *m* de entrada; (*fig*) empuje *m*. ~**r** *n* conductor *m*, chofer *m* (*LAm*). ~**r's license** *n* (*Amer*) *see* DRIVING LICENSE

drivel /'drɪvl/ *n* tonterías *fpl*

driving /'draɪvɪŋ/ *n* conducción *f*. ~ **licence** *n* permiso *m* de conducir, licencia *f* de conducción (*LAm*), licencia *f* (de manejar) (*Mex*). ~ **test** *n* examen *m* de conducir, examen *m* de manejar (*LAm*)

drizzle /'drɪzl/ *n* llovizna *f*. ●*vi* lloviznar

drone /drəʊn/ *n* zumbido *m*. ●*vi* zumbar

drool /dru:l/ *vi* babear

droop /dru:p/ *vi* inclinarse; (flowers) marchitarse

drop /drɒp/ *n* gota *f*; (*fall*) caída *f*; (*decrease*) descenso *m*. ●*vt* (*pt* **dropped**) dejar caer; (*lower*) bajar. ●*vi* caer. □ ~ **in on** *vt* pasar por casa de. □ ~ **off** *vi* (*sleep*) dormirse. □ ~ **out** *vi* retirarse; (student) abandonar los estudios. ~**out** *n* marginado *m*

drought /draʊt/ *n* sequía *f*

drove /drəʊv/ *see* DRIVE. ●*n* manada *f*

drown /draʊn/ *vt* ahogar. ●*vi* ahogarse

drowsy /'draʊzɪ/ *adj* soñoliento

drudgery /'drʌdʒərɪ/ *n* trabajo *m* pesado

drug /drʌg/ *n* droga *f*; (*Med*) medicamento *m*. ●*vt* (*pt* **drugged**) drogar. ~ **addict** *n* drogadicto *m*. ~**gist** *n* (*Amer*) farmacéutico *m*. ~**store** *n* (*Amer*) farmacia *f* (que vende otros artículos también)

drum /drʌm/ *n* tambor *m*; (*for oil*) bidón *m*. ●*vi* (*pt* **drummed**) tocar el tambor. ●*vt*. ~ **sth into s.o.** hacerle aprender algo a uno a fuerza de repetírselo. ~**mer** *n* tambor *m*; (*in group*) batería *f*. ~**s** *npl* batería *f*. ~**stick** *n* baqueta *f*; (*Culin*) muslo *m*

drunk /drʌŋk/ *see* DRINK. ●*adj* borracho. **get** ~ emborracharse. ●*n* borracho *m*. ~**ard** /-əd/ *n* borracho *m*. ~**en** *adj* borracho

dry /draɪ/ *adj* (**drier**, **driest**) seco. ●*vt* secar. ●*vi* secarse. □ ~ **up** *vi* (stream) secarse; (funds) agotarse. ~**-clean** *vt* limpiar en seco. ~**-cleaner's** tintorería *f*. ~**er** *n* *see* DRIER

DTD *abbrev* **Document Type Definition** DTD *m*

dual /'dju:əl/ *adj* doble. ~ **carriageway** *n* autovía *f*, carretera *f* de doble pista

dub /dʌb/ *vt* (*pt* **dubbed**) doblar (film)

dubious /'dju:bɪəs/ *adj* dudoso; (person) sospechoso

duchess /'dʌtʃɪs/ *n* duquesa *f*

duck /dʌk/ *n* pato *m*. ●*vt* sumergir; bajar (head). ●*vi* agacharse. ~**ling** /'dʌklɪŋ/ *n* patito *m*

duct /dʌkt/ *n* conducto *m*

dud /dʌd/ *adj* inútil; (cheque) sin fondos

due /dju:/ *adj* debido; (*expected*) esperado. ~ **to** debido a. ●*adv*. ~ **north** derecho hacia el norte. ~**s** *npl* derechos *mpl*

duel /'dju:əl/ *n* duelo *m*

duet /dju:'et/ *n* dúo *m*

duffel, **duffle** /'dʌfl/: ~ **bag** *n* bolsa *f* de lona. ~ **coat** *n* trenca *f*

dug /dʌg/ *see* DIG

duke /dju:k/ *n* duque *m*

dull /dʌl/ *adj* (**-er**, **-est**) (weather) gris; (colour) apagado; (person, play, etc) pesado; (sound) sordo

dumb /dʌm/ *adj* (**-er**, **-est**) mudo; [I] estúpido. □ **~ down** *vt* reducir el valor intelectual de. **~found** /dʌm'faʊnd/ *vt* pasmar

dummy /'dʌmɪ/ *n* muñeco *m*; (*of tailor*) maniquí *m*; (*for baby*) chupete *m*. ● *adj* falso. **~ run** prueba *f*

dump /dʌmp/ *vt* tirar, botar (*LAm*). ● *n* vertedero *m*; (*Mil*) depósito *m*; [I] lugar *m* desagradable. **be down in the ~s** estar deprimido

dumpling /'dʌmplɪŋ/ *n* bola *f* de masa hervida

Dumpster /'dʌmpstə(r)/ *n* (*Amer*, ®) contenedor *m* (para escombros)

dumpy /'dʌmpɪ/ *adj* (**-ier**, **-iest**) regordete

dunce /dʌns/ *n* burro *m*

dung /dʌŋ/ *n* (*manure*) estiércol *m*

dungarees /dʌŋgə'ri:z/ *npl* mono *m*, peto *m*

dungeon /'dʌndʒən/ *n* calabozo *m*

dunk /dʌŋk/ *vt* remojar

dupe /dju:p/ *vt* engañar. ● *n* inocentón *m*

duplicat|e /'dju:plɪkət/ *adj & n* duplicado (*m*). ● /'dju:plɪkeɪt/ *vt* duplicar; (*on machine*) reproducir. **~ing machine**, **~or** *n* multicopista *f*

durable /'djʊərəbl/ *adj* durable

duration /djʊ'reɪʃn/ *n* duración *f*

duress /djʊ'res/ *n*. **under ~** bajo coacción

during /'djʊərɪŋ/ *prep* durante

dusk /dʌsk/ *n* anochecer *m*

dust /dʌst/ *n* polvo *m*. ● *vt* quitar el polvo a; (*sprinkle*) espolvorear (**with** con). **~bin** *n* cubo *m* de la basura, bote *m* de la basura (*Mex*). **~ cloth** (*Amer*). **~er** *n* trapo *m*. **~jacket** *n* sobrecubierta *f*. **~man** /-mən/ *n* basurero *m*. **~pan** *n* recogedor *m*. **~y** *adj* (**-ier**, **-iest**) polvoriento

Dutch /dʌtʃ/ *adj* holandés. ● *n* (*language*) holandés *m*. **the ~** (*people*) los holandeses. **~man** /-mən/ *m* holandés *m*. **~woman** *n* holandesa *f*

duty /'dju:tɪ/ *n* deber *m*; (*tax*) derechos *mpl* de aduana. **on ~** de servicio. **~-free** /-'fri:/ *adj* libre de impuestos

duvet /'dju:veɪ/ *n* edredón *m*

DVD *abbr* (= **digital video disc**) DVD *m*

dwarf /dwɔ:f/ *n* (*pl* **-s** *or* **dwarves**) enano *m*

dwell /dwel/ *vi* (*pt* **dwelt** *or* **dwelled**) morar. □ **~ on** *vt* detenerse en. **~ing** *n* morada *f*

dwindle /'dwɪndl/ *vi* disminuir

dye /daɪ/ *vt* (*pres p* **dyeing**) teñir. ● *n* tinte *m*

dying /'daɪɪŋ/ *see* DIE

dynamic /daɪ'næmɪk/ *adj* dinámico. **~s** *npl* dinámica *f*

dynamite /'daɪnəmaɪt/ *n* dinamita *f*. ● *vt* dinamitar

dynamo /'daɪnəməʊ/ *n* (*pl* **-os**) dinamo *f*, dínamo *f*, dinamo *m* (*LAm*), dínamo *m* (*LAm*)

dynasty /'dɪnəstɪ/ *n* dinastía *f*

Ee

E *abbr* (= **East**) E

e

each /iːtʃ/ *adj* cada. ● *pron* cada uno. ~ **one** cada uno. ~ **other** uno a otro, el uno al otro. **they love ~ other** se aman

eager /ˈiːɡə(r)/ *adj* impaciente; (*enthusiastic*) ávido. ~**ness** *n* impaciencia *f*; (*enthusiasm*) entusiasmo *m*

eagle /ˈiːɡl/ *n* águila *f*

ear /ɪə(r)/ *n* oído *m*; (*outer*) oreja *f*; (*of corn*) espiga *f*. ~**ache** *n* dolor *m* de oído. ~**drum** *n* tímpano *m*

earl /ɜːl/ *n* conde *m*

early /ˈɜːlɪ/ *adj* (**-ier**, **-iest**) temprano; (*before expected time*) prematuro. ● *adv* temprano; (*ahead of time*) con anticipación

earn /ɜːn/ *vt* ganar; (*deserve*) merecer

earnest /ˈɜːnɪst/ *adj* serio. **in ~** en serio

earnings /ˈɜːnɪŋz/ *npl* ingresos *mpl*; (*Com*) ganancias *fpl*

ear: ~**phone** *n* audífono *m*. ~**ring** *n* pendiente *m*, arete *m* (*LAm*). ~**shot** *n*. **within ~shot** al alcance del oído

earth /ɜːθ/ *n* tierra *f*. **the E~** (*planet*) la Tierra. ● *vt* (*Elec*) conectar a tierra. ~**quake** *n* terremoto *m*

earwig /ˈɪəwɪɡ/ *n* tijereta *f*

ease /iːz/ *n* facilidad *f*; (*comfort*) tranquilidad *f*. **at ~** a gusto; (*Mil*) en posición de descanso. **ill at ~** molesto. **with ~** fácilmente. ● *vt* calmar; aliviar (pain). ● *vi* calmarse; (*lessen*) disminuir

easel /ˈiːzl/ *n* caballete *m*

easily /ˈiːzɪlɪ/ *adv* fácilmente

east /iːst/ *n* este *m*. ● *adj* este, oriental; (wind) del este. ● *adv* hacia el este.

Easter /ˈiːstə(r)/ *n* Semana *f* Santa; (*Relig*) Pascua *f* de Resurrección. ~ **egg** *n* huevo *m* de Pascua

east: ~**erly** /-əlɪ/ *adj* (wind) del este. ~**ern** /-ən/ *adj* este, oriental. ~**ward**/-wəd/, ~**wards** *adv* hacia el este

easy /ˈiːzɪ/ *adj* (**-ier**, **-iest**) fácil. ● *adv*. **go ~ on sth** [I] no pasarse con algo. **take it ~** tomarse las cosas con calma. ● *int* ¡despacio! ~ **chair** *n* sillón *m*. ~**going** /-ˈɡəʊɪŋ/ *adj* acomodadizo

eat /iːt/ *vt/i* (*pt* **ate**, *pp* **eaten**) comer. □ ~ **into** *vt* corroer. ~**er** *n* comedor *m*

eaves /iːvz/ *npl* alero *m*. ~**drop** *vi* (*pt* **-dropped**). ~**drop (on)** escuchar a escondidas

ebb /eb/ *n* reflujo *m*. ● *vi* bajar; (*fig*) decaer

ebola /iːˈbəʊlə/ *n* Ébola *m*

ebony /ˈebənɪ/ *n* ébano *m*

EC /iːˈsiː/ *abbr* (= **European Community**) CE *f* (Comunidad *f* Europea)

eccentric /ɪkˈsentrɪk/ *adj* & *n* excéntrico (*m*). ~**ity** /eksenˈtrɪsətɪ/ *n* excentricidad *f*

echo /ˈekəʊ/ *n* (*pl* **-oes**) eco *m*. ● *vi* hacer eco

eclipse /ɪˈklɪps/ *n* eclipse *m*. ● *vt* eclipsar

ecolog|ical /iːkəˈlɒdʒɪkl/ *adj* ecológico. ~**y** *n* ecología *f*

e-commerce /iːˈkɒmɜːs/ *n* comercio *m* electrónico

econom|ic /iːkəˈnɒmɪk/ *adj* económico; ~ **refugee** refugiado *m* económico. **~ical** *adj* económico. **~ics** *n* economía *f*. **~ist** /ɪ'kɒnəmɪst/ *n* economista *m & f*. **~ize** /ɪ'kɒnəmaɪz/ *vi* economizar. **~ize on sth** economizar algo. **~y** /ɪ'kɒnəmɪ/ *n* economía *f*

ecsta|sy /'ekstəsɪ/ *n* éxtasis *f*. **~tic** /ɪk'stætɪk/ *adj* extático

Ecuador /'ekwədɔ:(r)/ *n* Ecuador *m*. **~ean** /ekwə'dɔ:rɪən/ *adj & n* ecuatoriano (*m*)

edg|e /edʒ/ *n* borde *m*; (*of knife*) filo *m*; (*of town*) afueras *fpl*. **have the ~e on** 🅸 llevar la ventaja a. **on ~e** nervioso. • *vt* ribetear. • *vi* avanzar cautelosamente. **~eways** *adv* de lado. **~y** *adj* nervioso

edible /'edɪbl/ *adj* comestible

edit /'edɪt/ *vt* dirigir (newspaper); preparar una edición de (text); editar (film). **~ion** /ɪ'dɪʃn/ *n* edición *f*. **~or** *n* (*of newspaper*) director *m*; (*of text*) redactor *m*. **~orial** /edɪ'tɔ:rɪəl/ *adj* editorial. • *n* artículo *m* de fondo

Edinburgh Festival Es el principal acontecimiento cultural británico que, desde 1947, se celebra en agosto, en la capital de Escocia. El festival atrae a un gran número de visitantes y un aspecto muy importante del mismo son los espectáculos que no forman parte del programa oficial, que se conocen como *the Fringe*.

educat|e /'edʒʊkeɪt/ *vt* educar. **~ed** *adj* culto. **~ion** /-'keɪʃn/ *n* educación *f*; (*knowledge, culture*) cultura *f*. **~ional** /-'keɪʃənl/ *adj* instructivo

EC /i:i:'si:/ *abbr* (= **European Commission**) CE *f* (Comisión *f* Europea)

eel /i:l/ *n* anguila *f*

eerie /'ɪərɪ/ *adj* (**-ier, -iest**) misterioso

effect /ɪ'fekt/ *n* efecto *m*. **in ~** efectivamente. **take ~** entrar en vigor. **~ive** *adj* eficaz; (*striking*) impresionante; (*real*) efectivo. **~ively** *adv* eficazmente. **~iveness** *n* eficacia *f*

effeminate /ɪ'femɪnət/ *adj* afeminado

efficien|cy /ɪ'fɪʃənsɪ/ *n* eficiencia *f*; (*Mec*) rendimiento *m*. **~t** *adj* eficiente. **~tly** *adv* eficientemente

effort /'efət/ *n* esfuerzo *m*. **~less** *adj* fácil

e.g. /i:'dʒi:/ *abbr* (= **exempli gratia**) p.ej., por ejemplo

egg /eg/ *n* huevo *m*. □ **~ on** *vt* 🅸 incitar. **~cup** *n* huevera *f*. **~plant** *n* (*Amer*) berenjena *f*. **~shell** *n* cáscara *f* de huevo

ego /'i:gəʊ/ *n* (*pl* **-os**) yo *m*. **~ism** *n* egoísmo *m*. **~ist** *n* egoísta *m & f*. **~centric** /i:gəʊ'sentrɪk/ *adj* egocéntrico. **~tism** *n* egotismo *m*. **~tist** *n* egotista *m & f*

eh /eɪ/ *int* 🅸 ¡eh!

eiderdown /'aɪdədaʊn/ *n* edredón *m*

eight /eɪt/ *adj & n* ocho (*m*). **~een** /eɪ'ti:n/ *adj & n* dieciocho (*m*). **~eenth** *adj* decimoctavo. • *n* dieciochavo *m*. **~h** /eɪtθ/ *adj & n* octavo (*m*) **~ieth** /'eɪtɪəθ/ *adj* octogésimo. • *n* ochentavo *m*. **~y** /'eɪtɪ/ *adj & n* ochenta (*m*)

either /'aɪðə(r)/ *adj* cualquiera de los dos; (*negative*) ninguno de los dos; (*each*) cada. • *pron* uno u otro; (*with negative*) ni uno ni otro. • *adv* (*negative*) tampoco. • *conj* o. ~

Tuesday or Wednesday o el martes o el miércoles; (*with negative*) ni el martes ni el miércoles

eject /ɪ'dʒekt/ *vt* expulsar

eke /i:k/ *vt*. ~ **out** hacer alcanzar (resources). ~ **out a living** ganarse la vida a duras penas

e

elaborate /ɪ'læbərət/ *adj* complicado. •/ɪ'læbəreɪt/ *vt* elaborar. •/ɪ'læbəreɪt/ *vi* explicarse

elapse /ɪ'læps/ *vi* transcurrir

elastic /ɪ'læstɪk/ *adj* & *n* elástico (*m*). ~ **band** *n* goma *f* (elástica), liga *f* (*Mex*)

elat|ed /ɪ'leɪtɪd/ *adj* regocijado. ~**ion** /-ʃn/ *n* regocijo *m*

elbow /'elbəʊ/ *n* codo *m*. •*vt* dar un codazo a

elder /'eldə(r)/ *adj* mayor. •*n* mayor *m* & *f*; (*tree*) saúco *m*. ~**ly** /'eldəlɪ/ *adj* mayor, anciano

eldest /'eldɪst/ *adj* & *n* mayor (*m* & *f*)

elect /ɪ'lekt/ *vt* elegir. ~ **to do** decidir hacer. •*adj* electo. ~**ion** /-ʃn/ *n* elección *f*. ~**or** *n* elector *m*. ~**oral** *adj* electoral. ~**orate** /-ət/ *n* electorado *m*

electric /ɪ'lektrɪk/ *adj* eléctrico. ~**al** *adj* eléctrico. ~ **blanket** *n* manta *f* eléctrica. ~**ian** /ɪlek'trɪʃn/ *n* electricista *m* & *f*. ~**ity** /ɪlek'trɪsətɪ/ *n* electricidad *f*

electrify /ɪ'lektrɪfaɪ/ *vt* electrificar; (*fig*) electrizar

electrocute /ɪ'lektrəkju:t/ *vt* electrocutar

electrode /ɪ'lektrəʊd/ *n* electrodo *m*

electron /ɪ'lektrɒn/ *n* electrón *m*

electronic /ɪlek'trɒnɪk/ *adj* electrónico. ~ **mail** *n* correo *m* electrónico. ~**s** *n* electrónica *f*

elegan|ce /'elɪgəns/ *n* elegancia *f*. ~**t** *adj* elegante. ~**tly** *adv* elegantemente

element /'elɪmənt/ *n* elemento *m*. ~**ary** /-'mentrɪ/ *adj* elemental. ~**ary school** *n* (*Amer*) escuela *f* primaria

elephant /'elɪfənt/ *n* elefante *m*

elevat|e /'elɪveɪt/ *vt* elevar. ~**ion** /-'veɪʃn/ *n* elevación *f*. ~**or** *n* (*Amer*) ascensor *m*

eleven /ɪ'levn/ *adj* & *n* once (*m*). ~**th** *adj* undécimo. •*n* onceavo *m*

elf /elf/ *n* (*pl* **elves**) duende *m*

eligible /'elɪdʒəbl/ *adj* elegible. **be** ~ **for** tener derecho a

eliminat|e /ɪ'lɪmɪneɪt/ *vt* eliminar. ~**ion** /-'neɪʃn/ *n* eliminación *f*

élite /eɪ'li:t/ *n* elite *f*, élite *f*

ellip|se /ɪ'lɪps/ *n* elipse *f*. ~**tical** *adj* elíptico

elm /elm/ *n* olmo *m*

elope /ɪ'ləʊp/ *vi* fugarse con el amante

eloquen|ce /'eləkwəns/ *n* elocuencia *f*. ~**t** *adj* elocuente

El Salvador /el'sælvədɔ:(r)/ *n* El Salvador

else /els/ *adv*. **somebody** ~ otra persona. **everybody** ~ todos los demás. **nobody** ~ ningún otro, nadie más. **nothing** ~ nada más. **or** ~ o bien. **somewhere** ~ en otra parte. ~**where** *adv* en otra parte

elu|de /ɪ'lu:d/ *vt* eludir. ~**sive** /-sɪv/ *adj* esquivo

elves /elvz/ *see* ELF

emaciated /ɪ'meɪʃɪeɪtɪd/ *adj* consumido

email, e-mail /'i:meɪl/ *n* correo *m* electrónico, correo-e *m*. •*vt* mandar por correo electrónico, emailear. ~ **address** *n* casilla *f* electrónica, dirección *f* de correo

electrónico
emancipat|e /ɪ'mænsɪpeɪt/ *vt* emancipar. **~ion** /-'peɪʃn/ *n* emancipación *f*
embankment /ɪm'bæŋkmənt/ *n* terraplén *m*; (*of river*) dique *m*
embargo /ɪm'bɑ:gəʊ/ *n* (*pl* **-oes**) embargo *m*
embark /ɪm'bɑ:k/ *vi* embarcarse. **~ on** (*fig*) emprender. **~ation** /embɑ:'keɪʃn/ *n* embarque *m*
embarrass /ɪm'bærəs/ *vt* avergonzar. **~ed** *adj* avergonzado. **~ing** *adj* embarazoso. **~ment** *n* vergüenza *f*
embassy /'embəsɪ/ *n* embajada *f*
embellish /ɪm'belɪʃ/ *vt* adornar. **~ment** *n* adorno *m*
embers /'embəz/ *npl* ascuas *fpl*
embezzle /ɪm'bezl/ *vt* desfalcar. **~ment** *n* desfalco *m*
emblem /'embləm/ *n* emblema *m*
embrace /ɪm'breɪs/ *vt* abrazar; (*fig*) abarcar. •*vi* abrazarse. •*n* abrazo *m*
embroider /ɪm'brɔɪdə(r)/ *vt* bordar. **~y** *n* bordado *m*
embroil /ɪm'brɔɪl/ *vt* enredar
embryo /'embrɪəʊ/ *n* (*pl* **-os**) embrión *m*. **~nic** /-'ɒnɪk/ *adj* embrionario
emend /ɪ'mend/ *vt* enmendar
emerald /'emərəld/ *n* esmeralda *f*
emerge /ɪ'mɜ:dʒ/ *vi* salir. **~nce** /-əns/ *n* aparición *f*
emergency /ɪ'mɜ:dʒənsɪ/ *n* emergencia *f*; (*Med*) urgencia *f*. **in an ~** en caso de emergencia. **~ exit** *n* salida *f* de emergencia. **~ room** urgencias *fpl*
emigra|nt /'emɪgrənt/ *n* emigrante *m & f*. **~te** /'emɪgreɪt/ *vi* emigrar. **~tion** /-'greɪʃn/ *n* emigración *f*
eminen|ce /'emɪnəns/ *n* eminencia *f*. **~t** *adj* eminente.
emi|ssion /ɪ'mɪʃn/ *n* emisión *f*. **~t** *vt* (*pt* **emitted**) emitir
emoti|on /ɪ'məʊʃn/ *n* emoción *f*. **~onal** *adj* emocional; (person) emotivo; (*moving*) conmovedor. **~ve** /ɪ'məʊtɪv/ *adj* emotivo
empathy /'empəθɪ/ *n* empatía *f*
emperor /'empərə(r)/ *n* emperador *m*
empha|sis /'emfəsɪs/ *n* (*pl* **~ses** /-si:z/) énfasis *m*. **~size** /'emfəsaɪz/ *vt* enfatizar. **~tic** /ɪm'fætɪk/ *adj* (gesture) enfático; (assertion) categórico
empire /'empaɪə(r)/ *n* imperio *m*
empirical /ɪm'pɪrɪkl/ *adj* empírico
employ /ɪm'plɔɪ/ *vt* emplear. **~ee** /emplɔɪ'i:/ *n* empleado *m*. **~er** *n* patrón *m*. **~ment** *n* empleo *m*. **~ment agency** *n* agencia *f* de trabajo
empower /ɪm'paʊə(r)/ *vt* autorizar (**to do** a hacer)
empress /'emprɪs/ *n* emperatriz *f*
empty /'emptɪ/ *adj* vacío; (promise) vano. **on an ~y stomach** con el estómago vacío. •*n* ⓘ envase *m* (vacío). •*vt* vaciar. •*vi* vaciarse
emulate /'emjʊleɪt/ *vt* emular
emulsion /ɪ'mʌlʃn/ *n* emulsión *f*
enable /ɪ'neɪbl/ *vt*. **~ s.o. to do sth** permitir a uno hacer algo
enact /ɪ'nækt/ *vt* (*Jurid*) decretar; (*in theatre*) representar
enamel /ɪ'næml/ *n* esmalte *m*. •*vt* (*pt* **enamelled**) esmaltar
enchant /ɪn'tʃɑ:nt/ *vt* encantar. **~ing** *adj* encantador. **~ment** *n* encanto *m*
encircle /ɪn'sɜ:kl/ *vt* rodear

enclave /ˈenkleɪv/ *n* enclave *m*

enclos|e /ɪnˈkləʊz/ *vt* cercar (land); (*Com*) adjuntar. **~ed** *adj* (space) cerrado; (*Com*) adjunto. **~ure** /ɪnˈkləʊʒə(r)/ *n* cercamiento *m*

encode /ɪnˈkəʊd/ *vt* codificar, cifrar

e

encore /ˈɒŋkɔː(r)/ *int* ¡otra! ● *n* bis *m*, repetición *f*

encounter /ɪnˈkaʊntə(r)/ *vt* encontrar. ● *n* encuentro *m*

encourag|e /ɪnˈkʌrɪdʒ/ *vt* animar; (*stimulate*) fomentar. **~ement** *n* ánimo *m*. **~ing** *adj* alentador

encroach /ɪnˈkrəʊtʃ/ *vi*. **~ on** invadir (land); quitar (time)

encyclopaedi|a /ɪnsaɪkləˈpiːdɪə/ *n* enciclopedia *f*. **~c** *adj* enciclopédico

end /end/ *n* fin *m*; (*furthest point*) extremo *m*. **in the ~** por fin. **make ~s meet** poder llegar a fin de mes. **put an ~ to** poner fin a. **no ~ of** muchísimos. **on ~** de pie; (*consecutive*) seguido. ● *vt/i* terminar, acabar

endanger /ɪnˈdeɪndʒə(r)/ *vt* poner en peligro. **~ed** *adj* (species) en peligro

endearing /ɪnˈdɪərɪŋ/ *adj* simpático

endeavour /ɪnˈdevə(r)/ *n* esfuerzo *m*, intento *m*. ● *vi*. **~ to** esforzarse por

ending /ˈendɪŋ/ *n* fin *m*

endless /ˈendlɪs/ *adj* interminable

endorse /ɪnˈdɔːs/ *vt* endosar; (*fig*) aprobar. **~ment** *n* endoso *m*; (*fig*) aprobación *f*; (*Auto*) nota *f* de inhabilitación

endur|ance /ɪnˈdjʊərəns/ *n* resistencia *f*. **~e** /ɪnˈdjʊə(r)/ *vt* aguantar. **~ing** *adj* perdurable

enemy /ˈenəmɪ/ *n & a* enemigo (*m*)

energ|etic /enəˈdʒetɪk/ *adj* enérgico. **~y** /ˈenədʒɪ/ *n* energía *f*. **~y-efficient** *adj* energéticamente eficiente

enforce /ɪnˈfɔːs/ *vt* hacer cumplir (law); hacer valer (claim). **~d** *adj* forzado

engag|e /ɪnˈgeɪdʒ/ *vt* emplear (staff); captar (attention); (*Mec*) hacer engranar. ● *vi* (*Mec*) engranar. **~e in** dedicarse a. **~ed** *adj* prometido, comprometido (*LAm*); (*busy*) ocupado. **be ~ed** (*of phone*) estar comunicando, estar ocupado (*LAm*). **get ~ed** prometerse, comprometerse (*LAm*). **~ement** *n* compromiso *m*

engine /ˈendʒɪn/ *n* motor *m*; (*of train*) locomotora *f*. **~ driver** *n* maquinista *m*

engineer /endʒɪˈnɪə(r)/ *n* ingeniero *m*; (*mechanic*) mecánico *m*; (*Amer, Rail*) maquinista *m*. ● *vt* (*contrive*) fraguar. **~ing** *n* ingeniería *f*

England /ˈɪŋglənd/ *n* Inglaterra *f*

English /ˈɪŋglɪʃ/ *adj* inglés. ● *n* (*language*) inglés *m*. ● *npl*. **the ~** los ingleses. **~man** /-mən/ *n* inglés *m*. **~woman** *n* inglesa *f*

engrav|e /ɪnˈgreɪv/ *vt* grabar. **~ing** *n* grabado *m*

engrossed /ɪnˈgrəʊst/ *adj* absorto

engulf /ɪnˈgʌlf/ *vt* envolver

enhance /ɪnˈhɑːns/ *vt* realzar; aumentar (value)

enigma /ɪˈnɪgmə/ *n* enigma *m*. **~tic** /enɪgˈmætɪk/ *adj* enigmático

enjoy /ɪnˈdʒɔɪ/ *vt*. **I ~ reading** me gusta la lectura. **~ o.s.** divertirse. **~able** *adj* agradable. **~ment** *n* placer *m*

enlarge /ɪnˈlɑːdʒ/ *vt* agrandar;

(*Photo*) ampliar. ● *vi* agrandarse. ~ **upon** extenderse sobre. ~**ment** *n* (*Photo*) ampliación *f*

enlighten /ɪn'laɪtn/ *vt* ilustrar. ~**ment** *n*. **the E~ment** el siglo de la luces

enlist /ɪn'lɪst/ *vt* alistar; conseguir (support). ● *vi* alistarse

enliven /ɪn'laɪvn/ *vt* animar

enorm|ity /ɪ'nɔ:mətɪ/ *n* enormidad *f*. ~**ous** /ɪ'nɔ:məs/ *adj* enorme. ~**ously** *adv* enormemente

enough /ɪ'nʌf/ *adj & adv* bastante. ● *n* bastante *m*, suficiente *m*. ● *int* ¡basta!

enquir|e /ɪn'kwaɪə(r)/ *vt/i* preguntar. ~**e about** informarse de. ~**y** *n* pregunta *f*; (*investigation*) investigación *f*

enrage /ɪn'reɪdʒ/ *vt* enfurecer

enrol /ɪn'rəʊl/ *vt* (*pt* **enrolled**) inscribir, matricular (student). ● *vi* inscribirse, matricularse

ensue /ɪn'sju:/ *vi* seguir

ensure /ɪn'ʃʊə(r)/ *vt* asegurar

entail /ɪn'teɪl/ *vt* suponer; acarrear (expense)

entangle /ɪn'tæŋgl/ *vt* enredar. ~**ment** *n* enredo *m*

enter /'entə(r)/ *vt* entrar en, entrar a (*esp LAm*); presentarse a (competition); inscribirse en (race); (*write*) escribir. ● *vi* entrar

enterpris|e /'entəpraɪz/ *n* empresa *f*; (*fig*) iniciativa *f*. ~**ing** *adj* emprendedor

entertain /entə'teɪn/ *vt* entretener; recibir (guests); abrigar (ideas, hopes); (*consider*) considerar. ~**ing** *adj* entretenido. ~**ment** *n* entretenimiento *m*; (*show*) espectáculo *m*

enthral /ɪn'θrɔ:l/ *vt* (*pt* **enthralled**) cautivar

enthuse /ɪn'θju:z/ *vi*. ~ **over** entusiasmarse por

enthusias|m /ɪn'θju:zɪæzəm/ *n* entusiasmo *m*. ~**t** *n* entusiasta *m & f*. ~**tic** /-'æstɪk/ *adj* entusiasta. ~**tically** *adv* con entusiasmo

entice /ɪn'taɪs/ *vt* atraer

entire /ɪn'taɪə(r)/ *adj* entero. ~**ly** *adv* completamente. ~**ty** /ɪn'taɪərətɪ/ *n*. **in its ~ty** en su totalidad

entitle /ɪn'taɪtl/ *vt* titular; (*give a right*) dar derecho a. **be ~d to** tener derecho a. ~**ment** *n* derecho *m*

entity /'entətɪ/ *n* entidad *f*

entrails /'entreɪlz/ *npl* entrañas *fpl*

entrance /'entrəns/ *n* entrada *f*. ● /ɪn'trɑ:ns/ *vt* encantar

entrant /'entrənt/ *n* participante *m & f*; (*in exam*) candidato *m*

entreat /ɪn'tri:t/ *vt* suplicar. ~**y** *n* súplica *f*

entrenched /ɪn'trentʃt/ *adj* (position) afianzado

entrust /ɪn'trʌst/ *vt* confiar

entry /'entrɪ/ *n* entrada *f*

entwine /ɪn'twaɪn/ *vt* entrelazar

enumerate /ɪ'nju:məreɪt/ *vt* enumerar

envelop /ɪn'veləp/ *vt* envolver

envelope /'envələʊp/ *n* sobre *m*

enviable /'envɪəbl/ *adj* envidiable

envious /'envɪəs/ *adj* envidioso

environment /ɪn'vaɪərənmənt/ *n* medio *m* ambiente. ~**al** /-'mentl/ *adj* ambiental

envisage /ɪn'vɪzɪdʒ/ *vt* prever; (*imagine*) imaginar

envision /ɪn'vɪʒn/ *vt* (*Amer*) prever

envoy /'envɔɪ/ *n* enviado *m*

envy /'envɪ/ *n* envidia *f*. ● *vt* envidiar

enzyme /'enzaɪm/ *n* enzima *f*

ephemeral /ɪ'femərəl/ *adj*

efímero

epic /'epɪk/ *n* épica *f.* ●*adj* épico

epidemic /epɪ'demɪk/ *n* epidemia *f.* ●*adj* epidémico

epilep|sy /'epɪlepsɪ/ *n* epilepsia *f.* **~tic** /-'leptɪk/ *adj & n* epiléptico (*m*)

epilogue /'epɪlɒg/ *n* epílogo *m*

episode /'epɪsəʊd/ *n* episodio *m*

epitaph /'epɪtɑ:f/ *n* epitafio *m*

epitom|e /ɪ'pɪtəmɪ/ *n* personificación *f*, epítome *m*. **~ize** *vt* ser la personificación de

epoch /'i:pɒk/ *n* época *f*

equal /'i:kwəl/ *adj & n* igual (*m & f*). **~ to** (*a task*) a la altura de. ●*vt* (*pt* **equalled**) ser igual a; (*Math*) ser. **~ity** /ɪ'kwɒlətɪ/ *n* igualdad *f.* **~ize** *vt* igualar. ●*vi* (*Sport*) emapatar. **~izer** *n* (*Sport*) gol *m* del empate. **~ly** *adv* igualmente; (share) por igual

equation /ɪ'kweɪʒn/ *n* ecuación *f*

equator /ɪ'kweɪtə(r)/ *n* ecuador *m*. **~ial** /ekwə'tɔ:rɪəl/ *adj* ecuatorial

equilibrium /i:kwɪ'lɪbrɪəm/ *n* equilibrio *m*

equinox /'i:kwɪnɒks/ *n* equinoccio *m*

equip /ɪ'kwɪp/ *vt* (*pt* **equipped**) equipar. **~ sth with** proveer algo de. **~ment** *n* equipo *m*

equivalen|ce /ɪ'kwɪvələns/ *n* equivalencia *f.* **~t** *adj & n* equivalente (*m*). **be ~t to** equivaler

equivocal /ɪ'kwɪvəkl/ *adj* equívoco

era /'ɪərə/ *n* era *f*

eradicate /ɪ'rædɪkeɪt/ *vt* erradicar, extirpar

erase /ɪ'reɪz/ *vt* borrar. **~r** *n* goma *f* (de borrar)

erect /ɪ'rekt/ *adj* erguido. ●*vt* levantar. **~ion** /-ʃn/ *n* construcción *f*; (*physiology*) erección *f*

ero|de /ɪ'rəʊd/ *vt* erosionar. **~sion** /-ʒn/ *n* erosión *f*

erotic /ɪ'rɒtɪk/ *adj* erótico

err /ɜ:(r)/ *vi* errar; (*sin*) pecar

errand /'erənd/ *n* recado *m*, mandado *m* (*LAm*)

erratic /ɪ'rætɪk/ *adj* desigual; (person) voluble

erroneous /ɪ'rəʊnɪəs/ *adj* erróneo

error /'erə(r)/ *n* error *m*

erudit|e /'eru:daɪt/ *adj* erudito. **~ion** /-'dɪʃn/ *n* erudición *f*

erupt /ɪ'rʌpt/ *vi* entrar en erupción; (*fig*) estallar. **~ion** /-ʃn/ *n* erupción *f*

escalat|e /'eskəleɪt/ *vt* intensificar. ●*vi* intensificarse. **~ion** /-'leɪʃn/ *n* intensificación *f.* **~or** *n* escalera *f* mecánica

escapade /eskə'peɪd/ *n* aventura *f*

escap|e /ɪ'skeɪp/ *vi* escaparse. ●*vt* evitar. ●*n* fuga *f*; (*of gas, water*) escape *m*. **have a narrow ~e** escapar por un pelo. **~ism** /-ɪzəm/ *n* escapismo *m*

escort /'eskɔ:t/ *n* acompañante *m*; (*Mil*) escolta *f.* ●/ɪ'skɔ:t/ *vt* acompañar; (*Mil*) escoltar

Eskimo /'eskɪməʊ/ *n* (*pl* **-os** *or invar*) esquimal *m & f*

especial /ɪ'speʃl/ *adj* especial. **~ly** *adv* especialmente

espionage /'espɪənɑ:ʒ/ *n* espionaje *m*

Esq. /ɪ'skwaɪə(r)/ *abbr* (= **Esquire**) (*in address*) **E. Ashton, ~** Sr. Don E. Ashton

essay /'eseɪ/ *n* ensayo *m*; (*at school*) composición *f*

essence /'esns/ *n* esencia *f.* **in ~** esencialmente

essential /ɪ'senʃl/ *adj* esencial. ●*n* elemento *m* esencial. **~ly** *adv* esencialmente

establish /ɪ'stæblɪʃ/ *vt* establecer. **~ment** *n* establecimiento *m*. **the E~ment** los que mandan

estate /ɪ'steɪt/ *n* finca *f*; (*housing estate*) complejo *m* habitacional, urbanización *f*, fraccionamiento *m* (*Mex*); (*possessions*) bienes *mpl*. **~ agent** *n* agente *m* inmobiliario. **~ car** *n* ranchera *f*, (coche *m*) familiar *m*, camioneta *f* (*LAm*)

esteem /ɪ'sti:m/ *n* estima *f*

estimat|e /'estɪmət/ *n* cálculo *m*; (*Com*) presupuesto *m*. ●/'estɪmeɪt/ *vt* calcular. **~ion** /-'meɪʃn/ *n* estimación *f*; (*opinion*) opinión *f*

estranged /ɪs'treɪndʒd/ *adj* alejado

estuary /'estʃʊərɪ/ *n* estuario *m*

etc /et'setrə/ *abbr* (= **et cetera**) etc.

etching /'etʃɪŋ/ *n* aguafuerte *m*

etern|al /ɪ'tɜ:nl/ *adj* eterno. **~ity** /-ətɪ/ *n* eternidad *f*

ether /'i:θə(r)/ *n* éter *m*

ethic /'eθɪk/ *n* ética *f*. **~al** *adj* ético. **~s** *npl* ética *f*

ethnic /'eθnɪk/ *adj* étnico

etiquette /'etɪket/ *n* etiqueta *f*

etymology /etɪ'mɒlədʒɪ/ *n* etimología *f*

EU /i:'ju:/ *abbr* (**European Union**) UE (Unión Europea)

euphemism /'ju:fəmɪzəm/ *n* eufemismo *m*

euphoria /ju:'fɔ:rɪə/ *n* euforia *f*

euro /'jʊərəʊ/ *n* euro *m*

Europe /'jʊərəp/ *n* Europa *f*. **~an** /-'pɪən/ *adj & n* europeo (*m*). **~an Health Insurance Card** *n* Tarjeta *f* Sanitaria Europea. **~an Union** *n* Unión *f* Europea

euthanasia /ju:θə'neɪzɪə/ *n* eutanasia *f*

evacuat|e /ɪ'vækjʊeɪt/ *vt* evacuar; desocupar (building). **~ion** /-'eɪʃn/ *n* evacuación *f*

evade /ɪ'veɪd/ *vt* evadir

evalua|te /ɪ'væljʊeɪt/ *vt* evaluar. **~tion** /-'eɪʃn/ *vt* evaluación *f*

evangelical /i:væn'dʒelɪkl/ *adj* evangélico

evaporat|e /ɪ'væpəreɪt/ *vi* evaporarse. **~ion** /-'reɪʃn/ *n* evaporación *f*

evasi|on /ɪ'veɪʒn/ *n* evasión *f*. **~ve** /ɪ'veɪsɪv/ *adj* evasivo

eve /i:v/ *n* víspera *f*

even /'i:vn/ *adj* (*flat, smooth*) plano; (colour) uniforme; (distribution) equitativo; (number) par. **get ~ with** desquitarse con. ●*vt* nivelar. □ **~ up** *vt* equilibrar. ●*adv* aun, hasta, incluso. **~ if** aunque. **~ so** aun así. **not ~** ni siquiera

evening /'i:vnɪŋ/ *n* tarde *f*; (*after dark*) noche *f*. **~ class** *n* clase *f* nocturna

event /ɪ'vent/ *n* acontecimiento *m*; (*Sport*) prueba *f*. **in the ~ of** en caso de. **~ful** *adj* lleno de acontecimientos

eventual /ɪ'ventʃʊəl/ *adj* final, definitivo. **~ity** /-'ælətɪ/ *n* eventualidad *f*. **~ly** *adv* finalmente

ever /'evə(r)/ *adv* (*negative*) nunca, jamás; (*at all times*) siempre. **have you ~ been to Greece?** ¿has estado (alguna vez) en Grecia?. **~ after** desde entonces. **~ since** desde entonces. **~ so** [!] muy. **for ~** para siempre. **hardly ~** casi nunca. **~green** *adj* de hoja perenne. ●*n* árbol *m* de hoja perenne. **~lasting** *adj* eterno.

every /'evrɪ/ *adj* cada, todo. **~**

child todos los niños. **~ one** cada uno. **~ other day** un día sí y otro no. **~body** *pron* todos, todo el mundo. **~day** *adj* de todos los días. **~one** *pron* todos, todo el mundo. **~thing** *pron* todo. **~where** *adv* (*be*) en todas partes, (*go*) a todos lados

evict /ɪ'vɪkt/ *vt* desahuciar. **~ion** /-ʃn/ *n* desahucio *m*

eviden|ce /'evɪdəns/ *n* evidencia *f*; (*proof*) pruebas *fpl*; (*Jurid*) testimonio *m*; **give ~ce** prestar declaración. **~ce of** señales de. **in ~ce** visible. **~t** *adj* evidente. **~tly** *adv* evidentemente

evil /'i:vl/ *adj* malvado. ● *n* mal *m*

evo|cative /ɪ'vɒkətɪv/ *adj* evocador. **~ke** /ɪ'vəʊk/ *vt* evocar

evolution /i:və'lu:ʃn/ *n* evolución *f*

evolve /ɪ'vɒlv/ *vt* desarrollar. ● *vi* evolucionar

ewe /ju:/ *n* oveja *f*

exact /ɪg'zækt/ *adj* exacto. ● *vt* exigir (**from** a). **~ing** *adj* exigente. **~ly** *adv* exactamente

exaggerat|e /ɪg'zædʒəreɪt/ *vt* exagerar. **~ion** /-'reɪʃn/ *n* exageración *f*

exam /ɪg'zæm/ *n* examen *m*. **~ination** /ɪgzæmɪ'neɪʃn/ *n* examen *m*. **~ine** /ɪg'zæmɪn/ *vt* examinar; interrogar (witness). **~iner** *n* examinador *m*

example /ɪg'zɑ:mpl/ *n* ejemplo *m*. **for ~** por ejemplo. **make an ~ of s.o.** darle un castigo ejemplar a uno

exasperat|e /ɪg'zæspəreɪt/ *vt* exasperar. **~ing** *adj* exasperante. **~ion** /-'reɪʃn/ *n* exasperación *f*

excavat|e /'ekskəveɪt/ *vt* excavar. **~ion** /-'veɪʃn/ *n* excavación *f*

exceed /ɪk'si:d/ *vt* exceder. **~ingly** *adv* sumamente

excel /ɪk'sel/ *vi* (*pt* **excelled**) sobresalir. ● *vt*. **~ o.s.** lucirse. **~lence** /'eksələns/ *n* excelencia *f*. **~lent** *adj* excelente

except /ɪk'sept/ *prep* menos, excepto. **~ for** si no fuera por. ● *vt* exceptuar. **~ing** *prep* con excepción de

exception /ɪk'sepʃən/ *n* excepción *f*. **take ~ to** ofenderse por. **~al** *adj* excepcional. **~ally** *adv* excepcionalmente

excerpt /'eksɜ:pt/ *n* extracto *m*

excess /ɪk'ses/ *n* exceso *m*. ● /'ekses/ *adj* excedente. **~ fare** suplemento *m*. **~ luggage** exceso *m* de equipaje. **~ive** *adj* excesivo

exchange /ɪk'stʃeɪndʒ/ *vt* cambiar. ● *n* intercambio *m*; (*of money*) cambio *m*. **(telephone) ~** central *f* telefónica

excise /'eksaɪz/ *n* impuestos *mpl* interos. ● /ek'saɪz/ *vt* quitar

excit|able /ɪk'saɪtəbl/ *adj* excitable. **~e** /ɪk'saɪt/ *vt* emocionar; (*stimulate*) excitar. **~ed** *adj* entusiasmado. **get ~ed** entusiasmarse. **~ement** *n* emoción *f*; (*enthusiasm*) entusiasmo *m*. **~ing** *adj* emocionante

excla|im /ɪk'skleɪm/ *vi/t* exclamar. **~mation** /eksklə'meɪʃn/ *n* exclamación *f*. **~mation mark** *n* signo *m* de admiración *f*

exclu|de /ɪk'sklu:d/ *vt* excluir. **~sion** /-ʒən/ *n* exclusión *f*. **~sive** /ɪk'sklu:sɪv/ *adj* exclusivo; (club) selecto. **~sive of** excluyendo. **~sively** *adv* exclusivamente

excruciating /ɪk'skru:ʃɪeɪtɪŋ/ *adj* atroz, insoportable

excursion /ɪk'skɜ:ʃn/ *n* excursión *f*

excus|able /ɪk'skju:zəbl/ *adj* perdonable. **~e** /ɪk'skju:z/ *vt* perdonar. **~e from** dispensar de. **~e me!** ¡perdón! ● /ɪk'skju:s/ *n* excusa *f*

ex-directory /eksdɪ'rektərɪ/ *adj* que no figura en la guía telefónica, privado (*Mex*)

execut|e /'eksɪkju:t/ *vt* ejecutar. **~ion** /eksɪ'kju:ʃn/ *n* ejecución *f*. **~ioner** *n* verdugo *m*

executive /ɪg'zekjʊtɪv/ *adj & n* ejecutivo (*m*)

exempt /ɪg'zempt/ *adj* exento (from de). ● *vt* dispensar. **~ion** /-ʃn/ *n* exención *f*

exercise /'eksəsaɪz/ *n* ejercicio *m*. ● *vt* ejercer. ● *vi* hacer ejercicio. **~ book** *n* cuaderno *m*

exert /ɪg'zɜ:t/ *vt* ejercer. **~ o.s.** hacer un gran esfuerzo. **~ion** /-ʃn/ *n* esfuerzo *m*

exhale /eks'heɪl/ *vt/i* exhalar

exhaust /ɪg'zɔ:st/ *vt* agotar. ● *n* (*Auto*) tubo *m* de escape. **~ed** *adj* agotado. **~ion** /-stʃən/ *n* agotamiento *m*. **~ive** *adj* exhaustivo

exhibit /ɪg'zɪbɪt/ *vt* exponer; (*fig*) mostrar. ● *n* objeto *m* expuesto; (*Jurid*) documento *m*. **~ion** /eksɪ'bɪʃn/ *n* exposición. **~ionist** *n* exhibicionista *m & f*. **~or** /ɪg'zɪbɪtə(r)/ *n* expositor *m*

exhilarat|ing /ɪg'zɪləreɪtɪŋ/ *adj* excitante. **~ion** /-'reɪʃn/ *n* regocijo *m*

exhort /ɪg'zɔ:t/ *vt* exhortar

exile /'eksaɪl/ *n* exilio *m*; (*person*) exiliado *m*. ● *vt* desterrar

exist /ɪg'zɪst/ *vi* existir. **~ence** *n* existencia *f*. **in ~ence** existente

exit /'eksɪt/ *n* salida *f*

exorbitant /ɪg'zɔ:bɪtənt/ *adj* exorbitante

exorcis|e /'eksɔ:saɪz/ *vt* exorcizar. **~m** /-sɪzəm/ *n* exorcismo *m*. **~t** *n* exorcista *m & f*

exotic /ɪg'zɒtɪk/ *adj* exótico

expand /ɪk'spænd/ *vt* expandir; (*develop*) desarrollar. ● *vi* expandirse

expanse /ɪk'spæns/ *n* extensión *f*

expansion /ɪk'spænʃn/ *n* expansión *f*

expatriate /eks'pætrɪət/ *adj & n* expatriado (*m*)

expect /ɪk'spekt/ *vt* esperar; (*suppose*) suponer; (*demand*) contar con. **I ~ so** supongo que sí. **~ancy** *n* esperanza *f*. **life ~ancy** esperanza *f* de vida. **~ant** *adj* expectante. **~ant mother** *n* futura madre *f*

expectation /ekspek'teɪʃn/ *n* expectativa *f*

expedient /ɪk'spi:dɪənt/ *adj* conveniente. ● *n* expediente *m*

expedition /ekspɪ'dɪʃn/ *n* expedición *f*

expel /ɪk'spel/ *vt* (*pt* **expelled**) expulsar

expend /ɪk'spend/ *vt* gastar. **~able** *adj* prescindible. **~iture** /-ɪtʃə(r)/ *n* gastos *mpl*

expens|e /ɪk'spens/ *n* gasto *m*. **at s.o.'s ~e** a costa de uno. **~es** *npl* (*Com*) gastos *mpl*. **~ive** *adj* caro

experience /ɪk'spɪərɪəns/ *n* experiencia. ● *vt* experimentar. **~d** *adj* con experiencia; (driver) experimentado

experiment /ɪk'sperɪmənt/ *n* experimento *m*. ● *vi* experimentar. **~al** /-'mentl/ *adj* experimental

expert /'ekspɜ:t/ *adj & n* experto (*m*). **~ise** /ekspɜ:'ti:z/ *n* pericia *f*. **~ly** *adv* hábilmente

expir|e /ɪk'spaɪə(r)/ *vi* (passport, ticket) caducar; (contract) vencer. **~y** *n* vencimiento *m*, caducidad *f*

expla|in /ɪk'spleɪn/ *vt* explicar. **~nation** /eksplə'neɪʃn/ *n* explicación *f*. **~natory** /ɪks'plænətərɪ/ *adj* explicativo

e

explicit /ɪk'splɪsɪt/ *adj* explícito

explode /ɪk'spləʊd/ *vt* hacer explotar. ● *vi* estallar

exploit /'eksplɔɪt/ *n* hazaña *f*. ● /ɪk'splɔɪt/ *vt* explotar. **~ation** /eksplɔɪ'teɪʃn/ *n* explotación *f*

explor|ation /eksplə'reɪʃn/ *n* exploración *f*. **~atory** /ɪk'splɒrətrɪ/ *adj* exploratorio. **~e** /ɪk'splɔ:(r)/ *vt* explorar. **~er** *n* explorador *m*

explosi|on /ɪk'spləʊʒn/ *n* explosión *f*. **~ve** /-sɪv/ *adj & n* explosivo (*m*)

export /ɪk'spɔ:t/ *vt* exportar. ● /'ekspɔ:t/ *n* exportación *f*; (*item*) artículo *m* de exportación. **~er** /ɪks'pɔ:tə(r)/ exportador *m*

expos|e /ɪk'spəʊz/ *vt* exponer; (*reveal*) descubrir. **~ure** /-ʒə(r)/ *n* exposición *f*. **die of ~ure** morir de frío

express /ɪk'spres/ *vt* expresar. ● *adj* expreso; (letter) urgente. ● *adv* (*by express post*) por correo urgente. ● *n* (*train*) rápido *m*, expreso *m*. **~ion** *n* expresión *f*. **~ive** *adj* expresivo. **~ly** *adv* expresadamente. **~way** *n* (*Amer*) autopista *f*

expulsion /ɪk'spʌlʃn/ *n* expulsión *f*

exquisite /'ekskwɪzɪt/ *adj* exquisito

exten|d /ɪk'stend/ *vt* extender; (*prolong*) prolongar; ampliar (house). ● *vi* extenderse. **~sion** /-ʃn/ *n* extensión *f*; (*of road, time*) prolongación *f*; (*building*) anejo *m*. **~sive** /-sɪv/ *adj* extenso. **~sively** *adv* extensamente. **~t** *n* extensión *f*; (*fig*) alcance. **to a certain ~t** hasta cierto punto

exterior /ɪk'stɪərɪə(r)/ *adj & n* exterior (*m*)

exterminat|e /ɪk'stɜ:mɪneɪt/ *vt* exterminar. **~ion** /-'neɪʃn/ *n* exterminio *m*

external /ɪk'stɜ:nl/ *adj* externo

extinct /ɪk'stɪŋkt/ *adj* extinto. **~ion** /-ʃn/ *n* extinción *f*

extinguish /ɪk'stɪŋgwɪʃ/ *vt* extinguir. **~er** *n* extintor *m*, extinguidor *m* (*LAm*)

extol /ɪk'stəʊl/ *vt* (*pt* **extolled**) alabar

extort /ɪk'stɔ:t/ *vt* sacar por la fuerza. **~ion** /-ʃn/ *n* exacción *f*. **~ionate** /-ənət/ *adj* exorbitante

extra /'ekstrə/ *adj* de más. ● *adv* extraordinariamente. ● *n* suplemento *m*; (*Cinema*) extra *m & f*

extract /'ekstrækt/ *n* extracto *m*. ● /ɪk'strækt/ *vt* extraer. **~ion** /ɪk'strækʃn/ *n* extracción *f*

extradit|e /'ekstrədaɪt/ *vt* extraditar. **~ion** /-'dɪʃn/ *n* extradición *f*

extra: ~ordinary /ɪk'strɔ:dnrɪ/ *adj* extraordinario. **~-sensory** /ekstrə'sensərɪ/ *adj* extrasensorial

extravagan|ce /ɪk'strævəgəns/ *n* prodigalidad *f*; (*of gestures, dress*) extravagancia *f*. **~t** *adj* pródigo; (behaviour) extravagante. **~za** *n* gran espectáculo *m*

extrem|e /ɪk'stri:m/ *adj & n* extremo (*m*). **~ely** *adv* extremadamente. **~ist** *n* extremista *m & f*

extricate /'ekstrɪkeɪt/ *vt* desenredar, librar

extrovert /'ekstrəvɜ:t/ *n* extrovertido *m*

exuberan|ce /ɪg'zju:bərəns/ *n*

exuberancia *f.* **~t** *adj* exuberante

exude /ɪɡ'zjuːd/ *vt* rezumar

exult /ɪɡ'zʌlt/ *vi* exultar. **~ation** /egzʌl'teɪʃn/ *n* exultación *f*

eye /aɪ/ *n* ojo m. **keep an ~ on** no perder de vista. **see ~ to ~ with s.o.** estar de acuerdo con uno. ● *vt* (*pt* **eyed**, *pres p* **eyeing**) mirar. **~ball** *n* globo *m* ocular. **~brow** *n* ceja *f.* **~drops** *npl* colirio *m.* **~lash** *n* pestaña *f.* **~lid** *n* párpado *m.* **~-opener** *n* 🅘 revelación *f.* **~-shadow** *n* sombra *f* de ojos. **~sight** *n* vista *f.* **~sore** *n* (*fig, fam*) monstruosidad *f*, adefesio *m.* **~witness** *n* testigo *m* ocular

Ff

fable /'feɪbl/ *n* fábula *f*

fabric /'fæbrɪk/ *n* tejido *m*, tela *f*

fabricate /'fæbrɪkeɪt/ *vt* inventar. **~ation** /-'keɪʃn/ *n* invención *f*

fabulous /'fæbjʊləs/ *adj* fabuloso

facade /fə'sɑːd/ *n* fachada *f*

face /feɪs/ *n* cara *f*, rostro *m*; (*of watch*) esfera *f*, carátula *f* (*Mex*); (*aspect*) aspecto *m.* **~ down(wards)** boca abajo. **~ up(wards)** boca arriba. **in the ~ of** frente a. **lose ~** quedar mal. **pull ~s** hacer muecas. ● *vt* mirar hacia; (house) dar a; (*confront*) enfrentarse con. ● *vi* volverse. □ **~ up to** *vt* enfrentarse con. **~ flannel** *n* paño *m* (para lavarse la cara). **~less** *adj* anónimo. **~ lift** *n* cirugía *f* estética en la cara

facetious /fə'siːʃəs/ *adj* burlón

facial /'feɪʃl/ *adj* facial

facile /'fæsaɪl/ *adj* superficial, simplista

facilitate /fə'sɪlɪteɪt/ *vt* facilitar

facility /fə'sɪlɪtɪ/ *n* facilidad *f*

fact /fækt/ *n* hecho *m.* **as a matter of ~, in ~** en realidad, de hecho

faction /'fækʃn/ *n* facción *f*

factor /'fæktə(r)/ *n* factor *m*

factory /'fæktərɪ/ *n* fábrica *f*

factual /'fæktʃʊəl/ *adj* basado en hechos, factual

faculty /'fækəltɪ/ *n* facultad *f*

fad /fæd/ *n* manía *f*, capricho *m*

fade /feɪd/ *vi* (colour) desteñirse; (flowers) marchitarse; (light) apagarse; (memory, sound) desvanecerse

fag /fæɡ/ *n* (*fam, chore*) faena *f*; (*sl, cigarette*) cigarrillo *m*, pitillo *m*

Fahrenheit /'færənhaɪt/ *adj* Fahrenheit

fail /feɪl/ *vi* fracasar; (brakes) fallar; (*in an exam*) suspender, ser reprobado (*LAm*). **he ~ed to arrive** no llegó. ● *vt* suspender, ser reprobado en (*LAm*) (exam); suspender, reprobar (*LAm*) (candidate). ● *n.* **without ~** sin falta. **~ing** *n* defecto *m.* ● *prep.* **~ing that, ...** si eso no resulta.... **~ure** /'feɪljə(r)/ *n* fracaso *m*

faint /feɪnt/ *adj* (**-er, -est**) (*weak*) débil; (*indistinct*) indistinto. **feel ~** estar mareado. **the ~est idea** la más remota idea. ● *vi* desmayarse. ● *n* desmayo *m.* **~-hearted** /-'hɑːtɪd/ *adj* pusilánime, cobarde. **~ly** *adv* (*weakly*) débilmente; (*indistinctly*) indistintamente; (*slightly*) ligeramente

fair /feə(r)/ *adj* (**-er, -est**) (*just*) justo; (weather) bueno; (amount) razonable; (hair) rubio, güero (*Mex fam*); (skin) blanco. ● *adv* limpio. ● *n*

e

f

feria *f*. **~-haired** /-ˈheəd/ *adj* rubio, güero (*Mex fam*). **~ly** *adv* (*justly*) justamente; (*rather*) bastante. **~ness** *n* justicia *f*. **in all ~ness** sinceramente. **~ play** *n* juego *m* limpio. **~ trade** *n* comercio *m* justo

fairy /ˈfeərɪ/ *n* hada *f*. **~ story, ~ tale** *n* cuento *m* de hadas

faith /feɪθ/ *n* (*trust*) confianza *f*; (*Relig*) fe *f*. **~ful** *adj* fiel. **~fully** *adv* fielmente. **yours ~fully** (*in letters*) (le saluda) atentamente

fake /feɪk/ *n* falsificación *f*; (*person*) farsante *m*. ● *adj* falso. ● *vt* falsificar

falcon /ˈfɔːlkən/ *n* halcón *m*

Falkland Islands /ˈfɔːlklənd/ *npl*. **the Falkland Islands, the Falklands** las (Islas) Malvinas

fall /fɔːl/ *vi* (*pt* **fell**, *pp* **fallen**) caer; (*decrease*) bajar. ● *n* caída *f*; (*Amer, autumn*) otoño *m*; (*in price*) bajada *f*. □ **~ apart** *vi* deshacerse. □ **~ back on** *vt* recurrir a. □ **~ down** *vi* (*fall*) caerse. □ **~ for** *vt* ⓘ enamorarse de (person); dejarse engañar por (trick). □ **~ in** *vi* (*Mil*) formar filas. □ **~ off** *vi* caerse; (*diminish*) disminuir. □ **~ out** *vi* (*quarrel*) reñir (**with** con); (*drop out*) caerse; (*Mil*) romper filas. □ **~ over** *vi* caerse. *vt* tropezar con. □ **~ through** *vi* no salir adelante

fallacy /ˈfæləsɪ/ *n* falacia *f*

fallible /ˈfælɪbl/ *adj* falible

fallout /ˈfɔːlaʊt/ *n* lluvia *f* radiactiva. **~ shelter** *n* refugio *m* antinuclear

fallow /ˈfæləʊ/ *adj* en barbecho

false /fɔːls/ *adj* falso. **~ alarm** *n* falsa alarma. **~hood** *n* mentira *f*. **~ly** *adv* falsamente. **~ teeth** *npl* dentadura *f* postiza

falsify /ˈfɔːlsɪfaɪ/ *vt* falsificar

falter /ˈfɔːltə(r)/ *vi* vacilar

fame /feɪm/ *n* fama *f*. **~d** *adj* famoso

familiar /fəˈmɪlɪə(r)/ *adj* familiar. **the name sounds ~** el nombre me suena. **be ~ with** conocer. **~ity** /-ˈærətɪ/ *n* familiaridad *f*. **~ize** *vt* familiarizar

family /ˈfæməlɪ/ *n* familia *f*. ● *adj* de (la) familia, familiar. **~ tree** *n* árbol *m* genealógico

famine /ˈfæmɪn/ *n* hambre *f*, hambruna *f*

famished /ˈfæmɪʃt/ *adj* hambriento

famous /ˈfeɪməs/ *adj* famoso

fan /fæn/ *n* abanico *m*; (*Mec*) ventilador *m*; (*enthusiast*) aficionado *m*; (*of group, actor*) fan *m & f*; (*of sport, team*) hincha *m & f*. ● *vt* (*pt* **fanned**) abanicar; avivar (interest). □ **~ out** *vi* desparramarse en forma de abanico

fanatic /fəˈnætɪk/ *n* fanático *m*. **~al** *adj* fanático. **~ism** /-sɪzəm/ *n* fanatismo *m*

fan belt *n* correa *f* de ventilador, banda *f* del ventilador (*Mex*)

fanciful /ˈfænsɪfl/ *adj* (*imaginative*) imaginativo; (*impractical*) extravagante

fancy /ˈfænsɪ/ *n* imaginación *f*; (*liking*) gusto *m*. **take a ~ to** tomar cariño a (person); aficionarse a (thing). ● *adj* de lujo. ● *vt* (*imagine*) imaginar; (*believe*) creer; (*fam, want*) apetecer a. **~ dress** *n* disfraz *m*

fanfare /ˈfænfeə(r)/ *n* fanfarria *f*

fang /fæŋ/ *n* (*of animal*) colmillo *m*; (*of snake*) diente *m*

fantasize /ˈfæntəsaɪz/ *vi* fantasear

fantastic /fænˈtæstɪk/ *adj* fantástico

fantasy /ˈfæntəsɪ/ *n* fantasía *f*

far /fɑː(r)/ *adv* lejos; (*much*) mucho. **as ~ as** hasta. **as ~ as I know** que yo sepa. **by ~** con mucho. • *adj* (**further, furthest** *or* **farther, farthest**) lejano. **~ away** lejano

farc|e /fɑːs/ *n* farsa *f*. **~ical** *adj* ridículo

fare /feə(r)/ *n* (*on bus*) precio *m* del billete, precio *m* del boleto (*LAm*); (*on train, plane*) precio *m* del billete, precio *m* del pasaje (*LAm*); (*food*) comida *f*

Far East /fɑːrˈiːst/ *n* Extremo *or* Lejano Oriente *m*

farewell /feəˈwel/ *int & n* adiós (*m*)

far-fetched /fɑːˈfetʃt/ *adj* improbable

farm /fɑːm/ *n* granja *f*. • *vt* cultivar. □ **~ out** *vt* encargar (a terceros). • *vi* ser agricultor. **~er** *n* agricultor *m*, granjero *m*. **~house** *n* granja *f*. **~ing** *n* agricultura *f*. **~yard** *n* corral *m*

far: ~-off *adj* lejano. **~-reaching** /fɑːˈriːtʃɪŋ/ *adj* trascendental. **~-sighted** /fɑːˈsaɪtɪd/ *adj* con visión del futuro; (*Med, Amer*) hipermétrope

farther, farthest /ˈfɑːðə(r), ˈfɑːðəst/ *see* **FAR**

fascinat|e /ˈfæsɪneɪt/ *vt* fascinar. **~ed** *adj* fascinado. **~ing** *adj* fascinante. **~ion** /-ˈneɪʃn/ *n* fascinación *f*

fascis|m /ˈfæʃɪzəm/ *n* fascismo *m*. **~t** *adj & n* fascista (*m & f*)

fashion /ˈfæʃn/ *n* (*manner*) manera *f*; (*vogue*) moda *f*. **be in/out of ~** estar de moda/estar pasado de moda. **~able** *adj* de moda

fast /fɑːst/ *adj* (**-er, -est**) rápido; (clock) adelantado; (*secure*) fijo; (colours) sólido. • *adv* rápidamente; (*securely*) firmemente. **~ asleep** profundamente dormido. • *vi* ayunar. • *n* ayuno *m*

fasten /ˈfɑːsn/ *vt* sujetar; cerrar (case); abrochar (belt etc). • *vi* (case) cerrar; (belt etc) cerrarse. **~er, ~ing** *n* (*on box, window*) cierre *m*; (*on door*) cerrojo *m*

fat /fæt/ *n* grasa *f*. • *adj* (**fatter, fattest**) gordo; (meat) que tiene mucha grasa; (*thick*) grueso. **get ~** engordar

fatal /ˈfeɪtl/ *adj* mortal; (*fateful*) fatídico. **~ity** /fəˈtælətɪ/ muerto *m*. **~ly** *adv* mortalmente

fate /feɪt/ *n* destino *m*; (*one's lot*) suerte *f*. **~d** *adj* predestinado. **~ful** *adj* fatídico

father /ˈfɑːðə(r)/ *n* padre *m*. **~hood** *m* paternidad *f*. **~-in-law** *m* (*pl* **~s-in-law**) *m* suegro *m*. **~ly** *adj* paternal

fathom /ˈfæðəm/ *n* braza *f*. • *vt*. **~ (out)** comprender

fatigue /fəˈtiːg/ *n* fatiga *f*. • *vt* fatigar

fat|ten *vt*. **~ten (up)** cebar (animal). **~tening** *adj* que engorda. **~ty** *adj* graso, grasoso (*LAm*). • *n* ⓘ gordinflón *m*

fatuous /ˈfætjʊəs/ *adj* fatuo

faucet /ˈfɔːsɪt/ *n* (*Amer*) grifo *m*, llave *f* (*LAm*)

fault /fɔːlt/ *n* defecto *m*; (*blame*) culpa *f*; (*tennis*) falta *f*; (*in geology*) falla *f*. **at ~** culpable. • *vt* encontrarle defectos a. **~less** *adj* impecable. **~y** *adj* defectuoso

favour /ˈfeɪvə(r)/ *n* favor *m*. • *vt* favorecer; (*support*) estar a favor de; (*prefer*) preferir. **~able** *adj* favorable. **~ably** *adv* favorablemente. **~ite** *adj & n* preferido (*m*). **~itism** *n* favoritismo *m*

f

fawn /fɔ:n/ *n* cervato *m.* ●*adj* beige, beis. ●*vi.* ~ **on** adular

fax /fæks/ *n* fax *m.* ●*vt* faxear

fear /fɪə(r)/ *n* miedo *m.* ●*vt* temer. ~**ful** *adj* (*frightening*) espantoso; (*frightened*) temeroso. ~**less** *adj* intrépido. ~**some** /-səm/ *adj* espantoso

feasib|ility /fi:zə'bɪlətɪ/ *n* viabilidad *f.* ~**le** /'fi:zəbl/ *adj* factible; (*likely*) posible

feast /fi:st/ *n* (*Relig*) fiesta *f*; (*meal*) banquete *m*

feat /fi:t/ *n* hazaña *f*

feather /'feðə(r)/ *n* pluma *f.* ~**weight** *n* peso *m* pluma

feature /'fi:tʃə(r)/ *n* (*on face*) rasgo *m*; (*characteristic*) característica *f*; (*in newspaper*) artículo *m*; ~ **(film)** película *f* principal, largometraje *m.* ●*vt* presentar; (*give prominence to*) destacar

February /'februərɪ/ *n* febrero *m*

fed /fed/ *see* FEED

feder|al /'fedərəl/ *adj* federal. ~**ation** /fedə'reɪʃn/ *n* federación *f*

fed up *adj* ☐ harto (**with** de)

fee /fi:/ *n* (*professional*) honorarios *mpl*; (*enrolment*) derechos *mpl*; (*club*) cuota *f*

feeble /'fi:bl/ *adj* (**-er**, **-est**) débil

feed /fi:d/ *vt* (*pt* **fed**) dar de comer a; (*supply*) alimentar. ●*vi* comer. ●*n* (*for animals*) pienso *m*; (*for babies*) comida *f.* ~**back** *n* reacción *f*

feel /fi:l/ *vt* (*pt* **felt**) sentir; (*touch*) tocar; (*think*) considerar. **do you ~ it's a good idea?** ¿te parece buena idea? ~ **as if** tener la impresión de que. ~ **hot**/**hungry** tener calor/hambre. ~ **like** (*fam, want*) tener ganas de. ●*n* sensación *f.* **get the ~ of sth** acostumbrarse a algo. ~**er** *n* (*of insect*) antena *f.* ~**ing** *n* sentimiento *m*; (*physical*) sensación *f*

feet /fi:t/ *see* FOOT

feign /feɪn/ *vt* fingir

feint /feɪnt/ *n* finta *f*

fell /fel/ *see* FALL. ●*vt* derribar; talar (tree)

fellow /'feləʊ/ *n* ☐ tipo *m*; (*comrade*) compañero *m*; (*of society*) socio *m.* ~ **countryman** *n* compatriota *m.* ~ **passenger**/**traveller** *n* compañero *m* de viaje

felony /'felənɪ/ *n* delito *m* grave

felt /felt/ *n see* FEEL. ●*n* fieltro *m*

female /'fi:meɪl/ *adj* hembra; (voice, sex etc) femenino. ●*n* mujer *f*; (*animal*) hembra *f*

femini|ne /'femənɪn/ *adj & n* femenino (*m*). ~**nity** /-'nɪnətɪ/ *n* feminidad *f.* ~**st** *adj & n* feminista *m & f*

fenc|e /fens/ *n* cerca *f*, cerco *m* (*LAm*). ●*vt.* ~**e (in)** encerrar, cercar. ●*vi* (*Sport*) practicar la esgrima. ~**er** *n* esgrimidor *m.* ~**ing** *n* (*Sport*) esgrima *f*

fend /fend/ *vi.* ~ **for o.s.** valerse por sí mismo. □ ~ **off** *vt* defenderse de

fender /'fendə(r)/ *n* rejilla *f*; (*Amer, Auto*) guardabarros *m*, salpicadera *f* (*Mex*)

ferment /fə'ment/ *vt/i* fermentar. ~**ation** /-'teɪʃn/ *n* fermentación *f*

fern /fɜ:n/ *n* helecho *m*

feroci|ous /fə'rəʊʃəs/ *adj* feroz. ~**ty** /fə'rɒsətɪ/ *n* ferocidad *f*

ferret /'ferɪt/ *n* hurón *m.* ●*vi* (*pt* **ferreted**) ~ **about** husmear. ●*vt.* ~ **out** descubrir

ferry /'ferɪ/ *n* ferry *m.* ●*vt* transportar

fertil|e /'fɜ:taɪl/ *adj* fértil. ~**ity** /-'tɪlətɪ/ *n* fertilidad *f.* ~**ize**

/'fɜ:təlaɪz/ *vt* fecundar, abonar (soil). **~izer** *n* fertilizante *m*

ferv|ent /'fɜ:vənt/ *adj* ferviente. **~our** /-və(r)/ *n* fervor *m*

fester /'festə(r)/ *vi* enconarse

festival /'festəvl/ *n* fiesta *f*; (*of arts*) festival *m*

festiv|e /'festɪv/ *adj* festivo. **the ~e season** *n* las Navidades. **~ity** /fe'stɪvətɪ/ *n* festividad *f*

fetch /fetʃ/ *vt* (*go for*) ir a buscar; (*bring*) traer; (*be sold for*) venderse en. **~ing** *adj* atractivo

fête /feɪt/ *n* fiesta *f*. • *vt* festejar

fetish /'fetɪʃ/ *n* fetiche *m*

fetter /'fetə(r)/ *vt* encadenar

feud /fju:d/ *n* contienda *f*

feudal /'fju:dl/ *adj* feudal. **~ism** *n* feudalismo m

fever /'fi:və(r)/ *n* fiebre *f*. **~ish** *adj* febril

few /fju:/ *adj* pocos. **a ~ houses** algunas casas. •*n* pocos *mpl*. **a ~** unos (pocos). **a good ~**, **quite a ~** 🅸 muchos. **~er** *adj & n* menos. **~est** *adj* el menor número de

fiancé /fɪ'ɒnseɪ/ *n* novio *m*. **~e** /fɪ 'ɒnseɪ/ *n* novia *f*

fiasco /fɪ'æskəʊ/ *n* (*pl* **-os**) fiasco *m*

fib /fɪb/ *n* 🅸 mentirilla *f*. •*vi* 🅸 mentir, decir mentirillas

fibre /'faɪbə(r)/ *n* fibra *f*. **~glass** *n* fibra *f* de vidrio

fickle /'fɪkl/ *adj* inconstante

ficti|on /'fɪkʃn/ *n* ficción *f*. **(works of) ~** novelas *fpl*. **~onal** *adj* novelesco. **~tious** /fɪk'tɪʃəs/ *adj* ficticio

fiddle /'fɪdl/ *n* 🅸 violín *m*; (*fam, swindle*) trampa *f*. •*vt* 🅸 falsificar. **~ with** juguetear con

fidget /'fɪdʒɪt/ *vi* (*pt* **fidgeted**) moverse, ponerse nervioso. **~ with** juguetear con. •*n* persona *f* inquieta. **~y** *adj* inquieto

field /fi:ld/ *n* campo *m*. **~ day** *n*. **have a ~ day** hacer su agosto. **~ glasses** *npl* gemelos *mpl*. **F~ Marshal** *n* mariscal *m* de campo. **~ trip** *n* viaje *m* de estudio. **~work** *n* investigaciones *fpl* en el terreno

fiend /fi:nd/ *n* demonio *m*. **~ish** *adj* diabólico

fierce /fɪəs/ *adj* (**-er**, **-est**) feroz; (attack) violento. **~ly** *adv* (growl) con ferocidad; (fight) con fiereza

fiery /'faɪərɪ/ *adj* (**-ier**, **-iest**) ardiente; (temper) exaltado

fifteen /fɪf'ti:n/ *adj & n* quince (*m*). **~th** *adj* decimoquinto. •*n* quinceavo *m*

fifth /fɪfθ/ *adj & n* quinto (*m*)

fift|ieth /'fɪftɪəθ/ *adj* quincuagésimo. •*n* cincuentavo *m*. **~y** *adj & n* cincuenta (*m*). **~y-~y** *adv* mitad y mitad, a medias. •*adj*. **a ~y-~y chance** una posibilidad de cada dos

fig /fɪg/ *n* higo *m*

fight /faɪt/ *vi* (*pt* **fought**) luchar; (*quarrel*) disputar. •*vt* luchar contra. •*n* pelea *m*; (*struggle*) lucha *f*; (*quarrel*) disputa *f*; (*Mil*) combate *m*. □ **~ back** *vi* defenderse. □ **~ off** *vt* rechazar (attack); luchar contra (illness). **~er** *n* luchador *m*; (*aircraft*) avión *m* de caza. **~ing** *n* luchas *fpl*

figment /'fɪgmənt/ *n*. **~ of the imagination** producto *m* de la imaginación

figurative /'fɪgjʊrətɪv/ *adj* figurado

figure /'fɪgə(r)/ *n* (*number*) cifra *f*; (*person*) figura *f*; (*shape*) forma *f*; (*of woman*) tipo *m*. •*vt* imaginar;

f

(*Amer fam, reckon*) calcular. ● *vi* figurar. **that ~s** (*fam*) es lógico. □ **~ out** *vt* entender. **~head** *n* testaferro *m*, mascarón *m* de proa. **~ of speech** *n* figura *f* retórica

filch /fɪltʃ/ *vt* 🅸 hurtar

file /faɪl/ *n* (*tool, for nails*) lima *f*; (*folder*) carpeta *f*; (*set of papers*) expediente *m*; (*Comp*) archivo *m*; (*row*) fila *f*. **in single ~** en fila india. ● *vt* archivar (papers); limar (metal, nails). ● **~ in** *vi* entrar en fila. **~ past** *vt* desfilar ante

filing cabinet /ˈfaɪlɪŋ/ *n* archivador *m*

fill /fɪl/ *vt* llenar. ● *vi* llenarse. ● *n*. **eat one's ~** hartarse de comer. **have had one's ~ of** estar harto de □ **~ in** *vt* rellenar (form, hole). □ **~ out** *vt* rellenar (form). *vi* (*get fatter*) engordar. □ **~ up** *vt* llenar. *vi* llenarse

fillet /ˈfɪlɪt/ *n* filete *m*. ● *vt* (*pt* **filleted**) cortar en filetes (meat); quitar la espina a (fish)

filling /ˈfɪlɪŋ/ *n* (*in tooth*) empaste *m*, tapadura *f* (*Mex*). **~ station** *n* gasolinera *f*

film /fɪlm/ *n* película *f*. ● *vt* filmar. **~ star** *n* estrella *f* de cine

filter /ˈfɪltə(r)/ *n* filtro *m*. ● *vt* filtrar. ● *vi* filtrarse. **~-tipped** *adj* con filtro

filth /fɪlθ/ *n* mugre *f*. **~y** *adj* mugriento

fin /fɪn/ *n* aleta *f*

final /ˈfaɪnl/ *adj* último; (*conclusive*) decisivo. ● *n* (*Sport*) final *f*. **~s** *npl* (*Schol*) exámenes *mpl* de fin de curso

finale /fɪˈnɑːlɪ/ *n* final *m*

final|ist *n* finalista *m & f*. **~ize** *vt* ultimar. **~ly** *adv* (*lastly*) finalmente, por fin

financ|e /ˈfaɪnæns/ *n* finanzas *fpl*. ● *vt* financiar. **~ial** /faɪˈnænʃl/ *adj* financiero; (difficulties) económico

find /faɪnd/ *vt* (*pt* **found**) encontrar. **~ out** *vt* descubrir. ● *vi* (*learn*) enterarse. **~ings** *npl* conclusiones *fpl*

fine /faɪn/ *adj* (**-er**, **-est**) (*delicate*) fino; (*excellent*) excelente. ● *adv* muy bien. ● *n* multa *f*. ● *vt* multar. **~ arts** *npl* bellas artes *fpl*. **~ly** *adv* (*cut*) en trozos pequeños; (adjust) con precisión

finger /ˈfɪŋgə(r)/ *n* dedo *m*. ● *vt* tocar. **~nail** *n* uña *f*. **~print** *n* huella *f* digital. **~tip** *n* punta *f* del dedo

finish /ˈfɪnɪʃ/ *vt/i* terminar, acabar. **~ doing** terminar de hacer. ● *n* fin *m*; (*of race*) llegada *f*

finite /ˈfaɪnaɪt/ *adj* finito

Fin|land /ˈfɪnlənd/ *n* Finlandia *f*. **~n** *n* finlandés *m*. **~nish** *adj & n* finlandés (*m*)

fiord /fjɔːd/ *n* fiordo *m*

fir /fɜː(r)/ *n* abeto *m*

fire /faɪə(r)/ *n* fuego *m*; (*conflagration*) incendio *m*. ● *vt* disparar (gun); (*dismiss*) despedir; avivar (imagination). ● *vi* disparar. **~ alarm** *n* alarma *f* contra incendios. **~arm** *n* arma *f* de fuego. **~ brigade**, **~ department** (*Amer*) *n* cuerpo *m* de bomberos. **~ engine** *n* coche *m* de bomberos, carro *m* de bomberos (*Mex*). **~-escape** *n* escalera *f* de incendios. **~ extinguisher** *n* extintor *m*, extinguidor *m* (*LAm*). **~fighter** *n* bombero *m*. **~man** /-mən/ *n* bombero *m*. **~place** *n* chimenea *f*. **~side** *n* hogar *m*. **~ truck** *n* (*Amer*) *see* **~ ENGINE**. **~wood** *n* leña *f*. **~work** *n* fuego *m* artificial

firm /fɜːm/ *n* empresa *f*. ● *adj* (**-er**,

-est) firme. **~ly** *adv* firmemente

first /fɜ:st/ *adj* primero, (*before masculine singular noun*) primer. **at ~ hand** directamente. ● *n* primero *m*. ● *adv* primero; (*first time*) por primera vez. **~ of all** primero. **~ aid** *n* primeros auxilios *mpl*. **~ aid kit** *n* botiquín *m*. **~ class** /-'klɑ:s/ *adv* (travel) en primera clase. **~-class** *adj* de primera clase. **~ floor** *n* primer piso *m*; (*Amer*) planta *f* baja. **F~ Lady** *n* (*Amer*) Primera Dama *f*. **~ly** *adv* en primer lugar. **~ name** *n* nombre *m* de pila. **~-rate** /-'reɪt/ *adj* excelente

fish /fɪʃ/ *n* (*pl invar or* **-es**) pez *m*; (*as food*) pescado *m*. ● *vi* pescar. **go ~ing** ir de pesca. □ **~ out** *vt* sacar. **~erman** *n* pescador *m*. **~ing** *n* pesca *f*. **~ing pole** (*Amer*), **~ing rod** *n* caña *f* de pesca. **~monger** *n* pescadero *m*. **~ shop** *n* pescadería *f*. **~y** *adj* (smell) a pescado; (*fam, questionable*) sospechoso

fission /'fɪʃn/ *n* fisión *f*

fist /fɪst/ *n* puño *m*

fit /fɪt/ *adj* (**fitter, fittest**) (*healthy*) en forma; (*good enough*) adecuado; (*able*) capaz. ● *n* (*attack*) ataque; (*of clothes*) corte *m*. ● *vt* (*pt* **fitted**) (*adapt*) adaptar; (*be the right size for*) quedarle bien a; (*install*) colocar. ● *vi* encajar; (*in certain space*) caber; (clothes) quedarle bien a uno. □ **~ in** *vi* caber. **~ful** *adj* irregular. **~ness** *n* salud *f*; (*Sport*) (buena) forma *f* física. **~ting** *adj* apropiado. ● *n* (*of clothes*) prueba *f*. **~ting room** *n* probador *m*

five /faɪv/ *adj & n* cinco (*m*)

fix /fɪks/ *vt* fijar; (*mend, deal with*) arreglar. ● *n*. **in a ~** en un aprieto. **~ed** *adj* fijo. **~ture** /'fɪkstʃə(r)/ *n* (*Sport*) partido *m*

fizz /fɪz/ *vi* burbujear. ● *n* efervescencia *f*. **~le** /fɪzl/ *vi*. **~le out** fracasar. **~y** *adj* efervescente; (water) con gas

fjord /fjɔ:d/ *n* fiordo *m*

flabbergasted /'flæbəgɑ:stɪd/ *adj* estupefacto

flabby /'flæbɪ/ *adj* flojo

flag /flæg/ *n* bandera *f*. ● *vi* (*pt* **flagged**) (*weaken*) flaquear; (conversation) languidecer

flagon /'flægən/ *n* botella *f* grande, jarro *m*

flagpole /'flægpəʊl/ *n* asta *f* de bandera

flagrant /'fleɪgrənt/ *adj* flagrante

flair /fleə(r)/ *n* don *m* (**for** de)

flak|e /fleɪk/ *n* copo *m*; (*of paint, metal*) escama *f*. ● *vi* desconcharse. **~y** *adj* escamoso

flamboyant /flæm'bɔɪənt/ *adj* (clothes) vistoso; (manner) extravagante

flame /fleɪm/ *n* llama *f*. **go up in ~s** incendiarse

flamingo /flə'mɪŋgəʊ/ *n* (*pl* **-o(e)s** flamenco *m*

flammable /'flæməbl/ *adj* inflamable

flan /flæn/ *n* tartaleta *f*

flank /flænk/ *n* (*of animal*) ijada *f*; (*of person*) costado *m*; (*Mil, Sport*) flanco *m*

flannel /'flænl/ *n* franela *f*; (*for face*) paño *m* (para lavarse la cara).

flap /flæp/ *vi* (*pt* **flapped**) ondear; (wings) aletear. ● *vt* batir (wings); agitar (arms). ● *n* (*cover*) tapa *f*; (*of pocket*) cartera *f*; (*of table*) ala *f*. **get into a ~** 🅸 ponerse nervioso

flare /fleə(r)/ ● *n* llamarada *f*; (*Mil*)

f

bengala *f*; (*in skirt*) vuelo *m*. □ ~ **up** *vi* llamear; (fighting) estallar; (person) encolerizarse

flash /flæʃ/ • *vi* destellar. • *vt* (*aim torch*) dirigir; (*flaunt*) hacer ostentación de. ~ **past** pasar como un rayo. • *n* destello *m*; (*Photo*) flash *m*. ~**back** *n* escena *f* retrospectiva. ~**light** *n* (*Amer, torch*) linterna *f*. ~**y** *adj* ostentoso

f

flask /flɑ:sk/ *n* frasco *m*; (*vacuum flask*) termo *m*

flat /flæt/ *adj* (**flatter, flattest**) plano; (tyre) desinflado; (refusal) categórico; (fare, rate) fijo; (*Mus*) bemol. • *adv* (*Mus*) demasiado bajo. ~ **out** (*at top speed*) a toda velocidad. • *n* (*rooms*) apartamento *m*, piso *m*; [!] pinchazo *m*; (*Mus*) (*Auto, esp Amer*) bemol *m*. ~**ly** *adv* categóricamente. ~**ten** *vt* allanar, aplanar

flatter /flætə(r)/ *vt* adular. ~**ing** *adj* (person) lisonjero; (clothes) favorecedor. ~**y** *n* adulación *f*

flaunt /flɔ:nt/ *vt* hacer ostentación de

flavour /'fleɪvə(r)/ *n* sabor *m*. • *vt* sazonar. ~**ing** *n* condimento *m*

flaw /flɔ:/ *n* defecto *m*. ~**less** *adj* perfecto

flea /fli:/ *n* pulga *f*

fleck /flek/ *n* mancha *f*, pinta *f*

fled /fled/ *see* FLEE

flee /fli:/ *vi* (*pt* **fled**) huir. • *vt* huir de

fleece /fli:s/ *n* vellón *m*. • *vt* [!] desplumar

fleet /fli:t/ *n* flota *f*; (*of cars*) parque *m* móvil

fleeting /'fli:tɪŋ/ *adj* fugaz

Flemish /'flemɪʃ/ *adj* & *n* flamenco (*m*)

flesh /fleʃ/ *n* carne *f*. **in the** ~ en persona

flew /flu:/ *see* FLY

flex /fleks/ *vt* doblar; flexionar (muscle). • *n* (*Elec*) cable *m*

flexib|ility /fleksə'bɪlətɪ/ *n* flexibilidad *f*. ~**le** /'fleksəbl/ *adj* flexible

flexitime/'fleksɪtaɪm/, (*Amer*) **flextime** /'flekstaɪm/*n* horario *m* flexible

flick /flɪk/ *n* golpecito *m*. • *vt* dar un golpecito a. □ ~ **through** *vt* hojear

flicker /'flɪkə(r)/ *vi* parpadear. • *n* parpadeo *m*; (*of hope*) resquicio *m*

flies /flaɪz/ *npl* (*on trousers*) bragueta *f*

flight /flaɪt/ *n* vuelo *m*; (*fleeing*) huida *f*, fuga *f*. ~ **of stairs** tramo *m* de escalera *f*. **take (to)** ~ darse a la fuga. ~ **attendant** *n* (*male*) sobrecargo *m*, aeromozo *m* (*LAm*); (*female*) azafata *f*, aeromoza *f* (*LAm*). ~**-deck** *n* cubierta *f* de vuelo

flimsy /'flɪmzɪ/ *adj* (**-ier, -iest**) flojo, débil, poco sólido

flinch /flɪntʃ/ *vi* retroceder (**from** ante)

fling /flɪŋ/ *vt* (*pt* **flung**) arrojar. • *n* (*love affair*) aventura *f*; (*wild time*) juerga *f*

flint /flɪnt/ *n* pedernal *m*; (*for lighter*) piedra *f*

flip /flɪp/ *vt* (*pt* **flipped**) dar un golpecito a. • *n* golpecito *m*. □ ~ **through** *vt* hojear.

flippant /'flɪpənt/ *adj* poco serio

flipper /'flɪpə(r)/ *n* aleta *f*

flirt /flɜ:t/ *vi* coquetear. • *n* (*woman*) coqueta *f*; (*man*) coqueto *m*

flit /flɪt/ *vi* (*pt* **flitted**) revolotear

float /fləʊt/ *vi* flotar. • *vt* hacer flotar; introducir en Bolsa (company).

● *n* flotador *m*; (*cash*) caja *f* chica

flock /flɒk/ *n* (*of birds*) bandada *f*; (*of sheep*) rebaño *m*. ● *vi* congregarse

flog /flɒg/ *vt* (*pt* **flogged**) (*beat*) azotar; (*fam, sell*) vender

flood /flʌd/ *n* inundación *f*; (*fig*) avalancha *f*. ● *vt* inundar. ● *vi* (building etc) inundarse; (river) desbordar. **~light** *n* foco *m*. ● *vt* (*pt* **~lit**) iluminar (con focos)

floor /flɔ:(r)/ *n* suelo *m*; (*storey*) piso *m*; (*for dancing*) pista *f*. ● *vt* derribar; (*baffle*) confundir

flop /flɒp/ *vi* (*pt* **flopped**) dejarse caer pesadamente; (*fam, fail*) fracasar. ● *n* ⊡ fracaso *m*. **~py** *adj* flojo. ● *n see* **~PY DISK**. **~py disk** *n* disquete *m*, floppy (disk) *m*

floral /'flɔ:rəl/ *adj* floral

florid /'flɒrɪd/ *adj* florido

florist /'flɒrɪst/ *n* florista *m & f*

flounder /'flaʊndə(r)/ *vi* (*in water*) luchar para mantenerse a flote; (speaker) quedar sin saber qué decir

flour /flaʊə(r)/ *n* harina *f*

flourish /'flʌrɪʃ/ *vi* florecer; (business) prosperar. ● *vt* blandir. ● *n* ademán *m* elegante; (*in handwriting*) rasgo *m*. **~ing** *adj* próspero

flout /flaʊt/ *vt* burlarse de

flow /fləʊ/ *vi* fluir; (blood) correr; (*hang loosely*) caer. ● *n* flujo *m*; (*stream*) corriente *f*; (*of traffic, information*) circulación *f*. **~ chart** *n* organigrama *m*

flower /'flaʊə(r)/ *n* flor *f*. ● *vi* florecer, florear (*Mex*). **~ bed** *n* macizo *m* de flores. **~y** *adj* florido

flown /fləʊn/ *see* **FLY**

flu /flu:/ *n* gripe *f*

fluctuat|e /'flʌktjʊeɪt/ *vi* fluctuar. **~ion** /-'eɪʃn/ *n* fluctuación *f*

flue /flu:/ *n* tiro *m*

fluen|cy /'flu:ənsɪ/ *n* fluidez *f*. **~t** *adj* (style) fluido; (speaker) elocuente. **be ~t in a language** hablar un idioma con fluidez. **~tly** *adv* con fluidez

fluff /flʌf/ *n* pelusa *f*. **~y** *adj* (**-ier, -iest**) velloso

fluid /'flu:ɪd/ *adj & n* fluido (*m*)

flung /flʌŋ/ *see* **FLING**

fluorescent /flʊə'resnt/ *adj* fluorescente

flush /flʌʃ/ *vi* ruborizarse. ● *vt*. **~ the toilet** tirar de la cadena, jalarle a la cadena (*LAm*). ● *n* (*blush*) rubor *m*

fluster /'flʌstə(r)/ *vt* poner nervioso

flute /flu:t/ *n* flauta *f*

flutter /'flʌtə(r)/ *vi* ondear; (bird) revolotear. ● *n* (*of wings*) revoloteo *m*; (*fig*) agitación *f*

flux /flʌks/ *n* flujo *m*. **be in a state of ~** estar siempre cambiando

fly /flaɪ/ *vi* (*pt* **flew**, *pp* **flown**) volar; (passenger) ir en avión; (flag) flotar; (*rush*) correr. ● *vt* pilotar, pilotear (*LAm*) (aircraft); transportar en avión (passengers, goods); izar (flag). ● *n* mosca *f*; (*of trousers*) *see* **FLIES**. **~ing** *adj* volante. **~ing visit** visita *f* relámpago. ● *n* (*activity*) aviación *f*. **~leaf** *n* guarda *f*. **~over** *n* paso *m* elevado

foal /fəʊl/ *n* potro *m*

foam /fəʊm/ *n* espuma *f*. ● *vi* espumar. **~ rubber** *n* goma *f* espuma, hule *m* espuma (*Mex*)

fob /fɒb/ *vt* (*pt* **fobbed**). **~ sth off onto s.o.** (*palm off*) encajarle algo a uno

focal /'fəʊkl/ *adj* focal

focus /'fəʊkəs/ *n* (*pl* **-cuses** *or* **-ci** /-saɪ/) foco *m*; (*fig*) centro *m*. **in ~**

enfocado. **out of ~** desenfocado. ● *vt* (*pt* **focused**) enfocar (*fig*) concentrar. ● *vi* enfocar; (*fig*) concentrarse (**on** en)

fodder /'fɒdə(r)/ *n* forraje *m*

foe /fəʊ/ *n* enemigo *m*

foetus /'fi:təs/ *n* (*pl* **-tuses**) feto *m*

fog /fɒg/ *n* niebla *f*

fog|gy *adj* (**-ier, -iest**) nebuloso. **it is ~gy** hay niebla. **~horn** *n* sirena *f* de niebla

foible /'fɔɪbl/ *n* punto *m* débil

foil /fɔɪl/ *vt* (*thwart*) frustrar. ● *n* papel *m* de plata

foist /fɔɪst/ *vt* encajar (**on** a)

fold /fəʊld/ *vt* doblar; cruzar (arms). ● *vi* doblarse; (*fail*) fracasar. ● *n* pliegue *m*. (*for sheep*) redil *m*. **~er** *n* carpeta *f*. **~ing** *adj* plegable

foliage /'fəʊlɪɪdʒ/ *n* follaje *m*

folk /fəʊk/ *n* gente *f*. ● *adj* popular. **~lore** /-lɔ:(r)/ *n* folklore *m*. **~ music** *n* música *f* folklórica; (*modern*) música *f* folk. **~s** *npl* (*one's relatives*) familia *f*

follow /'fɒləʊ/ *vt/i* seguir. □ **~ up** *vt* seguir. **~er** *n* seguidor *m*. **~ing** *n* partidarios *mpl*. ● *adj* siguiente. ● *prep* después de

folly /'fɒlɪ/ *n* locura *f*

fond /fɒnd/ *adj* (**-er, -est**) (*loving*) cariñoso; (hope) vivo. **be ~ of s.o.** tener(le) cariño a uno. **be ~ of sth** ser aficionado a algo

fondle /'fɒndl/ *vt* acariciar

fondness /'fɒndnɪs/ *n* cariño *m*; (*for things*) afición *f*

font /fɒnt/ *n* pila *f* bautismal

food /fu:d/ *n* comida *f*. **~ processor** *n* robot *m* de cocina

fool /fu:l/ *n* idiota *m & f* ● *vt* engañar. □ **~ about** *vi* hacer payasadas. **~hardy** *adj* temerario. **~ish** *adj* tonto. **~ishly** *adv* tontamente. **~ishness** *n* tontería *f*. **~proof** *adj* infalible

foot /fʊt/ *n* (*pl* **feet**) pie *m*; (*measure*) pie *m* (= 30,48cm); (*of animal, furniture*) pata *f*. **get under s.o.'s feet** estorbar a uno. **on ~** a pie. **on/to one's feet** de pie. **put one's ~ in it** meter la pata. ● *vt* pagar (bill). **~age** /-ɪdʒ/ *n* (*of film*) secuencia *f*. **~-and-mouth disease** *n* fiebre *f* aftosa. **~ball** *n* (*ball*) balón *m*; (*game*) fútbol *m*; (*American ~ball*) fútbol *m* americano. **~baller** *n* futbolista *m & f*. **~bridge** *n* puente *m* para peatones. **~hills** *npl* estribaciones *fpl*. **~hold** *n* punto *m* de apoyo. **~ing** *n* pie *m*. **on an equal ~ing** en igualdad de condiciones. **~lights** *npl* candilejas *fpl*. **~man** /-mən/ *n* lacayo *m*. **~note** *n* nota *f* (al pie de la página). **~path** *n* (*in country*) senda *f*; (*in town*) acera *f*, banqueta *f* (*Mex*). **~print** *n* huella *f*. **~step** *n* paso *m*. **~wear** *n* calzado *m*

for /fɔ:(r)//fə(r)/

● *preposition*

····▸ (*intended for*) para. **it's ~ my mother** es para mi madre. **she works ~ a multinational** trabaja para una multinacional

····▸ (*on behalf of*) por. **I did it ~ you** lo hice por ti

 See entries **para** and **por** for further information

····▸ (*expressing purpose*) para. **I use it ~ washing the car** lo uso para limpiar el coche. **what ~?** ¿para qué?. **to go out ~ a meal** salir a comer

fuera

····➤ (*in favour of*) a favor de. **are you ~ or against the idea?** ¿estás a favor o en contra de la idea?

····➤ (*indicating cost, in exchage for*) por. **I bought it ~ 30 pounds** lo compré por 30 libras. **she left him ~ another man** lo dejó por otro. **thanks ~ everything** gracias por todo. **what's the Spanish ~ toad'?** ¿cómo se dice toad' en español?

····➤ (*expressing duration*) **he read ~ two hours** leyó durante dos horas. **how long are you going ~?** ¿por cuánto tiempo vas? **I've been waiting ~ three hours** hace tres horas que estoy esperando, llevo tres horas esperando

····➤ (*in the direction of*) para. **the train ~ Santiago** el tren para Santiago

● *conjunction* (*because*) porque, pues (*literary usage*). **she left at once, ~ it was getting late** se fue en seguida, porque or pues se hacía tarde

forage /'fɒrɪdʒ/ *vi* forrajear. ● *n* forraje *m*

forbade /fə'bæd/ *see* FORBID

forbearance /fɔː'beərəns/ *n* paciencia *f*

forbid /fə'bɪd/ *vt* (*pt* **forbade**, *pp* **forbidden**) prohibir (**s.o. to do** a uno hacer). **~ s.o. sth** prohibir algo a uno. **~ding** *adj* imponente

force /fɔːs/ *n* fuerza *f*. **by ~** a la fuerza. **come into ~** entrar en vigor. **the ~s** las fuerzas *fpl* armadas. ● *vt* forzar; (*compel*) obligar (**s.o. to do sth** a uno a hacer algo). **~ on** imponer a. **~ open** forzar. **~d** *adj* forzado. **~-feed** *vt* alimentar a la fuerza. **~ful** *adj* enérgico

forceps /'fɔːseps/ *n* fórceps *m*

forcibl|e /'fɔːsəbl/ *adj* a la fuerza. **~y** *adv* a la fuerza

ford /fɔːd/ *n* vado *m* ● *vt* vadear

fore /fɔː(r)/ *adj* anterior. ● *n*. **come to the ~** hacerse evidente

forearm /'fɔːrɑːm/ *n* antebrazo *m*

foreboding /fɔː'bəʊdɪŋ/ *n* presentimiento *m*

forecast /'fɔːkɑːst/ *vt* (*pt* **forecast**) pronosticar (weather); prever (result). ● *n* pronóstico *m*. **weather ~** pronóstico *m* del tiempo

forecourt /'fɔːkɔːt/ *n* patio *m* delantero

forefinger /'fɔːfɪŋgə(r)/ *n* (dedo *m*) índice *m*

forefront /'fɔːfrʌnt/ *n* vanguardia *f*. **in the ~** a la vanguardia

forego /fɔː'gəʊ/ *vt* (*pt* **forewent**, *pp* **foregone**) *see* FORGO

foregone /'fɔːgɒn/ *adj*. **~ conclusion** resultado *m* previsto

foreground /'fɔːgraʊnd/ *n*. **in the ~** en primer plano

forehead /'fɒrɪd/ *n* frente *f*

foreign /'fɒrən/ *adj* extranjero; (trade) exterior; (travel) al extranjero, en el extranjero. **~er** *n* extranjero *m*

foreman /'fɔːmən/ (*pl* **-men** /-mən/) *n* capataz *m*

foremost /'fɔːməʊst/ *adj* primero. ● *adv*. **first and ~** ante todo

forerunner /'fɔːrʌnə(r)/ *n* precursor *m*

foresee /fɔː'siː/ *vt* (*pt* **-saw**, *pp* **-seen**) prever. **~able** *adj* previsible

foresight /'fɔːsaɪt/ *n* previsión *f*

f

forest /ˈfɒrɪst/ *n* bosque *m*
forestall /fɔːˈstɔːl/ *vt* (*prevent*) prevenir; (*preempt*) anticiparse a
forestry /ˈfɒrɪstrɪ/ *n* silvicultura *f*
foretaste /ˈfɔːteɪst/ *n* anticipo *m*
foretell /fɔːˈtel/ *vt* (*pt* **foretold**) predecir
forever /fəˈrevə(r)/ *adv* para siempre; (*always*) siempre
forewarn /fɔːˈwɔːn/ *vt* advertir
forewent /fɔːˈwent/ *see* FOREGO
foreword /ˈfɔːwɜːd/ *n* prefacio *m*
forfeit /ˈfɔːfɪt/ *n* (*penalty*) pena *f*; (*in game*) prenda *f*. ●*vt* perder; perder el derecho a (property)
forgave /fəˈgeɪv/ *see* FORGIVE
forge /fɔːdʒ/ *n* fragua *f*. ●*vt* fraguar; (*copy*) falsificar. □ **~ ahead** *vi* adelantarse rápidamente. **~r** *n* falsificador *m*. **~ry** *n* falsificación *f*
forget /fəˈget/ *vt* (*pt* **forgot**, *pp* **forgotten**) olvidar, olvidarse de. ●*vi* olvidarse (**about** de). **I forgot** se me olvidó. **~ful** *adj* olvidadizo
forgive /fəˈgɪv/ *vt* (*pt* **forgave**, *pp* **forgiven**) perdonar. **~ s.o. for sth** perdonar algo a uno. **~ness** *n* perdón *m*
forgo /fɔːˈgəʊ/ *vt* (*pt* **forwent**, *pp* **forgone**) renunciar a
fork /fɔːk/ *n* tenedor *m*; (*for digging*) horca *f*; (*in road*) bifurcación *f*. ●*vi* (road) bifurcarse. □ **~ out** *vt* [I] desembolsar, aflojar [I]. **~lift truck** *n* carretilla *f* elevadora
forlorn /fəˈlɔːn/ *adj* (hope, attempt) desesperado; (smile) triste
form /fɔːm/ *n* forma *f*; (*document*) formulario *m*; (*Schol*) clase *f*. ●*vt* formar. ●*vi* formarse
formal /ˈfɔːml/ *adj* formal; (person) formalista; (dress) de etiqueta. **~ity** /-ˈmælətɪ/ *n* formalidad *f*. **~ly** *adv* oficialmente
format /ˈfɔːmæt/ *n* formato *m*. ●*vt* (*pt* **formatted**) (*Comp*) formatear
formation /fɔːˈmeɪʃn/ *n* formación *f*
former /ˈfɔːmə(r)/ *adj* anterior; (*first of two*) primero. ●*n*. **the ~** el primero *m*, la primera *f*, los primeros *mpl*, las primeras *fpl*. **~ly** *adv* antes
formidable /ˈfɔːmɪdəbl/ *adj* formidable
formula /ˈfɔːmjʊlə/ *n* (*pl* **-ae** /-iː/ *or* **-as**) fórmula *f*. **~te** /-leɪt/ *vt* formular
forsake /fəˈseɪk/ *vt* (*pt* **forsook**, *pp* **forsaken**) abandonar
fort /fɔːt/ *n* fuerte *m*
forth /fɔːθ/ *adv*. **and so ~** y así sucesivamente. **~coming** /-ˈkʌmɪŋ/ *adj* próximo, venidero; (*sociable*) comunicativo. **~right** *adj* directo. **~with** /-ˈwɪθ/ *adv* inmediatamente
fortieth /ˈfɔːtɪɪθ/ *adj* cuadragésimo. ●*n* cuadragésima parte *f*
fortnight /ˈfɔːtnaɪt/ *n* quince días *mpl*, quincena *f*. **~ly** *adj* bimensual. ●*adv* cada quince días
fortress /ˈfɔːtrɪs/ *n* fortaleza *f*
fortunate /ˈfɔːtʃənət/ *adj* afortunado. **be ~** tener suerte. **~ly** *adv* afortunadamente
fortune /ˈfɔːtʃuːn/ *n* fortuna *f*. **~-teller** *n* adivino *m*
forty /ˈfɔːtɪ/ *adj* & *n* cuarenta (*m*). **~ winks** un sueñecito
forum /ˈfɔːrəm/ *n* foro *m*
forward /ˈfɔːwəd/ *adj* (movement) hacia adelante; (*advanced*) precoz; (*pert*) impertinente. ●*n* (*Sport*) delantero *m*. ●*adv* adelante. **go ~** avanzar. ●*vt* hacer seguir (letter); enviar (goods). **~s** *adv* adelante
forwent /fɔːˈwent/ *see* FORGO
fossil /ˈfɒsl/ *adj* & *n* fósil (*m*)

foster /'fɒstə(r)/ *vt* (*promote*) fomentar; criar (child). ~ **child** *n* hijo *m* adoptivo

fought /fɔ:t/ *see* FIGHT

foul /faʊl/ *adj* (**-er**, **-est**) (smell) nauseabundo; (weather) pésimo; (person) asqueroso; (*dirty*) sucio; (language) obsceno. ●*n* (*Sport*) falta *f*. ●*vt* contaminar; (*entangle*) enredar. ~ **play** *n* (*Sport*) jugada *f* sucia; (*crime*) delito *m*

found /faʊnd/ *see* FIND. ●*vt* fundar.

foundation /faʊn'deɪʃn/ *n* fundación *f*; (*basis*) fundamento. (*cosmetic*) base *f* (de maquillaje). ~**s** *npl* (*of building*) cimientos *mpl*

founder /'faʊndə(r)/ *n* fundador *m*. ●*vi* (ship) hundirse

fountain /'faʊntɪn/ *n* fuente *f*. ~ **pen** *n* pluma *f* (estilográfica) *f*, estilográfica *f*

four /fɔ:(r)/ *adj* & *n* cuatro (*m*). ~**fold** *adj* cuádruple. ●*adv* cuatro veces. ~**some** /-səm/ *n* grupo *m* de cuatro personas ~**teen** /'fɔ:ti:n/ *adj* & *n* catorce (*m*). ~**teenth** *adj* & *n* decimocuarto (*m*). ~**th** /fɔ:θ/ *adj* & *n* cuarto (*m*). ~**-wheel drive** *n* tracción *f* integral

fowl /faʊl/ *n* ave *f*

fox /fɒks/ *n* zorro *m*, zorra *f*. ●*vt* [!] confundir

foyer /'fɔɪeɪ/ *n* (*of theatre*) foyer *m*; (*of hotel*) vestíbulo *m*

fraction /'frækʃn/ *n* fracción *f*

fracture /'fræktʃə(r)/ *n* fractura *f*. ●*vt* fracturar. ●*vi* fracturarse

fragile /'frædʒaɪl/ *adj* frágil

fragment /'frægmənt/ *n* fragmento *m*. ~**ary** /-ərɪ/ *adj* fragmentario

fragran|ce /'freɪgrəns/ *n* fragancia *f*. ~**t** *adj* fragante

frail /freɪl/ *adj* (**-er**, **-est**) frágil

frame /freɪm/ *n* (*of picture, door, window*) marco *m*; (*of spectacles*) montura *f*; (*fig, structure*) estructura *f*. ●*vt* enmarcar (picture); formular (plan, question); (*fam, incriminate unjustly*) incriminar falsamente. ~**work** *n* estructura *f*; (*context*) marco *m*

France /frɑ:ns/ *n* Francia *f*

frank /fræŋk/ *adj* franco. ●*vt* franquear. ~**ly** *adv* francamente

frantic /'fræntɪk/ *adj* frenético. ~ **with** loco de

fratern|al /frə'tɜ:nl/ *adj* fraternal. ~**ity** /frə'tɜ:nɪtɪ/ *n* fraternidad *f*; (*club*) asociación *f*. ~**ize** /'frætənaɪz/ *vi* fraternizar

fraud /frɔ:d/ *n* fraude *m*; (*person*) impostor *m*. ~**ulent** /-jʊlənt/ *adj* fraudulento

fraught /frɔ:t/ *adj* (*tense*) tenso. ~ **with** cargado de

fray /freɪ/ *n* riña *f*

freak /fri:k/ *n* fenómeno *m*; (*monster*) monstruo *m*. ●*adj* anormal. ~**ish** *adj* anormal

freckle /'frekl/ *n* peca *f*. ~**d** *adj* pecoso

free /fri:/ *adj* (**freer** /'fri:ə(r)/, **freest** /'fri:ɪst/) libre; (*gratis*) gratuito. ~ **of charge** gratis. ●*vt* (*pt* **freed**) (*set at liberty*) poner en libertad; (*relieve from*) liberar (**from/of** de); (*untangle*) desenredar. ~**dom** *n* libertad *f*. ~**hold** *n* propiedad *f* absoluta. ~ **kick** *n* tiro *m* libre. ~**lance** *adj* & *adv* por cuenta propia. ~**ly** *adv* libremente. ~**mason** *n* masón *m*. ~**-range** *adj* (eggs) de granja. ~ **speech** *n* libertad *f* de expresión. ~**style** *n* estilo *m* libre. ~**way** *n* (*Amer*) autopista *f*

freez|e /'fri:z/ *vt* (*pt* **froze**, *pp* **frozen**) helar; congelar (food, wages). • *vi* helarse; (*become motionless*) quedarse inmóvil. • *n* (*on wages, prices*) congelación *f.* **~er** *n* congelador *m.* **~ing** *adj* glacial. • *n.* **~ing (point)** punto *m* de congelación *f.* **below ~ing** bajo cero

freight /freɪt/ *n* (*goods*) mercancías *fpl.* **~er** *n* buque *m* de carga

French /frentʃ/ *adj* francés. • *n* (*language*) francés *m.* • *npl.* **the ~** (*people*) los franceses. **~ fries** *npl* patatas *fpl* fritas, papas *fpl* fritas (*LAm*). **~man** /-mən/ *n* francés *m.* **~ window** *n* puerta *f* ventana. **~woman** *f* francesa *f*

frenz|ied /'frenzɪd/ *adj* frenético. **~y** *n* frenesí *m*

frequency /'fri:kwənsɪ/ *n* frecuencia *f*

frequent /frɪ'kwent/ *vt* frecuentar. • /'fri:kwənt/ *adj* frecuente. **~ly** *adv* frecuentemente

fresh /freʃ/ *adj* (**-er**, **-est**) fresco; (*different, additional*) nuevo; (water) dulce. **~en** *vi* refrescar. □ **~en up** *vi* (person) refrescarse. **~er** *n* 🅸 *see* **~MAN**. **~ly** *adv* recientemente. **~man** *n* /-mən/ estudiante *m* de primer año. **~ness** *n* frescura *f*

fret /fret/ *vi* (*pt* **fretted**) preocuparse. **~ful** *adj* (*discontented*) quejoso; (*irritable*) irritable

friction /'frɪkʃn/ *n* fricción *f*

Friday /'fraɪdeɪ/ *n* viernes *m*

fridge /frɪdʒ/ *n* 🅸 frigorífico *m*, nevera *f*, refrigerador *m* (*LAm*)

fried /fraɪd/ *see* **FRY**. • *adj* frito

friend /frend/ *n* amigo *m.* **~liness** *n* simpatía *f.* **~ly** *adj* (**-ier**, **-iest**) simpático. **~ship** *n* amistad *f*

fries /fraɪz/ *npl see* **FRENCH FRIES**

frieze /fri:z/ *n* friso *m*

frigate /'frɪgət/ *n* fragata *f*

fright /fraɪt/ *n* miedo *m*; (*shock*) susto *m.* **~en** *vt* asustar. □ **~ off** *vt* ahuyentar. **~ened** *adj* asustado. **be ~ened** tener miedo (**of** de.) **~ful** *adj* espantoso, horrible. **~fully** *adv* terriblemente

frigid /'frɪdʒɪd/ *adj* frígido

frill /frɪl/ *n* volante *m*, olán *m* (*Mex*). **~s** *npl* (*fig*) adornos *mpl.* **with no ~s** sencillo

fringe /frɪndʒ/ *n* (*sewing*) fleco *m*; (*ornamental border*) franja *f*; (*of hair*) flequillo *m*, cerquillo *m* (*LAm*), fleco *m* (*Mex*); (*of area*) periferia *f*; (*of society*) margen *m*

fritter /'frɪtə(r)/ *vt.* □ **~ away** *vt* desperdiciar (time); malgastar (money)

frivol|ity /frɪ'vɒlətɪ/ *n* frivolidad *f.* **~ous** /'frɪvələs/ *adj* frívolo

fro /frəʊ/ *see* **TO AND FRO**

frock /frɒk/ *n* vestido *m*

frog /frɒg/ *n* rana *f.* **have a ~ in one's throat** tener carraspera. **~man** /-mən/ *n* hombre *m* rana. **~spawn** *n* huevos *mpl* de rana

frolic /'frɒlɪk/ *vi* (*pt* **frolicked**) retozar

from /frɒm//frəm/ *prep* de; (*indicating starting point*) desde; (*habit, conviction*) por; **~ then on** a partir de ahí

front /frʌnt/ *n* parte *f* delantera; (*of building*) fachada *f*; (*of clothes*) delantera *f*; (*Mil, Pol*) frente *f*; (*of book*) principio *m*; (*fig, appearance*) apariencia *f*; (*seafront*) paseo *m* marítimo, malecón *m* (*LAm*). **in ~ of** delante de. • *adj* delantero; (*first*) primero. **~al** *adj* frontal; (attack) de frente. **~ door** *n* puerta *f* principal

frontier /'frʌntɪə(r)/ *n* frontera *f*

front page *n* (*of newspaper*) primera plana *f*

frost /frɒst/ *n* (*freezing*) helada *f*; (*frozen dew*) escarcha *f*. **~bite** *n* congelación *f*. **~bitten** *adj* congelado. **~ed** *adj* (glass) esmerilado. **~ing** *n* (*Amer*) glaseado *m*. **~y** *adj* (weather) helado; (night) de helada; (*fig*) glacial

froth /frɒθ/ *n* espuma *f*. ● *vi* espumar. **~y** *adj* espumoso

frown /fraʊn/ *vi* fruncir el entrecejo ● *n* ceño *m*. □ **~ on** *vt* desaprobar.

froze /frəʊz/ *see* FREEZE. **~n** /'frəʊzn/ *see* FREEZE. ● *adj* congelado; (region) helado

frugal /'fru:gl/ *adj* frugal

fruit /fru:t/ *n* (*in botany*) fruto *m*; (*as food*) fruta *f*. **~ful** /'fru:tfl/ *adj* fértil; (*fig*) fructífero. **~ion** /fru:'ɪʃn/ *n*. **come to ~ion** realizarse. **~less** *adj* infructuoso. **~ salad** *n* macedonia *f* de frutas. **~y** *adj* que sabe a fruta

frustrat|e /frʌ'streɪt/ *vt* frustrar. **~ion** /-ʃn/ *n* frustración *f*. **~ed** *adj* frustrado. **~ing** *adj* frustrante

fry /fraɪ/ *vt* (*pt* **fried**) freír. ● *vi* freírse. **~ing pan** *n* sárten *f*, sartén *m* (*LAm*)

fudge /fʌdʒ/ *n* dulce *m* de azúcar

fuel /'fju:əl/ *n* combustible *m*

fugitive /'fju:dʒɪtɪv/ *adj* & *n* fugitivo (*m*)

fulfil /fʊl'fɪl/ *vt* (*pt* **fulfilled**) cumplir (con) (promise, obligation); satisfacer (condition); hacer realidad (ambition). **~ment** *n* (*of promise, obligation*) cumplimiento *m*; (*of conditions*) satisfacción *f*; (*of hopes, plans*) realización *f*

full /fʊl/ *adj* (**-er, -est**) lleno; (bus, hotel) completo; (account) detallado. **at ~ speed** a máxima velocidad. **be ~ (up)** (*with food*) no poder más. ● *n*. **in ~** sin quitar nada. **to the ~** completamente. **write in ~** escribir con todas las letras. **~back** *n* (*Sport*) defensa *m* & *f*. **~-blown** /fʊl'bləʊn/ *adj* verdadero. **~-fledged** /-'fledʒd/ *adj* (*Amer*) *see* FULLY-FLEDGED. **~ moon** *n* luna *f* llena. **~-scale** /-'skeɪl/ *adj* (drawing) de tamaño natural; (*fig*) amplio. **~ stop** *n* punto *m*. **~-time** *adj* (employment) de jornada completa. ● /-'taɪm/ *adv* a tiempo completo. **~y** *adv* completamente. **~-fledged** /-'fledʒd/ *adj* (chick) capaz de volar; (lawyer, nurse) hecho y derecho

fulsome /'fʊlsəm/ *adj* excesivo

fumble /'fʌmbl/ *vi* buscar (a tientas)

fume /fju:m/ *vi* despedir gases; (*fig, be furious*) estar furioso. **~s** *npl* gases *mpl*

fumigate /'fju:mɪgeɪt/ *vt* fumigar

fun /fʌn/ *n* (*amusement*) diversión *f*; (*merriment*) alegría *f*. **for ~** en broma. **have ~** divertirse. **make ~ of** burlarse de

function /'fʌŋkʃn/ *n* (*purpose, duty*) función *f*; (*reception*) recepción *f*. ● *vi* funcionar. **~al** *adj* funcional

fund /fʌnd/ *n* fondo *m*. ● *vt* financiar

fundamental /fʌndə'mentl/ *adj* fundamental. **~ist** *adj* & *n* fundamentalista (*m* & *f*)

funeral /'fju:nərəl/ *n* entierro *m*, funerales *mpl*. **~ director** *n* director *m* de pompas fúnebres

funfair /'fʌnfeə(r)/ *n* feria *f*; (*permanent*) parque *m* de atracciones, parque *m* de diversiones (*LAm*)

f

fungus /ˈfʌŋgəs/ *n* (*pl* **-gi**/-gaɪ/) hongo *m*

funnel /ˈfʌnl/ *n* (*for pouring*) embudo *m*; (*of ship*) chimenea *f*

funn|ily /ˈfʌnɪlɪ/ *adv* (*oddly*) curiosamente. **~y** *adj* (**-ier**, **-iest**) divertido, gracioso; (*odd*) curioso, raro

fur /fɜː(r)/ *n* pelo *m*; (*pelt*) piel *f*

furious /ˈfjʊərɪəs/ *adj* furioso. **~ly** *adv* furiosamente

furlough /ˈfɜːləʊ/ *n* (*Amer*) permiso *m*. **on ~** de permiso

furnace /ˈfɜːnɪs/ *n* horno *m*

furnish /ˈfɜːnɪʃ/ *vt* amueblar, amoblar (*LAm*); (*supply*) proveer. **~ings** *npl* muebles *mpl*, mobiliario *m*

furniture /ˈfɜːnɪtʃə(r)/ *n* muebles *mpl*, mobiliario *m*. **a piece of ~** un mueble

furrow /ˈfʌrəʊ/ *n* surco *m*

furry /ˈfɜːrɪ/ *adj* peludo

furthe|r /ˈfɜːðə(r)/ *adj* más lejano; (*additional*) nuevo. • *adv* más lejos; (*more*) además. • *vt* fomentar. **~rmore** *adv* además. **~st** *adj* más lejano. • *adv* más lejos

furtive /ˈfɜːtɪv/ *adj* furtivo

fury /ˈfjʊərɪ/ *n* furia *f*

fuse /fjuːz/ *vt* (*melt*) fundir; (*fig, unite*) fusionar. **~ the lights** fundir los plomos. • *vi* fundirse; (*fig*) fusionarse. • *n* fusible *m*, plomo *m*; (*of bomb*) mecha *f*. **~box** *n* caja *f* de fusibles

fuselage /ˈfjuːzəlɑːʒ/ *n* fuselaje *m*

fusion /ˈfjuːʒn/ *n* fusión *f*

fuss /fʌs/ *n* (*commotion*) jaleo *m*. **kick up a ~** armar un lío, armar una bronca. **make a ~ of** tratar con mucha atención. • *vi* preocuparse. **~y** *adj* (**-ier**, **-iest**) (*finicky*) remilgado; (*demanding*) exigente

futil|e /ˈfjuːtaɪl/ *adj* inútil, vano. **~ity** /fjuːˈtɪlətɪ/ *n* inutilidad *f*

futur|e /ˈfjuːtʃə(r)/ *adj* futuro. • *n* futuro *m*. **in ~e** de ahora en adelante. **~istic** /fjuːtʃəˈrɪstɪk/ *adj* futurista

fuzz /fʌz/ *n* pelusa *f*. **~y** *adj* (hair) crespo; (photograph) borroso

Gg

gab /gæb/ *n*. **have the gift of the ~** tener un pico de oro

gabardine /gæbəˈdiːn/ *n* gabardina *f*

gabble /ˈgæbl/ *vi* hablar atropelladamente

gable /ˈgeɪbl/ *n* aguilón *m*

gad /gæd/ *vi* (*pt* **gadded**). **~ about** callejear

gadget /ˈgædʒɪt/ *n* chisme *m*

Gaelic /ˈgeɪlɪk/ *adj & n* gaélico (*m*)

gaffe /gæf/ *n* plancha *f*, metedura *f* de pata, metida *f* de pata (*LAm*)

gag /gæg/ *n* mordaza *f*; (*joke*) chiste *m*. • *vt* (*pt* **gagged**) amordazar. • *vi* hacer arcadas

gaiety /ˈgeɪətɪ/ *n* alegría *f*

gaily /ˈgeɪlɪ/ *adv* alegremente

gain /geɪn/ *vt* ganar; (*acquire*) adquirir; (*obtain*) conseguir. • *vi* (clock) adelantar. • *n* ganancia *f*; (*increase*) aumento *m*

gait /geɪt/ *n* modo *m* de andar

gala /ˈgɑːlə/ *n* fiesta *f*. **~ performance** (función *f* de) gala *f*

galaxy /ˈgæləksɪ/ *n* galaxia *f*

gale /geɪl/ *n* vendaval *m*

gall /gɔːl/ *n* bilis *f*; (*fig*) hiel *f*; (*impudence*) descaro *m*

gallant /ˈgælənt/ *adj* (*brave*) valiente; (*chivalrous*) galante. **~ry** *n* valor *m*

gall bladder /'gɔ:lblædə(r)/ *n* vesícula *f* biliar

gallery /'gælərɪ/ *n* galería *f*

galley /'gælɪ/ *n* (*ship*) galera *f*; (*ship's kitchen*) cocina *f*. ~ **(proof)** *n* galerada *f*

gallivant /'gælɪvænt/ *vi* 🅸 callejear

gallon /'gælən/ *n* galón *m* (*imperial = 4,546l; Amer = 3,785l*)

gallop /'gæləp/ *n* galope *m*. ● *vi* (*pt* **galloped**) galopar

gallows /'gæləʊz/ *n* horca *f*

galore /gə'lɔ:(r)/ *adj* en abundancia

galvanize /'gælvənaɪz/ *vt* galvanizar

gambl|e /'gæmbl/ *vi* jugar. **~e on** contar con. ● *vt* jugarse. ● *n* (*venture*) empresa *f* arriesgada; (*bet*) apuesta *f*; (*risk*) riesgo *m*. **~er** *n* jugador *m*. **~ing** *n* juego *m*

game /geɪm/ *n* juego *m*; (*match*) partido *m*; (*animals, birds*) caza *f*. ● *adj* valiente. ~ **for** listo para. **~keeper** *n* guardabosque *m*. **~s** *n* (*in school*) deportes *mpl*

gammon /'gæmən/ *n* jamón *m* fresco

gamut /'gæmət/ *n* gama *f*

gander /'gændə(r)/ *n* ganso *m*

gang /gæŋ/ *n* pandilla *f*; (*of workmen*) equipo *m*. **~master** *n contratista de mano de obra indocumentada*. □ ~ **up** *vi* unirse (**on** contra)

gangling /'gæŋglɪŋ/ *adj* larguirucho

gangrene /'gæŋgri:n/ *n* gangrena *f*

gangster /'gæŋstə(r)/ *n* bandido *m*, gángster *m & f*

gangway /'gæŋweɪ/ *n* pasillo *m*; (*of ship*) pasarela *f*

gaol /dʒeɪl/ *n* cárcel *f*. **~er** *n* carcelero *m*

gap /gæp/ *n* espacio *m*; (*in fence, hedge*) hueco *m*; (*in time*) intervalo *m*; (*in knowledge*) laguna *f*; (*difference*) diferencia *f*

> *i* **gap year** En Gran Bretaña, es el periodo, entre el final de los estudios secundarios y el ingreso a la universidad, que muchos estudiantes destinan a obtener experiencia laboral relacionada con sus futuras carreras. Otros emprenden actividades no relacionadas con los estudios y para algunos es la oportunidad para ahorrar dinero o viajar.

gap|e /geɪp/ *vi* quedarse boquiabierto; (*be wide open*) estar muy abierto. **~ing** *adj* abierto; (*person*) boquiabierto

garage /'gærɑ:ʒ/ *n* garaje *m*, garage *m* (*LAm*), cochera *f* (*Mex*); (*petrol station*) gasolinera *f*; (*for repairs, sales*) taller *m*, garage *m* (*LAm*)

garbage /'gɑ:bɪdʒ/ *n* basura *f*. ~ **can** *n* (*Amer*) cubo *m* de la basura, bote *m* de la basura (*Mex*). ~ **collector**, ~ **man** *n* (*Amer*) basurero *m*

garble /'gɑ:bl/ *vt* tergiversar, embrollar

garden /'gɑ:dn/ *n* (*of flowers*) jardín *m*; (*of vegetables/fruit*) huerto *m*. ● *vi* trabajar en el jardín. **~er** /'gɑ:dnə(r)/ *n* jardinero *m*. **~ing** *n* jardinería *f*; (*vegetable growing*) horticultura *f*

gargle /'gɑ:gl/ *vi* hacer gárgaras

gargoyle /'gɑ:gɔɪl/ *n* gárgola *f*

garish /'geərɪʃ/ *adj* chillón

garland /ˈgɑːlənd/ *n* guirnalda *f*
garlic / ˈgɑːlɪk/ *n* ajo *m*
garment /ˈgɑːmənt/ *n* prenda *f* (de vestir)
garnish /ˈgɑːnɪʃ/ *vt* adornar, decorar. ● *n* adorno *m*
garret /ˈgærət/ *n* buhardilla *f*
garrison /ˈgærɪsn/ *n* guarnición *f*
garrulous /ˈgærələs/ *adj.* hablador
garter /ˈgɑːtə(r)/ *n* liga *f*

g

gas /gæs/ *n* (*pl* **gases**) gas *m*; (*anaesthetic*) anestésico *m*; (*Amer, petrol*) gasolina *f*. ● *vt* (*pt* **gassed**) asfixiar con gas
gash /gæʃ/ *n* tajo *m*. ● *vt* hacer un tajo de
gasket /ˈgæskɪt/ *n* junta *f*
gas: ~ **mask** *n* careta *f* antigás. ~ **meter** *n* contador *m* de gas
gasoline /ˈgæsəliːn/ *n* (*Amer*) gasolina *f*
gasp /gɑːsp/ *vi* jadear; (*with surprise*) dar un grito ahogado. ● *n* exclamación *f*, grito *m*
gas: ~ **ring** *n* hornillo *m* de gas. ~ **station** *n* (*Amer*) gasolinera *f*
gastric /ˈgæstrɪk/ *adj* gástrico
gate /geɪt/ *n* puerta *f*; (*of metal*) verja *f*; (*barrier*) barrera *f*
gate: ~**crash** *vt* colarse en. ~**crasher** *n* intruso *m* (que ha entrado sin ser invitado). ~**way** *n* puerta *f*
gather /ˈgæðə(r)/ *vt* reunir (people, things); (*accumulate*) acumular; (*pick up*) recoger; recoger (flowers); (*fig, infer*) deducir; (*sewing*) fruncir. ~ **speed** acelerar. ● *vi* (people) reunirse; (things) acumularse. ~**ing** *n* reunión *f*
gaudy /ˈgɔːdɪ/ *adj* (**-ier**, **-iest**) chillón
gauge /geɪdʒ/ *n* (*measurement*) medida *f*; (*Rail*) entrevía *f*; (*instrument*) indicador *m*. ● *vt* medir; (*fig*) estimar
gaunt /gɔːnt/ *adj* descarnado; (*from illness*) demacrado
gauntlet /ˈgɔːntlɪt/ *n*. **run the** ~ **of** aguantar el acoso de
gauze /gɔːz/ *n* gasa *f*
gave /geɪv/ *see* **GIVE**
gawky /ˈgɔːkɪ/ *adj* (**-ier**, **-iest**) torpe
gawp /gɔːp/ *vi*. ~ **at** mirar como un tonto
gay /geɪ/ *adj* (**-er**, **-est**) (*fam, homosexual*) homosexual, gay [!]; (*dated, joyful*) alegre
gaze /geɪz/ *vi*. ~ **(at)** mirar (fijamente). ● *n* mirada *f* (fija)
gazelle /gəˈzel/ *n* (*pl invar or* **-s**) gacela *f*
GB *abbr see* **GREAT BRITAIN**
gear /gɪə(r)/ *n* equipo *m*; (*Tec*) engranaje *m*; (*Auto*) marcha *f*, cambio *m*. **in** ~ engranado. **out of** ~ desengranado. **change** ~, **shift** ~ (*Amer*) cambiar de marcha. ● *vt* adaptar. ~**box** *n* (*Auto*) caja *f* de cambios
geese /giːs/ *see* **GOOSE**
gel /dʒel/ *n* gel *m*
gelatine /ˈdʒelətiːn/ *n* gelatina *f*
gelignite /ˈdʒelɪgnaɪt/ *n* gelignita *f*
gem /dʒem/ *n* piedra *f* preciosa
Gemini /ˈdʒemɪnaɪ/ *n* Géminis *mpl*
gender /ˈdʒendə(r)/ *n* género *m*
gene /dʒiːn/ *n* gen *m*, gene *m*
genealogy /dʒiːnɪˈælədʒɪ/ *n* genealogía *f*
general /ˈdʒenərəl/ *adj* general. ● *n* general *m*. **in** ~ en general. ~ **election** *n* elecciones *fpl* generales. ~**ization** /-ˈzeɪʃn/ *n* generalización

f. **~ize** *vt/i* generalizar. **~ knowledge** *n* cultura *f* general. **~ly** *adv* generalmente. **~ practitioner** *n* médico *m* de cabecera

generat|e /ˈdʒenəreɪt/ *vt* generar. **~ion** /-ˈreɪʃn/ *n* generación *f*. **~ion gap** *n* brecha *f* generacional. **~or** *n* generador *m*

genero|sity /dʒenəˈrɒsətɪ/ *n* generosidad *f*. **~us** /ˈdʒenərəs/ *adj* generoso; (*plentiful*) abundante

genetic /dʒɪˈnetɪk/ *adj* genético. **~s** *n* genética *f*

Geneva /dʒɪˈniːvə/ *n* Ginebra *f*

genial /ˈdʒiːnɪəl/ *adj* simpático, afable

genital /ˈdʒenɪtl/ *adj* genital. **~s** *npl* genitales *mpl*

genitive /ˈdʒenɪtɪv/ *adj* & *n* genitivo (*m*)

genius /ˈdʒiːnɪəs/ *n* (*pl* **-uses**) genio *m*

genocide /ˈdʒenəsaɪd/ *n* genocidio *m*

genome /ˈdʒiːnəʊm/ *n* genoma *m*

genre /ʒɑːŋr/ *n* género *m*

gent /dʒent/ *n* [I] señor *m*. **~s** *n* aseo *m* de caballeros

genteel /dʒenˈtiːl/ *adj* distinguido

gentl|e /ˈdʒentl/ *adj* (**-er**, **-est**) (person) dulce; (murmur, breeze) suave; (hint) discreto. **~eman** *n* señor *m*; (*well-bred*) caballero *m*. **~eness** *n* amabilidad *f*

genuine /ˈdʒenjʊɪn/ *adj* verdadero; (person) sincero

geograph|er /dʒɪˈɒgrəfə(r)/ *n* geógrafo *m*. **~ical** /dʒɪəˈgræfɪkl/ *adj* geográfico. **~y** /dʒɪˈɒgrəfɪ/ *n* geografía *f*

geolog|ical /dʒɪəˈlɒdʒɪkl/ *adj* geológico. **~ist** /dʒɪˈɒlədʒɪst/ *n* geólogo *m*. **~y** /dʒɪˈɒlədʒɪ/ *n* geología *f*

geometr|ic(al) /dʒɪəˈmetrɪk(l)/ *adj* geométrico. **~y** /dʒɪˈɒmətrɪ/ *n* geometría *f*

geranium /dʒəˈreɪnɪəm/ *n* geranio *m*

geriatric /dʒerɪˈætrɪk/ *adj* (patient) anciano; (ward) de geriatría. **~s** *n* geriatría *f*

germ /dʒɜːm/ *n* microbio *m*, germen *m*

German /ˈdʒɜːmən/ *adj* & *n* alemán (*m*). **~ic** /dʒɜːˈmænɪk/ *adj* germánico. **~ measles** *n* rubéola *f*. **~y** *n* Alemania *f*

germinate /ˈdʒɜːmɪneɪt/ *vi* germinar

gesticulate /dʒeˈstɪkjʊleɪt/ *vi* hacer ademanes, gesticular

gesture /ˈdʒestʃə(r)/ *n* gesto *m*, ademán *m*; (*fig*) gesto *m*. ● *vi* hacer gestos

get /get/

past **got;** past participle **got, gotten** (*Amer*); present participle **getting**

● *transitive verb*

····➤ (*obtain*) conseguir, obtener. **did you get the job?** ¿conseguiste el trabajo?

····➤ (*buy*) comprar. **I got it in the sales** lo compré en las rebajas

····➤ (*achieve, win*) sacar. **she got very good marks** sacó muy buenas notas

····➤ (*receive*) recibir. **I got a letter from Alex** recibí una carta de Alex

····➤ (*fetch*) ir a buscar. **~ your coat** vete a buscar tu abrigo

....➤(*experience*) llevarse. **I got a terrible shock** me llevé un shock espantoso
....➤(*fam, understand*) entender. **I don't ~ what you mean** no entiendo lo que quieres decir
....➤(*ask or persuade*) **to ~ s.o. to do sth** hacer que uno haga algo

Note that *hacer que* is followed by the subjunctive form of the verb

....➤(*cause to be done or happen*) **I must ~ this watch fixed** tengo que llevar a arreglar este reloj. **they got the roof mended** hicieron arreglar el techo

● *intransitive verb*

....➤(*arrive, reach*) llegar. **I got there late** llegué tarde. **how do you ~ to Paddington?** ¿cómo se llega a Paddington?
....➤(*become*) **to ~ tired** cansarse. **she got very angry** se puso furiosa. **it's ~ting late** se está haciendo tarde

➡ For translations of expressions such as **get better, get old** see entries **better, old** etc. See also **got**

....➤ **to get to do sth** (*manage to*) llegar a. **did you get to see him?** ¿llegaste a verlo? ▫ **get along** *vi* (*manage*) arreglárselas; (*progress*) hacer progresos. ▫ **get along with** *vt* llevarse bien con. ▫ **get at** *vt* (*reach*) llegar a; (*imply*) querer decir. ▫ **get away** *vi* salir; (*escape*) escaparse. ▫ **get back** *vi* volver. *vt* (*recover*) recobrar. ▫ **get by** *vi* (*manage*) arreglárselas; (*pass*) pasar. ▫ **get down** *vi* bajar. *vt* (*make depressed*) deprimir. ▫ **get in** *vi* entrar. ▫ **get into** *vt* entrar en; subir a (car) ▫ **get off** *vt* bajar(se) de (train etc). *vi* (*from train etc*) bajarse; (*Jurid*) salir absuelto. ▫ **get on** *vi* (*progress*) hacer progresos; (*succeed*) tener éxito. *vt* subirse a (train etc). ▫ **get on with** *vt* (*be on good terms with*) llevarse bien con; (*continue*) seguir con. ▫ **get out** *vi* salir. *vt* (*take out*) sacar. ▫ **get out of** *vt* (*fig*) librarse de. ▫ **get over** *vt* reponerse de (illness). ▫ **get round** *vt* soslayar (difficulty etc); engatusar (person). ▫ **get through** *vi* pasar; (*on phone*) comunicarse (**to** con). ▫ **get together** *vi* (*meet up*) reunirse. *vt* (*assemble*) reunir. ▫ **get up** *vi* levantarse; (*climb*) subir

geyser /ˈgiːzə(r)/ *n* géiser *m*
ghastly /ˈgɑːstlɪ/ *adj* (**-ier, -iest**) horrible
gherkin /ˈgɜːkɪn/ *n* pepinillo *m*
ghetto /ˈgetəʊ/ *n* (*pl* **-os**) gueto *m*
ghost /gəʊst/ *n* fantasma *m*. **~ly** *adj* espectral
giant /ˈdʒaɪənt/ *n* gigante *m*. ● *adj* gigantesco
gibberish /ˈdʒɪbərɪʃ/ *n* jerigonza *f*
gibe /dʒaɪb/ *n* pulla *f*
giblets /ˈdʒɪblɪts/ *npl* menudillos *mpl*
gidd|iness /ˈgɪdɪnɪs/ *n* vértigo *m*. **~y** *adj* (**-ier, -iest**) mareado. **be/feel ~y** estar/sentirse mareado
gift /gɪft/ *n* regalo *m*; (*ability*) don

m. **~ed** *adj* dotado de talento. **~-wrap** *vt* envolver para regalo

gigantic /dʒaɪ'gæntɪk/ *adj* gigantesco

giggle /'gɪgl/ *vi* reírse tontamente. ●*n* risita *f*

gild /gɪld/ *vt* dorar

gills /gɪlz/ *npl* agallas *fpl*

gilt /gɪlt/ *n* dorado *m*. ●*adj* dorado

gimmick /'gɪmɪk/ *n* truco *m*

gin / dʒɪn/ *n* ginebra *f*

ginger /'dʒɪndʒə(r)/ *n* jengibre *m*. ●*adj* rojizo. **he has ~ hair** es pelirrojo. **~bread** *n* pan *m* de jengibre

gipsy /'dʒɪpsɪ/ *n* gitano *m*

giraffe /dʒɪ'rɑ:f/ *n* jirafa *f*

girder /'gɜ:də(r)/ *n* viga *f*

girdle /'gɜ:dl/ *n* (*belt*) cinturón *m*; (*corset*) corsé *m*

girl /gɜ:l/ *n* chica *f*, muchacha *f*; (*child*) niña *f*. **~ band** *n* grupo *m* pop de chicas. **~friend** *n* amiga *f*; (*of boy*) novia *f*. **~ish** *adj* de niña; (boy) afeminado. **~ scout** *n* (*Amer*) exploradora *f*, guía *f*

giro /'dʒaɪrəʊ/ *n* (*pl* **-os**) giro *m* (bancario)

girth /gɜ:θ/ *n* circunferencia *f*

gist /dʒɪst/ *n* lo esencial

give /gɪv/ *vt* (*pt* **gave**, *pp* **given**) dar; (*deliver*) entregar; regalar (present); prestar (aid, attention). **~ o.s. to** darse a. ●*vi* dar; (*yield*) ceder; (*stretch*) dar de sí. ●*n* elasticidad *f*. □ **~ away** *vt* regalar; revelar (secret). □ **~ back** *vt* devolver. □ **~ in** *vi* ceder. □ **~ off** *vt* emitir. □ **~ out** *vt* distribuir. (*become used up*) agotarse. □ **~ up** *vt* renunciar a; (*yield*) ceder. **~ up doing sth** dejar de hacer algo. **~ o.s. up** entregarse (**to** a). *vi* rendirse. **~n** /'gɪvn/ *see* GIVE. ●*adj* dado. **~n name** *n* nombre *m* de pila

glacier /'glæsɪə(r)/ *n* glaciar *m*

glad /glæd/ *adj* contento. **be ~** alegrarse (**about** de). **~den** *vt* alegrar

gladly /'glædlɪ/ *adv* alegremente; (*willingly*) con mucho gusto

glamo|rous /'glæmərəs/ *adj* glamoroso. **~ur** /'glæmə(r)/ *n* glamour *m*

glance /glɑ:ns/ *n* ojeada *f*. ●*vi*. **~ at** dar un vistazo a

gland /glænd/ *n* glándula *f*

glar|e /gleə(r)/ *vi* (light) deslumbrar; (*stare angrily*) mirar airadamente. ●*n* resplandor *m*; (*stare*) mirada *f* airada. **~ing** *adj* deslumbrante; (*obvious*) manifiesto

glass /glɑ:s/ *n* (*material*) cristal *m*, vidrio *m*; (*without stem or for wine*) vaso *m*; (*with stem*) copa *f*; (*for beer*) caña *f*; (*mirror*) espejo *m*. **~es** *npl* (*spectacles*) gafas *fpl*, lentes *fpl* (*LAm*), anteojos *mpl* (*LAm*). **~y** *adj* vítreo

glaze /gleɪz/ *vt* poner cristal(es) *or* vidrio(s) a (windows, doors); vidriar (pottery). ●*vi*. **~ (over)** (eyes) vidriarse. ●*n* barniz *m*; (*for pottery*) esmalte *m*

gleam /gli:m/ *n* destello *m*. ●*vi* destellar

glean /gli:n/ *vt* espigar; recoger (information)

glee /gli:/ *n* regocijo *m*

glib /glɪb/ *adj* de mucha labia; (reply) fácil

glid|e /glaɪd/ *vi* deslizarse; (*plane*) planear. **~er** *n* planeador *m*. **~ing** *n* planeo *m*

glimmer /'glɪmə(r)/ *n* destello *m*. ●*vi* destellar

glimpse /glɪmps/ *n*. **catch a ~ of** vislumbrar, ver brevemente. ●*vt* vislumbrar

glint /glɪnt/ *n* destello *m*. ● *vi* destellar

glisten /'glɪsn/ *vi* brillar

glitter /'glɪtə(r)/ *vi* brillar. ● *n* brillo *m*

gloat /gləʊt/ *vi*. ~ **on/over** regodearse sobre

glob|al /gləʊbl/ *adj* (*worldwide*) mundial; (*all-embracing*) global. **~alization** *n* globalización *f*. **~al warming** *n* calentamiento *m* global. **~e** /gləʊb/ *n* globo *m*

gloom /glu:m/ *n* oscuridad *f*; (*sadness, fig*) tristeza *f*. **~y** *adj* (**-ier, -iest**) triste; (*pessimistic*) pesimista

glor|ify /'glɔ:rɪfaɪ/ *vt* glorificar. **~ious** /'glɔ:rɪəs/ *adj* espléndido; (deed, hero etc) glorioso. **~y** /'glɔ:rɪ/ *n* gloria *f*

gloss /glɒs/ *n* lustre *m*. ~ **(paint)** (pintura *f* al *or* de) esmalte *m*. □ ~ **over** *vt* (*make light of*) minimizar; (*cover up*) encubrir

glossary /'glɒsərɪ/ *n* glosario *m*

glossy /'glɒsɪ/ *adj* brillante

glove /glʌv/ *n* guante *m*. ~ **compartment** *n* (*Auto*) guantera *f*

glow /gləʊ/ *vi* brillar. ● *n* brillo *m*. **~ing** /'gləʊɪŋ/ *adj* incandescente; (account) entusiasta; (complexion) rojo

glucose /'glu:kəʊs/ *n* glucosa *f*

glue /glu:/ *n* cola *f*, goma *f* de pegar. ● *vt* (*pres p* **gluing**) pegar

glum /glʌm/ *adj* (**glummer, glummest**) triste

glutton /'glʌtn/ *n* glotón *m*

gnarled /nɑ:ld/ *adj* nudoso

gnash /næʃ/ *vt*. ~ **one's teeth** rechinar los dientes

gnat /næt/ *n* jején *m*, mosquito *m*

gnaw /nɔ:/ *vt* roer. ● *vi*. ~ **at** roer

gnome /nəʊm/ *n* gnomo *m*

go /gəʊ/

3rd pers sing present **goes;** past **went;** past participle **gone**

● *intransitive verb*

····> ir. **I'm going to France** voy a Francia. **to go shopping** ir de compras. **to go swimming** ir a nadar

····> (*leave*) irse. **we're going on Friday** nos vamos el viernes

····> (*work, function*) (engine, clock) funcionar

····> (*become*) **to go deaf** quedarse sordo. **to go mad** volverse loco. **his face went red** se puso colorado

····> (*stop*) (headache, pain) irse (+ *me/te/le*). **the pain's gone** se me ha ido el dolor

····> (*turn out, progress*) ir. **everything's going very well** todo va muy bien. **how did the exam go?** ¿qué tal te fue en el examen?

····> (*match, suit*) combinar. **the jacket and the trousers go well together** la chaqueta y los pantalones combinan bien.

····> (*cease to function*) (bulb, fuse) fundirse. **the brakes have gone** los frenos no funcionan

● *auxiliary verb* **to be going to** + *infinitive* ir a + *infinitivo*. **it's going to rain** va a llover. **she's going to win!** ¡va a ganar!

● *noun* (*pl* **goes**)

····> (*turn*) turno *m*. **you have three goes** tienes tres turnos. **it's your go** te toca a ti

····> (*attempt*) **to have a go at**

doing sth intentar hacer algo. **have another go** inténtalo de nuevo

····➤(*energy, drive*) empuje *m*. **she has a lot of go** tiene mucho empuje

····➤(*in phrases*) **I've been on the go all day** no he parado en todo el día. **to make a go of sth** sacar algo adelante □ **go across** *vt/vi* cruzar. □ **go after** *vi* perseguir. □ **go away** *vt* irse. □ **go back** *vi* volver. □ **go back on** *vt* faltar a (promise etc). □ **go by** *vi* pasar. □ **go down** *vi* bajar; (sun) ponerse. □ **go for** *vt* (*fam, attack*) atacar. □ **go in** *vi* entrar. □ **go in for** *vt* presentarse para (exam); participar en (competition). □ **go off** *vi* (*leave*) irse; (*go bad*) pasarse; (*explode*) estallar; (lights) apagarse. □ **go on** *vi* seguir; (*happen*) pasar; (*be switched on*) encenderse, prenderse (*LAm*). □ **go out** *vi* salir; (fire, light) apagarse. □ **go over** *vt* (*check*) revisar; (*revise*) repasar. □ **go through** *vt* pasar por; (*search*) registrar; (*check*) examinar. □ **go up** *vi/vt* subir. □ **go without** *vt* pasar sin

goad /gəʊd/ *vt* aguijonear

go-ahead /ˈgəʊəhed/ *n* luz *f* verde. ● *adj* dinámico

goal /gəʊl/ *n* (*Sport*) gol *m*; (*objective*) meta *f*. **~ie** /ˈgəʊlɪ/ *n* ⊞. **~keeper** *n* portero *m*, arquero *m* (*LAm*). **~post** *n* poste *m* de la portería, poste *m* del arco (*LAm*)

goat /gəʊt/ *n* cabra *f*

gobble /ˈgɒbl/ *vt* engullir

goblin /ˈgɒblɪn/ *n* duende *m*

god /gɒd/ *n* dios *m*. **G~** *n* Dios *m*. **~child** *n* ahijado *m*. **~-daughter** *n* ahijada *f*. **~dess** /ˈgɒdes/ *n* diosa *f*. **~father** *n* padrino *m*. **~forsaken** *adj* olvidado de Dios. **~mother** *n* madrina *f*. **~send** *n* beneficio *m* inesperado. **~son** *n* ahijado *m*

going /ˈgəʊɪŋ/ *n* camino *m*; (*racing*) (estado *m* del) terreno *m*. **it is slow/hard ~** es lento/difícil. ● *adj* (price) actual; (concern) en funcionamiento

gold /gəʊld/ *n* oro *m*. ● *adj* de oro. **~en** *adj* de oro; (*in colour*) dorado; (opportunity) único. **~en wedding** *n* bodas *fpl* de oro. **~fish** *n invar* pez *m* de colores. **~mine** *n* mina *f* de oro; (*fig*) fuente *f* de gran riqueza. **~-plated** /-ˈpleɪtɪd/ *adj* chapado en oro. **~smith** *n* orfebre *m*

golf /gɒlf/ *n* golf *m*. **~ ball** *n* pelota *f* de golf. **~ club** *n* palo *m* de golf; (*place*) club *m* de golf. **~course** *n* campo *m* de golf. **~er** *n* jugador *m* de golf

gondola /ˈgɒndələ/ *n* góndola *f*

gone /gɒn/ *see* GO. ● *adj* pasado. **~ six o'clock** después de las seis

gong /gɒŋ/ *n* gong(o) *m*

good /gʊd/ *adj* (**better, best**) bueno, (*before masculine singular noun*) buen. **~ afternoon** buenas tardes. **~ evening** (*before dark*) buenas tardes; (*after dark*) buenas noches. **~ morning** buenos días. **~ night** buenas noches. **as ~ as** (*almost*) casi. **feel ~** sentirse bien. **have a ~ time** divertirse. ● *n* bien *m*. **for ~** para siempre. **it is no ~ shouting** es inútil gritar *etc*. **~bye** /-ˈbaɪ/ *int* ¡adiós! ● *n* adiós *m*. **say ~bye to** despedirse de. **~-for-nothing** /-fənʌθɪŋ/ *adj & n* inútil (*m*). **G~ Friday** *n* Viernes *m* Santo. **~-looking**

/-ˈlʊkɪŋ/ *adj* guapo, buen mozo *m* (*LAm*), buena moza *f* (*LAm*). **~ness** *n* bondad *f*. **~ness!**, **~ness gracious!**, **~ness me!**, **my ~ness!** ¡Dios mío! **~s** *npl* mercancías *fpl*. **~will** /-ˈwɪl/ *n* buena voluntad *f*. **~y** *n* (*Culin, fam*) golosina *f*; (*in film*) bueno *m*

gooey /ˈguːɪ/ *adj* (**gooier**, **gooiest**) 🅸 pegajoso; (*fig*) sentimental

g

goofy /ˈguːfɪ/ *adj* (*Amer*) necio

google (®) /ˈguːgl/ *vt, vi* 🅸 googlear 🅸

goose /guːs/ *n* (*pl* **geese**) oca *f*, ganso *m*. **~berry** /ˈgʊzbərɪ/ *n* uva *f* espina, grosella *f* espinosa. **~-flesh** *n*, **~-pimples** *npl* carne *f* de gallina

gore /gɔː(r)/ *n* sangre *f*. ● *vt* cornear

gorge /gɔːdʒ/ *n* (*of river*) garganta *f*. ● *vt*. **~ o.s.** hartarse (**on** de)

gorgeous /ˈgɔːdʒəs/ *adj* precioso; (*splendid*) magnífico

gorilla /gəˈrɪlə/ *n* gorila *m*

gorse /gɔːs/ *n* aulaga *f*

gory /ˈgɔːrɪ/ *adj* (**-ier**, **-iest**) 🅸 sangriento

gosh /gɒʃ/ *int* ¡caramba!

go-slow /gəʊˈsləʊ/ *n* huelga *f* de celo, huelga *f* pasiva

gospel /ˈgɒspl/ *n* evangelio *m*

gossip /ˈgɒsɪp/ *n* (*chatter*) chismorreo *m*; (*person*) chismoso *m*. ● *vi* (*pt* **gossiped**) (*chatter*) chismorrear; (*repeat scandal*) contar chismes

got /gɒt/ *see* GET. **have ~** tener. **I've ~ to do it** tengo que hacerlo.

gotten /ˈgɒtn/ *see* GET

gouge /gaʊdʒ/ *vt* abrir (hole). □ **~ out** *vt* sacar

gourmet /ˈgʊəmeɪ/ *n* gastrónomo *m*

govern /ˈgʌvən/ *vt/i* gobernar. **~ess** *n* institutriz *f*. **~ment** *n* gobierno *m*. **~or** *n* gobernador *m*

gown /gaʊn/ *n* vestido *m*; (*of judge, teacher*) toga *f*

GP *abbr see* GENERAL PRACTITIONER

GPS *abbrev* **Global Positioning System** GPS *m*

grab /græb/ *vt* (*pt* **grabbed**) agarrar

grace /greɪs/ *n* gracia *f*. **~ful** *adj* elegante

gracious /ˈgreɪʃəs/ *adj* (*kind*) amable; (*elegant*) elegante

grade /greɪd/ *n* clase *f*, categoría *f*; (*of goods*) clase *f*, calidad *f*; (*on scale*) grado *m*; (*school mark*) nota *f*; (*Amer, class*) curso *m*, año *m*

gradient /ˈgreɪdɪənt/ *n* pendiente *f*, gradiente *f* (*LAm*)

gradual /ˈgrædʒʊəl/ *adj* gradual. **~ly** *adv* gradualmente, poco a poco

graduat|e /ˈgrædjʊət/ *n* (*Univ*) licenciado. ● /ˈgrædjʊeɪt/ *vi* licenciarse. **~ion** /-ˈeɪʃn/ *n* graduación *f*

graffiti /grəˈfiːtɪ/ *npl* graffiti *mpl*, pintadas *fpl*

graft /grɑːft/ *n* (*Med, Bot*) injerto *m*; (*Amer fam, bribery*) chanchullos *mpl*. ● *vt* injertar

grain /greɪn/ *n* grano *m*

gram /græm/ *n* gramo *m*

gramma|r /ˈgræmə(r)/ *n* gramática *f*. **~tical** /grəˈmætɪkl/ *adj* gramatical

gramme /græm/ *n* gramo *m*

grand /grænd/ *adj* (**-er**, **-est**) magnífico; (*fam, excellent*) estupendo. **~child** *n* nieto *m*. **~daughter** *n* nieta *f*. **~eur** /ˈgrændʒə(r)/ *n* grandiosidad *f*. **~father** *n* abuelo *m*. **~father clock** *n* reloj *m* de caja. **~iose** /ˈgrændɪəʊs/ *adj* grandioso.

~mother *n* abuela *f.* **~parents** *npl* abuelos *mpl.* **~ piano** *n* piano *m* de cola. **~son** *n* nieto *m.* **~stand** /'grænstænd/ *n* tribuna *f*

granite /'grænɪt/ *n* granito *m*

granny /'grænɪ/ *n* [I] abuela *f*

grant /grɑ:nt/ *vt* conceder; (*give*) donar; (*admit*) admitir (**that** que). **take for ~ed** dar por sentado. ● *n* concesión *f*; (*Univ*) beca *f*

granule /'grænu:l/ *n* gránulo *m*

grape /greɪp/ *n* uva *f.* **~fruit** *n invar* pomelo *m*, toronja *f* (*LAm*)

graph /grɑ:f/ *n* gráfica *f*

graphic /'græfɪk/ *adj* gráfico. **~s** *npl* diseño *m* gráfico; (*Comp*) gráficos *mpl*

grapple /'græpl/ *vi.* **~ with** forcejear con; (*mentally*) lidiar con

grasp /grɑ:sp/ *vt* agarrar. ● *n* (*hold*) agarro *m*; (*fig*) comprensión *f.* **~ing** *adj* avaro

grass /grɑ:s/ *n* hierba *f.* **~hopper** *n* saltamontes *m.* **~ roots** *npl* base *f* popular. ● *adj* de las bases. **~y** *adj* cubierto de hierba

grate /greɪt/ *n* rejilla *f*; (*fireplace*) chimenea *f.* ● *vt* rallar. ● *vi* rechinar; (*be irritating*) ser crispante

grateful /'greɪtfl/ *adj* agradecido. **~ly** *adv* con gratitud

grater /'greɪtə(r)/ *n* rallador *m*

gratif|ied /'grætɪfaɪd/ *adj* contento. **~y** /'grætɪfaɪ/ *vt* satisfacer; (*please*) agradar a. **~ying** *adj* agradable

grating /'greɪtɪŋ/ *n* reja *f*

gratitude /'grætɪtju:d/ *n* gratitud *f*

gratuitous /grə'tju:ɪtəs/ *adj* gratuito

gratuity /grə'tju:ətɪ/ *n* (*tip*) propina *f*

grave /greɪv/ *n* sepultura *f.* ● *adj* (**-er, -est**) (*serious*) grave

gravel /'grævl/ *n* grava *f*

gravely /'greɪvlɪ/ *adv* (*seriously*) seriamente; (*solemnly*) con gravedad

grave: ~stone *n* lápida *f.* **~yard** *n* cementerio *m*

gravitate /'grævɪteɪt/ *vi* gravitar

gravity /'grævətɪ/ *n* gravedad *f*

gravy /'greɪvɪ/ *n* salsa *f*

gray /greɪ/ *adj & n* (*Amer*) *see* GREY

graze /greɪz/ *vi* (*eat*) pacer. ● *vt* (*touch*) rozar; (*scrape*) raspar. ● *n* rasguño *m*

greas|e /gri:s/ *n* grasa *f.* ● *vt* engrasar. **~eproof paper** *n* papel *m* encerado *or* de cera. **~y** *adj* (hands) grasiento; (food) graso; (hair, skin) graso, grasoso (*LAm*)

great /greɪt/ *adj* (**-er, -est**) grande, (*before singular noun*) gran; (*fam, very good*) estupendo. **G~ Britain** *n* Gran Bretaña *f.* **~-grandfather** /-'grænfɑ:ðə(r)/ *n* bisabuelo *m.* **~-grandmother** /-'grænmʌðə(r)/ *n* bisabuela *f*, **~ly** *adv* (*very*) muy; (*much*) mucho

Greece /gri:s/ *n* Grecia *f*

greed /gri:d/ *n* avaricia *f*; (*for food*) glotonería *f.* **~y** *adj* avaro; (*for food*) glotón

Greek /gri:k/ *adj & n* griego (*m*)

green /gri:n/ *adj* (**-er, -est**) verde. ● *n* verde *m*; (*grass*) césped *m.* **~ belt** *n* zona *f* verde. **~ card** *n* (*Amer*) permiso *m* de residencia y trabajo. **~ery** *n* verdor *m.* **~gage** /-geɪdʒ/ *n* claudia *f.* **~grocer** *n* verdulero *m.* **~house** *n* invernadero *m.* **the ~house effect** el efecto invernadero. **~ light** *n* luz *f* verde. **~s** *npl* verduras *fpl*

g

Green Card En EE.UU., documento oficial que toda persona que no sea ciudadana norteamericana debe obtener para residir y trabajar en este país. En el Reino Unido, es el documento que se debe obtener de la compañía de seguros, cuando se lleva un automóvil al extranjero, a fin de que siga vigente la cobertura de la póliza.

greet /gri:t/ *vt* saludar; (*receive*) recibir. **~ing** *n* saludo *m*

gregarious /grɪ'geərɪəs/ *adj* gregario; (person) sociable

grenade /grɪ'neɪd/ *n* granada *f*

grew /gru:/ *see* GROW

grey /greɪ/ *adj* (**-er**, **-est**) gris. **have ~ hair** ser canoso. • *n* gris *m*. **~hound** *n* galgo *m*

grid /grɪd/ *n* reja *f*; (*Elec, network*) red *f*; (*on map*) cuadriculado *m*

grief /gri:f/ *n* dolor *m*. **come to ~** (person) acabar mal; (*fail*) fracasar

grievance /'gri:vns/ *n* queja *f* formal

grieve /gri:v/ *vt* apenar. • *vi* afligirse. **~ for** llorar

grievous /'gri:vəs/ *adj* doloroso; (*serious*) grave. **~ bodily harm** (*Jurid*) lesiones *fpl* (corporales) graves

grill /grɪl/ *n* parrilla *f*. • *vt* asar a la parrilla; (🅸, *interrogate*) interrogar

grille /grɪl/ *n* rejilla *f*

grim /grɪm/ *adj* (**grimmer**, **grimmest**) severo

grimace /'grɪməs/ *n* mueca *f*. • *vi* hacer muecas

grim|e /graɪm/ *n* mugre *f*. **~y** *adj* mugriento

grin /grɪn/ *vt* (*pt* **grinned**) sonreír. • *n* sonrisa *f* (abierta)

grind /graɪnd/ *vt* (*pt* **ground**) moler (coffee, corn etc); (*pulverize*) pulverizar; (*sharpen*) afilar; (*Amer*) picar, moler (meat)

grip /grɪp/ *vt* (*pt* **gripped**) agarrar; (*interest*) captar. • *n* (*hold*) agarro *m*; (*strength of hand*) apretón *m*; (*hairgrip*) horquilla *f*, pasador *m* (*Mex*). **come to ~s with** entender (subject)

grisly /'grɪzlɪ/ *adj* (**-ier**, **-iest**) horrible

gristle /'grɪsl/ *n* cartílago *m*

grit /grɪt/ *n* arenilla *f*; (*fig*) agallas *fpl*. • *vt* (*pt* **gritted**) echar arena en (road). **~ one's teeth** (*fig*) acorazarse

groan /grəʊn/ *vi* gemir. • *n* gemido *m*

grocer /'grəʊsə(r)/ *n* tendero *m*, abarrotero *m* (*Mex*). **~ies** *npl* comestibles *mpl*. **~y** *n* tienda *f* de comestibles, tienda *f* de abarrotes (*Mex*)

groggy /'grɒgɪ/ *adj* (*weak*) débil; (*unsteady*) inseguro; (*ill*) malucho

groin /grɔɪn/ *n* ingle *f*

groom /gru:m/ *n* mozo *m* de caballos; (*bridegroom*) novio *m*. • *vt* almohazar (horses); (*fig*) preparar

groove /gru:v/ *n* ranura *f*; (*in record*) surco *m*

grope /grəʊp/ *vi* (*find one's way*) moverse a tientas. **~ for** buscar a tientas

gross /grəʊs/ *adj* (**-er**, **-est**) (*coarse*) grosero; (*Com*) bruto; (*fat*) grueso; (*flagrant*) flagrante. • *n invar* gruesa *f*. **~ly** *adv* (*very*) enormemente

grotesque /grəʊ'tesk/ *adj* grotesco

ground /graʊnd/ *see* GRIND. • *n* suelo *m*; (*area*) terreno *m*; (*reason*) razón *f*; (*Amer, Elec*) toma *f* de tierra. ● *vt* fundar (theory); retirar del servicio (aircraft). **~s** *npl* jardines *mpl*; (*sediment*) poso *m*. **~ beef** *n* (*Amer*) carne *f* picada, carne *f* molida. **~ cloth** *n* (*Amer*) see **~SHEET**. **~ floor** *n* planta *f* baja. **~ing** *n* base *f*, conocimientos *mpl* (**in** de). **~less** *adj* infundado. **~sheet** *n* suelo *m* impermeable (de una tienda de campaña). **~work** *n* trabajo *m* preparatorio

group /gru:p/ *n* grupo *m*. ● *vt* agrupar. ● *vi* agruparse

grouse /graʊs/ *n invar* (*bird*) urogallo *m*. ● *vi* 🅘 rezongar

grovel /'grɒvl/ *vi* (*pt* **grovelled**) postrarse; (*fig*) arrastrarse

grow /grəʊ/ *vi* (*pt* **grew**, *pp* **grown**) crecer; (*become*) volverse, ponerse. ● *vt* cultivar. **~ a beard** dejarse (crecer) la barba. □ **~ up** *vi* hacerse mayor. **~ing** *adj* (quantity) cada vez mayor; (influence) creciente

growl /graʊl/ *vi* gruñir. ● *n* gruñido *m*

grown /grəʊn/ see **GROW**. ● *adj* adulto. **~-up** *adj* & *n* adulto (*m*)

growth /grəʊθ/ *n* crecimiento *m*; (*increase*) aumento *m*; (*development*) desarrollo *m*; (*Med*) bulto *m*, tumor *m*

grub /grʌb/ *n* (*larva*) larva *f*; (*fam, food*) comida *f*

grubby /'grʌbɪ/ *adj* (**-ier**, **-iest**) mugriento

grudg|e /grʌdʒ/ *vt* see **BEGRUDGE**. ● *n* rencilla *f*. **bear/have a ~e against s.o.** guardarle rencor a uno. **~ingly** *adv* de mala gana

gruelling /'gru:əlɪŋ/ *adj* agotador

gruesome /'gru:səm/ *adj* horrible

gruff /grʌf/ *adj* (**-er**, **-est**) (manners) brusco; (voice) ronco

grumble /'grʌmbl/ *vi* rezongar

grumpy /'grʌmpɪ/ *adj* (**-ier**, **-iest**) malhumorado

grunt /grʌnt/ *vi* gruñir. ● *n* gruñido *m*

guarant|ee /gærən'ti:/ *n* garantía *f*. ● *vt* garantizar. **~or** *n* garante *m* & *f*

guard /gɑ:d/ *vt* proteger; (*watch*) vigilar. ● *n* (*vigilance, Mil group*) guardia *f*; (*person*) guardia *m*; (*on train*) jefe *m* de tren. □ **~ against** *vt* evitar; protegerse contra (risk). **~ed** *adj* cauteloso. **~ian** /-ɪən/ *n* guardián *m*; (*of orphan*) tutor *m*

Guatemala /gwɑ:tə'mɑ:lə/ *n* Guatemala *f*. **~n** *adj* & *n* guatemalteco (*m*)

guer(r)illa /gə'rɪlə/ *n* guerrillero *m*. **~ warfare** *n* guerrilla *f*

guess /ges/ *vt* adivinar; (*Amer, suppose*) suponer. ● *n* conjetura *f*. **~work** *n* conjeturas *fpl*

guest /gest/ *n* invitado *m*; (*in hotel*) huésped *m*. **~house** *n* casa *f* de huéspedes

guffaw /gʌ'fɔ:/ *n* carcajada *f*. ● *vi* reírse a carcajadas

guidance /'gaɪdəns/ *n* (*advice*) consejos *mpl*; (*information*) información *f*

guide /gaɪd/ *n* (*person*) guía *m* & *f*; (*book*) guía *f*. **Girl G~** exploradora *f*, guía *f*. ● *vt* guiar. **~book** *n* guía *f*. **~ dog** *n* perro *m* guía, perro *m* lazarillo. **~d missile** *n* proyectil *m* teledirigido. **~lines** *npl* pauta *f*

guild /gɪld/ *n* gremio *m*

guile /gaɪl/ *n* astucia *f*

guillotine /'gɪləti:n/ *n* guillotina *f*

guilt /gɪlt/ *n* culpa *f*; (*Jurid*) culpabilidad *f*. **~y** *adj* culpable

guinea pig /'gɪnɪ/ *n* conejillo *m*

de Indias, cobaya *f*
guitar /gɪ'tɑ:(r)/ *n* guitarra *f*. **~ist** *n* guitarrista *m & f*
gulf /gʌlf/ *n* (*part of sea*) golfo *m*; (*gap*) abismo *m*
gull /gʌl/ *n* gaviota *f*
gullet /'gʌlɪt/ *n* garganta *f*, gaznate *m* [!]
gullible /'gʌləbl/ *adj* crédulo
gully /'gʌlɪ/ *n* (*ravine*) barranco *m*
gulp /gʌlp/ *vt*. □ ~ **(down)** tragarse de prisa. ● *vi* tragar saliva. ● *n* trago *m*
gum /gʌm/ *n* (*in mouth*) encía *f*; (*glue*) goma *f* de pegar; (*for chewing*) chicle *m*. ● *vt* (*pt* **gummed**) engomar
gun /gʌn/ *n* (*pistol*) pistola *f*; (*rifle*) fusil *m*, escopeta *f*; (*artillery piece*) cañón *m*. ● *vt* (*pt* **gunned**). □ ~ **down** *vt* abatir a tiros. **~fire** *n* tiros *mpl*
gun: ~man /-mən/ *n* pistolero *m*, gatillero *m* (*Mex*). **~powder** *n* pólvora *f*. **~shot** *n* disparo *m*
gurgle /'gɜ:gl/ *vi* (liquid) gorgotear; (baby) gorjear
gush /gʌʃ/ *vi*. ~ **(out)** salir a borbotones. ● *n* (*of liquid*) chorro *m*; (*fig*) torrente *m*
gusset /'gʌsɪt/ *n* entretela *f*
gust /gʌst/ *n* ráfaga *f*
gusto /'gʌstəʊ/ *n* entusiasmo *m*
gusty /'gʌstɪ/ *adj* borrascoso
gut /gʌt/ *n* intestino *m*. ● *vt* (*pt* **gutted**) destripar; (fire) destruir. **~s** *npl* tripas *fpl*; (*fam, courage*) agallas *fpl*
gutter /'gʌtə(r)/ *n* (*on roof*) canalón *m*, canaleta *f*; (*in street*) cuneta *f*; (*fig, slum*) arroyo *m*
guttural /'gʌtərəl/ *adj* gutural
guy /gaɪ/ *n* (*fam, man*) tipo *m* [!], tío *m* [!]
guzzle /'gʌzl/ *vt* (*drink*) chupar [!]; (*eat*) tragarse
gym /dʒɪm/ *n* [!] (*gymnasium*) gimnasio *m*; (*gymnastics*) gimnasia *f*
gymnasium /dʒɪm'neɪzɪəm/ *n* gimnasio *m*
gymnast /'dʒɪmnæst/ *n* gimnasta *m & f*. **~ics** /dʒɪm'næstɪks/ *npl* gimnasia *f*
gymslip /'dʒɪmslɪp/ *n* túnica *f* (de gimnasia)
gynaecolog|ist /gaɪnɪ'kɒlədʒɪst/ *n* ginecólogo *m*. **~y** *n* ginecología *f*
gypsy /'dʒɪpsɪ/ *n* gitano *m*
gyrate /dʒaɪə'reɪt/ *vi* girar

Hh

haberdashery /'hæbədæʃərɪ/ *n* mercería *f*; (*Amer, clothes*) ropa *f* y accesorios *mpl* para caballeros
habit /'hæbɪt/ *n* costumbre *f*; (*Relig, costume*) hábito *m*. **be in the ~ of** (+ *gerund*) tener la costumbre de (+ *infinitivo*), soler (+ *infinitivo*). **get into the ~ of** (+ *gerund*) acostumbrarse a (+ *infinitivo*)
habitable /'hæbɪtəbl/ *adj* habitable
habitat /'hæbɪtæt/ *n* hábitat *m*
habitation /hæbɪ'teɪʃn/ *n* habitación *f*
habitual /hə'bɪtjʊəl/ *adj* habitual; (liar) inveterado. **~ly** *adv* de costumbre
hack /hæk/ *n* (*old horse*) jamelgo

m; (*writer*) escritorzuelo *m*. ●*vt* cortar. **~er** *n* (*Comp*) pirata *m* informático

hackneyed /ˈhæknɪd/ *adj* manido

had /hæd/ *see* **HAVE**

haddock /ˈhædək/ *n invar* eglefino *m*

haemorrhage /ˈhemərɪdʒ/ *n* hemorragia *f*

haemorrhoids /ˈhemərɔɪdz/ *npl* hemorroides *fpl*

hag /hæg/ *n* bruja *f*

haggard /ˈhægəd/ *adj* demacrado

hail /heɪl/ *n* granizo *m*. ●*vi* granizar. ●*vt* (*greet*) saludar; llamar (taxi). □ **~ from** *vt* venir de. **~stone** *n* grano *m* de granizo

hair /heə(r)/ *n* pelo *m*. **~band** *n* cinta *f*, banda *f* (*Mex*). **~brush** *n* cepillo *m* (para el pelo). **~cut** *n* corte *m* de pelo. **have a ~cut** cortarse el pelo. **~do** *n* 🄸 peinado *m*. **~dresser** *n* peluquero *m*. **~dresser's (shop)** *n* peluquería *f*. **~-dryer** *n* secador *m*, secadora *f* (*Mex*). **~grip** *n* horquilla *f*, pasador *m* (*Mex*). **~pin** *n* horquilla *f*. **~pin bend** *n* curva *f* cerrada. **~-raising** *adj* espeluznante. **~spray** *n* laca *f*, fijador *m* (para el pelo). **~style** *n* peinado *m*. **~y** *adj* (**-ier**, **-iest**) peludo

half /hɑːf/ *n* (*pl* **halves**) mitad *f*. ●*adj* medio. **~ a dozen** media docena *f*. **~ an hour** media hora *f*. ●*adv* medio, a medias. **~-hearted** /-ˈhɑːtɪd/ *adj* poco entusiasta. **~-mast** /-ˈmɑːst/ *n*. **at ~-mast** a media asta. **~ term** *n* vacaciones *fpl* de medio trimestre. **~-time** *n* (*Sport*) descanso *m*, medio tiempo *m* (*LAm*). **~way** *adj* medio. ●*adv* a medio camino

hall /hɔːl/ *n* (*entrance*) vestíbulo *m*; (*for public events*) sala *f*, salón *m*. **~ of residence** residencia *f* universitaria, colegio *m* mayor. **~mark** /-mɑːk/ *n* (*on gold, silver*) contraste *m*; (*fig*) sello *m* (distintivo)

hallo /həˈləʊ/ *int see* **HELLO**

Hallowe'en /ˈhæləʊˈiːn/ *n* víspera *f* de Todos los Santos

hallucination /həluːsɪˈneɪʃn/ *n* alucinación *f*

halo /ˈheɪləʊ/ *n* (*pl* **-oes**) aureola *f*

halt /hɔːlt/ *n*. **come to a ~** pararse. ●*vt* parar. ●*vi* pararse

halve /hɑːv/ *vt* reducir a la mitad; (*divide into halves*) partir por la mitad

halves /hɑːvz/ *see* **HALF**

ham /hæm/ *n* jamón *m*

hamburger /ˈhæmbɜːgə(r)/ *n* hamburguesa *f*

hammer /ˈhæmə(r)/ *n* martillo *m*. ●*vt* martill(e)ar

hammock /ˈhæmək/ *n* hamaca *f*

hamper /ˈhæmpə(r)/ *n* cesta *f*. ●*vt* estorbar

hamster /ˈhæmstə(r)/ *n* hámster *m*

hand /ˈhænd/ *n* mano *f*; (*of clock, watch*) manecilla *f*; (*worker*) obrero *m*. **by ~** a mano. **lend a ~** echar una mano. **on ~** a mano. **on the one ~... on the other ~** por un lado... por otro. **out of ~** fuera de control. **to ~** a mano. ●*vt* pasar. □ **~ down** *vt* pasar. □ **~ in** *vt* entregar. □ **~ over** *vt* entregar. □ **~ out** *vt* distribuir. **~bag** *n* bolso *m*, cartera *f* (*LAm*), bolsa *f* (*Mex*). **~brake** *n* (*in car*) freno *m* de mano. **~cuffs** *npl* esposas *fpl*. **~ful** *n* puñado *m*; (*fam, person*) persona *f* difícil

handicap /ˈhændɪkæp/ *n* desventaja *f*; (*Sport*) hándicap *m*. **~ped** *adj* minusválido

handicraft /ˈhændɪkrɑ:ft/ *n* artesanía *f*

handkerchief /ˈhæŋkətʃɪf/ *n* (*pl* **-fs** *or* **-chieves** /-ˈtʃi:vz/) pañuelo *m*

handle /ˈhændl/ *n* (*of door*) picaporte *m*; (*of drawer*) tirador *m*; (*of implement*) mango *m*; (*of cup, bag, jug*) asa *f*. • *vt* manejar; (*touch*) tocar. **~bars** *npl* manillar *m*, manubrio *m* (*LAm*).

hand: ~out *n* folleto *m*; (*of money, food*) dádiva *f*. **~shake** *n* apretón *m* de manos

h

handsome /ˈhænsəm/ *adj* (*good-looking*) guapo, buen mozo, buena moza (*LAm*); (*generous*) generoso

handwriting /ˈhændraɪtɪŋ/ *n* letra *f*

handy /ˈhændɪ/ *adj* (**-ier**, **-iest**) (*useful*) práctico; (person) diestro; (*near*) a mano. **come in ~** venir muy bien. **~man** *n* hombre *m* habilidoso

hang /hæŋ/ *vt* (*pt* **hung**) colgar; (*pt* **hanged**) (*capital punishment*) ahorcar. • *vi* colgar; (clothing) caer. • *n*. **get the ~ of sth** coger el truco de algo. □ **~ about, ~ around** *vi* holgazanear. □ **~ on** *vi* (*wait*) esperar. □ **~ out** *vt* tender (washing). □ **~ up** *vi* (*also telephone*) colgar

hangar /ˈhæŋə(r)/ *n* hangar *m*

hang: ~er *n* (*for clothes*) percha *f*. **~-glider** *n* alta *f* delta, deslizador *m* (*Mex*). **~over** (*after drinking*) resaca *f*. **~-up** *n* 🅸 complejo *m*

hankie, hanky /ˈhæŋkɪ/ *n* 🅸 pañuelo *m*

haphazard /hæpˈhæzəd/ *adj* fortuito. **~ly** *adv* al azar

happen /ˈhæpən/ *vi* pasar, suceder, ocurrir. **if he ~s to come** si acaso viene. **~ing** *n* acontecimiento *m*

happ|ily /ˈhæpɪlɪ/ *adv* alegremente; (*fortunately*) afortunadamente. **~iness** *n* felicidad *f*. **~y** *adj* (**-ier**, **-iest**) feliz; (*satisfied*) contento

harass /ˈhærəs/ *vt* acosar. **~ment** *n* acoso *m*

harbour /ˈhɑ:bə(r)/ *n* puerto *m*

hard /hɑ:d/ *adj* (**-er**, **-est**) duro; (*difficult*) difícil. • *adv* (work) mucho; (*pull*) con fuerza. **~ done by** tratado injustamente. **~-boiled egg** /-ˈbɔɪld/ *n* huevo *m* duro. **~ disk** *n* disco *m* duro. **~en** *vt* endurecer. • *vi* endurecerse. **~-headed** /-ˈhedɪd/ *adj* realista

hardly /ˈhɑ:dlɪ/ *adv* apenas. **~ ever** casi nunca

hard: ~ness *n* dureza *f*. **~ship** *n* apuro *m*. **~ shoulder** *n* arcén *m*, acotamiento *m* (*Mex*). **~ware** *n* /-weə(r)/ ferretería *f*; (*Comp*) hardware *m*. **~ware store** *n* (*Amer*) ferretería *f*. **~-working** /-ˈwɜ:kɪŋ/ *adj* trabajador

hardy /ˈhɑ:dɪ/ *adj* (**-ier**, **-iest**) fuerte; (plants) resistente

hare /heə(r)/ *n* liebre *f*

hark /hɑ:k/ *vi* escuchar. □ **~ back to** *vt* volver a

harm /hɑ:m/ *n* daño *m*. **there is no ~ in asking** con preguntar no se pierde nada. • *vt* hacer daño a (person); dañar (thing); perjudicar (interests). **~ful** *adj* perjudicial. **~less** *adj* inofensivo

harmonica /hɑ:ˈmɒnɪkə/ *n* armónica *f*

harmon|ious /hɑ:ˈməʊnɪəs/ *adj* armonioso. **~y** /ˈhɑ:mənɪ/ *n* armonía *f*

harness /ˈhɑːnɪs/ *n* arnés *m*. ● *vt* poner el arnés a (horse); (*fig*) aprovechar

harp /hɑːp/ *n* arpa *f*. ● *vi*. ~ **on (about)** machacar (con)

harpoon /hɑːˈpuːn/ *n* arpón *m*

harpsichord /ˈhɑːpsɪkɔːd/ *n* clavicémbalo *m*, clave *m*

harrowing / ˈhærəʊɪŋ/ *adj* desgarrador

harsh /hɑːʃ/ *adj* (**-er**, **-est**) duro, severo; (light) fuerte; (climate) riguroso. **~ly** *adv* severamente. **~ness** *n* severidad *f*

harvest /ˈhɑːvɪst/ *n* cosecha *f*. ● *vt* cosechar

has /hæz/ *see* HAVE

hassle /ˈhæsl/ *n* [I] lío *m* [I], rollo *m* [I]. ● *vt* (*harass*) fastidiar

hast|e /heɪst/ *n* prisa *f*, apuro *m* (*LAm*). **make ~e** darse prisa. **~ily** /ˈheɪstɪlɪ/ *adv* de prisa. **~y** /ˈheɪstɪ/ *adj* (**-ier**, **-iest**) rápido; (*rash*) precipitado

hat /hæt/ *n* sombrero *m*

hatch /hætʃ/ *n* (*for food*) ventanilla *f*; (*Naut*) escotilla *f*. ● *vt* empollar (eggs); tramar (plot). ● *vi* salir del cascarón. **~back** *n* coche *m* con tres/cinco puertas; (*door*) puerta *f* trasera

hatchet /ˈhætʃɪt/ *n* hacha *f*

hat|e /heɪt/ *n* odio *m*. ● *vt* odiar. **~eful** *adj* odioso. **~red** /ˈheɪtrɪd/ *n* odio *m*

haughty /ˈhɔːtɪ/ *adj* (**-ier**, **-iest**) altivo

haul /hɔːl/ *vt* arrastrar; transportar (goods). ● *n* (*catch*) redada *f*; (*stolen goods*) botín *m*; (*journey*) recorrido *m*. **~age** /-ɪdʒ/ *n* transporte *m*. **~er** (*Amer*), **~ier** *n* transportista *m & f*

haunt /hɔːnt/ *vt* frecuentar; (ghost) rondar. ● *n* sitio *m* preferido. **~ed** *adj* (house) embrujado; (look) angustiado

have /hæv//həv, əv/

3rd person singular present **has**, past **had**

● *transitive verb*

⟶ tener. **I ~ three sisters** tengo tres hermanas. **do you ~ a credit card?** ¿tiene una tarjeta de crédito?

⟶ (*in requests*) **can I ~ a kilo of apples, please?** ¿me da un kilo de manzanas, por favor?

⟶ (*eat*) comer. **I had a pizza** comí una pizza

⟶ (*drink*) tomar. **come and ~ a drink** ven a tomar una copa

⟶ (*smoke*) fumar (cigarette)

⟶ (*hold, organize*) hacer (party, meeting)

⟶ (*get, receive*) **I had a letter from Tony yesterday** recibí una carta de Tony ayer. **we've had no news of her** no hemos tenido noticias suyas

⟶ (*illness*) tener (flu, headache). **to ~ a cold** estar resfriado, tener catarro

⟶ **to have sth done: we had it painted** lo hicimos pintar. **I had my hair cut** me corté el pelo

⟶ **to have it in for s.o.** tenerle manía a uno

● *auxiliary verb*

⟶ haber. **I've seen her already** ya la he visto, ya la vi (*LAm*)

⟶ **to have just done sth** acabar de hacer algo. **I've just**

h

seen her acabo de verla

····➤ **to have to do sth** tener que hacer algo. **I ~ to** *or* **I've got to go to the bank** tengo que ir al banco

····➤ (*in tag questions*) **you've met her, ~n't you?** ya la conoces, ¿no? *or* ¿verdad? *or* ¿no es cierto?

····➤ (*in short answers*) **you've forgotten something - have I?** has olvidado algo - ¿sí?

h

haven /'heɪvn/ *n* puerto *m*; (*refuge*) refugio *m*

haversack /'hævəsæk/ *n* mochila *f*

havoc /'hævək/ *n* estragos *mpl*

hawk /hɔ:k/ *n* halcón *m*

hawthorn /'hɔ:θɔ:n/ *n* espino *m*

hay /heɪ/ *n* heno *m*. **~ fever** *n* fiebre *f* del heno. **~stack** *n* almiar *m*. **~wire** *adj*. **go ~wire** (*plans*) desorganizarse; (machine) estropearse

hazard /'hæzəd/ *n* riesgo *m*. **~ous** *adj* arriesgado

haze /heɪz/ *n* neblina *f*

hazel /'heɪzl/ *n* avellano *m*. **~nut** *n* avellana *f*

hazy /'heɪzɪ/ *adj* (**-ier**, **-iest**) nebuloso

he /hi:/ *pron* él

head /hed/ *n* cabeza *f*; (*of family, government*) jefe *m*; (*of organization*) director *m*; (*of beer*) espuma *f*. **~s or tails** cara o cruz. ● *adj* principal. ● *vt* encabezar, cabecear (ball). □ **~ for** *vt* dirigirse a. **~ache** *n* dolor *m* de cabeza. **~er** *n* (*football*) cabezazo *m*. **~first** /-'fɜ:st/ *adv* de cabeza. **~ing** *n* título *m*, encabezamiento *m*. **~lamp** *n* faro *m*, foco *m* (*LAm*). **~land** /-lənd/ *n* promontorio *m*. **~line** *n* titular *m*. **the news ~lines** el resumen informativo. **~long** *adv* de cabeza; (*precipitately*) precipitadamente. **~master** *n* director *m*. **~mistress** *n* directora *f*. **~-on** /-'ɒn/ *adj & adv* de frente. **~phones** *npl* auriculares *mpl*, cascos *mpl*. **~quarters** /-'kwɔ:təz/ *n* (*of business*) oficina *f* central; (*Mil*) cuartel *m* general. **~strong** *adj* testarudo. **~teacher** /-'ti:tʃə(r)/ *n* director *m*. **~y** *adj* (**-ier**, **-iest**) (scent) embriagador

heal /hi:l/ *vt* curar. ● *vi* cicatrizarse

health /helθ/ *n* salud *f*. **~y** *adj* sano

heap /hi:p/ *n* montón *m*. ● *vt* amontonar.

hear /hɪə(r)/ *vt/i* (*pt* **heard** /hɜ:d/) oír. **~, ~!** ¡bravo! **~ about** oír hablar de. **~ from** recibir noticias de. **~ing** *n* oído *m*; (*Jurid*) vista *f*. **~ing-aid** *n* audífono *m*. **~say** *n* rumores *mpl*

hearse /hɜ:s/ *n* coche *m* fúnebre

heart / hɑ:t/ *n* corazón *m*. **at ~** en el fondo. **by ~** de memoria. **lose ~** descorazonarse. **~ache** *n* congoja *f*. **~ attack** *n* ataque *m* al corazón, infarto *m*. **~break** *n* congoja *f*. **~breaking** *adj* desgarrador. **~burn** *n* ardor *m* de estómago. **~felt** *adj* sincero

hearth /hɑ:θ/ *n* hogar *m*

heart: ~ily *adv* de buena gana. **~less** *adj* cruel. **~y** *adj* (*welcome*) caluroso; (meal) abundante

heat /hi:t/ *n* calor *m*; (*contest*) (prueba *f*) eliminatoria *f*. ● *vt* calentar. ● *vi* calentarse. **~ed** *adj* (*fig*) acalorado. **~er** *n* calentador *m*

heath /hi:θ/ *n* brezal *m*, monte *m*

heathen /'hi:ðn/ *n & a* pagano (*m*)

heather /'heðə(r)/ *n* brezo *m*

heat: ~ing *n* calefacción *f.* **~stroke** *n* insolación *f.* **~wave** *n* ola *f* de calor

heave /hi:v/ *vt* (*lift*) levantar; exhalar (sigh); (*fam, throw*) tirar. ● *vi* (*pull*) tirar, jalar (*LAm*); (*[!], retch*) dar arcadas

heaven /ˈhevn/ *n* cielo *m.* **~ly** *adj* celestial; (*astronomy*) celeste; (*fam, excellent*) divino

heav|ily /ˈhevɪlɪ/ *adv* pesadamente; (*smoke, drink*) mucho. **~y** *adj* (**-ier, -iest**) pesado; (rain) fuerte; (traffic) denso. **~yweight** *n* peso *m* pesado

heckle /ˈhekl/ *vt* interrumpir

hectic /ˈhektɪk/ *adj* febril

he'd /hi:d/ = **he had, he would**

hedge /hedʒ/ *n* seto *m* (vivo). ● *vi* escaparse por la tangente. **~hog** *n* erizo *m*

heed /hi:d/ *vt* hacer caso de. ● *n.* **take ~** tener cuidado

heel /hi:l/ *n* talón *m*; (*of shoe*) tacón *m*

hefty /ˈheftɪ/ *adj* (**-ier, -iest**) (*sturdy*) fuerte; (*heavy*) pesado

heifer /ˈhefə(r)/ *n* novilla *f*

height /haɪt/ *n* altura *f*; (*of person*) estatura *f*; (*of fame, glory*) cumbre *f.* **~en** *vt* elevar; (*fig*) aumentar

heir /eə(r)/ *n* heredero *m.* **~ess** *n* heredera *f.* **~loom** *n* reliquia *f* heredada

held /held/ *see* **HOLD**

helicopter /ˈhelɪkɒptə(r)/ *n* helicóptero *m*

hell /hel/ *n* infierno *m*

he'll /hi:l/ = **he will**

hello /həˈləʊ/ *int* ¡hola!; (*Telephone, caller*) ¡oiga!, ¡bueno! (*Mex*); (*Telephone, person answering*) ¡diga!, ¡bueno! (*Mex*). **say ~ to** saludar

helm /helm/ *n* (*Naut*) timón *m*

helmet /ˈhelmɪt/ *n* casco *m*

help /help/ *vt/i* ayudar. **he cannot ~ laughing** no puede menos de reír. **~ o.s. to** servirse. **it cannot be ~ed** no hay más remedio. ● *n* ayuda *f.* ● *int* ¡socorro! **~er** *n* ayudante *m.* **~ful** *adj* útil; (person) amable. **~ing** *n* porción *f.* **~less** *adj* (*unable to manage*) incapaz; (*defenceless*) indefenso

hem /hem/ *n* dobladillo *m*

hemisphere /ˈhemɪsfɪə(r)/ *n* hemisferio *m*

hen /hen/ *n* (*chicken*) gallina *f*; (*female bird*) hembra *f*

hence /hens/ *adv* de aquí. **~forth** *adv* de ahora en adelante

henpecked /ˈhenpekt/ *adj* dominado por su mujer

her /hɜ:(r)/ *pron* (*direct object*) la; (*indirect object*) le; (*after prep*) ella. **I know ~** la conozco. ● *adj* su, sus *pl*

herb /hɜ:b/ *n* hierba *f.* **~al** *adj* de hierbas

herd /hɜ:d/ *n* (*of cattle, pigs*) manada *f*; (*of goats*) rebaño *m.* ● *vt* arrear. **~ together** reunir

here /hɪə(r)/ *adv* aquí, acá (*esp LAm*). **~!** (*take this*) ¡tenga! **~abouts** /-əˈbaʊts/ *adv* por aquí. **~after** /-ˈɑ:ftə(r)/ *adv* en el futuro. **~by** /-ˈbaɪ/ *adv* por este medio

heredit|ary /hɪˈredɪtərɪ/ *adj* hereditario

here|sy /ˈherəsɪ/ *n* herejía *f.* **~tic** *n* hereje *m & f*

herewith /hɪəˈwɪð/ *adv* adjunto

heritage /ˈherɪtɪdʒ/ *n* herencia *f*; (*fig*) patrimonio *m.* **~ tourism** *n* turismo *m* cultural, turismo *m* patrimonial (*LAm*)

hermetically /hɜ:ˈmetɪklɪ/ *adv.* **~ sealed** herméticamente cerrado

h

hermit /ˈhɜːmɪt/ *n* ermitaño *m*, eremita *m*

hernia /ˈhɜːnɪə/ *n* hernia *f*

hero /ˈhɪərəʊ/ *n* (*pl* **-oes**) héroe *m*. **~ic** /hɪˈrəʊɪk/ *adj* heroico

heroin /ˈherəʊɪn/ *n* heroína *f*

hero: ~ine /ˈherəʊɪn/ *n* heroína *f*. **~ism** /ˈherəʊɪzm/ *n* heroismo *m*

heron /ˈherən/ *n* garza *f* (real)

herring /ˈherɪŋ/ *n* arenque *m*

hers /hɜːz/ *poss pron* (el) suyo *m*, (la) suya *f*, (los) suyos *mpl*, (las) suyas *fpl*

h

herself /hɜːˈself/ *pron* ella misma; (*reflexive*) se; (*after prep*) sí misma

he's /hiːz/ = **he is, he has**

hesit|ant /ˈhezɪtənt/ *adj* vacilante. **~ate** /-teɪt/ *vi* vacilar. **~ation** /-ˈteɪʃn/ *n* vacilación *f*

heterosexual /hetərəʊˈseksjʊəl/ *adj & n* heterosexual (*m & f*)

het up /hetˈʌp/ *adj* [I] nervioso

hew /hjuː/ *vt* (*pp* **hewed** *or* **hewn**) cortar; (*cut into shape*) tallar

hexagon /ˈheksəgən/ *n* hexágono *m*. **~al** /-ˈægənl/ *adj* hexagonal

hey /heɪ/ *int* ¡eh!; (*expressing dismay, protest*) ¡oye!

heyday /heɪdeɪ/ *n* apogeo *m*

hi /haɪ/ *int* [I] ¡hola!

hibernat|e /ˈhaɪbəneɪt/ *vi* hibernar. **~ion** /-ˈneɪʃn/ *n* hibernación *f*

hiccough, hiccup /ˈhɪkʌp/ *n* hipo *m*. **have (the) ~s** tener hipo. ● *vi* hipar

hide /haɪd/ *vt* (*pt* **hid**, *pp* **hidden**) esconder. ● *vi* esconderse. ● *n* piel *f*; (*tanned*) cuero *m*. **~-and-seek** /ˈhaɪdnsiːk/ *n*. **play ~-and-seek** jugar al escondite, jugar a las escondidas (*LAm*)

hideous /ˈhɪdɪəs/ *adj* (*dreadful*) horrible; (*ugly*) feo

hideout /ˈhaɪdaʊt/ *n* escondrijo *m*

hiding /ˈhaɪdɪŋ/ *n* ([I], *thrashing*) paliza *f*. **go into ~** esconderse. **~ place** *n* escondite *m*, escondrijo *m*

hierarchy /ˈhaɪərɑːkɪ/ *n* jerarquía *f*

hieroglyphics /haɪərəˈglɪfɪks/ *n* jeroglíficos *mpl*

hi-fi /ˈhaɪfaɪ/ *adj* de alta fidelidad. ● *n* equipo *m* de alta fidelidad, hi-fi *m*

high /haɪ/ *adj* (**-er**, **-est**) alto; (ideals) elevado; (wind) fuerte; (*fam, drugged*) drogado, colocado [I]; (voice) agudo; (meat) pasado. ● *n* alto nivel *m*. **a (new) ~** un récord. ● *adv* alto. **~er education** *n* enseñanza *f* superior. **~-handed** /-ˈhændɪd/ *adj* prepotente. **~ heels** *npl* zapatos *mpl* de tacón alto. **~lands** /-ləndz/ *npl* tierras *fpl* altas. **~-level** *adj* de alto nivel. **~light** *n* punto *m* culminante. ● *vt* destacar; (*Art*) realzar. **~ly** *adv* muy; (paid) muy bien. **~ly strung** *adj* nervioso. **H~ness** *n* (*title*) alteza *f*. **~-rise** *adj* (building) alto. **~ school** *n* (*Amer*) instituto *m*, colegio *m* secundario. **~ street** *n* calle *f* principal. **~-strung** *adj* (*Amer*) nervioso. **~way** *n* carretera *f*

> *i*
>
> **High School** En EE.UU., el último ciclo del colegio secundario, generalmente para alumnos de edades comprendidas entre los 14 y los 18 años. En Gran Bretaña, algunos colegios secundarios también reciben el nombre de *high schools*.

hijack /ˈhaɪdʒæk/ *vt* secuestrar. ● *n* secuestro *m*. **~er** *n* secuestrador

hike /haɪk/ *n* caminata *f*. ● *vi* ir de

caminata. **~r** *n* excursionista *m & f*

hilarious /hɪˈleərɪəs/ *adj* muy divertido

hill /hɪl/ *n* colina *f*; (*slope*) cuesta *f*. **~side** *n* ladera *f*. **~y** *adj* accidentado

hilt /hɪlt/ *n* (*of sword*) puño *m*. **to the ~** (*fig*) totalmente

him /hɪm/ *pron* (*direct object*) lo, le (*only Spain*); (*indirect object*) le; (*after prep*) él. **I know ~** lo/le conozco. **~self** *pron* él mismo; (*reflexive*) se; (*after prep*) sí mismo

hind|er /ˈhɪndə(r)/ *vt* estorbar. **~rance** /ˈhɪndrəns/ *n* obstáculo *m*

hindsight /ˈhaɪmsaɪt/ *n*. **with ~** retrospectivamente

Hindu /ˈhɪnduː/ *n & a* hindú (*m & f*). **~ism** *n* hinduismo *m*

hinge /hɪndʒ/ *n* bisagra *f*

hint /hɪnt/ *n* indirecta *f*; (*advice*) consejo *m*. • *vi* soltar una indirecta. **~ at** dar a entender

hip /hɪp/ *n* cadera *f*

hippie /ˈhɪpɪ/ *n* hippy *m & f*

hippopotamus /hɪpəˈpɒtəməs/ *n* (*pl* **-muses** *or* **-mi** /-maɪ/) hipopótamo *m*

hire /haɪə(r)/ *vt* alquilar (thing); contratar (person). • *n* alquiler *m*. **car ~** alquiler *m* de coches. **~ purchase** *n* compra *f* a plazos

his /hɪz/ *adj* su, sus *pl*. • *poss pron* (el) suyo *m*, (la) suya *f*, (los) suyos *mpl*, (las) suyas *fpl*

Hispan|ic /hɪˈspænɪk/ *adj* hispánico. • *n* (*Amer*) hispano *m*. **~ist** /ˈhɪspənɪst/ *n* hispanista *m & f*

hiss /hɪs/ *n* silbido. • *vt/i* silbar

histor|ian /hɪˈstɔːrɪən/ *n* historiador *m*. **~ic(al)** /hɪˈstɒrɪk(l)/ *adj* histórico. **~y** /ˈhɪstərɪ/ *n* historia *f*.

hit /hɪt/ *vt* (*pt* **hit**, *pres p* **hitting**) golpear (object); pegarle a (person); (*collide with*) chocar con; (*affect*) afectar. **~ it off with** hacer buenas migas con. □ **~ on** *vt* dar con. • *n* (*blow*) golpe *m*; (*success*) éxito *m*. (*Internet*) visita *f*

hitch /hɪtʃ/ *vt* (*fasten*) enganchar. • *n* (*snag*) problema *m*. **~ a lift, ~ a ride** (*Amer*) *see* **~HIKE**. **~hike** *vi* hacer autostop, hacer dedo, ir de aventón (*Mex*). **~hiker** *n* autoestopista *m & f*

hither /ˈhɪðə(r)/ *adv* aquí, acá. **~ and thither** acá y allá. **~to** *adv* hasta ahora

hit-or-miss /hɪtɔːˈmɪs/ *adj* (approach) poco científico

hive /haɪv/ *n* colmena *f*

hoard /hɔːd/ *vt* acumular. • *n* provisión *f*; (*of money*) tesoro *m*

hoarding /ˈhɔːdɪŋ/ *n* valla *f* publicitaria

hoarse /hɔːs/ *adj* (**-er, -est**) ronco. **~ly** *adv* con voz ronca

hoax /həʊks/ *n* engaño *m*. • *vt* engañar

hob /hɒb/ *n* (*of cooker*) hornillos *mpl*, hornillas *fpl* (*LAm*)

hobble /ˈhɒbl/ *vi* cojear, renguear (*LAm*)

hobby /ˈhɒbɪ/ *n* pasatiempo *m*. **~horse** *n* (*toy*) caballito *m* (de niño); (*fixation*) caballo *m* de batalla

hockey /ˈhɒkɪ/ *n* hockey *m*; (*Amer*) hockey *m* sobre hielo

hoe /həʊ/ *n* azada *f*. • *vt* (*pres p* **hoeing**) azadonar

hog /hɒg/ *n* (*Amer*) cerdo *m*. • *vt* (*pt* **hogged**) 🅘 acaparar

hoist /hɔɪst/ *vt* levantar; izar (flag). • *n* montacargas *m*

hold /həʊld/ *vt* (*pt* **held**) tener; (*grasp*) coger (*esp Spain*), agarrar; (*contain*) contener; mantener (interest); (*believe*) creer. ● *vi* mantenerse. ● *n* (*influence*) influencia *f*; (*Naut, Aviat*) bodega *f*. **get ~ of** agarrar; (*fig, acquire*) adquirir. □ **~ back** *vt* (*contain*) contener. □ **~ on** *vi* (*stand firm*) resistir; (*wait*) esperar. □ **~ on to** *vt* (*keep*) guardar; (*cling to*) agarrarse a. □ **~ out** *vt* (*offer*) ofrecer. *vi* (*resist*) resistir. □ **~ up** *vt* (*raise*) levantar; (*support*) sostener; (*delay*) retrasar; (*rob*) atracar. **~all** *n* bolsa *f* (de viaje). **~er** *n* tenedor *m*; (*of post*) titular *m*; (*wallet*) funda *f*. **~up** atraco *m*

h

hole /həʊl/ *n* agujero *m*; (*in ground*) hoyo *m*; (*in road*) bache *m*. ● *vt* agujerear

holiday /ˈhɒlɪdeɪ/ *n* vacaciones *fpl*; (*public*) fiesta *f*. **go on ~** ir de vacaciones. **~maker** *n* veraneante *m* & *f*

holiness /ˈhəʊlɪnɪs/ *n* santidad *f*

Holland /ˈhɒlənd/ *n* Holanda *f*

hollow /ˈhɒləʊ/ *adj* & *n* hueco (*m*)

holly /ˈhɒlɪ/ *n* acebo *m*

holocaust /ˈhɒləkɔːst/ *n* holocausto *m*

holster /ˈhəʊlstə(r)/ *n* pistolera *f*

holy /ˈhəʊlɪ/ *adj* (**-ier**, **-iest**) santo, sagrado. **H~ Ghost** *n*, **H~ Spirit** *n* Espíritu *m* Santo. **~ water** *n* agua *f* bendita

homage /ˈhɒmɪdʒ/ *n* homenaje *m*. **pay ~ to** rendir homenaje a

home /həʊm/ *n* casa *f*; (*for old people*) residencia *f* de ancianos; (*native land*) patria *f*. ● *adj* (cooking) casero; (*address*) particular; (background) familiar; (*Pol*) interior; (match) de casa. ● *adv*. **(at) ~** en casa. **~land** *n* patria *f*. **~land security** seguridad *f* nacional. **~less** *adj* sin hogar. **~ly** *adj* (**-ier**, **-iest**) casero; (*Amer, ugly*) feo. **~-made** *adj* hecho en casa. **~ page** *n* (*Comp*) página *f* frontal. **~sick** *adj*. **be ~sick** echar de menos a su familia/su país, extrañar a su familia/su país (*LAm*). **~ town** *n* ciudad *f* natal. **~work** *n* deberes *mpl*

homicide /ˈhɒmɪsaɪd/ *n* homicidio *m*

homoeopathic /həʊmɪəʊˈpæθɪk/ *adj* homeopático

homogeneous /hɒməʊˈdʒiːnɪəs/ *adj* homogéneo

homosexual /həʊməʊˈseksjʊəl/ *adj* & *n* homosexual (*m*)

honest /ˈɒnɪst/ *adj* honrado; (*frank*) sincero. **~ly** *adv* honradamente. **~y** *n* honradez *f*

honey /ˈhʌnɪ/ *n* miel *f*. **~comb** *n* panal *m*. **~moon** *n* luna *f* de miel. **~suckle** *n* madreselva *f*

honorary /ˈɒnərərɪ/ *adj* honorario

honour /ˈɒnə(r)/ *n* honor *m*. ● *vt* honrar; cumplir (con) (promise). **~able** *adj* honorable

hood /hʊd/ *n* capucha *f*; (*car roof*) capota *f*; (*Amer, car bonnet*) capó *m*, capote *m* (*Mex*)

hoodwink /ˈhʊdwɪŋk/ *vt* engañar

hoof /huːf/ *n* (*pl* **hoofs** *or* **hooves**) (*of horse*) casco *m*, pezuna *f* (*Mex*); (*of cow*) pezuña *f*

hook /hʊk/ *n* gancho *m*; (*on garment*) corchete *m*; (*for fishing*) anzuelo *m*. **let s.o. off the ~** dejar salir a uno del atolladero. **off the ~** (telephone) descolgado. ● *vt*. **~ed on** [I] adicto a. □ **~ up** *vt* enganchar. **~ed** *adj* (tool) en forma de gancho; (nose) aguileño

hookey /ˈhʊkɪ/ *n*. **play ~** (*Amer fam*) faltar a clase, hacer novillos

hooligan /ˈhuːlɪgən/ *n* vándalo *m*, gamberro *m*

hoop /hu:p/ *n* aro *m*

hooray /hʊ'reɪ/ *int & n* ¡viva! (*m*)

hoot /hu:t/ *n* (*of horn*) bocinazo *m*; (*of owl*) ululato *m*. ●*vi* tocar la bocina; (owl) ulular

Hoover /'hu:və(r)/ *n* (®) aspiradora *f*. ●*vt* pasar la aspiradora por, aspirar (*LAm*)

hooves /hu:vz/ *see* HOOF

hop /hɒp/ *vi* (*pt* **hopped**) saltar a la pata coja; (frog, rabbit) brincar, saltar; (bird) dar saltitos. ●*n* salto *m*; (*flight*) etapa *f*. **~(s)** (*plant*) lúpulo *m*

hope /həʊp/ *n* esperanza *f*. ●*vt/i* esperar. **~ for** esperar. **~ful** *adj* (*optimistic*) esperanzado; (*promising*) esperanzador. **~fully** *adv* con optimismo; (*it is hoped*) se espera. **~less** *adj* desesperado

horde /hɔ:d/ *n* horda *f*

horizon /hə'raɪzn/ *n* horizonte *m*

horizontal /hɒrɪ'zɒntl/ *adj* horizontal. **~ly** *adv* horizontalmente

hormone /'hɔ:məʊn/ *n* hormona *f*

horn /hɔ:n/ *n* cuerno *m*, asta *f*, cacho *m* (*LAm*); (*of car*) bocina *f*; (*Mus*) trompa *f*. **~ed** *adj* con cuernos

hornet /'hɔ:nɪt/ *n* avispón *m*

horoscope /'hɒrəskəʊp/ *n* horóscopo *m*

horrible /'hɒrəbl/ *adj* horrible

horrid /'hɒrɪd/ *adj* horrible

horrific /hə'rɪfɪk/ *adj* horroroso

horrify /'hɒrɪfaɪ/ *vt* horrorizar

horror /'hɒrə(r)/ *n* horror *m*

hors-d'oeuvre /ɔ:'dɜ:vr/ *n* (*pl* **-s** /-'dɜ:vr/ entremés *m*, botana *f* (*Mex*)

horse /hɔ:s/ *n* caballo *m*. **~back** *n*. **on ~back** a caballo. **~power** *n* (*unit*) caballo *m* (de fuerza). **~racing** *n* carreras *fpl* de caballos. **~shoe** *n* herradura *f*

horticultur|al /hɔ:tɪ'kʌltʃərəl/ *adj* hortícola. **~e** /'hɔ:tɪkʌltʃə(r)/ *n* horticultura *f*

hose /həʊz/ *n* manguera *f*, manga *f*. ●*vt*. **~ down** lavar (con manguera). **~pipe** *n* manga *f*

hosiery /'həʊzɪərɪ/ *n* calcetería *f*

hospice /'hɒspɪs/ *n* residencia *f* para enfermos desahuciados

hospitable /hɒ'spɪtəbl/ *adj* hospitalario

hospital /'hɒspɪtl/ *n* hospital *m*

hospitality /hɒspɪ'tælətɪ/ *n* hospitalidad *f*

host /həʊst/ *n* (*master of house*) anfitrión *m*; (*Radio, TV*) presentador *m*; (*multitude*) gran cantidad *f*; (*Relig*) hostia *f*

hostage /'hɒstɪdʒ/ *n* rehén *m*

hostel /'hɒstl/ *n* (*for students*) residencia *f*; (*for homeless people*) hogar *m*

hostess /'həʊstɪs/ *n* anfitriona *f*

hostil|e /'hɒstaɪl/ *adj* hostil. **~ity** /-'tɪlətɪ/ *n* hostilidad *f*

hot /hɒt/ *adj* (**hotter**, **hottest**) caliente; (weather, day) caluroso; (climate) cálido; (*Culin*) picante; (news) de última hora. **be/feel ~** tener calor. **get ~** calentarse. **it is ~** hace calor. **~bed** *n* (*fig*) semillero *m*

hotchpotch /'hɒtʃpɒtʃ/ *n* mezcolanza *f*

hot dog *n* perrito *m* caliente

hotel /həʊ'tel/ *n* hotel *m*. **~ier** /-ɪeɪ/*n* hotelero *m*

hot: ~house *n* invernadero *m*. **~plate** *n* placa *f*, hornilla *f* (*LAm*). **~-water bottle** /-'wɔ:tə(r)/ *n* bolsa *f* de agua caliente

hound /haʊnd/ *n* perro *m* de caza.

• *vt* perseguir

hour /aʊə(r)/ *n* hora *f*. **~ly** *adj* (rate) por hora. • *adv* (*every hour*) cada hora; (*by the hour*) por hora

house /haʊs/ *n* (*pl* **-s** /ˈhaʊzɪz/) casa *f*; (*Pol*) cámara *f*. • /haʊz/ *vt* alojar; (*keep*) guardar. **~hold** *n* casa *f*. **~holder** *n* dueño *m* de una casa. **~keeper** *n* ama *f* de llaves. **~maid** *n* criada *f*, mucama *f* (*LAm*). **~-proud** *adj* meticuloso. **~warming** (*party*) *n* fiesta de inauguración de una casa. **~wife** *n* ama *f* de casa. **~work** *n* tareas *fpl* domésticas

housing /ˈhaʊzɪŋ/ *n* alojamiento *m*. **~ development** (*Amer*), **~ estate** *n* complejo *m* habitacional, urbanización *f*

hovel /ˈhɒvl/ *n* casucha *f*

hover /ˈhɒvə(r)/ *vi* (bird, threat etc) cernerse; (*loiter*) rondar. **~craft** *n* (*pl invar or* **-crafts**) aerodeslizador *m*

how /haʊ/ *adv* cómo. **~ about a walk?** ¿qué te parece si damos un paseo? **~ are you?** ¿cómo está Vd? **~ do you do?** (*in introduction*) mucho gusto. **~ long?** (*in time*) ¿cuánto tiempo? **~ long is the room?** ¿cuánto mide de largo el cuarto? **~ often?** ¿cuántas veces?

however /haʊˈevə(r)/ *adv* (*nevertheless*) no obstante, sin embargo; (*with verb*) de cualquier manera que (+ *subjunctive*); (*with adjective or adverb*) por... que (+ *subjunctive*). **~ much it rains** por mucho que llueva

howl /haʊl/ *n* aullido. • *vi* aullar

hp *abbr see* **HORSEPOWER**

HP *abbr see* **HIRE-PURCHASE**

hub /hʌb/ *n* (*of wheel*) cubo *m*; (*fig*) centro *m*

hubcap /ˈhʌbkæp/ *n* tapacubos *m*

huddle /ˈhʌdl/ *vi* apiñarse

hue /hjuː/ *n* (*colour*) color *m*

huff /hʌf/ *n*. **be in a ~** estar enfurruñado

hug /hʌg/ *vt* (*pt* **hugged**) abrazar. • *n* abrazo *m*

huge /hjuːdʒ/ *adj* enorme. **~ly** *adv* enormemente

hulk /hʌlk/ *n* (*of ship*) barco *m* viejo

hull /hʌl/ *n* (*of ship*) casco *m*

hullo /həˈləʊ/ *int see* **HELLO**

hum /hʌm/ *vt/i* (*pt* **hummed**) (person) canturrear; (insect, engine) zumbar. • *n* zumbido *m*

human /ˈhjuːmən/ *adj & n* humano (*m*). **~ being** *n* ser *m* humano. **~e** /hjuːˈmeɪn/ *adj* humano. **~itarian** /hjuːmænɪˈteərɪən/ *adj* humanitario. **~ity** /hjuːˈmænətɪ/ *n* humanidad *f*

humbl|e /ˈhʌmbl/ *adj* (**-er**, **-est**) humilde. • *vt* humillar. **~y** *adv* humildemente

humdrum /ˈhʌmdrʌm/ *adj* monótono

humid /ˈhjuːmɪd/ *adj* húmedo. **~ity** /hjuːˈmɪdətɪ/ *n* humedad *f*

humiliat|e /hjuːˈmɪlɪeɪt/ *vt* humillar. **~ion** /-ˈeɪʃn/ *n* humillación *f*

humility /hjuːˈmɪlətɪ/ *n* humildad *f*

humongous /hjuːˈmʌŋgəs/ *adj* [I] de primera

humo|rist /ˈhjuːmərɪst/ *n* humorista *m & f*. **~rous** /-rəs/ *adj* humorístico. **~rously** *adv* con gracia. **~ur** /ˈhjuːmə(r)/ *n* humor *m*. **sense of ~ur** sentido *m* del humor

hump /hʌmp/ *n* (*of person, camel*) joroba *f*; (*in ground*) montículo *m*

hunch /hʌntʃ/ *vt* encorvar. ● *n* presentimiento *m*; (*lump*) joroba *f*. **~back** *n* jorobado *m*

hundred /'hʌndrəd/ *adj* ciento, (*before noun*) cien. **one ~ and ninety-eight** ciento noventa y ocho. **two ~** doscientos. **three ~ pages** trescientas páginas. **four ~** cuatrocientos. **five ~** quinientos. ● *n* ciento *m*. **~s of** centenares de. **~th** *adj & n* centésimo (*m*). **~weight** *n* 50,8kg; (*Amer*) 45,36kg

hung /hʌŋ/ *see* HANG

Hungar|ian /hʌŋ'geərɪən/ *adj & n* húngaro (*m*). **~y** /'hʌŋgəri/ *n* Hungría *f*

hung|er /'hʌŋgə(r)/ *n* hambre *f*. ● *vi*. **~er for** tener hambre de. **~rily** /'hʌŋgrəlɪ/ *adv* ávidamente. **~ry** *adj* (**-ier**, **-iest**) hambriento. **be ~ry** tener hambre

hunk /hʌŋk/ *n* (buen) pedazo *m*

hunt /hʌnt/ *vt* cazar. ● *vi* cazar. **~ for** buscar. ● *n* caza *f*. **~er** *n* cazador *m*. **~ing** *n* caza *f*. **go ~ing** ir de caza

hurl /hɜ:l/ *vt* lanzar

hurrah/hʊ'rɑ:/, **hurray** /hʊ'reɪ/ *int & n* ¡viva! (*m*)

hurricane /'hʌrɪkən/ *n* huracán *m*

hurr|ied /'hʌrɪd/ *adj* apresurado. **~iedly** *adv* apresuradamente. **~y** *vi* darse prisa, apurarse (*LAm*). ● *vt* meter prisa a, apurar (*LAm*). ● *n* prisa *f*. **be in a ~y** tener prisa, estar apurado (*LAm*)

hurt /hɜ:t/ *vt* (*pt* **hurt**) hacer daño a, lastimar (*LAm*). **~ s.o.'s feelings** ofender a uno. ● *vi* doler. **my head ~s** me duele la cabeza. **~ful** *adj* hiriente

hurtle /'hɜ:tl/ *vt* ir volando. ● *vi*. **~ along** mover rápidamente

husband /'hʌzbənd/ *n* marido *m*, esposo *m*

hush /hʌʃ/ *vt* acallar. ● *n* silencio *m*. □ **~ up** *vt* acallar (affair). **~-hush** *adj* ⊡ super secreto

husk /hʌsk/ *n* cáscara *f*

husky /'hʌskɪ/ *adj* (**-ier**, **-iest**) (*hoarse*) ronco

hustle /'hʌsl/ *vt* (*jostle*) empujar. ● *vi* (*hurry*) darse prisa, apurarse (*LAm*). ● *n* empuje *m*

hut /hʌt/ *n* cabaña *f*

hutch /hʌtʃ/ *n* conejera *f*

hybrid /'haɪbrɪd/ *adj & n* híbrido (*m*)

hydrangea /haɪ'dreɪmdʒə/ *n* hortensia *f*

hydrant /'haɪdrənt/ *n*. **(fire) ~** *n* boca *f* de riego, boca *f* de incendios (*LAm*)

hydraulic /haɪ'drɔ:lɪk/ *adj* hidráulico

hydroelectric /haɪdrəʊɪ'lektrɪk/ *adj* hidroeléctrico

hydrofoil /'haɪdrəfɔɪl/ *n* hidrodeslizador *m*

hydrogen /'haɪdrədʒən/ *n* hidrógeno *m*

hyena /haɪ'i:nə/ *n* hiena *f*

hygien|e /'haɪdʒi:n/ *n* higiene *f*. **~ic** /haɪ'dʒi:nɪk/ *adj* higiénico

hymn /hɪm/ *n* himno *m*

hyper... /'haɪpə(r)/ *pref* hiper...

hyphen /'haɪfn/ *n* guión *m*. **~ate** /-eɪt/ *vt* escribir con guión

hypno|sis /hɪp'nəʊsɪs/ *n* hipnosis *f*. **~tic** /-'nɒtɪk/ *adj* hipnótico. **~tism** /'hɪpnətɪzəm/ *n* hipnotismo *m*. **~tist** /'hɪpnətɪst/ *n* hipnotista *m & f*. **~tize** /'hɪpnətaɪz/ *vt* hipnotizar

hypochondriac /haɪpə'kɒndrɪæk/ *n* hipocondríaco *m*

hypocri|sy /hɪ'pɒkrəsɪ/ *n* hipocresía *f.* ~**te** /ˈhɪpəkrɪt/ *n* hipócrita *m & f.* ~**tical** /hɪpəˈkrɪtɪkl/ *adj* hipócrita

hypodermic /haɪpəˈdɜːmɪk/ *adj* hipodérmico. •*n* hipodérmica *f*

hypothe|sis /haɪˈpɒθəsɪs/ *n* (*pl* **-theses**/-siːz/) hipótesis *f.* ~**tical** /-əˈθetɪkl/ *adj* hipotético

hysteri|a /hɪˈstɪərɪə/ *n* histerismo *m.* ~**cal** /-ˈterɪkl/ *adj* histérico. ~**cs** /hɪˈsterɪks/ *npl* histerismo *m.* **have** ~**cs** ponerse histérico; (*laugh*) morir de risa

Ii

I /aɪ/ *pron* yo

ice /aɪs/ *n* hielo *m.* •*vt* helar; glasear (cake). •*vi.* ~ **(up)** helarse, congelarse. ~**berg** /-bɜːg/ *n* iceberg *m.* ~ **box** *n* (*compartment*) congelador; (*Amer fam, refrigerator*) frigorífico *m*, refrigerador *m* (*LAm*). ~**cream** *n* helado *m.* ~ **cube** *n* cubito *m* de hielo

Iceland /ˈaɪslənd/ *n* Islandia *f*

ice: ~ **lolly** polo *m*, paleta *f* helada (*LAm*). ~ **rink** *n* pista *f* de hielo. ~ **skating** *n* patinaje *m* sobre hielo

icicle /ˈaɪsɪkl/ *n* carámbano *m*

icing /ˈaɪsɪŋ/ *n* glaseado *m*

icon /ˈaɪkɒn/ *n* icono *m*

icy /ˈaɪsɪ/ *adj* (**-ier**, **-iest**) helado; (*fig*) glacial

I'd /aɪd/ = **I had, I would**

idea /aɪˈdɪə/ *n* idea *f*

ideal /aɪˈdɪəl/ *adj & n* ideal (*m*). ~**ism** *n* idealismo *m.* ~**ist** *n* idealista *m &·f.* ~**istic** /-ˈlɪstɪk/ *adj* idealista. ~**ize** *vt* idealizar. ~**ly** *adv* idealmente

identical /aɪˈdentɪkl/ *adj* idéntico. ~ **twins** *npl* gemelos *mpl* idénticos, gemelos *mpl* (*LAm*)

identif|ication /aɪdentɪfɪˈkeɪʃn/ *n* identificación *f.* ~**y** /aɪˈdentɪfaɪ/ *vt* identificar. •*vi.* ~**y with** identificarse con

identity /aɪˈdentɪtɪ/ *n* identidad *f.* ~ **card** *n* carné *m* de identidad. ~ **theft** *n* robo *m* de identidad

ideolog|ical /aɪdɪəˈlɒdʒɪkl/ *adj* ideológico. ~**y** /aɪdɪˈɒlədʒɪ/ *n* ideología *f*

idiocy /ˈɪdɪəsɪ/ *n* idiotez *f*

idiom /ˈɪdɪəm/ *n* locución *f.* ~**atic** /-ˈmætɪk/ *adj* idiomático

idiot /ˈɪdɪət/ *n* idiota *m & f.* ~**ic** /-ˈɒtɪk/ *adj* idiota

idle /ˈaɪdl/ *adj* (**-er**, **-est**) ocioso; (*lazy*) holgazán; (*out of work*) desocupado; (machine) parado. •*vi* (engine) andar al ralentí. ~**ness** *n* ociosidad *f*; (*laziness*) holgazanería *f*

idol /ˈaɪdl/ *n* ídolo *m.* ~**ize** *vt* idolatrar

idyllic /ɪˈdɪlɪk/ *adj* idílico

i.e. *abbr* (= **id est**) es decir

if /ɪf/ *conj* si

igloo /ˈɪgluː/ *n* iglú *m*

ignit|e /ɪgˈnaɪt/ *vt* encender. •*vi* encenderse. ~**ion** /-ˈnɪʃn/ *n* ignición *f*; (*Auto*) encendido *m.* ~**ion key** *n* llave *f* de contacto

ignoramus /ɪgnəˈreɪməs/ *n* (*pl* **-muses**) ignorante

ignoran|ce /ˈɪgnərəns/ *n* ignorancia *f.* ~**t** *adj* ignorante

ignore /ɪgˈnɔː(r)/ *vt* no hacer caso de; hacer caso omiso de (warning)

ill /ɪl/ *adj* enfermo. •*adv* mal. •*n* mal *m*

I'll /aɪl/ = **I will**

ill: ~-advised /-əd'vaɪzd/ *adj* imprudente. **~ at ease** /-ət'i:z/ *adj* incómodo. **~-bred** /-'bred/ *adj* mal educado

illegal /ɪ'li:gl/ *adj* ilegal

illegible /ɪ'ledʒəbl/ *adj* ilegible

illegitima|cy /ɪlɪ'dʒɪtɪməsɪ/ *n* ilegitimidad *f.* **~te** /-ət/ *adj* ilegítimo

illitera|cy /ɪ'lɪtərəsɪ/ *n* analfabetismo *m.* **~te** /-ət/ *adj* analfabeto

illness /'ɪlnɪs/ *n* enfermedad *f*

illogical /ɪ'lɒdʒɪkl/ *adj* ilógico

illuminat|e /ɪ'lu:mɪneɪt/ *vt* iluminar. **~ion** /-'neɪʃn/ *n* iluminación *f*

illus|ion /ɪ'lu:ʒn/ *n* ilusión *f.* **~sory** /-sərɪ/ *adj* ilusorio

illustrat|e /'ɪləstreɪt/ *vt* ilustrar. **~ion** /-'streɪʃn/ *n* ilustración *f*; (*example*) ejemplo *m*

illustrious /ɪ'lʌstrɪəs/ *adj* ilustre

ill will /ɪl'wɪl/ *n* mala voluntad *f*

I'm /aɪm/ = **I am**

image /'ɪmɪdʒ/ *n* imagen *f.* **~ry** *n* imágenes *fpl*

imagin|able /ɪ'mædʒɪnəbl/ *adj* imaginable. **~ary** *adj* imaginario. **~ation** /-'neɪʃn/ *n* imaginación *f.* **~ative** *adj* imaginativo. **~e** /ɪ 'mædʒɪn/ *vt* imaginar(se)

imbalance /ɪm'bæləns/ *n* desequilibrio *m*

imbecile /'ɪmbəsi:l/ *n* imbécil *m & f*

imitat|e /'ɪmɪteɪt/ *vt* imitar. **~ion** /-'teɪʃn/ *n* imitación *f.* ● *adj* de imitación. **~or** *n* imitador *m*

immaculate /ɪ'mækjʊlət/ *adj* inmaculado

immatur|e /ɪmə'tjʊə(r)/ *adj* inmaduro. **~ity** *n* inmadurez *f*

immediate /ɪ'mi:dɪət/ *adj* inmediato. **~ly** *adv* inmediatamente. ● *conj* en cuanto (+ *subjunctive*)

immens|e /ɪ'mens/ *adj* inmenso. **~ely** *adv* inmensamente; (*fam, very much*) muchísimo

immers|e /ɪ'mɜ:s/ *vt* sumergir. **~ion** /-ʃn/ *n* inmersión *f.* **~ion heater** *n* calentador *m* de inmersión

immigra|nt /'ɪmɪgrənt/ *adj & n* inmigrante (*m & f*). **~tion** /-'greɪʃn/ *n* inmigración *f*

imminent /'ɪmɪnənt/ *adj* inminente

immobil|e /ɪ'məʊbaɪl/ *adj* inmóvil. **~ize** /-bɪlaɪz/ *vt* inmovilizar. **~izer** /-bɪlaɪzə(r)/ *n* inmovilizador *m*

immoderate /ɪ'mɒdərət/ *adj* inmoderado

immodest /ɪ'mɒdɪst/ *adj* inmodesto

immoral /ɪ'mɒrəl/ *adj* inmoral. **~ity** /ɪmə'rælətɪ/ *n* inmoralidad *f*

immortal /ɪ'mɔ:tl/ *adj* inmortal. **~ity** /-'tælətɪ/ *n* inmortalidad *f.* **~ize** *vt* inmortalizar

immun|e /ɪ'mju:n/ *adj* inmune (**to** a). **~ity** *n* inmunidad *f.* **~ization** /ɪmjʊnaɪ'zeɪʃn/ *n* inmunización *f.* **~ize** /'ɪmjʊnaɪz/ *vt* inmunizar

imp /ɪmp/ *n* diablillo *m*

impact /'ɪmpækt/ *n* impacto *m*

impair /ɪm'peə(r)/ *vt* perjudicar

impale /ɪm'peɪl/ *vt* atravesar (**on** con)

impart /ɪm'pɑ:t/ *vt* comunicar (news); impartir (knowledge)

impartial /ɪm'pɑ:ʃl/ *adj* imparcial. **~ity** /-ɪ'ælətɪ/ *n* imparcialidad *f*

impassable /ɪm'pɑ:səbl/ *adj* (road) intransitable

impassive /ɪm'pæsɪv/ *adj* impasible

impatien|ce /ɪmˈpeɪʃəns/ *n* impaciencia *f*. **~t** *adj* impaciente. **get ~t** impacientarse. **~tly** *adv* con impaciencia

impeccable /ɪmˈpekəbl/ *adj* impecable

impede /ɪmˈpiːd/ *vt* estorbar

impediment /ɪmˈpedɪmənt/ obstáculo *m*. **(speech) ~** *n* defecto *m* del habla

impending /ɪmˈpendɪŋ/ *adj* inminente

impenetrable /ɪmˈpenɪtrəbl/ *adj* impenetrable

imperative /ɪmˈperətɪv/ *adj* imprescindible. ● *n* (*Gram*) imperativo *m*

imperceptible /ɪmpəˈseptəbl/ *adj* imperceptible

imperfect /ɪmˈpɜːfɪkt/ *adj* imperfecto. **~ion** /ɪmpəˈfekʃn/ *n* imperfección *f*

imperial /ɪmˈpɪərɪəl/ *adj* imperial. **~ism** *n* imperialismo *m*

impersonal /ɪmˈpɜːsənl/ *adj* impersonal

impersonat|e /ɪmˈpɜːsəneɪt/ *vt* hacerse pasar por; (*mimic*) imitar. **~ion** /-ˈneɪʃn/ *n* imitación *f*. **~or** *n* imitador *m*

impertinen|ce /ɪmˈpɜːtɪnəns/ *n* impertinencia *f*. **~t** *adj* impertinente

impervious /ɪmˈpɜːvɪəs/ *adj*. **~ to** impermeable a

impetuous /ɪmˈpetjʊəs/ *adj* impetuoso

impetus /ˈɪmpɪtəs/ *n* ímpetu *m*

implacable /ɪmˈplækəbl/ *adj* implacable

implant /ɪmˈplɑːnt/ *vt* implantar

implement /ˈɪmplɪmənt/ *n* instrumento *m*, implemento *m* (*LAm*). ● /ˈɪmplɪment/ *vt* implementar

implementation /ɪmplɪmenˈteɪʃn/ *n* implementación *f*

implicat|e /ˈɪmplɪkeɪt/ *vt* implicar. **~ion** /-ˈkeɪʃn/ *n* implicación *f*

implicit /ɪmˈplɪsɪt/ *adj* (*implied*) implícito; (*unquestioning*) absoluto

implore /ɪmˈplɔː(r)/ *vt* implorar

imply /ɪmˈplaɪ/ *vt* (*involve*) implicar; (*insinuate*) dar a entender, insinuar

impolite /ɪmpəˈlaɪt/ *adj* mal educado

import /ɪmˈpɔːt/ *vt* importar. ● /ˈɪmpɔːt/ *n* importación *f*; (*item*) artículo *m* de importación; (*meaning*) significación *f*

importan|ce /ɪmˈpɔːtəns/ *n* importancia *f*. **~t** *adj* importante

importer /ɪmˈpɔːtə(r)/ *n* importador *m*

impos|e /ɪmˈpəʊz/ *vt* imponer. ● *vi*. **~e on** abusar de la amabilidad de. **~ing** *adj* imponente. **~ition** /ɪmpəˈzɪʃn/ *n* imposición *f*; (*fig*) abuso *m*

impossib|ility /ɪmpɒsəˈbɪlətɪ/ *n* imposibilidad *f*. **~le** /ɪmˈpɒsəbl/ *adj* imposible

impostor /ɪmˈpɒstə(r)/ *n* impostor *m*

impoten|ce /ˈɪmpətəns/ *n* impotencia *f*. **~t** *adj* impotente

impound /ɪmˈpaʊnd/ *vt* confiscar

impoverished /ɪmˈpɒvərɪʃt/ *adj* empobrecido

impractical /ɪmˈpræktɪkl/ *adj* poco práctico

impregnable /imˈpregnəbl/ *adj* inexpugnable

impregnate /ˈɪmpregneɪt/ *vt* impregnar (**with** con, de)

impress /ɪmˈpres/ *vt* impresionar; (*make good impression*) causar una buena impresión a. ● *vi* impresionar

impression /ɪm'preʃn/ *n* impresión *f*. **~able** *adj* impresionable. **~ism** *n* impresionismo *m*

impressive /ɪm'presɪv/ *adj* impresionante

imprint /'ɪmprɪnt/ *n* impresión *f*. ● /ɪm'prɪnt/ *vt* imprimir

imprison /ɪm'prɪzn/ *vt* encarcelar. **~ment** *n* encarcelamiento *m*

improbab|ility /ɪmprɒbə'bɪlətɪ/ *n* improbabilidad *f*. **~le** /ɪm'prɒbəbl/ *adj* improbable

impromptu /ɪm'prɒmptju:/ *adj* improvisado. ● *adv* de improviso

improper /ɪm'prɒpə(r)/ *adj* impropio; (*incorrect*) incorrecto

improve /ɪm'pru:v/ *vt* mejorar. ● *vi* mejorar. **~ment** *n* mejora *f*

improvis|ation /ɪmprəvaɪ'zeɪʃn/ *n* improvisación *f*. **~e** /'ɪmprəvaɪz/ *vt/i* improvisar

impuden|ce /'ɪmpjʊdəns/ *n* insolencia *f*. **~t** *adj* insolente

impuls|e /'ɪmpʌls/ *n* impulso *m*. **on ~e** sin reflexionar. **~ive** *adj* irreflexivo

impur|e /ɪm'pjʊə(r)/ *adj* impuro. **~ity** *n* impureza *f*

in /ɪn/ *prep* en; (*within*) dentro de. **~ a firm manner** de una manera terminante. **~ an hour('s time)** dentro de una hora. **~ doing** al hacer. **~ so far as** en la medida en que. **~ the evening** por la tarde. **~ the rain** bajo la lluvia. **~ the sun** al sol. **one ~ ten** uno de cada diez. **the best ~ the world** el mejor del mundo. ● *adv* (*inside*) dentro; (*at home*) en casa. **come ~** entrar. ● *n*. **the ~s and outs of** los detalles de

inability /ɪnə'bɪlətɪ/ *n* incapacidad *f*

inaccessible /ɪnæk'sesəbl/ *adj* inaccesible

inaccura|cy /ɪn'ækjʊrəsɪ/ *n* inexactitud *f*. **~te** /-ət/ *adj* inexacto

inactiv|e /ɪn'æktɪv/ *adj* inactivo. **~ity** /-'tɪvətɪ/ *n* inactividad *f*

inadequa|cy /ɪn'ædɪkwəsɪ/ *adj* insuficiencia *f*. **~te** /-ət/ *adj* insuficiente

inadvertently /ɪnəd'vɜ:təntlɪ/ *adv* sin querer

inadvisable /ɪnəd'vaɪzəbl/ *adj* desaconsejable

inane /ɪ'neɪn/ *adj* estúpido

inanimate /ɪn'ænɪmət/ *adj* inanimado

inappropriate /ɪnə'prəʊprɪət/ *adj* inoportuno

inarticulate /ɪnɑ:'tɪkjʊlət/ *adj* incapaz de expresarse claramente

inattentive /ɪnə'tentɪv/ *adj* desatento

inaudible /ɪn'ɔ:dəbl/ *adj* inaudible

inaugurate /ɪ'nɔ:gjʊreɪt/ *vt* inaugurar

inborn /'ɪnbɔ:n/ *adj* innato

inbred /ɪn'bred/ *adj* (*inborn*) innato; (social group) endogámico

Inc /ɪŋk/ *abbr* (*Amer*) (= **Incorporated**) S.A., Sociedad Anónima

incalculable /ɪn'kælkjʊləbl/ *adj* incalculable

incapable /ɪn'keɪpəbl/ *adj* incapaz

incapacit|ate /ɪnkə'pæsɪteɪt/ *vt* incapacitar. **~y** *n* incapacidad *f*

incarcerate /ɪn'kɑ:səreɪt/ *vt* encarcelar

incarnat|e /ɪn'kɑ:nət/ *adj* encarnado. **~ion** /-'neɪʃn/ *n* encarnación *f*

incendiary /ɪn'sendɪərɪ/ *adj* incendiario. **~ bomb** bomba *f* incendiaria

incense /ˈɪnsens/ *n* incienso *m*. ● /ɪnˈsens/ *vt* enfurecer

incentive /ɪnˈsentɪv/ *n* incentivo *m*

incessant /ɪnˈsesnt/ *adj* incesante. **~ly** *adv* sin cesar

incest /ˈɪnsest/ *n* incesto *m*. **~uous** /ɪnˈsestjʊəs/ *adj* incestuoso

inch /ɪntʃ/ *n* pulgada *f*; (= *2,54cm*). ● *vi*. **~ forward** avanzar lentamente

incidence /ˈɪnsɪdəns/ *n* frecuencia *f*

incident /ˈɪnsɪdənt/ *n* incidente *m*

incidental /ɪnsɪˈdentl/ *adj* (effect) secundario; (*minor*) incidental. **~ly** *adv* a propósito

incinerat|e /ɪnˈsɪnəreɪt/ *vt* incinerar. **~or** *n* incinerador *m*

incision /ɪnˈsɪʒn/ *n* incisión *f*

incite /ɪnˈsaɪt/ *vt* incitar. **~ment** *n* incitación *f*

inclination /ɪnklɪˈneɪʃn/ *n* inclinación *f*. **have no ~ to** no tener deseos de

incline /ɪnˈklaɪn/ *vt* inclinar. **be ~d to** tener tendencia a. ● *vi* inclinarse. ● /ˈɪnklaɪn/ *n* pendiente *f*

inclu|de /ɪnˈkluːd/ *vt* incluir. **~ding** *prep* incluso. **~sion** /-ʒn/ *n* inclusión *f*. **~sive** /-sɪv/ *adj* inclusivo

incognito /ɪnkɒgˈniːtəʊ/ *adv* de incógnito

incoherent /ɪnkəʊˈhɪərənt/ *adj* incoherente

incom|e /ˈɪnkʌm/ *n* ingresos *mpl*. **~e tax** *n* impuesto *m* sobre la renta. **~ing** *adj* (tide) ascendente

incomparable /ɪnˈkɒmpərəbl/ *adj* incomparable

incompatible /ɪnkəmˈpætəbl/ *adj* incompatible

incompeten|ce /ɪnˈkɒmpɪtəns/ *n* incompetencia *f*. **~t** *adj* incompetente

incomplete /ɪnkəmˈpliːt/ *adj* incompleto

incomprehensible /ɪnkɒmprɪˈhensəbl/ *adj* incomprensible

inconceivable /ɪnkənˈsiːvəbl/ *adj* inconcebible

inconclusive /ɪnkənˈkluːsɪv/ *adj* no concluyente

incongruous /ɪnˈkɒŋgrʊəs/ *adj* incongruente

inconsiderate /ɪnkənˈsɪdərət/ *adj* desconsiderado

inconsisten|cy /ɪnkənˈsɪstənsɪ/ *n* inconsecuencia *f*. **~t** *adj* inconsecuente. **be ~t with** no concordar con

inconspicuous /ɪnkənˈspɪkjʊəs/ *adj* que no llama la atención. **~ly** *adv* sin llamar la atención

incontinent /ɪnˈkɒntɪnənt/ *adj* incontinente

inconvenien|ce /ɪnkənˈviːnɪəns/ *adj* inconveniencia *f*; (*drawback*) inconveniente *m*. **~t** *adj* inconveniente

incorporate /ɪnˈkɔːpəreɪt/ *vt* incorporar; (*include*) incluir; (*Com*) constituir (en sociedad)

incorrect /ɪnkəˈrekt/ *adj* incorrecto

increas|e /ˈɪnkriːs/ *n* aumento *m* (**in** de). ● /ɪnˈkriːs/ *vt/i* aumentar. **~ing** /ɪnˈkriːsɪŋ/ *adj* creciente. **~ingly** *adv* cada vez más

incredible /ɪnˈkredəbl/ *adj* increíble

incredulous /ɪnˈkredjʊləs/ *adj* incrédulo

incriminat|e /ɪnˈkrɪmɪneɪt/ *vt* incriminar. **~ing** *adj* comprometedor

incubat|e /'ɪŋkjʊbeɪt/ *vt* incubar. **~ion** /-'beɪʃn/ *n* incubación *f*. **~or** *n* incubadora *f*

incur /ɪn'kɜ:(r)/ *vt* (*pt* **incurred**) incurrir en; contraer (debts)

incurable /ɪn'kjʊərəbl/ *adj* (disease) incurable; (romantic) empedernido

indebted /ɪn'detɪd/ *adj*. **be ~ to s.o.** estar en deuda con uno

indecen|cy /ɪn'di:snsɪ/ *n* indecencia *f*. **~t** *adj* indecente

indecisi|on /ɪndɪ'sɪʒn/ *n* indecisión *f*. **~ve** /-'saɪsɪv/ *adj* indeciso

indeed /ɪn'di:d/ *adv* en efecto; (*really?*) ¿de veras?

indefinable /ɪndɪ'faɪnəbl/ *adj* indefinible

indefinite /ɪn'defɪnət/ *adj* indefinido. **~ly** *adv* indefinidamente

indelible /ɪn'delɪbl/ *adj* indeleble

indemni|fy /ɪn'demnɪfaɪ/ *vt* (*insure*) asegurar; (*compensate*) indemnizar. **~ty** /-ətɪ/ *n* (*insurance*) indemnidad *f*; (*payment*) indemnización *f*

indent /ɪn'dent/ *vt* sangrar (text). **~ation** /-'teɪʃn/ *n* mella *f*

independen|ce /ɪndɪ'pendəns/ *n* independencia *f*. **~t** *adj* independiente. **~tly** *adv* independientemente

in-depth /ɪn'depθ/ *adj* a fondo

indescribable /ɪndɪ'skraɪbəbl/ *adj* indescriptible

indestructible /ɪndɪ'strʌktəbl/ *adj* indestructible

indeterminate /ɪndɪ'tɜ:mɪnət/ *adj* indeterminado

index /'ɪndeks/ *n* (*pl* **indexes**) (*in book*) índice *m*; (*pl* **indexes** *or* **indices**) (*Com, Math*) índice *m*. ● *vt* poner índice a; (*enter in index*) poner en un índice. **~ finger** *n* (dedo *m*) índice *m*. **~-linked** /-'lɪŋkt/ *adj* indexado

India /'ɪndɪə/ *n* la India. **~n** *adj & n* indio (*m*)

indicat|e /'ɪndɪkeɪt/ *vt* indicar. **~ion** /-'keɪʃn/ *n* indicación *f*. **~ive** /ɪn'dɪkətɪv/ *adj & n* indicativo (*m*). **~or** /'ɪndɪkeɪtə(r)/ *n* indicador *m*; (*Auto*) intermitente *m*

indices /'ɪndɪsi:z/ *see* **INDEX**

indict /ɪn'daɪt/ *vt* acusar. **~ment** *n* acusación *f*

indifferen|ce /ɪn'dɪfrəns/ *n* indiferencia *f*. **~t** *adj* indiferente; (*not good*) mediocre

indigesti|ble /ɪndɪ'dʒestəbl/ *adj* indigesto. **~on** /-tʃən/ *n* indigestión *f*

indigna|nt /ɪn'dɪgnənt/ *adj* indignado. **~tion** /-'neɪʃn/ *n* indignación *f*

indirect /ɪndɪ'rekt/ *adj* indirecto. **~ly** *adv* indirectamente

indiscre|et /ɪndɪ'skri:t/ *adj* indiscreto. **~tion** /-'kreʃn/ *n* indiscreción *f*

indiscriminate /ɪndɪ'skrɪmɪnət/ *adj* indistinto. **~ly** *adv* indistintamente

indispensable /ɪndɪ'spensəbl/ *adj* indispensable, imprescindible

indisposed /ɪndɪ'spəʊzd/ *adj* indispuesto

indisputable /ɪndɪ'spju:təbl/ *adj* indiscutible

indistinguishable /ɪndɪ'stɪŋgwɪʃəbl/ *adj* indistinguible (**from** de)

individual /ɪndɪ'vɪdjʊəl/ *adj* individual. ● *n* individuo *m*. **~ly** *adv* individualmente

indoctrinat|e /ɪn'dɒktrɪmeɪt/ *vt* adoctrinar. **~ion** /-'neɪʃn/ *n* adoctrinamiento *m*

indolen|ce /'ɪndələns/ *n* indolen-

cia *f.* ~**t** *adj* indolente
indomitable /ɪn'dɒmɪtəbl/ *adj* indómito
indoor /'ɪndɔ:(r)/ *adj* interior; (clothes etc) de casa; (*covered*) cubierto. ~**s** *adv* dentro, adentro (*LAm*)
induc|e /ɪn'dju:s/ *vt* inducir. ~**ement** *n* incentivo *m*
indulge /ɪn'dʌldʒ/ *vt* satisfacer (desires); complacer (person). ● *vi.* ~ **in** permitirse. ~**nce** /-əns/ *n* (*of desires*) satisfacción *f*; (*extravagance*) lujo *m.* ~**nt** *adj* indulgente
industrial /ɪn'dʌstrɪəl/ *adj* industrial; (unrest) laboral. ~**ist** *n* industrial *m & f.* ~**ized** *adj* industrializado
industrious /ɪn'dʌstrɪəs/ *adj* trabajador
industry /'ɪndəstrɪ/ *n* industria *f*; (*zeal*) aplicación *f*
inebriated /ɪ'ni:brɪeɪtɪd/ *adj* beodo, ebrio
inedible /ɪn'edɪbl/ *adj* incomible
ineffective /ɪnɪ'fektɪv/ *adj* ineficaz; (person) incompetente
ineffectual /ɪnɪ'fektjʊəl/ *adj* ineficaz
inefficien|cy /ɪnɪ'fɪʃnsɪ/ *n* ineficacia *f*; (*of person*) incompetencia *f.* ~**t** *adj* ineficaz; (person) incompetente
ineligible /ɪn'elɪdʒəbl/ *adj* inelegible. **be** ~ **for** no tener derecho a
inept /ɪ'nept/ *adj* inepto
inequality /ɪnɪ'kwɒlətɪ/ *n* desigualdad *f*
inert /ɪ'nɜ:t/ *adj* inerte. ~**ia** /ɪ'nɜ:ʃə/ *n* inercia *f*
inescapable /ɪnɪ'skeɪpəbl/ *adj* ineludible
inevitabl|e /ɪn'evɪtəbl/ *adj* inevitable. ● *n.* **the** ~**e** lo inevitable. ~**y** *adv* inevitablemente
inexact /ɪnɪg'zækt/ *adj* inexacto
inexcusable /ɪnɪk'skju:səbl/ *adj* imperdonable
inexpensive /ɪnɪk'spensɪv/ *adj* económico, barato
inexperience /ɪnɪk'spɪərɪəns/ *n* falta *f* de experiencia. ~**d** *adj* inexperto
inexplicable /ɪnɪk'splɪkəbl/ *adj* inexplicable
infallib|ility /ɪnfælə'bɪlətɪ/ *n* infalibilidad *f.* ~**le** /ɪn'fæləbl/ *adj* infalible
infam|ous /'ɪnfəməs/ *adj* infame. ~**y** *n* infamia *f*
infan|cy /'ɪnfənsɪ/ *n* infancia *f.* ~**t** *n* niño *m.* ~**tile** /'ɪnfəntaɪl/ *adj* infantil
infantry /'ɪnfəntrɪ/ *n* infantería *f*
infatuat|ed /ɪn'fætjʊeɪtɪd/ *adj.* **be** ~**ed with** estar encaprichado con. ~**ion** /-'eɪʃn/ *n* encaprichamiento *m*
infect /ɪn'fekt/ *vt* infectar; (*fig*) contagiar. ~ **s.o. with sth** contagiarle algo a uno. ~**ion** /-ʃn/ *n* infección *f.* ~**ious** /-ʃəs/ *adj* contagioso
infer /ɪn'fɜ:(r)/ *vt* (*pt* **inferred**) deducir
inferior /ɪn'fɪərɪə(r)/ *adj & n* inferior (*m & f*). ~**ity** /-'ɒrətɪ/ *n* inferioridad *f*
inferno /ɪn'fɜ:nəʊ/ *n* (*pl* **-os**) infierno *m*
infertil|e /ɪn'fɜ:taɪl/ *adj* estéril. ~**ity** /-'tɪlətɪ/ *n* esterilidad *f*
infest /ɪn'fest/ *vt* infestar
infidelity /ɪnfɪ'delətɪ/ *n* infidelidad *f*
infiltrat|e /'ɪnfɪltreɪt/ *vt* infiltrarse en. ● *vi* infiltrarse. ~**or** *n* infiltrado *m*
infinite /'ɪnfɪnət/ *adj* infinito. ~**ly**

adv infinitamente

infinitesimal /ɪnfɪnɪ'tesɪml/ *adj* infinitesimal

infinitive /ɪn'fɪnətɪv/ *n* infinitivo *m*

infinity /ɪn'fɪnətɪ/ *n* (*infinite distance*) infinito *m*; (*infinite quantity*) infinidad *f*

infirm /ɪn'fɜ:m/ *adj* enfermizo. **~ity** *n* enfermedad *f*

inflam|e /ɪn'fleɪm/ *vt* inflamar. **~mable** /ɪn'flæməbl/ *adj* inflamable. **~mation** /-ə'meɪʃn/ *n* inflamación *f*

inflat|e /ɪn'fleɪt/ *vt* inflar. **~ion** /-ʃn/ *n* inflación *f*. **~ionary** *adj* inflacionario

inflection /ɪn'flekʃn/ *n* inflexión *f*

inflexible /ɪn'fleksəbl/ *adj* inflexible

inflict /ɪn'flɪkt/ *vt* infligir (**on** a)

influen|ce /'ɪnflʊəns/ *n* influencia *f*. **under the ~ce** (*fam, drunk*) borracho. • *vt* influir (en). **~tial** /-'enʃl/ *adj* influyente

influenza /ɪnflʊ'enzə/ *n* gripe *f*

influx /'ɪnflʌks/ *n* afluencia *f*

inform /ɪn'fɔ:m/ *vt* informar. **keep ~ed** tener al corriente. • *vi*. **~ on s.o.** delatar a uno

informal /ɪn'fɔ:ml/ *adj* informal; (language) familiar. **~ity** /-'mælətɪ/ *n* falta *f* de ceremonia. **~ly** *adv* (*casually*) de manera informal; (*unofficially*) informalmente

inform|ation /ɪnfə'meɪʃn/ *n* información *f*. **~ation technology** *n* informática *f*. **~ative** *adj* /ɪn 'fɔ:mətɪv/ informativo. **~er** /ɪb 'fɔ:mə(r)/ *n* informante *m*

infrared /ɪnfrə'red/ *adj* infrarrojo

infrequent /ɪn'fri:kwənt/ *adj* poco frecuente. **~ly** *adv* raramente

infringe /ɪn'frɪndʒ/ *vt* infringir. **~ on** violar. **~ment** *n* violación *f*

infuriat|e /ɪn'fjʊərɪeɪt/ *vt* enfurecer. **~ing** *adj* exasperante

ingen|ious /ɪn'dʒi:nɪəs/ *adj* ingenioso. **~uity** /ɪndʒɪ'nju:ətɪ/ *n* ingeniosidad *f*

ingot /'ɪŋgət/ *n* lingote *m*

ingrained /ɪn'greɪnd/ *adj* (*belief*) arraigado

ingratiate /ɪn'greɪʃɪeɪt/ *vt*. **~ o.s. with** congraciarse con

ingratitude /ɪn'grætɪtju:d/ *n* ingratitud *f*

ingredient /ɪn'gri:dɪənt/ *n* ingrediente *m*

ingrowing/'ɪngrəʊɪŋ/, **ingrown** /'ɪngrəʊn/ *adj*. **~ nail** *n* uñero *m*, uña *f* encarnada

inhabit /ɪn'hæbɪt/ *vt* habitar. **~able** *adj* habitable. **~ant** *n* habitante *m*

inhale /ɪn'heɪl/ *vt* aspirar. • *vi* (*when smoking*) aspirar el humo. **~r** *n* inhalador *m*

inherent /ɪn'hɪərənt/ *adj* inherente. **~ly** *adv* intrínsecamente

inherit /ɪn'herɪt/ *vt* heredar. **~ance** /-əns/ *n* herencia *f*

inhibit /ɪn'hɪbɪt/ *vt* inhibir. **~ed** *adj* inhibido. **~ion** /-'bɪʃn/ *n* inhibición *f*

inhospitable /ɪnhə'spɪtəbl/ *adj* (place) inhóspito; (person) inhospitalario

inhuman /ɪn'hju:mən/ *adj* inhumano. **~e** /ɪnhju:'meɪn/ *adj* inhumano. **~ity** /ɪnhju:'mænətɪ/ *n* inhumanidad *f*

initial /ɪ'nɪʃl/ *n* inicial *f*. • *vt* (*pt* **initialled**) firmar con iniciales. • *adj* inicial. **~ly** *adv* al principio

initiat|e /ɪ'nɪʃɪeɪt/ *vt* iniciar; promover (scheme etc). **~ion** /-'eɪʃn/ *n* iniciación *f*

i

initiative /ɪ'nɪʃətɪv/ *n* iniciativa *f*. **on one's own ~** por iniciativa propia. **take the ~** tomar la iniciativa

inject /ɪn'dʒekt/ *vt* inyectar. **~ion** /-ʃn/ *n* inyección *f*

injur|e /'ɪndʒə(r)/ *vt* herir. **~y** *n* herida *f*

injustice /ɪn'dʒʌstɪs/ *n* injusticia *f*

ink /ɪŋk/ *n* tinta *f*. **~well** *n* tintero *m*. **~y** *adj* manchado de tinta

inland /'ɪnlənd/ *adj* interior. ●/ɪn'lænd/ *adv* tierra adentro. **I~ Revenue** /'ɪnlənd/ *n* Hacienda *f*

i

in-laws /'ɪnlɔ:z/ *npl* parientes *mpl* políticos

inlay /ɪn'leɪ/ *vt* (*pt* **inlaid**) taracear, incrustar. ●/'ɪnleɪ/ *n* taracea *f*, incrustación *f*

inlet /'ɪnlet/ *n* (*in coastline*) ensenada *f*; (*of river, sea*) brazo *m*

inmate /'ɪnmeɪt/ *n* (*of asylum*) interno *m*; (*of prison*) preso *m*

inn /ɪn/ *n* posada *f*

innate /ɪ'neɪt/ *adj* innato

inner /'ɪnə(r)/ *adj* interior; (*fig*) íntimo. **~most** *adj* más íntimo. **~ tube** *n* cámara *f*

innocen|ce /'ɪnəsns/ *n* inocencia *f*. **~t** *adj* & *n* inocente (*m* & *f*)

innocuous /ɪ'nɒkjʊəs/ *adj* inocuo

innovat|e /'ɪnəveɪt/ *vi* innovar. **~ion** /-'veɪʃn/ *n* innovación *f*. **~ive** /'ɪnəvətɪv/ *adj* innovador. **~or** *n* innovador *m*

innuendo /ɪnju:'endəʊ/ *n* (*pl* **-oes**) insinuación *f*

innumerable /ɪ'nju:mərəbl/ *adj* innumerable

inoculat|e /ɪ'nɒkjʊleɪt/ *vt* inocular. **~ion** /-'leɪʃn/ *n* inoculación *f*

inoffensive /ɪnə'fensɪv/ *adj* inofensivo

inopportune /ɪn'ɒpətju:n/ *adj* inoportuno

input /'ɪnpʊt/ *n* aportación *f*, aporte *m* (*LAm*); (*Comp*) entrada *f*. ●*vt* (*pt* **input**, *pres p* **inputting**) entrar (data)

inquest /'ɪnkwest/ *n* investigación *f* judicial

inquir|e /ɪn'kwaɪə(r)/ *vt/i* preguntar. **~e about** informarse de. **~y** *n* pregunta *f*; (*investigation*) investigación *f*

inquisition /ɪnkwɪ'zɪʃn/ *n* inquisición *f*

inquisitive /ɪn'kwɪzətɪv/ *adj* inquisitivo

insan|e /ɪn'seɪn/ *adj* loco. **~ity** /ɪn'sænətɪ/ *n* locura *f*

insatiable /ɪn'seɪʃəbl/ *adj* insaciable

inscri|be /ɪn'skraɪb/ *vt* inscribir (letters); grabar (design). **~ption** /-ɪpʃn/ *n* inscripción *f*

inscrutable /ɪn'skru:təbl/ *adj* inescrutable

insect /'ɪnsekt/ *n* insecto *m*. **~icide** /ɪn'sektɪsaɪd/ *n* insecticida *f*

insecur|e /ɪnsɪ'kjʊə(r)/ *adj* inseguro. **~ity** *n* inseguridad *f*

insensitive /ɪn'sensətɪv/ *adj* insensible

inseparable /ɪn'sepərəbl/ *adj* inseparable

insert /'ɪnsɜ:t/ *n* materia *f* insertada. ●/ɪn'sɜ:t/ *vt* insertar. **~ion** /ɪn'sɜ:ʃn/ *n* inserción *f*

inside /ɪn'saɪd/ *n* interior *m*. **~ out** al revés; (*thoroughly*) a fondo. ●*adj* interior. ●*adv* dentro, adentro (*LAm*). ●*prep* dentro de. **~s** *npl* tripas *fpl*

insight /'ɪnsaɪt/ *n* perspicacia *f*. **gain an ~ into** llegar a comprender bien

insignificant /ɪnsɪɡ'nɪfɪkənt/ *adj* insignificante

insincer|e /ɪnsɪn'sɪə(r)/ *adj* poco sincero. **~ity** /-'serətɪ/ *n* falta *f* de sinceridad

insinuat|e /ɪn'sɪnjʊeɪt/ *vt* insinuar. **~ion** /-'eɪʃn/ *n* insinuación *f*

insipid /ɪn'sɪpɪd/ *adj* insípido

insist /ɪn'sɪst/ *vt* insistir (**that** en que). ●*vi* insistir. **~ on** insistir en. **~ence** /-əns/ *n* insistencia *f*. **~ent** *adj* insistente. **~ently** *adv* con insistencia

insolen|ce /'ɪnsələns/ *n* insolencia *f*. **~t** *adj* insolente

insoluble /ɪn'sɒljʊbl/ *adj* insoluble

insolvent /ɪn'sɒlvənt/ *adj* insolvente

insomnia /ɪn'sɒmnɪə/ *n* insomnio *m*. **~c** /-ɪæk/ *n* insomne *m & f*

inspect /ɪn'spekt/ *vt* (*officially*) inspeccionar; (*look at closely*) revisar, examinar . **~ion** /-ʃn/ *n* inspección *f*. **~or** *n* inspector *m*; (*on train, bus*) revisor *m*, inspector *m* (*LAm*)

inspir|ation /ɪnspə'reɪʃn/ *n* inspiración *f*. **~e** /ɪn'spaɪə(r)/ *vt* inspirar. **~ing** *adj* inspirador

instability /ɪnstə'bɪlətɪ/ *n* inestabilidad *f*

install /ɪn'stɔ:l/ *vt* instalar. **~ation** /-ə'leɪʃn/ *n* instalación *f*

instalment /ɪn'stɔ:lmənt/ *n* (*payment*) plazo *m*; (*of publication*) entrega *f*; (*of radio, TV serial*) episodio *m*

instance /'ɪnstəns/ *n* ejemplo *m*; (*case*) caso *m*. **for ~** por ejemplo. **in the first ~** en primer lugar

instant /'ɪnstənt/ *adj* instantáneo. ●*n* instante *m*. **~aneous** /ɪnstən'teɪmɪəs/ *adj* instantáneo

instead /ɪn'sted/ *adv* en cambio. **~ of** en vez de, en lugar de

instigat|e /'ɪnstɪɡeɪt/ *vt* instigar. **~ion** /-'ɡeɪʃn/ *n* instigación *f*

instinct /'ɪnstɪŋkt/ *n* instinto *m*. **~ive** *adj* instintivo

institut|e /'ɪnstɪtju:t/ *n* instituto *m*. ●*vt* instituir; iniciar (enquiry etc). **~ion** /-'tju:ʃn/ *n* institución *f*. **~ional** *adj* institucional

instruct /ɪn'strʌkt/ *vt* instruir; (*order*) mandar. **~ s.o. in sth** enseñar algo a uno. **~ion** /-ʃn/ *n* instrucción *f*. **~ions** *npl* (*for use*) modo *m* de empleo. **~ive** *adj* instructivo. **~or** *n* instructor *m*

instrument /'ɪnstrəmənt/ *n* instrumento *m*. **~al** /ɪnstrə'mentl/ *adj* instrumental. **be ~al in** jugar un papel decisivo en

insubordinat|e /ɪnsə'bɔ:dɪnət/ *adj* insubordinado. **~ion** /-'neɪʃn/ *n* insubordinación *f*

insufferable /ɪn'sʌfərəbl/ *adj* (person) insufrible; (heat) insoportable

insufficient /ɪnsə'fɪʃnt/ *adj* insuficiente

insular /'ɪnsjʊlə(r)/ *adj* insular; (*narrow-minded*) estrecho de miras

insulat|e /'ɪnsjʊleɪt/ *vt* aislar. **~ion** /-'leɪʃn/ *n* aislamiento *m*

insulin /'ɪnsjʊlɪn/ *n* insulina *f*

insult /ɪn'sʌlt/ *vt* insultar. ●/'ɪnsʌlt/ *n* insulto *m*. **~ing** /ɪn'sʌltɪŋ/ *adj* insultante

insur|ance /ɪn'ʃʊərəns/ *n* seguro *m*. **~e** /ɪn'ʃʊə(r)/ *vt* (*Com*) asegurar; (*Amer*) *see* **ENSURE**

insurmountable /ɪnsə'maʊntəbl/ *adj* insuperable

intact /ɪn'tækt/ *adj* intacto

integral /'ɪntɪɡrəl/ *adj* integral

integrat|e /'ɪntɪɡreɪt/ *vt* integrar. ●*vi* integrarse. **~ion** /-'ɡreɪʃn/ *n* integración *f*

integrity /ɪn'tegrətɪ/ *n* integridad *f*

intellect /'ɪntəlekt/ *n* intelecto *m.* **~ual** /ɪntə'lektʃʊəl/ *adj & n* intelectual (*m*)

intelligen|ce /ɪn'telɪdʒəns/ *n* inteligencia *f.* **~t** *adj* inteligente. **~tly** *adv* inteligentemente

intelligible /ɪn'telɪdʒəbl/ *adj* inteligible

intend /ɪn'tend/ *vt.* **~ to do** pensar hacer

intens|e /ɪn'tens/ *adj* intenso; (person) apasionado. **~ely** *adv* intensamente; (*very*) sumamente. **~ify** /-ɪfaɪ/ *vt* intensificar. ● *vi* intensificarse. **~ity** /-ɪtɪ/ *n* intensidad *f*

intensive /ɪn'tensɪv/ *adj* intensivo. **~ care** *n* cuidados *mpl* intensivos

intent /ɪn'tent/ *n* propósito *m.* ● *adj* atento. **~ on** absorto en. **~ on doing** resuelto a hacer

intention /ɪn'tenʃn/ *n* intención *f.* **~al** *adj* intencional

intently /ɪn'tentlɪ/ *adv* atentamente

interact /ɪntər'ækt/ *vi* relacionarse. **~ion** /-ʃn/ *n* interacción *f*

intercept /ɪntə'sept/ *vt* interceptar. **~ion** /-ʃn/ *n* interceptación *f*

interchange /ɪntə'tʃeɪndʒ/ *vt* intercambiar. ● /'ɪntətʃeɪndʒ/ *n* intercambio *m;* (*road junction*) cruce *m.* **~able** /-'tʃeɪndʒəbl/ *adj* intercambiable

intercity /ɪntə'sɪtɪ/ *adj* rápido interurbano *m*

intercourse /'ɪntəkɔ:s/ *n* trato *m;* (*sexual*) acto *m* sexual

interest /'ɪntrest/ *n* interés *m.* ● *vt* interesar. **~ed** *adj* interesado. **be ~ed in** interesarse por. **~ing** *adj* interesante

interface /'ɪntəfeɪs/ interfaz *m & f;* (*interaction*) interrelación *f*

interfere /ɪntə'fɪə(r)/ *vi* entrometerse. **~ in** entrometerse en. **~ with** afectar (a); interferir (radio). **~nce** /-rəns/ *n* intromisión *f;* (*Radio*) interferencia *f*

interior /ɪn'tɪərɪə(r)/ *adj & n* interior (*m*)

interjection /ɪntə'dʒekʃn/ *n* interjección *f*

interlude /'ɪntəlu:d/ *n* intervalo *m;* (*theatre, music*) interludio *m*

intermediary /ɪntə'mi:dɪərɪ/ *adj & n* intermediario (*m*)

interminable /ɪn'tɜ:mɪnəbl/ *adj* interminable

intermittent /ɪntə'mɪtnt/ *adj* intermitente. **~ly** *adv* con discontinuidad

intern /ɪn'tɜ:n/ *vt* internar. ● /'ɪntɜ:n/ *n* (*Amer, doctor*) interno *m*

internal /ɪn'tɜ:nl/ *adj* interno. **~ly** *adv* internamente. **I~ Revenue Service** *n* (*Amer*) Hacienda *f*

international /ɪntə'næʃənl/ *adj* internacional

Internet /'ɪntənet/ *n.* **the ~** el Internet

interpret /ɪn'tɜ:prɪt/ *vt/i* interpretar. **~ation** /-'teɪʃn/ *n* interpretación *f.* **~er** *n* intérprete *m & f*

interrogat|e /ɪn'terəgeɪt/ *vt* interrogar. **~ion** /-'geɪʃn/ *n* interrogatorio *m.* **~ive** /-'rɒgətɪv/ *adj* interrogativo

interrupt /ɪntə'rʌpt/ *vt/i* interrumpir. **~ion** /-ʃn/ *n* interrupción *f*

intersect /ɪntə'sekt/ *vt* cruzar. ● *vi* (roads) cruzarse; (*geometry*) intersecarse. **~ion** /-ʃn/ *n* (*roads*) cruce *m*; (*geometry*) intersección *f*

intersperse /ɪntə'spɜ:s/ *vt* intercalar

interstate (highway) /'ɪntəsteɪt/ *n* (*Amer*) carretera *f* interestal

intertwine /ɪntə'twaɪn/ *vt* entrelazar. ● *vi* entrelazarse

interval /'ɪntəvl/ *n* intervalo *m*; (*theatre*) descanso *m*. **at ~s** a intervalos

interven|e /ɪntə'vi:n/ *vi* intervenir. **~tion** /-'venʃn/ *n* intervención *f*

interview /'ɪntəvju:/ *n* entrevista *f*. ● *vt* entrevistar. **~ee** /-'i:/ *n* entrevistado *m*. **~er** *n* entrevistador *m*

intestine /ɪn'testɪn/ *n* intestino *m*

intimacy /'ɪntɪməsɪ/ *n* intimidad *f*

intimate /'ɪntɪmət/ *adj* íntimo. ● /'ɪntɪmeɪt/ *vt* (*state*) anunciar; (*imply*) dar a entender. **~ly** /'ɪntɪmətlɪ/ *adv* íntimamente

intimidat|e /ɪn'tɪmɪdeɪt/ *vt* intimidar. **~ion** /-'deɪʃn/ *n* intimidación *f*

into/'ɪntu://'ɪntə/ *prep* en; (translate) a

intolerable /ɪn'tɒlərəbl/ *adj* intolerable

intoleran|ce /ɪn'tɒlərəns/ *n* intolerancia *f*. **~t** *adj* intolerante

intoxicat|e /ɪn'tɒksɪkeɪt/ *vt* embriagar; (*Med*) intoxicar. **~ed** *adj* ebrio. **~ing** *adj* (substance) estupefaciente. **~ion** /-'keɪʃn/ *n* embriaguez *f*; (*Med*) intoxicación *f*

intransitive /ɪn'trænsɪtɪv/ *adj* intransitivo

intravenous /ɪntrə'vi:nəs/ *adj* intravenoso

intrepid /ɪn'trepɪd/ *adj* intrépido

intrica|cy /'ɪntrɪkəsɪ/ *n* complejidad *f*. **~te** /-ət/ *adj* complejo

intrigu|e /ɪn'tri:g/ *vt/i* intrigar. ● /'ɪntri:g/ *n* intriga *f*. **~ing** /ɪn'tri:gɪŋ/ *adj* intrigante

intrinsic /ɪn'trɪnsɪk/ *adj* intrínseco. **~ally** *adv* intrínsecamente

introduc|e /ɪntrə'dju:s/ *vt* introducir; presentar (person). **~tion** /ɪntrə'dʌkʃn/ *n* introducción *f*; (*to person*) presentación *f*. **~tory** /ɪntrə'dʌktərɪ/ *adj* preliminar; (course) de introducción

introvert /'ɪntrəvɜ:t/ *n* introvertido *m*

intru|de /ɪn'tru:d/ *vi* entrometerse; (*disturb*) importunar. **~der** *n* intruso *m*. **~sion** /-ʒn/ *n* intrusión *f*. **~sive** /-sɪv/ *adj* impertinente

intuiti|on /ɪntju:'ɪʃn/ *n* intuición *f*. **~ve** /ɪn'tju:ɪtɪv/ *adj* intuitivo

inundat|e /'ɪnʌndeɪt/ *vt* inundar. **~ion** /-'deɪʃn/ *n* inundación *f*

invade /ɪn'veɪd/ *vt* invadir. **~r** *n* invasor *m*

invalid /'ɪnvəlɪd/ *n* inválido *m*. ● /ɪn'vælɪd/ *adj* inválido. **~ate** /ɪn'vælɪdeɪt/ *vt* invalidar

invaluable /ɪn'væljʊəbl/ *adj* inestimable, invalorable (*LAm*)

invariabl|e /ɪn'veərɪəbl/ *adj* invariable. **~y** *adv* invariablemente

invasion /ɪn'veɪʒn/ *n* invasión *f*

invent /ɪn'vent/ *vt* inventar. **~ion** /-'venʃn/ *n* invención *f*. **~ive** *adj* inventivo. **~or** *n* inventor *m*

inventory /'ɪnvəntrɪ/ *n* inventario *m*

invertebrate /ɪn'vɜ:tɪbrət/ *n* invertebrado *m*

inverted commas /ɪnvɜ:tɪd 'kɒməz/*npl* comillas *fpl*

invest /ɪn'vest/ *vt* invertir. ● *vi*. **~ in** invertir en

investigat|e /ɪn'vestɪgeɪt/ *vt* investigar. **~ion** /-'geɪʃn/ *n* investigación *f*. **under ~ion** sometido a examen. **~or** *n* investigador *m*

investment /ɪn'vestmənt/ inversión *f*

investor /ɪn'vestə(r)/ inversionista *m & f*

inveterate /ɪn'vetərət/ *adj* inveterado

invidious /ɪn'vɪdɪəs/ *adj* (*hateful*) odioso; (*unfair*) injusto

invigorating /ɪn'vɪgəreɪtɪŋ/ *adj* vigorizante; (*stimulating*) estimulante

i

invincible /ɪn'vɪnsɪbl/ *adj* invencible

invisible /ɪn'vɪzəbl/ *adj* invisible

invit|ation /ɪnvɪ'teɪʃn/ *n* invitación *f*. **~e** /ɪn'vaɪt/ *vt* invitar; (*ask for*) pedir. ● /'ɪnvaɪt/ *n* [I] invitación *f*. **~ing** /ɪn'vaɪtɪŋ/ *adj* atrayente

invoice /'ɪnvɔɪs/ *n* factura *f*. ● *vt*. **~ s.o. (for sth)** pasarle a uno factura (por algo)

involuntary /ɪn'vɒləntərɪ/ *adj* involuntario

involve /ɪn'vɒlv/ *vt* (*entail*) suponer; (*implicate*) implicar. **~d in** envuelto en. **~d** *adj* (*complex*) complicado. **~ment** *n* participación *f*; (*relationship*) enredo *m*

inward /'ɪnwəd/ *adj* interior. ● *adv* hacia adentro. **~s** *adv* hacia dentro

iodine /'aɪədi:n/ *n* yodo *m*

ion /'aɪən/ *n* ion *m*

iota /aɪ'əʊtə/ *n* (*amount*) pizca *f*

IOU /aɪəʊ'ju:/ *abbr* (= **I owe you**) pagaré *m*

IQ *abbr* (= **intelligence quotient**) CI *m*, cociente *m* intelectual

Iran /ɪ'rɑ:n/ *n* Irán *m*. **~ian** /ɪ'reɪmɪən/ *adj & n* iraní (*m*)

Iraq /ɪ'rɑ:k/ *n* Irak *m*. **~i** *adj & n* iraquí (*m & f*)

irate /aɪ'reɪt/ *adj* colérico

Ireland /'aɪələnd/ *n* Irlanda *f*

iris /'aɪərɪs/ *n* (*of eye*) iris *m*; (*flower*) lirio *m*

Irish /'aɪərɪʃ/ *adj* irlandés. ● *n* (*language*) irlandés *m*. *npl*. **the ~** (*people*) los irlandeses. **~man** /-mən/ *n* irlandés *m*. **~woman** *n* irlandesa *f*

iron /'aɪən/ *n* hierro *m*; (*appliance*) plancha *f*. ● *adj* de hierro. ● *vt* planchar. □ **~ out** *vt* allanar

ironic /aɪ'rɒnɪk/ *adj* irónico. **~ally** *adv* irónicamente

ironing board /'aɪənɪŋ/ *n* tabla *f* de planchar, burro *m* de planchar (*Mex*)

iron: ~monger /-mʌŋgə(r)/ *n* ferretero *m*. **~monger's** *n* ferretería *f*

irony /'aɪərənɪ/ *n* ironía *f*

irrational /ɪ'ræʃənl/ *adj* irracional

irrefutable /ɪrɪ'fju:təbl/ *adj* irrefutable

irregular /ɪ'regjʊlə(r)/ *adj* irregular. **~ity** /-'lærətɪ/ *n* irregularidad *f*

irrelevan|ce /ɪ'reləvəns/ *n* irrelevancia *f*. **~t** *adj* irrelevante

irreparable /ɪ'repərəbl/ *adj* irreparable

irreplaceable /ɪrɪ'pleɪsəbl/ *adj* irreemplazable

irresistible /ɪrɪ'zɪstəbl/ *adj* irresistible

irrespective /ɪrɪ'spektɪv/ *adj*. **~ of** sin tomar en cuenta

irresponsible /ɪrɪ'spɒnsəbl/ *adj* irresponsable

irretrievable /ɪrɪ'tri:vəbl/ *adj* irrecuperable

irreverent /ɪ'revərənt/ *adj* irreverente

irrevocable /ɪ'revəkəbl/ *adj* irrevocable

irrigat|e /'ɪrɪgeɪt/ *vt* regar, irrigar. **~ion** /-'geɪʃn/ *n* riego *m*, irrigación *f*

irritable /'ɪrɪtəbl/ *adj* irritable

irritat|e /'ɪrɪteɪt/ *vt* irritar. **~ed** *adj* irritado. **~ing** *adj* irritante. **~ion** /-'teɪʃn/ *n* irritación *f*

IRS *abbr* (*Amer*) *see* **INTERNAL REVENUE SERVICE**

is /ɪz/ *see* **BE**

ISDN *abbr* (**Integrated Services Digital Network**) RDSI

Islam /'ɪzlɑːm/ *n* el Islam. **~ic** /ɪz'læmɪk/ *adj* islámico

island /'aɪlənd/ *n* isla *f*. **~er** *n* isleño *m*

isolat|e /'aɪsəleɪt/ *vt* aislar. **~ion** /-'leɪʃn/ *n* aislamiento *m*

Israel /'ɪzreɪl/ *n* Israel *m*. **~i** /ɪz'reɪlɪ/ *adj & n* israelí (*m*)

issue /'ɪʃuː/ *n* tema *m*, asunto *m*; (*of magazine etc*) número *m*; (*of stamps, bank notes*) emisión *f*; (*of documents*) expedición *f*. **take ~ with** discrepar de. ● *vt* hacer público (statement); expedir (documents); emitir (stamps etc); prestar (library book)

it /ɪt/ *pronoun*

....> (*as subject*) *generally not translated*. **it's huge** es enorme. **where is it?** ¿dónde está?. **it's all lies** son todas mentiras

....> (*as direct object*) lo (*m*), la (*f*). **he read it to me** me lo/la leyó. **give it to me** dámelo/dámela

....> (*as indirect object*) le. **I gave it another coat of paint** le di otra mano de pintura

....> (*after a preposition*) *generally not translated*. **there's nothing behind it** no hay nada detrás

! Note, however, that in some cases *él* or *ella* must be used e.g. **he picked up the spoon and hit me with it** *agarró la cuchara y me golpeó con ella*

....> (*at door*) **who is it?** ¿quién es?. **it's me** soy yo; (*on telephone*) **who is it, please?** ¿quién habla, por favor?; (*before passing on to sb else*) ¿de parte de quién, por favor? **it's Carol** soy Carol (*Spain*), habla Carol

....> (*in impersonal constructions*) **it is well known that ...** bien se sabe que ... **it's five o'clock** son las cinco. **so it seems** así parece

....> **that's it** (*that's right*) eso es; (*that's enough, that's finished*) ya está

Italian /ɪ'tæljən/ *adj & n* italiano (*m*)

italics /ɪ'tælɪks/ *npl* (letra *f*) cursiva *f*

Italy /'ɪtəlɪ/ *n* Italia *f*

itch /ɪtʃ/ *n* picazón *f*. ● *vi* picar. **I'm ~ing to** estoy que me muero por. **my arm ~es** me pica el brazo. **~y** *adj* que pica. **I've got an ~y nose** me pica la nariz

it'd /ɪtəd/ = **it had, it would**

item /'aɪtəm/ *n* artículo *m*; (*on agenda*) punto *m*. **news ~** *n* noticia *f*. **~ize** *vt* detallar

itinerary /aɪ'tɪnərərɪ/ *n* itinerario *m*

it'll /'ɪtl/ = **it will**

its /ɪts/ *adj* su, sus (*pl*). ● *pron* (el)

suyo *m*, (la) suya *f*, (los) suyos *mpl*, (las) suyas *fpl*

it's /ɪts/ = **it is, it has**

itself /ɪt'self/ *pron* él mismo, ella misma, ello mismo; (*reflexive*) se; (*after prep*) sí mismo, sí misma

I've /aɪv/ = **I have**

ivory /'aɪvərɪ/ *n* marfil *m*. ~ **tower** *n* torre *f* de marfil

ivy /'aɪvɪ/ *n* hiedra *f*

> **Ivy League - the** El grupo de universidades más antiguas y respetadas de EE.UU. Situadas al noreste del país, son: Harvard, Yale, Columbia, Cornell, Dartmouth College, Brown, Princeton y Pensylvania. El término proviene de la hiedra que crece en los antiguos edificios de estos establecimientos.

Jj

jab /dʒæb/ *vt* (*pt* **jabbed**) pinchar; (*thrust*) hurgonear. ● *n* pinchazo *m*

jack /dʒæk/ *n* (*Mec*) gato *m*; (*socket*) enchufe *m* hembra; (*Cards*) sota *f*. □ ~ **up** *vt* alzar con gato

jackal /'dʒækl/ *n* chacal *m*

jackdaw /'dʒækdɔ:/ *n* grajilla *f*

jacket /'dʒækɪt/ *n* chaqueta *f*; (*casual*) americana *f*, saco *m* (*LAm*); (*Amer*, *of book*) sobrecubierta *f*; (*of record*) funda *f*, carátula *f*

jack: ~ knife *vi* (lorry) plegarse. **~pot** *n* premio *m* gordo. **hit the ~pot** sacar el premio gordo

jade /dʒeɪd/ *n* (*stone*) jade *m*

jagged /'dʒægɪd/ *adj* (edge, cut) irregular; (rock) recortado

jaguar /'dʒægjʊə(r)/ *n* jaguar *m*

jail /dʒeɪl/ *n* cárcel *m*, prisión *f*. ● *vt* encarcelar. **~er** *n* carcelero *m*. **~house** *n* (*Amer*) cárcel *f*

jam /dʒæm/ *vt* (*pt* **jammed**) interferir con (radio); atestar (road). ~ **sth into sth** meter algo a la fuerza en algo. ● *vi* (brakes) bloquearse; (machine) trancarse. ● *n* mermelada *f*; (*fam, situation*) apuro *m*

jangle /'dʒæŋgl/ *n* sonido *m* metálico (y áspero). ● *vi* hacer ruido (metálico)

janitor /'dʒænɪtə(r)/ *n* portero *m*

January /'dʒænjʊərɪ/ *n* enero *m*

Japan /dʒə'pæn/ *n* (el) Japón *m*. **~ese** /dʒæpə'ni:z/ *adj & n invar* japonés (*m*)

jar /dʒɑ:(r)/ *n* tarro *m*, bote *m*. ● *vi* (*pt* **jarred**) (clash) desentonar. ● *vt* sacudir

jargon /'dʒɑ:gən/ *n* jerga *f*

jaundice /'dʒɔ:ndɪs/ *n* ictericia *f*

jaunt /dʒɔ:nt/ *n* excursión *f*

jaunty /'dʒɔ:ntɪ/ *adj* (**-ier**, **-iest**) garboso

jaw /dʒɔ:/ *n* mandíbula *f*. **~s** *npl* fauces *fpl*. **~bone** *n* mandíbula *f*, maxilar *m*; (*of animal*) quijada *f*

jay /dʒeɪ/ *n* arrendajo *m*. **~walk** *vi* cruzar la calle descuidadamente. **~walker** *n* peatón *m* imprudente

jazz /dʒæz/ *n* jazz *m*. □ ~ **up** *vt* animar. **~y** *adj* chillón

jealous /dʒeləs/ *adj* celoso; (*envious*) envidioso. **~y** *n* celos *mpl*

jeans /dʒi:nz/ *npl* vaqueros *mpl*, jeans *mpl*, tejanos *mpl*, pantalones *mpl* de mezclilla (*Mex*)

Jeep (*P*), **jeep** /dʒi:p/ *n* Jeep *m* (*P*)

jeer /dʒɪə(r)/ *vi*. ~ **at** mofarse de;

(*boo*) abuchear. • *n* burla *f*; (*boo*) abucheo *m*

Jell-O /'dʒeləʊ/ *n* (*P*) (*Amer*) gelatina *f* (con sabor a frutas)

jelly /dʒelɪ/ *n* (*clear jam*) jalea *f*; (*pudding*) *see* **Jell-O**; (*substance*) gelatina *f*. **~fish** *n* (*pl invar or* **-es**) medusa *f*

jeopardize /'dʒepədaɪz/ *vt* arriesgar

jerk /dʒɜ:k/ *n* sacudida *f*; (*sl, fool*) idiota *m & f*. • *vt* sacudir

jersey /'dʒɜ:zɪ/ *n* (*pl* **-eys**) jersey *m*, suéter *m*, pulóver *m*

jest /dʒest/ *n* broma *f*. • *vi* bromear

Jesus /'dʒi:zəs/ *n* Jesús *m*

jet /dʒet/ *n* (*stream*) chorro *m*; (*plane*) avión *m* (con motor a reacción); (*mineral*) azabache *m*. **~-black** /-'blæk/ *adj* azabache negro *a invar*. **~ lag** *n* jet lag *m*, desfase *f* horario. **have ~ lag** estar desfasado. **~-propelled** /-prə'peld/ *adj* (de propulsión) a reacción

jettison /'dʒetɪsn/ *vt* echar al mar; (*fig, discard*) deshacerse de

jetty /'dʒetɪ/ *n* muelle *m*

Jew /dʒu:/ *n* judío *m*

jewel /'dʒu:əl/ *n* joya *f*. **~ler** *n* joyero *m*. **~lery** *n* joyas *fpl*

Jewish /'dʒu:ɪʃ/ *adj* judío

jiffy /'dʒɪfɪ/ *n* momentito *m*. **do sth in a ~** hacer algo en un santiamén

jig /dʒɪg/ *n* (*dance*) giga *f*

jigsaw /'dʒɪgsɔ:/ *n*. **~ (puzzle)** rompecabezas *m*

jilt /dʒɪlt/ *vt* dejar plantado

jingle /'dʒɪŋgl/ *vt* hacer sonar. • *vi* tintinear. • *n* tintineo *m*; (*advert*) jingle *m* (publicitario)

job /dʒɒb/ *n* empleo *m*, trabajo *m*; (*piece of work*) trabajo *m*. **it is a good ~ that** menos mal que. **~less** *adj* desempleado

jockey /'dʒɒkɪ/ *n* jockey *m*

jocular /'dʒɒkjʊlə(r)/ *adj* jocoso

jog /dʒɒg/ *vt* (*pt* **jogged**) empujar; refrescar (memory). • *vi* hacer footing, hacer jogging. **~er** *n* persona *f* que hace footing. **~ging** *n* footing *m*, jogging *m*. **go ~ging** salir a hacer footing *or* jogging

join /dʒɔɪn/ *vt* (*link*) unir; hacerse socio de (club); hacerse miembro de (political group); alistarse en (army); reunirse con (another person). • *n* juntura. • *vi*. **~ together** (parts) unirse; (roads etc) empalmar; (rivers) confluir. □ **~ in** *vi* participar (en). □ **~ up** *vi* (*Mil*) alistarse. **~er** *n* carpintero *m*

joint /dʒɔɪnt/ *adj* conjunto. • *n* (*join*) unión *f*, junta *f*; (*in limbs*) articulación *f*. (*Culin*) trozo *m* de carne (para asar). **out of ~** descoyuntado. **~ account** *n* cuenta *f* conjunta. **~ly** *adv* conjuntamente. **~ owner** *n* copropietario *m*.

joist /dʒɔɪst/ *n* viga *f*

jok|e /dʒəʊk/ *n* (*story*) chiste *m*; (*practical joke*) broma *f*. • *vi* bromear. **~er** *n* bromista *m & f*; (*Cards*) comodín *m*. **~y** *adj* jocoso

jolly /'dʒɒlɪ/ *adj* (**-ier**, **-iest**) alegre. • *adv* [I] muy

jolt /dʒɒlt/ *vt* sacudir. • *vi* (vehicle) dar una sacudida. • *n* sacudida *f*

jostle /'dʒɒsl/ *vt* empujar. • *vi* empujarse

jot /dʒɒt/ *n* pizca *f*. • *vt* (*pt* **jotted**). □ **~ down** *vt* apuntar (rápidamente). **~ter** *n* bloc *m*

journal /'dʒɜ:nl/ *n* (*diary*) diario *m*; (*newspaper*) periódico *m*; (*magazine*) revista *f*. **~ism** *n* periodismo *m*. **~ist** *n* periodista *m & f*

J

journey /ˈdʒɜːnɪ/ *n* viaje *m.* **go on a ~** hacer un viaje. ●*vi* viajar

jovial /ˈdʒəʊvɪəl/ *adj* jovial

joy /dʒɔɪ/ *n* alegría *f.* **~ful** *adj* feliz. **~ous** *adj* feliz. **~rider** *n* joven *m* que roba un coche para dar una vuelta. **~stick** *n* (*in aircraft*) palanca *f* de mando; (*Comp*) mando *m*, joystick *m*

jubila|nt /ˈdʒuːbɪlənt/ *adj* jubiloso. **~tion** /-ˈleɪʃn/ *n* júbilo *m*

jubilee /ˈdʒuːbɪliː/ *n* aniversario *m* especial

Judaism /ˈdʒuːdeɪɪzəm/ *n* judaísmo *m*

j

judge /dʒʌdʒ/ *n* juez *m.* ●*vt* juzgar. **~ment** *n* juicio *m*

judicia|l /dʒuːˈdɪʃl/ *adj* judicial. **~ry** /-ərɪ/ *n* judicatura *f*

judo /ˈdʒuːdəʊ/ *n* judo *m*

jug /dʒʌg/ *n* jarra *f*

juggernaut /ˈdʒʌgənɔːt/ *n* camión *m* grande

juggle /ˈdʒʌgl/ *vi* hacer malabarismos. ●*vt* hacer malabarismos con. **~r** *n* malabarista *m & f*

juic|e /dʒuːs/ *n* jugo *m*, zumo *m.* **~y** *adj* jugoso, zumoso; (story etc) 🄸 picante

jukebox /ˈdʒuːkbɒks/ *n* máquina *f* de discos, rocola *f* (*LAm*)

July /dʒuːˈlaɪ/ *n* julio *m*

jumble /ˈdʒʌmbl/ *vt.* **~ (up)** mezclar. ●*n* (*muddle*) revoltijo *m.* **~ sale** *n* venta *f* de objetos usados *m*

jumbo /ˈdʒʌmbəʊ/ *adj* gigante. **~ jet** *n* jumbo *m*

jump /dʒʌmp/ *vt* saltar. **~ rope** (*Amer*) saltar a la comba, saltar a la cuerda. **~ the gun** obrar prematuramente. **~ the queue** colarse. ●*vi* saltar; (*start*) sobresaltarse; (prices) alzarse. **~ at an opportunity** apresurarse a aprovechar una oportunidad. ●*n* salto *m*; (*start*) susto *m*; (*increase*) aumento *m.* **~er** *n* jersey *m*, suéter *m*, pulóver *m*; (*Amer, dress*) pichi *m*, jumper *m & f* (*LAm*). **~er cables** (*Amer*), **~ leads** *npl* cables *mpl* de arranque. **~ rope** (*Amer*) comba *f*, cuerda *f*, reata *f* (*Mex*). **~suit** *n* mono *m.* **~y** *adj* nervioso

junction /ˈdʒʌŋkʃn/ *n* (*of roads, rails*) cruce *m*; (*Elec*) empalme *m*

June /dʒuːn/ *n* junio *m*

jungle /ˈdʒʌŋgl/ *n* selva *f*, jungla *f*

junior /ˈdʒuːnɪə(r)/ *adj* (*in age*) más joven (**to** que); (*in rank*) subalterno. ●*n* menor *m*

junk /dʒʌŋk/ *n* trastos *mpl* viejos; (*worthless stuff*) basura *f.* ●*vt* 🄸 tirar. **~ food** *n* comida *f* basura, alimento *m* chatarra (*Mex*). **~ie** /ˈdʒʌnkɪ/ *n* 🄸 drogadicto *m*, yonqui *m & f* 🄸. **~ mail** *n* propaganda *f* que se recibe por correo. **~ shop** *n* tienda *f* de trastos viejos

junta /ˈdʒʌntə/ *n* junta *f* militar

Jupiter /ˈdʒuːpɪtə(r)/ *n* Júpiter *m*

jurisdiction /dʒʊərɪsˈdɪkʃn/ *n* jurisdicción *f*

jur|or /ˈdʒʊərə(r)/ *n* (miembro *m* de un) jurado *m.* **~y** *n* jurado *m*

just /dʒʌst/ *adj* (*fair*) justo. ●*adv* exactamente, justo; (*barely*) justo; (*only*) sólo, solamente. **~ as tall** tan alto (**as** como). **~ listen!** ¡escucha! **he has ~ arrived** acaba de llegar, recién llegó (*LAm*)

justice /ˈdʒʌstɪs/ *n* justicia *f.* **J~ of the Peace** juez *m* de paz

justif|iable /dʒʌstɪˈfaɪəbl/ *adj* justificable. **~iably** *adv* con razón. **~ication** /dʒʌstɪfɪˈkeɪʃn/ *n* justificación *f.* **~y** /ˈdʒʌstɪfaɪ/ *vt* justificar

jut /dʒʌt/ *vi* (*pt* **jutted**). **~ (out)**

sobresalir

juvenile /ˈdʒuːvənaɪl/ *adj* juvenil; (*childish*) infantil. ●*n* (*Jurid*) menor *m & f*

Kk

kaleidoscope /kəˈlaɪdəskəʊp/ *n* caleidoscopio *m*

kangaroo /kæŋgəˈruː/ *n* canguro *m*

karate /kəˈrɑːtɪ/ *n* kárate *m*, karate *m* (*LAm*)

keel /kiːl/ *n* (*of ship*) quilla *f*. □ **~ over** *vi* volcar(se)

keen /kiːn/ *adj* (**-er**, **-est**) (interest, feeling) vivo; (wind, mind, analysis) penetrante; (eyesight) agudo; (*eager*) entusiasta. **I'm ~ on golf** me encanta el golf. **he's ~ on Shostakovich** le gusta Shostakovich. **~ly** *adv* vivamente; (*enthusiastically*) con entusiasmo. **~ness** *n* intensidad *f*; (*enthusiasm*) entusiasmo *m*.

keep /kiːp/ *vt* (*pt* **kept**) guardar; cumplir (promise); tener (shop, animals); mantener (family); observar (rule); (*celebrate*) celebrar; (*delay*) detener; (*prevent*) impedir. ●*vi* (food) conservarse; (*remain*) quedarse; (*continue*) seguir. **~ doing** seguir haciendo. ●*n* subsistencia *f*; (*of castle*) torreón *m*. **for ~s** 🄸 para siempre. □ **~ back** *vt* retener. ●*vi* no acercarse. □ **~ in** *vt* no dejar salir. □ **~ off** *vt* mantenerse alejado de (land). **'~ off the grass'** 'prohibido pisar el césped'. □ **~ on** *vi* seguir. **~ on doing sth** seguir haciendo. □ **~ out** *vt* no dejar entrar. □ **~ up** *vt* mantener. □ **~ up with** *vt* estar al día en

kennel /ˈkenl/ *n* casa *f* del perro; (*Amer, for boarding*) residencia *f* canina. **~s** *n invar* residencia *f* canina

kept /kept/ *see* KEEP

kerb /kɜːb/ *n* bordillo *m* (de la acera), borde *m* de la banqueta (*Mex*)

kerosene /ˈkerəsiːn/ *n* queroseno *m*

ketchup /ˈketʃʌp/ *n* salsa *f* de tomate

kettle /ˈketl/ *n* pava *f*, tetera *f* (para calentar agua)

key /kiː/ *n* llave *f*; (*of computer, piano*) tecla *f*; (*Mus*) tono *m*. **be off ~** no estar en el tono. ●*adj* clave. □ **~ in** *vt* teclear. **~board** *n* teclado *m*. **~hole** *n* ojo *m* de la cerradura. **~ring** *n* llavero *m*

khaki /ˈkɑːkɪ/ *adj* caqui

kick /kɪk/ *vt* dar una patada a (person); patear (ball). ●*vi* dar patadas; (horse) cocear. ●*n* patada *f*; (*of horse*) coz *f*; (*fam, thrill*) placer *m*. □ **~ out** *vt* 🄸 echar. □ **~ up** *vt* armar (fuss etc). **~off** *n* (*Sport*) saque *m* inicial. **~ start** *vt* arrancar (con el pedal de arranque) (engine)

kid /kɪd/ *n* (*young goat*) cabrito *m*; (*fam, child*) niño *m*, chaval *m*, escuincle *m* (*Mex*). ●*vt* (*pt* **kidded**) tomar el pelo a. ●*vi* bromear

kidnap /ˈkɪdnæp/ *vt* (*pt* **kidnapped**) secuestrar. **~per** *n* secuestrador *m*. **~ping** *n* secuestro *m*

kidney /ˈkɪdnɪ/ *n* riñón *m*

kill /kɪl/ *vt* matar; (*fig*) acabar con. ●*n* matanza *f*. □ **~ off** *vt* matar. **~er** *n* asesino *m*. **~ing** *n* matanza *f*; (*murder*) asesinato *m*. **make a**

~ing (*fig*) hacer un gran negocio

kiln /kɪln/ *n* horno *m*

kilo /'ki:ləʊ/ *n* (*pl* **-os**) kilo *m*. **~gram(me)** /'kɪləgræm/ *n* kilogramo *m*. **~metre**/'kɪləmi:tə(r)/, /kɪ'lɒmɪtə(r)/ *n* kilómetro *m*. **~watt** /'kɪləwɒt/ *n* kilovatio *m*

kilt /kɪlt/ *n* falda *f* escocesa

kin /kɪn/ *n* familiares *mpl*

kind /kaɪnd/ *n* tipo *m*, clase *f*. **~ of** (*fam, somewhat*) un poco. **in ~** en especie. **be two of a ~** ser tal para cual. ● *adj* amable

kindergarten /'kɪndəgɑ:tn/ *n* jardín *m* de infancia

kind-hearted /kaɪnd'hɑ:tɪd/ *adj* bondadoso

k

kindle /'kɪndl/ *vt* encender

kind|ly *adj* (**-ier, -iest**) bondadoso. ● *adv* amablemente; (*please*) haga el favor de. **~ness** *n* bondad *f*; (*act*) favor *m*

king /kɪŋ/ *n* rey *m*. **~dom** *n* reino *m*. **~fisher** *n* martín *m* pescador. **~-size(d)** *adj* extragrande

kink /kɪŋk/ *n* (*in rope*) vuelta *f*, curva *f*; (*in hair*) onda *f*. **~y** *adj* [!] pervertido

kiosk /'ki:ɒsk/ *n* quiosco *m*

kipper /'kɪpə(r)/ *n* arenque *m* ahumado

kiss /kɪs/ *n* beso *m*. ● *vt* besar. ● *vi* besarse

kit /kɪt/ *n* avíos *mpl*. **tool ~** caja *f* de herramientas. □ **~ out** *vt* (*pt* **kitted**) equipar

kitchen /'kɪtʃɪn/ *n* cocina *f*

kite /kaɪt/ *n* cometa *f*, papalote *m* (*Mex*)

kitten /'kɪtn/ *n* gatito *m*

knack /næk/ *n* truco *m*

knapsack /'næpsæk/ *n* mochila *f*

knead /ni:d/ *vt* amasar

knee /ni:/ *n* rodilla *f*. **~cap** *n* rótula *f*

kneel /ni:l/ *vi* (*pt* **kneeled** *or* **knelt**). **~ (down)** arrodillarse; (*be on one's knees*) estar arrodillado

knelt /nelt/ *see* KNEEL

knew /nju:/ *see* KNOW

knickers /'nɪkəz/ *npl* bragas *fpl*, calzones *mpl* (*LAm*), pantaletas *fpl* (*Mex*)

knife /naɪf/ *n* (*pl* **knives**) cuchillo *m*. ● *vt* acuchillar

knight /naɪt/ *n* caballero *m*; (*Chess*) caballo *m*. ● *vt* conceder el título de Sir a. **~hood** *n* título *m* de Sir

knit /nɪt/ *vt* (*pt* **knitted** *or* **knit**) hacer, tejer (*LAm*). ● *vi* tejer, hacer punto. **~ one's brow** fruncir el ceño. **~ting** *n* tejido *m*, punto *m*. **~ting needle** *n* aguja *f* de hacer punto, aguja *f* de tejer

knives /naɪvz/ *see* KNIFE

knob /nɒb/ *n* botón *m*; (*of door, drawer etc*) tirador *m*. **~bly** *adj* nudoso

knock /nɒk/ *vt* golpear; (*criticize*) criticar. ● *vi* golpear; (*at door*) llamar, golpear (*LAm*). ● *n* golpe *m*. □ **~ about** *vt* maltratar. □ **~ down** *vt* derribar; atropellar (person). □ **~ off** *vt* hacer caer. ● *vi* (*fam, finish work*) terminar, salir del trabajo. □ **~ out** *vt* (*by blow*) dejar sin sentido; (*eliminate*) eliminar. □ **~ over** *vt* tirar; atropellar (person). **~er** *n* aldaba *f*. **~-kneed** /-'ni:d/ *adj* patizambo. **~out** *n* (*Boxing*) nocaut *m*

knot /nɒt/ *n* nudo *m*. ● *vt* (*pt* **knotted**) anudar

know /nəʊ/ *vt* (*pt* **knew**) saber; (*be acquainted with*) conocer. **let s.o. ~ sth** decirle algo a uno;

(*warn*) avisarle algo a uno. ● *vi* saber. ~ **how to do sth** saber hacer algo. ~ **about** entender de (cars etc). ~ **of** saber de. ● *n*. **be in the** ~ estar enterado. ~**-all** *n n* sabelotodo *m & f*. ~**-how** *n* know-how *m*, conocimientos *mpl* y experiencia. ~**ingly** *adv* a sabiendas. ~**-it-all** *n* (*Amer*) *see* ~-ALL

knowledge /'nɒlɪdʒ/ *n* saber *m*; (*awareness*) conocimiento *m*; (*learning*) conocimientos *mpl*. ~**able** *adj* informado

known /nəʊn/ *see* KNOW. ● *adj* conocido

knuckle /'nʌkl/ *n* nudillo *m*. □ ~ **under** *vi* someterse

Korea /kə'rɪə/ *n* Corea *f*. ~**n** *adj & n* coreano (*m*)

kudos /'kju:dɒs/ *n* prestigio *m*

L

lab /læb/ *n* 🄸 laboratorio *m*

label /'leɪbl/ *n* etiqueta *f*. ● *vt* (*pt* **labelled**) poner etiqueta a; (*fig, describe as*) tachar de

laboratory /lə'bɒrətərɪ/ *n* laboratorio *m*

laborious /lə'bɔ:rɪəs/ *adj* penoso

labour /'leɪbə(r)/ *n* trabajo *m*; (*workers*) mano *f* de obra; (*Med*) parto *m*. **in** ~ de parto. ● *vi* trabajar. ● *vt* insistir en. **L**~ *n* el partido *m* laborista. ● *adj* laborista. ~**er** *n* peón *m*

lace /leɪs/ *n* encaje *m*; (*of shoe*) cordón *m*, agujeta *f* (*Mex*). ● *vt* (*fasten*) atar

lacerate /'læsəreɪt/ *vt* lacerar

lack /læk/ *n* falta *f*. **for** ~ **of** por falta de. ● *vt* faltarle a uno. **he** ~**s confidence** le falta confianza en sí mismo. ~**ing** *adj*. **be** ~**ing** faltar. **be** ~**ing in** no tener

lad /læd/ *n* muchacho *m*

ladder /'lædə(r)/ *n* escalera *f* (de mano); (*in stocking*) carrera *f*. ● *vt* hacerse una carrera en. ● *vi* hacérsele una carrera a

laden /'leɪdn/ *adj* cargado (**with** de)

ladle /'leɪdl/ *n* cucharón *m*

lady /'leɪdɪ/ *n* señora *f*. **young** ~ señorita *f*. ~**bird** *n*, ~**bug** *n* (*Amer*) mariquita *f*, catarina *f* (*Mex*). ~**-in-waiting** *n* dama *f* de honor. ~**like** *adj* fino

lag /læg/ *vi* (*pt* **lagged**). ~ (**behind**) retrasarse. ● *vt* revestir (pipes). ● *n* (*interval*) intervalo *m*

lager /'lɑ:gə(r)/ *n* cerveza *f* (rubia)

lagging /'lægɪŋ/ *n* revestimiento *m*

lagoon /lə'gu:n/ *n* laguna *f*

laid /leɪd/ *see* LAY

lain /leɪn/ *see* LIE[1]

lair /leə(r)/ *n* guarida *f*

lake /leɪk/ *n* lago *m*

lamb /læm/ *n* cordero *m*

lame /leɪm/ *adj* (**-er, -est**) cojo, rengo (*LAm*); (excuse) pobre, malo

lament /lə'ment/ *n* lamento *m*. ● *vt* lamentar. ~**able** /'læməntəbl/ *adj* lamentable

lamp /læmp/ *n* lámpara *f*

lamp: ~**post** *n* farol *m*. ~**shade** *n* pantalla *f*

lance /lɑ:ns/ *n* lanza *f*

land /lænd/ *n* tierra *f*; (*country*) país *m*; (*plot*) terreno *m*. ● *vt* desembarcar; (*obtain*) conseguir; dar (blow). ● *vi* (*from ship*) desembarcar; (aircraft) aterrizar. □ ~ **up** *vi* ir a parar. ~**ing** *n* desembarque *m*; (*by aircraft*) aterrizaje *m*; (*top of stairs*) descanso *m*. ~**lady** *n* casera *f*; (*of inn*) dueña *f*. ~**lord** *n* casero *m*, dueño *m*; (*of inn*) dueño *m*. ~**mark** *n* punto *m* destacado. ~**scape** /-skeɪp/ *n* paisaje *m*. ~**slide** *n* desprendimiento *m* de tierras; (*Pol*) victoria *f* arrolladora

lane /leɪn/ *n* (*path, road*) camino *m*, sendero *m*; (*strip of road*) carril *m*

language /ˈlæŋgwɪdʒ/ *n* idioma *m*; (*speech, style*) lenguaje *m*

lank /læŋk/ *adj* (hair) lacio. ~**y** *adj* (**-ier**, **-iest**) larguirucho

lantern /ˈlæntən/ *n* linterna *f*

lap /læp/ *n* (*of body*) rodillas *fpl*; (*Sport*) vuelta *f*. □ ~ **up** *vt* (*pt* **lapped**) beber a lengüetazos; (*fig*) aceptar con entusiasmo. ● *vi* (waves) chapotear

lapel /ləˈpel/ *n* solapa *f*

lapse /læps/ *vi* (*decline*) degradarse; (*expire*) caducar; (time) transcurrir. ~ **into silence** callarse. ● *n* error *m*; (*of time*) intervalo *m*

laptop /ˈlæptɒp/ *n*. ~ **(computer)** laptop *m*, portátil *m*

lard /lɑːd/ *n* manteca *f* de cerdo

larder /ˈlɑːdə(r)/ *n* despensa *f*

large /lɑːdʒ/ *adj* (**-er**, **-est**) grande, (*before singular noun*) gran. ● *n*. **at** ~ en libertad. ~**ly** *adv* en gran parte

lark /lɑːk/ *n* (*bird*) alondra *f*; (*joke*) broma *f*; (*bit of fun*) travesura *f*. □ ~ **about** *vt* hacer el tonto [!]

larva /ˈlɑːvə/ *n* (*pl* **-vae**/-viː/) larva *f*

laser /ˈleɪzə(r)/ *n* láser *m*. ~ **beam** *n* rayo *m* láser. ~ **printer** *n* impresora *f* láser

lash /læʃ/ *vt* azotar. □ ~ **out** *vi* atacar. ~ **out against** *vt* atacar. ● *n* latigazo *m*; (*eyelash*) pestaña *f*; (*whip*) látigo *m*

lashings /ˈlæʃɪŋz/ *npl*. ~ **of** (*fam*, *cream etc*) montones de

lass /læs/ *n* muchacha *f*

lasso /læˈsuː/ *n* (*pl* **-os**) lazo *m*

last /lɑːst/ *adj* último; (week etc) pasado. ~ **Monday** el lunes pasado. ~ **night** anoche. ● *adv* por último; (*most recently*) la última vez. **he came** ~ llegó el último. ● *n* último *m*; (*remainder*) lo que queda. ~ **but one** penúltimo. **at (long)** ~ por fin. ● *vi/t* durar. □ ~ **out** *vi* sobrevivir. ~**ing** *adj* duradero. ~**ly** *adv* por último

latch /lætʃ/ *n* pestillo *m*

late /leɪt/ *adj* (**-er**, **-est**) (*not on time*) tarde; (*recent*) reciente; (*former*) antiguo, ex. **be** ~ llegar tarde. **in** ~ **July** a fines de julio. **the** ~ **Dr Phillips** el difunto Dr. Phillips. ● *adv* tarde. ~**ly** *adv* últimamente

latent /ˈleɪtnt/ *adj* latente

later /ˈleɪtə(r)/ *adv* más tarde

lateral /ˈlætərəl/ *adj* lateral

latest /ˈleɪtɪst/ *adj* último. ● *n*. **at the** ~ a más tardar

lathe /leɪð/ *n* torno *m*

lather /ˈlɑːðə(r)/ *n* espuma *f*

Latin /ˈlætɪn/ *n* (*language*) latín *m*. ● *adj* latino. ~ **America** *n* América *f* Latina, Latinoamérica *f*. ~ **American** *adj & n* latinoamericano *f*

latitude /ˈlætɪtjuːd/ *n* latitud *m*

latter /ˈlætə(r)/ *adj* último; (*of two*) segundo. ● *n*. **the** ~ éste *m*, ésta *f*, éstos *mpl*, éstas *fpl*

laugh /lɑːf/ *vi* reír(se). ~ **at** reírse de. ● *n* risa *f*. ~**able** *adj* ridículo. ~**ing stock** *n* hazmerreír *m*. ~**ter**

n risas *fpl*

launch /lɔːntʃ/ *vt* lanzar; botar (new vessel). ● *n* lanzamiento *m*; (*of new vessel*) botadura; (*boat*) lancha *f* (a motor). **~ing pad**, **~ pad** *n* plataforma *f* de lanzamiento

laund|er /ˈlɔːndə(r)/ *vt* lavar (y planchar). **~erette** /-et/, **L~romat** /ˈlɔːndrəmæt/ (*Amer*) (*P*) *n* lavandería *f* automática. **~ry** *n* (*place*) lavandería *f*; (*dirty clothes*) ropa *f* sucia; (*clean clothes*) ropa *f* limpia

lava /ˈlɑːvə/ *n* lava *f*

lavatory /ˈlævətərɪ/ *n* (cuarto *m* de) baño *m*. **public ~** servicios *mpl*, baños *mpl* (*LAm*)

lavish /ˈlævɪʃ/ *adj* (lifestyle) de derroche; (*meal*) espléndido; (*production*) fastuoso. ● *vt* prodigar (**on** a)

law /lɔː/ *n* ley *f*; (*profession, subject of study*) derecho *m*. **~ and order** *n* orden *m* público. **~ court** *n* tribunal *m*

lawn /lɔːn/ *n* césped *m*, pasto *m* (*LAm*). **~mower** *n* cortacésped *f*, cortadora *f* de pasto (*LAm*)

lawsuit /ˈlɔːsuːt/ *n* juicio *m*

lawyer /ˈlɔjə(r)/ *n* abogado *m*

lax /læks/ *adj* descuidado; (morals etc) laxo

laxative /ˈlæksətɪv/ *n* laxante *m*

lay /leɪ/ *see* LIE. ● *vt* (*pt* **laid**) poner (also table, eggs); tender (trap); formar (plan). **~ hands on** echar mano a. **~ hold of** agarrar. ● *adj* (*non-clerical*) laico; (opinion etc) profano. □ **~ down** *vt* dejar a un lado; imponer (condition). □ **~ into** *vt* ☒ dar una paliza a. □ **~ off** *vt* despedir (worker). *vi* ◫ terminar. □ **~ on** *vt* (*provide*) proveer. □ **~ out** *vt* (*design*) disponer; (*display*) exponer; gastar (money). **~about** *n* holgazán. **~-by** *n* área *f* de reposo

layer /ˈleɪə(r)/ *n* capa *f*

layette /leɪˈet/ *n* canastilla *f*

layman /ˈleɪmən/ *n* (*pl* **-men**) lego *m*

layout /ˈleɪaʊt/ *n* disposición *f*

laz|e /leɪz/ *vi* holgazanear; (*relax*) descansar. **~iness** *n* pereza *f*. **~y** *adj* perezoso. **~ybones** *n* holgazán *m*

lead¹ /liːd/ *vt* (*pt* **led**) conducir; dirigir (team); llevar (life); encabezar (parade, attack). **I was led to believe that ...** me dieron a entender que .... ● *vi* (*go first*) ir delante; (*in race*) aventajar. ● *n* mando *m*; (*clue*) pista *f*; (*leash*) correa *f*; (*wire*) cable *m*. **be in the ~** llevar la delantera

lead² /led/ *n* plomo *m*; (*of pencil*) mina *f*. **~ed** *adj* (fuel) con plomo

lead: /liːd/ **~er** *n* jefe *m*; (*Pol*) líder *m & f*; (*of gang*) cabecilla *m*. **~ership** *n* dirección *f*. **~ing** *adj* principal; (*in front*) delantero

leaf /liːf/ *n* (*pl* **leaves**) hoja *f*. □ **~ through** *vi* hojear **~let** /ˈliːflɪt/ *n* folleto *m*. **~y** *adj* frondoso

league /liːg/ *n* liga *f*. **be in ~ with** estar aliado con

leak /liːk/ *n* (*hole*) agujero *m*; (*of gas, liquid*) escape *m*; (*of information*) filtración *f*; (*in roof*) gotera *f*; (*in boat*) vía *f* de agua. ● *vi* gotear; (liquid) salirse; (boat) hacer agua. ● *vt* perder; filtrar (information). **~y** *adj* (receptacle) agujereado; (roof) que tiene goteras

lean /liːn/ (*pt* **leaned** *or* **leant** /lent/) *vt* apoyar. ● *vi* inclinarse. □ **~ against** *vt* apoyarse en. □ **~ on** *vt* apoyarse en. □ **~ out** *vt* asomarse (**of** a). □ **~ over** *vi* inclinarse ● *adj* (**-er, -est**) (person) delgado;

(animal) flaco; (meat) magro. ~**ing** *adj* inclinado. ~**-to** *n* colgadizo *m*

leap /li:p/ *vi* (*pt* **leaped** *or* **leapt** /lept/) saltar. ● *n* salto *m*. ~**frog** *n*. **play** ~**frog** saltar al potro, jugar a la pídola, brincar al burro (*Mex*). ● *vi* (*pt* **-frogged**) saltar. ~ **year** *n* año *m* bisiesto

learn /lɜ:n/ *vt/i* (*pt* **learned** *or* **learnt**) aprender (**to do** a hacer). ~**ed** /-ɪd/ *adj* culto. ~**er** *n* principiante *m* & *f*; (*apprentice*) aprendiz *m*. ~**ing** *n* saber *m*. ~**ing curve** *n* curva *f* del aprendizaje

lease /li:s/ *n* arriendo *m*. ● *vt* arrendar

leash /li:ʃ/ *n* correa *f*

least /li:st/ *adj* (*smallest amount of*) mínimo; (*slightest*) menor; (*smallest*) más pequeño. ● *n*. **the** ~ lo menos. **at** ~ por lo menos. **not in the** ~ en absoluto. ● *adv* menos

leather /'leðə(r)/ *n* piel *f*, cuero *m*

leave /li:v/ *vt* (*pt* **left**) dejar; (*depart from*) salir de. ~ **alone** dejar de tocar (thing); dejar en paz (person). ● *vi* marcharse; (train) salir. ● *n* permiso *m*. □ ~ **behind** *vt* dejar. □ ~ **out** *vt* omitir. □ ~ **over** *vt*. **be left over** quedar. **on** ~ (*Mil*) de permiso

leaves /li:vz/ *see* LEAF

lecture /'lektʃə(r)/ *n* conferencia *f*; (*Univ*) clase *f*; (*rebuke*) sermón *m*. ● *vi* dar clase. ● *vt* (*scold*) sermonear. ~**r** *n* conferenciante *m* & *f*, conferencista *m* & *f* (*LAm*); (*Univ*) profesor *m* universitario

led /led/ *see* LEAD[1]

ledge /ledʒ/ *n* cornisa *f*; (*of window*) alféizar *m*

leek /li:k/ *n* puerro *m*

leer /'lɪə(r)/ *vi*. ~ **at** mirar impúdicamente. ● *n* mirada impúdica *f*

left /left/ *see* LEAVE. *adj* izquierdo. ● *adv* a la izquierda. ● *n* izquierda *f*. ~**-handed** /-'hændɪd/ *adj* zurdo. ~ **luggage** *n* consigna *f*. ~**overs** *npl* restos *mpl*. ~**-wing** /-'wɪŋ/ *adj* izquierdista

leg /leg/ *n* pierna *f*; (*of animal, furniture*) pata *f*; (*of pork*) pernil *m*; (*of lamb*) pierna *f*; (*of journey*) etapa *f*. **on its last** ~**s** en las últimas. **pull s.o.'s** ~ [!] tomarle el pelo a uno

legacy /'legəsɪ/ *n* herencia *f*

legal /'li:gl/ *adj* (*permitted by law*) lícito; (*recognized by law*) legítimo; (system etc) jurídico. ~**ity** /li:'gælətɪ/ *n* legalidad *f*. ~**ize** *vt* legalizar. ~**ly** *adv* legalmente

legend /'ledʒənd/ *n* leyenda *f*. ~**ary** *adj* legendario

legible /'ledʒəbl/ *adj* legible

legislat|e /'ledʒɪsleɪt/ *vi* legislar. ~**ion** /-'leɪʃn/ *n* legislación *f*

legitimate /lɪ'dʒɪtɪmət/ *adj* legítimo

leisure /'leʒə(r)/ *n* ocio *m*. **at your** ~ cuando le venga bien. ~**ly** *adj* lento, pausado

lemon /'lemən/ *n* limón *m*. ~**ade** /-'neɪd/ *n* (*fizzy*) gaseosa *f* (de limón); (*still*) limonada *f*

lend /lend/ *vt* (*pt* **lent**) prestar. ~**ing** *n* préstamo *m*

length /leŋθ/ *n* largo *m*; (*of time*) duración *f*; (*of cloth*) largo *m*. **at** ~ (*at last*) por fin. **at (great)** ~ detalladamente. ~**en** /'leŋθən/ *vt* alargar. ● *vi* alargarse. ~**ways** *adv* a lo largo. ~**y** *adj* largo

lenient /'li:nɪənt/ *adj* indulgente

lens /lens/ *n* lente *f*; (*of camera*) objetivo *m*. **(contact)** ~**es** *npl* (*optics*) lentillas *fpl*, lentes *mpl* de

contacto (*LAm*)
lent /lent/ *see* **LEND**
Lent /lent/ *n* cuaresma *f*
Leo /'li:əʊ/ *n* Leo *m*
leopard /'lepəd/ *n* leopardo *m*
leotard /'li:ətɑ:d/ *n* malla *f*
lesbian /'lezbɪən/ *n* lesbiana *f*. • *adj* lesbiano
less /les/ *adj & n & adv & prep* menos. ~ **than** menos que; (*with numbers*) menos de. ~ **and** ~ cada vez menos. **none the** ~ sin embargo. ~**en** *vt/i* disminuir
lesson /'lesn/ *n* clase *f*
lest /lest/ *conj* no sea que (+ *subjunctive*)
let /let/ *vt* (*pt* **let**, *pres p* **letting**) dejar; (*lease*) alquilar. ~ **me do it** déjame hacerlo. • *modal verb*. ~**'s go!** ¡vamos!, ¡vámonos! ~**'s see** (vamos) a ver. ~**'s talk**/**drink** hablemos/bebamos. □ ~ **down** *vt* bajar; (*deflate*) desinflar; (*fig*) defraudar. □ ~ **go** *vt* soltar. □ ~ **in** *vt* dejar entrar. □ ~ **off** *vt* disparar (gun); (*cause to explode*) hacer explotar; hacer estallar (firework); (*excuse*) perdonar. □ ~ **out** *vt* dejar salir. □ ~ **through** *vt* dejar pasar. □ ~ **up** *vi* disminuir. ~**down** *n* desilusión *f*
lethal /'li:θl/ *adj* (dose, wound) mortal; (weapon) mortífero
letharg|ic /lɪ'θɑ:dʒɪk/ *adj* letárgico. ~**y** /'leθədʒɪ/ *n* letargo *m*
letter /'letə(r)/ *n* (*of alphabet*) letra *f*; (*written message*) carta *f*. ~ **bomb** *n* carta *f* bomba. ~**box** *n* buzón *m*. ~**ing** *n* letras *fpl*
lettuce /'letɪs/ *n* lechuga *f*
let-up /'letʌp/ *n* interrupción *f*
leukaemia /lu:'ki:mɪə/ *n* leucemia *f*
level /'levl/ *adj* (*flat, even*) plano, parejo (*LAm*); (spoonful) raso. ~ **with** (*at same height*) al nivel de. • *n* nivel *m*. • *vt* (*pt* **levelled**) nivelar; (*aim*) apuntar. ~ **crossing** *n* paso *m* a nivel, crucero *m* (*Mex*)
lever /'li:və(r)/ *n* palanca *f*. • *vt* apalancar. ~ **open** abrir haciendo palanca. ~**age** /-ɪdʒ/ *n* apalancamiento *m*
levy /'levɪ/ *vt* imponer (tax). • *n* impuesto *m*
lewd /lu:d/ *adj* (**-er**, **-est**) lascivo
liab|ility /laɪə'bɪlətɪ/ *n* responsabilidad *f*; (*fam, disadvantage*) lastre *m*. ~**ilities** *npl* (*debts*) deudas *fpl*. ~**le** /'laɪəbl/ *adj*. **be** ~**le to do** tener tendencia a hacer. ~**le for** responsable de. ~**le to** susceptible de; expuesto a (fine)
liais|e /lɪ'eɪz/ *vi* actuar de enlace (**with** con). ~**on** /-ɒn/ *n* enlace *m*
liar /'laɪə(r)/ *n* mentiroso *m*
libel /'laɪbl/ *n* difamación *f*. • *vt* (*pt* **libelled**) difamar (por escrito)
liberal /'lɪbərəl/ *adj* liberal; (*generous*) generoso. **L**~ (*Pol*) del Partido Liberal. • *n* liberal *m & f*. ~**ly** *adv* liberalmente; (*generously*) generosamente
liberat|e /'lɪbəreɪt/ *vt* liberar. ~**ion** /-'reɪʃn/ *n* liberación *f*
liberty /'lɪbətɪ/ *n* libertad *f*. **take liberties** tomarse libertades. **take the** ~ **of** tomarse la libertad de
Libra /'li:brə/ *n* Libra *f*
librar|ian /laɪ'breərɪən/ *n* bibliotecario *m*. ~**y** /'laɪbrərɪ/ *n* biblioteca *f*

Library of Congress La biblioteca nacional de EEUU, situada en Washington DC. Fundada por el Congreso *Congress*, alberga más de ochenta millones de libros en 470 idiomas, y otros objetos.

lice /laɪs/ *see* LOUSE
licence /'laɪsns/ *n* licencia *f*, permiso *m*
license /'laɪsns/ *vt* autorizar. ●*n* (*Amer*) *see* LICENCE. ~ **number** *n* (*Amer*) (número *m* de) matrícula *f*. ~ **plate** *n* (*Amer*) matrícula *f*, placa *f* (*LAm*)
lick /lɪk/ *vt* lamer; (*sl, defeat*) dar una paliza a. ●*n* lametón *m*
licorice /'lɪkərɪs/ *n* (*Amer*) regaliz *m*
lid /lɪd/ *n* tapa *f*; (*eyelid*) párpado *m*
lie[1] /laɪ/ *vi* (*pt* **lay**, *pp* **lain**, *pres p* **lying**) echarse, tenderse; (*be in lying position*) estar tendido; (*be*) estar, encontrarse. ~ **low** quedarse escondido. □ ~ **down** *vi* echarse, tenderse
lie[2] /laɪ/ *n* mentira *f*. ●*vi* (*pt* **lied**, *pres p* **lying**) mentir
lie-in /laɪ'ɪn/ *n*. **have a** ~ quedarse en la cama
lieutenant /lef'tenənt/ *n* (*Mil*) teniente *m*
life /laɪf/ *n* (*pl* **lives**) vida *f*. ~ **belt** *n* salvavidas *m*. ~**boat** *n* lancha *f* de salvamento; (*on ship*) bote *m* salvavidas. ~**buoy** *n* boya *f* salvavidas. ~ **coach** *n* coach *m* & *f* personal. ~**guard** *n* salvavidas *m* & *f*, socorrista *m* & *f*. ~ **jacket** *n* chaleco *m* salvavidas. ~**less** *adj* sin vida. ~**like** *adj* verosímil. ~**line** *n* cuerda *f* de salvamento; (*fig*) tabla *f* de salvación. ~**long** *adj* de toda la vida. ~ **preserver** *n* (*Amer, buoy*) *see* ~BUOY; (*jacket*) *see* ~ JACKET. ~ **ring** *n* (*Amer*) *see* ~ BELT. ~**saver** *n* (*person*) salvavidas *m* & *f*; (*fig*) salvación *f*. ~**-size(d)** *adj* (de) tamaño natural. ~**time** *n* vida *f*. ~ **vest** *n* (*Amer*) *see* ~ JACKET
lift /lɪft/ *vt* levantar. ●*vi* (*fog*) disiparse. ●*n* ascensor *m*. **give a** ~ **to s.o.** llevar a uno en su coche, dar aventón a uno (*Mex*). □ ~ **up** *vt* levantar. ~**-off** *n* despegue *m*
light /laɪt/ *n* luz *f*; (*lamp*) lámpara *f*, luz *f*; (*flame*) fuego *m*. **come to** ~ salir a la luz. **have you got a** ~**?** ¿tienes fuego? **the** ~**s** *npl* (*traffic signals*) el semáforo; (*on vehicle*) las luces. ●*adj* (**-er**, **-est**) (*in colour*) claro; (*not heavy*) ligero. ●*vt* (*pt* **lit** *or* **lighted**) encender, prender (*LAm*); (*illuminate*) iluminar. ●*vi* encenderse, prenderse (*LAm*). ~ **up** *vt* iluminar. ●*vi* iluminarse. ~ **bulb** *n* bombilla *f*, foco *m* (*Mex*). ~**en** *vt* (*make less heavy*) aligerar, alivianar (*LAm*); (*give light to*) iluminar; (*make brighter*) aclarar. ~**er** *n* (*for cigarettes*) mechero *m*, encendedor *m*. ~**-hearted** /-'hɑ:tɪd/ *adj* alegre. ~**house** *n* faro *m*. ~**ly** *adv* ligeramente
lightning /'laɪtnɪŋ/ *n*. **flash of** ~ relámpago *m*. ●*adj* relámpago
lightweight *adj* ligero, liviano (*LAm*)
like /laɪk/ *adj* parecido. ●*prep* como. ●*conj* [I] como. ●*vt*. **I** ~ **chocolate** me gusta el chocolate. **they** ~ **swimming** (a ellos) les gusta nadar. **would you** ~ **a coffee?** ¿quieres un café?. ~**able** *adj* simpático.
like|lihood /'laɪklɪhʊd/ *n* probabilidad *f*. ~**ly** *adj* (**-ier**, **-iest**) probable. **he is** ~**ly to come** es probable que venga. ●*adv* probablemente. **not** ~**ly!** ¡ni hablar! ~**n** *vt* comparar (**to** con, a). ~**ness** *n* parecido *m*. **be a good** ~**ness** parecerse mucho. ~**wise**

adv (*also*) también; (*the same way*) lo mismo

liking /ˈlaɪkɪŋ/ *n* (*for thing*) afición *f*; (*for person*) simpatía *f*

lilac /ˈlaɪlək/ *adj* lila. ●*n* lila *f*; (*color*) lila *m*

lily /ˈlɪlɪ/ *n* lirio *m*; (*white*) azucena *f*

limb /lɪm/ *n* miembro *m*. **out on a ~** aislado

lime /laɪm/ *n* (*white substance*) cal *f*; (*fruit*) lima *f*. **~light** *n*. **be in the ~light** ser el centro de atención

limerick /ˈlɪmərɪk/ *n* quintilla *f* humorística

limit /ˈlɪmɪt/ *n* límite *m*. ●*vt* limitar. **~ation** /-ˈteɪʃn/ *n* limitación *f*. **~ed** *adj* limitado. **~ed company** *n* sociedad *f* anónima

limousine /ˈlɪməziːn/ *n* limusina *f*

limp /lɪmp/ *vi* cojear, renguear (*LAm*). ●*n* cojera *f*, renguera *f* (*LAm*). **have a ~** cojear. ●*adj* (**-er**, **-est**) flojo

linden /ˈlɪndn/ *n* (*Amer*) tilo *m*

line /laɪn/ *n* línea *f*; (*track*) vía *f*; (*wrinkle*) arruga *f*; (*row*) fila *f*; (*of poem*) verso *m*; (*rope*) cuerda *f*; (*of goods*) surtido *m*; (*Amer, queue*) cola *f*. **stand in ~** (*Amer*) hacer cola. **get in ~** (*Amer*) ponerse en la cola.. **cut in ~** (*Amer*) colarse. **in ~ with** de acuerdo con. ●*vt* forrar (skirt, box); bordear (streets etc). □ **~ up** *vi* alinearse; (*in queue*) hacer cola. *vt* (*form into line*) poner en fila; (*align*) alinear. **~d** /laɪnd/ *adj* (paper) con renglones; (*with fabric*) forrado

linen /ˈlɪnɪn/ *n* (*sheets etc*) ropa *f* blanca; (*material*) lino *m*

liner /ˈlaɪnə(r)/ *n* (*ship*) transatlántico *m*

linger /ˈlɪŋgə(r)/ *vi* tardar en marcharse. **~ (on)** (smells etc) persistir. □ **~ over** *vt* dilatarse en

lingerie /ˈlænʒərɪ/ *n* lencería *f*

linguist /ˈlɪŋgwɪst/ *n* políglota *m* & *f*; lingüista *m* & *f*. **~ic** /lɪŋˈgwɪstɪk/ *adj* lingüístico. **~ics** *n* lingüística *f*

lining /ˈlaɪnɪŋ/ *n* forro *m*

link /lɪŋk/ *n* (*of chain*) eslabón *m*; (*connection*) conexión *f*; (*bond*) vínculo *m*; (*transport, telecommunications*) conexión *f*, enlace *m*. ●*vt* conectar; relacionar (facts, events). □ **~ up** *vt/i* conectar

lino /ˈlaɪnəʊ/ *n* (*pl* **-os**) linóleo *m*

lint /lɪnt/ *n* (*Med*) hilas *fpl*

lion /ˈlaɪən/ *n* león *m*. **~ess** /-nɪs/ *n* leona *f*

lip /lɪp/ *n* labio *m*; (*edge*) borde *m*. **~read** *vi* leer los labios. **~salve** *n* crema *f* para los labios. **~ service** *n*. **pay ~ service to** aprobar de boquilla, aprobar de los dientes para afuera (*Mex*). **~stick** *n* lápiz *m* de labios

liqueur /lɪˈkjʊə(r)/ *n* licor *m*

liquid /ˈlɪkwɪd/ *adj* & *n* líquido (*m*)

liquidate /ˈlɪkwɪdeɪt/ *vt* liquidar

liquidize /ˈlɪkwɪdaɪz/ *vt* licuar. **~r** *n* licuadora *f*

liquor /ˈlɪkə(r)/ *n* bebidas *fpl* alcohólicas

liquorice /ˈlɪkərɪs/ *n* regaliz *m*

liquor store *n* (*Amer*) tienda *f* de bebidas alcohólicas

lisp /lɪsp/ *n* ceceo *m*. **speak with a ~** cecear. ●*vi* cecear

list /lɪst/ *n* lista *f*. ●*vt* hacer una lista de; (*enter in a list*) inscribir. ●*vi* (*ship*) escorar

listen /ˈlɪsn/ *vi* escuchar. **~ in (to)** escuchar. **~ to** escuchar. **~er** *n* oyente *m* & *f*

listless /ˈlɪstlɪs/ *adj* apático

lit /lɪt/ *see* LIGHT

literacy /ˈlɪtərəsɪ/ *n* alfabetismo *m*

literal /ˈlɪtərəl/ *adj* literal. **~ly** *adv* literalmente

literary /ˈlɪtərərɪ/ *adj* literario

literate /ˈlɪtərət/ *adj* alfabetizado

literature /ˈlɪtərətʃə(r)/ *n* literatura *f*; (*fig*) folletos *mpl*

lithe /laɪð/ *adj* ágil

litre /ˈliːtə(r)/ *n* litro *m*

litter /ˈlɪtə(r)/ *n* basura *f*; (*of animals*) camada *f*. ● *vt* ensuciar; (*scatter*) esparcir. **~ed with** lleno de. **~ bin** *n* papelera *f*. **~bug**, **~ lout** *n* persona *f* que tira basura en lugares públicos

little /ˈlɪtl/ *adj* pequeño; (*not much*) poco. **a ~ water** un poco de agua. ● *pron* poco, poca. **a ~** un poco. ● *adv* poco. **~ by ~** poco a poco. **~ finger** *n* (dedo *m*) meñique *m*

l

live /lɪv/ *vt/i* vivir. □ **~ down** *vt* lograr borrar. □ **~ off** *vt* vivir a costa de (family, friends); (*feed on*) alimentarse de. □ **~ on** *vt* (*feed o.s. on*) vivir de. *vi* (memory) seguir presente; (tradition) seguir existiendo. □ **~ up** *vt*. **~ it up** [I] darse la gran vida. □ **~ up to** *vt* vivir de acuerdo con; cumplir (promise). ● /laɪv/ *adj* vivo; (wire) con corriente; (broadcast) en directo

livelihood /ˈlaɪvlɪhʊd/ *n* sustento *m*

lively /ˈlaɪvlɪ/ *adj* (**-ier**, **-iest**) vivo

liven up /ˈlaɪvn/ *vt* animar. ● *vi* animar(se)

liver /ˈlɪvə(r)/ *n* hígado *m*

lives /laɪvz/ *see* LIFE

livestock /ˈlaɪvstɒk/ *n* animales *mpl* (de cría); (*cattle*) ganado *m*

livid /ˈlɪvɪd/ *adj* lívido; (*fam, angry*) furioso

living /ˈlɪvɪŋ/ *adj* vivo. ● *n* vida *f*. **make a ~** ganarse la vida. **~ room** *n* salón *m*, sala *f* (de estar), living *m* (*LAm*)

lizard /ˈlɪzəd/ *n* lagartija *f*; (*big*) lagarto *m*

load /ləʊd/ *n* (*also Elec*) carga *f*; (*quantity*) cantidad *f*; (*weight, strain*) peso *m*. **~s of** [I] montones de. ● *vt* cargar. **~ed** *adj* cargado

loaf /ləʊf/ *n* (*pl* **loaves**) pan *m*; (*stick of bread*) barra *f* de pan. ● *vi*. **~ (about)** holgazanear

loan /ləʊn/ *n* préstamo *m*. **on ~** prestado. ● *vt* prestar

loath|e /ləʊð/ *vt* odiar. **~ing** *n* odio *m* (**of** a). **~esome** /-səm/ *adj* repugnante

lobby /ˈlɒbɪ/ *n* vestíbulo *m*; (*Pol*) grupo *m* de presión. ● *vt* ejercer presión sobre. ● *vi*. **~ for sth** ejercer presión para obtener algo

lobe /ləʊb/ *n* lóbulo *m*

lobster /ˈlɒbstə(r)/ *n* langosta *f*, bogavante m

local /ˈləʊkl/ *adj* local. **~ (phone) call** llamada *f* urbana. ● *n* (*fam, pub*) bar *m*. **the ~s** los vecinos *mpl*. **~ government** *n* administración *f* municipal. **~ity** /-ˈkælətɪ/ *n* localidad *f*. **~ization** *n* localización *f*. **~ly** *adv* (live, work) en la zona

locat|e /ləʊˈkeɪt/ *vt* (*situate*) situar, ubicar (*LAm*); (*find*) localizar, ubicar (*LAm*). **~ion** /-ʃn/ *n* situación *f*, ubicación *f* (*LAm*). **on ~ion** fuera del estudio. **to film on ~ion in Andalusia** rodar en Andalucía

lock /lɒk/ *n* (*of door etc*) cerradura *f*; (*on canal*) esclusa *f*; (*of hair*) mechón *m*. ● *vt* cerrar con llave. ● *vi* cerrarse con llave. □ ~ **in** *vt* encerrar. □ ~ **out** *vt* cerrar la puerta a. □ ~ **up** *vt* encerrar (person); cerrar con llave (building)

locker /ˈlɒkə(r)/ *n* armario *m*, locker *m* (*LAm*). ~ **room** *n* (*Amer*) vestuario *m*, vestidor *m* (*Mex*)

locket /ˈlɒkɪt/ *n* medallón *m*

lock: ~out /ˈlɒkaʊt/ *n* cierre *m* patronal, paro *m* patronal (*LAm*). **~smith** *n* cerrajero *m*

locomotive /ləʊkəˈməʊtɪv/ *n* locomotora *f*

lodg|e /lɒdʒ/ *n* (*of porter*) portería *f*. ● *vt* alojar; presentar (complaint). **~er** *n* huésped *m*. **~ings** *n* alojamiento *m*; (*room*) habitación *f* alquilada

loft /lɒft/ *n* desván *m*, altillo *m* (*LAm*)

lofty /ˈlɒftɪ/ *adj* (**-ier**, **-iest**) elevado; (*haughty*) altanero

log /lɒg/ *n* (*of wood*) tronco *m*; (*as fuel*) leño *m*; (*record*) diario *m*. **sleep like a** ~ dormir como un tronco. ● *vt* (*pt* **logged**) registrar. □ ~ **in**, ~ **on** *vi* (*Comp*) entrar (al sistema). □ ~ **off**, ~ **out** *vi* (*Comp*) salir (del sistema)

logarithm /ˈlɒgərɪðəm/ *n* logaritmo *m*

loggerheads /ˈlɒgəhedz/ *npl*. **be at** ~ **with** estar a matar con

logic /ˈlɒdʒɪk/ *adj* lógica *f*. **~al** *adj* lógico. **~ally** *adv* lógicamente

logistics /ləˈdʒɪstɪks/ *n* logística *f*. ● *npl* (*practicalities*) problemas *mpl* logísticos

logo /ˈləʊgəʊ/ *n* (*pl* **-os**) logo *m*

loin /lɔɪn/ *n* (*Culin*) lomo *m*. **~s** *npl* entrañas *fpl*

loiter /ˈlɔɪtə(r)/ *vi* perder el tiempo

loll /lɒl/ *vi* repantigarse

loll|ipop /ˈlɒlɪpɒp/ *n* pirulí *m*. **~y** *n* polo *m*, paleta *f* (helada) (*LAm*)

London /ˈlʌndən/ *n* Londres *m*. ● *adj* londinense. **~er** *n* londinense *m & f*

lone /ləʊn/ *adj* solitario. **~ly** *adj* (**-ier**, **-iest**) solitario. **feel ~ly** sentirse muy solo. **~r** *n* solitario *m*. **~some** /-səm/ *adj* solitario

long /lɒŋ/ *adj* (**-er**, **-est**) largo. **a ~ time** mucho tiempo. **how ~ is it?** ¿cuánto tiene de largo? ● *adv* largo/mucho tiempo. **as ~ as** (*while*) mientras; (*provided that*) con tal que (+ *subjunctive*). **before ~** dentro de poco. **so ~!** ¡hasta luego! **so ~ as** (*provided that*) con tal que (+ *subjunctive*). □ ~ **for** *vi* anhelar. ~ **to do** estar deseando hacer. **~-distance** /-ˈdɪstəns/ *adj* de larga distancia. **~-distance phone call** llamada *f* de larga distancia, conferencia *f*. **~er** *adv*. **no ~er** ya no. **~-haul** /-ˈhɔːl/ *adj* de larga distancia. **~ing** *n* anhelo *m*, ansia *f*

longitude /ˈlɒŋgɪtjuːd/ *n* longitud *f*

long: ~ jump *n* salto *m* de longitud. **~-playing record** *n* elepé *m*. **~-range** *adj* de largo alcance. **~-sighted** /-ˈsaɪtɪd/ *adj* hipermétrope. **~-term** *adj* a largo plazo. **~-winded** /-ˈwɪndɪd/ *adj* prolijo

loo /luː/ *n* [I] váter *m*, baño *m* (*LAm*)

look /lʊk/ *vt* mirar; representar (age). ● *vi* mirar; (*seem*) parecer; (*search*) buscar. ● *n* mirada *f*; (*appearance*) aspecto *m*. **good ~s** belleza *f*. □ ~ **after** *vt* cuidar (person); (*be responsible for*) encargarse de. □ ~ **at** *vt* mirar; (*consider*) considerar. □ ~ **down on** *vt* despreciar. □~ **for** *vt* buscar. □~ **forward to** *vt* esperar con ansia. □~ **into** *vt* investigar. □~ **like** *vt* parecerse a. □~ **on** *vi* mirar. □~ **out** *vi* tener cuidado. □~ **out for** *vt* buscar; (*watch*) tener cuidado con. □~ **round** *vi* volver la cabeza. □~ **through** *vt* hojear. □~ **up** *vt* buscar (word); (*visit*) ir a ver. □~ **up to** *vt* admirar. ~**-alike** *n* 🅸 doble *m & f*. ~**out** *n* (*Mil, person*) vigía *m*. **be on the ~out for** andar a la caza de. ~**s** *npl* belleza *f*

loom /lu:m/ *n* telar *m*. ● *vi* aparecerse

looney, loony /'lu:nɪ/ *adj & n* 🆇 chiflado (*m*) 🅸, loco (*m*)

loop /lu:p/ *n* (*shape*) curva *f* ; (*in string*) lazada *f*. ● *vt* hacer una lazada con. ~**hole** *n* (*in rule*) escapatoria *f*

loose /lu:s/ *adj* (**-er**, **-est**) suelto; (garment, thread, hair) flojo; (*inexact*) vago; (*not packed*) suelto. **be at a ~ end** no tener nada que hacer. ~**ly** *adv* sueltamente; (*roughly*) aproximadamente. ~**n** *vt* aflojar

loot /lu:t/ *n* botín *m*. ● *vt/i* saquear. ~**er** *n* saqueador *m*

lop /lɒp/ *vt* (*pt* **lopped**). ~ **off** cortar

lop-sided /-'saɪdɪd/ *adj* ladeado

lord /lɔ:d/ *n* señor *m*; (*British title*) lord *m*. **(good) L~!** ¡Dios mío! **the L~** el Señor. **the (House of) L~s** la Cámara de los Lores

lorry /'lɒrɪ/ *n* camión *m*. ~ **driver** *n* camionero *m*

lose /lu:z/ *vt/i* (*pt* **lost**) perder. ~**r** *n* perdedor *m*

loss /lɒs/ *n* pérdida *f*. **be at a ~** estar perplejo. **be at a ~ for words** no encontrar palabras

lost /lɒst/ *see* LOSE. ● *adj* perdido. **get ~** perderse. ~ **property** *n*, ~ **and found** (*Amer*) oficina *f* de objetos perdidos

lot /lɒt/ *n* (*fate*) suerte *f*; (*at auction*) lote *m*; (*land*) solar *m*. **a ~ (of)** muchos. **quite a ~ of** 🅸 bastante. ~**s (of)** 🅸 muchos. **they ate the ~** se lo comieron todo

lotion /'ləʊʃn/ *n* loción *f*

lottery /'lɒtərɪ/ *n* lotería *f*

loud /laʊd/ *adj* (**-er**, **-est**) fuerte; (*noisy*) ruidoso; (*gaudy*) chillón. **out ~** en voz alta. ~**hailer** /-'heɪlə(r)/ *n* megáfono *m*. ~**ly** *adv* (speak) en voz alta; (shout) fuerte; (complain) a voz en grito. ~**speaker** /-'spi:kə(r)/ *n* altavoz *m*, altoparlante *m* (*LAm*)

lounge /laʊndʒ/ *vi* repantigarse. ● *n* salón *m*, sala *f* (de estar), living *m* (*LAm*)

lous|e /laʊs/ *n* (*pl* **lice**) piojo *m*. ~**y** /'laʊzɪ/ *adj* (**-ier**, **-iest**) (*sl*, *bad*) malísimo

lout /laʊt/ *n* patán *m*

lov|able /'lʌvəbl/ *adj* adorable. ~**e** /lʌv/ *n* amor *m*; (*tennis*) cero *m*. **be in ~e (with)** estar enamorado (de). **fall in ~e (with)** enamorarse (de). ● *vt* querer, amar (person). **I ~e milk** me encanta la leche. ~**e affair** *n* aventura *f*, amorío *m*

lovely /'lʌvlɪ/ *adj* (**-ier**, **-iest**) (appearance) precioso, lindo (*LAm*); (person) encantador, amoroso (*LAm*)

lover /'lʌvə(r)/ *n* amante *m & f*

loving /'lʌvɪŋ/ *adj* cariñoso

low /ləʊ/ *adj & adv* (**-er**, **-est**) bajo. ● *vi* (cattle) mugir. ~**er** *vt* bajar. ~**er o.s.** envilecerse. ~**-level** *adj* a bajo nivel. ~**ly** *adj* (**-ier**, **-iest**) humilde

loyal /'lɔɪəl/ *adj* leal, fiel. **~ty** *n* lealtad *f*. **~ty card** tarjeta *f* de fidelidad

lozenge /'lɒzɪndʒ/ *n* (*shape*) rombo *m*; (*tablet*) pastilla *f*

LP *abbr* (= **long-playing record**) elepé *m*

Ltd /'lɪmɪtɪd/ *abbr* (= **Limited**) S.A., Sociedad Anónima

lubricate /'lu:brɪkeɪt/ *vt* lubricar

lucid /'lu:sɪd/ *adj* lúcido

luck /lʌk/ *n* suerte *f*. **good ~!** ¡(buena) suerte! **~ily** *adv* por suerte. **~y** *adj* (**-ier**, **-iest**) (*person*) con suerte. **be ~y** tener suerte. **~y number** número *m* de la suerte

lucrative /'lu:krətɪv/ *adj* lucrativo

ludicrous /'lu:dɪkrəs/ *adj* ridículo

lug /lʌg/ *vt* (*pt* **lugged**) 🅸 arrastrar

luggage /'lʌgɪdʒ/ *n* equipaje *m*. **~ rack** *n* rejilla *f*

lukewarm /'lu:kwɔ:m/ *adj* tibio; (*fig*) poco entusiasta

lull /lʌl/ *vt* (*soothe, send to sleep*) adormecer; (*calm*) calmar. ● *n* periodo *m* de calma

lullaby /'lʌləbaɪ/ *n* canción *f* de cuna

lumber /'lʌmbə(r)/ *n* trastos *mpl* viejos; (*wood*) maderos *mpl*. ● *vt*. **~ s.o. with sth** 🅸 endilgar algo a uno. **~jack** *n* leñador *m*

luminous /'lu:mɪnəs/ *adj* luminoso

lump /'lʌmp/ *n* (*swelling*) bulto *m*; (*as result of knock*) chichón *m*; (*in liquid*) grumo *m*; (*of sugar*) terrón *m*. ● *vt*. **~ together** agrupar. **~ it** 🅸 aguantarse. **~ sum** *n* suma *f* global. **~y** *adj* (sauce) grumoso; (mattress, cushions) lleno de protuberancias

lunacy /'lu:nəsɪ/ *n* locura *f*

lunar /'lu:nə(r)/ *adj* lunar

lunatic /'lu:nətɪk/ *n* loco *m*

lunch /lʌntʃ/ *n* comida *f*, almuerzo *m*. **have ~** comer, almorzar

luncheon /'lʌntʃən/ *n* comida *f*, almuerzo *m*. **~ voucher** *n* vale *m* de comida

lung /lʌŋ/ *n* pulmón *m*

lunge /lʌndʒ/ *n* arremetida *f*. ● *vi*. **~ at** arremeter contra

lurch /lɜ:tʃ/ *vi* tambalearse. ● *n*. **leave in the ~** dejar plantado

lure /ljʊə(r)/ *vt* atraer

lurid /'ljʊərɪd/ *adj* (colour) chillón; (*shocking*) morboso

lurk /lɜ:k/ *vi* merodear; (*in ambush*) estar al acecho

luscious /'lʌʃəs/ *adj* delicioso

lush /lʌʃ/ *adj* exuberante

lust /lʌst/ *n* lujuria *f*; (*craving*) deseo *m*. ● *vi*. **~ after** codiciar

lute /lu:t/ *n* laúd *m*

Luxembourg, **Luxemburg** /'lʌksəmbɜ:g/ *n* Luxemburgo *m*

luxuriant /lʌg'zjʊərɪənt/ *adj* exuberante

luxur|ious /lʌg'zjʊərɪəs/ *adj* lujoso. **~y** /'lʌkʃərɪ/ *n* lujo *m*. ● *adj* de lujo

lying /'laɪɪŋ/ *see* LIE[1], LIE[2]. ● *n* mentiras *fpl*. ● *adj* mentiroso

lynch /lɪntʃ/ *vt* linchar

lyric /'lɪrɪk/ *adj* lírico. **~al** *adj* lírico. **~s** *npl* letra *f*

Mm

MA /em'eɪ/ *abbr see* **Master**

mac /mæk/ *n* ⓘ impermeable *m*

macabre /mə'kɑːbrə/ *adj* macabro

macaroni /mækə'rəʊnɪ/ *n* macarrones *mpl*

mace /meɪs/ *n* (*staff*) maza *f*; (*spice*) macis *f*. **M~** (*P*) (*Amer*) gas *m* para defensa personal

machine /mə'ʃiːn/ *n* máquina *f*. **~ gun** *n* ametralladora *f*. **~ry** *n* maquinaria *f*; (*working parts, fig*) mecanismo *m*

mackintosh /'mækɪntɒʃ/ *n* impermeable *m*

macro /'mækrəʊ/ *n* (*pl* **-os**) (*Comp*) macro *m*

macrobiotic /mækrəʊbaɪ'ɒtɪk/ *adj* macrobiótico

mad /mæd/ *adj* (**madder, maddest**) loco; (*fam, angry*) furioso. **be ~ about** estar loco por

madam /'mædəm/ *n* señora *f*

mad: ~cap *adj* atolondrado. **~ cow disease** *f* enfermedad *f* de las vacas locas. **~den** *vt* (*make mad*) enloquecer; (*make angry*) enfurecer

made /meɪd/ *see* **make**. **~-to-measure** hecho a (la) medida

mad: ~house *n* manicomio *m*. **~ly** *adv* (*interested, in love etc*) locamente; (*frantically*) como un loco. **~man** /-mən/ *n* loco *m*. **~ness** *n* locura *f*

Madonna /mə'dɒnə/ *n*. **the ~** (*Relig*) la Virgen

maestro /'maɪstrəʊ/ *n* (*pl* **maestri** /-striː/ *or* **-os**) maestro *m*

Mafia /'mæfɪə/ *n* mafia *f*

magazine /mægə'ziːn/ *n* revista *f*; (*of gun*) recámara *f*

magenta /mə'dʒentə/ *adj* magenta, morado

maggot /'mægət/ *n* gusano *m*

magic /'mædʒɪk/ *n* magia *f*. ● *adj* mágico. **~al** *adj* mágico. **~ian** /mə'dʒɪʃn/ *n* mago *m*

magistrate /'mædʒɪstreɪt/ *n* juez *m* que conoce de faltas y asuntos civiles de menor importancia

magnet /'mægnɪt/ *n* imán *m*. **~ic** /-'netɪk/ *adj* magnético; (*fig*) lleno de magnetismo. **~ism** *n* magnetismo *m*. **~ize** *vt* imantar, magnetizar

magnif|ication /mægnɪfɪ'keɪʃn/ *n* aumento *m*. **~y** /'mægnɪfaɪ/ *vt* aumentar. **~ying glass** *n* lupa *f*

magnificen|ce /mæg'nɪfɪsns/ *adj* magnificencia *f*. **~t** *adj* magnífico

magnitude /'mægnɪtjuːd/ *n* magnitud *f*

magpie /'mægpaɪ/ *n* urraca *f*

mahogany /mə'hɒgənɪ/ *n* caoba *f*

maid /meɪd/ *n* (*servant*) criada *f*, sirvienta *f*; (*girl, old use*) doncella *f*. **old ~** solterona *f*

maiden /'meɪdn/ *n* doncella *f*. ● *adj* (voyage) inaugural. **~ name** *n* apellido *m* de soltera

mail /meɪl/ *n* correo *m*; (*armour*) (cota *f* de) malla *f*. ● *adj* correo. ● *vt* echar al correo (letter); (*send*) enviar por correo. **~box** *n* (*Amer*) buzón m. **~ing list** *n* lista *f* de direcciones. **~man** /-mən/ *n* (*Amer*) cartero *m*. **~ order** *n* venta *f* por correo

maim /meɪm/ *vt* mutilar

main /meɪn/ *n*. **(water/gas) ~** cañería *f* principal. **in the ~** en su mayor parte. **the ~s** *npl* (*Elec*) la red *f* de suministro. ● *adj* principal. **~ course** *n* plato *m* principal, plato *m* fuerte. **~ frame** *n* (*Comp*) unidad *f* central. **~land** *n*. **the ~land** la masa territorial de un país excluyendo sus islas. ● *adj*. **~land China** (la) China continental. **~ly** *adv* principalmente. **~ road** *n* carretera *f* principal. **~stream** *adj* (culture) establecido. **~ street** *n* calle *f* principal

maint|ain /meɪn'teɪn/ *vt* mantener. **~enance** /'meɪntənəns/ *n* mantenimiento *m*

maisonette /meɪzə'net/ *n* (*small house*) casita *f*; (*part of house*) dúplex *m*

maize /meɪz/ *n* maíz *m*

majestic /mə'dʒestɪk/ *adj* majestuoso

majesty /'mædʒəstɪ/ *n* majestad *f*

major /'meɪdʒə(r)/ *adj* (*important*) muy importante; (*Mus*) mayor. **a ~ road** una calle prioritaria. ● *n* comandante *m* & *f*, mayor *m* & *f* (*LAm*). ● *vi*. **~ in** (*Amer, Univ*) especializarse en

Majorca /mə'jɔ:kə/ *n* Mallorca *f*

majority /mə'dʒɒrətɪ/ *n* mayoría *f*. ● *adj* mayoritario

make /meɪk/ *vt* (*pt* **made**) hacer; (*manufacture*) fabricar; ganar (money); tomar (decision); llegar a (destination). **~ s.o. do sth** obligar a uno a hacer algo. **be made of** estar hecho de. **I ~ it two o'clock** yo tengo las dos. **~ believe** fingir. **~ do** (*manage*) arreglarse. **~ do with** (*content o.s.*) contentarse con. **~ it** llegar; (*succeed*) tener éxito. ● *n* marca *f*. **~ for** *vt* dirigirse a. **~ good** *vt* compensar; (*repair*) reparar. □ **~ off** *vi* escaparse (**with** con). □ **~ out** *vt* distinguir; (*understand*) entender; (*write out*) hacer; (*assert*) dar a entender. *vi* (*cope*) arreglárselas. □ **~ up** *vt* (*constitute*) formar; (*prepare*) preparar; inventar (story); **~ it up** (*become reconciled*) hacer las paces. **~ up (one's face)** maquillarse. □ **~ up for** *vt* compensar. **~-believe** *adj* fingido, simulado. *n* ficción *f*. **~over** *n* (*Amer*) maquillaje *m*. **~r** *n* fabricante *m* & *f*. **~shift** *adj* (*temporary*) provisional, provisorio (*LAm*); (*improvised*) improvisado. **~up** *n* maquillaje *m*. **put on ~up** maquillarse.

making /'meɪkɪŋ/ *n*. **he has the ~s of** tiene madera de. **in the ~** en vías de formación

maladjusted /mælə'dʒʌstɪd/ *adj* inadaptado

malaria /mə'leərɪə/ *n* malaria *f*, paludismo *m*

Malaysia /mə'leɪzɪə/ *n* Malasia *f*. **~n** *adj* & *n* malaisio (*m*)

male /meɪl/ *adj* macho; (voice, attitude) masculino. ● *n* macho *m*; (*man*) varón *m*

malevolent /mə'levələnt/ *adj* malévolo

malfunction /mæl'fʌŋkʃn/ *vi* fallar, funcionar mal

malic|e /'mælɪs/ *n* mala intención *f*, maldad *f*. **bear s.o. ~e** guardar rencor a uno. **~ious** /mə'lɪʃəs/ *adj* malintencionado. **~iously** *adv* con malevolencia

malignant /mə'lɪgnənt/ *adj* maligno

mallet /'mælɪt/ *n* mazo *m*

malnutrition /mælnju:'trɪʃn/ *n* desnutrición *f*

malpractice /mæl'præktɪs/ *n* mala práctica *f* (en el ejercicio de una profesión)

malt /mɔːlt/ *n* malta *f*

Malt|a /ˈmɔːltə/ *n* Malta *f.* **~ese** /-ˈtiːz/ *adj & n* maltés (*m*)

mammal /ˈmæml/ *n* mamífero *m*

mammoth /ˈmæməθ/ *n* mamut *m.* •*adj* gigantesco

man /mæn/ *n* (*pl* **men** /men/) hombre *m*; (*Chess*) pieza *f.* **~ in the street** hombre *m* de la calle. •*vt* (*pt* **manned**) encargarse de (switchboard); tripular (ship); servir (guns)

manacles /ˈmænəklz/ *n* (*for wrists*) esposas *fpl*; (*for legs*) grillos *mpl*

manag|e /ˈmænɪdʒ/ *vt* dirigir; administrar (land, finances); (*handle*) manejar. •*vi* (*Com*) dirigir; (*cope*) arreglárselas. **~e to do** lograr hacer. **~eable** *adj* (task) posible de alcanzar; (size) razonable. **~ement** *n* dirección *f.* **~er** *n* director *m*; (*of shop*) encargado *m*; (*of soccer team*) entrenador *m*, director *m* técnico (*LAm*). **~eress** /-ˈres/ *n* encargada *f.* **~erial** /-ˈdʒɪərɪəl/ *adj* directivo, gerencial (*LAm*). **~ing director** *n* director *m* ejecutivo

mandate /ˈmændeɪt/ *n* mandato *m*

mandatory /ˈmændətərɪ/ *adj* obligatorio

mane /meɪn/ *n* (*of horse*) crin(es) *f*(*pl*); (*of lion*) melena *f*

mangle /ˈmæŋgl/ *n* rodillo *m* (escurridor). •*vt* destrozar

man: ~handle *vt* mover a pulso; (*treat roughly*) maltratar. **~hole** *n* registro *m.* **~hood** *n* madurez *f*; (*quality*) virilidad *f.* **~-hour** *n* hora *f* hombre. **~-hunt** *n* persecución *f*

mania /ˈmeɪnɪə/ *n* manía *f.* **~c** /-ɪæk/ *n* maníaco *m*

manicure /ˈmænɪkjʊə(r)/ *n* manicura *f*, manicure *f* (*LAm*)

manifest /ˈmænɪfest/ *adj* manifiesto. •*vt* manifestar. **~ation** /-ˈsteɪʃn/ *n* manifestación *f*

manifesto /mænɪˈfestəʊ/ *n* (*pl* **-os**) manifiesto *m*

manipulat|e /məˈnɪpjʊleɪt/ *vt* manipular. **~ion** /-ˈleɪʃn/ *n* manipulación *f.* **~ive** /-lətɪv/ *adj* manipulador

man: ~kind *n* humanidad *f.* **~ly** *adj* viril. **~-made** *adj* artificial

manner /ˈmænə(r)/ *n* manera *f*; (*demeanour*) actitud *f*; (*kind*) clase *f.* **~ed** *adj* amanerado. **~s** *npl* modales *mpl*, educación *f.* **bad ~s** mala educación

manoeuvre /məˈnuːvə(r)/ *n* maniobra *f.* •*vt/i* maniobrar

manor /ˈmænə(r)/ *n.* **~ house** casa *f* solariega

manpower *n* mano *f* de obra

mansion /ˈmænʃn/ *n* mansión *f*

man: ~-size(d) *adj* grande. **~slaughter** *n* homicidio *m* sin premeditación

mantelpiece /ˈmæntlpiːs/ *n* repisa *f* de la chimenea

manual /ˈmænjʊəl/ *adj* manual. •*n* (*handbook*) manual *m*

manufacture /mænjʊˈfæktʃə(r)/ *vt* fabricar. •*n* fabricación *f.* **~r** *n* fabricante *m & f*

manure /məˈnjʊə(r)/ *n* estiércol *m*

manuscript /ˈmænjʊskrɪpt/ *n* manuscrito *m*

many /ˈmenɪ/ *adj & pron* muchos, muchas. **~ people** mucha gente. **a great/good ~** muchísimos. **how ~?** ¿cuántos? **so ~** tantos. **too ~** demasiados

map /mæp/ *n* mapa *m*; (*of streets etc*) plano *m*

mar /mɑ:(r)/ *vt* (*pt* **marred**) estropear

marathon /ˈmærəθən/ *n* maratón *m* & *f*

marble /ˈmɑ:bl/ *n* mármol *m*; (*for game*) canica *f*

march /mɑ:tʃ/ *vi* (*Mil*) marchar. **~ off** *vi* irse. ●*n* marcha *f*

March /mɑ:tʃ/ *n* marzo *m*

march-past /ˈmɑ:tʃpɑ:st/ *n* desfile *m*

mare /meə(r)/ *n* yegua *f*

margarine /mɑ:dʒəˈri:n/ *n* margarina *f*

margin /ˈmɑ:dʒɪn/ *n* margen *f*. **~al** *adj* marginal

marijuana /mærɪˈhwɑ:nə/ *n* marihuana *f*

marina /məˈri:nə/ *n* puerto *m* deportivo

marine /məˈri:n/ *adj* marino. ●*n* (*sailor*) infante *m* de marina

marionette /mærɪəˈnet/ *n* marioneta *f*

marital status /mærɪtl ˈsteɪtəs/ *n* estado *m* civil

mark /mɑ:k/ *n* marca *f*; (*stain*) mancha *f*; (*Schol*) nota *f*; (*target*) blanco *m*. ●*vt* (*indicate*) señalar, marcar; (*stain*) manchar; corregir (exam). **~ time** marcar el paso. □**~ out** *vt* (*select*) señalar; (*distinguish*) distinguir. **~ed** *adj* marcado. **~edly** /-kɪdlɪ/ *adv* marcadamente. **~er** *n* marcador *m*. **~er (pen)** *n* rotulador *m*, marcador *m* (*LAm*)

market /ˈmɑ:kɪt/ *n* mercado *m*. **on the ~** en venta. ●*vt* comercializar. **~ garden** *n* huerta *f*. **~ing** *n* marketing *m*

marking /ˈmɑ:kɪŋ/ *n* marcas *fpl*; (*on animal, plant*) mancha *f*

marksman /ˈmɑ:ksmən/ *n* (*pl* **-men**) tirador *m*. **~ship** *n* puntería *f*

marmalade /ˈmɑ:məleɪd/ *n* mermelada *f* (de cítricos)

maroon /məˈru:n/ *adj* & *n* granate (*m*). ●*vt* abandonar (en una isla desierta)

marquee /mɑ:ˈki:/ *n* toldo *m*, entoldado *m*; (*Amer, awning*) marquesina *f*

marriage /ˈmærɪdʒ/ *n* matrimonio *m*; (*ceremony*) casamiento *m*

married /ˈmærɪd/ *adj* casado; (life) conyugal

marrow /ˈmærəʊ/ *n* (*of bone*) tuétano *m*; (*vegetable*) calabaza *f* verde alargada. **~ squash** *n* (*Amer*) calabaza *f* verde alargada

marry /ˈmærɪ/ *vt* casarse con; (*give or unite in marriage*) casar. ●*vi* casarse. **get married** casarse (**to** con)

Mars /mɑ:z/ *n* Marte *m*

marsh /mɑ:ʃ/ *n* pantano *m*

marshal /ˈmɑ:ʃl/ *n* (*Mil*) mariscal *m*; (*Amer, police chief*) jefe *m* de policía. ●*vt* (*pt* **marshalled**) reunir; poner en orden (thoughts)

marsh: ~mallow /-ˈmæləʊ/ *n* malvavisco *m*, bombón *m* (*LAm*). **~y** *adj* pantanoso

martial /ˈmɑ:ʃl/ *adj* marcial. **~ arts** *npl* artes *fpl* marciales. **~ law** *n* ley *f* marcial

martyr /ˈmɑ:tə(r)/ *n* mártir *m* & *f*

marvel /ˈmɑ:vl/ *n* maravilla *f*. ●*vi* (*pt* **marvelled**) maravillarse (**at** de). **~lous** *adj* maravilloso

Marxis|m /ˈmɑ:ksɪzəm/ *n* marxismo *m*. **~t** *adj* & *n* marxista (*m* & *f*)

marzipan /ˈmɑ:zɪpæn/ *n* mazapán *m*

mascara /mæˈskɑ:rə/ *n* rímel® *m*

mascot /ˈmæskɒt/ *n* mascota *f*

masculin|e /ˈmæskjʊlɪn/ *adj & n* masculino (*m*). **~ity** /-ˈlɪnətɪ/ *n* masculinidad *f*

mash /mæʃ/ *n* (*Brit* 🄸, *potatoes*) puré *m* de patatas, puré *m* de papas (*LAm*). ● *vt* hacer puré de, moler (*Mex*). **~ed potatoes** *n* puré *m* de patatas, puré *m* de papas (*LAm*)

mask /mɑːsk/ *n* máscara *f*; (*Sport*) careta *f*. ● *vt* ocultar

masochis|m /ˈmæsəkɪzəm/ *n* masoquismo *m*. **~t** *n* masoquista *m* & *f*. **~tic** /-ˈkɪstɪk/ *adj* masoquista

mason /ˈmeɪsn/ *n* (*stone* ~) mampostero *m*. **M~** (*freemason*) masón *m*. **~ry** /ˈmeɪsnrɪ/ *n* albañilería *f*

masquerade /mɑːskəˈreɪd/ *n* mascarada *f*. ● *vi*. ~ **as** hacerse pasar por

m

mass /mæs/ *n* masa *f*; (*Relig*) misa *f*; (*large quantity*) montón *m*. **the ~es** las masas. ● *vi* concentrarse

massacre /ˈmæsəkə(r)/ *n* masacre *f*, matanza *f*. ● *vt* masacrar

mass|age /ˈmæsɑːʒ/ *n* masaje *m*. ● *vt* masajear. **~eur** /mæˈsɜː(r)/ *n* masajista *m*. **~euse** /mæˈsɜːz/ *n* masajista *f*

massive /ˈmæsɪv/ *adj* masivo; (*heavy*) macizo; (*huge*) enorme

mass: ~ media *n* medios *mpl* de comunicación. **~-produce** /-prəˈdjuːs/ *vt* fabricar en serie

mast /mɑːst/ *n* mástil *m*; (*for radio, TV*) antena *f* repetidora

master /ˈmɑːstə(r)/ *n* amo *m*; (*expert*) maestro *m*; (*in secondary school*) profesor *m*; (*of ship*) capitán *m*; (*master copy*) original *m*. **~'s degree** master *m*, maestría *f*. **M~ of Arts (MA)** poseedor *m* de una maestría en folosofía y letras. **M~ of Science (MSc)** poseedor *m* de una maestría en ciencias. ● *vt* llegar a dominar. **~ key** *n* llave *f* maestra. **~mind** *n* cerebro *m*. ● *vt* dirigir. **~piece** *n* obra *f* maestra. **~stroke** *n* golpe *m* de maestro. **~y** *n* dominio *m*; (*skill*) maestría *f*

masturbat|e /ˈmæstəbeɪt/ *vi* masturbarse. **~ion** /-ˈbeɪʃn/ *n* masturbación *f*

mat /mæt/ *n* estera *f*; (*at door*) felpudo *m*. ● *adj* (*Amer*) *see* **MATT**

match /mætʃ/ *n* (*Sport*) partido *m*; (*for fire*) cerilla *f*, fósforo *m* (*LAm*), cerillo *m* (*Mex*); (*equal*) igual *m*. ● *vt* emparejar; (*equal*) igualar; (clothes, colours) hacer juego con. ● *vi* hacer juego. **~box** *n* caja *f* de cerillas, caja *f* de fósforos (*LAm*), caja *f* de cerillos (*Mex*). **~ing** *adj* que hace juego. **~stick** *n* cerilla *f*, fósforo *m* (*LAm*), cerillo *m* (*Mex*)

mate /meɪt/ *n* (*of person*) pareja *f*; (*of animals, male*) macho *m*; (*of animals, female*) hembra *f*; (*assistant*) ayudante *m*; (🄸, *friend*) amigo *m*, cuate *m* (*Mex*); (*Chess*) (jaque *m*) mate *m*. ● *vi* aparearse

material /məˈtɪərɪəl/ *n* material *m*; (*cloth*) tela *f*. ● *adj* material. **~istic** /-ˈlɪstɪk/ *adj* materialista. **~ize** *vi* materializarse. **~s** *npl* materiales *mpl*

matern|al /məˈtɜːnl/ *adj* maternal. **~ity** /-ətɪ/ *n* maternidad *f*. ● *adj* (ward) de obstetricia; (clothes) premamá, de embarazada

math /mæθ/ *n* (*Amer*) *see* **MATHS**

mathematic|ian /mæθəməˈtɪʃn/ *n* matemático *m*. **~al** /-ˈmætɪkl/ *adj* matemático. **~s** /-ˈmætɪks/ *n* matemática(s) *f(pl)*

maths /mæθs/ *n* matemática(s) *f(pl)*

matinée, **matinee** /'mætɪneɪ/ *n* (*Theatre*) función *f* de tarde; (*Cinema*) primera sesión *f* (de la tarde)

matrices /'meɪtrɪsi:z/ *see* **MATRIX**

matriculat|e /mə'trɪkjʊleɪt/ *vi* matricularse. **~ion** /-'leɪʃn/ *n* matrícula *f*

matrimon|ial /mætrɪ'məʊnɪəl/ *adj* matrimonial. **~y** /'mætrɪmənɪ/ *n* matrimonio *m*

matrix /'meɪtrɪks/ *n* (*pl* **matrices**) matriz *f*

matron /'meɪtrən/ *n* (*married, elderly*) matrona *f*; (*in school*) ama *f* de llaves; (*former use, in hospital*) enfermera *f* jefe

matt, **matte** (*Amer*) /mæt/ *adj* mate

matted /'mætɪd/ *adj* enmarañado y apelmazado

matter /'mætə(r)/ *n* (*substance*) materia *f*; (*affair*) asunto *m*; (*pus*) pus *m*. **as a ~ of fact** en realidad. **no ~** no importa. **what is the ~?** ¿qué pasa? **to make ~s worse** para colmo (de males). • *vi* importar. **it doesn't ~** no importa. **~-of-fact** /-əv'fækt/ *adj* (person) práctico

mattress /'mætrɪs/ *n* colchón *m*

matur|e /mə'tjʊə(r)/ *adj* maduro. • *vi* madurar. **~ity** *n* madurez *f*

maudlin /'mɔ:dlɪn/ *adj* llorón

maul /mɔ:l/ *vt* atacar (y herir)

mauve /məʊv/ *adj & n* malva (*m*)

maverick /'mævərɪk/ *n* inconformista *m & f*

maxim /'mæksɪm/ *n* máxima *f*

maxim|ize /'mæksɪmaɪz/ *vt* maximizar. **~um** /-əm/ *adj & n* máximo (*m*)

may /meɪ/,

past **might**

auxiliary verb

····➤ (*expressing possibility*) **he ~ come** puede que venga, es posible que venga. **it ~ be true** puede ser verdad. **she ~ not have seen him** es posible que *or* puede que no lo haya visto

····➤ (*asking for or giving permission*) **~ I smoke?** ¿puedo fumar?, ¿se puede fumar? **~ I have your name and address, please?** ¿quiere darme su nombre y dirección, por favor?

····➤ (*expressing a wish*) **~ he be happy** que sea feliz

····➤ (*conceding*) **he ~ not have much experience, but he's very hardworking** no tendrá mucha experiencia, pero es muy trabajador. **that's as ~ be** puede ser

····➤ **I ~ as well stay** más vale quedarme

May /meɪ/ *n* mayo *m*

maybe /'meɪbɪ/ *adv* quizá(s), tal vez, a lo mejor

May Day *n* el primero de mayo

mayhem /'meɪhem/ *n* caos *m*

mayonnaise /meɪə'neɪz/ *n* mayonesa *f*, mahonesa *f*

mayor /meə(r)/ *n* alcalde *m*, alcaldesa *f*. **~ess** /-ɪs/ *n* alcaldesa *f*

maze /meɪz/ *n* laberinto *m*

me /mi:/ *pron* me; (*after prep*) mí. **he knows ~** me conoce. **it's ~** soy yo

meadow /'medəʊ/ *n* prado *m*, pradera *f*

meagre /'mi:gə(r)/ *adj* escaso

meal /miːl/ *n* comida *f*. **~time** *n* hora *f* de comer

mean /miːn/ *vt* (*pt* **meant**) (*intend*) tener la intención de, querer; (*signify*) querer decir, significar. **~ to do** tener la intención de hacer. **~ well** tener buenas intenciones. **be meant for** estar destinado a. ●*adj* (**-er, -est**) (*miserly*) tacaño; (*unkind*) malo; (*Math*) medio. ●*n* media *f*; (*average*) promedio *m*

meander /mɪˈændə(r)/ *vi* (river) serpentear

meaning /ˈmiːnɪŋ/ *n* sentido *m*. **~ful** *adj* significativo. **~less** *adj* sin sentido

meanness /ˈmiːnnɪs/ *n* (*miserliness*) tacañería *f*; (*unkindness*) maldad *f*

m

means /miːnz/ *n* medio *m*. **by ~ of** por medio de, mediante. **by all ~** por supuesto. **by no ~** de ninguna manera. ●*npl* (*wealth*) medios *mpl*, recursos *mpl*. **~ test** *n* investigación *f* de ingresos

meant /ment/ *see* **MEAN**

meantime /ˈmiːntaɪm/ *adv* mientras tanto, entretanto. ●*n*. **in the ~** mientras tanto, entretanto

meanwhile /ˈmiːnwaɪl/ *adv* mientras tanto, entretanto

measl|es /ˈmiːzlz/ *n* sarampión *m*. **~y** /ˈmiːzlɪ/ *adj* [!] miserable

measure /ˈmeʒə(r)/ *n* medida *f*; (*ruler*) regla *f*. ●*vt/i* medir. □ **~ up to** *vt* estar a la altura de. **~ment** *n* medida *f*

meat /miːt/ *n* carne *f*. **~ball** *n* albóndiga *f*. **~y** *adj* (taste, smell) a carne; (soup, stew) con mucha carne

mechan|ic /mɪˈkænɪk/ *n* mecánico *m*. **~ical** *adj* mecánico. **~ics** *n* mecánica *f*. **~ism** /ˈmekənɪzəm/ *n* mecanismo *m*. **~ize** /ˈmekənaɪz/ *vt* mecanizar

medal /ˈmedl/ *n* medalla *f*. **~list** /ˈmedəlɪst/ *n* medallista *m & f*. **be a gold ~list** ganar una medalla de oro

meddle /ˈmedl/ *vi* meterse, entrometerse (**in** en). **~ with** (*tinker*) toquetear

media /ˈmiːdɪə/ *see* **MEDIUM**. ●*npl*. **the ~** los medios de comunicación

mediat|e /ˈmiːdɪeɪt/ *vi* mediar. **~ion** /-ˈeɪʃn/ *n* mediación *f*. **~or** *n* mediador *m*

medical /ˈmedɪkl/ *adj* médico; (student) de medicina. ●*n* revisión *m* médica

medicat|ed /ˈmedɪkeɪtɪd/ *adj* medicinal. **~ion** /-ˈkeɪʃn/ *n* medicación *f*

medicin|al /mɪˈdɪsɪnl/ *adj* medicinal. **~e** /ˈmedsɪn/ *n* medicina *f*

medieval /medɪˈiːvl/ *adj* medieval

mediocre /miːdɪˈəʊkə(r)/ *adj* mediocre

meditat|e /ˈmedɪteɪt/ *vi* meditar. **~ion** /-ˈteɪʃn/ *n* meditación *f*

Mediterranean /medɪtəˈreɪnɪən/ *adj* mediterráneo. ●*n*. **the ~** el Mediterráneo

medium /ˈmiːdɪəm/ *n* (*pl* **media**) medio *m*. **happy ~** término *m* medio. ●*adj* mediano. **~-size(d)** /-saɪz(d)/ *adj* de tamaño mediano

medley /ˈmedlɪ/ *n* (*Mus*) popurrí *m*; (*mixture*) mezcla *f*

meek /miːk/ *adj* (**-er, -est**) dócil

meet /miːt/ *vt* (*pt* **met**) encontrar; (*bump into s.o.*) encontrarse con; (*fetch*) ir a buscar; (*get to know, be introduced to*) conocer. ●*vi* encontrarse; (*get to know*) conocerse; (*have meeting*) reunirse. **~ up** *vi* encontrarse (**with** con). ▫ **~ with** *vt* ser recibido con; (*Amer, meet*) encontrarse con. **~ing** *n* reunión *f*; (*accidental between two people*) encuentro *m*

megabyte /'megəbaɪt/ *n* (*Comp*) megabyte *m*, megaocteto *m*

megaphone /'megəfəʊn/ *n* megáfono *m*

melanchol|ic /melən'kɒlɪk/ *adj* melancólico. **~y** /'melənkɒlɪ/ *n* melancolía *f*. ● *adj* melancólico

mellow /'meləʊ/ *adj* (**-er, -est**) (fruit) maduro; (sound) dulce; (colour) tenue; (person) apacible

melodrama /'melədrɑːmə/ *n* melodrama *m*. **~tic** /melədrə'mætɪk/ *adj* melodramático

melody /'melədɪ/ *n* melodía *f*

melon /'melən/ *n* melón *m*

melt /melt/ *vt* (*make liquid*) derretir; fundir (metals). ● *vi* (*become liquid*) derretirse; (metals) fundirse. ▫ **~ down** *vt* fundir

member /'membə(r)/ *n* miembro *m & f*; (*of club*) socio *m*. **~ of staff** empleado *m*. **M~ of Congress** *n* (*Amer*) miembro *m & f* del Congreso. **M~ of Parliament** *n* diputado *m*. **~ship** *n* calidad *f* de socio; (*members*) socios *mpl*, membresía *f* (*LAm*)

membrane /'membreɪn/ *n* membrana *f*

memento /mɪ'mentəʊ/ *n* (*pl* **-os** *or* **-oes**) recuerdo *m*

memo /'meməʊ/ *n* (*pl* **-os**) memorándum *m*, memo *m*

memoir /'memwɑː(r)/ *n* memoria *f*

memorable /'memərəbl/ *adj* memorable

memorandum /memə'rændəm/ *n* (*pl* **-ums** *or* **-da** /-də/) memorándum *m*

memorial /mɪ'mɔːrɪəl/ *n* monumento *m*. ● *adj* conmemorativo

memor|ize /'meməraɪz/ *vt* aprender de memoria. **~y** /'memərɪ/ *n* (*faculty*) memoria *f*; (*thing remembered*) recuerdo *m*. **from ~y** de memoria. **in ~y of** a la memoria de

men /men/ *see* MAN

menac|e /'menəs/ *n* amenaza *f*; (*fam, nuisance*) peligro *m* público. ● *vt* amenazar. **~ing** *adj* amenazador

mend /mend/ *vt* reparar; arreglar (garment). **~ one's ways** enmendarse. ● *n* remiendo *m*. **be on the ~** ir mejorando

menfolk /'menfəʊk/ *n* hombres *mpl*

menial /'miːnɪəl/ *adj* servil

meningitis /menɪn'dʒaɪtɪs/ *n* meningitis *f*

menopause /'menəpɔːz/ *n* menopausia *f*

menstruat|e /'menstrʊeɪt/ *vi* menstruar. **~ion** /-'eɪʃn/ *n* menstruación *f*

mental /'mentl/ *adj* mental; (hospital) psiquiátrico. **~ity** /-'tælətɪ/ *n* mentalidad *f*. **~ly** *adv* mentalmente. **be ~ly ill** ser un enfermo mental

mention /'menʃn/ *vt* mencionar. **don't ~ it!** ¡no hay de qué! ● *n* mención *f*

mentor /'mentɔː(r)/ *n* mentor *m*

menu /'menjuː/ *n* menú *m*

meow /mɪ'aʊ/ *n & vi see* MEW

mercenary /'mɜːsɪnərɪ/ *adj & n* mercenario (*m*)

merchandise /'mɜːtʃəndaɪz/ *n* mercancías *fpl*, mercadería *f* (*LAm*)

merchant /'mɜːtʃənt/ *n* comerciante *m*. ● *adj* (ship, navy) mercante. ~ **bank** *n* banco *m* mercantil

merci|ful /'mɜ:sɪfl/ *adj* misericordioso. **~less** *adj* despiadado

mercury /'mɜ:kjʊrɪ/ *n* mercurio *m*. **M~** (*planet*) Mercurio *m*

mercy /'mɜ:sɪ/ *n* compasión *f*. **at the ~ of** a merced de

mere /mɪə(r)/ *adj* simple. **~ly** *adv* simplemente

merge /mɜ:dʒ/ *vt* unir; fusionar (companies). ● *vi* unirse; (companies) fusionarse. **~r** *n* fusión *f*

meridian /mə'rɪdɪən/ *n* meridiano *m*

meringue /mə'ræŋ/ *n* merengue *m*

merit /'merɪt/ *n* mérito *m*. ● *vt* (*pt* **merited**) merecer

mermaid /'mɜ:meɪd/ *n* sirena *f*

m

merr|ily /'merəlɪ/ *adv* alegremente. **~iment** /'merɪmənt/ *n* alegría *f*. **~y** /'merɪ/ *adj* (**-ier**, **-iest**) alegre. **make ~** divertirse. **~y-go-round** *n* tiovivo *m*, carrusel *m* (*LAm*). **~y-making** *n* jolgorio *m*

mesh /meʃ/ *n* malla *f*

mesmerize /'mezməraɪz/ *vt* hipnotizar; (*fascinate*) cautivar

mess /mes/ *n* desorden *m*; (*dirt*) suciedad *f*; (*Mil*) rancho *m*. **make a ~ of** estropear. □ **~ up** *vt* desordenar; (*dirty*) ensuciar; estropear (plans). □ **~ about** *vi* tontear. □ **~ with** *vt* (*tinker with*) manosear

mess|age /'mesɪdʒ/ *n* mensaje *m*; (*when phoning*) recado *m*. **~enger** /'mesɪndʒə(r)/ *n* mensajero *m*

Messiah /mɪ'saɪə/ *n* Mesías *m*

Messrs /'mesəz/ *npl*. **~ Smith** los señores Smith, los Sres. Smith

messy /'mesɪ/ *adj* (**-ier**, **-iest**) en desorden; (*dirty*) sucio

met /met/ *see* MEET

metabolism /mɪ'tæbəlɪzəm/ *n* metabolismo *m*

metal /'metl/ *n* metal. ● *adj* de metal. **~lic** /mə'tælɪk/ *adj* metálico

metaphor /'metəfə(r)/ *n* metáfora *f*. **~ical** /-'fɒrɪkl/ *adj* metafórico

mete /mi:t/ *vt*. **~ out** repartir; dar (punishment)

meteor /'mi:tɪə(r)/ *n* meteoro *m*. **~ic** /-'ɒrɪk/ *adj* meteórico. **~ite** /'mi:tɪəraɪt/ *n* meteorito *m*

meteorolog|ical /mi:tɪərə'lɒdʒɪkl/ *adj* meteorológico. **~ist** /-'rɒlədʒɪst/ *n* meteorólogo *m*. **~y** /-'rɒlədʒɪ/ *n* meteorología *f*

meter /'mi:tə(r)/ *n* contador *m*, medidor *m* (*LAm*); (*Amer*) *see* METRE

method /'meθəd/ *n* método *m*. **~ical** /mɪ'θɒdɪkl/ *adj* metódico. **M~ist** /'meθədɪst/ *adj & n* metodista (*m & f*)

methylated /'meθɪleɪtɪd/ *adj*. **~ spirit(s)** *n* alcohol *m* desnaturalizado

meticulous /mɪ'tɪkjʊləs/ *adj* meticuloso

metre /'mi:tə(r)/ *n* metro *m*

metric /'metrɪk/ *adj* métrico

metropoli|s /mɪ'trɒpəlɪs/ *n* metrópoli(s) *f*

mettle /'metl/ *n*. **be on one's ~** (*fig*) estar dispuesto a dar lo mejor de sí

mew /mju:/ *n* maullido *m*. ● *vi* maullar

Mexic|an /'meksɪkən/ *adj & n* mejicano (*m*), mexicano (*m*). **~o** /-kəʊ/ *n* Méjico *m*, México *m*

miaow /mi:'aʊ/ *n & vi see* MEW

mice /maɪs/ *see* MOUSE

mickey /'mɪkɪ/ *n*. **take the ~ out of** Ⓘ tomar el pelo a

micro... /ˈmaɪkrəʊ/ *pref* micro...
microbe /ˈmaɪkrəʊb/ *n* microbio *m*
micro: ~chip *n* pastilla *f*. **~film** *n* microfilme *m*. **~light** *n* aeroligero *m*. **~phone** *n* micrófono *m*. **~processor** /-ˈprəʊsesə(r)/ *n* microprocesador *m*. **~scope** *n* microscopio *m*. **~scopic** /-ˈskɒpɪk/ *adj* microscópico. **~wave** *n* microonda *f*. **~wave oven** *n* horno *m* de microondas
mid- /mɪd/ *pref*. **in ~ air** en pleno aire. **in ~ March** a mediados de marzo
midday /mɪdˈdeɪ/ *n* mediodía *m*
middl|e /ˈmɪdl/ *adj* de en medio. ● *n* medio *m*. **in the ~e of** en medio de. **~e-aged** /-ˈeɪdʒd/ *adj* de mediana edad. **M~e Ages** *npl* Edad *f* Media. **~e class** *n* clase *f* media. **~e-class** *adj* de la clase media. **M~e East** *n* Oriente *m* Medio. **~eman** *n* intermediario *m*. **~e name** *n* segundo nombre *m*. **~ing** *adj* regular
midge /mɪdʒ/ *n* mosquito *m*
midget /ˈmɪdʒɪt/ *n* enano *m*. ● *adj* minúsculo
Midlands /ˈmɪdləndz/ *npl* región *f* central de Inglaterra
midnight /ˈmɪdnaɪt/ *n* medianoche *f*
midriff /ˈmɪdrɪf/ *n* diafragma *m*
midst /mɪdst/ *n*. **in our ~** entre nosotros. **in the ~ of** en medio de
midsummer /mɪdˈsʌmə(r)/ *n* pleno verano *m*; (*solstice*) solsticio *m* de verano
midway /mɪdˈweɪ/ *adv* a mitad de camino
Midwest /ˈmɪdˈwest/ región *f* central de los EE.UU.
midwife /ˈmɪdwaɪf/ *n* comadrona *f*, partera *f*
midwinter /mɪdˈwɪntə(r)/ *n* pleno invierno *m*
might /maɪt/ *see* MAY. ● *n* (*strength*) fuerza *f*; (*power*) poder *m*. **~y** *adj* (*strong*) fuerte; (*powerful*) poderoso. ● *adv* [I] muy
migraine /ˈmi:greɪn/ *n* jaqueca *f*
migra|nt /ˈmaɪgrənt/ *adj* migratorio. ● *n* (*person*) emigrante *m* & *f*. **~te** /maɪˈgreɪt/ *vi* emigrar. **~tion** /-ˈgreɪʃn/ *n* migración *f*
mild /maɪld/ *adj* (**-er**, **-est**) (person) afable; (climate) templado; (*slight*) ligero; (taste, manner) suave
mildew /ˈmɪldju:/ *n* moho *m*; (*on plants*) mildeu *m*, mildiu *m*
mildly /ˈmaɪldlɪ/ *adv* (*gently*) suavemente; (*slightly*) ligeramente
mile /maɪl/ *n* milla *f*. **~s better** [I] mucho mejor. **~s too big** [I] demasiado grande. **~age** /-ɪdʒ/ *n* (*loosely*) kilometraje *m*. **~ometer** /maɪˈlɒmɪtə(r)/ *n* (*loosely*) cuentakilómetros *m*. **~stone** *n* mojón *m*; (*event, stage, fig*) hito *m*
militant /ˈmɪlɪtənt/ *adj* & *n* militante (*m* & *f*)
military /ˈmɪlɪtərɪ/ *adj* militar
militia /mɪˈlɪʃə/ *n* milicia *f*
milk /mɪlk/ *n* leche *f*. ● *adj* (product) lácteo; (chocolate) con leche. ● *vt* ordeñar (cow). **~man** /-mən/ *n* lechero *m*. **~ shake** *n* batido *m*, (leche *f*) malteada *f* (*LAm*), licuado *m* con leche (*LAm*). **~y** *adj* lechoso. **M~y Way** *n* Vía *f* Láctea
mill /mɪl/ *n* molino *m*; (*for coffee, pepper*) molinillo *m*; (*factory*) fábrica *f* de tejidos de algodón. ● *vt* moler. □ **~ about, mill around** *vi* dar vueltas

m

millennium /mɪˈlenɪəm/ *n* (*pl* **-ia** /-ɪə/ *or* **-iums**) milenio *m*

miller /ˈmɪlə(r)/ *n* molinero *m*

milli... /ˈmɪlɪ/ *pref* mili... **~gram(me)** *n* miligramo *m*. **~metre** *n* milímetro *m*

milliner /ˈmɪlɪnə(r)/ *n* sombrerero *m*

million /ˈmɪlɪən/ *n* millón *m*. **a ~ pounds** un millón de libras. **~aire** /-ˈeə(r)/ *n* millonario *m*

millstone /ˈmɪlstəʊn/ *n* muela *f* (de molino); (*fig, burden*) carga *f*

mime /maɪm/ *n* mímica *f*. ●*vt* imitar, hacer la mímica de. ●*vi* hacer la mímica

mimic /ˈmɪmɪk/ *vt* (*pt* **mimicked**) imitar. ●*n* imitador *m*. **~ry** *n* imitación *f*

mince /mɪns/ *vt* picar, moler (*LAm*) (meat). **not to ~ matters/words** no andar(se) con rodeos. ●*n* carne *f* picada, carne *f* molida (*LAm*). **~ pie** *n* pastelito *m* de Navidad (pastelito relleno de picadillo de frutos secos). **~r** *n* máquina *f* de picar carne, máquina *f* de moler carne (*LAm*)

m

mind /maɪnd/ *n* mente *f*; (*sanity*) juicio *m*. **to my ~** a mi parecer. **be on one's mind** preocuparle a uno. **make up one's ~** decidirse. ●*vt* (*look after*) cuidar (de); atender (shop). **~ the steps!** ¡cuidado con las escaleras! **never ~ him** no le hagas caso. **I don't ~ the noise** no me molesta el ruido. **would you ~ closing the door?** ¿le importaría cerrar la puerta? ●*vi*. **never ~** no importa, no te preocupes. **I don't ~** (*don't object*) me da igual. **do you ~ if I smoke?** ¿le importa si fumo? **~ful** *adj* atento (**of** a). **~less** *adj* (activity) mecánico; (violence) ciego

mine¹ /maɪn/ *poss pron* (*sing*) mío, mía; (*pl*) míos, mías. **it is ~** es mío. **~ are blue** los míos/las mías son azules. **a friend of ~** un amigo mío/una amiga mía

mine² /maɪn/ *n* mina *f*; (*Mil*) mina *f*. ●*vt* extraer. **~field** *n* campo *m* de minas. **~r** *n* minero *m*

mineral /ˈmɪnərəl/ *adj* & *n* mineral (*m*). **~ water** *n* agua *f* mineral

mingle /ˈmɪŋgl/ *vi* mezclarse

mini... /ˈmɪnɪ/ *pref* mini...

miniature /ˈmɪnɪtʃə(r)/ *n* miniatura *f*. ●*adj* en miniatura

mini: ~bus *n* microbús *m*. **~cab** *n* taxi *m* (que se pide por teléfono)

minim|al /ˈmɪnɪml/ *adj* mínimo. **~ize** *vt* reducir al mínimo. **~um** /-məm/ *adj* & *n* (*pl* **-ima** /-mə/) mínimo (*m*)

mining /ˈmaɪnɪŋ/ *n* minería *f*. ●*adj* minero

miniskirt /ˈmɪnɪskɜːt/ *n* minifalda *f*

minist|er /ˈmɪnɪstə(r)/ *n* ministro *m*, secretario *m* (*Mex*); (*Relig*) pastor *m*. **~erial** /-ˈstɪərɪəl/ *adj* ministerial. **~ry** *n* ministerio *m*, secretaría *f* (*Mex*)

mink /mɪŋk/ *n* visón *m*

minor /ˈmaɪnə(r)/ *adj* (*also Mus*) menor; (injury) leve; (change) pequeño; (operation) de poca importancia. ●*n* menor *m* & *f* de edad. **~ity** /maɪˈnɒrətɪ/ *n* minoría *f*. ●*adj* minoritario

minstrel /ˈmɪnstrəl/ *n* juglar *m*

mint /mɪnt/ *n* (*plant*) menta *f*; (*sweet*) pastilla *f* de menta; (*Finance*) casa *f* de la moneda. **in ~ condition** como nuevo. ●*vt* acuñar

minus /ˈmaɪnəs/ *prep* menos; (*fam, without*) sin. ●*n* (*sign*) menos *m*. **five ~ three is two** cinco menos tres is igual a dos. **~ sign** *n* (signo *m* de) menos *m*

minute¹ /ˈmɪnɪt/ *n* minuto *m*. **the ~s** *npl* (*of meeting*) el acta *f*

minute² /maɪˈnjuːt/ *adj* diminuto; (*detailed*) minucioso

mirac|le /ˈmɪrəkl/ *n* milagro *m*. **~ulous** /mɪˈrækjʊləs/ *adj* milagroso

mirage /ˈmɪrɑːʒ/ *n* espejismo *m*

mirror /ˈmɪrə(r)/ *n* espejo *m*; (*driving ~*) (espejo *m*) retrovisor *m*. •*vt* reflejar

mirth /mɜːθ/ *n* regocijo *m*; (*laughter*) risas *fpl*

misapprehension /mɪsæprɪˈhenʃn/ *n* malentendido *m*

misbehav|e /mɪsbɪˈheɪv/ *vi* portarse mal. **~iour** *n* mala conducta

miscalculat|e /mɪsˈkælkjʊleɪt/ *vt/i* calcular mal. **~ion** /-ˈleɪʃn/ *n* error *m* de cálculo

miscarr|iage /ˈmɪskærɪdʒ/ *n* aborto *m* espontáneo. **~iage of justice** *n* injusticia *f*. **~y** *vi* abortar

miscellaneous /mɪsəˈleɪnɪəs/ *adj* heterogéneo

mischie|f /ˈmɪstʃɪf/ *n* (*foolish conduct*) travesura *f*; (*harm*) daño *m*. **get into ~f** hacer travesuras. **make ~f** causar daños. **~vous** /ˈmɪstʃɪvəs/ *adj* travieso; (grin) pícaro

misconception /mɪskənˈsepʃn/ *n* equivocación *f*

misconduct /mɪsˈkɒndʌkt/ *n* mala conducta *f*

misdeed /mɪsˈdiːd/ *n* fechoría *f*

misdemeanour /mɪsdɪˈmiːnə(r)/ *n* delito *m* menor, falta *f*

miser /ˈmaɪzə(r)/ *n* avaro *m*

miserable /ˈmɪzərəbl/ *adj* (*sad*) triste; (*in low spirits*) abatido; (*wretched, poor*) mísero; (weather) pésimo

miserly /ˈmaɪzəlɪ/ *adj* avariento

misery /ˈmɪzərɪ/ *n* (*unhappiness*) tristeza *f*; (*pain*) sufrimiento *m*

misfire /mɪsˈfaɪə(r)/ *vi* fallar

misfit /ˈmɪsfɪt/ *n* inadaptado *m*

misfortune /mɪsˈfɔːtʃuːn/ *n* desgracia *f*

misgiving /mɪsˈgɪvɪŋ/ *n* recelo *m*

misguided /mɪsˈgaɪdɪd/ *adj* equivocado

mishap /ˈmɪshæp/ *n* percance *m*

misinform /mɪsɪnˈfɔːm/ *vt* informar mal

misinterpret /mɪsɪnˈtɜːprɪt/ *vt* interpretar mal

misjudge /mɪsˈdʒʌdʒ/ *vt* juzgar mal; (*miscalculate*) calcular mal

mislay /mɪsˈleɪ/ *vt* (*pt* **mislaid**) extraviar, perder

mislead /mɪsˈliːd/ *vt* (*pt* **misled** /mɪsˈled/) engañar. **~ing** *adj* engañoso

mismanage /mɪsˈmænɪdʒ/ *vt* administrar mal. **~ment** *n* mala administración *f*

misplace /mɪsˈpleɪs/ *vt* (*lose*) extraviar, perder

misprint /ˈmɪsprɪnt/ *n* errata *f*

miss /mɪs/ *vt* (*fail to hit*) no dar en; (*regret absence of*) echar de menos, extrañar (*LAm*); perder (train, party); perder (chance). **~ the point** no comprender. •*vi* errar el tiro, fallar; (bullet) no dar en el blanco. •*n* fallo *m*, falla *f* (*LAm*); (*title*) señorita *f*. □ **~ out** *vt* saltarse (line). **~out on sth** perderse algo

misshapen /mɪsˈʃeɪpən/ *adj* deforme

missile /ˈmɪsaɪl/ *n* (*Mil*) misil *m*

missing /ˈmɪsɪŋ/ *adj* (*lost*) perdido. **be ~** faltar. **go ~** desaparecer. **~ person** desaparecido *m*

mission /ˈmɪʃn/ *n* misión *f.* **~ary** /ˈmɪʃənərɪ/ *n* misionero *m*

mist /mɪst/ *n* neblina *f*; (*at sea*) bruma *f.* ▫ **~ up** *vi* empañarse

mistake /mɪˈsteɪk/ *n* error *m*. **make a ~** cometer un error. **by ~** por error. • *vt* (*pt* **mistook**, *pp* **mistaken**) confundir. **~ for** confundir con. **~n** /-ən/ *adj* equivocado. **be ~n** equivocarse

mistletoe /ˈmɪsltəʊ/ *n* muérdago *m*

mistreat /mɪsˈtri:t/ *vt* maltratar

mistress /ˈmɪstrɪs/ *n* (*of house*) señora *f*; (*lover*) amante *f*

mistrust /mɪsˈtrʌst/ *vt* desconfiar de. • *n* desconfianza *f.* **~ful** *adj* desconfiado

m

misty /ˈmɪstɪ/ *adj* (**-ier**, **-iest**) neblinoso; (day) de neblina. **it's ~** hay neblina

misunderstand /mɪsʌndəˈstænd/ *vt* (*pt* **-stood**) entender mal. **~ing** *n* malentendido *m*

misuse /mɪsˈju:z/ *vt* emplear mal; malversar (funds). • /mɪsˈju:s/ *n* mal uso *m*; (*unfair use*) abuso *m*; (*of funds*) malversación *f*

mite /maɪt/ *n* (*insect*) ácaro *m*

mitten /ˈmɪtn/ *n* mitón *m*

mix /mɪks/ *vt* mezclar. • *vi* mezclarse; (*go together*) combinar. **~ with** tratarse con (people). • *n* mezcla *f.* ▫ **~ up** *vt* mezclar; (*confuse*) confundir. **~ed** *adj* (school etc) mixto; (*assorted*) mezclado. **be ~ed up** estar confuso. **~er** *n* (*Culin*) batidora *f*; (*TV, machine*) mezcladora *f.* **~ture** /ˈmɪkstʃə(r)/ *n* mezcla *f.* **~-up** *n* lío *m*

moan /məʊn/ *n* gemido *m*. • *vi* gemir; (*complain*) quejarse (**about** de)

moat /məʊt/ *n* foso *m*

mob /mɒb/ *n* turba *f.* • *vt* (*pt* **mobbed**) acosar

mobil|e /ˈməʊbaɪl/ *adj* móvil. **~e home** *n* caravana *f* fija, trailer *m* (*LAm*). **~e (phone)** *n* (teléfono *m*) móvil *m*, (teléfono *m*) celular *m* (*LAm*). • *n* móvil *m*. **~ize** /ˈməʊbɪlaɪz/ *vt* movilizar. • *vi* movilizarse

mock /mɒk/ *vt* burlarse de. • *adj* (anger) fingido; (exam) de práctica. **~ery** /ˈmɒkərɪ/ *n* burla *f.* **make a ~ery of sth** ridiculizar algo

model /ˈmɒdl/ *n* (*example*) modelo *m*; (*mock-up*) maqueta *f*; (*person*) modelo *m*. • *adj* (*exemplary*) modelo; (car etc) en miniatura. • *vt* (*pt* **modelled**) modelar. **~ s.o. on s.o.** tomar a uno como modelo

modem /ˈməʊdem/ *n* (*Comp*) módem *m*

moderat|e /ˈmɒdərət/ *adj & n* moderado (*m*). • /ˈmɒdəreɪt/ *vt* moderar. **~ely** /ˈmɒdərətlɪ/ *adv* (*fairly*) medianamente. **~ion** /-ˈreɪʃn/ *n* moderación *f.* **in ~ion** con moderación

modern /ˈmɒdn/ *adj* moderno. **~ize** *vt* modernizar

modest /ˈmɒdɪst/ *adj* modesto. **~y** *n* modestia *f*

modif|ication /mɒdɪfɪˈkeɪʃn/ *n* modificación *f.* **~y** /-faɪ/ *vt* modificar

module /ˈmɒdju:l/ *n* módulo *m*

moist /mɔɪst/ *adj* (**-er**, **-est**) húmedo. **~en** /ˈmɔɪsn/ *vt* humedecer

moistur|e /ˈmɔɪstʃə(r)/ *n* humedad *f.* **~ize** *vt* hidratar. **~izer**, **~izing cream** *n* crema *f* hidratante

mole /məʊl/ *n* (*animal*) topo *m*; (*on skin*) lunar *m*

molecule /ˈmɒlɪkjuːl/ *n* molécula *f*

molest /məˈlest/ *vt* abusar (sexualmente) de

mollify /ˈmɒlɪfaɪ/ *vt* aplacar

mollusc /ˈmɒləsk/ *n* molusco *m*

mollycoddle /ˈmɒlɪkɒdl/ *vt* mimar

molten /ˈməʊltən/ *adj* fundido; (lava) líquido

mom /mɒm/ *n* (*Amer*, [!]) mamá *f* [!]

moment /ˈməʊmənt/ *n* momento *m*. **at the ~** en este momento. **for the ~** de momento. **~ary** /ˈməʊməntərɪ/ *adj* momentáneo

momentous /məˈmentəs/ *adj* trascendental

momentum /məˈmentəm/ *n* momento *m*; (*speed*) velocidad *f*

mommy /ˈmɒmɪ/ *n* (*Amer*, *fam*) mamá *m* [!]

monarch /ˈmɒnək/ *n* monarca *m*. **~y** *n* monarquía *f*

monastery /ˈmɒnəstərɪ/ *n* monasterio *m*

Monday /ˈmʌndeɪ/ *n* lunes *m*

money /ˈmʌnɪ/ *n* dinero *m*, plata *f* (*LAm*). **~box** *n* hucha *f*, alcancía *f* (*LAm*). **~ order** *n* giro *m* postal

mongrel /ˈmʌŋgrəl/ *n* perro *m* mestizo, chucho *m* [!]

monitor /ˈmɒnɪtə(r)/ *n* (*Tec*) monitor *m*. • *vt* observar (elections); seguir (progress); (*electronically*) monitorizar, escuchar

monk /mʌŋk/ *n* monje *m*. **~fish** *n* rape *m*

monkey /ˈmʌŋkɪ/ *n* mono *m*. **~-nut** *n* cacahuete *m*, cacahuate *m* (*Mex*), maní *m* (*LAm*). **~wrench** *n* llave *f* inglesa

mono /ˈmɒnəʊ/ *n* monofonía *f*

monologue /ˈmɒnəlɒg/ *n* monólogo *m*

monopol|ize /məˈnɒpəlaɪz/ *vt* monopolizar; acaparar (conversation). **~y** *n* monopolio *m*

monoton|e /ˈmɒnətəʊn/ *n* tono *m* monocorde. **~ous** /məˈnɒtənəs/ *adj* monótono. **~y** *n* monotonía *f*

monsoon /mɒnˈsuːn/ *n* monzón *m*

monst|er /ˈmɒnstə(r)/ *n* monstruo *m*. **~rous** /-strəs/ *adj* monstruoso

month /mʌnθ/ *n* mes *m*. **£200 a ~** 200 libras mensuales *or* al mes. **~ly** *adj* mensual. **~ly payment** mensualidad *f*, cuota *f* mensual (*LAm*). • *adv* mensualmente

monument /ˈmɒnjʊmənt/ *n* monumento *m*. **~al** /-ˈmentl/ *adj* monumental

moo /muː/ *n* mugido *m*. • *vi* mugir

mood /muːd/ *n* humor *m*. **be in a good/bad ~** estar de buen/mal humor. **~y** *adj* (**-ier**, **-iest**) temperamental; (*bad-tempered*) malhumorado

moon /muːn/ *n* luna *f*. **~light** *n* luz *f* de la luna. **~lighting** *n* pluriempleo *m*. **~lit** *adj* iluminado por la luna; (night) de luna

moor /mʊə(r)/ *n* páramo *m*; (*of heather*) brezal *m*. • *vt* amarrar. **~ing** *n* (*place*) amarradero *m*. **~ings** *npl* (*ropes*) amarras *fpl*

moose /muːs/ *n invar* alce *m* americano

mop /mɒp/ *n* fregona *f*, trapeador *m* (*LAm*). **~ of hair** pelambrera *f*. • *vt* (*pt* **mopped**). **~ (up)** limpiar

mope /məʊp/ *vi* estar abatido

moped /ˈməʊped/ *n* ciclomotor *m*

moral /ˈmɒrəl/ *adj* moral. ●*n* (*of tale*) moraleja *f*
morale /məˈrɑːl/ *n* moral *f*
moral|ity /məˈrælətɪ/ *n* moralidad *f*. **~ly** *adv* moralmente. **~s** *npl* moralidad *f*
morbid /ˈmɔːbɪd/ *adj* morboso
more /mɔː(r)/ *adj* más. **two ~ bottles** dos botellas más. ●*pron* más. **you ate ~ than me** comiste más que yo. **some ~** más. **~ than six** más de seis. **the ~ he has, the ~ he wants** cuánto más tiene, más quiere. ●*adv* más. **~ and ~** cada vez más. **~ or less** más o menos. **once ~** una vez más. **she doesn't live here any ~** ya no vive aquí. **~over** /mɔːˈrəʊvə(r)/ *adv* además
morgue /mɔːg/ *n* depósito *m* de cadáveres, morgue *f* (*LAm*)

m

morning /ˈmɔːnɪŋ/ *n* mañana *f*; (*early hours*) madrugada *f*. **at 11 o'clock in the ~** a las once de la mañana. **in the ~** por la mañana, en la mañana (*LAm*). **tomorrow/yesterday ~** mañana/ayer por la mañana *or* (*LAm*) en la mañana. **(good) ~!** ¡buenos días!
Moroc|can /məˈrɒkən/ *adj* & *n* marroquí (*m* & *f*). **~o** /-kəʊ/ *n* Marruecos *m*
moron /ˈmɔːrɒn/ *n* imbécil *m* & *f*
morose /məˈrəʊs/ *adj* taciturno
Morse /mɔːs/ *n* Morse *m*. **in ~ (code)** *n* en (código) morse
morsel /ˈmɔːsl/ *n* bocado *m*
mortal /ˈmɔːtl/ *adj* & *n* mortal (*m*). **~ity** /-ˈtælətɪ/ *n* mortalidad *f*
mortar /ˈmɔːtə(r)/ *n* (*all senses*) mortero *m*
mortgage /ˈmɔːgɪdʒ/ *n* hipoteca *f*. ●*vt* hipotecar
mortify /ˈmɔːtɪfaɪ/ *vt* darle mucha vergüenza a
mortuary /ˈmɔːtjʊərɪ/ *n* depósito *m* de cadáveres, morgue *f* (*LAm*)
mosaic /məʊˈzeɪk/ *n* mosaico *m*
mosque /mɒsk/ *n* mezquita *f*
mosquito /mɒsˈkiːtəʊ/ *n* (*pl* **-oes**) mosquito *m*, zancudo *m* (*LAm*)
moss /mɒs/ *n* musgo *m*
most /məʊst/ *adj* la mayoría de, la mayor parte de. **~ days** casi todos los días. ●*pron* la mayoría, la mayor parte. **at ~** como máximo. **make the ~ of** aprovechar al máximo. ●*adv* más; (*very*) muy; (*Amer, almost*) casi. **~ly** *adv* principalmente
MOT *n*. **~ (test)** ITV *f*, inspección *f* técnica de vehículos
motel /məʊˈtel/ *n* motel *m*
moth /mɒθ/ *n* mariposa *f* de la luz, palomilla *f*; (*in clothes*) polilla *f*
mother /ˈmʌðə(r)/ *n* madre *f*. ● *vt* mimar. **~-in-law** *n* (*pl* **~s-in-law**) suegra *f*. **~land** *n* patria *f*. **~ly** *adj* maternal. **~-of-pearl** *n* nácar *m*, madreperla *f*. **M~'s Day** *n* el día *m* de la Madre. **~-to-be** *n* futura madre *f*. **~ tongue** *n* lengua *f* materna
motif /məʊˈtiːf/ *n* motivo *m*
motion /ˈməʊʃn/ *n* movimiento *m*; (*proposal*) moción *f*. **put** *or* **set in ~** poner algo en marcha. ●*vt/i*. **~ (to) s.o. to** hacerle señas a uno para que. **~less** *adj* inmóvil
motiv|ate /ˈməʊtɪveɪt/ *vt* motivar. **~ation** /-ˈveɪʃn/ *n* motivación *f*. **~e** /ˈməʊtɪv/ *n* motivo *m*
motley /ˈmɒtlɪ/ *adj* variopinto
motor /ˈməʊtə(r)/ *n* motor *m*. ●*adj* motor; (*fem*) motora, motriz. **~ bike** *n* ☐ motocicleta *f*, moto *f* ☐. **~ boat** *n* lancha *f* a motor. **~ car** *n* automóvil *m*. **~ cycle** *n* motocicleta *f*. **~cyclist** *n* motoci-

clista *m & f.* **~ing** *n* automovilismo *m.* **~ist** *n* automovilista *m & f.* **~way** *n* autopista *f*

motto /'mɒtəʊ/ *n* (*pl* **-oes**) lema *m*

mould /məʊld/ *n* molde *m*; (*fungus*) moho *m.* •*vt* moldear; formar (character). **~ing** *n* (*on wall etc*) moldura *f.* **~y** *adj* mohoso

moult /məʊlt/ *vi* mudar de pelo/piel/plumas

mound /maʊnd/ *n* montículo *m*; (*pile, fig*) montón *m*

mount /maʊnt/ *vt* montar (horse); engarzar (gem); preparar (attack). •*vi* subir, crecer. •*n.* montura *f*; (*mountain*) monte *m.* □ **~ up** *vi* irse acumulando

mountain /'maʊntɪn/ *n* montaña *f.* **~eer** /maʊntɪ'nɪə(r)/ *n* alpinista *m & f.* **~eering** *n* alpinismo *m.* **~ous** *adj* montañoso

mourn /mɔːn/ *vt* llorar. •*vi* lamentarse. **~ for s.o.** llorar a uno. **~er** *n* doliente *m & f.* **~ful** *adj* triste. **~ing** *n* duelo *m*, luto *m.* **be in ~ing** estar de duelo

mouse /maʊs/ *n* (*pl* **mice**) ratón *m.* **~trap** *n* ratonera *f*

mousse /muːs/ *n* (*Culin*) mousse *f or m*; (*for hair*) mousse *f*

moustache /mə'stɑːʃ/ *n* bigote *m*

mouth /maʊθ/ *n* boca *f*; (*of cave*) entrada *f*; (*of river*) desembocadura *f.* **~ful** *n* bocado *m.* **~-organ** *n* armónica *f.* **~wash** *n* enjuague *m* bucal

move /muːv/ *vt* mover; (*relocate*) trasladar; (*with emotion*) conmover; (*propose*) proponer. **~ the television** cambiar de lugar la televisión. **~ house** mudarse de casa. •*vi* moverse; (*be in motion*) estar en movimiento; (*take action*) tomar medidas. •*n* movimiento *m*; (*in game*) jugada *f*; (*player's turn*) turno *m*; (*removal*) mudanza *f.* □ **~ away** *vi* alejarse. □ **~ in** *vi* instalarse. **~ in with s.o.** irse a vivir con uno. □ **~ over** *vi* correrse. **~ment** *n* movimiento *m*

movie /'muːvɪ/ *n* (*Amer*) película *f.* **the ~s** *npl* el cine. **~ camera** *n* (*Amer*) tomavistas *m*, filmadora *f* (*LAm*)

moving /'muːvɪŋ/ *adj* en movimiento; (*touching*) conmovedor

mow /məʊ/ *vt* (*pt* **mowed** *or* **mown** /məʊn/) cortar (lawn); segar (hay). □ **~ down** *vt* acribillar. **~er** *n* (*for lawn*) cortacésped *m*

MP *abbr see* **Member of Parliament**

Mr /'mɪstə(r)/ *abbr* (*pl* **Messrs**) (= **Mister**) Sr. **~ Coldbeck** Sr. Coldbeck

Mrs /'mɪsɪz/ *abbr* (*pl* **Mrs**) (= **Missis**) Sra. **~ Andrews** Sra. Andrews

Ms /mɪz/ *abbr* (title of married or unmarried woman)

MSc *abbr see* **Master**

much /mʌtʃ/ *adj & pron* mucho, mucha. •*adv* mucho; (*before pp*) muy. **~ as** por mucho que. **~ the same** más o menos lo mismo. **how ~?** ¿cuánto?. **so ~** tanto. **too ~** demasiado

muck /mʌk/ *n* estiércol *m*; (*fam, dirt*) mugre *f.* □ **~ about** *vi* 🄸 tontear

mud /mʌd/ *n* barro *m*, lodo *m*

muddle /'mʌdl/ *vt* embrollar. •*n* desorden *m*; (*mix-up*) lío *m.* □ **~ through** *vi* salir del paso

muddy *adj* lodoso; (hands etc) cubierto de lodo. **~guard** *n* guardabarros *m*, salpicadera *f* (*Mex*)

muffle /'mʌfl/ *vt* amortiguar (sound). **~r** *n* (*scarf*) bufanda *f*;

(*Amer, Auto*) silenciador *m*

mug /mʌg/ *n* taza *f* (*alta y sin platillo*), tarro *m* (*Mex*); (*for beer*) jarra *f*; (*fam, face*) cara *f*, jeta *f* ☒; (*fam, fool*) idiota *m & f*. ● *vt* (*pt* **mugged**) asaltar. **~ger** *n* asaltante *m & f*. **~ging** *n* asalto *m*

muggy /ˈmʌgɪ/ *adj* bochornoso

mule /mju:l/ *n* mula *f*

mull /mʌl/ (*Amer*). **~ over** *vt* reflexionar sobre

multi|coloured /mʌltɪˈkʌləd/ *adj* multicolor. **~national** /-ˈnæʃənl/ *adj & n* multinacional (*f*)

multipl|e /ˈmʌltɪpl/ *adj* múltiple. ● *n* múltiplo *m*. **~ication** /mʌltɪplɪˈkeɪʃn/ *n* multiplicación *f*. **~y** /ˈmʌltɪplaɪ/ *vt* multiplicar. ● *vi* (*Math*) multiplicar; (*increase*) multiplicarse

multitude /ˈmʌltɪtju:d/ *n*. **a ~ of problems** múltiples problemas

mum /mʌm/ *n* ⓘ mamá *f* ⓘ

mumble /ˈmʌmbl/ *vt* mascullar. ● *vi* hablar entre dientes

mummy /ˈmʌmɪ/ *n* (*fam, mother*) mamá *f* ⓘ; (*archaeology*) momia *f*

mumps /mʌmps/ *n* paperas *fpl*

munch /mʌntʃ/ *vt/i* mascar

mundane /mʌnˈdeɪn/ *adj* mundano

municipal /mju:ˈnɪsɪpl/ *adj* municipal

mural /ˈmjʊərəl/ *adj & n* mural (*f*)

murder /ˈmɜ:də(r)/ *n* asesinato *m*. ● *vt* asesinar. **~er** *n* asesino *m*

murky /ˈmɜ:kɪ/ *adj* (**-ier**, **-iest**) turbio

murmur /ˈmɜ:mə(r)/ *n* murmullo *m*. ● *vt/i* murmurar

musc|le /ˈmʌsl/ *n* músculo *m*. **~ular** /ˈmʌskjʊlə(r)/ *adj* muscular; (arm, body) musculoso

muse /mju:z/ *vi* meditar (**on** sobre)

museum /mju:ˈzɪəm/ *n* museo *m*

mush /mʌʃ/ *n* papilla *f*

mushroom /ˈmʌʃrʊm/ *n* champiñón *m*; (*in botany*) seta *f*. ● *vi* aparecer como hongos

mushy /ˈmʌʃɪ/ *adj* blando

music /ˈmju:zɪk/ *n* música *f*. **~al** *adj* musical. **be ~** tener sentido musical. ● *n* musical *m*. **~ian** /mju:ˈzɪʃn/ *n* músico *m*

Muslim /ˈmʊzlɪm/ *adj & n* musulmán (*m*)

mussel /ˈmʌsl/ *n* mejillón *m*

must /mʌst/ *modal verb* deber, tener que; (*expressing supposition*) deber (de). **he ~ be old** debe (de) ser viejo. **I ~ have done it** debo (de) haberlo hecho. ● *n*. **be a ~** ser imprescindible

mustache /ˈmʌstæʃ/ *n* (*Amer*) bigote *m*

mustard /ˈmʌstəd/ *n* mostaza *f*

muster /ˈmʌstə(r)/ *vt* reunir

musty /ˈmʌstɪ/ *adj* (**-ier**, **-iest**) que huele a humedad

mutation /mju:ˈteɪʃn/ *n* mutación *f*

mute /mju:t/ *adj* mudo

mutilate /ˈmju:tɪleɪt/ *vt* mutilar

mutiny /ˈmju:tɪnɪ/ *n* motín *m*. ● *vi* amotinarse

mutter /ˈmʌtə(r)/ *vt/i* murmurar

mutton /ˈmʌtn/ *n* carne *f* de ovino

mutual /ˈmju:tʃʊəl/ *adj* mutuo; (*fam, common*) común

muzzle /ˈmʌzl/ *n* (*snout*) hocico *m*; (*device*) bozal *m*

my /maɪ/ *adj* (*sing*) mi; (*pl*) mis

myself /maɪˈself/ *pron* (*reflexive*) me; (*used for emphasis*) yo mismo *m*, yo misma *f*. **I cut ~** me corté. **I made it ~** lo hice yo mismo/ misma. **I was by ~** estaba solo/ sola

myster|ious /mɪˈstɪərɪəs/ *adj* misterioso. **~y** /ˈmɪstərɪ/ *n* misterio *m*

mystical /ˈmɪstɪkl/ *adj* místico

mystify /ˈmɪstɪfaɪ/ *vt* dejar perplejo

mystique /mɪˈstiːk/ *n* mística *f*

myth /mɪθ/ *n* mito *m*. **~ical** *adj* mítico. **~ology** /mɪˈθɒlədʒɪ/ *n* mitología *f*

Nn

N *abbr* (= **north**) N

nab /næb/ *vt* (*pt* **nabbed**) (*sl, arrest*) pescar; (*snatch*) agarrar

nag /næg/ *vt* (*pt* **nagged**) fastidiar; (*scold*) estarle encima a. ● *vi* criticar

nail /neɪl/ *n* clavo *m*; (*of finger, toe*) uña *f*. **~ polish** esmalte *m* para las uñas. ● *vt*. **~ (down)** clavar

naive /naɪˈiːv/ *adj* ingenuo

naked /ˈneɪkɪd/ *adj* desnudo. **to the ~ eye** a simple vista

name /neɪm/ *n* nombre *m*; (*of book, film*) título *m*; (*fig*) fama *f*. **my ~ is Chris** me llamo Chris. **good ~** buena reputación. ● *vt* ponerle nombre a; (*appoint*) nombrar. **a man ~d Jones** un hombre llamado Jones. **she was ~d after** *or* (*Amer*) **for her grandmother** le pusieron el nombre de su abuela. **~less** *adj* anónimo. **~ly** *adv* a saber. **~sake** *n* (*person*) tocayo *m*

nanny /ˈnænɪ/ *n* niñera *f*

nap /næp/ *n* (*sleep*) sueñecito *m*; (*after lunch*) siesta *f*. **have a ~** echarse un sueño

napkin /ˈnæpkɪn/ *n* servilleta *f*

nappy /ˈnæpɪ/ *n* pañal *m*

narcotic /nɑːˈkɒtɪk/ *adj & n* narcótico (*m*)

narrat|e /nəˈreɪt/ *vt* narrar. **~ive** /ˈnærətɪv/ *n* narración *f*. **~or** /nəˈreɪtə(r)/ *n* narrador *m*

narrow /ˈnærəʊ/ *adj* (**-er, -est**) estrecho, angosto (*LAm*). **have a ~ escape** salvarse de milagro. ● *vt* estrechar; (*limit*) limitar. ● *vi* estrecharse. **~ly** *adv* (*just*) por poco. **~-minded** /-ˈmaɪndɪd/ *adj* de miras estrechas

nasal /ˈneɪzl/ *adj* nasal; (voice) gangoso

nasty /ˈnɑːstɪ/ *adj* (**-ier, -iest**) desagradable; (*spiteful*) malo (**to** con); (taste, smell) asqueroso; (cut) feo

nation /ˈneɪʃn/ *n* nación *f*

national /ˈnæʃənl/ *adj* nacional. ● *n* ciudadano *m*. **~ anthem** *n* himno *m* nacional. **~ism** *n* nacionalismo *m*. **~ity** /næʃəˈnælətɪ/ *n* nacionalidad *f*. **~ize** *vt* nacionalizar. **~ly** *adv* a escala nacional

> **National Trust** Fundación británica cuyo objetivo es la conservación de lugares de interés histórico o de belleza natural. Se financia mediante legados y subvenciones privadas. Es la mayor propietaria de tierras de Gran Bretaña. En Escocia, es independiente y recibe el nombre de *National Trust for Scotland*.

nationwide /ˈneɪʃnwaɪd/ *adj & adv* a escala nacional

native /ˈneɪtɪv/ *n* natural *m & f*. **be**

a ~ **of** ser natural de. ● *adj* nativo; (country, town) natal; (language) materno; (plant, animal) autóctono. **N~ American** indio *m* americano

nativity /nəˈtɪvətɪ/ *n.* **the N~** la Natividad *f*

NATO /ˈneɪtəʊ/ *abbr* (= **North Atlantic Treaty Organization**) OTAN *f*

natter /ˈnætə(r)/ 🅸 *vi* charlar. ● *n* charla *f*

natural /ˈnætʃərəl/ *adj* natural. ~ **history** *n* historia *f* natural. **~ist** *n* naturalista *m & f*. **~ized** *adj* (citizen) naturalizado. **~ly** *adv* (*of course*) naturalmente; (*by nature*) por naturaleza

nature /ˈneɪtʃə(r)/ *n* naturaleza *f*; (*of person*) carácter *m*; (*of things*) naturaleza *f*

naught /nɔːt/ *n* cero *m*

naughty /ˈnɔːtɪ/ *adj* (**-ier, -iest**) malo, travieso

nause|a /ˈnɔːzɪə/ *n* náuseas *fpl*. **~ous** /-ɪəs/ *adj* nauseabundo

nautical /ˈnɔːtɪkl/ *adj* náutico. ~ **mile** *n* milla *f* marina

naval /ˈneɪvl/ *adj* naval; (officer) de marina

nave /neɪv/ *n* nave *f*

navel /ˈneɪvl/ *n* ombligo *m*

naviga|ble /ˈnævɪgəbl/ *adj* navegable. **~te** /ˈnævɪgeɪt/ *vt* navegar por (sea etc); gobernar (ship). ● *vi* navegar. **~tion** /-ˈgeɪʃn/ *n* navegación *f*. **~tor** *n* oficial *m & f* de derrota

navy /ˈneɪvɪ/ *n* marina *f* de guerra. ~ **(blue)** *a & n* azul (*m*) marino

NE *abbr* (= **north-east**) NE

near /ˈnɪə(r)/ *adv* cerca. **draw ~** acercarse. ● *prep.* ~ **(to)** cerca de. **go ~ (to) sth** acercarse a algo. ● *adj* cercano. ● *vt* acercarse a. **~by** *adj* cercano. **~ly** *adv* casi. **he ~ly died** por poco se muere, casi se muere. **not ~ly** ni con mucho. **~sighted** /-ˈsaɪtɪd/ *adj* miope, corto de vista

neat /niːt/ *adj* (**-er, -est**) (person) pulcro; (room etc) bien arreglado; (*ingenious*) hábil; (whisky, gin) solo; ; (*Amer fam, great*) fantástico 🅸. **~ly** *adv* pulcramente; (organized) cuidadosamente

necessar|ily /nesəˈserɪlɪ/ *adv* necesariamente. **~y** /ˈnesəserɪ/ *adj* necesario

necessit|ate /nəˈsesɪteɪt/ *vt* exigir. **~y** /nɪˈsesətɪ/ *n* necesidad *f*. **the bare ~ies** lo indispensable

neck /nek/ *n* (*of person, bottle, dress*) cuello *m*; (*of animal*) pescuezo *m*. ~ **and** ~ a la par, parejos (*LAm*). **~lace** /ˈnekləs/ *n* collar *m*. **~line** *n* escote *m*

nectar /ˈnektə(r)/ *n* néctar *m*

nectarine /ˈnektərɪn/ *n* nectarina *f*

née /neɪ/ *adj* de soltera

need /niːd/ *n* necesidad *f* (**for** de). ● *vt* necesitar; (*demand*) exigir. **you ~ not speak** no tienes que hablar

needle /ˈniːdl/ *n* aguja *f*. ● *vt* (*fam, annoy*) pinchar

needless /ˈniːdlɪs/ *adj* innecesario

needlework /ˈniːdlwɜːk/ *n* labores *fpl* de aguja; (*embroidery*) bordado *m*

needy /ˈniːdɪ/ *adj* (**-ier, -iest**) necesitado

negative /ˈnegətɪv/ *adj* negativo. ● *n* (*of photograph*) negativo *m*; (*no*) negativa *f*

neglect /nɪˈglekt/ *vt* descuidar (house); desatender (children); no cumplir con (duty). ● *n* negligencia

f. **(state of)** ~ abandono *m.* **~ful** *adj* negligente
neglig|ence /'neglɪdʒəns/ *n* negligencia *f*, descuido *m.* **~ent** *adj* negligente. **~ible** /'neglɪdʒəbl/ *adj* insignificante
negotia|ble /nɪ'gəʊʃəbl/ *adj* negociable. **~te** /nɪ'gəʊʃɪeɪt/ *vt/i* negociar. **~tion** /-'eɪʃn/ *n* negociación *f.* **~tor** *n* negociador *m*
neigh /neɪ/ *vi* relinchar
neighbour /'neɪbə(r)/ *n* vecino *m.* **~hood** *n* vecindad *f*, barrio *m.* **in the ~hood of** alrededor de. **~ing** *adj* vecino
neither /'naɪðə(r)/ *adj.* **~ book** ninguno de los libros. ● *pron* ninguno, -na. ● *conj.* **neither...nor** ni...ni. **~ do I** yo tampoco
neon /'ni:ɒn/ *n* neón *m.* ● *adj* (lamp etc) de neón
nephew /'nevju:/ *n* sobrino *m*
Neptune /'neptju:n/ *n* Neptuno *m*
nerv|e /nɜ:v/ *n* nervio *m*; (*courage*) valor *m*; (*calm*) sangre *f* fría; (*fam, impudence*) descaro *m.* **~es** *npl* (*before exams etc*) nervios *mpl.* **get on s.o.'s ~es** ponerle los nervios de punta a uno. **~e-racking** *adj* exasperante. **~ous** /'nɜ:vəs/ *adj* nervioso. **be/feel ~ous** estar nervioso. **~ousness** *n* nerviosismo *m.* **~y** /'nɜ:vɪ/ *adj* nervioso; (*Amer fam*) descarado
nest /nest/ *n* nido *m.* ● *vi* anidar
nestle /'nesl/ *vi* acurrucarse
net /net/ *n* red *f.* **the N~** (*Comp*) la Red. ● *vt* (*pt* **netted**) pescar (*con red*) (fish). ● *adj* neto. **~ball** *n especie de baloncesto*
Netherlands /'neðələndz/ *npl.* **the ~** los Países Bajos
netting /'netɪŋ/ *n* redes *fpl.* **wire ~** tela *f* metálica
nettle /'netl/ *n* ortiga *f*
network /'netwɜ:k/ *n* red *f*; (*TV*) cadena *f*
neuro|sis /njʊə'rəʊsɪs/ *n* (*pl* **-oses** /-si:z/) neurosis *f.* **~tic** /-'rɒtɪk/ *adj & n* neurótico (*m*)
neuter /'nju:tə(r)/ *adj & n* neutro (*m*). ● *vt* castrar (animals)
neutral /'nju:trəl/ *adj* neutral; (colour) neutro; (*Elec*) neutro. **~ (gear)** (*Auto*) punto *m* muerto. **~ize** *vt* neutralizar
neutron /'nju:trɒn/ *n* neutrón *m*
never /nevə(r)/ *adv* nunca; (*more emphatic*) jamás; (*fam, not*) no. **~ again** nunca más. **he ~ smiles** no sonríe nunca, nunca sonríe. **I ~ saw him** 🅸 no lo vi. **~-ending** *adj* interminable. **~theless** /-ðə'les/ *adv* sin embargo, no obstante
new /nju:/ *adj* (**-er**, **-est**) nuevo. **~born** *adj* recién nacido. **~comer** *n* recién llegado *m.* **~fangled** /-'fæŋgld/ *adj* (*pej*) moderno. **~ly** *adv* recién. **~ly-weds** *npl* recién casados *mpl*
news /nju:z/ *n.* **a piece of ~** una noticia. **good/bad ~** buenas/malas noticias. **the ~** (*TV, Radio*) las noticias. **~agent** *n* vendedor *m* de periódicos. **~caster** *n* locutor *m.* **~dealer** *n* (*Amer*) *see* **~AGENT**. **~flash** *n* información *f* de última hora. **~letter** *n* boletín *m*, informativo *m.* **~paper** *n* periódico *m*, diario *m.* **~reader** *n* locutor *m*
newt /nju:t/ *n* tritón *m*
New Year /nju:'jɪə(r)/ *n* Año *m* Nuevo. **N~'s Day** *n* día *m* de Año Nuevo. **N~'s Eve** *n* noche *f* vieja, noche *f* de fin de Año
New Zealand /njʊ:'zi:lənd/ *n* Nueva Zeland(i)a *f*
next /nekst/ *adj* próximo; (week,

month etc) que viene, próximo; (*adjoining*) vecino; (*following*) siguiente. • *adv* luego, después. ~ **to** al lado de. **when you see me ~** la próxima vez que me veas. ~ **to nothing** casi nada. ~ **door** al lado (**to** de). **~-door** *adj* de al lado. ~ **of kin** *n* familiar(es) *m(pl)* más cercano(s)

nib /nɪb/ *n* plumilla *f*

nibble /ˈnɪbl/ *vt/i* mordisquear. • *n* mordisco *m*

Nicaragua /nɪkəˈrægjʊə/ *n* Nicaragua *f*. **~n** *adj & n* nicaragüense (*m & f*)

nice /naɪs/ *adj* (**-er**, **-est**) agradable; (*likeable*) simpático; (*kind*) amable; (weather, food) bueno. **we had a ~ time** lo pasamos bien. **~ly** *adv* (*kindly*) amablemente; (*politely*) con buenos modales

niche /nɪtʃ, niːʃ/ *n* nicho *m*

n **nick** /nɪk/ *n* corte *m* pequeño. **in the ~ of time** justo a tiempo. • *vt* (*sl, steal*) afanar ☒

nickel /ˈnɪkl/ *n* (*metal*) níquel *m*; (*Amer*) moneda *f* de cinco centavos

nickname /ˈnɪkneɪm/ *n* apodo *m*. • *vt* apodar

nicotine /ˈnɪkətiːn/ *n* nicotina *f*

niece /niːs/ *n* sobrina *f*

niggling /ˈnɪglɪŋ/ *adj* (doubt) constante

night /naɪt/ *n* noche *f*; (*evening*) tarde *f*. **at ~** por la noche, de noche. **good ~** ¡buenas noches! • *adj* nocturno, de noche. **~cap** *n* (*drink*) bebida *f* (tomada antes de acostarse). **~club** *n* club *m* nocturno. **~dress** *n* camisón *m*. **~fall** *n* anochecer *m*. **~gown**, **~ie** /ˈnaɪtɪ/ ☐ *n* camisón *m*. **~life** *n* vida *f* nocturna. **~ly** *adj* de todas las noches. **~mare** *n* pesadilla *f*. **~ school** *n* escuela *f* nocturna. **~-time** *n* noche *f*. **~watchman** *n* sereno *m*

nil /nɪl/ *n* nada *f*; (*Sport*) cero *m*

nimble /ˈnɪmbl/ *adj* (**-er**, **-est**) ágil

nine /naɪn/ *adj & n* nueve (*m*). **~teen** /naɪnˈtiːn/ *adj & n* diecinueve (*m*). **~teenth** *adj* decimonoveno. • *n* diecinueveavo *m*. **~tieth** /ˈnaɪntɪəθ/ *adj* nonagésimo. • *n* noventavo *m*. **~ty** *adj & n* noventa (*m*)

ninth /ˈnaɪnθ/ *adj & n* noveno (*m*)

nip /nɪp/ *vt* (*pt* **nipped**) (*pinch*) pellizcar; (*bite*) mordisquear. • *vi* (*fam, rush*) correr

nipple /ˈnɪpl/ *n* (*of woman*) pezón *m*; (*of man*) tetilla *f*; (*of baby's bottle*) tetina *f*, chupón *m* (*Mex*)

nippy /ˈnɪpɪ/ *adj* (**-ier**, **-iest**) (*fam, chilly*) fresquito

nitrogen /ˈnaɪtrədʒən/ *n* nitrógeno *m*

no /nəʊ/ *adj* ninguno, (*before masculine singular noun*) ningún. **I have ~ money** no tengo dinero. **there's ~ food left** no queda nada de comida. **it has ~ windows** no tiene ventanas. **I'm ~ expert** no soy ningún experto. **~ smoking** prohibido fumar. **~ way!** ☐ ¡ni hablar! • *adv & int* no. • *n* (*pl* **noes**) no *m*

noble /ˈnəʊbl/ *adj* (**-er**, **-est**) noble. **~man** /-mən/ *n* noble *m*

nobody /ˈnəʊbədɪ/ *pron* nadie. **there's ~ there** no hay nadie

nocturnal /nɒkˈtɜːnl/ *adj* nocturno

nod /nɒd/ *vt* (*pt* **nodded**). **~ one's head** asentir con la cabeza. • *vi* (*in agreement*) asentir con la cabeza; (*in greeting*) saludar con la cabeza.

▫ **~ off** *vi* dormirse

nois|e /nɔɪz/ *n* ruido *m*. **~ily** *adv* ruidosamente. **~y** *adj* (**-ier**, **-iest**) ruidoso. **it's too ~y here** hay demasiado ruido aquí

nomad /ˈnəʊmæd/ *n* nómada *m & f*. **~ic** /-ˈmædɪk/ *adj* nómada

no man's land *n* tierra *f* de nadie

nominat|e /ˈnɒmɪneɪt/ *vt* (*put forward*) proponer; postular (*LAm*); (*appoint*) nombrar. **~ion** /-ˈneɪʃn/ *n* nombramiento *m*; (*Amer, Pol*) proclamación *f*

non-... /nɒn/ *pref* no ...

nonchalant /ˈnɒnʃələnt/ *adj* despreocupado

non-committal /nɒnkəˈmɪtl/ *adj* evasivo

nondescript /ˈnɒndɪskrɪpt/ *adj* anodino

none /nʌn/ *pron* ninguno, ninguna. **there were ~ left** no quedaba ninguno/ninguna. **~ of us** ninguno de nosotros. ● *adv* no, de ninguna manera. **he is ~ the happier** no está más contento

nonentity /nɒˈnentətɪ/ *n* persona *f* insignificante

non-existent /nɒnɪgˈzɪstənt/ *adj* inexistente

nonplussed /nɒnˈplʌst/ *adj* perplejo

nonsens|e /ˈnɒnsns/ *n* tonterías *fpl*, disparates *mpl*. **~ical** /-ˈsensɪkl/ *adj* disparatado

non-smoker /nɒnˈsməʊkə(r)/ *n* no fumador *m*. **I'm a ~** no fumo

non-stop /nɒnˈstɒp/ *adj* (train) directo; (flight) sin escalas. ● *adv* sin parar; (*by train*) directamente; (*by air*) sin escalas

noodles /ˈnu:dlz/ *npl* fideos *mpl*

nook /nʊk/ *n* rincón *m*

noon /nu:n/ *n* mediodía *m*

no-one /ˈnəʊwʌn/ *pron* nadie

noose /nu:s/ *n* soga *f*

nor /nɔ:(r)/ *conj* ni, tampoco. **neither blue ~ red** ni azul ni rojo. **he doesn't play the piano, ~ do I** no sabe tocar el piano, ni yo tampoco

norm /nɔ:m/ *n* norma *f*

normal /ˈnɔ:ml/ *adj* normal. **~cy** *n* (*Amer*) normalidad *f*. **~ity** /-ˈmælətɪ/ *n* normalidad *f*. **~ly** *adv* normalmente

north /nɔ:θ/ *n* norte *m*. ● *adj* norte. ● *adv* hacia el norte. **N~ America** *n* América *f* del Norte, Norteamérica *f*. **N~ American** *adj & n* norteamericano (*m*). **~east** *n* nor(d)este *m*. ● *adj* nor(d)este. ● *adv* (go) hacia el nor(d)este. **it's ~east of Leeds** está al nor(d)este de Leeds. **~erly** /ˈnɔ:ðəlɪ/ *adj* (wind) del norte. **~ern** /ˈnɔ:ðən/ *adj* del norte. **~erner** *n* norteño *m*. **N~ern Ireland** *n* Irlanda *f* del Norte. **N~ Sea** *n* mar *m* del Norte. **~ward** /ˈnɔ:θwəd/, **~wards** *adv* hacia el norte. **~west** *n* noroeste *m*. ● *adj* noroeste. ● *adv* hacia el noroeste

Norw|ay /ˈnɔ:weɪ/ *n* Noruega *f*. **~egian** /-ˈwi:dʒən/ *adj & n* noruego (*m*)

nose /nəʊz/ *n* nariz *f*. **~bleed** *n* hemorragia *f* nasal. **~dive** *vi* descender en picado, descender en picada (*LAm*)

nostalgi|a /nɒˈstældʒə/ *n* nostalgia *f*. **~c** *adj* nostálgico

nostril /ˈnɒstrɪl/ *n* ventana *f* de la nariz *f*

nosy /ˈnəʊzɪ/ *adj* (**-ier**, **-iest**) 🄸 entrometido, metiche (*LAm*)

not /nɒt/

Cuando **not** va precedido del verbo auxiliar **do** or **have** o de un verbo modal como **should** etc, se suele emplear la forma contraída **don't, haven't, shouldn't** etc

adverb

····➤no. **I don't know** no sé. **~ yet** todavía no. **~ me** yo no

····➤(*replacing a clause*) **I suppose ~** supongo que no. **of course ~** por supuesto que no. **are you going to help me or ~?** ¿me vas a ayudar o no?

····➤(*emphatic*) ni. **~ a penny more!** ¡ni un penique más!

····➤(*in phrases*) **certainly ~** de ninguna manera . **~ you again!** ¡tú otra vez!

n

notabl|e /'nəʊtəbl/ *adj* notable; (author) distinguido. **~y** /'nəʊtəblɪ/ *adv* notablemente; (*in particular*) particularmente

notch /nɒtʃ/ *n* muesca *f.* □ **~ up** *vt* apuntarse

note /nəʊt/ *n* (*incl Mus*) nota *f*; (*banknote*) billete *m.* **take ~s** tomar apuntes. ●*vt* (*notice*) observar; (*record*) anotar. □ **~ down** *vt* apuntar. **~book** *n* cuaderno *m.* **~d** *adj* célebre. **~paper** *n* papel *m* de carta(s)

nothing /'nʌθɪŋ/ *pron* nada. **he eats ~** no come nada. **for ~** (*free*) gratis; (*in vain*) en vano. **~ else** nada más. **~ much happened** no pasó gran cosa. **he does ~ but complain** no hace más que quejarse

notice /'nəʊtɪs/ *n* (*sign*) letrero *m*; (*item of information*) anuncio *m*; (*notification*) aviso *m*; (*of termination of employment*) preaviso *m*; **~ (of dismissal)** despido *m.* **take ~ of** hacer caso a (person). ●*vt* notar. ●*vi* darse cuenta. **~able** *adj* perceptible. **~ably** *adv* perceptiblemente. **~board** *n* tablón *m* de anuncios, tablero *m* de anuncios (*LAm*)

notif|ication /nəʊtɪfɪ'keɪʃn/ *n* notificación *f.* **~y** /'nəʊtɪfaɪ/ *vt* informar; (*in writing*) notificar. **~y s.o. of sth** comunicarle algo a uno

notion /'nəʊʃn/ *n* (*concept*) concepto *m*; (*idea*) idea *f*

notorious /nəʊ'tɔ:rɪəs/ *adj* notorio

notwithstanding /nɒtwɪθ'stændɪŋ/ *prep* a pesar de. ●*adv* no obstante

nougat /'nu:gɑ:/ *n* turrón *m*

nought /nɔ:t/ *n* cero *m*

noun /naʊn/ *n* sustantivo *m*, nombre *m*

nourish /'nʌrɪʃ/ *vt* alimentar. **~ment** *n* alimento *m*

novel /'nɒvl/ *n* novela *f.* ●*adj* original, novedoso. **~ist** *n* novelista *m & f.* **~ty** *n* novedad *f*

November /nəʊ'vembə(r)/ *n* noviembre *m*

novice /'nɒvɪs/ *n* principiante *m & f*

now /naʊ/ *adv* ahora. **~ and again**, **~ and then** de vez en cuando. **right ~** ahora mismo. **from ~ on** a partir de ahora. ●*conj.* **~ (that)** ahora que. **~adays** /'naʊədeɪz/ *adv* hoy (en) día

nowhere /'nəʊweə(r)/ *adv* por ninguna parte, por ningún lado; (*after motion towards*) a ninguna

parte, a ningún lado
nozzle /'nɒzl/ *n* (*on hose*) boca *f*; (*on fire extinguisher*) boquilla *f*
nuance /'njuɑ:ns/ *n* matiz *m*
nuclear /'nju:klɪə(r)/ *adj* nuclear
nucleus /'nju:klɪəs/ *n* (*pl* **-lei** /-lɪaɪ/) núcleo *m*
nude /nju:d/ *adj & n* desnudo (*m*). **in the ~** desnudo
nudge /nʌdʒ/ *vt* codear (ligeramente). ●*n* golpe *m* (suave) con el codo
nudi|st /'nju:dɪst/ *n* nudista *m & f*. **~ty** /'nju:dətɪ/ *n* desnudez *f*
nuisance /'nju:sns/ *n* (*thing, event*) molestia *f*, fastidio *m*; (*person*) pesado *m*
null /nʌl/ *adj* nulo
numb /nʌm/ *adj* entumecido. **go ~** entumecerse ●*vt* entumecer
number /'nʌmbə(r)/ *n* número *m*; (*telephone number*) número *m* de teléfono. **a ~ of people** varias personas. ●*vt* numerar; (*count, include*) contar. **~plate** *n* matrícula *f*, placa *f* (*LAm*)
numer|al /'nju:mərəl/ *n* número *m*. **~ical** /nju:'merɪkl/ *adj* numérico. **~ous** /'nju:mərəs/ *adj* numeroso
nun /nʌn/ *n* monja *f*
nurse /nɜ:s/ *n* enfermero *m*, enfermera *f*; (*nanny*) niñera *f*. ●*vt* cuidar; abrigar (hope etc)
nursery /'nɜ:sərɪ/ *n* (*for plants*) vivero *m*; (*day ~*) guardería *f*. **~ rhyme** *n* canción *f* infantil. **~ school** *n* jardín *m* de infancia, jardín *m* infantil (*LAm*)
nursing home /'nɜ:sɪŋ/ *n* (*for older people*) residencia *f* de ancianos (con mayor nivel de asistencia médica)
nut /nʌt/ *n* fruto *m* seco (*nuez, almendra, avellana etc*); (*Tec*) tuerca *f*. **~case** *n* 🄸 chiflado *m*. **~crackers** *npl* cascanueces *m*. **~meg** /-meg/ *n* nuez *f* moscada
nutri|ent /'nju:trɪənt/ *n* nutriente *m*. **~tion** /nju:'trɪʃn/ *n* nutrición *f*. **~tious** /nju:'trɪʃəs/ *adj* nutritivo
nuts /nʌts/ *adj* (*fam, crazy*) chiflado
nutshell /'nʌtʃel/ *n* cáscara *f* de nuez. **in a ~** en pocas palabras
NW *abbr* (= **north-west**) NO
nylon /'naɪlɒn/ *n* nylon *m*

Oo

oaf /əʊf/ *n* zoquete *m*
oak /əʊk/ *n* roble *m*
OAP /əʊeɪ'pi:/ *abbr* (= **old-age pensioner**) *n* pensionista *m & f*, pensionado *m*
oar /ɔ:(r)/ *n* remo *m*
oasis /əʊ'eɪsɪs/ *n* (*pl* **oases** /-si:z/) oasis *m*
oath /əʊθ/ *n* juramento *m*
oat|meal /'əʊtmi:l/ *n* harina *f* de avena; (*Amer, flakes*) avena *f* (*en copos*). **~s** /əʊts/ *npl* avena *f*
obedien|ce /əʊ'bi:dɪəns/ *n* obediencia *f*. **~t** *adj* obediente. **~tly** *adv* obedientemente
obes|e /əʊ'bi:s/ *adj* obeso. **~ity** *n* obesidad *f*
obey /əʊ'beɪ/ *vt/i* obedecer
obituary /ə'bɪtʃʊərɪ/ *n* nota *f* necrológica, obituario *m*
object /'ɒbdʒɪkt/ *n* objeto *m*; (*aim*) objetivo *m*. ●/əb'dʒekt/ *vi* oponerse (**to** a). **~ion** /əb'dʒekʃn/ *n* obje-

n
o

ción *f*. **~ionable** *adj* censurable; (*unpleasant*) desagradable. **~ive** /əb'dʒektɪv/ *adj & n* objetivo (*m*)

oblig|ation /ɒblɪ'geɪʃn/ *n* obligación *f*. **be under an ~ation to** estar obligado a. **~atory** /ə'blɪgətrɪ/ *adj* obligatorio. **~e** /ə'blaɪdʒ/ *vt* obligar. **I'd be much ~ed if you could help me** le quedaría muy agradecido si pudiera ayudarme. ● *vi* hacer un favor. **~ing** *adj* atento

oblique /ə'bli:k/ *adj* oblicuo

obliterate /ə'blɪtəreɪt/ *vt* arrasar; (*erase*) borrar

oblivio|n /ə'blɪvɪən/ *n* olvido *m*. **~us** /-vɪəs/ *adj* (*unaware*) inconsciente (**to, of** de)

oblong /'ɒblɒŋ/ *adj* oblongo. ● *n* rectángulo *m*

obnoxious /əb'nɒkʃəs/ *adj* odioso

oboe /'əʊbəʊ/ *n* oboe *m*

obscen|e /əb'si:n/ *adj* obsceno. **~ity** /əb'senətɪ/ *n* obscenidad *f*

O

obscur|e /əb'skjʊə(r)/ *adj* oscuro. ● *vt* ocultar; impedir ver claramente (issue). **~ity** *n* oscuridad *f*

obsequious /əb'si:kwɪəs/ *adj* servil

observ|ant /əb'zɜ:vənt/ *adj* observador. **~ation** /ɒbzə'veɪʃn/ *n* observación *f*. **~atory** /əb'zɜ:vətrɪ/ *n* observatorio *m*. **~e** /əb'zɜ:v/ *vt* observar. **~er** *n* observador *m*

obsess /əb'ses/ *vt* obsesionar. **~ed** /əb'sest/ *adj* obsesionado. **~ion** /-ʃn/ *n* obsesión *f*. **~ive** *adj* obsesivo

obsolete /'ɒbsəli:t/ *adj* obsoleto

obstacle /'ɒbstəkl/ *n* obstáculo *m*

obstina|cy /'ɒbstɪnəsɪ/ *n* obstinación *f*. **~te** /-ət/ *adj* obstinado. **~tely** *adv* obstinadamente

obstruct /əb'strʌkt/ *vt* obstruir; bloquear (traffic). **~ion** /-ʃn/ *n* obstrucción *f*

obtain /əb'teɪn/ *vt* conseguir, obtener. **~able** *adj* asequible

obtrusive /əb'tru:sɪv/ *adj* (presence) demasiado prominente; (noise) molesto

obtuse /əb'tju:s/ *adj* obtuso

obvious /'ɒbvɪəs/ *adj* obvio. **~ly** *adv* obviamente

occasion /ə'keɪʒn/ *n* ocasión *f*. **~al** *adj* esporádico. **~ally** *adv* de vez en cuando

occult /ɒ'kʌlt/ *adj* oculto

occup|ant /'ɒkjʊpənt/ *n* ocupante *m & f*. **~ation** /ɒkjʊ'peɪʃn/ *n* ocupación *f*. **~ier** /'ɒkjʊpaɪə(r)/ *n* ocupante *m & f*. **~y** /'ɒkjʊpaɪ/ *vt* ocupar. **keep o.s. ~ied** entretenerse

occur /ə'kɜ:(r)/ *vi* (*pt* **occurred**) tener lugar, ocurrir; (change) producirse; (*exist*) encontrarse. **it ~red to me that** se me ocurrió que. **~rence** /ə'kʌrəns/ *n* (*incidence*) incidencia *f*. **it is a rare ~rence** no es algo frecuente

ocean /'əʊʃn/ *n* océano *m*

o'clock /ə'klɒk/ *adv*. **it is 7 ~** son las siete. **it's one ~** es la una

octagon /'ɒktəgən/ *n* octágono *m*

octave /'ɒktɪv/ *n* octava *f*

October /ɒk'təʊbə(r)/ *n* octubre *m*

octopus /'ɒktəpəs/ *n* (*pl* **-puses**) pulpo *m*

odd /ɒd/ *adj* (**-er, -est**) extraño, raro; (number) impar; (*one of pair*) desparejado. **smoke the ~ cigarette** fumarse algún que otro cigarillo. **fifty-~** unos cincuenta, cincuenta y pico. **the ~ one out** la excepción. **~ity** *n* (*thing*) rareza *f*;

(*person*) bicho *m* raro. **~ly** *adv* de una manera extraña. **~ly enough** por extraño que parezca. **~ment** *n* retazo *m*. **~s** *npl* probabilidades *fpl*; (*in betting*) apuesta *f*. **be at ~s** estar en desacuerdo. **~s and ends** *mpl* ⓘ cosas *fpl* sueltas

odious /'əʊdɪəs/ *adj* odioso

odometer /ɒ'dɒmətə(r)/ *n* (*Amer*) cuentakilómetros *m*

odour /'əʊdə(r)/ *n* olor *m*

of /ɒv//əv/ *preposition*

- de. **a pound of cheese** una libra de queso. **it's made of wood** es de madera. **a girl of ten** una niña de diez años
- (*in dates*) de. **the fifth of November** el cinco de noviembre
- (*Amer, when telling the time*) **it's ten (minutes) of five** son las cinco menos diez, son diez para las cinco (*LAm*)

! **of** is not translated in cases such as the following: **a colleague of mine** *un colega mío;* **there were six of us** *éramos seis;* **that's very kind of you** *es Ud muy amable*

off /ɒf/ *prep* (*from*) de. **he picked it up ~ the floor** lo recogió del suelo; (*distant from*) **just ~ the coast of Texas** a poca distancia de la costa de Tejas. **2 ft ~ the ground** a dos pies del suelo; (*absent from*) **I've been ~ work for a week** hace una semana que no voy a trabajar. • *adv* (*removed*) **the lid was ~** la tapa no estaba puesta; (*distant*) **some way ~** a cierta distancia; (*leaving*) **I'm ~** me voy; (*switched off*) (light, TV) apagado; (water) cortado; (*cancelled*) (match) cancelado; (*not on duty*) (day) libre. • *adj*. **be ~** (meat) estar malo, estar pasado; (milk) estar cortado. **~-beat** *adj* poco convencional. **~ chance** *n*. **on the ~ chance** por si acaso

i **off-licence** En el Reino Unido, es una tienda que tiene licencia para vender bebidas alcohólicas que se deben consumir fuera del local. Abren cuando los bares y *pubs* están cerrados y también suelen vender bebidas no alcohólicas, tabaco, golosinas etc. A menudo alquilan vasos y copas para fiestas, etc.

offen|ce /ə'fens/ *n* (*breach of law*) infracción *f*; (*criminal* **~ce**) delito *m*; (*cause of outrage*) atentado *m*; (*Amer, attack*) ataque *m*. **take ~ce** ofenderse. **~d** *vt* ofender. **~der** *n* delincuente *m & f*. **~sive** /-sɪv/ *adj* ofensivo; (*disgusting*) desagradable

offer /'ɒfə(r)/ *vt* ofrecer. **~ to do sth** ofrecerse a hacer algo. • *n* oferta *f*. **on ~** de oferta

offhand /ɒf'hænd/ *adj* (*brusque*) brusco. **say sth in an ~ way** decir algo a la ligera. • *adv* de improviso

office /'ɒfɪs/ *n* oficina *f*; (*post*) cargo *m*. **doctor's ~** (*Amer*) consultorio *m*, consulta *m*. **~ block** *n* edificio *m* de oficinas **~r** *n* oficial *m & f*; (*police* **~r**) policía *m & f*; (*as form of address*) agente

offici|al /ə'fɪʃl/ *adj* oficial. • *n* funcionario *m* del Estado; (*of party, union*) dirigente *m & f*. **~ally** *adv* oficialmente. **~ous** /ə'fɪʃəs/ *adj* oficioso

offing /'ɒfɪŋ/ *n*. **in the ~** en perspectiva

off: ~-licence *n* tienda *f* de vinos y licores. **~-putting** *adj* (*disconcerting*) desconcertante; (*disagreeable*) desagradable. **~set** *vt* (*pt* **-set**, *pres p* **-setting**) compensar. **~shore** *adj* (breeze) que sopla desde la tierra; (drilling) offshore; (well) submarino. ● *adv* a un lugar de mano de obra barata. **~side** /ɒf'saɪd/ *adj* (*Sport*) fuera de juego. **~spring** *n invar* prole *f*. **~-stage** /-'steɪdʒ/ *adv* fuera del escenario. **~-white** *adj* color hueso

often /'ɒfn/ *adv* a menudo, con frecuencia. **how ~?** ¿con qué frecuencia? **more ~** con más frecuencia

ogle /'əʊgl/ *vt* comerse con los ojos

ogre /'əʊgə(r)/ *n* ogro *m*

oh /əʊ/ *int* ¡ah!; (*expressing dismay*) ¡ay!

oil /ɔɪl/ *n* aceite *m*; (*petroleum*) petróleo *m*. ● *vt* lubricar. **~field** *n* yacimiento *m* petrolífero. **~ painting** *n* pintura *f* al óleo; (*picture*) óleo *m*. **~ rig** *n* plataforma *f* petrolífera. **~y** *adj* (substance) oleaginoso; (food) aceitoso

ointment /'ɔɪntmənt/ *n* ungüento *m*

OK /əʊ'keɪ/ *int* ¡vale!, ¡de acuerdo!, ¡bueno! (*LAm*). ● *adj* **~, thanks** bien, gracias. **the job's ~** el trabajo no está mal

old /əʊld/ *adj* (**-er**, **-est**) viejo; (*not modern*) antiguo; (*former*) antiguo; **an ~ friend** un viejo amigo. **how ~ is she?** ¿cuántos años tiene? **she is ten years ~** tiene diez años. **his ~er sister** su hermana mayor. **~ age** *n* vejez *f*. **~-fashioned** /-'fæʃənd/ *adj* anticuado

olive /'ɒlɪv/ *n* aceituna *f*.

Olympic /ə'lɪmpɪk/ *adj* olímpico. **the ~s** *npl*, **the ~ Games** *npl* los Juegos Olímpicos

omelette /'ɒmlɪt/ *n* tortilla *f* francesa, omelette *m* (*LAm*)

omen /'əʊmen/ *n* agüero *m*

omi|ssion /ə'mɪʃn/ *n* omisión *f*. **~t** /əʊ'mɪt/ *vt* (*pt* **omitted**) omitir

on /ɒn/ *prep* en, sobre; (*about*) sobre. **~ foot** a pie. **~ Monday** el lunes. **~ seeing** al ver. **I heard it ~ the radio** lo oí por la radio. ● *adv* (*light etc*) encendido, prendido (*LAm*); (*machine*) en marcha; (*tap*) abierto. **~ and ~** sin cesar. **and so ~** y así sucesivamente. **have a hat ~** llevar (puesto) un sombrero. **further ~** un poco más allá. **what's ~ at the Odeon?** ¿qué dan en el Odeon? **go ~** continuar. **later ~** más tarde

once /wʌns/ *adv* una vez; (*formerly*) antes. **at ~** inmediatamente. **~ upon a time there was...** érase una vez.... **~ and for all** de una vez por todas. ● *conj* una vez que

one /wʌn/ *adj* uno, (*before masculine singular noun*) un. **the ~ person I trusted** la única persona en la que confiaba. ● *n* uno *m*. **~ by ~** uno a uno.. ● *pron* uno (*m*), una (*f*). **the blue ~** el/la azul. **this ~** éste/ésta. **~ another** el uno al otro

onerous /'ɒnərəs/ *adj* (task) pesado

one: ~self /-'self/ *pron* (*reflexive*) se; (*after prep*) sí (mismo); (*emphatic use*) uno mismo, una misma. **by ~self** solo. **~-way** *adj* (street) de sentido único; (ticket) de ida, sencillo

onion /'ʌnɪən/ *n* cebolla *f*

online /ɒn'laɪn/ *adj* en línea

onlooker /ˈɒnlʊkə(r)/ *n* espectador *m*

only /ˈəʊnlɪ/ *adj* único. **she's an ~ child** es hija única. ●*adv* sólo, solamente. **~ just** (*barely*) apenas. **I've ~ just arrived** acabo de llegar. ●*conj* pero, sólo que

onset /ˈɒnset/ *n* comienzo *m*; (*of disease*) aparición *f*

onshore /ˈɒnʃɔ:(r)/ *adj* (breeze) que sopla desde el mar; (oil field) en tierra

onslaught /ˈɒnslɔ:t/ *n* ataque *m*

onus /ˈəʊnəs/ *n* responsabilidad *f*

onward(s) /ˈɒnwəd(z)/ *adj & adv* hacia adelante

ooze /u:z/ *vt/i* rezumar

opaque /əʊˈpeɪk/ *adj* opaco

open /ˈəʊpən/ *adj* abierto; (question) discutible. ●*n*. **in the ~** al aire libre. ●*vt/i* abrir. **~ing** *n* abertura *f*; (*beginning*) principio *m*. **~ly** *adv* abiertamente. **~-minded** /-ˈmaɪndɪd/ *adj* de actitud abierta

> **Open University** La universidad a distancia británica, fundada en 1969. La enseñanza se imparte fundamentalmente por correspondencia, mediante materiales impresos, material enviado por internet y programas de televisión emitidos por la BBC. También hay cursos de verano a los que los alumnos deben asistir. No se exigen calificaciones académicas para su ingreso.

opera /ˈɒprə/ *n* ópera *f*

operate /ˈɒpəreɪt/ *vt* manejar, operar (*Mex*) (machine). ●*vi* funcionar; (company) operar. **~ (on)** (*Med*) operar (a)

operatic /ɒpəˈrætɪk/ *adj* operístico

operation /ɒpəˈreɪʃn/ *n* operación *f*; (*Mec*) funcionamiento *m*; (*using of machine*) manejo *m*. **he had an ~** lo operaron. **in ~** en vigor. **~al** *adj* operacional

operative /ˈɒpərətɪv/ *adj*. **be ~** estar en vigor

operator *n* operador *m*

opinion /əˈpɪnɪən/ *n* opinión *f*. **in my ~** en mi opinión, a mi parecer

opponent /əˈpəʊnənt/ *n* adversario *m*; (*in sport*) contrincante *m & f*

opportun|e /ˈɒpətju:n/ *adj* oportuno. **~ist** /ɒpəˈtju:nɪst/ *n* oportunista *m & f*. **~ity** /ɒpəˈtju:nətɪ/ *n* oportunidad *f*

oppos|e /əˈpəʊz/ *vt* oponerse a. **be ~ed to** oponerse a, estar en contra de. **~ing** *adj* opuesto. **~ite** /ˈɒpəzɪt/ *adj* (*contrary*) opuesto; (*facing*) de enfrente. ●*n*. **the ~ite** lo contrario. **quite the ~ite** al contrario. ●*adv* enfrente. ●*prep* enfrente de. **~ite number** *n* homólogo *m*. **~ition** /ɒpəˈzɪʃn/ *n* oposición *f*; (*resistance*) resistencia *f*

oppress /əˈpres/ *vt* oprimir. **~ion** /-ʃn/ *n* opresión *f*. **~ive** *adj* (*cruel*) opresivo; (heat) sofocante

opt /ɒpt/ *vi*. **~ to** optar por. □**~ out** *vi* decidir no tomar parte

optic|al /ˈɒptɪkl/ *adj* óptico. **~ian** /ɒpˈtɪʃn/ *n* óptico *m*

optimis|m /ˈɒptɪmɪzəm/ *n* optimismo *m*. **~t** *n* optimista *m & f*. **~tic** /-ˈmɪstɪk/ *adj* optimista

option /ˈɒpʃn/ *n* opción *f*. **~al** *adj* facultativo

or /ɔ:(r)/ *conj* o; (*before* o- *and* ho-) u; (*after negative*) ni. **~ else** si no, o bien

oral /ˈɔ:rəl/ *adj* oral. ●*n* ☐ examen *m* oral

O

orange /'ɒrɪndʒ/ *n* naranja *f*; (*colour*) naranja *m*. ● *adj* naranja. **~ade** /-'eɪd/ *n* naranjada *f*

orbit /'ɔ:bɪt/ *n* órbita *f*. ● *vt* orbitar

orchard /'ɔ:tʃəd/ *n* huerto *m*

orchestra /'ɔ:kɪstrə/ *n* orquesta *f*; (*Amer, in theatre*) platea *f*. **~l** /-'kestrəl/ *adj* orquestal. **~te** /-eɪt/ *vt* orquestar

orchid /'ɔ:kɪd/ *n* orquídea *f*

ordain /ɔ:'deɪn/ *vt* (*Relig*) ordenar; (*decree*) decretar

ordeal /ɔ:'di:l/ *n* dura prueba *f*

order /'ɔ:də(r)/ *n* orden *m*; (*Com*) pedido *m*; (*command*) orden *f*. **in ~ that** para que. **in ~ to** para. ● *vt* (*command*) ordenar, mandar; (*Com*) pedir; (*in restaurant*) pedir, ordenar (*LAm*); encargar (book); llamar, ordenar (*LAm*) (taxi). **~ly** *adj* ordenado. ● *n* camillero *m*

ordinary /'ɔ:dɪnrɪ/ *adj* corriente; (*average*) medio; (*mediocre*) ordinario

ore /ɔ:(r)/ *n* mena *f*

organ /'ɔ:gən/ *n* órgano *m*

organ|ic /ɔ:'gænɪk/ *adj* orgánico. **~ism** /'ɔ:gənɪzəm/ *n* organismo *m*. **~ist** /'ɔ:gənɪst/ *n* organista *m & f*. **~ization** /ɔ:gənaɪ'zeɪʃn/ *n* organización *f*. **~ize** /'ɔ:gənaɪz/ *vt* organizar. **~izer** *n* organizador *m*

orgasm /'ɔ:gæzəm/ *n* orgasmo *m*

orgy /'ɔ:dʒɪ/ *n* orgía *f*

Orient /'ɔ:rɪənt/ *n* Oriente *m*. **~al** /-'entl/ *adj* oriental

orientat|e /'ɔ:rɪənteɪt/ *vt* orientar. **~ion** /-'teɪʃn/ *n* orientación *f*

origin /'ɒrɪdʒɪn/ *n* origen *m*. **~al** /ə'rɪdʒənl/ *adj* original. **~ally** *adv* originariamente. **~ate** /ə'rɪdʒɪneɪt/ *vi*. **~ate from** provenir de

ornament /'ɔ:nəmənt/ *n* adorno *m*. **~al** /-'mentl/ *adj* de adorno

ornate /ɔ:'neɪt/ *adj* ornamentado; (style) recargado

ornithology /ɔ:nɪ'θɒlədʒɪ/ *n* ornitología *f*

orphan /'ɔ:fn/ *n* huérfano *m*. ● *vt*. **be ~ed** quedar huérfano. **~age** /-ɪdʒ/ *n* orfanato *m*

orthodox /'ɔ:θədɒks/ *adj* ortodoxo

oscillate /'ɒsɪleɪt/ *vi* oscilar

ostentatious /ɒsten'teɪʃəs/ *adj* ostentoso

osteopath /'ɒstɪəpæθ/ *n* osteópata *m & f*

ostracize /'ɒstrəsaɪz/ *vt* hacerle vacío a

ostrich /'ɒstrɪtʃ/ *n* avestruz *m*

other /'ʌðə(r)/ *adj & pron* otro. **~ than** aparte de. **the ~ one** el otro. **~wise** *adv* de lo contrario, si no

otter /'ɒtə(r)/ *n* nutria *f*

ouch /aʊtʃ/ *int* ¡ay!

ought /ɔ:t/ *modal verb*. **I ~ to see it** debería verlo. **he ~ to have done it** debería haberlo hecho

ounce /aʊns/ *n* onza *f* (= *28.35 gr.*)

our /'aʊə(r)/ *adj* (*sing*) nuestro, nuestra, (*pl*) nuestros, nuestras. **~s** /'aʊəz/ *poss pron* (*sing*) nuestro, nuestra; (*pl*) nuestros, nuestras. **~s is red** el nuestro es rojo. **a friend of ~s** un amigo nuestro. **~selves** /-'selvz/ *pron* (*reflexive*) nos; (*used for emphasis and after prepositions*) nosotros mismos, nosotras mismas. **we behaved ~selves** nos portamos bien. **we did it ~selves** lo hicimos nosotros mismos/nosotras mismas

oust /aʊst/ *vt* desbancar; derrocar (government)

out /aʊt/ *adv* (*outside*) fuera, afuera

(*LAm*). (*not lighted, not on*) apagado; (*in blossom*) en flor; (*in error*) equivocado. **he's ~** (*not at home*) no está; **be ~ to** estar resuelto a. **~ of** *prep* (*from inside*) de; (*outside*) fuera, afuera (*LAm*). **five ~ of six** cinco de cada seis. **made ~ of** hecho de. **we're ~ of bread** nos hemos quedado sin pan. **~break** *n* (*of war*) estallido *m*; (*of disease*) brote *m*. **~burst** *n* arrebato *m*. **~cast** *n* paria *m & f*. **~come** *n* resultado *m*. **~cry** *n* protesta *f*. **~dated** /-'deɪtɪd/ *adj* anticuado. **~do** /-'du:/ *vt* (*pt* **-did**, *pp* **-done**) superar. **~door** *adj* (clothes) de calle; (pool) descubierto. **~doors** /-'dɔ:z/ *adv* al aire libre

outer /'aʊtə(r)/ *adj* exterior

out: ~fit *n* equipo *m*; (*clothes*) conjunto *m*. **~going** *adj* (minister etc) saliente; (*sociable*) abierto. **~goings** *npl* gastos *mpl*. **~grow** /-'grəʊ/ *vt* (*pt* **-grew**, *pp* **-grown**) crecer más que (person). **he's ~grown his new shoes** le han quedado pequeños los zapatos nuevos. **~ing** *n* excursión *f*

outlandish /aʊt'lændɪʃ/ *adj* extravagante

out: ~law *n* forajido *m*. ● *vt* proscribir. **~lay** *n* gastos *mpl*. **~let** *n* salida *f*; (*Com*) punto *m* de venta; (*Amer, Elec*) toma *f* de corriente. **~line** *n* contorno *m*; (*summary*) resumen *m*; (*plan of project*) esquema *m*.● *vt* trazar; (*summarize*) esbozar. **~live** /-'lɪv/ *vt* sobrevivir a. **~look** *n* perspectivas *fpl*; (*attitude*) punto *m* de vista. **~lying** *adj* alejado. **~number** /-'nʌmbə(r)/ *vt* superar en número. **~-of-date** *adj* (ideas) desfasado; (clothes) pasado de moda. **~patient** *n* paciente *m* externo. **~post** *n* avanzada *f*. **~put** *n* producción *f*; (*of machine, worker*) rendimiento *m*. **~right** *adv* completamente; (*frankly*) abiertamente; (kill) en el acto. ● *adj* completo; (refusal) rotundo. **~set** *n* principio *m*. **~side** *adj & n* exterior (*m*). **at the ~** como máximo. ● /-'saɪd/ *adv* fuera, afuera (*LAm*). ● *prep* fuera de. **~size** *adj* de talla gigante. **~skirts** *npl* afueras *fpl*. **~spoken** /-'spəʊkn/ *adj* directo, franco. **~standing** /-'stændɪŋ/ *adj* excepcional; (debt) pendiente. **~stretched** /aʊt'stretʃt/ *adj* extendido. **~strip** /-'strɪp/ *vt* (*pt* **-stripped**) (*run faster than*) tomarle la delantera a; (*exceed*) sobrepasar. **~ward** /-wəd/ *adj* (appearance) exterior; (sign) externo; (journey) de ida. **~wardly** *adv* por fuera, exteriormente. **~(s)** *adv* hacia afuera. **~weigh** /-'weɪ/ *vt* ser mayor que. **~wit** /-'wɪt/ *vt* (*pt* **-witted**) burlar

oval /'əʊvl/ *adj* ovalado, oval. ● *n* óvalo *m*

> **Oval Office** El Despacho Oval es el despacho oficial del Presidente de los Estados Unidos, ubicado en el ala oeste de la Casa Blanca. La forma oval fue determinada por George Washington, lo que le permitiría tener contacto visual con todos durante las reuniones. Originariamente, quería que todas las habitaciones de la Casa Blanca fueran ovales, pero pronto comprendió que este diseño era poco práctico.

ovary /'əʊvərɪ/ *n* ovario *m*

ovation /əʊ'veɪʃn/ *n* ovación *f*

oven /'ʌvn/ *n* horno *m*

over /ˈəʊvə(r)/ *prep* por encima de; (*across*) al otro lado de; (*during*) durante; (*more than*) más de. ~ **and above** por encima de. ●*adv* por encima; (*ended*) terminado; (*more*) más; (*in excess*) de sobra. ~ **again** otra vez. ~ **and** ~ una y otra vez. ~ **here** por aquí. ~ **there** por allí. **all** ~ (*finished*) acabado; (*everywhere*) por todas partes

over... /ˈəʊvə(r)/ *pref* excesivamente, demasiado

over: ~**all** /-ˈɔːl/ *adj* global; (length, cost) total. ●*adv* en conjunto. ●/ˈəʊvərɔːl/ *n*, ~**alls** *npl* mono *m*, overol *m* (*LAm*); (*Amer, dungarees*) peto *m*, overol *m*. ~**awe** /-ˈɔː/ *vt* intimidar. ~**balance** /-ˈbæləns/ *vi* perder el equilibrio. ~**bearing** /-ˈbeərɪŋ/ *adj* dominante. ~**board** *adv* (throw) por la borda. ~**cast** /-ˈkɑːst/ *adj* (day) nublado; (sky) cubierto. ~**charge** /-ˈtʃɑːdʒ/ *vt* cobrarle de más a. ~**coat** *n* abrigo *m*. ~**come** /-ˈkʌm/ *vt* (*pt* **-came**, *pp* **-come**) superar, vencer. ~**crowded** /-ˈkraʊdɪd/ *adj* abarrotado (de gente). ~**do** /-ˈduː/ *vt* (*pt* **-did**, *pp* **-done**) exagerar; (*Culin*) recocer. ~**dose** *n* sobredosis *f*. ~**draft** *n* descubierto *m*. ~**draw** /-ˈdrɔː/ *vt* (*pt* **-drew**, *pp* **-drawn**) girar en descubierto. **be** ~**drawn** tener un descubierto. ~**due** /-ˈdjuː/ *adj*. **the book is a month** ~**due** el plazo de devolución del libro venció hace un mes. ~**estimate** /-ˈestɪmeɪt/ *vt* sobreestimar. ~**flow** /-ˈfləʊ/ *vi* desbordarse. ●*n* /-fləʊ/ (*excess*) exceso *m*; (*outlet*) rebosadero *m*. ~**flow car park** *n* estacionamento *m* extra (*LAm*), aparcamiento *m* extra (*Esp*). ~**grown** /-ˈgrəʊn/ *adj* demasiado grande; (garden) lleno de maleza. ~**haul** /-ˈhɔːl/ *vt* revisar. ●/-hɔːl/ *n* revisión *f*. ~**head** /-ˈhed/ *adv* por encima. ●/-hed/ *adj* de arriba. ~**heads** /-hedz/ *npl*, ~**head** *n* (*Amer*) gastos *mpl* indirectos. ~**hear** /-ˈhɪə(r)/ *vt* (*pt* **-heard**) oír por casualidad. ~**joyed** /-ˈdʒɔɪd/ *adj* encantado. ~**land** *a*/*adv* por tierra. ~**lap** /-ˈlæp/ *vi* (*pt* **-lapped**) traslaparse. ~**leaf** /-ˈliːf/ *adv* al dorso. ~**load** /-ˈləʊd/ *vt* sobrecargar. ~**look** /-ˈlʊk/ *vt* (room) dar a; (*not notice*) pasar por alto; (*disregard*) disculpar. ~**night** /-ˈnaɪt/ *adv* durante la noche. **stay** ~**night** quedarse a pasar la noche. ●*adj* (journey) de noche; (stay) de una noche. ~**pass** *n* paso *m* elevado, paso *m* a desnivel (*Mex*). ~**pay** /-ˈpeɪ/ *vt* (*pt* **-paid**) pagar demasiado. ~**power** /-ˈpaʊə(r)/ *vt* dominar (opponent); (emotion) abrumar. ~**powering** /-ˈpaʊərɪŋ/ *adj* (smell) muy fuerte; (desire) irrestible. ~**priced** /-ˈpraɪst/ *adj* demasiado caro. ~**rated** /-ˈreɪtɪd/ *adj* sobrevalorado. ~**react** /-rɪˈækt/ *vi* reaccionar en forma exagerada. ~**ride** /-ˈraɪd/ *vt* (*pt* **-rode**, *pp* **-ridden**) invalidar. ~**riding** /-ˈraɪdɪŋ/ *adj* dominante. ~**rule** /-ˈruːl/ *vt* anular; rechazar (objection). ~**run** /-ˈrʌn/ *vt* (*pt* **-ran**, *pp* **-run**, *pres p* **-running**) invadir; exceder (limit). ~**seas** /-ˈsiːz/ *adj* (trade) exterior; (investments) en el exterior; (visitor) extranjero. ●*adv* al extranjero. ~**see** /-ˈsiː/ *vt* (*pt* **-saw**, *pp* **-seen**) supervisar. ~**seer** /-sɪə(r)/ *n* capataz *m* & *f*, supervisor *m*. ~**shadow** /-ˈʃædəʊ/ *vt* eclipsar. ~**shoot** /-ˈʃuːt/ *vt* (*pt* **-shot**) excederse. ~**sight** *n* descuido *m*. ~**sleep** /-ˈsliːp/ *vi* (*pt*

-slept) quedarse dormido. **~step** /-'step/ *vt* (*pt* **-stepped**) sobrepasar. **~step the mark** pasarse de la raya

overt /'əʊvɜːt/ *adj* manifiesto

over: **~take** /-'teɪk/ *vt/i* (*pt* **-took**, *pp* **-taken**) sobrepasar; (*Auto*) adelantar, rebasar (*Mex*). **~throw** /-'θrəʊ/ *vt* (*pt* **-threw**, *pp* **-thrown**) derrocar. **~time** *n* horas *fpl* extra

overture /'əʊvətjʊə(r)/ *n* obertura *f*

over: **~turn** /-'tɜːn/ *vt* darle la vuelta a. ●*vi* volcar. **~weight** /-'weɪt/ *adj* demasiado gordo. **be ~weight** pesar demasiado. **~whelm** /-'welm/ *vt* aplastar; (*with emotion*) abrumar. **~whelming** *adj* aplastante; (*fig*) abrumador. **~work** /-'wɜːk/ *vt* hacer trabajar demasiado. ●*vi* trabajar demasiado. ●*n* agotamiento *m*

ow|e /əʊ/ *vt* deber. **~ing to** debido a

owl /aʊl/ *n* búho *m*

own /əʊn/ *adj* propio. **my ~ house** mi propia casa. ●*pron.* **it's my ~** es mío (propio)/mía (propia). **on one's ~** solo. **get one's ~ back** 🄸 desquitarse. ●*vt* tener. □ **~ up** *vi.* 🄸 confesarse culpable. **~er** *n* propietario *m*, dueño *m*. **~ership** *n* propiedad *f*

oxygen /'ɒksɪdʒən/ *n* oxígeno *m*

> ***i*** **Oxbridge** Término usado para referirse conjuntamente a las universidades más antiguas y de más prestigio en el Reino Unido; Oxford y Cambridge, especialmente cuando se quiere destacar el ambiente de privilegio con el que se las relaciona. Últimamente se han hecho grandes esfuerzos para atraer a estudiantes de todos los medios sociales.

oyster /'ɔɪstə(r)/ *n* ostra *f*

p *abbr* (= **pence, penny**) penique(s) (*m*(*pl*))

p. (*pl* **pp.**) (= **page**) pág., p.

pace /peɪs/ *n* paso *m*. **keep ~ with s.o.** seguirle el ritmo a uno. ●*vi.* **~ up and down** andar de un lado para otro. **~maker** *n* (*runner*) liebre *f*; (*Med*) marcapasos *m*

Pacific /pə'sɪfɪk/ *n*. **the ~ (Ocean)** el (Océano) Pacífico *m*

pacif|ist /'pæsɪfɪst/ *n* pacifista *m & f*. **~y** /'pæsɪfaɪ/ *vt* apaciguar

pack /pæk/ *n* fardo *m*; (*of cigarettes*) paquete *m*, cajetilla *f*; (*of cards*) baraja *f*; (*of hounds*) jauría *f*; (*of wolves*) manada *f*. **a ~ of lies** una sarta de mentiras. ●*vt* empaquetar; hacer (suitcase); (*press down*) apisonar. ●*vi* hacer la maleta, empacar (*LAm*). **~age** /-ɪdʒ/ *n* paquete *m*. **~age holiday** *n* vacaciones *fpl* organizadas. **~ed** /pækt/ *adj* lleno (de gente). **~et** /'pækɪt/ *n* paquete *m*

pact /pækt/ *n* pacto *m*, acuerdo *m*

pad /pæd/ *n* (*for writing*) bloc *m*. **shoulder ~s** hombreras *fpl*. ●*vt* (*pt* **padded**) rellenar

paddle /'pædl/ *n* pala *f*. ●*vi* mojarse los pies; (*in canoe*) remar (con pala)

paddock /'pædək/ *n* prado *m*

O P

padlock /'pædlɒk/ *n* candado *m*. ● *vt* cerrar con candado

paed|iatrician /pi:dɪə'trɪʃn/ *n* pediatra *m & f*. **~ophile** /'pi:dəfaɪl/ *n* pedófilo *m*

pagan /'peɪgən/ *adj & n* pagano (*m*)

page /peɪdʒ/ *n* página *f*; (*attendant*) paje *m*; (*in hotel*) botones *m*. ● *vt* llamar por megafonía/por buscapersonas, vocear (*LAm*)

paid /peɪd/ *see* PAY. ● *adj*. **put ~ to** [I] acabar con

pail /peɪl/ *n* balde *m*, cubo *m*

pain /peɪn/ *n* dolor *m*. **I have a ~ in my back** me duele la espalda. *m*. **be in ~** tener dolores. **be a ~ in the neck** [I] ser un pesado; (*thing*) ser una lata. ● *vt* doler. **~ful** *adj* doloroso. **it's very ~ful** duele mucho. **~-killer** *n* analgésico *m*. **~less** *adj* indoloro. **~staking** /'peɪnzteɪkɪŋ/ *adj* concienzudo

paint /peɪnt/ *n* pintura *f*. ● *vt/i* pintar. **~er** *n* pintor *m*. **~ing** *n* (*medium*) pintura *f*; (*picture*) cuadro *m*

pair /peə(r)/ *n* par *m*; (*of people*) pareja *f*. **a ~ of trousers** unos pantalones. □ **~off, ~ up** *vi* formar parejas

pajamas /pə'dʒɑ:məz/ *npl* (*Amer*) pijama *m*

Pakistan /pɑ:kɪ'stɑ:n/ *n* Pakistán *m*. **~i** *adj & n* paquistaní (*m & f*)

pal /pæl/ *n* [I] amigo *m*

palace /'pælɪs/ *n* palacio *m*

palat|able /'pælətəbl/ *adj* agradable. **~e** /'pælət/ *n* paladar *m*

pale /peɪl/ *adj* (**-er**, **-est**) pálido. **go ~, turn ~** palidecer. **~ness** *n* palidez *f*

Palestin|e /'pælɪstaɪn/ *n* Palestina *f*. **~ian** /-'stɪnɪən/ *adj & n* palestino (*m*)

palette /'pælɪt/ *n* paleta *f*

palm /pɑ:m/ *n* palma *f*. □ **~ off** *vt* encajar (on a). **P~ Sunday** *n* Domingo *m* de Ramos

palpable /'pælpəbl/ *adj* palpable

palpitat|e /'pælpɪteɪt/ *vi* palpitar. **~ion** /-'teɪʃn/ *n* palpitación *f*

pamper /'pæmpə(r)/ *vt* mimar

pamphlet /'pæmflɪt/ *n* folleto *m*

pan /pæn/ *n* cacerola *f*; (*for frying*) sartén *f*

panacea /pænə'sɪə/ *n* panacea *f*

Panama /'pænəmɑ:/ *n* Panamá *m*. **~nian** /-'meɪnɪən/ *adj & n* panameño (*m*)

pancake /'pænkeɪk/ *n* crep(e) *m*, panqueque *m* (*LAm*)

panda /'pændə/ *n* panda *m*

pandemonium /pændɪ'məʊnɪəm/ *n* pandemonio *m*

pander /'pændə(r)/ *vi*. **~ to s.o.** consentirle los caprichos a uno

pane /peɪn/ *n* vidrio *m*, cristal *m*

panel /'pænl/ *n* panel *m*; (*group of people*) jurado *m*. **~ling** *n* paneles *mpl*

pang /pæŋ/ *n* punzada *f*

panic /'pænɪk/ *n* pánico *m*. ● *vi* (*pt* **panicked**) dejarse llevar por el pánico. **~-stricken** *adj* aterrorizado

panoram|a /pænə'rɑ:mə/ *n* panorama *m*. **~ic** /-'ræmɪk/ *adj* panorámico

pansy /'pænzɪ/ *n* (*flower*) pensamiento *m*

pant /pænt/ *vi* jadear

panther /'pænθə(r)/ *n* pantera *f*

panties /'pæntɪz/ *npl* bragas *fpl*, calzones *mpl* (*LAm*), pantaletas *fpl* (*Mex*)

pantihose /'pæntɪhəʊz/ *npl* *see* PANTYHOSE

pantomime /'pæntəmaɪm/ *n* pantomima *f*

pantry /ˈpæntrɪ/ *n* despensa *f*
pants /pænts/ *npl* (*man's*) calzoncillos *mpl*; (*woman's*) bragas *fpl*, calzones *mpl* (*LAm*), pantaletas *fpl* (*Mex*); (*Amer, trousers*) pantalones *mpl*
pantyhose /ˈpæntɪhəʊz/ *npl* (*Amer*) panty *m*, medias *fpl*, pantimedias *fpl* (*Mex*)
paper /ˈpeɪpə(r)/ *n* papel *m*; (*newspaper*) diario *m*, periódico *m*; (*exam*) examen *m*; (*document*) documento *m*. ● *vt* empapelar, tapizar (*Mex*). **~back** *n* libro *m* en rústica. **~ clip** *n* sujetapapeles *m*, clip *m*. **~weight** *n* pisapapeles *m*. **~work** *n* papeleo *m*, trabajo *m* administrativo
parable /ˈpærəbl/ *n* parábola *f*
parachut|e /ˈpærəʃuːt/ *n* paracaídas *m*. ● *vi* saltar en paracaídas. **~ist** *n* paracaidista *m & f*
parade /pəˈreɪd/ *n* desfile *m*; (*Mil*) formación *f*. ● *vi* desfilar. ● *vt* hacer alarde de
paradise /ˈpærədaɪs/ *n* paraíso *m*
paraffin /ˈpærəfɪn/ *n* queroseno *m*
paragraph /ˈpærəgrɑːf/ *n* párrafo *m*
Paraguay /ˈpærəgwaɪ/ *n* Paraguay *m*. **~an** *adj & n* paraguayo (*m*)
parallel /ˈpærəlel/ *adj* paralelo. ● *n* paralelo *m*; (*line*) paralela *f*
paraly|se /ˈpærəlaɪz/ *vt* paralizar. **~sis** /pəˈræləsɪs/ *n* (*pl* **-ses** /-siːz/) parálisis *f*
parameter /pəˈræmɪtə(r)/ *n* parámetro *m*
paranoia /pærəˈnɔɪə/ *n* paranoia *f*
parapet /ˈpærəpɪt/ *n* parapeto *m*
paraphernalia /pærəfəˈneɪlɪə/ *n* trastos *mpl*
parasite /ˈpærəsaɪt/ *n* parásito *m*
paratrooper /ˈpærətruːpə(r)/ *n* paracaidista *m* (del ejército)
parcel /ˈpɑːsl/ *n* paquete *m*
parch /pɑːtʃ/ *vt* resecar. **be ~ed** 🅘 estar muerto de sed
parchment /ˈpɑːtʃmənt/ *n* pergamino *m*
pardon /ˈpɑːdn/ *n* perdón *m*; (*Jurid*) indulto *m*. **I beg your ~** perdón. **(I beg your) ~?** ¿cómo?, ¿mande? (*Mex*). ● *vt* perdonar; (*Jurid*) indultar. **~ me?** (*Amer*) ¿cómo?
parent /ˈpeərənt/ *n* (*father*) padre *m*; (*mother*) madre *f*. **my ~s** mis padres. **~al** /pəˈrentl/ *adj* de los padres
parenthesis /pəˈrenθəsɪs/ *n* (*pl* **-theses** /-siːz/) paréntesis *m*
parenthood /ˈpeərənthʊd/ *n* el ser padre/madre
Paris /ˈpærɪs/ *n* París *m*
parish /ˈpærɪʃ/ *n* parroquia *f*; (*municipal*) distrito *m*. **~ioner** /pəˈrɪʃənə(r)/ *n* feligrés *m*
park /pɑːk/ *n* parque *m*. **~-and-ride** estacionamiento *m* disuasorio (*LAm*), aparcamiento *m* disuasorio (*Esp*). ● *vt/i* aparcar, estacionar (*LAm*)
parking: /ˈpɑːkɪŋ/ *n*: **~ lot** *n* (*Amer*) aparcamiento *m*, estacionamiento *m* (*LAm*). **~ meter** *n* parquímetro *m*
parkway /ˈpɑːkweɪ/ *n* (*Amer*) carretera *f* ajardinada
parliament /ˈpɑːləmənt/ *n* parlamento *m*. **~ary** /-ˈmentrɪ/ *adj* parlamentario

Parliament El Parlamento británico, el más alto organismo legislativo. Está formado por la Cámara de los Lores y la Cámara de los Comunes. La

P

primera, consta de 703 miembros, en la mayoría nombrados, con un número de cargos hereditarios, lo que es objeto de reforma en la actualidad. La Cámara de los Comunes consta de 659 miembros elegidos por el pueblo. Ver ▹Dáil Éireann, ▹Scottish Parliament, ▹Welsh Assembly.

parlour /ˈpɑːlə(r)/ *n* salón *m*
parochial /pəˈrəʊkɪəl/ *adj* (*fig*) provinciano
parody /ˈpærədɪ/ *n* parodia *f.* • *vt* parodiar
parole /pəˈrəʊl/ *n* libertad *f* condicional
parrot /ˈpærət/ *n* loro *m*, papagayo *m*
parsley /ˈpɑːslɪ/ *n* perejil *m*
parsnip /ˈpɑːsnɪp/ *n* pastinaca *f*
part /pɑːt/ *n* parte *f*; (*of machine*) pieza *f*; (*of serial*) episodio *m*; (*in play*) papel *m*; (*Amer, in hair*) raya *f.* **take ~ in** tomar parte en, participar en. **for the most ~** en su mayor parte. • *adv* en parte. • *vt* separar. • *vi* separarse. ▫ **~ with** *vt* desprenderse de
partial /ˈpɑːʃl/ *adj* parcial. **be ~ to** tener debilidad por. **~ly** *adv* parcialmente
participa|nt /pɑːˈtɪsɪpənt/ *n* participante *m & f.* **~te** /-peɪt/ *vi* participar. **~tion** /-ˈpeɪʃn/ *n* participación *f*
particle /ˈpɑːtɪkl/ *n* partícula *f*
particular /pəˈtɪkjʊlə(r)/ *adj* particular; (*precise*) meticuloso; (*fastidious*) quisquilloso. **in ~** en particular. • *n* detalle *m.* **~ly** *adv* particularmente; (*specifically*) específicamente
parting /ˈpɑːtɪŋ/ *n* despedida *f*; (*in hair*) raya *f.* • *adj* de despedida
partition /pɑːˈtɪʃn/ *n* partición *f*; (*wall*) tabique *m.* • *vt* dividir
partly /ˈpɑːtlɪ/ *adv* en parte
partner /ˈpɑːtnə(r)/ *n* socio *m*; (*Sport*) pareja *f.* **~ship** *n* asociación *f*; (*Com*) sociedad *f*
partridge /ˈpɑːtrɪdʒ/ *n* perdiz *f*
part-time /pɑːtˈtaɪm/ *adj & adv* a tiempo parcial, de medio tiempo (*LAm*)
party /ˈpɑːtɪ/ *n* reunión *f*, fiesta *f*; (*group*) grupo *m*; (*Pol*) partido *m*; (*Jurid*) parte *f*
pass /pɑːs/ *vt* (*hand, convey*) pasar; (*go past*) pasar por delante de; (*overtake*) adelantar, rebasar (*Mex*); (*approve*) aprobar (exam, bill, law); pronunciar (judgement). • *vi* pasar; (pain) pasarse; (*Sport*) pasar la pelota. ▫ **~ away** *vi* fallecer. ▫ **~ down** *vt* transmitir. ▫ **~ out** *vi* desmayarse. ▫ **~ round** *vt* distribuir. ▫ **~ up** *vt* 🅘 dejar pasar. • *n* (*permit*) pase *m*; (*ticket*) abono *m*; (*in mountains*) puerto *m*, desfiladero *m*; (*Sport*) pase *m*; (*in exam*) aprobado *m.* **make a ~ at** 🅘 intentar besar. **~able** *adj* pasable; (road) transitable
passage /ˈpæsɪdʒ/ *n* (*voyage*) travesía *f*; (*corridor*) pasillo *m*; (*alleyway*) pasaje *m*; (*in book*) pasaje *m*
passenger /ˈpæsɪndʒə(r)/ *n* pasajero *m*
passer-by /pɑːsəˈbaɪ/ *n* (*pl* **passers-by**) transeúnte *m & f*
passion /ˈpæʃn/ *n* pasión *f.* **~ate** /-ət/ *adj* apasionado. **~ately** *adv* apasionadamente
passive /ˈpæsɪv/ *adj* pasivo
Passover /ˈpɑːsəʊvə(r)/ *n* Pascua *f* de los hebreos

pass: ~port *n* pasaporte *m*. **~word** *n* contraseña *f*

past /pɑːst/ *adj* anterior; (life) pasado; (week, year) último. **in times ~** en tiempos pasados. ●*n* pasado *m*. **in the ~** (*formerly*) antes, antiguamente. ●*prep* por delante de; (*beyond*) más allá de. **it's twenty ~ four** son las cuatro y veinte. ●*adv*. **drive ~** pasar en coche. **go ~** pasar

paste /peɪst/ *n* pasta *f*; (*glue*) engrudo *m*; (*wallpaper* ~) pegamento *m*; (*jewellery*) estrás *m*

pastel /'pæstl/ *adj & n* pastel (*m*)

pasteurize /'pɑːstʃəraɪz/ *vt* pasteurizar

pastime /'pɑːstaɪm/ *n* pasatiempo *m*

pastry /'peɪstrɪ/ *n* masa *f*; (*cake*) pastelito *m*

pasture /'pɑːstʃə(r)/ *n* pasto(s) *mpl*

pasty /'pæstɪ/ *n* empanadilla *f*, empanada *f* (*LAm*)

pat /pæt/ *vt* (*pt* **patted**) darle palmaditas. ●*n* palmadita *f*; (*of butter*) porción *f*

patch /pætʃ/ *n* (*on clothes*) remiendo *m*, parche *m*; (*over eye*) parche *m*. **a bad ~** una mala racha. ●*vt* remendar. □ **~ up** *vt* hacerle un arreglo a

patent /'peɪtnt/ *adj* patente. ●*n* patente *f*. ●*vt* patentar. **~ leather** *n* charol *m*. **~ly** *adv*. **it's ~ly obvious that...** está clarísimo que...

patern|al /pə'tɜːnl/ *adj* paterno. **~ity** /-ətɪ/ *n* paternidad *f*

path /pɑːθ/ *n* (*pl* **-s**/pɑːðz/) sendero *m*; (*Sport*) pista *f*; (*of rocket*) trayectoria *f*; (*fig*) camino *m*

pathetic /pə'θetɪk/ *adj* (*pitiful*) patético; (excuse) pobre. **don't be so ~** no seas tan pusilánime

patien|ce /'peɪʃns/ *n* paciencia *f*. **~t** *adj & n* paciente (*m & f*). **be ~t with s.o.** tener paciencia con uno. **~tly** *adv* pacientemente

patio /'pætɪəʊ/ *n* (*pl* **-os**) patio *m*

patriot /'pætrɪət/ *n* patriota *m & f*. **~ic** /-'ɒtɪk/ *adj* patriótico. **~ism** *n* patriotismo *m*

patrol /pə'trəʊl/ *n* patrulla *f*. ●*vt/i* patrullar

patron /'peɪtrən/ *n* (*of the arts*) mecenas *m & f*; (*of charity*) patrocinador *m*; (*customer*) cliente *m & f*. **~age** /'pætrənɪdʒ/ *n* (*sponsorship*) patrocinio *m*; (*of the arts*) mecenazgo *m*. **~ize** /'pætrənaɪz/ *vt* ser cliente de; (*fig*) tratar con condescendencia. **~izing** *adj* condescendiente

pattern /'pætn/ *n* diseño *m*; (*sample*) muestra *f*; (*in dressmaking*) patrón *m*

paunch /pɔːntʃ/ *n* panza *f*

pause /pɔːz/ *n* pausa *f*. ●*vi* hacer una pausa

pave /peɪv/ *vt* pavimentar; (*with flagstones*) enlosar. **~ment** *n* pavimento *m*; (*at side of road*) acera *f*, banqueta *f* (*Mex*)

paving stone /'peɪvɪŋstəʊn/ *n* losa *f*

paw /pɔː/ *n* pata *f*

pawn /pɔːn/ *n* (*Chess*) peón *m*; (*fig*) títere *m*. ●*vt* empeñar. **~broker** *n* prestamista *m & f*

pay /peɪ/ *vt* (*pt* **paid**) pagar; prestar (attention); hacer (compliment, visit). **~ cash** pagar al contado. ●*vi* pagar; (*be profitable*) rendir. ●*n* paga *f*. **in the ~ of** al servicio de. □ **~ back** *vt* devolver; pagar (loan). □ **~ in** *vt* ingresar, depositar (*LAm*). □ **~ off** *vt* cancelar, saldar (debt). *vi* valer la pena. □ ~ **up** *vi* pagar. ~**able** *adj* pagadero. ~**ment** *n* pago *m*. ~**roll** *n* nómina *f*

pea /pi:/ *n* guisante *m*, arveja *f* (*LAm*), chícharo *m* (*Mex*)

peace /pi:s/ *n* paz *f*. ~ **of mind** tranquilidad *f*. ~**ful** *adj* tranquilo. ~**maker** *n* conciliador *m*

peach /pi:tʃ/ *n* melocotón *m*, durazno *m* (*LAm*)

peacock /'pi:kɒk/ *n* pavo *m* real

peak /pi:k/ *n* cumbre *f*; (*of career*) apogeo *m*; (*maximum*) máximo *m*. ~ **hours** *npl* horas *fpl* de mayor demanda (o consumo etc)

peal /pi:l/ *n* repique *m*. ~**s of laughter** risotadas *fpl*

peanut /'pi:nʌt/ *n* cacahuete *m*, maní *m* (*LAm*), cacahuate *m* (*Mex*)

pear /peə(r)/ *n* pera *f*. ~ **(tree)** peral *m*

pearl /pɜ:l/ *n* perla *f*

peasant /'peznt/ *n* campesino *m*

peat /pi:t/ *n* turba *f*

pebble /'pebl/ *n* guijarro *m*

P **peck** /pek/ *vt* picotear. ● *n* picotazo *m*; (*kiss*) besito *m*

peculiar /pɪ'kju:lɪə(r)/ *adj* raro; (*special*) especial. ~**ity** /-'ærətɪ/ *n* rareza *f*; (*feature*) particularidad *f*

pedal /'pedl/ *n* pedal *m*. ● *vi* pedalear

pedantic /pɪ'dæntɪk/ *adj* pedante

peddle /'pedl/ *vt* vender por las calles

pedestal /'pedɪstl/ *n* pedestal *m*

pedestrian /pɪ'destrɪən/ *n* peatón *m*. ~ **crossing** paso *m* de peatones. ● *adj* pedestre; (*dull*) prosaico

pedigree /'pedɪgri:/ linaje *m*; (*of animal*) pedigrí *m*. ● *adj* (animal) de raza

peek /pi:k/ *vi* mirar a hurtadillas

peel /pi:l/ *n* piel *f*, cáscara *f*. ● *vt* pelar (fruit, vegetables). ● *vi* pelarse

peep /pi:p/ *vi*. ~ **at** echarle un vistazo a. ● *n* (*look*) vistazo *m*; (*bird sound*) pío *m*

peer /pɪə(r)/ *vi* mirar. ~ **at** escudriñar. ● *n* (*equal*) par *m* & *f*; (*contemporary*) coetáneo *m*; (*lord*) par *m*. ~**age** /-ɪdʒ/ *n* nobleza *f*

peg /peg/ *n* (*in ground*) estaca *f*; (*on violin*) clavija *f*; (*for washing*) pinza *f*; (*hook*) gancho *m*; (*for tent*) estaquilla *f*. **off the** ~ de confección. ● *vt* (*pt* **pegged**) sujetar (*con estacas, etc*); fijar (precios)

pejorative /pɪ'dʒɒrətɪv/ *adj* peyorativo, despectivo

pelican /'pelɪkən/ *n* pelícano *m*

pellet /'pelɪt/ *n* bolita *f*; (*for gun*) perdigón *m*

pelt /pelt/ *n* pellejo *m*. ● *vt*. ~ **s.o. with sth** lanzarle algo a uno. ● *vi*. ~ **with rain,** ~ **down** llover a cántaros

pelvis /'pelvɪs/ *n* pelvis *f*

pen /pen/ (*for writing*) pluma *f*; (*ballpoint*) bolígrafo *m*; (*sheep* ~) redil *m*; (*cattle* ~) corral *m*

penal /'pi:nl/ *adj* penal. ~**ize** *vt* sancionar. ~**ty** /'penltɪ/ *n* pena *f*; (*fine*) multa *f*; (*in soccer*) penalty *m*; (*in US football*) castigo *m*. ~**ty kick** *n* (*in soccer*) penalty *m*

penance /'penəns/ *n* penitencia *f*

pence /pens/ *see* PENNY

pencil /'pensl/ *n* lápiz *m*. ● *vt* (*pt* **pencilled**) escribir con lápiz. ~**-sharpener** *n* sacapuntas *m*

pendulum /'pendjʊləm/ *n* péndulo *m*

penetrat|e /'penɪtreɪt/ *vt/i* penetrar. ~**ing** *adj* penetrante. ~**ion**

/-'treɪʃn/ *n* penetración *f*

penguin /'peŋgwɪn/ *n* pingüino *m*

penicillin /penɪ'sɪlɪn/ *n* penicilina *f*

peninsula /pə'nɪnsjʊlə/ *n* península *f*

penis /'pi:nɪs/ *n* pene *m*

pen: ~knife /'pennaɪf/ *n* (*pl* **pen-knives**) navaja *f*. **~-name** *n* seudónimo *m*

penn|iless /'penɪlɪs/ *adj* sin un céntimo. **~y** /'penɪ/ *n* (*pl* **pennies** *or* **pence**) penique *m*

pension /'penʃn/ *n* pensión *f*; (*for retirement*) pensión *f* de jubilación. **~er** *n* jubilado *m*

pensive /'pensɪv/ *adj* pensativo

Pentecost /'pentɪkɒst/ *n* Pentecostés *m*

penthouse /'penthaʊs/ *n* penthouse *m*

pent-up /pent'ʌp/ *adj* reprimido; (*confined*) encerrado

penultimate /pen'ʌltɪmət/ *adj* penúltimo

people /'pi:pl/ *npl* gente *f*; (*citizens*) pueblo *m*. **~ say (that)** se dice que, dicen que. **English ~** los ingleses. **young ~** los jóvenes. **the ~** (*nation*) el pueblo. ● *vt* poblar

pepper /'pepə(r)/ *n* pimienta *f*; (*vegetable*) pimiento *m*. ● *vt* (*intersperse*) salpicar (**with** de). **~box** *n* (*Amer*) pimentero *m*. **~corn** *n* grano *m* de pimienta. **~mint** *n* menta *f*; (*sweet*) caramelo *m* de menta. **~pot** *n* pimentero *m*

per /pɜ:(r)/ *prep* por. **~ annum** al año. **~ cent** *see* PERCENT. **~ head** por cabeza, por persona. **ten miles ~ hour** diez millas por hora

perceive /pə'si:v/ *vt* percibir; (*notice*) darse cuenta de

percent, per cent /pə'sent/ *n* (*no pl*) porcentaje *m*. ● *adv* por ciento. **~age** /-ɪdʒ/ *n* porcentaje *m*

percepti|ble /pə'septəbl/ *adj* perceptible. **~on** /-ʃn/ *n* percepción *f*. **~ve** /-tɪv/ *adj* perspicaz

perch /pɜ:tʃ/ *n* (*of bird*) percha *f*; (*fish*) perca *f*. ● *vi* (bird) posarse. **~ on** (person) sentarse en el borde de

percolat|e /'pɜ:kəleɪt/ *vi* filtrarse. **~or** *n* cafetera *f* eléctrica

percussion /pə'kʌʃn/ *n* percusión *f*

perfect /'pɜ:fɪkt/ *adj* perfecto; (place, day) ideal. ● /pə'fekt/ *vt* perfeccionar. **~ion** /pə'fekʃn/ *n* perfección *f*. **to ~ion** a la perfección. **~ly** /'pɜ:fɪktlɪ/ *adv* perfectamente

perform /pə'fɔ:m/ *vt* desempeñar (function, role); ejecutar (task); realizar (experiment); representar (*play*); (*Mus*) interpretar. **~ an operation** (*Med*) operar. ● *vi* (actor) actuar; (musician) tocar; (*produce results*) (vehicle) responder; (company) rendir. **~ance** /-əns/ *n* ejecución *f*; (*of play*) representación *f*; (*of actor, musician*) interpretación *f*; (*of team*) actuación *f*; (*of car*) rendimiento *m*. **~er** *n* (*actor*) actor *m*; (*entertainer*) artista *m & f*

perfume /'pɜ:fju:m/ *n* perfume *m*

perhaps /pə'hæps/ *adv* quizá(s), tal vez, a lo mejor

peril /'perəl/ *n* peligro *m*. **~ous** *adj* arriesgado, peligroso

perimeter /pə'rɪmɪtə(r)/ *n* perímetro *m*

period /'pɪərɪəd/ *n* período *m*; (*in history*) época *f*; (*lesson*) clase *f*; (*Amer, Gram*) punto *m*; (*menstruation*) período *m*, regla *f*. ● *adj* de (la) época. **~ic** /-'ɒdɪk/ *adj* periódico. **~ical** /pɪərɪ'ɒdɪkl/ *n* revista *f*.

~**ically** *adv* periódico
peripher|al /pəˈrɪfərəl/ *adj* secundario; (*Comp*) periférico. ~**y** /pəˈrɪfərɪ/ *n* periferia *f*
perish /ˈperɪʃ/ *vi* perecer; (*rot*) deteriorarse. ~**able** *adj* perecedero. ~**ing** *adj* 🅸 glacial
perjur|e /ˈpɜːdʒə(r)/ *vr.* ~**e o.s.** perjurarse. ~**y** *n* perjurio *m*
perk /pɜːk/ *n* gaje *m*. □ ~ **up** *vt* reanimar. *vi* reanimarse
perm /pɜːm/ *n* permanente *f*. ● *vt.* have one's hair ~**ed** hacerse la permanente
permanen|ce /ˈpɜːmənəns/ *n* permanencia *f*. ~**t** *adj* permanente. ~**tly** *adv* permanentemente
permissible /pəˈmɪsəbl/ *adj* permisible
permission /pəˈmɪʃn/ *n* permiso *m*
permit /pəˈmɪt/ *vt* (*pt* **permitted**) permitir. ● /ˈpɜːmɪt/ *n* permiso *m*
peroxide /pəˈrɒksaɪd/ *n* peróxido *m*
perpendicular /pɜːpənˈdɪkjʊlə(r)/ *adj* & *n* perpendicular (*f*)
perpetrat|e /ˈpɜːpɪtreɪt/ *vt* cometer. ~**or** *n* autor *m*
perpetua|l /pəˈpetʃʊəl/ *adj* perpetuo. ~**te** /pəˈpetʃʊeɪt/ *vt* perpetuar
perplex /pəˈpleks/ *vt* dejar perplejo. ~**ed** *adj* perplejo
persecut|e /ˈpɜːsɪkjuːt/ *vt* perseguir. ~**ion** /-ˈkjuːʃn/ *n* persecución *f*
persever|ance /pɜːsɪˈvɪərəns/ *n* perseverancia *f*. ~**e** /pɜːsɪˈvɪə(r)/ *vi* perseverar, persistir
Persian /ˈpɜːʃn/ *adj* persa. **the** ~ **Gulf** *n* el golfo Pérsico
persist /pəˈsɪst/ *vi* persistir. ~**ence** /-əns/ *n* persistencia *f*. ~**ent** *adj* persistente; (*continual*) continuo
person /ˈpɜːsn/ *n* persona *f*. **in** ~ en persona. ~**al** *adj* personal; (call) particular; (property) privado. ~**al assistant** *n* secretario *m* personal. ~**ality** /-ˈnælətɪ/ *n* personalidad *f*. ~**ally** *adv* personalmente. ~**nel** /pɜːsəˈnel/ *n* personal *m*. **P**~ (*department*) sección *f* de personal
perspective /pəˈspektɪv/ *n* perspectiva *f*
perspir|ation /pɜːspəˈreɪʃn/ *n* transpiración *f*. ~**e** /pəsˈpaɪə(r)/ *vi* transpirar
persua|de /pəˈsweɪd/ *vt* convencer, persuadir. ~**e s.o. to do sth** convencer a uno para que haga algo. ~**sion** *n* /-ʃn/ persuasión *f*. ~**sive** /-sɪv/ *adj* persuasivo
pertinent /ˈpɜːtɪnənt/ *adj* pertinente. ~**ly** *adv* pertinentemente
perturb /pəˈtɜːb/ *vt* perturbar
Peru /pəˈruː/ *n* el Perú *m*
peruse /pəˈruːz/ *vt* leer cuidadosamente
Peruvian /pəˈruːvɪan/ *adj* & *n* peruano (*m*)
perver|se /pəˈvɜːs/ *adj* retorcido; (*stubborn*) obstinado. ~**sion** *n* perversión *f*. ~**t** /pəˈvɜːt/ *vt* pervertir. ● /ˈpɜːvɜːt/ *n* pervertido *m*
pessimis|m /ˈpesɪmɪzəm/ *n* pesimismo *m*. ~**t** *n* pesimista *m* & *f*. ~**tic** /-ˈmɪstɪk/ *adj* pesimista
pest /pest/ *n* plaga *f*; (🅸, *person, thing*) peste *f*
pester /ˈpestə(r)/ *vt* importunar
pesticide /ˈpestɪsaɪd/ *n* pesticida *f*
pet /pet/ *n* animal *m* doméstico; (*favourite*) favorito *m*. ● *adj* preferido. **my** ~ **hate** lo que más odio. ● *vt* (*pt* **petted**) acariciar
petal /ˈpetl/ *n* pétalo *m*

petition /pɪ'tɪʃn/ *n* petición *f*
pet name *n* apodo *m*
petrified /'petrɪfaɪd/ *adj* (*terrified*) muerto de miedo; (rock) petrificado
petrol /'petrəl/ *n* gasolina *f*. **~ pump** *n* surtidor *m*. **~ station** *n* gasolinera *f*. **~ tank** *n* depósito *m* de gasolina **~eum** /pɪ'trəʊlɪəm/ *n* petróleo *m*.
petticoat /'petɪkəʊt/ *n* enagua *f*; (*slip*) combinación *f*
petty /'petɪ/ *adj* (**-ier**, **-iest**) insignificante; (*mean*) mezquino. **~y cash** *n* dinero *m* para gastos menores
petulant /'petjʊlənt/ *adj* irritable
pew /pju:/ *n* banco *m* (de iglesia)
phantom /'fæntəm/ *n* fantasma *m*
pharma|ceutical /fɑ:mə'sju:tɪkl/ *adj* farmacéutico. **~cist** /'fɑ:məsɪst/ *n* farmacéutico *m*. **~cy** /'fɑ:məsɪ/ *n* farmacia *f*
phase /feɪz/ *n* etapa *f*. □ **~ out** *vt* retirar progresivamente
PhD *abbr* (= **Doctor of Philosophy**) *n* doctorado *m*; (*person*) Dr., Dra.
pheasant /'feznt/ *n* faisán *m*
phenomen|al /fɪ'nɒmɪnl/ *adj* fenomenal. **~on** /-mən/ *n* (*pl* **-ena** /-ɪnə/) fenómeno *m*
philistine /'fɪlɪstaɪn/ *adj* & *n* filisteo (*m*)
philosoph|er /fɪ'lɒsəfə(r)/ *n* filósofo *m*. **~ical** /-ə'sɒfɪkl/ *adj* filosófico. **~y** /fɪ'lɒsəfɪ/ *n* filosofía *f*
phlegm /flem/ *n* flema *f*. **~atic** /fleg'mætɪk/ *adj* flemático
phobia /'fəʊbɪə/ *n* fobia *f*
phone /fəʊn/ *n* 🅸 teléfono *m*. ●*vt/i* llamar (por teléfono). **~ back** (*call again*) volver a llamar; (*return call*) llamar (más tarde). **~ book** *n* guía *f* telefónica, directorio *m* (*LAm*). **~ booth**, **~ box** *n* cabina *f* telefónica. **~ call** *n* llamada *f* (telefónica). **~ card** *n* tarjeta *f* telefónica. **~ number** *n* número *m* de teléfono
phonetic /fə'netɪk/ *adj* fonético. **~s** *n* fonética *f*
phoney /'fəʊnɪ/ *adj* (**-ier**, **-iest**) 🅸 falso
phosph|ate /'fɒsfeɪt/ *n* fosfato *m*. **~orus** /'fɒsfərəs/ *n* fósforo *m*
photo /'fəʊtəʊ/ *n* (*pl* **-os**) 🅸 foto *f*. **take a ~** sacar una foto. **~copier** /-kɒpɪə(r)/ *n* fotocopiadora *f*. **~copy** *n* fotocopia *f*. ●*vt* fotocopiar. **~genic** /-'dʒenɪk/ *adj* fotogénico. **~graph** /-grɑ:f/ *n* fotografía *f*. ●*vt* fotografiar, sacarle una fotografía a. **~grapher** /fə'tɒgrəfə(r)/ *n* fotógrafo *m*. **~graphic** /-'græfɪk/ *adj* fotográfico. **~graphy** /fə'tɒgrəfɪ/ *n* fotografía *f*
phrase /freɪz/ *n* frase *f*. ●*vt* expresar. **~ book** *n* manual *m* de conversación
physi|cal /'fɪzɪkl/ *adj* físico. **~cian** /fɪ'zɪʃn/ *n* médico *m*. **~cist** /'fɪzɪsɪst/ *n* físico *m*. **~cs** /'fɪzɪks/ *n* física *f*. **~ology** /fɪzɪ'ɒlədʒɪ/ *n* fisiología *f*. **~otherapist** /fɪzɪəʊ'θerəpɪst/ *n* fisioterapeuta *m* & *f*. **~otherapy** /fɪzɪəʊ'θerəpɪ/ *n* fisioterapia *f*. **~que** /fɪ'zi:k/ *n* físico *m*
pian|ist /'pɪənɪst/ *n* pianista *m* & *f*. **~o** /pɪ'ænəʊ/ *n* (*pl* **-os**) piano *m*
pick /pɪk/ (*tool*) pico *m*. ●*vt* escoger; cortar (flowers); recoger (fruit, cotton); abrir con una ganzúa (lock). **~ a quarrel** buscar camorra. **~ holes in** criticar. □ **~ on** *vt* meterse con. □ **~ out** *vt* escoger; (*identify*) reconocer. □ **~ up** *vt* re-

P

coger; (*lift*) levantar; (*learn*) aprender; adquirir (habit, etc); contagiarse de (illness). ● *vi* mejorar; (sales) subir. **~axe** *n* pico *m*

picket /'pɪkɪt/ *n* (*group*) piquete *m*. **~ line** *n* piquete *m*. ● *vt* formar un piquete frente a

pickle /'pɪkl/ *n* (*in vinegar*) encurtido *m*; (*Amer, gherkin*) pepinillo *m*; (*relish*) salsa *f* (*a base de encurtidos*). ● *vt* encurtir

pick: ~pocket *n* carterista *m & f*. **~-up** *n* (*truck*) camioneta *f*

picnic /'pɪknɪk/ *n* picnic *m*

picture /'pɪktʃə(r)/ *n* (*painting*) cuadro *m*; (*photo*) foto *f*; (*drawing*) dibujo *m*; (*illustration*) ilustración *f*; (*film*) película *f*; (*fig*) descripción *f*. ● *vt* imaginarse. **~sque** /-'resk/ *adj* pintoresco

pie /paɪ/ *n* empanada *f*; (*sweet*) pastel *m*, tarta *f*

piece /pi:s/ *n* pedazo *m*, trozo *m*; (*part of machine*) pieza *f*; (*coin*) moneda *f*; (*in chess*) figura *f*. **a ~ of advice** un consejo. **a ~ of furniture** un mueble. **a ~ of news** una noticia. **take to ~s** desmontar. □ **~ together** *vt* juntar. **~meal** *adj* gradual; (*unsystematic*) poco sistemático. ● *adv* poco a poco

pier /pɪə(r)/ *n* muelle *m*; (*with amusements*) paseo con atracciones sobre un muelle

pierc|e /pɪəs/ *vt* perforar. **~ing** *adj* penetrante

piety /'paɪətɪ/ *n* piedad *f*

pig /pɪg/ *n* cerdo *m*, chancho *m* (*LAm*)

pigeon /'pɪdʒɪn/ *n* paloma *f*; (*Culin*) pichón *m*. **~-hole** *n* casillero *m*; (*fig*) casilla *f*

piggy /'pɪgɪ/ *n* cerdito *m*. **~back** *n*. **give s.o. a ~back** llevar a uno a cuestas. **~ bank** *n* hucha *f*

pig-headed /-'hedɪd/ *adj* terco

pigment /'pɪgmənt/ *n* pigmento *m*

pig|sty /'pɪgstaɪ/ *n* pocilga *f*. **~tail** *n* (*plait*) trenza *f*; (*bunch*) coleta *f*

pike /paɪk/ *n invar* (*fish*) lucio *m*

pilchard /'pɪltʃəd/ *n* sardina *f*

pile /paɪl/ *n* (*heap*) montón *m*; (*of fabric*) pelo *m*. ● *vt* amontonar. **~ it on** exagerar. ● *vi* amontonarse. □ **~ up** *vt* amontonar. ● *vi* amontonarse. **~s** /paɪlz/ *npl* (*Med*) almorranas *fpl*. **~-up** *n* choque *m* múltiple

pilgrim /'pɪlgrɪm/ *n* peregrino. **~age** /-ɪdʒ/ *n* peregrinación *f*

pill /pɪl/ *n* pastilla *f*

pillar /'pɪlə(r)/ *n* columna *f*. **~ box** *n* buzón *m*

pillow /'pɪləʊ/ *n* almohada *f*. **~case** *n* funda *f* de almohada

pilot /'paɪlət/ *n* piloto *m*. ● *vt* pilotar. **~ light** *n* fuego *m* piloto

pimple /'pɪmpl/ *n* grano *m*, espinilla *f* (*LAm*)

pin /pɪn/ *n* alfiler *m*; (*Mec*) perno *m*. **~s and needles** hormigueo *m*. ● *vt* (*pt* **pinned**) prender con alfileres; (*fix*) sujetar

PIN /pɪn/ *n* (= **personal identification number**) NIP *m*

pinafore /'pɪnəfɔ:(r)/ *n* delantal *m*. **~ dress** *n* pichi *m*, jumper *m & f* (*LAm*)

pincers /'pɪnsəz/ *npl* tenazas *fpl*

pinch /pɪntʃ/ *vt* pellizcar; (*fam, steal*) hurtar. ● *vi* (shoe) apretar. ● *n* pellizco *m*; (*small amount*) pizca *f*. **at a ~** si fuera necesario

pine /paɪn/ *n* pino *m*. ● *vi*. **~ for sth** suspirar por algo. □ **~ away** *vi*

languidecer de añoranza. **~apple** /'paınæpl/ *n* piña *f*
ping-pong /'pıŋpɒŋ/ *n* ping-pong *m*
pink /pıŋk/ *adj & n* rosa (*m*), rosado (*m*)
pinnacle /'pınəkl/ *n* pináculo *m*
pin: ~point *vt* determinar con precisión *f*. **~stripe** *n* raya *f* fina
pint /paınt/ *n* pinta *f* (*= 0.57 litros*)
pioneer /paıə'nıə(r)/ *n* pionero *m*
pious /'paıəs/ *adj* piadoso
pip /pıp/ *n* (*seed*) pepita *f*; (*time signal*) señal *f*
pipe /paıp/ *n* tubo *m*; (*Mus*) caramillo *m*; (*for smoking*) pipa *f*. ● *vt* llevar por tuberías. **~-dream** *n* ilusión *f*. **~line** *n* conducto *m*; (*for oil*) oleoducto *m*. **in the ~line** en preparación *f*
piping /'paıpıŋ/ *n* tubería *f*. ● *adv*. **~ hot** muy caliente, hirviendo
pira|cy /'paıərəsı/ *n* piratería *f*. **~te** /'paıərət/ *n* pirata *m*
Pisces /'paısi:z/ *n* Piscis *m*
piss /pıs/ *vi* ☒ mear. □ **~ off** *vi* ☒. **~ off!** ¡vete a la mierda! **~ed** /pıst/ *adj* (☒, *drunk*) como una cuba; (*Amer, fed up*) cabreado
pistol /'pıstl/ *n* pistola *f*
piston /'pıstən/ *n* pistón *m*
pit /pıt/ *n* hoyo *m*; (*mine*) mina *f*; (*Amer, in fruit*) hueso *m*
pitch /pıtʃ/ *n* (*substance*) brea *f*; (*degree*) grado *m*; (*Mus*) tono *m*; (*Sport*) campo *m*. ● *vt* (*throw*) lanzar; armar (tent). ● *vi* (ship) cabecear. **~-black** /-'blæk/ *adj* oscuro como boca de lobo. **~er** *n* jarra *f*
pitfall /'pıtfɔ:l/ *n* trampa *f*
pith /pıθ/ *n* (*of orange, lemon*) médula *f*; (*fig*) meollo *m*
pitiful /'pıtıfl/ *adj* lastimoso
pittance /'pıtns/ *n* miseria *f*
pity /'pıtı/ *n* lástima *f*, pena *f*; (*compassion*) piedad *f*. **it's a ~ you can't come** es una lástima que no puedas venir. ● *vt* tenerle lástima a
pivot /'pıvət/ *n* pivote *m*. ● *vi* pivotar; (*fig*) depender (**on** de)
placard /'plækɑ:d/ *n* pancarta *f*; (*sign*) letrero *m*
placate /plə'keıt/ *vt* apaciguar
place /pleıs/ *n* lugar *m*; (*seat*) asiento *m*; (*in firm, team*) puesto *m*; (*fam, house*) casa *f*. **feel out of ~** sentirse fuera de lugar. **take ~** tener lugar. ● *vt* poner, colocar; (*identify*) identificar. **be ~d** (*in race*) colocarse. **~-mat** *n* mantel *m* individual
placid /'plæsıd/ *adj* plácido
plague /pleıg/ *n* peste *f*; (*fig*) plaga *f*. ● *vt* atormentar
plaice /pleıs/ *n invar* platija *f*
plain /pleın/ *adj* (**-er, -est**) (*clear*) claro; (*simple*) sencillo; (*candid*) franco; (*ugly*) feo. **in ~ clothes** de civil. ● *adv* totalmente. ● *n* llanura *f*. **~ly** *adv* claramente; (*frankly*) francamente; (*simply*) con sencillez
plaintiff /'pleıntıf/ *n* demandante *m & f*
plait /plæt/ *vt* trenzar. ● *n* trenza *f*
plan /plæn/ *n* plan *m*; (*map*) plano *m*; (*of book, essay*) esquema *f*. ● *vt* (*pt* **planned**) planear; planificar (strategies). **I'm ~ning to go to Greece** pienso ir a Grecia
plane /pleın/ *n* (*tree*) plátano *m*; (*level*) nivel *m*; (*aircraft*) avión *m*; (*tool*) cepillo *m*. ● *vt* cepillar
planet /'plænıt/ *n* planeta *m*. **~ary** *adj* planetario
plank /plæŋk/ *n* tabla *f*
planning /'plænıŋ/ *n* planificación *f*. **family ~** planificación fami-

P

liar. **town ~** urbanismo *m*

plant /plɑ:nt/ *n* planta *f*; (*Mec*) maquinaria *f*; (*factory*) fábrica *f*. ● *vt* plantar; (*place in position*) colocar. **~ation** /plæn'teɪʃn/ *n* plantación *f*

plaque /plæk/ *n* placa *f*

plasma /'plæzmə/ *n* plasma *m*

plaster /'plɑ:stə(r)/ *n* yeso *m*; (*on walls*) revoque *m*; (*sticking plaster*) tirita *f* (®), curita *f* (®) (*LAm*); (*for setting bones*) yeso *m*, escayola *f*. ● *vt* revocar; rellenar con yeso (cracks)

plastic /'plæstɪk/ *adj & n* plástico (*m*)

Plasticine /'plæstɪsi:n/ *n* (®) plastilina *f* (®)

plastic surgery /plæstɪk 'sɜ:dʒərɪ/ *n* cirugía *f* estética

plate /pleɪt/ *n* plato *m*; (*of metal*) chapa *f*; (*silverware*) vajilla *f* de plata; (*in book*) lámina *f*. ● *vt* recubrir (**with** de)

platform /'plætfɔ:m/ *n* plataforma *f*; (*Rail*) andén *m*

P

platinum /'plætɪnəm/ *n* platino *m*

platitude /'plætɪtju:d/ *n* lugar *m* común

platonic /plə'tɒnɪk/ *adj* platónico

plausible /'plɔ:zəbl/ *adj* verosímil; (person) convincente

play /pleɪ/ *vt* jugar a (game, cards); jugar a, jugar (*LAm*) (football, chess); tocar (instrument); (*act role*) representar el papel de. ● *vi* jugar. ● *n* juego *m*; (*drama*) obra *f* de teatro. □ **~ down** *vt* minimizar. □ **~ up** *vi* [I] (child) dar guerra; (car, TV) no funcionar bien. **~er** *n* jugador *m*; (*Mus*) músico *m*. **~ful** *adj* juguetón. **~ground** *n* parque *m* de juegos infantiles; (*in school*) patio *m* de recreo. **~group** *n* jardín *m* de la infancia. **~ing card** *n* naipe *m*. **~ing field** *n* campo *m* de deportes. **~pen** *n* corralito *m*. **~wright** /-raɪt/ *n* dramaturgo *m*

plc *abbr* (= **public limited company**) S.A.

plea /pli:/ *n* súplica *f*; (*excuse*) excusa *f*; (*Jurid*) defensa *f*

plead /pli:d/ *vt* (*Jurid*) alegar; (*as excuse*) pretextar. ● *vi* suplicar. **~ with** suplicarle a. **~ guilty** declararse culpable

pleasant /'pleznt/ *adj* agradable

pleas|e /pli:z/ *int* por favor. ● *vt* complacer; (*satisfy*) contentar. ● *vi* agradar; (*wish*) querer. **~ed** *adj* (*satisfied*) satisfecho; (*happy*) contento. **~ed with** satisfecho de. **~ing** *adj* agradable; (*news*) grato. **~ure** /'pleʒə(r)/ *n* placer *m*

pleat /pli:t/ *n* pliegue *m*

pledge /pledʒ/ *n* cantidad *f* prometida

plent|iful /'plentɪfl/ *adj* abundante. **~y** /'plentɪ/ *n* abundancia *f*. ● *pron*. **~y of** muchos, -chas; (*of sth uncountable*) mucho, -cha

pliable /'plaɪəbl/ *adj* flexible

pliers /'plaɪəz/ *npl* alicates *mpl*

plight /plaɪt/ *n* situación *f* difícil

plimsolls /'plɪmsəlz/ *npl* zapatillas *fpl* de lona

plod /plɒd/ *vi* (*pt* **plodded**) caminar con paso pesado

plot /plɒt/ *n* complot *m*; (*of novel etc*) argumento *m*; (*piece of land*) parcela *f*. ● *vt* (*pt* **plotted**) tramar; (*mark out*) trazar. ● *vi* conspirar

plough /plaʊ/ *n* arado *m*. ● *vt/i* arar. □ **~ into** *vt* estrellarse contra. □ **~ through** *vt* avanzar laboriosamente por

ploy /plɔɪ/ *n* treta *f*

pluck /plʌk/ *vt* arrancar; depilarse

(eyebrows); desplumar (bird). **~ up courage to** armarse de valor para. ● *n* valor *m*. **~y** *adj* (**-ier**, **-iest**) valiente

plug /plʌg/ *n* (*in bath*) tapón *m*; (*Elec*) enchufe *m*; (*spark* ~) bujía *f*. ● *vt* (*pt* **plugged**) tapar; (*fam, advertise*) hacerle propaganda a. □ **~ in** *vt* (*Elec*) enchufar. **~hole** *n* desagüe *m*

plum /plʌm/ *n* ciruela *f*

plumage /ˈpluːmɪdʒ/ *n* plumaje *m*

plumb|er /ˈplʌmə(r)/ *n* fontanero *m*, plomero *m* (*LAm*). **~ing** *n* instalación *f* sanitaria, instalación *f* de cañerías

plume /pluːm/ *n* pluma *f*

plump /plʌmp/ *adj* (**-er**, **-est**) rechoncho

plunge /plʌndʒ/ *vt* hundir (knife); (*in water*) sumergir; (*into state, condition*) sumir. ● *vi* zambullirse; (*fall*) caer. ● *n* zambullida *f*

plural /ˈplʊərəl/ *n* plural *m*. ● *adj* en plural

plus /plʌs/ *prep* más. ● *adj* positivo. ● *n* signo *m* de más; (*fig*) ventaja *f*

plush /plʌʃ/ *adj* lujoso

Pluto /ˈpluːtəʊ/ *n* Plutón *m*

plutonium /pluːˈtəʊnɪəm/ *n* plutonio *m*

ply /plaɪ/ *vt* manejar (tool); ejercer (trade). **~ s.o. with drink** dar continuamente de beber a uno. **~wood** *n* contrachapado *m*

p.m. *abbr* (= **post meridiem**) de la tarde

pneumatic drill /njuːˈmætɪk/ *adj* martillo *m* neumático

pneumonia /njuːˈməʊnjə/ *n* pulmonía *f*

poach /pəʊtʃ/ *vt* escalfar (egg); cocer (fish etc); (*steal*) cazar furtivamente. **~er** *n* cazador *m* furtivo

PO box /piːˈəʊ/ *n* Apdo. postal

pocket /ˈpɒkɪt/ *n* bolsillo *m*; (*of air, resistance*) bolsa *f*. ● *vt* poner en el bolsillo. **~book** *n* (*notebook*) libro *m* de bolsillo; (*Amer, wallet*) cartera *f*; (*Amer, handbag*) bolso *m*, cartera *f* (*LAm*), bolsa *f* (*Mex*). **~ money** *n* dinero *m* de bolsillo, mesada *f* (*LAm*)

pod /pɒd/ *n* vaina *f*

poem /ˈpəʊɪm/ *n* poema *f*

poet /ˈpəʊɪt/ *n* poeta *m*. **~ic** /-ˈetɪk/ *adj* poético. **~ry** /ˈpəʊɪtrɪ/ *n* poesía *f*

poignant /ˈpɔɪnjənt/ *adj* conmovedor

point /pɔɪnt/ *n* (*dot, on scale*) punto *m*; (*sharp end*) punta *f*; (*in time*) momento *m*; (*statement*) observación; (*on agenda, in discussion*) punto *m*; (*Elec*) toma *f* de corriente. **to the ~** pertinente. **up to a ~** hasta cierto punto. **be on the ~ of** estar a punto de. **get to the ~** ir al grano. **there's no ~ (in) arguing** no sirve de nada discutir. ● *vt* (*aim*) apuntar; (*show*) indicar. ● *vi* señalar. **~ at/to sth** señalar algo. □ **~ out** *vt* señalar. **~-blank** *adj & adv* a quemarropa. **~ed** *adj* (*chin, nose*) puntiagudo; (*fig*) mordaz. **~less** *adj* inútil

poise /pɔɪz/ *n* porte *m*; (*composure*) desenvoltura *f*

poison /ˈpɔɪzn/ *n* veneno *m*. ● *vt* envenenar. **~ous** *adj* venenoso; (chemical etc) tóxico

poke /pəʊk/ *vt* empujar; atizar (fire). ● *vi* hurgar; (*pry*) meterse. ● *n* golpe *m*. □ **~ about** *vi* fisgonear. **~r** /ˈpəʊkə(r)/ *n* atizador *m*; (*Cards*) póquer *m*

poky /ˈpəʊkɪ/ *adj* (**-ier**, **-iest**) diminuto

Poland /ˈpəʊlənd/ *n* Polonia *f*

polar /ˈpəʊlə(r)/ *adj* polar. **~ bear** *n* oso *m* blanco

pole /pəʊl/ *n* palo *m*; (*fixed*) poste *m*; (*for flag*) mástil *m*; (*in geography*) polo *m*

police /pəˈliːs/ *n* policía *f*. **~man** /-mən/ *n* policía *m*, agente *m*. **~ station** *n* comisaría *f*. **~woman** *n* policía *f*, agente *f*

policy /ˈpɒlɪsɪ/ *n* política *f*; (*insurance*) póliza *f* (de seguros)

polish /ˈpɒlɪʃ/ *n* (*for shoes*) betún *m*; (*furniture* **~**) cera *f* para muebles; (*floor* **~**) abrillantador *m* de suelos; (*shine*) brillo *m*; (*fig*) finura *f*. ● *vt* darle brillo a; limpiar (shoes); (*refine*) pulir. ▫ **~ off** *vt* despachar. **~ed** *adj* pulido

Polish /ˈpəʊlɪʃ/ *adj & n* polaco (*m*)

polite /pəˈlaɪt/ *adj* cortés. **~ly** *adv* cortésmente. **~ness** *n* cortesía *f*

politic|al /pəˈlɪtɪkl/ *adj* político. **~ian** /pɒlɪˈtɪʃn/ *n* político *m*. **~s** /ˈpɒlətɪks/ *n* política *f*

poll /pəʊl/ *n* elección *f*; (*survey*) encuesta *f*. ● *vt* obtener (votes)

pollack /ˈpɒlæk/ *n* abadejo *m*

pollen /ˈpɒlən/ *n* polen *m*

polling booth *n* cabina *f* de votar

pollut|e /pəˈluːt/ *vt* contaminar. **~ion** /-ʃn/ *n* contaminación *f*

polo /ˈpəʊləʊ/ *n* polo *m*. **~ neck** *n* cuello *m* vuelto

poly|styrene /pɒlɪˈstaɪriːn/ *n* poliestireno *m*. **~thene** /ˈpɒlɪθiːn/ *n* plástico, polietileno *m*

pomp /pɒmp/ *n* pompa *f*. **~ous** *adj* pomposa

pond /pɒnd/ *n* (*natural*) laguna *f*; (*artificial*) estanque *m*

ponder /ˈpɒndə(r)/ *vt* considerar. **~ous** *adj* pesado

pony /ˈpəʊnɪ/ *n* poni *m*. **~-tail** *n* cola *f* de caballo

poodle /ˈpuːdl/ *n* caniche *m*

pool /puːl/ *n* charca *f*; (*artificial*) estanque *m*; (*puddle*) charco *m*. (*common fund*) fondos *mpl* comunes; (*snooker*) billar *m* americano. **(swimming) ~** *n* piscina *f*, alberca *f* (*Mex*). **~s** *npl* quinielas *fpl*. ● *vt* aunar

poor /pʊə(r)/ *adj* (**-er**, **-est**) pobre; (quality, diet) malo. **be in ~ health** estar mal de salud. **~ly** *adj* 🅸 malito. ● *adv* mal

pop /pɒp/ *n* (*Mus*) música *f* pop; (*Amer fam, father*) papá *m*. ● *vt* (*pt* **popped**) hacer reventar; (*put*) poner. ▫ **~ in** *vi* (*visit*) pasar por. ▫ **~ out** *vi* saltar; (person) salir un rato. ▫ **~ up** *vi* surgir, aparecer

popcorn /ˈpɒpkɔːn/ *n* palomitas *fpl*

pope /pəʊp/ *n* papa *m*

poplar /ˈpɒplə(r)/ *n* álamo *m* (blanco)

poppy /ˈpɒpɪ/ *n* amapola *f*

popular /ˈpɒpjʊlə(r)/ *adj* popular. **~ity** /-ˈlærətɪ/ *n* popularidad *f*. **~ize** *vt* popularizar

populat|e /ˈpɒpjʊleɪt/ *vt* poblar. **~ion** /-ˈleɪʃn/ *n* población *f*

pop-up /ˈpɒpʌp/ *n* ventana *f* emergente, pop-up *m*

porcelain /ˈpɔːsəlɪn/ *n* porcelana *f*

porch /pɔːtʃ/ *n* porche *m*

porcupine /ˈpɔːkjʊpaɪn/ *n* puerco *m* espín

pore /pɔː(r)/ *n* poro *m*

pork /pɔːk/ *n* carne *f* de cerdo *m*, carne *f* de puerco *m* (*Mex*)

porn /pɔːn/ *n* 🅸 pornografía *f*. **~ographic** /-əˈgræfɪk/ *adj* pornográfico. **~ography** /pɔːˈnɒgrəfɪ/ *n* pornografía *f*

porpoise /'pɔːpəs/ *n* marsopa *f*

porridge /'pɒrɪdʒ/ *n* avena *f* (*cocida*)

port /pɔːt/ *n* puerto *m*; (*Naut*) babor *m*; (*Comp*) puerto *m*; (*Culin*) oporto *m*

portable /'pɔːtəbl/ *adj* portátil

porter /'pɔːtə(r)/ *n* (*for luggage*) maletero *m*; (*concierge*) portero *m*

porthole /'pɔːthəʊl/ *n* portilla *f*

portion /'pɔːʃn/ *n* porción *f*; (*part*) parte *f*

portrait /'pɔːtrɪt/ *n* retrato *m*

portray /pɔː'treɪ/ *vt* representar. **~al** *n* representación *f*

Portug|al /'pɔːtjʊgl/ *n* Portugal *m*. **~uese** /-'giːz/ *adj* & *n* portugués (*m*)

pose /pəʊz/ *n* pose *f*, postura *f*. ● *vt* representar (threat); plantear (problem, question). ● *vi* posar. **~ as** hacerse pasar por

posh /pɒʃ/ *adj* 🄸 elegante

position /pə'zɪʃn/ *n* posición *f*; (*job*) puesto *m*; (*situation*) situación *f*. ● *vt* colocar

positive /'pɒzətɪv/ *adj* positivo; (*real*) auténtico; (*certain*) seguro. ● *n* (*Photo*) positiva *f*. **~ly** *adv* positivamente

possess /pə'zes/ *vt* poseer. **~ion** /-ʃn/ *n* posesión *f*; (*Jurid*) bien *m*. **~ive** *adj* posesivo

possib|ility /pɒsə'bɪlətɪ/ *n* posibilidad *f*. **~le** /'pɒsəbl/ *adj* posible. **~ly** *adv* posiblemente

post /pəʊst/ *n* (*pole*) poste *m*; (*job*) puesto *m*; (*mail*) correo *m*. ● *vt* echar al correo (letter); (*send*) enviar por correo. **keep s.o. ~ed** mantener a uno al corriente

post... /pəʊst/ *pref* post, pos

post: ~age /-ɪdʒ/ /-ɪdʒ/ *n* franqueo *m*. **~al** *adj* postal. **~al order** *n* giro *m* postal. **~ box** *n* buzón *m*. **~card** *n* (tarjeta *f*) postal *f*. **~code** *n* código *m* postal

poster /'pəʊstə(r)/ *n* cartel *m*, póster *m*

posterity /pɒs'terətɪ/ *n* posteridad *f*

posthumous /'pɒstjʊməs/ *adj* póstumo

post: ~man /-mən/ *n* cartero *m*. **~mark** *n* matasellos *m*

post mortem /pəʊst'mɔːtəm/ *n* autopsia *f*

post office *n* oficina *f* de correos, correos *mpl*, correo *m* (*LAm*)

postpone /pəʊst'pəʊn/ *vt* aplazar, posponer. **~ment** *n* aplazamiento *m*

postscript /'pəʊstskrɪpt/ *n* posdata *f*

posture /'pɒstʃə(r)/ *n* postura *f*

posy /'pəʊzɪ/ *n* ramillete *m*

pot /pɒt/ *n* (*for cooking*) olla *f*; (*for jam, honey*) tarro *m*; (*for flowers*) tiesto *m*; (*in pottery*) vasija *f*. **~s and pans** cacharros *mpl*

potato /pə'teɪtəʊ/ *n* (*pl* **-oes**) patata *f*, papa *f* (*LAm*)

potent /'pəʊtnt/ *adj* potente; (drink) fuerte

potential /pəʊ'tenʃl/ *adj* & *n* potencial (*m*). **~ly** *adv* potencialmente

pot: ~hole *n* cueva *f* subterránea; (*in road*) bache *m*. **~holing** *n* espeleología *f*

potion /'pəʊʃn/ *n* poción *f*

pot-shot *n* tiro *m* al azar

potter /'pɒtə(r)/ *n* alfarero *m*. ● *vi* hacer pequeños trabajos agradables. **~y** *n* (*pots*) cerámica *f*; (*workshop, craft*) alfarería *f*

potty /'pɒtɪ/ *adj* (**-ier**, **-iest**) 🄸

P

chiflado. ● *n* orinal *m*
pouch /paʊtʃ/ *n* bolsa *f* pequeña; (*for correspondence*) valija *f*
poultry /'pəʊltrɪ/ *n* aves *fpl* de corral
pounce /paʊns/ *vi* saltar. ~ **on** abalanzarse sobre
pound /paʊnd/ *n* (*weight*) libra *f* (= *454g*); (*money*) libra *f* (esterlina); (*for cars*) depósito *m*. ● *vt* (*crush*) machacar. ● *vi* aporrear; (heart) palpitar; (sound) retumbar
pour /pɔ:(r)/ *vt* verter; echar (salt). ~ **(out)** servir (drink). ● *vi* (blood) manar; (water) salir; (*rain*) llover a cántaros. □ ~ **out** *vi* (people) salir en tropel. ~**ing** *adj*. ~**ing rain** lluvia *f* torrencial
pout /paʊt/ *vi* hacer pucheros
poverty /'pɒvətɪ/ *n* pobreza *f*
powder /'paʊdə(r)/ *n* polvo *m*; (*cosmetic*) polvos *mpl*. ● *vt* empolvar. ~ **one's face** ponerse polvos en la cara. ~**y** *adj* como polvo
power /'paʊə(r)/ *n* poder *m*; (*energy*) energía *f*; (*electricity*) electricidad *f*; (*nation*) potencia *f*. ● *vt*. ~**ed by** impulsado por ~ **cut** *n* apagón *m*. ~**ed** *adj* con motor. ~**ful** *adj* poderoso. ~**less** *adj* impotente. ~ **plant**, ~**-station** *n* central *f* eléctrica
PR = **public relations**
practicable /'præktɪkəbl/ *adj* practicable
practical /'præktɪkl/ *adj* práctico. ~ **joke** *n* broma *f*. ~**ly** *adv* prácticamente
practi|ce /'præktɪs/ *n* práctica *f*; (*custom*) costumbre *f*; (*exercise*) ejercicio *m*; (*Sport*) entrenamiento *m*; (*clients*) clientela *f*. **he's out of** ~**ce** le falta práctica. **in** ~**ce** (*in fact*) en la práctica. ~**se** /'præktɪs/ *vt* practicar; ensayar (act); ejercer (profession). ● *vi* practicar; (professional) ejercer. ~**tioner** /-'tɪʃənə(r)/ *n* médico *m*
prairie /'preərɪ/ *n* pradera *f*
praise /preɪz/ *vt* (*Relig*) alabar; (*compliment*) elogiar. ● *n* (*credit*) elogios *mpl*. ~**worthy** *adj* loable
pram /præm/ *n* cochecito *m*
prank /præŋk/ *n* travesura *f*
prawn /prɔ:n/ *n* gamba *f*, camarón *m* (*LAm*)
pray /preɪ/ *vi* rezar (**for** por). ~**er** /preə(r)/ *n* oración *f*
pre.. /pri:/ *pref* pre...
preach /pri:tʃ/ *vt/i* predicar. ~**er** *n* predicador *m*; (*Amer, minister*) pastor *m*
pre-arrange /pri:ə'reɪndʒ/ *vt* concertar de antemano
precarious /prɪ'keərɪəs/ *adj* precario. ~**ly** *adv* precariamente
precaution /prɪ'kɔ:ʃn/ *n* precaución *f*
precede /prɪ'si:d/ *vt* preceder. ~**nce** /'presədəns/ *n* precedencia *f*. ~**nt** /'presədənt/ *n* precedente *m*
preceding /prɪ'si:dɪŋ/ *adj* anterior
precept /'pri:sept/ *n* precepto *m*
precinct /'pri:sɪŋkt/ *n* recinto *m*; (*Amer, police district*) distrito *m* policial; (*Amer, voting district*) circunscripción *f*. **pedestrian** ~ zona *f* peatonal. ~**s** (*of city*) límites *mpl*
precious /'preʃəs/ *adj* precioso. ● *adv* 🅸 muy
precipice /'presɪpɪs/ *n* precipicio *m*
precipitate /prɪ'sɪpɪteɪt/ *vt* precipitar. ● /prɪ'sɪpɪtət/ *n* precipitado *m*. ● /prɪ'sɪpɪtət/ *adj* precipitado
precis|e /prɪ'saɪs/ *adj* (*accurate*)

exacto; (*specific*) preciso; (*meticulous*) minucioso. **~ely** *adv* con precisión. **~!** ¡exacto! **~ion** /-'sɪʒn/ *n* precisión *f*

preclude /prɪ'klu:d/ *vt* excluir

precocious /prɪ'kəʊʃəs/ *adj* precoz. **~ly** *adv* precozmente

preconce|ived /pri:kən'si:vd/ *adj* preconcebido. **~ption** /-'sepʃn/ *n* preconcepción *f*

precursor /pri:'kɜ:sə(r)/ *n* precursor *m*

predator /'predətə(r)/ *n* depredador *m*. **~y** *adj* predador

predecessor /'pri:dɪsesə(r)/ *n* predecesor *m*, antecesor *m*

predicament /prɪ'dɪkəmənt/ *n* aprieto *m*

predict /prɪ'dɪkt/ *vt* predecir. **~ion** /-ʃn/ *n* predicción *f*

preen /pri:n/ *vt* arreglar. **~ o.s.** atildarse

prefab /'pri:fæb/ *n* ⊡ casa *f* prefabricada. **~ricated** /-'fæbrɪkeɪtɪd/ *adj* prefabricado

preface /'prefəs/ *n* prefacio *m*; (*to event*) prólogo *m*

prefect /'pri:fekt/ *n* (*Schol*) monitor *m*; (*official*) prefecto *m*

prefer /prɪ'fɜ:(r)/ *vt* (*pt* **preferred**) preferir. **~ sth to sth** preferir algo a algo. **~able** /'prefrəbl/ *adj* preferible. **~ence** /'prefrəns/ *n* preferencia *f*. **~ential** /-ə'renʃl/ *adj* preferente

pregnan|cy /'pregnənsɪ/ *n* embarazo *m*. **~t** *adj* embarazada

prehistoric /pri:hɪ'stɒrɪk/ *adj* prehistórico

prejudge /pri:'dʒʌdʒ/ *vt* prejuzgar

prejudice /'predʒʊdɪs/ *n* prejuicio *m*. ● *vt* predisponer; (*harm*) perjudicar. **~d** *adj* lleno de prejuicios

preliminary /prɪ'lɪmɪnərɪ/ *adj* preliminar

prelude /'prelju:d/ *n* preludio *m*

premature /'premətjʊə(r)/ *adj* prematuro

premeditated /pri:'medɪteɪtɪd/ *adj* premeditado

premier /'premɪə(r)/ *n* (*Pol*) primer ministro *m*

première /'premɪeə(r)/ *n* estreno *m*

premise /'premɪs/ *n* premisa *f*. **~s** /'premɪsɪz/ *npl* local *m*. **on the ~s** en el local

premium /'pri:mɪəm/ *n* (*insurance* **~**) prima *f* de seguro. **be at a ~** escasear

premonition /pri:mə'nɪʃn/ *n* premonición *f*, presentimiento *m*

preoccup|ation /pri:ɒkjʊ'peɪʃn/ *n* (*obsession*) obsesión *f*; (*concern*) preocupación *f*. **~ied** /-'ɒkjʊpaɪd/ *adj* absorto; (*worried*) preocupado

preparat|ion /prepə'reɪʃn/ *n* preparación *f*. **~ions** *npl* preparativos *mpl*. **~ory** /prɪ'pærətrɪ/ *adj* preparatorio

prepare /prɪ'peə(r)/ *vt* preparar. ● *vi* prepararse. ● *adj* preparado (*willing*). **be ~d to** estar dispuesto a

preposition /prepə'zɪʃn/ *n* preposición *f*

preposterous /prɪ'pɒstərəs/ *adj* absurdo

prerequisite /pri:'rekwɪzɪt/ *n* requisito *m* esencial

prerogative /prɪ'rɒgətɪv/ *n* prerrogativa *f*

Presbyterian /prezbɪ'tɪərɪən/ *adj* & *n* presbiteriano (*m*)

prescri|be /prɪ'skraɪb/ *vt* prescribir; (*Med*) recetar. **~ption** /-'ɪpʃn/ *n* (*Med*) receta *f*

presence /'prezns/ *n* presencia *f*. **~ of mind** presencia *f* de ánimo

present /'preznt/ *n* (*gift*) regalo *m*; (*current time*) presente *m*. **at ~** actualmente. **for the ~** por ahora. ● *adj* presente. ● /prɪ'zent/ *vt* presentar; (*give*) obsequiar. **~ s.o. with** obsequiar a uno con. **~able** /prɪ'zentəbl/ *adj* presentable. **~ation** /prezn'teɪʃn/ *n* presentación *f*; (*ceremony*) ceremonia *f* de entrega. **~er** /prɪ'zentə(r)/ *n* presentador *m*. **~ly** /'prezntlɪ/ *adv* dentro de poco

preserv|ation /prezə'veɪʃn/ *n* conservación *f*. **~ative** /prɪ'zɜːvətɪv/ *n* conservante *m*. **~e** /prɪ'zɜːv/ *vt* conservar; (*maintain*) mantener; (*Culin*) hacer conserva de. ● *n* coto *m*; (*jam*) confitura *f*. **wildlife ~e** (*Amer*) reserva *f* de animales

preside /prɪ'zaɪd/ *vi* presidir. **~ over** presidir

presiden|cy /'prezɪdənsɪ/ *n* presidencia *f*. **~t** *n* presidente *m*. **~tial** /-'denʃl/ *adj* presidencial

press /pres/ *vt* apretar; prensar (grapes); (*put pressure on*) presionar; (*iron*) planchar. **be ~ed for time** andar escaso de tiempo. ● *vi* apretar; (time) apremiar; (*fig*) urgir. ● *n* (*Mec, newspapers*) prensa *f*; (*printing*) imprenta *f*. □ **~ on** *vi* seguir adelante (with con). **~ conference** *n* rueda *f* de prensa. **~ cutting** *n* recorte *m* de periódico. **~ing** *adj* urgente. **~-up** *n* flexión *f*, fondo *m*

pressur|e /'preʃə(r)/ *n* presión *f*. ● *vt* presionar. **~e-cooker** *n* olla *f* a presión. **~ize** *vt* presionar

prestig|e /pre'stiːʒ/ *n* prestigio *m*. **~ious** /-'stɪdʒəs/ *adj* prestigioso

presum|ably /prɪ'zjuːməblɪ/ *adv*. **~...** supongo que..., me imagino que... **~e** /prɪ'zjuːm/ *vt* suponer. **~ptuous** /prɪ'zʌmptʃʊəs/ *adj* impertinente

presuppose /priːsə'pəʊz/ *vt* presuponer

preten|ce /prɪ'tens/ *n* fingimiento *m*; (*claim*) pretensión *f*; (*pretext*) pretexto *m*. **~d** /-'tend/ *vt/i* fingir. **~sion** /-'tenʃən/ *n* pretensión *f*. **~tious** /-'tenʃəs/ *adj* pretencioso

pretext /'priːtekst/ *n* pretexto *m*

pretty /'prɪtɪ/ *adj* (**-ier**, **-iest**) *adv* bonito, lindo (*esp LAm*)

prevail /prɪ'veɪl/ *vi* predominar; (*win*) prevalecer. □ **~ on** *vt* persuadir

prevalen|ce /'prevələns/ *n* (*occurrence*) preponderancia *f*; (*predominance*) predominio *m*. **~t** *adj* extendido

prevent /prɪ'vent/ *vt* (*hinder*) impedir; (*forestall*) prevenir, evitar. **~ion** /-ʃn/ *n* prevención *f*. **~ive** *adj* preventivo

preview /'priːvjuː/ *n* preestreno *m*; (*trailer*) avance *m*

previous /'priːvɪəs/ *adj* anterior. **~ to** antes de. **~ly** *adv* antes

prey /preɪ/ *n* presa *f*. **bird of ~** ave *f* de rapiña

price /praɪs/ *n* precio *m*. ● *vt* fijar el precio de. **~less** *adj* inestimable; (*fam, amusing*) muy divertido. **~y** *adj* [!] carito

prick /prɪk/ *vt/i* pinchar. ● *n* pinchazo *m*

prickl|e /'prɪkl/ *n* (*thorn*) espina *f*; (*of animal*) púa *f*; (*sensation*) picor *m*. **~y** *adj* espinoso; (animal) con púas; (*touchy*) quisquilloso

pride /praɪd/ *n* orgullo *m*. ● *vr*. **~ o.s. on** enorgullecerse de

priest /priːst/ *n* sacerdote *m*. **~hood** *n* sacerdocio *m*

prim /prɪm/ *adj* (**primmer**, **primmest**) mojigato; (*affected*) remilgado

primar|ily /ˈpraɪmərɪlɪ/ *adv* en primer lugar. **~y** /ˈpraɪmərɪ/ *adj* (*principal*) primordial; (*first, basic*) primario. **~ school** *n* escuela *f* primaria

prime /praɪm/ *vt* cebar (gun); (*prepare*) preparar; aprestar (surface). ● *adj* principal; (*first rate*) excelente. **~ minister** *n* primer ministro *m*. ● *n*. **be in one's ~** estar en la flor de la vida. **~r** *n* (*paint*) imprimación *f*

primeval /praɪˈmiːvl/ *adj* primigenio

primitive /ˈprɪmɪtɪv/ *adj* primitivo

primrose /ˈprɪmrəʊz/ *n* primavera *f*

prince /prɪns/ *n* príncipe *m*. **~ss** /prɪnˈses/ *n* princesa *f*

principal /ˈprɪnsəpl/ *adj* principal. ● *n* (*of school*) director *m*; (*of university*) rector *m*. **~ly** /ˈprɪnsɪpəlɪ/ *adv* principalmente

principle /ˈprɪnsəpl/ *n* principio *m*. **in ~** en principio. **on ~** por principio

print /prɪnt/ *vt* imprimir; (*write in capitals*) escribir con letras de molde. **~ed matter** impresos *mpl*. ● *n* (*characters*) letra *f*; (*picture*) grabado *m*; (*Photo*) copia *f*; (*fabric*) estampado *m*. **in ~** (*published*) publicado; (*available*) a la venta. **out of ~** agotado. **~er** /ˈprɪntə(r)/ *n* impresor *m*; (*machine*) impresora *f*. **~ing** *n* impresión *f*; (*trade*) imprenta *f*. **~out** *n* listado *m*

prion /ˈpraɪɒn/ *n* prión *m*

prior /ˈpraɪə(r)/ *n* prior *m*. ● *adj* previo. **~ to** antes de. **~ity** /praɪˈɒrətɪ/ *n* prioridad *f*. **~y** *n* priorato *m*

prise /praɪz/ *vt*. **~ open** abrir haciendo palanca

prison /ˈprɪzn/ *n* cárcel *m*. **~er** *n* prisionero *m*; (*in prison*) preso *m*; (*under arrest*) detenido *m*. **~ officer** *n* funcionario *m* de prisiones

priva|cy /ˈprɪvəsɪ/ *n* privacidad *f*. **~te** /ˈpraɪvɪt/ *adj* privado; (*confidential*) personal; (lessons, house) particular. **in ~te** en privado; (*secretly*) en secreto. ● *n* soldado *m* raso. **~te detective** *n* detective *m* & *f* privado. **~tely** *adv* en privado. **~tion** /praɪˈveɪʃn/ *n* privación *f*

privilege /ˈprɪvəlɪdʒ/ *n* privilegio *m*. **~d** *adj* privilegiado. **be ~d to** tener el privilegio de

prize /praɪz/ *n* premio *m*. ● *adj* (idiot etc) de remate. ● *vt* estimar

pro /prəʊ/ *n*. **~s and cons** los pros *m* y los contras

probab|ility /prɒbəˈbɪlətɪ/ *n* probabilidad *f*. **~le** /ˈprɒbəbl/ *adj* probable. **~ly** *adv* probablemente

probation /prəˈbeɪʃn/ *n* período *m* de prueba; (*Jurid*) libertad *f* condicional

probe /prəʊb/ *n* sonda *f*; (*fig*) investigación *f*. ● *vt* sondar. ● *vi*. **~ into** investigar

problem /ˈprɒbləm/ *n* problema *m*. ● *adj* difícil. **~atic** /-ˈmætɪk/ *adj* problemático

procedure /prəˈsiːdʒə(r)/ *n* procedimiento *m*

proceed /prəˈsiːd/ *vi* proceder; (*move forward*) avanzar. **~ings** *npl* (*report*) actas *fpl*; (*Jurid*) proceso *m*. **~s** /ˈprəʊsiːdz/ *npl*. **the ~s** lo recaudado

process /ˈprəʊses/ *n* proceso *m*. **in the ~ of** en vías de. ● *vt* tratar; revelar (photo); tramitar (order).

P

~ion /prəˈseʃn/ *n* desfile *m*; (*Relig*) procesión *f*. **~or** *n* procesador *m*. **food ~** procesador *m* de alimentos

procla|im /prəˈkleɪm/ *vt* proclamar. **~mation** /prɒkləˈmeɪʃn/ *n* proclamación *f*

procure /prəˈkjʊə(r)/ *vt* obtener

prod /prɒd/ *vt* (*pt* **prodded**) (*with sth sharp*) pinchar; (*with elbow*) darle un codazo a. ● *n* (*with sth sharp*) pinchazo *m*; (*with elbow*) codazo *m*

produc|e /prəˈdjuːs/ *vt* producir; surtir (effect); sacar (gun); producir (film); poner en escena (play). ● /ˈprɒdjuːs/ *n* productos *mpl*. **~er** /prəˈdjuːsə(r)/ *n* (*TV, Cinema*) productor *m*; (*in theatre*) director *m*; (*manufacturer*) fabricante *m & f*. **~t** /ˈprɒdʌkt/ *n* producto *m*. **~tion** /prəˈdʌkʃn/ *n* (*manufacture*) fabricación *f*; (*output*) producción *f*; (*of play*) producción *f*. **~tive** /prəˈdʌktɪv/ *adj* productivo. **~tivity** /prɒdʌkˈtɪvətɪ/ *n* productividad *f*

P **profess** /prəˈfes/ *vt* profesar; (*pretend*) pretender. **~ion** /-ˈfeʃn/ *n* profesión *f*. **~ional** *adj & n* profesional (*m & f*). **~or** /-ˈfesə(r)/ *n* catedrático *m*; (*Amer*) profesor *m*

proficien|cy /prəˈfɪʃənsɪ/ *n* competencia *f*. **~t** *adj* competente

profile /ˈprəʊfaɪl/ *n* perfil *m*

profit /ˈprɒfɪt/ *n* (*Com*) ganancia *f*; (*fig*) provecho *m*. ● *vi*. **~ from** sacar provecho de. **~able** *adj* provechoso

profound /prəˈfaʊnd/ *adj* profundo. **~ly** *adv* profundamente

profus|e /prəˈfjuːs/ *adj* profuso. **~ely** *adv* profusamente

prognosis /prɒgˈnəʊsɪs/ *n* (*pl* **-oses**) pronóstico *m*

program /ˈprəʊgræm/ *n* (*Comp*) programa *m*; (*Amer, course*) curso *m*. **~me** /ˈprəʊgræm/ *n* programa *m*. ● *vt* (*pt* **-med**) programar. **~mer** *n* programador *m*

progress /ˈprəʊgres/ *n* progreso *m*; (*development*) desarrollo *m*. **make ~** hacer progresos. **in ~** en curso. ● /prəˈgres/ *vi* hacer progresos; (*develop*) desarrollarse. **~ion** /prəˈgreʃn/ *n* progresión *f*; (*advance*) evolución *f*. **~ive** /prəˈgresɪv/ *adj* progresivo; (*reforming*) progresista. **~ively** *adv* progresivamente

prohibit /prəˈhɪbɪt/ *vt* prohibir; (*prevent*) impedir. **~ive** *adj* prohibitivo

project /prəˈdʒekt/ *vt* proyectar. ● *vi* (*stick out*) sobresalir. ● /ˈprɒdʒekt/ *n* proyecto *m*; (*Schol*) trabajo *m*; (*Amer, housing ~*) complejo *m* de viviendas subvencionadas. **~or** /prəˈdʒektə(r)/ *n* proyector *m*

prolific /prəˈlɪfɪk/ *adj* prolífico

prologue /ˈprəʊlɒg/ *n* prólogo *m*

prolong /prəˈlɒŋ/ *vt* prolongar

prom /prɒm/ *n* (*Amer*) baile *m* del colegio. **~enade** /prɒməˈnɑːd/ *n* paseo *m* marítimo. ● *vi* pasearse.

i

Prom En EE.UU. un *prom* es un baile que se celebra para los estudiantes que terminan el *High School*. En Londres *the Proms* son una serie de conciertos de música clásica, durante los cuales una gran parte del público permanece de pie. Tienen lugar en el *Albert Hall* en el verano, durante ocho semanas. Oficialmente, son conocidos como los *Henry Wood Promenade Concerts*, en memoria de su fundador.

prominen|ce /'prɒmɪnəns/ *n* prominencia *f*; (*fig*) importancia *f*. **~t** *adj* prominente; (*important*) importante; (*conspicuous*) destacado

promiscu|ity /prɒmɪ'skju:ətɪ/ *n* promiscuidad *f*. **~ous** /prə'mɪskjʊəs/ *adj* promiscuo

promis|e /'prɒmɪs/ *n* promesa *f*. • *vt/i* prometer. **~ing** *adj* prometedor; (future) halagüeño

promot|e /prə'məʊt/ *vt* promover; promocionar (product); (*in rank*) ascender. **~ion** /-'məʊʃn/ *n* promoción *f*; (*in rank*) ascenso *m*

prompt /prɒmpt/ *adj* rápido; (*punctual*) puntual. • *adv* en punto. • *n* (*Comp*) presto *m*. • *vt* incitar; apuntar (actor). **~ly** *adv* puntualmente

prone /prəʊn/ *adj* (tendido) boca abajo. **be ~ to** ser propenso a

pronoun /'prəʊnaʊn/ *n* pronombre *m*

pronounc|e /prə'naʊns/ *vt* pronunciar; (*declare*) declarar. **~ement** *n* declaración *f*. **~ed** *adj* pronunciado; (*noticeable*) marcado

pronunciation /prənʌnsɪ'eɪʃn/ *n* pronunciación *f*

proof /pru:f/ *n* prueba *f*, pruebas *fpl*; (*of alcohol*) graduación *f* normal. • *adj*. **~ against** a prueba de. **~-reading** *n* corrección *f* de pruebas

propaganda /prɒpə'gændə/ *n* propaganda *f*

propagate /'prɒpəgeɪt/ *vt* propagar. • *vi* propagarse

propel /prə'pel/ *vt* (*pt* **propelled**) propulsar. **~ler** *n* hélice *f*

proper /'prɒpə(r)/ *adj* correcto; (*suitable*) apropiado; (*Gram*) propio; (*fam, real*) verdadero. **~ly** *adv* correctamente; (eat, work) bien

property /'prɒpətɪ/ *n* propiedad *f*; (*things owned*) bienes *mpl*. • *adj* inmobiliario

prophe|cy /'prɒfəsɪ/ *n* profecía *f*. **~sy** /'prɒfɪsaɪ/ *vt/i* profetizar. **~t** /'prɒfɪt/ *n* profeta *m*. **~tic** /prə'fetɪk/ *adj* profético

proportion /prə'pɔ:ʃn/ *n* proporción *f*. **~al** *adj*, **~ate** /-ət/ *adj* proporcional

propos|al /prə'pəʊzl/ *n* propuesta *f*; (*of marriage*) proposición *f* matrimonial. **~e** /prə'pəʊz/ *vt* proponer. • *vi*. **~e to s.o.** hacerle una oferta de matrimonio a una. **~ition** /prɒpə'zɪʃn/ *n* propuesta *f*; (*offer*) oferta *f*

proprietor /prə'praɪətə(r)/ *n* propietario *m*

pro rata /'prəʊ'rɑ:tə/ *adv* a prorrata

prose /prəʊz/ *n* prosa *f*

prosecut|e /'prɒsɪkju:t/ *vt* procesar (**for** por); (*carry on*) proseguir. **~ion** /-'kju:ʃn/ *n* proceso *m*. **the ~** (*side*) la acusación. **~or** *n* fiscal *m & f*; (*in private prosecutions*) abogado *m* de la acusación

prospect /'prɒspekt/ *n* (*possibility*) posibilidad *f* (**of** de); (*situation envisaged*) perspectiva *f*. **~s** (*chances*) perspectivas *fpl*. **~ive** /prə'spektɪv/ *adj* posible; (*future*) futuro. **~or** /prə'spektə(r)/ *n* prospector *m*. **~us** /prə'spektəs/ *n* folleto *m* informativo

prosper /'prɒspə(r)/ *vi* prosperar. **~ity** /-'sperətɪ/ *n* prosperidad *f*. **~ous** *adj* próspero

prostitut|e /'prɒstɪtju:t/ *n* prostituta *f*. **~ion** /-'tju:ʃn/ *n* prostitución *f*

prostrate /'prɒstreɪt/ *adj* postrado

protagonist /prəˈtægənɪst/ *n* protagonista *m & f*

protect /prəˈtekt/ *vt* proteger. **~ion** /-ʃn/ *n* protección *f*. **~ive** *adj* protector. **~or** *n* protector *m*

protein /ˈprəʊtiːn/ *n* proteína *f*

protest /ˈprəʊtest/ *n* protesta *f*. **in ~ (against)** en señal de protesta (contra). **under ~** bajo protesta. • /prəˈtest/ *vt/i* protestar

Protestant /ˈprɒtɪstənt/ *adj & n* protestante (*m & f*)

protester /prəˈtestə(r)/ *n* manifestante *m & f*

protocol /ˈprəʊtəkɒl/ *n* protocolo *m*

protrud|e /prəˈtruːd/ *vi* sobresalir. **~ing** *adj* (chin) prominente. **~ing eyes** ojos saltones

proud /praʊd/ *adj* orgulloso. **~ly** *adv* con orgullo; (*arrogantly*) orgullosamente

prove /pruːv/ *vt* probar; demostrar (loyalty). • *vi* resultar. **~n** *adj* probado

P

proverb /ˈprɒvɜːb/ *n* refrán *m*, proverbio *m*

provide /prəˈvaɪd/ *vt* proporcionar; dar (accommodation). **~ s.o. with sth** proveer a uno de algo. • *vi*. **~ for** (*allow for*) prever; mantener (person). **~d** *conj*. **~d (that)** con tal de que, siempre que

providen|ce /ˈprɒvɪdəns/ *n* providencia *f*. **~tial** /-ˈdenʃl/ *adj* providencial

providing /prəˈvaɪdɪŋ/ *conj*. **~ that** con tal de que, siempre que

provinc|e /ˈprɒvɪns/ *n* provincia *f*; (*fig*) competencia *f*. **~ial** /prəˈvɪnʃl/ *adj* provincial

provision /prəˈvɪʒn/ *n* provisión *f*; (*supply*) suministro *m*; (*stipulation*) disposición *f*. **~s** *npl* provisiones *fpl*, víveres *mpl*. **~al** *adj* provisional

provo|cation /prɒvəˈkeɪʃn/ *n* provocación *f*. **~cative** /-ˈvɒkətɪv/ *adj* provocador. **~ke** /prəˈvəʊk/ *vt* provocar

prow /praʊ/ *n* proa *f*

prowess /ˈpraʊɪs/ *n* destreza *f*; (*valour*) valor *m*

prowl /praʊl/ *vi* merodear. **~er** *n* merodeador *m*

proximity /prɒkˈsɪmətɪ/ *n* proximidad *f*

prude /pruːd/ *n* mojigato *m*

pruden|ce /ˈpruːdəns/ *n* prudencia *f*. **~t** *adj* prudente. **~tly** *adv* prudentemente

prudish /ˈpruːdɪʃ/ *adj* mojigato

prune /pruːn/ *n* ciruela *f* pasa. • *vt* podar

pry /praɪ/ *vi* curiosear. **~ into sth** entrometerse en algo. *vt* (*Amer*) *see* PRISE

PS *n* (*postscript*) P.D.

psalm /sɑːm/ *n* salmo *m*

psychiatr|ic /saɪkɪˈætrɪk/ *adj* psiquiátrico. **~ist** /saɪˈkaɪətrɪst/ *n* psiquiatra *m & f*. **~y** /saɪˈkaɪətrɪ/ *n* psiquiatría *f*

psychic /ˈsaɪkɪk/ *adj* para(p)sicológico

psycho|analysis /saɪkəʊəˈnæləsɪs/ *n* (p)sicoanálisis *m*. **~logical** /saɪkəˈlɒdʒɪkl/ *adj* (p)sicológico. **~logist** /saɪˈkɒlədʒɪst/ *n* (p)sicólogo *m*. **~logy** /saɪˈkɒlədʒɪ/ *n* (p)sicología *f*. **~therapy** /-ˈθerəpɪ/ *n* (p)sicoterapia *f*

pub /pʌb/ *n* bar *m*

pub En Gran Bretaña, establecimiento donde se vende cerveza y otras bebidas (alcohólicas y no alcohólicas) para consumir en el local. *Pub* es la forma abreviada de *public house*. Suelen ofrecer comidas y una variedad de juegos, especialmente dardos, billar etc. Recientemente, las horas en que pueden abrir dependen de la licencia, siendo lo normal de 11 - 23 horas.

puberty /'pju:bətɪ/ *n* pubertad *f*

pubic /'pju:bɪk/ *adj* pubiano, púbico

public /'pʌblɪk/ *adj* público. **~an** *n* tabernero *m*. **~ation** /-'keɪʃn/ *n* publicación *f*. **~ holiday** *n* día *m* festivo, día *m* feriado (*LAm*). **~ house** *n* bar *m*. **~ity** /pʌb'lɪsətɪ/ *n* publicidad *f*. **~ize** /'pʌblɪsaɪz/ *vt* hacer público. **~ly** *adv* públicamente. **~ school** *n* colegio *m* privado; (*Amer*) instituto *m*, escuela *f* pública

public school En Inglaterra y Gales, un colegio privado para alumnos de edades comprendidas entre los 13 y 18 años. La mayoría de estos colegios tiene régimen de internado y a menudo son mixtos. En EE.UU. y Escocia, el término se utiliza para referirse a un colegio estatal.

publish /'pʌblɪʃ/ *vt* publicar. **~er** *n* editor *m*. **~ing** *n* publicación *f*. **~ing house** editorial *f*

pudding /'pʊdɪŋ/ *n* postre *m*; (*steamed*) budín *m*

puddle /'pʌdl/ *n* charco *m*

Puerto Ric|an /pwɜ:təʊ'ri:kən/ *adj & n* portorriqueño (*m*), puertorriqueño (*m*). **~o** /-əʊ/ *n* Puerto Rico *m*

puff /pʌf/ *n* (*of wind*) ráfaga *f*; (*of smoke*) nube *f*; (*action*) soplo *m*; (*on cigarette*) chupada *f*, calada *f*. ● *vt/i* soplar. **~ at** dar chupadas a (pipe). **~ out** (*swell up*) inflar, hinchar. **~ed** *adj* (*out of breath*) sin aliento. **~ paste** (*Amer*), **~ pastry** *n* hojaldre *m*. **~y** *adj* hinchado

pull /pʊl/ *vt* tirar de, jalar (*LAm*); desgarrarse (muscle). **~ a face** hacer una mueca. **~ a fast one** hacer una mala jugada. ● *vi* tirar, jalar (*LAm*). **~ at** tirar de, jalar (*LAm*). ● *n* tirón *m*, jalón *m* (*LAm*); (*pulling force*) fuerza *f*; (*influence*) influencia *f*. □ **~ away** *vi* (*Auto*) alejarse. □ **~ back** *vi* retirarse. □ **~ down** *vt* echar abajo (building); (*lower*) bajar. □ **~ in** *vi* (*Auto*) parar. □ **~ off** *vt* (*remove*) quitar; (*achieve*) conseguir. □ **~ out** *vt* sacar; retirar (team). *vi* (*Auto*) salirse. □ **~ through** *vi* recobrar la salud. □ **~ up** *vi* (*Auto*) parar. *vt* (*uproot*) arrancar; (*reprimand*) regañar

pullover /'pʊləʊvə(r)/ *n* suéter *m*, pulóver *m*, jersey *m*

pulp /pʌlp/ *n* pulpa *f*; (*for paper*) pasta *f*

pulpit /'pʊlpɪt/ *n* púlpito *m*

pulse /pʌls/ *n* (*Med*) pulso *m*; (*Culin*) legumbre *f*

pummel /'pʌml/ *vt* (*pt* **pummelled**) aporrear

pump /pʌmp/ *n* bomba *f*; (*for petrol*) surtidor *m*. ● *vt* sacar con una bomba. □ **~ up** *vt* inflar

pumpkin /'pʌmpkɪn/ *n* calabaza *f*

pun /pʌn/ *n* juego *m* de palabras

punch /pʌntʃ/ *vt* darle un puñetazo a; (*perforate*) perforar; hacer (hole). ● *n* puñetazo *m*; (*vigour*) fuerza *f*; (*device*) perforadora *f*; (*drink*) ponche *m*. **~ in** *vi* (*Amer*) fichar (*al entrar al trabajo*). **~ out** *vi* (*Amer*) fichar (*al salir del trabajo*)

punctual /ˈpʌŋktʃʊəl/ *adj* puntual. **~ity** /-ˈælətɪ/ *n* puntualidad *f.* **~ly** *adv* puntualmente

punctuat|e /ˈpʌŋkʃʊeɪt/ *vt* puntuar. **~ion** /-ˈeɪʃn/ *n* puntuación *f*

puncture /ˈpʌŋktʃə(r)/ *n* (*in tyre*) pinchazo *m.* **have a ~** pinchar. ● *vt* pinchar. ● *vi* pincharse

punish /ˈpʌnɪʃ/ *vt* castigar. **~ment** *n* castigo *m*

punk /pʌŋk/ *n* punk *m & f*, punki *m & f*; (*Music*) punk *m*; (*Amer, hoodlum*) vándalo *m*

punt /pʌnt/ *n* (*boat*) batea *f.* **~er** *n* apostante *m & f*

puny /ˈpju:nɪ/ *adj* (**-ier, -iest**) enclenque

pup /pʌp/ *n* cachorro *m*

pupil /ˈpju:pl/ *n* alumno *m*; (*of eye*) pupila *f*

puppet /ˈpʌpɪt/ *n* marioneta *f*, títere *m*; (*glove ~*) títere *m*

puppy /ˈpʌpɪ/ *n* cachorro *m*

purchase /ˈpɜ:tʃəs/ *vt* adquirir. ● *n* adquisición *f.* **~r** *n* comprador *m*

pur|e /ˈpjʊə(r)/ *adj* (**-er, -est**) puro. **~ity** *n* pureza *f*

purgatory /ˈpɜ:gətrɪ/ *n* purgatorio *m*

purge /pɜ:dʒ/ *vt* purgar. ● *n* purga *f*

purif|ication /pjʊərɪfɪˈkeɪʃn/ *n* purificación *f.* **~y** /ˈpjʊərɪfaɪ/ *vt* purificar

purist /ˈpjʊərɪst/ *n* purista *m & f*

puritan /ˈpjʊərɪtən/ *n* puritano *m.* **~ical** /-ˈtænɪkl/ *adj* puritano

purple /ˈpɜ:pl/ *adj* morado. ● *n* morado *m*, púrpura *f*

purport /pəˈpɔ:t/ *vt.* **~ to be** pretender ser

purpose /ˈpɜ:pəs/ *n* propósito *m*; (*determination*) resolución *f.* **on ~** a propósito. **serve a ~** servir de algo. **~ful** *adj* (*resolute*) resuelto. **~ly** *adv* a propósito

purr /pɜ:(r)/ *vi* ronronear

purse /pɜ:s/ *n* monedero *m*; (*Amer*) bolso *m*, cartera *f* (*LAm*), bolsa *f* (*Mex*)

pursu|e /pəˈsju:/ *vt* perseguir, continuar con (course of action). **~it** /pəˈsju:t/ *n* persecución *f*; (*pastime*) actividad *f*

pus /pʌs/ *n* pus *m*

push /pʊʃ/ *vt* empujar; apretar (*button*). ● *vi* empujar. ● *n* empujón *m*; (*effort*) esfuerzo *m.* □ **~ back** *vt* hacer retroceder. □ **~ off** *vi* ⊠ largarse. **~chair** *n* sillita *f* de paseo, carreola *f* (*Mex*). **~y** *adj* (*pej*) ambicioso

pussy /ˈpʊsɪ/ (*pl* **-sies**), **pussycat** /ˈpʊsɪkæt/ *n* ⊡ minino *m*

put /pʊt/ *vt* (*pt* **put**, *pres p* **putting**) poner; (*with care, precision*) colocar; (*inside sth*) meter; (*express*) decir. □ **~ across** *vt* comunicar. □ **~ away** *vt* guardar. □ **~ back** *vt* volver a poner; retrasar (clock). □ **~ by** *vt* guardar; ahorrar (money). □ **~ down** *vt* (*on a surface*) dejar; colgar (phone); (*suppress*) sofocar; (*write*) apuntar; (*kill*) sacrificar. □ **~ forward** *vt* presentar (plan); proponer (candidate); adelantar (clocks); adelantar (meeting). □ **~ in** *vt* (*instal*) poner; presentar (claim). □ **~ in for** *vt* solicitar. □ **~ off** *vt* aplazar, posponer; (*disconcert*) desconcertar. □ **~ on** *vt* (*wear*) ponerse; poner (CD, music); encender (light). □ **~ out** *vt* (*extinguish*) apagar; (*inconvenience*) incomodar; extender (hand); (*disconcert*) desconcertar. □ **~ through** *vt* (*phone*) poner, pasar (to con). □ **~ up** *vt* levantar; aumentar (rent); subir (price); poner (sign); alojar (guest). ▫ **~ up with** *vt* aguantar, soportar

putrid /ˈpjuːtrɪd/ *adj* putrefacto

putt /pʌt/ *n* (*golf*) golpe *m* suave

puzzl|e /ˈpʌzl/ *n* misterio *m*; (*game*) rompecabezas *m*. ● *vt* dejar perplejo. **~ed** *adj* (expression) de desconcierto. **I'm ~ed about it** me tiene perplejo. **~ing** *adj* incomprensible; (*odd*) curioso

pygmy /ˈpɪgmɪ/ *n* pigmeo *m*

pyjamas /pəˈdʒɑːməz/ *npl* pijama *m*, piyama *m or f* (*LAm*)

pylon /ˈpaɪlɒn/ *n* pilón *m*

pyramid /ˈpɪrəmɪd/ *n* pirámide *f*

python /ˈpaɪθn/ *n* pitón *m*

Qq

quack /kwæk/ *n* (*of duck*) graznido *m*; (*person*) charlatán *m*. **~ doctor** *n* curandero *m*

quadrangle /ˈkwɒdræŋgl/ *n* cuadrilátero *m*

quadruped /ˈkwɒdrʊped/ *n* cuadrúpedo *m*

quadruple /ˈkwɒdrʊpl/ *adj & n* cuádruplo (*m*). ● *vt* cuadruplicar

quagmire /ˈkwægmaɪə(r)/ *n* lodazal *m*

quail /kweɪl/ *n* codorniz *f*

quaint /kweɪnt/ *adj* (**-er, -est**) pintoresco; (*odd*) curioso

quake /kweɪk/ *vi* temblar. ● *n* ! terremoto *m*

qualif|ication /kwɒlɪfɪˈkeɪʃn/ *n* título *m*; (*requirement*) requisito *m*; (*ability*) capacidad *f*; (*Sport*) clasificación *f*; (*fig*) reserva *f*. **~ied** /ˈkwɒlɪfaɪd/ *adj* cualificado; (*with degree, diploma*) titulado; (*competent*) capacitado. **~y** /ˈkwɒlɪfaɪ/ *vt* calificar; (*limit*) limitar. ● *vi* titularse; (*Sport*) clasificarse. **~y for sth** (*be entitled to*) tener derecho a algo

qualit|ative /ˈkwɒlɪtətɪv/ *adj* cualitativo. **~y** /ˈkwɒlɪtɪ/ *n* calidad *f*; (*attribute*) cualidad *f*

qualm /kwɑːm/ *n* reparo *m*

quandary /ˈkwɒndrɪ/ *n* dilema *m*

quanti|fy /ˈkwɒntɪfaɪ/ *vt* cuantificar. **~ty** /-tɪ/ *n* cantidad *f*

quarantine /ˈkwɒrəntiːn/ *n* cuarentena *f*. ● *vt* poner en cuarentena

quarrel /ˈkwɒrəl/ *n* pelea *f*. ● *vi* (*pt* **quarrelled**) pelearse, discutir. **~some** /-səm/ *adj* pendenciero

quarry /ˈkwɒrɪ/ *n* (*excavation*) cantera *f*; (*prey*) presa *f*

quart /kwɔːt/ *n* cuarto *m* de galón

quarter /ˈkwɔːtə(r)/ *n* cuarto *m*; (*of year*) trimestre *m*; (*district*) barrio *m*. **a ~ of an hour** un cuarto de hora. ● *vt* dividir en cuartos; (*Mil*) acuartelar. **~-final** *n* cuarto *m* de final. **~ly** *adj* trimestral. ● *adv* trimestralmente

quartz /kwɔːts/ *n* cuarzo *m*

quay /kiː/ *n* muelle *m*

queasy /ˈkwiːzɪ/ *adj* mareado

queen /kwiːn/ *n* reina *f*. **~ mother** *n* reina *f* madre

queer /kwɪə(r)/ *adj* (**-er, -est**) extraño

quench /kwentʃ/ *vt* quitar (thirst); sofocar (desire)

query /ˈkwɪərɪ/ *n* pregunta *f*. ● *vt* preguntar; (*doubt*) poner en duda

quest /kwest/ *n* busca *f*

question /ˈkwestʃən/ *n* pregunta *f*; (*for discussion*) cuestión *f*. **in ~** en cuestión. **out of the ~** imposi-

p q

ble. **without ~** sin duda. • *vt* hacer preguntas a; (police etc) interrogar; (*doubt*) poner en duda. **~able** *adj* discutible. **~ mark** *n* signo *m* de interrogación. **~naire** /-ˈneə(r)/ *n* cuestionario *m*

queue /kjuː/ *n* cola *f*. • *vi* (*pres p* **queuing**) hacer cola

quibble /ˈkwɪbl/ *vi* discutir; (*split hairs*) sutilizar

quick /kwɪk/ *adj* (**-er**, **-est**) rápido. **be ~!** ¡date prisa! • *adv* rápido. **~en** *vt* acelerar. • *vi* acelerarse. **~ly** *adv* rápido. **~sand** *n* arena *f* movediza. **~-tempered** /-ˈtempəd/ *adj* irascible

quid /kwɪd/ *n invar* [I] libra *f* (esterlina)

quiet /ˈkwaɪət/ *adj* (**-er**, **-est**) tranquilo; (*silent*) callado; (*discreet*) discreto. • *n* tranquilidad *f*. • *vt/i* (*Amer*) *see* **QUIETEN**. **~en** *vt* calmar. • *n* calmarse. **~ly** *adv* tranquilamente; (*silently*) silenciosamente; (*discreetly*) discretamente. **~ness** *n* tranquilidad *f*

quilt /kwɪlt/ *n* edredón *m*. **~ed** *adj* acolchado

quintet /kwɪnˈtet/ *n* quinteto *m*

quirk /kwɜːk/ *n* peculiaridad *f*

quit /kwɪt/ *vt* (*pt* **quitted**) dejar. **~ doing** (*Amer, cease*) dejar de hacer. • *vi* (*give in*) abandonar; (*stop*) parar; (*resign*) dimitir

quite /kwaɪt/ *adv* bastante; (*completely*) totalmente; (*really*) verdaderamente. **~ (so!)** ¡claro! **~ a few** bastante

quits /kwɪts/ *adj*. **be ~** estar en paz. **call it ~** darlo por terminado

quiver /ˈkwɪvə(r)/ *vi* temblar

quiz /kwɪz/ *n* (*pl* **quizzes**) serie *f* de preguntas; (*game*) concurso *m*. • *vt* (*pt* **quizzed**) interrogar. **~zical** *adj* burlón

quota /ˈkwəʊtə/ *n* cuota *f*

quot|ation /kwəʊˈteɪʃn/ *n* cita *f*; (*price*) presupuesto *m*. **~ation marks** *npl* comillas *fpl*. **~e** /kwəʊt/ *vt* citar; (*Com*) cotizar. • *n* [I] cita *f*; (*price*) presupuesto *m*. **in ~es** *npl* entre comillas

Rr

rabbi /ˈræbaɪ/ *n* rabino *m*

rabbit /ˈræbɪt/ *n* conejo *m*

rabi|d /ˈræbɪd/ *adj* feroz; (dog) rabioso. **~es** /ˈreɪbiːz/ *n* rabia *f*

race /reɪs/ *n* (*in sport*) carrera *f*; (*ethnic group*) raza *f*. • *vt* hacer correr (horse). • *vi* (*run*) correr, ir corriendo; (*rush*) ir de prisa. **~course** *n* hipódromo *m*. **~horse** *n* caballo *m* de carreras. **~ relations** *npl* relaciones *fpl* raciales. **~track** *n* hipódromo *m*

racial /ˈreɪʃl/ *adj* racial

racing /ˈreɪsɪŋ/ *n* carreras *fpl*. **~ car** *n* coche *m* de carreras

racis|m /ˈreɪsɪzəm/ *n* racismo *m*. **~t** *adj & n* racista (*m & f*)

rack[1] /ræk/ *n* (*shelf*) estante *m*; (*for luggage*) rejilla *f*; (*for plates*) escurreplatos *m*. • *vt*. **~ one's brains** devanarse los sesos

rack[2] /ræk/ *n*. **go to ~ and ruin** quedarse en la ruina

racket /ˈrækɪt/ *n* (*for sports*) raqueta; (*din*) alboroto *m*; (*swindle*) estafa *f*. **~eer** /-əˈtɪə(r)/ *n* estafador *m*

racy /ˈreɪsɪ/ *adj* (**-ier**, **-iest**) vivo

radar /ˈreɪdɑː(r)/ *n* radar *m*

radian|ce /ˈreɪdɪəns/ *n* resplandor *m*. **~t** *adj* radiante

radiat|e /ˈreɪdɪeɪt/ *vt* irradiar. ● *vi* divergir. **~ion** /-ˈeɪʃn/ *n* radiación *f*. **~or** *n* radiador *m*

radical /ˈrædɪkl/ *adj & n* radical (*m*)

radio /ˈreɪdɪəʊ/ *n* (*pl* **-os**) radio *f or m*. ● *vt* transmitir por radio. **~active** /reɪdɪəʊˈæktɪv/ *adj* radiactivo. **~activity** /-ˈtɪvətɪ/ *n* radiactividad *f*

radish /ˈrædɪʃ/ *n* rábano *m*

radius /ˈreɪdɪəs/ *n* (*pl* **-dii** /-dɪaɪ/) radio *m*

raffle /ˈræfl/ *n* rifa *f*

raft /rɑːft/ *n* balsa *f*

rafter /ˈrɑːftə(r)/ *n* cabrio *m*

rag /ræg/ *n* andrajo *m*; (*for wiping*) trapo *m*. **in ~s** (person) andrajoso

rage /reɪdʒ/ *n* rabia *f*; (*fashion*) moda *f*. ● *vi* estar furioso; (storm) bramar

ragged /ˈrægɪd/ *adj* (person) andrajoso; (clothes) hecho jirones

raid /reɪd/ *n* (*Mil*) incursión *f*; (*by police etc*) redada *f*; (*by thieves*) asalto *m*. ● *vt* (*Mil*) atacar; (police) hacer una redada en; (thieves) asaltar. **~er** *n* invasor *m*; (*thief*) ladrón *m*

rail /reɪl/ *n* barandilla *f*; (*for train*) riel *m*; (*rod*) barra *f*. **by ~** por ferrocarril. **~ing** *n* barandilla *f*; (*fence*) verja *f*. **~road** *n* (*Amer*), **~way** *n* ferrocarril *m*. **~way station** *n* estación *f* de ferrocarril

rain /reɪn/ *n* lluvia *f*. ● *vi* llover. **~bow** /-bəʊ/ *n* arco *m* iris. **~coat** *n* impermeable *m*. **~fall** *n* precipitación *f*. **~y** *adj* (**-ier**, **-iest**) lluvioso

raise /reɪz/ *vt* levantar; (*breed*) criar; obtener (money etc); formular (question); plantear (problem); subir (price). ● *n* (*Amer*) aumento *m*

raisin /ˈreɪzn/ *n* (uva *f*) pasa *f*

rake /reɪk/ *n* rastrillo *m*. ● *vt* rastrillar; (*search*) buscar en. □ **~ up** *vt* remover

rally /ˈrælɪ/ *vt* reunir; (*revive*) reanimar. ● *n* reunión *f*; (*Auto*) rally *m*

ram /ræm/ *n* carnero *m*. ● *vt* (*pt* **rammed**) (*thrust*) meter por la fuerza; (*crash into*) chocar con

RAM /ræm/ *n* (*Comp*) RAM *f*

rambl|e /ˈræmbl/ *n* excursión *f* a pie. ● *vi* ir de paseo; (*in speech*) divagar. □ **~e on** *vi* divagar. **~er** *n* excursionista *m & f*. **~ing** *adj* (speech) divagador

ramp /ræmp/ *n* rampa *f*

rampage /ræmˈpeɪdʒ/ *vi* alborotarse. ● /ˈræmpeɪdʒ/ *n*. **go on the ~** alborotarse

ramshackle /ˈræmʃækl/ *adj* desvencijado

ran /ræn/ *see* **RUN**

ranch /rɑːntʃ/ *n* hacienda *f*

random /ˈrændəm/ *adj* hecho al azar; (*chance*) fortuito. ● *n*. **at ~** al azar

rang /ræŋ/ *see* **RING**[2]

range /reɪndʒ/ *n* alcance *m*; (*distance*) distancia *f*; (*series*) serie *f*; (*of mountains*) cordillera *f*; (*extent*) extensión *f*; (*Com*) surtido *m*; (*stove*) cocina *f* económica. ● *vi* extenderse; (*vary*) variar. **~r** *n* guarda bosque *m*

rank /ræŋk/ *n* posición *f*, categoría *f*; (*row*) fila *f*; (*for taxis*) parada *f*. **the ~ and file** la masa *f*. **~s** *npl* soldados *mpl* rasos. ● *adj* (**-er**, **-est**) (*smell*) fétido; (*fig*) completo. ● *vt* clasificar. ● *vi* clasificarse

ransack /ˈrænsæk/ *vt* registrar; (*pillage*) saquear

ransom /ˈrænsəm/ *n* rescate *m*.

r

hold s.o. to ~ exigir rescate por uno. •*vt* rescatar; (*redeem*) redimir

rant /rænt/ *vi* despotricar

rap /ræp/ *n* golpe *m* seco. •*vt/i* (*pt* **rapped**) golpear

rape /reɪp/ *vt* violar. •*n* violación *f*

rapid /ˈræpɪd/ *adj* rápido. **~s** *npl* rápidos *mpl*

rapist /ˈreɪpɪst/ *n* violador *m*

raptur|e /ˈræptʃə(r)/ *n* éxtasis *m*. **~ous** /-rəs/ *adj* extático

rare /reə(r)/ *adj* (**-er**, **-est**) raro; (*Culin*) poco hecho. **~fied** /ˈreərɪfaɪd/ *adj* enrarecido. **~ly** *adv* raramente

raring /ˈreərɪŋ/ *adj* ⊡. **~ to** impaciente por

rarity /ˈreərətɪ/ *n* rareza *f*

rascal /ˈrɑːskl/ *n* granuja *m* & *f*

rash /ræʃ/ *adj* (**-er**, **-est**) precipitado, imprudente. •*n* erupción *f*

rasher /ˈræʃə(r)/ *n* loncha *f*

rashly /ˈræʃlɪ/ *adv* precipitadamente, imprudentemente

rasp /rɑːsp/ *n* (*file*) escofina *f*

raspberry /ˈrɑːzbrɪ/ *n* frambuesa *f*

r

rat /ræt/ *n* rata *f*

rate /reɪt/ *n* (*ratio*) proporción *f*; (*speed*) velocidad *f*; (*price*) precio *m*; (*of interest*) tipo *m*. **at any ~** de todas formas. **at this ~** así. **~s** *npl* (*taxes*) impuestos *mpl* municipales. •*vt* valorar; (*consider*) considerar; (*Amer, deserve*) merecer. •*vi* ser considerado

rather /ˈrɑːðə(r)/ *adv* mejor dicho; (*fairly*) bastante; (*a little*) un poco. •*int* claro. **I would ~ not** prefiero no

rating /ˈreɪtɪŋ/ *n* clasificación *f*; (*sailor*) marinero *m*; (*number, TV*) índice *m*

ratio /ˈreɪʃɪəʊ/ *n* (*pl* **-os**) proporción *f*

ration /ˈræʃn/ *n* ración *f*. **~s** *npl* (*provisions*) víveres *mpl*. •*vt* racionar

rational /ˈræʃənəl/ *adj* racional. **~ize** *vt* racionalizar

rattle /ˈrætl/ *vi* traquetear. •*vt* (*shake*) agitar; ⊡ desconcertar. •*n* traqueteo *m*; (*toy*) sonajero *m*. □ **~ off** *vt* (*fig*) decir de corrida

raucous /ˈrɔːkəs/ *adj* estridente

ravage /ˈrævɪdʒ/ *vt* estragar

rave /reɪv/ *vi* delirar; (*in anger*) despotricar. **~ about sth** poner a algo por las nubes

raven /ˈreɪvn/ *n* cuervo *m*

ravenous /ˈrævənəs/ *adj* voraz; (person) hambriento. **be ~** morirse de hambre

ravine /rəˈviːn/ *n* barranco *m*

raving /ˈreɪvɪŋ/ *adj*. **~ mad** loco de atar

ravishing /ˈrævɪʃɪŋ/ *adj* (*enchanting*) encantador

raw /rɔː/ *adj* (**-er**, **-est**) crudo; (sugar) sin refinar; (*inexperienced*) inexperto. **~ deal** *n* tratamiento *m* injusto, injusticia *f*. **~ materials** *npl* materias *fpl* primas

ray /reɪ/ *n* rayo *m*

raze /reɪz/ *vt* arrasar

razor /ˈreɪzə(r)/ *n* navaja *f* de afeitar; (*electric*) maquinilla *f* de afeitar

Rd /rəʊd/ *abbr* (= **Road**) C/, Calle *f*

re /riː/ *prep* con referencia a. •*pref* re.

reach /riːtʃ/ *vt* alcanzar; (*extend*) extender; (*arrive at*) llegar a; (*achieve*) lograr; (*hand over*) pasar, dar. •*vi* extenderse. •*n* alcance *m*. **within ~ of** al alcance de; (*close to*) a corta distancia de. □ **~ out** *vi* alargar la mano

react /rɪ'ækt/ *vi* reaccionar. **~ion** /rɪ'ækʃn/ *n* reacción *f*. **~ionary** *adj* & *n* reaccionario (*m*). **~or** /rɪ'æktə(r)/ *n* reactor *m*

read /ri:d/ *vt* (*pt* **read** /red/) leer; (*study*) estudiar; (*interpret*) interpretar. ●*vi* leer; (instrument) indicar. □ **~ out** *vt* leer en voz alta. **~able** *adj* (*clear*) legible. **~er** *n* lector *m*

readily /'redɪlɪ/ *adv* (*willingly*) de buena gana; (*easily*) fácilmente

reading /'ri:dɪŋ/ *n* lectura *f*

readjust /ri:ə'dʒʌst/ *vt* reajustar. ●*vi* readaptarse (**to** a)

ready /'redɪ/ *adj* (**-ier**, **-iest**) listo, preparado. **get ~** prepararse. **~-made** *adj* confeccionado

real /rɪəl/ *adj* verdadero. ●*adv* (*Amer fam*) verdaderamente. **~ estate** *n* bienes *mpl* raíces, propiedad *f* inmobiliaria. **~ estate agent** *see* REALTOR. **~ism** *n* realismo *m*. **~ist** *n* realista *m* & *f*. **~istic** /-'lɪstɪk/ *adj* realista. **~ity** /rɪ'ælətɪ/ *n* realidad *f*. **~ization** /rɪəlaɪ'zeɪʃn/ *n* comprensión *f*. **~ize** /'rɪəlaɪz/ *vt* darse cuenta de; (*fulfil, Com*) realizar. **~ly** /'rɪəlɪ/ *adv* verdaderamente

realm /relm/ *n* reino *m*

realtor /'ri:əltə(r)/ *n* (*Amer*) agente *m* inmobiliario

reap /ri:p/ *vt* segar; (*fig*) cosechar

reappear /ri:ə'pɪə(r)/ *vi* reaparecer

rear /rɪə(r)/ *n* parte *f* de atrás. ●*adj* posterior, trasero. ●*vt* (*bring up, breed*) criar. ● *vi* **~ (up)** (horse) encabritarse

rearguard /'rɪəgɑ:d/ *n* retaguardia *f*

rearrange /ri:ə'reɪndʒ/ *vt* arreglar de otra manera

reason /'ri:zn/ *n* razón *f*, motivo *m*. **within ~** dentro de lo razonable. ●*vi* razonar. **~able** *adj* razonable. **~ing** *n* razonamiento *m*

reassur|ance /ri:ə'ʃʊərəns/ *n* promesa *f* tranquilizadora; (*guarantee*) garantía *f*. **~e** /ri:ə'ʃʊə(r)/ *vt* tranquilizar

rebate /'ri:beɪt/ *n* (*discount*) rebaja *f*

rebel /'rebl/ *n* rebelde *m* & *f*. ●/rɪ'bel/ *vi* (*pt* **rebelled**) rebelarse. **~lion** /rɪ'belɪən/ *n* rebelión *f*. **~lious** *adj* rebelde

rebound /rɪ'baʊnd/ *vi* rebotar; (*fig*) recaer. ● /'ri:baʊnd/ *n* rebote *m*

rebuff /rɪ'bʌf/ *vt* rechazar. ●*n* desaire *m*

rebuild /ri:'bɪld/ *vt* (*pt* **rebuilt**) reconstruir

rebuke /rɪ'bju:k/ *vt* reprender. ●*n* reprimenda *f*

recall /rɪ'kɔ:l/ *vt* (*call s.o. back*) llamar; (*remember*) recordar. ●*n* /'ri:kɔ:l/ (*of goods, ambassador*) retirada *f*; (*memory*) memoria *f*

recap /'ri:kæp/ *vt/i* (*pt* **recapped**) ▣ resumir

recapitulate /ri:kə'pɪtʃʊleɪt/ *vt/i* resumir

recapture /ri:'kæptʃə(r)/ *vt* recobrar; (*recall*) hacer revivir

recede /rɪ'si:d/ *vi* retroceder

receipt /rɪ'si:t/ *n* recibo *m*. **~s** *npl* (*Com*) ingresos *mpl*

receive /rɪ'si:v/ *vt* recibir. **~r** *n* (*of stolen goods*) perista *m* & *f*; (*part of phone*) auricular *m*

recent /'ri:snt/ *adj* reciente. **~ly** *adv* recientemente

recept|ion /rɪ'sepʃn/ *n* recepción *f*; (*welcome*) acogida *f*. **~ionist** *n* recepcionista *m* & *f*. **~ive** /-tɪv/ *adj* receptivo

recess /rɪ'ses/ *n* hueco *m*; (*holiday*)

r

vacaciones *fpl.* **~ion** /rɪˈseʃn/ *n* recesión *f*

recharge /riːˈtʃɑːdʒ/ *vt* cargar de nuevo, recargar

recipe /ˈresəpɪ/ *n* receta *f.* **~ book** *n* libro *m* de cocina

recipient /rɪˈsɪpɪənt/ *n* recipiente *m & f*; (*of letter*) destinatario *m*

recit|al /rɪˈsaɪtl/ *n* (*Mus*) recital *m.* **~e** /rɪˈsaɪt/ *vt* recitar; (*list*) enumerar

reckless /ˈreklɪs/ *adj* imprudente. **~ly** *adv* imprudentemente

reckon /ˈrekən/ *vt/i* calcular; (*consider*) considerar; (*think*) pensar. □ **~ on** *vt* (*rely*) contar con

reclaim /rɪˈkleɪm/ *vt* reclamar; recuperar (land)

reclin|e /rɪˈklaɪn/ *vi* recostarse. **~ing** *adj* acostado; (seat) reclinable

recluse /rɪˈkluːs/ *n* ermitaño *m*

recogni|tion /rekəgˈnɪʃn/ *n* reconocimiento *m.* **beyond ~tion** irreconocible. **~ze** /ˈrekəgnaɪz/ *vt* reconocer

recoil /rɪˈkɔɪl/ *vi* retroceder. ● /ˈriːkɔɪl/ *n* (*of gun*) culatazo *m*

recollect /rekəˈlekt/ *vt* recordar. **~ion** /-ʃn/ *n* recuerdo *m*

recommend /rekəˈmend/ *vt* recomendar. **~ation** /-ˈdeɪʃn/ *n* recomendación *f*

reconcil|e /ˈrekənsaɪl/ *vt* reconciliar (people); conciliar (facts). **~e o.s.** resignarse (to a). **~iation** /-sɪlɪˈeɪʃn/ *n* reconciliación *f*

reconnaissance /rɪˈkɒnɪsns/ *n* reconocimiento *m*

reconnoitre /rekəˈnɔɪtə(r)/ *vt* (*pres p* **-tring**) (*Mil*) reconocer

re: ~consider /riːkənˈsɪdə(r)/ *vt* volver a considerar. **~construct** /riːkənˈstrʌkt/ *vt* reconstruir

record /rɪˈkɔːd/ *vt* (*in register*) registrar; (*in diary*) apuntar; (*Mus*) grabar. ● /ˈrekɔːd/ *n* (*document*) documento *m*; (*of events*) registro *m*; (*Mus*) disco *m*; (*Sport*) récord *m.* **off the ~** en confianza. **~er** /rɪˈkɔːdə(r)/ *n* registrador *m*; (*Mus*) flauta *f* dulce. **~ing** /rɪˈkɔːdɪŋ/ *n* grabación *f.* **~-player** /ˈrekɔːd-/ *n* tocadiscos *m* invar

recount /rɪˈkaʊnt/ *vt* contar, relatar

re-count /ˈriːkaʊnt/ *vt* volver a contar; recontar (votes). ● /ˈriːkaʊnt/ *n* (*Pol*) recuento *m*

recover /rɪˈkʌvə(r)/ *vt* recuperar. ● *vi* reponerse. **~y** *n* recuperación *f*

recreation /rekrɪˈeɪʃn/ *n* recreo *m.* **~al** *adj* de recreo

recruit /rɪˈkruːt/ *n* recluta *m.* ● *vt* reclutar; contratar (staff). **~ment** *n* reclutamiento *m*

rectang|le /ˈrektæŋgl/ *n* rectángulo *m.* **~ular** /-ˈtæŋgjʊlə(r)/ *adj* rectangular

rectify /ˈrektɪfaɪ/ *vt* rectificar

rector /ˈrektə(r)/ *n* párroco *m*; (*of college*) rector *m.* **~y** *n* rectoría *f*

recuperat|e /rɪˈkuːpəreɪt/ *vt* recuperar. ● *vi* reponerse. **~ion** /-ˈreɪʃn/ *n* recuperación *f*

recur /rɪˈkɜː(r)/ *vi* (*pt* **recurred**) repetirse. **~rence** /rɪˈkʌrns/ *n* repetición *f.* **~rent** /rɪˈkʌrənt/ *adj* repetido

recycle /riːˈsaɪkl/ *vt* reciclar

red /red/ *adj* (**redder, reddest**) rojo. ● *n* rojo. **be in the ~** estar en números rojos. **~den** *vi* enrojecerse. **~dish** *adj* rojizo

redecorate /riːˈdekəreɪt/ *vt* pintar de nuevo

rede|em /rɪˈdiːm/ *vt* redimir. **~mption** /-ˈdempʃn/ *n* redención *f*

red: ~-handed /-'hændɪd/ *adj.* **catch s.o. ~handed** agarrar a uno con las manos en la masa. **~ herring** *n* (*fig*) pista *f* falsa. **~-hot** *adj* al rojo vivo. **~ light** *n* luz *f* roja

redo /ri:'du:/ *vt* (*pt* **redid**, *pp* **redone**) rehacer

redouble /rɪ'dʌbl/ *vt* redoblar

red tape /red'teɪp/ *n* (*fig*) papeleo *m*

reduc|e /rɪ'dju:s/ *vt* reducir; aliviar (pain). ● *vi* (*Amer, slim*) adelgazar. **~tion** /rɪ'dʌkʃn/ *n* reducción *f*

redundan|cy /rɪ'dʌndənsɪ/ *n* superfluidad *f*; (*unemployment*) despido *m*. **~t** superfluo. **she was made ~t** la despidieron por reducción de plantilla

reed /ri:d/ *n* caña *f*; (*Mus*) lengüeta *f*

reef /ri:f/ *n* arrecife *m*

reek /ri:k/ *n* mal olor *m*. ● *vi*. **~ (of)** apestar a

reel /ri:l/ *n* carrete *m*. ● *vi* dar vueltas; (*stagger*) tambalearse. □ **~ off** *vt* (*fig*) enumerar

refectory /rɪ'fektərɪ/ *n* refectorio *m*

refer /rɪ'fɜ:(r)/ *vt* (*pt* **referred**) remitir. ● *vi* referirse. **~ to** referirse a; (*consult*) consultar. **~ee** /refə'ri:/ *n* árbitro *m*; (*for job*) referencia *f*. ● *vi* (*pt* **refereed**) arbitrar. **~ence** /'refrəns/ *n* referencia *f*. **~ence book** *n* libro *m* de consulta. **in ~ to, with ~ to** con referencia a; (*Com*) respecto a. **~endum** /refə'rendəm/ *n* (*pl* **-ums** *or* **-da**) referéndum *m*

refill /ri:'fɪl/ *vt* volver a llenar. ● /'ri:fɪl/ *n* recambio *m*

refine /rɪ'faɪn/ *vt* refinar. **~d** *adj* refinado. **~ry** /-ərɪ/ *n* refinería *f*

reflect /rɪ'flekt/ *vt* reflejar. ● *vi* reflejarse; (*think*) reflexionar. □ **~ badly upon** perjudicar. **~ion** /-ʃn/ *n* reflexión *f*; (*image*) reflejo *m*. **~or** *n* reflector *m*

reflex /'ri:fleks/ *adj & n* reflejo (*m*). **~ive** /rɪ'fleksɪv/ *adj* (*Gram*) reflexivo

reform /rɪ'fɔ:m/ *vt* reformar. ● *vi* reformarse. ● *n* reforma *f*

refrain /rɪ'freɪn/ *n* estribillo *m*. ● *vi* abstenerse (**from** de)

refresh /rɪ'freʃ/ *vt* refrescar. **~ing** *adj* refrescante. **~ments** *npl* (*food and drink*) refrigerio *m*

refrigerat|e /rɪ'frɪdʒəreɪt/ *vt* refrigerar. **~or** *n* frigorífico *m*, refrigerador *m* (*LAm*)

refuel /ri:'fju:əl/ *vt/i* (*pt* **refuelled**) repostar

refuge /'refju:dʒ/ *n* refugio *m*. **take ~** refugiarse. **~e** /refjʊ'dʒi:/ *n* refugiado *m*

refund /rɪ'fʌnd/ *vt* reembolsar. ● /'ri:fʌnd/ *n* reembolso *m*

refusal /rɪ'fju:zl/ *n* negativa *f*

refuse /rɪ'fju:z/ *vt* rehusar. ● *vi* negarse. ● /'refju:s/ *n* residuos *mpl*

refute /rɪ'fju:t/ *vt* refutar

regain /rɪ'geɪn/ *vt* recobrar

regal /'ri:gl/ *adj* real

regard /rɪ'gɑ:d/ *vt* considerar; (*look at*) contemplar. **as ~s** en lo que se refiere a. ● *n* (*consideration*) consideración *f*, (*esteem*) estima *f*. **~s** *npl* saludos *mpl*. **kind ~s** recuerdos. **~ing** *prep* en lo que se refiere a. **~less** *adv* a pesar de todo. **~less of** sin tener en cuenta

regatta /rɪ'gætə/ *n* regata *f*

regime /reɪ'ʒi:m/ *n* régimen *m*

regiment /'redʒɪmənt/ *n* regimiento *m*. **~al** /-'mentl/ *adj* del regimiento

r

region /'ri:dʒən/ *n* región *f*. **in the ~ of** alrededor de. **~al** *adj* regional

register /'redʒɪstə(r)/ *n* registro *m*. ● *vt* registrar; matricular (vehicle); declarar (birth); certificar (letter); facturar (luggage). ● *vi* (*enrol*) inscribirse; (*fig*) producir impresión

registrar /redʒɪ'strɑ:(r)/ *n* secretario *m* del registro civil; (*Univ*) secretario *m* general

registration /redʒɪ'streɪʃn/ *n* registro *m*; (*in register*) inscripción *f*. **~ number** *n* (*Auto*) (número de) matrícula *f*

registry /'redʒɪstrɪ/ *n*. **~ office** *n* registro *m* civil

regret /rɪ'gret/ *n* pesar *m*; (*remorse*) arrepentimiento *m*. ● *vt* (*pt* **regretted**) lamentar. **I ~ that** siento (que). **~table** *adj* lamentable

regula|r /'regjʊlə(r)/ *adj* regular; (*usual*) habitual. ● *n* ⊡ cliente *m* habitual. **~rity** /-'lærətɪ/ *n* regularidad *f*. **~rly** *adv* con regularidad. **~te** /'regjʊleɪt/ *vt* regular. **~tion** /-'leɪʃn/ *n* regulación *f*; (*rule*) regla *f*

rehears|al /rɪ'hɜ:sl/ *n* ensayo *m*. **~e** /rɪ'hɜ:s/ *vt* ensayar

reign /reɪn/ *n* reinado *m*. ● *vi* reinar

reindeer /'reɪndɪə(r)/ *n invar* reno *m*

reinforce /ri:ɪn'fɔ:s/ *vt* reforzar. **~ment** *n* refuerzo *m*

reins /reɪnz/ *npl* riendas *fpl*

reiterate /ri:'ɪtəreɪt/ *vt* reiterar

reject /rɪ'dʒekt/ *vt* rechazar. ● /'ri:dʒekt/ *n* producto *m* defectuoso. **~ion** /rɪ'dʒekʃn/ *n* rechazo *m*; (*after job application*) respuesta *f* negativa

rejoice /rɪ'dʒɔɪs/ *vi* regocijarse

rejoin /rɪ'dʒɔɪn/ *vt* reunirse con

rejuvenate /rɪ'dʒu:vəneɪt/ *vt* rejuvenecer

relapse /rɪ'læps/ *n* recaída *f*. ● *vi* recaer; (*into crime*) reincidir

relat|e /rɪ'leɪt/ *vt* contar; (*connect*) relacionar. ● *vi* relacionarse (**to** con). **~ed** *adj* emparentado; (ideas etc) relacionado. **~ion** /rɪ'leɪʃn/ *n* relación *f*; (*person*) pariente *m & f*. **~ionship** *n* relación *f*; (*blood tie*) parentesco *m*; (*affair*) relaciones *fpl*. **~ive** /'relətɪv/ *n* pariente *m & f*. ● *adj* relativo. **~ively** *adv* relativamente

relax /rɪ'læks/ *vt* relajar. ● *vi* relajarse. **~ation** /-'seɪʃn/ *n* relajación *f*; (*rest*) descanso *m*; (*recreation*) recreo *m*. **~ing** *adj* relajante

relay /'ri:leɪ/ *n* relevo *m*. **~ (race)** *n* carrera *f* de relevos. ● /rɪ'leɪ/ *vt* transmitir

release /rɪ'li:s/ *vt* soltar; poner en libertad (prisoner); estrenar (film); (*Mec*) soltar; publicar (news). ● *n* liberación *f*; (*of film*) estreno *m*; (*record*) disco *m* nuevo

relent /rɪ'lent/ *vi* ceder. **~less** *adj* implacable; (*continuous*) incesante

relevan|ce /'reləvəns/ *n* pertinencia *f*. **~t** *adj* pertinente

relia|bility /rɪlaɪə'bɪlətɪ/ *n* fiabilidad *f*. **~ble** /rɪ'laɪəbl/ *adj* (person) de confianza; (car) fiable. **~nce** /rɪ'laɪəns/ *n* dependencia *f*; (*trust*) confianza *f*. **~nt** /rɪ'laɪənt/ *adj* confiado

relic /'relɪk/ *n* reliquia *f*

relie|f /rɪ'li:f/ *n* alivio *m*; (*assistance*) socorro *m*. **be on ~f** (*Amer*) recibir prestaciones de la seguridad social. **~ve** /rɪ'li:v/ *vt* aliviar; (*take over from*) relevar. **~ved** *adj* ali-

viado. **feel ~ved** sentir un gran alivio
religio|n /rɪ'lɪdʒən/ *n* religión *f*. **~us** /rɪ'lɪdʒəs/ *adj* religioso
relinquish /rɪ'lɪnkwɪʃ/ *vt* abandonar, renunciar
relish /'relɪʃ/ *n* gusto *m*; (*Culin*) salsa *f*. ● *vt* saborear
reluctan|ce /rɪ'lʌktəns/ *n* desgana *f*. **~t** *adj* mal dispuesto. **be ~t to** no tener ganas de. **~tly** *adv* de mala gana
rely /rɪ'laɪ/ *vi*. **~ on** contar con; (*trust*) fiarse de; (*depend*) depender
remain /rɪ'meɪn/ *vi* (*be left*) quedar; (*stay*) quedarse; (*continue to be*) seguir. **~der** *n* resto *m*. **~s** *npl* restos *mpl*; (*left-overs*) sobras *fpl*
remand /rɪ'mɑ:nd/ *vt*. **~ in custody** mantener bajo custodia. ● *n*. **on ~** en prisión preventiva
remark /rɪ'mɑ:k/ *n* observación *f*. ● *vt* observar. **~able** *adj* notable
remarry /ri:'mærɪ/ *vi* volver a casarse
remedy /'remədɪ/ *n* remedio *m*. ● *vt* remediar
remember /rɪ'membə(r)/ *vt* acordarse de, recordar. ● *vi* acordarse
remind /rɪ'maɪnd/ *vt* recordar. **~er** *n* recordatorio *m*
reminisce /remɪ'nɪs/ *vi* rememorar los viejos tiempos. **~nces** /-ənsɪz/ *npl* recuerdos *mpl*. **~nt** /-'nɪsnt/ *adj*. **be ~nt of** recordar
remnant /'remnənt/ *n* resto *m*; (*of cloth*) retazo *m*; (*trace*) vestigio *m*
remorse /rɪ'mɔ:s/ *n* remordimiento *m*. **~ful** *adj* arrepentido. **~less** *adj* implacable
remote /rɪ'məʊt/ *adj* remoto. **~ control** *n* mando *m* a distancia. **~ly** *adv* remotamente
remov|able /rɪ'mu:vəbl/ *adj* (*detachable*) de quita y pon; (handle) desmontable. **~al** *n* eliminación *f*; (*from house*) mudanza *f*. **~e** /rɪ'mu:v/ *vt* quitar; (*dismiss*) destituir; (*get rid of*) eliminar
render /'rendə(r)/ *vt* rendir (homage); prestar (help etc). **~ sth useless** hacer que algo resulte inútil
rendezvous /'rɒndɪvu:/ *n* (*pl* **-vous**/-vu:z/) cita *f*
renegade /'renɪgeɪd/ *n* renegado
renew /rɪ'nju:/ *vt* renovar; (*resume*) reanudar. **~al** *n* renovación *f*
renounce /rɪ'naʊns/ *vt* renunciar a
renovat|e /'renəveɪt/ *vt* renovar. **~ion** /-'veɪʃn/ *n* renovación *f*
renown /rɪ'naʊn/ *n* renombre *m*. **~ed** *adj* de renombre
rent /rent/ *n* alquiler *m*. ● *vt* alquilar. **~al** *n* alquiler *m*. **car ~** (*Amer*) alquiler *m* de coche
renunciation /rɪnʌnsɪ'eɪʃn/ *n* renuncia *f*
reopen /ri:'əʊpən/ *vt* volver a abrir. ● *vi* reabrirse
reorganize /ri:'ɔ:gənaɪz/ *vt* reorganizar
rep /rep/ *n* (*Com*) representante *m* & *f*
repair /rɪ'peə(r)/ *vt* arreglar, reparar; arreglar (clothes, shoes). ● *n* reparación *f*; (*patch*) remiendo *m*. **in good ~** en buen estado. **it's beyond ~** ya no tiene arreglo
repatriat|e /ri:'pætrɪeɪt/ *vt* repatriar
repay /ri:'peɪ/ *vt* (*pt* **repaid**) reembolsar; pagar (debt); corresponder a (kindness). **~ment** *n* pago *m*
repeal /rɪ'pi:l/ *vt* revocar. ● *n* revo-

cación *f*

repeat /rɪ'pi:t/ *vt* repetir. ● *vi* repetir(se). ● *n* repetición *f*. **~edly** *adv* repetidas veces

repel /rɪ'pel/ *vt* (*pt* **repelled**) repeler. **~lent** *adj* repelente

repent /rɪ'pent/ *vi* arrepentirse. **~ant** *adj* arrepentido

repercussion /ri:pə'kʌʃn/ *n* repercusión *f*

repertoire /'repətwɑ:(r)/ *n* repertorio *m*

repetit|ion /repɪ'tɪʃn/ *n* repetición *f*. **~ious** /-'tɪʃəs/ *adj*, **~ive** /rɪ'petətɪv/ *adj* repetitivo

replace /rɪ'pleɪs/ *vt* reponer; cambiar (battery); (*take the place of*) sustituir. **~ment** *n* sustitución *f*; (*person*) sustituto *m*

replay /'ri:pleɪ/ *n* (*Sport*) repetición *f* del partido; (*recording*) repetición *f* inmediata

replenish /rɪ'plenɪʃ/ *vt* reponer

replica /'replɪkə/ *n* réplica *f*

reply /rɪ'plaɪ/ *vt/i* responder, contestar. **~ to sth** responder a algo, contestar algo. ● *n* respuesta *f*

report /rɪ'pɔ:t/ *vt* (reporter) informar sobre; informar de (accident); (*denounce*) denunciar. ● *vi* informar; (*present o.s.*) presentarse. ● *n* informe *m*; (*Schol*) boletín *m* de notas; (*rumour*) rumor *m*; (*in newspaper*) reportaje *m*. **~ card** (*Amer*) *n* boletín *m* de calificaciones. **~edly** *adv* según se dice. **~er** *n* periodista *m* & *f*, reportero *m*

reprehensible /reprɪ'hensəbl/ *adj* reprensible

represent /reprɪ'zent/ *vt* representar. **~ation** /-'teɪʃn/ *n* representación *f*. **~ative** *adj* representativo. ● *n* representante *m* & *f*; (*Amer, in government*) diputado *m*

repress /rɪ'pres/ *vt* reprimir. **~ion** /-ʃn/ *n* represión *f*. **~ive** *adj* represivo

reprieve /rɪ'pri:v/ *n* indulto *m*; (*fig*) respiro *m*. ● *vt* indultar

reprimand /'reprɪmɑ:nd/ *vt* reprender. ● *n* reprensión *f*

reprisal /rɪ'praɪzl/ *n* represalia *f*

reproach /rɪ'prəʊtʃ/ *vt* reprochar. ● *n* reproche *m*. **~ful** *adj* de reproche

reproduc|e /ri:prə'dju:s/ *vt* reproducir. ● *vi* reproducirse. **~tion** /-'dʌkʃn/ *n* reproducción *f*. **~tive** /-'dʌktɪv/ *adj* reproductor

reprove /rɪ'pru:v/ *vt* reprender

reptile /'reptaɪl/ *n* reptil *m*

republic /rɪ'pʌblɪk/ *n* república *f*. **~an** *adj* & *n* republicano (*m*). **R~** *a* & *n* (*in US*) republicano (*m*)

repugnan|ce /rɪ'pʌgnəns/ *n* repugnancia *f*. **~t** *adj* repugnante

repuls|e /rɪ'pʌls/ *vt* rechazar, repulsar. **~ion** /-ʃn/ *n* repulsión *f*. **~ive** *adj* repulsivo

reput|able /'repjʊtəbl/ *adj* acreditado, reputado. **~ation** /repjʊ'teɪʃn/ *n* reputación *f*

request /rɪ'kwest/ *n* petición *f*. ● *vt* pedir

require /rɪ'kwaɪə(r)/ *vt* requerir; (*need*) necesitar; (*demand*) exigir. **~d** *adj* necesario. **~ment** *n* requisito *m*

rescue /'reskju:/ *vt* rescatar, salvar. ● *n* rescate *m*. **~r** *n* salvador *m*

research /rɪ'sɜ:tʃ/ *n* investigación *f*. ● *vt* investigar. **~er** *n* investigador *m*

resembl|ance /rɪ'zembləns/ *n* parecido *m*. **~e** /rɪ'zembl/ *vt* parecerse a

resent /rɪ'zent/ *vt* guardarle rencor a (person). **she ~ed his suc-**

cess le molestaba que él tuviera éxito. **~ful** *adj* resentido. **~ment** *n* resentimiento *m*

reserv|ation /rezə'veɪʃn/ *n* reserva *f*; (*booking*) reserva *f*. **~e** /rɪ'zɜːv/ *vt* reservar. ● *n* reserva *f*; (*in sports*) suplente *m & f*. **~ed** *adj* reservado. **~oir** /'rezəvwɑː(r)/ *n* embalse *m*

reshuffle /riː'ʃʌfl/ *n* (*Pol*) reorganización *f*

residen|ce /'rezɪdəns/ *n* residencia *f*. **~t** *adj & n* residente (*m & f*). **~tial** /rezɪ'denʃl/ *adj* residencial

residue /'rezɪdjuː/ *n* residuo *m*

resign /rɪ'zaɪn/ *vt/i* dimitir. **~ o.s. to** resignarse a. **~ation** /rezɪg'neɪʃn/ *n* resignación *f*; (*from job*) dimisión *f*. **~ed** *adj* resignado

resilien|ce /rɪ'zɪlɪəns/ *n* elasticidad *f*; (*of person*) resistencia *f*. **~t** *adj* elástico; (person) resistente

resin /'rezɪn/ *n* resina *f*

resist /rɪ'zɪst/ *vt* resistir. ● *vi* resistirse. **~ance** *n* resistencia *f*. **~ant** *adj* resistente

resolut|e /'rezəluːt/ *adj* resuelto. **~ion** /-'luːʃn/ *n* resolución *f*

resolve /rɪ'zɒlv/ *vt* resolver. **~ to do** resolver a hacer. ● *n* resolución *f*

resort /rɪ'zɔːt/ *n* recurso *m*; (*place*) lugar *m* turístico. **in the last ~** como último recurso. □ **~ to** *vt* recurrir a.

resource /rɪ'sɔːs/ *n* recurso *m*. **~ful** *adj* ingenioso

respect /rɪ'spekt/ *n* (*esteem*) respeto *m*; (*aspect*) respecto *m*. **with ~ to** con respecto a. ● *vt* respetar. **~able** *adj* respetable. **~ful** *adj* respetuoso. **~ive** *adj* respectivo. **~ively** *adv* respectivamente

respiration /respə'reɪʃn/ *n* respiración *f*

respite /'respaɪt/ *n* respiro *m*

respon|d /rɪ'spɒnd/ *vi* responder. **~se** /rɪ'spɒns/ *n* respuesta *f*; (*reaction*) reacción *f*

responsib|ility /rɪspɒnsə'bɪlətɪ/ *n* responsabilidad *f*. **~le** /rɪ'spɒnsəbl/ *adj* responsable; (job) de responsabilidad. **~ly** *adv* con formalidad

responsive /rɪ'spɒnsɪv/ *adj* que reacciona bien. **~ to** sensible a

rest /rest/ *vt* descansar; (*lean*) apoyar. ● *vi* descansar; (*lean*) apoyarse. ● *n* descanso *m*; (*Mus*) pausa *f*; (*remainder*) resto *m*, lo demás; (*people*) los demás, los otros *mpl*. **to have a ~** tomarse un descanso. □ **~ up** *vi* (*Amer*) descansar

restaurant /'restərɒnt/ *n* restaurante *m*

rest: ~ful *adj* sosegado. **~ive** *adj* impaciente. **~less** *adj* inquieto

restor|ation /restə'reɪʃn/ *n* restablecimiento *m*; (*of building, monarch*) restauración *f*. **~e** /rɪ'stɔː(r)/ *vt* restablecer; restaurar (building); devolver (confidence, health)

restrain /rɪ'streɪn/ *vt* contener. **~ o.s.** contenerse. **~ed** *adj* (*moderate*) moderado; (*in control of self*) comedido. **~t** *n* restricción *f*; (*moderation*) compostura *f*

restrict /rɪ'strɪkt/ *vt* restringir. **~ion** /-ʃn/ *n* restricción *f*. **~ive** *adj* restrictivo

rest room *n* (*Amer*) baño *m*, servicio *m*

result /rɪ'zʌlt/ *n* resultado *m*. **as a ~ of** como consecuencia de. ● *vi*. **~ from** resultar de. **~ in** dar como resultado

resume /rɪ'zjuːm/ *vt* reanudar. ● *vi* reanudarse

résumé /'rezjʊmeɪ/ *n* resumen *m*;

(*Amer, CV*) currículum *m*, historial *m* personal
resurrect /rezə'rekt/ *vt* resucitar. **~ion** /-ʃn/ *n* resurrección *f*
resuscitat|e /rɪ'sʌsɪteɪt/ *vt* resucitar. **~ion** /-'teɪʃn/ *n* resucitación *f*
retail /'ri:teɪl/ *n* venta *f* al por menor. •*adj & adv* al por menor. •*vt* vender al por menor. •*vi* venderse al por menor. **~er** *n* minorista *m & f*
retain /rɪ'teɪn/ *vt* retener; conservar (heat)
retaliat|e /rɪ'tælɪeɪt/ *vi* desquitarse; (*Mil*) tomar represalias. **~ion** /-'eɪʃn/ *n* represalias *fpl*
retarded /rɪ'tɑ:dɪd/ *adj* retrasado
rethink /ri:'θɪŋk/ *vt* (*pt* **rethought**) reconsiderar
reticen|ce /'retɪsns/ *n* reticencia *f*. **~t** *adj* reticente
retina /'retɪnə/ *n* retina *f*
retinue /'retɪnju:/ *n* séquito *m*
retir|e /rɪ'taɪə(r)/ *vi* (*from work*) jubilarse; (*withdraw*) retirarse; (*go to bed*) acostarse. **~ed** *adj* jubilado. **~ement** *n* jubilación *f*. **~ing** *adj* retraído
retort /rɪ'tɔ:t/ *vt/i* replicar. •*n* réplica *f*
retrace /ri:'treɪs/ *vt*. **~ one's steps** volver sobre sus pasos
retract /rɪ'trækt/ *vt* retirar (statement). •*vi* retractarse
retrain /ri:'treɪn/ *vi* hacer un curso de reciclaje
retreat /rɪ'tri:t/ *vi* retirarse. •*n* retirada *f*; (*place*) refugio *m*
retrial /ri:'traɪəl/ *n* nuevo juicio *m*
retriev|al /rɪ'tri:vl/ *n* recuperación *f*. **~e** /rɪ'tri:v/ *vt* recuperar. **~er** *n* (*dog*) perro *m* cobrador
retro|grade /'retrəgreɪd/ *adj* retrógrado. **~spect** /-spekt/ *n*. **in ~** en retrospectiva. **~spective** /-'spektɪv/ *adj* retrospectivo
return /rɪ'tɜ:n/ *vi* volver, regresar; (symptom) reaparecer. •*vt* devolver; corresponder a (affection). •*n* regreso *m*, vuelta *f*; (*Com*) rendimiento *m*; (*to owner*) devolución *f*. **in ~ for** a cambio de. **many happy ~s!** ¡feliz cumpleaños! **~ ticket** *n* billete *m or* (*LAm*) boleto *m* de ida y vuelta, boleto *m* redondo (*Mex*). **~s** *npl* (*Com*) ingresos *mpl*
reun|ion /ri:'ju:nɪən/ *n* reunión *f*. **~ite** /ri:ju:'naɪt/ *vt* reunir
rev /rev/ *n* (*Auto, fam*) revolución *f*. •*vt/i*. **~ (up)** (*pt* **revved**) (*Auto, fam*) acelerar(se)
reveal /rɪ'vi:l/ *vt* revelar. **~ing** *adj* revelador
revel /'revl/ *vi* (*pt* **revelled**) tener un jolgorio. **~ in** deleitarse en. **~ry** *n* jolgorio *m*
revelation /revə'leɪʃn/ *n* revelación *f*
revenge /rɪ'vendʒ/ *n* venganza *f*. **take ~** vengarse. •*vt* vengar
revenue /'revənju:/ *n* ingresos *mpl*
revere /rɪ'vɪə(r)/ *vt* venerar. **~nce** /'revərəns/ *n* reverencia *f*.
Reverend /'revərənd/ *adj* reverendo
reverent /'revərənt/ *adj* reverente
reverie /'revərɪ/ *n* ensueño *m*
revers|al /rɪ'vɜ:sl/ *n* inversión *f*. **~e** /rɪ'vɜ:s/ *adj* inverso. •*n* contrario *m*; (*back*) revés *m*; (*Auto*) marcha *f* atrás. •*vt* invertir; anular (decision); (*Auto*) dar marcha atrás a. •*vi* (*Auto*) dar marcha atrás
revert /rɪ'vɜ:t/ *vi*. **~ to** volver a; (*Jurid*) revertir a
review /rɪ'vju:/ *n* revisión *f*; (*Mil*)

revista *f*; (*of book, play, etc*) crítica *f*. ●*vt* examinar (situation); reseñar (book, play, etc); (*Amer, for exam*) repasar

revis|e /rɪ'vaɪz/ *vt* revisar; (*Schol*) repasar. **~ion** /rɪ'vɪʒn/ *n* revisión *f*; (*Schol*) repaso *m*

revive /rɪ'vaɪv/ *vt* resucitar (person)

revolt /rɪ'vəʊlt/ *vi* sublevarse. ●*n* revuelta *f*. **~ing** *adj* asqueroso

revolution /revə'lu:ʃn/ *n* revolución *f*. **~ary** *adj & n* revolucionario (*m*). **~ize** *vt* revolucionar

revolv|e /rɪ'vɒlv/ *vi* girar. **~er** *n* revólver *m*. **~ing** /rɪ'vɒlvɪŋ/ *adj* giratorio

revue /rɪ'vju:/ *n* revista *f*

revulsion /rɪ'vʌlʃn/ *n* asco *m*

reward /rɪ'wɔ:d/ *n* recompensa *f*. ●*vt* recompensar. **~ing** *adj* gratificante

rewrite /ri:'raɪt/ *vt* (*pt* **rewrote**, *pp* **rewritten**) volver a escribir *or* redactar; (*copy out*) escribir otra vez

rhetoric /'retərɪk/ *n* retórica *f*. **~al** /rɪ'tɒrɪkl/ *adj* retórico

rheumatism /'ru:mətɪzəm/ *n* reumatismo *m*

rhinoceros /raɪ'nɒsərəs/ *n* (*pl* **-oses** *or invar*) rinoceronte *m*

rhubarb /'ru:bɑ:b/ *n* ruibarbo *m*

rhyme /raɪm/ *n* rima *f*; (*poem*) poesía *f*. ●*vt/i* rimar

rhythm /'rɪðəm/ *n* ritmo *m*. **~ic(al)** /'rɪðmɪk(l)/ *adj* rítmico

rib /rɪb/ *n* costilla *f*

ribbon /'rɪbən/ *n* cinta *f*

rice /raɪs/ *n* arroz *m*. **~ pudding** *n* arroz con leche

rich /rɪtʃ/ *adj* (**-er**, **-est**) rico. ●*n* ricos *mpl*. **~es** *npl* riquezas *fpl*

ricochet /'rɪkəʃeɪ/ *vi* rebotar

rid /rɪd/ *vt* (*pt* **rid**, *pres p* **ridding**) librar (of de). **get ~ of** deshacerse de. **~dance** /'rɪdns/ *n*. **good ~dance!** ¡adiós y buen viaje!

ridden /'rɪdn/ *see* **RIDE**

riddle /'rɪdl/ *n* acertijo *m*. ●*vt* acribillar. **be ~d with** estar lleno de

ride /raɪd/ *vi* (*pt* **rode**, *pp* **ridden**) (*on horseback*) montar a caballo; (*go*) ir (en bicicleta, a caballo etc). ●*vt* montar a (horse); ir en (bicycle); (*Amer*) ir en (bus, train); recorrer (distance). ●*n* (*on horse*) cabalgata *f*; (*in car*) paseo *m* en coche. **take s.o. for a ~** ⊡ engañarle a uno. **~r** *n* (*on horse*) jinete *m*; (*cyclist*) ciclista *m & f*

ridge /rɪdʒ/ *n* (*of hills*) cadena *f*; (*hilltop*) cresta *f*

ridicul|e /'rɪdɪkju:l/ *n* burlas *fpl*. ●*vt* ridiculizar. **~ous** /rɪ'dɪkjʊləs/ *adj* ridículo

rife /raɪf/ *adj* difundido

rifle /'raɪfl/ *n* fusil *m*

rift /rɪft/ *n* grieta *f*; (*fig*) ruptura *f*

rig /rɪg/ *vt* (*pt* **rigged**) (*pej*) amañar. ●*n* (*at sea*) plataforma *f* de perforación. □ **~ up** *vt* improvisar

right /raɪt/ *adj* (answer) correcto; (*morally*) bueno; (*not left*) derecho; (*suitable*) adecuado. **be ~** (person) tener razón; (clock) estar bien. **it is ~** (*just, moral*) es justo. **put ~** rectificar. **the ~ person for the job** la persona indicada para el puesto. ●*n* (*entitlement*) derecho *m*; (*not left*) derecha *f*; (*not evil*) bien *m*. **~ of way** (*Auto*) prioridad *f*. **be in the ~** tener razón. **on the ~** a la derecha. ●*vt* enderezar; (*fig*) reparar. ●*adv* a la derecha; (*directly*) derecho; (*completely*) completamente. **~ angle** *n* ángulo *m* recto.

~ **away** *adv* inmediatamente. ~**eous** /ˈraɪtʃəs/ *adj* recto; (cause) justo. ~**ful** /ˈraɪtfl/ *adj* legítimo. ~**-handed** /-ˈhændɪd/ *adj* diestro. ~**-hand man** *n* brazo *m* derecho. ~**ly** *adv* justamente. ~ **wing** *adj* (*Pol*) derechista

rigid /ˈrɪdʒɪd/ *adj* rígido

rig|orous /ˈrɪgərəs/ *adj* riguroso. ~**our** /ˈrɪgə(r)/ *n* rigor *m*

rim /rɪm/ *n* borde *m*; (*of wheel*) llanta *f*; (*of glasses*) montura *f*

rind /raɪnd/ *n* corteza *f*; (*of fruit*) cáscara *f*

ring[1] /rɪŋ/ *n* (*circle*) círculo *m*; (*circle of metal etc*) aro *m*; (*on finger*) anillo *m*; (*on finger with stone*) sortija *f*; (*Boxing*) cuadrilátero *m*; (*bullring*) ruedo *m*; (*for circus*) pista *f*; • *vt* cercar

ring[2] /rɪŋ/ *n* (*of bell*) toque *m*; (*tinkle*) tintineo *m*; (*telephone call*) llamada *f*. • *vt* (*pt* **rang**, *pp* **rung**) hacer sonar; (*telephone*) llamar por teléfono. ~ **the bell** tocar el timbre. • *vi* sonar. ~ **back** *vt/i* volver a llamar. □ ~ **up** *vt* llamar por teléfono

ring: ~**leader** /ˈrɪŋliːdə(r)/ *n* cabecilla *m & f*. ~ **road** *n* carretera *f* de circunvalación

r

rink /rɪŋk/ *n* pista *f*

rinse /rɪns/ *vt* enjuagar. • *n* aclarado *m*; (*of dishes*) enjuague *m*; (*for hair*) tintura *f* (no permanente)

riot /ˈraɪət/ *n* disturbio *m*; (*of colours*) profusión *f*. **run** ~ desenfrenarse. • *vi* causar disturbios

rip /rɪp/ *vt* (*pt* **ripped**) rasgar. • *vi* rasgarse. • *n* rasgón *m*. □ ~ **off** *vt* (*pull off*) arrancar; (⊠, *cheat*) robar

ripe /raɪp/ *adj* (**-er**, **-est**) maduro. ~**n** /ˈraɪpn/ *vt/i* madurar

rip-off /ˈrɪpɒf/ *n* ⊠ timo *m*

ripple /ˈrɪpl/ *n* (*on water*) onda *f*

ris|e /raɪz/ *vi* (*pt* **rose**, *pp* **risen**) subir; (sun) salir; (river) crecer; (prices) subir; (land) elevarse; (*get up*) levantarse. • *n* subida *f*; (*land*) altura *f*; (*increase*) aumento *m*; (*to power*) ascenso *m*. **give** ~**e to** ocasionar. ~**er** *n*. **early** ~**er** *n* madrugador *m*. ~**ing** *n*. • *adj* (sun) naciente; (number) creciente; (prices) en alza

risk /rɪsk/ *n* riesgo *m*. • *vt* arriesgar. ~**y** *adj* (**-ier**, **-iest**) arriesgado

rite /raɪt/ *n* rito *m*

ritual /ˈrɪtʃʊəl/ *adj & n* ritual (*m*)

rival /ˈraɪvl/ *adj & n* rival (*m*). ~**ry** *n* rivalidad *f*

river /ˈrɪvə(r)/ *n* río *m*

rivet /ˈrɪvɪt/ *n* remache *m*. ~**ing** *adj* fascinante

road /rəʊd/ *n* (*in town*) calle *f*; (*between towns*) carretera *f*; (*route, way*) camino *m*. ~ **map** *n* mapa *m* de carreteras. ~**side** *n* borde *m* de la carretera. ~**works** *npl* obras *fpl*. ~**worthy** *adj* (vehicle) apto para circular

roam /rəʊm/ *vi* vagar

roar /rɔː(r)/ *n* rugido *m*; (*laughter*) carcajada *f*. • *vt/i* rugir. ~ **past** (vehicles) pasar con estruendo. ~ **with laughter** reírse a carcajadas. ~**ing** *adj* (trade etc) activo

roast /rəʊst/ *vt* asar; tostar (coffee). • *adj & n* asado (*m*). ~ **beef** *n* rosbif *m*

rob /rɒb/ *vt* (*pt* **robbed**) atracar, asaltar (bank); robarle a (person). ~ **of** (*deprive of*) privar de. ~**ber** *n* ladrón *m*; (*of bank*) atracador *m*. ~**bery** *n* robo *m*; (*of bank*) atraco *m*

robe /rəʊb/ *n* bata *f*; (*Univ etc*)

toga *f*
robin /'rɒbɪn/ *n* petirrojo *m*
robot /'rəʊbɒt/ *n* robot *m*
robust /rəʊ'bʌst/ *adj* robusto
rock /rɒk/ *n* roca *f*; (*crag, cliff*) peñasco *m*. ● *vt* mecer; (*shake*) sacudir. ● *vi* mecerse; (*shake*) sacudirse. ● *n* (*Mus*) música *f* rock. **~-bottom** /-'bɒtəm/ *adj* 🄸 bajísimo
rocket /'rɒkɪt/ *n* cohete *m*
rock: ~ing-chair *n* mecedora *f*. **~y** *adj* (**-ier**, **-iest**) rocoso; (*fig, shaky*) bamboleante
rod /rɒd/ *n* vara *f*; (*for fishing*) caña *f*; (*metal*) barra *f*
rode /rəʊd/ *see* RIDE
rodent /'rəʊdnt/ *n* roedor *m*
rogue /rəʊg/ *n* pícaro *m*
role /rəʊl/ *n* papel *m*
roll /rəʊl/ *vt* hacer rodar; (*roll up*) enrollar; allanar (lawn); aplanar (pastry). ● *vi* rodar; (ship) balancearse; (*on floor*) revolcarse. **be ~ing in money** 🄸 nadar en dinero ● *n* rollo *m*; (*of ship*) balanceo *m*; (*of drum*) redoble *m*; (*of thunder*) retumbo *m*; (*bread*) panecillo *m*, bolillo *m* (*Mex*). □ **~ over** *vi* (*turn over*) dar una vuelta. □ **~ up** *vt* enrollar; arremangar (sleeve). *vi* 🄸 llegar. **~-call** *n* lista *f*
roller /'rəʊlə(r)/ *n* rodillo *m*; (*wheel*) rueda *f*; (*for hair*) rulo *m*. **R~ blades** *npl* (*P*) patines *mpl* en línea. **~-coaster** *n* montaña *f* rusa. **~-skate** *n* patín *m* de ruedas. **~-skating** patinaje *m* (*sobre ruedas*)
rolling /'rəʊlɪŋ/ *adj* ondulado. **~-pin** *n* rodillo *m*
ROM /rɒm/ *n* (= **read-only memory**) ROM *f*
Roman /'rəʊmən/ *adj* & *n* romano (*m*). **~ Catholic** *adj* & *n* católico (*m*) (romano)
romance /rəʊ'mæns/ *n* novela *f* romántica; (*love*) amor *m*; (*affair*) aventura *f*
Romania /ruː'meɪnɪə/ *n* Rumania *f*, Rumanía *f*. **~n** *adj* & *n* rumano (*m*)
romantic /rəʊ'mæntɪk/ *adj* romántico
Rome /'rəʊm/ *n* Roma *f*
romp /rɒmp/ *vi* retozar
roof /ruːf/ *n* techo *m*, tejado *m*; (*of mouth*) paladar *m*. ● *vt* techar. **~rack** *n* baca *f*. **~top** *n* tejado *m*
rook /rʊk/ *n* grajo *m*; (*in chess*) torre *f*
room /ruːm/ *n* cuarto *m*, habitación *f*; (*bedroom*) dormitorio *m*; (*space*) espacio *m*; (*large hall*) sala *f*. **~y** *adj* espacioso
roost /ruːst/ *vi* posarse. **~er** *n* gallo *m*
root /ruːt/ *n* raíz *f*. **take ~** echar raíces; (idea) arraigarse. ● *vi* echar raíces. **~ about** *vi* hurgar. □ **~ for** *vt* 🄸 alentar. □ **~ out** *vt* extirpar
rope /rəʊp/ *n* cuerda *f*. **know the ~s** estar al corriente. ● *vt* atar; (*Amer, lasso*) enlazar. □ **~ in** *vt* agarrar
rose[1] /rəʊz/ *n* rosa *f*; (*nozzle*) roseta *f*
rose[2] /rəʊz/ *see* RISE
rosé /'rəʊzeɪ/ *n* (vino *m*) rosado *m*
rot /rɒt/ *vt* (*pt* **rotted**) pudrir. ● *vi* pudrirse. ● *n* putrefacción *f*
rota /'rəʊtə/ *n* lista *f* (de turnos)
rotary /'rəʊtərɪ/ *adj* rotatorio
rotat|e /rəʊ'teɪt/ *vt* girar; (*change round*) alternar. ● *vi* girar; (*change round*) alternarse. **~ion** /-ʃn/ *n* rotación *f*
rote /rəʊt/ *n*. **by ~** de memoria
rotten /'rɒtn/ *adj* podrido; 🄸 pé-

simo Ⅱ; (weather) horrible
rough /rʌf/ *adj* (**-er**, **-est**) áspero; (person) tosco; (*bad*) malo; (ground) accidentado; (*violent*) brutal; (*approximate*) aproximado; (diamond) bruto. ● *adv* duro. ~ **copy**, ~ **draft** borrador *m*. ● *vt*. ~ **it** vivir sin comodidades. ~**age** /ˈrʌfɪdʒ/ *n* fibra *f*. ~**-and-ready** *adj* improvisado. ~**ly** *adv* bruscamente; (*more or less*) aproximadamente
roulette /ru:ˈlet/ *n* ruleta *f*
round /raʊnd/ *adj* (**-er**, **-est**) redondo. ● *n* círculo *m*; (*of visits, drinks*) ronda *f*; (*of competition*) vuelta *f*; (*Boxing*) asalto *m*. ● *prep* alrededor de. ● *adv* alrededor. ~ **about** (*approximately*) aproximadamente. **come** ~ **to**, **go** ~ **to** (*a friend etc*) pasar por casa de. ● *vt* doblar (corner). □ ~ **off** *vt* terminar; redondear (number). □ ~ **up** *vt* rodear (cattle); hacer una redada de (suspects). ~**about** *n* tiovivo *m*, carrusel *m* (*LAm*); (*for traffic*) glorieta *f*, rotonda *f*. ● *adj* in directo. ~ **trip** *n* viaje *m* de ida y vuelta. ~**-up** *n* resumen *m*; (*of suspects*) redada *f*
rous|e /raʊz/ *vt* despertar. ~**ing** *adj* enardecedor
route /ru:t/ *n* ruta *f*; (*Naut, Aviat*) rumbo *m*; (*of bus*) línea *f*
routine /ru:ˈti:n/ *n* rutina *f*. ● *adj* rutinario
row¹ /rəʊ/ *n* fila *f*. ● *vi* remar
row² /raʊ/ *n* (*fam, noise*) bulla *f* Ⅱ; (*quarrel*) pelea *f*. ● *vi* Ⅱ pelearse
rowboat /ˈrəʊbəʊt/ (*Amer*) *n* bote *m* de remos
rowdy /ˈraʊdɪ/ *adj* (**-ier**, **-iest**) *n* escandaloso, alborotador
rowing /ˈrəʊɪŋ/ *n* remo *m*. ~ **boat** *n* bote *m* de remos
royal /ˈrɔɪəl/ *adj* real. ~**ist** *adj & n* monárquico (*m*). ~**ly** *adv* magníficamente. ~**ty** *n* realeza *f*
rub /rʌb/ *vt* (*pt* **rubbed**) frotar. □ ~ **out** *vt* borrar
rubber /ˈrʌbə(r)/ *n* goma *f*, caucho *m*, hule *m* (*Mex*); (*eraser*) goma *f* (de borrar). ~ **band** *n* goma *f* (elástica). ~**-stamp** *vt* (*fig*) autorizar. ~**y** *adj* parecido al caucho
rubbish /ˈrʌbɪʃ/ *n* basura *f*; (*junk*) trastos *mpl*; (*fig*) tonterías *fpl*. ~ **bin** *n* cubo *m* de la basura, bote *m* de la basura (*Mex*). ~**y** *adj* sin valor
rubble /ˈrʌbl/ *n* escombros *mpl*
ruby /ˈru:bɪ/ *n* rubí *m*
rucksack /ˈrʌksæk/ *n* mochila *f*
rudder /ˈrʌdə(r)/ *n* timón *m*
rude /ru:d/ *adj* (**-er**, **-est**) grosero, mal educado; (*improper*) indecente; (*brusque*) brusco. ~**ly** *adv* groseramente. ~**ness** *n* mala educación *f*
rudimentary /ru:dɪˈmentrɪ/ *adj* rudimentario
ruffian /ˈrʌfɪən/ *n* rufián *m*
ruffle /ˈrʌfl/ *vt* despeinar (hair); arrugar (clothes)
rug /rʌg/ *n* alfombra *f*, tapete *m* (*Mex*); (*blanket*) manta *f* de viaje
rugged /ˈrʌgɪd/ *adj* (coast) escarpado; (landscape) escabroso
ruin /ˈru:ɪn/ *n* ruina *f*. ● *vt* arruinar; (*spoil*) estropear
rul|e /ru:l/ *n* regla *f*; (*Pol*) dominio *m*. **as a** ~ por regla general. ● *vt* gobernar; (*master*) dominar; (*Jurid*) dictaminar. ~**e out** *vt* descartar. ~**ed paper** *n* papel *m* rayado. ~**er** *n* (*sovereign*) soberano *m*; (*leader*) gobernante *m & f*; (*measure*) regla *f*. ~**ing** *adj* (class) dirigente. ● *n* decisión *f*
rum /rʌm/ *n* ron *m*

rumble /'rʌmbl/ *vi* retumbar; (stomach) hacer ruidos

rummage /'rʌmɪdʒ/ *vi* hurgar

rumour /'ru:mə(r)/ *n* rumor *m*. ● *vt*. **it is ~ed that** se rumorea que

rump steak /rʌmpsteɪk/ *n* filete *m* de cadera

run /rʌn/ *vi* (*pt* **ran**, *pp* **run**, *pres p* **running**) correr; (water) correr; (*function*) funcionar; (*melt*) derretirse; (makeup) correrse; (colour) desteñir; (bus etc) circular; (*in election*) presentarse. ● *vt* correr (race); dirigir (business); correr (risk); (*move, pass*) pasar; tender (wire); preparar (bath). **~ a temperature** tener fiebre. ● *n* corrida *f*, carrera *f*; (*outing*) paseo *m* (en coche); (*ski*) pista *f*. **in the long ~** a la larga. **be on the ~** estar prófugo. □ **~ away** *vi* huir, escaparse. □ **~ down** *vi* bajar corriendo; (battery) descargarse. *vt* (*Auto*) atropellar; (*belittle*) denigrar. □ **~ in** *vi* entrar corriendo. □ **~ into** *vt* toparse con (friend); (*hit*) chocar con. □ **~ off** *vt* sacar (copies). □ **~ out** *vi* salir corriendo; (liquid) salirse; (*fig*) agotarse. □ **~ out of** *vt* quedarse sin. □ **~ over** *vt* (*Auto*) atropellar. □ **~ through** *vt* (*review*) ensayar; (*rehearse*) repasar. □ **~ up** *vt* ir acumulando (bill). *vi* subir corriendo. **~away** *n* fugitivo *m*. **~ down** *adj* (person) agotado

rung[1] /rʌŋ/ *n* (*of ladder*) peldaño *m*

rung[2] /rʌŋ/ *see* RING

run: ~ner /'rʌnə(r)/ *n* corredor *m*; (*on sledge*) patín *m*. **~ner bean** *n* judía *f* escarlata. **~nerup** *n*. **be ~er-up** quedar en segundo lugar. **~ning** *n*. **be in the ~ning** tener posibilidades de ganar. ● *adj* (water) corriente; (commentary) en directo. **four times ~ning** cuatro veces seguidas. **~ny** /'rʌnɪ/ *adj* líquido; (nose) que moquea. **~way** *n* pista *f* de aterrizaje

rupture /'rʌptʃə(r)/ *n* ruptura *f*. ● *vt* romper

rural /'rʊərəl/ *adj* rural

ruse /ru:z/ *n* ardid *m*

rush /rʌʃ/ *n* (*haste*) prisa *f*; (*crush*) bullicio *m*; (*plant*) junco *m*. ● *vi* precipitarse. ● *vt* apresurar; (*Mil*) asaltar. **~-hour** *n* hora *f* punta, hora *f* pico (*LAm*)

Russia /'rʌʃə/ *n* Rusia *f*. **~n** *adj* & *n* ruso (*m*)

rust /rʌst/ *n* orín *m*. ● *vt* oxidar. ● *vi* oxidarse

rustle /'rʌsl/ *vt* hacer susurrar; (*Amer*) robar. ● *vi* susurrar □ **~ up** *vt* 🄸 preparar.

rust: ~proof *adj* inoxidable. **~y** (**-ier**, **-iest**) oxidado

rut /rʌt/ *n* surco *m*. **be in a ~** estar anquilosado

ruthless /'ru:θlɪs/ *adj* despiadado

rye /raɪ/ *n* centeno *m*

Ss

S *abbr* (= **south**) S

sabot|age /'sæbətɑ:ʒ/ *n* sabotaje *m*. ● *vt* sabotear. **~eur** /-'tɜ:(r)/ *n* saboteador *m*

saccharin /'sækərɪn/ *n* sacarina *f*

sachet /'sæʃeɪ/ *n* bolsita *f*

sack /sæk/ *n* saco *m*. **get the ~** 🄸 ser despedido. ● *vt* 🄸 despedir, echar

sacrament /ˈsækrəmənt/ *n* sacramento *m*

sacred /ˈseɪkrɪd/ *adj* sagrado

sacrifice /ˈsækrɪfaɪs/ *n* sacrificio *m.* ● *vt* sacrificar

sacrileg|e /ˈsækrɪlɪdʒ/ *n* sacrilegio *m.* **~ious** /-ˈlɪdʒəs/ *adj* sacrílego

sad /sæd/ *adj* (**sadder, saddest**) triste. **~den** *vt* entristecer

saddle /ˈsædl/ *n* silla *f* de montar. ● *vt* ensillar (horse). **~ s.o. with sth** (*fig*) endilgarle algo a uno

sadist /ˈseɪdɪst/ *n* sádico *m.* **~tic** /səˈdɪstɪk/ *adj* sádico

sadly /ˈsædlɪ/ *adv* tristemente; (*fig*) desgraciadamente. **~ness** *n* tristeza *f*

safe /seɪf/ *adj* (**-er, -est**) seguro; (*out of danger*) salvo; (*cautious*) prudente. **~ and sound** sano y salvo. ● *n* caja *f* fuerte. **~ deposit** *n* caja *f* de seguridad. **~guard** *n* salvaguardia *f.* ● *vt* salvaguardar. **~ly** *adv* sin peligro; (*in safe place*) en lugar seguro. **~ty** *n* seguridad *f.* **~ty belt** *n* cinturón *m* de seguridad. **~ty pin** *n* imperdible *m*

sag /sæg/ *vi* (*pt* **sagged**) (ceiling) combarse; (bed) hundirse

saga /ˈsɑːgə/ *n* saga *f*

Sagittarius /sædʒɪˈteərɪəs/ *n* Sagitario *m*

said /sed/ *see* SAY

sail /seɪl/ *n* vela *f*; (*trip*) paseo *m* (en barco). **set ~** zarpar. ● *vi* navegar; (*leave*) partir; (*Sport*) practicar la vela; (*fig*) deslizarse. **go ~ing** salir a navegar. *vt* gobernar (boat). **~boat** *n* (*Amer*) barco *m* de vela. **~ing** *n* (*Sport*) vela *f.* **~ing boat** *n*, **~ing ship** *n* barco *m* de vela. **~or** *n* marinero *m*

saint /seɪnt//sənt/ *n* santo *m.* **~ly** *adj* santo

sake /seɪk/ *n.* **for the ~ of** por. **for God's ~** por el amor de Dios

salad /ˈsæləd/ *n* ensalada *f.* **~ bowl** *n* ensaladera *f.* **~ dressing** *n* aliño *m*

salary /ˈsælərɪ/ *n* sueldo *m*

sale /seɪl/ *n* venta *f*; (*at reduced prices*) liquidación *f.* **for ~** (*sign*) se vende. **be for ~** estar a la venta. **be on ~** (*Amer, reduced*) estar en liquidación. **~able** *adj* vendible. (*for sale*) estar a la venta. **~s clerk** *n* (*Amer*) dependiente *m*, dependienta *f.* **~sman** /-mən/ *n* vendedor *m*; (*in shop*) dependiente *m.* **~swoman** *n* vendedora *f*; (*in shop*) dependienta *f*

saliva /səˈlaɪvə/ *n* saliva *f*

salmon /ˈsæmən/ *n invar* salmón *m*

saloon /səˈluːn/ *n* (*on ship*) salón *m*; (*Amer, bar*) bar *m*; (*Auto*) turismo *m*

salt /sɔːlt/ *n* sal *f.* ● *vt* salar. **~ cellar** *n* salero *m.* **~y** *adj* salado

salute /səˈluːt/ *n* saludo *m.* ● *vt* saludar. ● *vi* hacer un saludo

Salvadorean, Salvadorian /sælvəˈdɔːrɪən/ *adj & n* salvadoreño (*m*)

salvage /ˈsælvɪdʒ/ *vt* salvar

salvation /sælˈveɪʃn/ *n* salvación *f*

same /seɪm/ *adj* igual (as que); (*before noun*) mismo (as que). **at the ~ time** al mismo tiempo. ● *pron.* **the ~** lo mismo. **all the ~** de todas formas. ● *adv.* **the ~** igual

sample /ˈsɑːmpl/ *n* muestra *f.* ● *vt* degustar (food)

sanct|ify /ˈsæŋktɪfaɪ/ *vt* santificar. **~ion** /ˈsæŋkʃn/ *n* sanción *f.* ● *vt* sancionar. **~uary** /ˈsæŋktʃʊərɪ/ *n* (*Relig*) santuario *m*; (*for wildlife*) reserva *f*; (*refuge*) asilo *m*

sand /sænd/ *n* arena *f*. ● *vt* pulir (floor). □ ~ **down** *vt* lijar (wood)

sandal /'sændl/ *n* sandalia *f*

sand: ~**castle** *n* castillo *m* de arena. ~**paper** *n* papel *m* de lija. ● *vt* lijar. ~**storm** *n* tormenta *f* de arena

sandwich /'sænwɪdʒ/ *n* bocadillo *m*, sandwich *m*. ● *vt*. **be** ~**ed between** (person) estar apretujado entre

sandy /'sændɪ/ *adj* arenoso

sane /seɪn/ *adj* (-**er**, -**est**) (person) cuerdo; (*sensible*) sensato

sang /sæŋ/ *see* SING

sanitary /'sænɪtrɪ/ *adj* higiénico; (system etc) sanitario. ~ **towel**, ~ **napkin** *n* (*Amer*) compresa *f* (higiénica)

sanitation /sænɪ'teɪʃn/ *n* higiene *f*; (*drainage*) sistema *m* sanitario

sanity /'sænɪtɪ/ *n* cordura *f*

sank /sæŋk/ *see* SINK

Santa (Claus) /'sæntə(klɔːz)/ *n* Papá *m* Noel

sap /sæp/ *n* (*in plants*) savia *f*. ● (*pt* **sapped**) minar

sapling /'sæplɪŋ/ *n* árbol *m* joven

sapphire /'sæfaɪə(r)/ *n* zafiro *m*

sarcas|m /'sɑːkæzəm/ *n* sarcasmo *m*. ~**tic** /-'kæstɪk/ *adj* sarcástico

sardine /sɑː'diːn/ *n* sardina *f*

sash /sæʃ/ *n* (*over shoulder*) banda *f*; (*round waist*) fajín *m*.

sat /sæt/ *see* SIT

SAT *abbr* (*Amer*) (**Scholastic Aptitude Test**); (*Brit*) (**Standard Assessment Task**)

satchel /'sætʃl/ *n* cartera *f*

satellite /'sætəlaɪt/ *n* & *a* satélite (*m*). ~ **TV** *n* televisión *f* por satélite

satin /'sætɪn/ *n* raso *m*. ● *adj* de raso

satir|e /'sætaɪə(r)/ *n* sátira *f*. ~**ical** /sə'tɪrɪkl/ *adj* satírico. ~**ize** /'sætəraɪz/ *vt* satirizar

satis|faction /sætɪs'fækʃn/ *n* satisfacción *f*. ~**factorily** /-'fæktərɪlɪ/ *adv* satisfactoriamente. ~**factory** /-'fæktərɪ/ *adj* satisfactorio. ~**fy** /'sætɪsfaɪ/ *vt* satisfacer; (*convince*) convencer. ~**fying** *adj* satisfactorio

satphone /'sætfəʊn/ *n* teléfono *m* satélite

saturat|e /'sætʃəreɪt/ *vt* saturar. ~**ed** *adj* saturado; (*drenched*) empapado

Saturday /'sætədeɪ/ *n* sábado *m*

Saturn /'sætən/ *n* Saturno *m*

sauce /sɔːs/ *n* salsa *f*; (*cheek*) descaro *m*. ~**pan** /'sɔːspən/ *n* cazo *m*, cacerola *f*. ~**r** /'sɔːsə(r)/ *n* platillo *m*

saucy /'sɔːsɪ/ *adj* (-**ier**, -**iest**) descarado

Saudi /'saʊdɪ/ *adj* & *n* saudita (*m* & *f*). ~ **Arabia** /-ə'reɪbɪə/ *n* Arabia *f* Saudí

sauna /'sɔːnə/ *n* sauna *f*

saunter /'sɔːntə(r)/ *vi* pasearse

sausage /'sɒsɪdʒ/ *n* salchicha *f*

savage /'sævɪdʒ/ *adj* salvaje; (*fierce*) feroz. ● *n* salvaje *m* & *f*. ● *vt* atacar. ~**ry** *n* ferocidad *f*

sav|e /seɪv/ *vt* (*rescue*) salvar; ahorrar (money, time); (*prevent*) evitar; (*Comp*) guardar. ● *n* (*football*) parada *f*. ● *prep* salvo, excepto. □ ~**e up** *vi/t* ahorrar. ~**er** *n* ahorrador *m*. ~**ing** *n* ahorro *m*. ~**ings** *npl* ahorros *mpl*

saviour /'seɪvɪə(r)/ *n* salvador *m*

savour /'seɪvə(r)/ *vt* saborear. ~**y** *adj* (*appetizing*) sabroso; (*not sweet*) no dulce

S

saw[1] /sɔː/ *see* **SEE**[1]
saw[2] /sɔː/ *n* sierra *f.* •*vt* (*pt* **sawed**, *pp* **sawn**) serrar. **~dust** *n* serrín *m.* **~n** /sɔːn/ *see* **SAW**[2]
saxophone /'sæksəfəʊn/ *n* saxofón *m*, saxófono *m*
say /seɪ/ *vt/i* (*pt* **said** /sed/) decir; rezar (prayer). •*n*. **have a ~** expresar una opinión; (*in decision*) tener voz en capítulo. **have no ~** no tener ni voz ni voto. **~ing** *n* refrán *m*
scab /skæb/ *n* costra *f*; (*fam, blackleg*) esquirol *m*
scaffolding /'skæfəldɪŋ/ *n* andamios *mpl*
scald /skɔːld/ *vt* escaldar
scale /skeɪl/ *n* (*also Mus*) escala *f*; (*of fish*) escama *f.* •*vt* (*climb*) escalar. **~ down** *vt* reducir (a escala) (drawing); recortar (operation). **~s** *npl* (*for weighing*) balanza *f*, peso *m*
scallion /'skæljən/ *n* (*Amer*) cebolleta *f*
scalp /skælp/ *vt* quitar el cuero cabelludo a. •*n* cuero *m* cabelludo
scamper /'skæmpə(r)/ *vi*. **~ away** irse correteando
scan /skæn/ *vt* (*pt* **scanned**) escudriñar; (*quickly*) echar un vistazo a; (radar) explorar
scandal /'skændl/ *n* escándalo *m*; (*gossip*) chismorreo *m.* **~ize** *vt* escandalizar. **~ous** *adj* escandaloso
Scandinavia /skændɪ'neɪvɪə/ *n* Escandinavia *f.* **~n** *adj & n* escandinavo (*m*)
scant /skænt/ *adj* escaso. **~y** *adj* (**-ier**, **-iest**) escaso
scapegoat /'skeɪpgəʊt/ *n* cabeza *f* de turco
scar /skɑː(r)/ *n* cicatriz *f*
scarc|e /skeəs/ *adj* (**-er**, **-est**) escaso. **be ~e** escasear. **make o.s. ~e** ⊡ mantenerse lejos. **~ely** *adv* apenas. **~ity** *n* escasez *f*
scare /'skeə(r)/ *vt* asustar. **be ~d** tener miedo. **be ~d of sth** tenerle miedo a algo. •*n* susto *m.* **~crow** *n* espantapájaros *m*
scarf /skɑːf/ *n* (*pl* **scarves**) bufanda *f*; (*over head*) pañuelo *m*
scarlet /'skɑːlət/ *adj* escarlata *f.* **~ fever** *n* escarlatina *f*
scarves /skɑːvz/ *see* **SCARF**
scary /'skeərɪ/ *adj* (**-ier**, **-iest**) que da miedo
scathing /'skeɪðɪŋ/ *adj* mordaz
scatter /'skætə(r)/ *vt* (*throw*) esparcir; (*disperse*) dispersar. •*vi* dispersarse. **~ed** /'skætəd/ *adj* disperso; (*occasional*) esporádico
scavenge /'skævɪndʒ/ *vi* escarbar (en la basura)
scenario /sɪ'nɑːrɪəʊ/ *n* (*pl* **-os**) perspectiva *f*; (*of film*) guión *m*
scen|e /siːn/ *n* escena *f*; (*sight*) vista *f*; (*fuss*) lío *m.* **behind the ~es** entre bastidores. **~ery** /'siːnərɪ/ *n* paisaje *m*; (*in theatre*) decorado *m.* **~ic** /'siːnɪk/ *adj* pintoresco
scent /sent/ *n* olor *m*; (*perfume*) perfume *m*; (*trail*) pista *f.* •*vt* intuir; (*make fragrant*) perfumar
sceptic /'skeptɪk/ *n* escéptico *m.* **~al** *adj* escéptico. **~ism** /-sɪzəm/ *n* escepticismo *m*
sceptre /'septə(r)/ *n* cetro *m*
schedule /'ʃedjuːl, 'skedjuːl/ *n* programa *f*; (*timetable*) horario *m.* **behind ~** atrasado. **it's on ~** va de acuerdo a lo previsto. •*vt* proyectar. **~d flight** *n* vuelo *m* regular
scheme /skiːm/ *n* proyecto *m*; (*plot*) intriga *f.* •*vi* (*pej*) intrigar
schizophrenic /skɪtsə'frenɪk/ *adj & n* esquizofrénico (*m*)
scholar /'skɒlə(r)/ *n* erudito *m.*

~ly *adj* erudito. **~ship** *n* erudición *f*; (*grant*) beca *f*

school /sku:l/ *n* escuela *f*; (*Univ*) facultad *f*. ● *adj* (age, holidays, year) escolar. ● *vt* instruir; (*train*) capacitar. **~boy** *n* colegial *m*. **~girl** *n* colegiala *f*. **~ing** *n* instrucción *f*. **~master** *n* (*primary*) maestro *m*; (*secondary*) profesor *m*. **~mistress** *n* (*primary*) maestra *f*; (*secondary*) profesora *f*. **~teacher** *n* (*primary*) maestro *m*; (*secondary*) profesor *m*

scien|ce /'saɪəns/ *n* ciencia *f*. **study ~ce** estudiar ciencias. **~ce fiction** *n* ciencia *f* ficción. **~tific** /-'tɪfɪk/ *adj* científico. **~tist** /'saɪəntɪst/ *n* científico *m*

scissors /'sɪsəz/ *npl* tijeras *fpl*

scoff /skɒf/ *vt* 🄸 zamparse. ● *vi*. **~ at** mofarse de

scold /skəʊld/ *vt* regañar

scoop /sku:p/ *n* pala *f*; (*news*) primicia *f*. □ **~ out** *vt* sacar; excavar (hole)

scooter /'sku:tə(r)/ *n* escúter *m*; (*for child*) patinete *m*

scope /skəʊp/ *n* alcance *m*; (*opportunity*) oportunidad *f*

scorch /skɔ:tʃ/ *vt* chamuscar. **~ing** *adj* 🄸 de mucho calor

score /skɔ:(r)/ *n* tanteo *m*; (*Mus*) partitura *f*; (*twenty*) veintena *f*. **on that ~** en cuanto a eso. **know the ~** 🄸 saber cómo son las cosas. ● *vt* marcar (goal); anotarse (points); (*cut, mark*) rayar; conseguir (success). ● *vi* marcar

scorn /skɔ:n/ *n* desdén *m*. ● *vt* desdeñar. **~ful** *adj* desdeñoso

Scorpio /'skɔ:pɪəʊ/ *n* Escorpio *m*, Escorpión *m*

scorpion /'skɔ:pɪən/ *n* escorpión *m*

Scot /skɒt/ *n* escocés *m*. **~ch** /skɒtʃ/ *n* whisky *m*, güisqui *m*

> **Scottish Parliament** El Parlamento Escocés fue establecido en Edinburgo en 1999. Tiene competencia legislativa y ejecutiva en los asuntos internos de Escocia y poderes tributarios limitados. Los *MSPs* (*Members of the Scottish Parliament*) son 129, de los cuales 73 son elegidos directamente y el resto mediante el sistema de representación proporcional.

scotch /skɒtʃ/ *vt* frustrar; acallar (rumours)

Scotch tape *n* (*Amer*) celo *m*, cinta *f* Scotch

Scot: ~land /'skɒtlənd/ *n* Escocia *f*. **~s** *adj* escocés. **~tish** *adj* escocés

scoundrel /'skaʊndrəl/ *n* canalla *f*

scour /'skaʊə(r)/ *vt* fregar; (*search*) registrar. **~er** *n* estropajo *m*

scourge /skɜ:dʒ/ *n* azote *m*

scout /skaʊt/ *n* explorador *m*. **Boy S~** explorador *m*

scowl /skaʊl/ *n* ceño *m* fruncido. ● *vi* fruncir el ceño

scram /skræm/ *vi* 🄸 largarse

scramble /'skræmbl/ *vi* (*clamber*) gatear. ● *n* (*difficult climb*) subida *f* difícil; (*struggle*) rebatiña *f*. **~d egg** *n* huevos *mpl* revueltos

scrap /skræp/ *n* pedacito *m*; (*fam, fight*) pelea *f*. ● *vt* (*pt* **scrapped**) desechar. **~book** *n* álbum *m* de recortes. **~s** *npl* sobras *fpl*

scrape /skreɪp/ *n* (*fig*) apuro *m*. ● *vt* raspar; (*graze*) rasparse; (*rub*) rascar. □ **~ through** *vi/t* aprobar por los pelos (exam). □ **~ together** *vt* reunir. **~r** *n* rasqueta *f*

scrap: ~heap *n* montón *m* de deshechos. **~ yard** *n* chatarrería *f*

scratch /skrætʃ/ *vt* rayar (furniture, record); (*with nail etc*) arañar; rascarse (itch). ● *vi* arañar. ● *n* rayón *m*; (*from nail etc*) arañazo *m*. **start from ~** empezar desde cero. **be up to ~** dar la talla

scrawl /skrɔːl/ *n* garabato *m*. ● *vt/i* garabatear

scream /skriːm/ *vt/i* gritar. ● *n* grito *m*

screech /skriːtʃ/ *vi* chillar; (brakes etc) chirriar. ● *n* chillido *m*; (*of brakes etc*) chirrido *m*

screen /skriːn/ *n* pantalla *f*; (*folding*) biombo *m*. ● *vt* (*hide*) ocultar; (*protect*) proteger; proyectar (film)

screw /skruː/ *n* tornillo *m*. ● *vt* atornillar. □ **~ up** *vt* atornillar; entornar (eyes); torcer (face); (*sl, ruin*) fastidiar. **~driver** *n* destornillador *m*

scribble /ˈskrɪbl/ *vt/i* garrabatear. ● *n* garrabato *m*

script /skrɪpt/ *n* escritura *f*; (*of film etc*) guión *m*

scroll /skrəʊl/ *n* rollo *m* (de pergamino). □ **~ down** *vi* retroceder la pantalla. □ **~ up** *vi* avanzar la pantalla

scrounge /skraʊndʒ/ *vt/i* gorronear. **~r** *n* gorrón *m*

scrub /skrʌb/ *n* (*land*) maleza *f*. ● *vt/i* (*pt* **scrubbed**) fregar

scruff /skrʌf/ *n*. **by the ~ of the neck** por el pescuezo. **~y** *adj* (**-ier, -iest**) desaliñado

scrup|le /ˈskruːpl/ *n* escrúpulo *m*. **~ulous** /-jʊləs/ *adj* escrupuloso

scrutin|ize /ˈskruːtɪnaɪz/ *vt* escudriñar; inspeccionar (document). **~y** /ˈskruːtɪnɪ/ *n* examen *m* minucioso

scuffle /ˈskʌfl/ *n* refriega *f*

sculpt /skʌlpt/ *vt/i* esculpir. **~or** *n* escultor *m*. **~ure** /-tʃə(r)/ *n* escultura *f*. ● *vt/i* esculpir

scum /skʌm/ *n* espuma *f*; (*people, pej*) escoria *f*

scupper /ˈskʌpə(r)/ *vt* echar por tierra (plans)

scurry /ˈskʌrɪ/ *vi* corretear

scuttle /ˈskʌtl/ *n* cubo *m* del carbón. ● *vt* barrenar (ship). ● *vi*. **~ away** escabullirse rápidamente

scythe /saɪð/ *n* guadaña *f*

SE *abbr* (= **south-east**) SE

sea /siː/ *n* mar *m*. **at ~** en el mar; (*fig*) confuso. **by ~** por mar. **~food** *n* mariscos *mpl*. **~ front** *n* paseo *m* marítimo, malecón *m* (*LAm*). **~gull** *n* gaviota *f*. **~horse** *n* caballito *m* de mar

seal /siːl/ *n* sello *m*; (*animal*) foca *f*. ● *vt* sellar

sea level *n* nivel *m* del mar

sea lion *n* león *m* marino

seam /siːm/ *n* costura *f*; (*of coal*) veta *f*

seaman /ˈsiːmən/ *n* (*pl* **-men**) marinero *m*

seamy /ˈsiːmɪ/ *adj* sórdido

seance /ˈseɪɑːns/ *n* sesión *f* de espiritismo

search /sɜːtʃ/ *vt* registrar; buscar en (records). ● *vi* buscar. ● *n* (*for sth*) búsqueda *f*; (*of sth*) registro *m*; (*Comp*) búsqueda *f*. **in ~ of** en busca de. □ **~ for** *vt* buscar. **~ engine** *n* buscador *m*. **~ing** *adj* penetrante. **~light** *n* reflector *m*. **~ party** *n* partida *f* de rescate

sea: ~shore *n* orilla *f* del mar. **~sick** *adj* mareado. **be ~sick** marearse. **~side** *n* playa *f*

season /ˈsiːzn/ *n* estación *f*; (*period*) temporada *f*. **high/low ~**

temporada *f* alta/baja. ● *vt* (*Culin*) sazonar. **~al** *adj* estacional; (demand) de estación. **~ed** *adj* (*fig*) avezado. **~ing** *n* condimento *m*. **~ ticket** *n* abono *m* (de temporada)

seat /si:t/ *n* asiento *m*; (*place*) lugar *m*; (*in cinema, theatre*) localidad *f*; (*of trousers*) fondillos *mpl*. **take a ~** sentarse. ● *vt* sentar; (*have seats for*) (auditorium) tener capacidad para; (bus) tener asientos para. **~belt** *n* cinturón *m* de seguridad

sea: ~ trout *n* reo *m*. **~-urchin** *n* erizo *m* de mar. **~weed** *n* alga *f* marina. **~worthy** *adj* en condiciones de navegar

seclu|ded /sɪ'klu:dɪd/ *adj* aislado

second /'sekənd/ *adj & n* segundo (*m*). **on ~ thoughts** pensándolo bien. ● *adv* (*in race etc*) en segundo lugar. ● *vt* secundar. **~s** *npl* (*goods*) artículos *mpl* de segunda calidad; (*fam, more food*) **have ~s** repetir. ● /sɪ'kɒnd/ *vt* (*transfer*) trasladar temporalmente. **~ary** /'sekəndrɪ/ *adj* secundario. **~ary school** *n* instituto *m* (de enseñanza secundaria)

second: ~-class *adj* de segunda (clase). **~-hand** *adj* de segunda mano. **~ly** *adv* en segundo lugar. **~-rate** *adj* mediocre

secre|cy /'si:krəsɪ/ *n* secreto *m*. **~t** *adj & n* secreto (*m*). **in ~t** en secreto

secretar|ial /sekrə'teərɪəl/ *adj* de secretario; (course) de secretariado. **~y** /'sekrətrɪ/ *n* secretario *m*. **S~y of State** (*in UK*) ministro *m*: (*in US*) secretario *m* de Estado

secretive /'si:krɪtɪv/ *adj* reservado

sect /sekt/ *n* secta *f*. **~arian** /-'teərɪən/ *adj* sectario

section /'sekʃn/ *n* sección *f*; (*part*) parte *f*

sector /'sektə(r)/ *n* sector *m*

secular /'sekjʊlə(r)/ *adj* secular

secur|e /sɪ'kjʊə(r)/ *adj* seguro; (shelf) firme. ● *vt* asegurar; (*obtain*) obtener. **~ely** *adv* seguramente. **~ity** *n* seguridad *f*; (*for loan*) garantía *f*

sedat|e /sɪ'deɪt/ *adj* reposado. ● *vt* sedar. **~ion** /sɪ'deɪʃn/ *n* sedación *f*. **~ive** /'sedətɪv/ *adj & n* sedante (*m*)

sediment /'sedɪmənt/ *n* sedimento *m*

seduc|e /sɪ'dju:s/ *vt* seducir. **~er** *n* seductor *m*. **~tion** /sɪ'dʌkʃn/ *n* seducción *f*. **~tive** /sɪ'dʌktɪv/ *adj* seductor

see /si:/ ● *vt* (*pt* **saw**, *pp* **seen**) ver; (*understand*) comprender; (*escort*) acompañar. **~ing that** visto que. **~ you later!** ¡hasta luego! ● *vi* ver. □ **~ off** *vt* (*say goodbye to*) despedirse de. □ **~ through** *vt* llevar a cabo; calar (person). □ **~ to** *vt* ocuparse de

seed /si:d/ *n* semilla *f*; (*fig*) germen *m*; (*Amer, pip*) pepita *f*. **go to ~** granar; (*fig*) echarse a perder. **~ling** *n* planta *f* de semillero. **~y** *adj* (**-ier**, **-iest**) sórdido

seek /si:k/ *vt* (*pt* **sought**) buscar; pedir (approval). □ **~ out** *vt* buscar

seem /si:m/ *vi* parecer

seen /si:n/ *see* SEE

seep /si:p/ *vi* filtrarse

see-saw /'si:sɔ:/ *n* balancín *m*

seethe /si:ð/ *vi* (*fig*) estar furioso. **I was seething with anger** me hervía la sangre

see-through /'si:θru:/ *adj* transparente

segment /'segmənt/ *n* segmento

m; (*of orange*) gajo *m*

segregat|e /'segrɪgeɪt/ *vt* segregar. **~ion** /-'geɪʃn/ *n* segregación *f*

seiz|e /si:z/ *vt* agarrar; (*Jurid*) incautar. **~e on** *vt* aprovechar (chance). □ **~e up** *vi* (*Tec*) agarrotarse. **~ure** /'si:ʒə(r)/ *n* incautación *f*; (*Med*) ataque *m*

seldom /'seldəm/ *adv* rara vez

select /sɪ'lekt/ *vt* escoger; (*Sport*) seleccionar. ● *adj* selecto; (*exclusive*) exclusivo. **~ion** /-ʃn/ *n* selección *f*. **~ive** *adj* selectivo

self /self/ *n* (*pl* **selves**). **he's his old ~ again** vuelve a ser el de antes. **~-addressed** *adj* con el nombre y la dirección del remitente. **~-catering** *adj* con facilidades para cocinar. **~-centred** *adj* egocéntrico. **~-confidence** *n* confianza *f* en sí mismo. **~-confident** *adj* seguro de sí mismo. **~-conscious** *adj* cohibido. **~-contained** *adj* independiente. **~-control** *n* dominio *m* de sí mismo. **~-defence** *n* defensa *f* propia. **~-employed** *adj* que trabaja por cuenta propia. **~-evident** *adj* evidente. **~-important** *adj* presumido. **~-indulgent** *adj* inmoderado. **~-interest** *n* interés *m* (personal). **~ish** *adj* egoísta. **~ishness** *n* egoísmo *m*. **~-pity** *n* autocompasión. **~-portrait** *n* autorretrato *m*. **~-respect** *n* amor *m* propio. **~-righteous** *adj* santurrón. **~-sacrifice** *n* abnegación *f*. **~-satisfied** *adj* satisfecho de sí mismo. **~-serve** (*Amer*), **~-service** *adj* & *n* autoservicio (*m*). **~-sufficient** *adj* independiente

sell /sel/ *vt* (*pt* **sold**) vender. ● *vi* venderse. □ **~ off** *vt* liquidar. **~ out** *vi*. **we've sold out of gloves** los guantes están agotados. **~-by date** *n* fecha *f* límite de venta. **~er** *n* vendedor *m*

Sellotape /'seləteɪp/ *n* (®) celo *m*, cinta *f* Scotch

sell-out /'selaʊt/ *n* (*performance*) éxito *m* de taquilla; (*fam, betrayal*) capitulación *f*

semblance /'sembləns/ *n* apariencia *f*

semester /sɪ'mestə(r)/ *n* (*Amer*) semestre *m*

semi... /'semɪ/ *pref* semi...

semi|breve /-bri:v/ *n* redonda *f*. **~circle** *n* semicírculo *m*. **~colon** /-'kəʊlən/ *n* punto *m* y coma. **~-detached** /-dɪ'tætʃt/ *adj* (house) adosado. **~final** /-'faɪnl/ *n* semifinal *f*

seminar /'semɪnɑ:(r)/ *n* seminario *m*

senat|e /'senɪt/ *n* senado *m*. **the S~e** (*Amer*) el Senado. **~or** /-ətə(r)/ *n* senador *m*

send /send/ *vt/i* (*pt* **sent**) mandar, enviar. □ **~ away** *vt* despedir. □ **~ away for** *vt* pedir (por correo). □ **~ for** *vt* enviar a buscar. □ **~ off for** *vt* pedir (por correo). □ **~ up** *vt* 🅸 parodiar. **~er** *n* remitente *m*. **~-off** *n* despedida *f*

senile /'si:naɪl/ *adj* senil

senior /'si:nɪə(r)/ *adj* mayor; (*in rank*) superior; (partner etc) principal. ● *n* mayor *m* & *f*. **~ citizen** *n* jubilado *m*. **~ high school** *n* (*Amer*) colegio *m* secundario. **~ity** /-'ɒrətɪ/ *n* antigüedad *f*

sensation /sen'seɪʃn/ *n* sensación *f*. **~al** *adj* sensacional

sens|e /sens/ *n* sentido *m*; (*common sense*) juicio *m*; (*feeling*) sensación *f*. **make ~e** *vt* tener sentido. **make ~e of sth** entender algo. **~eless** *adj* sin sentido. **~ible**

/'sensəbl/ *adj* sensato; (clothing) práctico. **~itive** /'sensɪtɪv/ *adj* sensible; (*touchy*) susceptible. **~itivity** /-'tɪvətɪ/ *n* sensibilidad *f*. **~ual** /'senʃʊəl/ *adj* sensual. **~uous** /'sensʊəs/ *adj* sensual

sent /sent/ *see* **SEND**

sentence /'sentəns/ *n* frase *f*; (*judgment*) sentencia *f*; (*punishment*) condena *f*. ● *vt*. **~ to** condenar a

sentiment /'sentɪmənt/ *n* sentimiento *m*; (*opinion*) opinión *f*. **~al** /-'mentl/ *adj* sentimental. **~ality** /-'tæləti/ *n* sentimentalismo *m*

sentry /'sentrɪ/ *n* centinela *f*

separa|ble /'sepərəbl/ *adj* separable. **~te** /'sepərət/ *adj* separado; (*independent*) independiente. ● *vt* /'sepəreɪt/ separar. ● *vi* separarse. **~tely** /'sepərətlɪ/ *adv* por separado. **~tion** /-'reɪʃn/ *n* separación *f*. **~tist** /'sepərətɪst/ *n* separatista *m & f*

September /sep'tembə(r)/ *n* se(p)tiembre *m*

septic /'septɪk/ *adj* séptico

sequel /'si:kwəl/ *n* continuación *f*; (*later events*) secuela *f*

sequence /'si:kwəns/ *n* sucesión *f*; (*of film*) secuencia *f*

Serb /sɜ:b/ *adj & n see* **SERBIAN**. **~ia** /'sɜ:bɪə/ *n* Serbia *f* **~ian** *adj & n* serbio (*m*)

serenade /serə'neɪd/ *n* serenata *f* ● *vt* dar serenata a

serene /sɪ'ri:n/ *adj* sereno

sergeant /'sɑ:dʒənt/ *n* sargento *m*

serial /'sɪərɪəl/ *n* serie *f*. **~ize** *vt* serializar

series /'sɪəri:z/ *n* serie *f*

serious /'sɪərɪəs/ *adj* serio. **~ly** *adv* seriamente; (*ill*) gravemente. **take ~ly** tomar en serio

sermon /'sɜ:mən/ *n* sermón *m*

serum /'sɪərəm/ *n* (*pl* **-a**) suero *m*

servant /'sɜ:vənt/ *n* criado *m*

serve /sɜ:v/ *vt* servir; servir a (country); cumplir (sentence). **~ as** servir de. **it ~s you right** ¡bien te lo mereces! ● *vi* servir; (*in tennis*) sacar. ● *n* (*in tennis*) saque *m*. **~r** *n* (*Comp*) servidor *m*

service /'sɜ:vɪs/ *n* servicio *m*; (*of car etc*) revisión *f*. ● *vt* revisar (car etc). **~ charge** *n* (*in restaurant*) servicio *m*. **~s** *npl* (*Mil*) fuerzas *fpl* armadas. **~ station** *n* estación *f* de servicio

serviette /sɜ:vɪ'et/ *n* servilleta *f*

servile /'sɜ:vaɪl/ *adj* servil

session /'seʃn/ *n* sesión *f*

set /set/ *vt* (*pt* **set**, *pres p* **setting**) poner; poner en hora (clock etc); fijar (limit etc); (*typeset*) componer. **~ fire to** prender fuego a. **~ free** *vt* poner en libertad. ● *vi* (sun) ponerse; (jelly) cuajarse. ● *n* serie *f*; (*of cutlery etc*) juego *m*; (*tennis*) set *m*; (*TV, Radio*) aparato *m*; (*in theatre*) decorado *m*; (*of people*) círculo *m*. ● *adj* fijo. **be ~ on** estar resuelto a. □ **~ back** *vt* (*delay*) retardar; (*fam, cost*) costar. □ **~ off** *vi* salir. *vt* hacer sonar (alarm); hacer explotar (bomb). □ **~ out** *vt* exponer (argument). *vi* (*leave*) salir. □ **~ up** *vt* establecer. **~back** *n* revés *m*

settee /se'ti:/ *n* sofá *m*

setting /'setɪŋ/ *n* (*of dial, switch*) posición *f*

settle /'setl/ *vt* (*arrange*) acordar; arreglar (matter); resolver (dispute); pagar (bill); saldar (debt). ● *vi* (*live*) establecerse. □ **~ down** *vi* calmarse; (*become more responsible*) sentar (la) cabeza. □ **~ for** *vt* aceptar. □ **~ up** *vi* arreglar cuentas. **~ment** *n* establecimiento *m*; (*agreement*) acuerdo *m*; (*of debt*) liquidación *f*; (*colony*) colonia *f*. **~r** *n* colono *m*

set: ~-to *n* pelea *f*. **~-up** *n* [I] sistema *m*; (*con*) tinglado *m*

seven /ˈsevn/ *adj & n* siete (*m*). **~teen** /sevnˈtiːn/ *adj & n* diecisiete (*m*). **~teenth** *adj* decimoséptimo. ● *n* diecisietavo *m*. **~th** *adj & n* séptimo (*m*). **~tieth** /ˈsevəntɪɪθ/ *adj* septuagésimo. ● *n* setentavo *m*. **~ty** /ˈsevntɪ/ *adj & n* setenta (*m*)

sever /ˈsevə(r)/ *vt* cortar; (*fig*) romper

several /ˈsevrəl/ *adj & pron* varios

sever|e /sɪˈvɪə(r)/ *adj* (**-er**, **-est**) severo; (*serious*) grave; (weather) riguroso. **~ely** *adv* severamente. **~ity** /sɪˈverətɪ/ *n* severidad *f*; (*seriousness*) gravedad *f*

sew /səʊ/ *vt/i* (*pt* **sewed**, *pp* **sewn**, *or* **sewed**) coser. □ **~ up** *vt* coser

sew|age /ˈsuːɪdʒ/ *n* aguas *fpl* residuales. **~er** /ˈsuːə(r)/ *n* cloaca *f*

sewing /ˈsəʊɪŋ/ *n* costura *f*. **~-machine** *n* máquina *f* de coser

sewn /səʊn/ *see* **SEW**

sex /seks/ *n* sexo *m*. **have ~** tener relaciones sexuales. ● *adj* sexual. **~ist** *adj & n* sexista (*m & f*). **~ual** /ˈsekʃʊəl/ *adj* sexual. **~ual intercourse** *n* relaciones *fpl* sexuales. **~uality** /-ˈælətɪ/ *n* sexualidad *f*. **~y** *adj* (**-ier**, **-iest**) excitante, sexy, provocativo

shabby /ˈʃæbɪ/ *adj* (**-ier**, **-iest**) (clothes) gastado; (person) pobremente vestido

shack /ʃæk/ *n* choza *f*

shade /ʃeɪd/ *n* sombra *f*; (*of colour*) tono *m*; (*for lamp*) pantalla *f*; (*nuance*) matiz *m*; (*Amer, over window*) persiana *f*

shadow /ˈʃædəʊ/ *n* sombra *f*. ● *vt* (*follow*) seguir de cerca a. **~y** *adj* (*fig*) vago

shady /ˈʃeɪdɪ/ *adj* (**-ier**, **-iest**) sombreado; (*fig*) turbio; (character) sospechoso

shaft /ʃɑːft/ *n* (*of arrow*) astil *m*; (*Mec*) eje *m*; (*of light*) rayo *m*; (*of lift, mine*) pozo *m*

shaggy /ˈʃægɪ/ *adj* (**-ier**, **-iest**) peludo

shake /ʃeɪk/ *vt* (*pt* **shook**, *pp* **shaken**) sacudir; agitar (bottle); (*shock*) desconcertar. **~ hands with** estrechar la mano a. **~ one's head** negar con la cabeza; (*Amer, meaning yes*) asentir con la cabeza. ● *vi* temblar. □ **~ off** *vi* deshacerse de. ● *n* sacudida *f*

shaky /ˈʃeɪkɪ/ *adj* (**-ier**, **-iest**) tembloroso; (table etc) inestable

shall /ʃæl/ *modal verb*. **we ~ see** veremos. **~ we go to the cinema?** ¿vamos al cine?

shallow /ˈʃæləʊ/ *adj* (**-er**, **-est**) poco profundo; (*fig*) superficial

sham /ʃæm/ *n* farsa *f*. ● *adj* fingido

shambles /ˈʃæmblz/ *npl* (*fam, mess*) caos *m*

shame /ʃeɪm/ *n* (*feeling*) vergüenza *f*. **what a ~!** ¡qué lástima! ● *vt* avergonzar. **~ful** *adj* vergonzoso. **~less** *adj* desvergonzado

shampoo /ʃæmˈpuː/ *n* champú *m*. ● *vt* lavar

shan't /ʃɑːnt/ = **shall not**

shape /ʃeɪp/ *n* forma *f*. ● *vt* formar; determinar (future). ● *vi* tomar forma. **~less** *adj* informe

share /ʃeə(r)/ *n* porción *f*; (*Com*) acción *f*. ● *vt* compartir; (*divide*) dividir. ● *vi* compartir. **~ in sth** participar en algo. □ **~ out** *vt* repartir. **~holder** *n* accionista *m & f*. **~-out**

S

n reparto *m*

shark /ʃɑːk/ *n* tiburón *m*

sharp /ʃɑːp/ *adj* (**-er**, **-est**) (knife etc) afilado; (pin etc) puntiagudo; (pain, sound) agudo; (taste) ácido; (bend) cerrado; (contrast) marcado; (*clever*) listo; (*Mus*) sostenido. ● *adv* en punto. **at seven o'clock ~** a las siete en punto. ● *n* (*Mus*) sostenido *m*. **~en** *vt* afilar; sacar punta a (pencil). **~ener** *n* (*Mec*) afilador *m*; (*for pencils*) sacapuntas *m*. **~ly** *adv* bruscamente

shatter /'ʃætə(r)/ *vt* hacer añicos. **he was ~ed by the news** la noticia lo dejó destrozado. ● *vi* hacerse añicos. **~ed** /'ʃætəd/*adj* (*exhausted*) agotado

shav|e /ʃeɪv/ *vt* afeitar, rasurar (*Mex*). ● *vi* afeitarse, rasurarse (*Mex*). ● *n* afeitada *f*, rasurada *f* (*Mex*). **have a ~e** afeitarse. **~er** *n* maquinilla *f* (de afeitar). **~ing brush** *n* brocha *f* de afeitar. **~ing cream** *n* crema *f* de afeitar

shawl /ʃɔːl/ *n* chal *m*

she /ʃiː/ *pron* ella

sheaf /ʃiːf/ *n* (*pl* **sheaves** /ʃiːvz/) gavilla *f*

shear /ʃɪə(r)/ *vt* (*pp* **shorn** *or* **sheared**) esquilar. **~s** /ʃɪəz/ *npl* tijeras *fpl* grandes

shed /ʃed/ *n* cobertizo *m*. ● *vt* (*pt* **shed**, *pres p* **shedding**) perder; derramar (tears); despojarse de (clothes). **~ light on** arrojar luz sobre

she'd /ʃiː(ə)d/ = **she had, she would**

sheep /ʃiːp/ *n invar* oveja *f*. **~dog** *n* perro *m* pastor. **~ish** *adj* avergonzado

sheer /ʃɪə(r)/ *adj* (*as intensifier*) puro; (*steep*) perpendicular

sheet /ʃiːt/ *n* sábana *f*; (*of paper*) hoja *f*; (*of glass*) lámina *f*; (*of ice*) capa *f*

shelf /ʃelf/ *n* (*pl* **shelves**) estante *m*. **a set of shelves** unos estantes

shell /ʃel/ *n* concha *f*; (*of egg*) cáscara *f*; (*of crab, snail, tortoise*) caparazón *m or f*; (*explosive*) proyectil *m*, obús *m*. ● *vt* pelar (peas etc); (*Mil*) bombardear

she'll /'ʃiː(ə)l/ = **she had, she would**

shellfish /'ʃelfɪʃ/ *n invar* marisco *m*; (*collectively*) mariscos *mpl*

shelter /'ʃeltə(r)/ *n* refugio *m*. **take ~** refugiarse. ● *vt* darle cobijo a (fugitive); (*protect from weather*) resguardar. ● *vi* refugiarse. **~ed** /'ʃeltəd/ *adj* (spot) abrigado; (life) protegido

shelv|e /ʃelv/ *vt* (*fig*) dar carpetazo a. **~ing** *n* estantería *f*

shepherd /'ʃepəd/ *n* pastor *m*. **~ess** /-'des/ *n* pastora *f*

sherbet /'ʃɜːbət/ *n* (*Amer, water ice*) sorbete *m*

sheriff /'ʃerɪf/ *n* (*in US*) sheriff *m*

sherry /'ʃerɪ/ *n* (vino *m* de) jerez *m*

she's /ʃiːz/ = **she is, she has**

shield /ʃiːld/ *n* escudo *m*. ● *vt* proteger

shift /ʃɪft/ *vt* cambiar; correr (furniture etc). ● *vi* (wind) cambiar; (attention, opinion) pasar a; (*Amer, change gear*) cambiar de velocidad. ● *n* cambio *m*; (*work*) turno *m*; (*workers*) tanda *f*. **~y** *adj* (**-ier**, **-iest**) furtivo

shilling /'ʃɪlɪŋ/ *n* chelín *m*

shimmer /'ʃɪmə(r)/ *vi* rielar, relucir

shin /ʃɪn/ *n* espinilla *f*

shine /ʃaɪn/ *vi* (*pt* **shone**) brillar.

•*vt* sacar brillo a. ~ **a light on sth** alumbrar algo con una luz. •*n* brillo *m*

shingle /'ʃɪŋgl/ *n* (*pebbles*) guijarros *mpl*

shin|ing /'ʃaɪnɪŋ/ *adj* brillante. **~y** /'ʃaɪnɪ/ *adj* (**-ier**, **-iest**) brillante

ship /ʃɪp/ *n* barco *m*, buque *m*. •*vt* (*pt* **shipped**) transportar; (*send*) enviar; (*load*) embarcar. **~building** *n* construcción *f* naval. **~ment** *n* envío *m*. **~ping** *n* transporte *m*; (*ships*) barcos *mpl*. **~shape** *adj* limpio y ordenado. **~wreck** *n* naufragio *m*. **~wrecked** *adj* naufragado. **be ~wrecked** naufragar. **~yard** *n* astillero *m*

shirk /ʃɜːk/ *vt* esquivar

shirt /ʃɜːt/ *n* camisa *f*. **in ~-sleeves** en mangas de camisa

shit /ʃɪt/ *n & int* (*vulgar*) mierda *f*. •*vi* (*vulgar*) (*pt* **shat**, *pres p* **shitting**) cagar

shiver /'ʃɪvə(r)/ *vi* temblar. •*n* escalofrío *m*

shoal /ʃəʊl/ *n* banco *m*

shock /ʃɒk/ *n* (*of impact*) choque *m*; (*of earthquake*) sacudida *f*; (*surprise*) shock *m*; (*scare*) susto *m*; (*Elec*) descarga *f*; (*Med*) shock *m*. **get a ~** llevarse un shock. •*vt* escandalizar; (*apall*) horrorizar. **~ing** *adj* escandaloso; ⓘ espantoso

shod /ʃɒd/ *see* SHOE

shoddy /'ʃɒdɪ/ *adj* (**-ier**, **-iest**) mal hecho, de pacotilla

shoe /ʃuː/ *n* zapato *m*; (*of horse*) herradura *f*. •*vt* (*pt* **shod**, *pres p* **shoeing**) herrar (horse). **~horn** *n* calzador *m*. **~lace** *n* cordón *m* (de zapato). ~ **polish** *n* betún *m*

shone /ʃɒn/ *see* SHINE

shoo /ʃuː/ *vt* ahuyentar

shook /ʃʊk/ *see* SHAKE

shoot /ʃuːt/ *vt* (*pt* **shot**) disparar; rodar (film). •*vi* (*hunt*) cazar. •*n* (*of plant*) retoño *m*. □ **~ down** *vt* derribar. □ **~ out** *vi* (*rush*) salir disparado. □ **~ up** *vi* (prices) dispararse; (*grow*) crecer mucho

shop /ʃɒp/ *n* tienda *f*. **go to the ~s** ir de compras. **talk ~** hablar del trabajo. •*vi* (*pt* **shopping**) hacer compras. **go ~ping** ir de compras. □ **~ around** *vi* buscar el mejor precio. ~ **assistant** *n* dependiente *m*, dependienta *f*, empleado *m*, empleada *f* (*LAm*). **~keeper** *n* comerciante *m*, tendero *m*. **~lifter** *n* ladrón *m* (que roba en las tiendas). **~lifting** *n* hurto *m* (en las tiendas). **~per** *n* comprador *m*. **~ping** *n* (*purchases*) compras *fpl*. **do the ~ping** hacer la compra, hacer el mandado (*Mex*). **~ping bag** *n* bolsa *f* de la compra. **~ping cart** *n* (*Amer*) carrito *m* (de la compra). **~ping centre**, **~ping mall** (*Amer*) *n* centro *m* comercial. **~ping trolley** *n* carrito *m* de la compra. ~ **steward** *n* enlace *m* sindical. ~ **window** *n* escaparate *m*, vidriera *f* (*LAm*), aparador *m* (*Mex*)

shore /ʃɔː(r)/ *n* orilla *f*

shorn /ʃɔːn/ *see* SHEAR

short /ʃɔːt/ *adj* (**-er**, **-est**) corto; (*not lasting*) breve; (person) bajo; (*curt*) brusco. **a ~ time ago** hace poco. **be ~ of time/money** andar corto de tiempo/dinero. **Mick is ~ for Michael** Mick es el diminutivo de Michael. •*adv* (stop) en seco. **we never went ~ of food** nunca nos faltó comida. •*n*. **in ~** en resumen. **~age** /-ɪdʒ/ *n* escasez *f*, falta *f*. **~bread** *n* galleta *f* (de mantequilla). ~ **circuit** *n* cortocircuito *m*. **~coming** *n* defecto *m*. ~ **cut** *n* atajo *m*. **~en** *vt* acortar.

~**hand** *n* taquigrafía *f*. ~**ly** *adv* (*soon*) dentro de poco. ~**ly before midnight** poco antes de la medianoche. ~**s** *npl* pantalones *m* cortos, shorts *mpl*; (*Amer, underwear*) calzoncillos *mpl*. ~**-sighted** /-'saɪtɪd/*adj* miope

shot /ʃɒt/ *see* **SHOOT**. ●*n* (*from gun*) disparo *m*; tiro *m*; (*in soccer*) tiro *m*, disparo *m*; (*in other sports*) tiro *m*; (*Photo*) foto *f*. **be a good/poor** ~ ser un buen/mal tirador. **be off like a** ~ salir disparado. ~**gun** *n* escopeta *f*

should /ʃʊd, ʃəd/ *modal verb*. **I** ~ **go** debería ir. **you** ~**n't have said that** no deberías haber dicho eso. **I** ~ **like to see her** me gustaría verla. **if he** ~ **come** si viniese

shoulder /'ʃəʊldə(r)/ *n* hombro *m*. ●*vt* cargar con (responsibility); ponerse al hombro (burden). ~**blade** *n* omóplato *m*

shout /ʃaʊt/ *n* grito *m*. ●*vt/i* gritar. ~ **at s.o.** gritarle a uno

shove /ʃʌv/ *n* empujón *m*. ●*vt* empujar; (*fam, put*) poner. ●*vi* empujar. □ ~ **off** *vi* [I] largarse

shovel /'ʃʌvl/ *n* pala *f*. ●*vt* (*pt* **shovelled**) palear (coal); espalar (snow)

show /ʃəʊ/ *vt* (*pt* **showed**, *pp* **shown**) mostrar; (*put on display*) exponer; poner (film). **I'll** ~ **you to your room** lo acompaño a su cuarto. ●*vi* (*be visible*) verse. ●*n* muestra *f*; (*exhibition*) exposición *f*; (*in theatre*) espectáculo *m*; (*on TV, radio*) programa *m*; (*ostentation*) pompa *f*. **be on** ~ estar expuesto. □ ~ **off** *vt* (*pej*) lucir, presumir de. *vi* presumir, lucirse. □ ~ **up** *vi* (*be visible*) notarse; (*arrive*) aparecer. *vt* (*reveal*) poner de manifiesto; (*embarrass*) hacer quedar mal. ~**case** *n* vitrina *f*. ~**down** *n* confrontación *f*

shower /'ʃaʊə(r)/ *n* (*of rain*) chaparrón *m*; (*for washing*) ducha *f*. **have a** ~, **take a** ~ ducharse. ●*vi* ducharse

showjumping *n* concursos *mpl* hípicos.

shown /ʃəʊn/ *see* **SHOW**

show: ~**-off** *n* fanfarrón *m*. ~**room** *n* sala *f* de exposición *f*. ~**y** *adj* (**-ier**, **-iest**) llamativo; (*attractive*) ostentoso

shrank /ʃræŋk/ *see* **SHRINK**

shred /ʃred/ *n* pedazo *m*; (*fig*) pizca *f*. ●*vt* (*pt* **shredded**) hacer tiras; destruir, triturar (documents). ~**der** *n* (*for paper*) trituradora *f*; (*for vegetables*) cortadora *f*

shrewd /ʃru:d/ *adj* (**-er**, **-est**) astuto

shriek /ʃri:k/ *n* chillido *m*; (*of pain*) alarido *m*. ●*vt/i* chillar

shrift /ʃrɪft/ *n*. **give s.o. short** ~ despachar a uno con brusquedad. **give sth short** ~ desestimar algo de plano

shrill /ʃrɪl/ *adj* agudo

shrimp /ʃrɪmp/ *n* gamba *f*, camarón *m* (*LAm*); (*Amer, large*) langostino *m*

shrine /ʃraɪn/ *n* (*place*) santuario *m*; (*tomb*) sepulcro *m*

shrink /ʃrɪŋk/ *vt* (*pt* **shrank**, *pp* **shrunk**) encoger. ●*vi* encogerse; (amount) reducirse; retroceder (recoil)

shrivel /'ʃrɪvl/ *vi* (*pt* **shrivelled**). ~ **(up)** (plant) marchitarse; (fruit) resecarse y arrugarse

shroud /ʃraʊd/ *n* mortaja *f*; (*fig*) velo *m*. ●*vt* envolver

Shrove /ʃrəʊv/ *n*. ~ **Tuesday** *n* martes *m* de carnaval

S

shrub /ʃrʌb/ *n* arbusto *m*

shrug /ʃrʌg/ *vt* (*pt* **shrugged**) encogerse de hombros

shrunk /ʃrʌŋk/ *see* SHRINK. **~en** *adj* encogido

shudder /ˈʃʌdə(r)/ *vi* estremecerse. ● *n* estremecimiento *m*

shuffle /ˈʃʌfl/ *vi* andar arrastrando los pies. ● *vt* barajar (cards). **~ one's feet** arrastrar los pies

shun /ʃʌn/ *vt* (*pt* **shunned**) evitar

shunt /ʃʌnt/ *vt* cambiar de vía

shush /ʃʊʃ/ *int* ¡chitón!

shut /ʃʌt/ *vt* (*pt* **shut**, *pres p* **shutting**) cerrar. ● *vi* cerrarse. ● *adj*. **be ~** estar cerrado. □ **~ down** *vt/i* cerrar. □ **~ up** *vt* cerrar; [I] hacer callar. *vi* callarse. **~ter** *n* contraventana *f*; (*Photo*) obturador *m*

shuttle /ˈʃʌtl/ *n* lanzadera *f*; (*by air*) puente *m* aéreo; (*space* **~**) transbordador *m* espacial. ● *vi*. **~ (back and forth)** ir y venir. **~cock** *n* volante *m*. **~ service** *n* servicio *m* de enlace

shy /ʃaɪ/ *adj* (**-er**, **-est**) tímido. ● *vi* (*pt* **shied**) asustarse. **~ness** *n* timidez *f*

sick /sɪk/ *adj* enfermo; (humour) negro; (*fam*, *fed up*) harto. **be ~** estar enfermo; (*vomit*) vomitar. **be ~ of** (*fig*) estar harto de. **feel ~** sentir náuseas. **get ~** (*Amer*) caer enfermo, enfermarse (*LAm*). **~ leave** *n* permiso *m* por enfermedad, baja *f* por enfermedad. **~ly** /ˈsɪklɪ/ *adj* (**-lier**, **-liest**) enfermizo; (taste, smell etc) nauseabundo. **~ness** /ˈsɪknɪs/ *n* enfermedad *f*

side /saɪd/ *n* lado *m*; (*of hill*) ladera *f*; (*of person*) costado *m*; (*team*) equipo *m*; (*fig*) parte *f*. **~ by ~** uno al lado del otro. **take ~s** tomar partido. ● *adj* lateral. □ **~ with** *vt* ponerse de parte de. **~board** *n* aparador *m*. **~ dish** *n* acompañamiento *m*. **~-effect** *n* efecto *m* secundario; (*fig*) consecuencia *f* indirecta. **~line** *n* actividad *f* suplementaria. **~ road** *n* calle *f* secundaria. **~-step** *vt* eludir. **~-track** *vt* desviar del tema. **~walk** *n* (*Amer*) acera *f*, vereda *f* (*LAm*), banqueta *f* (*Mex*). **~ways** *adj* & *adv* de lado

siding /ˈsaɪdɪŋ/ *n* apartadero *m*

sidle /ˈsaɪdl/ *vi*. **~ up to s.o.** acercarse furtivamente a uno

siege /siːdʒ/ *n* sitio *m*

sieve /sɪv/ *n* tamiz *m*. ● *vt* tamizar, cernir

sift /sɪft/ *vt* tamizar, cernir. ● *vi*. **~ through sth** pasar algo por el tamiz

sigh /saɪ/ *n* suspiro. ● *vi* suspirar

sight /saɪt/ *n* vista *f*; (*spectacle*) espectáculo *m*; (*on gun*) mira *f*. **at first ~** a primera vista. **catch ~ of** ver; (*in distance*) avistar. **lose ~ of** perder de vista. **see the ~s** visitar los lugares de interés. **within ~ of** (*near*) cerca de. ● *vt* ver; divisar (land). **~-seeing** *n*. **go ~** ir a visitar los lugares de interés. **~seer** /-siːə(r)/ *n* turista *m* & *f*

sign /saɪn/ *n* (*indication*) señal *f*, indicio *m*; (*gesture*) señal *f*, seña *f*; (*notice*) letrero *m*; (*astrological*) signo *m*. ● *vt* firmar. □ **~ on** *vi* (*for unemployment benefit*) anotarse para recibir el seguro de desempleo

signal /ˈsɪgnəl/ *n* señal *f*. ● *vt* (*pt* **signalled**) señalar. ● *vi*. **~ (to s.o.)** hacer señas (a uno); (*Auto*) poner el intermitente, señalizar

signature /ˈsɪgnətʃə(r)/ *n* firma *f*. **~ tune** *n* sintonía *f*

significan|ce /sɪg'nɪfɪkəns/ *n* importancia *f*. **~t** *adj* (*important*) importante; (fact) significativo

signify /'sɪgnɪfaɪ/ *vt* significar

signpost /'saɪnpəʊst/ *n* señal *f*, poste *m* indicador

silen|ce /'saɪləns/ *n* silencio *m*. ● *vt* hacer callar. **~cer** *n* (*on gun and on car*) silenciador *m*. **~t** *adj* silencioso; (film) mudo. **remain ~t** quedarse callado. **~tly** *adv* silenciosamente

silhouette /sɪlu:'et/ *n* silueta *f*. ● *vt*. **be ~d** perfilarse (**against** contra)

silicon /'sɪlɪkən/ *n* silicio *m*. **~ chip** *n* pastilla *f* de silicio

silk /sɪlk/ *n* seda *f*. **~y** *adj* (*of silk*) de seda; (*like silk*) sedoso

silly /'sɪlɪ/ *adj* (**-ier**, **-iest**) tonto

silt /sɪlt/ *n* cieno *m*

silver /'sɪlvə(r)/ *n* plata *f*. ● *adj* de plata. **~-plated** *adj* bañado en plata, plateado. **~ware** /-weə(r)/ *n* platería *f*

SIM card *n* tarjeta *f* SIM

simil|ar /'sɪmɪlə(r)/ *adj* parecido, similar. **~arity** /-'lærətɪ/ *n* parecido *m*. **~arly** *adv* de igual manera. **~e** /'sɪmɪlɪ/ *n* símil *m*

simmer /'sɪmə(r)/ *vt/i* hervir a fuego lento. □ **~ down** *vi* calmarse

simpl|e /'sɪmpl/ *adj* (**-er**, **-est**) sencillo, simple; (person) (*humble*) simple; (*backward*) simple. **~e-minded** /-'maɪndɪd/ *adj* ingenuo. **~icity** /-'plɪsetɪ/ *n* simplicidad *f*, sencillez *f*. **~ify** /'sɪmplɪfaɪ/ *vt* simplificar. **~y** *adv* sencillamente, simplemente; (*absolutely*) realmente

simulate /'sɪmjʊleɪt/ *vt* simular

simultaneous /sɪml'teɪnɪəs/ *adj* simultáneo. **~ly** *adv* simultáneamente

sin /sɪn/ *n* pecado *m*. ● *vi* (*pt* **sinned**) pecar

since /sɪns/

● *preposition* desde. **he's been living here ~ 1991** vive aquí desde 1991. **~ Christmas** desde Navidad. **~ then** desde entonces. **I haven't been feeling well ~ Sunday** desde el domingo que no me siento bien. **how long is it ~ your interview?** ¿cuánto (tiempo) hace de la entrevista?

● *adverb* desde entonces. **I haven't spoken to her ~** no he hablado con ella desde entonces

● *conjunction*

····▸ desde que. **I haven't seen her ~ she left** no la he visto desde que se fue. **~ coming to Manchester** desde que vine (*or* vino *etc*) a Manchester. **it's ten years ~ he died** hace diez años que se murió

····▸ (*because*) como, ya que. **~ it was quite late, I decided to stay** como *or* ya que era bastante tarde, decidí quedarme

sincer|e /sɪn'sɪə(r)/ *adj* sincero. **~ely** *adv* sinceramente. **yours ~ely**, **~ely (yours)** (*in letters*) (saluda) a usted atentamente. **~ity** /-'serətɪ/ *n* sinceridad *f*

sinful /'sɪnfl/ *adj* (person) pecador; (act) pecaminoso

sing /sɪŋ/ *vt/i* (*pt* **sang**, *pp* **sung**) cantar

singe /sɪndʒ/ *vt* (*pres p* **singeing**) chamuscar

singer /'sɪŋə(r)/ *n* cantante *m & f*

single /'sɪŋgl/ *adj* solo; (*not*

double) sencillo; (*unmarried*) soltero; (bed, room) individual, de una plaza (*LAm*); (ticket) de ida, sencillo. **not a ~ house** ni una sola casa. **every ~ day** todos los días sin excepción. ●*n* (*ticket*) billete *m* sencillo, boleto *m* de ida (*LAm*). □ **~ out** *vt* escoger; (*distinguish*) distinguir. **~-handed** /-'hændɪd/ *adj & adv* sin ayuda. **~s** *npl* (*Sport*) individuales *mpl*

singular /'sɪŋgjʊlə(r)/ *n* singular *f*. ●*adj* singular; (*unusual*) raro; (noun) en singular

sinister /'sɪnɪstə(r)/ *adj* siniestro

sink /sɪŋk/ *vt* (*pt* **sank**, *pp* **sunk**) hundir. ●*vi* hundirse. ●*n* fregadero *m* (*Amer, in bathroom*) lavabo *m*, lavamanos *m*. □ **~ in** *vi* penetrar

sinner /'sɪnə(r)/ *n* pecador *m*

sip /sɪp/ *n* sorbo *m*. ●*vt* (*pt* **sipped**) sorber

siphon /'saɪfən/ *n* sifón *m*. **~ (out)** sacar con sifón. □ **~ off** *vt* desviar (money).

sir /sɜ:(r)/ *n* señor *m*. **S~** *n* (*title*) sir *m*. **Dear S~,** (*in letters*) De mi mayor consideración:

siren /'saɪərən/ *n* sirena *f*

sister /'sɪstə(r)/ *n* hermana *f*; (*nurse*) enfermera *f* jefe. **~-in-law** *n* (*pl* **~s-in-law**) cuñada *f*

sit /sɪt/ *vi* (*pt* **sat**, *pres p* **sitting**) sentarse; (committee etc) reunirse en sesión. **be ~ting** estar sentado. ●*vt* sentar; hacer (exam). □ **~ back** *vi* (*fig*) relajarse. □ **~ down** *vi* sentarse. **be ~ting down** estar sentado. □ **~ up** *vi* (*from lying*) incorporarse; (*straighten back*) ponerse derecho. **~-in** *n* (*strike*) encierro *m*, ocupación *f*

site /saɪt/ *n* emplazamiento *m*; (*piece of land*) terreno *m*; (*archaeological*) yacimiento *m*. **building ~** *n* solar *m*. ●*vt* situar

sit: ~ting *n* sesión *f*; (*in restaurant*) turno *m*. **~ting room** *n* sala *f* de estar, living *m*

situat|e /'sɪtjʊeɪt/ *vt* situar. **~ion** /-'eɪʃn/ *n* situación *f*

six /sɪks/ *adj & n* seis (*m*). **~teen** /sɪk'sti:n/ *adj & n* dieciséis (*m*). **~teenth** *adj* decimosexto. ●*n* dieciseisavo *m*. **~th** *adj & n* sexto (*m*). **~tieth** /'sɪkstɪɪθ/ *adj* sexagésimo. ●*n* sesentavo *m*. **~ty** /'sɪkstɪ/ *adj & n* sesenta (*m*)

size /saɪz/ *n* tamaño *m*; (*of clothes*) talla *f*; (*of shoes*) número *m*; (*of problem, operation*) magnitud *f*. **what ~ do you take?** (*clothes*) ¿qué talla tiene?; (*shoes*) ¿qué número calza?. □ **~ up** *vt* 🄸 evaluar (problem); calar (person)

sizzle /'sɪzl/ *vi* crepitar

skat|e /skeɪt/ *n* patín *m*. ●*vi* patinar. **~eboard** *n* monopatín *m*, patineta *f* (*Mex*). **~er** *n* patinador *m*. **~ing** *n* patinaje *m*. **~ing-rink** *n* pista *f* de patinaje

skeleton /'skelɪtn/ *n* esqueleto *m*. **~ key** *n* llave *f* maestra

sketch /sketʃ/ *n* (*drawing*) dibujo *m*; (*rougher*) esbozo *m*; (*TV, Theatre*) sketch *m*. ●*vt* esbozar. ●*vi* dibujar. **~y** *adj* (**-ier**, **-iest**) incompleto

ski /ski:/ *n* (*pl* **skis**) esquí *m*. ●*vi* (*pt* **skied**, *pres p* **skiing**) esquiar. **go ~ing** ir a esquiar

skid /skɪd/ *vi* (*pt* **skidded**) patinar. ●*n* patinazo *m*

ski: ~er *n* esquiador *m*. **~ing** *n* esquí *m*

skilful /'skɪlfl/ *adj* diestro

ski-lift /'ski:lɪft/ *n* telesquí *m*

skill /skɪl/ *n* habilidad *f*; (*technical*) destreza *f*. **~ed** *adj* hábil; (worker) cualificado

skim /skɪm/ *vt* (*pt* **skimmed**) espumar (soup); desnatar, descremar (milk); (*glide over*) pasar casi rozando. ~ **milk** (*Amer*), ~**med milk** *n* leche *f* desnatada, leche *f* descremada. ~ **through** *vt* leer por encima

skimp /skɪmp/ *vi*. ~ **on sth** escatimar algo. ~**y** *adj* (**-ier**, **-iest**) escaso; (skirt, dress) brevísimo

skin /skɪn/ *n* piel *f*. ●*vt* (*pt* **skinned**) despellejar. ~**-deep** *adj* superficial. ~**-diving** *n* submarinismo *m*. ~**ny** *adj* (**-ier**, **-iest**) flaco

skip /skɪp/ *vi* (*pt* **skipped**) *vi* saltar; (*with rope*) saltar a la comba, saltar a la cuerda. ●*vt* saltarse (chapter); faltar a (class). ●*n* brinco *m*; (*container*) contenedor *m* (para escombros). ~**per** *n* capitán *m*. ~**ping-rope**, ~**rope** (*Amer*) *n* comba *f*, cuerda *f* de saltar, reata *f* (*Mex*)

skirmish /'skɜːmɪʃ/ *n* escaramuza *f*

skirt /skɜːt/ *n* falda *f*. ●*vt* bordear; (*go round*) ladear. ~**ing-board** *n* rodapié *m*, zócalo *m*

skittle /'skɪtl/ *n* bolo *m*

skive off /skaɪv/ (*vi* 🄸, *disappear*) escurrir el bulto; (*stay away from work*) no ir a trabajar

skulk /skʌlk/ *vi* (*hide*) esconderse. ~ **around** *vi* merodear

skull /skʌl/ *n* cráneo *m*; (*remains*) calavera *f*

sky /skaɪ/ *n* cielo *m*. ~**lark** *n* alondra *f*. ~**light** *n* tragaluz *m*. ~ **marshal** *n* guardia *m* armado a bordo. ~**scraper** *n* rascacielos *m*

slab /slæb/ *n* (*of concrete*) bloque *m*; (*of stone*) losa *f*

slack /slæk/ *adj* (**-er**, **-est**) flojo; (person) poco aplicado; (period) de poca actividad. ●*vi* flojear. ~**en** *vt* aflojar. ●*vi* (person) descansar. ▫ ~**en off** *vt/i* aflojar

slain /sleɪn/ *see* SLAY

slake /sleɪk/ *vt* apagar

slam /slæm/ *vt* (*pt* **slammed**). ~ **the door** dar un portazo. ~ **the door shut** cerrar de un portazo. ~ **on the brakes** pegar un frenazo; (*sl*, *criticize*) atacar violentamente. ●*vi* cerrarse de un portazo

slander /'slɑːndə(r)/ *n* calumnia *f*. ●*vt* difamar

slang /slæŋ/ *n* argot *m*

slant /slɑːnt/ *vt* inclinar. ●*n* inclinación *f*

slap /slæp/ *vt* (*pt* **slapped**) (*on face*) pegarle una bofetada a; (*put*) tirar. ~ **s.o. on the back** darle una palmada a uno en la espalda. ●*n* bofetada *f*; (*on back*) palmada *f*. ●*adv* de lleno. ~**dash** *adj* descuidado; (work) chapucero

slash /slæʃ/ *vt* acuchillar; (*fig*) rebajar drásticamente. ●*n* cuchillada *f*

slat /slæt/ *n* tablilla *f*

slate /sleɪt/ *n* pizarra *f*. ●*vt* 🄸 poner por los suelos

slaughter /'slɔːtə(r)/ *vt* matar salvajemente; matar (animal). ●*n* carnicería *f*; (*of animals*) matanza *f*

slave /sleɪv/ *n* esclavo *m*. ●*vi* ~ **(away)** trabajar como un negro. ~**-driver** *n* 🄸 negrero *m*. ~**ry** /-ərɪ/ *n* esclavitud *f*

slay /sleɪ/ *vt* (*pt* **slew**, *pp* **slain**) dar muerte a

sleazy /'sliːzɪ/ *adj* (**-ier**, **-iest**) 🄸 sórdido

sled /sled/ (*Amer*), **sledge** /sledʒ/ *n* trineo *m*

sledge-hammer *n* mazo *m*, almádena *f*

S

sleek /sli:k/ *adj* (**-er**, **-est**) liso, brillante

sleep /sli:p/ *n* sueño *m*. **go to ~** dormirse. • *vi* (*pt* **slept**) dormir. • *vt* poder alojar. **~er** *n* (*on track*) traviesa *f*, durmiente *m*. **be a light/heavy ~er** tener el sueño ligero/pesado. **~ing bag** *n* saco *m* de dormir. **~ing pill** *n* somnífero *m*. **~less** *adj*. **have a ~less night** pasar la noche en blanco. **~walk** *vi* caminar dormido. **~y** *adj* (**-ier**, **-iest**) soñoliento. **be/feel ~y** tener sueño

sleet /sli:t/ *n* aguanieve *f*

sleeve /sli:v/ *n* manga *f*; (*for record*) funda *f*, carátula *f*. **up one's ~** en reserva. **~less** *adj* sin mangas

sleigh /sleɪ/ *n* trineo *m*

slender /ˈslendə(r)/ *adj* delgado; (*fig*) escaso

slept /slept/ *see* **SLEEP**

slew /slu:/ *see* **SLAY**

slice /slaɪs/ *n* (*of ham*) lonja *f*; (*of bread*) rebanada *f*; (*of meat*) tajada *f*; (*of cheese*) trozo *m*; (*of sth round*) rodaja *f*. • *vt* cortar (en rebanadas, tajadas etc)

slick /slɪk/ *adj* (performance) muy pulido. • *n*. (**oil**) **~** marea *f* negra

S

slid|e /slaɪd/ *vt* (*pt* **slid**) deslizar. • *vi* (*intentionally*) deslizarse; (*unintentionally*) resbalarse. • *n* resbalón *m*; (*in playground*) tobogán *m*, resbaladilla *f* (*Mex*); (*for hair*) pasador *m*, broche *m* (*Mex*); (*Photo*) diapositiva *f*. **~ing scale** *n* escala *f* móvil

slight /slaɪt/ *adj* (**-er**, **-est**) ligero; (*slender*) delgado. • *vt* desairar. • *n* desaire *m*. **~est** *adj* mínimo. **not in the ~est** en absoluto. **~ly** *adv* un poco, ligeramente

slim /slɪm/ *adj* (**slimmer**, **slimmest**) delgado. • *vi* (*pt* **slimmed**) (*become slimmer*) adelgazar; (*diet*) hacer régimen

slim|e /slaɪm/ *n* limo *m*; (*of snail, slug*) baba *f*. **~y** *adj* viscoso; (*fig*) excesivamente obsequioso

sling /slɪŋ/ *n* (*Med*) cabestrillo *m*. • *vt* (*pt* **slung**) lanzar

slip /slɪp/ *vt* (*pt* **slipped**) deslizar. **~ s.o.'s mind** olvidársele a uno. • *vi* resbalarse. **it ~ped out of my hands** se me resbaló de las manos. **he ~ped out the back door** se deslizó por la puerta trasera • *n* resbalón *m*; (*mistake*) error *m*; (*petticoat*) combinación *f*; (*paper*) trozo *m*. **give s.o. the ~** lograr zafarse de uno. **~ of the tongue** *n* lapsus *m* linguae. □ **~ away** *vi* escabullirse. □ **~ up** *vi* [!] equivocarse

slipper /ˈslɪpə(r)/ *n* zapatilla *f*

slippery /ˈslɪpərɪ/ *adj* resbaladizo

slip: ~ road *n* rampa *f* de acceso. **~shod** /ˈslɪpʃɒd/ *adj* descuidado. **~-up** *n* [!] error *m*

slit /slɪt/ *n* raja *f*; (*cut*) corte *m*. • *vt* (*pt* **slit**, *pres p* **slitting**) rajar; (*cut*) cortar

slither /ˈslɪðə(r)/ *vi* deslizarse

slobber /ˈslɒbə(r)/ *vi* babear

slog /slɒg/ *vt* (*pt* **slogged**) golpear. • *vi* caminar trabajosamente. • *n* golpetazo *m*; (*hard work*) trabajo *m* penoso. □ **~ away** *vi* sudar tinta [!]

slogan /ˈsləʊgən/ *n* eslogan *m*

slop /slɒp/ *vt* (*pt* **slopped**) derramar. • *vi* derramarse

slop|e /sləʊp/ *vi* inclinarse. • *vt* inclinar. • *n* declive *m*, pendiente *f*. **~ing** *adj* inclinado

sloppy /ˈslɒpɪ/ *adj* (**-ier**, **-iest**) (work) descuidado; (person) des-

aliñado
slosh /slɒʃ/ *vi* 🅸 chapotear
slot /slɒt/ *n* ranura *f.* ● *vt* (*pt* **slotted**) encajar
slot-machine *n* distribuidor *m* automático; (*for gambling*) máquina *f* tragamonedas
slouch /slaʊtʃ/ *vi* andar cargado de espaldas; (*in chair*) repanchigarse
Slovak /'sləʊvæk/ *adj & n* eslovaco (*m*). **~ia** *n* Eslovaquia *f*
slovenly /'slʌvnlɪ/ *adj* (work) descuidado; (person) desaliñado
slow /sləʊ/ *adj* (**-er, -est**) lento. **be ~** (clock) estar atrasado. **in ~ motion** a cámara lenta. ● *adv* despacio. ● *vt* retardar. ● *vi* ir más despacio. ▫ **~ down, ~ up** *vt* retardar. *vi* ir más despacio. **~ly** *adv* despacio, lentamente
sludge /slʌdʒ/ *n* fango *m*
slug /slʌg/ *n* babosa *f.* **~gish** *adj* lento
slum /slʌm/ *n* barrio *m* bajo
slumber /'slʌmbə(r)/ *vi* dormir
slump /slʌmp/ *n* baja *f* repentina; (*in business*) depresión *f.* ● *vi* desplomarse
slung /slʌŋ/ *see* SLING
slur /slɜ:(r)/ *vt* (*pt* **slurred**). **~ one's words** arrastrar las palabras. ● *n.* **a racist ~** un comentario racista
slush /slʌʃ/ *n* nieve *f* medio derretida. **~ fund** *n* fondo *m* de reptiles
sly /slaɪ/ *adj* (**slyer, slyest**) (*crafty*) astuto. ● *n.* **on the ~** a hurtadillas. **~ly** *adv* astutamente
smack /smæk/ *n* manotazo *m.* ● *adv* 🅸 **~ in the middle** justo en el medio. **he went ~ into a tree** se dio contra un árbol. ● *vt* pegarle a (con la mano)
small /smɔ:l/ *adj* (**-er, -est**) pequeño, chico (*LAm*). ● *n.* **the ~ of the back** la región lumbar. **~ ads** *npl* anuncios *mpl* (clasificados), avisos *mpl* (clasificados) (*LAm*). **~ change** *n* suelto *m.* **~pox** /-pɒks/ *n* viruela *f.* **~ talk** *n* charla *f* sobre temas triviales
smart /smɑ:t/ *adj* (**-er, -est**) elegante; (*clever*) listo; (*brisk*) rápido. ● *vi* escocer. ▫ **~en up** *vt* arreglar. *vi* (person) mejorar su aspecto, arreglarse. **~ly** *adv* elegantemente; (*quickly*) rápidamente
smash /smæʃ/ *vt* romper; (*into little pieces*) hacer pedazos; batir (record). ● *vi* romperse; (*collide*) chocar (**into** con). ● *n* (*noise*) estrépito *m*; (*collision*) choque *m*; (*in sport*) smash *m.* ▫ **~ up** *vt* destrozar. **~ing** *adj* 🅸 estupendo
smattering /'smætərɪŋ/ *n* nociones *fpl*
smear /smɪə(r)/ *vt* untar (**with** de); (*stain*) manchar (**with** de); (*fig*) difamar. ● *n* mancha *f*
smell /smel/ *n* olor *m*; (*sense*) olfato *m.* ● *vt* (*pt* **smelt**) oler; (animal) olfatear. ● *vi* oler. **~ of sth** oler a algo. **~y** *adj* maloliente. **be ~y** oler mal
smelt /smelt/ *see* SMELL. ● *vt* fundir
smile /smaɪl/ *n* sonrisa *f.* ● *vi* sonreír. **~ at s.o.** sonreírle a uno
smirk /smɜ:k/ *n* sonrisita *f* (de suficiencia etc)
smith /smɪθ/ *n* herrero *m*
smithereens /smɪðə'ri:nz/ *npl.* **smash sth to ~** hacer algo añicos
smock /smɒk/ *n* blusa *f*, bata *f*
smog /smɒg/ *n* smog *m*
smok|e /sməʊk/ *n* humo *m.* ● *vt* fumar (tobacco); ahumar (food).

● *vi* fumar. **~less** *adj* que arde sin humo. **~er** *n* fumador *m*. **~y** *adj* (room) lleno de humo

smooth /smu:ð/ *adj* (**-er**, **-est**) (texture/stone) liso; (skin) suave; (movement) suave; (sea) tranquilo. ● *vt* alisar. □ **~ out** *vt* allanar (problems). **~ly** *adv* suavemente; (*without problems*) sin problemas

smother /'smʌðə(r)/ *vt* asfixiar (person). **~ s.o. with kisses** cubrir a uno de besos

smoulder /'sməʊldə(r)/ *vi* arder sin llama

smudge /smʌdʒ/ *n* borrón *m*. ● *vi* tiznarse

smug /smʌg/ *adj* (**smugger**, **smuggest**) pagado de sí mismo; (expression) de suficiencia

smuggl|e /'smʌgl/ *vt* pasar de contrabando. **~er** *n* contrabandista *m & f*. **~ing** *n* contrabando *m*

snack /snæk/ *n* tentempié *m*. **~ bar** *n* cafetería *f*

snag /snæg/ *n* problema *m*

snail /sneɪl/ *n* caracol *m*. **at a ~'s pace** a paso de tortuga

snake /sneɪk/ *n* culebra *f*, serpiente *f*

snap /snæp/ *vt* (*pt* **snapped**) (*break*) romper. **~ one's fingers** chasquear los dedos. ● *vi* romperse; (dog) intentar morder; (*say*) contestar bruscamente. **~ at** (dog) intentar morder; (*say*) contestar bruscamente. ● *n* chasquido *m*; (*Photo*) foto *f*. ● *adj* instantáneo. □ **~ up** *vt* no dejar escapar (offer). **~py** *adj* (**-ier**, **-iest**) Ⓘ rápido. **make it ~py!** ¡date prisa! **~shot** *n* foto *f*

snare /sneə(r)/ *n* trampa *f*

snarl /snɑ:l/ *vi* gruñir

snatch /snætʃ/ *vt*. **~ sth from s.o.** arrebatarle algo a uno; (*steal*) robar. ● *n* (*short part*) fragmento *m*

sneak /sni:k/ *n* soplón *m*. ● *vi* (*past & pp* **sneaked** *or* Ⓘ **snuck**) **~ in** entrar a hurtadillas. **~ off** escabullirse. **~ers** /'sni:kəz/ *npl* zapatillas *fpl* de deporte. **~y** *adj* artero

sneer /snɪə(r)/ *n* expresión *f* desdeñosa. ● *vi* hacer una mueca de desprecio. **~ at** hablar con desprecio a

sneeze /sni:z/ *n* estornudo *m*. ● *vi* estornudar

snide /snaɪd/ *adj* insidioso

sniff /snɪf/ *vt* oler. ● *vi* sorberse la nariz

snigger /'snɪgə(r)/ *n* risilla *f*. ● *vi* reírse (por lo bajo)

snip /snɪp/ *vt* (*pt* **snipped**) dar un tijeretazo a. ● *n* tijeretazo *m*

sniper /'snaɪpə(r)/ *n* francotirador *m*

snippet /'snɪpɪt/ *n* (*of conversation*) trozo *m*. **~s of information** datos *mpl* aislados

snivel /'snɪvl/ *vi* (*pt* **snivelled**) lloriquear

snob /snɒb/ *n* esnob *m & f*. **~bery** *n* esnobismo *m*. **~bish** *adj* esnob

snooker /'snu:kə(r)/ *n* snooker *m*

snoop /snu:p/ *vi* Ⓘ husmear

snooze /snu:z/ *n* sueñecito *m*. ● *vi* dormitar

snore /snɔ:(r)/ *n* ronquido *m*. ● *vi* roncar

snorkel /'snɔ:kl/ *n* esnórkel *m*

snort /snɔ:t/ *n* bufido *m*. ● *vi* bufar

snout /snaʊt/ *n* hocico *m*

snow /snəʊ/ *n* nieve *f*. ● *vi* nevar. **be ~ed in** estar aislado por la nieve. **be ~ed under with work** estar agobiado de trabajo. **~ball** *n* bola *f* de nieve. **~drift** *n* nieve *f* amontonada. **~fall** *n* nevada *f*.

~flake *n* copo *m* de nieve. **~man** *n* muñeco *m* de nieve. **~plough** *n* quitanieves *m*. **~storm** *n* tormenta *f* de nieve. **~y** *adj* (day, weather) nevoso; (landscape) nevado

snub /snʌb/ *vt* (*pt* **snubbed**) desairar. ● *n* desaire *m*. **~-nosed** *adj* chato

snuck /snʌk/ *see* SNEAK

snuff out /snʌf/ *vt* apagar (candle)

snug /snʌg/ *adj* (**snugger**, **snuggest**) cómodo; (*tight*) ajustado

snuggle (up) /'snʌgl/ *vi* acurrucarse

so /səʊ/ *adv* (*before a or adv*) tan; (*thus*) así; **and ~ on, and ~ forth** etcétera (etcétera). **I think ~** creo que sí. **or ~** más o menos. **~ long!** ¡hasta luego! ● *conj* (*therefore*) así que. **~ am I** yo también. **~ as to** para. **~ far** *adv* (*time*) hasta ahora. **~ far as I know** que yo sepa. **~ that** *conj* para que.

soak /səʊk/ *vt* remojar. ● *vi* remojarse. □ **~ in** *vi* penetrar. □ **~ up** *vt* absorber. **~ing** *adj* empapado.

so-and-so /'səʊənsəʊ/ *n* fulano *m*

soap /səʊp/ *n* jabón *m*. ● *vt* enjabonar. **~ opera** *n* telenovela *f*, culebrón *m*. **~ powder** *n* jabón *m* en polvo. **~y** *adj* jabonoso

soar /sɔ:(r)/ *vi* (bird/plane) planear; (*rise*) elevarse; (price) dispararse. **~ing** *adj* (inflation) galopante

sob /sɒb/ *n* sollozo *m*. ● *vi* (*pt* **sobbed**) sollozar

sober /'səʊbə(r)/ *adj* (*not drunk*) sobrio

so-called /'səʊkɔ:ld/ *adj* denominado; (expert) supuesto

soccer /'sɒkə(r)/ *n* fútbol *m*, futbol *m* (*Mex*)

sociable /'səʊʃəbl/ *adj* sociable

social /'səʊʃl/ *adj* social; (*sociable*) sociable. **~ism** *n* socialismo *m*. **~ist** *adj* & *n* socialista (*m* & *f*). **~ize** *vt* socializar. **~ security** *n* seguridad *f* social. **~ worker** *n* asistente *m* social

society /sə'saɪətɪ/ *n* sociedad *f*

sociolog|ical /səʊsɪə'lɒdʒɪkl/ *adj* sociológico. **~ist** /-'ɒlədʒɪst/ *n* sociólogo *m*. **~y** /-'ɒlədʒɪ/ *n* sociología *f*

sock /sɒk/ *n* calcetín *m*

socket /'sɒkɪt/ *n* (*of joint*) hueco *m*; (*of eye*) cuenca *f*; (*wall plug*) enchufe *m*; (*for bulb*) portalámparas *m*

soda /'səʊdə/ *n* soda *f*. **~-water** *n* soda *f*

sodium /'səʊdɪəm/ *n* sodio *m*

sofa /'səʊfə/ *n* sofá *m*

soft /sɒft/ *adj* (**-er**, **-est**) blando; (light, colour) suave; (*gentle*) dulce, tierno; (*not strict*) blando. **~ drink** *n* refresco *m*. **~en** /'sɒfn/ *vt* ablandar; suavizar (skin). ● *vi* ablandarse. **~ly** *adv* dulcemente; (speak) bajito. **~ware** /-weə(r)/ *n* software *m*

soggy /'sɒgɪ/ *adj* (**-ier**, **-iest**) empapado

soil /sɔɪl/ *n* tierra *f*; (*Amer*, *dirt*) suciedad *f*. ● *vt* ensuciar

solar /'səʊlə(r)/ *adj* solar

sold /səʊld/ *see* SELL

solder /'sɒldə(r)/ *vt* soldar

soldier /'səʊldʒə(r)/ *n* soldado *m*. □ **~ on** *vi* 🅸 seguir al pie del cañon

sole /səʊl/ *n* (*of foot*) planta *f*; (*of shoe*) suela *f*. ● *adj* único, solo. **~ly** *adv* únicamente

solemn /'sɒləm/ *adj* solemne

solicitor /sə'lɪsɪtə(r)/ *n* abogado *m*; (*notary*) notario *m*

solid /'sɒlɪd/ *adj* sólido; (gold etc)

macizo; (*unanimous*) unánime; (meal) sustancioso. ● *n* sólido *m*. **~s** *npl* alimentos *mpl* sólidos. **~arity** /sɒlɪ'dærətɪ/ *n* solidaridad *f*. **~ify** /sə'lɪdɪfaɪ/ *vi* solidificarse

solitary /'sɒlɪtrɪ/ *adj* solitario

solitude /'sɒlɪtju:d/ *n* soledad *f*

solo /'səʊləʊ/ *n* (*pl* **-os**) (*Mus*) solo *m*. **~ist** *n* solista *m & f*

solstice /'sɒlstɪs/ *n* solsticio *m*

solu|ble /'sɒljʊbl/ *adj* soluble. **~tion** /sə'lu:ʃn/ *n* solución *f*

solve /sɒlv/ *vt* solucionar (problem); resolver (mystery). **~nt** /-vənt/ *adj & n* solvente (*m*)

sombre /'sɒmbə(r)/ *adj* sombrío

some /sʌm//səm/

● *adjective*

····➤ (*unspecified number*) unos, unas. **he ate ~ olives** comió unas aceitunas

····➤ (*unspecified amount*) *not translated*. **I have to buy ~ bread** tengo que comprar pan. **would you like ~ coffee?** ¿quieres café?

····➤ (*certain, not all*) algunos, -nas. **I like ~ modern writers** algunos escritores modernos me gustan

····➤ (*a little*) algo de. **I eat ~ meat, but not much** como algo de carne, pero no mucho

····➤ (*considerable amount of*) **we've known each other for ~ time** ya hace tiempo que nos conocemos

····➤ (*expressing admiration*) **that's ~ car you've got!** ¡vaya coche que tienes!

● *pronoun*

····➤ (*a number of things or people*) algunos, -nas, unos, unas. **~ are mine and ~ aren't** algunos *or* unos son míos y otros no. **aren't there any apples? we bought ~ yesterday** ¿no hay manzanas? compramos algunas ayer

····➤ (*part of an amount*) **he wants ~** quiere un poco. **~ of what he said** parte *or* algo de lo que dijo

····➤ (*certain people*) algunos, -nas. **~ say that...** algunos dicen que...

● *adverb*

····➤ (*approximately*) unos, unas, alrededor de. **there were ~ fifty people there** había unas cincuenta personas, había alrededor de cincuenta personas

some: ~body /-bədɪ/ *pron* alguien. **~how** *adv* de algún modo. **~how or other** de una manera u otra. **~one** *pron* alguien

somersault /'sʌməsɔ:lt/ *n* salto *m* mortal. ● *vi* dar un salto mortal

some: ~thing *pron* algo *m*. **~thing like** (*approximately*) alrededor de. **~time** *adj* ex. ● *adv* algún día. **~time next week** un día de la semana que viene. **~times** *adv* a veces. **~what** *adv* un tanto. **~where** *adv* en alguna parte, en algún lado

son /sʌn/ *n* hijo *m*

sonata /sə'nɑ:tə/ *n* sonata *f*

song /sɒŋ/ *n* canción *f*

sonic /'sɒnɪk/ *adj* sónico

son-in-law /'sʌnɪnlɔ:/ *n* (*pl* **sons-in-law**) yerno *m*

sonnet /'sɒnɪt/ *n* soneto *m*

son of a bitch *n* (*pl* **sons of bitches**) (*esp Amer sl*) hijo *m* de puta

soon /su:n/ *adv* (**-er**, **-est**) pronto; (*in a short time*) dentro de poco. **~ after** poco después. **~er or later** tarde o temprano. **as ~ as** en cuanto; **as ~ as possible** lo antes posible. **the ~er the better** cuanto antes mejor

soot /sʊt/ *n* hollín *m*

sooth|e /su:ð/ *vt* calmar; aliviar (pain). **~ing** *adj* (medicine) calmante; (words) tranquilizador

sooty /'sʊtɪ/ *adj* cubierto de hollín

sophisticated /sə'fɪstɪkeɪtɪd/ *adj* sofisticado; (*complex*) complejo

sophomore /'sɒfəmɔ:(r)/ *n* (*Amer*) estudiante *m & f* de segundo curso (en la universidad)

sopping /'sɒpɪŋ/ *adj*. **~ (wet)** empapado

soppy /'sɒpɪ/ *adj* (**-ier**, **-iest**) [!] sentimental

soprano /sə'prɑ:nəʊ/ *n* (*pl* **-os**) soprano *f*

sordid /'sɔ:dɪd/ *adj* sórdido

sore /'sɔ:(r)/ *adj* (**-er**, **-est**) dolorido; (*Amer fam, angry*) **be ~ at s.o.** estar picado con uno. **~ throat** *n* dolor *m* de garganta. **I've got a ~ throat** me duele la garganta. ● *n* llaga *f*.

sorrow /'sɒrəʊ/ *n* pena *f*, pesar *m*

sorry /'sɒrɪ/ *adj* (**-ier**, **-ier**) arrepentido; (*wretched*) lamentable. **I'm ~** lo siento. **be ~ for s.o.** (*pity*) compadecer a uno. **I'm ~ you can't come** siento que no puedas venir. **say ~** pedir perdón. **~!** (*apologizing*) ¡lo siento! ¡perdón!. **~?** (*asking s.o. to repeat*) ¿cómo?

sort /sɔ:t/ *n* tipo *m*, clase *f*; (*fam, person*) tipo *m*. **a ~ of** una especie de. ● *vt* clasificar. □ **~ out** *vt* (*organize*) ordenar; organizar (finances); (*separate out*) separar; solucionar (problem)

so-so /'səʊsəʊ/ *adj* regular

soufflé /'su:fleɪ/ *n* suflé *m*

sought /sɔ:t/ *see* **SEEK**

soul /səʊl/ *n* alma *f*

sound /saʊnd/ *n* sonido *m*; (*noise*) ruido *m*. ● *vt* tocar. ● *vi* sonar; (*seem*) parecer (**as if** que). **it ~s interesting** suena interesante.. ● *adj* (**-er**, **-est**) sano; (argument) lógico; (*secure*) seguro. ● *adv*. **~ asleep** profundamente dormido. **~ barrier** *n* barrera *f* del sonido. **~ly** *adv* sólidamente; (*asleep*) profundamente. **~proof** *adj* insonorizado. **~track** *n* banda *f* sonora

soup /su:p/ *n* sopa *f*

sour /'saʊə(r)/ *adj* (**-er**, **-est**) agrio; (milk) cortado

source /sɔ:s/ *n* fuente *f*

south /saʊθ/ *n* sur *m*. ● *adj* sur *a invar*; (wind) del sur. ● *adv* (go) hacia el sur. **it's ~ of** está al sur de. **S~ Africa** *n* Sudáfrica *f*. **S~ America** *n* América *f* (del Sur), Sudamérica *f*. **S~ American** *adj & n* sudamericano (*m*). **~-east** *n* sudeste *m*, sureste *m*. **~erly** /'sʌðəlɪ/ (wind) del sur. **~ern** /'sʌðən/ *adj* del sur, meridional. **~erner** *n* sureño *m*. **~ward** /-wəd/, **~wards** *adv* hacia el sur. **~-west** *n* sudoeste *m*, suroeste *m*

souvenir /su:və'nɪə(r)/ *n* recuerdo *m*

sovereign /'sɒvrɪn/ *n & a* soberano (*m*)

Soviet /'səʊvɪət/ *adj* (*History*) soviético. **the ~ Union** *n* la Unión *f* Soviética

sow[1] /səʊ/ *vt* (*pt* **sowed**, *pp* **sowed** *or* **sown** /səʊn/) sembrar

sow² /saʊ/ *n* cerda *f*
soy (*esp Amer*), **soya** /'sɔɪə/ *n*. **~ bean** *n* soja *f*
spa /spɑ:/ *n* balneario *m*
space /speɪs/ *n* espacio *m*; (*room*) espacio *m*, lugar *m*. ●*adj* (research etc) espacial. ●*vt* espaciar. □ **~ out** *vt* espaciar. **~craft**, **~ship** *n* nave *f* espacial
spade /speɪd/ *n* pala *f*. **~s** *npl* (*Cards*) picas *fpl*
spaghetti /spə'getɪ/ *n* espaguetis *mpl*
Spain /speɪn/ *n* España *f*
spam /spæm/ *n* (*Comp*) correo *m* basura
span /spæn/ *n* (*of arch*) luz *f*; (*of time*) espacio *m*; (*of wings*) envergadura *f*. ●*vt* (*pt* **spanned**) extenderse sobre. ●*adj see* **SPICK**
Spaniard /'spænjəd/ *n* español *m*
spaniel /'spænjəl/ *n* spaniel *m*
Spanish /'spænɪʃ/ *adj* español; (*language*) castellano, español. ●*n* (*language*) castellano *m*, español *m*. *npl*. **the ~** (*people*) los españoles
spank /spæŋk/ *vt* pegarle a (en las nalgas)
spanner /'spænə(r)/ *n* llave *f*
spare /speə(r)/ *vt*. **if you can ~ the time** si tienes tiempo. **can you ~ me a pound?** ¿tienes una libra que me des? **~ no effort** no escatimar esfuerzos. **have money to ~** tener dinero de sobra. ●*adj* (*not in use*) de más; (*replacement*) de repuesto; (*free*) libre. **~ (part)** *n* repuesto *m*. **~ room** *n* cuarto *m* de huéspedes. **~ time** *n* tiempo *m* libre. **~ tyre** *n* neumático *m* de repuesto
sparingly /'speərɪŋlɪ/ *adv* (use) con moderación
spark /spɑ:k/ *n* chispa *f*. ●*vt* provocar (criticism); suscitar (interest). **~ing plug** *n* (*Auto*) bujía *f*
sparkl|e /'spɑ:kl/ *vi* centellear. ●*n* destello *m*. **~ing** *adj* centelleante; (wine) espumoso
spark plug *n* (*Auto*) bujía *f*
sparrow /'spærəʊ/ *n* gorrión *m*
sparse /spɑ:s/ *adj* escaso. **~ly** *adv* escasamente
spasm /'spæzəm/ *n* espasmo *m*; (*of cough*) acceso *m*. **~odic** /-'mɒdɪk/ *adj* espasmódico; (*Med*) irregular
spat /spæt/ *see* **SPIT**
spate /speɪt/ *n* racha *f*
spatial /'speɪʃl/ *adj* espacial
spatter /'spætə(r)/ *vt* salpicar (**with** de)
spawn /spɔ:n/ *n* huevas *fpl*. ●*vt* generar. ●*vi* desovar
speak /spi:k/ *vt/i* (*pt* **spoke**, *pp* **spoken**) hablar. **~ for s.o.** hablar en nombre de uno. □ **~ up** *vi* hablar más fuerte. **~er** *n* (*in public*) orador *m*; (*loudspeaker*) altavoz *m*; (*of language*) hablante *m & f*
spear /spɪə(r)/ *n* lanza *f*. **~head** *vt* (*lead*) encabezar
special /'speʃl/ *adj* especial. **~ist** /'speʃəlɪst/ *n* especialista *m & f*. **~ity** /-ɪ'ælətɪ/ *n* especialidad *f*. **~ization** /-əlaɪ'zeɪʃn/ *n* especialización *f*. **~ize** /-əlaɪz/ *vi* especializarse. **~ized** *adj* especializado. **~ly** *adv* especialmente. **~ty** *n* (*Amer*) especialidad *f*
species /'spi:ʃi:z/ *n* especie *f*
specif|ic /spə'sɪfɪk/ *adj* específico. **~ically** *adv* específicamente; (state) explícitamente. **~ication** /-ɪ'keɪʃn/ *n* especificación *f*. **~y** /'spesɪfaɪ/ *vt* especificar
specimen /'spesɪmɪn/ *n* muestra *f*

S

speck /spek/ *n* (*of dust*) mota *f*; (*in distance*) punto *m*

specs /speks/ *npl* 🅸 *see* **SPECTACLES**

spectac|le /ˈspektəkl/ *n* espectáculo *m*. **~les** *npl* gafas *fpl*, lentes *fpl* (*LAm*), anteojos *mpl* (*LAm*). **~ular** /-ˈtækjʊlə(r)/ *adj* espectacular

spectator /spekˈteɪtə(r)/ *n* espectador *m*

spectr|e /ˈspektə(r)/ *n* espectro *m*. **~um** /ˈspektrəm/ *n* (*pl* **-tra** /-trə/) espectro *m*; (*of views*) gama *f*

speculat|e /ˈspekjʊleɪt/ *vi* especular. **~ion** /-ˈleɪʃn/ *n* especulación *f*. **~or** *n* especulador *m*

sped /sped/ *see* **SPEED**

speech /spi:tʃ/ *n* (*faculty*) habla *f*; (*address*) discurso *m*. **~less** *adj* mudo

speed /spi:d/ *n* velocidad *f*; (*rapidity*) rapidez *f*. •*vi* (*pt* **speeded**) (*drive too fast*) ir a exceso de velocidad. ▫ **~ off, ~ away** (*pt* **sped**) *vi* alejarse a toda velocidad. ▫ **~ by** (*pt* **sped**) *vi* (time) pasar volando. ▫ **~ up** (*pt* **speeded**) *vt* acelerar. *vi* acelerarse. **~boat** *n* lancha *f* motora. **~ camera** *n* cámara *f* de control de velocidad. **~ dating** *n* cita *f* flash, speed dating *m*. **~ limit** *n* velocidad *f* máxima. **~ometer** /spi:ˈdɒmɪtə(r)/ *n* velocímetro *m*. **~way** *n* (*Amer*) autopista *f*. **~y** *adj* (**-ier**, **-iest**) rápido

spell /spel/ *n* (*magic*) hechizo *m*; (*of weather, activity*) período *m*. **go through a bad ~** pasar por una mala racha. •*vt/i* (*pt* **spelled** *or* **spelt**) escribir. ▫ **~ out** *vt* deletrear; (*fig*) explicar. **~ checker** *n* corrector *m* ortográfico. **~ing** *n* ortografía *f*

spellbound /ˈspelbaʊnd/ *adj* embelesado

spelt /spelt/ *see* **SPELL**

spend /spend/ *vt* (*pt* **spent** /spent/) gastar (money); pasar (time); dedicar (care). •*vi* gastar dinero

sperm /spɜ:m/ *n* (*pl* **sperms** *or* **sperm**) esperma *f*; (*individual*) espermatozoide *m*

spew /spju:/ *vt/i* vomitar

spher|e /sfɪə(r)/ *n* esfera *f*. **~ical** /ˈsferɪkl/ *adj* esférico

spice /spaɪs/ *n* especia *f*

spick /spɪk/ *adj*. **~ and span** limpio y ordenado

spicy /ˈspaɪsɪ/ *adj* picante

spider /ˈspaɪdə(r)/ *n* araña *f*

spik|e /spaɪk/ *n* (*of metal etc*) punta *f*. **~y** *adj* puntiagudo

spill /spɪl/ *vt* (*pt* **spilled** *or* **spilt**) derramar. •*vi* derramarse. **~ over** *vi* (container) desbordarse; (liquid) rebosar

spin /spɪn/ *vt* (*pt* **spun**, *pres p* **spinning**) hacer girar; hilar (wool); centrifugar (washing). •*vi* girar. •*n*. **give sth a ~** hacer girar algo. **go for a ~** (*Auto*) ir a dar un paseo en coche

spinach /ˈspɪnɪdʒ/ *n* espinacas *fpl*

spindly /ˈspɪndlɪ/ *adj* larguirucho

spin-drier /spɪnˈdraɪə(r)/ *n* centrifugadora *f* (de ropa)

spine /spaɪn/ *n* columna *f* vertebral; (*of book*) lomo *m*; (*on animal*) púa *f*. **~less** *adj* (*fig*) sin carácter

spinning wheel /ˈspɪnɪŋ/ *n* rueca *f*

spin-off /ˈspɪnɒf/ *n* resultado *m* indirecto; (*by-product*) producto *m* derivado

spinster /ˈspɪnstə(r)/ *n* soltera *f*

spiral /ˈspaɪərəl/ *adj* espiral;

(shape) de espiral. • *n* espiral *f*. • *vi* (*pt* **spiralled**) (unemployment) escalar; (prices) dispararse. ~ **staircase** *n* escalera *f* de caracol

spire /'spaɪə(r)/ *n* aguja *f*

spirit /'spɪrɪt/ *n* espíritu *m*. **be in good** ~**s** estar animado. **in low** ~**s** abatido. ~**ed** *adj* animado, fogoso. ~**s** *npl* (*drinks*) bebidas *fpl* alcohólicas (de alta graduación). ~**ual** /'spɪrɪtjʊəl/ *adj* espiritual

spit /spɪt/ *vt* (*pt* **spat** *or* (*Amer*) **spit**, *pres p* **spitting**) escupir. • *vi* escupir. **it's** ~**ting** caen algunas gotas. • *n* saliva *f*; (*for roasting*) asador *m*

spite /spaɪt/ *n* rencor *m*. **in** ~ **of** a pesar de. • *vt* fastidiar. ~**ful** *adj* rencoroso

spittle /'spɪtl/ *n* baba *f*

splash /splæʃ/ *vt* salpicar. • *vi* (person) chapotear. • *n* salpicadura *f*. **a** ~ **of paint** un poco de pintura. □ ~ **about** *vi* chapotear. □ ~ **down** *vi* (spacecraft) amerizar. □ ~ **out** *vi* gastarse un dineral (**on** en)

splend|id /'splendɪd/ *adj* espléndido. ~**our** /-ə(r)/ *n* esplendor *m*

splint /splɪnt/ *n* tablilla *f*

splinter /'splɪntə(r)/ *n* astilla *f*. • *vi* astillarse

S

split /splɪt/ *vt* (*pt* **split**, *pres p* **splitting**) partir; fisionar (atom); reventar (trousers); (*divide*) dividir. • *vi* partirse; (*divide*) dividirse. **a** ~**ting headache** un dolor de cabeza espantoso. • *n* (*in garment*) descosido *m*; (*in wood, glass*) rajadura *f*. □ ~ **up** *vi* separarse. ~ **second** *n* fracción *f* de segundo

splutter /'splʌtə(r)/ *vi* chisporrotear; (person) farfullar

spoil /spɔɪl/ *vt* (*pt* **spoilt** *or* **spoiled**) estropear, echar a perder; (*indulge*) consentir, malcriar. ~**s** *npl* botín *m*. ~**-sport** *n* aguafiestas *m* & *f*

spoke[1] /spəʊk/ *see* **SPEAK**

spoke[2] /spəʊk/ *n* (*of wheel*) rayo *m*

spoken /spəʊkən/ *see* **SPEAK**

spokesman /'spəʊksmən/ *n* (*pl* **-men**) portavoz *m*

sponge /spʌndʒ/ *n* esponja *f*. • *vt* limpiar con una esponja. ~ **off**, ~ **on** *vt* vivir a costillas de. ~ **cake** *n* bizcocho *m*

sponsor /'spɒnsə(r)/ *n* patrocinador *m*; (*of the arts*) mecenas *m* & *f*; (*surety*) garante *m*. • *vt* patrocinar. ~**ship** *n* patrocinio *m*; (*of the arts*) mecenazgo *m*

spontaneous /spɒn'teɪnɪəs/ *adj* espontáneo. ~**ously** *adv* espontáneamente

spoof /spu:f/ *n* [I] parodia *f*

spooky /'spu:kɪ/ *adj* (**-ier**, **-iest**) [I] espeluznante

spool /spu:l/ *n* carrete *m*

spoon /spu:n/ *n* cuchara *f*. ~**ful** *n* cucharada *f*

sporadic /spə'rædɪk/ *adj* esporádico

sport /spɔ:t/ *n* deporte *m*. ~**s car** *n* coche *m* deportivo. ~**s centre** *n* centro *m* deportivo. ~**sman** /-mən/ *n*, (*pl* **-men**), ~**swoman** *n* deportista *m* & *f*

spot /spɒt/ *n* mancha *f*; (*pimple*) grano *m*; (*place*) lugar *m*; (*in pattern*) lunar *m*. **be in a** ~ [I] estar en apuros. **on the** ~ allí mismo; (decide) en ese mismo momento. • *vt* (*pt* **spotted**) manchar; (*fam, notice*) ver, divisar; descubrir (mistake). ~ **check** *n* control *m* hecho al azar. ~**less** *adj* (clothes) impecable; (house) limpísimo. ~**light** *n* reflector *m*; (*in theatre*) foco *m*.

~ted *adj* moteado; (material) de lunares. **~ty** *adj* (**-ier, -iest**) (skin) lleno de granos; (youth) con la cara llena de granos

spouse /spaʊz/ *n* cónyuge *m & f*

spout /spaʊt/ *n* pico *m*; (*jet*) chorro *m*

sprain /spreɪn/ *vt* hacerse un esguince en. ● *n* esguince *m*

sprang /spræŋ/ *see* **SPRING**

spray /spreɪ/ *n* (*of flowers*) ramillete *m*; (*from sea*) espuma *f*; (*liquid in spray form*) espray *m*; (*device*) rociador *m*. ● *vt* rociar

spread /spred/ *vt* (*pt* **spread**) (*stretch, extend*) extender; desplegar (wings); difundir (idea, news). **~ butter on a piece of toast** untar una tostada con mantequilla. ● *vi* extenderse; (disease) propagarse; (idea, news) difundirse. ● *n* (*of ideas*) difusión *f*; (*of disease, fire*) propagación *f*; (*fam, feast*) festín *m*. □ **~ out** *vi* (*move apart*) desplegarse

spree /spriː/ *n*. **go on a shopping ~** ir de expedición a las tiendas

sprightly /ˈspraɪtlɪ/ *adj* (**-ier, -iest**) vivo

spring /sprɪŋ/ *n* (*season*) primavera *f*; (*device*) resorte *m*; (*in mattress*) muelle *m*, resorte *m* (*LAm*); (*elasticity*) elasticidad *f*; (*water*) manantial *m*. ● *adj* primaveral. ● *vi* (*pt* **sprang**, *pp* **sprung**) saltar; (*issue*) brotar. **~ from sth** (problem) provenir de algo. □ **~ up** *vi* surgir. **~board** *n* trampolín *m*. **~-clean** /-ˈkliːn/ *vi* hacer una limpieza general. **~ onion** *n* cebolleta *f*. **~time** *n* primavera *f*. **~y** *adj* (**-ier, -iest**) (mattress, grass) mullido

sprinkle /ˈsprɪŋkl/ *vt* salpicar; (*with liquid*) rociar. ● *n* salpicadura *f*; (*of liquid*) rociada *f*. **~r** *n* regadera *f*

sprint /sprɪnt/ *n* carrera *f* corta. ● *vi* (*Sport*) esprintar; (*run fast*) correr. **~er** *n* corredor *m*

sprout /spraʊt/ *vi* brotar. ● *n* brote *m*. **(Brussels) ~s** *npl* coles *fpl* de Bruselas

sprung /sprʌŋ/ *see* **SPRING**

spud /spʌd/ *n* 🅸 patata *f*, papa *f* (*LAm*)

spun /spʌn/ *see* **SPIN**

spur /spɜː(r)/ *n* espuela *f*; (*stimulus*) acicate *m*. **on the ~ of the moment** sin pensarlo. ● *vt* (*pt* **spurred**). **~ (on)** espolear; (*fig*) estimular

spurn /spɜːn/ *vt* desdeñar; (*reject*) rechazar

spurt /spɜːt/ *vi* (liquid) salir a chorros. ● *n* chorro *m*; (*of activity*) racha *f*

spy /spaɪ/ *n* espía *m & f*. ● *vt* descubrir, ver. ● *vi* espiar. **~ on s.o.** espiar a uno

squabble /ˈskwɒbl/ *vi* reñir

squad /skwɒd/ *n* (*Mil*) pelotón *m*; (*of police*) brigada *f*; (*Sport*) equipo *m*. **~ car** *m* coche *m* patrulla. **~ron** /ˈskwɒdrən/ *n* (*Mil, Aviat*) escuadrón *m*; (*Naut*) escuadra *f*

squalid /ˈskwɒlɪd/ *adj* miserable

squall /skwɔːl/ *n* turbión *m*

squalor /ˈskwɒlə(r)/ *n* miseria *f*

squander /ˈskwɒndə(r)/ *vt* derrochar; desaprovechar (opportunity)

square /skweə(r)/ *n* cuadrado *m*; (*in town*) plaza *f*. ● *adj* cuadrado; (meal) decente; (*fam, old-fashioned*) chapado a la antigua. ● *vt* (*settle*) arreglar; (*Math*) elevar al cuadrado. ● *vi* (*agree*) cuadrar. □ **~ up** *vi* arreglar cuentas (**with** con). **~ly** *adv* directamente

squash /skwɒʃ/ *vt* aplastar; (*sup-*

press) acallar. ● *n*. **it was a terrible** ~ íbamos (*or* iban) terriblemente apretujados; (*drink*) **orange** ~ naranjada *f*; (*Sport*) squash *m*; (*vegetable*) calabaza *f*. ~**y** *adj* blando

squat /skwɒt/ *vi* (*pt* **squatted**) ponerse en cuclillas; (*occupy illegally*) ocupar sin autorización. ● *adj* rechoncho y bajo. ~**ter** *n* ocupante *m & f* ilegal, okupa *m & f*

squawk /skwɔːk/ *n* graznido *m*. ● *vi* graznar

squeak /skwiːk/ *n* chillido *m*; (*of door*) chirrido *m*. ● *vi* chillar; (door) chirriar; (shoes) crujir. ~**y** *adj* chirriante

squeal /skwiːl/ *n* chillido *m* ● *vi* chillar

squeamish /ˈskwiːmɪʃ/ *adj* impresionable, delicado

squeeze /skwiːz/ *vt* apretar; exprimir (lemon etc). ● *vi*. ~ **in** meterse. ● *n* estrujón *m*; (*of hand*) apretón *m*

squid /skwɪd/ *n* calamar *m*

squiggle /ˈskwɪgl/ *n* garabato *m*

squint /skwɪnt/ *vi* bizquear; (*trying to see*) entrecerrar los ojos. ● *n* estrabismo *m*

squirm /skwɜːm/ *vi* retorcerse

squirrel /ˈskwɪrəl/ *n* ardilla *f*

squirt /skwɜːt/ *vt* (liquid) echar un chorro de. ● *vi* salir a chorros. ● *n* chorrito *m*

St /sənt/ *abbr* (= **saint**) /sənt/ S, San(to); (= **street**) C/, Calle *f*

stab /stæb/ *vt* (*pt* **stabbed**) apuñalar. ● *n* puñalada *f*; (*pain*) punzada *f*. **have a** ~ **at sth** intentar algo

stabili|ty /stəˈbɪlətɪ/ *n* estabilidad *f*. ~**ze** /ˈsteɪbɪlaɪz/ *vt/i* estabilizar

stable /ˈsteɪbl/ *adj* (**-er**, **-est**) estable. ● *n* caballeriza *f*, cuadra *f*

stack /stæk/ *n* montón *m*. ● *vt*. ~ (**up**) amontonar

stadium /ˈsteɪdɪəm/ *n* (*pl* **-diums** *or* **-dia** /-dɪə/) estadio *m*

staff /stɑːf/ *n* (*stick*) palo *m*; (*employees*) personal *m*. **teaching** ~ personal *m* docente. **a member of** ~ un empleado

stag /stæg/ *n* ciervo *m*. ~**-night**, ~**-party** *n* (*before wedding*) fiesta *f* de despedida de soltero; (*men-only party*) fiesta *f* para hombres

stage /steɪdʒ/ *n* (*in theatre*) escenario *f*; (*platform*) plataforma *f*; (*phase*) etapa *f*. **the** ~ (*profession, medium*) el teatro. ● *vt* poner en escena (play); (*arrange*) organizar; (*pej*) orquestar. ~**coach** *n* diligencia *f*

stagger /ˈstægə(r)/ *vi* tambalearse. ● *vt* dejar estupefacto; escalonar (holidays etc). ~**ing** *adj* asombroso

stagna|nt /ˈstægnənt/ *adj* estancado. ~**te** /stægˈneɪt/ *vi* estancarse

staid /steɪd/ *adj* serio, formal

stain /steɪn/ *vt* manchar; (*colour*) teñir. ● *n* mancha *f*; (*dye*) tintura *f*. ~**ed glass window** *n* vidriera *f* de colores. ~**less steel** *n* acero *m* inoxidable. ~ **remover** *n* quitamanchas *m*

stair /steə(r)/ *n* escalón *m*. ~**s** *npl* escalera *f*. ~**case**, ~**way** *n* escalera *f*

stake /steɪk/ *n* estaca *f*; (*wager*) apuesta *f*; (*Com*) intereses *mpl*. **be at** ~ estar en juego. ● *vt* estacar; jugarse (reputation). ~ **a claim** reclamar

stala|ctite /ˈstæləktaɪt/ *n* estalactita *f*. ~**gmite** /ˈstæləgmaɪt/ *n* estalagmita *f*

stale /steɪl/ *adj* (**-er**, **-est**) no fresco; (bread) duro; (smell) viciado. **~mate** *n* (*Chess*) ahogado *m*; (*deadlock*) punto *m* muerto

stalk /stɔ:k/ *n* tallo *m*. ● *vt* acechar. ● *vi* irse indignado

stall /stɔ:l/ *n* (*in stable*) compartimiento *m*; (*in market*) puesto *m*. **~s** *npl* (*in theatre*) platea *f*, patio *m* de butacas. ● *vt* parar (engine). ● *vi* (engine) pararse; (*fig*) andar con rodeos

stallion /ˈstæljən/ *n* semental *m*

stalwart /ˈstɔ:lwət/ *adj* (supporter) leal, incondicional

stamina /ˈstæmɪnə/ *n* resistencia *f*

stammer /ˈstæmə(r)/ *vi* tartamudear. ● *n* tartamudeo *m*

stamp /stæmp/ *vt* (*with feet*) patear; (*press*) estampar; (*with rubber stamp*) sellar; (*fig*) señalar. ● *vi* dar patadas en el suelo. ● *n* sello *m*, estampilla *f* (*LAm*), timbre *m* (*Mex*); (*on passport*) sello *m*; (*with foot*) patada *f*; (*mark*) marca *f*, señal *f*. □ **~ out** *vt* (*fig*) erradicar. **~ed addressed envelope** *n* sobre *m* franqueado con su dirección

stampede /stæmˈpi:d/ *n* estampida *f*. ● *vi* salir en estampida

stance /stɑ:ns/ *n* postura *f*

stand /stænd/ *vi* (*pt* **stood**) estar de pie, estar parado (*LAm*); (*rise*) ponerse de pie, pararse; (*be*) encontrarse; (*Pol*) presentarse como candidato (**for** en). **the offer ~s** la oferta sigue en pie. **~ to reason** ser lógico. ● *vt* (*endure*) soportar; (*place*) colocar. **~ a chance** tener una posibilidad. ● *n* posición *f*, postura *f*; (*for lamp etc*) pie *m*, sostén *m*; (*at market*) puesto *m*; (*booth*) quiosco *m*; (*Sport*) tribuna *f*. **make a ~ against sth** oponer resistencia a algo. □ **~ back** *vi* apartarse. □ **~ by** *vi* estar preparado. *vt* (*support*) apoyar. □ **~ down** *vi* retirarse. □ **~ for** *vt* significar. □ **~ in for** *vt* suplir a. □ **~ out** *vi* destacarse. □ **~ up** *vi* ponerse de pie, pararse (*LAm*). □ **~ up for** *vt* defender. **~ up for oneself** defenderse. □ **~ up to** *vt* resistir a

standard /ˈstændəd/ *n* norma *f*; (*level*) nivel *m*; (*flag*) estandarte *m*. ● *adj* estándar *a invar*, normal. **~ize** *vt* estandarizar. **~ lamp** *n* lámpara *f* de pie. **~s** *npl* principios *mpl*

stand: ~-by *n* (*at airport*) standby *m*. **be on ~-by** (police) estar en estado de alerta. **~-in** *n* suplente *m & f*. **~ing** *adj* de pie, parado (*LAm*); (*permanent*) permanente *f*. ● *n* posición *f*; (*prestige*) prestigio *m*. **~off** *n* (*Amer, draw*) empate *m*; (*deadlock*) callejón *m* sin salida. **~point** *n* punto *m* de vista. **~still** *n*. **be at a ~still** estar paralizado. **come to a ~still** (vehicle) parar; (city) quedar paralizado

stank /stæŋk/ see STINK

staple /ˈsteɪpl/ *adj* principal. ● *n* grapa *f*. ● *vt* sujetar con una grapa. **~r** *n* grapadora *f*

star /stɑ:(r)/ *n* (*incl Cinema, Theatre*) estrella *f*; (*asterisk*) asterisco *m*. ● *vi* (*pt* **starred**). **~ in a film** protagonizar una película. **~board** *n* estribor *m*.

starch /stɑ:tʃ/ *n* almidón *m*; (*in food*) fécula *f*. ● *vt* almidonar. **~y** (food) *adj* a base de féculas

stardom /ˈstɑ:dəm/ *n* estrellato *m*

stare /steə(r)/ *n* mirada *f* fija. ● *vi*. **~ (at)** mirar fijamente

starfish /ˈstɑ:fɪʃ/ *n* estrella *f* de mar

stark /stɑ:k/ *adj* (**-er, -est**) escueto. ● *adv* completamente

starling /ˈstɑ:lɪŋ/ *n* estornino *m*

starry /ˈstɑːrɪ/ *adj* estrellado

start /stɑːt/ *vt* empezar, comenzar; encender (engine); arrancar (car); (*cause*) provocar; abrir (business). • *vi* empezar; (car etc) arrancar; (*jump*) dar un respingo. **to ~ with** (*as linker*) para empezar. **~ off by doing sth** empezar por hacer algo. • *n* principio *m*; (*Sport*) ventaja *f*; (*jump*) susto *m*. **make an early ~** (*on journey*) salir temprano. **~er** *n* (*Auto*) motor *m* de arranque; (*Culin*) primer plato *m*. **~ing-point** *n* punto *m* de partida

startle /ˈstɑːtl/ *vt* asustar

starv|ation /stɑːˈveɪʃn/ *n* hambre *f*, inanición *f*. **~e** /stɑːv/ *vt* hacer morir de hambre. • *vi* morirse de hambre. **I'm ~ing** me muero de hambre

state /steɪt/ *n* estado *m*. **be in a ~** estar agitado. **the S~** los Estados *mpl* Unidos. • *vt* declarar; expresar (views); (*fix*) fijar. • *adj* del Estado; (*Schol*) público; (*with ceremony*) de gala. **~ly** *adj* (**-ier**, **-iest**) majestuoso. **~ly home** *n* casa *f* solariega. **~ment** *n* declaración *f*; (*account*) informe *m*. **~sman** /-mən/ *n* estadista *m*

S

> **state school** En Gran Bretaña, colegio estatal de educación gratuita, financiado directa o indirectamente por el gobierno. Abarca la educación primaria y secundaria, colegios especializados, *comprehensives* etc.

static /ˈstætɪk/ *adj* estacionario. • *n* (*interference*) estática *f*

station /ˈsteɪʃn/ *n* estación *f*; (*on radio*) emisora *f*; (*TV*) canal *m*. • *vt* colocar; (*Mil*) estacionar. **~ary** *adj* estacionario. **~er's (shop)** *n* papelería *f*. **~ery** *n* artículos *mpl* de papelería. **~ wagon** *n* (*Amer*) ranchera *f*, (coche *m*) familiar *m*, camioneta *f* (*LAm*)

statistic /stəˈtɪstɪk/ *n* estadística *f*. **~al** *adj* estadístico. **~s** *n* (*science*) estadística *f*

statue /ˈstætʃuː/ *n* estatua *f*

stature /ˈstætʃə(r)/ *n* talla *f*, estatura *f*

status /ˈsteɪtəs/ *n* posición *f* social; (*prestige*) categoría *f*; (*Jurid*) estado *m*

statut|e /ˈstætʃuːt/ *n* estatuto *m*. **~ory** /-ʊtrɪ/ *adj* estatutario

staunch /stɔːnʃ/ *adj* (**-er**, **-est**) leal

stave /ˈsteɪv/ *n* (*Mus*) pentagrama *m*. □ **~ off** *vt* evitar

stay /steɪ/ *n* (*of time*) estancia *f*, estadía *f* (*LAm*); (*Jurid*) suspensión *f*. • *vi* quedarse; (*reside*) alojarse. **I'm ~ing in a hotel** estoy en un hotel. □ **~ in** *vi* quedarse en casa. □ **~ up** *vi* quedarse levantado

stead /sted/ *n*. **in s.o.'s ~** en lugar de uno. **stand s.o. in good ~** resultarle muy útil a uno. **~ily** *adv* firmemente; (*regularly*) regularmente. **~y** *adj* (**-ier**, **-iest**) firme; (*regular*) regular; (flow) continuo; (worker) serio

steak /steɪk/ *n*. **a ~** un filete. **some ~** carne para guisar

steal /stiːl/ *vt* (*pt* **stole**, *pp* **stolen**) robar. **~ in** *vi* entrar a hurtadillas

stealth /stelθ/ *n*. **by ~** sigilosamente. **~y** *adj* sigiloso

steam /stiːm/ *n* vapor *m*. **let off ~** (*fig*) desahogarse. • *vt* (*cook*) cocer al vapor. • *vi* echar vapor. □ **~ up** *vi* empañarse. **~ engine** *n* máquina *f* de vapor. **~er** *n* (*ship*) barco *m* de vapor. **~roller** *n* apisonadora *f.* ~**y** *adj* lleno de vapor

steel /sti:l/ *n* acero *m.* ● *vt.* ~ **o.s.** armarse de valor. ~ **industry** *n* industria *f* siderúrgica

steep /sti:p/ ● *adj* (**-er, -est**) empinado; (increase) considerable; (price) ⊡ excesivo

steeple /'sti:pl/ *n* aguja *f*, campanario *m*

steeply /'sti:plɪ/ *adv* abruptamente; (increase) considerablemente

steer /stɪə(r)/ *vt* dirigir; gobernar (ship). ● *vi* (*in ship*) estar al timón. ~ **clear of** evitar. ~**ing** *n* (*Auto*) dirección *f.* ~**ing wheel** *n* volante *m*

stem /stem/ *n* (*of plant*) tallo *m*; (*of glass*) pie *m*; (*of word*) raíz *f.* ● *vt* (*pt* **stemmed**) contener (bleeding). ● *vi.* ~ **from** provenir de

stench /stentʃ/ *n* hedor *m*

stencil /'stensl/ *n* plantilla *f*

stenographer /ste'nɒgrəfə(r)/ *n* estenógrafo *m*

step /step/ *vi* (*pt* **stepped**). ~ **in sth** pisar algo. □ ~ **aside** *vi* hacerse a un lado. □ ~ **down** *vi* retirarse. □ ~ **in** *vi* (*fig*) intervenir. □ ~ **up** *vt* intensificar; redoblar (security). ● *n* paso *m*; (*stair*) escalón *m*; (*fig*) medida *f.* **take** ~**s** tomar medidas. **be in** ~ llevar el paso. **be out of** ~ no llevar el paso. ~**brother** *n* hermanastro *m.* ~**daughter** *n* hijastra *f.* ~**father** *n* padrastro *m.* ~**ladder** *n* escalera *f* de tijera. ~**mother** *n* madrastra *f.* ~**ping-stone** *n* peldaño *m.* ~**sister** *n* hermanastra *f.* ~**son** *n* hijastro *m*

stereo /'sterɪəʊ/ *n* (*pl* **-os** estéreo *m.* ● *adj* estéreo *a invar.* ~**type** *n* estereotipo *m*

steril|e /'steraɪl/ *adj* estéril. ~**ize** /'sterɪlaɪz/ *vt* esterilizar

sterling /'stɜ:lɪŋ/ *n* libras *fpl* esterlinas. ● *adj* (pound) esterlina

stern /stɜ:n/ *n* (*of boat*) popa *f.* ● *adj* (**-er, -est**) severo

stethoscope /'steθəskəʊp/ *n* estetoscopio *m*

stew /stju:/ *vt/i* guisar. ● *n* estofado *m*, guiso *m*

steward /'stjʊu:əd/ *n* administrador *m*; (*on ship*) camarero *m*; (*air steward*) sobrecargo *m*, aeromozo *m* (*LAm*). ~**ess** /-'des/ *n* camarera *f*; (*on aircraft*) auxiliar *f* de vuelo, azafata *f*

stick /stɪk/ *n* palo *m*; (*for walking*) bastón *m*; (*of celery etc*) tallo *m.* ● *vt* (*pt* **stuck**) (*glue*) pegar; (*fam, put*) poner; (*thrust*) clavar; (*fam, endure*) soportar. ● *vi* pegarse; (*jam*) atascarse. □ ~ **out** *vi* sobresalir. □ ~ **to** *vt* ceñirse a. □ ~ **up for** *vt* ⊡ defender. ~**er** *n* pegatina *f.* ~**ing plaster** *n* esparadrapo *m*; (*individual*) tirita *f*, curita *f* (*LAm*). ~**ler** /'stɪklə(r)/ *n.* **be a** ~**ler for** insistir en. ~**y** /'stɪkɪ/ *adj* (**-ier, -iest**) (surface) pegajoso; (label) engomado

stiff /stɪf/ *adj* (**-er, -est**) rígido; (joint, fabric) tieso; (muscle) entumecido; (*difficult*) difícil; (manner) estirado; (drink) fuerte. **have a** ~ **neck** tener tortícolis. ~**en** *vi* (*become rigid*) agarrotarse; (*become firm*) endurecerse. ~**ly** *adv* rígidamente

stifl|e /'staɪfl/ *vt* sofocar. ~**ing** *adj* sofocante

stiletto (heel) /stɪ'letəʊ/ *n* (*pl* **-os**) tacón *m* de aguja

still /stɪl/ *adj* inmóvil; (*peaceful*) tranquilo; (drink) sin gas. **sit** ~, **stand** ~ quedarse tranquilo. ● *adv* todavía, aún; (*nevertheless*) sin embargo. **~born** *adj* nacido muerto. **~ life** *n* (*pl* **-s**) bodegón *m*. **~ness** *n* tranquilidad *f*

stilted /'stɪltɪd/ *adj* rebuscado; (conversation) forzado

stilts /stɪlts/ *npl* zancos *mpl*

stimul|ant /'stɪmjʊlənt/ *n* estimulante *m*. **~ate** /-leɪt/ *vt* estimular. **~ation** /-'leɪʃn/ *n* estímulo *m*. **~us** /-əs/ *n* (*pl* **-li** /-laɪ/) estímulo *m*

sting /stɪŋ/ *n* picadura *f*; (*organ*) aguijón *m*. ● *vt/i* (*pt* **stung**) picar

stingy /'stɪndʒɪ/ *adj* (**-ier**, **-iest**) tacaño

stink /stɪŋk/ *n* hedor *m*. ● *vi* (*pt* **stank** *or* **stunk**, *pp* **stunk**) apestar, oler mal

stipulat|e /'stɪpjʊleɪt/ *vt/i* estipular. **~ion** /-'leɪʃn/ *n* estipulación *f*

stir /stɜ:(r)/ *vt* (*pt* **stirred**) remover, revolver; (*move*) agitar; estimular (imagination). ● *vi* moverse. **~ up trouble** armar lío [I]. ● *n* revuelo *m*, conmoción *f*

stirrup /'stɪrəp/ *n* estribo *m*

stitch /stɪtʃ/ *n* (*in sewing*) puntada *f*; (*in knitting*) punto *m*; (*pain*) dolor *m* costado. **be in ~es** [I] desternillarse de risa. ● *vt* coser

S **stock** /stɒk/ *n* (*Com, supplies*) existencias *fpl*; (*Com, variety*) surtido *m*; (*livestock*) ganado *m*; (*Culin*) caldo *m*. **~s and shares**, **~s and bonds** (*Amer*) acciones *fpl*. **out of ~** agotado. **take ~ of sth** (*fig*) hacer un balance de algo. ● *adj* estándar *a invar*; (*fig*) trillado. ● *vt* surtir, abastecer (**with** de). □ **~ up** *vi* abastecerse (**with** de). **~broker** /-brəʊkə(r)/ *n* corredor *m* de bolsa. **S~ Exchange** *n* bolsa *f*. **~ing** *n* media *f*. **~pile** *n* reservas *fpl*. ● *vt* almacenar. **~-still** *adj* inmóvil. **~-taking** *n* (*Com*) inventario *m*. **~y** *adj* (**-ier**, **-iest**) bajo y fornido

stodgy /'stɒdʒɪ/ (**-dgier**, **-dgiest**) *adj* pesado

stoke /stəʊk/ *vt* echarle carbón (*or* leña) a

stole /stəʊl/ *see* **STEAL**

stolen /'stəʊlən/ *see* **STEAL**

stomach /'stʌmək/ *n* estómago *m*. ● *vt* soportar. **~-ache** *n* dolor *m* de estómago

ston|e /stəʊn/ *n* piedra *f*; (*in fruit*) hueso *m*; (*weight*, *pl* **stone**) unidad de peso equivalente a 14 libras o 6,35 kg. ● *adj* de piedra. ● *vt* apedrear. **~e-deaf** *adj* sordo como una tapia. **~y** *adj* (silence) sepulcral

stood /stʊd/ *see* **STAND**

stool /stu:l/ *n* taburete *m*

stoop /stu:p/ *vi* agacharse; (*fig*) rebajarse. ● *n*. **have a ~** ser cargado de espaldas

stop /stɒp/ *vt* (*pt* **stopped**) (*halt, switch off*) parar; (*cease*) terminar; (*prevent*) impedir; (*interrupt*) interrumpir. **~ doing sth** dejar de hacer algo. **~ it!** ¡basta ya! ● *vi* (bus) parar, detenerse; (clock) pararse. **it's ~ped raining** ha dejado de llover. ● *n* (*bus etc*) parada *f*; (*break on journey*) parada *f*. **put a ~ to sth** poner fin a algo. **come to a ~** detenerse. **~gap** *n* remedio *m* provisional. **~over** *n* escala *f*. **~page** /'stɒpɪdʒ/ *n* suspensión *f*, paradero *m* (*LAm*); (*of work*) huelga *f*, paro *m* (*LAm*); (*interruption*) interrupción *f*. **~per** *n* tapón *m*. **~watch** *n* cronómetro *m*

storage /'stɔ:rɪdʒ/ *n* almacenamiento *m*

store /stɔ:(r)/ *n* provisión *f*; (*depot*) almacén *m*; (*Amer, shop*) tienda *f*; (*fig*) reserva *f*. **in ~** en reserva. ●*vt* (*for future*) poner en reserva; (*in warehouse*) almacenar. □ **~ up** *vt* (*fig*) ir acumulando. **~keeper** *n* (*Amer*) tendero *m*, comerciante *m & f*. **~room** *n* almacén *m*; (*for food*) despensa *f*

storey /ˈstɔːrɪ/ *n* (*pl* **-eys**) piso *m*, planta *f*

stork /stɔːk/ *n* cigüeña *f*

storm /stɔːm/ *n* tempestad *f*. ●*vi* rabiar. ●*vt* (*Mil*) asaltar. **~y** *adj* tormentoso; (sea, relationship) tempestuoso

story /ˈstɔːrɪ/ *n* historia *f*; (*in newspaper*) artículo *m*; (*rumour*) rumor *m*; (🅘, *lie*) mentira *f*, cuento *m*. **~-teller** *n* cuentista *m & f*

stout /staʊt/ *adj* (**-er**, **-est**) robusto, corpulento. ●*n* cerveza *f* negra

stove /stəʊv/ *n* estufa *f*

stow /stəʊ/ *vt* guardar; (*hide*) esconder. □ **~ away** *vi* viajar de polizón. **~away** *n* polizón *m & f*

straggl|e /ˈstrægl/ *vi* rezagarse. **~y** *adj* desordenado

straight /streɪt/ *adj* (**-er**, **-est**) recto; (*tidy*) en orden; (*frank*) franco; (hair) lacio; (🅘, *conventional*) convencional. **be ~** estar derecho. ●*adv* (sit up) derecho; (*direct*) directamente; (*without delay*) inmediatamente. **~ away** en seguida, inmediatamente. **~ on** todo recto. **~ out** sin rodeos. ●*n* recta *f*. **~en** *vt* enderezar. □ **~en up** *vt* ordenar. **~forward** /-ˈfɔːwəd/ *adj* franco; (*easy*) sencillo

strain /streɪn/ *n* (*tension*) tensión *f*; (*injury*) torcedura *f*. ●*vt* forzar (voice, eyesight); someter a demasiada tensión (relations); (*sieve*) colar. **~ one's back** hacerse daño en la espalda. **~ a muscle** hacerse un esguince. **~ed** *adj* forzado; (relations) tirante. **~er** *n* colador *m*. **~s** *npl* (*Mus*) acordes *mpl*

strait /streɪt/ *n* estrecho *m*. **be in dire ~s** estar en grandes apuros. **~jacket** *n* camisa *f* de fuerza

strand /strænd/ *n* (*thread*) hebra *f*. **a ~ of hair** un pelo. ●*vt*. **be ~ed** (ship) quedar encallado. **I was left ~ed** me abandonaron a mi suerte

strange /streɪndʒ/ *adj* (**-er**, **-est**) raro, extraño; (*not known*) desconocido. **~ly** *adv* de una manera rara. **~ly enough** aunque parezca mentira. **~r** *n* desconocido *m*; (*from another place*) forastero *m*

strangle /ˈstræŋgl/ *vt* estrangular

strap /stræp/ *n* correa *f*; (*of garment*) tirante *m*. ●*vt* (*pt* **strapped**) atar con una correa

strat|egic /strəˈtiːdʒɪk/ *adj* estratégico. **~egy** /ˈstrætədʒɪ/ *n* estrategia *f*

straw /strɔː/ *n* paja *f*; (*drinking* **~**) pajita *f*, paja *f*, popote *m* (*Mex*). **the last ~** el colmo. **~berry** /-bərɪ/ *n* fresa *f*; (*large*) fresón *m*

stray /streɪ/ *vi* (*wander away*) apartarse; (*get lost*) extraviarse; (*deviate*) desviarse (**from** de). ●*adj* (animal) (*without owner*) callejero; (*lost*) perdido. ●*n* (*without owner*) perro *m*/gato *m* callejero; (*lost*) perro *m*/gato *m* perdido

streak /striːk/ *n* lista *f*, raya *f*; (*in hair*) reflejo *m*; (*in personality*) veta *f*

stream /striːm/ *n* arroyo *m*; (*current*) corriente *f*. **a ~ of abuse** una sarta de insultos. ●*vi* correr. □ **~ out** *vi* (people) salir en tropel. **~er** *n* (*paper*) serpentina *f*; (*banner*) banderín *m*. **~line** *vt* dar línea aerodinámica a; (*simplify*) racionalizar. **~lined** *adj* aerodinámico

street /stri:t/ *n* calle *f*. **~car** *n* (*Amer*) tranvía *m*. **~ lamp** *n* farol *m*. **~ map**, **~ plan** *n* plano *m*

strength /streŋθ/ *n* fuerza *f*; (*of wall etc*) solidez *f*. **~en** *vt* reforzar (wall); fortalecer (muscle)

strenuous /'strenjʊəs/ *adj* enérgico; (*arduous*) arduo; (*tiring*) fatigoso

stress /stres/ *n* énfasis *f*; (*Gram*) acento *m*; (*Mec, Med, tension*) tensión *f*. • *vt* insistir en

stretch /stretʃ/ *vt* estirar; (*extend*) extender; forzar (truth); estirar (resources). • *vi* estirarse; (*when sleepy*) desperezarse; (*extend*) extenderse; (*be elastic*) estirarse. • *n* (*period*) período *m*; (*of road*) tramo *m*. **at a ~** sin parar. □ **~ out** *vi* (person) tenderse. **~er** *n* camilla *f*

strict /strɪkt/ *adj* (**-er**, **-est**) estricto; (secrecy) absoluto. **~ly** *adv* con severidad; (rigorously) terminantemente. **~ly speaking** en rigor

stridden /strɪdn/ *see* STRIDE

stride /straɪd/ *vi* (*pt* **strode**, *pp* **stridden**) andar a zancadas. • *n* zancada *f*. **take sth in one's ~** tomarse algo con calma. **~nt** /'straɪdnt/ *adj* estridente

strife /straɪf/ *n* conflicto *m*

strike /straɪk/ *vt* (*pt* **struck**) golpear; encender (match); encontrar (gold, oil); (clock) dar. **it ~s me as odd** me parece raro. • *vi* golpear; (*go on strike*) declararse en huelga; (*be on strike*) estar en huelga; (*attack*) atacar; (clock) dar la hora. • *n* (*of workers*) huelga *f*, paro *m*; (*attack*) ataque *m*. **come out on ~** ir a la huelga. □ **~ off**, **~ out** *vt* tachar. **~ up a friendship** trabar amistad. **~r** *n* huelguista *m & f*; (*Sport*) artillero *m*

striking /'straɪkɪŋ/ *adj* (resemblance) sorprendente; (colour) llamativo

string /strɪŋ/ *n* cordel *m*, mecate *m* (*Mex*); (*Mus*) cuerda *f*; (*of lies, pearls*) sarta *f*; (*of people*) sucesión *f*. □ **~ along** *vt* [I] engañar

stringent /'strɪndʒənt/ *adj* riguroso

strip /strɪp/ *vt* (*pt* **stripped**) desnudar (person); deshacer (bed). • *vi* desnudarse. • *n* tira *f*; (*of land*) franja *f*. **~ cartoon** *n* historieta *f*

stripe /straɪp/ *n* raya *f*. **~d** *adj* a rayas, rayado

strip lighting *n* luz *f* fluorescente

strive /straɪv/ *vi* (*pt* **strove**, *pp* **striven**). **~ to** esforzarse por

strode /strəʊd/ *see* STRIDE

stroke /strəʊk/ *n* golpe *m*; (*in swimming*) brazada *f*; (*Med*) ataque *m* de apoplejía; (*of pen etc*) trazo *m*; (*of clock*) campanada *f*; (*caress*) caricia *f*. **a ~ of luck** un golpe de suerte. • *vt* acariciar

stroll /strəʊl/ *vi* pasearse. • *n* paseo *m*. **~er** *n* (*Amer*) sillita *f* de paseo, cochecito *m*

strong /strɒŋ/ *adj* (**-er**, **-est**) fuerte. **~hold** *n* fortaleza *f*; (*fig*) baluarte *m*. **~ly** *adv* (*greatly*) fuertemente; (protest) enérgicamente; (*deeply*) profundamente. **~room** *n* cámara *f* acorazada

strove /strəʊv/ *see* STRIVE

struck /strʌk/ *see* STRIKE

structur|al /'strʌktʃərəl/ *adj* estructural. **~e** /'strʌktʃə(r)/ *n* estructura *f*

struggle /'strʌgl/ *vi* luchar; (*thrash around*) forcejear. • *n* lucha *f*

strum /strʌm/ *vt* (*pt* **strummed**)

rasguear

strung /strʌŋ/ *see* STRING

strut /strʌt/ *n* (*in building*) puntal *m*. ● *vi* (*pt* **strutted**) pavonearse

stub /stʌb/ *n* (*of pencil, candle*) cabo *m*; (*counterfoil*) talón *m*; (*of cigarette*) colilla. □ ~ **out** (*pt* **stubbed**) *vt* apagar

stubble /'stʌbl/ *n* rastrojo *m*; (*beard*) barba *f* de varios días

stubborn /'stʌbən/ *adj* terco

stuck /stʌk/ *see* STICK. ● *adj*. **the drawer is** ~ el cajón se ha atascado. **the door is** ~ la puerta se ha atrancado. ~**-up** *adj* 🅸 estirado

stud /stʌd/ *n* tachuela *f*; (*for collar*) gemelo *m*.

student /'stju:dənt/ *n* estudiante *m & f*; (*at school*) alumno *m*. ~ **driver** *n* (*Amer*) persona que está aprendiendo a conducir

studio /'stju:dɪəʊ/ *n* (*pl* **-os**) estudio *m*. ~ **apartment**, ~ **flat** *n* estudio *m*

studious /'stju:dɪəs/ *adj* estudioso

study /'stʌdɪ/ *n* estudio *m*. ● *vt/i* estudiar

stuff /stʌf/ *n* 🅸 cosas *fpl*. **what's this** ~ **called?** ¿cómo se llama esta cosa?. ● *vt* rellenar; disecar (animal); (*cram*) atiborrar; (*put*) meter de prisa. ~ **o.s.** 🅸 darse un atracón. ~**ing** *n* relleno *m*. ~**y** *adj* (**-ier, -iest**) mal ventilado; (*old-fashioned*) acartonado. **it's** ~**y in here** está muy cargado el ambiente

stumbl|e /'stʌmbl/ *vi* tropezar. ~**e across**, ~**e on** *vt* dar con. ~**ing-block** *n* tropiezo *m*, impedimento *m*

stump /stʌmp/ *n* (*of limb*) muñón *m*; (*of tree*) tocón *m*

stun /stʌn/ *vt* (*pt* **stunned**) (*daze*) aturdir; (*bewilder*) dejar atónito. ~**ning** *adj* sensacional

stung /stʌŋ/ *see* STING

stunk /stʌŋk/ *see* STINK

stunt /stʌnt/ *n* 🅸 ardid *m* publicitario. ● *vt* detener, atrofiar. ~**ed** *adj* (*growth*) atrofiado; (*body*) raquítico. ~**man** *n* especialista *m*. ~**woman** *n* especialista *f*

stupendous /stju:'pendəs/ *adj* estupendo

stupid /'stju:pɪd/ *adj* (*foolish*) tonto; (*unintelligent*) estúpido. ~**ity** /-'pɪdətɪ/ *n* estupidez *f*. ~**ly** *adv* estúpidamente

stupor /'stju:pə(r)/ *n* estupor *m*

sturdy /'stɜ:dɪ/ *adj* (**-ier, -iest**) robusto

stutter /'stʌtə(r)/ *vi* tartamudear. ● *n* tartamudeo *m*

sty /staɪ/ *n* (*pl* **sties**) pocilga *f*; (*Med*) orzuelo *m*

styl|e /staɪl/ *n* estilo *m*; (*fashion*) moda *f*; (*design, type*) diseño *m*. **in** ~ a lo grande. ● *vt* diseñar. ~**ish** *adj* elegante. ~**ist** *n* estilista *m & f*. **hair** ~**ist** estilista *m & f*

stylus /'staɪləs/ *n* (*pl* **-uses**) aguja *f* (de tocadiscos)

suave /swɑ:v/ *adj* elegante y desenvuelto

subconscious /sʌb'kɒnʃəs/ *adj & n* subconsciente (*m*)

subdivide /sʌbdɪ'vaɪd/ *vt* subdividir

subdued /səb'dju:d/ *adj* apagado

subject /'sʌbdʒɪkt/ *adj* sometido. ~ **to** sujeto a. ● *n* (*theme*) tema *m*; (*Schol*) asignatura *f*, materia *f* (*LAm*); (*Gram*) sujeto *m*; (*Pol*) súbdito *m*. ● /səb'dʒekt/ *vt* someter. ~**ive** /səb'dʒektɪv/ *adj* subjetivo

subjunctive /səb'dʒʌŋktɪv/ *adj &*

n subjuntivo (*m*)

sublime /sə'blaɪm/ *adj* sublime

submarine /sʌbmə'ri:n/ *n* submarino *m*

submerge /səb'mɜ:dʒ/ *vt* sumergir. ● *vi* sumergirse

submi|ssion /səb'mɪʃn/ *n* sumisión *f*. **~t** /səb'mɪt/ *vt* (*pt* **submitted**) (*subject*) someter; presentar (application). ● *vi* rendirse

subordinate /sə'bɔ:dɪnət/ *adj & n* subordinado (*m*). ● /sə'bɔ:dɪneɪt/ *vt* subordinar

subscri|be /səb'skraɪb/ *vi* suscribir. **~be to** suscribirse a (magazine). **~ber** *n* suscriptor *m*. **~ption** /-rɪpʃn/ *n* (*to magazine*) suscripción *f*

subsequent /'sʌbsɪkwənt/ *adj* posterior, subsiguiente. **~ly** *adv* posteriormente

subside /səb'saɪd/ *vi* (land) hundirse; (flood) bajar; (storm, wind) amainar. **~nce** /'sʌbsɪdəns/ *n* hundimiento *m*

subsidiary /səb'sɪdɪərɪ/ *adj* secundario; (subject) complementario. ● *n* (*Com*) filial

subsid|ize /'sʌbsɪdaɪz/ *vt* subvencionar, subsidiar (*LAm*). **~y** /'sʌbsədɪ/ *n* subvención *f*, subsidio *m*

substance /'sʌbstəns/ *n* sustancia *f*

substandard /sʌb'stændəd/ *adj* de calidad inferior

substantial /səb'stænʃl/ *adj* (*sturdy*) sólido; (meal) sustancioso; (*considerable*) considerable

substitut|e /'sʌbstɪtju:t/ *n* (*person*) substituto *m*; (*thing*) sucedáneo *m*. ● *vt/i* sustituir. **~ion** /-'tju:ʃn/ *n* sustitución *f*

subterranean /sʌbtə'reɪnjən/ *adj* subterráneo

subtitle /'sʌbtaɪtl/ *n* subtítulo *m*

subtle /'sʌtl/ *adj* (**-er**, **-est**) sutil; (*tactful*) discreto. **~ty** *n* sutileza *f*

subtract /səb'trækt/ *vt* restar. **~ion** /-ʃn/ *n* resta *f*

suburb /'sʌbɜ:b/ *n* barrio *m* residencial de las afueras, colonia *f*. **the ~s** las afueras *fpl*. **~an** /sə'bɜ:bən/ *adj* suburbano. **~ia** /sə'bɜ:bɪə/ *n zonas residenciales de las afueras de una ciudad*

subversive /səb'vɜ:sɪv/ *adj* subversivo

subway /'sʌbweɪ/ *n* paso *m* subterráneo; (*Amer*) metro *m*

succeed /sək'si:d/ *vi* (plan) dar resultado; (person) tener éxito. **~ in doing** lograr hacer. ● *vt* suceder

success /sək'ses/ *n* éxito *m*. **~ful** *adj* (person) de éxito, exitoso (*LAm*). **the ~ful applicant** el candidato que obtenga el puesto. **~fully** *adj* satisfactoriamente. **~ion** /-ʃn/ *n* sucesión *f*. **for 3 years in ~ion** durante tres años consecutivos. **in rapid ~ion** uno tras otro. **~ive** *adj* sucesivo. **~or** *n* sucesor *m*

succulent /'sʌkjʊlənt/ *adj* suculento

succumb /sə'kʌm/ *vi* sucumbir

such /sʌtʃ/ *adj* tal (+ *noun*), tan (+ *adj*). **~ a big house** una casa tan grande. ● *pron* tal. **~ and ~** tal o cual. **~ as** como. **~ as it is** tal como es

suck /sʌk/ *vt* chupar (sweet, thumb); sorber (liquid). □ **~ up** *vt* (vacuum cleaner) aspirar; (pump) succionar. □ **~ up to** *vt* [F] dar coba a. **~er** *n* (*plant*) chupón *m*; (*fam, person*) imbécil *m*

suckle /sʌkl/ *vt* amamantar

suction /'sʌkʃn/ *n* succión *f*

S

sudden /'sʌdn/ *adj* repentino. **all of a ~** de repente. **~ly** *adv* de repente

suds /sʌds/ *npl* espuma *f* de jabón

sue /su:/ *vt* (*pres p* **suing**) demandar (**for** por)

suede /sweɪd/ *n* ante *m*

suet /'su:ɪt/ *n* sebo *m*

suffer /'sʌfə(r)/ *vt* sufrir; (*tolerate*) aguantar. ● *vi* sufrir; (*be affected*) resentirse

suffic|e /sə'faɪs/ *vi* bastar. **~ient** /sə'fɪʃnt/ *adj* suficiente, bastante. **~iently** *adv* (lo) suficientemente

suffix /'sʌfɪks/ *n* (*pl* **-ixes**) sufijo *m*

suffocat|e /'sʌfəkeɪt/ *vt* asfixiar. ● *vi* asfixiarse. **~ion** /-'keɪʃn/ *n* asfixia *f*

sugar /'ʃʊgə(r)/ *n* azúcar *m* & *f*. **~ bowl** *n* azucarero *m*. **~y** *adj* azucarado.

suggest /sə'dʒest/ *vt* sugerir. **~ion** /-tʃən/ *n* sugerencia *f*

suicid|al /su:ɪ'saɪdl/ *adj* suicida. **~e** /'su:ɪsaɪd/ *n* suicidio *m*. **commit ~e** suicidarse

suit /su:t/ *n* traje *m*; (*woman's*) traje *m* de chaqueta; (*Cards*) palo *m*; (*Jurid*) pleito *m*. ● *vt* venirle bien a, convenirle a; (clothes) quedarle bien a; (*adapt*) adaptar. **be ~ed to** (thing) ser apropiado para. **I'm not ~ed to this kind of work** no sirvo para este tipo de trabajo. **~able** *adj* apropiado, adecuado. **~ably** *adv* (dressed) apropiadamente; (qualified) adecuadamente. **~case** *n* maleta *f*, valija *f* (*LAm*)

suite /swi:t/ *n* (*of furniture*) juego *m*; (*of rooms*) suite *f*

sulk /sʌlk/ *vi* enfurruñarse

sullen /'sʌlən/ *adj* hosco

sulphur /'sʌlfə(r)/ *n* azufre *m*. **~ic acid** /sʌl'fjʊərɪk/ *n* ácido *m* sulfúrico

sultan /'sʌltən/ *n* sultán *m*

sultana /sʌl'tɑ:nə/ *n* pasa *f* de Esmirna

sultry /'sʌltrɪ/ *adj* (**-ier**, **-iest**) (weather) bochornoso; (*fig*) sensual

sum /sʌm/ *n* (*of money*) suma *f*, cantidad *f*; (*Math*) suma *f*. ● □ **~ up** (*pt* **summed**) *vt* resumir. ● *vi* recapitular

summar|ily /'sʌmərɪlɪ/ *adv* sumariamente. **~ize** *vt* resumir. **~y** *n* resumen *m*

summer /'sʌmə(r)/ *n* verano *m*. **~ camp** *n* (*in US*) colonia *f* de vacaciones. **~time** *n* verano *m*. **~y** *adj* veraniego

> **i** **summer camp** En EE.UU., es el campamento de verano, aspecto muy importante en la vida de muchos niños. Las actividades al aire libre se practican en un ambiente natural entre las que se incluyen natación, montañismo, supervivencia al aire libre. En estos campamentos miles de estudiantes trabajan como supervisores.

summit /'sʌmɪt/ *n* (*of mountain*) cumbre *f*. **~ conference** *n* conferencia *f* cumbre

summon /'sʌmən/ *vt* llamar; convocar (meeting, s.o. to meeting); (*Jurid*) citar. □ **~ up** *vt* armarse de. **~s** *n* (*Jurid*) citación *f*. ● *vt* citar

sumptuous /'sʌmptjʊəs/ *adj* suntuoso

sun /sʌn/ *n* sol *m*. **~bathe** *vi* tomar el sol, asolearse (*LAm*). **~beam** *n* rayo *m* de sol. **~burn** *n* quemadura *f* de sol. **~burnt** *adj* quemado por el sol

Sunday /'sʌndeɪ/ *n* domingo *m*

sunflower /ˈsʌnflaʊə(r)/ *n* girasol *m*

sung /sʌŋ/ *see* SING

sunglasses /ˈsʌnglɑːsɪz/ *npl* gafas *fpl* de sol, lentes *mpl* de sol (*LAm*)

sunk /sʌŋk/ *see* SINK. **~en** /ˈsʌŋkən/ ● *adj* hundido

sun: ~light *n* luz *f* del sol. **~ny** *adj* (**-ier**, **-iest**) (day) de sol; (*place*) soleado. **it is ~ny** hace sol. **~rise** *n*. **at ~rise** al amanecer. salida *f* del sol. **~roof** *n* techo *m* corredizo. **~set** *n* puesta *f* del sol. **~shine** *n* sol *m*. **~stroke** *n* insolación *f*. **~tan** *n* bronceado *m*. **get a ~tan** broncearse. **~tan lotion** *n* bronceador *m*

super /ˈsuːpə(r)/ *adj* [I] genial, super *a invar*

superb /suːˈpɜːb/ *adj* espléndido

supercilious /suːpəˈsɪlɪəs/ *adj* desdeñoso

superficial /suːpəˈfɪʃl/ *adj* superficial

superfluous /suːˈpɜːflʊəs/ *adj* superfluo

superhighway /ˈsuːpəhaɪweɪ/ *n* (*Amer, Auto*) autopista *f*; (*Comp*) **information ~** autopista *f* de la comunicación

superhuman /suːpəˈhjuːmən/ *adj* sobrehumano

superintendent /suːpərɪn ˈtendənt/ *n* director *m*; (*Amer, of building*) portero *m*; (*of police*) comisario *m*; (*in US*) superintendente *m & f*

superior /suːˈpɪərɪə(r)/ *adj & n* superior (*m*). **~ity** /-ˈɒrətɪ/ *n* superioridad *f*

superlative /suːˈpɜːlətɪv/ *adj* inigualable. ● *n* superlativo *m*

supermarket /ˈsuːpəmɑːkɪt/ *n* supermercado *m*

supernatural /suːpəˈnætʃrəl/ *adj* sobrenatural

superpower /ˈsuːpəpaʊə(r)/ *n* superpotencia *f*

supersede /suːpəˈsiːd/ *vt* reemplazar, sustituir

supersonic /suːpəˈsɒnɪk/ *adj* supersónico

superstitio|n /suːpəˈstɪʃn/ *n* superstición *f*. **~us** *adj* /-əs/ supersticioso

supervis|e /ˈsuːpəvaɪz/ *vt* supervisar. **~ion** /-ˈvɪʒn/ *n* supervisión *f*. **~or** *n* supervisor *m*

supper /ˈsʌpə(r)/ *n* cena *f* (*ligera*), comida *f* (*ligera*) (*LAm*)

supple /sʌpl/ *adj* flexible

supplement /ˈsʌplɪmənt/ *n* suplemento *m*; (*to diet, income*) complemento *m*. ● *vt* complementar (diet, income). **~ary** /-ˈmentərɪ/ *adj* suplementario

suppl|ier /səˈplaɪə(r)/ *n* (*Com*) proveedor *m*. **~y** /səˈplaɪ/ *vt* suministrar; proporcionar (information). **~y s.o. with sth** (equipment) proveer a uno de algo; (*in business*) abastecer a uno de algo. ● *n* suministro *m*. **~y and demand** oferta *f* y demanda. **~ies** *npl* provisiones *mpl*, víveres *mpl*; (*Mil*) pertrechos *mpl*. **office ~ies** artículos *mpl* de oficina

support /səˈpɔːt/ *vt* (*hold up*) sostener; (*back*) apoyar; mantener (family). ● *n* apoyo *m*; (*Tec*) soporte *m*. **~er** *n* partidario *m*; (*Sport*) hincha *m & f*

suppos|e /səˈpəʊz/ *vt* suponer, imaginarse; (*think*) creer. **I'm ~ed to start work at nine** se supone que tengo que empezar a trabajar a las nueve. **~edly** *adv* supuestamente. **~ition** /sʌpəˈzɪʃn/ *n* suposición *f*

suppress /sə'pres/ *vt* reprimir (feelings); sofocar (rebellion). **~ion** /-ʃn/*n* represión *f*

suprem|acy /suː'preməsɪ/ *n* supremacía *f.* **~e** /suː'priːm/ *adj* supremo

sure /ʃʊə(r)/ *adj* (**-er**, **-est**) seguro. **make ~ that** asegurarse de que. ● *adv* ¡claro!. **~ly** *adv* (*undoubtedly*) seguramente; (*gladly*) desde luego. **~ly you don't believe that!** ¡no te creerás eso! **~ty** /-ətɪ/ *n* garantía *f*

surf /sɜːf/ *n* oleaje *m*; (*foam*) espuma *f.* ● *vi* hacer surf. ● *vt* (*Comp*) surfear, navegar

surface /'sɜːfɪs/ *n* superficie *f.* ● *adj* superficial. ● *vt* recubrir (**with** de). ● *vi* salir a la superficie; (problems) aflorar

surfboard /'sɜːfbɔːd/ *n* tabla *f* de surf

surfeit /'sɜːfɪt/ *n* exceso *m*

surf: ~er *n* surfista *m* & *f*; (*Internet*) navegador *m*. **~ing** *n* surf *m*

surge /sɜːdʒ/ *vi* (crowd) moverse en tropel; (sea) hincharse. ● *n* oleada *f*; (*in demand, sales*) aumento *m*

surg|eon /'sɜːdʒən/ *n* cirujano *m*. **~ery** *n* cirugía *f*; (*consulting room*) consultorio *m*; (*consulting hours*) consulta *f*. **~ical** *adj* quirúrgico

surly /'sɜːlɪ/ *adj* (**-ier**, **-iest**) hosco

surmise /sə'maɪz/ *vt* conjeturar

surmount /sə'maʊnt/ *vt* superar

surname /'sɜːneɪm/ *n* apellido *m*

surpass /sə'pɑːs/ *vt* superar

surplus /'sɜːpləs/ *adj* & *n* excedente (*m*)

surpris|e /sə'praɪz/ *n* sorpresa *f.* ● *vt* sorprender. **~ed** *adj* sorprendido. **~ing** *adj* sorprendente. **~ingly** *adv* sorprendentemente

surrender /sə'rendə(r)/ *vt* entregar. ● *vi* rendirse. ● *n* rendición *f*

surreptitious /sʌrəp'tɪʃəs/ *adj* furtivo

surround /sə'raʊnd/ *vt* rodear; (*Mil*) rodear, cercar. **~ing** *adj* circundante. **~ings** *npl* alrededores *mpl*; (*environment*) ambiente *m*

surveillance /sɜː'veɪləns/ *n* vigilancia *f*

survey /'sɜːveɪ/ *n* inspección *f*; (*report*) informe *m*; (*general view*) vista *f* general. ● /sə'veɪ/ *vt* inspeccionar; (*measure*) medir; (*look at*) contemplar. **~or** *n* topógrafo *m*, agrimensor *m*; (*of building*) perito *m*

surviv|al /sə'vaɪvl/ *n* supervivencia *f.* **~e** /sə'vaɪv/ *vt/i* sobrevivir. **~or** *n* superviviente *m* & *f*

susceptible /sə'septəbl/ *adj*. **~ to** propenso a

suspect /sə'spekt/ *vt* sospechar; sospechar de (person). ● /'sʌspekt/ *adj* & *n* sospechoso (*m*)

suspen|d /sə'spend/ *vt* suspender. **~ders** *npl* (*Amer, braces*) tirantes *mpl*. **~se** /-s/ *n* (*in film etc*) suspense *m*, suspenso *m* (*LAm*). **keep s.o. in ~se** mantener a uno sobre ascuas. **~sion** /-ʃn/ *n* suspensión *f.* **~sion bridge** *n* puente *m* colgante

suspici|on /sə'spɪʃn/ *n* (*belief*) sospecha *f*; (*mistrust*) desconfianza *f*. **~ous** /-ʃəs/ *adj* desconfiado; (*causing suspicion*) sospechoso

sustain /sə'steɪn/ *vt* sostener; mantener (conversation, interest); (*suffer*) sufrir

SW *abbr* (= **south-west**) SO

swab /swɒb/ *n* (*specimen*) muestra *f*, frotis *m*

swagger /ˈswægə(r)/ *vi* pavonearse

swallow /ˈswɒləʊ/ *vt/i* tragar. ● *n* trago *m*; (*bird*) golondrina *f*

swam /swæm/ *see* **SWIM**

swamp /swɒmp/ *n* pantano *m*, ciénaga *f*. ● *vt* inundar. **~y** *adj* pantanoso

swan /swɒn/ *n* cisne *m*

swap /swɒp/ *vt/i* (*pt* **swapped**) intercambiar. **~ sth for sth** cambiar algo por algo. ● *n* cambio *m*

swarm /swɔːm/ *n* enjambre *m*. ● *vi* (bees) enjambrar; (*fig*) hormiguear

swarthy /ˈswɔːðɪ/ *adj* (**-ier**, **-iest**) moreno

swat /swɒt/ *vt* (*pt* **swatted**) matar (*con matamoscas etc*)

sway /sweɪ/ *vi* balancearse; (*gently*) mecerse. ● *vt* (*influence*) influir en

swear /sweə(r)/ *vt/i* (*pt* **swore**, *pp* **sworn**) jurar. **~word** *n* palabrota *f*

sweat /swet/ *n* sudor *m*, transpiración *f*. ● *vi* sudar

sweat|er /ˈswetə(r)/ *n* jersey *m*, suéter *m*. **~shirt** *n* sudadera *f*. **~suit** *n* (*Amer*) chándal *m*, equipo *m* de deportes

S

swede /swiːd/ *n* nabo *m* sueco

Swede /swiːd/ *n* sueco *m*. **~n** /ˈswiːdn/ *n* Suecia *f*. **~ish** *adj* sueco. ● *n* (*language*) sueco *m*. ● *npl*. **the ~** (*people*) los suecos

sweep /swiːp/ *vt* (*pt* **swept**) barrer; deshollinar (chimney). ● *vi* barrer. ● *n* barrido *m*. **~ away** *vt* (*carry away*) arrastrar; (*abolish*) erradicar. **~er** *n* barrendero *m*. **~ing** *adj* (gesture) amplio; (changes) radical; (statement) demasiado general

sweet /swiːt/ *adj* (**-er**, **-est**) dulce; (*fragrant*) fragante; (*pleasant*) agradable; (*kind, gentle*) dulce; (*cute*) rico. **have a ~ tooth** ser dulcero. ● *n* caramelo *m*, dulce *m* (*Mex*); (*dish*) postre *m*. **~en** *vt* endulzar. **~heart** *n* enamorado *m*; (*as form of address*) amor *m*. **~ly** *adv* dulcemente. **~ potato** *n* boniato *m*, batata *f*, camote *m LAm*

swell /swel/ *vt* (*pt* **swelled**, *pp* **swollen** *or* **swelled**) hinchar; (*increase*) aumentar. ● *vi* hincharse; (*increase*) aumentar. ● *adj* (*Amer fam*) fenomenal. ● *n* (*of sea*) oleaje *m*. **~ing** *n* hinchazón *m*

sweltering /ˈsweltərɪŋ/ *vi* sofocante

swept /swept/ *see* **SWEEP**

swerve /swɜːv/ *vi* virar bruscamente

swift /swɪft/ *adj* (**-er**, **-est**) veloz, rápido; (reply) rápido. ● *n* (*bird*) vencejo *m*. **~ly** *adv* rápidamente

swig /swɪg/ *vt* (*pt* **swigged**) 🄸 beber a grandes tragos. ● *n* 🄸 trago *m*

swim /swɪm/ *vi* (*pt* **swam**, *pp* **swum**) nadar. ● *n* baño *m*. **~mer** *n* nadador *m*. **~ming** *n* natación *f*. **~ming bath(s)** *n(pl)* piscina *f* cubierta, alberca *f* techada (*Mex*). **~ming pool** *n* piscina *f*, alberca *f* (*Mex*). **~ming trunks** *npl* bañador *m*, traje *m* de baño **~suit** *n* traje *m* de baño, bañador *m*

swindle /ˈswɪndl/ *vt* estafar. ● *n* estafa *f*. **~r** *n* estafador *m*

swine /swaɪn/ *npl* cerdos *mpl*. ● *n* (*pl* **swine**) (*fam, person*) canalla *m* & *f*. **~ fever** *n* fiebre *f* porcina

swing /swɪŋ/ *vt* (*pt* **swung**) balancear; (*object on rope*) hacer oscilar. ● *vi* (*dangle*) balancearse; (*swing on a swing*) columpiarse; (pendulum) oscilar. ~ **open/shut** abrirse/cerrarse. ●*n* oscilación *f*, vaivén *m*; (*seat*) columpio *m*; (*in opinion*) cambio *m*. **in full** ~ en plena actividad

swipe /swaɪp/ *vt* darle un golpe a; (*fam, snatch*) birlar. ●*n* golpe *m*

Swiss /swɪs/ *adj* suizo (*m*). ●*npl*. **the** ~ los suizos

switch /swɪtʃ/ *n* (*Elec*) interruptor *m*; (*exchange*) intercambio *m*; (*Amer, Rail*) agujas *fpl*. ●*vt* cambiar; (*deviate*) desviar. □ ~ **off** *vt* (*Elec*) apagar (light, TV, heating); desconectar (electricity). □ ~ **on** *vt* encender, prender (*LAm*); arrancar (engine). ~**board** *n* centralita *f*

Switzerland /'swɪtsələnd/ *n* Suiza *f*

swivel /'swɪvl/ *vi* (*pt* **swivelled**) girar. ●*vt* hacer girar

swollen /'swəʊlən/ *see* **SWELL**. ●*adj* hinchado

swoop /swu:p/ *vi* (bird) abatirse; (police) llevar a cabo una redada. ●*n* (*of bird*) descenso *m* en picado *or* (*LAm*) en picada; (*by police*) redada *f*

sword /sɔ:d/ *n* espada *f*

swore /swɔ:(r)/ *see* **SWEAR**

sworn /swɔ:n/ *see* **SWEAR**. ●*adj* (enemy) declarado; (statement) jurado

swot /swɒt/ *vt/i* (*pt* **swotted**) (*Schol, fam*) empollar, estudiar como loco. ●*n* (*Schol, fam*) empollón *m*, matado *m* (*Mex*)

swum /swʌm/ *see* **SWIM**

swung /swʌŋ/ *see* **SWING**

syllable /'sɪləbl/ *n* sílaba *f*

syllabus /'sɪləbəs/ *n* (*pl* **-buses**) plan *m* de estudios; (*of a particular subject*) programa *m*

symbol /'sɪmbl/ *n* símbolo *m*. ~**ic(al)** /-'bɒlɪk(l)/ *adj* simbólico. ~**ism** *n* simbolismo *m*. ~**ize** *vt* simbolizar

symmetr|ical /sɪ'metrɪkl/ *adj* simétrico. ~**y** /'sɪmətrɪ/ *n* simetría *f*

sympath|etic /sɪmpə'θetɪk/ *adj* comprensivo; (*showing pity*) compasivo. ~**ize** /'sɪmpəθaɪz/ *vi* comprender; (*commiserate*) ~**ize with s.o.** compadecer a uno. ~**y** /'sɪmpəθɪ/ *n* comprensión *f*; (*pity*) compasión *f*; (*condolences*) pésame *m*

symphony /'sɪmfənɪ/ *n* sinfonía *f*

symptom /'sɪmptəm/ *n* síntoma *m*. ~**atic** /-'mætɪk/ *adj* sintomático

synagogue /'sɪnəgɒg/ *n* sinagoga *f*

synchronize /'sɪŋkrənaɪz/ *vt* sincronizar

syndicate /'sɪndɪkət/ *n* agrupación *f*; (*Amer, TV*) agencia *f* de distribución periodística

synonym /'sɪnənɪm/ *n* sinónimo *m*. ~**ous** /-'nɒnɪməs/ *adj* sinónimo

syntax /'sɪntæks/ *n* sintaxis *f*

synthesi|s /'sɪnθəsɪs/ *n* (*pl* **-theses** /-si:z/) síntesis *f*. ~**ze** /-aɪz/ *vt* sintetizar

synthetic /sɪn'θetɪk/ *adj* sintético

syringe /'sɪrɪndʒ/ *n* jeringa *f*, jeringuilla *f*

syrup /'sɪrəp/ *n* (*sugar solution*) almíbar *m*; (*with other ingredients*) jarabe *m*; (*medicine*) jarabe *m*

system /'sɪstəm/ *n* sistema *m*, método *m*; (*Tec, Mec, Comp*) sistema *m*. **the digestive** ~ el aparato digestivo. ~**atic** /-ə'mætɪk/ *adj* sistemático. ~**atically** /-ə'mætɪklɪ/ *adv* sistemáticamente. ~**s analyst** *n* analista *m & f* de sistemas

Tt

tab /tæb/ *n* (*flap*) lengüeta *f*; (*label*) etiqueta *f*

table /'teɪbl/ *n* mesa *f*; (*list*) tabla *f*. **~cloth** *n* mantel *m*. **~ mat** *n* salvamanteles *m*. **~spoon** *n* cuchara *f* grande; (*measure*) cucharada *f* (grande)

tablet /'tæblɪt/ *n* pastilla *f*; (*pill*) comprimido *m*

table tennis *n* tenis *m* de mesa, ping-pong *m*

tabloid /'tæblɔɪd/ *n* tabloide *m*

taboo /tə'bu:/ *adj & n* tabú (*m*)

tacit /'tæsɪt/ *adj* tácito

taciturn /'tæsɪtɜ:n/ *adj* taciturno

tack /tæk/ *n* tachuela *f*; (*stitch*) hilván *m*. ● *vt* clavar con tachuelas; (*sew*) hilvanar. ● *vi* (*Naut*) virar □ **~ on** *vt* añadir.

tackle /'tækl/ *n* (*equipment*) equipo *m*; (*soccer*) entrada *f* fuerte; (*US football, Rugby*) placaje *m*. **fishing ~** aparejo *m* de pesca. ● *vt* abordar (problem); (*in soccer*) entrarle a; (*in US football, Rugby*) placar

tacky /'tækɪ/ *adj* pegajoso

tact /tækt/ *n* tacto *m*. **~ful** *adj* diplomático

tactic|al /'tæktɪkl/ *adj* táctico. **~s** *npl* táctica *f*

tactless /'tæktləs/ *adj* indiscreto

tadpole /'tædpəʊl/ *n* renacuajo *m*

tag /tæg/ *n* (*label*) etiqueta *f*. □ **~ along** (*pt* **tagged**) *vt* 🅸 seguir

tail /teɪl/ *n* (*of horse, fish, bird*) cola *f*; (*of dog, pig*) rabo *m*. **~s** *npl* (*tailcoat*) frac *m*; (*of coin*) cruz *f*. ● *vt* seguir. □ **~ off** *vi* disminuir.

tailor /'teɪlə(r)/ *n* sastre *m*. **~ed** /'teɪləd/ *adj* entallado. **~-made** *n* hecho a (la) medida

taint /teɪnt/ *vt* contaminar

take /teɪk/ *vt* (*pt* **took**, *pp* **taken**) tomar, coger (*esp Spain*), agarrar (*esp LAm*); (*capture*) capturar; (*endure*) aguantar; (*require*) requerir; llevar (time); tomar (bath); tomar (medicine); (*carry*) llevar; aceptar (cheque). **I ~ a size 10** uso la talla 14. □ **~ after** *vt* parecerse a. □ **~ away** *vt* llevarse; (*confiscate*) quitar. □ **~ back** *vt* retirar (statement etc). □ **~ in** *vt* achicar (garment); (*understand*) asimilar; (*deceive*) engañar. □ **~ off** *vt* (*remove*) quitar, sacar; quitarse (shoes, jacket); (*mimic*) imitar. *vi* (aircraft) despegar. □ **~ on** *vt* contratar (employee). □ **~ out** *vt* sacar. □ **~ over** *vt* tomar posesión de; hacerse cargo de (job). *vi* (*assume control*) asumir el poder. □ **~ up** *vt* empezar a hacer (hobby); aceptar (challenge); subir (hem); llevar (time); ocupar (space). ● *n* (*Cinema*) toma *f*. **~-off** *n* despegue *m*. **~-over** *n* (*Com*) absorción *f*

takings /'teɪkɪŋz/ *npl* recaudación *f*; (*at box office*) taquilla *f*

talcum powder /'tælkəm/ *n* polvos *mpl* de talco, talco *m* (*LAm*)

tale /teɪl/ *n* cuento *m*

talent /'tælənt/ *n* talento *m*. **~ed** *adj* talentoso

talk /tɔ:k/ *vt/i* hablar. **~ to s.o.** hablar con uno. **~ about** hablar de. ● *n* conversación *f*; (*lecture*) charla *f*. □ **~ over** *vt* discutir. **~ative** /-ətɪv/ *adj* hablador

tall /tɔ:l/ *adj* (**-er**, **-est**) alto. **~ story** *n* 🅸 cuento *m* chino

tally /'tælɪ/ *vi* coincidir (**with** con)

talon /'tælən/ *n* garra *f*

t

tambourine /tæmbəˈriːn/ *n* pandereta *f*

tame /teɪm/ *adj* (**-er**, **-est**) (animal) (*by nature*) manso; (*tamed*) domado. ● *vt* domar (wild animal)

tamper /ˈtæmpə(r)/ *vi*. ~ **with** tocar; (*alter*) alterar, falsificar

tampon /ˈtæmpɒn/ *n* tampón *m*

tan /tæn/ *vi* (*pt* **tanned**) broncearse. ● *n* bronceado *m*. **get a** ~ broncearse. ● *adj* habano

tang /tæŋ/ *n* sabor *m* fuerte

tangent /ˈtændʒənt/ *n* tangente *f*

tangerine /tændʒəˈriːn/ *n* mandarina *f*

tangible /ˈtændʒəbl/ *adj* tangible

tangle /ˈtæŋgl/ *vt* enredar. **get ~d (up)** enredarse. ● *n* enredo *m*, maraña *f*

tango /ˈtæŋgəʊ/ *n* (*pl* **-os**) tango *m*

tank /tæŋk/ *n* depósito *m*; (*Auto*) tanque *m*; (*Mil*) tanque *m*

tanker /ˈtæŋkə(r)/ *n* (*ship*) buque *m* cisterna; (*truck*) camión *m* cisterna

tantrum /ˈtæntrəm/ *n* berrinche *m*, rabieta *f*

tap /tæp/ *n* grifo *m*, llave *f* (*LAm*); (*knock*) golpecito *m*. ● *vt* (*pt* **tapped**) (*knock*) dar un golpecito en; interceptar (phone). ● *vi* dar golpecitos (**on** en). ~ **dancing** *n* claqué *m*

tape /teɪp/ *n* cinta *f*; (*Med*) esparadrapo *m*. ● *vt* (*record*) grabar. **~-measure** *n* cinta *f* métrica

taper /ˈteɪpə(r)/ *vt* afilar. ● *vi* afilarse. □ ~ **off** *vi* disminuir

tape recorder *n* magnetofón *m*, magnetófono *m*

tapestry /ˈtæpɪstrɪ/ *n* tapiz *m*

tar /tɑː(r)/ *n* alquitrán *m*. ● *vt* (*pt* **tarred**) alquitranar

target /ˈtɑːgɪt/ *n* blanco *m*; (*fig*) objetivo *m*

tarmac /ˈtɑːmæk/ *n* pista *f*. **T~** *n* (*Amer*, ®) asfalto *m*

tarnish /ˈtɑːnɪʃ/ *vt* deslustrar; empañar (reputation)

tart /tɑːt/ *n* pastel *m*; (*individual*) pastelillo *m*; (*sl*, *woman*) prostituta *f*, fulana *f* ▣. ● *vt*. ~ **o.s. up** ▣ engalanarse. ● *adj* (**-er**, **-est**) ácido

tartan /ˈtɑːtn/ *n* tartán *m*, tela *f* escocesa

task /tɑːsk/ *n* tarea *f*. **take to** ~ reprender

tassel /ˈtæsl/ *n* borla *f*

tast|e /teɪst/ *n* sabor *m*, gusto *m*; (*liking*) gusto *m*. ● *vt* probar. ● *vi*. **~e of** saber a. **~eful** *adj* de buen gusto. **~eless** *adj* soso; (*fig*) de mal gusto. **~y** *adj* (**-ier**, **-iest**) sabroso

tat /tæt/ *see* TIT FOR TAT

tatter|ed /ˈtætəd/ *adj* hecho jirones. **~s** /ˈtætəz/ *npl* andrajos *mpl*

tattoo /tæˈtuː/ *n* (*on body*) tatuaje *m*. ● *vt* tatuar

tatty /ˈtætɪ/ *adj* (**-ier**, **-iest**) gastado, estropeado

taught /tɔːt/ *see* TEACH

taunt /tɔːnt/ *vt* provocar mediante burlas. ● *n* pulla *f*

Taurus /ˈtɔːrəs/ *n* Tauro *m*

taut /tɔːt/ *adj* tenso

tavern /ˈtævən/ *n* taberna *f*

tax /tæks/ *n* impuesto *m*. ● *vt* imponer contribuciones a (person); gravar (thing); (*strain*) poner a prueba. **~able** *adj* imponible. **~ation** /-ˈseɪʃn/ *n* impuestos *mpl*; (*system*) sistema *m* tributario. ~ **collector** *n* recaudador *m* de impuestos. **~-free** *adj* libre de impuestos

taxi /'tæksɪ/ *n* (*pl* **-is**) taxi *m*. ● *vi* (*pt* **taxied**, *pres p* **taxiing**) (aircraft) rodar por la pista

taxpayer /'tækspeɪə(r)/ *n* contribuyente *m & f*

tea /ti:/ *n* té *m*; (*afternoon tea*) merienda *f*, té *m*. **~ bag** *n* bolsita *f* de té

teach /ti:tʃ/ *vt* (*pt* **taught**) dar clases de, enseñar (subject); dar clase a (person). **~ school** (*Amer*) dar clase(s) en un colegio. ● *vi* dar clase(s). **~er** *n* profesor *m*; (*primary*) maestro *m*. **~ing** *n* enseñanza *f*. ● *adj* docente

tea: ~cup *n* taza *f* de té. **~ leaf** *n* hoja *f* de té

team /ti:m/ *n* equipo *m*. □ **~ up** *vi* asociarse (**with** con). **~ work** *n* trabajo *m* de equipo

teapot /'ti:pɒt/ *n* tetera *f*

tear¹ /teə(r)/ *vt* (*pt* **tore**, *pp* **torn**) romper, rasgar. ● *vi* romperse, rasgarse. ● *n* rotura *f*; (*rip*) desgarrón *m*. □ **~ along** *vi* ir a toda velocidad. □ **~ apart** *vt* desgarrar. □ **~ off**, **~ out** *vt* arrancar. □ **~ up** *vt* romper

tear² /tɪə(r)/ *n* lágrima *f*. **be in ~s** estar llorando. **~ful** *adj* lloroso (farewell) triste. **~ gas** *n* gas *m* lacrimógeno

tease /ti:z/ *vt* tomarle el pelo a

tea: ~ set *n* juego *m* de té. **~spoon** *n* cucharita *f*, cucharilla *f*; (*amount*) cucharadita *f*

teat /ti:t/ *n* (*of animal*) tetilla *f*; (*for bottle*) tetina *f*

tea towel /'ti:taʊəl/ *n* paño *m* de cocina

techni|cal /'teknɪkl/ *adj* técnico. **~cality** *n* /-'kælətɪ/ *n* detalle *m* técnico. **~cally** *adv* técnicamente. **~cian** /tek'nɪʃn/ *n* técnico *m*. **~que** /tek'ni:k/ *n* técnica *f*

technolog|ical /teknə'lɒdʒɪkl/ *adj* tecnológico. **~y** /tek'nɒlədʒɪ/ *n* tecnología *f*

teddy bear /'tedɪ/ *n* osito *m* de peluche

tedi|ous /'ti:dɪəs/ *adj* tedioso. **~um** /'ti:dɪəm/ *n* tedio *m*

teem /ti:m/ *vi* abundar (**with** en), estar repleto (**with** de)

teen|age /'ti:neɪdʒ/ *adj* adolescente; (*for teenagers*) para jóvenes. **~ager** *n* adolescente *m & f*. **~s** /ti:nz/ *npl* adolescencia *f*

teeny /'ti:nɪ/ *adj* (**-ier**, **-iest**) Ⓘ chiquito

teeter /'ti:tə(r)/ *vi* balancearse

teeth /ti:θ/ *see* TOOTH. **~e** /ti:ð/ *vi*. **he's ~ing** le están saliendo los dientes. **~ing troubles** *npl* (*fig*) problemas *mpl* iniciales

tele|communications /telɪkəmju:nɪ'keɪʃnz/ *npl* telecomunicaciones *fpl*. **~gram** /'telɪgræm/ *n* telegrama *m*. **~pathic** /telɪ'pæθɪk/ *adj* telepático. **~pathy** /tə'lepəθɪ/ *n* telepatía *f*

telephon|e /'telɪfəʊn/ *n* teléfono *m*. ● *vt* llamar por teléfono. **~e booth**, **~e box** *n* cabina *f* telefónica. **~e call** *n* llamada *f* telefónica. **~ card** *n* tarjeta *f* telefónica. **~e directory** *n* guía *f* telefónica. **~e exchange** *n* central *f* telefónica. **~ist** /tɪ'lefənɪst/ *n* telefonista *m & f*

tele|sales /'telɪseɪlz/ *npl* televentas *fpl*. **~scope** *n* telescopio *m*. **~scopic** /-'skɒpɪk/ *adj* telescópico. **~text** *n* teletex(to) *m*. **~working** *n* teletrabajo *m*

televis|e /'telɪvaɪz/ *vt* televisar. **~ion** /'telɪvɪʒn/ *n* (*medium*) televisión *f*. **~ion (set)** *n* televisor *m*

telex /'teleks/ *n* télex *m*

tell /tel/ *vt* (*pt* **told**) decir; contar (story, joke); (*distinguish*) distinguir. ~ **the difference** notar la diferencia. ~ **the time** decir la hora. ● *vi* (*produce an effect*) tener efecto; (*know*) saber. □ ~ **off** *vt* regañar. ~**ing** *adj* revelador. ~**-tale** *n* soplón *m*. ● *adj* revelador

telly /'telɪ/ *n* ⓘ tele *f*

temp /temp/ *n* empleado *m* eventual *or* temporal

temper /'tempə(r)/ *n* (*mood*) humor *m*; (*disposition*) carácter *m*; (*fit of anger*) cólera *f*. **be in a** ~ estar furioso. **lose one's** ~ perder los estribos. ~**ament** /'temprəmənt/ *n* temperamento *m*. ~**amental** /-'mentl/ *adj* temperamental. ~**ate** /'tempərət/ *adj* templado. ~**ature** /'temprɪtʃə(r)/ *n* temperatura *f*. **have a** ~**ature** tener fiebre

tempestuous /tem'pestjʊəs/ *adj* tempestuoso

temple /'templ/ *n* templo *m*; (*of head*) sien *f*

tempo /'tempəʊ/ *n* (*pl* **-os** *or* **tempi**) ritmo *m*

temporar|ily /'tempərərəlɪ/ *adv* temporalmente, temporariamente (*LAm*). ~**y** /'tempərərɪ/ *adj* temporal, provisional; (job) eventual, temporal

tempt /tempt/ *vt* tentar. ~**ation** /-'teɪʃn/ *n* tentación *f*. ~**ing** *adj* tentador

ten /ten/ *adj & n* diez (*m*)

tenaci|ous /tɪ'neɪʃəs/ *adj* tenaz. ~**ty** /tɪ'næsətɪ/ *n* tenacidad *f*

tenan|cy /'tenənsɪ/ *n* inquilinato *m*. ~**t** *n* inquilino *m*, arrendatorio *m*

tend /tend/ *vi*. ~ **to** tender a. ● *vt* cuidar (de). ~**ency** /'tendənsɪ/ *n* tendencia *f*

tender /'tendə(r)/ *adj* tierno; (*painful*) sensible. ● *n* (*Com*) oferta *f*. **legal** ~ *n* moneda *f* de curso legal. ● *vt* ofrecer, presentar. ~**ly** *adv* tiernamente

tendon /'tendən/ *n* tendón *m*

tennis /'tenɪs/ *n* tenis *m*

tenor /'tenə(r)/ *n* tenor *m*

tens|e /tens/ *adj* (**-er**, **-est**) (*taut*) tenso, tirante; (person) tenso. ● *n* (*Gram*) tiempo *m*. ~**ion** /'tenʃn/ *n* tensión *f*; (*between two parties*) conflicto *m*

tent /tent/ *n* tienda *f* (de campaña), carpa *f* (*LAm*)

tentacle /'tentəkl/ *n* tentáculo *m*

tentative /'tentətɪv/ *adj* (plan) provisional; (offer) tentativo; (person) indeciso

tenterhooks /'tentəhʊks/ *npl*. **be on** ~ estar en ascuas

tenth /tenθ/ *adj & n* décimo (*m*)

tenuous /'tenjʊəs/ *adj* (claim) poco fundado; (link) indirecto

tenure /'tenjʊə(r)/ *n* tenencia *f*; (*period of office*) ejercicio *m*

tepid /'tepɪd/ *adj* tibio

term /tɜ:m/ *n* (*of time*) período *m*; (*Schol*) trimestre *m*; (*word etc*) término *m*. ~**s** *npl* condiciones *fpl*; (*Com*) precio *m*. **on good**/**bad** ~**s** en buenas/malas relaciones. ● *vt* calificar de

termin|al /'tɜ:mɪnl/ *adj* terminal. ● *n* (*transport*) terminal *f*; (*Comp, Elec*) terminal *m*. ~**ate** /-eɪt/ *vt* poner fin a; poner término a (contract); (*Amer, fire*) despedir. ● *vi* terminarse. ~**ology** /-'nɒlədʒɪ/ *n* terminología *f*

terrace /'terəs/ *n* terraza *f*; (*houses*) hilera *f* de casas

terrain /tə'reɪn/ *n* terreno *m*

terrestrial /tɪ'restrɪəl/ *adj* terrestre

terribl|e /'terəbl/ *adj* espantoso. **~y** *adv* terriblemente

terrif|ic /tə'rɪfɪk/ *adj* (*fam, excellent*) estupendo; (*fam, huge*) enorme. **~ied** /'terɪfaɪd/ *adj* aterrorizado. **~y** /'terɪfaɪ/ *vt* aterrorizar. **~ying** *adj* aterrador

territor|ial /terɪ'tɔːrɪəl/ *adj* territorial. **~y** /'terɪtrɪ/ *n* territorio *m*

terror /'terə(r)/ *n* terror *m*. **~ism** *n* terrorismo *m*. **~ist** *n* terrorista *m & f*. **~ize** *vt* aterrorizar

terse /tɜːs/ *adj* seco, lacónico

test /test/ *n* (*of machine, drug*) prueba *f*; (*exam*) prueba *f*, test *m*; (*of blood*) análisis *m*; (*for eyes, hearing*) examen *m*. ● *vt* probar, poner a prueba (product); hacerle una prueba a (student); evaluar (knowledge); examinar (sight)

testament /'testəmənt/ *n* (*will*) testamento *m*. **Old/New T~** Antiguo/Nuevo Testamento

testicle /'testɪkl/ *n* testículo *m*

testify /'testɪfaɪ/ *vt* atestiguar. ● *vi* declarar

testimon|ial /testɪ'məʊnɪəl/ *n* recomendación *f*. **~y** /'testɪmənɪ/ *n* testimonio *m*

test: ~ match *n* partido *m* internacional. **~ tube** *n* tubo *m* de ensayo, probeta *f*

t

tether /'teðə(r)/ *vt* atar. ● *n*. **be at the end of one's ~** no poder más

text /tekst/ *n* texto *m*. ● *vt* mandar un mensaje a. **~book** *n* libro *m* de texto

textile /'tekstaɪl/ *adj & n* textil (*m*)

texture /'tekstʃə(r)/ *n* textura *f*

Thames /temz/ *n* Támesis *m*

than /ðæn, ðən/ *conj* que; (*with quantity*) de

thank /θæŋk/ *vt* darle las gracias a, agradecer. **~ you** gracias. **~ful** *adj* agradecido. **~fully** *adv* (*happily*) gracias a Dios. **~less** *adj* ingrato. **~s** *npl* agradecimiento *m*. **~s!** 🄸 ¡gracias!. **~s to** gracias a

Thanksgiving (Day) /θæŋks 'gɪvɪŋ/ *n* (*in US*) el día de Acción de Gracias

that /ðæt, ðət/ *adj* (*pl* **those**) ese, aquel, esa, aquella. ● *pron* (*pl* **those**) ése, aquél, ésa, aquélla. **~** is es decir. **~'s not true** eso no es cierto. **~'s why** por eso. **is ~ you?** ¿eres tú? **like ~** así. ● *adv* tan. ● *rel pron* que; (*with prep*) el que, la que, el cual, la cual. ● *conj* que

thatched /θætʃt/ *adj* (roof) de paja; (cottage) con techo de paja

thaw /θɔː/ *vt* descongelar. ● *vi* descongelarse; (snow) derretirse. ● *n* deshielo *m*

the *definite article*

····➤ el (*m*), la (*f*), los (*mpl*), las (*fpl*). **~ building** el edificio. **~ windows** las ventanas

! Feminine singular nouns beginning with a stressed or accented *a* or *ha* take the article *el* instead of *la*, e.g. **~ soul** *el alma;* **~ axe** *el hacha;* **~ eagle** *el águila*

Note that when *el* follows the prepositions *de* and *a*, it combines to form *del* and *al*, e.g. **of ~ group** *del grupo.* **I went to ~ bank** *fui al banco*

····➤ (*before an ordinal number in*

names, titles) *not translated*. **Henry ~ Eighth** Enrique Octavo. **Elizabeth ~ Second** Isabel Segunda

....➤ (*in abstractions*) lo. **~ impossible** lo imposible

theatr|e /'θɪətə(r)/ *n* teatro *m*; (*Amer, movie theater*) cine *m*. **~ical** /-'ætrɪkl/ *adj* teatral

theft /θeft/ *n* hurto *m*

their /ðeə(r)/ *adj* su, sus *pl*. **~s** /ðeəz/ *poss pron* (el) suyo *m*, (la) suya *f*, (los) suyos *mpl*, (las) suyas *fpl*

them /ðem, ðəm/ *pron* (*accusative*) los *m*, las *f*; (*dative*) les; (*after prep*) ellos *m*, ellas *f*

theme /θi:m/ *n* tema *m*. **~ park** *n* parque *m* temático. **~ song** *n* motivo *m* principal

themselves /ðəm'selvz/ *pron* ellos mismos *m*, ellas mismas *f*; (*reflexive*) se; (*after prep*) sí mismos *m*, sí mismas *f*

then /ðen/ *adv* entonces; (*next*) luego, después. **by ~** para entonces. **now and ~** de vez en cuando. **since ~** desde entonces. ● *adj* entonces

theology /θɪ'ɒlədʒɪ/ *n* teología *f*

theor|etical /θɪə'retɪkl/ *adj* teórico. **~y** /'θɪərɪ/ *n* teoría *f*

therap|eutic /θerə'pju:tɪk/ *adj* terapéutico. **~ist** /'θerəpɪst/ *n* terapeuta *m & f*. **~y** /θerəpɪ/ *n* terapia *f*

there /ðeə(r)/ *adv* ahí; (*further away*) allí, ahí; (*less precise, further*) allá. **~ is, ~ are** hay. **~ it is** ahí está. **down ~** ahí abajo. **up ~** ahí arriba. ● *int*. **~! that's the last box** ¡listo! ésa es la última caja. **~, ~, don't cry!** vamos, no llores. **~abouts** *adv* por ahí. **~fore** /-fɔ:(r)/ *adv* por lo tanto.

thermometer /θə'mɒmɪtə(r)/ *n* termómetro *m*

Thermos /'θɜ:məs/ *n* (®) termo *m*

thermostat /'θɜ:məstæt/ *n* termostato *m*

thesaurus /θɪ'sɔ:rəs/ *n* (*pl* **-ri**/-raɪ/) diccionario *m* de sinónimos

these /ði:z/ *adj* estos, estas. ● *pron* éstos, éstas

thesis /'θi:sɪs/ *n* (*pl* **theses**/-si:z/) tesis *f*

they /ðeɪ/ *pron* ellos *m*, ellas *f*. **~ say that** dicen *or* se dice que

they'd /ðeɪ(ə)d/ = **they had, they would**

they'll /ðeɪl/ = **they will**

they're /ðeɪə(r)/ = **they are**

they've /ðeɪv/ = **they have**

thick /θɪk/ *adj* (**-er, -est**) (layer, sweater) grueso, gordo; (sauce) espeso; (fog, smoke) espeso, denso; (fur) tupido; (*fam, stupid*) burro. ● *adv* espesamente, densamente. ● *n*. **in the ~ of** en medio de. **~en** *vt* espesar. ● *vi* espesarse. **~et** /-ɪt/ *n* matorral *m*. **~ness** *n* (*of fabric*) grosor *m*; (*of paper, wood, wall*) espesor *m*

thief /θi:f/ *n* (*pl* **thieves** /θi:vz/) ladrón *m*

thigh /θaɪ/ *n* muslo *m*

thimble /'θɪmbl/ *n* dedal *m*

thin /θɪn/ *adj* (**thinner, thinnest**) (person) delgado, flaco; (layer, slice) fino; (hair) ralo

thing /θɪŋ/ *n* cosa *f*. **it's a good ~ (that)...** menos mal que.... **just the ~** exactamente lo que se necesita. **poor ~!** ¡pobrecito!

think /θɪŋk/ *vt* (*pt* **thought**) pensar, creer. ● *vi* pensar (**about** en); (*carefully*) reflexionar; (*imagine*) imaginarse. **I ~ so** creo que sí. **~ of s.o.** pensar en uno. **I hadn't**

thought of that eso no se me ha ocurrido. **~ over** *vt* pensar bien. **~ up** *vt* idear, inventar. **~er** *n* pensador *m*. **~-tank** *n* gabinete *m* estratégico

third /θɜːd/ *adj* tercero, (*before masculine singular noun*) tercer. ●*n* tercio *m*, tercera parte *f*. **~ (gear)** *n* (*Auto*) tercera *f*. **~-rate** *adj* muy inferior. **T~ World** *n* Tercer Mundo *m*

thirst /θɜːst/ *n* sed *f*. **~y** *adj* sediento. **be ~y** tener sed

thirt|een /θɜːˈtiːn/ *adj & n* trece (*m*). **~teenth** *adj* decimotercero. ●*n* treceavo *m* **~ieth** /ˈθɜːtɪəθ/ *adj* trigésimo. ●*n* treintavo *m*. **~y** /ˈθɜːtɪ/ *adj & n* treinta (*m*)

this /ðɪs/ *adj* (*pl* **these**) este, esta. **~ one** éste, ésta. ●*pron* (*pl* **these**) éste, ésta, esto. **like ~** así

thistle /ˈθɪsl/ *n* cardo *m*

thong /θɒŋ/ *n* correa *f*; (*Amer, sandal*) chancla *f*

thorn /θɔːn/ *n* espina *f*. **~y** *adj* espinoso

thorough /ˈθʌrə/ *adj* (investigation) riguroso; (cleaning etc) a fondo; (person) concienzudo. **~bred** /-bred/ *adj* de pura sangre. **~fare** *n* vía *f* pública; (*street*) calle *f*. **no ~fare** prohibido el paso. **~ly** *adv* (clean) a fondo; (examine) minuciosamente; (*completely*) perfectamente

those /ðəʊz/ *adj* esos, esas, aquellos, aquellas. ●*pron* ésos, ésas, aquéllos, aquéllas

though /ðəʊ/ *conj* aunque. ●*adv* sin embargo. **as ~** como si

thought /θɔːt/ *see* **THINK**. ●*n* pensamiento *m*; (*idea*) idea *f*. **~ful** *adj* pensativo; (*considerate*) atento. **~fully** *adv* pensativamente; (*considerately*) atentamente. **~less** *adj* desconsiderado

thousand /ˈθaʊznd/ *adj & n* mil (*m*). **~th** *adj & n* milésimo (*m*)

thrash /θræʃ/ *vt* azotar; (*defeat*) derrotar

thread /θred/ *n* hilo *m*; (*of screw*) rosca *f*. ●*vt* enhebrar (needle); ensartar (beads). **~bare** *adj* gastado, raído

threat /θret/ *n* amenaza *f*. **~en** *vt/i* amenazar. **~ening** *adj* amenazador

three /θriː/ *adj & n* tres (*m*). **~fold** *adj* triple. ●*adv* tres veces

threshold /ˈθreʃhəʊld/ *n* umbral *m*

threw /θruː/ *see* **THROW**

thrift /θrɪft/ *n* economía *f*, ahorro *m*. **~y** *adj* frugal

thrill /θrɪl/ *n* emoción *f*. ●*vt* emocionar. **~ed** *adj* contentísimo (**with** con). **~er** *n* (*book*) libro *m* de suspense *or* (*LAm*) suspenso; (*film*) película *f* de suspense *or* (*LAm*) suspenso. **~ing** *adj* emocionante

thriv|e /θraɪv/ *vi* prosperar. **~ing** *adj* próspero

throat /θrəʊt/ *n* garganta *f*

throb /θrɒb/ *vi* (*pt* **throbbed**) palpitar; (*with pain*) dar punzadas; (engine) vibrar. **~bing** *adj* (pain) punzante

throes /θrəʊz/ *npl*. **be in one's death ~** estar agonizando

throne /θrəʊn/ *n* trono *m*

throng /θrɒŋ/ *n* multitud *f*

throttle /ˈθrɒtl/ *n* (*Auto*) acelerador *m* (*que se acciona con la mano*). ●*vt* estrangular

through /θruː/ *prep* por, a través de; (*during*) durante; (*by means of*) a través de; (*Amer, until and including*) **Monday ~ Friday** de lunes a viernes. ●*adv* de parte a parte, de un lado a otro; (*entirely*) completamente; (*to the end*) hasta el final. **be ~** (*finished*) haber terminado. ●*adj* (train etc) directo. **no ~ road** calle sin salida. **~out** /-'aʊt/ *prep* por todo; (*time*) durante todo. **~out his career** a lo largo de su carrera

throve /θrəʊv/ *see* THRIVE

throw /θrəʊ/ *vt* (*pt* **threw**, *pp* **thrown**) tirar, aventar (*Mex*); lanzar (grenade, javelin); (*disconcert*) desconcertar; 🅸 hacer, dar (party). ●*n* (*of ball*) tiro *m*; (*of dice*) tirada *f*. □ **~ away** *vt* tirar. □ **~ up** *vi* (*vomit*) vomitar.

thrush /θrʌʃ/ *n* tordo *m*

thrust /θrʌst/ *vt* (*pt* **thrust**) empujar; (*push in*) clavar. ●*n* empujón *m*; (*of sword*) estocada *f*

thud /θʌd/ *n* ruido *m* sordo

thug /θʌg/ *n* matón *m*

thumb /θʌm/ *n* pulgar *m*. ●*vt*. **~ a lift** ir a dedo. **~tack** *n* (*Amer*) chincheta *f*, tachuela *f*, chinche *f* (*Mex*)

thump /θʌmp/ *vt* golpear. ●*vi* (heart) latir fuertemente. ●*n* golpazo *m*

thunder /'θʌndə(r)/ *n* truenos *mpl*, (*of traffic*) estruendo *m*. ●*vi* tronar. **~bolt** *n* rayo *m*. **~storm** *n* tormenta *f* eléctrica. **~y** *adj* con truenos

Thursday /'θɜːzdeɪ/ *n* jueves *m*

thus /ðʌs/ *adv* así

thwart /θwɔːt/ *vt* frustrar

tic /tɪk/ *n* tic *m*

tick /tɪk/ *n* (*sound*) tic *m*; (*insect*) garrapata *f*, (*mark*) marca *f*, visto *m*, palomita *f* (*Mex*); (*fam, instant*) momentito *m*. ●*vi* hacer tictac. ●*vt*. **~ (off)** marcar

ticket /'tɪkɪt/ *n* (*for bus, train*) billete *m*, boleto *m* (*LAm*); (*for plane*) pasaje *m*, billete *m*; (*for theatre, museum*) entrada *f*; (*for baggage, coat*) ticket *m*; (*fine*) multa *f*. **~ collector** *n* revisor *m*. **~ office** *n* (*transport*) mostrador *m* de venta de billetes *or* (*LAm*) boletos; (*in theatre*) taquilla *f*, boletería *f* (*LAm*)

tickl|e /'tɪkl/ *vt* hacerle cosquillas a. ●*n* cosquilleo *m*. **~ish** /'tɪklɪʃ/ *adj*. **be ~ish** tener cosquillas

tidal wave /'taɪdl/ *n* maremoto *m*

tide /taɪd/ *n* marea *f*. **high/low ~** marea alta/baja. □ **~ over** *vt* ayudar a salir de un apuro

tid|ily /'taɪdɪlɪ/ *adv* ordenadamente. **~iness** *n* orden *m*. **~y** *adj* (**-ier**, **-iest**) ordenado. ●*vt/i* **~y (up)** ordenar, arreglar

tie /taɪ/ *vt* (*pres p* **tying**) atar, amarrar (*LAm*); hacer (knot). ●*vi* (*Sport*) empatar. ●*n* (*constraint*) atadura *f*; (*bond*) lazo *m*; (*necktie*) corbata *f*; (*Sport*) empate *m*. **~ in with** *vt* concordar con. □ **~ up** *vt* atar. **be ~d up** (*busy*) estar ocupado

tier /tɪə(r)/ *n* hilera *f* superpuesta; (*in stadium etc*) grada *f*; (*of cake*) piso *m*

tiger /'taɪgə(r)/ *n* tigre *m*

tight /taɪt/ *adj* (**-er**, **-est**) (clothes) ajustado, ceñido; (*taut*) tieso; (control) estricto; (knot, nut) apretado; (*fam, drunk*) borracho. **~en** *vt* apretar. □ **~en up** *vt* hacer más estricto. **~-fisted** /-'fɪstɪd/ *adj* tacaño. **~ly** *adv* bien, fuerte; (fastened) fuertemente. **~rope** *n* cuerda *f* floja. **~s** *npl* (*for ballet etc*) leotardo(s) *m(pl)*; (*pantyhose*) medias *fpl*

tile /taɪl/ *n* (*decorative*) azulejo *m*; (*on roof*) teja *f*; (*on floor*) baldosa *f*.

● *vt* azulejar; tejar (roof); embaldosar (floor)

till /tɪl/ *prep* hasta. ● *conj* hasta que. ● *n* caja *f.* ● *vt* cultivar

tilt /tɪlt/ *vt* inclinar. ● *vi* inclinarse. ● *n* inclinación *f*

timber /'tɪmbə(r)/ *n* madera *f* (*para construcción*)

time /taɪm/ *n* tiempo *m*; (*moment*) momento *m*; (*occasion*) ocasión *f*; (*by clock*) hora *f*; (*epoch*) época *f*; (*rhythm*) compás *m*. **at ~s** a veces. **for the ~ being** por el momento. **from ~ to ~** de vez en cuando. **have a good ~** divertirse, pasarlo bien. **in a year's ~** dentro de un año. **in no ~** en un abrir y cerrar de ojos. **in ~** a tiempo; (*eventually*) con el tiempo. **arrive on ~** llegar a tiempo. **it's ~ we left** es hora de irnos. ● *vt* elegir el momento; cronometrar (race). **~ bomb** *n* bomba *f* de tiempo. **~ly** *adj* oportuno. **~r** *n* cronómetro *m*; (*Culin*) avisador *m*; (*with sand*) reloj *m* de arena; (*Elec*) interruptor *m* de reloj. **~s** /'taɪmz/ *prep*. **2 ~s 4 is 8** 2 (multiplicado) por 4 son 8. **~table** *n* horario *m*

timid /'tɪmɪd/ *adj* tímido; (*fearful*) miedoso

tin /tɪn/ *n* estaño *m*; (*container*) lata *f*. **~ foil** *n* papel *m* de estaño

tinge /tɪndʒ/ *vt*. **be ~d with sth** estar matizado de algo. ● *n* matiz *m*

tingle /'tɪŋgl/ *vi* sentir un hormigueo

tinker /'tɪŋkə(r)/ *vi*. **~ with** juguetear con

tinkle /'tɪŋkl/ *vi* tintinear

tinned /tɪnd/ *adj* en lata, enlatado

tin opener *n* abrelatas *m*

tint /tɪnt/ *n* matiz *m*

tiny /'taɪnɪ/ *adj* (**-ier**, **-iest**) minúsculo, diminuto

tip /tɪp/ *n* punta *f*. ● *vt* (*pt* **tipped**) (*tilt*) inclinar; (*overturn*) volcar; (*pour*) verter; (*give gratuity to*) darle (una) propina a. □ **~ off** *vt* avisar. □ **~ out** *vt* verter. □ **~ over** *vi* caerse. *n* propina *f*; (*advice*) consejo *m* (práctico); (*for rubbish*) vertedero *m*. **~ped** *adj* (cigarette) con filtro

tipsy /'tɪpsɪ/ *adj* achispado

tiptoe /'tɪptəʊ/ *n*. **on ~** de puntillas

tiptop /'tɪptɒp/ *adj* ◻ de primera. **in ~ condition** en excelente estado

tire /'taɪə(r)/ *n* (*Amer*) see TYRE. ● *vt* cansar. ● *vi* cansarse. **~d** /'taɪəd/ *adj* cansado. **get ~d** cansarse. **~d of** harto de. **~d out** agotado. **~less** *adj* incansable; (efforts) inagotable. **~some** /-səm/ *adj* (person) pesado; (task) tedioso

tiring /'taɪərɪŋ/ *adj* cansado, cansador (*LAm*)

tissue /'tɪʃu:/ *n* (*of bones, plants*) tejido *m*; (*paper handkerchief*) pañuelo *m* de papel. **~ paper** *n* papel *m* de seda

tit /tɪt/ *n* (*bird*) paro *m*; (◻, *breast*) teta *f*

titbit /'tɪtbɪt/ *n* exquisitez *f*

tit for tat *n*: **it was ~** fue ojo por ojo, diente por diente

title /'taɪtl/ *n* título *m*

to /tu:, tə/ *prep* a; (*towards*) hacia; (*in order to*) para; (*as far as*) hasta; (*of*) de. **give it ~ me** dámelo. **what did you say ~ him?** ¿qué le dijiste?; **I don't want ~** no quiero. **it's twenty ~ seven** (*by clock*) son las siete menos veinte, son veinte para las siete (*LAm*). ● *adv*. **pull ~**

cerrar. ~ **and fro** *adv* de un lado a otro

toad /təʊd/ *n* sapo *m*. **~stool** *n* hongo *m* (*no comestible*)

toast /təʊst/ *n* pan *m* tostado, tostadas *fpl*; (*drink*) brindis *m*. **a piece of ~** una tostada, un pan tostado (*Mex*). **drink a ~ to** brindar por. ● *vt* (*Culin*) tostar; (*drink to*) brindar por. **~er** *n* tostadora *f* (eléctrica), tostador *m*

tobacco /təˈbækəʊ/ *n* tabaco *m*. **~nist** /-ənɪst/ *n* estanquero *m*

toboggan /təˈbɒgən/ *n* tobogán *m*

today /təˈdeɪ/ *n & adv* hoy (*m*)

toddler /ˈtɒdlə(r)/ *n* niño *m* pequeño (entre un año y dos años y medio de edad)

toe /təʊ/ *n* dedo *m* (del pie); (*of shoe*) punta *f*. **big ~** dedo *m* gordo (del pie). **on one's ~s** (*fig*) alerta. ● *vt*. **~ the line** acatar la disciplina

TOEFL - Test of English as a Foreign Language

Un examen que, a la hora de solicitar el ingreso a una universidad americana, evalúa el dominio del inglés de aquellos estudiantes cuya lengua materna no es este idioma.

toffee /ˈtɒfɪ/ *n* toffee *m* (golosina hecha con azúcar y mantequilla)

together /təˈgeðə(r)/ *adv* juntos; (*at same time*) a la vez. **~ with** junto con

toil /tɔɪl/ *vi* afanarse. ● *n* trabajo *m* duro

toilet /ˈtɔɪlɪt/ *n* servicio *m*, baño *m* (*LAm*). **~ paper** *n* papel *m* higiénico. **~ries** /ˈtɔɪlɪtrɪz/ *npl* artículos *mpl* de tocador. **~ roll** *n* rollo *m* de papel higiénico

token /ˈtəʊkən/ *n* muestra *f*; (*voucher*) vale *m*; (*coin*) ficha *f*. ● *adj* simbólico

told /təʊld/ *see* TELL

tolera|ble /ˈtɒlərəbl/ *adj* tolerable; (*not bad*) pasable. **~nce** /ˈtɒlərəns/ *n* tolerancia *f*. **~nt** *adj* tolerante. **~te** /-reɪt/ *vt* tolerar. **~tion** /-ˈreɪʃən/ *n* tolerancia *f*

toll /təʊl/ *n* (*on road*) peaje *m*, cuota *f* (*Mex*). **death ~** número *m* de muertos. **~ call** *n* (*Amer*) llamada *f* interurbana, conferencia *f*. ● *vi* doblar, tocar a muerto

tomato /təˈmɑːtəʊ/ *n* (*pl* **-oes**) tomate *m*, jitomate *m* (*Mex*)

tomb /tuːm/ *n* tumba *f*, sepulcro *m*. **~stone** *n* lápida *f*

tomorrow /təˈmɒrəʊ/ *n & adv* mañana (*f*). **see you ~!** ¡hasta mañana!

ton /tʌn/ *n* tonelada *f* (= *1,016kg*). **~s of** [!] montones de. **metric ~** tonelada *f* (métrica) (= *1,000kg*)

tone /təʊn/ *n* tono *m*. □ **~ down** *vt* atenuar; moderar (language). **~-deaf** *adj* que no tiene oído (musical)

tongs /tɒŋz/ *npl* tenacillas *fpl*

tongue /tʌŋ/ *n* lengua *f*. **say sth ~ in cheek** decir algo medio burlándose. **~-tied** *adj* cohibido. **~-twister** *n* trabalenguas *m*

tonic /ˈtɒnɪk/ *adj* tónico. ● *n* (*Med, fig*) tónico *m*. **~ (water)** *n* tónica *f*

tonight /təˈnaɪt/ *adv & n* esta noche (*f*); (*evening*) esta tarde (*f*)

tonne /tʌn/ *n* tonelada *f* (métrica)

tonsil /ˈtɒnsl/ *n* amígdala *f*. **~litis** /-ˈlaɪtɪs/ *n* amigdalitis *f*

too /tuː/ *adv* (*excessively*) demasiado; (*also*) también. **I'm not ~ sure** no estoy muy seguro. **~ many** demasiados. **~ much**

t

demasiado

took /tʊk/ *see* **TAKE**

tool /tu:l/ *n* herramienta *f*

tooth /tu:θ/ *n* (*pl* **teeth**) diente *m*; (*molar*) muela *f*. **~ache** *n* dolor *m* de muelas. **~brush** *n* cepillo *m* de dientes. **~paste** *n* pasta *f* dentífrica, pasta *f* de dientes. **~pick** *n* palillo *m* (de dientes)

top /tɒp/ *n* parte *f* superior, parte *f* de arriba; (*of mountain*) cima *f*; (*of tree*) copa *f*; (*of page*) parte *f* superior; (*lid, of bottle*) tapa *f*; (*of pen*) capuchón *m*; (*spinning* ~) trompo *m*, peonza *f*. **be ~ of the class** ser el primero de la clase. **from ~ to bottom** de arriba abajo. **on ~ of** encima de; (*besides*) además de. ● *adj* más alto; (shelf) superior; (speed) máximo; (*in rank*) superior; (*leading*) más destacado. ● *vt* (*pt* **topped**) cubrir; (*exceed*) exceder. **~ floor** *n* último piso *m*. □ **~ up** *vt* llenar; (mobile phone) recargar el saldo. **~ hat** *n* chistera *f*. **~-heavy** /-'hevɪ/ *adj* inestable (por ser más pesado en su parte superior)

topic /'tɒpɪk/ *n* tema *m*. **~al** *adj* de actualidad

topless /tɒples/ *adj* topless

topple /'tɒpl/ *vi* (*Pol*) derribar; (*overturn*) volcar. ● *vi* caerse

top secret /tɒp'si:krɪt/ *adj* secreto, reservado

t

torch /tɔ:tʃ/ *n* linterna *f*; (*flaming*) antorcha *f*

tore /tɔ:(r)/ *see* **TEAR**[1]

torment /'tɔ:ment/ *n* tormento *m*. ● /tɔ:'ment/ *vt* atormentar

torn /tɔ:n/ *see* **TEAR**[1]

tornado /tɔ:'neɪdəʊ/ *n* (*pl* **-oes**) tornado *m*

torpedo /tɔ:'pi:dəʊ/ *n* (*pl* **-oes**) torpedo *m*. ● *vt* torpedear

torrent /'tɒrənt/ *n* torrente *m*. **~ial** /tə'renʃl/ *adj* torrencial

torrid /'tɒrɪd/ *adj* tórrido; (affair) apasionado

tortoise /'tɔ:təs/ *n* tortuga *f*. **~shell** *n* carey *m*

tortuous /'tɔ:tjʊəs/ *adj* tortuoso

torture /'tɔ:tʃə(r)/ *n* tortura *f*. ● *vt* torturar

toss /tɒs/ *vt* tirar, lanzar (ball); (*shake*) sacudir. ● *vi*. **~ and turn** (*in bed*) dar vueltas

tot /tɒt/ *n* pequeño *m*; (*fam, of liquor*) trago *m*. ● *vt* (*pt* **totted**). **~ up** 🅸 sumar

total /'təʊtl/ *adj & n* total (*m*). ● *vt* (*pt* **totalled**) ascender a un total de; (*add up*) totalizar. **~itarian** /təʊtælɪ'teərɪən/ *adj* totalitario. **~ly** *adv* totalmente

totter /'tɒtə(r)/ *vi* tambalearse

touch /tʌtʃ/ *vt* tocar; (*move*) conmover; (*concern*) afectar. ● *vi* tocar; (wires) tocarse. ● *n* toque *m*; (*sense*) tacto *m*; (*contact*) contacto *m*. **be/get/stay in ~ with** estar/ponerse/mantenerse en contacto con. □ **~ down** *vi* (aircraft) aterrizar. □ **~ up** *vt* retocar. **~ing** *adj* enternecedor. **~y** *adj* quisquilloso

tough /tʌf/ *adj* (**-er**, **-est**) duro; (*strong*) fuerte, resistente; (*difficult*) difícil; (*severe*) severo. **~en**. **~ (up)** *vt* endurecer; hacer más fuerte (person)

tour /tʊə(r)/ *n* viaje *m*; (*visit*) visita *f*; (*excursion*) excursión *f*; (*by team etc*) gira *f*. **be on ~** estar de gira. ● *vt* recorrer; (*visit*) visitar. **~ guide** *n* guía de turismo

touris|m /'tʊərɪzəm/ *n* turismo *m*. **~t** /'tʊərɪst/ *n* turista *m & f*. ● *adj* turístico. **~t office** *n* oficina *f* de turismo

tournament /ˈtɔːnəmənt/ *n* torneo *m*

tousle /ˈtaʊzl/ *vt* despeinar

tout /taʊt/ *vi*. ~ **(for)** solicitar

tow /təʊ/ *vt* remolcar. ● *n* remolque *m*

toward(s) /təˈwɔːd(z)/ *prep* hacia. **his attitude ~ her** su actitud para con ella

towel /ˈtaʊəl/ *n* toalla *f*

tower /ˈtaʊə(r)/ *n* torre *f*. ● *vi*. ~ **above** (building) descollar sobre; (person) destacar sobre. ~ **block** *n* edificio *m* or bloque *m* de apartamentos. ~**ing** *adj* altísimo; (rage) violento

town /taʊn/ *n* ciudad *f*; (*smaller*) pueblo *m*. **go to ~** [!] no escatimar dinero. ~ **hall** *n* ayuntamiento *m*

toxic /ˈtɒksɪk/ *adj* tóxico

toy /tɔɪ/ *n* juguete *m*. □ ~ **with** *vt* juguetear con (object); darle vueltas a (idea). ~**shop** *n* juguetería *f*

trac|e /treɪs/ *n* señal *f*, rastro *m*. ● *vt* trazar; (*draw*) dibujar; (*with tracing paper*) calcar; (*track down*) localizar. ~**ing paper** *n* papel *m* de calcar

track /træk/ *n* pista *f*, huellas *fpl*; (*path*) sendero *m*; (*Sport*) pista *f*. **the ~(s)** la vía férrea; (*Rail*) vía *f*. **keep ~ of** seguirle la pista a (person). ● *vt* seguirle la pista a. □ ~ **down** *vt* localizar. ~ **suit** *n* equipo *m* (de deportes) chándal *m*

tract /trækt/ *n* (*land*) extensión *f*; (*pamphlet*) tratado *m* breve

traction /ˈtrækʃn/ *n* tracción *f*

tractor /ˈtræktə(r)/ *n* tractor *m*

trade /treɪd/ *n* comercio *m*; (*occupation*) oficio *m*; (*exchange*) cambio *m*; (*industry*) industria *f*. ● *vt*. ~ **sth for sth** cambiar algo por algo. ● *vi* comerciar. □ ~ **in** *vt* (*give in part-exchange*) entregar como parte del pago. ~ **mark** *n* marca *f* (de fábrica). ~**r** *n* comerciante *m* & *f*. ~ **union** *n* sindicato *m*

tradition /trəˈdɪʃn/ *n* tradición *f*. ~**al** *adj* tradicional

traffic /ˈtræfɪk/ *n* tráfico *m*. ● *vi* (*pt* **trafficked**) comerciar (**in** en). ~ **circle** *n* (*Amer*) glorieta *f*, rotonda *f*. ~ **island** *n* isla *f* peatonal. ~ **jam** *n* embotellamiento *m*, atasco *m*. ~ **lights** *npl* semáforo *m*. ~ **warden** *n* guardia *m*, controlador *m* de tráfico

trag|edy /ˈtrædʒɪdɪ/ *n* tragedia *f*. ~**ic** /ˈtrædʒɪk/ *adj* trágico

trail /treɪl/ *vi* arrastrarse; (*lag*) rezagarse. ● *vt* (*track*) seguir la pista de. ● *n* (*left by animal, person*) huellas *fpl*; (*path*) sendero *m*. **be on the ~ of s.o./sth** seguir la pista de uno/algo ~**er** *n* remolque *m*; (*Amer, caravan*) caravana *f*, rulot *m*; (*film*) avance *m*

train /treɪn/ *n* (*Rail*) tren *m*; (*of events*) serie *f*; (*of dress*) cola *f*. ● *vt* capacitar (employee); adiestrar (soldier); (*Sport*) entrenar; educar (voice); guiar (plant); amaestrar (animal). ● *vi* estudiar; (*Sport*) entrenarse. ~**ed** *adj* (*skilled*) cualificado, calificado; (doctor) diplomado. ~**ee** /treɪˈniː/ *n* aprendiz *m*; (*Amer, Mil*) recluta *m* & *f*. ~**er** *n* (*Sport*) entrenador *m*; (*of animals*) amaestrador *m*. ~**ers** *mpl* zapatillas *fpl* de deporte. ~**ing** *n* capacitación *f*; (*Sport*) entrenamiento *m*

trait /treɪ(t)/ *n* rasgo *m*

traitor /ˈtreɪtə(r)/ *n* traidor *m*

tram /træm/ *n* tranvía *m*

tramp /træmp/ *vi*. ~ **(along)** caminar pesadamente. ● *n* vagabundo *m*

trample /'træmpl/ *vt* pisotear. ● *vi.* ~ on pisotear

trampoline /'træmpəli:n/ *n* trampolín *m*

trance /trɑ:ns/ *n* trance *m*

tranquil /'træŋkwɪl/ *adj* tranquilo. **~lity** /-'kwɪlətɪ/ *n* tranquilidad *f*; (*of person*) serenidad *f*. **~lize** /'træŋkwɪlaɪz/ *vt* sedar, dar un sedante a. **~lizer** *n* sedante *m*, tranquilizante *m*

transaction /træn'zækʃən/ *n* transacción *f*, operación *f*

transatlantic /trænzət'læntɪk/ *adj* transatlántico

transcend /træn'send/ *vt* (*go beyond*) exceder

transcript /'trænskrɪpt/ *n* transcripción *f*

transfer /træns'fɜ:(r)/ *vt* (*pt* **transferred**) trasladar; traspasar (player); transferir (funds, property); pasar (call). ● *vi* trasladarse. ● /'trænsfɜ:(r)/ *n* traslado *m*; (*of player*) traspaso *m*; (*of funds, property*) transferencia *f*; (*paper*) calcomanía *f*

transform /træns'fɔ:m/ *vt* transformar. **~ation** /-ə'meɪʃn/ *n* transformación *f*. **~er** *n* transformador *m*

transfusion /træns'fju:ʒn/ *n* transfusión *f*

transient /'trænzɪənt/ *adj* pasajero

transistor /træn'zɪstə(r)/ *n* transistor *m*

transit /'trænsɪt/ *n* tránsito *m*. **~ion** /træn'zɪʒn/ *n* transición *f*. **~ive** /'trænsɪtɪv/ *adj* transitivo

translat|e /trænz'leɪt/ *vt* traducir. **~ion** /-ʃn/ *n* traducción *f*. **~or** *n* traductor *m*

transmission /træns'mɪʃn/ *n* transmisión *f*

transmit /trænz'mɪt/ *vt* (*pt* **transmitted**) transmitir. **~ter** *n* transmisor *m*

transparen|cy /træns'pærənsɪ/ *n* transparencia *f*; (*Photo*) diapositiva *f*. **~t** *adj* transparente

transplant /træns'plɑ:nt/ *vt* trasplantar. ● /'trænsplɑ:nt/ *n* trasplante *m*

transport /træn'spɔ:t/ *vt* transportar. ● /'trænspɔ:t/ *n* transporte *m*. **~ation** /-'teɪʃn/ *n* transporte *m*

trap /træp/ *n* trampa *f*. ● *vt* (*pt* **trapped**) atrapar; (*jam*) atascar; (*cut off*) bloquear. **~door** *n* trampilla *f*

trapeze /trə'pi:z/ *n* trapecio *m*

trash /træʃ/ *n* basura *f*; (*Amer, worthless people*) escoria *f*. ~ **can** *n* (*Amer*) cubo *m* de la basura, bote *m* de la basura (*Mex*). **~y** *adj* (souvenir) de porquería; (magazine) malo

travel /'trævl/ *vi* (*pt* **travelled**) viajar; (vehicle) desplazarse. ● *vt* recorrer. ● *n* viajes *mpl*. ~ **agency** *n* agencia *f* de viajes. **~ler** *n* viajero *m*. **~ler's cheque** *n* cheque *m* de viaje *or* viajero. **~ling expenses** *npl* gastos *mpl* de viaje

trawler /'trɔ:lə(r)/ *n* barca *f* pesquera

tray /treɪ/ *n* bandeja *f*

treacher|ous *adj* traidor; (*deceptive*) engañoso. **~y** *n* traición *f*

treacle /'tri:kl/ *n* melaza *f*

tread /tred/ *vi* (*pt* **trod**, *pp* **trodden**) pisar. ~ **on sth** pisar algo. ~ **carefully** andarse con cuidado. ● *n* (*step*) paso *m*; (*of tyre*) banda *f* de rodamiento

treason /'tri:zn/ *n* traición *f*

treasur|e /'treʒə(r)/ *n* tesoro *m*.

~ed /'treʒəd/ *adj* (possession) preciado. **~er** /'treʒərə(r)/ *n* tesorero *m*. **~y** *n* erario *m*, tesoro *m*. **the T~y** el fisco, la hacienda pública. **Department of the T~y** (*in US*) Departamento *m* del Tesoro

treat /tri:t/ *vt* tratar; (*Med*) tratar. **~ s.o.** (*to meal etc*) invitar a uno. ● *n* placer *m*; (*present*) regalo *m*

treatise /'tri:tɪz/ *n* tratado *m*

treatment /'tri:tmənt/ *n* tratamiento *m*

treaty /'tri:tɪ/ *n* tratado *m*

treble /'trebl/ *adj* triple; (clef) de sol; (voice) de tiple. ● *vt* triplicar. ● *vi* triplicarse. ● *n* tiple *m & f*

tree /tri:/ *n* árbol *m*

trek /trek/ *n* caminata *f*. ● *vi* (*pt* **trekked**) caminar

trellis /'trelɪs/ *n* enrejado *m*

tremble /'trembl/ *vi* temblar

tremendous /trɪ'mendəs/ *adj* formidable; (*fam, huge*) tremendo. **~ly** *adv* tremendamente

tremor /'tremə(r)/ *n* temblor *m*

trench /trentʃ/ *n* zanja *f*; (*Mil*) trinchera *f*

trend /trend/ *n* tendencia *f*; (*fashion*) moda *f*. **~y** *adj* (**-ier**, **-iest**) ⊡ moderno

trepidation /trepɪ'deɪʃn/ *n* inquietud *f*

trespass /'trespəs/ *vi*. **~ on** entrar sin autorización (en propiedad ajena). **~er** *n* intruso *m*

trial /'traɪəl/ *n* prueba *f*; (*Jurid*) proceso *m*, juicio *m*; (*ordeal*) prueba *f* dura. **by ~ and error** por ensayo y error. **be on ~** estar a prueba; (*Jurid*) estar siendo procesado

triang|le /'traɪæŋgl/ *n* triángulo *m*. **~ular** /-'æŋgjʊlə(r)/ *adj* triangular

trib|al /'traɪbl/ *adj* tribal. **~e** /traɪb/ *n* tribu *f*

tribulation /trɪbjʊ'leɪʃn/ *n* tribulación *f*

tribunal /traɪ'bju:nl/ *n* tribunal *m*

tributary /'trɪbjʊtrɪ/ *n* (*of river*) afluente *m*

tribute /'trɪbju:t/ *n* tributo *m*; (*acknowledgement*) homenaje *m*. **pay ~ to** rendir homenaje a

trick /trɪk/ *n* trampa *f*, ardid *m*; (*joke*) broma *f*; (*feat*) truco *m*; (*in card games*) baza *f*. **play a ~ on** gastar una broma a. ● *vt* engañar. **~ery** *n* engaño *m*

trickle /'trɪkl/ *vi* gotear. **~ in** (*fig*) entrar poco a poco

trickster /'trɪkstə(r)/ *n* estafador *m*

tricky /'trɪkɪ/ *adj* delicado, difícil

tricycle /'traɪsɪkl/ *n* triciclo *m*

tried /traɪd/ *see* **TRY**

trifl|e /'traɪfl/ *n* nimiedad *f*; (*Culin*) postre de bizcocho, jerez, frutas y nata. ● *vi*. □ **~e with** *vt* jugar con. **~ing** *adj* insignificante

trigger /'trɪgə(r)/ *n* (*of gun*) gatillo *m*. ● *vt*. **~ (off)** desencadenar

trim /trɪm/ *adj* (**trimmer**, **trimmest**) (*slim*) esbelto; (*neat*) elegante. ● *vt* (*pt* **trimmed**) (*cut*) recortar; (*adorn*) adornar. ● *n* (*cut*) recorte *m*. **in ~** en buen estado. **~mings** *npl* recortes *mpl*

trinity /'trɪnɪtɪ/ *n*. **the (Holy) T~** la (Santísima) Trinidad

trinket /'trɪŋkɪt/ *n* chuchería *f*

trio /'tri:əʊ/ *n* (*pl* **-os**) trío *m*

trip /trɪp/ (*pt* **tripped**) *vt* **~ (up)** hacerle una zancadilla a, hacer tropezar ● *vi* tropezar. ● *n* (*journey*) viaje *m*; (*outing*) excursión *f*; (*stumble*) traspié *m*

tripe /traɪp/ *n* callos *mpl*, mondongo *m* (*LAm*), pancita *f* (*Mex*); (*fam, nonsense*) paparruchas *fpl*

triple /'trɪpl/ *adj* triple. ●*vt* triplicar. ●*vi* triplicarse. **~t** /'trɪplɪt/ *n* trillizo *m*

triplicate /'trɪplɪkət/ *adj* triplicado. **in ~** por triplicado

tripod /'traɪpɒd/ *n* trípode *m*

trite /traɪt/ *adj* trillado

triumph /'traɪʌmf/ *n* triunfo *m*. ●*vi* triunfar (**over** sobre). **~al** /-'ʌmfl/ *adj* triunfal. **~ant** /-'ʌmfnt/ *adj* (troops) triunfador; (moment) triunfal; (smile) de triunfo

trivial /'trɪvɪəl/ *adj* insignificante; (concerns) trivial. **~ity** /-'ælətɪ/ *n* trivialidad *f*

trod, trodden /trɒd, trɒdn/ *see* **TREAD**

trolley /'trɒlɪ/ *n* (*pl* **-eys**) carretón *m*; (*in supermarket, airport*) carrito *m*; (*for food, drink*) carrito *m*, mesa *f* rodante. **~ car** *n* (*Amer*) tranvía *f*

trombone /trɒm'bəʊn/ *n* trombón *m*

troop /tru:p/ *n* compañía *f*; (*of cavalry*) escuadrón *m*. ●*vi*. **~ in** entrar en tropel. **~ out** salir en tropel. **~er** *n* soldado *m* de caballería; (*Amer, state police officer*) agente *m* & *f*. **~s** *npl* (*Mil*) tropas *fpl*

trophy /'trəʊfɪ/ *n* trofeo *m*

tropic /'trɒpɪk/ *n* trópico *m*. **~al** *adj* tropical. **~s** *npl* trópicos *mpl*

trot /trɒt/ *n* trote *m*. ●*vi* (*pt* **trotted**) trotar

trouble /'trʌbl/ *n* problemas *mpl*; (*awkward situation*) apuro *m*; (*inconvenience*) molestia *f*. **be in ~** estar en apuros. **get into ~** meterse en problemas. **look for ~** buscar camorra. **take the ~ to do sth** molestarse en hacer algo. ●*vt* (*bother*) molestar; (*worry*) preocupar. **~-maker** *n* alborotador *m*. **~some** /-səm/ *adj* problemático. **~ spot** *n* punto *m* conflictivo

trough /trɒf/ *n* (*for drinking*) abrevadero *m*; (*for feeding*) comedero *m*

troupe /tru:p/ *n* compañía *f* teatral

trousers /'traʊzəz/ *npl* pantalón *m*, pantalones *mpl*

trout /traʊt/ *n* (*pl* **trout**) trucha *f*

trowel /'traʊəl/ *n* (*garden*) desplantador *m*; (*for mortar*) paleta *f*

truant /'tru:ənt/ *n*. **play ~** hacer novillos

truce /tru:s/ *n* tregua *f*

truck /trʌk/ *n* camión *m*; (*Rail*) vagón *m*, furgón *m*; (*Amer, vegetables, fruit*) productos *mpl* de la huerta. **~ driver**, **~er** (*Amer*) *n* camionero *m*. **~ing** *n* transporte *m* por carretera

trudge /trʌdʒ/ *vi* andar penosamente

true /tru:/ *adj* (**-er, -est**) verdadero; (story, account) verídico; (friend) auténtico, de verdad. **~ to sth/s.o.** fiel a algo/uno. **be ~** ser cierto. **come ~** hacerse realidad

truffle /'trʌfl/ *n* trufa *f*; (*chocolate*) trufa *f* de chocolate

truly /'tru:lɪ/ *adv* verdaderamente; (*sincerely*) sinceramente. **yours ~** (*in letters*) cordiales saludos

trump /trʌmp/ *n* (*Cards*) triunfo *m*; (*fig*) baza *f*

trumpet /'trʌmpɪt/ *n* trompeta *f*. **~er** *n* trompetista *m* & *f*, trompeta *m* & *f*

truncheon /'trʌntʃən/ *n* porra *f*

trunk /trʌŋk/ *n* (*of tree*) tronco *m*; (*box*) baúl *m*; (*of elephant*) trompa *f*; (*Amer, Auto*) maletero *m*, cajuela *f* (*Mex*). **~s** *npl* bañador *m*, traje *m* de baño

truss /trʌs/ *vt.* **truss (up)** *vt* atar

trust /trʌst/ *n* confianza *f*; (*money, property*) fondo *m* de inversiones; (*institution*) fundación *f*. **on ~** a ojos cerrados; (*Com*) al fiado. ●*vi*. **~ in s.o./sth** confiar en uno/algo. ●*vt* confiar en; (*in negative sentences*) fiarse; (*hope*) esperar. **~ed** *adj* leal. **~ee** /trʌ'sti:/ *n* fideicomisario *m*. **~ful** *adj* confiado. **~ing** *adj* confiado. **~worthy**, **~y** *adj* digno de confianza

truth /tru:θ/ *n* (*pl* **-s** /tru:ðz/) verdad *f*; (*of account, story*) veracidad *f*. **~ful** *adj* veraz.

try /traɪ/ *vt* (*pt* **tried**) intentar; probar (food, product); (*be a strain on*) poner a prueba; (*Jurid*) procesar. **~ to do sth** tratar de hacer algo, intentar hacer algo. **~ not to forget** procura no olvidarte. ●*n* tentativa *f*, prueba *f*; (*Rugby*) ensayo *m*. □ **~ on** *vt* probarse (garment). □ **~ out** *vt* probar. **~ing** *adj* duro; (*annoying*) molesto

tsar /zɑ:(r)/ *n* zar *m*

T-shirt /'ti:ʃɜ:t/ *n* camiseta *f*

tub /tʌb/ *n* cuba *f*; (*for washing clothes*) tina *f*; (*bathtub*) bañera *f*; (*for ice cream*) envase *m*, tarrina *f*

tuba /'tju:bə/ *n* tuba *f*

tubby /'tʌbɪ/ *adj* (**-ier**, **-iest**) rechoncho

tube /tju:b/ *n* tubo *m*; (*fam, Rail*) metro *m*; (*Amer fam, television*) tele *f*. **inner ~** *n* cámara *f* de aire

tuberculosis /tju:bɜ:kjʊ'ləʊsɪs/ *n* tuberculosis *f*

tub|ing /'tju:bɪŋ/ *n* tubería *f*. **~ular** /-jʊlə(r)/ *adj* tubular

tuck /tʌk/ *n* (*fold*) jareta *f*. ●*vt* plegar; (*put*) meter. □ **~ in(to)** *vi* (*fam, eat*) ponerse a comer. □ **~ up** *vt* arropar (child)

Tuesday /'tju:zdeɪ/ *n* martes *m*

tuft /tʌft/ *n* (*of hair*) mechón *m*; (*of feathers*) penacho *m*; (*of grass*) mata *f*

tug /tʌg/ *vt* (*pt* **tugged**) tirar de. ●*vi*. **~ at sth** tirar de algo. ●*n* tirón *m*; (*Naut*) remolcador *m*. **~-of-war** *n* juego de tira y afloja

tuition /tju:'ɪʃn/ *n* clases *fpl*

tulip /'tju:lɪp/ *n* tulipán *m*

tumble /'tʌmbl/ *vi* caerse. ●*n* caída *f*. **~down** *adj* en ruinas. **~-drier** *n* secadora *f*. **~r** *n* (*glass*) vaso *m* (*de lados rectos*)

tummy /'tʌmɪ/ *n* 🅸 barriga *f*

tumour /'tju:mə(r)/ *n* tumor *m*

tumult /'tju:mʌlt/ *n* tumulto *m*. **~uous** /-'mʌltjʊəs/ *adj* (applause) apoteósico

tuna /'tju:nə/ *n* (*pl* **tuna**) atún *m*

tune /tju:n/ *n* melodía *f*; (*piece*) tonada *f*. **be in ~** estar afinado. **be out of ~** estar desafinado. ●*vt* afinar, sintonizar (radio, TV); (*Mec*) poner a punto. ●*vi*. **~ in (to)** sintonizar (con). □ **~ up** *vt/i* afinar. **~ful** *adj* melodioso. **~r** *n* afinador *m*; (*Radio*) sintonizador *m*

tunic /'tju:nɪk/ *n* túnica *f*

tunnel /'tʌnl/ *n* túnel *m*. ●*vi* (*pt* **tunnelled**) abrir un túnel

turban /'tɜ:bən/ *n* turbante *m*

turbine /'tɜ:baɪn/ *n* turbina *f*

turbo /'tɜ:bəʊ/ *n* (*pl* **-os**) turbo(compresor) *m*

turbulen|ce /'tɜ:bjʊləns/ *n* turbulencia *f*. **~t** *adj* turbulento

turf /tɜ:f/ *n* (*pl* **turfs** *or* **turves**) césped *m*; (*segment of grass*) tepe *m*. □ **~ out** *vt* 🅸 echar

turgid /'tɜ:dʒɪd/ *adj* (language) ampuloso

t

turkey /ˈtɜːkɪ/ *n* (*pl* **-eys**) pavo *m*
Turk|ey /ˈtɜːkɪ/ *f* Turquía *f*. **~ish** *adj & n* turco (*m*)
turmoil /ˈtɜːmɔɪl/ *n* confusión *f*
turn /tɜːn/ *vt* hacer girar; volver (head, page); doblar (corner); (*change*) cambiar; (*deflect*) desviar. **~ sth into sth** convertir *or* transformar algo en algo. • *vi* (handle) girar, dar vueltas; (person) volverse, darse la vuelta. **~ right** girar *or* doblar *or* torcer a la derecha. **~ red** ponerse rojo. **~ into sth** convertirse en algo. • *n* vuelta *f*; (*in road*) curva *f*; (*change*) giro *m*; (*sequence*) turno *m*; (*fam, of illness*) ataque *m*. **good ~** favor *m*. **in ~** a su vez. □ **~ down** *vt* (*fold*) doblar; (*reduce*) bajar; (*reject*) rechazar. □ **~ off** *vt* cerrar (tap); apagar (light, TV, etc). *vi* (*from road*) doblar. □ **~ on** *vt* abrir (tap); encender, prender (*LAm*) (light etc). □ **~ out** *vt* apagar (light etc). *vi* (*result*) resultar. □ **~ round** *vi* darse la vuelta. □ **~ up** *vi* aparecer. *vt* (*find*) encontrar; levantar (collar); subir (hem); acortar (trousers); poner más fuerte (gas). **~ed-up** *adj* (nose) respingón. **~ing** *n* (*in town*) bocacalle *f*. **we've missed the ~ing** nos hemos pasado la calle (*or* carretera). **~ing-point** *n* momento *m* decisivo.
turnip /ˈtɜːnɪp/ *n* nabo *m*
turn: ~over *n* (*Com*) facturación *f*; (*of staff*) movimiento *m*. **~pike** *n* (*Amer*) autopista *f* de peaje. **~stile** *n* torniquete *m*. **~table** *n* platina *f*. **~-up** *n* (*of trousers*) vuelta *f*, valenciana *f* (*Mex*)
turquoise /ˈtɜːkwɔɪz/ *adj & n* turquesa (*f*)
turret /ˈtʌrɪt/ *n* torrecilla *f*

turtle /ˈtɜːtl/ *n* tortuga *f* de mar; (*Amer, tortoise*) tortuga *f*
turves /tɜːvz/ *see* **TURF**
tusk /tʌsk/ *n* colmillo *m*
tussle /ˈtʌsl/ *n* lucha *f*
tutor /ˈtjuːtə(r)/ *n* profesor *m* particular
tuxedo /tʌkˈsiːdəʊ/ *n* (*pl* **-os**) (*Amer*) esmoquin *m*, smoking *m*
TV /tiːˈviː/ *n* televisión *f*, tele *f* [I]
twang /twæŋ/ *n* tañido *m*; (*in voice*) gangueo *m*
tweet /twiːt/ *n* piada *f*. • *vi* piar
tweezers /ˈtwiːzəz/ *npl* pinzas *fpl*
twel|fth /twelfθ/ *adj* duodécimo. • *n* doceavo *m*. **~ve** /twelv/ *adj & n* doce (*m*)
twent|ieth /ˈtwentɪəθ/ *adj* vigésimo. • *n* veinteavo *m*. **~y** /ˈtwentɪ/ *adj & n* veinte (*m*)
twice /twaɪs/ *adv* dos veces. **~ as many people** el doble de gente
twiddle /ˈtwɪdl/ *vt* (hacer) girar
twig /twɪg/ *n* ramita *f*. • *vi* (*pt* **twigged**) [I] caer, darse cuenta
twilight /ˈtwaɪlaɪt/ *n* crepúsculo *m*
twin /twɪn/ *adj & n* gemelo (*m*), mellizo (*m*) (*LAm*)
twine /twaɪn/ *n* cordel *m*, bramante *m*
twinge /twɪndʒ/ *n* punzada *f*; (*of remorse*) punzada *f*
twinkle /ˈtwɪŋkl/ *vi* centellear. • *n* centelleo *m*; (*in eye*) brillo *m*
twirl /twɜːl/ *vt* (hacer) girar. • *vi* girar. • *n* vuelta *f*
twist /twɪst/ *vt* retorcer; (*roll*) enrollar; girar (knob); tergiversar (words); (*distort*) retorcer. **~ one's ankle** torcerse el tobillo. • *vi* (rope, wire) enrollarse; (road, river) serpentear. • *n* torsión *f*; (*curve*)

vuelta *f*

twit /twɪt/ *n* [I] imbécil *m*

twitch /twɪtʃ/ *vi* moverse. ● *n* tic *m*

twitter /ˈtwɪtə(r)/ *vi* gorjear

two /tu:/ *adj & n* dos (*m*). **~-bit** *adj* (*Amer*) de tres al cuarto. **~-faced** *adj* falso, insincero. **~fold** *adj* doble. ● *adv* dos veces. **~pence** /ˈtʌpəns/ *n* dos peniques *mpl*. **~-piece (suit)** *n* traje *m* de dos piezas. **~-way** *adj* (traffic) de doble sentido

tycoon /taɪˈku:n/ *n* magnate *m*

tying /ˈtaɪɪŋ/ *see* TIE

type /taɪp/ *n* tipo *m*. ● *vt/i* escribir a máquina. **~-cast** *adj* (actor) encasillado. **~script** *n* texto *m* mecanografiado, manuscrito *m* (de una obra, novela etc). **~writer** *n* máquina *f* de escribir. **~written** *adj* escrito a máquina, mecanografiado

typhoon /taɪˈfu:n/ *n* tifón *m*

typical /ˈtɪpɪkl/ *adj* típico. **~ly** *adv* típicamente

typify /ˈtɪpɪfaɪ/ *vt* tipificar

typi|ng /ˈtaɪpɪŋ/ *n* mecanografía *f*. **~st** *n* mecanógrafo *m*

tyran|nical /tɪˈrænɪkl/ *adj* tiránico. **~ny** /ˈtɪrənɪ/ *n* tiranía *f*. **~t** /ˈtaɪərənt/ *n* tirano *m*

tyre /ˈtaɪə(r)/ *n* neumático *m*, llanta *f* (*LAm*)

Uu

udder /ˈʌdə(r)/ *n* ubre *f*

UFO /ˈju:fəʊ/ *abbr* (= **unidentified flying object**) OVNI *m* (objeto volante no identificado)

ugly /ˈʌglɪ/ *adj* (**-ier**, **-iest**) feo

UK /ju:ˈkeɪ/ *abbr* (= **United Kingdom**) Reino *m* Unido

Ukraine /ju:ˈkreɪn/ *n* Ucrania *f*

ulcer /ˈʌlsə(r)/ *n* úlcera *f*; (*external*) llaga *f*

ultimate /ˈʌltɪmət/ *adj* (*eventual*) final; (*utmost*) máximo. **~ly** *adv* en última instancia; (*in the long run*) a la larga

ultimatum /ʌltɪˈmeɪtəm/ *n* (*pl* **-ums**) ultimátum *m*

ultra... /ˈʌltrə/ *pref* ultra... **~violet** /-ˈvaɪələt/ *adj* ultravioleta

umbilical cord /ʌmˈbɪlɪkl/ *n* cordón *m* umbilical

umbrella /ʌmˈbrelə/ *n* paraguas *m*

umpire /ˈʌmpaɪə(r)/ *n* árbitro *m*. ● *vt* arbitrar

umpteen /ˈʌmpti:n/ *adj* [I] tropecientos [I]. **~th** *adj* [I] enésimo

un... /ʌn/ *pref* in..., des..., no, poco, sin

UN /ju:ˈen/ *abbr* (= **United Nations**) ONU *f* (Organización de las Naciones Unidas)

unable /ʌnˈeɪbl/ *adj*. **be ~ to** no poder; (*be incapable of*) ser incapaz de

unacceptable /ʌnəkˈseptəbl/ *adj* (behaviour) inaceptable; (terms) inadmisible

unaccompanied /ʌnə'kʌmpənɪd/ *adj* (luggage) no acompañado; (person, instrument) solo; (singing) sin acompañamiento

unaccustomed /ʌnə'kʌstəmd/ *adj* desacostumbrado. **be ~ to** *adj* no estar acostumbrado a

unaffected /ʌnə'fektɪd/ *adj* natural

unaided /ʌn'eɪdɪd/ *adj* sin ayuda

unanimous /ju:'nænɪməs/ *adj* unánime. **~ly** *adv* unánimemente; (elect) por unanimidad

unarmed /ʌn'ɑ:md/ *adj* desarmado

unattended /ʌnə'tendɪd/ *adj* sin vigilar

unattractive /ʌnə'træktɪv/ *adj* poco atractivo

unavoidabl|e /ʌnə'vɔɪdəbl/ *adj* inevitable. **~y** *adv.* **I was ~y delayed** no pude evitar llegar tarde

unaware /ʌnə'weə(r)/ *adj.* **be ~ of** ignorar, no ser consciente de. **~s** /-eəz/ *adv* desprevenido

unbearabl|e /ʌn'beərəbl/ *adj* insoportable, inaguantable. **~y** *adv* inaguantablemente

unbeat|able /ʌn'bi:təbl/ *adj* (quality) insuperable; (team) invencible. **~en** *adj* no vencido; (record) insuperado

unbelievabl|e /ʌnbɪ'li:vəbl/ *adj* increíble. **~y** *adv* increíblemente

unbiased /ʌn'baɪəst/ *adj* imparcial

unblock /ʌn'blɒk/ *vt* desatascar

unbolt /ʌn'bəʊlt/ *vt* descorrer el pestillo de

unborn /ʌn'bɔ:n/ *adj* que todavía no ha nacido

unbreakable /ʌn'breɪkəbl/ *adj* irrompible

unbroken /ʌn'brəʊkən/ *adj* (*intact*) intacto; (*continuous*) ininterrumpido

unbutton /ʌn'bʌtn/ *vt* desabotonar, desabrochar

uncalled-for /ʌn'kɔ:ldfɔ:(r)/ *adj* fuera de lugar

uncanny /ʌn'kænɪ/ *adj* (**-ier**, **-iest**) raro, extraño

uncertain /ʌn'sɜ:tn/ *adj* incierto; (*hesitant*) vacilante. **be ~ of/about sth** no estar seguro de algo. **~ty** *n* incertidumbre *f*

uncharitable /ʌn'tʃærɪtəbl/ *adj* severo

uncivilized /ʌn'sɪvɪlaɪzd/ *adj* incivilizado

uncle /'ʌŋkl/ *n* tío *m*

> **i** **Uncle Sam** Es la típica personificación de EE.UU., en que éste es representado por un hombre de barba blanca, vestido con los colores nacionales y con un sombrero de copa adornado con estrellas. Es posible que la imagen se haya extraído del cartel de reclutamiento, en 1917, que llevaba la leyenda: "A Ud. lo necesito".

unclean /ʌn'kli:n/ *adj* impuro

unclear /ʌn'klɪə(r)/ *adj* poco claro

uncomfortable /ʌn'kʌmfətəbl/ *adj* incómodo

uncommon /ʌn'kɒmən/ *adj* poco común

uncompromising /ʌn'kɒmprəmaɪzɪŋ/ *adj* intransigente

unconcerned /ʌnkən'sɜ:nd/ *adj* indiferente

unconditional /ʌnkən'dɪʃənl/ *adj* incondicional

unconnected /ʌnkə'nektɪd/ *adj* (*unrelated*) sin conexión. **the**

events are ~ estos acontecimientos no guardan ninguna relación (entre sí)

unconscious /ʌnˈkɒnʃəs/ *adj* (*Med*) inconsciente. **~ly** *adv* inconscientemente

unconventional /ʌnkənˈvenʃənl/ *adj* poco convencional

uncork /ʌnˈkɔːk/ *vt* descorchar

uncouth /ʌnˈkuːθ/ *adj* zafio

uncover /ʌnˈkʌvə(r)/ *vt* destapar; revelar (plot, scandal)

undaunted /ʌnˈdɔːntɪd/ *adj* impertérrito

undecided /ʌndɪˈsaɪdɪd/ *adj* indeciso

undeniabl|e /ʌndɪˈnaɪəbl/ *adj* innegable. **~y** *adv* sin lugar a dudas

under /ˈʌndə(r)/ *prep* debajo de; (*less than*) menos de; (heading) bajo; (*according to*) según; (*expressing movement*) por debajo de. ● *adv* debajo, abajo

under... *pref* sub...

under: ~carriage *n* tren *m* de aterrizaje. **~charge** *vt* /-ˈtʃɑːdʒ/ cobrarle de menos a. **~clothes** *npl* ropa *f* interior. **~coat**, **~coating** (*Amer*) *n* (*paint*) pintura *f* base; (*first coat*) primera mano *f* de pintura. **~cover** *adj* /-ˈkʌvə(r)/ secreto. **~current** *n* corriente *f* submarina. **~dog** *n*. **the ~dog** el que tiene menos posibilidades. **the ~dogs** *npl* los de abajo. **~done** *adj* /-ˈdʌn/ (meat) poco hecho. **~estimate** /-ˈestɪmeɪt/ *vt* (*underrate*) subestimar. **~fed** /-ˈfed/ *adj* subalimentado. **~foot** /-ˈfʊt/ *adv* debajo de los pies. **~go** *vt* (*pt* **-went**, *pp* **-gone**) sufrir. **~graduate** /-ˈgrædjʊət/ *n* estudiante *m* universitario (no licenciado). **~ground** /-ˈgraʊnd/ *adv* bajo tierra; (*in secret*) clandestinamente. ● /-graʊnd/ *adj* subterráneo; (*secret*) clandestino. ● *n* metro *m*. **~growth** *n* maleza *f*. **~hand** /-ˈhænd/ *adj* (*secret*) clandestino; (*deceptive*) fraudulento. **~lie** /-ˈlaɪ/ *vt* (*pt* **-lay**, *pp* **-lain**, *pres p* **-lying**) subyacer a. **~line** /-ˈlaɪn/ *vt* subrayar. **~lying** /-ˈlaɪɪŋ/ *adj* subyacente. **~mine** /-ˈmaɪn/ *vt* socavar. **~neath** /-ˈniːθ/ *prep* debajo de, abajo de (*LAm*). ● *adv* por debajo. **~paid** /-ˈpeɪd/ *adj* mal pagado. **~pants** *npl* calzoncillos *mpl*. **~pass** *n* paso *m* subterráneo; (*for traffic*) paso *m* inferior. **~privileged** /-ˈprɪvəlɪdʒd/ *adj* desfavorecido. **~rate** /-ˈreɪt/ *vt* subestimar. **~rated** /-ˈreɪtɪd/ *adj* no debidamente apreciado. **~shirt** *n* (*Amer*) camiseta *f* (interior).

understand /ʌndəˈstænd/ *vt* (*pt* **-stood**) entender; (*empathize with*) comprender, entender. ● *vi* entender, comprender. **~able** *adj* comprensible. **~ing** *adj* comprensivo. ● *n* (*grasp*) entendimiento *m*; (*sympathy*) comprensión *f*; (*agreement*) acuerdo *m*

under: ~statement *n* subestimación *f*. **~take** /-ˈteɪk/ (*pt* **-took**, *pp* **-taken**) emprender (task); asumir (responsibility). **~take to do sth** comprometerse a hacer algo. **~taker** *n* director *m* de pompas fúnebres. **~taking** /-ˈteɪkɪŋ/ *n* empresa *f*; (*promise*) promesa *f*. **~tone** *n*. **in an ~tone** en voz baja. **~value** /-ˈvæljuː/ *vt* subvalorar. **~water** /-ˈwɔːtə(r)/ *adj* submarino. ● *adv* debajo del agua. **~wear** *n* ropa *f* interior. **~weight** /-ˈweɪt/ *adj* de peso más bajo que el normal. **~went** /-ˈwent/ see UNDERGO.

~**world** *n* (*criminals*) hampa *f*. ~**write** /-'raɪt/ *vt* (*pt* **-wrote**, *pp* **-written**) (*Com*) asegurar; (*guarantee financially*) financiar

undeserved /ʌndɪ'zɜ:vd/ *adj* inmerecido

undesirable /ʌndɪ'zaɪərəbl/ *adj* indeseable

undignified /ʌn'dɪgnɪfaɪd/ *adj* indecoroso

undisputed /ʌndɪs'pju:tɪd/ *adj* (champion) indiscutido; (facts) innegable

undo /ʌn'du:/ *vt* (*pt* **-did**, *pp* **-done**) desabrochar (button, jacket); abrir (zip); desatar (knot, laces)

undoubted /ʌn'daʊtɪd/ *adj* indudable. ~**ly** *adv* indudablemente, sin duda

undress /ʌn'dres/ *vt* desvestir, desnudar. • *vi* desvestirse, desnudarse

undue /ʌn'dju:/ *adj* excesivo

undulate /'ʌndjʊleɪt/ *vi* ondular

unduly /ʌn'dju:lɪ/ *adv* excesivamente

unearth /ʌn'ɜ:θ/ *vt* desenterrar; descubrir (document)

unearthly /ʌn'ɜ:θlɪ/ *adj* sobrenatural. **at an ~ hour** a estas horas intempestivas

uneasy /ʌn'i:zɪ/ *adj* incómodo

uneconomic /ʌni:kə'nɒmɪk/ *adj* poco económico

uneducated /ʌn'edjʊkeɪtɪd/ *adj* sin educación

unemploy|ed /ʌnɪm'plɔɪd/ *adj* desempleado, parado. ~**ment** *n* desempleo *m*, paro *m*

unending /ʌn'endɪŋ/ *adj* interminable, sin fin

unequal /ʌn'i:kwəl/ *adj* desigual

unequivocal /ʌnɪ'kwɪvəkl/ *adj* inequívoco

unethical /ʌn'eθɪkl/ *adj* poco ético, inmoral

uneven /ʌn'i:vn/ *adj* desigual

unexpected /ʌnɪk'spektɪd/ *adj* inesperado; (result) imprevisto. ~**ly** *adv* (arrive) de improviso; (happen) de forma imprevista

unfair /ʌn'feə(r)/ *adj* injusto; improcedente (dismissal). ~**ly** *adv* injustamente

unfaithful /ʌn'feɪθfl/ *adj* infiel

unfamiliar /ʌnfə'mɪlɪə(r)/ *adj* desconocido. **be ~ with** desconocer

unfasten /ʌn'fɑ:sn/ *vt* desabrochar (clothes); (*untie*) desatar

unfavourable /ʌn'feɪvərəbl/ *adj* desfavorable

unfeeling /ʌn'fi:lɪŋ/ *adj* insensible

unfit /ʌn'fɪt/ *adj*. **I'm ~** no estoy en forma. **~ for human consumption** no apto para el consumo

unfold /ʌn'fəʊld/ *vt* desdoblar; desplegar (wings); (*fig*) revelar. • *vi* (leaf) abrirse; (events) desarrollarse

unforeseen /ʌnfɔ:'si:n/ *adj* imprevisto

unforgettable /ʌnfə'getəbl/ *adj* inolvidable

unforgivable /ʌnfə'gɪvəbl/ *adj* imperdonable

unfortunate /ʌn'fɔ:tʃənət/ *adj* desafortunado; (*regrettable*) lamentable. ~**ly** *adv* desafortunadamente; (*stronger*) por desgracia, desgraciadamente

unfounded /ʌn'faʊndɪd/ *adj* infundado

unfriendly /ʌn'frendlɪ/ *adj* poco amistoso; (*stronger*) antipático

unfurl /ʌn'fɜːl/ *vt* desplegar

ungainly /ʌn'gemlɪ/ *adj* desgarbado

ungrateful /ʌn'greɪtfl/ *adj* desagradecido, ingrato

unhapp|iness /ʌn'hæpmes/ *n* infelicidad *f*, tristeza *f*. **~y** *adj* (**-ier, -iest**) infeliz, triste; (*unsuitable*) inoportuno. **be ~y about sth** no estar contento con algo

unharmed /ʌn'hɑːmd/ *adj* (person) ileso

unhealthy /ʌn'helθɪ/ *adj* (**-ier, -iest**) (person) de mala salud; (complexion) enfermizo; (conditions) poco saludable

unhurt /ʌn'hɜːt/ *adj* ileso

unification /juːnɪfɪ'keɪʃn/ *n* unificación *f*

uniform /'juːnɪfɔːm/ *adj & n* uniforme (*m*). **~ity** /-'fɔːmətɪ/ *n* uniformidad *f*

unify /'juːnɪfaɪ/ *vt* unir

unilateral /juːnɪ'lætərəl/ *adj* unilateral

unimaginable /ʌnɪ'mædʒɪnəbl/ *adj* inimaginable

unimaginative /ʌnɪ'mædʒɪnətɪv/ *adj* (person) poco imaginativo

unimportant /ʌnɪm'pɔːtnt/ *adj* sin importancia

uninhabited /ʌnɪn'hæbɪtɪd/ *adj* deshabitado; (island) despoblado

unintelligible /ʌnɪn'telɪdʒəbl/ *adj* ininteligible

unintentional /ʌnɪn'tenʃənl/ *adj* involuntario

union /'juːnjən/ *n* unión *f*; (*trade union*) sindicato *m*; (*student ~*) asociación *f* de estudiantes. **U~ Jack** *n* bandera *f* del Reino Unido

unique /juː'niːk/ *adj* único

unison /'juːnɪsn/ *n*. **in ~** al unísono

unit /'juːnɪt/ *n* unidad *f*; (*of furniture etc*) módulo *m*; (*in course*) módulo *m*

unite /juː'naɪt/ *vt* unir. ● *vi* unirse. **U~d Kingdom** *n* Reino *m* Unido. **U~d Nations** *n* Organización *f* de las Naciones Unidas (ONU). **U~d States (of America)** *n* Estados *mpl* Unidos (de América)

unity /'juːnɪtɪ/ *n* unidad *f*

univers|al /juːnɪ'vɜːsl/ *adj* universal. **~e** /'juːnɪvɜːs/ *n* universo *m*

university /juːnɪ'vɜːsətɪ/ *n* universidad *f*. ● *adj* universitario

unjust /ʌn'dʒʌst/ *adj* injusto. **~ified** /-ɪfaɪd/ *adj* injustificado

unkind /ʌn'kaɪnd/ *adj* poco amable; (*cruel*) cruel; (remark) hiriente

unknown /ʌn'nəʊn/ *adj* desconocido

unlawful /ʌn'lɔːfl/ *adj* ilegal

unleaded /ʌn'ledɪd/ *adj* (fuel) sin plomo

unleash /ʌn'liːʃ/ *vt* soltar

unless /ʌn'les, ən'les/ *conj* a menos que, a no ser que

unlike /ʌn'laɪk/ *prep* diferente de. (*in contrast to*) a diferencia de. **~ly** *adj* improbable

unlimited /ʌn'lɪmɪtɪd/ *adj* ilimitado

unlisted /ʌn'lɪstɪd/ *adj* (*Amer*) que no figura en la guía telefónica, privado (*Mex*)

unload /ʌn'ləʊd/ *vt* descargar

unlock /ʌn'lɒk/ *vt* abrir (con llave)

unluck|ily /ʌn'lʌkɪlɪ/ *adv* desgraciadamente. **~y** *adj* (**-ier, -iest**) (person) sin suerte, desafortunado. **be ~y** tener mala suerte; (*bring bad luck*) traer mala suerte

unmarried /ʌn'mærɪd/ *adj*

soltero

unmask /ʌn'mɑ:sk/ *vt* desenmascarar

unmentionable /ʌn'menʃənəbl/ *adj* inmencionable

unmistakable /ʌnmɪ'steɪkəbl/ *adj* inconfundible

unnatural /ʌn'nætʃərəl/ *adj* poco natural; (*not normal*) anormal

unnecessar|ily /ʌn'nesəsərɪlɪ/ *adv* innecesariamente. **~y** *adj* innecesario

unnerve /ʌn'nɜ:v/ *vt* desconcertar

unnoticed /ʌn'nəʊtɪst/ *adj* inadvertido

unobtainable /ʌnəb'teɪnəbl/ *adj* imposible de conseguir

unobtrusive /ʌnəb'tru:sɪv/ *adj* discreto

unofficial /ʌnə'fɪʃl/ *adj* no oficial. **~ly** *adv* extraoficialmente

unpack /ʌn'pæk/ *vt* sacar las cosas de (bags); deshacer, desempacar (*LAm*) (suitcase). ● *vi* deshacer las maletas, desempacar (*LAm*)

unpaid /ʌn'peɪd/ *adj* (work) no retribuido, no remunerado; (leave) sin sueldo

unperturbed /ʌnpə'tɜ:bd/ *adj* impasible. **he carried on ~** siguió sin inmutarse

unpleasant /ʌn'pleznt/ *adj* desagradable

unplug /ʌn'plʌg/ *vt* desenchufar

unpopular /ʌn'pɒpjʊlə(r)/ *adj* impopular

unprecedented /ʌn'presɪdentɪd/ *adj* sin precedentes

unpredictable /ʌnprɪ'dɪktəbl/ *adj* imprevisible

unprepared /ʌnprɪ'peəd/ *adj* no preparado; (*unready*) desprevenido

unprofessional /ʌnprə'feʃənəl/ *adj* poco profesional

unprofitable /ʌn'prɒfɪtəbl/ *adj* no rentable

unprotected /ʌnprə'tektɪd/ *adj* sin protección; (sex) sin el uso de preservativos

unqualified /ʌn'kwɒlɪfaɪd/ *adj* sin título; (*fig*) absoluto

unquestion|able /ʌn'kwestʃənəbl/ *adj* incuestionable, innegable. **~ing** *adj* (obedience) ciego; (loyalty) incondicional

unravel /ʌn'rævl/ *vt* (*pt* **unravelled**) desenredar; desentrañar (mystery)

unreal /ʌn'rɪəl/ *adj* irreal. **~istic** /-'lɪstɪk/ *adj* poco realista

unreasonable /ʌn'ri:zənəbl/ *adj* irrazonable

unrecognizable /ʌnrekəg'naɪzəbl/ *adj* irreconocible

unrelated /ʌnrɪ'leɪtɪd/ *adj* (facts) no relacionados (entre sí); (people) no emparentado

unreliable /ʌnrɪ'laɪəbl/ *adj* (person) informal; (machine) poco fiable; (information) poco fidedigno

unrepentant /ʌnrɪ'pentənt/ *adj* impenitente

unrest /ʌn'rest/ *n* (*discontent*) descontento *m*; (*disturbances*) disturbios *mpl*

unrivalled /ʌn'raɪvld/ *adj* incomparable

unroll /ʌn'rəʊl/ *vt* desenrollar. ● *vi* desenrollarse

unruffled /ʌn'rʌfld/ (person) sereno

unruly /ʌn'ru:lɪ/ *adj* (class) indisciplinado; (child) revoltoso

unsafe /ʌn'seɪf/ *adj* inseguro

unsatisfactory /ʌnsætɪs'fæktərɪ/ *adj* insatisfactorio

unsavoury /ʌn'seɪvərɪ/ *adj* desagradable
unscathed /ʌn'skeɪðd/ *adj* ileso
unscheduled /ʌn'ʃedju:ld/ *adj* no programado, no previsto
unscrew /ʌn'skru:/ *vt* destornillar; desenroscar (lid)
unscrupulous /ʌn'skru:pjʊləs/ *adj* inescrupuloso
unseemly /ʌn'si:mlɪ/ *adj* indecoroso
unseen /ʌn'si:n/ *adj* (danger) oculto; (*unnoticed*) sin ser visto
unselfish /ʌn'selfɪʃ/ *adj* (act) desinteresado; (person) nada egoísta
unsettle /ʌn'setl/ *vt* desestabilizar (situation); alterar (plans). **~d** *adj* agitado; (weather) inestable; (*undecided*) pendiente (de resolución)
unshakeable /ʌn'ʃeɪkəbl/ *adj* inquebrantable
unshaven /ʌn'ʃeɪvn/ *adj* sin afeitar, sin rasurar (*Mex*)
unsightly /ʌn'saɪtlɪ/ *adj* feo
unskilled /ʌn'skɪld/ *adj* (work) no especializado; (worker) no cualificado, no calificado
unsociable /ʌn'səʊʃəbl/ *adj* insociable
unsolved /ʌn'sɒlvd/ *adj* no resuelto; (murder) sin esclarecerse
unsophisticated /ʌnsə'fɪstɪkeɪtɪd/ *adj* sencillo
unsound /ʌn'saʊnd/ *adj* poco sólido
unspecified /ʌn'spesɪfaɪd/ *adj* no especificado
unstable /ʌn'steɪbl/ *adj* inestable
unsteady /ʌn'stedɪ/ *adj* inestable, poco firme
unstuck /ʌn'stʌk/ *adj* despegado. **come ~** despegarse; (*fail*) fracasar
unsuccessful /ʌnsək'sesfʊl/ *adj* (attempt) infructuoso. **be ~** no tener éxito, fracasar
unsuitable /ʌn'su:təbl/ *adj* (clothing) poco apropiado, poco adecuado; (time) inconveniente. **she is ~ for the job** no es la persona indicada para el trabajo
unsure /ʌn'ʃʊə(r)/ *adj* inseguro
unthinkable /ʌn'θɪŋkəbl/ *adj* inconcebible
untid|iness /ʌn'taɪdɪnəs/ *n* desorden *m*. **~y** *adj* (**-ier**, **-iest**) desordenado; (appearance, writing) descuidado
untie /ʌn'taɪ/ *vt* desatar, desamarrar (*LAm*)
until /ən'tɪl, ʌn'tɪl/ *prep* hasta. ● *conj* hasta que
untold /ʌn'təʊld/ *adj* incalculable
untouched /ʌn'tʌtʃt/ *adj* intacto
untried /ʌn'traɪd/ *adj* no probado
untrue /ʌn'tru:/ *adj* falso
unused /ʌn'ju:zd/ *adj* nuevo. ● /ʌn'ju:st/ *adj*. **~ to** no acostumbrado a
unusual /ʌn'ju:ʒʊəl/ *adj* poco común, poco corriente. **it's ~ to see so many people** es raro ver a tanta gente. **~ly** *adv* excepcionalmente, inusitadamente
unveil /ʌn'veɪl/ *vt* descubrir
unwanted /ʌn'wɒntɪd/ *adj* superfluo; (child) no deseado
unwelcome /ʌn'welkəm/ *adj* (news) poco grato; (guest) inoportuno
unwell /ʌn'wel/ *adj* indispuesto
unwieldy /ʌn'wi:ldɪ/ *adj* pesado y difícil de manejar
unwilling /ʌn'wɪlɪŋ/ *adj* mal dispuesto. **be ~** no querer
unwind /ʌn'waɪnd/ *vt* (*pt* **unwound**) desenrollar. ● *vi* (*fam*,

relax) relajarse

unwise /ʌn'waɪz/ *adj* poco sensato

unworthy /ʌn'wɜːðɪ/ *adj* indigno

unwrap /ʌn'ræp/ *vt* (*pt* **unwrapped**) desenvolver

unwritten /ʌn'rɪtn/ *adj* no escrito; (agreement) verbal

up /ʌp/ *adv* arriba; (*upwards*) hacia arriba; (*higher*) más arriba. **~ here** aquí arriba. **~ there** allí arriba. **~ to** hasta. **he's not ~ yet** todavía no se ha levantado. **be ~ against** enfrentarse con. **come ~** subir. **go ~** subir. **he's not ~ to the job** no tiene las condiciones necesarias para el trabajo. **it's ~ to you** depende de ti. **what's ~?** ¿qué pasa? ● *prep.* **go ~ the stairs** subir la escalera. **it's just ~ the road** está un poco más allá. ● *vt* (*pt* **upped**) aumentar. ● *n.* **~s and downs** *npl* altibajos *mpl*; (*of life*) vicisitudes *fpl*. **~bringing** /'ʌpbrɪŋɪŋ/ *n* educación *f*. **~date** /ʌp'deɪt/ *vt* poner al día. **~grade** /ʌp'greɪd/ *vt* elevar de categoría (person); mejorar (equipment). **~heaval** /ʌp'hiːvl/ *n* trastorno *m*. **~hill** /ʌp'hɪl/ *adv* cuesta arriba. **~hold** /ʌp'həʊld/ *vt* (*pt* **upheld**) mantener (principle); confirmar (decision). **~holster** /ʌp'həʊlstə(r)/ *vt* tapizar. **~holstery** *n* tapicería *f*. **~keep** *n* mantenimiento *m*. **~-market** /ʌp'mɑːkɪt/ *adj* de categoría

upon /ə'pɒn/ *prep* sobre. **once ~ a time** érase una vez

upper /'ʌpə(r)/ *adj* superior. **~ class** *n* clase *f* alta

up:: **~right** *adj* vertical; (citizen) recto. **place sth ~right** poner algo de pie. **~rising** /'ʌpraɪzɪŋ/ *n* levantamiento *m*. **~roar** *n* tumulto *m*

upset /ʌp'set/ *vt* (*pt* **upset**, *pres p* **upsetting**) (*hurt*) disgustar; (*offend*) ofender; (*distress*) alterar; desbaratar (plans). ● *adj* (*hurt*) disgustado; (*distressed*) alterado; (*offended*) ofendido; (*disappointed*) desilusionado. ● /'ʌpset/ *n* trastorno *m*. **have a stomach ~** estar mal del estómago

up: **~shot** *n* resultado *m*. **~side down** /ʌpsaɪd'daʊn/ *adv* al revés (*con la parte de arriba abajo*); (*in disorder*) patas arriba. **turn sth ~side down** poner algo boca abajo. **~stairs** /ʌp'steəz/ *adv* arriba. **go ~stairs** subir. ● /'ʌpsteəz/ *adj* de arriba. **~start** *n* advenedizo *m*. **~state** *adv* (*Amer*). **I live ~state** vivo en el norte del estado. **~stream** /ʌp'striːm/ *adv* río arriba. **~take** *n*. **be quick on the ~take** agarrar las cosas al vuelo. **~-to-date** /ʌptə'deɪt/ *adj* al día; (news) de última hora. **~turn** *n* repunte *m*, mejora *f*. **~ward** /'ʌpwəd/ *adj* (movement) ascendente; (direction) hacia arriba. ● *adv* hacia arriba. **~wards** *adv* hacia arriba

uranium /jʊ'reɪnɪəm/ *n* uranio *m*

Uranus /'jʊərənəs//jʊə'reɪnəs/ *n* Urano *m*

urban /'ɜːbən/ *adj* urbano

urchin /'ɜːtʃɪn/ *n* pilluelo *m*

urge /ɜːdʒ/ *vt* instar. **~ s.o. to do sth** instar a uno a que haga algo. ● *n* impulso *m*; (*wish, whim*) ganas *fpl*. □ **~ on** *vt* animar

urgen|cy /'ɜːdʒənsɪ/ *n* urgencia *f*. **~t** *adj* urgente. **~tly** *adv* urgentemente, con urgencia

urin|ate /'jʊərɪmeɪt/ *vi* orinar. **~e** /'jʊərɪn/ *n* orina *f*

Uruguay /jʊərəgwaɪ/ *n* Uruguay

m. **~an** *adj & n* uruguayo (*m*)

us /ʌs, əs/ *pron* nos; (*after prep*) nosotros *m*, nosotras *f*

US(A) /juːes'eɪ/ *abbr* (= **United States (of America)**) EE.UU. (*only written*), Estados *mpl* Unidos

usage /'juːzɪdʒ/ *n* uso *m*

use /juːz/ *vt* usar; utilizar (service, facilities); consumir (fuel). ● /juːs/ *n* uso *m*, empleo *m*. **be of ~** servir. **it is no ~** es inútil. □ **~ up** *vt* agotar, consumir. **~d** /juːzd/ *adj* usado. ● /juːst/ *v mod* **~ to. he ~d to say** decía, solía decir. **there ~d to be** (antes) había. ● *adj*/juːst/. **be ~d to** estar acostumbrado a. **~ful** /'juːsfl/ *adj* útil. **~fully** *adv* útilmente. **~less** *adj* inútil; (person) incompetente. **~r** /-zə(r)/ *n* usuario *m*. **drug ~** *n* consumidor *m* de drogas

usher /'ʌʃə(r)/ *n* (*in theatre etc*) acomodador *m*. □ **~ in** *vt* hacer pasar; marcar el comienzo de (new era). **~ette** /-'ret/ *n* acomodadora *f*

USSR *abbr* (*History*) (= **Union of Soviet Socialist Republics**) URSS

usual /'juːʒʊəl/ *adj* usual; (*habitual*) acostumbrado, habitual; (place, route) de siempre. **as ~** como de costumbre, como siempre. **~ly** *adv* normalmente. **he ~ly wakes up early** suele despertarse temprano

utensil /juː'tensl/ *n* utensilio *m*

utilize /'juːtɪlaɪz/ *vt* utilizar

utmost /'ʌtməʊst/ *adj* sumo. ● *n*. **do one's ~** hacer todo lo posible (to para)

utter /'ʌtə(r)/ *adj* completo. ● *vt* pronunciar (word); dar (cry). **~ly** *adv* totalmente

U-turn /'juːtɜːn/ *n* cambio *m* de sentido

Vv

vacan|cy /'veɪkənsɪ/ *n* (*job*) vacante *f*; (*room*) habitación *f* libre. **~t** *adj* (building) desocupado; (seat) libre; (post) vacante; (look) ausente

vacate /və'keɪt/ *vt* dejar

vacation /və'keɪʃn/ *n* (*Amer*) vacaciones *fpl*. **go on ~** ir de vacaciones. **~er** *n* (*Amer*) veraneante *m & f*

vaccin|ate /'væksɪmeɪt/ *vt* vacunar. **~ation** /-'neɪʃn/ *n* vacunación *f*. **~e** /'væksiːn/ *n* vacuna *f*

vacuum /'vækjʊəm/ *n* vacío *m*. **~ cleaner** *n* aspiradora *f*

vagina /və'dʒaɪnə/ *n* vagina *f*

vague /veɪg/ *adj* (**-er**, **-est**) vago; (outline) borroso; (person, expression) despistado. **~ly** *adv* vagamente

vain /veɪn/ *adj* (**-er**, **-est**) vanidoso; (*useless*) vano. **in ~** en vano

Valentine's Day /'væləntaɪnz/ *n* el día de San Valentín

valiant /'vælɪənt/ *adj* valeroso

valid /'vælɪd/ *adj* válido. **~ate** /-eɪt/ *vt* dar validez a; validar (contract). **~ity** /-'ɪdətɪ/ *n* validez *f*

valley /'vælɪ/ *n* (*pl* **-eys**) valle *m*

valour /'vælə(r)/ *n* valor *m*

valu|able /'væljʊəbl/ *adj* valioso. **~ables** *npl* objetos *mpl* de valor. **~ation** /-'eɪʃn/ *n* valoración *f*. **~e** /'væljuː/ *n* valor *m*. ● *vt* valorar; tasar, valorar, avaluar (*LAm*) (property). **~e added tax** *n* impuesto *m* sobre el valor añadido

valve /vælv/ *n* válvula *f*

vampire /'væmpaɪə(r)/ *n*

vampiro *m*

van /væn/ *n* furgoneta *f*, camioneta *f*; (*Rail*) furgón *m*

vandal /ˈvændl/ *n* vándalo *m*. **~ism** *n* vandalismo *m*. **~ize** *vt* destruir

vanilla /vəˈnɪlə/ *n* vainilla *f*

vanish /ˈvænɪʃ/ *vi* desaparecer

vanity /ˈvænɪtɪ/ *n* vanidad *f*. **~ case** *n* neceser *m*

vapour /ˈveɪpə(r)/ *n* vapor *m*

varia|ble /ˈveərɪəbl/ *adj* variable. **~nce** /-əns/ *n*. **at ~ce** en desacuerdo. **~nt** *n* variante *f*. **~tion** /-ˈeɪʃn/ *n* variación *f*

vari|ed /ˈveərɪd/ *adj* variado. **~ety** /vəˈraɪətɪ/ *n* variedad *f*. **~ety show** *n* espectáculo *m* de variedades. **~ous** /ˈveərɪəs/ *adj* (*several*) varios; (*different*) diversos

varnish /ˈvɑːnɪʃ/ *n* barniz *m*; (*for nails*) esmalte *m*. ●*vt* barnizar; pintar (nails)

vary /ˈveərɪ/ *vt/i* variar

vase /vɑːz/, (*Amer*) /veɪs/ *n* (*for flowers*) florero *m*; (*ornamental*) jarrón *m*

vast /vɑːst/ *adj* vasto, extenso; (size) inmenso. **~ly** *adv* infinitamente

vat /væt/ *n* cuba *f*

VAT /viːeɪˈtiː/ *abbr* (= **value added tax**) IVA *m*

vault /vɔːlt/ *n* (*roof*) bóveda *f*; (*in bank*) cámara *f* acorazada; (*tomb*) cripta *f*. ●*vt/i* saltar

VCR *n* = **videocassette recorder**

VDU *n* = **visual display unit**

veal /viːl/ *n* ternera *f*

veer /vɪə(r)/ *vi* dar un viraje, virar

vegeta|ble /ˈvedʒɪtəbl/ *adj* vegetal. ●*n* verdura *f*. **~rian** /vedʒɪˈteərɪən/ *adj & n* vegetariano (*m*). **~tion** /vedʒɪˈteɪʃn/ *n* vegetación *f*

vehement /ˈviːəmənt/ *adj* vehemente. **~tly** *adv* con vehemencia

vehicle /ˈviːɪkl/ *n* vehículo *m*

veil /veɪl/ *n* velo *m*

vein /veɪn/ *n* vena *f*; (*in marble*) veta *f*

velocity /vɪˈlɒsɪtɪ/ *n* velocidad *f*

velvet /ˈvelvɪt/ *n* terciopelo *m*

vendetta /venˈdetə/ *n* vendetta *f*

vend|ing machine /ˈvendɪŋ/ *n* distribuidor *m* automático. **~or** /ˈvendə(r)/ *n* vendedor *m*

veneer /vəˈnɪə(r)/ *n* chapa *f*, enchapado *m*; (*fig*) barniz *m*, apariencia *f*

venerate /ˈvenəreɪt/ *vt* venerar

venereal /vəˈnɪərɪəl/ *adj* venéreo

Venetian blind /vəˈniːʃn/ *n* persiana *f* veneciana

Venezuela /venəˈzweɪlə/ *n* Venezuela *f*. **~n** *adj & n* venezolano (*m*)

vengeance /ˈvendʒəns/ *n* venganza *f*. **with a ~** (*fig*) con ganas

venom /ˈvenəm/ *n* veneno *m*. **~ous** *adj* venenoso

vent /vent/ *n* (conducto *m* de) ventilación; (*air ~*) respiradero *m*. **give ~ to** dar rienda suelta a. ●*vt* descargar

ventilat|e /ˈventɪleɪt/ *vt* ventilar. **~ion** /-ˈleɪʃn/ *n* ventilación *f*

ventriloquist /venˈtrɪləkwɪst/ *n* ventrílocuo *m*

venture /ˈventʃə(r)/ *n* empresa *f*. ●*vt* aventurar. ●*vi* atreverse

venue /ˈvenjuː/ *n* (*for concert*) lugar *m* de actuación

Venus /ˈviːnəs/ *n* Venus *m*

veranda /vəˈrændə/ *n* galería *f*

verb /vɜːb/ *n* verbo *m*. **~al** *adj*

verbal

verdict /ˈvɜ:dɪkt/ *n* veredicto *m*; (*opinion*) opinión *f*

verge /vɜ:dʒ/ *n* borde *m*. □ **~ on** *vt* rayar en

verify /ˈverɪfaɪ/ *vt* (*confirm*) confirmar; (*check*) verificar

vermin /ˈvɜ:mɪn/ *n* alimañas *fpl*

versatil|e /ˈvɜ:sətaɪl/ *adj* versátil. **~ity** /-ˈtɪlətɪ/ *n* versatilidad *f*

verse /vɜ:s/ *n* estrofa *f*; (*poetry*) poesías *fpl*. **~d** /vɜ:st/ *adj*. **be well-~ed in** ser muy versado en. **~ion** /ˈvɜ:ʃn/ *n* versión *f*

versus /ˈvɜ:səs/ *prep* contra

vertebra /ˈvɜ:tɪbrə/ *n* (*pl* **-brae** /-bri:/) vértebra *f*. **~te** /-brət/ *n* vertebrado *m*

vertical /ˈvɜ:tɪkl/ *adj & n* vertical (*f*). **~ly** *adv* verticalmente

vertigo /ˈvɜ:tɪgəʊ/ *n* vértigo *m*

verve /vɜ:v/ *n* brío *m*

very /ˈverɪ/ *adv* muy. **~ much** muchísimo. **~ well** muy bien. **the ~ first** el primero de todos. ● *adj* mismo. **the ~ thing** exactamente lo que hace falta

vessel /ˈvesl/ *n* (*receptacle*) recipiente *m*; (*ship*) navío *m*, nave *f*

vest /vest/ *n* camiseta *f*; (*Amer*) chaleco *m*.

vestige /ˈvestɪdʒ/ *n* vestigio *m*

vet /vet/ *n* veterinario *m*; (*Amer fam, veteran*) veterano *m*. ● *vt* (*pt* **vetted**) someter a investigación (applicant)

veteran /ˈvetərən/ *n* veterano *m*

veterinary /ˈvetərɪnərɪ/ *adj* veterinario. **~ surgeon** *n* veterinario *m*

veto /ˈvi:təʊ/ *n* (*pl* **-oes**) veto *m*. ● *vt* vetar

vex /veks/ *vt* fastidiar

via /ˈvaɪə/ *prep* por, por vía de

viable /ˈvaɪəbl/ *adj* viable

viaduct /ˈvaɪədʌkt/ *n* viaducto *m*

vibrat|e /vaɪˈbreɪt/ *vt/i* vibrar. **~ion** /-ʃn/ *n* vibración *f*

vicar /ˈvɪkə(r)/ *n* párroco *m*. **~age** /-rɪdʒ/ *n* casa *f* del párroco

vice /vaɪs/ *n* vicio *m*; (*Tec*) torno *m* de banco

vice versa /vaɪsɪˈvɜ:sə/ *adv* viceversa

vicinity /vɪˈsɪnɪtɪ/ *n* vecindad *f*. **in the ~ of** cerca de

vicious /ˈvɪʃəs/ *adj* (attack) feroz; (dog) fiero; (rumour) malicioso. **~ circle** *n* círculo *m* vicioso

victim /ˈvɪktɪm/ *n* víctima *f*. **~ize** *vt* victimizar

victor /ˈvɪktə(r)/ *n* vencedor *m*

Victorian /vɪkˈtɔ:rɪən/ *adj* victoriano

victor|ious /vɪkˈtɔ:rɪəs/ *adj* (army) victorioso; (team) vencedor. **~y** /ˈvɪktərɪ/ *n* victoria *f*

video /ˈvɪdɪəʊ/*n* (*pl* **-os**) vídeo *m*, video *m* (*LAm*). **~ camera** *n* videocámara *f*. **~(cassette) recorder** *n* magnetoscopio *m*. **~tape** *n* videocassette *f*

vie /vaɪ/ *vi* (*pres p* **vying**) rivalizar

Vietnam /vjetˈnæm/ *n* Vietnam *m*. **~ese** *adj & n* vietnamita (*m & f*)

view /vju:/ *n* vista *f*; (*mental survey*) visión *f* de conjunto; (*opinion*) opinión *f*. **in my ~** a mi juicio. **in ~ of** en vista de. **on ~** expuesto. ● *vt* ver (scene, property); (*consider*) considerar. **~er** *n* (*TV*) televidente *m & f*. **~finder** *n* visor *m*. **~point** *n* punto *m* de vista

vigil|ance *n* vigilancia *f*. **~ant** *adj* vigilante

vigo|rous /ˈvɪgərəs/ *adj* enérgico;

(growth) vigoroso. **~ur** /ˈvɪgə(r)/ *n* vigor *m*

vile /vaɪl/ *adj* (*base*) vil; (food) asqueroso; (weather, temper) horrible

village /ˈvɪlɪdʒ/ *n* pueblo *m*; (*small*) aldea *f*. **~r** *n* vecino *m* del pueblo; (*of small village*) aldeano *m*

villain /ˈvɪlən/ *n* maleante *m* & *f*; (*in story etc*) villano *m*

vindicate /ˈvɪndɪkeɪt/ *vt* justificar

vindictive /vɪnˈdɪktɪv/ *adj* vengativo

vine /vaɪn/ *n* (*on ground*) vid *f*; (*climbing*) parra *f*

vinegar /ˈvɪnɪgə(r)/ *n* vinagre *m*

vineyard /ˈvɪnjəd/ *n* viña *f*

vintage /ˈvɪntɪdʒ/ *n* (*year*) cosecha *f*. • *adj* (wine) añejo; (car) de época

vinyl /ˈvaɪnɪl/ *n* vinilo *m*

viola /vɪˈəʊlə/ *n* viola *f*

violat|e /ˈvaɪəleɪt/ *vt* violar. **~ion** /-ˈleɪʃn/ *n* violación *f*

violen|ce /ˈvaɪələns/ *n* violencia *f*. **~t** *adj* violento. **~tly** *adv* violentamente

violet /ˈvaɪələt/ *adj* & *n* violeta (*f*); (*colour*) violeta (*m*)

violin /ˈvaɪəlɪn/ *n* violín *m*. **~ist** *n* violinista *m* & *f*

VIP /vi:aɪˈpi:/ *abbr* (= **very important person**) VIP *m*

viper /ˈvaɪpə(r)/ *n* víbora *f*

V **virgin** /ˈvɜ:dʒɪn/ *adj* & *n* virgen (*f*)

Virgo /ˈvɜ:gəʊ/ *n* Virgo *f*

virile /ˈvɪraɪl/ *adj* viril

virtual /ˈvɜ:tʃʊəl/ *adj*. **traffic is at a ~ standstill** el tráfico está prácticamente paralizado. **~ reality** *n* realidad *f* virtual. **~ly** *adv* prácticamente

virtue /ˈvɜ:tʃu:/ *n* virtud *f*. **by ~ of** en virtud de

virtuous /ˈvɜ:tʃʊəs/ *adj* virtuoso

virulent /ˈvɪrʊlənt/ *adj* virulento

virus /ˈvaɪərəs/ *n* (*pl* **-uses**) virus *m*

visa /ˈvi:zə/ *n* visado *m*, visa *f* (*LAm*)

vise /vaɪs/ *n* (*Amer*) torno *m* de banco

visib|ility /vɪzɪˈbɪlətɪ/ *n* visibilidad *f*. **~le** /ˈvɪzɪbl/ *adj* visible; (sign, improvement) evidente

vision /ˈvɪʒn/ *n* visión *f*; (*sight*) vista *f*

visit /ˈvɪzɪt/ *vt* visitar; hacer una visita a (person). • *vi* hacer visitas. **~ with s.o.** (*Amer*) ir a ver a uno. • *n* visita *f*. **pay s.o. a ~** hacerle una visita a uno. **~or** *n* visitante *m* & *f*; (*guest*) visita *f*

visor /ˈvaɪzə(r)/ *n* visera *f*

visual /ˈvɪʒʊəl/ *adj* visual. **~ize** *vt* imaginar(se); (*foresee*) prever

vital /ˈvaɪtl/ *adj* (*essential*) esencial; (factor) de vital importancia; (organ) vital. **~ity** /vaɪˈtælətɪ/ *n* vitalidad *f*

vitamin /ˈvɪtəmɪn/ *n* vitamina *f*.

vivacious /vɪˈveɪʃəs/ *adj* vivaz

vivid /ˈvɪvɪd/ *adj* vivo. **~ly** *adv* intensamente; (*describe*) gráficamente

vivisection /vɪvɪˈsekʃn/ *n* vivisección *f*

vocabulary /vəˈkæbjʊlərɪ/ *n* vocabulario *m*

vocal /ˈvəʊkl/ *adj* vocal. **~ist** *n* cantante *m* & *f*

vocation /vəʊˈkeɪʃn/ *n* vocación *f*. **~al** *adj* profesional

vociferous /vəˈsɪfərəs/ *adj* vociferador

vogue /vəʊg/ *n* moda *f*, boga *f*

voice /vɔɪs/ *n* voz *f.* ● *vt* expresar

void /vɔɪd/ *adj* (*not valid*) nulo. ● *n* vacío *m*

volatile /ˈvɒlətaɪl/ *adj* volátil; (*person*) imprevisible

volcan|ic /vɒlˈkænɪk/ *adj* volcánico. **~o** /vɒlˈkeɪnəʊ/ *n* (*pl* **-oes**) volcán *m*

volley /ˈvɒlɪ/ *n* (*pl* **-eys**) (*of gunfire*) descarga *f* cerrada; (*sport*) volea *f.* **~ball** *n* vóleibol *m*

volt /vəʊlt/ *n* voltio *m.* **~age** /-ɪdʒ/ *n* voltaje *m*

volume /ˈvɒlju:m/ *n* volumen *m*; (*book*) tomo *m*

voluntar|ily /ˈvɒləntərəlɪ/ *adv* voluntariamente. **~y** *adj* voluntario; (organization) de beneficencia

volunteer /vɒlənˈtɪə(r)/ *n* voluntario *m.* ● *vt* ofrecer. ● *vi.* **~ (to)** ofrecerse (a)

vomit /ˈvɒmɪt/ *vt/i* vomitar. ● *n* vómito *m*

voracious /vəˈreɪʃəs/ *adj* voraz

vot|e /vəʊt/ *n* voto *m*; (*right*) derecho *m* al voto; (*act*) votación *f.* ● *vi* votar. **~er** *n* votante *m & f.* **~ing** *n* votación *f*

vouch /vaʊtʃ/ *vi.* **~ for s.o.** responder por uno. **~er** /-ə(r)/ *n* vale *m*

vow /vaʊ/ *n* voto *m.* ● *vi* jurar

vowel /ˈvaʊəl/ *n* vocal *f*

voyage /ˈvɔɪɪdʒ/ *n* viaje *m*; (*by sea*) travesía *f*

vulgar /ˈvʌlgə(r)/ *adj* (*coarse*) grosero, vulgar; (*tasteless*) de mal gusto. **~ity** /-ˈgærətɪ/ *n* vulgaridad *f*

vulnerable /ˈvʌlnərəbl/ *adj* vulnerable

vulture /ˈvʌltʃə(r)/ *n* buitre *m*

vying /ˈvaɪɪŋ/ *see* VIE

Ww

W *abbr* (= **West**) O

wad /wɒd/ *n* (*of notes*) fajo *m*; (*tied together*) lío *m*; (*papers*) montón *m*

waddle /ˈwɒdl/ *vi* contonearse

wade /weɪd/ *vi* caminar (*por el agua etc*)

wafer /ˈweɪfə(r)/ *n* galleta *f* de barquillo

waffle /ˈwɒfl/ *n* 🅸 palabrería *f.* ● *vi* 🅸 divagar; (*in essay, exam*) meter paja 🅸. ● *n* (*Culin*) gofre *m*, wafle *m* (*LAm*)

waft /wɒft/ *vi* flotar

wag /wæg/ *vt* (*pt* **wagged**) menear. ● *vi* menearse

wage /weɪdʒ/ *n* sueldo *m.* **~s** *npl* salario *m*, sueldo *m.* **~r** *n* apuesta *f*

waggle /ˈwægl/ *vt* menear. ● *vi* menearse

wagon /ˈwægən/ *n* carro *m*; (*Rail*) vagón *m*; (*Amer, delivery truck*) furgoneta *f* de reparto

wail /weɪl/ *vi* llorar

waist /weɪst/ *n* cintura *f.* **~coat** *n* chaleco *m.* **~line** *n* cintura *f*

wait /weɪt/ *vi* esperar; (*at table*) servir. **~ for** esperar. **~ on s.o.** atender a uno. ● *vt* (*await*) esperar (chance, turn). **~ table** (*Amer*) servir a la mesa. **I can't ~ to see him** me muero de ganas de verlo. ● *n* espera *f.* **lie in ~** acechar

waiter /ˈweɪtə(r)/ *n* camarero *m*, mesero *m* (*LAm*)

wait: ~ing-list *n* lista *f* de espera. **~ing-room** *n* sala *f* de espera

waitress /ˈweɪtrɪs/ *n* camarera *f*,

mesera *f* (*LAm*)

waive /weɪv/ *vt* renunciar a

wake /weɪk/ *vt* (*pt* **woke**, *pp* **woken**) despertar. ● *vi* despertarse. ● *n* (*Naut*) estela *f*. **in the ~ of** como resultado de. □ **~ up** *vt* despertar. *vi* despertarse

Wales /weɪlz/ *n* (el país de) Gales

walk /wɔ:k/ *vi* andar, caminar; (*not ride*) ir a pie; (*stroll*) pasear. ● *vt* andar por (streets); llevar de paseo (dog). ● *n* paseo *m*; (*long*) caminata *f*; (*gait*) manera *f* de andar. □ **~ out** *vi* salir; (workers) declararse en huelga. □ **~ out on** *vt* abandonar. **~er** *n* excursionista *m & f*

walkie-talkie /wɔ:kɪ'tɔ:kɪ/ *n* walkie-talkie *m*

walk: ~ing-stick *n* bastón *m*. **W~man** /-mən/ *n* Walkman *m* (*P*). **~-out** *n retirada en señal de protesta*; (*strike*) abandono *m* del trabajo

wall /wɔ:l/ *n* (*interior*) pared *f*; (*exterior*) muro *m*

Wall Street Una calle en Manhattan, Nueva York, donde se encuentran la Bolsa neoyorquina y las sedes de muchas instituciones financieras. Cuando se habla de *Wall Street*, a menudo se está refiriendo a esas instituciones.

wallet /'wɒlɪt/ *n* cartera *f*, billetera *f*

wallop /'wɒləp/ *vt* (*pt* **walloped**) 🅸 darle un golpazo a.

wallow /'wɒləʊ/ *vi* revolcarse

wallpaper /'wɔ:lpeɪpə(r)/ *n* papel *m* pintado

walnut /'wɔ:lnʌt/ *n* nuez *f*; (*tree*) nogal *m*

walrus /'wɔ:lrəs/ *n* morsa *f*

waltz /wɔ:ls/ *n* vals *m*. ● *vi* valsar

wand /wɒnd/ *n* varita *f* (mágica)

wander /'wɒndə(r)/ *vi* vagar; (*stroll*) pasear; (*digress*) divagar. ● *n* vuelta *f*, paseo *m*. **~er** *n* trotamundos *m*

wane /weɪn/ *vi* (moon) menguar; (interest) decaer. ● *n*. **be on the ~** (popularity) estar decayendo

wangle /'wæŋgl/ *vt* 🅸 agenciarse

want /wɒnt/ *vt* querer; (*need*) necesitar. ● *vi*. **~ for** carecer de. ● *n* necesidad *f*; (*lack*) falta *f*. **~ed** *adj* (criminal) buscado

war /wɔ:(r)/ *n* guerra *f*. **at ~** en guerra

warble /'wɔ:bl/ *vi* trinar, gorjear

ward /wɔ:d/ *n* (*in hospital*) sala *f*; (*child*) pupilo *m*. □ **~ off** *vt* conjurar (danger); rechazar (attack)

warden /'wɔ:dn/ *n* guarda *m*

warder /'wɔ:də(r)/ *n* celador *m* (*de una cárcel*)

wardrobe /'wɔ:drəʊb/ *n* armario *m*; (*clothes*) guardarropa *f*, vestuario *m*

warehouse /'weəhaʊs/ *n* depósito *m*, almacén *m*

wares /weəz/ *npl* mercancía(s) *f(pl)*

war: ~fare *n* guerra *f*. **~head** *n* cabeza *f*, ojiva *f*

warm /wɔ:m/ *adj* (**-er**, **-est**) (water, day) tibio, templado; (room) caliente; (climate, wind) cálido; (clothes) de abrigo; (welcome) caluroso. **be ~** (person) tener calor. **it's ~ today** hoy hace calor. ● *vt*. **~ (up)** calentar (room); recalentar (food); (*fig*) animar. ● *vi*. **~ (up)** calentarse; (*fig*) animarse. **~-blooded** /-'blʌdɪd/ *adj* de sangre caliente. **~ly** *adv* (*heartily*) calurosamente. **~th** *n* calor *m*; (*of colour, atmosphere*) calidez *f*

warn /wɔːn/ *vt* advertir. **~ing** *n* advertencia *f*; (*notice*) aviso *m*

warp /wɔːp/ *vt* alabear. **~ed** /ˈwɔːpt/ *adj* (wood) alabeado; (mind) retorcido

warrant /ˈwɒrənt/ *n* orden *f* judicial; (*search* ~) orden *f* de registro; (*for arrest*) orden *f* de arresto. ● *vt* justificar. **~y** *n* garantía *f*

warrior /ˈwɒrɪə(r)/ *n* guerrero *m*

warship /ˈwɔːʃɪp/ *n* buque *m* de guerra

wart /wɔːt/ *n* verruga *f*

wartime /ˈwɔːtaɪm/ *n* tiempo *m* de guerra

wary /ˈweərɪ/ *adj* (**-ier**, **-iest**) cauteloso. **be ~ of** recelar de

was /wəz, wɒz/ *see* BE

wash /wɒʃ/ *vt* lavar; fregar, lavar (*LAm*) (floor). **~ one's face** lavarse la cara. ● *vi* lavarse. ● *n* (*in washing machine*) lavado *m*. **have a ~** lavarse. **I gave the car a ~** lavé el coche. □ **~ out** *vt* (*clean*) lavar; (*rinse*) enjuagar. □ **~ up** *vi* fregar los platos, lavar los trastes (*Mex*); (*Amer, wash face and hands*) lavarse. **~able** *adj* lavable. **~basin**, **~bowl** (*Amer*) *n* lavabo *m*. **~er** *n* arandela *f*. **~ing** *n* lavado *m*; (*dirty clothes*) ropa *f* para lavar; (*wet clothes*) ropa *f* lavada. **do the ~ing** lavar la ropa, hacer la colada. **~ing-machine** *n* máquina *f* de lavar, lavadora *f*. **~ing-powder** *n* jabón *m* en polvo. **~ing-up** *n*. **do the ~ing-up** lavar los platos, fregar (los platos). **~ing-up liquid** *n* lavavajillas *m*. **~out** *n* 🅸 desastre *m*. **~room** *n* (*Amer*) baños *mpl*, servicios *mpl*

wasp /wɒsp/ *n* avispa *f*

waste /weɪst/ ● *adj* (matter) de desecho; (land) (*barren*) yermo; (*uncultivated*) baldío. ● *n* (*of materials*) desperdicio *m*; (*of time*) pérdida *f*; (*refuse*) residuos *mpl*. ● *vt* despilfarrar (electricity, money); desperdiciar (talent, effort); perder (time). ● *vi*. **~-disposal unit** *n* trituradora *f* de desperdicios. **~ful** *adj* poco económico; (person) despilfarrador. **~-paper basket** *n* papelera *f*

watch /wɒtʃ/ *vt* mirar; observar (person, expression); ver (TV); (*keep an eye on*) vigilar; (*take heed*) tener cuidado con. ● *vi* mirar. ● *n* (*observation*) vigilancia *f*; (*period of duty*) guardia *f*; (*timepiece*) reloj *m*. **~ out** *vi* (*be careful*) tener cuidado; (*look carefully*) estarse atento. **~dog** *n* perro *m* guardián. **~man** /-mən/ *n* (*pl* **-men**) vigilante *m*.

water /ˈwɔːtə(r)/ *n* agua *f*. ● *vt* regar (plants etc). ● *vi* (eyes) llorar. **make s.o.'s mouth ~** hacérsele la boca agua, hacérsele agua la boca (*LAm*). **~ down** *vt* diluir; aguar (wine). **~-colour** *n* acuarela *f*. **~cress** *n* berro *m*. **~fall** *n* cascada *f*; (*large*) catarata *f*. **~ing-can** *n* regadera *f*. **~ lily** *n* nenúfar *m*. **~logged** /-lɒgd/ *adj* anegado; (shoes) empapado. **~proof** *adj* impermeable; (watch) sumergible. **~-skiing** *n* esquí *m* acuático. **~tight** *adj* hermético; (boat) estanco; (argument) irrebatible. **~way** *n* canal *m* navegable. **~y** *adj* acuoso; (eyes) lloroso

watt /wɒt/ *n* vatio *m*

wave /weɪv/ *n* onda *f*; (*of hand*) señal *f*; (*fig*) oleada *f*. ● *vt* agitar; (*curl*) ondular (hair). ● *vi* (*signal*) hacer señales con la mano; ondear (flag). **~band** *n* banda *f* de frecuencia. **~length** *n* longitud *f* de onda

waver /'weɪvə(r)/ *vi* (*be indecisive*) vacilar; (*falter*) flaquear

wavy /'weɪvɪ/ *adj* (**-ier**, **-iest**) ondulado

wax /wæks/ *n* cera *f*. ●*vi* (moon) crecer. **~work** *n* figura *f* de cera. **~works** *npl* museo *m* de cera

way /weɪ/ *n* (*route*) camino *m*; (*manner*) manera *f*, forma *f*, modo *m*; (*direction*) dirección *f*; (*habit*) costumbre *f*. **it's a long ~ from here** queda muy lejos de aquí. **be in the ~** estorbar. **by the ~** a propósito. **either ~** de cualquier manera. **give ~** (*collapse*) ceder, romperse; (*Auto*) ceder el paso. **in a ~** en cierta manera. **in some ~s** en ciertos modos. **make ~** dejar paso a. **no ~!** ¡ni hablar! **on my ~ to** de camino a. **out of the ~** remoto; (*extraordinary*) fuera de lo común. **that ~** por allí. **this ~** por aquí. **~ in** *n* entrada *f*. **~lay** /weɪ'leɪ/ *vt* (*pt* **-laid**) abordar. **~ out** *n* salida *f*. **~-out** *adj* ultramoderno, original. **~s** *npl* costumbres *fpl*

we /wi:/ *pron* nosotros *m*, nosotras *f*

weak /wi:k/ *adj* (**-er**, **-est**) débil; (structure) poco sólido; (performance, student) flojo; (coffee) poco cargado; (solution) diluido; (beer) suave; (*pej*) aguado. **~en** *vt* debilitar. ●*vi* (resolve) flaquear. **~ling** *n* alfeñique *m*. **~ness** *n* debilidad *f*

wealth /welθ/ *n* riqueza *f*. **~y** *adj* (**-ier**, **-iest**) rico

W

weapon /'wepən/ *n* arma *f*. **~s of mass destruction** armas de destrucción masiva

wear /weə(r)/ *vt* (*pt* **wore**, *pp* **worn**) llevar; vestirse de (black, red, etc); (*usually*) usar. **I've got nothing to ~** no tengo nada que ponerme. ●*vi* (*through use*) gastarse; (*last*) durar. ●*n* uso *m*; (*damage*) desgaste *m*; **~ and tear** desgaste *m* natural. □ **~ out** *vt* gastar; (*tire*) agotar. *vi* gastarse

weary /'wɪərɪ/ *adj* (**-ier**, **-iest**) cansado. ●*vt* cansar. ●*vi* cansarse. **~ of** cansarse de

weather /'weðə(r)/ *n* tiempo *m*. **what's the ~ like?** ¿qué tiempo hace?. **the ~ was bad** hizo mal tiempo. **be under the ~** 🄸 no andar muy bien 🄸. ●*vt* (*survive*) sobrellevar. **~-beaten** *adj* curtido. **~ forecast** *n* pronóstico *m* del tiempo. **~-vane** *n* veleta *f*

weave /wi:v/ *vt* (*pt* **wove**, *pp* **woven**) tejer; entretejer (threads). **~ one's way** abrirse paso. ●*vi* (person) zigzaguear; (road) serpentear. **~r** *n* tejedor *m*

web /web/ *n* (*of spider*) telaraña *f*; (*of intrigue*) red *f*. **~ page** *n* página web. **~ site** *n* sitio web *m*

wed /wed/ *vt* (*pt* **wedded**) casarse con. ●*vi* casarse.

we'd /wi:d//wɪəd/ = **we had**, **we would**

wedding /'wedɪŋ/ *n* boda *f*, casamiento *m*. **~-cake** *n* pastel *m* de boda. **~-ring** *n* anillo *m* de boda

wedge /wedʒ/ *n* cuña *f*

Wednesday /'wenzdeɪ/ *n* miércoles *m*

wee /wi:/ *adj* 🄸 pequeñito. ●*n*. **have a ~** 🄸 hacer pis 🄸

weed /wi:d/ *n* mala hierba *f*. ●*vt* desherbar. □ **~ out** *vt* eliminar. **~killer** *n* herbicida *m*. **~y** *adj* (person) enclenque; (*Amer*, *lanky*) larguirucho 🄸

week /wi:k/ *n* semana *f*. **~day** *n* día *m* de semana. **~end** *n* fin *m* de semana. **~ly** *adj* semanal. ●*n* semanario *m*. ● *adv* semanalmente

weep /wi:p/ *vi* (*pt* **wept**) llorar

weigh /weɪ/ *vt/i* pesar. ~ **anchor** levar anclas. □ ~ **down** *vt* (*fig*) oprimir. □ ~ **up** *vt* pesar; (*fig*) considerar

weight /weɪt/ *n* peso *m*; (*sport*) pesa *f*. **put on** ~ engordar. **lose** ~ adelgazar. ~**-lifting** *n* halterofilia *f*, levantamiento *m* de pesos

weir /wɪə(r)/ *n* presa *f*

weird /wɪəd/ *adj* (**-er**, **-est**) raro, extraño; (*unearthly*) misterioso

welcom|e /'welkəm/ *adj* bienvenido. **you're** ~**e!** (*after thank you*) ¡de nada! ● *n* bienvenida *f*; (*reception*) acogida *f*. ● *vt* dar la bienvenida a; (*appreciate*) alegrarse de. ~**ing** *adj* acogedor

weld /weld/ *vt* soldar. ● *n* soldadura *f*. ~**er** *n* soldador *m*

welfare /'welfeə(r)/ *n* bienestar *m*; (*aid*) asistencia *f* social. **W**~ **State** *n* estado *m* benefactor

well /wel/ *adv* (**better**, **best**) bien. ~ **done!** ¡muy bien!, ¡bravo! **as** ~ también. **as** ~ **as** además de. **we may as** ~ **go tomorrow** más vale que vayamos mañana. **do** ~ (*succeed*) tener éxito. **very** ~ muy bien. ● *adj* bien. **I'm very** ~ estoy muy bien. ● *int* (*introducing, continuing sentence*) bueno; (*surprise*) ¡vaya!; (*indignation, resignation*) bueno. ~ **I never!** ¡no me digas! ● *n* pozo *m*

we'll /wi:l//wɪəl/ = **we will**

well: ~**-behaved** /-bɪ'heɪvd/ *adj* que se porta bien, bueno. ~**-educated** /-'edjʊkeɪtɪd/ *adj* culto.

wellington (boot) /'welɪŋtən/ *n* bota *f* de goma *or* de agua; (*Amer, short boot*) botín *m*

well: ~**-known** /-'nəʊn/ *adj* conocido. ~ **off** *adj* adinerado. ~**-stocked** /-'stɒkt/ *adj* bien provisto. ~**-to-do** /-tə'du:/ *adj* adinerado

Welsh /welʃ/ *adj & n* galés (*m*). **the** ~ *n* los galeses

> **Welsh Assembly** La Asamblea Nacional de Gales empezó a funcionar, en Cardiff, en 1999. Tiene poderes limitados, por lo que no puede imponer impuestos. Consta de 60 miembros o *AMs* (*Assembly Members*); 40 elegidos directamente y el resto, de las listas regionales, mediante el sistema de representación proporcional.

went /went/ *see* **GO**

wept /wept/ *see* **WEEP**

were /wɜ:(r), wə(r)/ *see* **BE**

we're /wɪə(r)/ = **we are**

west /west/ *n* oeste *m*. **the W**~ el Occidente *m*. ● *adj* oeste; (wind) del oeste. ● *adv* (go) hacia el oeste, al oeste. **it's** ~ **of York** está al oeste de York. ~**erly** /-əlɪ/ *adj* (wind) del oeste. ~**ern** /-ən/ *adj* occidental. ● *n* (*film*) película *f* del Oeste. ~**erner** *n* occidental *m & f*. **W**~ **Indian** *adj & n* antillano (*m*). **W**~ **Indies** *npl* Antillas *fpl*. ~**ward(s)** /-wəd(z)/,

wet /wet/ *adj* (**wetter**, **wettest**) mojado; (*rainy*) lluvioso; (*fam, person*) soso. '~ **paint**' 'pintura fresca'. **get** ~ mojarse. **he got his feet** ~ se mojó los pies. ● *vt* (*pt* **wetted**) mojar; (*dampen*) humedecer. ~ **o.s.** orinarse. ~**back** *n* espalda *f* mojada. ~ **blanket** *n* aguafiestas *m & f*. ~ **suit** *n* traje *m* de neopreno

we've /wiːv/ = **we have**

whack /wæk/ *vt* [I] golpear. ●*n* [I] golpe *m*.

whale /weɪl/ *n* ballena *f*. **we had a ~ of a time** [I] lo pasamos bomba [I]

wham /wæm/ *int* ¡zas!

wharf /wɔːf/ *n* (*pl* **wharves** *or* **wharfs**) muelle *m*

what /wɒt/

●*adjective*

····➤(*in questions*) qué. **~ perfume are you wearing?** ¿qué perfume llevas?. **~ colour are the walls?** ¿de qué color son las paredes?

····➤(*in exclamations*) qué. **~ a beautiful house!** ¡qué casa más linda!. **~ a lot of people!** ¡cuánta gente!

····➤(*in indirect speech*) qué. **I'll ask him ~ bus to take** le preguntaré qué autobús hay que tomar. **do you know ~ time it leaves?** ¿sabes a qué hora sale?

●*pronoun*

····➤(*in questions*) qué. **~ is it?** ¿qué es? **~ for?** ¿para qué?. **~'s the problem?** ¿cuál es el problema? **~'s he like?** ¿cómo es? **what?** (*say that again*) ¿cómo?, ¿qué?

····➤(*in indirect questions*) qué. **I didn't know ~ to do** no sabía qué hacer

····➤(*relative*) lo que. **I did ~ I could** hice lo que pude. **~ I need is a new car** lo que necesito es un coche nuevo

····➤(*in phrases*) **~ about me?** ¿y yo qué? **~ if she doesn't come?** ¿y si no viene?

whatever /wɒt'evə(r)/ *adj* cualquiera. ●*pron* (todo) lo que, cualquier cosa que

whatsoever /wɒtsəʊ'evə(r)/ *adj & pron* = **whatever**

wheat /wiːt/ *n* trigo *m*

wheel /wiːl/ *n* rueda *f*. **at the ~** al volante. ●*vt* empujar (bicycle etc); llevar (en silla de ruedas etc) (person). **~barrow** *n* carretilla *f*. **~chair** *n* silla *f* de ruedas

wheeze /wiːz/ *vi* respirar con dificultad

when /wen/ *adv* cuándo. ●*conj* cuando. **~ever** /-'evə(r)/ *adv* (*every time that*) cada vez que, siempre que; (*at whatever time*) **we'll go ~ever you're ready** saldremos cuando estés listo

where /weə(r)/ *adv & conj* donde; (*interrogative*) dónde. **~ are you going?** ¿adónde vas? **~ are you from?** ¿de dónde eres?. **~abouts** /-əbaʊts/ *adv* en qué parte. ●*n* paradero *m*. **~as** /-'æz/ *conj* por cuanto; (*in contrast*) mientras (que). **~ver** /weər'evə(r)/ *adv* (*in questions*) dónde; (*no matter where*) en cualquier parte. ●*conj* donde (+ *subjunctive*), dondequiera (+ *subjunctive*)

whet /wet/ *vt* (*pt* **whetted**) abrir (appetite)

whether /'weðə(r)/ *conj* si. **I don't know ~ she will like it** no sé si le gustará. **~ you like it or not** te guste o no te guste

which /wɪtʃ/ *adj* (*in questions*) (*sing*) qué, cuál; (*pl*) qué, cuáles. **~ one** cuál. **~ one of you** cuál de ustedes. ●*pron* (*in questions*) (*sing*) cuál; (*pl*) cuáles; (*relative*) que; (*object*) el cual, la cual, lo cual, los cuales, las cuales. **~ever** /-'evə(r)/

adj cualquier. ●*pron* cualquiera que, el que, la que; (*in questions*) cuál; (*pl*) cuáles

while /waɪl/ *n* rato *m*. **a ~ ago** hace un rato. ●*conj* mientras; (*although*) aunque. ▫**~ away** *vt* pasar (time)

whilst /waɪlst/ *conj see* **WHILE**

whim /wɪm/ *n* capricho *m*

whimper /ˈwɪmpə(r)/ *vi* gimotear. ●*n* quejido *m*

whine /waɪn/ *vi* (person) gemir; (child) lloriquear; (dog) aullar

whip /wɪp/ *n* látigo *m*; (*for punishment*) azote *m*. ●*vt* (*pt* **whipped** /wɪpt/) fustigar, pegarle a (*con la fusta*) (horse); azotar (person); (*Culin*) batir

whirl /wɜːl/ *vi* girar rápidamente. **~pool** *n* remolino *m*. **~wind** *n* torbellino *m*

whirr /wɜː(r)/ *n* zumbido *m*. ●*vi* zumbar

whisk /wɪsk/ *vt* (*Culin*) batir. ●*n* (*Culin*) batidor *m*. **~ away** llevarse

whisker /ˈwɪskə(r)/ *n* pelo *m*. **~s** *npl* (*of cat etc*) bigotes *mpl*

whisky /ˈwɪskɪ/ *n* whisky *m*, güisqui *m*

whisper /ˈwɪspə(r)/ *vt* susurrar. ●*vi* cuchichear. ●*n* susurro *m*

whistle /ˈwɪsl/ *n* silbido *m*; (*loud*) chiflado *m*; (*instrument*) silbato *m*, pito *m*. ●*vi* silbar; (*loudly*) chiflar

white /waɪt/ *adj* (**-er**, **-est**) blanco. **go ~** ponerse pálido. ●*n* blanco; (*of egg*) clara *f*. **~ coffee** *n* café *m* con leche. **~-collar worker** *n* empleado *m* de oficina. **~ elephant** *n* objeto *m* inútil y costoso. **~-hot** *adj* (metal) al rojo blanco. **~ lie** *n* mentirijilla *f*. **~n** *vt/i* blanquear. **~wash** *n* cal *f*; (*cover-up*) tapadera *f* 🅸. ●*vt* blanquear, encalar

Whitsun /ˈwɪtsn/ *n* Pentecostés *m*

whiz /wɪz/ *vi* (*pt* **whizzed**). **~ by**, **~ past** pasar zumbando. **~-kid** *n* 🅸 lince *m* 🅸

who /huː/ *pron* (*in questions*) quién; (*pl*) quiénes; (*as relative*) que; **the girl ~ lives there** la chica que vive allí. **those ~ can't come tomorrow** los que no puedan venir mañana. **~ever** /huːˈevə(r)/ *pron* quienquiera que; (*interrogative*) quién

whole /həʊl/ *adj*. **the ~ country** todo el país. **there's a ~ bottle left** queda una botella entera. ●*n* todo *m*, conjunto *m*; (*total*) total *m*. **on the ~** en general. **~-hearted** /-ˈhɑːtɪd/ *adj* (support) incondicional; (approval) sin reservar. **~meal** *adj* integral. **~sale** *n* venta *f* al por mayor. ●*adj & adv* al por mayor. **~some** /-səm/ *adj* sano

wholly /ˈhəʊlɪ/ *adv* completamente

whom /huːm/ *pron* que, a quien; (*in questions*) a quién

whooping cough /ˈhuːpɪŋ/ *n* tos *f* convulsa

whore /hɔː(r)/ *n* puta *f*

whose /huːz/ *pron* de quién; (*pl*) de quiénes. ●*adj* (*in questions*) de quién; (*pl*) de quiénes; (*relative*) cuyo; (*pl*) cuyos

why /waɪ/ *adv* por qué. **~ not?** ¿por qué no? **that's ~ I couldn't go** por eso no pude ir. ●*int* ¡vaya!

wick /wɪk/ *n* mecha *f*

wicked /ˈwɪkɪd/ *adj* malo; (*mischievous*) travieso; (*fam, very bad*) malísimo

wicker /ˈwɪkə(r)/ *n* mimbre *m & f*. ●*adj* de mimbre. **~work** *n* artículos *mpl* de mimbre

wicket /ˈwɪkɪt/ *n* (*cricket*) rastrillo *m*

wide /waɪd/ *adj* (**-er**, **-est**) ancho; (range, experience) amplio; (*off target*) desviado. **it's four metres ~** tiene cuatro metros de ancho. ● *adv*. **open ~!** abra bien la boca. **~ awake** *adj* completamente despierto; (*fig*) despabilado. **I left the door ~ open** dejé la puerta abierta de par en par. **~ly** *adv* extensamente; (*believed*) generalmente; (*different*) muy. **~n** *vt* ensanchar. ● *vi* ensancharse. **~spread** *adj* extendido; (*fig*) difundido

widow /ˈwɪdəʊ/ *n* viuda *f*. **~er** *n* viudo *m*.

width /wɪdθ/ *n* anchura *f*. **in ~** de ancho

wield /wiːld/ *vt* manejar; ejercer (power)

wife /waɪf/ *n* (*pl* **wives**) mujer *f*, esposa *f*

wig /wɪg/ *n* peluca *f*

wiggle /ˈwɪgl/ *vt* menear. ● *vi* menearse

wild /waɪld/ *adj* (**-er**, **-est**) (animal) salvaje; (flower) silvestre; (country) agreste; (*enraged*) furioso; (idea) extravagante; (*with joy*) loco. **a ~ guess** una conjetura hecha totalmente al azar. **I'm not ~ about the idea** la idea no me enloquece. ● *adv* en estado salvaje. **run ~** (children) criarse como salvajes. **~s** *npl* regiones *fpl* salvajes. **~erness** /ˈwɪldənɪs/ *n* páramo *m*. **~fire** *n*. **spread like ~fire** correr como un reguero de pólvora. **~-goose chase** *n* empresa *f* inútil. **~life** *n* fauna *f*. **~ly** *adv* violentamente; (*fig*) locamente

will /wɪl/

● *auxiliary verb*

past **would;** contracted forms **I'll, you'll, etc = I will, you will, etc.; won't = will not**

····➤ (*talking about the future*)

! The Spanish future tense is not always the first option for translating the English future tense. The present tense of *ir + a + verb* is commonly used instead, particularly in Latin American countries. **he'll be here on Tuesday** *estará el martes, va a estar el martes;* **she won't agree** *no va a aceptar, no aceptará*

····➤ (*in invitations and requests*) **~ you have some wine?** ¿quieres (un poco de) vino? **you'll stay for dinner, won't you?** te quedas a cenar, ¿no?

····➤ (*in tag questions*) **you ~ be back soon, won't you?** vas a volver pronto, ¿no?

····➤ (*in short answers*) **will it be ready by Monday? - yes, it ~** ¿estará listo para el lunes? - sí

● *noun*

····➤ (*mental power*) voluntad *f*

····➤ (*document*) testamento *m*

willing /ˈwɪlɪŋ/ *adj* complaciente. **~ to** dispuesto a. **~ly** *adv* de buena gana

willow /ˈwɪləʊ/ *n* sauce *m*

will-power /ˈwɪlpaʊə(r)/ *n* fuerza *f* de voluntad

wilt /wɪlt/ *vi* marchitarse

win /wɪn/ *vt* (*pt* **won**, *pres p* **winning**) ganar; (*achieve, obtain*) conseguir. ● *vi* ganar. ● *n* victoria *f*. ▫ ~ **over** *vt* ganarse a

wince /wɪns/ *vi* hacer una mueca de dolor

winch /wɪntʃ/ *n* cabrestante *m*. ● *vt* levantar con un cabrestante

wind[1] /wɪnd/ *n* viento *m*; (*in stomach*) gases *mpl*. ~ **instrument** instrumento *m* de viento. ● *vt* dejar sin aliento

wind[2] /waɪnd/ *vt* (*pt* **wound**) (*wrap around*) enrollar; dar cuerda a (clock etc). ● *vi* (road etc) serpentear. ▫ ~ **up** *vt* dar cuerda a (watch, clock); (*fig*) terminar, concluir

winding /ˈwaɪndɪŋ/ *adj* tortuoso

windmill /ˈwɪndmɪl/ *n* molino *m* (de viento)

window /ˈwɪndəʊ/ *n* ventana *f*; (*in shop*) escaparate *m*, vitrina *f* (*LAm*), vidriera *f* (*LAm*), aparador *m* (*Mex*); (*of vehicle, booking-office*) ventanilla *f*; (*Comp*) ventana *f*, window *m*. ~ **box** *n* jardinera *f*. **~-shop** *vi* mirar los escaparates. **~sill** *n* alféizar *m or* repisa *f* de la ventana

wine /waɪn/ *n* vino *m*. **~-cellar** *n* bodega *f*. **~glass** *n* copa *f* de vino. **~-growing** *n* vinicultura *f*. ● *adj* vinícola. ~ **list** *n* lista *f* de vinos. **~-tasting** *n* cata *f* de vinos

wing /wɪŋ/ *n* ala *f*; (*Auto*) aleta *f*. **under one's** ~ bajo la protección de uno. **~er** *n* (*Sport*) ala *m & f*. **~s** *npl* (*in theatre*) bastidores *mpl*

wink /wɪŋk/ *vi* guiñar el ojo; (light etc) centellear. ● *n* guiño *m*. **not to sleep a** ~ no pegar ojo

win: ~ner *n* ganador *m*. **~ning-post** *n* poste *m* de llegada. **~nings** *npl* ganancias *fpl*

wint|er /ˈwɪntə(r)/ *n* invierno *m*. ● *vi* invernar. **~ry** *adj* invernal

wipe /waɪp/ *vt* limpiar, pasarle un trapo a; (*dry*) secar. ~ **one's nose** limpiarse la nariz. ● *n*. **give sth a** ~ limpiar algo, pasarle un trapo a algo. ▫ ~ **out** *vt* (*cancel*) cancelar; (*destroy*) destruir; (*obliterate*) borrar. ▫ ~ **up** *vt* limpiar

wir|e /ˈwaɪə(r)/ *n* alambre *m*; (*Elec*) cable *m*. **~ing** *n* instalación *f* eléctrica

wisdom /ˈwɪzdəm/ *n* sabiduría *f*. ~ **tooth** *n* muela *f* del juicio

wise /waɪz/ *adj* (**-er**, **-est**) sabio; (*sensible*) prudente; (decision, choice) acertado. **~ly** *adv* sabiamente; (*sensibly*) prudentemente

wish /wɪʃ/ *n* deseo *m*; (*greeting*) saludo *m*. **make a** ~ pedir un deseo. **best ~es, John** (*in letters*) saludos de John, un abrazo de John. ● *vt* desear. ~ **s.o. well** desear buena suerte a uno. **I ~ I were rich** ¡ojalá fuera rico! **he ~ed he hadn't told her** lamentó habérselo dicho. **~ful thinking** *n* ilusiones *fpl*

wistful /ˈwɪstfl/ *adj* melancólico

wit /wɪt/ *n* gracia *f*; (*intelligence*) ingenio *m*. **be at one's ~s' end** no saber más qué hacer

witch /wɪtʃ/ *n* bruja *f*. **~craft** *n* brujería *f*.

with /wɪð/ *prep* con; (*cause, having*) de. **come ~ me** ven conmigo. **take it ~ you** llévalo contigo; (*formal*) llévelo consigo. **the man ~ the beard** el hombre de la barba. **trembling ~ fear** temblando de miedo

withdraw /wɪðˈdrɔː/ *vt* (*pt* **withdrew**, *pp* **withdrawn**) retirar. ● *vi* apartarse. **~al** *n* retirada *f*. **~n** *adj* (person) retraído

wither /ˈwɪðə(r)/ *vi* marchitarse

withhold /wɪðˈhəʊld/ *vt* (*pt* **withheld**) retener; (*conceal*) ocultar (**from** a)

within /wɪˈðɪn/ *prep* dentro de. ● *adv* dentro. **~ sight** a la vista

without /wɪˈðaʊt/ *prep* sin. **~ paying** sin pagar

withstand /wɪðˈstænd/ *vt* (*pt* **-stood**) resistir

witness /ˈwɪtnɪs/ *n* testigo *m*; (*proof*) testimonio *m*. ● *vt* presenciar; atestiguar (signature). **~-box** *n* tribuna *f* de los testigos

witt|icism /ˈwɪtɪsɪzəm/ *n* ocurrencia *f*. **~y** /ˈwɪtɪ/ *adj* (**-ier**, **-iest**) gracioso

wives /waɪvz/ *see* **WIFE**

wizard /ˈwɪzəd/ *n* hechicero *m*

wizened /ˈwɪznd/ *adj* arrugado

wobbl|e /ˈwɒbl/ *vi* (chair) tambalearse; (bicycle) bambolearse; (voice, jelly, hand) temblar. **~y** *adj* (chair etc) cojo

woe /wəʊ/ *n* aflicción *f*

woke/wəʊk/, **woken** /ˈwəʊkən/ *see* **WAKE**

wolf /wʊlf/ *n* (*pl* **wolves** /wʊlvz/) lobo *m*

woman /ˈwʊmən/ *n* (*pl* **women**) mujer *f*

womb /wu:m/ *n* matriz *f*

women /ˈwɪmɪn/ *npl see* **WOMAN**

won /wʌn/ *see* **WIN**

W **wonder** /ˈwʌndə(r)/ *n* maravilla *f*; (*bewilderment*) asombro *m*. **no ~** no es de extrañarse (**that** que). ● *vt* (*ask oneself*) preguntarse. **I ~ whose book this is** me pregunto de quién será este libro; (*in polite requests*) **I ~ if you could help me?** ¿me podría ayudar? **~ful** *adj* maravilloso. **~fully** *adv* maravillosamente

won't /wəʊnt/ = **will not**

wood /wʊd/ *n* madera *f*; (*for burning*) leña *f*; (*area*) bosque *m*. **~ed** *adj* poblado de árboles, boscoso. **~en** *adj* de madera. **~land** *n* bosque *m*. **~wind** /-wɪnd/ *n* instrumentos *mpl* de viento de madera. **~work** *n* carpintería *f*; (*in room etc*) maderaje *m*. **~worm** *n* carcoma *f*. **~y** *adj* leñoso

wool /wʊl/ *n* lana *f*. **pull the ~ over s.o.'s eyes** engañar a uno. **~len** *adj* de lana. **~ly** *adj* (**-ier**, **-iest**) de lana; (*unclear*) vago. ● *n* jersey *m*

word /wɜ:d/ *n* palabra *f*; (*news*) noticia *f*. **by ~ of mouth** de palabra. **I didn't say a ~** yo no dije nada. **in other ~s** es decir. ● *vt* expresar. **~ing** *n* redacción *f*; (*of question*) formulación *f*. **~ processor** *n* procesador *m* de textos. **~y** *adj* prolijo

wore /wɔ:(r)/ *see* **WEAR**

work /wɜ:k/ *n* trabajo *m*; (*arts*) obra *f*. **be out of ~** estar sin trabajo, estar desocupado. ● *vt* hacer trabajar; manejar (machine). ● *vi* trabajar; (machine) funcionar; (student) estudiar; (drug etc) surtir efecto. □ **~ off** *vt* desahogar. □ **~ out** *vt* resolver (problem); (*calculate*) calcular; (*understand*) entender. ● *vi* (*succeed*) salir bien; (*Sport*) entrenarse. □ **~ up** *vt*. **get ~ed up** exaltarse. **~able** *adj* (project, solution) factible. **~er** *n* trabajador *m*; (*manual*) obrero *m*; (*in office, bank*) empleado *m*. **~ing** *adj* (day) laborable; (clothes etc) de trabajo. **in ~ing order** en estado de funcionamiento. **~ing class** *n* clase *f* obrera. **~ing-class** *adj* de la clase obrera. **~man** /-mən/ *n* (*pl* **-men**) obrero *m*. **~manship** *n* destreza *f*. **~s** *npl* (*building*) fábrica *f*; (*Mec*) mecanismo *m*. **~shop** *n* taller *m*

world /wɜːld/ *n* mundo *m*. **out of this ~** maravilloso. ● *adj* mundial. **W~ Cup** *n*. **the W~ Cup** la Copa del Mundo. **~ly** *adj* mundano. **~wide** *adj* universal. **W~ Wide Web** *n* World Wide Web *m*

worm /wɜːm/ *n* gusano *m*, lombriz *f*

worn /wɔːn/ *see* **WEAR**. ● *adj* gastado. **~-out** *adj* gastado; (person) rendido

worr|ied /ˈwʌrɪd/ *adj* preocupado. **~y** /ˈwʌrɪ/ *vt* preocupar; (*annoy*) molestar. ● *vi* preocuparse. ● *n* preocupación *f*. **~ying** *adj* inquietante

worse /wɜːs/ *adj* peor. **get ~** empeorar. ● *adv* peor; (*more*) más. **~n** *vt/i* empeorar

worship /ˈwɜːʃɪp/ *n* culto *m*; (*title*) Su Señoría. ● *vt* (*pt* **worshipped**) adorar

worst /wɜːst/ *adj* peor. **he's the ~ in the class** es el peor de la clase. ● *adv* peor. ● *n*. **the ~** lo peor

worth /wɜːθ/ *n* valor *m*. ● *adj*. **be ~** valer. **it's ~ trying** vale la pena probarlo. **it was ~ my while** (me) valió la pena. **~less** *adj* sin valor. **~while** /-ˈwaɪl/ *adj* que vale la pena. **~y** /ˈwɜːðɪ/ *adj* meritorio; (*respectable*) respetable; (*laudable*) loable

would /wʊd/ *modal verb*. (*in conditional sentences*) **~ you go?** ¿irías tú? **he ~ come if he could** vendría si pudiera; (*in reported speech*) **I thought you'd forget** pensé que te olvidarías; (*in requests, invitations*) **~ you come here, please?** ¿quieres venir aquí? **~ you switch the television off?** ¿podrías apagar la televisión?; (*be prepared to*) **he ~n't listen to me** no me quería escuchar

wound[1] /wuːnd/ *n* herida *f*. ● *vt* herir

wound[2] /waʊnd/ *see* **WIND**[2]

wove, woven /wəʊv, ˈwəʊvn/ *see* **WEAVE**

wow /waʊ/ *int* ¡ah!

wrangle /ˈræŋgl/ *vi* reñir. ● *n* riña *f*

wrap /ræp/ *vt* (*pt* **wrapped**) envolver. ● *n* bata *f*; (*shawl*) chal *m*. **~per** *n*, **~ping** *n* envoltura *f*

wrath /rɒθ/ *n* ira *f*

wreak /riːk/ *vt* sembrar. **~ havoc** causar estragos

wreath /riːθ/ *n* (*pl* **-ths** /-ðz/) corona *f*

wreck /rek/ *n* (*ship*) restos *mpl* de un naufragio; (*vehicle*) restos *mpl* de un avión siniestrado. **be a nervous ~** tener los nervios destrozados. ● *vt* provocar el naufragio de (ship); destrozar (car); (*Amer, demolish*) demoler; (*fig*) destrozar. **~age** /-ɪdʒ/ *n* restos *mpl*; (*of building*) ruinas *fpl*

wrench /rentʃ/ *vt* arrancar; (*sprain*) desgarrarse; dislocarse (joint). ● *n* tirón *m*; (*emotional*) dolor *m* (causado por una separación); (*tool*) llave *f* inglesa

wrestl|e /ˈresl/ *vi* luchar. **~er** *n* luchador *m*. **~ing** *n* lucha *f*

wretch /retʃ/ *n* (*despicable person*) desgraciado *m*; (*unfortunate person*) desdichado *m* & *f*. **~ed** /-ɪd/ *adj* desdichado; (weather) horrible

wriggle /ˈrɪgl/ *vi* retorcerse. **~**

out of escaparse de
wring /rɪŋ/ *vt* (*pt* **wrung**) retorcer (neck). ~ **out of** (*obtain from*) arrancar. □ ~ **out** *vt* retorcer
wrinkl|e /'rɪŋkl/ *n* arruga *f*. ● *vt* arrugar. ● *vi* arrugarse. ~**y** *adj* arrugado
wrist /rɪst/ *n* muñeca *f*. ~**watch** *n* reloj *m* de pulsera
writ /rɪt/ *n* orden *m* judicial
write /raɪt/ *vt/i* (*pt* **wrote**, *pp* **written**, *pres p* **writing**) escribir. □ ~ **down** *vt* anotar. □ ~ **off** *vt* cancelar (debt). ~**-off** *n*. **the car was a ~-off** el coche fue declarado un siniestro total. ~**r** *n* escritor *m*
writhe /raɪð/ *vi* retorcerse
writing /'raɪtɪŋ/ *n* (*script*) escritura *f*; (*handwriting*) letra *f*. **in** ~ por escrito. ~**s** *npl* obra *f*, escritos *mpl*. ~ **desk** *n* escritorio *m*. ~ **pad** *n* bloc *m*. ~ **paper** *n* papel *m* de escribir
written /'rɪtn/ *see* WRITE
wrong /rɒŋ/ *adj* equivocado, incorrecto; (*not just*) injusto; (*mistaken*) equivocado. **be** ~ no tener razón; (*be mistaken*) equivocarse. **what's ~?** ¿qué pasa? **it's ~ to steal** robar está mal. **what's ~ with that?** ¿qué hay de malo en eso?. ● *adv* mal. **go** ~ equivocarse; (plan) salir mal. ● *n* injusticia *f*; (*evil*) mal *m*. **in the** ~ equivocado. ● *vt* ser injusto con. ~**ful** *adj* injusto. ~**ly** *adv* mal; (*unfairly*) injustamente
wrote /rəʊt/ *see* WRITE
wrought iron /rɔːt/ *n* hierro *m* forjado
wrung /rʌŋ/ *see* WRING
wry /raɪ/ *adj* (**wryer**, **wryest**) irónico. **make a ~ face** torcer el gesto

xerox /'zɪərɒks/ *vt* fotocopiar, xerografiar
Xmas /'krɪsməs/ *n abbr* (**Christmas**) Navidad *f*
X-ray /'eksreɪ/ *n* (*ray*) rayo *m* X; (*photograph*) radiografía *f*. ~**s** *npl* rayos *mpl*. ● *vt* hacer una radiografía de
xylophone /'zaɪləfəʊn/ *n* xilofón *m*, xilófono *m*

yacht /jɒt/ *n* yate *m*. ~**ing** *n* navegación *f* a vela
yank /jæŋk/ *vt* Ⓘ tirar de (*violentamente*)
Yankee /'jæŋkɪ/ *n* Ⓘ yanqui *m* & *f*
yap /jæp/ *vi* (*pt* **yapped**) (dog) ladrar (*con ladridos agudos*)
yard /jɑːd/ *n* patio *m*; (*Amer, garden*) jardín *m*; (*measurement*) yarda *f* (= *0.9144 metre*)
yarn /jɑːn/ *n* hilo *m*; (*fam, tale*) cuento *m*
yawn /jɔːn/ *vi* bostezar. ● *n* bostezo *m*
yeah /jeə/ *adv* Ⓘ sí
year /jɪə(r)/ *n* año *m*. **be three ~s old** tener tres años. ~**ly** *adj* anual. ● *adv* cada año
yearn /'jɜːn/ *vi*. ~ **to do sth** anhelar hacer algo. ~ **for sth** añorar

algo. **~ing** *n* anhelo *m*, ansia *f*

yeast /ji:st/ *n* levadura *f*

yell /jel/ *vi* gritar. ● *n* grito *m*

yellow /ˈjeləʊ/ *adj & n* amarillo (*m*)

yelp /jelp/ *n* gañido *m*. ● *vi* gañir

yes /jes/ *int & n* sí (*m*)

yesterday /ˈjestədeɪ/ *adv & n* ayer (*m*). **the day before ~** anteayer *m*. **~ morning** ayer por la mañana, ayer en la mañana (*LAm*)

yet /jet/ *adv* todavía, aún; (*already*) ya. **as ~** hasta ahora; (*as a linker*) sin embargo. ● *conj* pero

Yiddish /ˈjɪdɪʃ/ *n* yídish *m*

yield /ji:ld/ *vt* (*surrender*) ceder; producir (crop/mineral); dar (results). ● *vi* ceder. **'yield'** (*Amer, traffic sign*) ceda el paso. ● *n* rendimiento *m*

yoga /ˈjəʊgə/ *n* yoga *m*

yoghurt /ˈjɒgət/ *n* yogur *m*

yoke /jəʊk/ *n* (*fig also*) yugo *m*

yokel /ˈjəʊkl/ *n* palurdo *m*

yolk /jəʊk/ *n* yema *f* (de huevo)

you /ju:/ *pronoun*

····➤ (*as the subject*) (*familiar form*) (*sing*) tú, vos (*River Plate and parts of Central America*); (*pl*) vosotros, -tras (*Spain*), ustedes (*LAm*); (*formal*) (*sing*) usted; (*pl*) ustedes

> **!** In Spanish the subject pronoun is usually only used to give emphasis or mark contrast.

····➤ (*as the direct object*) (*familiar form*) (*sing*) te; (*pl*) os (*Spain*), los, las (*LAm*); (*formal*) (*sing*) lo *or* (*Spain*) le, la; (*pl*) los *or* (*Spain*) les, las. **I love ~** te quiero

····➤ (*as the indirect object*) (*familiar form*) (*sing*) te; (*pl*) os (*Spain*), les (*LAm*); (*formal*) (*sing*) le; (*pl*) les. **I sent ~ the book yesterday** te mandé el libro ayer

> **!** The pronoun *se* replaces the indirect object pronoun *le* or *les* when the latter is used with the direct object pronoun (*lo, la* etc), e.g. **I gave it to ~** *se lo di*

····➤ (*when used after a preposition*) (*familiar form*) (*sing*) ti, vos (*River Plate and parts of Central America*); (*pl*) vosotros, -tras (*Spain*), ustedes (*LAm*); (*formal*) (*sing*) usted; (*pl*) ustedes

····➤ (*generalizing*) uno, tú (*esp Spain*). **~ feel very proud** uno se siente muy orgulloso, te sientes muy orgulloso (*esp Spain*). **~ have to be patient** hay que tener paciencia

you'd/ju:d/, /jʊəd/ = **you had**, **you would**

you'll/ju:l/, /jʊəl/ = **you will**

young /jʌŋ/ *adj* (**-er**, **-est**) joven. **my ~er sister** mi hermana menor. **he's a year ~er than me** tiene un año menos que yo. **~ lady** *n* señorita *f*. **~ man** *n* joven *m*. **~ster** /-stə(r)/ *n* joven *m*

your /jɔ:(r)/ *adj* (*belonging to one person*) (*sing, familiar*) tu; (*pl, familiar*) tus; (*sing, formal*) su; (*pl, formal*) sus; (*belonging to more than one person*) (*sing, familiar*) vuestro, -tra, su (*LAm*); (*pl, familiar*) vuestros, -tras, sus (*LAm*); (*sing, formal*) su; (*pl, formal*) sus

you're/jʊə(r)/, /jɔ:(r)/ = **you are**

yours /jɔːz/ *poss pron* (*belonging to one person*) (*sing, familiar*) tuyo, -ya; (*pl, familiar*) tuyos, -yas; (*sing, formal*) suyo, -ya; (*pl, formal*) suyos, -yas. (*belonging to more than one person*) (*sing, familiar*) vuestro, -tra; (*pl, familiar*) vuestros, -tras, suyos, -yas (*LAm*); (*sing, formal*) suyo, -ya; (*pl, formal*) suyos, -yas. **an aunt of ~** una tía tuya/suya; **~ is here** el tuyo/la tuya/el suyo/la suya está aquí

yoursel|f /jɔːˈself/ *pron* (*reflexive*). (*emphatic use*) 🅸 tú mismo, tú misma; (*formal*) usted mismo, usted misma. **describe ~f** descríbete; (*Ud form*) descríbase. **stop thinking about ~f** 🅸 deja de pensar en tí mismo; (*formal*) deje de pensar en sí mismo. **by ~f** solo, sola. **~ves** /jɔːˈselvz/ *pron* vosotros mismos, vosotras mismas (*familiar*), ustedes mismos, ustedes mismas (*LAm familiar*), ustedes mismos, ustedes mismas (*formal*); (*reflexive*). **behave ~ves** ¡portaos bien! (*familiar*), ¡pórtense bien! (*formal, LAm familiar*). **by ~ves** solos, solas

youth /juːθ/ *n* (*pl* **youths** /juːðz/) (*early life*) juventud *f*; (*boy*) joven *m*; (*young people*) juventud *f*. **~ful** *adj* joven, juvenil. **~ hostel** *n* albergue *m* juvenil

you've/juːv/ = **you have**

Yugoslav /ˈjuːgəslɑːv/ *adj & n* yugoslavo (*m*). **~ia** /-ˈslɑːvɪə/ *n* Yugoslavia *f*

Zz

zeal /ziːl/ *n* fervor *m*, celo *m*

zeal|ot /ˈzelət/ *n* fanático *m*. **~ous** /-əs/ *adj* ferviente; (*worker*) que pone gran celo en su trabajo

zebra /ˈzebrə/ *n* cebra *f*. **~ crossing** *n* paso *m* de cebra

zenith /ˈzenɪθ/ *n* cenit *m*

zero /ˈzɪərəʊ/ *n* (*pl* **-os**) cero *m*

zest /zest/ *n* entusiasmo *m*; (*peel*) cáscara *f*

zigzag /ˈzɪgzæg/ *n* zigzag *m*. ●*vi* (*pt* **zigzagged**) zigzaguear

zilch /zɪltʃ/ *n* 🆇 nada de nada

zinc /zɪŋk/ *n* cinc *m*

zip /zɪp/ *n* cremallera *f*, cierre *m* (*LAm*), zíper *m* (*Mex*). ●*vt*. **~ (up)** cerrar (la cremallera). **Z~ code** *n* (*Amer*) código *m* postal. **~ fastener** *n* cremallera *f*. **~per** *n/vt see* ZIP

zodiac /ˈzəʊdɪæk/ *n* zodíaco *m*, zodiaco *m*

zombie /ˈzɒmbɪ/ *n* zombi *m & f*

zone /zəʊn/ *n* zona *f*. **time ~** *n* huso *m* horario

zoo /zuː/ *n* zoo *m*, zoológico *m*. **~logical** /zuːəˈlɒdʒɪkl/ *adj* zoológico. **~logist** /zuːˈɒlədʒɪst/ *n* zoólogo *m*. **~logy** /zuːˈɒlədʒɪ/ *n* zoología *f*

zoom /zuːm/. □ **~ in** *vi* (*Photo*) hacer un zoom in (**on** sobre). □ **~ past** *vi/t* pasar zumbando. **~ lens** *n* teleobjetivo *m*, zoom *m*

zucchini /zʊˈkiːnɪ/ *n* (*invar or* **~s**) (*Amer*) calabacín *m*

Numbers/números

zero	**0**	cero
one (first)	**1**	uno (primero)
two (second)	**2**	dos (segundo)
three (third)	**3**	tres (tercero)
four (fourth)	**4**	cuatro (cuarto)
five (fifth)	**5**	cinco (quinto)
six (sixth)	**6**	seis (sexto)
seven (seventh)	**7**	siete (séptimo)
eight (eighth)	**8**	ocho (octavo)
nine (ninth)	**9**	nueve (noveno)
ten (tenth)	**10**	diez (décimo)
eleven (eleventh)	**11**	once (undécimo)
twelve (twelfth)	**12**	doce (duodécimo)
thirteen (thirteenth)	**13**	trece (decimotercero)
fourteen (fourteenth)	**14**	catorce (decimocuarto)
fifteen (fifteenth)	**15**	quince (decimoquinto)
sixteen (sixteenth)	**16**	dieciséis (decimosexto)
seventeen (seventeenth)	**17**	diecisiete (decimoséptimo)
eighteen (eighteenth)	**18**	dieciocho (decimoctavo)
nineteen (nineteenth)	**19**	diecinueve (decimonoveno)
twenty (twentieth)	**20**	veinte (vigésimo)
twenty-one (twenty-first)	**21**	veintiuno (vigésimo primero)
twenty-two (twenty-second)	**22**	veintidós (vigésimo segundo)
twenty-three (twenty-third)	**23**	veintitrés (vigésimo tercero)
twenty-four (twenty-fourth)	**24**	veinticuatro (vigésimo cuarto)
twenty-five (twenty-fifth)	**25**	veinticinco (vigésimo quinto)
twenty-six (twenty-sixth)	**26**	veintiséis (vigésimo sexto)
thirty (thirtieth)	**30**	treinta (trigésimo)

thirty-one (thirty-first)	**31**	treinta y uno (trigésimo primero)
forty (fortieth)	**40**	cuarenta (cuadragésimo)
fifty (fiftieth)	**50**	cincuenta (quincuagésimo)
sixty (sixtieth)	**60**	sesenta (sexagésimo)
seventy (seventieth)	**70**	setenta (septuagésimo)
eighty (eightieth)	**80**	ochenta (octogésimo)
ninety (ninetieth)	**90**	noventa (nonagésimo)
a/one hundred (hundredth)	**100**	cien (centésimo)
a/one hundred and one (hundred and first)	**101**	ciento uno (centésimo primero)
two hundred (two hundredth)	**200**	doscientos (ducentésimo)
three hundred (three hundredth)	**300**	trescientos (tricentésimo)
four hundred (four hundredth)	**400**	cuatrocientos (cuadringentésimo)
five hundred (five hundredth)	**500**	quinientos (quingentésimo)
six hundred (six hundredth)	**600**	seiscientos (sexcentésimo)
seven hundred (seven hundredth)	**700**	setecientos (septingentésimo)
eight hundred (eight hundredth)	**800**	ochocientos (octingentésimo)
nine hundred (nine hundredth)	**900**	novecientos (noningentésimo)
a/one thousand (thousandth)	**1000**	mil (milésimo)
two thousand (two thousandth)	**2000**	dos mil (dos milésimo)
a/one million (millionth)	**1,000,000**	un millón (millonésimo)

Verbos irregulares ingleses

Infinitivo	*Pretérito*	*Participio pasado*
be	was	been
bear	bore	borne
beat	beat	beaten
become	became	become
begin	began	begun
bend	bent	bent
bet	bet, betted	bet, betted
bid	bade, bid	bidden, bid
bind	bound	bound
bite	bit	bitten
bleed	bled	bled
blow	blew	blown
break	broke	broken
breed	bred	bred
bring	brought	brought
build	built	built
burn	burnt, burned	burnt, burned
burst	burst	burst
buy	bought	bought
catch	caught	caught
choose	chose	chosen
cling	clung	clung
come	came	come
cost	cost, costed (*vt*)	cost, costed
cut	cut	cut
deal	dealt	dealt
dig	dug	dug
do	did	done
draw	drew	drawn
dream	dreamt, dreamed	dreamt, dreamed
drink	drank	drunk

Infinitivo	*Pretérito*	*Participio pasado*
drive	drove	driven
eat	ate	eaten
fall	fell	fallen
feed	fed	fed
feel	felt	felt
fight	fought	fought
find	found	found
flee	fled	fled
fly	flew	flown
freeze	froze	frozen
get	got	got, gotten *US*
give	gave	given
go	went	gone
grow	grew	grown
hang	hung, hanged	hung, hanged
have	had	had
hear	heard	heard
hide	hid	hidden
hit	hit	hit
hold	held	held
hurt	hurt	hurt
keep	kept	kept
kneel	knelt	knelt
know	knew	known
lay	laid	laid
lead	led	led
lean	leaned, leant	leaned, leant
learn	learnt, learned	learnt, learned
leave	left	left
lend	lent	lent
let	let	let
lie	lay	lain

Infinitivo	*Pretérito*	*Participio pasado*
lose	lost	lost
make	made	made
mean	meant	meant
meet	met	met
pay	paid	paid
put	put	put
read	read	read
ride	rode	ridden
ring	rang	rung
rise	rose	risen
run	ran	run
say	said	said
see	saw	seen
seek	sought	sought
sell	sold	sold
send	sent	sent
set	set	set
sew	sewed	sewn, sewed
shake	shook	shaken
shine	shone	shone
shoe	shod	shod
shoot	shot	shot
show	showed	shown
shut	shut	shut
sing	sang	sung
sink	sank	sunk
sit	sat	sat
sleep	slept	slept
sling	slung	slung
smell	smelt, smelled	smelt, smelled
speak	spoke	spoken
spell	spelled, spelt	spelled, spelt
spend	spent	spent
spit	spat	spat
spoil	spoilt, spoiled	spoilt, spoiled
spread	spread	spread
spring	sprang	sprung
stand	stood	stood
steal	stole	stolen
stick	stuck	stuck
sting	stung	stung
stride	strode	stridden
strike	struck	struck
swear	swore	sworn
sweep	swept	swept
swell	swelled	swollen, swelled
swim	swam	swum
swing	swung	swung
take	took	taken
teach	taught	taught
tear	tore	torn
tell	told	told
think	thought	thought
throw	threw	thrown
thrust	thrust	thrust
tread	trod	trodden
under-stand	under-stood	understood
wake	woke	woken
wear	wore	worn
win	won	won
write	wrote	written

Spanish verbs

Regular verbs:

● in **-ar** (*e.g.* **comprar**)
Present; compr|o, **~as, ~a, ~amos, ~áis, ~an**
Future: comprar|é, **~ás, ~á, ~emos, ~éis, ~án**
Imperfect: compr|aba, **~abas, ~aba, ~ábamos, ~abais, ~aban**
Preterite: compr|é, **~aste, ~ó, ~amos, ~asteis, ~aron**
Present subjunctive: compr|e, **~es, ~e, ~emos, ~éis, ~en**
Imperfect subjunctive: compr|ara, **~aras, ~ara, ~áramos, ~arais, ~aran**
compr|ase, **~ases, ~ase, ~ásemos, ~aseis, ~asen**
Conditional: comprar|ía, **~ías, ~ía, ~íamos, ~íais, ~ían**
Present participle: comprando
Past participle: comprado
Imperative: compra, comprad

● in **-er** (*e.g.* **beber**)
Present: beb|o, **~es, ~e, ~emos, ~éis, ~en**
Future: beber|é, **~ás, ~á, ~emos, ~éis, ~án**
Imperfect: beb|ía, **~ías, ~ía, ~íamos, ~íais, ~ían**
Preterite: beb|í, **~iste, ~ió, ~imos, ~isteis, ~ieron**
Present subjunctive: beb|a, **~as, ~a, ~amos, ~áis, ~an**
Imperfect subjunctive: beb|iera, **~ieras, ~iera, ~iéramos, ~ierais, ~ieran**
beb|iese, **~ieses, ~iese, ~iésemos, ~ieseis, ~iesen**
Conditional: beber|ía, **~ías, ~ía, ~íamos, ~íais, ~ían**
Present participle: bebiendo
Past participle: bebido
Imperative: bebe, bebed

● in **-ir** (*e.g.* **vivir**)
Present: viv|o, **~es, ~e, ~imos, ~ís, ~en**
Future: vivir|é, **~ás, ~á, ~emos, ~éis, ~án**
Imperfect: viv|ía, **~ías, ~ía, ~íamos, ~íais, ~ían**
Preterite: viv|í, **~iste, ~ió, ~imos, ~isteis, ~ieron**
Present subjunctive: viv|a, **~as, ~a, ~amos, ~áis, ~an**
Imperfect subjunctive: viv|iera, **~ieras, ~iera, ~iéramos, ~ierais, ~ieran**
viv|iese, **~ieses, ~iese, ~iésemos, ~ieseis, ~iesen**
Conditional: vivir|ía, **~ías, ~ía, ~íamos, ~íais, ~ían**
Present participle: viviendo
Past participle: vivido
Imperative: vive, vivid

Irregular verbs:

[1] cerrar

Present: cierro, cierras, cierra, cerramos, cerráis, cierran
Present subjunctive: cierre, cierres, cierre, cerremos, cerréis, cierren
Imperative: cierra, cerrad

[2] contar, mover

Present: cuento, cuentas, cuenta, contamos, contáis, cuentan
muevo, mueves, mueve, movemos, movéis, mueven
Present subjunctive: cuente, cuentes, cuente, contemos, contéis, cuenten
mueva, muevas, mueva, movamos, mováis, muevan
Imperative: cuenta, contad
mueve, moved

[3] jugar

Present: juego, juegas, juega, jugamos, jugáis, juegan
Preterite: jugué, jugaste, jugó, jugamos, jugasteis, jugaron
Present subjunctive: juegue, juegues, juegue, juguemos, juguéis, jueguen

[4] sentir

Present: siento, sientes, siente, sentimos, sentís, sienten
Preterite: sentí, sentiste, sintió, sentimos, sentisteis, sintieron
Present subjunctive: sienta, sientas, sienta, sintamos, sintáis, sientan
Imperfect subjunctive: sint|iera, **~ieras, ~iera, ~iéramos, ~ierais, ~ieran**
sint|iese, **~ieses, ~iese, ~iésemos, ~ieseis, ~iesen**
Present participle: sintiendo
Imperative: siente, sentid

[5] pedir

Present: pido, pides, pide, pedimos, pedís, piden
Preterite: pedí, pediste, pidió, pedimos, pedisteis, pidieron
Present subjunctive: pid|a, **~as, ~a, ~amos, ~áis, ~an**
Imperfect subjunctive: pid|iera, **~ieras, ~iera, ~iéramos, ~ierais, ~ieran**
pid|iese, **~ieses, ~iese, ~iésemos, ~ieseis, ~iesen**
Present participle: pidiendo
Imperative: pide, pedid

[6] dormir

Present: duermo, duermes, duerme, dormimos, dormís, duermen
Preterite: dormí, dormiste, durmió, dormimos, dormisteis, durmieron
Present subjunctive: duerma, duermas, duerma, durmamos, durmáis, duerman
Imperfect subjunctive: durm|iera, **~ieras, ~iera, ~iéramos, ~ierais, ~ieran**
durm|iese, **~ieses, ~iese, ~iésemos, ~ieseis, ~iesen**
Present participle: durmiendo
Imperative: duerme, dormid

[7] dedicar

Preterite: dediqué, dedicaste, dedicó, dedicamos, dedicasteis, dedicaron
Present subjunctive: dediqu|e, **~es, ~e, ~emos, ~éis, ~en**

[8] delinquir

Present: delinco, delinques, delinque, delinquimos, delinquís, delinquen
Present subjunctive: delinc|a, **~as, ~a, ~amos, ~áis, ~an**

[9] vencer, esparcir

Present: venzo, vences, vence, vencemos, vencéis, vencen
esparzo, esparces, esparce, esparcimos, esparcís, esparcen

Present subjunctive: venz|a, **~as, ~a, ~amos, ~áis, ~an**
esparz|a, **~as, ~a, ~amos, ~áis, ~an**

[10] rechazar

Preterite: rechacé, rechazaste, rechazó, rechazamos, rechazasteis, rechazaron
Present subjunctive: rechac|e, **~es, ~e, ~emos, ~éis, ~en**

[11] conocer, lucir

Present: conozco, conoces, conoce, conocemos, conocéis, conocen
luzco, luces, luce, lucimos, lucís, lucen
Present subjunctive: conozc|a, **~as, ~a, ~amos, ~áis, ~an**
luzc|a, **~as, ~a, ~amos, ~áis, ~an**

[12] pagar

Preterite: pagué, pagaste, pagó, pagamos, pagasteis, pagaron
Present subjunctive: pagu|e, **~es, ~e, ~emos, ~éis, ~en**

[13] distinguir

Present: distingo, distingues, distingue, distinguimos, distinguís, distinguen
Present subjunctive: disting|a, **~as, ~a, ~amos, ~áis, ~an**

[14] acoger, afligir

Present: acojo, acoges, acoge, acogemos, acogéis, acogen
aflijo, afliges, aflige, afligimos, afligís, afligen
Present subjunctive: acoj|a, **~as, ~a, ~amos, ~áis, ~an**
aflij|a, **~as, ~a, ~amos, ~áis, ~an**

[15] averiguar

Preterite: averigüé, averiguaste, averiguó, averiguamos, averiguasteis, averiguaron
Present subjunctive: averigü|e, **~es, ~e, ~emos, ~éis, ~en**

[16] agorar

Present: agüero, agüeras, agüera, agoramos, agoráis, agüeran
Present subjunctive: agüere, agüeres, agüere, agoremos, agoréis, agüeren
Imperative: agüera, agorad

[17] huir

Present: huyo, huyes, huye, huimos, huís, huyen
Preterite: huí, huiste, huyó, huimos, huisteis, huyeron
Present subjunctive: huy|a, **~as, ~a, ~amos, ~áis, ~an**
Imperfect subjunctive: huy|era, **~eras, ~era, ~éramos, ~erais, ~eran**
huy|ese, **~eses, ~ese, ~ésemos, ~eseis, ~esen**
Present participle: huyendo
Imperative: huye, huid

[18] creer

Preterite: creí, creíste, creyó, creímos, creísteis, creyeron
Imperfect subjunctive: crey|era, **~eras, ~era, ~éramos, ~erais, ~eran**
crey|ese, **~eses, ~ese, ~ésemos, ~eseis, ~esen**
Present participle: creyendo
Past participle: creído

[19] argüir

Present: arguyo, arguyes, arguye, argüimos, argüís, arguyen
Preterite: argüí, argüiste, arguyó, argüimos, argüisteis, arguyeron
Present subjunctive: arguy|a, **~as, ~a, ~amos, ~áis, ~an**
Imperfect subjunctive: arguy|era, **~eras, ~era, ~éramos, ~erais, ~eran**
arguy|ese, **~eses, ~ese, ~ésemos, ~eseis, ~esen**
Present participle: arguyendo
Imperative: arguye, argüid

[20] vaciar

Present: vacío, vacías, vacía, vaciamos, vaciáis, vacían
Present subjunctive: vacíe, vacíes, vacíe, vaciemos, vaciéis, vacíen
Imperative: vacía, vaciad

[21] acentuar

Present: acentúo, acentúas, acentúa, acentuamos, acentuáis, acentúan
Present subjunctive: acentúe, acentúes, acentúe, acentuemos, acentuéis, acentúen
Imperative: acentúa, acentuad

[22] atañer, engullir

Preterite: atañ|i, **~iste, ~ó, ~imos, ~isteis, ~eron**
engull|í **~iste, ~ó, ~imos, ~isteis, ~eron**
Imperfect subjunctive: atañera, **~eras, ~era, ~éramos, ~erais, ~eran**
atañese, **~eses, ~ese, ~ésemos, ~eseis, ~esen**
engull|era, **~eras, ~era, ~éramos, ~erais, ~eran**
engull|ese, **~eses, ~ese, ~ésemos, ~eseis, ~esen**
Present participle: atañendo
engullendo

[23] aislar, aullar

Present: aíslo, aíslas, aísla, aislamos, aisláis, aíslan
aúllo, aúllas, aúlla, aullamos aulláis, aúllan
Present subjunctive: aísle, aísles, aísle, aislemos, aisléis, aíslen
aúlle, aúlles, aúlle, aullemos, aulléis, aúllen
Imperative: aísla, aislad
aúlla, aullad

[24] abolir

Present: abolimos, abolís
Present subjunctive: not used
Imperative: abolid

[25] andar

Preterite: anduv|e, **~iste, ~o, ~imos, ~isteis, ~ieron**
Imperfect subjunctive: anduv|iera, **~ieras, ~iera, ~iéramos, ~ierais, ~ieran**
anduv|iese, **~ieses, ~iese, ~iésemos, ~ieseis, ~iesen**

[26] dar

Present: doy, das, da, damos, dais, dan
Preterite: di, diste, dio, dimos, disteis, dieron
Present subjunctive: dé, des, dé, demos, deis, den
Imperfect subjunctive: diera, dieras, diera, diéramos, dierais, dieran diese, dieses, diese, diésemos, dieseis, diesen

[27] estar

Present: estoy, estás, está, estamos, estáis, están
Preterite: estuv|e, **~iste, ~o, ~imos, ~isteis, ~ieron**
Present subjunctive: esté, estés, esté, estemos, estéis, estén
Imperfect subjunctive: estuv|iera, **~ieras, ~iera, ~iéramos, ~ierais, ~ieran**
estuv|iese, **~ieses, ~iese, ~iésemos, ~ieseis, ~iesen**
Imperative: está, estad

[28] caber

Present: quepo, cabes, cabe, cabemos, cabéis, caben
Future: cabr|é, **~ás, ~á, ~emos, ~éis, ~án**
Preterite: cup|e, **~iste, ~o, ~imos, ~isteis, ~ieron**
Present subjunctive: quep|a, **~as, ~a, ~amos, ~áis, ~an**
Imperfect subjunctive: cup|iera, **~ieras, ~iera, ~iéramos, ~ierais, ~ieran**
cup|iese, **~ieses, ~iese, ~iésemos, ~ieseis, ~iesen**
Conditional: cabr|ía, **~ías, ~ía, ~íamos, ~íais, ~ían**

[29] caer

Present: caigo, caes, cae, caemos, caéis, caen
Preterite: caí, caiste, cayó, caímos, caísteis, cayeron
Present subjunctive: caig|a, **~as, ~a, ~amos, ~áis, ~an**
Imperfect subjunctive: cay|era, **~eras, ~era, ~éramos, ~erais, ~eran**
cay|ese, **~eses, ~ese, ~ésemos, ~eseis, ~esen**
Present participle: cayendo
Past participle: caído

[30] haber

Present: he, has, ha, hemos, habéis, han
Future: habr|é **~ás, ~á, ~emos, ~éis, ~án**
Preterite: hub|e, **~iste, ~o, ~imos, ~isteis, ~ieron**
Present subjunctive: hay|a, **~as, ~a, ~amos, ~áis, ~an**
Imperfect subjunctive: hub|iera, **~ieras, ~iera, ~iéramos, ~ierais, ~ieran**
hub|iese, **~ieses, ~iese, ~iésemos, ~ieseis, ~iesen**
Conditional: habr|ía, **~ías, ~ía, ~íamos, ~íais, ~ían**
Imperative: he, habed

[31] hacer

Present: hago, haces, hace, hacemos, hacéis, hacen
Future: har|é, **~ás, ~á, ~emos, ~éis, ~án**
Preterite: hice, hiciste, hizo, hicimos, hicisteis, hicieron
Present subjunctive: hag|a, **~as, ~a, ~amos, ~áis, ~an**
Imperfect subjunctive: hic|iera, **~ieras, ~iera, ~iéramos, ~ierais, ~ieran**
hic|iese, **~ieses, ~iese, ~iésemos, ~ieseis, ~iesen**
Conditional: har|ía, **~ías, ~ía, ~íamos, ~íais, ~ían**
Past participle: hecho
Imperative: haz, haced

[32] placer

Present subjunctive: plazca
Imperfect subjunctive: placiera, placiese

[33] poder

Present: puedo, puedes, puede, podemos, podéis, pueden
Future: podr|é, **~ás, ~á, ~emos, ~éis, ~án**
Preterite: pud|e, **~iste, ~o, ~imos, ~isteis, ~ieron**
Present subjunctive: pueda, puedas, pueda, podamos, podáis, puedan
Imperfect subjunctive: pud|iera, **~ieras, ~iera, ~iéramos, ~ierais, ~ieran**
pud|iese, **~ieses, ~iese, ~iésemos, ~ieseis, ~iesen**
Conditional: podr|ía, **~ías, ~ía, ~íamos, ~íais, ~ían**
Past participle: pudiendo

[34] poner

Present: pongo, pones, pone, ponemos, ponéis, ponen
Future: pondr|é, **~ás, ~á, ~emos, ~éis, ~án**
Preterite: pus|e, **~iste, ~o, ~imos, ~isteis, ~ieron**
Present subjunctive: pong|a, **~as, ~a, ~amos, ~áis, ~an**
Imperfect subjunctive: pus|iera, **~ieras, ~iera, ~iéramos, ~ierais, ~ieran**
pus|iese, **~ieses, ~iese, ~iésemos, ~ieseis, ~iesen**
Conditional: pondr|ía, **~ías, ~ía, ~íamos, ~íais, ~ían**
Past participle: puesto
Imperative: pon, poned

[35] querer

Present: quiero, quieres, quiere, queremos, queréis, quieren
Future: querr|é, **~ás, ~á, ~emos, ~éis, ~án**
Preterite: quis|e, **~iste, ~o, ~imos, ~isteis, ~ieron**
Present subjunctive: quiera, quieras, quiera, queramos, queráis, quieran
Imperfect subjunctive: quis|iera, **~ieras, ~iera, ~iéramos, ~ierais, ~ieran**
quis|iese, **~ieses, ~iese, ~iésemos, ~ieseis, ~iesen**
Conditional: querr|ía, **~ías, ~ía, ~íamos, ~íais, ~ían**
Imperative: quiere, quered

[36] raer

Present: raigo/rayo, raes, rae, raemos, raéis, raen
Preterite: raí, raíste, rayó, raímos, raísteis, rayeron
Present subjunctive: raig|a, **~as, ~a, ~amos, ~áis, ~an** ray|a, **~as, ~a, ~amos, ~áis, ~an**
Imperfect subjunctive: ray|era, **~eras, ~era, ~éramos, ~erais, ~eran**
ray|ese, **~eses, ~ese, ~ésemos, ~eseis, ~esen**
Present participle: rayendo
Past participle: raído

[37] roer

Present: roo, roes, roe, roemos, roéis, roen
Preterite: roí, roíste, royó, roímos, roísteis, royeron
Present subjunctive: ro|a, **~as, ~a, ~amos, ~áis, ~an**
Imperfect subjunctive: roy|era, **~eras, ~era, ~éramos, ~erais, ~eran**
roy|ese, **~eses, ~ese, ~ésemos, ~eseis, ~esen**
Present participle: royendo
Past participle: roído

[38] saber

Present: sé, sabes, sabe, sabemos, sabéis, saben
Future: sabr|é, **~ás, ~á, ~emos, ~éis, ~án**
Preterite: sup|e, **~iste, ~o, ~imos, ~isteis, ~ieron**
Present subjunctive: sep|a, **~as, ~a, ~amos, ~áis, ~an**
Imperfect subjunctive: sup|iera, **~ieras, ~iera, ~iéramos, ~ierais, ~ieran** sup|iese, **~ieses, ~iese, ~iésemos, ~ieseis, ~iesen**
Conditional: sabr|ía, **~ías, ~ía, ~íamos, ~íais, ~ían**

[39] ser

Present: soy, eres, es, somos, sois, son
Imperfect: era, eras, era, éramos, erais, eran
Preterite: fui, fuiste, fue, fuimos, fuisteis, fueron
Present subjunctive: se|a, **~as, ~a, ~amos, ~áis, ~an**
Imperfect subjunctive: fu|era, **~eras, ~era, ~éramos, ~erais, ~eran** fu|ese, **~eses, ~ese, ~ésemos, ~eseis, ~esen**
Imperative: sé, sed

[40] tener

Present: tengo, tienes, tiene, tenemos, tenéis, tienen
Future: tendr|é, **~ás, ~á, ~emos, ~éis, ~án**
Preterite: tuv|e, **~iste, ~o, ~imos, ~isteis, ~ieron**
Present subjunctive: teng|a, **~as, ~a, ~amos, ~áis, ~an**
Imperfect subjunctive: tuv|iera, **~ieras, ~iera, ~iéramos, ~ierais, ~ieran** tuv|iese, **~ieses, ~iese, ~iésemos, ~ieseis, ~iesen**
Conditional: tendr|ía, **~ías, ~ía, ~íamos, ~íais, ~ían**
Imperative: ten, tened

[41] traer

Present: traigo, traes, trae, traemos, traéis, traen
Preterite: traj|e, **~iste, ~o, ~imos, ~isteis, ~eron**
Present subjunctive: traig|a, **~as, ~a, ~amos, ~áis, ~an**
Imperfect subjunctive: traj|era, **~eras, ~era, ~éramos, ~erais, ~eran** traj|ese, **~eses, ~ese, ~ésemos, ~eseis, ~esen**
Present participle: trayendo
Past participle: traído

[42] valer

Present: valgo, vales, vale, valemos, valéis, valen
Future: vald|ré, **~ás, ~á, ~emos, ~éis, ~án**
Present subjunctive: valg|a, **~as, ~a, ~amos, ~áis, ~an**
Conditional: vald|ría, **~ías, ~ía, ~íamos, ~íais, ~ían**
Imperative: vale, valed

[43] ver

Present: veo, ves, ve, vemos, veis, ven
Imperfect: ve|ía, **~ías, ~ía, ~íamos, ~íais, ~ían**
Preterite: vi, viste, vio, vimos, visteis, vieron
Present subjunctive: ve|a, **~as, ~a, ~amos, ~áis, ~an**
Past participle: visto

[44] yacer

Present: yazco, yaces, yace, yacemos, yacéis, yacen
Present subjunctive: yazc|a, **~as, ~a, ~amos, ~áis, ~an**
Imperative: yace, yaced

[45] asir

Present: asgo, ases, ase, asimos, asís, asen
Present subjunctive: asg|a, **~as, ~a, ~amos, ~áis, ~an**

[46] decir

Present: digo, dices, dice, decimos, decís, dicen
Future: dir|é, **~ás, ~á, ~emos, ~éis, ~án**
Preterite: dij|e, **~iste, ~o, ~imos, ~isteis, ~eron**
Present subjunctive: dig|a, **~as, ~a, ~amos, ~áis, ~an**
Imperfect subjunctive: dij|era, **~eras, ~era, ~éramos, ~erais, ~eran**
dij|ese, **~eses, ~ese, ~ésemos, ~eseis, ~esen**
Conditional: dir|ía, **~ías, ~ía, ~íamos, ~íais, ~ían**
Present participle: dicho
Imperative: di, decid

[47] reducir

Present: reduzco, reduces, reduce, reducimos, reducís, reducen
Preterite: reduj|e, **~iste, ~o, ~imos, ~isteis, ~eron**
Present subjunctive: reduzc|a, **~as, ~a, ~amos, ~áis, ~an**
Imperfect subjunctive: reduj|era, **~eras, ~era, ~éramos, ~erais, ~eran**
reduj|ese, **~eses, ~ese, ~ésemos, ~eseis, ~esen**

[48] erguir

Present: yergo, yergues, yergue, erguimos, erguís, yerguen
Preterite: erguí, erguiste, irguió, erguimos, erguisteis, irguieron
Present subjunctive: yerg|a, **~as, ~a, ~amos, ~áis, ~an**
Imperfect subjunctive: irgu|iera, **~ieras, ~iera, ~iéramos, ~ierais, ~ieran**
irgu|iese, **~ieses, ~iese, ~iésemos, ~ieseis, ~iesen**
Present participle: irguiendo
Imperative: yergue, erguid

[49] ir

Present: voy, vas, va, vamos, vais, van
Imperfect: iba, ibas, iba, íbamos, ibais, iban
Preterite: fui, fuiste, fue, fuimos, fuisteis, fueron
Present subjunctive: vay|a, **~as, ~a, ~amos, ~áis, ~an**
Imperfect subjunctive: fu|era, **~eras, ~era, ~éramos, ~erais, ~eran**
fu|ese, **~eses, ~ese, ~ésemos, ~eseis, ~esen**
Present participle: yendo
Imperative: ve, id

[50] oír

Present: oigo, oyes, oye, oímos, oís, oyen
Preterite: oí, oíste, oyó, oímos, oísteis, oyeron
Present subjunctive: oig|a, **~as, ~a, ~amos, ~áis, ~an**
Imperfect subjunctive: oy|era, **~eras, ~era, ~éramos, ~erais, ~eran**

oy|ese, **~eses, ~ese, ~ésemos, ~eseis, ~esen**
Present participle: oyendo
Past participle: oído
Imperative: oye, oíd

[51] reír

Present: río, ríes, ríe, reímos, reís, ríen
Preterite: reí, reíste, rió, reímos, reísteis, rieron
Present subjunctive: ría, rías, ría, riamos, riáis, rían
Present participle: riendo
Past participle: reído
Imperative: ríe, reíd

[52] salir

Present: salgo, sales, sale, salimos, salís, salen
Future: saldr|é, **~ás, ~á, ~emos, ~éis, ~án**
Present subjunctive: salg|a, **~as, ~a, ~amos, ~áis, ~an**
Conditional: saldr|ía, **~ías, ~ía, ~íamos, ~íais, ~ían**
Imperative: sal, salid

[53] venir

Present: vengo, vienes, viene, venimos, venís, vienen
Future: vendr|é, **~ás, ~á, ~emos, ~éis, ~án**
Preterite: vin|e, **~iste, ~o, ~imos, ~isteis, ~ieron**
Present subjunctive: veng|a, **~as, ~a, ~amos, ~áis, ~an**
Imperfect subjunctive: vin|iera, **~ieras, ~iera, ~iéramos, ~ierais, ~ieran** vin|iese, **~ieses, ~iese, ~iésemos, ~ieseis, ~iesen**
Conditional: vendr|ía, **~ías, ~ía, ~íamos, ~íais, ~ían**
Present participle: viniendo
Imperative: ven, venid

Abbreviations/Abreviaturas

adjective	*adj*	adjetivo
abbreviation	*abbr/abrev*	abreviatura
adverb	*adv*	adverbio
American	*Amer*	americano
motoring	*Auto*	automóvil
British	*Brit*	británico
commerce	*Com*	comercio
computing	*Comp*	informática
conjunction	*conj*	conjunción
cookery	*Culin*	cocina
electricity	*Elec*	electricidad
Spain	*Esp*	España
feminine	*f*	femenino
familiar	*fam*	familiar
figurative	*fig*	figurado
philosophy	*Fil*	filosofía
photography	*Foto*	fotografía
grammar	*Gram*	gramática
interjection	*int*	interjección
invariable	*invar*	invariable
legal, law	*Jurid*	jurídico
Latin American	*LAm*	latinoamericano
masculine	*m*	masculino
mathematics	*Mat(h)*	matemáticas
mechanics	*Mec*	mecánica
medicine	*Med*	medicina
Mexico	*Mex*	México